Contested Continent

The Oxford History of the United States

David M. Kennedy, *General Editor*

PETER C. MANCALL
CONTESTED CONTINENT
The Struggle for North America, c. 1000–1680

ROBERT MIDDLEKAUFF
THE GLORIOUS CAUSE
The American Revolution, 1763–1789

GORDON S. WOOD
EMPIRE OF LIBERTY
A History of the Early Republic, 1789–1815

DANIEL WALKER HOWE
WHAT HATH GOD WROUGHT
The Transformation of America, 1815–1848

JAMES M. MCPHERSON
BATTLE CRY OF FREEDOM
The Civil War Era

RICHARD WHITE
THE REPUBLIC FOR WHICH IT STANDS
The United States during Reconstruction and the Gilded Age, 1865–1896

DAVID M. KENNEDY
FREEDOM FROM FEAR
The American People in Depression and War, 1929–1945

JAMES T. PATTERSON
GRAND EXPECTATIONS
The United States, 1945–1974

JAMES T. PATTERSON
RESTLESS GIANT
The United States from Watergate to Bush v. Gore

GEORGE C. HERRING
FROM COLONY TO SUPERPOWER
U.S. Foreign Relations since 1776

CONTESTED CONTINENT

The Struggle for North America, c. 1000–1680

PETER C. MANCALL

OXFORD
UNIVERSITY PRESS

OXFORD
UNIVERSITY PRESS

Oxford University Press is a department of the University of Oxford.
It furthers the University's objective of excellence in research, scholarship,
and education by publishing worldwide. Oxford is a registered trade mark of
Oxford University Press in the UK and in certain other countries.

Published in the United States of America by Oxford University Press
198 Madison Avenue, New York, NY 10016, United States of America.

CIP data is on file with the Library of Congress

ISBN 9780195372786

Printed by Sheridan Books, Inc., United States of America

The manufacturer's authorized representative in the EU for product safety is
Oxford University Press España S.A. of Parque Empresarial San Fernando de Henares,
Avenida de Castilla, 2 – 28830 Madrid (www.oup.es/en or product.safety@oup.com).
OUP España S.A. also acts as importer into Spain of products made by the manufacturer.

FSC
www.fsc.org
MIX
Paper | Supporting responsible forestry
FSC® C008955

For Lisa

What is an American?

—Hector St. John de Crèvecoeur, *Letters from an American Farmer* (1782)

Acknowledgments

"No man is an island," the English poet John Donne wrote in 1624. Neither, he might have added, is an author. Everyone who has the luxury to write a book, especially one as long as *Contested Continent*, has been able to complete their projects because of support from friends, colleagues, and institutions. This book would not have happened without the help of many others.

It began with an invitation from David Kennedy, the editor of the Oxford History of the United States series, and Susan Ferber, my editor at the press. In the years that followed, I had many conversations with both, especially David, about the contents of this volume as well as its style and range. *Contested Continents*, which is now the first volume of the renowned series, ends long before there was a United States, and much of the action takes place in regions that never became part of the modern nation. How to make a book that begins at the end of the first millennium of the Common Era and ends almost a century before the Revolution fit into such a series required astute historical instincts. I am fortunate indeed to have had two master stylists attend to this book, long in both length and gestation.

During the years I conducted research and wrote, I received unflagging assistance from the University of Southern California, which supported my research time and provided funding for assistants, and the Huntington Library, my intellectual home. At USC I want to especially thank Steve Kay and Amber Miller for their constant support while I worked in the office of the Dean of Dornsife College; Amy Braden, program director of the USC-Huntington Early Modern Studies Institute, who helped me keep this book on track; and Bill Deverell, a perpetual source of guidance and friendship. Roy Ritchie, Steve Hindle, and Sue Juster, the three directors of research at the Huntington while I worked on this book, provided the best intellectual climate for sustained research and writing I have ever experienced. I was very lucky indeed to have been the Harmsworth Professor at Oxford University during the 2019–2020 academic year, where I received extraordinary hospitality and support at both The Queen's College and the Rothermere American Institute; and to have been the Robert C. Ritchie Distinguished Fellow at the Huntington for 2023–2024. Those years spent free from other academic responsibilities allowed me time to shape this narrative.

I am delighted to have an opportunity to name the many research assistants at USC and elsewhere who have helped me over the years. I want to thank Maddie Adams, Julia Brown-Bernstein, Himani Boompally, Lauren Dodds, Ellen Dooley, Joyce Fienman, Lance Good, Megan Hansford, Alex Hofmann, Serena Jarwala, Emily Johnson, Emily Levine, Azriel Linder, Mallory Novikoff, Will Orr, Jenna Ross, Marissa Roy, Mira Schulman, Avery Wendell, and Madeline White. In addition, I have benefited from assistance and insights from some of my current and former PhD students, including Karin Amundsen, Michael Block, Christophe Boucher, Harrison Diskin, John Grigg, Cynthia Ingham, Keith Pluymers, Martha Robinson, Hannah Ryan, and Rebecca Simpson-Menzies.

In addition, I would like to thank the extraordinary production support I received while transforming a long manuscript into a polished book. In particular, I thank Rebecca Wrenn, whose vivid maps provide necessary geographical context for much of the story I tell in these pages. Rachel Ruisard coordinated production of the book at Oxford, along with Amy Whitmer, the production editor; copy editor Sue Warga; Birgitte Necessary, who produced the index; and proofreader James Fraleigh.

During the years I was writing I had the good fortune to speak to many audiences about parts of this book, including at the McNeil Center for Early American Studies at the University of Pennsylvania, where I delivered the Mellon Distinguished Lectures in the Humanities in 2012, which later became the basis for *Nature and Culture in the Early Modern Atlantic* (Penn, 2018); Oxford University, where I delivered my inaugural Harmsworth lecture, followed by a vigorous seminar at the Rothermere American Institute; the Cambridge University American history seminar; the Bosworth Memorial Lecture at Yale University; the Omohundro Institute's Council Lecture; and an intensive review of early chapters of the first half of the book at the Omohundro Institute. In addition, I worked out preliminary versions of parts of this book in articles including "Pigs for Historians: *Changes in the Land* and Beyond" (*William and Mary Quarterly*, 2010); "The Raw and the Cold: Five English Sailors in

Sixteenth-Century Nunavut" (*William and Mary Quarterly*, 2013); "Thinking with James Bay: Crees, English, and Cold" (*Northeastern Naturalist*, 2017); "The Age of Failure" (*Early American Literature*, 2021); "Sir Francis Drake's Date with Destiny" (*Alta*, 2022); "Was the 1623 Poisoning of 200 Native Americans One of the Continent's First War Crimes?" (*Smithsonian Magazine*, 2023); and "Disappointment, Grievance, and Violence in Early Virginia" (*William and Mary Quarterly*, 2023). I especially want to thank Chris Grasso and Josh Piker at the *WMQ* for helping me develop the pieces published there. In places I have also drawn on some of my previous books, including *Hakluyt's Promise: An Elizabethan's Quest for an English America* (Yale, 2007); *Fatal Journey: The Final Expedition of Henry Hudson—A Tale of Mutiny and Murder in the Arctic* (Basic Books, 2009); and *The Trials of Thomas Morton: An Anglican Lawyer, His Puritan Foes, and the Battle for a New England* (Yale, 2019).

Over the years I have accumulated many scholarly debts, and I am happy to offer this public acknowledgment of insights from (in alphabetical order) Rolena Adorno, Zara Anishlansin, Steve Aron, Alice Baumgartner, Luis Corteguera, Liz Ellis, Julia Gaffield, Anne Goldgar, Mark Hanna, John Harpham, Jim Horn, Grace Mallon, Jennifer Morgan, Laura Nelson, Sarah Pearsall, Carla Pestana, Nathan Perl-Rosenthal, Nick Radburn, Danny Richter (who provided crucial help for Latin translations), Steve Ross, Ann Schofield, Jake Soll, Marta Vicente, Amy Watson, Jennifer Wells, Juliet Wiersema, Karin Wulf, Ann Marie Yasin, and Mike Zuckerman. Deirdre Mullane, my phenomenal longtime agent, provided encouragement and guidance over the many years since she helped arrange this book. I regret that Bernard Bailyn and John Elliott, two scholars who shaped my understanding of this era and its central questions in many generous conversations, are not able to see the final product. Many friends and colleagues went well above any reasonable request to help me answer the innumerable questions I had while writing. Among them are Emily Berquist, Steve Hackel, Dana Murillo Velasco, and Sherry Velasco, who deepened my understanding of early modern Spanish America; Daniela Bleichmar, my guide to the early modern visual world; Nathalie Caron, who hosted me multiple times in Paris, including for a month-long graduate seminar at the Sorbonne in March 2024; Nicholas Canny, my guide to all things about early modern Ireland; Alison Games, who sharpened my argument so many times; Julia Lewandoski, who shared her continent-spanning research about Indigenous communities over countless conversations; Bob Lockhart, with whom I have worked for years to develop the Early Modern Americas series at Penn; Mary Beth Norton, to whom I turned time and again, especially on issues relating to gender in early America; Colin Calloway and Daniel K. Richter, who each read much of the manuscript and showed me how to make it better; Brett Rushforth, who generously shared much of his research about France and the Atlantic world; Carole Shammas, who helped bring me to Los Angeles and has been my close intellectual partner ever since; and Lindsay O'Neill and Vanessa Wilkie, who answered every question I ever had about the early modern English world and pointed me toward valuable archives.

Beyond those colleagues I want to offer my deepest thanks to Lou Masur and Doug Greenberg, trusty guides to the American past. Steve Pincus shared his own in-the-works history of the British Empire and found time to do a close reading of much of my book. I spoke every week for years with five creative early Americanists who helped me shape my arguments: Trevor Burnard, Lige Gould, Ed Gray, Eric Hinderaker, and Mark Peterson. I am very saddened that Ed and Trevor are not around to see how this all worked out. I am sorry, too, that my parents, Jackie and Elliott Mancall, who were so excited that I was writing this book, are also not here to see it in print. Fortunately, my brother Andrew can bear familial witness.

Many of the stories I tell in these pages focused on families, some no doubt happy and many, as Tolstoy told us, rather less contented. Luckily for me, I wrote this book with unending support from my own family, especially my brilliant children, Sophie and Nicholas Mancall-Bitel, who have lived with this project since they were teenagers. I dedicate this book to Lisa Bitel, intellectual soulmate and forever editor, without whom it would not exist.

Contents

Part II: Colonies

Part III: Fractures

Maps

Editor's Introduction

"In the beginning, all the world was America."

With those words penned in 1689, some two centuries after Columbus's Caribbean landfall, John Locke (in his *Second Treatise on Government*) testified to the persistent European fantasy that the New World, North America in particular, was a vacant, pristine wilderness, a hushed and fallow continent serenely awaiting the quickening hand of European civilization.

In this, the first chronological volume of the *Oxford History of the United States* series, Peter Mancall puts that stubborn delusion to rest once and for all. Assiduously mining the rich literature on Indigenous Americans that has flourished in recent decades, he limns a vivid portrait of the vitality and diversity—and the conspicuous environmental savvy—of precontact North American peoples, as well as their ongoing struggles with the European newcomers penetrating inexorably and ever more deeply into the continent's interior.

Mancall artfully captures the staggering blow to the European mind as it struggled to make sense of reports that lands and humans previously unimagined lay beyond the Atlantic sea's western horizon. It is telling that Florentine explorer Amerigo Vespucci in 1503 coined the capaciously expansive term *mundus novus* (new world) to describe the continents that came to bear his name—not merely "new places" or "new peoples," but a new *world*, a vast, varied, and vibrant panorama of nature and man inexplicably unaccounted for in the two great sources of Renaissance-era intellectual authority: the Bible and the writings of classical antiquity.

For their part, Native Americans were no less stunned by the appearance in their ancient homelands of disruptive adventurers unmentioned in their lore and legends. Small wonder that so much mutual bafflement, fear, misunderstanding—and often barbarous violence—attended the initial encounters between the myriad peoples whose stories Mancall so colorfully recounts. And, as he convincingly argues, their repeated interactions created new *worlds*, not just for Europeans but for Africans and Native Americans as well. Their complex relationships over the centuries that Mancall addresses set much of the template and historical background for the remarkably diverse society that would one day be the United States.

Contrary to much popular understanding, then and later, time had not stood still for those original Americans. As the cultivation of maize (corn) spread outward from the Valley of Mexico, several North American Indigenous peoples had developed sophisticated cultures well before 1492, notably including the Mound-Building societies stretching from the Mississippi Valley to the Atlantic seaboard and the Puebloans in the present-day southwestern United States.

Then came the Europeans—and soon enough, along with them, enslaved Africans. Though North America lay at the northernmost edge of the transatlantic slave trade, ultimately receiving less than 4 percent of the more than ten million Africans brought mainly to Brazil and the Caribbean, *Contested Continent* convincingly documents how their presence in these early days laid the foundation for the slave system that would plague the continent for centuries thereafter.

Among the many virtues of *Contested Continent* is its refreshing emphasis on the environmental impacts of the "Columbian Exchange"—the physical collisions and transoceanic migration of biota that transformed landscapes, habitats, diets, and lifeways in North America and around the entire Atlantic basin, with consequences that would reverberate for centuries to come. Environmental history as a distinct field of inquiry is scarcely two scholarly generations old; Mancall deploys his matchless mastery of its methods and findings to open novel perspectives on countless episodes across the centuries of his story.

Contested Continent spans a much longer arc of time than any other volume in the Oxford History of the United States series. And it encompasses the histories of a plethora of widely diverse persons, peoples, places, and themes, from Columbus and the Spanish conquistadores imposing their will (and their pathogens) on Caribs and Tainos in the 1490s to Hernán Cortés conquering the Aztecs in 1521 and Álvar Núñez Cabeza de Vaca surviving unspeakable trials of body and spirit wandering from 1528 to 1536 across the parched landscape from Galveston to Tenochtitlán (Mexico City). Here also readers will encounter Algonquian-speakers Manteo and Wanchese wintering at Sir Walter Ralegh's London estate in 1584; Juan de Oñate y Salazar mercilessly mutilating the Acoma Puebloans in 1599; Captain John Smith struggling to rescue the starving Jamestown settlers in 1608; John Winthrop leading the Massachusetts Bay colonists ashore in 1630; and the several ill-fated attempts to find the fabled "Northwest Passage" by the likes of indomitable mariners John Cabot, Jacques Cartier, Martin Frobisher, Humphrey Gilbert, and Henry Hudson.

Mancall also superbly illuminates the tangled tale of the great-power rivalries that were so momentous for the continent's future. By 1600, from Florida and New Mexico southward, most of the New World lay firmly within the grip of imperial Spain. Then, heralding the coming century of colonization and conflict that *Contested Continent* so dramatically describes, three European powers planted three primitive outposts in three distant corners of North America within three years of one another: the Spanish at Sante Fe in 1610, the French at Quebec in 1608, and, most consequentially for the future United States, the English at Jamestown in 1607.

Indeed, even as the era covered in the following pages came to a close, it was unclear whether *any* of the European colonizers would predominate—or even survive. Across the New World as a whole, more enslaved Africans than Europeans had arrived in the previous two centuries. In North America, native peoples still outnumbered both Black and white intruders, and they remained formidably powerful. As Mancall's concluding chapters brilliantly demonstrate, a series of eruptions in the century's last decades gave emphatic punctuation to the great theme announced in his book's title: that North America in 1680 remained hotly contested despite centuries of exploration, exploitation, and slaughter—and even as John Locke and others continued to invoke its supposedly unspoiled, primeval character. New England in 1675 endured a bloody Indigenous uprising against English colonists, known as King Philip's War or Metacom's Rebellion. Along the shores of Chesapeake Bay, desperate hinterland colonists led by Nathaniel Bacon burned the Virginia capital in 1676 and forced the governor to flee, an outbreak that triggered a fateful decision to begin replacing troublesome white workers with enslaved Africans. Four years later, Puebloan rebels in New Mexico murderously drove their Spanish masters from the colony.

Those outbreaks bore ferocious witness to the enduring presence of Indigenous peoples, the intensification of imperial contestation, the accumulating costs of colonization, and the vexed future of North American slavery, as well as the accelerating conflicts among the colonists themselves.

It has been said that the assumption of inevitability is the assassin of the historical imagination. In Peter Mancall's sweeping, magisterial account of this formative epoch in North American history he shuns any suggestion of inevitability and brings to bear an impressively original scholarly imagination. He compels the reader to contemplate that several nascent narratives were in play as his story comes to its climax around 1680. Who could then say with confidence which would prevail?

The sprawling expanses of time and distance that *Contested Continent* addresses, along with its daunting bounty of topics and an uncommonly large and varied cast of characters, pose particularly sharp challenges for the historian. Peter Mancall has fully and creatively risen to that challenge. He has accomplished the near-impossible task of weaving a welter of disparate historical raw material—including anthropological and archaeological evidence from peoples who left few if any written records behind—into a coherent and captivating story of an era that foreshadowed and shaped so much of what was to follow. He offers a persuasive argument that understanding origins is the indispensable key to understanding endings—and that this era constitutes nothing less than a foundational prologue to the history of the future United States. *Contested Continent* also serves as a fitting prologue to the entire Oxford History of the United States series. Peter Mancall has crafted an admirably ambitious work that surpassingly fulfills the *Oxford History*'s goal of bringing the most comprehensive and current historical scholarship to experts and general readers alike.

David M. Kennedy

Glossary

Adelantado: governor of a Spanish territory
"By turf and twig": a ceremony to mark the transfer of title, also known as "livery of seisin"
Cacique: an Indigenous chief or leader
Encomienda: a grant to an individual in Spanish territory enabling the holder to demand labor or tribute from Indigenous peoples. The holder of such a title was an *encomendero*
Ingenio: a water mill used to process sugar cane
Inter caetera: bull of Pope Alexander VI of 1493 granting title of lands in the Western Hemisphere and creating an imaginary line to divide Spanish from Portuguese claims
Mita: mandatory labor system developed in the Andes
Partus sequitur ventrem: legal principle dictating that the status of a child is determined by whether the mother was free or enslaved
Pinnace: a small ship used to explore coastlines or to communicate between larger vessels
Repartimiento: a system of forced labor imposed by Spanish colonizers on Indigenous peoples
Sachem: a paramount chief of a group of Native peoples
Sagamore: a paramount chief of a single group
Shallop: a small ship often carried on board a larger vessel and used to explore shallow waters
Weroance, werowance: a commander or chief subordinate to a sachem

Note on Spelling

In places, *Contested Continent* has silently modernized texts following the guidelines in Frank Friedel, ed., *Harvard Guide to American History* (Cambridge, MA: Harvard University Press, 1974), 27–32.

Abbreviations

AAS	American Antiquarian Society
AHR	*American Historical Review*
Avalon	The Avalon Project: Documents in Law, History, and Diplomacy, Yale Law School
CO	Colonial Office papers, TNA
DRCHNY	E. B. O'Callaghan, ed., *Documents Relative to the Colonial History of the State of New York*, 10 vols. (Albany, NY, 1853–1887).
EA	John Alden et al., eds., *European Americana: A Chronological Guide to Works Printed in Europe Relating to the Americas, 1493–1776*, 6 vols. (New York: Readex Books, 1980–1996).
FP	Ferrar Papers, Magdalene College, Cambridge (available online as Virginia Company Archives).
HAHR	*Hispanic American Historical Review*
Hak. Soc.	Works Issued by the Hakluyt Society
HBC	Hudson Bay Company
HCA	High Court of Admiralty; the HCA papers are in TNA
HEH	Henry E. Huntington Library
Hening, *Statutes*	William W. Hening, ed., *The Statutes at Large . . . of all the laws of Virginia*, 13 vols. (Richmond, 1809–1823).
JAH	*Journal of American History*
JR	*The Jesuit Relations and Allied Documents*, ed. Reuben G. Thwaites, 73 vols. (Cleveland: Burrows Bros., 1896–1901).
MHS	Massachusetts Historical Society

NAW	David B. Quinn, et al., ed., *New American World: A Documentary History of North America to 1612*, 5 vols. (New York: Arno, 1979).
NEHGR	*New England Historical and Genealogical Register*
NEQ	*New England Quarterly*
PMHB	*Pennsylvania Magazine of History and Biography*
QCL	Queen's College Library, Oxford
RAC	Royal Africa Company
RVC	*Records of the Virginia Company of London*, ed. Susan M. Kingsbury, 4 vols. (Washington, DC: Government Printing Office, 1906).
SPG	Society for the Propagation of the Gospel in Foreign Parts
TNA	The National Archives (formerly Public Record Office), Kew
VMHB	*Virginia Magazine of History and Biography*
WIC	Geoctrooieerde Westindische Compagnie, the Dutch West India Company
WMQ	*William and Mary Quarterly*

Prologue

On April 9, 1585, Manteo and Wanchese, Algonquian-speakers from the Outer Banks of modern-day North Carolina, boarded ship at Plymouth on England's southern coast. They were among the six hundred or so travelers crowded together on seven vessels bound for the American coastline. The European voyagers aimed to establish a colony in what some believed to be a pristine New World. Manteo, a son of an elite Croatoan family, and Wanchese, a Roanoke native, were going home.

Manteo and Wanchese had come to England in 1584 alongside travelers who had reconnoitered the Carolina coast that year. The pair had spent the winter in London at Durham House as guests of Sir Walter Ralegh, a favorite of Queen Elizabeth I. Visitors to the house sometimes gawked when they encountered the two Indigenous Americans. But not their fellow voyager Thomas Harriot, who was then twenty-four or twenty-five years old. In Durham House, a mansion built in the thirteenth century, Wanchese, Manteo, and Harriot had learned how to speak to one another. Harriot even produced a short version of a preliminary word list, which was likely the first time that anyone had written down an Algonquian language.[1]

The Algonquians proved to be brilliant tutors, expert guides to territory that would have otherwise been unintelligible to visitors from the European rim of the Atlantic. *Pagatowr*, they taught Harriot, was the word for maize, the most important crop along the Outer Banks in the sixteenth century. Their people also cultivated pumpkins and gourds, along with sunflowers that grew six feet high and could be used to make both soup and bread. Local Algonquian-speakers grew *uppówac* (tobacco),

1. "Algonquin Alphabet, 1585," Personal Papers of Thomas Harriot, Westminster School Archive and Collections, https://collections.westminster.org.uk/index.php/gb-2014-ws-05-har-01; *"Brief Lives," chiefly of Contemporaries, set down by John Aubrey, between the Years 1669 & 1696*, ed. Andrew Clark (Oxford: Clarendon Press, 1898), 284–285.

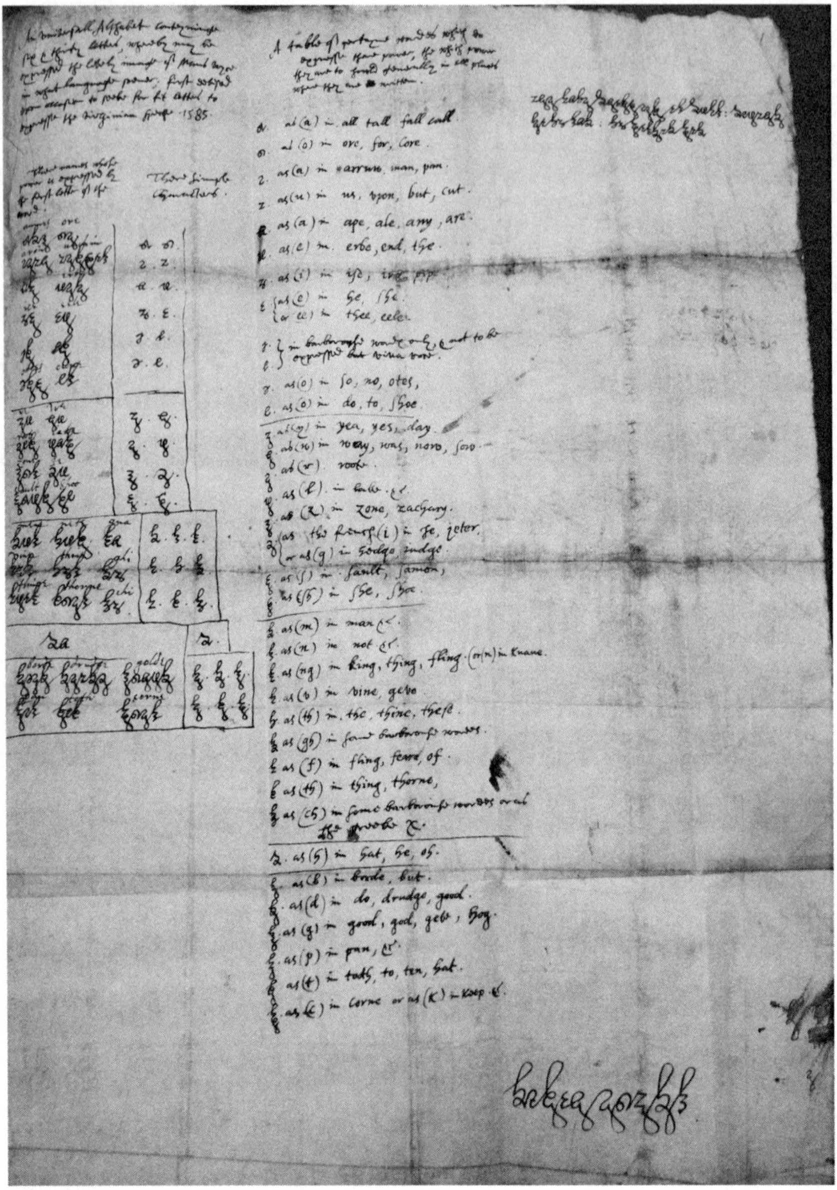

Thomas Harriot's "Algonquin Alphabet," produced with his Carolina Algonquian collaborators, represented what the seventeenth-century English antiquarian John Aubrey would later call "an alphabet he had contrived for the American language." "Algonquin Alphabet," Personal Papers of Thomas Harriot, Westminster School Archive and Collections. Reproduced by kind assistance of the Governing Body of Westminster School.

drying its leaves and smoking it through clay pipes. The Carolina Algonquians believed that *uppówac* had sacred powers. They offered it to their gods, sometimes by drying the plant and crushing the leaves to make a powder they could throw in the air. The gods reciprocated: they quelled dangerous waters for those at sea, lured fish into weirs, and protected those facing risks. Harriot soon published his observations that the Carolina Algonquians "sowed and husbanded" maize and tobacco, using the same terminology that English observers applied to their farms at home. The climate also seemed temperate enough to import plants that grew at similar latitudes in Europe, including sugar cane.[2]

English artist John White traveled on the same expedition with Harriot, Manteo, and Wanchese. White was an astute observer of American nature, including the myriad species of fish and shellfish to be found in the shallow waters off the barrier islands. His watercolors reveal a densely populated and carefully curated world that was far from the prelapsarian Eden imagined by previous English travelers. Like Harriot, White documented how these Carolina Algonquians had cleared fields, constructed houses and fences, felled large trees, built weirs, organized towns, fashioned effective hunting weapons, designated spots for religious rituals, and erected effigies in their fields to propitiate their deities and scare off ravenous birds.[3]

Harriot's writings and White's images came together in 1590 in a volume published in four languages by Flemish engraver Theodor de Bry in Frankfurt am Main. In addition to the English version, de Bry printed a German version for his local audience, a translation possibly intended for the French Protestant minority, and a Latin edition for the international community of scholars. The book sharply challenged Europeans' understandings of a supposedly unsettled North America.

The landscape that Harriot described and White painted bore the marks of longtime settlement. Maize, so central to the regional economy, had been cultivated in North America for over five hundred years, as Indigenous people had moved cobs northward from Mexico. The shrubs and small trees that edged their fields, another sign of their deliberate

2. "The first voyage made to the coastes of America," in Richard Hakluyt, *Principall Navigations, Voiages and Discoveries of the English Nation* (London, 1589), 728–733; Thomas Harriot, *A Briefe and True Report of the New Found Land of Virginia* (orig. pub. London, 1588; Frankfurt am Main, 1590), 11–16; David B. Quinn, *Set Fair for Roanoke: Voyages and Colonies, 1584–1606* (Chapel Hill: University of North Carolina Press, 1985), 232–236.

3. Paul Hulton and David B. Quinn, eds., *The American Drawings of John White, 1577–1590*, 2 vols. (Chapel Hill: University of North Carolina Press, 1964), esp. plates 31, 35, and 42.

land management, regularly attracted deer from the region's native herds. Yet despite evidence of intensive human sculpting of the landscape, many Europeans, following a tradition that dated back to Columbus's first voyage, persisted in believing that North America was a wilderness, all but wholly devoid of human presence.

Harriot also learned that many Carolina Algonquians had been stricken by an ailment previously unknown to them, quite possibly smallpox. The arrival of the illness at around the time of the appearance of English travelers led the Algonquians to link the migrants with the malady. Their belief that the appearance of Europeans produced calamity signaled the accumulating costs of conquest and colonization.

"And the Egyptians vexed us, and troubled us," taught Deuteronomy 26:6, "and laded us with cruel bondage." For many Native Americans, as well as Africans transported against their will in the early modern era, Europeans acted like biblical villains even though many traveled to the Western Hemisphere to flee their own persecution.

Manteo, Wanchese, and Harriot may not have agreed on many things. But each of them understood that human migrations across the Atlantic Ocean would forever alter life in North America. Yet none could foresee the enormous depth and range of the changes to come.

Preface

In 1000 CE, there was no America. By the time this book's account concludes, in 1680, it surely and consequentially existed. The pages that follow explain how and why an entity now known simply as "America" came to be and how its tumultuous history shaped the birth, a century after this book ends, of the United States.

Trying to find the origins of "America" is not a new pursuit. In 1782, French traveler J. Hector St. John de Crèvecoeur asked, "What is an American?" Crèvecoeur declared that "he is either an European or the descendant of an European; hence that strange mixture of blood, which you will find in no other country." He offered an example of a man whose "grandfather was an Englishman, whose wife was Dutch, whose son married a French woman, and whose present four sons have now four wives of different nations. *He* is an American." Casting off the "prejudices and manners" of Europe, this man absorbed the values of the continent, becoming "an American by being received in the broad lap of our great Alma Mater."[1]

Crèvecoeur's slender volume, *Letters from an American Farmer*, became an immediate publishing sensation across Europe. His work has remained popular and in print for over two hundred years. But on the question of who was an American, his ideas and mine are far apart. Despite his confident assertion, there was no single kind of American before 1680 or, for that matter, thereafter. This book aims to show how the territory that became America, and eventually the United States, reflected the experiences of millions of Indigenous women and men as well as Africans and Europeans. Together, these peoples altered much of the environment of a continent that stretched between the Atlantic and the Pacific. European migrants traveled for different reasons, including their search for new places to practice their faith unmolested, to advance the political agenda of their home country, or to pursue economic gain. Enslaved Africans enjoyed no similar choices. Native peoples, too, had no choice about the

1. J. Hector St. John de Crèvecoeur, *Letters from an American Farmer* (London, 1782), 51–53.

arrival of newcomers, though they responded with resilience to the intruders in their homelands.

There is no shortage of books about early American history that lead readers along a journey from the age of Christopher Columbus to that of George Washington. Like those works, this one offers unexpected twists and turns. Much of what happened from c. 1000 CE to 1680, the chronological boundaries of this book, came to define the American experience, including the rise of a booming transatlantic economy based on the extraction of abundant American natural resources, the central role European migrants and their descendants played in the enslavement of Africans, the displacement of Indigenous peoples, and the spread of self-governing polities where many people enjoyed religious liberty. None of those developments was inevitable. Nor did sweeping changes occur quickly. By 1680, after a series of revolts rocked colonies along the Atlantic coast as well as in New Mexico, the later success of Europeans was hardly certain. On the mainland, Indigenous peoples still far outnumbered people of European descent. Only in the Caribbean were there more immigrants than Natives, a consequence not of Europeans' ability to sustain their own populations but of the countless ships that brought enslaved Africans to Barbados, Jamaica, and other islands dominated by plantation agriculture.

Books about America often begin around 1492. This one has a significantly earlier starting date because what happened in the approximately five hundred years before Columbus's journeys shaped much of what would happen in the next 250 years, including the spread of maize agriculture across the Americas and the wholesale forced migration of enslaved peoples. Around the turn of the first Christian millennium, unknown Indigenous people brought Mexican maize to the Mississippi Valley, spawning the creation of a city of at least thirty thousand at Cahokia. At about the same moment, Norse sailors arrived in Newfoundland—the first known contact between Europeans and Native Americans. Those northern European men and women soon abandoned their plans to establish communities in what they called Vinland. But they maintained two settlements on the west coast of Greenland for about five hundred years. During those centuries, news about seemingly infinite schools of cod in the northwest Atlantic Ocean spread to Europe, eventually luring fishing crews from western Europe. The accumulation of such knowledge about the Western Hemisphere proved far more important than the modest and short-lived community the Norse established in Newfoundland around 1020 CE. Circulation of travelers' accounts, which accelerated when printing technology spread across Europe starting in the mid-fifteenth century, enticed Europeans to think about a world that few of them knew about before 1492.

Long after the Norse abandoned Greenland, some Portuguese began to purchase the bodies of captured Africans, transporting them against their will to toil on sugar plantations on mid-Atlantic islands. While the institution of slavery long predated Columbus and existed across much of the world, only in the fifteenth century did Europeans devise the practice of large-scale, systemic, commercially driven, and racially defined enslavement that altered the lives of millions across the four continents bordering the Atlantic. These unrelated developments—the expansion of maize farming, the rise and fall of Norse colonial aspirations, the spread of printing technology across Europe, and the forced relocation of enslaved Africans—begin the story told in *Contested Continent*.

Despite the impact of maize and the earliest development of the Atlantic slave trade, the pace of change in the pre-Columbian era was glacial compared to what happened after 1492. One need not valorize or condemn Christopher Columbus to recognize that his voyages opened a new chapter in the history of the Americas and, indeed, the entire world. Environmental historian Alfred Crosby has described the far-ranging transatlantic movement of biota—humans, livestock, plants, rodents, bacteria, and viruses—as the "Columbian Exchange." Put simply, the transfer of American plants to Eurasia led to population growth, while the passage of pathogens westward inflicted demographic catastrophe on Indigenous Americans. Physical anthropologists and historians have estimated that the Native population of the Americas declined by perhaps 90 percent from 1492 to 1800. Yet during the entire period covered in this book Indigenous peoples across North America continued to outnumber Europeans and Africans. That was true even in the narrow band where lay the thirteen colonies that together would rebel against Britain in 1776.

Columbus's journeys devastated the Tainos of the West Indies, but another aspect of his experience proved just as important. Columbus's reports almost immediately circulated in print. His first account, known as the Barcelona Letter after the city where it was published in 1493, announced what he saw to a European reading public eager for news about what lay beyond the boundaries of their world. By publicizing what he had seen, Columbus established a model that proved as decisive in the future of the hemisphere as the commodities he eventually brought home. The spread of information about the continent conjured an "America" that sparked the dreams of many Europeans looking for a better future. Their quest for a better life led to nightmares for the less powerful who met disease-bearing travelers or were already living as captives—and for whom passage on the seas proved a one-way ticket to a harsh existence and shortened life.

No single pattern defined Indigenous responses to colonization or European plans, in part because of the diversity of the five hundred or so Native peoples in North America. Nor was there initially a single European plan. At first, European colonial ventures fell into four types. The first type, practiced in the Arctic and in much of the interior of the Southwest, involved small groups bent on exploration. Their goal was not to remain but instead to gather intelligence about local resources and Indigenous peoples and send it back to authorities. The second—evident in the English colonial efforts at Roanoke, Avalon, Sagadahoc, New Plymouth, Virginia, and Massachusetts, the French effort in Quebec, and the Spanish settlement in Hispaniola—involved the transportation of groups of Europeans to an American territory with the idea of establishing a permanent community. The third sort involved religious missionaries, typically in relatively small numbers, committed to working for the salvation of those they deemed infidels. They hoped to bring new souls to Christendom and then, if all worked out, create village-based economies that would rely on Native workers to produce exportable commodities. This was the model that the Spanish deployed in Florida and in the land of the Puebloan peoples and that the French pursued in the St. Lawrence Valley. The fourth model was a commercial venture—the establishment of a satellite of an enterprise housed in Europe and staffed by individuals whose primary goal was to extract commodities. This was how the English operated the East India, Levant, and Muscovy companies, and how the Dutch used the West India Company (WIC) to create its export-oriented communities in Pernambuco (in present-day Brazil) and at the mouth of the Hudson River.

The success or failure of each of these ventures depended on luck—many ships sank crossing the Atlantic—and on the disposition of the Native peoples who inhabited the places where Europeans hoped to create their new societies. Some Indigenous groups proved adept at resisting conquest and colonization, especially in places where Native leaders or communities had already risen to positions of prominence before the first colonizers appeared on their shores. Impressive legacies of earlier civilizations could still be seen, notably mounds that rose to nearly a hundred feet at Cahokia, in present-day southern Illinois, the largest city north of Tenochtitlán (modern Mexico City), or the thousand-foot-long Serpent Mound in today's central Ohio, or Moundville, on the banks of the Black Warrior River in Alabama, where twenty-nine large mounds were arrayed around a plaza. After the decline of ancient Mississippian civilizations responsible for such durable alterations of the landscape, novel alliances emerged, especially in areas where the adoption of maize agriculture facilitated new economic practices. Charismatic leaders chose whether to trade with newcomers or to push back against the entreaties of would-be colonizers. Europeans often failed, especially in eastern North America, because they were unable to establish sustainable ties to local Indigenous peoples who possessed valuable knowledge about the environment—where to find fresh water, for example—as well as the location of valuable natural resources. Colonizers repeatedly found themselves in precarious situations, their fates dependent not on the possession of lethal arms or pathogens but instead on the decisions made by host communities.

Similarly, the enslavement of Africans, a central feature of the early American experience, did not occur in all places equally. Some African leaders, notably those along the continent's Atlantic shores, had established commercial relationships with Europeans before 1492. They established trade because they wanted specific goods, including European-style cloth, copper, alcohol, and firearms, which they could obtain only from sailors who arrived by sea. To get those goods, they offered up what they had, including elephant ivory, spices, gold—and people. Europeans wanted men and women to tend to the burgeoning plantations that colonizers created across the Caribbean and near shorelines in territory stretching from Chesapeake Bay to Pernambuco and Bahia in Brazil and to the islands of the greater Caribbean.[2]

Before 1680, Africans or American-born women and men with African ancestry constituted relatively small percentages of the population in mainland British colonies—probably around 7 percent in the English colonies along Chesapeake Bay, where the first documented captive Angolans had arrived in 1619. But in the Caribbean and parts of the South American coast stretching from modern Venezuela to Brazil, enslaved Africans or creoles constituted a substantial proportion, and sometimes a majority, of the population. Barbados, unpopulated when the English arrived, became a model for enslavement in territory far away from Chesapeake Bay.[3]

2. Toby Mintz, *A Fistful of Shells: West Africa from the Rise of the Slave Trade to the Age of Revolution* (Chicago: University of Chicago Press, 2019), 114–120; David Northrup, *Africa's Discovery of Europe, 1450–1850* (New York: Oxford University Press, 2002), 50–56.

3. Ira Berlin, *Many Thousands Gone: The First Two Centuries of Slavery in North America* (Cambridge, MA: Harvard University Press, 1998), 369–371 (table 1); Lorena S. Walsh, *Motives of Honor, Pleasure, and Profit: Plantation Management in the Colonial Chesapeake, 1607–1763* (Chapel Hill: University of North Carolina. Press for the Omohundro Institute,

Together, Indigenous Americans, Europeans, and Africans created societies in North America that only partially resembled what had existed before these Atlantic peoples encountered each other. These emergent societies differed from one region to another, with politics, religion, economics, and culture all reflecting the blend of peoples inhabiting specific locales. New social arrangements also drew on the deep histories of peoples who met each other.[4] The ability to govern one's own community, celebrated by earlier generations of American historians, did not look the same across the continent, nor did the creation of what became the House of Burgesses in Virginia in 1619 mark the origins of self-government on the continent. Long before any Europeans arrived, Indigenous peoples inhabited self-governing communities, with locally recognized leaders and long-lasting diplomatic and economic alliances with other Native peoples.

Religious practice similarly differed. From 1620 to 1642, over twenty-two thousand English dissenters crossed the ocean to seek spiritual freedom, a familiar part of the story of what became the United States. Many others chose to sail from Europe in pursuit of better economic prospects. But no stark differences divided God-fearing puritans, on the one hand, from Mammon-thirsty planters, on the other. Some European travelers, more bent on extracting natural resources than establishing communities, never intended to stay. Their goals differed from those of Europeans who crossed the Atlantic to establish permanent communities but who often failed, for reasons discussed in the pages that follow. Although they differed in their goals, the vast majority of European migrants believed that Indigenous Americans would, sooner or later, adopt Christianity and European economic practices. Even devout dissenters understood the importance of participating in trade and developing local economies with ties to Native communities. Edward Winslow, who arrived in New Plymouth aboard the *Mayflower* acutely aware of the need to find lucrative exports, believed that the colonists could send home a substantial number of fish. If that was the case, as he wrote in a 1624 promotional tract, "religion and profit jump together" in New England.[5]

Despite a rich documentary record, there is much in this era of North American history that remains elusive. No first-person accounts tell of daily life in Cahokia or any other ancient Mississippian civilization. After

2010), 203; and see David Eltis and David Richardson, *Atlas of the Transatlantic Slave Trade* (New Haven, CT: Yale University Press, 2010), 196–203.

4. See Daniel K. Richter, *Before the Revolution: America's Ancient Pasts* (Cambridge, MA: Harvard University Press, 2011), 3–63.
5. E[dward] W[inslow], *Good Newes from New-England: Or, A true Relation of things very remarkable at the Plantation of Plimoth in New-England* (London, 1624), 63–64.

its prodigious rise, Cahokia collapsed in the mid-thirteenth century and its population dispersed amid an ecological catastrophe. Not until the seventeenth century would a community north of the Rio Grande ever count more than a few thousand members other than on the rare and fleeting occasions when groups came together for major celebrations or diplomatic sessions. Towns tended to be small. Most people, free and enslaved alike, lived in rural areas.

From a bird's-eye view of the continent, a perspective common among European cartographers who wanted to lay claim to vast territories, North America seemed like a placid place. But violence was common and often personal. When a European planter shackled an enslaved African, others nearby witnessed the confinement. When Indigenous and colonial soldiers faced off in battle, they fought face-to-face. Hatchets, knives, and arrows all tore through human flesh more frequently than bullets. Invaders captured children and murdered their parents or older siblings. Captors often enslaved their enemies. Such atrocities happened across the early modern world, so in some ways there is nothing unique about these incidents in the Western Hemisphere. Only after 1650 did anything resembling constabulary forces arise in North America—and their goal was less the quelling of daily violence than the suppression of incipient rebellion by enslaved women and men. Peaceful relations within any community relied on obedience to common codes of behavior. Those who challenged such authorities—Quakers who refused to disavow their religious beliefs, enslaved Africans who sought to protect themselves from the brutalities and indignities of involuntary servitude, Indigenous peoples who stood up to European colonizers eager to take their land—might face death for their actions.

The pages that follow trace historical developments crucial to the eventual founding of the United States even if they took place beyond its modern borders. It is impossible to tell the story of slavery in America and its central role in the Atlantic economy without considering Barbados, Bermuda, Jamaica, and Providence Island. It is just as impossible to describe the impact of Europeans on Native peoples and the American environment without examining encounters in the silver-rich town of Parral (in the modern Mexican state of Chihuahua) and along the shores of Hudson Bay. The pursuit of religious liberty, long a mainstay of histories of the United States, stretched from the dissenting Protestant community of Leiden in the 1610s to the anti-Catholic uprising in New Mexico in 1680. American commodities that changed the world could be harvested in some places but not others because of differences in climate, not because of whatever polity laid claim to a region. European claims to American territory, central in any telling of the early history of what became a nation, often existed only on paper. The grand fantasies embedded in many European maps became visual scripts to propel conquest and colonization. That did not make them accurate renderings of complicated landscapes.

Early American history has long been popularized through specific dates: 1492 (Columbus crossing the Atlantic), 1607 (the founding of Jamestown), 1619 (the first African slaves on mainland North America), 1620 (the arrival of the Pilgrims at the Wampanoag town of Patuxet, which the newcomers called New Plymouth). While these moments mattered and shaped much of what followed, each also has a complex backstory. The stories that we tend to remember obscure the moments that we often ignore or forget, including the narratives of many failed European (and particularly English) efforts to control parts of North America. But those failures, which might be reinterpreted as Indigenous victories, mattered as much as the more famous moments—not only as reminders that non-Europeans regularly shaped what happened in North America but also because disappointment taught other Europeans how to survive and, with patience and often malice, succeed.

Europeans frequently missed the fact that the inviting landscapes they viewed had long been shaped by Native residents. But few could have ignored the changes in relations between humans and the environment after 1492, when Europeans became eager to procure maize, tobacco, fish, furs, and sugar. Those economic demands contributed mightily to environmental, social, political, and cultural changes.

Promoters of colonization sought to attract Europeans looking for a new start. However sincere their plans to improve the lives of Europeans, for decades, even centuries, not enough women and men chose to cross the Atlantic Ocean to satisfy the economic cravings of those eager to extract wealth from the Western Hemisphere. By the early seventeenth century, many English, Dutch, French, Spanish, and Portuguese planters and investors in North America came to believe that they needed enslaved Africans to provide necessary labor, mimicking a pattern that Europeans had imposed farther south in the sixteenth century. Within fifty years of first contact, bound laborers became a growing share of the migrants sailing westward across the Atlantic. Before 1580, enslaved women and men totaled one-quarter of the migrants who sailed west across the Atlantic. From 1580 to 1700, more than six of every ten oceanic travelers were enslaved.[6] The expanding transatlantic slave trade transformed coastal west-central

6. The percentage of enslaved continued to grow; by 1820, captive African men and women accounted for 80 percent of all migrants who had boarded ships to cross the Atlantic since 1500—many thousands never surviving the journey. See David Eltis, *The*

Africa, much of the continental Western Hemisphere, and the islands that lay in between.

Few of these developments could have been anticipated, even by those who played leading roles in colonization schemes. The continent that beckoned immigrants, from those hauling maize to Cahokia to Europeans seeking religious freedom in Pennsylvania, offered abundant opportunities to some. But hundreds of thousands of people paid a high price to satisfy the expansionist dreams of a wealthy and powerful minority of the basin's population.

Contested Continent tells the story of seven hundred years in three distinct eras, each accompanied by a portfolio of images. The first concentrates on the centuries-long process of mutual discovery when peoples on four continents—North America, South America, Europe, and Africa—became increasingly entangled in long-distance relationships. This era of learning about each other gave way to one of European conquest and colonization throughout the Western Hemisphere. During this long era, from the late sixteenth to the mid-seventeenth centuries, Europeans concentrated less on explorations—though intrepid sailors and their backers still sought new places—and more on establishing overseas outposts of their home nations. This era dominates the first chapters of most written histories of the United States, which makes sense since the modern nation owed so much to the Europeans who had established colonies. Although the era of colonization continued—some argue that it continues still today—the generation after the middle of the seventeenth century witnessed widespread turbulence that in some places threatened the confident dreams of colony builders. In Barbados, then the most profitable English colony in the Western Hemisphere, enslaved Africans plotted a murderous rebellion in 1675. In New England in the same year, pent-up frustrations and fear for the future inspired a region-wide Indigenous uprising against English colonists, known variously as King Philip's War or Metacom's Rebellion. Along the shores of Chesapeake Bay, poorer, hinterland colonial farmers led by Nathaniel Bacon and fueled by grievance against Virginia's ruling elite burned the capital in 1676 and forced the governor to flee. Four years later, religiously inspired rebels in New Mexico drove Spaniards out of the colony and repudiated all signs of Christianity or European material culture. North America in 1680 hardly looked like a place where Europeans were destined to triumph. Chance

Rise of African Slavery in the Americas (Cambridge: Cambridge University Press, 2000), 11 (table 1.2); Eltis and Richardson, *Atlas of the Transatlantic Slave Trade*, xvii.

and contingency, not divine will or even dogged determination, enabled many colonists to survive. It was often catastrophe, experienced or narrowly averted, that taught the survivors and their supporters across the ocean what they needed to do if they wanted to claim the continent as their own.

During the centuries between the turn of the first millennium of the Common Era and 1680, the chronological boundaries of *Contested Continent*, multiple peoples struggled to control portions of North America. The epic violence that characterized the end of this period serves as more than epitaph for the deadly nature of conflicts in the generations following 1492. The brutal spasms of murderous rage that devastated long-standing communities as the seventeenth century wore on bear witness to a signifying feature of North America before 1680. No matter how stable communities appeared to observers, no one could know what the next day would bring. Later, well after 1680, life in North America became more predictable, especially when Europeans solidified their control over the eastern portions of the continent. But that durability did not yet exist even in areas Europeans claimed. The struggle for North America had begun, but it had not yet been resolved.

Amerigo Vespucci, whose name would soon demarcate the Western Hemisphere on European maps, believed that he, Columbus, and other travelers from the eastern shores of the Atlantic had discovered a *mundus novus*—a new world. He was wrong. It was countless encounters from the mid-fifteenth century onward among the many peoples chronicled in these pages that created a new world—one that was often brutally contested.

Part I

Discoveries

1

1450

In 1556, a Venetian scholar and civil servant named Giovanni Battista Ramusio, the secretary to the Council of Ten, the governing body of the Serene Republic of Venice, edited a massive collection of travel reports about territory from Canada to Peru. In his preface to the volume, Ramusio wrote that "it is possible to find public houses full of those ropes, through which the person who is in charge of them can tell the past events, although they are far in the past, in the same way as we do with our letters."[1] He was referring to khipu (or quipu), knotted strings that Spanish conquerors had seen in Peru. His observations circulated widely, along with the first European engraving of maize. Among the readers of his work were Europeans who promoted the colonization of North America. For this audience, Ramusio's description had a point more important than his recognition of the utility of khipu. From the start, Europeans knew that the Americas were home to extensive settlements with complex histories. To succeed, they would need to discover what the Natives knew.

Ramusio bore witness to the impact of three revolutions that had already begun to transform the Atlantic world and laid the foundations for the next 250 years. An agricultural revolution altered diets, first in the Western Hemisphere and then across the Atlantic basin. It began with the cultivation of maize (*Zea mays*) in the Valley of Mexico thousands of years earlier. Not long before the turn of the first Christian millennium, Indigenous Americans brought cobs northward to the fertile soils at the confluence of the Mississippi and Missouri Rivers. There local peoples planted maize along with beans and squash, the "three sisters" of North American horticulture. The combination of plants provided nutrition that enabled communities to grow and prevented diseases, such as pellagra, which can result from overreliance on niacin-poor

1. "Se ne trovano case publiche piene di dette corde, con le quai facilme[n]te da ad inte[n]der coluí, che n'ha il carico, le cose passate, ben che elle siano di molta eta avanti di lui: si come noi facciamo con le nostre lettere." Giovanni Battista Ramusio, *Terzo Volume Della Navigationi et Viaggi* (Venice, 1556), 4r.

corn.[2] With a predictable food supply, the area's Natives soon began to change their lifestyles, not only along the Mississippi but also in the Southwest, where agriculture enabled sedentary settlements. Cities, already a fixture of the Central American landscape, appeared in North America where local populations relied on agriculture, as was the case at Cahokia, as well as Acoma, about sixty miles west of modern-day Albuquerque. When maize cultivation spread, new opportunities arose for those who decided to embrace horticulture. Since most Indigenous communities relied on women to plant, tend, and harvest maize and other crops, female authority extended far wider in North America than in most of the Old World.

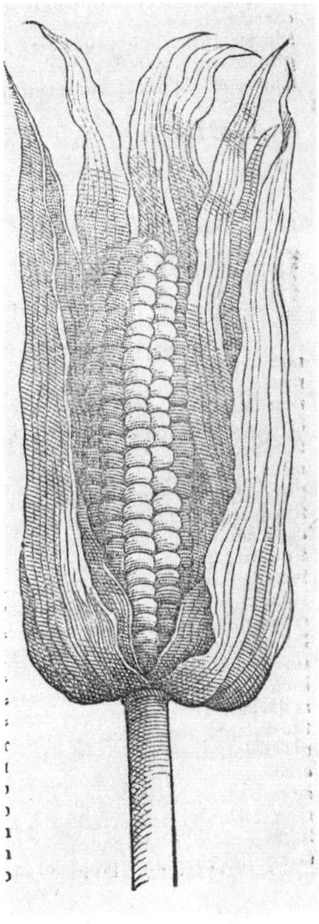

This 1556 engraving of maize appeared in the third volume of Giovanni Batista Ramusio's *Navigationi et Viaggi*, the first major collection of European travel narratives about the Western Hemisphere. The book would eventually help convince other Europeans, especially the English, to make regular investments in North American colonies. Courtesy of the John Carter Brown Library.

2. Daniel K. Richter, *Before the Revolution: America's Ancient Pasts* (Cambridge, MA: Harvard University Press, 2011), 13–23; Jane E. Buikstra, "Diet and Disease in Late Prehistory," in John W. Verano and Douglas H. Ubelaker, eds., *Disease and Demography in the Americas* (Washington, DC: Smithsonian Institution Press, 1992), 87–101.

Maize transformed American economies at the same time that sugar production, having earlier migrated from South Asia to the eastern shores of the Mediterranean basin, altered the eastern shores of the Atlantic. Within two hundred years of European Crusaders bringing it back from their eleventh- to fourteenth-century quests to the Middle East, proponents of sugar farming, confronted by the fact that the crop could grow only in warm climates, created sugar plantations as far afield as the Azores, Madeira, and the Canary Islands. Unlike maize, sugar was a labor-intensive crop. Those who wanted to profit from the growing European demand for sweetness needed to find laborers to work in hot fields, a pursuit that led by the middle decades of the fifteenth century to the enslavement of Africans.[3]

These agricultural developments unfolded while a shipping revolution accelerated Europeans' ability to cross wide expanses of open water. Improved ship design, better rigging, and compasses enabled some Europeans to sail ever farther out into the Atlantic. They also sailed on ships large enough to carry more cannons, providing a crucial advantage in any potential conflict. By the middle of the fifteenth century, Portuguese mariners regularly launched expeditions to Africa's Guinea Coast. They traded European cloth and livestock; they captured or purchased enslaved Africans, most of them prisoners seized by rival communities. Enslavers put the majority of these captives to work planting and harvesting cane. Others transformed the plant into molasses and sugar, dangerous pursuits in an age when one could lose an arm in a mill or die when a boiler exploded.[4]

American corn and cane sugar attracted Europeans' interest. Their ships enabled them to move commodities across the Atlantic. Enslaved Africans provided a growing proportion of labor to produce these crops. The revolutions in agriculture, transportation, and labor supply spawned sweeping political, technological, and social change.

In the five centuries following the expansion of maize cultivation into the Mississippi Valley, the peoples of the Atlantic basin altered their landscapes to adapt to new opportunities. Some of those changes, including

3. See Alfred W. Crosby, *Ecological Imperialism: The Biological Expansion of Europe, 900–1900* (Cambridge: Cambridge University Press, 1986), 67, 77–78; Sidney W. Mintz, *Sweetness and Power: The Place of Sugar in Modern History* (New York: Viking, 1985), 19–150.

4. See J. H. Parry, *The Discovery of the Sea* (Berkeley: University of California Press, 1981), 38–48; Carlo M. Cipolla, *Guns, Sails and Empires: Technological Innovation and the Early Phases of European Expansion, 1400–1700* (New York: Pantheon, 1965), 76–89; John Thornton, *Africa and Africans in the Making of the Atlantic World, 1400–1800*, 2nd ed. (Cambridge: Cambridge University Press, 1998), 72–97; Crosby, *Ecological Imperialism*, 105–107.

maize agriculture, became permanent. But others proved more transitory, such as the centuries-long Norse flirtation with northeastern North America. The first European foray into the Western Hemisphere left barely a trace on the land, a reminder, if one is necessary, that the arrival of Europeans in North America did not necessarily mean that colonization would follow, much less have a permanent impact on the continent's peoples.

In 1450, the Native population of America north of the Rio Grande stood between 1.9 and 5 million.[5] The population of northern and central Mesoamerica was probably between 5 and 15 million, and the Amazon basin likely was home to 1.5 to 2 million occupants.[6] Hispaniola, the most populous island in the Caribbean, likely had at least 200,000 and possibly more than 400,000 residents, though it was so densely populated that the sixteenth-century Dominican friar Bartolomé de Las Casas thought that 3 million people lived there when Spaniards arrived.[7] The population of Hawai'i stood at approximately half a million.[8] In all, the Western Hemisphere had perhaps 50 million residents and possibly as many as 72 million.[9] By comparison, Britain and Ireland together likely numbered about 3 million, with 12 million inhabiting the area encompassing modern

5. Douglas H. Ubelaker, "North American Indian Population Size," in Verano and Ubelaker, eds., *Disease and Demography*, 169–176; Alan Taylor, *American Colonies* (New York: Viking, 2001), 40.
6. For Mexico: Robert McCaa, "The Peopling of Mexico from Origins to Revolution," in Michael R. Haines and Richard H. Steckels, eds., *A Population History of North America* (Cambridge: Cambridge University Press, 2000), 253. For the Amazon: Betty J. Meggers, "Prehistoric Population Density in the Amazon Basin," in Verano and Ubelaker, eds., *Disease and Demography*, 253. McCaa's estimate is for the Mexican population in 1519, before the period of population decreases on the mainland.
7. Massimo Livi Bacci, "Return to Hispaniola: Reassessing a Demographic Catastrophe," *HAHR* 83 (2003), 3–51; Andrés Reséndez, *The Other Slavery: The Uncovered Story of Indian Enslavement in the Americas* (Boston: Houghton Mifflin, 2016), 16; Juan José Ponce Vázquez, *Islanders and Empire: Smuggling and Political Defiance in Hispaniola, 1580–1690* (Cambridge: Cambridge University Press, 2020), 25n4.
8. Patrick V. Kirch, *On the Road of the Winds: An Archaeological History of the Pacific Islands Before European Contact*, rev. ed. (Berkeley: University of California Press, 2017), 259.
9. Taylor, *American Colonies*, 40. Estimates of pre-contact population have varied over time, based on the techniques anthropologists and demographers have employed; see Ubelaker, "North American Indian Population Size." For the estimate of 72 million, see Russell Thornton, *American Indian Holocaust and Survival: Population History Since 1492* (Norman: University of Oklahoma Press, 1987); see also Douglas H. Ubelaker, "North American Indian Population Size, A.D. 1500 to 1985," *American Journal of Physical Anthropology* 77 (1988), 289–294.

France and the Low Countries, 7.5 million in Germany and Scandinavia, and 19 million in the area now encompassing Iberia, Italy, Greece, and the Balkans. The European population, devastated by the Black Death of the mid-fourteenth century, stood around 50 million in all, likely about the same size as the population of Africa. The number of Europeans was almost one-third less than it had been in 1340.[10]

Most North Americans, like Europeans at the same time, inhabited small communities, with material cultures reflecting the places where they lived and their contact with others. Virtually none lived in complete isolation.[11] Across much of the continent, groups often moved during the year, normally to maximize access to resources such as migratory fish, to seasonal farming spots, or to congregate for trade or religious ceremonies. But even those who dispersed after an autumn harvest to shift from tending crops to capturing fish and game did not scatter randomly across the landscape. Instead, they moved in small groups to winter hunting territories.

Although seasonal migration was common, such practices were not universal. In the Southwest, for example, Puebloan peoples developed irrigation systems to maximize their water supply so they could spend most of the year in one place. Native peoples in Florida and coastal California also tended to remain in one area throughout the year, taking advantage of local resources and often trading with nearby communities to gain access to a wider range of goods.[12] Indigenous Hawaiians, the descendants of Polynesians who had mastered the challenges of crossing the Pacific Ocean, arrived in the archipelago sometime between approximately 1000 and the mid-thirteenth century. Once there, residents created ties between the islands, expanded family connections, shared economic practices and architectural ideas, built large heiaus along their coasts, and created a political hierarchy that stretched beyond any specific island. Their movements likely remained confined to inter-island journeys rather than the kind of long-distance travel that had led their ancestors to the

10. J. C. Russell, "Population in Europe, 500–1500," in Carlo M. Cipolla, ed., *The Fontana Economic History of Europe* (Glasgow: Fontana, 1972), 36.

11. See Ann M. Carlos, "The Country They Built: Dynamic and Complex Indigenous Economies in North America Before 1492," *Journal of Economic History* 83 (2023), 319–358.

12. Neal Salisbury, "The Indians' Old World: Native Americans and the Coming of Europeans," *WMQ* 53 (1996), 435–458; Natale Zappia, *Traders and Raiders: The Indigenous World of the Colorado Basin, 1540–1859* (Chapel Hill: University of North Carolina Press, 2014); Dale Hutchinson et al., "Regional Variation in the Pattern of Maize Adoption and Use in Florida and Georgia," *American Antiquity* 63 (1998), 397–416.

archipelago. Residents mastered the various ecosystems on land and in the surrounding seas, where catching different maritime animals required adaptations in fishing techniques depending on the depth of the water and whether it was on the windward or leeward side of an island.[13]

Native oral history, a rich archaeological record, and written reports from the early period of European contact together reveal the complexities of Indigenous American communities before Europeans arrived. Those first Americans had no equivalent of the European printing press, but that did not impede long-distance communication. Those who lived near modern Narragansett Bay and Long Island Sound drilled holes in quahog shells and strung them together to make wampum, which moved from hand to hand, communicating messages from one community to another. Across the West, Natives recorded events and history with pictographs painted on animal skins or on the face of cliffs and petroglyphs carved into rocks. As many as 12,000 sites have rock art that predates the arrival of Europeans, with some dating back as far as 3000 BCE.[14] Hundreds of rock paintings, for example, can be found on islands in Minnesota's Lake of the Woods. "They refer to a spiritual geography," Louise Erdrich, an Ojibwe writer, has noted, "and are meant to provide teaching and dream guides to generations of Anishinaabeg." They provide visual clues to Ojibwemowin, "a language of memory, an oral language, passed on by community but not written."[15] As Kiowa scholar N. Scott Momaday observed, "The New World is ancient."[16]

While Europeans commented frequently that Indigenous peoples of North America had no writing, they understood that Americans' illiteracy was not a sign of ignorance. "The Gaspesians do not know how to read nor how to write," Recollect missionary Chrestien Le Clercq wrote in his

13. See Patrick V. Kirch, "When Did the Polynesians Settle Hawaii? A Review of 150 Years of Scholarly Inquiry and a Tentative Answer," *Hawaiian Archaeology* 12 (2011), 3–26; Kirch, *On the Road of the Winds*, 258–268; Patrick V. Kirch, *Feathered Gods and Fishhooks: An Introduction to Hawaiian Archaeology and Prehistory* (Honolulu: University of Hawai'i Press, 1997), 199–214; K. Ann Horsburgh and Mark D. McCoy, "Dispersal, Isolation, and Interaction in the Islands of Polynesia: A Critical Review of Archaeological and Genetic Evidence," *Diversity* 9, no. 3 (2017), 37; Timothy M. Rieth et al., "The 13th Century Polynesian Colonization of Hawai'i Island," *Journal of Archaeological Science* 38 (2011), 2740–2749.
14. Colin G. Calloway, *One Vast Winter Count: The Native American West Before Lewis and Clark* (Lincoln: University of Nebraska Press, 2003), 4–5.
15. Louise Erdrich, *Books and Islands in Ojibwe Country* (Washington, DC: National Geographic, 2003), quotations at 50 and 86.
16. N. Scott Momaday, "The Becoming of the Native: Man in America Before Columbus," in Alvin M. Josephy Jr., ed., *America in 1492: The World of the Indian Peoples Before the Arrival of Columbus* (New York: Alfred A. Knopf, 1992), 14.

history of the Mi'kmaqs (or Micmacs) in the 1670s. But, he added, they "have, nevertheless, enough understanding and memory to learn how to do both if only they were willing to give the necessary application." Much of their knowledge impressed him. As he and other Europeans learned, Indigenous scholars possessed accurate information about the movement of stars, especially constellations they called Mouhinne (Great Bear) and Mouhinchiche (Little Bear).[17]

The Mi'kmaqs' intellectual universe reflected their understanding of a specific place—the coastal ranges of the modern-day Maritime Provinces of Canada, including Newfoundland and Labrador, and the adjacent interior. Other places proved far more daunting to Europeans than these relatively temperate coasts. The Crees (or Omushkegos) who lived around James Bay inhabited an environment that many Europeans found difficult, yet they had lived in the region for at least a thousand years before Europeans arrived.[18] They succeeded by understanding how to predict changing seasons and to maximize available resources. Their year began in March, when the first bald eagle returned, so the Crees called the month Mekisseu-Apehem or Eagle Moon. There followed months named after other animal appearances or behavior—Goose Moon (Niscock-Apeshem) in April because the gray goose came then; Frog Moon (Atheak-Apeshem) in May when those reptiles started to croak, and so on. Other names of months commemorated geese's egg-laying time (May), young geese taking wing (August), the time when caribou lost their antlers (September), and the arrival of winter—from rivers freezing in November to severe cold in January.[19] Regional place-names likewise reflected an awareness of the physical world. Ki-chi-na-me-kos-ka-hi-gan means "the lake that has the largest lake trout" (and is still known as Big Trout Lake). Moo-zoo-ni-mi-nis-tic, also known as Moose Factory, translates as "a location plentiful in moose."

17. Chrestian Le Clercq, *New Relation of Gaspesia: With the Customs and Religion of the Gaspesian Indians*, trans. William F. Ganong (Toronto: Champlain Society, 1910), 125, 135. Farther south, in territory that never became the United States, there was a rich written tradition, not only in the khipu kept by Incan peoples but also detailed records produced by Mexica; see Camilla Townsend, *Fifth Sun: A New History of the Aztecs* (Oxford: Oxford University Press, 2019) and Camilla Townsend, *The Annals of Native America: How the Nahuas of Colonial Mexico Kept Their History Alive* (Oxford: Oxford University Press, 2016).

18. Crees, who continue to occupy territory stretching from Hudson and James Bays to the Rocky Mountains, have lived in the area for at least 1,500 years and perhaps as long as 5,000 years; see V. P. Lyntwyn, *Muskekowuck Athinuwick: Original People of the Great Swampy Land* (Winnipeg: University of Manitoba Press, 2002), 36–39; G. Whiteman, "The Impact of Economic Development in James Bay, Canada," *Organization and Environment* 17 (2004), 426.

19. Lyntwyn, *Muskekowuck Athinuwick*, 82.

One outcropping was called Peawanuk, or "flint," because of the presence of the stone there.[20] Cree dictionaries identify over fifty words relating to particular experiences of snow and less than a handful referring to farming.[21]

For the Crees, like every other community, language and custom reflected an elaborate set of specific rituals designed to maintain one's place in the world.[22] Rules needed to be obeyed throughout the hunt, not only in the preparatory stages. If hunters left blood on the snow, they would offend Ciiwetinsuu, the North Wind spirit who was believed to have control of the movements of animals hunted in the winter. To avoid infractions, hunters brushed clean snow on top of the blood. Further, since female animals killed in winter were often pregnant, Cree hunters developed specific rules for handling the remains of a victim's fetus. Hunters would peel off the fat of the mother's intestine and place it in the mouth of the fetus with the belief that the ritual would please the supernatural deities controlling the movement of game, which would in turn provide animals with fat on them in subsequent hunts.[23] Such vital knowledge remained alive from one generation to the next, shared by women and girls as well as men and boys.[24]

20. Louis Bird, *Telling Our Stories: Omushkego Legends and Histories from Hudson Bay* (Peterborough, ON: Broadview Press, 2005), 26–29.
21. A. Wolvengray, comp., *Nēhiyawēwin: Itwēwina: Cree: Words*, 2 vols. (Regina: University of Regina Press, 2001); E. Waugh, N. LeClaire, and G. Cardinal, eds., *Alberta Elders' Cree Dictionary* (Edmonton: University of Alberta Press, 1998); *Nehiyaw Masinahikan: Online Cree Dictionary*, www.creedictionary.com (accessed February 4, 2017).
22. See, e.g., J. M. Cooper, "The Northern Algonquian Supreme Being," *Primitive Man* 6 (1933), 46, 49, 52–57, 60–61; Adrian Tanner, *Bringing Home Animals: Religious Ideology and Mode of Production of the Mistassini Cree Hunters* (New York: St. Martin's Press, 1979), 108–135, 141–143; and cf. R. J. Preston, *Cree Narrative*, 2nd ed. (Montreal: McGill-Queen's University Press, 2002), 78–173.
23. Tanner, *Bringing Home Animals*, 146–147.
24. K. Ohmagari and F. Berkes, "Transmission of Indigenous Knowledge and Bush Skills Among the Western James Cree Women of Subarctic Canada," *Human Ecology* 25 (1997), 203, 206, 216–217; see also R. Brightman, *Grateful Prey: Rock Cree Human-Animal Relationships* (Berkeley: University of California Press, 1973). Ancient knowledge of local ecology provided benefits that continue to the present day; see M. Rapinski et al., "Adipogenic Activity of Wild Populations of *Rhododendron groenlandicum*, a Medicinal Shrub from the James Bay Cree Traditional Pharmacopeia," *Evidence-Based Complementary and Alternative Medicine*, 2015, art. 492458; A. Nachar et al., "The Action of Antidiabetic Plants of the Canadian James Bay Cree Traditional Pharmacopeia on Key Enzymes of Hepatic Glucose Homeostasis," *Evidence-Based Complementary and Alternative Medicine*, 2013, 189819.

By c. 1000 CE, Indigenous peoples across the Americas had developed economies based on utilizing local resources with culturally acceptable practices. Though there is no evidence of trade connecting Native Americans with peoples across either the Pacific Ocean or the Atlantic, goods moved far across the North American continent along well-established trade routes. Unlike the economic systems created by Europeans, this Native commerce likely consisted of a series of short-distance exchanges. Wampum made from shells native to Narragansett Bay and Long Island Sound spread across much of the interior to peoples who had no direct access to the Atlantic coast. In exchange, those who proffered wampum received goods to which they otherwise had no access, such as the hides of certain animals or stones used for decoration or as tools. Tribute systems facilitated the circulation of rare or prestige goods among Indigenous peoples.[25]

The first corn cobs arrived in the Southwest at least 4,000 years ago.[26] Unlike in the Valley of Mexico, where cultivation of the crop had led to a population explosion, maize had a more limited impact west of the 100th meridian because annual rainfall was typically only eleven to sixteen inches. Still, by c. 1000 CE, residents of Acoma and other Ancestral Puebloan communities developed irrigation systems that allowed for year-round occupation without the need to migrate in search of food. Acoma bore witness to the success of this Indigenous knowledge: built on top of a mesa that rises over 350 feet from the valley floor below, it has been continuously occupied since at least the fourteenth century and quite possibly much longer. To be sure, Southwestern irrigation systems were at times incapable of sustaining local communities, including those in Chaco Canyon, which likely collapsed in the twelfth century because of an inability to manage water in times of drought. But the people did not disappear. Instead, migrants from urban centers like Chaco dispersed, with some likely joining the mobile communities of bison hunters on the Plains.[27]

25. See Neal Salisbury, *Manitou and Providence: Indians, Europeans, and the Making of New England* (New York: Oxford University Press, 1982), 148–152; Christopher L. Miller and George R. Hammell, "A New Perspective on Indian-White Contact: Cultural Symbols and Colonial Trade," *JAH* 73 (1986), 311–328; Stephen R. Potter, *Commoners, Tribute, and Chiefs: The Development of Algonquian Culture in the Potomac Valley* (Charlottesville: University of Virginia Press, 1993), 17–18; Daniel K. Richter, "Tsenacommacah and the Atlantic World," in Peter C. Mancall, ed., *The Atlantic World and Virginia, 1550–1624* (Chapel Hill: University of North Carolina Press for the Omohundro Institute for Early American History and Culture, 2007), 29–65.

26. Rute R. da Fonseca, "The Origin and Evolution of Maize in the Southwestern United States," *Nature Plants: Letters*, January 8, 2015, 14003; Logan Kistler et al., "Multiproxy Evidence Highlights a Complex Evolutionary Legacy of Maize in South America," *Science* 362 (2018), 1309–1313.

27. Juliana Barr, "There's No Such Thing as 'Prehistory': What the Longue Durée of Caddo and Pueblo History Tells Us About Colonial America," *WMQ* 74 (2017), 203–240;

Acoma, seen here in a late nineteenth-century photograph, has existed on the top of a mesa since around 1200 CE, making it the longest-settled community within the territorial limits of the United States. Courtesy of the Huntington Library, San Marino, California.

People known now as Mississippians built Cahokia, the largest city in pre-contact North America (near modern-day East St. Louis, Illinois), on the table-flat lands near the confluence of the Mississippi and Missouri Rivers. The city had perhaps 10,000 people at its core and another 20,000 to 30,000 living nearby. Monk's Mound, the largest structure, took hundreds of thousands of hours of labor to construct, and the supplies for building it came from many miles away. Goods buried in graves suggest that there was a strict social and political hierarchy in the region and that its largest buildings may have been constructed by enslaved peoples. The presence of Cahokia-style ceramics in communities hundreds of miles distant places the city at the hub of an extensive trade network, which

Pekka Hämäläinen, "The Politics of Grass, European Expansion, Ecological Change, and Indigenous Power in the Southwest Borderlands," *WMQ* 67 (2010), 173–208; John A. McClelland, "Revisiting Hohokam Paleodemography," *American Antiquity* 80 (2015), 492–510; Alan H. Simmons, "New Evidence for the Early Use of Cultigens in the American Southwest," *American Antiquity* 51 (1986), 73–89; Edgar Proctor Hunt, *The Origin Myth of Acoma Pueblo*, ed. Peter Nabokov (New York: Penguin, 2015), xi–xvi; Lynne Sebastian, *The Chaco Anasazi: Sociopolitical Evolution in the Prehistoric Southwest* (Cambridge: Cambridge University Press, 1992), 138–141; Brian Fagan, *Chaco Canyon: Archaeologists Explore the Lives of an Ancient Society* (New York: Oxford University Press, 2005), 18–22.

moved goods from the northern plains and the Atlantic coast into the continent's interior. The presence in Cahokia's graves of executed women, many of them young, suggests that female captives were especially at risk in these centralized societies, where elites, their power maintained through their apparent connection to divine forces, determined who would be sacrificed in rituals. Bodily remains at Cahokia and other Mississippian ritual centers, with bones and teeth different from those of elite members found in elaborate graves such as Moundville, suggest that these were captives taken in war in other places.[28]

Cahokia thrived for perhaps 200 to 300 years. But a series of devastating droughts parched its once-fertile fields in the middle decades of the thirteenth century. Then sometime around 1250 a mega-storm dumped too much water for the earth to contain, washing away the remains of countless fields. Together, these climatic events made it more difficult to sustain a large population, and the residents of Cahokia dispersed.[29] Like the great cities of Mesoamerica (such as Tenochtitlán, Chichén Itza, and Palenque), Cahokia blossomed because those in control of the city organized enormous expenditures of labor to sustain it for over two centuries. But its most important legacy was providing a model for the long-term benefits of maize cultivation.

Many émigrés from Cahokia traveled to the south and east as well as to the west. By 1400, Etzanoa, a cluster of related villages on the border of modern Kansas and Arkansas, housed up to 20,000 maize-growing people. Living in more dispersed communities and with no apparent desire to build the large mounds that formed the visual heart of Cahokia, they never had the labor demands a ruling elite had imposed on others. Rather than disappearing, these Mississippians formed the origins of the modern Wichita nation.[30]

The rulers of Cahokia likely relied on enslaved labor to build the city's mounds, but the institution of forced bondage existed in parts of the continent even where there were no major public works. Enslavement of

28. T. R. Pauketat, *Ancient Cahokia and the Mississippians* (Cambridge: Cambridge University Press, 2004); Christina Snyder, *Slavery in Indian Country: The Changing Face of Captivity in Early America* (Cambridge, MA: Harvard University Press, 2010), 14–28; Thomas E. Anderson, *Cahokia and the Archaeology of Power* (Tuscaloosa: University of Alabama Press, 1997).

29. A. J. White et al., "Fecal Stanols Show Simultaneous Flooding and Seasonal Precipitation Change Correlate with Cahokia's Population Decline," *Proceedings of the National Academy of Sciences* 116 (2019), 5461–5466.

30. M. R. Balthus et al., "Diasporic Connections: Cahokia and the Greater Southeast," *Journal of Archaeological Method Theory* 27 (2020), 1–6; Donald J. Blakeslee, "The Miguel Map Revisited," *Plains Anthropologist* 63 (2018), 67–84.

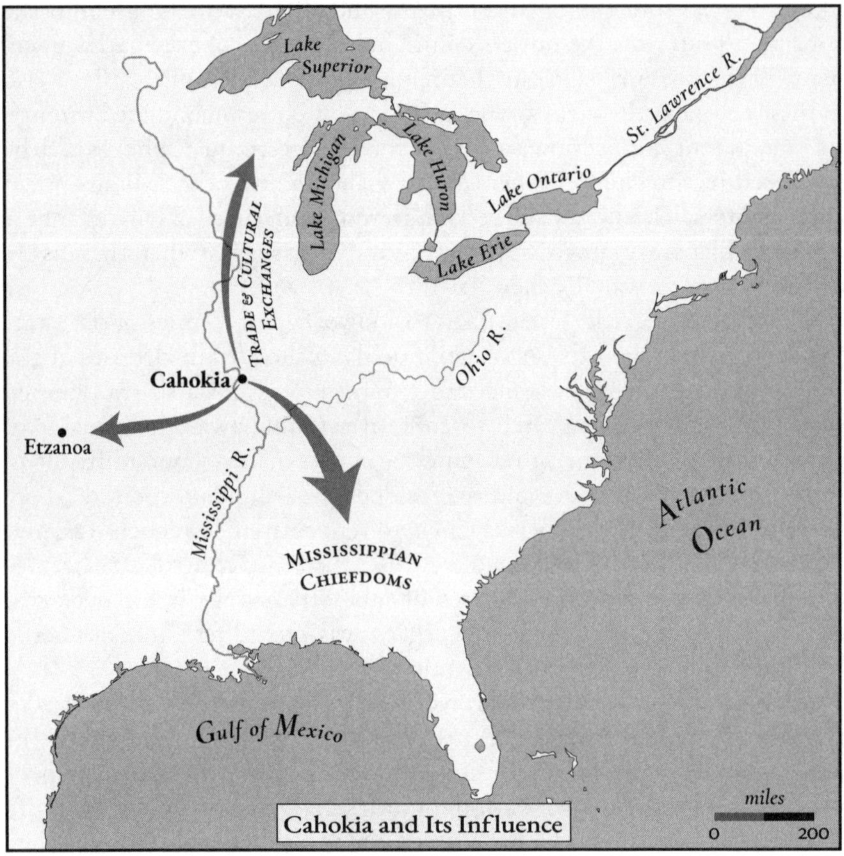

Cahokia and Its Influence

war captives was a common practice in the Great Lakes and northern Midwest. The area, later called the Pays d'en Haut by French colonizers, was home to clusters of Indigenous peoples who spoke related Algonquian languages: Cree-Monsoni-Assiniboine, Fox-Sauk-Kickapoo, Miami-Illinois, Ojibwa-Ottawa-Potawatomi, and Sioux. Despite language variations, these peoples saw the utility of capturing, keeping, and trading enslaved prisoners.[31]

Enslavement across the Pays d'en Haut was about power, not productivity. Communities developed specific rituals associated with taking captives, often subjecting victims to physical suffering while deciding

31. Brett Rushforth, *Bonds of Alliance: Indigenous and Atlantic Slaveries in New France* (Chapel Hill: University of North Carolina Press for the Omohundro Institute of Early American History and Culture, 2012), 20–23.

whether to execute them or force them into subordinate status. Captors sometimes marked captives by biting off part of their ears or nose or burning them with spears. They stripped their prisoners. They made them sing before coming into town to erase their former culture and make them more suitable to be enslaved. Sometimes a captive became an adoptive member of a family to replace a lost child, though likely without the sentimental attachment. Linguistic practices confirmed the association of captivity and enslavement with property and power. *Awakaan* was an Anishinaabe term for both "captive" and "dog." A seventeenth-century Jesuit who had spent enough time in the region to produce an 800-page dictionary explained that the Anishinaabe term *nit'aouakara* meant both "I make him my slave" and "I make him my dog." Ottawas spoke of *nit'aouakan* and Illinois of *nitaïa*—each meaning either "my dog" or "my slave." Before heading into combat, Sioux and Illinois men sang about their intent to bring enslaved captives back with them. As property, the enslaved could also be traded, as many were in diplomatic meetings across the Pays d'en Haut. But unlike forms of bondage that Europeans practiced, the status of being enslaved did not pass to any children they might bear.[32]

After Cahokia's fall, new economic practices evolved, especially east of the Mississippi River. Over time, with their population growing, these agriculturalists formed new groups such as the Choctaws.[33] Maize spread into the Northeast as well. South of the Kennebec-Saco watershed, maize, beans, and squash became common among Algonquian- and Iroquoian-speaking peoples. Like others who relied on farming, they needed to determine the optimal time to put seeds in the ground. Well before 1450, women and men studied the movement of the Pleiades. When the constellation reached a designated point, they knew it was likely past the time for any new frosts.[34] Communities gathered in the spring, with men typically clearing fields and women planting seeds. During the following months, women tended to the crops while men fished, hunted, or gathered supplies for their houses. After the autumn harvest, communities tended to disperse, leaving few if any people behind at the farming site. From November to April, family groups inhabited smaller communities, with men hunting, a practice made easier when

32. Rushforth, *Bonds of Alliance*, 15–71.
33. Patricia Galloway, *Choctaw Genesis, 1500–1700* (Lincoln: University of Nebraska Press, 1998).
34. Lynn Ceci, "Watchers of the Pleiades: Ethnoastronomy Among Native Cultivators in Northeastern North America," *Ethnohistory* 25 (1978), 301–317.

deer and fur-bearing animals left their footprints in the snow and hunters developed snowshoes to track them.[35]

The Cahokian experience demonstrated that the production of maize allowed Indigenous communities to store food efficiently and diversify their economies. In many towns, women boiled freshly picked corn in large ceramic pots, many of them also likely produced by female artisans. Dried kernels could be ground and turned into bread, or treated with lye to make what European colonists came to call hominy. Across the maize-growing areas women wove plant fibers into baskets, an often time-consuming task vital for the living and, based on intricate textiles in graves, for the dead to be able to continue productive work in the next life.[36] They also made pots to store grain, often carving or painting them with patterns that signified relations or a local community. Those who possessed surpluses could trade with those who were unable to plant or uninterested in doing so. Men supplemented women's agricultural work by hunting and fishing. Protein harvested from forests, rivers, and coastlines enriched Indigenous maize-based diets, perhaps accounting for a phenomenon that many European visitors noticed in the sixteenth century: Native Americans, especially in eastern North America, tended to have larger bodies than Europeans.[37]

After the dispersal of Cahokia, the heirs of the Mississippians tended to create smaller communities, with a chiefly elite dominating local politics. Chiefdoms typically had a central town and outlying satellite settle-

35. See, e.g., Daniel K. Richter, *The Ordeal of the Longhouse: The Peoples of the Iroquois League in the Era of European Colonization* (Chapel Hill: University of North Carolina Press/Institute for Early American History and Culture, 1992), 13–29; Peter C. Mancall, *Valley of Opportunity: Economic Culture Along the Upper Susquehanna, 1700–1800* (Ithaca, NY: Cornell University Press, 1991), 27–46; Thomas M. Wickman, *Snowshoe Country: An Environmental and Cultural History of Winter in the Early American Northeast* (Cambridge: Cambridge University Press, 2018).
36. Penelope P. Drooker, "The Fabric of Power: Textiles in Mississippian Politics and Ritual," in Gregory A. Waselkov and Marvin T. Smith, eds., *Forging Southeastern Identities: Social Archaeology, Ethnohistory, and Folklore of the Mississippian to Early Historic South* (Tuscaloosa: University of Alabama Press, 2017), 16–40. Algonquian-speaking peoples referred to hominy as *sagamite* or *rockahomonie*; Mexica called it *atole*; Choctaws called it *tafala*. See Betty Fussell, *The Story of Corn* (New York: Alfred Knopf, 1992), 195–200.
37. For Indigenous lifeways after the dispersal of Cahokia, see Robbie Ethridge, "Navigating the Mississippian World: Infrastructure in the Sixteenth-Century Native South," in Waselkov and Smith, eds., *Forging Southeastern Identities*, 62–84; on body sizes, see Richard H. Steckel and Jerome C. Rose, "Native Americans in North America," in Richard H. Steckel and Jerome C. Rose, eds., *The Backbone of History: Health and Nutrition in the Western Hemisphere* (Cambridge: Cambridge University Press, 2002), 403–405.

ments. While tensions existed between dispersed chiefdoms, actual violence tended to be relatively small-scale, likely because prevailing juridical customs often emphasized the importance of reconciliation rather than revenge, a notion of justice that could also be found in other parts of the Americas.[38]

Still, communities did war against each other. Victors often took captives, whom they put through a series of ritual tests and beatings. Captors often killed adult men, more commonly enslaved women, and adopted children. Although the Mississippian world was just as riven with hostilities as much of Europe at the time, the scale of conflict minimized casualties. Alliances formed between chiefdoms allowed political elites to gather hundreds of fighters to battle a common enemy, though normally warfare did not produce large numbers of casualties. Though the Southeast became a meeting ground for individuals from Algonquian, Caddoan, Iroquoian, Muskogean, Timucuan, and Siouan language families, individuals found ways to communicate across linguistic barriers. Generations of contact had enabled groups to learn new technologies from others, including the best ways to burn out the inside of a large tree to make a canoe, the ubiquitous and durable watercraft of the Mississippi Valley and the Southeast.[39]

The dynamism evident in eastern North America after the dispersal of Cahokia could be seen elsewhere too. Farther west, Native peoples created trade routes that reached from the islands off the shore of southern California to the Colorado basin. Traders exchanged acorns, seeds, pine nuts, and yucca for artisan-produced baskets and cotton. Maize growers traded for deerskins. Crucially, Indigenous peoples in the Southwest adapted to environmental change that reached across the region in the last decades of the fifteenth century and prompted migrations from the once livable shorelines of Lake Cahuilla (straddling the present-day California-Mexico border) toward the Colorado basin. These migrations altered regional trade patterns. Mojaves adapted pottery techniques employed by Maricopas and stored acorns and beans in gourds that had come from Quechans. Tongva and Chumash from present-day California brought beads made from shells of mollusks in the genus *Olivella*, to

38. See, e.g., Nicole Eustace, *Covered with Night: A Story of Murder and Justice in Early America* (New York: Norton/Liveright, 2021).

39. See Snyder, *Slavery in Indian Country*, 13–45; Wayne E. Lee, *The Cutting-Off Way: Indigenous Warfare in Eastern North America, 1500–1800* (Chapel Hill: University of North Carolina Press, 2023); James M. Crawford, *The Mobilian Trade Language* (Knoxville: University of Tennessee Press, 1978); Peter H. Wood, "Missing the Boat: Ancient Dugout Canoes in the Mississippi-Missouri Watershed," *Early American Studies* 16 (2018), 197–254.

Akimel O'odham, Hopis, and Zuñis in the Colorado basin, who in turn wove cotton textiles they shipped westward. Within dispersed communities only certain people produced goods for export. Women dominated the production of baskets, with a skilled artisan producing six each year. A village that might have 100 to 300 residents could afford to trade 150 to 450 baskets a year, virtually all of them bearing the distinctive style of their creator. Aesthetic ideas traveled Native roads and trails. So did news of travelers, especially if they looked different from or acted differently than those who long inhabited the region.[40]

Europeans who later described Indigenous economic practices in eastern North America tended to believe that they had always existed, not recognizing that it was the arrival of maize in the thirteenth or fourteenth century that had enabled the spread of farms, encouraged population growth, and reshaped the landscape to make it seem more familiar to those who crossed the Atlantic. By 1450, mixed agriculture/hunting economies in eastern North America were old, but they were not ancient. Indigenous names often referred to localized resources, some presumably predating the arrival of maize, providing speakers with a map that provided guidance throughout the year to well-known places with defined, if unmarked, borders.[41]

At approximately the same time that farmers carried the first cobs into the Mississippi Valley, some Europeans were also expanding their horizons and moving into new territories. Among the most avid of these migrants were the Norse, who descended from their Scandinavian homeland into Britain and Ireland at the end of the eighth century. In 787, an English scribe reported that the "first three ships of the Northmen from the land of robbers" arrived. A local sheriff mounted his horse to meet them, planning to bring them to the king. The newcomers murdered him. "These were," the annalist wrote, "the first ships of the Danish men that sought the land of the English nation." Observers recoiled in horror when Norse invaders created "lamentable havoc," as one put it in 793, "by rapine and slaughter."[42] "Never before has such terror appeared in Britain as we have now suffered from a pagan race," Alcuin of York wrote to

40. Zappia, *Traders and Raiders*, 7 (range of trade goods), 25–26 (languages), 29–30 (trade fairs), 31 (Mojave trade), 38–47 (*olivella*, baskets).

41. William Cronon, *Changes in the Land: Indians, Colonists, and the Ecology of New England* (New York: Hill and Wang, 1983), 19–53; Salisbury, "Indians' Old World," 435–458; Kathleen Bragdon, *Native Peoples of Southern New England, 1500–1650* (Norman: University of Oklahoma Press, 1999), 89; Renée Fossett, "Mapping Inuktut: Inuit Views of the Real World," in Jennifer S. H. Brown and Elizabeth Vibert, eds., *Reading Beyond Words: Contexts for Native History* (Peterborough, ON: Broadview Press, 1996), 74–94.

42. "The Anglo-Saxon Chronicle: Eighth Century," Avalon, years 787, 793.

Ethelred, the king of Northumbria, after the Norse attack on the monastery at Lindisfarne, the "Holy Island" off the Northumberland coast. The invaders splattered the church of St. Cuthbert "with the blood of the priests of God, despoiled of all its ornaments; a place more venerable than all in Britain is given as prey to pagan peoples."[43] In 794 an annalist in Ulster reported "devastation of all the islands of Britain by heathens," while others wrote about attacks across Britain and Ireland, including the destruction of monasteries.[44]

These Norse invaders came from a culture with long exposure to other peoples. As early as the ninth century Norse fur traders had contacted Saamis (or Sámi), the Indigenous peoples of the far north, whom English scholars often referred to as Lapps or Laplanders. Christian missionaries who arrived in the region recognized the numinous powers of Saami shrines and built churches on top of them, a strategy that clerics had used in other European Christian frontiers.[45] Norse merchants purchased walrus ivory and walrus hides (the latter ideal for making ship's ropes) from these northern neighbors, integrating them into a commercial system that stretched as far south as the Arabic Caliphate.[46] An eastern trade route ran from modern Finland through Sweden and deep into Russia. Norse traders acquired a bronze statue of the Buddha from northern India, beads from the Middle East, and thousands of coins minted by Anglo-Saxons, Germans, or Islamic peoples. The Norse saw their neighbors as potential trade partners, not their territory as a likely region for colonization.[47]

43. Alcuin to Ethelred, after June 8, 793, in Dorothy Whitelock, ed., *English Historical Documents c. 500–1042*, 2nd ed. (New York: Oxford University Press, 1979), 842–844, quotation at 842.

44. "Anglo-Saxon Chronicle," year 794; see also Seán Mac Air and Gearóid Mac Niocaill, eds., *The Annals of Ulster (to A.D. 1131), Part I: Text and Translation* (Dublin: Dublin Institute for Advanced Studies, 1983), 251–253 (years 794–798), 263 (807), 267 (811), 269 (813), 277 (821), 281 (823–824), 283 (825).

45. Noel Broadbent, *Lapps and Labyrinths: Saami Prehistory, Colonization, and Cultural Resilience* (Washington, DC: Smithsonian Institution Press, 2010), 159, 30, 163, 4, 177, 211–215, 213.

46. *Ohthere's Voyages: A Late 9th-Century Account of Voyages Along the Coasts of Norway and Denmark and Its Cultural Context*, ed. Janet Bately and Anton Englert (Roskilde, Norway: Viking Ship Museum, 2007), 46; *Two Voyagers at the Court of King Alfred*, trans. Christine E. Fell (York: William Sessions, 1984), 43–54; Anders Winroth, *The Age of the Vikings* (Princeton, NJ: Princeton University Press, 2014), 112–113; Berte Philippsen et al., "Single-Year Radiocarbon Dating Anchors Viking Age Trade Cycles in Time," *Nature* 601 (2022), 392–395.

47. Torstein Edgren, "The Eastern Route: Finland in the Viking Age," in William W. Fitzhugh and Elisabeth I. Ward, eds., *Vikings: The North Atlantic Saga* (Washington, DC: Smithsonian Institution Press, 2000), 103–115.

In Ireland, the Norse chose to remain as settlers. During their conquering raids, Norse hauled off treasures. Staying put required a different strategy. They set up a *longphort* or harbor at Dublin, which they maintained until at least the start of the twelfth century. Norse migrants traveled down the east coast of Ireland, establishing communities at Wexford and Waterford. By the late ninth century, they had also colonized the Orkney Islands, the Hebrides, territory stretching from Northumbria through East Anglia, and the west coast of Scotland and England, forcing conquered peoples to live under the Danelaw. The Norse erected fortified towns at Leicester, Lincoln, and Nottingham. By the time Anglo-Normans crossed the Irish Sea in 1166, the Norse had become integrated into Irish society.[48]

But the Norse era of long-distance travel and colonization did not end on Irish shores. By the end of the ninth century CE, some Norse began to explore the North Atlantic. Yet when they contemplated new journeys to the west, they realized the dangers they faced. They were too far north to use the North Star to guide them, which meant that celestial observation provided little information. Everyone who sailed into the open ocean feared what they called *hafvilla*, the loss of all sense of direction at sea, which would lead to death. The Norse were brave, but they were seeking better lives, not a path to Helgafjell, a sacred mountain where the souls of the dead migrated, or Valhalla, the storied realm in the skies where warriors prepared for a final battle.[49] Still, some hardy souls among them overcame any anxiety and reached Iceland before the turn of the first Christian millennium, clearing aboriginal forests that have yet to regrow to their earlier size.[50] Rather than sail to the south and across potentially warmer seas, the Norse instead moved westward from one coastline to another: from Iceland to the east coast of Greenland, and then around the peninsula and across the modern Davis Strait to Nunavut. They kept land in sight as they sailed southward, first to Labrador and then across the relatively small water gap to Newfoundland.

48. Colleen E. Batey and John Sheehan, "Viking Expansion and Cultural Blending in Britain and Ireland," in Fitzhugh and Ward, eds., *Vikings*, 127–141.
49. See Crosby, *Ecological Imperialism*, 50–57.
50. On the long-term ecological impacts of the Norse in Iceland, see Kevin P. Smith, "Landnám: The Settlement of Iceland in Archaeological and Historical Perspective," *World Archaeology* 26 (1995), 319–347; Ian Y. Ashworth and Edgar Jackson, "Sagas as Evidence of Early Deforestation in Iceland," *Canadian Geographer* 14 (1970), 158–166; Henry Fountain, "Vikings Razed the Forests. Can Iceland Regrow Them?," *New York Times*, October 20, 2017. While most Norse who lived on Greenland scavenged driftwood for their needs, wealthier households obtained wood from Europe and North America, another sign of early ecological change; see Lísabet Guðmundsdóttir, "Timber Imports to Norse Greenland: Lifeline or Luxury?," *Antiquity* 97 (2023), 454–471.

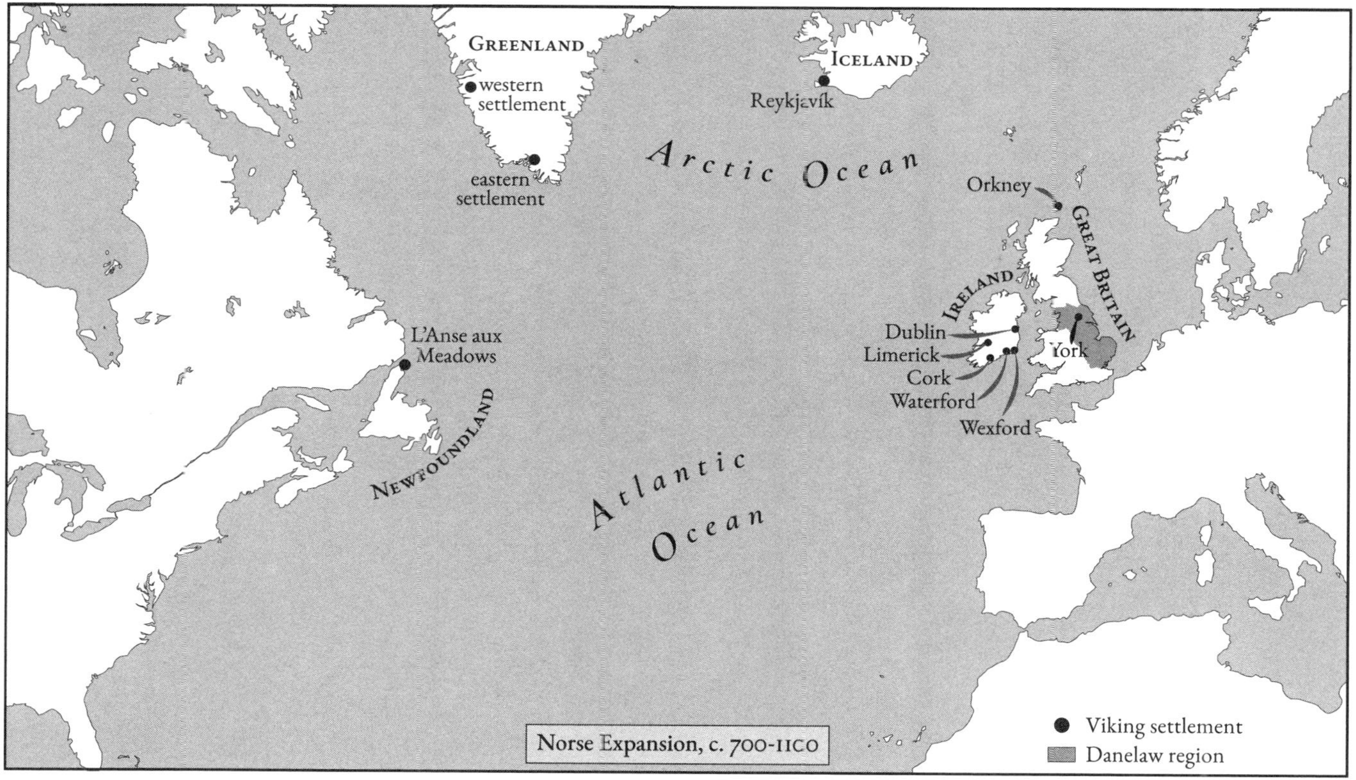

Norse Expansion, c. 700-1100

The earliest written record of Norse reaching North America survives in a late eleventh-century manuscript by a German cleric known as Adam of Bremen, who revealed how Europeans centuries before Columbus integrated information about distant places into their knowledge of the world. Like other scholars, Adam had read classical literature, including works by Solinus, Sallust, and Virgil, all of whom had offered their readers a view of the world beyond Europe's borders. From such works he concluded that Amazons—women warriors who supposedly sliced off one breast so they could launch their arrows more effectively—roamed the earth, as did dog-headed people (known as cynocephali) and cannibals (anthropophagi). He was not alone. Writers described alleged human and quasi-human beings residing at the edges of the known world, often inhabiting territories just beyond the reach of Europeans.[51]

Adam gathered a great deal of knowledge about the North Atlantic. "Beyond Norway," he wrote, "which is the farthermost northern country, you will find no human habitation, nothing but ocean, terrible to look upon and limitless, encircling the whole world." He described the Orkneys and an island once called "Thule." "This Thule is now called Iceland," he noted, "from the ice which binds the ocean." Even by this time there were already substantial populations of humans and livestock there, but no agriculture. The archbishop of Bremen appointed a priest to carry his views to the residents of this distant outpost.[52]

Beyond Iceland lay Greenland, perhaps a week's sailing distance. "The people there," Adam wrote, "are greenish from the salt water, whence, too, that region gets its name." They were formidable, prone to launch attacks on passing ships. There were other islands as well, including what he called "Helgeland," likely a part of northern Norway but possibly a

51. Adam, a tireless chronicler, had arrived in Bremen between May 1066 and April 1067 but did not complete his book, the *Gesta Hammaburgensis ecclesiae pontificum*, for at least fourteen years. Once it was complete, other scribes copied it, though the surviving texts do not match in all details. For biographical details, see Adam of Bremen, *History of the Archbishops of Hamburg-Bremen*, trans. Francis J. Tschan (New York: Columbia University Press, 1959), xiii–xvi. Despite similarities between what Adam wrote and accounts by later chroniclers of the world beyond Europe's boundaries, there is no evidence that Columbus had ever heard of him. For the larger intellectual context in which Adam worked, see Rudolf Wittkower, "Marvels of the East: A Study in the History of Monsters," *Journal of the Warburg and Courtauld Institutes* 5 (1941), 159–157; Carolyn Walker Bynum, "Wonder," *AHR* 102 (1997), 1–17; Robert Bartlett, *The Natural and the Supernatural in the Middle Ages* (Cambridge: Cambridge University Press, 2008), 94–110; Konrad [of Megenberg], [*Buch de Nature*], [Augsburg, 1475], HEH 85861; James S. Romm, *The Edges of the Earth in Ancient Thought: Geography, Exploration, and Fiction* (Princeton, NJ: Princeton University Press, 1992).

52. Adam of Bremen, *History of the Archbishops*, 215–218.

reference to Helluland, perhaps modern Baffin Island. Adam reported that the people who knew this place were amazed by the endless day of the summer solstice and the darkness of the winter, which residents attributed to supernatural forces.[53]

Adam wrote too about a place he knew as Vinland, where Danish travelers claimed to have seen wild vines that could produce wine. But his informants, including a Danish king, offered no information about territory farther west. According to the king, "no habitable land is found in that ocean" beyond that island, because "every place beyond it is full of impenetrable ice and intense darkness," a report that echoed that of fifth-century encyclopedist Martianus Capella, who had written that "the sea is congealed after one day's navigation." Adam added that Prince Harold of Norway had tried to sail into those waters but turned back when he eyed "the darksome bounds of a failing world." He retraced his route home, escaping "the vast pit of the abyss."[54]

In the decades after Adam's passing, information about North America circulated in sagas, a genre that blended history, folklore, and myth. The late twelfth-century *Grœndlinga Saga* included the claim that a Norse explorer named Bjarni Herjolfsson had seen Vinland around the turn of the first Christian millennium. As was common practice at a time when only a small percentage of any European population could read (and fewer still could write), information circulated orally. So, it is no surprise that Herjolfsson told others what he had seen, and they spread news even farther. Other witnesses appeared as well, including a Norseman from Iceland named Audun whose adventures took him across the North Atlantic, from Greenland to Denmark. Audun came home with a polar bear, likely the first creature from the Western Hemisphere to arrive in Europe, which he gave to the Danish king in the mid- to late eleventh century.[55]

53. Adam of Bremen, *History of the Archbishops*, 218–219.
54. Adam of Bremen, *History of the Archbishops*, 219–220.
55. *The Vinland Sagas*, trans. Magnus Magnusson and Hermann Pálsson (Harmondsworth, Middlesex: Penguin Classics, 1965), 25. The *Grœndlinga Saga* circulated for almost two hundred years before a scribe memorialized it on vellum in Iceland at some point between 1382 and 1395. The book was in the hands of a farming family for hundreds of years, then in the possession of the king of Denmark, and since the seventeenth century it has been in the Royal Library in Copenhagen. See *Vinland Sagas*, 29–30, 32. That polar bear was only one non-European animal to arrive home with an explorer. Fauna from across the Old World had appeared earlier in western Europe, as even Shakespeare knew; see *Romeo and Juliet*, act V, scene 1, ll. 42–43. Elsewhere, an Egyptian crocodile hung from the rafters of the cathedral in Seville beginning in 1260 and Pope Leo X kept a menagerie at the Vatican in the early sixteenth century. The crocodile eventually deteriorated; a wooden replica hangs there now. See Lorraine Daston and

Sometime around 1127, an Iceland-born historian named Ari Thorgilsson attributed the success of the early settlements in Greenland to Erik Thorvaldsson (known as Erik the Red), noting that the Norse explorer and his companions found old kayaks on the eastern and western shorelines along with stone tools. The evidence led him to conclude that "the people who had been there before were of the same kind as those who inhabit Vinland and whom the Greenlanders call Skraelings." In the words of modern translators, the closest meaning would be "wretch," or perhaps "savage."[56] That act of naming signified much about how the Norse would view their colonization of the North Atlantic.

More than likely, the "Skraelings" were Beothuks, an Indigenous people whose culture developed in Newfoundland long before any European arrived. Native peoples had lived in the region for perhaps four millennia before any *knörr* (Norse merchant ship) arrived. The oldest human-made remains in the region date from about 3000 BCE. These little-known Native peoples earlier lived in coastal Labrador and then migrated across the relatively narrow Strait of Belle Isle. From there they moved south along the coast, developing an economy based on harvesting local sea mammals, primarily small whales, porpoises, and walrus. They crafted harpoons to kill seals and fish, which they also captured with nets. Stone axes suggest that they sometimes moved inland and used local trees for fuel and housing. Graves along the west coast of the northern peninsula of Newfoundland contain tools fashioned from antlers and bone. The archaeological record suggests that these people either left Newfoundland or for an unknown reason disappeared by about 1050 BCE. In the years that followed, other groups migrated from the north. The physical remains of their settlements suggest that they were Inuit whose material practices reflected traditions that existed earlier in Labrador. This population reached its peak between 250 and 500 CE but disappeared by 950. A third northern group, known as Thule Eskimo, later migrated southward, well after the arrival of the Norse. By then Newfoundland had become home to Native peoples from other regions too, likely attracted to a region where they could fish and hunt caribou. They buried family members

Katherine Park, *Wonders and the Order of Nature, 1150–1750* (New York: Zone Books, 1998), 84; Silvio A. Bedoni, *The Pope's Elephant* (Manchester, UK: Carcanet, 1997); Spencer J. Weinreich, "Thinking with Crocodiles: An Iconic Animal at the Intersection of Early-Modern Religion and Natural Philosophy," *Early Science and Medicine* 20 (2015), 209–240 (with reference to *Romeo and Juliet* at 227n70).

56. *Vinland Sagas*, 26–27. Some scholars believe the term has never been properly translated, though all seem to agree that it was a pejorative; see Winroth, *Age of the Vikings*, 68.

with goods including red ochre, an effigy of a whale carved in stone, and bone pendants, so the dead could thrive in the next realm.[57]

The Beothuks and the Norse likely met in the opening years of the eleventh century when a Norseman named Leif, the son of Erik the Red, outfitted a *knörr* in Greenland and sailed westward. The ship, which was probably around fifty feet long, carried a crew of thirty-five, including a German named Tyrkir. The saga reported that the *knörr* landed along the coastline of the territory the Norse had spotted earlier. "There was no grass to be seen," the saga noted, "and the hinterland was covered with great glaciers." Between the ocean and the glaciers was nothing but rock. Deeming this a "worthless country," they continued their way. Before they left they named the place Helluland—"slab land"—reflecting the dominant feature of the landscape; foxes could be found, but the visitors saw no other animals. They sailed south by southwest and soon arrived at modern-day Labrador. The sailors were impressed by the dense woods and an environment more inviting than what they had seen before, including white sandy beaches and gentle slopes. They called this place Markland, or "Forest-Land."[58]

It was more inviting than Helluland, but not welcoming enough for them to stay. The Norse set off again. Within two days they spotted modern Newfoundland. From first sight this seemed more promising, even its morning dew. "The first thing they did," the saga noted, "was to get some of it on their hands and put it to their lips, and to them it seemed the sweetest thing they had ever tasted." After figuring out how to protect their boat in a region with the world's largest tidal shifts, they decided to remain for the winter. The biggest salmon that any of them had ever seen

57. Ingeborg Marshall, *A History and Ethnography of the Beothuk* (Montreal: McGill-Queen's University Press, 1996), 254–263; see also James A. Tuck, "European-Native Contacts in the Strait of Belle Isle, Labrador," in Louwrens Hacquebord and Richard Vaughan, eds., *Between Greenland and America: Cross Cultural Contacts and the Environment in the Baffin Bay Area* (Groningen: Arctic Center, University of Groningen, 1987); Douglas T. Robbins, "'Newfoundland Dorset' Culture?," in *Paleo-Eskimo Cultures in Newfoundland, Labrador and Ungava*, Reports in Archaeology 1 (St. John's: Memorial University of Newfoundland, 1986), 119–124; Frank G. Speck, *Beothuk and Micmac*, Indian Notes and Monographs 22 (New York: Museum of the American Indian/Heye Foundation, 1922); for reliance on marine resources in the Northwest Atlantic, see Matthew R. Bahar, *Storm of the Sea: Indians and Empires in the Atlantic's Age of Sail* (New York: Oxford University Press, 2019), 31.

58. *Vinland Sagas*, 54–55, 94. On the timing of the arrival, see Margot Kultems et al., "Evidence for European Presence in the Americas in AD 1021," *Nature* 601 (2022), 388–390.

ran up the stream, providing them with a constant source of protein. They brought livestock with them, which prospered on the rich grasses growing near the shoreline. Employing strategies that they brought from home, they constructed walls using stone and turf, which they likely covered with tarps. Soon they set about exploring the land, leaving about one-half of the sailors at their camp.[59]

All went well until Tyrkir disappeared. Leif took his possible loss hard since he had a family connection with the German. But soon enough Tyrkir returned from the woods, babbling and "rolling his eyes in all directions and pulling faces, and no one could understand what he was saying." He finally calmed down and told them he had found grapevines. Leif named the place Vinland (or Vineland) "after its natural qualities." It was in the months that followed that the Norse likely established a community at L'Anse aux Meadows, at the northernmost point of modern Newfoundland. There they learned of the region's other abundant resources, including flocks of eider ducks so thick on the ground that it proved hard to walk without crushing eggs. "It is beautiful here," one announced. "Here I should like to make my home."[60]

When some of the Norse returned after a winter exploring the territory, they discovered three kayaks pulled up on the shoreline, each providing shelter to three men. Without any recorded reason, the Norse attacked. They caught and murdered eight of the nine, while the other paddled off. Soon the main group of Norse realized that many kayaks were coming their way. But rather than fight, these Natives looked to trade. The Natives wanted metal weapons, but the Norse only offered red cloth in exchange for animal skins. Commerce continued until the visitors had nothing left to sell.[61]

The next time the locals arrived things went less well. According to one saga, the Beothuks shot arrows at the intruders. The Natives killed one, but his death did not drive the Norse away. Instead, they remained for another winter. With spring came the ripening of the grapes. The Norse gathered what they could and set off to Greenland to tell what had happened.[62]

In the years that followed, other Norse sailed across the North Atlantic toward Vinland. Surviving documents at times blend the fabulous with the mundane, including one instance in which a dead man spoke to his

59. *Vinland Sagas*, 56.
60. *Vinland Sagas*, 56–60, 95.
61. *Vinland Sagas*, 60, 99.
62. *Vinland Sagas*, 60–61. According to Erik's saga, Thorvald was struck in the groin by an arrow shot by a uniped, a creature embedded in Norse mythology; see *Vinland Sagas*, 102.

wife and another in which a Norse woman believed she had spoken to a Native woman in Vinland who then disappeared. Scattered from place to place are reports about encounters with Indigenous Americans. One part of the *Grændliga Saga* describes a journey by sixty men and five women from Norway to Vinland. This crew brought livestock with them, including a bull, and "intended to make a permanent settlement there if possible." The unfenced livestock found abundant grass to eat and "soon the male beasts became very frisky and difficult to manage." Violence between Indigenous and Europeans percolated through the sagas. During an encounter in Markland the Norse kidnapped two boys. They taught them their language and baptized them.[63]

At some point in the twelfth or thirteenth century, the Norse gave up their desire to maintain a settlement at Vinland. Why? The Norse believed that each colony they established was dependent on the place that sent migrants. By this logic, Iceland survived because it continued to serve needs for the Norse at home, though environmental changes produced by deforestation might have limited Norse interest in going there. Greenland persisted, in part because the Norse were able to grow enough fodder to feed the cattle they brought there. They also did not have to travel far from their two settlements to hunt walrus, whose tusks and hides found ready markets at home. But the Norse presence became precarious with the onset of the Little Ice Age in the thirteenth century; this period ended the climatic regime known as the "little optimum," which had begun in the mid-tenth century and warmed waters and thawed fjords that had previously been impassable. By the fourteenth century Greenland became colder than at any time in the previous millennium. Chillier times shortened the growing season and made it more difficult to bring in food for cattle. By then the colonists had likely also overhunted nearby walrus, so they had to travel farther to find the animals, an added risk in a changing climate. When the waters cooled, Norse routes to Vinland became more difficult. By 1500, they had abandoned Greenland.[64]

In the mid-fourteenth century the Black Death hit Europe, killing perhaps one-third of the population. In the northern reaches of the continent, and especially in Iceland, the death rate was even higher since human communities relied on livestock, and the plague reduced the number of people who could tend to animals. As a result, famine followed pestilence in these colder areas. While it is conceivable that the Norse might still have

63. *Vinland Sagas*, 63–67, 100–103.

64. Eleanor Barraclough, *Embers of the Hands: Hidden Histories of the Viking Age* (New York: W. W. Norton, 2024), 103–105, 208–211, 217–219; Crosby, *Ecological Imperialism*, 54.

maintained Vinland had they had sufficient economic motivation, the lure of its woods, vines, and fish diminished when Europeans gained access to other areas. Other Europeans discovered the cod-rich shores of North America and soon undermined the Norse market. Vinland could never escape its dependence on Greenland, which at its height had between 1,500 and 6,000 Norse. After the mid-fourteenth century, there were not enough voyages from Norway to Iceland or from Iceland to Greenland to sustain the two primary settlements there. In the end, Vinland was too far from its home population in Norway to be sustained. There were too many challenges for many of the Norse in Vinland, and ample work opportunities available back in Norway in the aftermath of the Black Death.[65]

The Norse did not lack the will to establish colonies in North America. Rather, they faced a looming environmental crisis—the Little Ice Age—and tried to establish an arc of influence across the North Atlantic without advantages that other Europeans later possessed. Because Norse populations at home and abroad tended to be small, there was no chance for lethal diseases like smallpox to become endemic. This meant that Norse who made it to Vinland and Greenland were healthy, not bearers of disease. Just as important, despite their immersion into long-distance trade across Europe, the Iberian navigational revolution never reached northern Europe while the Norse were still pursuing opportunities west of Iceland. Only in the fourteenth century did European artisans and shipwrights, taking advantage of navigational innovations based in part on their ability to use the North Star to guide them in open waters, figure out how to make larger ships capable of transporting hundreds across the ocean rather than the relatively small numbers who could cram together on a *knörr*. Still, news about the vast cod schools in the northern Atlantic spread by the early fourteenth century, encouraging fishing crews to sail deeper into the ocean. Within a century, cod was becoming more common among consumers across southern Europe.[66] Environment, technology, and culture, which had given the Norse a head start on European encounters in the Western Hemisphere, limited their options just when the Spanish and Portuguese began to expand their horizons under ambitious leaders who supported vigorous programs of ship design and construction.

65. Crosby, *Ecological Imperialism*, 50–54; Winroth, *Age of the Vikings*, 60–69, with population estimate at 62; Sam White, *A Cold Welcome: The Little Ice Age and Europe's Encounter with North America* (Cambridge, MA: Harvard University Press, 2017), 2–4.
66. See Richard C. Hoffman, *The Catch: An Environmental History of Medieval European Fisheries* (Cambridge: Cambridge University Press, 2023), 16–17.

The Norse gave up on Vinland. Yet their influence on North America did not disappear. Instead, it would be the descendants of the Norse who had colonized parts of Ireland and Britain and others who had gone to France (where they established the dominance of Norman culture) who began to articulate an ideology of colonization that would eventually propel many Europeans across the Atlantic. Under different historical circumstances, these Europeans, not the Norse, found the motivation to send explorers, then soldiers, and then colonists west, especially after Iberians had revealed the potential of such expeditions.

At around the same time that the Indigenous of the Mississippi Valley began to cultivate maize, Europeans who had ventured to the Middle East discovered a fondness for sugar—"an unsuspected and inestimable present from Heaven," as one medieval chronicler wrote. By the thirteenth century, Antwerp emerged as the most important refining center in Europe.[67] By then, Europeans had learned about the Canary Islands, an archipelago about sixty-five miles off the coast of West Africa peopled by Guanches, the descendants of Africans who might have arrived as much as 2,500 years earlier. For at least 1,200 years after the first century of the Common Era, there were no known contacts between these islands and anyone in Africa or Europe. In 1325, Genoese sailors landed on Lanzarote, part of the archipelago. The Genoese expedition revived interest, prompting excursions from Florence, Majorca, and Catalonia. In 1341, Portuguese sailors returned home to Lisbon with dye wood, animal skins, and fish oil. They also brought back four captives. In 1344, with information about the islands growing with each expedition, royal officials in Castile obtained a papal grant to the islands. In the years that followed, missionaries erected a bishopric on Grand Canary. Other Europeans arrived less interested in converting souls than in making a profit. By the end of the century, some of them had begun to capture and sell some of the islands' Indigenous population. The development extended an earlier slave trade, which had been based on buying and selling sub-Saharan war captives.[68]

67. Mintz, *Sweetness and Power*, 19–31; William D. Phillips Jr., "Sugar in Iberia," in Stuart B. Schwartz, ed., *Tropical Babylons: Sugar and the Making of the Atlantic World, 1450–1680* (Chapel Hill: University of North Carolina Press, 2004), 27–41; Charles Verlinden, *The Beginnings of Modern Colonization: Eleven Essays with an Introduction*, trans. Yvonne Freccero (Ithaca, NY: Cornell University Press, 1970), quotation at 18.

68. Emily Berquist Soule, "From Africa to the Ocean Sea: Atlantic Slavery in the Origins of the Spanish Empire," *Atlantic Studies* 15 (2018), 18–20; John Thornton, *Africa and Africans in the Making of the Atlantic World, 1400–1800*, 2nd ed. (Cambridge: Cambridge University Press, 1998), 72–125.

The institution of slavery had a long history across much of the Old World. Ever since antiquity, victors in battle had captured defeated foes or seized their land. By the middle decades of the fifteenth century, Europeans victorious in war tended to take their enemies' real property, the model that the Norse had employed centuries earlier in much of Britain and parts of the continent. But they also enslaved their enemies, keeping them as property for a certain period of time. Across Spain, enslavers enforced a system known as *partus sequitur ventrem* (literally, "offspring follows the belly"), meaning that an individual inherited the status of the mother. If a free man forced himself on an enslaved woman, their child would be his property unless he had freed her before the infant's birth. In west central Africa, the region where Atlantic slave traders plied their noxious trade and later shipped captive women, men, and children to the Western Hemisphere, enslaved peoples became a form of mobile property sold by one party to another. Law codes defined the enslaved as analogous to children who never grew up and hence remained under the control of the person claiming ownership in the way a parent controlled the fate of a child. In an age before modern concepts of "race," the participation of Africans in the trade needs to be understood as members of one community or nation capturing enemies, often in wartime. The term "slave" came from the kidnapping and sale of Slavs in similar contexts. A slave was an outsider, a stranger.[69]

During the fifteenth century, slave merchants in Portugal and Spain provided bound men and women who toiled, often for wages, alongside hired workers on rural farms, urban docks, and in artisans' shops. Those who could not afford to purchase a slave sometimes pooled their resources to obtain an enslaved individual who would work for more than one owner. Enslaved women typically performed domestic duties within households, where many suffered from sexual assault. Some owners forced women to work as prostitutes in parts of cities designated as *la pobla* or the *bordel*, though laws intended to prevent anyone from selling the bodies of Muslim women meant that enslavers risked authorities confiscating these women and then liberating them. Despite the laws, women who

69. *Las Siete Partidas*, ed. Robert I. Burns (Philadelphia: University of Pennsylvania Press, 2001), 4:977. As historian Saidiya Hartman has written, "Contrary to popular belief, Africans did not sell their brothers and sisters into slavery. They sold strangers: those outside the web of kin and clan relationships, nonmembers of the polity, foreigners and barbarians at the outskirts of their country, and lawbreakers expelled from society." Hartman, *Lose Your Mother: A Journey Along the Atlantic Slave Route* (New York: Farrar, Straus and Giroux, 2007), quotation at 5.

defied enslavers faced great risks. Deponents in legal trials testified that owners whipped and beat them if they resisted.[70]

Some African societies also had long maintained similar ideas about captives. Visitors to the court of Mali, the richest city-state in its region, marveled at its rulers' displays of wealth, including the ritual display of golden weapons and enslaved Turks and others purchased in Mediterranean markets. Sales of enslaved numbered up to 1,000 a month in Kano in modern Nigeria.[71]

Across western Africa, notions of private property differed from those in Europe. Rival kingdoms fought intense wars, but when they were over, the bodies of humans, not land, changed hands. This commodification of the body facilitated Europeans' ability to acquire enslaved Africans. Rather than needing to engage in bloody battles to acquire slaves, a risky strategy when Europeans were outnumbered and far from home, they instead realized that they could offer goods in exchange for people already taken captive. More to the point, as Portuguese enslavers recognized by the 1450s, they had limited capacity to profit by going to war. For Africans victorious in conflicts with others, enslaved captives were a form of moveable capital that could be exchanged for other goods, such as European weaponry, or horses. The coastal slave trade skirted Saharan traders, enabling African kings along the shore to establish trade directly with the Portuguese. Soon enough, the lure of rare objects or livestock became an accelerant. Seeking more European commodities, some Africans had ever greater incentive to capture and enslave others. As chronicler Gomes Eanes de Zurara recognized in 1445, the Portuguese would earn more through "trafficking and bargaining of merchants than by bravery and toil in arms."[72]

The Genoese and Portuguese crews that reached the Canary Islands and hauled goods home sailed on caravels, a vessel that European shipwrights had seen plying the waters of the eastern Mediterranean. For those who wanted to sail farther into the ocean, caravels offered a number of advantages over the *knörr*. Most important, they were broader and could hold more cargo. An average caravel was about seventy-five to

70. Debra Blumenthal, *Enemies and Familiars: Slavery and Mastery in Fifteenth Century Valencia* (Ithaca, NY: Cornell University Press, 2009), 80–121.

71. Toby Green, *A Fistful of Shells: West Africa from the Rise of the Slave Trade to the Age of Revolution* (Chicago: University of Chicago Press, 2019), 35–52.

72. Thornton, *Africa and Africans*, 72–125; Herman L. Bennett, *African Kings and Black Slaves: Sovereignty and Dispossession in the Early Modern Atlantic* (Philadelphia: University of Pennsylvania Press, 2019), 67–69; Gomes Eanes de Zurara, *The Chronicle of the Discovery and Conquest of Guinea*, ed. Charles R. Beazley and Edgar Prestage, Hak. Soc., 1st Ser., 95 and 100 (London: Hakluyt Society, 1896–1899), 2:289.

eighty feet long, though some were as little as forty feet and others as large as a hundred feet. Merchants and companies with a primary interest in deep-sea fishing would sail on a *caravela de pescar*, which had limited storage space. Those who wanted ships to transport enslaved humans fitted out a *caravela tilhada*, which had more decks and hence more space to hold captives as well as livestock.[73] Ship designers also developed new strategies for sails, adding a third mast, which gave captains more flexibility at sea by reducing the need to lower the main sail. The caravel and the carrack, a similar ship that developed later in the fifteenth century, provided the kind of durability and comfort that encouraged potential investors to fund their construction, stock their holds with goods for the voyage (and to trade in other locales), and recruit a crew.[74] Advances in navigational tools mattered too, including new designs for a mariner's compass in the 1420s that allowed a ship's navigator to be able to know the location of magnetic north while at sea, a crucial tool during days when clouds obscured the sun and stars.[75] More reliable ships and better tools to navigate at sea encouraged Iberians to travel more frequently and more extensively—including to the Canaries, Madeira, and the Azores.

In the early fifteenth century, Spanish and Portuguese claimants vied for control of the islands. The Castilians employed two French military commanders to lead an expedition to find the location of a mythical "River of Gold." Unable to locate the precious mineral, the interlopers concluded that the best profits could be found in capture and enslavement. In 1434 and 1435, Pope Eugenius IV, aware that enslavement of baptized Canary Islanders defeated Rome's hopes, threatened excommunication for anyone who tried to enslave Natives on any islands where missionaries had already staked a claim. But Vatican aspirations did not derail others, notably the Portuguese.[76]

In 1441, a group of Portuguese caravels returned to Lagos. Among those who greeted them was Infante Dom Henrique, better known as Prince

73. Peter Russell, *Prince Henry "The Navigator": A Life* (New Haven, CT: Yale University Press, 2000), 228–229.
74. Clinton R. Edwards, "Design and Construction of Fifteenth-Century Iberian Ships: A Review," *Mariner's Mirror* 78 (1992), 419–432; Martin M. Elbl, "The Portuguese Caravel and European Shipbuilding: Phases of Development and Diversity," *Revista da Universidade de Coimbra* 33 (1985), 543–572.
75. Frederic C. Lane, "The Economic Meaning of the Invention of the Compass," *AHR* 68 (1963), 605–617; see also E. G. R. Taylor, *The Haven-Finding Art: A History of Navigation from Odysseus to Captain Cook* (London: Hollis and Carter, 1956).
76. See Eugene IV's bulls *Creator omnium* (1434) and *Sicut dudum* (1435); Berquist Soule, "From Africa to the Ocean Sea," 20–22.

Henry the Navigator. The crews unloaded a small number of African captives. The moment enthralled the forty-seven-year-old Henry, giddy at the prospect of converting pagans to Christianity. Henry's superficial joy at the imminent conversion of souls masked the cruelty of the spectacle. The greatest benefits, one chronicler soon wrote, went to the Africans, "for though their bodies were now brought into subjection, that was a small matter in comparison of their souls, which would now possess true freedom for evermore."[77] The Portuguese typically painted crosses on the sails, creating the visual imagery that Henry wanted: a ship bringing the promise of salvation to the West African coast.[78]

Three years later, Portuguese enslavers captured 240 Idzagen (Sanhadja) between Cape Blanco and Cape Timiris. They arrived at Lagos on August 6, greeted by Henry astride his horse, eager to receive his royal due of one-fifth (his *quinto*) of the enslaved. He oversaw the auction, witnessing first-hand the destruction of African families. Mothers endured whipping to protect the bodies of their children who had tried to flee back to them. Whatever the level of physical and psychological abuse, the enslavers, with their prince's approval, justified the auctions as part of a divinely sanctioned effort to save heathen souls. The following year an even larger crowd gathered at the docks in Lisbon to watch another auction. An observer reported that there was no criticism but only praise for the wisdom and guidance of the virtuous prince.

Henry had not invented the slave trade. In the 1260s, the Byzantine emperor Michael VIII Paleologus opened the Black Sea to slave traders from Venice, Genoa, and the Mamluk kingdom, which controlled modern Syria and Egypt. But the Portuguese prince reoriented it to the great advantage of his nation. Portuguese slave traders soon increased their efforts to meet the demands of the booming cities of Seville (under the crown of Castile) and Valencia (under the rule of the Aragon crown). Eager to support the cause, Pope Nicholas V issued a new bull (*Romanus pontifex*) in January 1455 granting Henry and the Portuguese a monopoly on trade to Africa. The pontiff saw the edict as necessary to reward a favored subject and to clarify potential conflicts with other European claimants, notably Castile. The bull acknowledged the slave trade, which the Vatican saw as an acceptable step toward the conversion of "enemies to Christ." Within four years the prince became an avid promoter of direct Portuguese involvement in the trade. What had begun as a trade in enslaved Canary Islanders had, in little more than a century, launched the

77. Bennett, *African Kings and Black Slaves*, 3–5, quotation at 4.
78. Russell, *Prince Henry*, 226–227.

Atlantic slave trade. The shift happened quickly. Portuguese explorers landed on Madeira in 1425 and soon set fires to clear its thick forests to make it suitable for agriculture. By 1443 these new settlers had begun to import enslaved Africans. By 1460, Portuguese bent on harvesting resources of mid-Atlantic islands traded one horse for seven enslaved humans.[79]

The establishment of a set rate for the purchase of enslaved Africans reflected agreement between the African lords who controlled territory along the Guinea Coast and the Portuguese who arrived on their caravels. At first, these Europeans thought that the most efficient way to gather captives would be to go to war. But almost immediately those on the shoreline recognized the authority and power of African leaders. Rather than fight, the visitors instead turned to trade and diplomacy, accepting guidelines established by African kings. The raids of the 1440s soon gave way to commerce, a reflection of African sovereignty and agency.[80]

By the mid-fifteenth century, maize farmers had spread across eastern North America. They never met the Norse, who had given up their American aspirations without encountering agricultural communities. But those who bore the crops eastward altered the landscape of much of the continent, including territory where non-Norse Europeans would later arrive at the edge of lands transformed by Indigenous farmers. Those changes in the landscape would soon beckon Europeans, including many who knew about and already profited from the trade in enslaved humans.

79. Russell, *Prince Henry*, 239–263; Hannah Barker, *That Most Precious Merchandise: The Mediterranean Trade in Black Sea Slaves, 1260–1500* (Philadelphia: University of Pennsylvania Press, 2019), esp. 121–151; [Nicholas V], *Romanus pontifex*, January 8, 1455, https://www.papalencyclicals.net/nicholo5/romanus-pontifex.htm.

80. See Bennett, *African Kings and Black Slaves*, 60–74; David Hancock, *Oceans of Wine: Madeira and the Emergence of American Trade and Taste* (New Haven, CT: Yale University Press, 2009), 2–5, 8–11.

2

"People Without Number"

In 1500 Christopher Columbus, back in Spain after his third voyage to the West Indies, announced to one of Queen Isabella's favorites that he had, with divine guidance, "subdued another world" and brought it under the dominion of the Castilian monarchs. As a result, he reported, "Spain, that used to be called poor, is now the most wealthy of kingdoms." Despite his achievement, he grumbled, he had not received the rewards he deserved.[1] He seemed oblivious to the fact that it was his own actions in the Caribbean that had limited the rewards he thought he deserved.

By the time Columbus articulated his grievance, Europeans had spent almost a decade trying to understand the significance of their encounter with the Western Hemisphere, a part of the world that the ancient writers in what was becoming known as the Old World had never imagined. Europeans also wrestled with the aftermath of the Black Death, which undermined traditional mores and perhaps made some of them more willing to explore new opportunities than they may have been earlier.[2] Columbus's journey, and especially the reports that it generated, came at a momentous time for Europeans, who had embraced an information revolution with the spread of printing technology and had begun to recognize the profits to come from the enslavement of Africans. These developments on the eastern shores of the Atlantic basin shaped the ways that Spaniards, and the other Europeans who followed them, would come to embrace the conquest of the Americas, with devastating consequences for the Indigenous who met invaders when they arrived on their shores.

1. R. H. Major, trans. and ed., *Selected Letters of Christopher Columbus*, Hak. Soc., 1st Ser., 43 (London: Hakluyt Society, 1870), quotation at 170.
2. See David Herlihy, *The Black Death and the Transformation of the West* (Cambridge, MA: Harvard University Press, 1997).

In 1492, Tainos dominated Hispaniola, Puerto Rico, Jamaica, the Bahamas, and most of Cuba.[3] Two other peoples also resided in the Caribbean: the Guanahatabeys, who controlled western Cuba, and the Kalinagos, who populated the Lesser Antilles. While modern anthropologists have labeled them all "Taino," particular groups bore their own names, such as the Lucayo, who lived in the Bahamas, and the Borinquen of Puerto Rico. The term "Taino" translated as "noble" or "good," or at least that is how the first Spanish understood it, differentiating them from Kalinagos, or Island-Caribs.[4]

The Tainos inhabited individual towns, numbering as many as 2,000 residents. They constructed wooden houses with thatched roofs, a technology that would not have been out of place across most of rural Europe at the time. Tainos slept on hammocks, devices that fascinated European observers, who perhaps concluded that they were more comfortable than many beds they had at home. Each settlement had an internal political system with a cacique at the top, who sat on a carved wooden *duho*, which resembled a European throne. Men or women could govern politics in a town, a reflection of egalitarian relations in a matrilineal society. Nearby towns formed together into what anthropologists have called "district chiefdoms," with one of the local chiefs in a superior position over others. The Spanish recognized a two-tiered social structure dividing commoners from nobles. None had a status equivalent to the enslaved that Europeans knew at home. Local architectural practice reflected the division. Those with less property inhabited smaller, multi-family buildings known as *caney*, while those further up the social scale lived in *bohio*, which were larger though similarly built.[5]

Tainos tended to walk around naked or wear minimal cotton clothing—a loincloth for men and a short skirt (*nagua*) for women. It was common for Tainos to paint themselves for rituals and to wear jewelry. Many of their bodily ornaments contained gold, with caciques at times bearing

3. For the range of population estimates, see Massimo Livi-Bacci, "Return to Hispaniola: Reassessing a Demographic Catastrophe," *HAHR* 83 (2003), 7–8; Kathleen Deagan and José María Cruxent, *Columbus's Outpost Among the Taínos: Spain and America at Las Isabela, 1493–1498* (New Haven, CT: Yale University Press, 2002), 24; Peggy Liss, *Isabel the Queen: Life and Times*, rev. ed. (Philadelphia: University of Pennsylvania Press, 2004), 334–335.
4. Irving Rouse, *The Tainos: Rise and Decline of the People Who Greeted Columbus* (New Haven, CT: Yale University Press, 1992), 5–7; Erin W. Stone, *Captives of Conquest: Slavery in the Early Modern Spanish Caribbean* (Philadelphia: University of Pennsylvania Press, 2021), 13–14; Tessa Murphy, *The Creole Archipelago: Race and Borders in the Colonial Caribbean* (Philadelphia: University of Pennsylvania Press, 2021), 20–24.
5. Rouse, *Tainos*, 9; Deagan and Cruxent, *Columbus's Outpost*, 32.

guanín, which blended gold with copper. The Tainos did not refine copper but instead maintained trade relations with Indigenous on the mainland, a sign of long-distance economic activity. Taino artisans worked with bones, shells, stone, feathers, and wood. Those of higher social standing might be seen wearing masks known as *guaíza*, which took the shape of a human face.[6]

The size of the island populations reflected the Tainos' successful agricultural regime. Women performed much of the labor on farms. Unlike Indigenous on the mainland whose economies depended on maize, Tainos cultivated root crops: cassava (which they called *casavi*) and sweet potatoes (*batata*). They built earthen mounds (*conuco*), which hedged against erosion and facilitated drainage, two developments that enabled Tainos to maintain their crops in the ground longer than otherwise would have been possible. Tainos had maize too, but it was a subsidiary food source. They gathered wild plants and fruits, cultivated pineapples, and grew tobacco, a plant found across much of the Western Hemisphere. They were also expert at fishing, catching birds, and hunting their islands' native animals, practices that survived for generations after 1492.[7]

The central figures in Taino religious practices were deities and ancestral spirits, known as *cemíes* (sing. *cemí*, also *zemi*). Locals placed portable physical representations of *cemíes* at the edge of sacred sites as well as in towns. Since individuals could own multiple *cemí* representations, there might have been 4 million such items on Hispaniola alone at the time of Columbus's arrival. Recognizing the links between the world of the spirits and the passing of their relatives, Tainos often carved *cemíes* out of human bone, possibly from an ancestor, though they could also be fashioned from pottery, wood, stone, and shells. Because they possessed powers, the *cemíes* were handed down in families for generations. Though the Spanish often had difficulty comprehending the nuanced belief systems of the Tainos, some of the earliest visitors made efforts to understand the nature of local spiritual practices, including differences among the *cemíes*. They understood that elites had more elaborate burials than others, though family members used the bones to make *cemíes* regardless of social rank. The *cemíes* also played a role in rituals that incorporated purging and taking snuff (*cohoba*) through a specifically designed forked tube.[8]

6. Rouse, *Tainos*, 9–12.
7. Rouse, *Tainos*, 12–13; "Histoire Naturelle des Indes" (aka the Drake Manuscript), ff. 81r–124v, Morgan Library.
8. Ramón Pané, *An Account of the Antiquities of the Indians*, trans. Susan Griswold (Durham, NC: Duke University Press, 1999), 25–30; Rouse, *Tainos*, 12–17; Stone, *Captives of Conquest*, 15–16.

In the autumn of 1492, the communities that Tainos had spent generations developing faced a test they never anticipated.

In 1450, Portuguese merchants had learned that melegueta pepper, which they called grains of paradise, could be found south of the Gambia River. They labeled this territory, modern Liberia and Sierra Leone, the Melegueta Coast. But this, however desirable, was not the only plant that Europeans wanted. After the middle of the fifteenth century, Spanish and Portuguese sailors searched for a feasible route via the water around southern Africa and toward South Asia, eager to find a quick route to the Spice Islands of the Southwest Pacific, where they could stock up on raw goods to make medicine: cinnamon, cloves, nutmeg, and various kinds of peppers. Portuguese merchants, like others in Europe, wanted to break the monopoly of Venetian spice traders, who had long controlled the overland route to the Pacific. In 1488, explorer Bartolomeu Dias brought news to Lisbon that he had traveled around the Cape of Good Hope and found an open sea that could reach South Asia. Among those enthralled with the possibility was the Genoese mariner Christopher Columbus, whose search for royal patrons led him to send his brother Bartholomew as far as the English court of Henry VII. The king supported the plan but by the time news reached Spain the explorer had already found other supporters. In 1492, Isabella, queen of Castile and León since 1474, and her husband, Ferdinand of Aragon, agreed to finance Columbus's plan.[9]

Columbus arrived at the royal court at an auspicious moment. Less than two decades earlier, warfare had broken out on the Iberian Peninsula after the death in 1475 of the Castilian king Henry IV. His passing led to a constitutional crisis when his (alleged) daughter Joanna and his half-sister Isabella each believed she was the rightful heir. Unable to resolve the situation peacefully, the parties battled in the War of the Castilian Succession for four years. The 1479 Treaty of Alcáçovas clarified that Isabella along with Ferdinand would take Castile, while the Portuguese would have control over the Atlantic and the rights to Africa and territory lying to the east. The Portuguese also ceded the Canary Islands, the scene of their relatively recent economic success in launching the slave trade, to the Spanish. In 1481, Pope Sixtus IV issued *Aeterni regis*, a bull that reinforced Nicholas V's *Romanus pontifex* of 1455 and embodied the

9. Paul Freedman, *Out of the East: Spices and the Medieval Imagination* (New Haven, CT: Yale University Press, 2008), 12, 193–214; "The offer of the discoverie of the West Indies by Christopher Columbus to King Henrie the seventh in the yeere 1488," in Richard Hakluyt, *The Principall Navigations, Voiages, and Discoveries of the English Nation* (London, 1589), 507–509.

principles of the 1479 treaty. That agreement, which soothed political relations in southern Europe, reinforced the idea that the Vatican claimed authority over monarchs across Christendom even when their territorial claims included regions, such as much of Africa, where the faith was either nonexistent or rare. Indeed, Rome's insistence that its policies included the people who had never converted, the doctrine of *extra ecclesiam nulla salus* (no salvation outside the church), predated the arrival of Portuguese enslavers on the Guinea Coast. This long-pedigreed ideology allowed a succession of early modern popes to intrude in relations between Iberian monarchs who battled over African bodies.[10]

Columbus departed from Granada on May 12, 1492, bent on both economic and spiritual gain. In his mind, Jesus's evangels would have agreed that there existed "many peoples [who] were lost, falling into idolatry and accepting false and harmful religions." By contrast, Ferdinand and Isabella, "as Catholic Christians and Princes, lovers and promoters of the Holy Christian faith, and enemies of the false doctrine of Mahomet and of all idolatries and heresies," recognized the importance of solidifying Christendom. In case everlasting glory was not enough on this quest to find a more rapid route to spices of the Southwest Pacific, Columbus sailed off believing that he and his heirs would govern any previously unknown lands in perpetuity.[11]

Columbus's mission to the west came at the same moment as the Spanish celebrated victories over Muslims, in the Reconquista, and Jews. Christian rulers had battled Muslims on the Iberian peninsula since the eighth century and finally prevailed when Ferdinand and Isabella laid claim to Granada. That same year, Spain's rulers also announced the Alhambra Decree, or the Edict of the Expulsion, authorizing the removal of Jews from the lands of Castile and Aragon—territory that Jews had inhabited for over a thousand years. The 175,000 Jews who fled the kingdom left behind others who—at least in public—were willing to renounce

10. Herman L. Bennett, *African Kings and Black Slaves: Sovereignty and Dispossession in the Early Modern Atlantic* (Philadelphia: University of Pennsylvania Press, 2019), 5, 54–58, 122–125.

11. Oliver Dunn and James E. Kelley Jr., trans., *The Diario of Christopher Columbus's First Voyage to America, 1492–1493* (Norman: University of Oklahoma Press, 1989) [hereafter Columbus, *Diario*], 17–19. Columbus's original diary and a copy that he commissioned for it have both disappeared. What survives is a version from the 1530s in the hand of Bartolomé de Las Casas, a Dominican friar who would later become one of the most important chroniclers of the earliest period of Spanish colonization in the Americas. For the history of the manuscript and the surviving copy, see Columbus, *Diario*, 3–5.

their faith.[12] The crown also devised a system for paying tribute known as the encomienda, which would remain a feature of the Spanish administration of territory long after 1492. These developments—expulsion, forced conversion, and tribute payments—set the intellectual and institutional stage for Columbus's journey. He went exploring at a time when a unified Christian church based in Rome had become ascendant.

In early August 1492, the *Santa Maria*, *Pinta*, and *Niña* set off first for the Canary Islands, a familiar place to resupply ships and attend to problems such as the imperfect rigging on the *Pinta*. Columbus tried to keep track of his progress, but in this age before an accurate sea clock he had no way to measure longitude. Still, unlike the Norse, he could use the North Star, which hung low over the horizon, as a guide on his journey to the south and west.[13]

After departing the Canaries on September 6, Columbus was careful to measure how far they traveled and the plants and creatures they saw: green plants floating in the water, crabs, various birds, and dolphins, including some killed by sailors on the *Niña*. On October 5 they sailed into a school of flying fish, many of which flew onto the decks.[14] On the night of October 11, some of the sailors caught their first sight of what might be land. They lowered some of their sails, a common practice to prevent them from traveling too quickly toward an unknown coastline. Their caution was timely. On Friday the twelfth they spotted the Bahamas. Soon they saw nude figures on the shoreline. Columbus and a small armed retinue paddled to shore, where they planted the royal banner and two flags, one with an *F* for Ferdinand and the other with a *Y* for Ysabel (Isabella). Each had a green cross on the back. Columbus called over his captains so that they could witness him taking "possession of the said

12. Karoline P. Cook, *Forbidden Passages: Muslims and Moriscos in Colonial Spanish America* (Philadelphia: University of Pennsylvania Press, 2016), 11–13.
13. On the lack of a way to measure longitude, see Dava Sobel, *Longitude: The True Story of a Lone Genius Who Solved the Greatest Scientific Problem of His Times* (New York: Walker, 1995); on the advantages that Columbus had over the Norse, see Alfred W. Crosby, *Ecological Imperialism: The Biological Expansion of Europe, 900–1900* (Cambridge: Cambridge University Press, 1986), 54–55; for Columbus referring to the navigators using the North Star as a reference point, see his *Diario*, 33–35; for the rerigging of the *Pinta*, see Columbus, *Diario*, 25n; for the promise to track his progress, see *Diario*, 21; for his decision to sail south as well as west, see Nicolás Wey Gómez, *The Tropics of Empire: Why Columbus Sailed South to the Indies* (Cambridge, MA: MIT Press, 2008).
14. Columbus, *Diario*, 51.

island for the king and for the queen his lords."[15] Columbus believed that the Tainos, as his chronicler Bartolomé de Las Casas later reported, "would be better freed [from error] and converted to our Holy Faith by love than by force." To advance his agenda he gave them glass beads and red caps, which created an initial sense of goodwill among the Tainos. Soon after, some of the locals swam to the launches and offered the Spanish cotton, parrots, and javelins tipped with fish teeth.[16]

Columbus claimed that the Tainos welcomed the Spanish and offered various goods, but he believed they were "a people very poor in everything." He soon saw an opening for the Spanish to colonize the islands in the region and enslave residents. "They should be good and intelligent servants," he wrote, "for I see that they say very quickly everything that is said to them; and I believe they would become Christians very easily, for it seemed to me that they had no religion." He arranged to kidnap six of them so that his patrons could meet them and so "they may learn to speak," presumably meaning that they would be able to learn Spanish. In doing so, he embraced an idea then circulating in Spain that, as linguist Antonio de Nebrija wrote that year, "language was always a companion of the empire."[17]

Throughout the expedition, Columbus was convinced he had reached Asia. On October 21, less than ten days after he had arrived, the Tainos told him of a place they called Colba, which had, so he wrote, "many and very large ships and many traders." He concluded that this must be Cipango, an island that Marco Polo had reported lay east of the mainland of Asia and that many scholars presume meant Japan. That island had to be close to his destination. As he wrote, "I have already decided to go to the mainland and to the city of Quinsay and to give Your Highnesses' letters to the Grand Khan and to ask for, and to come with, a reply."[18] Columbus understood that Polo in the late thirteenth century had described the Japanese as having abundant stores of gold and pearls. His belief that these riches could be found in the Caribbean made sense as long as he continued to think that he had reached the Southwest Pacific—and if he took at face value Polo's report, which may have reached him if Queen Isabella had shared her manuscript copy of his *Travels*, which she had in an Aragonese translation in the period between Columbus getting

15. Columbus, *Diario*, 33–35, 37–39, 51, 63–65.
16. Columbus, *Diario*, 65–67.
17. Columbus, *Diario*, 67–69; Antonio de Nebrija, *Gramática de la lengua castellana* (1492), https://www.loc.gov/item/2021667003/.
18. Columbus, *Diario*, 109.

royal permission to travel west and the time of his departure.[19] Reading such a text would have aligned with Columbus's practice of examining scholarly treatises that might give insights into territories far from Europe.[20]

Despite his continued inability to grasp that he had not reached his intended destination, Columbus was an enthusiastic observer. He wrote that the fish and trees were more wondrous than those Iberians had ever seen before; that the islanders produced cotton but kept no livestock; and that there were enough deep harbors "for as many ships as there are in the whole of Christendom." Although he was unable to communicate with Tainos, he convinced himself that the Indigenous people he met thought the Iberians were divine. As he put it, an elderly man swam out to one of the boats and "called to all the men and women: Come see the men who came from the heavens." The man implored his compatriots to bring food and drink to the visitors, which they did, "giving thanks to God, throwing themselves on the ground." The Tainos wanted him to come ashore, but Columbus demurred, fearing that a large reef might doom his ship. He had little fear of the Tainos. He had kidnapped seven by that point and concluded that they could not defend their own land. He could enslave many if he had the soldiers, he observed, "because with 50 men all of them could be held in subjection and can be made to do whatever one might wish." He believed that many of them would convert to Christianity "very quickly because they are of very good understanding."[21]

Columbus behaved like previous European travelers to distant places. He collected evidence, gathered specimens to send home, and described what he saw through analogies to places and items that Europeans would recognize.[22] He also tapped into another theme of European travel narra-

19. See *The Travels of Marco Polo*, trans. Ronald Latham (London: Penguin, 1958), 243–244. As one expert on the narrative put it, Polo's "two brief chapters" on Japan "can without exaggeration be described as nonsense, yet it was to be immensely fruitful nonsense," and these were "the only western reference to Japan before the sixteenth century." See John Larimer, *Marco Polo and the Discovery of the World* (New Haven, CT: Yale University Press, 1999), 94–95, 156–157.

20. As Stephen Greenblatt put it, "The sightings are important only in relation to what Columbus already knows and what he can write about them on the basis of that knowledge." See Stephen Greenblatt, *Marvelous Possessions: The Wonder of the New World* (Chicago: University of Chicago Press, 1992), 86–90, quotation at 88.

21. Columbus, *Diario*, 75 (harbors, "heavens," "captives"), 89 (conversion).

22. Columbus, *Diario*, 93, 111. The strategy of analogous reasoning was common in the early modern era; see Anthony Pagden, *The Fall of Natural Man: The American Indian and the Origins of Comparative Ethnology* (Cambridge: Cambridge University Press, 1982), 1–4, and Donald F. Lach, *Asia in the Making of Europe*, vol. I, *The Century of Discovery* (Chicago: University of Chicago Press, 1965), 2:686–687.

tives: the idea that distant places held wonders.[23] Europeans had long debated the idea of the marvelous and what it meant. That discussion emerged whenever a traveler returned and rushed to a printer with tales of the great surprises to be found abroad. Columbus's reporting echoed that tendency. Parrot flocks blocked out the sun, he claimed. He estimated there were a thousand kinds of fragrant trees, each with its own fruit.[24] Among the wonders he sought were spices, including pepper and cinnamon that he had carried with him from Castile. He claimed that the Tainos recognized the plants and "said by signs" that much was to be found nearby. Similarly, he pulled out pearls and gold. Again, the Tainos responded that they could find such riches in a place they called Bohío. He also thought they told him about islands populated with deadly cyclopes and cynocephali, dog-headed men. Fortunately for him, none of those monsters was in sight. Columbus reported only that those he met "are very gentle and very timid, naked, as has been said before, without weapons and without law"—innocents inhabiting a paradise of fertile fields, untold mineral wealth, and abundant marvels.[25]

This was a decisive moment for these visiting sailors. Europeans had long believed that monsters roamed territory far to their east and south. This was no mere series of outlandish folk tales but accepted facts that had been documented since antiquity. One map after another depicted monsters on lands far from Europe and swimming across every known body of water. European cartographers, after reading the works of cosmographers, squeezed *monstra marina* into almost every open space on their maps.[26] Finding people, not monsters, meant that Europeans could convert Indigenous to Christianity since they were human, though within a generation of Columbus's return that recognition would fly in the face of those who believed that Americans should be enslaved.[27] For the moment, the belief in the humanity of Tainos and other Americans meant, for Columbus, that Indigenous could become Christians—which

23. See Caroline Walker Bynum, "Wonder," *AHR* 102 (1997), 1–26.
24. Columbus, *Diario*, 105–107, 111.
25. Columbus, *Diario*, 133.
26. Rudolf Wittkower, "Marvels of the East: A Study in the History of Monsters," *Journal of the Warburg and Courtauld Institutes* 5 (1942), 159–197; Surekha Davies, *Renaissance Ethnography and the Invention of the Human: New Worlds, Maps, and Monsters* (Cambridge: Cambridge University Press, 2016); Chet Van Duzer, *Sea Monsters on Medieval and Renaissance Maps* (London: British Library, 2013); Joseph Nigg, *Sea Monsters: A Voyage Around the World's Most Beguiling Map* (Chicago: University of Chicago Press, 2013); Peter C. Mancall, *Nature and Culture in the Early Modern Atlantic* (Philadelphia: University of Pennsylvania Press, 2018), 5–10.
27. See Paul III, "Sublimus Deus: On the Enslavement and Evangelization of Indians," 1537, Papal Encyclicals Online.

should not be too difficult since they already believed in higher powers—and would also become trade partners providing spices, gold, and pearls.[28]

When he reached Hispaniola in mid-December, Columbus reminded his men not to harm its residents. He believed that Ferdinand and Isabella "will make all of them Christians" and that they had become the monarchs' subjects, another way of taking possession for the Iberians. Hispaniola's naked people, the explorer claimed, believed that the Spanish had come from heaven "and that the realms of the kings of Castile were in the heavens and not in this world." Rumors swirled about endless deposits of gold.[29]

On Christmas Eve the *Santa Maria* ran aground on a sandbank and could not be rescued. Rather than fret, Columbus boarded the *Niña* and ordered that the planks from his destroyed flagship be used to build a fort on the northern coast of Hispaniola. He named the fort Navidad and claimed that it gave the Spanish a substantial base from which to learn even more about the island, extract its resources, and convert its residents.[30] When it was time to go home Columbus left thirty-nine men behind in the fort, with ample provisions for their survival and goods to trade for gold. He departed on January 4, the beginning of a journey that would eventually take him to Seville. On March 15 he arrived at the harbor where he had started his expedition some seven months earlier. Upon hearing that the monarchs were in Barcelona, he decided to go there to deliver his news.[31]

During his journey homeward Columbus composed a letter for the public. He knew that European printers would be eager to spread his report. In the half century since German printer Johan Gutenberg had, in 1440, begun to print texts on his press using quickly made moveable type, European publishers had produced editions of 30,000 to 35,000 different books, each with a print run of about 500 copies. Some appeared in multiple editions, but there were between 10,000 and 15,000 unique texts. Taken together, European printers had already manufactured 20 million books.[32]

28. Columbus, *Diario*, 141–147.
29. Columbus, *Diario*, 231, 233, 249, 263, 273.
30. For the wreck and Columbus's response, see *Diario*, 277–291, and Arthur Davies, "The Loss of the Santa Maria on Christmas Day, 1492," *AHR* 58 (1953), 854–865.
31. Columbus, *Diario*, 301–303 (men left behind), 401 (return).
32. Lucien Febvre and Henri-Jean Martin, *The Coming of the Book: The Impact of Printing, 1450–1800*, trans. David Gerard (London: NLB, 1976), 248.

Into this swelling sea of books came Columbus's account, which launched its own information revolution across the eastern shores of the Atlantic. He boasted that he reached the Indies in twenty days and "discovered a great many islands inhabited by people without number: and of them all I have taken possession" on behalf of Ferdinand and Isabella "by proclamation and with the royal flag extended, and I was not opposed." He acknowledged that the Tainos—*los īdios* (Indians), as he called them—had already named the places where they lived. The first island he had seen they called Guanaham. He renamed it San Salvador. From then on, he put other names on the emerging Iberian map of the Caribbean: Santa María de Concepcíon, Ferrandina, Isabella, Juana, "and so to each a new name." It was the first of what would be hundreds of acts of Europeans claiming to discover and hence possess already inhabited places.[33]

Time and again Columbus emphasized the bounty he observed. "La Española is a marvel," he wrote. It boasted the commodities that he knew would entice his readers: gold and other minerals, spices, clean water, fruit-bearing trees, and access to the markets of the Great Khan. He provided his readers with the first European description of Indigenous Americans, emphasizing their near nudity, lack of potent weapons, and "hopelessly timorous" nature. They were so innocent that, he claimed, he had to prevent his men from taking advantage of naive innocents who would take shreds of cloth or broken pieces of a wine cask in exchange for whatever they possessed. Though the Tainos lacked what he saw as a proper conception of religious practice, he believed that they had already made strides toward conversion by communicating with the newcomers in an improvised sign language.[34]

Columbus offered comments that revealed him to be well versed in contemporary understandings of the peoples of the world. "Until now," he wrote, "I have not found any monstrous men in these islands, as many had thought," likely a reference to his reading of ancient compilers of encyclopedias or the widely recopied travel narrative of the fourteenth-century English knight Sir John Mandeville. These authorities had terrified their readers with vivid descriptions of monsters lying beyond Christendom. He acknowledged that there were human-flesh-eaters on some islands, but he never saw them with his own eyes. Such potential

33. Mauricio Obregón, *The Columbus Papers: The Barcelona Letter of 1493, the Landfall Controversy, and the Indian Guides* (New York: Macmillan, 1991), 65; Patricia Seed, *Ceremonies of Possession in Europe's Conquest of the New World, 1492–1640* (Cambridge: Cambridge University Press, 1992); Allan Greer, *Property and Dispossession: Natives, Empires and Land in Early Modern North America* (Cambridge: Cambridge University Press, 2018), 117–131, 192–202.

34. Obregón, *Columbus Papers*, 65–67.

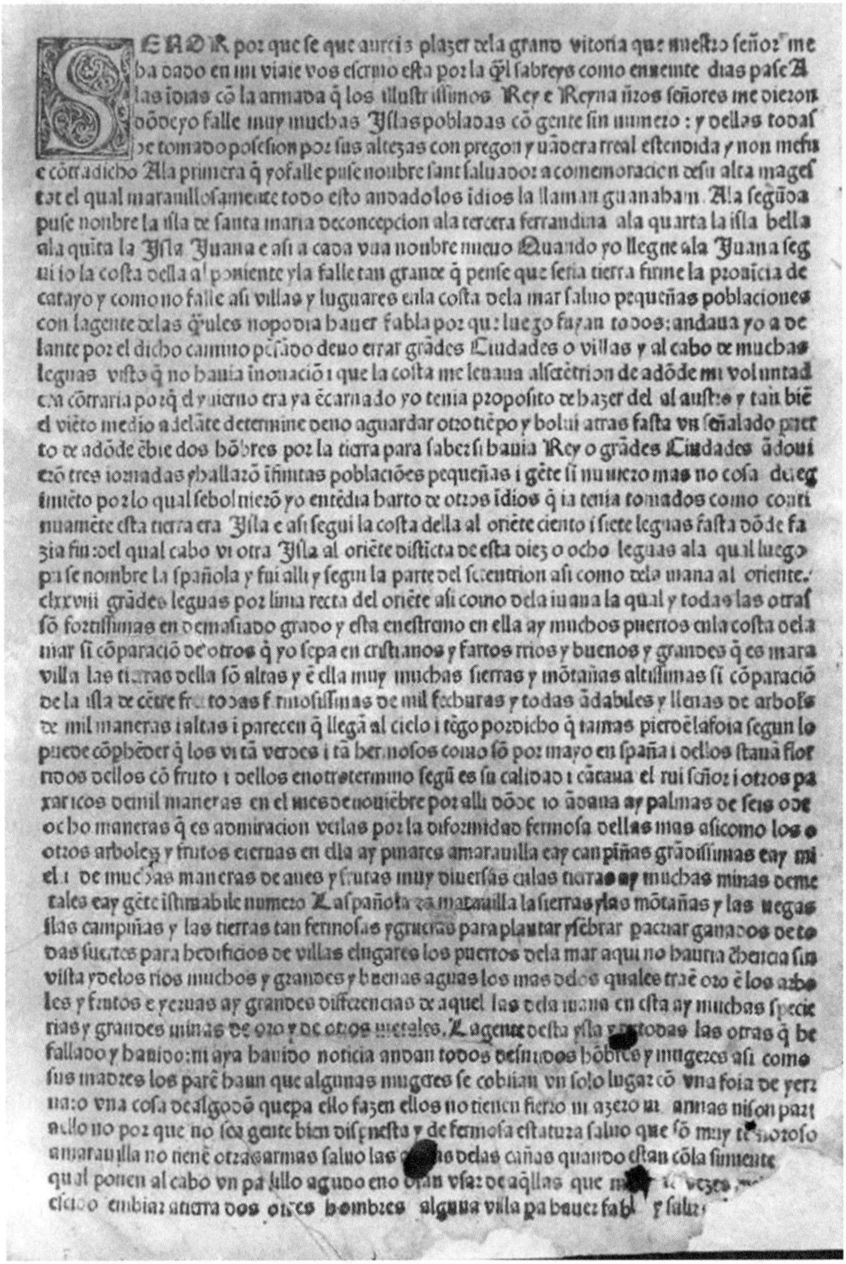

SEÑOR por que se que aureis plazer dela grand vitoria que nuestro señor me
ha dado en mi viaje vos escrivo esta por la q̃l sabreys como en treinte dias pase A
las idias cõ la armada q̃ los illustrissimos Rey e Reyna ñros señores me dieron
dõde yo falle muy muchas Yslas pobladas cõ gente sin numero : y dellas todas
he tomado posesion por sus altezas con pregon y vãdera real estendida y non mefu
e cõtradicho Ala primera q̃ yo falle puse nonbre sant saluador a comemoracion desu alta mages
tat el qual maravillosamente todo esto andado los idios la llaman guanahani. Ala segũda
puse nonbre la isla de santa maria deconcepcion ala tercera ferrandina ala quarta la isla bella
ala quita la Ysla Juana e asi a cada vna nonbre nuevo Quando yo llegue ala Juana seg
ui io la costa della al poniente y la falle tan grande q̃ pense que seria tierra firme la provicia de
catayo y como no falle asi villas y luguares enla costa dela mar saluo pequeñas poblaciones
con lagente delas q̃ules nopodia haver fabla por que luego fuyan todos: andava yo a de
lante por el dicho camino pẽsando deno errar grãdes Ciudades o villas y al cabo de muchas
leguas visto q̃ no havia inovaciõ i que la costa me levava alsetẽtrion de adõde mi voluntad
era cõtraria porq̃ el yvierno era ya ẽcarnado yo tenia proposito de hazer del al austro y tan biẽ
el viẽto medio adelãte determine deno aguardar otro tiẽpo y bolui atras fasta vn señalado puer
to de adõde ẽbie dos hõbres por la tierra para saber si havia Rey o grãdes Ciudades ãdovi
erõ tres iornadas y hallarõ ĩfinitas poblaciões pequeñas i gẽte si numero mas no cosa de reg
imiẽto por lo qual se bolvierõ yo entẽdia harto de otros idios q̃ ia tenia tomados como conti
nuamẽte esta tierra era Ysla e asi segui la costa della al oriẽte ciento i siete leguas fasta dõde fa
zia fin: del qual cabo vi otra Ysla al oriẽte distĩcta de esta diez o ocho leguas ala qual luego
puse nombre la spañola y fui alli y segui la parte del setentrion asi como dela iuana al oriente.
clxxviii grãdes leguas por linia recta del oriẽte asi como dela iuana la qual y todas las otras
sõ fortissimas en demasiado grado y esta enestremo en ella ay muchos puertos enla costa dela
mar si cõparaciõ de otros q̃ yo sepa en cristianos y fartos rios y buenos y grandes q̃ es mara
villa las tierras della sõ altas y ẽ ella muy muchas sierras y mõtañas altissimas si cõparaciõ
dela isla de cetrefrey todas fermosissimas de mil fechuras y todas ãdables y llenas de arboles
de mil maneras i altas i parecen q̃ llegã al cielo i tẽgo por dicho q̃ iamas pierdẽ la foia segun lo
puede cõprehẽder q̃ los vi tã verdes i tã hermosos como sõ por mayo en spaña i dellos stavã flor
idos dellos cõ fruto i dellos enotro termino segũ es su calidad i cãtava el ruiseñor i otros pa
xaricos de mil maneras en el mes de noviẽbre por alli dõde io ãdava ay palmas de seis o de
ocho maneras q̃ es admiracion verlas por la diformidad fermosa dellas mas asi como los o
tros arboles y frutos eiervas en ella ay pinares amaravilla e ay canpiñas grãdissimas e ay mi
el i de muchas maneras de aves y frutas muy diversas enlas tierras ay muchas minas deme
tales e ay gẽte istimabile numero La spañola es maravilla la sierras y las mõtañas y las vegas
ilas campiñas y las tierras tan fermosas y gruesas para plantar y sebrar pacer ganados de to
das suertes para hedificios de villas elugares los puertos dela mar aqui no havria chrẽencia sin
vista y delos rios muchos y grandes y buenas aguas los mas delos quales traẽ oro ẽ los arbo
les y frutos e yervas ay grandes differencias de aquellas dela iuana en esta ay muchas specie
rias y grandes minas de oro y de otros metales. La gente desta ysla y de todas las otras q̃ he
fallado y havido: ni aya havido noticia andan todos desnudos hõbres y mugeres asi como
sus madres los parẽ haun que algunas mugeres se cobijan vn solo lugar cõ vna foia de yerv
a: o vna cosa dealgodõ que pa ello fazen ellos no tienen fierro ni azero ni armas ni son par
a ello no por que no sea gente bien dispuesta y de fermosa estatura saluo que sõ muy te[...]oroso
amaravilla no tienẽ otras armas saluo las [...]as delas cañas quando estan cõla simiente
qual ponen al cabo vn palillo agudo e no [...]an vsar de aq̃llas que m[...] [...] vezes [...]
[...] embiar atierra dos o tres hombres alguna villa pa haver fab[...] y salir[...]

The first news about Columbus's 1492 voyage spread across Europe in a very brief, unillustrated tract published in Barcelona the following year. The news it contained raced across the continent when other printers translated the text. Rare Book Division, New York Public Library.

dangers meant little compared to the cornucopia he had found: gold, cotton, aloe, mastic (a resin used in medicine that was then available only on the Aegean island of Chios), and possibly also cinnamon and rhubarb, plants that had widely reported medicinal properties. Ferdinand and Isabella could also have "as many slaves as they order loaded, who will be idolaters." He repeatedly described his journey as a crucial stage in Christian history.[35]

Columbus, delayed by bad weather, reached Lisbon a month after he wrote the text. On March 14, he sent the letter to his sovereigns.[36] Before year's end it had been translated from Spanish into Latin and Catalan. Printers rushed out copies. Three editions appeared in Rome in 1493 alone. Other Latin editions appeared from printers in Antwerp and Paris.[37] A printer in Basel also produced an edition, which included woodblock illustrations created by an artist who had never seen the Western Hemisphere but created images based on Columbus's words. In simple visual language, the unnamed artist depicted two Europeans on a small launch approaching a shoreline and encountering naked Tainos, all of whom shrink at the prospect of the meeting. That same year Ferdinando Almeida, the bishop of Ceuta, published a letter he wrote to Pope Alexander VI praising Ferdinand, loyal servant of the Vatican, "who has increased the race of humanity since new peoples have been found" as well as adding new knowledge of "those islands of which we were, until now, unaware."[38]

35. Obregón, *Columbus Papers*, 68; Nancy G. Siraisi, *Medieval and Early Renaissance Medicine: An Introduction to Knowledge and Practice* (Cambridge: Cambridge University Press, 1990). On Columbus and Mandeville, see *The Travels of Sir John Mandeville*, trans C. W. R. D. Moseley (Harmondsworth: Penguin, 1983), 9, 31–32; Felipe Fernández-Armesto, *Columbus* (Oxford: Oxford University Press, 1991), 38–39.
36. Obregón, *Columbus Papers*, 69.
37. *EA*, I:1–2.
38. Ferdinando Almeida, *Ad Alexandrum VI* (Rome, 1493[?]); *EA*, I:1. The crucial passage: "Ille inquam Rex est, fama super aetheram notus, quem novis repertis hominibus ampliasse hominum genus. Quem novis additis terrarum orbi plurimisque a nobis disiunctis insulis: orbem ipsam propagasse et ipsius auspitio illas quas penitus ignorabamas certas, ac nobis notas rediddit" (That man, I declare, is the King, known in renown above the aether, who has increased the race of humanity since new peoples have been found; [the king] who has increased the globe itself, by the addition of new islands to the earth's orb, many of them disjoined from us, and on his own auspices, those islands of which we were, until now, unaware, he has made them known to us). Translation by Daniel Richter.

This engraving from one of the earliest editions of Columbus's letter announcing his discovery graphically summarized the explorer's view of Tainos, whom he described as uncivilized and timid, evident in their nudity and efforts to recoil from the arriving Europeans. From Basel, 1494 edition. Courtesy of the Huntington Library, San Marino, California.

News about Columbus's journey spread with alacrity if not accuracy. Accounts raced through Italian city-states. On April 21 Giocomo Trotti, an advisor to the duke of Ferrara, wrote to his patron from Milan to tell him about the return of Columbus, who, "because the world being round," had sailed westward to reach Asia. He noted that the Spanish had captured some of the Tainos to act as interpreters, a plan that worked when "the said captives went through the houses of the villages and towns saying that a man sent by God had come into those parts. For this reason, all those people, being of good faith, swore close love and friendship with Columbus and his men." He mentioned the presence of gold, aloe, and pepper and that the Natives walked around naked.[39] The next day Luca Fancelli, a student of the renowned Florentine architect Filippo Brunelleschi, wrote that Columbus had reached the Indies in sixteen days and found there generous, naked people inhabiting lush islands that could provide gold.[40] Two days later, Allegretto Allegretti, the commissioner general of the Sienese Republic, wrote in his diary that the Spanish king had "discovered many islands again this year, that is, in the Canaries, beyond the Pillars of Hercules." Allegretti, who claimed that the mariner returned with thirty captives, insisted that he gathered this information "by way of several letters from our merchants in Spain, and by word of mouth from several people." If he is to be believed, news about Columbus's findings outpaced the spread of the published letter.[41] Information about Hispaniola almost immediately reached Milan and Venice. Historians integrated American news into their narratives, at times adding details borrowed from tales of ancient Amazon warriors and rumors of cannibals.[42]

On May 3, 1493, Pope Alexander VI realized that he needed to weigh in on the news coming from Spain. In the bull known as *Inter caetera*, he praised Ferdinand and Isabella for their efforts to strengthen the church, which included the Reconquista and expelling the Moors and Jews from

39. Geoffrey Symcox, ed., *Italian Reports on America, 1493–1522: Letters, Dispatches, and Papal Bulls*, Repertorium Columbianum X (Turnhout, Belgium: Brepols, 2001), 27–28.
40. Symcox, ed., *Italian Reports on America, 1493–1522: Letters, Dispatches, and Papal Bulls*, 28–29.
41. Luciano Formisano and Geoffrey Symcox, eds., *Italian Reports on America, 1493–1522: Accounts by Contemporary Observers*, Repertorium Columbianum XII (Turnhout, Belgium: Brepols, 2002), 28.
42. Taddeo Vimercati to the duke of Milan, April 27, 1493, and annals of Domenico Malipiero and the historian Giacomo Filippo Foresti da Bergamo, who included these details in his *Novissie hystoriarum omnium repercussions*, published in Venice in 1503. See Formisano and Symcox, eds., *Italian Reports on America, 1493–1522: Accounts by Contemporary Observers*, 27–29.

Granada the previous year. He acknowledged that Columbus had discovered islands that had not yet "been found by others" and praised the Castilians for their commitment to spreading the faith in these distant lands. To facilitate that effort, he granted to the monarchs of Castile and León and their heirs "each and every said land and island thus unknown, both those already found by your envoys and those yet to be found, and which are not at present established under the temporal domination of any Christian lords." The Iberians would have the authority to govern these lands. But Alexander understood that the Portuguese had also been active in the Atlantic and "have also found and acquired other islands similarly in the regions of Africa, Guinea, and El Mina by an apostolic grant made to them." These Iberians were to possess the same rights as the Spanish would to the west. With a second bull he established a line that ran from one pole to the other that "would lie "one hundred leagues to the south and west from any of the islands which are commonly called the Azores and Cape Verde," as long as these islands "were not possessed in actuality by any Christian king or ruler" as of December 25, 1492. With this act, the pope divided the areas available to the Spanish from those to be claimed by the Portuguese.[43]

While Columbus's report had generated intense interest, the issue that it posed to the Vatican was not complicated. Ever since the middle of the fourteenth century, popes had been issuing bulls that related to reports of Portuguese explorers who had traveled to Africa. Yet by interpreting the Iberians' action as a missionary endeavor, Alexander stretched the original intent of both Columbus and the monarchs. What they had in mind was a commercial enterprise—getting to the East Indies more quickly than any other European had managed to accomplish. Once on the islands, and crucially in his public report, Columbus recognized that they had crossed into a religious borderland with peoples unknown to Europeans and unfamiliar with the practices of Christianity. The pope seized on the discovery because it provided him with yet more souls to bring into the fold of the universal church.[44]

43. Alexander VI, "Inter cetera" 1, and Alexander VI, "Inter cetera" 2, in Symcox, ed., *Italian Reports on America, 1493–1522: Letters, Dispatches, and Papal Bulls*, 31–34, 39–43, 36–37; William D. Phillips and Carla Rahn Phillips, *The Worlds of Christopher Columbus* (Cambridge: Cambridge University Press, 1992), 187–188; Luis Wekcmann-Muñoz, "The Alexandrine Bulls of 1493: Pseudo-Asiatic Documents," in Fredi Chiapelli, ed., *First Images of America: The Impact of the New World on the Old* (Berkeley: University of California Press, 1976), 1:202.

44. Symcox, ed., *Italian Reports on America, 1493–1522: Letters, Dispatches, and Papal Bulls*, 10; Weckman-Muñoz, "Alexandrine Bulls of 1493," 1:205–206.

Within a year of the explorer's return, Florentine cleric Giuliano Dati, the bishop of Sierra Leone, rephrased Columbus's letter in a poem published in Rome and Florence. One edition of Dati's poem included illustrations of monsters, which the engraver remained convinced were in existence even though Columbus never mentioned them.[45] By the end of the century, translations of Columbus's letter as well as other versions of Dati's version had appeared from publishers in Strasbourg, Valladolid, Florence, Heidelberg, Augsburg, Nuremberg, Venice, Pavia, Lübeck, Ferrara, Bologna, Burgos, Brescia, and Milan as well as continuing to appear in printers' works from Rome and Basel.[46]

Despite Columbus twice mentioning the fact that he met humans, not monsters, in the Caribbean, even his firsthand account was insufficient to eradicate long-held European ideas about the so-called monstrous races, as can be seen in this engraving from Florentine cleric and poet Giuliano Dati's verse rendering of the explorer's first published report. From *La lettera dellisole che ha Trovato nouvamente el re dispagna* (Florence, 1495). Courtesy of the Huntington Library, San Marino, California.

45. Giuliano Dati, *La lettera dellisole che ha trovato nuovamente il Re dispagna* (Florence, 1493); for a facsimile and translation, see Martin Davies, ed., *Columbus in Italy: An Italian Versification of the Letter on the Discovery of the New World* (London: British Library, 1991).
46. *EA*, I:2–3.

In late May 1493, Ferdinand and Isabella sent Columbus warrants enabling him to use their authority to gather the ships and equipment he would need for a new expedition. Their contract established Columbus as "our admiral of the Ocean Sea and our viceroy and governor of the islands and the mainland of the Ocean Sea that are in the region of the Indies." They gave him the authority to select those who would administer the colonies and the ability to commandeer ships from those otherwise unwilling to contribute to the cause. The monarchs emphasized their desire to convert Tainos "to our Holy Catholic Faith, since they have neither dogma nor worship." To do so, they instructed Columbus, echoing linguist Antonio de Nebrija, to teach Spanish to any Indigenous who sailed to Spain.[47]

Brandishing these privileges, Columbus returned to the Indies in late 1493 in a flotilla of seventeen ships carrying 1,200 to 1,500 men, many of them peasants hoping to create farms or work in mines. The expedition also included artisans, physicians, seventeen notaries, three royal treasury officials, two royal scribes, and at least twelve religious—but no women. The preparations reveal that the Spaniards intended to move quickly from a moment of exploration to launching a colony, which Columbus planned to situate on Hispaniola. In some ways, this voyage proved less auspicious than the first. The travelers reported that they discovered seven islands populated by cannibals, thereby cementing a trope that would stubbornly persist for years to come. But the newcomers possessed sufficient military strength to overcome the danger, offering those they found the option of abandoning the consumption of human flesh or becoming enslaved.[48]

More worrisome, the sailors discovered that the men they had left behind on Hispaniola among the allegedly timid Tainos had been killed. At first they presumed that the Tainos had murdered them, but eventually Columbus learned that the Spaniards had turned on each other. Reassured that the Tainos could become their allies, Columbus and his men established an alliance with a local king named Guacanagarí. Soon the Spanish were shipping gold homeward. "By their labors," Pavia-based

47. *The Book of Privileges Issued to Christopher Columbus by King Fernando and Queen Isabel, 1492–1502*, ed. and trans. Helen Nader, Repertorium Columbianum II (Berkeley: University of California Press, 1996) (hereafter *Book of Privileges*), 79–85, quotation at 84 (admiral); Deagan and Cruzent, *Columbus's Outpost*, quotation at 16.

48. Niccolò Scillacio, *De Insulis meridian atque Indici maris . . . nuper inventis* [*The Islands Recently Discovered in the Southern and Indian Seas*] (Pavia, [1494?]), translation in Formisano and Symcox, ed., *Italian Reports on America, 1493–1522: Accounts by Contemporary Observers*, 38–41; see also the letter of Giovanni de' Bardi of April 19, 1494, in Symcox, ed., *Italian Reports on America, 1493–1522: Letters, Dispatches, and Papal Bulls*, 44; Deagan and Cruxent, *Columbus's Outpost*, 18–21.

scholar Nicolò Scillacio soon wrote, "the kingdom of the Spaniards had been mightily increased, unknown lands had been occupied, and countless nations taken into the empire, far-flung lands stretching out to the west, beyond the equator and the burning heat of the zodiac, and peoples had been encountered in droves who lived scattered about without laws, and who could be quickly brought to the religion of Christ." Columbus, joyful at these developments, sent twelve caravels back to Spain to share the good fortune. He remained behind to supervise the construction of the new walled city he labeled La Isabela, from which ships bearing beeswax, ginger, cinnamon, and aloe would sail for Spain.[49]

While the caravels sailed eastward, representatives of the Spanish and Portuguese monarchs had come to an agreement about the resources of the West Indies. Following the pope's order of 1493, the nations on June 7, 1494, signed the Treaty of Tordesillas, which quickly redefined Europeans' understanding of the Atlantic basin. It established a line 370 leagues west of the Cape Verde Islands (c. 46° 30′ W longitude), giving the Spanish all territory to its west but reserving to the Portuguese all lands, including islands, that lay to its east—territory, Europeans soon learned, that included Brazil.[50]

Columbus again departed for Spain on March 10, 1496. That same year his brother Bartholomew established the foundations for Santo Domingo, which would become the longest continually occupied European colonial city in the Western Hemisphere and, according to contemporary Europeans, a base for expanding Christendom.[51] On this expedition Columbus concluded that he had found the location of the Earthly Paradise, another reading of an American landscape to make it conform to his prior study of scripture and ancient texts.[52]

Among those who remained behind at Hispaniola was a Spanish monk named Ramón Pané, who lived among the Tainos to learn their language and beliefs as part of his effort to convert the newly colonized. Pané understood that the Tainos worshipped "the heavens, planets, and stars." They also inhabited islands where demonic forces appeared at night as "phantasms and visions" and where the Tainos "senselessly make simula-

49. Deagan and Cruxent, *Columbus's Outpost*, 21–22; Scillacio, *De Insults*, 43–48; Luciano Gallinari, ed., *Diego Alvarez Chanca, Medico de Cristofero Colombo* (Cagliari, Italy: Istituto sui Rapporti Italo-Iberici, 1992), 243–244, 266–268; Geoffrey Symcox and Blair Sullivan, eds., *Columbus and the Enterprise of the Indies* (Boston: Bedford/St. Martin's, 2005), 157–159.

50. Treaty between Spain and Portugal concluded at Tordesillas, June 7, 1494, Avalon.

51. Formisano and Symcox, eds., *Italian Reports on America, 1493–1522: Accounts by Contemporary Observers*, 48–49.

52. See Greenblatt, *Marvelous Possessions*, 78–79.

cra which they gather together to worship." The Native residents taught Pané how humans had come into the world, offering versions of cosmogony that incorporated nightingales, plum trees, ants, and a woodpecker. Pané thought the story reminded him of the ancient Myrmidons, who—according to Greek historians—"were descended from ants." He learned about a sacred cave, decorated with *cemíes*, where "the sun and moon issued forth from there to illuminate the world." Elders kept these origin stories alive.[53]

In addition to providing the first European assessment of any American religion, Pané was also the first to describe healing practices in the Indies. Given the extraordinary efforts Europeans had made to extract medical benefits from the natural world, his description would have no doubt attracted attention, especially in the aftermath of the earliest reports of the *materia medica* that could be harvested in the Indies. Unlike the physician Chanca, Pané instead wrote about what he saw as the trickery practiced on credulous people by charlatans. The healers claimed an ability to communicate with the *cemíes* and provided an herb to patients that sent them into "a frenzy" and caused them to "moan like drunken men." Pané claimed that the Tainos used various practices with alleged medicinal power, including sucking on stones, blowing on the bodies of the ill, and massaging a sick person's lower extremities, to persuade the innocent that they could drive disease from human bodies.[54]

Pané's observations about Taino practice constituted a new kind of European testimony. Columbus's public report created the idea of America as a place to extract raw materials to advance economic interests. Pané's writing advanced a necessary corollary: if Tainos (or, by implication, other Indigenous) did not accept European ways, it was because they remained dupes of charlatans. By this reckoning, such people perhaps did not deserve the natural resources they possessed.

Spaniards were not quite ready to embrace the complete dispossession of the Tainos. Their reluctance emerged during Columbus's third voyage, which arrived at Trinidad on August 1, 1498. Four days later he dispatched an exploratory venture westward, toward what he hoped would be the mainland. The situation deteriorated for Columbus, who was soon accused of poor management and cruel treatment of the Tainos. News of his malfeasance reached Spain and prompted the monarchs to send Francisco de Bobadilla to Santo Domingo to arrest the alleged malefactors.

53. Formisano and Symcox, eds., *Italian Reports on America, 1493–1522: Accounts by Contemporary Observers*, 63–66.

54. Formisano and Symcox, eds., *Italian Reports on America, 1493–1522: Accounts by Contemporary Observers*, 66.

The Admiral of the Ocean Seas arrived in Spain in chains in October 1500, though Ferdinand and Isabella released him after two months in captivity.

News that Columbus had captured and enslaved West Indians perturbed Isabella. Once Columbus had claimed Taino homelands as her territory, the inhabitants became her subjects and, by her reckoning, could not be enslaved. "What power of mine," the queen wondered, "has the Admiral to give anyone my vassals?" Columbus managed to find a way around her logic, arguing that enslaving cannibals or war captives should be permissible since existing canon law, as well as the Castilian legal code, permitted it. To advance his cause, he shipped eight Kalinagos, seen by him as enemies of Spaniards, to Seville. If he could establish the legitimacy of their enslavement, then by his logic this would open the possibility of enslaving Tainos, a task he had already embraced with enthusiasm.[55] While that debate unfolded, the pope issued the bull *Eximie devotionis* in November 1501, which allowed Ferdinand and Isabella to tax both Indigenous and colonists to provide support for churches and priests.[56]

While he was still in Spain, Columbus decided the time had come to make what became his most grandiose claims about his role in recent events. What had begun as a commercial venture had taken on a religious meaning it initially lacked. Once back home, Columbus dug deeply into Scripture as well as the works of subsequent theologians including St. Augustine and a French cardinal and astrologer named Pierre d'Ailly, who had died in 1420, as well as classical authorities. He then produced a text that bore the title *Book or collection of auctoritates* [authoritative writings], *sayings, opinions, and prophecies concerning the need to recover the Holy City and Mount Zion, and the finding and conversion of the islands and of all peoples and nations.* Columbus's son Ferdinand gave the book, which Columbus quite likely took with him on his next journey to the West Indies, a simpler name: *Book of Prophecies*.[57]

55. Liss, *Isabel the Queen*, 329, 334–335; Instructions to Columbus, April 23, 1497, *Book of Privileges*, 106; J. H. Elliott, *Empires of the Atlantic World: Britain and Spain in America, 1492–1830* (New Haven, CT: Yale University Press, 2006), 97–98; Stone, *Captives of Conquest*, 8.
56. Symcox, ed., *Italian Reports on America, 1493–1522: Letters, Dispatches, and Papal Bulls*, 58–59.
57. *The Book of Prophecies*, ed. Roberto Rusconi, trans. Blair Sullivan, Repertorium Columbianum IV (Berkeley: University of California Press, 1997), 5 (title), 33 (taking the book on the fourth voyage). The original manuscript can be found at the

Returning to the model he had employed in the published letter of 1493, Columbus again addressed this book as a letter to Isabella and Ferdinand. What followed departed from that precursor, reading less like a finished argument than like a commonplace book—a hodgepodge of references to Columbus's own experiences, thoughts, and extracts from a remarkable range of sources. Unlike his published letter of 1493, this was a private book with a specific audience: the monarchs who had only recently released him from prison. He needed to regain their support if he was to complete his mission, which by then meant more to him than finding a water route to the Spice Islands or even harvesting the natural resources of the Indies. Columbus had in mind nothing less than, as he put it, the "restitution of the holy temple to the holy Church Militant."[58]

Columbus had come to this exalted sense of his world-historical significance from his own experience. By his reckoning, he had been sailing the Atlantic for forty years and had "personally sailed to all the known regions." He believed he had been endowed by God with great intelligence as well as natural seamanship abilities, which he combined with study of geometry, history, philosophy, cosmography, and astrology as well as "the mental and physical dexterity required to draw spherical maps of cities, rivers and mountains, islands and ports, with everything in its proper place." Columbus understood what every subsequent European explorer of the Americas recognized: their achievements far from home would be meaningless unless they could find a way to communicate what they saw to those in Europe who could support additional ventures and provide rewards for what they accomplished. He believed his careful study and lifelong experience had made him the ideal vessel for expanding the reach of his homeland, and because of this he deserved royal support. "Who could doubt," he asked, "that this flash of understanding was the work of the Holy Spirit, as well as my own?"[59]

Columbus knew he had become a less-than-favored subject of the crowns of Aragon and Castile. He had been trying to regain the privileges that had been taken from him when he was imprisoned and sent homeward at the end of his third voyage. He knew that others had spoken ill of him, castigating him for being "an uneducated man, an uninformed sailor, an ordinary person." He compared his struggles with those of St. Matthew and biblical prophets, and he embraced the legacy of Isaiah, who "was not just a prophet, but also an evangelist; he put all his efforts into describing

Biblioteca Columbina y Capitular in Seville; for a description of the text, see *Book of Prophecies*, 35–48.

58. *Book of Prophecies*, 67.

59. *Book of Prophecies*, 67–69.

the future and calling all people to our holy Catholic faith." If he had more time to complete his vision, he would fulfill the prophecy of the Italian theologian, mystic, and prophet Joachim of Fiore, who had died at the dawn of the thirteenth century and had "predicted that someone from Spain would recover the wealth of Zion."[60]

In the *Book of Prophecies*, Columbus cast himself as the ultimate agent of the next stage of biblical history. The Reconquista and the expulsion of the Jews and Muslims bolstered his opinion. He wove himself into a series of biblical excerpts and likened his life to the ancients. In fevered prose he drew from the books of Obadiah, Micah, Jeremiah, Genesis, First Chronicles, Ecclesiastes, Psalms, and Isaiah to create a spiritual geography that pivoted on a holy mountain and islands.[61] "During the last years of the world, the time will come in which the Ocean sea will loosen the bounds and a large landmass will appear," he wrote, adding that a "new sailor like the one named Tiphys," who had guided Jason, "will discover a new world, and then Thule will no longer be the most remote land."[62]

In the years of his exile, then, Columbus was consumed with reading holy signs. Where was the entrance to Mount Zion? What did it mean that he had found so many islands scattered so far from the Old World? He had evolved from a man obsessed with worldly gain to one driven to find the route to God's holiest places. What he needed was to return to the Indies, this time not in pursuit of a way to the Pacific but instead to explore the holy geography of this scripturally defined region.[63]

Columbus got his chance when his patrons decided he had earned one more opportunity, which he embraced as "high admiral of the Ocean Sea, viceroy, and governor general of the islands and mainland of Asia and the Indies," a privileged subject of an ever-expansive Castilian empire.[64] He led four ships from Cádiz on May 9, 1502. The expedition did not go well. While he was still in Spain, Isabella had transferred the governorship of the Indies to Nicolás de Ovando, who took up residence on Hispaniola,

60. *Book of Prophecies*, 161–169 (restitution), 73 (Matthew and Isiah), 317 (Joachim).

61. *Book of Prophecies*, 77, 165 (Reconquista), 289, 79 (biblical parallels), 241, 335–339 (spiritual geography).

62. *Book of Prophecies*, 291–293, quotation at 291.

63. See Columbus to Nicolò Oderigo, March 21, 1502, in *Book of Prophecies*, 172. As one of Columbus's most astute biographers has written, the "most disturbing feature of Columbus's mental state at this time was that he sought to circumvent the fact of his failure by senselessly affirming that he had succeeded." His "obstinate reversion to falsehoods marks the virtual end of Columbus's intellectual development, the triumph of obsession under the influence of ill fortune." Felipe Fernández-Armesto, *Columbus on Himself* (Indianapolis, IN: Hackett, 2010), 219.

64. Columbus to the Directors of the Bank of St. George, April 2, 1502, in *Book of Privileges*, 189.

the largest Spanish settlement in the Caribbean. Columbus arrived there on June 29, but Ovando refused to let him land even though Columbus told him that a hurricane was forming. Ovando was so confident Columbus was wrong that he sent a fleet to Spain. Twenty-five ships with their crews disappeared in the storm. For his part, Columbus sailed to Honduras, finally reaching the mainland that had eluded him up to that point. He traveled to Panama and traded with Natives there, and then sailed again for Hispaniola. But the intervening months had taken a toll on his ships. Two were so worm-eaten that they could not be put to sea, which left him with only two of his original vessels. They managed to reach as far as Jamaica but could get no farther. Columbus and some of his men, separated from those rotten hulls, reached Hispaniola on large canoes paddled by Tainos. After spending the summer of 1504 on Hispaniola, he departed for home, arriving at Sanlúcar de Barrameda on November 7. Less than three weeks later Isabella died. Columbus ended his days in Valladolid, where he succumbed to illness on May 20, 1506.

By the time of his death, Columbus's experiences had shifted the history of the Americas. Unlike the Norse, Columbus promulgated tales of encounters in the Americas that circulated widely in print, farther than Icelandic sagas ever managed to do. Columbus inspired the passions of Europeans who saw financial gain if they could bring American resources to European consumers. While Columbus could not have known it, some of those who pursued those resources—the gold to fill state coffers or paint church interiors, the plants that expanded the catalog of European *materia medica*, the souls brought into Christendom by eager priests who measured their success by each person accepting the word of the European God, the fame that would come from additional explorations and placing one's name on a map—also brought infectious diseases with them, though there is no evidence of major epidemics during Columbus's lifetime.

Just as decisively, Columbus and his men introduced a new kind of slavery into the Western Hemisphere. Unlike the forced labor evident in locales like Cahokia, the Spanish created a system in the Caribbean in which one's freedom could be taken by a newcomer who used raw power to force men, women, and children into perpetual service. In the first years of the new century, as a result of allocations of Tainos to colonizers desperate to find gold, the Indigenous population, suffering from famine, assaults, and possibly diseases that Spanish observers did not describe, took a sharp downturn. By 1514 there were perhaps only 26,000 Tainos still alive even though many Spanish, frustrated by the administration of the island, had left for more promising opportunities, including in Cuba. Smallpox arrived in December 1518 and the epidemic lasted four months. At that point, Spanish observers realized that there would be no way to utilize Tainos as a labor force. By the early 1520s, the Tainos had almost vanished.[65] Those sold into bondage were the first of 70,000 documented enslaved Indigenous in the Caribbean basin—though the real number may have reached 650,000.[66]

By the time Columbus died the Spanish had planted a colonial infrastructure in the Caribbean. Over time it would become increasingly durable and alter the fates of every individual—American, European, and African—who landed there. But those islands were no longer the sole area of European interest.

Soon after Columbus's return from his third expedition, the Portuguese explorer Amerigo Vespucci, with support from Ferdinand of Aragon, led an exploratory journey into the waters south of those seen by Columbus. Vespucci, who had earlier helped Columbus prepare for his third journey, returned from his voyage of 1499–1500 with news of the resources and peoples of modern-day Guiana and Brazil. He also came back having reached a conclusion that had eluded Columbus: South America was a continent, not an island. "After sailing continuously for about four hundred leagues along the coast," Vespucci wrote, "we concluded that this was a continental land" because "many times we chanced to see various animals, such as lions, deer, roe deer, boars, rabbits and other land animals not found on islands, but only on the mainland." He thought he had found an extension of Asia that no European had ever known, "a continent in those southern regions that is inhabited by more numerous peoples and animals than in our Europe, or Asia or Africa." Getting to the Spice Islands would involve navigating around what Vespucci announced in print, following the strategy Columbus had employed in 1493, as a *mundus novus*—a "new world." He subsequently made two more journeys, sponsored by King Manoel I of Portugal, describing territory that fell to the east of the line determined by the Treaty of Tordesillas. Vespucci was a brilliant self-promoter, extolling the importance of his exploits in printed books. As his reputation spread, Europeans began to refer to the Western Hemisphere as the Americas in Vespucci's honor.[67]

65. Livi-Bacci, "Return to Hispaniola," 4–6, 34, 38–44.

66. Stone, *Captives of Conquest*, 7; Nancy E. Van Deusen, *Global Indios: The Indigenous Struggle for Justice in Sixteenth-Century Spain* (Durham, NC: Duke University Press, 2015), 2.

67. Martin Lehmann, "Amerigo Vespucci and His Alleged Awareness of America as a Separate Land Mass," *Imago Mundi* 65 (2013), 15–24, quotations at 18 and 19.

News of Vespucci's discoveries quickly spread across the continent by word of mouth, letters, and in print. In 1504 his *Mundus novus* became a printing sensation, with an edition appearing in Venice, two in Augsburg, and another in Rome, with translations of his writings appearing in 1505 in Latin, German, and Italian, from printers in Nuremberg, Strasbourg, Augsburg, Rostock, Florence, Cologne, Antwerp, Leipzig, Basel, and Munich as well as an edition in Czech printed in Pilsen.[68] Mounting evidence suggested that the Americas contained the human and natural resources needed for European glory. One of those who paid attention was Juan Ponce de León.

On February 23, 1512, Ferdinand II of Spain issued a patent to Ponce de León, who had by then served as governor of the eastern portion of Hispaniola and then of Puerto Rico. But in 1511 he had lost that position when the Council of Spain decided to reorganize the administration of the islands, specifically to grant authority to Columbus's sons, a plan that Columbus had suggested at the time of his first voyage. The new patent granted Ponce de León the authority to explore only waters north of already claimed Spanish islands. He sought a rumored island called Beniny, one of many islands in the Atlantic that Europeans had either seen from a distance or vaguely heard about. If he found it, he would become *adelantado* (governor) and rule that land for the rest of his life, as long as he abided by certain provisions. For the first twelve years he had to give one-tenth of his revenue to the king, who would appoint someone to handle the "allotment of the Indians"—the sale of Native peoples into slavery and their distribution. Ferdinand also laid a claim to a share of any gold or other minerals found on Beniny and forbade Ponce de León from taking along any individuals "who are foreigners from outside our domains and seigniories."[69]

The patent authorizing Ponce de León's exploration remains the earliest account that survives for Spanish expectations about what to do when the scope of their raids extended beyond those accomplished by Columbus during his four voyages. At its core, the patent emphasized ideas that by then had become embedded in Spanish conceptions of the Western Hemisphere—specifically, that they would control the fate of all Native peoples they encountered, their agents had the right to extract natural resources, and those who sailed abroad had to share their revenues with

68. See, e.g., Amerigo Vespucci, *Petri Francisci de Medicis Salutem plurimam* (Paris, 1503) (HEH 19286); *EA*, I:7–9. Three editions of Vespucci's *Mundus novus* appeared in 1504, printed in Venice, Augsburg, and Rome, with editions appearing the next year from printers in Cologne, Antwerp, and Nuremberg.

69. T. Frederick Davis, "Ponce de Leon's First Voyage and Discovery of Florida," *Florida Historical Society Quarterly* 14 (1935), 9–14.

their patrons. The still (to the Europeans) unknown parts of the Americas existed to satisfy their habits and tastes. Gold, souls, and human labor existed to be harvested. The Spanish did not anticipate the large-scale migration of Europeans across the Atlantic, a notion that would become central to others' plans for the Americas. Exploitation, not settlement, remained their goal.

The patent that Ponce de León received required that he write a report about Beniny. The Spanish understood that it was not enough to land at a place and lay claim to it. By publishing accounts of what could be found in such a place, they could inscribe their possession on European maps, thereby further establishing their control over distant territory while ignoring the fact that these lands had occupants. This was crucial in an age when no European monarch or state had the resources to defend far-flung territories from potential invaders. Better, as the Spanish knew, to establish a claim and hope that other Europeans would avoid the territory when they planned their own journeys.

When Ferdinand offered Ponce de León this patent in 1512, he presumed that other Europeans would be the source of possible danger because, to that point, no Indigenous American group had been able to mount an effective opposition to Spanish claimants. That situation would change when the Spanish undertook to conquer the vast lands of the Mexica, which in the 1510s lay under the control of the Aztec ruler Moctezuma II. But the siege and conquest of Tenochtitlán by the conquistador Hernán Cortés, which would occur from 1519 to 1521, lay in the future. In 1512, the Spanish had yet to encounter any powerful resistance to their actions—despite Columbus and his followers enslaving Tainos and hauling off whatever natural resources they wanted. Seen from this moment, the conquest and colonization of the as yet undetected island of Beniny seemed a straightforward task that could be entrusted to a loyal and experienced governor.

On March 3, 1513, Ponce de León set sail from Puerto Rico.[70] On the night of April 2 he dropped anchor about two and a half miles (one Spanish league) from shore. He failed to find a harbor like those the Spanish had found in the West Indies. While he presumed that he was running along the outer banks of yet another island, the sailors took

70. The original documents for Ponce de León's voyages have long been lost; the earliest surviving account can be found in Antonio de Herrera, *Historia General de los hechos de los Castellanos en las Islasi tierra firme del Mar oceano* [General history of the events of the Castilians on the islands and the mainland of the Ocean Sea] (Madrid, 1601); see also John Hann, "Juan Ponce de León in Florida: A Translation of the Antonio de Herrera Account," 2009, in the John H. Hann Collection of Colonial Records at the University of Florida, https://ufdc.ufl.edu/AA00038903/00001/pdf/0.

account of an inviting territory of level lands and dense forests. Ponce de León, following the practice that the Iberians had used since Columbus's first voyage, landed and claimed possession of the territory. He described it as the Feast of Flowers—Pascua Florida.[71]

Ponce de León and his crew were likely just off the shore of modern-day Melbourne Beach, a long spit of land on Florida's east side that lacks a natural harbor.[72] Several days later they sailed southward and eventually came upon a small town. Ponce de León, according to the later chronicler Antonio de Herrera, "went ashore, called by the Indians, who immediately tried to take the boat, the oars, and the [Spaniards'] arms." They shot arrows made from "sharpened bones and fish spines" that struck two of Ponce de León's men. Despite the setback, Ponce de León and some of his men went in search of fresh water the next day. They met a group of about sixty and, following Columbus's model, captured one of them "so that he might learn the language." Ponce de León named a stream La Cruz, and he and his men fashioned a cross from stones and left it there with an inscription. But the water proved undrinkable, and the Spanish took to their ships and continued to sail south. On May 15, the Feast of the Holy Spirit, they named a cluster of rocks Los Martires—possibly one of the Florida Keys—because, "seen from a distance, the rocks as they rose to view appeared like men who were suffering."[73]

In the days that followed, the Spanish went around the southern tip of the peninsula and eventually made it as far north as modern Charlotte Harbor, where they likely met a group of Indigenous called Calusas, who had mastered the shallow waters and built canals to facilitate canoe travel long before the Spanish arrived. After about three weeks the Spanish turned back, sailed to the coast of Cuba, and then in early July headed back toward Florida and the Bahamas.[74] Sometimes they fought with the Natives, but other times they traded with them. One time they captured four women, though Herrera did not explain what happened other than that the Spanish destroyed two canoes, presumably to stop others from

71. Davis, "Ponce de Leon's Voyages," 16–17.

72. Juan Ponce de Leon landing site, Brevard Board of County Commissioners, https://www.brevardfl.gov/ParksAndRecreation/ParksByCity/ParksInMelbourneBeach/PonceDeLeon (accessed November 23, 2023).

73. Herrera added that the name made sense since many others had succumbed there in the years since Ponce de León's voyage; see Davis, "Ponce de Leon's Voyages," 17–19; Hann, "Juan Ponce de León in Florida."

74. Jerald T. Milanich, "Water World," *Archaeology* 57, no. 5 (2004), 46–50; William H. Marquandt, "The Development of Cultural Complexity in Southwest Florida: Elements of a Critique," *Southeastern Archaeology* 5 (1986), 63070; see the map in Davis, "Ponce de Leon's Voyages," 26.

recapturing them. On another occasion, they got into a major skirmish, killing an unknown number and capturing four more—two of whom Ponce de León sent home with word that the Natives had killed one of the Spaniards but still wanted to make an accord. In trade, they gathered poor-quality gold (*guanín*) and "skins," which might have meant deerskins but could have referred to the pelts of some of the region's fur-bearing mammals. On the fourth of June they met one local who could speak Spanish. Herrera wrote that the sailors believed "he must be from Hispaniola or from another island of those inhabited by the Spaniards." Day after day they tried to figure out what resources they could extract. On June 21 they approached a series of rocks they called Las Tortugas, and there they hauled in 160 tortoises, fourteen seals, and an unknown number of pelicans.[75]

By late July, Ponce de León and his men set sail for Puerto Rico. Herrera did not mention if they still had captives with them, or what had happened to the four women they had taken. For his part, Ponce de León was not sure if he had found Beniny or had just been coasting around a large island. He wanted to keep exploring because he had heard about "the wealth of this island, and especially of that particular spring so the Indians said that restores men from aged men to youths, the which he had not been able to find, by reason of shoals and currents and contrary weather." Unable to go on his own, he sent others to search for it. After his return to San Juan those he had dispatched arrived and told him that they had found the island but "not the spring." They told him that the island was large and covered with woodlands and springs. "The discovery by Juan Ponce of La Florida so ended," Herrera concluded, "without knowledge that it was the mainland." It would be years before the Spanish realized where he had landed.[76]

75. Davis, "Ponce de Leon's Voyages," 19–23.
76. Davis, "Ponce de Leon's Voyages," 23.

3

"Canada"

During the late 1490s, while Columbus, his sons, and their allies were laying the foundations for Spanish expansion to the mainland, European monarchs began to entertain proposals from explorers who hoped to sail to the South Sea via the northern reaches of the Atlantic. Among them was the Venetian-born mariner Zuan Cabuto (or Giovanni Caboto, later known as John Cabot), who took up Columbus's original goal of finding a water route from western Europe to the Spice Islands. Possibly living in Spain when Columbus returned in 1493, Cabot understood that he needed powerful patrons. After being rebuffed by both Spanish and Portuguese officials when he suggested that the best route to the east could be found by traveling west in the far north, he obtained an audience with Henry VII in 1496. The English king, perhaps regretting that he had been unable to support Christopher Columbus after his brother Bartholomew's earlier visit to England, proved amenable to Cabot's plan. The Venetian captain funded by an English monarch sailed west from Bristol on May 20, 1497, commanding a vessel with about twenty in his crew, including his son Sebastian.[1]

When Cabot pitched his plan to Henry VII, he argued that the shorter distance to be traveled would give the English a decided advantage over the Spanish. His plan made sense when looking at a globe. But he failed to consider the prevailing currents and winds, which made travel westward across the North Atlantic—where water was especially frigid because of the Little Ice Age—more difficult than transiting the southerly seas.

On June 22, 1497, about six weeks after their departure, the explorers sighted land. Like Columbus five years earlier, Cabot took possession through enacting specific rituals, which included a declaration that the territory was possessed by Henry VII. They noticed fishing nets on the

1. Peter E. Pope, *The Many Landfalls of John Cabot* (Toronto: University of Toronto Press, 1997), 13–20; "The offer of the discoverie of the West Indies by Christopher Columbus to King Henrie the seventh in the yere 1488," in Richard Hakluyt, *The Principall Navigations, Voiages, and Discoveries of the English Nation* (London, 1589), 507–509.

shore but saw no inhabitants. Cabot and the others had performed their theatrics in front of no one on the ground—but when they got home they publicized their action to the audience that really mattered: their royal sponsor. After exploring the coastline of modern Newfoundland or Nova Scotia—the documents are ambiguous—the English returned to England, arriving in Bristol on August 6. The mariners told the merchants of the rich fisheries they had encountered. In February 1498, an enthusiastic Henry provided Cabot with a royal ship and crew for a second mission. Cabot departed in May in a flotilla of five ships. One turned back early to Bristol and the other four disappeared. One of them probably had John Cabot on board. His son Sebastian, in all likelihood, remained in Bristol.[2]

In 1502, Sebastian sailed into the northwestern Atlantic. During the journey, he captured three Inuit men. When Cabot arrived in London with his prisoners, English observers offered remarks about these visitors' appearance and behavior. The prisoners were, one witness noted, "clothed in beastes skinnes, and eate raw fleshe." They could not communicate with their English captors. They acted like "bruite beastes" and seemed irredeemably savage. But within a few years of their arrival these three adopted English dress and language, a rapid cultural evolution in the eyes of the Europeans. News of the swift conversion was recorded first in a city chronicle and would become a fixture in English writings about North America.[3]

2. In the words of one manuscript edition of Polydore Vergil's *Anglica Historia*, written in 1512–1513, Cabot never came home and "is believed to have found the new lands nowhere but on the very bottom of the ocean, to which he is thought to have descended together with his boat, the victim himself of that self-same ocean; since after that voyage he was never seen again anywhere." See James A. Williamson, ed., *The Cabot Voyages and Bristol Discovery Under Henry VII*, Hak. Soc., 2nd Ser., 120 (Cambridge: Cambridge University Press, 1962), 224–225.

3. The initial description was in Robert Fabian's Chronicle of London, which Richard Hakluyt used when he retold the story in *Divers voyages touching the discoverie of America and the Ilands adjacent* (London, 1582), sig. A3[r]–[v]; see also John Stow, *The Chronicles of England, from Brute unto this present yeare of Christ, 1580* (London, [1580]), 875. There remains ambiguity about the origins of these men, who might have come to England with the younger Cabot or possibly on a mission sponsored by an unknown group of Bristol merchants. For the different possibilities, see David B. Quinn, "Sources for the Ethnography of Northeastern North America to 1611," Canadian Ethnology Service Paper No. 76, (Ottawa, 1981), 112–113; Williamson, ed., *Cabot Voyages*, 220–223; Pope, *The Many Landfalls of John Cabot*, 42; and Alden T. Vaughan, *Transatlantic Indians: American Indians in Britain, 1500–1776* (Cambridge: Cambridge University Press, 2006), 11. For the earliest European representation of Inuit drawn from life, see W. C. Sturtevant et al., "The First Inuit Depiction by Europeans," *Études/Inuit/Studies* 4 (1980), 47–49.

The alleged cultural conversion of the three Inuit stood in stark contrast to the experience of most Europeans who went in search of the resources of the northwestern Atlantic and an opening to a water route that would take them to the Spice Islands of the southwestern Pacific. Virtually all travelers learned quickly that this corner of North America posed problems that no one knew how to solve.

Even before Sebastian Cabot set out to retrace the journey of his father, other Europeans had begun to sail into the northwestern Atlantic. On October 28, 1499, King Manoel I of Portugal, using the authority he claimed under the Treaty of Tordesillas, offered a patent to João Fernandes, an explorer from the island of Terceira, to "seek out and discover at his own expense some islands lying in our sphere of influence." If he succeeded, he would be due the same profit and honor as the governors of other mid-Atlantic islands claimed by the Portuguese, including Madeira.[4] On May 12, 1500, Manoel granted another patent to Gaspar Corte Real, a courtier who had been funding his own exploratory journeys.[5]

Before the members of the Corte Real family were able to establish the claim and their putative colonies, a company of investors from Bristol and the Azores, then a Portuguese colony, requested a patent to enable them to explore the same region and establish trade there.[6] But the group, under the Bristol merchant Richard Warde, turned, like Cabot, to Henry VII, not Manoel I. The English monarch granted them the authority "to find, recover, discover and search out whatever islands, countries, regions or provinces of heathens and infidels, in whatever part of the world they may lie, which before this time were and at present are unknown to Christians." Once they got to such a place, they were to "set up our banners and ensigns in any town, city, castle, island or mainland." They had the authority to "enter and seize" these places and "possess and subdue" the locality and its residents. Henry's patentees would have the authority to govern any newly claimed land, including the ability to punish colonists who sexually assaulted Native women, committed murder, or stole from Indigenous people. The king added some restrictions relating to licensing and trade to protect the crown's interest but allowed colonizers

4. "Letters Patent from King Emmanuel to John Fernandez, October 23, 1499," in Henry P. Biggar, ed., *The Precursors of Jacques Cartier, 1497–1534* (Ottawa: Government Printing Bureau, 1911), 31–32.
5. "Grant to Gaspar Corte Real of Any Island, Islands, or Mainland He May Discover or Find," in Biggar, ed., *Precursors*, 35–37.
6. "Petition of Certain Merchants to Henry VII for the Issue of Letters Patent for Discovery of Trade, March 19, 1501," in Biggar, ed., *Precursors*, 40.

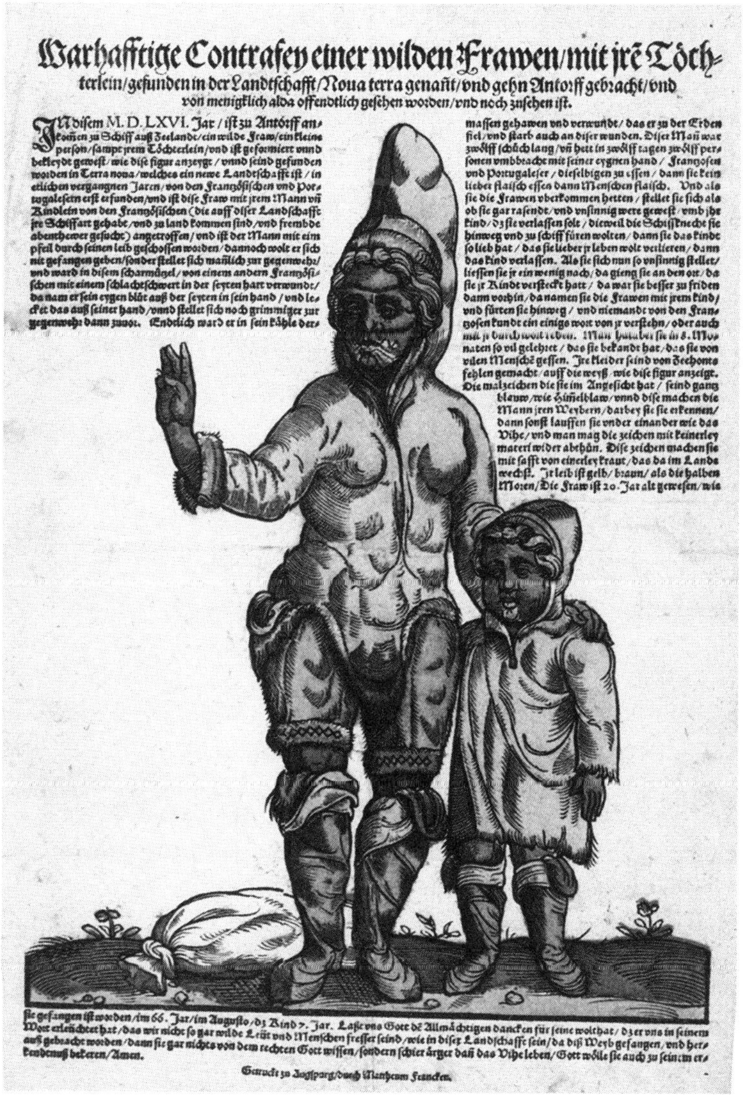

The first European representation of Inuit appeared in Augsburg in 1567, apparently to advertise the appearance of a woman and her child on display. The text claims that the mother's spouse was twelve feet tall and had killed perhaps a dozen French and Portuguese before some intrepid explorers felled him. Sailors took the survivors to Antwerp and then to Augsburg, an early example of how Indigenous Americans fascinated Europeans, who seemingly felt no hesitation about treating these alleged cannibals like other exotic specimens from distant places. Wikimedia Commons.

to sell resources extracted from this distant territory anywhere in England.[7]

These early patents suggest the territorial ambiguity of lands sighted by the Cabots, who were themselves still interested in exploring and making a profit in these northern waters. The looming contest, which would soon include French explorers, was only one of the elements that made European encounters in this region different from those in the West Indies. Columbus and the hundreds of Spaniards who sailed to the Caribbean only rarely faced the real possibility of dying because of an inability to understand their surroundings. The opposite conditions existed in the north, where Europeans, whatever they thought about competition with each other, regularly encountered problems that could be surmounted only with local expertise. Ignoring the Indigenous residents of the various coastlines where their battered vessels found refuge after the crossing led to failure. But those able to establish positive ties with local peoples realized that there was much to be extracted from this region that would find ready markets in Europe.

In mid-1500, Manoel I sponsored a second mission to establish his claim to lands that Cabot had described but that the Portuguese monarch insisted belonged to him per the terms of the Treaty of Tordesillas. Unlike its predecessor, the second voyage produced far more knowledge. On October 17, 1501, Albert Cantino, an agent of the duke of Ferrara, wrote to his patron with details he had gathered from a Portuguese crew that had just returned. He wrote that they sailed week after week, surviving in part on fresh water gathered atop icebergs during the summer.[8]

Once they were on land, the troubles they had faced at sea disappeared. Yet even the natural bounty they found in North America proved insufficient to entice others to follow in their wake. Cantino did not know the

7. "In regard to the grant to Richard Warde and others," in Biggar, ed., *Precursors*, 50–59, quotations at 51. Almost two years later the king issued a revised license, giving these authorities to Hugh Eliot and two of Warde's partners, leaving it open for the first group to work with Eliot; see the license, dated December 9, 1502, in Biggar, ed., *Precursors*, 81–91.

8. "Cantino to the Duke of Ferrara, October 17, 1501," in Biggar, ed., *Precursors*, 63–64. Cantino could not have understood the process, but these Portuguese were the beneficiaries of what happens as a result of brine extrusion—essentially the way that water molecules in an iceberg force salt out, which makes the water that is within an iceberg or that runs down its sides when it melts among the purest on Earth; for the process, see R. A. Lake and E. L. Lewis, "Salt Rejection by Sea Ice During Growth," *Journal of Geophysical Research* 75 (1970), 583–597; W. S. Reeburgh, "Fluxes Associated with Brine Motion in Growing Sea Ice," *Polar Biology* 3 (1984), 29–33.

fate of the other ship, which had taken a different course homeward. Soon after, at some unspecified date, he smuggled a Portuguese map to the duke of Ferrara. A small patch in the northwest corner reflected the arrival of Corte Real and others in territory that was still mostly unmapped by Europeans.[9]

By 1511, after two of the Corte Real brothers had disappeared at sea,[10] the Portuguese decided that the time had come to establish their presence in what they called Tierra Nova—Newfoundland to the English. In October, Queen Joanna authorized a Catalonian-born commander named John de Agramonte to set up a trading factory there and, if he returned, another in Portugal to process the resources he brought home. Knowing all too well the tragedies that had befallen Portuguese ships, she gave him the approval to hire two Bretons or others who "belong to some other nation which has been there," a recognition that the Portuguese had not been able to prevent other Europeans from exploring these seas.[11] Ferdinand, for one, did not accept the idea that this northern territory belonged to Spain's Iberian rival. He invited Sebastian Cabot to come to his court to provide evidence about routes to the "island of the Codfish."[12]

Two years later the monks at the Breton abbey of Beauport, overlooking the harbor at Paimpol, arranged with the residents of a nearby island called Bréhat to get fish from Newfoundland, a sign that fishing crews working the outer banks of northern North America had already begun to alter diets in western Europe.[13] Within a decade Basque fishing ships were regularly going back and forth from Brittany to Newfoundland, which profited French farmers and victuallers who provisioned the growing number of ships.[14] English king Henry VII supported a 1521 expedition

9. "Cantino to the Duke of Ferrara, October 17, 1501," and "Pietro Pasqualigo to the Signiory of Venice, October 18, 1501," in Biggar, ed., *Precursors*, 64, 66–67. The so-called Cantino planisphere or world map is in the Biblioteca Universitaria Estense in Modena, Italy; see Derek Hayes, *Historical Atlas of Canada* (Seattle: University of Washington Press, 2002), 20–21.

10. See the grants to the Corte Real family in Biggar, ed., *Precursors*, 69–70, 94–96, 143–144.

11. "Warrant to John de Agramonte, October 8/29, 1511," in Biggar, ed., *Precursors*, 107–111, quotation at 107.

12. The king sent the invitation on September 13, 1512; see Biggar, ed., *Precursors*, 116.

13. The agreement, dated December 14–17, 1514, is in Biggar, ed., *Precursors*, 118–123; for the larger context, see also Joseph Lehuenen, "The Role of Basque, Breton and Norman Cod Fishermen in the Discovery of North America from the XVIth to the End of the XVIIIth Century," *Arctic* 37 (1984), 520–527.

14. See, e.g., the agreement between local farmers and the mayor of Bayonne dated March 6, 1521, which allowed for the provision of cider produced in orchards outside of the city for transatlantic voyages, in Biggar, ed., *Precursors*, 125–127.

to the region, believing that explorers might find commodities to enrich his realm.[15]

The European push toward the northwestern Atlantic evoked the emerging reality of the post-1492 Atlantic basin. Europeans who could gather resources because they had connections at court or to local municipalities and trading companies found ways to finance expeditions and head into waters that European cartographers poorly understood. Rumors swirled about the possible riches to be found, fueled in part by what had become a kind of insurance plan: even those who failed to find a passage across the continent or wealth on land could still bring back cod.[16] By 1527, according to the crew of an English ship that improbably arrived in the port at Mona Island, a Spanish territory near Hispaniola, there were "50 Spanish, French and Portuguese fishing-vessels" in Newfoundland that year.[17]

Establishing a permanent European presence in the north had obvious benefits for those who could cross the Atlantic and transport their wares back home. There was much in the early reports that encouraged investments in such ventures, including the details about lush forests, bountiful populations of game, fertile soils, and endless schools of fish. Each report brought home from a French, Portuguese, English, Basque, or Spanish sailor had the potential to expand knowledge about what could be found for those who could manage the risks. Cartographers who listened to these reports integrated the news on their charts. The anonymous creators of what is now known as the Atlas Miller (1519) drew on the accounts generated by the Corte Real family to create a fantastic version of the northwestern Atlantic, a place dominated by fur-bearing animals and thick forests. For countless Europeans looking for new sources of fur and for wood to make masts for their ships, the news meant that one did not need to find gold or other hidden treasure to make an expedition viable. Brazil, after all, had become known for its parrots and, soon after, its dyewood. Seen from that context, the northwestern reaches of the Atlantic—at least those free of the dangers of icebergs—promised new avenues for wealth. Those who looked at world maps believed the north might hold another advantage: somewhere there might be a route that connected the Atlantic to the Pacific, the fabled Northwest Passage. The

15. See the patent from Manoel I to the Portuguese courtier John Alvarez Fagundes, May 22, 1521, and the subscription to support an English expedition dated March 1 and April 9, 1521, in Biggar, ed., *Precursors*, 129–131, 134–142.

16. See Biggar, ed., *Precursors*, 159–165.

17. Their statement can be found in Biggar, ed., *Precursors*, 167.

Europeans who found it would earn fame and fortune that could rival Columbus's before his fall from grace.

By the early 1520s, interest in finding the Northwest Passage had spread across western Europe. Even Spaniards who were already reaping profits in the Caribbean and New Spain hoped to find the Northwest Passage and a quicker route to the Spice Islands. Their most notable effort failed in 1523, though the king understood that every place Spanish explorers found would lie within Spain's territory per the terms of the Tordesillas agreement.[18] Around the same time, an English crew reached Newfoundland but was short of supplies and had a deadly encounter with unnamed Indigenous. Eager to put the dangers of the north behind them, they sailed south down the Atlantic coast, eventually stopping at the Spanish ports of Mona and later Santo Domingo to refresh their supplies.[19] After they left, Spanish authorities in Santo Domingo concluded that the English had not been so much looking for provisions as spying on them. Charles V came to the same conclusion when he heard about the visit, writing too late that he had wished the Audiencia of Santo Domingo, the administrative body established to provide royal oversight in the Caribbean, would have prevented the English from returning home with precious information at a time when, he observed, "we are at war with the king of England."[20] Still others eyed North America too, including Florentine silk merchants living in Lyon who in 1523 pooled their resources to support a mission to find a water route to Cathay.[21]

On their own, these ventures amounted to little. But in 1523, the last ship of the Portuguese explorer Ferdinand Magellan, who had been commissioned by the Spanish to discover where the Spice Islands fell under the terms of the 1494 treaty, straggled home. Four years earlier, Magellan had set out with a flotilla of five ships carrying a total of 270 men toward the Pacific. The mission suffered a series of calamities even before Magellan was killed on Mactan Island in the Philippines in March 1521.

18. See Biggar, ed., *Precursors*, 145–159; for the importance of spices, see Nancy G. Siraisi, *Medieval and Early Renaissance Medicine: An Introduction to Knowledge and Practice* (Chicago: University of Chicago Press, 1990); for the voyage, which attracted considerable attention by learned chroniclers including Oviedo, Peter Martyr, Antonio Galvão, and Antonio de Herrera, see *NAW*, 1:273–276.

19. The original is Audiencia de Santo Domingo, est. 53, cajon 1, leg. 9, AGI, printed in full in *Colección de Documentos inéditos relativos et Descubrimiento*, 1st Ser., XL: 305–354; an excerpt is in Biggar, ed., *Precursors*, 173–177.

20. *NAW*, 1:205–206.

21. The agreement, dated March 23, 1523, is in *NAW*, 1:280.

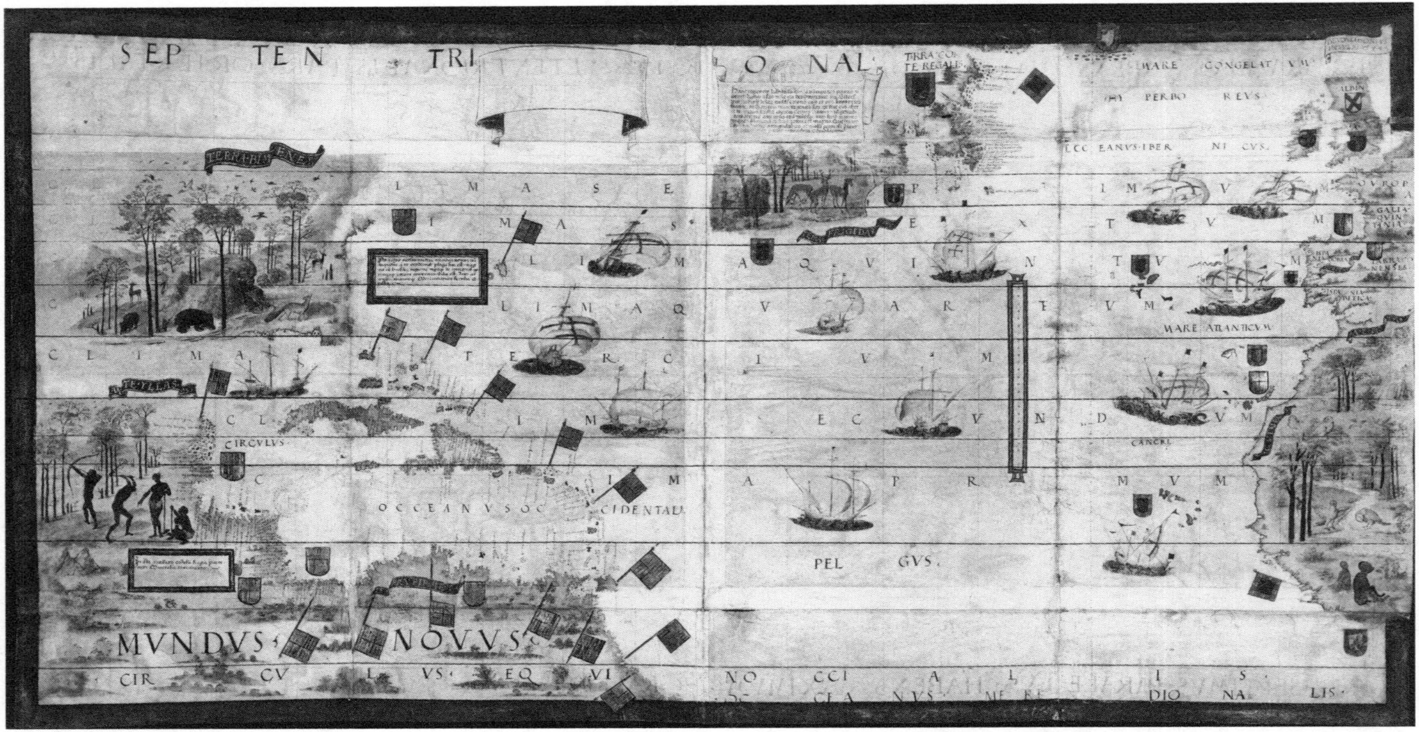

By the early years of the sixteenth century, Europeans had begun to circulate images of the lands ringing the Atlantic, including this French map, part of the so-called Atlas Miller, based on the expedition of the Corte Real family. Bibliothèque Nationale de France, World Digital Library.

The dwindling number of survivors sailed for Europe through the Indian Ocean and then around the Cape of Good Hope. Only seventeen of the original men on the expedition made it home. Despite their loss of ships and personnel, their return brought immediate acclaim.[22]

Buoyed by a new sense of possibility, merchants and monarchs sought more opportunities abroad. Among them was French king Francis I, who, goaded by the mercantile communities of Rouen and Lyon, hired veteran Italian explorer Giovanni da Verrazzano, who had emigrated to Dieppe early in the century, to lead an expedition westward in 1524 to the Pacific.[23] Despite storms that forced a return to France soon after their departure and another that threatened them after they resupplied their expedition in Madeira, they reached Cape Fear (in modern North Carolina) about seven weeks after their departure. Indigenous inhabitants, possibly Carolina Algonquians, offered food, a routine gesture of hospitality.[24]

In nearby forests the newcomers found fragrant varietals, including cypress, palms, laurels, and others "unknown in our Europe." There were other riches there too, including gold, abundant stocks of game, and large flocks of birds to be hunted. Verrazano praised the salubrious climate, fresh air, moderate temperatures, calm seas, and lack of dangers for mariners since the coastline was sand, not rocky—though this also meant, he realized, that they could not find a harbor nearby, meaning that all ventures on land would require shallops to transport people and goods to and from larger ships. He admired the Natives who rushed into crashing seas to rescue a young sailor who almost drowned and their ability to make canoes and snares to capture birds. One day, the visitors captured a boy and took him along on the journey. They sailed along the northeast coastline, exploring modern-day New York Harbor, Cape Cod, and Maine. Along the way, Verrazzano remarked time and again that the Natives he met offered the Europeans hospitality. He wrote about the Natives' high-quality wooden houses, each of which had twenty-five to thirty residents,

22. See Antonio Pigafetta, *Le Voyage et navigation faict par les Espaignolz es isles de Mollucques* (Paris, [c. 1525]); Antonio Pigafetta, *Magellan's Voyage: A Narrative Account of the First Navigation*, trans. and ed. R.A. Skelton (New Haven, CT: Yale University Press, 1969).

23. The original of this manuscript has disappeared, but Ramusio printed a version in 1556 and Hakluyt an English translation in 1582; for the publishing history, see Allesandro Bacchiani, "Giovannia Da Verrazano and His Discoveries in North America 1524: According to the Unpublished Contemporaneous Cellere Codex of Rome Italy," trans. Edward H. Hall, in *Annual Report of the American Scenic and Historic Preservation Society* (Albany, NY [?], 1910) [hereafter "Verrazano 1524"], 141–178, and *NAW*, 1:281.

24. One version of the manuscript referred to Sinarian as part of China; "Verrazano 1524," 180–182. The expedition departed on January 17 and spotted land around March 10.

and the availability of excellent harbors. The unnamed Indigenous he met moved with the seasons to maximize their hunting, fishing, and maize farming, employing "the rising of the Pleiades, and many customs derived from the ancients" to determine the time to plant their crops. He found them long-lived and generous, especially to family members. The sailors turned for home when they reached the territory they thought had been sighted by Cabot.[25]

Verrazzano had gone in search of the passage and failed to find it. But at a time when European monarchs and patrons wanted to discover other economic prospects, such as the existence of exportable natural resources, he understood that success in the north would mean understanding the cultures of locals, including their religious beliefs. He observed that "they have neither religion nor law, nor know a First Cause or Author, nor worship the sky, stars, sun or moon or other planets, nor have any species of idolatry, nor did we learn that they make sacrifices or other prayers; nor that their villages had temples or churches for prayer." Verrazano believed that his expedition had helped advance "the sacred word of the evangelist." He invoked Psalm 19: "Their sound has gone out into all the earth." Verrazzano had done his job. Others needed to follow.[26]

He never mentioned what happened to the child he kidnapped.

In 1527 Robert Thorne, an English merchant who spent most of his adult life in Seville, wrote to Henry VIII, who at age eighteen in 1509 had assumed the throne upon his father's death. Thorne had not seen the waters that English and other sailors had plied in the generation since the first word of Columbus's arrival in the West Indies spread across the continent. But in those years when new reports about the Western Hemisphere came off the presses with ever greater frequency, Thorne made a point of becoming an expert on everything related to the changes in the Atlantic basin. His location put him in an ideal position to provide the English court with information that might have been more difficult to locate in England even in an age when printers and spies alike were eager to spill all their news as soon as possible. Thorne understood the rhetorical tricks necessary to goad a monarch, noting that any ruler who failed to support Atlantic explorations could be seen as weak to his people.[27]

25. "Verrazano 1524," 182–185 (praise for region), 186–194 (local residents), 195–197 (return).
26. "Verrazano 1524," 198–202.
27. Robert Thorne, "A declaration of the Indies and lands discovered, and subdued unto the Emperour, the king of Portingall," in Hakuyt, *Principall Navigations*, 250.

Over the previous generation, Thorne reminded Henry VIII, all that had been known before about the vastness of the world had been turned upside down as scholars and courtiers struggled to make sense of the dizzying rush of information about the Western Hemisphere arriving in Europe. Thorne drew on his experience as a merchant when he emphasized that the people of the West and of the East were eager to be in more regular contact with each other. The desire to control trade across the globe had pushed Europeans to explore the Atlantic in search of a quicker route to the South Sea. The only limit to their ambition was geographical reality: explorers stopped when "they could passe no farther by reason of the great seas." English sailors had already brought glory to the realm. But it was not yet enough.[28]

Having watched one ship after another spill its cargo and secrets when they arrived in Spain, Thorne came to a truth that had been hiding in plain sight. The expansion of any European realm did not take an enormous up-front investment. Instead, "with a small number of ships there may be discovered divers New lands and kingdoms, in which without doubt" the king "shall winne perpetuall glory, and your subjects infinite profite." The question that remained was simple: where could the English go to maximize their chances of acquiring new valuable territory? "There is," he noted, "one way to discover, which is into the North." The Spanish and Portuguese had already found and claimed the rest. By contrast, the north remained unclaimed, at least as he saw it, either ignorant or dismissive of the claims that explorers since Cabot had already made to northern territory. England's location closer to the northern parts of the Western Hemisphere than other Europeans meant the English could expand their territory with modest cost, a small number of travelers, and little risk. This might encourage some, a generation after Columbus's expeditions, to consider missions that made the transition from extracting wealth to creating colonies. But at the moment, Thorne still emphasized the importance of trade. With greater expertise in northern waters, he believed that English sailors would be adept at finding their way past the pole and into the South Sea, where he presumed the water would be warmer and the passage to East Asia easier. Once there they could come home by retracing their steps or sailing through the Strait of Magellan. Either way, wealth beckoned: gold, spices, balms, jewels. In this vision, North America would be where the English could extract resources but not yet a place to plant colonies.[29]

28. Thorne, "Declaration of the Indies," 250.
29. Thorne, "Declaration of the Indies," 250–251.

Thorne believed that the only legitimate competitors for the English were the Spanish and Portuguese, each of whom, he acknowledged, had sorted out their differences with Rome and each other. But the discoveries made by the Cabots already gave the English a superior right to northern lands. Thorne compiled his knowledge of this geography on a map, which he included in his text. While that chart had little impact at first, the image and Thorne's words would later play a decisive role in prodding the English to dedicate resources toward American exploration.[30]

On April 20, 1534, Jacques Cartier left the Breton port at Saint-Malo, his hometown, bound for the northwest coast of North America. Like Verrazzano, Cartier left with the support of King Francis I, who financed his mission to find the Northwest Passage.[31] Unlike the others, he would soon discover just how important Indigenous populations would be, both for his expedition's survival and in redefining his—and, by extension, other Europeans'—aspirations for the northwest shores of the Atlantic and the largest river that fed into the ocean.

Saint-Malo, adjacent to a deep-water harbor, had its origins in the Roman occupation of northwest Gaul in the first century BCE. In the sixth century CE Brendan, the Irish saint long associated with travel into the Atlantic, established a monastery there.[32] One of his followers was a Welsh migrant named Maclou, who became St. Malo. By Cartier's time, the town had attracted fishing crews increasingly engaged in long-distance voyages. It is possible that sailors there had connections with the residents of Bréhat, the nearby island that provided fish from North America

30. "The booke made by the right worshipfull M. Robert Thorne," in Richard Hakluyt, *The Principall Navigations, Voiages and Discoveries of the English Nation* (London, 1589), 252–258.

31. *The Voyages of Jacques Cartier*, introduction by by Ramsay Cook (Toronto: University of Toronto Press, 1993) [hereafter *Cartier*], 117. The original manuscript for this journey no longer survives; the earliest printing was by Ramusio in Venice in 1556 in his *Navigationi et Viaggi*; the publishing history is in *Cartier*, x–xi.

32. Brendan (c. 489–570/583) traveled at least as far as the Orkney and Shetland Islands as well as Brittany, but despite earlier claims that he had reached North America, his surviving narrative of his exploits provides no proof. Still, the English scientist John Dee in 1580 claimed that the Irish saint had traveled across the Atlantic, and added to the claims that the English could make to the Western Hemisphere. The younger Richard Hakluyt, for his part, ignored Brendan, but did include a note about the Welsh traveler Madoc, whom Hakluyt believed was the earliest traveler from Britain across the Atlantic. See John J. O'Meara, *The Voyage of Saint Brendan: Journey to the Promised Land* (orig. pub. 1976; Gerrards Cross, Buckinghamshire: Colin Smythe, 2017), xi–xii (Dee); Hakluyt, *Principall Navigations*, 506–507.

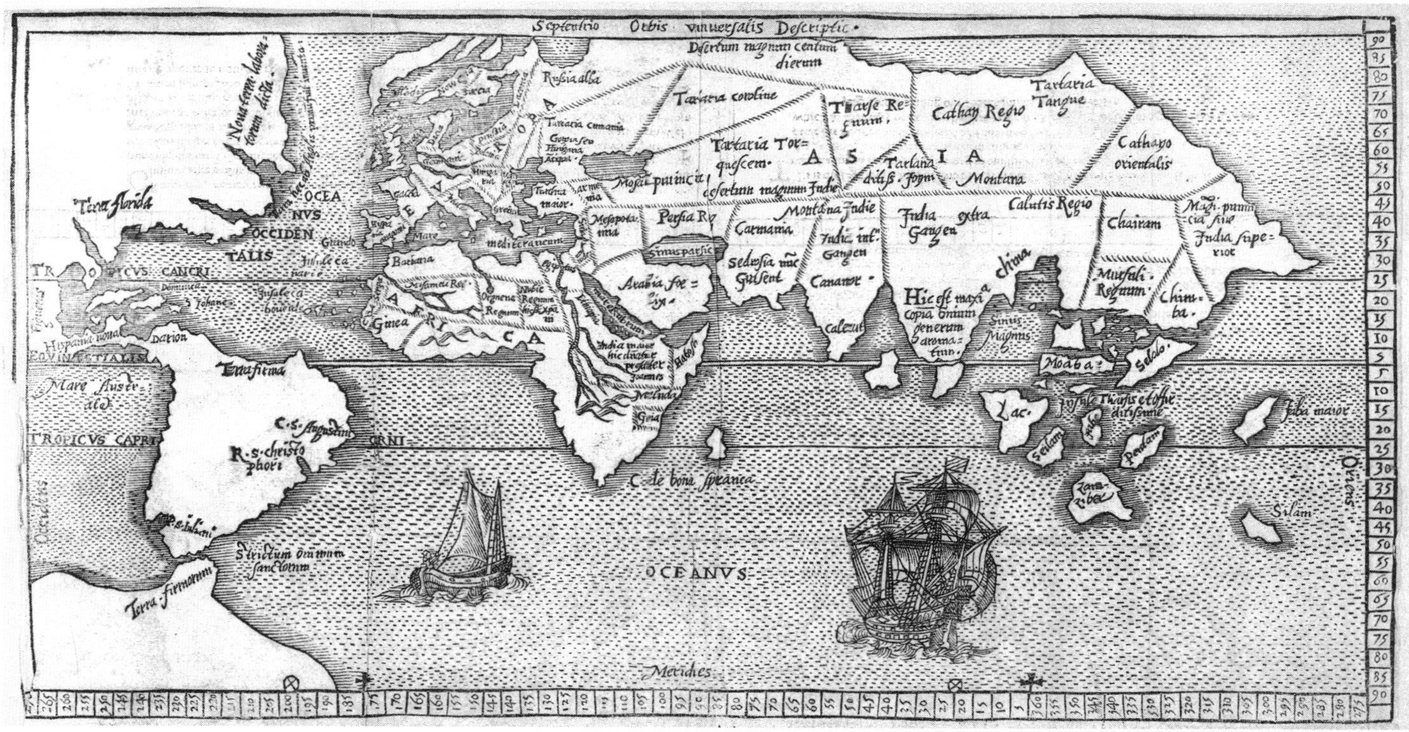

In 1528 English merchant Robert Thorne sent this map, which he obtained in Seville, to one of Henry VIII's ambassadors. The map made the crossing between Britain and North America seem relatively short, an idea promoted by some who wanted the English to launch expeditions across the Atlantic. From Richard Hakluyt, *Divers voyages touching the discovery of America and the ilands adjacent* (London, 1582). Courtesy of the John Carter Brown Library.

to the abbey at Beauport, which was about twenty miles by water due west from Saint-Malo.[33]

When he set off to the west, the forty-three-year-old Cartier already had a good idea about where he was going and his purpose.[34] It is possible, even likely, that he had seen one of the six surviving manuscript versions of a 1527 map of northeastern North America created by Diogo Ribiero, the Portuguese-born Spanish royal cosmographer. Ribiero had mentioned the cod fishery, but he was more impressed by the lack of gold or other valuable potential exports. "The country was discovered by the English," he wrote about Labrador, "and there is nothing there worth having."[35]

It took Cartier and the sixty others on this mission about three weeks to reach Newfoundland, which they sighted on May 10. They harvested birds on modern Funk Island, including great auks. Nearby islands hosted puffins and eider ducks. Mostly the sailors fished, finding the potential of the littoral more promising than what appeared to be an untillable landscape. "I am rather inclined to believe that this is the land that God gave to Cain," Cartier observed, making a reference to Genesis 4:12, describing the infertile land that awaited Abel's murderer. Soon after the French explorers met Natives, presumably Beothuks who had come to the coast to hunt for seals. Cartier called them "wild and savage folk."[36]

The mariners ascended the Gulf of St. Lawrence, the primary waterway that provided oceangoing ships access to territory that local speakers referred to as *kanata*, using an Iroquoian word that refers to clusters of houses. Cartier, who altered the name to Canada, believed that the gulf had to be the opening to the Northwest Passage. Like other Europeans, Cartier took note of local resources, notably islands with enormous bird populations; meadows with wild oats, peas as fine as those grown in Brittany, strawberries, gooseberries, and herbs; and fauna including foxes, bears, and walrus. At Chaleur Bay he thought the trees were so large they could be masts on 300-ton vessels. While there they were approached by fifty small boats bearing Indigenous, presumably Mi'kmaqs, who had arrived to trade. "They showed a marvelously great pleasure in possessing and obtaining these iron wares and other commodities," Cartier reported.[37] On a subsequent occasion, Cartier and his colleagues eased some of their

33. Carl Selmer, ed., *Navigatio sancti Brendani abbatis from Early Latin Manuscripts* (Notre Dame, IN: University of Notre Dame Press, 1959).

34. A later court document revealed that Cartier was born in 1491; see H. P. Biggar, ed., *A Collection of Documents Relating to Jacques Cartier and the Sieur de Roberval*, Publications of the Public Archives of Canada no. 14 (Ottawa: Public Archives of Canada, 1930), 492.

35. Quoted in Hayes, *Historical Atlas of Canada*, 23.

36. *Cartier*, 9–12.

37. *Cartier*, 13–14 (resources), 17–18 (harbors), 19 (thick trees), 3 (his ships), 20–21 (trade).

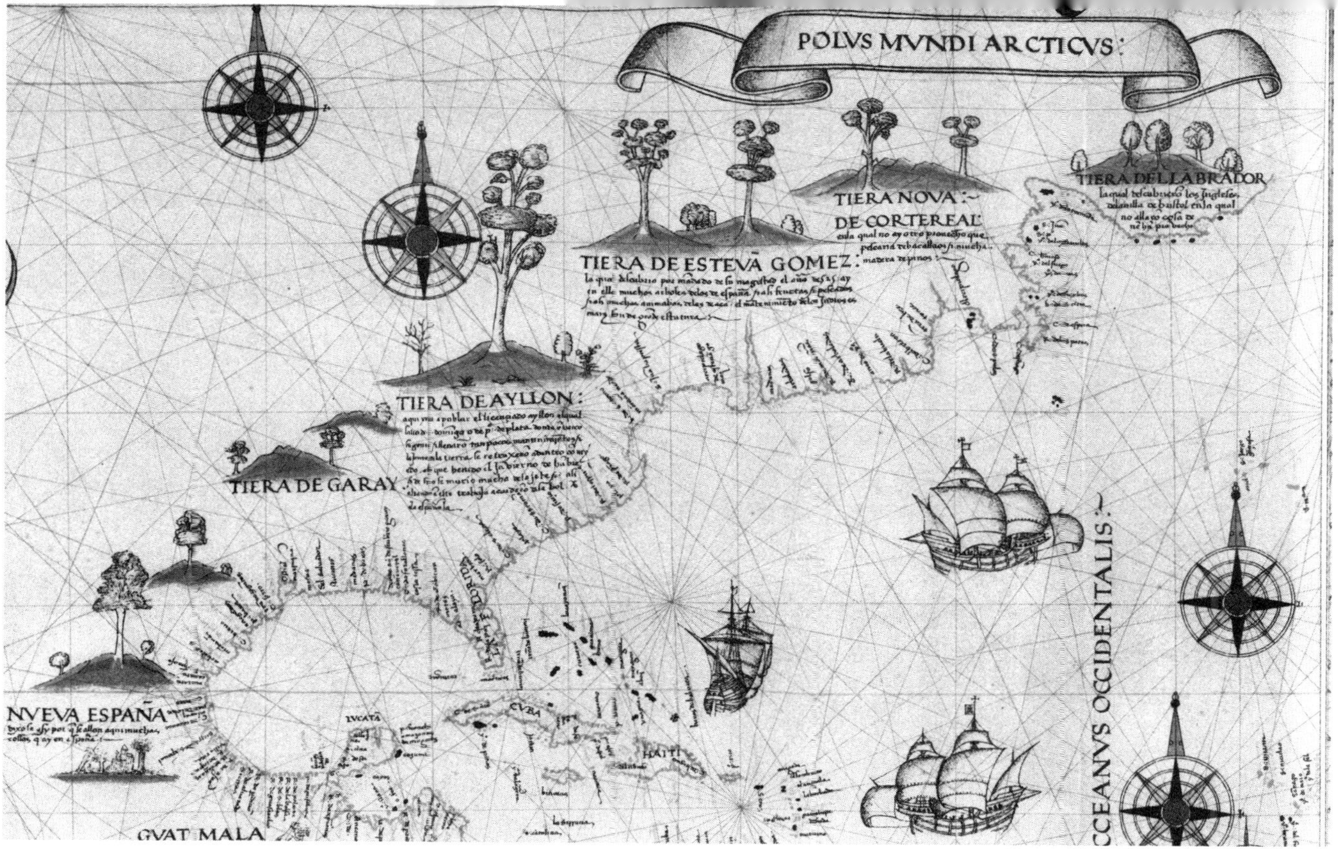

Spanish cartographer Diego Ribiero integrated information about American explorations onto his world map in 1529. He mentioned the great schools of cod to be found near Newfoundland and that modern-day New England had rich forests, but no gold had been found there. Detail of the New World portion of Diego Ribiero's world map of 1529. Library of Congress Geography and Map Division, 85690293.

exploratory disappointment by trading with an even larger group, which included women as well as men. Cartier could not interpret various ritual acts performed by the Natives, but the behavior he witnessed at the trading session convinced him that "these people would be easy to convert to our holy faith. He was less sanguine about a group of 200 the French met on the Gaspé Peninsula, a sign that even as a newcomer he drew distinctions among Indigenous based on his assessment of the possibility of transforming them into trade partners or Christians.[38]

Cartier had his men place a thirty-foot wooden cross at the entrance to the harbor, "under the crossbar of which we fixed a shield with three *fleurs-de-lys* in relief, and above it a wooden board, engraved in large Gothic characters, where was written, 'VIVE LE ROY DE FRANCE.' " After putting up the cross, the French fell to their knees, joined hands, and "worshipp[ed] it before them, and made signs to them, looking up and pointing towards heaven, that by means of this we had our redemption." Soon after, Cartier met Donnacona, a St. Lawrence headman from Stadacona (modern Quebec City). After trying to communicate through signs, the travelers told Donnacona that they were going to take two of his sons, Taignoagny and Dom Agaya, to France. To demonstrate that the French would treat them well, the visitors put the boys "in shirts and ribbons and in red caps, and put a little brass chain round the neck of each, at which they were greatly pleased," Cartier wrote. The crew gave Donnacona another hatchet and two more knives. The next day Donnacona brought fish to the boys and made signs indicating that "they would not pull down the cross, delivering at the same time several harangues which," Cartier admitted, "we did not understand."[39]

The French sailed off toward Anticosti Island. After debating whether they should still look for the passage, the travelers concluded that winter would soon approach and lock them in for winter. They opted to return home. They reached the anchorage at Blanc Sablon on August 9, stayed for a week, and then sailed homeward. On September 5, 1534, almost five months after they had left, the crew arrived in Saint-Malo. Cartier immediately began to share the news of his discoveries and the fact that he had claimed a previously unknown piece of the American mainland for France. In the spring, the king promised to support the next journey. By then, Cartier had already begun to teach Donnacona's sons how to speak and live like French men.[40]

38. *Cartier*, 22–25.

39. *Cartier*, 25–27.

40. *Cartier*, 118, 121, 127–132.

On May 19, 1534—less than nine months after his return—Cartier departed Saint-Malo again to return to the St. Lawrence. This time he saw the exploration and possible colonization of North America as a vital part of a mission to preserve and extend true Christian faith in the aftermath of the Reformation, the religious revolution that shaped the European competition for America and its resources. All peoples could know truth, but to a Catholic like Cartier there were dangerous Protestant heretics who threatened the work of the true God. At this moment, he wrote, "we see how the wicked Lutherans, apostates and imitators of Mahomet" stood in opposition to "the princes of Christendom and the true pillars of the Catholic church." In a message to his own king, he singled out "the Catholic king of Spain" who had supported missionizing efforts that had brought "innumerable peoples" into the faith in the West Indies and the American mainland. The French exploration of Canada would be the next logical step in this divinely sanctioned drama.[41]

Cartier commanded the 120-ton flagship called *La Grande Hermyne*, as well as two smaller vessels. There were sixty-nine men on this expedition, including an apothecary, a barber, six carpenters, and trumpeter Pierre Marquier—the kinds of travelers one would take to launch a colony. Also on board were Donnacona's two sons, Taignoagny and Dom Agaya.[42] The vessels plied a similar course as the year before, but this time Cartier, taking a page from Columbus's playbook, put new names on islands they passed: St. William's Islands, St. Martha's Islands, St. German's Islands, and St. Nicholas's Harbor, where the men set up a cross to use as a marker. Like other Europeans who had engaged in similar acts in the Western Hemisphere, Cartier was trying to sacralize a landscape that was already sacred and naming places that already bore names. His acts were not random. They christened St. William's Islands to mark the feast day of St. William, who had been a bishop near Saint-Malo, and St. Martha's Islands because they arrived there on her feast day. Only occasionally did they break from this practice—for example, on the day they named L'Isle de Bascuz after the Roman god Bacchus.[43]

On this journey, Cartier demonstrated that he had learned much about how the French could succeed along the St. Lawrence. While finding the passage remained crucial, he recognized the profits to be made from local supplies of copper and the abundant natural resources that could supply a new community. But he knew too that success hinged on maintaining

41. *Cartier*, 36–38.
42. *Cartier*, 122–124.
43. *Cartier*, 40 (St. William's and St. Martha's), 41 (St. German's), 42 (St. Nicholas), 52 (Bascuz).

good relations with Donnacona and his people. That meant giving and receiving gifts as well as hoping that the sons would speak well of their time in France. To his great relief, they told their father what they had "seen in France, and the good treatment meted out to them there."[44]

In Stadacona, the situation became more vexed. The young men shared some of what they had learned in France. Taignoagny "began to speak and repeated three times 'Jesus,' 'Jesus,' 'Jesus,' lifting his eyes towards heaven," Cartier reported. "Then Dom Agaya called out 'Jesus,' 'Maria,' 'Jacques Cartier,' " again looking upward. Then they informed the explorer that their god Cudouagny had instructed them to tell the French that there would be deadly snow and ice at Hochelaga (modern Montreal) and none of them would survive. "At this point we began to laugh," Cartier reported, "and to tell them that their god Cudouagny was a mere fool who did not know what he was saying." Despite French assurances that "Jesus would keep them safe from the cold if they would trust in him," Donnaconna and his sons refused to join the mission upriver.[45]

During the journey, the travelers passed fishing cabins and at one point met a group—Cartier did not identify them—who offered them an eight- or nine-year-old girl and a two- or three-year-old boy. The boy was too young, the French replied, but they took the girl with them and offered presents to those who presented her to them. When they reached Hochelaga, Cartier estimated that a thousand residents came out to greet them. Cartier saw a landscape he found as impressive as any in France. Soon they reached extensive corn fields close to a mountain the French labeled Mont Royal. In the middle of the fields was Hochelaga, a circular village, Cartier reported, "completely enclosed by a wooden palisade in three tiers like a pyramid." There were fifty longhouses within the walls, each of them fifty paces long and twelve wide. Each was subdivided into "many rooms and chambers," surrounding an opening in the middle where the residents kept a fire going. Families resided and stored maize in their own rooms. The area provided all the fish, eels, and animals they needed to supplement their grain.[46]

Soon Agouhanna, the local headman, arrived. Cartier estimated that he was about fifty years old. He was unable to walk, so others carried him to the meeting. After greeting Cartier in a way that made the Frenchman feel welcome, Agouhanna then extended his arms and legs "as if he thereby expected to be cured and healed." Cartier rubbed his legs and his arms, and Agouhanna gave him a red headband he had been wearing. Soon the

44. *Cartier*, 45–51.
45. *Cartier*, 51–56.
46. *Cartier*, 56–63.

afflicted of the city swarmed in—some blind in one or both eyes, "others lame or impotent and others again so extremely old that their eyelids hung down to their cheeks." All of them wanted Cartier to lay his hands on them too; "one would have thought," he wrote, "Christ had come down to earth to heal them." Cartier read the Bible to them, starting with the Gospel of St. John, making the sign of the cross, and trying to teach them about the passion, baptism, and redemption in words they did not understand and signs they had likely never seen before. When he was done, he offered more presents and ordered his companions to blow their trumpets "and other musical instruments"—which were among the goods that he had hauled across the ocean.[47]

After exiting the palisaded city, the French traveling party ascended Mont Royal, studied a landscape that looked unpromising for further exploration, and decided to return home.[48] On October 11, when the travelers reached the harbor at Ste. Croix, they discovered that those they had left behind had erected a wooden fort and taken the armor from their ships and placed it on land "pointing every way, and in a good state to defend us against the whole country-side." The image was so arresting that an unknown artist added it to a painted map of the region in 1547.[49] The next day Donnacona, Taignoagny, and Dom Agaya invited Cartier to visit their home. The French explorer and the Stadaconans discussed their religious views, with the brothers acting as interpreters. When they were done, the explorer promised to return with priests bearing holy oil to baptize the Stadaconans.[50]

But it proved too late in the year for the French to cross the ocean. Thick ice gripped their ships and deep snow covered the frozen land. Worse still, as the winter wore on, the French became ill. Cartier presumed that it was the Natives who had brought disease among them. But his men were suffering from scurvy, not a contagious pathogen. Its symptoms horrified those who watched the suffering, which killed five of the French and made most others so weak that they could barely take care of themselves. When one died, they performed an autopsy on his body, perhaps the first ever undertaken by Europeans in the Western Hemisphere. Cartier had never seen anything like the shriveled white heart in this victim, the gangrene in his lungs, and a spleen that looked like "it had been rubbed on a rough stone." Twenty-five of Cartier's 110 men succumbed

47. *Cartier*, 63–64.
48. *Cartier*, 64–66.
49. Vallard Atlas, HM 29, f. 9, HEH.
50. *Cartier*, 68–69.

that winter. As the disease spread among them, Cartier feared he might never make it back to France.[51]

With the disease still raging, Cartier took a walk outside their fort. There he encountered Dom Agaya. Cartier knew that the Stadaconan had at one point also been ill with this disease, "for one of his legs about the knee had swollen to the size of a two-year-old baby," his gums had rotted, and his teeth had "gone bad." Yet now Dom Agaya appeared at the French encampment in good health. How, Cartier asked, had he made his recovery? Dom Agaya informed the captain that there was a local tree, which they called *anedda*, with leaves that could be boiled to produce a juice, which the afflicted should drink. They should also take the remnants and place them as a poultice on their lesions. Dom Agaya asked two local women to gather branches and bring them to the French. The women then showed them how to produce the medicine. The drink brought immediate relief to the afflicted. Cartier added that some of the crew had had syphilis and "were by this medicine cured completely." That tree, Cartier wrote, "produced such a result that had all the doctors of Louvain and Montpellier been there, with all the drugs of Alexandria, they could not have done so much in a year as did this tree in eight days." At the start of the epidemic Cartier thought that the best way to combat the disease was to erect a shrine of the Virgin and say Mass in front of it. By the end, he realized it was the residents of Stadacona who had saved them—though Cartier, as was typical of Europeans who recounted their story in published books, gave thanks to God for delivering a miracle.[52]

The society the French visited differed substantially from what Cartier knew from his home. Women performed most of the agricultural labor, a stark contrast to gender roles in France. Indigenous men hunted deer, bear, and other animals, fished for the astonishing variety of creatures in the water, and captured birds, which could be found in an abundance that baffled Europeans. Cartier learned that they had a plant that they dried, pulverized, put in a "hollow instrument," set alight, and then sucked "at the other end to such an extent that they fill their bodies so full of smoke that it streams out of their mouths and nostrils as from a chimney." The Stadaconans told the French that this kept them warm "and in good health" and so they took it with them wherever they went. "We made a trial of this smoke," Cartier reported. "When it is in one's mouth, one would think one had taken powdered pepper, it is so hot." His description was among the earliest descriptions that Europeans had of tobacco. Despite the differences between these St. Lawrence Iroquoians and the

51. *Cartier*, 76–79.
52. *Cartier*, 77 (shrine), 79–80 (cure).

French, Cartier believed that the newcomers "could easily be molded in the way one would wish."[53]

The next step in French plans for the region necessitated cementing positive relations with the St. Lawrence Iroquoians. Toward that end, Cartier hoped to bring Donnacona and his two sons back with him so that Donnacona "might relate and tell to the king all he had seen in the west of the wonders of the world, for he assured us that he had been to the land of the Saguenay where there are immense quantities of gold, rubies, and other rich things, and that the men there are white as in France and go clothed in woolens." The headman had also told the French that he seen people who lacked an anus "and other marvels too long to relate." Cartier wanted Donnacona to go with him, then, to provide proof of the existence of the monstrous races, peoples whom Europeans continued to believe existed beyond their reach. Cartier extended the idea: the monsters were not to be found along the St. Lawrence but instead were located up the Saguenay River. Donnacona would become proof of both the malleability of Indigenous Canadians, who could convert to French ways, and of the inherited body of knowledge that Europeans still possessed.[54]

When it was time to leave, Cartier managed to lure Donnacona, his two sons, two other men, and five women onto his ship. Donnacona told his community that Cartier had promised to return him and the others in a year. Before the ship lifted its anchor, the Stadaconans offered twenty-four strings of wampum, "which is the most valuable article they possess in this world," Cartier reported, "for they attach more value to it than to gold or silver." Local women brought maize, fish, and meat for the journey. In exchange, Cartier gave Donnacona eight hatchets, knives, beads, and two brass kettles, which the headman left in the possession of his wives. Perhaps he knew that those kettles could be carved up and the strips of metal attached to the end of arrows and spears, thereby making them sharper and lighter than the stone or bone heads that they normally used. The French, their numbers diminished, decided to leave one of their ships behind. That too proved a boon to the Stadaconans, who went to the battered hull and pulled out the nails, which they then used to fashion tools.[55]

On May 6, 1535, the French departed from the harbor at Ste. Croix. In the weeks that followed they sailed past Cape Breton and Newfoundland,

53. *Cartier*, 69–70.

54. *Cartier*, 82.

55. *Cartier*, 83, 85–86; for the Indigenous uses of such goods, see Calvin Martin, "The Four Lives of a Micmac Copper Pot," *Ethnohistory* 22 (1975), 111–133.

meeting French and Breton fishing crews that had arrived for the summer cod season. They arrived at Saint-Malo in mid-July.[56] Little is known about the fate of most of these travelers. In September 1538 the king sent a payment of fifty crowns to Cartier as back pay "and for the food and upkeep of a certain number of savage people whom he has fed and kept at our order for two years now."[57] On March 25, 1539, three of the Indigenous received baptism. The October 17, 1540, commission for Cartier's third voyage mentioned that he had previously brought back "several valuable commodities" as well as "a certain number whom We have kept for a long time and instructed in our said holy faith with our said subjects." The use of the present tense here suggests that at least some of the Stadaconans were still alive.[58]

Once in France, Donnacona learned to speak French and converted to Christianity. According to André Thevet, the royal cosmographer for Francis I, Donnacona lived in France for four years, which was long enough for him to teach Cartier (or perhaps Thevet himself) about Indigenous beliefs.[59] Francis I told a Portuguese visitor that he too had spoken with Donnacona and that the headman had told him about a city with gold mines and coveted spices. Francis added that he hoped to build a fort on the Saguenay River, which could be used as a base for a lucrative fur-trading operation, a continuation of the European idea that North America remained more important as a source of potential riches than a locale for colonization.[60]

In 1541, Cartier launched his third expedition toward the St. Lawrence.[61] Before he left, he and his wife, Catherine Des Granges, signed their will, a sign perhaps that he had developed a greater sense of the dangers any

56. *Cartier*, 86–89; João Fernando Lagarto to John III, January 22, [1539 or 1540], *NAW*, 1:329; Biggar, ed., *Cartier and Roberval*, 75.
57. The king's order, dated September 22, 1538, is in *Cartier*, 125.
58. *Cartier*, 134–135.
59. As Thevet put it: "Ce qui nous a fait entrendre le Seigneur du païs de Canada, nommé Donaco[na] Aguanna, qui est mort en France bon Chrestien, parlant François, pour y avoir esté nourry quatre ans." Thevet, *Les Singularitez de la France Antarctique, autrement nommée Amerique* (Paris, 1558), 152. For the context of Thevet's remarks, see Roger Schlesinger and Arthur P. Stabler, eds., *André Thevet's North America: A Sixteenth-Century View* (Kingston, ON: McGill-Queen's University Press, 1986).
60. *NAW*, 1:328–329.
61. In his account, Cartier wrote that they sailed in 1540. But it had to have been 1541 since the Portuguese ambassador to France had learned about the expedition from some of the men who had returned to Saint-Malo in October 1541; see *NAW*, 1:334.

transatlantic passage posed.[62] By then, Donnacona and eight of the Stadaconans had died. The survivor was a ten-year-old girl, who might have been the girl whom Cartier had been given in 1535, but her fate remains unknown.[63] This time the king paid for five ships, which he put under the direction of both Cartier and a nobleman named Jean-François de La Rocque de Roberval. Cartier oversaw the construction of the ships at Saint-Malo, filled them with two years' worth of provisions, and offered passage to a couple of imprisoned gentlemen who had committed murder, for whom the voyage would be a way to do penance. Roberval sailed two months later, having obtained a pair of armed vessels in Rouen. A Spanish spy then in Saint-Malo reported that Cartier left with "400 mariners and twenty master pilots" along with twenty men to build boats once they got there. Roberval carried 300 soldiers along with ten barbers, ten priests, sixty carpenters and masons, and three doctors. The supplies on this journey reveal that the French had begun to think of the St. Lawrence Valley as an extension of the realm of Francis I, a place where French might live in the future as well as a source of American exports.[64] Rumors swirled in Saint-Malo whenever fishermen returned, with witnesses deposed by local authorities eager to find out what was happening in the St. Lawrence Valley.[65]

After a three-month passage, Cartier sailed into the harbor at Ste. Croix and waited for Roberval to arrive. As they waited, Agona, whom Donnacona had (in Cartier's telling) appointed to be the headman while he was abroad, arrived with six or seven canoes "with many women and children." Agona asked what had happened to Donnacona. Cartier told him the truth: he "was dead in France, and that his body rested in the earth." And then he lied about the other Stadaconans he had taken to France: "The rest stayed there as great Lords, and were married, and would not returne backe to their Countrey."[66]

62. *Cartier*, 156–158.

63. *Cartier*, xxxix; "The third voyage of discovery made by Captaine Jacques Cartier, 1540, unto the Countreys of Canada, Hochelaga, and Saguenay," in Richard Hakluyt, *The Principal Navigations, Voyages, Traffiques and Discoveries of the English Nation* (London, 1598–1600), III:232. In 1553, while Cartier was still alive, a captive from near Newfoundland was baptized in Saint-Malo, but it is likely that this individual was from a later voyage since Cartier was not mentioned in the provincial record. See Biggar, ed., *Cartier and Roberval*, 524–525.

64. *NAW*, 1:331; *Cartier*, 152–153 (spy report), 139 (convicts).

65. See, e.g., the depositions of Robert Lefant, Martin de Actalecu, and Clemente de Odelica in Biggar, ed., *Cartier and Roberval*, 447–464.

66. *NAW*, 1:331; "The third voyage of discovery made by . . . Cartier," III:233.

While the French laborers built their encampment, Cartier took two ships to Hochelaga. He deposited two French boys there, hoping that they would learn the local language, and also left gifts for a local headman. Then he set off for Saguenay, following a map that local residents had made with small sticks. During this expedition, Cartier was unable to replicate good relations with Indigenous, perhaps because of Donnacona's death. He ordered the French to secure their fort at Ste. Croix. Roberval finally arrived with six ships, meeting Cartier at Newfoundland in June 1542. The new commander headed up the St. Lawrence while Cartier sailed for home.[67]

Roberval, his vessels clad in heavy armor, proceeded to the outpost. But during the winter of 1542–1543, fifty of those on the expedition perished from disease. In the summer of 1543, Roberval welcomed a small party he had dispatched to find Saguenay, only to learn that one of their vessels had broken up and eight of the French drowned. The Natives provided Roberval with some assistance at first, but eventually it was not enough, and so he returned to France.[68] From then until the late 1550s, Roberval schemed to establish mines in Canada, pursuing the dreams of the secret treasure of Saguenay.[69]

French authorities, having become enticed by the possibility of establishing a colony along the St. Lawrence, gathered testimony from men who had gone to fish off the coast of Newfoundland. They also deposed Cartier and Roberval about what had happened after the collapse of the colonial plan.[70] Rather than signal a start to a new commitment, the return of the two instead marked a retreat from the St. Lawrence. Cartier appeared from time to time in provincial and church records, and he was in Saint-Malo when plague ripped through the port in 1548.[71] He died around five in the morning on September 1, 1557. Other than his occasional testimony about his conflict with Roberval and being asked about navigational matters, he never again played a substantial role in the French effort to claim the St. Lawrence. Roberval likely died in 1561. His dreams were no closer to coming true than Cartier's, despite persistent

67. "The third voyage of discovery made by . . . Cartier," 233–234.
68. See *Cartier*, 107–113.
69. On Roberval's efforts to establish mines see Biggar, ed., *Cartier and Roberval*, 494–498, 505–521, 552–555.
70. Biggar, ed., *Cartier and Roberval*, 477–489.
71. Biggar, ed., *Cartier and Roberval*, 476 (Portuguese), 467–468, 472, 486, 491, 498–501, 521–522, 536–537, 492–493 (plague); *Cartier*, 171–176 (court case).

rumors in Saint-Malo that Cartier had "discovered the world and all the Indies."[72]

After Cartier's death, his nephew Jacques Noël searched the ancient mariner's possessions. He turned up a "certaine book made in maner of a sea Chart" in Cartier's hand. That book contained an outline of the St. Lawrence River, which his nephew called the "River of Canada." Among other things, it provided the location of rapids and waterfalls that made travel treacherous. Noël added that he had seen on this map words written in the hand of Jacques Cartier: "By the people of Canada and Hochelaga it was said, That here is the land of Saguenay, which is rich and wealthy in precious stone." On the same map, near a place a hundred leagues to the southwest, was Cartier's other comment: "Here in this Countrey are Cinnamon and Cloves, which they call in their language Canodeta."[73]

In the years that followed, several maps of the St. Lawrence circulated in France. More than one included a depiction of Cartier, his hand extended, greeting Indigenous residents, including possibly Donnacona. In 1556, a Venetian cartographer named Giacomo Gastaldi produced an illustration of Hochelaga to accompany the narrative of Cartier's second journey in the third volume of Ramusio's *Navigatione et Viaggi*. In this illustration, the Natives of this St. Laurentian city inhabit an orderly, palisaded community. Their fields lie nearby. Indigenous perch atop the walls, ready to guard their community from any enemies. In the foreground, Cartier can be seen, bearded as always, with his extended hand grasped by an unidentified Native man. Saint-Malo, with its maze of ancient medieval streets, would have seemed chaotic by contrast.[74]

These maps could be read as a sign that the French had hoped to establish better relations with the Natives than the Spanish had in the West Indies as well as a sign of their hope to establish a colony. But these cartographers signaled a deep truth. Europeans in the northeastern reaches of North America would die without Indigenous help. Cartier and Roberval had high hopes—to find the Northwest Passage, to harvest the

72. Biggar, ed., *Cartier and Roberval*, 551 (death of Cartier), 547 (navigation), 555n (Roberval's death); letter from Nantes to the Portuguese ambassador at the Court of France November 12, 1541, in *NAW*, 1:335.

73. *Cartier*, 105–106.

74. See Gayle K. Brunelle, "Images of Empire: Francis I and His Cartographers," in Martin Grosman et al., eds., *Princes and Princely Culture, 1450–1650* (Leiden: Brill, 2003), 81–102; Helen Wallis, ed., *The Maps and Text of the Boke of Idrography Presented by Jean Rotz to Henry VIII Now in the British Library* (Oxford: Oxford University Press, 1981); Hayes, *Historical Atlas of Canada*, 25–26, 29.

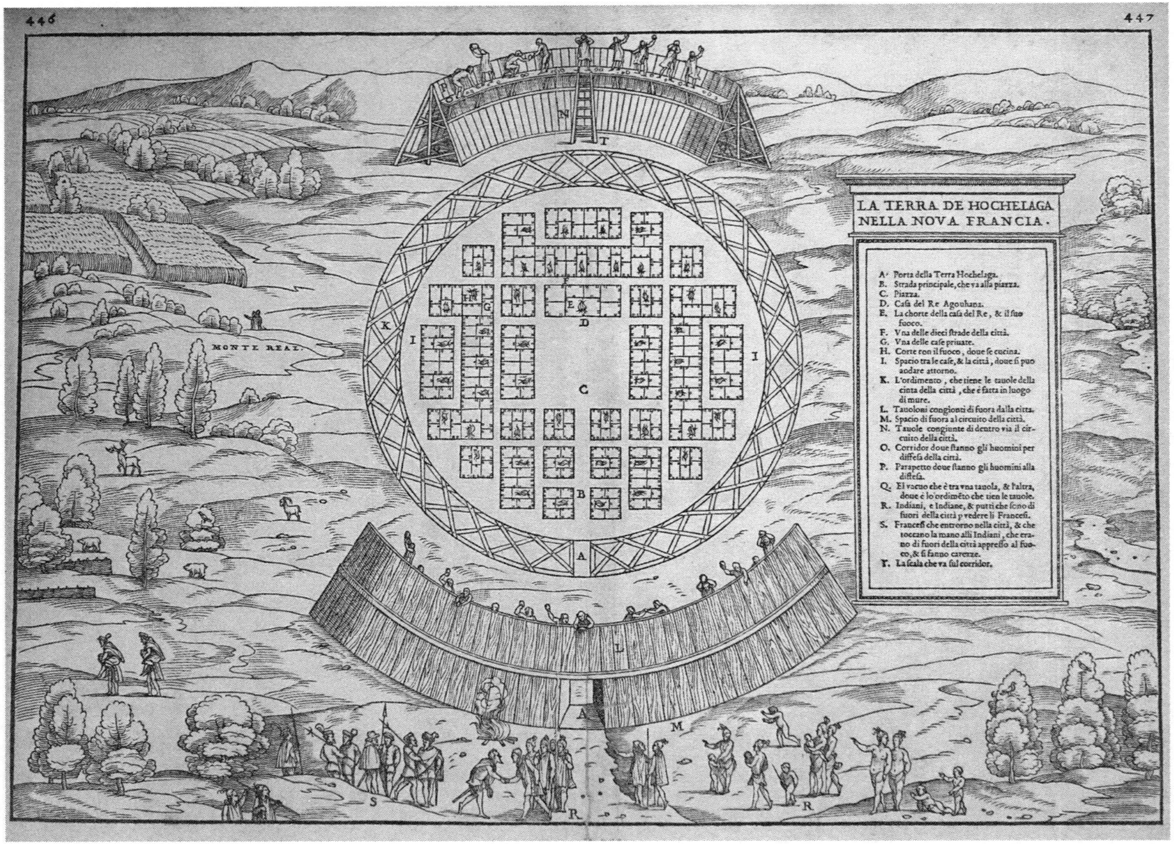

Italian mapmaker Giacomo Gastaldi's map of Hochelaga, which geographer Giovanni Battista Ramusio included in a massive compilation of travel accounts, emphasized both the orderly layout of the city and the positive relations between its inhabitants and French explorers, an idea epitomized by the handshake near the bottom. Courtesy of the Huntington Library, San Marino, California.

wealth of Saguenay, to convert Indigenous, and to extend their king's territory. But just like the parade of Europeans who had sailed into northern waters before them—the Cabots, the Corte Reals, and Verrazzano—they too failed. None of these Europeans proved capable of establishing durable relationships with the Beothuks, Mi'kmaqs, Wendats, Haudenosaunee, or St. Lawrence Iroquoians they met. And none could understand how to build a city that could rival Stadacona.[75]

French, Portuguese, and English mapmakers believed they codified reality when they depicted American lands as European possessions. But this was a fiction. The explorers' presence in Canada was as ephemeral as the blowing of trumpets or erecting of crosses in meaningless rituals of possession.

75. See Bruce G. Trigger, *The Children of Aataentsic* (Montreal: McGill-Queen's University Press, 1976), 1:178–181.

4

The Lost Colony of Chicora

During the decade that stretched from the late 1510s to the late 1520s, Spanish officials sponsored colonizing missions to the North American mainland, a territory that until that point lay entirely in Indigenous hands. Though much had changed since the dispersal of the Mississippians at Cahokia, the achievements of those who once dwelled there remained visible in a broad arc from modern-day Kansas to the Atlantic. The most important legacy of the rise of those Mound-Builders was the dispersal of farming based on the three sisters—maize, beans, and squash.

Although Spaniards were aware of the importance of agriculture from what they had seen in the West Indies, maize was less enticing than the prospect of expanding the arc of their own influence in the Western Hemisphere. Having resolved their dispute with the Portuguese over the American boundaries of their respective claims, Spanish monarchs and their courtiers laid plans to establish colonies on the mainland. The area that first drew their attention was the Valley of Mexico and the enormous city of Tenochtitlán, modern Mexico City, a metropolis as bustling as any to be found in Europe. If they could conquer the city, they believed, they would be able to expand their influence across Mexico and, they hoped, farther to the south and north. The high stakes led Spaniards to transport soldiers and horses across the Atlantic in preparation for a contest that was sure to be more difficult than the Columbian seizure of islands in the Caribbean. The conquest of Mexico, launched in 1519, became the decisive moment in the solidification of Spanish power in the Western Hemisphere, inspiring dreams of imperial expansion that would prompt would-be empire builders to seek new arenas in the Americas—including a return to lands not far from those explored by Ponce de Leon. Spaniards headed back to that region convinced that strategies developed to conquer Indigenous Americans in the Caribbean and then in Mexico would enable them to succeed wherever their agents, following the precedent of Columbus, laid claim to new territory on the American mainland. But as they learned, the fate of any would-be imperialists' plans hinged on the Indigenous peoples they encountered and the newcomers' ability to navigate in uncertain diplomatic waters—a task that became charged with renewed intensity after religious debates took on an unprecedented force within Europe.

Political disputes and wars had set Native peoples against each other in the Valley of Mexico and territory nearby long before any Spaniard knew about the Western Hemisphere. Bitter and sustained battles erupted after the death in 1426 of Tezozomoc, the king of the Mexica (Aztec) city of Axcapotxalco. During his reign, he had managed to bring order and peace to extensive territory since his accession in 1370. A new era of conflict enveloped the region in the fifteenth century. Indigenous chroniclers wrote about brutal warfare that lasted for about sixty years until the Mexica ruler of Tenochtitlán, the Acolhua leader of Texcoco, and the Tepanec king of Tlacopan formed an alliance in 1431. The alliance prevented the kinds of warfare that had proved so bloody earlier, but it did not mean that these empires were equal. During the fifteenth century, the Mexicas gathered enough wealth to transform the five-and-a-half-square-mile island in the middle of a vast lake into the wealthiest city in the hemisphere. By the time Columbus arrived in the Caribbean, the city of Tenochtitlán had perhaps 50,000 residents, with another 50,000 Mexica populating the fertile countryside nearby. They had created a commercial juggernaut in a valley that by then contained about 1.5 million people. But their gathering wealth aroused jealousy among others, especially the countless thousands paying tribute to the Mexicas. The tensions erupted into war in 1473. By the time it ended, the Mexica under their king Axayacatl had grown even more powerful. He died relatively young in 1481, possibly in battle. After two decades of rule by members of his family, a new Mexica king named Moctezuma Xocoyotl (or Moctezuma the Younger, or Moctezuma II) ascended to the throne in 1502. He immediately launched an ambitious administrative program to bring thirty-eight provinces under his direct control by placing his emissaries in each. Their primary task was to make sure that tribute owed to the Mexicas would be paid when due.[1]

Tenochtitlán bloomed under Moctezuma II. Architects designed streets for a building campaign that transformed the island city into distinctive districts. Noble (*pilli*) and commoner (*macehualli*) families coexisted, with the latter paying tribute to the former and providing the labor to produce what elites demanded. Merchants in local markets sold

1. Camilla Townsend, *Fifth Sun: A New History of the Aztecs* (New York: Oxford University Press, 2019), 41–73.

precious goods including jade, gold, turquoise, and brightly colored feathers, the last of which artisans wove into intricate and eye-catching tapestries or paintings. Some specialized in the sale of cloth, others in ceramic dishes, copper tools, rope, dyes, or nets. Consumers could choose their next meal from caged animals and birds, buy tortillas, and see a physician who drew on extensive knowledge of local plants to ease their afflictions. Jurists populated local courts and teachers offered instruction to future warriors, priests, and merchants. Poets and singers entertained while scholars maintained the history of the realm—and kept careful track of the tribute paid by outlying communities in precious stones, jaguar skins, crops, and feathers. Local palaces housed scribes who kept records of daily transactions. All residents, from the grandest to the poorest, walked along streets dominated by pyramids where religious maintained the rituals to keep the Mexica in good standing with the deities who governed their world.[2]

Moctezuma tried to govern through an organized system and to avoid violence. Yet despite his best efforts, his authority waned beyond Tenochtitlán. In the countryside, potential enemies bided their time, waiting for reason and opportunity to rebalance power. At the same time, Mexica raiding parties roved in search of their own opportunities. One of those parties entered the town of Coatzacoalas, southeast of modern Veracruz, and captured residents, including girls. They soon traded one of them, the daughter of a noble family, to some Maya in Xicallanco, a port renowned for its cluster of merchants who facilitated commerce among and between Indigenous communities. From there someone sold her to the Chontal Maya, who took her to Potonchan, a prominent community along the Tabasco River. No document recorded her birth name, nor did she ever tell Spaniards what it was.[3]

In 1517, this young woman was living among the Chontal when Francisco Hernández de Córdoba arrived from Cuba to explore the Yucatán Peninsula. Rumors of his arrival traveled much faster than Spaniards weighed down by armor. Tensions flared immediately when the Spaniards reached Potonchan. Chontol warriors, whose traditional cloth, spears, and arrows were no match for the invaders' metal shields and guns but who greatly outnumbered the visitors, drove the explorers away. Although the Chontol Maya had prevailed at first, another exploratory

2. Townsend, *Fifth Sun*, 72–84; "Tenochtitlan, 1521," map, 1550, Library of Congress, https://www.loc.gov/item/2021668313/; on Indigenous records of tribute payments and keeping accounts, see Daniela Bleichmar, "History in Pictures: Translating the Codex Mendoza," *Art History* 38 (2015), 682–701.

3. Townsend, *Fifth Sun*, 84–87.

party, led by Juan de Grijalva, arrived the following year. They knew to avoid the largest concentration of Chontol Maya at Potonchan. Instead of landing, they sent a delegation aboard canoes, including a young man who was able to speak to these Maya. He told them they were in search of gold, which the people of Potonchan heard as meaning that the Spaniards were yet another tribute-seeking group, perhaps no different from the Mexica who had been eager to seize what they had. The Chontal, through this interpreter, told the Spaniards that they would fare better in Mexica territory to the west. After some brief trading, the explorers sailed off.[4]

On February 18, 1519, Hernán Cortés, who had gathered information from Spaniards who had been to the Yucatán, led ten ships out of Cuba bound for the American mainland. When he set sail, Diego Velázquez, the governor of Cuba, was awaiting an appointment as *adelantado*, which would have liberated him from the authority of Christopher Columbus's son Diego, who had inherited his father's title and powers. As *adelantado*, Velázquez would have had the authority to mount a colonizing expedition on the mainland. In the absence of that title, he permitted Cortés to go in search of earlier explorers who had not yet returned, permission that fell far short of approving conquest and colonization. Still, aware that no one could know exactly what the explorer would find, the governor included a clause in the contract authorizing Cortés to exercise power beyond that of an explorer as long as he worked in "the service of God and their highnesses." Cortés, like Velásquez, was aware that changes in the court in Madrid following the coronation of Charles V meant that he might have a moment to advance his own dreams if he acted quickly—and basically ignored the limitations in his contract.[5]

Less than three weeks later, Cortés arrived at Potonchan—looking not to explore, the premise of his agreement with the governor, but to invade. Violence erupted almost immediately, with groups of Maya warriors defending their land from the armored Spaniards. The conquistadores had military advantages, including horses they rode into battle. On a single day they slew at least 200 Maya, a higher death toll than the Chontal had ever experienced in war. The Chontal sued for peace. In the negotiations to end the conflict, they sent the Spaniards twenty enslaved girls and women. A priest sprinkled holy water on each and gave each a new name. The daughter of the noble family of Coatzacoalas became Marina. Cortés offered her to Hernández de Puertocarrero, a relative of a noble family, who assaulted her. She may or may not have been sexually attacked

4. Townsend, *Fifth Sun*, 87–88.
5. J. H. Elliott, "Cortés, Velázquez and Charles V," in Anthony Pagden, trans., *Hernán Cortés: Letters from Mexico* (New Haven, CT: University Press, 1986) [hereafter Cortés, *Letters from Mexico*], xi–xxxvii.

during the years of her enslavement among the Maya, but this time there was no doubt.[6]

Living among the Spaniards, Marina met Jerónimo de Aguilar, a Spaniard who had survived a shipwreck eight years earlier only to be enslaved by the Yucatec Maya. Cortés ransomed Aguilar as quickly as possible, knowing that someone who could speak to the Maya would be of use. In the weeks that followed, Aguilar and Marina talked frequently, with him teaching her at least the rudiments of Spanish. Cortés saw that, between them, the Spaniard formerly enslaved by the Yucatec Maya and the daughter of an elite Mexica-speaking family held by Puertocarrero could enable him to communicate with Indigenous, either to resolve wars or to enlist them as allies in what soon became his relentless quest to conquer the Mexica and capture Tenochtitlán. The conquistador relied on information he gleaned from both to learn about Moctezuma's enemies.[7]

On Palm Sunday, 1519, Cortés and his soldiers sailed off from Potonchan and within a week landed at modern Veracruz. There they encountered Moctezuma's spies, a small number among the many representatives of his reign that the emperor had dispatched across the lands well beyond the valley of Mexico. Cortés captured one and sent Aguilar to interview him. But the Spaniard knew no Nahuatl. Marina, who sailed with Puertocarro and Cortés, stepped forward to speak with the captive. Cortés quickly realized her utility and promised her great wealth if she would help him against the Mexica, an offer too good to be true for a woman who had been sold into slavery by the Mexica. She and Aguilar together met with Moctezuma's spies, telling them that Cortés was eager to meet their king. The spies, after learning what they could about the newcomers, soon headed back to Tenochtitlán. The Spaniards, growing more impressed with Marina, began to refer to her as "Doña Marina," using an honorific title befitting such a valued member of their community. Soon enough this became "Malintzin," another honorific form, and eventually "Malinche."[8]

6. Townsend, *Fifth Sun*, 89–91; Bernal Diaz, *The Conquest of New Spain*, trans. J. M. Cohen (New York: Penguin, [1963]), 85–88 and passim. As Frances Kartunnen has explained, "Once in Spanish hands, the women were summarily baptized and distributed to provide the men with sexual services. This juxtaposition of a Christian sacrament with rape is jarring to our sensibilities, but the sixteenth-century Spaniards, Bernal Diaz included, were quite frank about it." See Kartunnen, "Rethinking Malinche," in Susan Schroeder et al., eds., *Indian Women of Early Mexico* (Norman: University of Oklahoma Press, 1997), 291–312, quotation at 301–302.
7. Townsend, *Fifth Sun*, 91–92.
8. Townsend, *Fifth Sun*, 92–95; Camilla Townsend, *Malintzin's Choices: An Indian Woman in the Conquest of Mexico* (Albuquerque: University of New Mexico Press, 2006), 55, 72–84.

With information about the Mexica in hand, Cortés laid out a plan for his army of several hundred to take a city of many thousands. He realized that the best strategy would be to become allies with powerful nations opposed to the Mexica. The most likely were the Tlaxcala. But shared enmity alone did not mean that a partnership would unfold. Instead, as the conquistador realized, he first had to defeat the Tlaxcala in battle. While making his plans he settled on two decisive actions. First, he dispatched Puertocarrero to Spain with the hope that the nobleman would gain royal authority for Cortés to conquer the Mexica. That plan had the added benefit of getting Malinche back to his side. Second, fearing that his own men might abandon him given what had to have seemed like staggering odds against them, he ordered his own ships to be beached—not destroyed, but sufficiently damaged to prevent anyone from beating a hasty retreat.[9]

At summer's end, Cortés led his soldiers into Tlaxcala. They found a breach in the formidable nine-foot-tall stone wall that surrounded their territory. Soon after, Tlaxcala warriors descended on them hundreds, in all likelihood, though Cortés would later claim there were thousands. In the days of battle that followed, scores of Tlaxcalas fell, along with a smaller number of Spaniards. Unable to figure out a way forward, Cortés came to rely on Malinche, a native of Coatzacoalcos, a town that had long had commercial ties among the Tlaxcala. Soon enough she facilitated discussions that produced the alliance that Cortés knew he needed. Still harboring hatred toward the Mexica, hundreds of Tlaxcala soldiers agreed to join the conquistador's march to Tenochtitlán. Their numbers likely tripled the men in arms under Cortés's command.[10]

Even before he reached Tenochtitlán, Cortés had laid claim to the territory in the name of Charles V. He did so, following precedent that other Spaniards had established after 1492, with a scribe and other witnesses present to mark his assertion of Spanish ownership. But Cortés also betrayed Velázquez's directions that he was only to explore the region and establish trade routes. Instead, he intended to settle the territory and place it under his leadership. On June 28, he and his followers incorporated a town to be called Villa Rica de Vera Cruz, whose residents quickly named him *alcalde mayor*. Cortés believed that this act liberated him from any restrictions Velásquez had put on him. The Cuban governor had hoped that he himself would perhaps claim Mexico for Charles V and expand his

9. Townsend, *Fifth Sun*, 100–101; Diaz, *Conquest of New Spain*, 130–131.
10. Townsend, *Fifth Sun*, 101–104.

own wealth and authority. Cortés, a master of protocol, usurped any such claim. Freed from the order to explore and trade, Cortés launched what became the first European military conquest of a substantial mainland American community.[11]

On August 8, Cortés, 300 conquistadores, and their new Tlaxcalan allies began their march toward Tenochtitlán. Over the next three months, the invaders began to remake the Mexican countryside. They tossed aside what they saw as relics of idolatry and erected crosses in Indigenous holy spaces. They formed alliances with Indigenous peoples who had become alienated from Moctezuma. In early November they reached the outskirts of the city. News of their approach had spread well before their arrival. Many of the city's leaders came to greet them, as did Moctezuma himself. The Spaniard offered Moctezuma a necklace of cut glass and pearls, and the Mexica ruler offered two in exchange, one made of red shells and the other bearing eight golden shrimp. Once in the city, Moctezuma offered his father's onetime palace for the visitors to use during what he presumably believed would be a limited stay. Soon after, the two men met again. The Spanish believed that Moctezuma, in a speech that perhaps the newcomers did not fully grasp or chose to misunderstand despite Malinche's efforts as a translator, saw Cortés and his followers as the heirs of the Nahuas who had returned to reclaim their homeland. Cortés seized on this interpretation. "I replied to all he said as I thought most fitting," he wrote in his letter to Charles, "especially in making him believe that Your Majesty was he whom they were expecting." Six days later, according to Cortés, conquistadores kidnapped Moctezuma, seeing his captive body as a visible sign that the Spanish now possessed the Mexica's empire.[12]

Not surprisingly, the Mexica did not accept the Spanish view of what had transpired. While Moctezuma, at least in Cortés's eyes, accepted his subordinate status, others refused. They soon turned on the conquistadores, forcing them out of the city. Cortés, following the logic of Spanish ceremonies of possession, believed that the Mexica had become rebels against his legitimate role as the ruler of Mexico in his capacity of serving as an emissary of Charles V. The conquistador and his supporters, who included Tlaxcalans eager to cast Moctezuma and his allies aside, launched a war that lasted for fourteen months. In May 1520, amid the conflict,

11. J. H. Elliott, *Empires of the Atlantic World: Britain and Spain in America, 1492–1830* (New Haven, CT: Yale University Press, 2006), 3–4.

12. Cortés, *Letters from Mexico*, 84–90, quotation at 86–87; Elliott, *Empires of the Atlantic World*, 4–5. For what happened during the period when the Spanish conquistador and the Aztec leader coexisted for 235 days, see Matthew Restall, *When Montezuma Met Cortés: The True Story of the Meeting That Changed History* (New York: HarperCollins, 2018), 211–228.

Cortés led a contingent back to the coast to repel a group of Spaniards who had come under orders from Velázquez to return him to Cuba for insubordination. He left Pedro de Alvarado in charge during his absence. After prevailing near the coast, Cortés convinced those who had come to arrest him to instead join the campaign in Tenochtitlán. Upon their return they discovered that Alvarado had massacred Mexicas during a festival, which prompted a new round of attacks on the conquistadores and their allies. The Spaniards convinced Moctezuma to try to quell the crowds assaulting the Spanish compound. However, the Mexicas soon died—at the hands of Mexicas, according to the Spanish, but at those of the conquistadores, according to Indigenous. In negotiations that followed, Cortés and his followers agreed to leave the city and return their stolen plunder, an agreement that Cuitláhuac, who had replaced Moctezuma as *tlatoani* (ruler) after he was kidnapped, seemed to accept.

But during their exodus at the start of July, the Spanish came under withering attack while trying to escape on causeways already damaged by previous fighting. "God alone knows how dangerous and difficult it was," Cortés wrote to the king, "for each time I turned on the enemy I came back full of arrows and bruised by stones. For as there was water on both sides they attacked in safety with no fear of those who were fleeing to the land." The Spanish and their Indigenous allies finally escaped, but at a high cost. "We discovered that 150 Spaniards had died in the rout and forty-five horses and more than two thousand Indians, who had helped the Spaniards," Cortés lamented, adding that Moctezuma's children and other lords they had held captive also perished. The Spaniards never forgot what they soon called their *noche triste*—their "night of sorrows."[13]

While the would-be conquerors suffered a setback, Cortés and his allies never left Mexico. Just as they regrouped to plot a new strategy, smallpox appeared in the middle of October. The epidemic lasted for two months, devastating the Mexica, who had no prior exposure to the virus, unlike the Spaniards, most of whom survived the scourge. Among the dead was Cuitláhuac, who likely perished from the disease on December 4. Months of renewed fighting in the spring of 1521 culminated in Spanish victory on August 13 when Cuauhtémoc, who had taken control after Cuitláhuac's death, surrendered to Cortés. The conquistador claimed victory over the Mexica and laid the foundation for what would soon become the viceroyalty of New Spain.[14]

13. Cortés, *Letters from Mexico*, 138–139.
14. Cortés, *Letters from Mexico*, 164–165; Elliott, *Empires of the Atlantic World*, 5.

Cortés understood that expanding the king's empire and profiting while doing so required adhering to what had already become a code for colonization. Scribes recorded the alleged transfer of Mexica territory to the invaders. Spanish military authorities, aware that they were outnumbered by Indigenous, looked for allies among the Native peoples they met, figuring—correctly, in the case of the Mexicas—that those who rose to the top of the political order might have many enemies looking for a chance to claim power for themselves. Conquistadores, following Cortés's explicit directions, hoped to undermine Indigenous belief systems by destroying icons. "They must know that there was only one God, Lord of all things," Cortés wrote. "And I told them all I knew about this to dissuade them from their idolatry and bring them to the knowledge of God our Saviour." Conquistadores felled those who stood against the invaders, either through killing them in war or by enslaving them, which he did "to strike fear into" others who resisted and to "impose a great and cruel punishment" without which "they would never be reformed." Cortés understood too that he should solidify Spanish desire for Mexican wealth, which he did in detailed letters to Charles V that described the treasures and marvels of Moctezuma's Tenochtitlán. In an echo of Columbus's initial strategy, Cortés knew that just as important as all his actions in the Western Hemisphere was garnering public attention back home with a narrative that increased demand for Mexico and its goods while promoting the legend of its author. As early as 1522, within a year of the conquest of Mexico, European printers began to print the long letters that Cortés had written to Charles V. A Spanish edition of Cortés's second letter, which detailed the conquest and the wonders of Tenochtitlán, appeared in Spanish in Seville first, with editions in French (printed in Antwerp) and Italian (in Milan) following within the same year, and other reports appearing by 1524 from publishers in Saragossa and Venice. These works spread news of Cortés's actions across Europe.[15]

While Cortés offered his readers a somewhat sanitized version of the violence during the conquest, Indigenous chroniclers dwelled on the Spaniards' actions, keeping alive the memory of the horrors they had suffered. As one later recalled, in May 1520, when Cortés was out of the city on a military campaign, Pedro de Alvarado, the deputy governor, launched

15. Cortés described these actions in his second letter; for quotations, see Cortés, *Letters from Mexico*, 106 (destruction of idols) and 146 (enslavement). For 1522: *Carta de la relacion . . . d'las tierras y provincias sin cuento que han descubierto nuevamente enel Yucatan del año* (Seville); *Des marches, ysle et pays trouvees et conquise par le capitaines du tres illustre . . . Charle. V* (Antwerp); and *Nova de le isole & terra ferma novamente trovate in India* (Milan). For imprints for the next three years, see *EA*, 1:25–28.

an attack on the city's Great Temple during the Feast of Uitzilopochtli, when Mexica had gathered to honor their god Texcatilpoca. Spanish soldiers blocked the exits and then entered the courtyard "to slay them." As the chronicler recalled, the soldiers entered, each one bearing a

> leather shield, some, each one, with his iron-studded shield, and each with his iron sword. Thereupon they surrounded the dancers. Thereupon they went among the drums. Then they struck the drummer's arms; they severed both his hands; then they struck his neck. Far off did his neck [and head] go to fall. Then they all pierced the people with iron lances and they struck them each with iron swords. Or some they slashed open their backs: then their entrails gushed out. Of some they cut their heads to pieces; they absolutely pulverized their heads; their heads were absolutely pulverized. And some they struck on the shoulder; they split openings, they broke openings in their bodies. Of some they struck repeatedly the shanks; of some they struck repeatedly the thighs; of some they struck the belly; then their entrails gushed forth. And when in vain one would run, he would only drag his intestines like something raw as he tried to escape. Nowhere could he go. And him who tried to go out they there struck; they stabbed him.

A few managed to escape, including some who raced to other temples and others who pretended they were dead. But most had no chance. "The blood of the brave warriors ran like water," the chronicler continued; "it was as if it lay slippery. And a foul odor rose and spread from the blood. And the intestines were as if dragged out." The conquistadores left the courtyard to hunt for survivors. "Everywhere they went making thrusts as they searched, in case someone had taken refuge. They went everywhere." The "slaughter in the Sacred Patio" lasted for three hours, another recorded, with invaders killing spectators after they had murdered the musicians.[16]

Cortés's conquest had its most immediate impact in the Valley of Mexico. But in the years after 1521, Spanish authorities expanded their control by forcing Indigenous who survived into tributary relationships while they captured and enslaved others, echoing the strategy other Spaniards had employed in Hispaniola. Large numbers of the enslaved were women quickly forced to become sex slaves, a fact that Spanish observers recognized at the time. So did Mexica. One Nahuatl report noted that conquistadores searching for gold subjected men and women to degrading examinations. "With the women they looked everywhere, in

16. Bernardino de Sahagún, *General History of the Things of New Spain: Florentine Codex*, 2nd ed., trans. and ed. Arthur J.O. Anderson and Charles E. Dibble, School of American Research Monograph Series (Salt Lake City: University of Utah Press, 1981), 12:55–56; Miguel León-Portilla, *The Broken Spears: The Aztec Account of the Conquest of Mexico* (Boston: Beacon, 1962), 131.

their vaginas, up their skirts," the commentator wrote, adding that Spaniards "picked out and took the beautiful women, with yellow bodies."[17]

The war brought ecological change that exacerbated human suffering. Spaniards eager to establish a colony imported livestock, especially sheep, which soon devoured Mexican fields, reducing the amount of food available to Indigenous communities. Malnutrition rendered Native bodies even more susceptible to diseases, increasing the mortality of later epidemics.[18] By the mid-1530s, Spanish claims stretched deep into the Andes, as well as to Potosí (in present-day Bolivia), where they knew they could mine silver. Colonial officials in New Spain also extended their reach northward, developing aspirations for further exploration, extraction of resources, and perhaps even the creation of colonies beyond the Rio Grande. In the years to come, that decision would propel Spaniards into sparsely populated territory, where the strategies they had employed in the conquest proved far less efficient.

On October 31, 1517, only a few months after Spaniards sailing from Cuba had begun to explore the Yucatán Peninsula, the German theologian Martin Luther launched what quickly became the gravest threat to the Vatican since its emergence as the center of Christianity in the West. That day Luther, a professor at the University of Wittenberg, went to a local church and posted a list of ninety-five "theses" he thought worthy of debate. His primary concern was the sale of indulgences and Rome's disinterest in curbing a practice that Christians with capital had used for generations to hasten their progress to Heaven. He was enraged by Pope Leo X's decision in 1515 to issue a bull (*Sacrosanctis*) to sell indulgences to raise funds needed to complete St. Peter's Basilica, a massive building project begun seventy years earlier. The Vatican's brazen act could not, Luther thought, be accepted as normal practice. As he and others raised their voices, Leo X at first brushed off their protests as mere squabbling among learned men. But as the pope would soon learn, Luther and those who embraced his moralistic cause recognized that they could use printing presses to accelerate their critique—first across the German-speaking states of central Europe, and then far beyond.[19]

17. Restall, *When Montezuma Met Cortés*, 306–311, quotation at 309.
18. See David W. Jones, "Virgin Soils Revisited," *WMQ*, 3rd Ser., 60 (2003), 703–742; Elinor Melville, *A Plague of Sheep: Environmental Consequences of the Conquest of Mexico* (Cambridge: Cambridge University Press, 1997).
19. Diarmaid MacCulloch, *The Reformation: A History* (New York: Viking Penguin, 2003), 120–124.

Within five years, Luther's protest had prompted thousands to join the cause to reform the workings of the church. To many Europeans, especially in rural areas, the critique brought to the surface economic discontent that had existed for generations but to that point had had no obvious way to link inchoate grievance to an organized movement. Luther and other Protestants gave them the language they needed, including in 1523 when Luther published *On Secular Authority: How Far Does the Obedience Owed to It Extend?* Though Luther did not intend to launch a revolution, the words he and his allies circulated created social upheaval across the continent.

By the mid-1520s, rebellions against princes aligned with the church exploded in modern southwest Germany, Austria, and Switzerland, with violence spreading as far as Hungary and Poland. Peasants lashed out at those who owned land, including clerics at wealthy cathedrals, college churches, and monasteries that had countless tenants on their properties. They attacked Jews too, whom rebels saw as allies of monarchs. Luther, himself an antisemite, was sufficiently chastened by what his words had encouraged that he sought to distance himself from the violence in a book he published with the unsubtle title *Against the Murderous, Thieving Hordes of Peasants*. By then the war was in full swing. The peasants faced brutal opposition. Better-armed emperors and elites deployed professional soldiers, many of them former mercenaries, who killed at least 70,000—and possibly as many as 100,000—of the rebels.[20]

The so-called Peasants' War ebbed quickly, but not the critique of Rome, which would eventually transform religious practice in central Europe, Denmark, Norway, Sweden, and, most important for the Americas, England. There would never again be a unified Christendom. Instead, the Protestant Reformation and the Roman-allied responses it elicited solidified the theological notion of *cuius regio, eius religio*—where one comes from determines one's religious faith.[21] At a time when close observers of European explorers' travels to the Western Hemisphere fantasized about the countless numbers of heathens who would expand the body of Christ on Earth, this doctrine intensified national rivalries. As many Europeans recognized, the Western Hemisphere was an ideal arena to simultaneously advance their economic and religious agendas. Clerics on both sides of the confessional divide helped princes gild their greed with high moral purpose.

20. MacCulloch, *The Reformation*, 157–162; Lyndal Roper, *Summer of Fire and Blood: The German Peasants' War* (New York: Basic Books, 2025), 1.

21. MacCulloch, *The Reformation*, 163–164.

As the conquest of Tenochtitlán was winding down in 1521 and just as competing religious tracts spread through Europe, two Spanish pilots left Hispaniola looking for Indigenous Americans to capture and sell into slavery to work the gold fields of the island. They headed for what they called the Islas Lucayas—the modern Bahamas—which they also called *las islas inútiles* or "the useless islands." The islands lacked value to the Spanish because they had no valuable natural resources other than their potentially enslavable Native inhabitants. Contemporary observers estimated that Spaniards captured between 15,000 and 40,000, likely a severe undercounting. The result of this widespread confinement and exile was no mystery: by the early 1520s there were no Indigenous Bahamians remaining to be captured.[22] Chronicler Peter Martyr concluded that the Bahamas were already "deserted" because "large numbers of the wretched islanders were transported to the gold-mines of Hispaniola and Fernandina, when the native inhabitants there were exterminated, exhausted by disease and famine, as well as excessive labour," an aspect of the Spanish conquest that he was "ashamed" to mention but felt compelled to record for posterity.[23]

In 1521, the two Spanish ships sailed north. The captain of one of them, Pedro de Quejo, spotted land on June 24, 1521, the feast day of John the Baptist. They went ashore at modern Winyah Bay, north of modern Charleston, South Carolina, laying claim to the land for the Spanish king. In honor of that first martyr, who preached and baptized people at the Jordan River, they named a river they found the Jordán. Unbeknownst to Quejo, spotters on the caravel commanded by Francisco Gordillo, which had lost sight of Quejo's ship during the voyage, had also seen the coast. When Gordillo heard that Quejo had claimed the land, he had his men fashion a cross from a red cedar to establish his prior claim. Despite their contest over who had the right of conquest by virtue of discovery, the two commanders decided to cooperate when it came to establishing relations with the local Indigenous.[24]

22. Andrés Reséndez, *The Other Slavery: The Uncovered Story of Indian Enslavement in America* (Boston: Houghton Mifflin Harcourt, 2016), 42–45; Erin W. Stone, *Captives of Conquest: Slavery in the Early Modern Spanish Caribbean* (Philadelphia: University of Pennsylvania Press, 2021), 48–49.
23. *De Obe Novo: The Eight Decades of Peter Martyr D'Anghera*, trans. France A. MacNutt (New York: G. P. Putnam's Sons, 1912), 2:255; see also Garcilaso de la Vega, the Inca, "La Florida," in *The De Soto Chronicles: The Expedition of Hernando de Soto to North America in 1539–1543*, ed. Lawrence A. Clayton, Vernon J. Knight Jr., and Edward C. Moore (Tuscaloosa: University of Alabama Press, 1993), and David J. Weber, *The Spanish Frontier in North America* (New Haven, CT: Yale University Press, 1992), 35–36.
24. *NAW*, 1:248.

Residents, unable to understand the Spanish who had arrived at the bay, exchanged presents with the newcomers. Within weeks, the visitors managed to lure sixty Indigenous onto their ships. Historian Francisco López de Gómera, spinning a story he thought portrayed the Spanish in a positive light, claimed that the local cacique offered fifty of his people because he was so astonished at the clothing the Spaniards wore. With the Natives on board, the visitors sailed off, in possession of slaves to justify the rationale for their original voyage. The raiders also took freshwater pearls. They sailed back toward Santo Domingo, but Gordillo's ship—without its pilot, who had taken a spot on Quejo's caravel—never arrived. Once the surviving ship landed, its crew apparently distributed the enslaved, scavenged for food among the corpses of donkeys and dogs, and then faded away. The last known among these Spaniards was dead by 1526.

In the late seventeenth century, Peruvian-born historian Garcilaso de la Vega, often known as Garcilaso the Inca, wrote that the loss of the ship on the return voyage had a devastating impact. In addition to those who drowned, the survivors "allowed themselves to die of sadness and hunger, for they refused to eat from anger at the deception that had been practiced upon them under color of friendship." The Spanish came to call the place on the mainland where the two vessels had landed Chicora. Despite an initial encounter that eventually proved fatal to virtually every Spaniard who was there, the earliest reports encouraged scores of both Spaniards and French to try to conquer the region.[25]

Although the Spaniards perished, at least one of the captives survived. He soon became enslaved to Lucas Vásquez de Ayllón, a jurist on the Royal Council of the Indies, the highest appellate court in Spanish America, who was then living in Santo Domingo. Ayllón took him to Spain, where he was baptized, as Peter Martyr wrote, "under the Christian name of Francisco united to the surname of his native country, Chicorana." He was, the chronicler reported, "not devoid of intelligence. He understands readily and has learned the Spanish tongue quite well." This American became a source of information about the resources of the Western

25. *NAW*, 1:248; Paul E. Hoffman, *A New Andalucia and a Way to the Orient: The American Southeast During the Sixteenth Century* (Baton Rouge: Louisiana State University Press, 1990), 3–17; Paul E. Hoffman, "The Chicora Legend and Franco-Spanish Rivalry in La Florida," *Florida Historical Quarterly* 62 (1984), 419–438; Garcilosa de la Vega, "La Florida," 2:64–65; see also Justin Winsor, ed., *Narrative and Critical History of America* (Boston: Houghton Mifflin, 1886), II:238–241; J. H. Elliott, "The Iberian Atlantic and Virginia," in Peter C. Mancall, ed., *The Atlantic World and Virginia, 1550–1625* (Chapel Hill: University of North Carolina Press/Omohundro Institute for Early American History and Culture, 2007), 543–544; and Samuel Eliot Morison, *European Discovery of America: The Northern Voyages* (New York: Oxford University Press, 1971), 332–334.

Hemisphere and the customs and practices of the Native peoples of the Atlantic coast.[26]

Ayllón soon sought a patent to establish a Spanish colony at Chicora and planned to establish a colony there.[27] The area he had in mind was already well populated by Indigenous, likely part of the group known as Cusabo, who hunted large deer herds, kept birds, grew corn, and gathered potatoes; extracted medicine from local plants; and harvested fruit, vines, and spices. Like Europeans, local Natives paraded in processions multiple times each year, often bearing a carved ritual statue. European observers likened their rites to those of the ancient Greeks and added that they smoked a local plant, presumably tobacco, in their rituals.[28]

In 1524, Ayllón returned to Santo Domingo to gather people and supplies for his colony. By the next year, he was ready to launch his new community with the permission of Charles V. Having just learned that the Spanish expedition to find the Northwest Passage had failed, the king was especially eager to expand his realm's presence on the mainland. Peter Martyr noted that the entire nation supported the venture because Spaniards were "so keen about novelties that people go eagerly anywhere they are called by a nod or a whistle, in the hope of bettering their condition, and are ready to sacrifice what they have for what they hope." Peter Martyr soon died, having never learned what happened to the planned colony, which Ayllón intended to name San Miguel de Gualdape.[29]

Ayllón recruited 500 or so migrants, including women and children, a sign that he had in mind a self-sustaining colony. The traveling party likely included enslaved Africans as well.[30] As the venture began, Ayllón's flagship sank, with the loss of valuable stores needed to launch a European-style colony: seeds, plant cuttings, Old World livestock (pigs, cattle, and sheep), and maize. But the loss did not doom the effort since San Miguel de Gualdape, at a latitude of 33°N, sat on level lowlands adjoining a rich

26. *De Obe Novo*, 2:258–259.

27. *NAW*, 1:249–254. Others disputed Ayllón's rights. Juan Ortiz de Matienzo, who had been a financial supporter of Quexos (or Quejos), filed claims indicating that he possessed rights to the land; see *NAW*, 1:254–260.

28. *NAW*, 1:266–270.

29. Garcilosa de la Vega, "La Florida," 2:65; *De Orbe Novo*, 2:269–270. Peter Martyr's complete history was published posthumously in Alcalá de Henares in 1530; see *EA*, 1:33. The documents are vague about the exact location of this colony, though it seems likely that the River Jourdán reached the Atlantic around 32°N and Gualdape perhaps north of the modern Savannah River; see *NAW*, 1:260.

30. Jane Landers, "Africans and Native Americans on the Spanish Florida Frontier," in Matthew Restall, ed., *Beyond Black and Red: African-Native Relations in Colonial Latin America* (Albuquerque: University of New Mexico Press, 2005), 54–55; Weber, *Spanish Frontier*, 36–37.

estuary where colonists could find a wide variety of fish and shellfish. The town was to be the first Spaniards established in territory that would eventually become the United States.[31]

As in other tidal rivers along the East Coast, ships built to cross an ocean could only sail in at high tide. When the tide receded, they would sink into the muck. This inconvenient environment also was ideal for the pathogens that cause ailments such as typhoid and dysentery. The colonists who survived the journey quickly ate through most of their provisions. To make matters worse, they had arrived in October, far too late in the year to plant their own crops. Famine raced through the nascent community, as did diseases that often followed dearth. Such ailments killed Ayllón and many others. Some died in bitter winter cold, including seven who froze to death on one ship and another who died from frostbite. When the Spanish suffered, the enslaved seized an opportunity. They joined forces with nearby Guales, the Native residents of the modern-day Georgia and northern Florida coastlines, and set fire to the colonists' buildings. Within six weeks, 350 Spaniards lay dead. The survivors boarded ships bound for Hispaniola. They bore tales of the harrowing conditions that could face any European trying to establish a colony in La Florida.[32]

Despite all the promise, including the idea that the Native inhabitants possessed religious ideas that might become adapted to Christian practice, Ayllón's colony failed. Writing near the end of the century, Garcilaso de la Vega saw the demise of the venture as the final judgment on colonizers who had betrayed the Indigenous peoples they needed for their survival. In his view, the Natives entertained the newcomers when they arrived "for three or four days and assured them of their friendship," but then "killed them one night and made a sudden assault at dawn upon the few Spaniards who had remained with [Ayllón] on the coast to guard the ships." The Indigenous were triumphant. "Having killed and wounded most of them," he wrote, "they forced them, broken and defeated, to embark and go back to Santo Domingo, thereby avenging the Indians of

31. See [Diego Ribera], "Carta universal en que se contiene todo lo que del mundo se ha descubierto fasta agora," Geography and Map Division, Smithsonian Institution, https://www.loc.gov/resource/g3200.ct002450?r=-0.067,-0.089,1.111,0.649,0 (accessed July 28, 2025).

32. *NAW*, 1:263 (cold), 264 (fish); Sam White, *A Cold Welcome: The Little Ice Age and Europe's Encounter with North America* (Cambridge, MA: Harvard University Press, 2017), 33–35; Hoffman, *New Andalucia*, 60–76; Douglas T. Peck, "Lucas Vásquez de Ayllón's Doomed Colony of San Miguel de Gualdape," *Georgia Historical Quarterly* 85 (2001), 183–198; Guy Cameron and Stephen Vermette, "The Role of Extreme Cold in the Failure of the San Miguel de Gualdape Colony," *Georgia Historical Quarterly* 96 (2012), 291–307; Weber, *Spanish Frontier*, 37.

the previous expedition."[33] Oviedo laid blame for the failure on a deadly mixture of greed and ignorance. Rather than find gold, he wrote, "they usually find tears and death for their bodies and great hardship and danger for their souls."[34]

The failure of the Spanish community at Chicora stands in stark contrast to Cortés's success only a few years earlier. By some logic, Spanish success in Mexico, publicized by printers at home, should have established a model for subsequent triumphs across the Western Hemisphere. What could explain the divergent fortunes of these two Spanish colonizing ventures? The answer lies in both local circumstances and strategic concerns. Spaniards learned early about the wealth of the Mexica, so they saw that conquering the Valley of Mexico would produce immediate profits. Those earlier estimates proved accurate. Conquistadores' plunder of Tenochtitlán produced hoards of gold, silver, and other treasures, the kind of return that justified investment in military invasion by armored soldiers and their horses. But it was not only military superiority that aided Cortés. Smallpox proved just as important as any sword- or gun-bearing soldier. Cortés and his allies also possessed strategic instincts that enabled his victory—including building ships to lay siege to the city after warfare had damaged many of the causeways that connected it to the mainland.[35]

Just as important, Cortés benefited from political rivalries that had divided Indigenous peoples in Mexico long before the arrival of Spaniards. He exploited those pre-existing hatreds when he formed an alliance with the Tlaxcalans. He was also an unwitting beneficiary of Malinche's own experience. The embitterment she felt from the early capture and sale into enslavement lingered with her. So too perhaps did her animosity toward Puertocarrero, but Cortés dispatched him, promised her rewards, and eventually had a son with her. The fact that he was still married to a Spanish woman he had left in Cuba likely bothered her, especially when the spouse moved to New Spain. Still, her value to the Spanish only grew over time, not only through her role in interpreting for Cortés but also in training others to carry out similar functions in the future.[36]

Ayllón and his companions in Winyah Bay lacked almost all these advantages. They had arrived seeking slaves, an act that no doubt

33. Garcilosa de la Vega, "La Florida," 2:66.
34. *NAW*, 1:262–264.
35. See Townsend, *Fifth Sun*, 107–128.
36. Townsend, *Fifth Sun*, 138–139.

immediately enraged Cusabos, Guales, and other Indigenous who lived along or near the coast. Unlike the Mexica, these Native communities were far smaller and decentralized. There was no figure comparable to Moctezuma whose defeat would signal the loss of a large population and, just as crucial, no figure around whom Indigenous opposition might have formed. Cortés and his invading army plundered supply houses. In comparison, though the Indigenous of the Carolina coast grew maize, the Spaniards never found sufficient stores to keep them alive while they established farms. The shortage of food they experienced mirrored not the victors of the conquest of Mexico but instead its victims. Like Native Mexicas who succumbed to disease, so did hungry Spaniards in Carolina. By living in small towns rather than a centralized city, Indigenous reduced the chance that a virus like smallpox would spread quickly. For their part, Spaniards learned too late that establishing a colony even in a relatively mild temperate region would require either arriving early enough in the year to plant crops or establishing positive relations with nearby Indigenous to provide them with food while they awaited their own harvest.

In the end, the Spaniards who survived to tell the sorry tale of Chicora provided clues to how Europeans could succeed in North America. The first of those messages: survival depended on understanding the environment and the peoples who lived there. It was a lesson that many Europeans, not only Spaniards, struggled to learn during the sixteenth century.

5

Entradas

In 1547, Álvar Núñez Cabeza de Vaca met Gonzalo Fernández de Oviedo at the Spanish court. Cabeza de Vaca was one of the four survivors of a mission led by Pánfilo de Narváez, a Spanish conquistador who had had a patent to "discover and conquer and settle the said territories that are from the Río de las Palmas to the cape of what is called La Florida."[1] Oviedo was the royal chronicler of the Indies, a position he had held since 1532. He was nearing completion of his epic work, the *Historia General y Natural de las Indias*, which he had begun in 1535. He was—along with the Dominican friar Bartolomé de Las Casas and Pietro Martire d'Anghierra (Peter Martyr), the chronicler for Charles V's Council of the Indies—one of the major historians of the earliest decades of the Spanish colonization of the West Indies and parts of the mainland, notably New Spain and Peru. Oviedo had mastered an enormous amount of information, ranging from politics to natural history. But Cabeza de Vaca had something that Oviedo needed: the most detailed account of North America stemming from the first Spanish effort to expand upon the information derived from Ponce de Leon's tour of La Florida. In an age when laying claim to American territory necessitated understanding its history—including the history of Europeans who had been among the first from their continent to spot new vistas—Oviedo needed to learn what Cabeza de Vaca could teach him.

The Narváez expedition to explore La Florida had come amid ever-expanding explorations to places no European had seen before. Spanish explorer Vasco Núñez de Balboa landed in Panama in 1517, returning home two years later with news about the narrow isthmus that separated the Gulf of Mexico from the Pacific Ocean. The year he returned, Hernan Cortés set off from Cuba and initiated the destruction of the Aztec empire and the death of Moctezuma. His letters to the king describing

1. Rolena Adorno and Patrick Charles Pautz, eds. and trans., *The Narrative of Cabeza de Vaca* (Lincoln: University of Nebraska Press, 1999), 7 (hereafter *Narrative of Cabeza de Vaca*).

Mexico began to appear in print in 1522.[2] Portuguese explorer Ferdinand Magellan set off on his journey to circumnavigate the planet in 1519. Some of those who left on that expedition arrived in Europe four years later, bearing news of distant places. They also brought back word that Magellan had been killed in the Philippines after a dispute with a local leader. Venturing into unknown lands and seas could be deadly, as the well-known demise of Ayllón's colony of Chicora demonstrated. To advance their mission, Spaniards needed to understand what they might encounter in territory that would eventually form the southern tier of the United States.[3]

Cabeza da Vaca knew of these efforts before he left. In the years that followed his return, the Spanish launched two other North American *entradas*—expeditions into territory that was unknown to them. In 1539 Hernando de Soto set off on a journey that took him farther north into La Florida, which incorporated not only the present-day state but also land that reached hundreds of miles to the north and west. Over the next four years he and his associates wended their way through the Southeast, eventually reaching modern east Tennessee. Even before news of de Soto's journey had reached Spanish authorities, Francisco Vásquez de Coronado, who had been the governor of Nueva Galicia (modern-day northwest Mexico), set out on a journey in search of the fabled seven cities of Cíbola, rumored to be a source of immense wealth—an idea that might have seemed reasonable given what Francisco Pizarro and his troops had been able to steal from the Incans only a few years earlier. The Spanish feared they might already be too late. Ferdinand and Isabella had heard from one informant that Sebastian Cabot and investors from Bristol had received permission from Henry VII to find both "the island of Brazil and the Seven Cities."[4] Further, a legend on the so-called Paris map of c. 1490–1493 demarcating land west of Europe noted: "Here is the island called the Island of the Seven Cities, a colony now peopled by the Portuguese: it is

2. Cortés, *Carta de relacion embiada a su. S. Majestad* (Seville, 1522); *Des marches, ysles et pays trouvees et conquise par les capitaines du tres illustres* (Antwerp, 1522); *Nove de isole & terra ferma novamente trovate in India* (Milan, 1522). For the surviving manuscripts and publishing history, see Hernan Cortés, *Letters from Mexico*, trans. and ed. Anthony Pagden (New Haven, CT: Yale University Press, 1986), liii–lx.

3. Three editions of Transylvanus Maximilianus's recounting of Magellan's voyage appeared the year the survivors returned to Europe as *De Moluccis insulis*, published in Cologne and Paris in 1523, and *Epistola, de admirabili & novissima Hispanorum in Orientem navigatione*, printed that year in Rome, with another edition of this imprint appearing in Rome again in 1524.

4. Dispatch of Pedro de Ayala to Ferdinand and Isabella, July 25, 1498, in Henry P. Biggar, ed., *The Precursors of Jacques Cartier, 1497–1534* (Ottawa: Government Printing Bureau, 1911), 28.

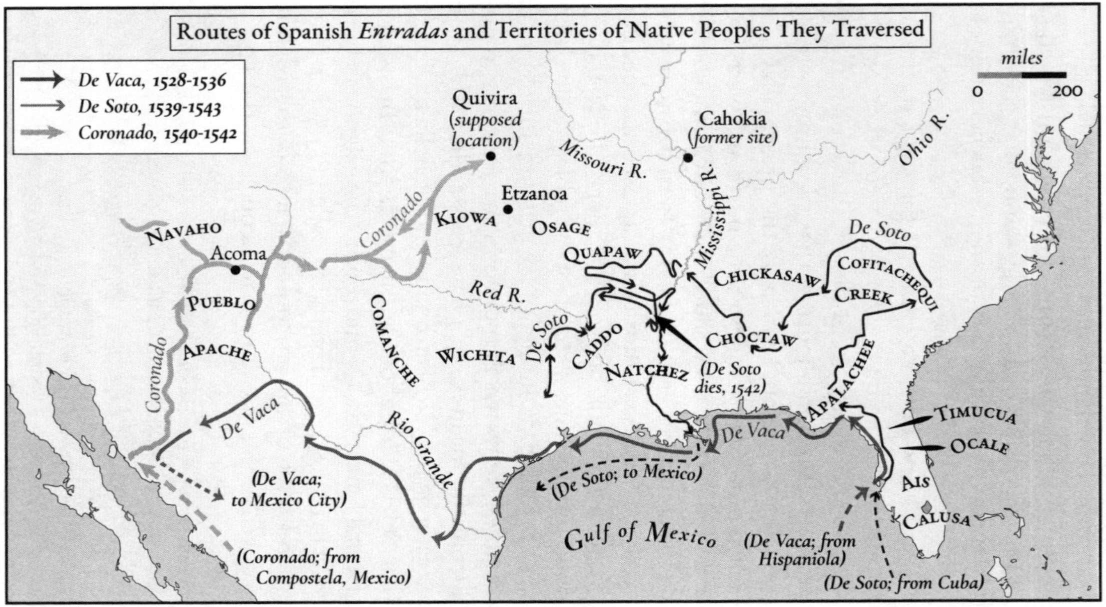
Routes of Spanish Entradas and Territories of Native Peoples They Traversed
De Vaca, 1528-1536
De Soto, 1539-1543
Coronado, 1540-1542
miles
0
200
Quivira
(supposed location)
Etzanoa
Cahokia
(former site)
Missouri R.
Mississippi R.
Ohio R.
Red R.
Rio Grande
Gulf of Mexico
Navaho
Acoma
Pueblo
Apache
Comanche
Kiowa
Osage
Wichita
Quapaw
Caddo
Natchez
Chickasaw
Choctaw
Creek
Cofitachequi
Apalachee
Timucua
Ocale
Ais
Calusa
Coronado
De Soto
De Vaca
(De Soto dies, 1542)
(De Vaca; to Mexico City)
(Coronado; from Compostela, Mexico)
(De Soto; to Mexico)
(De Vaca; from Hispaniola)
(De Soto; from Cuba)

said from a report by Spanish ship-boys, that silver is found in the sand."[5] Coronado got as far as present-day Kansas.

The legacy of these North American journeys lingered for generations. Thomas Jefferson, in 1787, instructed Thomas Mann Rudolph Jr., a young man trying to determine his future course of study, that it would be good to learn Spanish since "the antient part of American history is written chiefly in Spanish."[6] He meant that the earliest texts relating to American history in the post-Columbian world originated in Spanish. But had Jefferson thought about his own experiences more critically, especially the time he dug through Indigenous graves in Virginia,[7] he would have realized that the most ancient history of America had been etched in stone, constructed with adobe and slate, recorded on notched sticks, drilled into mollusk shells, beaten into the ground from regular migrations and hunting routes, and told from one generation to another long before the first Spanish visitor reached the continent.

On June 17, 1527, within a year of the demise of the Chicora settlement, explorer Panfilo Narváez led a five-ship flotilla with 600 men out of Sanlúcar de Barrameda, a port at the mouth of the Guadalquivir River, bound for the Caribbean. Among those on board was Cabeza de Vaca, a native of the Spanish town of Jerez de la Frontera, who had risen to prominence through a series of military positions. A loyal servant of King Ferdinand, he fought first in North Africa and then in Italy, where he was among those trying to defend territory acquired by the Aragonese crown. After Ferdinand's death, he served with distinction in the service of Charles I of Spain (who also held the title of Charles V of the Holy Roman

5. *NAW*, 1:145; Charles de la Roncière, *La Carte de Cristophe Colomb* (Paris, 1924), 27–28. The three islands are faintly visible far to the west of Ireland, on a longitude slightly west of the mid-Atlantic islands that Europeans had already colonized. The map, discovered by Roncière in 1924 (see the article in the *New York Times* on April 6, 1924), is in the Bibliothèque Nationale in Paris.
6. Jefferson to Randolph Jr., July 6, 1787, in *The Papers of Thomas Jefferson*, ed. Julian Boyd et al. (Princeton, NJ: Princeton University Press, 1950–), 11:558; see also *Narrative of Cabeza de Vaca*, 1.
7. Jefferson dismissed the significance of the remains of Indigenous peoples, writing: "I know of no such thing existing as an Indian monument: for I would not honour with that name arrow points, stone hatchets, stone pipes, and half-shapen images." That observation did not stop him from digging into a barrow tomb, which he then described; see Jefferson, *Notes on the State of Virginia*, ed. William Peden (Chapel Hill: University of North Carolina Press for the Institute of Early American History and Culture 1955), 97–100, quotation at 100.

Empire), including military service against the French. The expedition included five priests to help bring more souls into Christendom.[8]

The Spanish landed first at Santo Domingo, in the modern Dominican Republic, one of the largest colonial ports in the West Indies. Colonists there convinced about 140 of the travelers to remain. The diminished crew then landed in Santiago on the southern coast of Cuba, where they gathered more horses, men, and supplies and picked up an additional vessel. Soon after they landed, a Spanish gentleman named Vasco Porcallo convinced Narváez to send two ships to Trinidad, a distance of about 300 miles, where he could get yet more provisions for the expedition. Narváez stayed behind with four ships, and Cabeza de Vaca went on the journey instead. When they arrived in Trinidad the ship pilots remained on board, as did Cabeza de Vaca. One of the captains paddled to shore just before a hurricane arrived.[9]

After the storm passed, Cabeza de Vaca and the other survivors surveyed the scene. His two ships were gone, along with perhaps sixty of the travelers and twenty of their horses. The thirty survivors scavenged for food amid the devastation. Eventually Narváez and the four other ships, which had managed to weather the hurricane, arrived. Narváez, realizing the extent of the psychological turmoil among his men, opted to spend the winter in the nearby port of Jagua on the Bay of Cienfuegos. They set sail again in late February 1528. Again, strong storms hindered their progress, but they reached the west coast of Florida on April 12.[10]

The Spanish had arrived in the homeland of the Tocobagas. Soon the Natives, after having provided venison and fish to the newcomers, paddled off, at least temporarily. In their absence, the explorers inspected their houses, which they called by the Taino name *buhíos*. One of them was so large that Cabeza de Vaca believed it could hold 300 people. The Spanish also found fishing nets, including one with a golden rattle. The next day Narváez raised a standard and took possession of the territory in the name of Charles V, signaling the Spaniards' intent to keep the land, likely for a colony. After the Tocobagas returned they implored the newcomers to leave, but the Indigenous left again without taking any action against the visitors.[11]

Cabeza de Vaca and a contingent of forty men, including the venture's mine inspector, explored the region, heading north until they reached what was probably modern Tampa Bay, which the Spanish soon named

8. *Narrative of Cabeza de Vaca*, 3–4, 48.
9. *Narrative of Cabeza de Vaca*, 3–4, 48–51.
10. *Narrative of Cabeza de Vaca*, 51–53.
11. *Narrative of Cabeza de Vaca*, 53–55.

Bahía de la Cruz—the Bay of the Cross. The next day the group returned to the main camp, where Cabeza de Vaca learned that Narváez had decided to search for a different port, splitting the surviving Spaniards into two groups. After the ship left, the same contingent that had gone north decamped again, this time heading inland. Soon they met—and captured—four locals, who took the visitors to their nearby fields.[12]

The maize was not ripe yet, but something else caught the Spaniards' attention: "crates belonging to Castilian merchants, and in each one of them was the body of a dead man, and the bodies were covered with painted deer hides." The commissary, who was along on the exploratory journey, saw what he thought was "a type of idolatry, and he burned the crates with the bodies in them," an action that would later cause consternation since cremation was not deemed appropriate for Christian bodies and some of the visitors believed that the dead were Spanish. In addition to the crates, the explorers found feathers, gold, and linen cloth that they thought must have come from New Spain. Though they could communicate only through sign language, the Spaniards concluded that more riches could be found in the territory of the Apalachees.[13]

Back at the ships, Narváez asked the others what they should do. His initial thought was to lead an expedition into the interior and to send the ships down the coast until they found the as-yet-undiscovered port they had heard about. During the discussion, Cabeza de Vaca launched into what might have been the most revealing moment of self-awareness of any European who had arrived in North America to that point. "I responded that it seemed to me that by no means should [the governor] leave the ships without first assuring that they remained in a secure and inhabited port," he began,

> and that he should take notice that the pilots were not convinced, nor were they all affirming the same thing, nor did they know where they were, and that beyond all this, the horses were in such condition that we could not make use of them in any need that might present itself, and that above all we were traveling mute, that is, without interpreters, through an area where we could hardly make ourselves understood by the Indians or learn about the land what we desired to know, and that we were entering into a land about which we had no information, nor did we know what it was like, nor what was stored in it, nor by what people it was populated, nor in which part of it we were located, and that beyond all this, we did not have adequate provisions to enter a place of which we were ignorant, because having seen the stores of the ships, no more than a pound of hardtack and another of salt pork could be given to each

12. *Narrative of Cabeza de Vaca*, 55.
13. *Narrative of Cabeza de Vaca*, 56–57.

> man as a ration to take in exploring the land, and that in my opinion we should set sail and go to seek a port and a land better for settling, since what we had seen was in itself as unpopulated and as poor as any place that had been discovered in those parts.

Despite repeated pleading, Cabeza de Vaca lost the argument. Narváez decided to travel inland with a contingent of 300, including 40 on horseback. Cabeza de Vaca was among them. The Tocobaga captives led them away from the shallow, oyster-rich waters of the bay and toward their hoped-for gold. As they marched along, the Spaniards had difficulty traversing low-lying paths often blocked by large trees felled by lightning and high winds. Knowing they would be lost on their own, they continued to capture Natives when they found them, pressing them into service.[14]

They arrived at the thriving town of Apalachee, which had forty thatched houses set in clearings in an otherwise forbidding landscape of thick woods and murky swamps. The Apalachees were successful maize farmers who dried and stored their surplus corn. Deer, hares, rabbits, mountain lions, bears, and the common opossum roamed the land, while the skies and shorelines had ample herons, ducks, geese, partridges, sparrow hawks, and falcons. But while there were promising signs that this could be a place to remain, the Spanish could master neither the landscape, where they kept being impeded by lagoons and fallen trees, nor the locals, whom they battled off and on. After twenty-five days the visitors fled southward toward a place the Spanish called Aute, a perilous nine-day journey away. The destination must have seemed even farther when Apalachees shot arrows at the visitors, killing one of them.[15]

The trek undid the intruders. Narváez decided that the Spanish needed to get to the coast, build boats, and sail off, an unrealistic plan given their lack of the tools, iron, pitch, and ropes they would need to put a durable craft together. To make matters worse, they were starving. Periodic raids on the fields of Aute got them some maize, but the travelers became so desperate that they ate almost all their horses. Conflict with unidentified Indigenous people brought more deaths when Natives killed ten Spaniards gathering shellfish. Despite the long odds, the bedraggled venturers managed to lash together five rafts, each capable of carrying about fifty men. They set off from a place they called the Bay of Horses on these improvised rafts, "placing ourselves," as Cabeza de Vaca put it, "in a sea so treacherous, and without any one of us who went having any knowledge of the art of navigation."[16]

14. *Narrative of Cabeza de Vaca*, 56–64.
15. *Narrative of Cabeza de Vaca*, 65–69.
16. *Narrative of Cabeza de Vaca*, 72–74.

Calamity soon struck. Five died after trying to slake their thirst with seawater. The travelers encountered Indigenous but could not sustain positive relations with any of them. Eventually Narváez declared their mission over, telling Cabeza de Vaca that "it was no longer time for one man to rule another, that each one should do whatever seemed best to him in order to save his own life, [and] that he intended so to do it." The governor sailed off. Cabeza de Vaca never saw him again. The chronicler and a group of about eighty others, including an enslaved African named Estevâncio or Esteban, managed to reach an island in modern Galveston Bay they called Malhado—the Isle of Ill Fate. Soon their numbers dropped to fifteen. They remained there for four years, learning from the Indigenous residents who knew the best places to gather oysters and feasted seasonally on prickly pears.[17]

While on the island, Cabeza de Vaca learned that these Natives venerated healers, who were apparently all male, above all other members of the community. They were the only ones able to have up to three wives. When a healer died, the others cremated the body and then pulverized any remaining bones, which went to the family members a year later so they could be mixed with water and drunk. Cabeza de Vaca mocked their healing rituals, which he claimed involved blowing on infections or sores, placing special stones on the body, and cauterization. But Indigenous believed that Cabeza de Vaca, who survived diseases that felled others, possessed healing powers. The Spaniard resorted to what he knew: he made the sign of the cross over the afflicted, prayed the Ave Maria and Pater Noster, and beseeched "our Lord God that he grant them health and move them to treat us well."[18]

During his time on Malhado, Cabeza de Vaca took snails, conch, and "beads of the sea"—presumably pearls—to inland communities and brought back hides, red ocher, flints, and tassels fashioned from deer hair. Among the Natives, he wrote, "I was very well known; when they saw me and I brought them the things they needed, they were greatly pleased." While he managed to become integrated into an Indigenous trade network, the other Spaniards from the expedition fared worse. Only three of his original companions were still alive, he learned. Others had died of hunger or of cold, or had drowned. Some unidentified Natives had murdered two "for their own amusement" and killed two others "because of a dream."[19]

17. *Narrative of Cabeza de Vaca*, 74–82—salt water (76), Narváez (77), 86–87, 90–93, 95, 108 (prickly pears).
18. *Narrative of Cabeza de Vaca*, 93–94.
19. *Narrative of Cabeza de Vaca*, 96–99, 101–103.

In 1534, Cabeza de Vaca and his three surviving companions headed inland. They suffered from mosquito swarms, which he surmised made them look like lepers. But such suffering was a minor price to pay to learn about the natural bounty of the region, especially its herds of bison. Natives fashioned robes, shields, and shoes from the animal, which they followed along a trail that he believed stretched for 1,200 miles. At an Avavares town in modern-day south Texas, Cabeza de Vaca recognized some with whom he had traded when he was still on the island. They spoke Spanish and welcomed the refugees, hoping that they could cure those suffering from "a malady of the head." Castillo, one of Cabeza de Vaca's companions, made the sign of the cross over one of the afflicted, who apparently suffered no more. For their seeming cures, the town's residents paid the Spaniards with so many prickly pears and so much venison that they did not know where to store it. Over the next eight months, word of the newcomers' miraculous healing abilities spread through the region, bringing yet more stricken victims eager for cures. Following each healing, the Spanish received yet more gifts from the families of their patients, including highly valued flints. As they left, each group pled with the Spanish and their god to keep them well. "They departed the most contented people in the world," Cabeza de Vaca declared, "having given us all the best things they had." He claimed that every Native benefited from their actions.[20]

Cabeza de Vaca and his associates left the Avavares during the prickly pear season of 1535 and wandered on a northwest course toward the Rio Grande Valley. During their migration they met one group after another, learning local customs. They became intoxicated through smoking one plant, quite likely tobacco. At each stop, the Indigenous treated the visitors well. One group led them through more than 150 miles of desolate and unpopulated lands of the Sierra Madre Oriental. They crossed modern southwest Texas, determined to reach the Pacific. Eventually they broke off from the Rio Grande and headed west. They encountered one community where residents offered them coral that likely came from the Pacific and possessed what was probably turquoise. These Natives had traded parrot feathers and other plumes for the stones, a sign that they had trade connections that extended south into New Spain as well as north to where the rare stone could be found. Cabeza de Vaca found other Indigenous who already knew Spanish, which helped him learn that there had been many more Natives in the region but they had fled to escape

20. *Narrative of Cabeza de Vaca*, 107–121, quotation at 119.

Spanish slave raids from the south. They would rather die, he claimed, than be hauled off in chains.[21]

Cabeza de Vaca soon met the enslavers, who tried to convince the small party to help them capture Natives. Pleased to find other Christians, the chronicler and his allies at first acted as intermediaries. They convinced 600 Natives to come to the site, many of them carrying as much maize as they could manage. But the Indigenous soon learned the truth about the Spaniards from the south. According to Cabeza de Vaca, they distrusted these men bent on enslaving them and instead put their faith in the travelers who walked through the desert rather than those who had arrived on horses and armed with lances.[22]

In May 1536, Cabeza de Vaca and his weary companions reached the Gulf of California. Their reputation, so he claimed, had preceded them, and they were greeted by Natives offering feathers, turquoise, and beads. Cabeza de Vaca encouraged religious conversion, telling them that Christians could not be enslaved but they would need to build churches to ensure their future. The visitors baptized Indigenous children. Cabeza de Vaca informed Charles V that he believed they would remain Christians and that the Spanish, having a clear sense of what could be found across the breadth of La Florida, would harvest both great riches and innumerable souls.[23]

Eventually Cabeza de Vaca made his way to Tenochtitlán. He and the two surviving Spaniards set sail on a mission that took them to Bermuda and the Azores before arriving in Lisbon on August 9, 1537.[24] Estevâncio, still enslaved, remained behind. The four had survived a grueling *entrada* that had begun in the Bay of the Cross, spanned the northern coast of the Gulf of Mexico, spent five years in Galveston Bay, walked across much of southern Texas and northern Mexico and up the Rio Grande into modern New Mexico, then went overland to the Pacific coast and southward to Compostela before reaching Tenochtitlán. They had established no colony, but they had provided details that could benefit those who followed. Within five years, the first printed version of his narrative appeared; another edition followed in 1555.[25]

21. *Narrative of Cabeza de Vaca*, 123–124, 130–132, 144, 152–154, 156, 158.
22. *Narrative of Cabeza de Vaca*, 160–163.
23. *Narrative of Cabeza de Vaca*, 165–168, quotations at 165 and 167.
24. *Narrative of Cabeza de Vaca*, 169, 172–173; the route can be seen in *Narrative of Cabeza de Vaca*, 38–39.
25. *La Relacion que dio Alvar Nuñez Cabeça de Vaca de lo acaesido enlas Indias enla armade donde y va por governado Pamphilo de Narbaez* (Medina del Campo, 1542); *La relacion y comentarios del governador Alvar Nuñez Cabeça de Vaca, de lo acaescido en las dos jornados que hizo a las Indias* (Valladolid, 1555).

Born in Jerez de los Caballeros sometime around the dawn of the new century—his exact birthdate is unknown—Hernando de Soto had left home as a teenager to join an expedition to Panama led by Pedro Arias de Avila. Once there, he embraced the violent practices of the conquistadores, participating in attacks on Indigenous communities. Probably before turning twenty, he formed a company with Juan Ponce de León and Francisco Compañón. By 1519 he had received a land grant from Compañón for part of a Panamanian town called Natá. Four years later de Soto left Panama to join an expedition into present-day Nicaragua under the guidance of Francisco Hernández de Córdoba. In exchange for his efforts, he received encomiendas, mining rights, and slaves in a settlement called León. Compañón died there, leaving the nascent company in the hands of de Soto and Ponce de León. In 1530, Ponce de León and de Soto got a contract to provide horses for Pizarro's Andean campaign, which de Soto also joined. He was among the invaders to meet the Incan emperor Atahualpa, and he remained in Peru as the lieutenant governor of Cuzco until returning to Spain in 1535. By the time he landed he had amassed a fortune and gained access to the court.[26]

In the spring of 1537, de Soto petitioned Charles V for new American ventures. On April 20, the king granted him authority "to conquer and settle the Province of Rio de las Palmas to Florida," the territory that had previously been granted to Narváez, whom the king knew was dead, as well as the territory on the mainland that had been promised to Ayllón, also dead. If he succeeded, de Soto would be able to claim land that stretched for 200 leagues—about 500 miles—along a coastline, with the exact location to be chosen by de Soto, who would then be the *adelantado* (governor) of this territory. He would need to build three stone forts to protect the best harbors in this region and cover the cost of transporting priests to spread the faith to Indigenous. In addition, de Soto would become the governor of Cuba. He could take fifty enslaved Africans to Cuba and then onto the mainland, with the provision that at least one-third of them were women. Charles V also promised de Soto half of all the treasure that the explorer found in Indigenous graves and temples, a clause no doubt based on the vast wealth the Spanish had stolen in Tenochtitlán and from royal sites in the Andes. For the next stage of the colonization of La Florida, conquistadores under de Soto's command had

26. See the letter from Pizarro (July 27, 1534) and the cedula from the king (December 7, 1537) in Lawrence A. Clayton et al., eds., The *De Soto Chronicles: The Expedition of Hernando de Soto to North America in 1539–1543* (Tuscaloosa: University of Alabama Press, 1993), 1:467–469; David J. Weber, *The Spanish Frontier in North America* (New Haven, CT: Yale University Press, 1992), 49–50.

the authority to eradicate every vestige of Native religious practice with the understanding that they would make strenuous efforts to convert Indigenous to Christianity.[27]

De Soto led ten ships out of Sanlúcar de Barrameda in early April 1538, after having gathered intelligence from Cabeza de Vaca. Following a year in Cuba, he departed for the mainland in mid-May 1539, possibly landing near Tampa Bay. He had about 215 to 240 horses and 600 men under his command.[28] Over the next three years he guided them through much of the modern Southeast of the United States on an *entrada* that stretched 4,000 miles across eleven current states. Unlike Cabeza de Vaca, de Soto left no account of his journey. But three others—an anonymous author known as the Gentleman of Elvas, a conquistador named Luys Hernández de Biedma, and a man named Rodrigo Rangel—provided detailed reports of a conquistador in command of an army bent, first, on subjugating Indigenous and, second, on converting them to be Christian residents of a new Spanish colony. Adopting the religion of the invaders would not protect converts from suffering abuse at the hands of the invaders.[29]

Soon after getting to La Florida, the Spanish wandered into the town of Ucita. The residents had pearl necklaces and lived in wooden houses with palm leaf roofs. The Spanish destroyed the local buildings, constructed their own houses where the previous dwellings had stood, and cleared the thick forest around the town to make it more defensible. De Soto planned to enslave his captives, but those they had first kidnapped escaped.[30]

What happened at Ucita became a tragic predictor of actions that De Soto and his men would repeat time and again. Not long after their landing, the Spanish arrived at the territory where Narváez had become lost and disoriented. De Soto's men recommended that he turn back to the known shoreline, but the conquistador pushed on. On September 10, 1540, they captured the cacique of Caliquen. As they progressed, they encountered others, including the residents of Napetuca, a Timucuan settlement where the cacique was a cousin of De Soto's captive. Hearing rumors that the Spanish were going to be attacked, De Soto prepared for battle. Soon 400 warriors bearing bows and arrows surrounded the

27. *De Soto Chronicles*, 1:358–364; "The Account by a Gentleman of Elvas," trans. and ed. James Alexander Robertson, in *De Soto Chronicles*, 1:47.

28. *De Soto Chronicles*, 1:6 (Cabeza de Vaca), 1:57 (expedition), 1:185n47 (location).

29. Rangel's version, likely based on a diary, survives in the words of the historian Gonzalo Fernández de Oviedo y Valdés, who apparently interviewed Rangel in Santo Domingo where, as royal historian of the Indies, Oviedo gathered materials for Spanish authorities. See *De Soto Chronicles*, 1:225 (Biedma), 255 (Rangel).

30. *De Soto Chronicles*, 1:57–58.

Spanish. They sent two emissaries asking for the release of the captive. De Soto responded by launching a surprise attack, killing thirty to forty, prompting others to flee into nearby lakes, where they sheltered under lily leaves. Most eventually resurfaced, but twelve remained. De Soto sent troops to capture the dozen who refused to surrender, enlisting captives from Parocoxi to drag them out. The Spaniards put them in chains and distributed the now-enslaved captives "among the Christians for their service," according to the Gentleman of Elvas. When violence erupted, De Soto ordered any captives not yet enslaved to be staked in a plaza. He then had the Parocoxi captives kill them with arrows.[31]

Violence beset the expedition regularly, in part because De Soto presumed he was entering into places where he was unknown. But word of his *entrada* had spread far faster among Indigenous residents than he could have imagined. The cacique of Cutifachiqui had heard about abuses that De Soto's men had committed during their time in the region and pondered not providing guides or food to the Spanish. In response, De Soto captured and paraded the cacique across hundreds of miles, achieving his primary goal of obtaining resources from the Indigenous he met. While encounters could be peaceful and some local caciques provided hospitality, more often than not meetings turned vicious. Even De Soto's own chroniclers detailed the conquistadores' brutal murders and thefts. The march southward into Atahachi served as a prelude to a pitched battle in the fortified town of Mabila in modern central Alabama. There, reeling from an assault by perhaps 5,000 warriors who had hidden themselves within the town's eighty or so houses surrounding an open plaza, De Soto's men set the town alight and used their lances to murder those who tried to escape. Despite launching a fierce counterattack, many residents burned to death or suffocated. The Spanish lost 22 men and 7 horses, with another 150 men and 29 horses wounded. The battle took a huge toll among the Atahachi, who lost 2,500 to 3,000 during the nine-hour battle. The Spanish kept some of the women alive to enslave them, forcing them to tend to the wounded. In terms of lives lost, it proved to be one of the most lethal encounters between Europeans and Indigenous in North America in the sixteenth century.[32]

As he cut his bloody path through the lands of the Timucuan-speakers, De Soto understood that if news of this violence reached Cuba it would

31. *De Soto Chronicles*, 1:66–69.

32. *De Soto Chronicles*, 1:230, 85–88, 99–104, 235–236, 109–110; David E. Duncan, *Hernando de Soto: A Savage Quest in the Americas* (New York: Crown, 1995), 370–384; Charles Hudson, *Knights of Spain, Warriors of the Sun: Hernando de Soto and the South's Ancient Chiefdoms* (Athens: University of Georgia Press, 1997), 232–249.

deter potential colonists from the settlement he planned to launch. His reckoning reflected the facts of Spanish plans and migration patterns. The shift from exploration and trade to settlement, bloodily perfected by Cortés, hinged on luring Spaniards to the mainland. For De Soto, the only possible supply of migrants would be found in the islands, and most likely in Cuba, the place he knew best. But how could he possibly attract men and women if they heard about the turmoil he caused? His fears increased after the massacre at Mabila. If an account of the mayhem escaped, the Gentleman of Elvas wrote, only the discovery of gold or silver would lure colonists.[33]

In early May, De Soto and his men reached the Mississippi at a town called Guachoya. The conquistador realized that he was ill and would likely die soon. Shortly before he took to his bed, he sent a message to a local cacique claiming that, as the Gentleman of Elvas put it, "he was the son of the sun and that wherever he went all obeyed him and did him service."[34]

After his death, De Soto's men buried him. But then, fearing what would happen if Indigenous found his body, disinterred him, wrapped his remains in blankets along with a great deal of sand, paddled into the river, and sank his body. Suspecting he was dead, one cacique offered up two of his own slaves to be beheaded so they could join the conquistador on his journey. Luis de Moscoso, who had taken command, told his host that De Soto was still alive but had gone on a mission to the sun; the cacique spared the lives of the two men. Moscoso soon put De Soto's property up for auction. At the time of his death, his estate in La Florida amounted to two male slaves, two female slaves, three horses, and 700 pigs. The Spanish who had money bought up what they could and soon feasted on the pigs and then tried to escape the region. It took them fifty-two days to get to the Spanish settlement at Pánuco, on the coast of the Gulf of Mexico south of the Rio de las Palmas. Three hundred and eleven of De Soto's men survived their three-year *entrada*, leaving behind battered but resilient Native communities whose residents, like others across the Southeast, had withstood a planned invasion. Some, like the residents of Mabila, had paid a high price for foiling prospects for a colony.[35]

Before he departed Tenochtitlán for Lisbon, Cabeza de Vaca conveyed what happened on his *entrada* to Cortés and Antonio de Mendoza, viceroy

33. *De Soto Chronicles*, 1:104.
34. *De Soto Chronicles*, 1:133–134, 211n241.
35. *De Soto Chronicles*, 1:138–139, 148–158, 164 (trip to Panico), 217n320 (survivors).

of New Spain. The report convinced the imperial authorities to launch another expedition. Cortés selected Francisco Vásquez de Coronado to lead the journey. Before he left, the explorer gathered as much information as he could. Among his informants was Estevâncio.[36] Coronado thought he would find a wealthy province called Topira where residents bedecked in gold and emeralds would convert to Christianity and accept the Spanish king as their own in exchange for being left in peace. They would be good subjects, unlike nearby Chichimecas, who Coronado believed engaged in human sacrifice. The wealth of the fabled city of Cibola made any risk acceptable.[37]

Coronado set off in January 1540. After stopping at Culiacán, which marked the northernmost outpost of New Spain, he led a team of 340 soldiers and perhaps 300 Natives into the homeland of the Apaches and then farther north into Zuñi territory. They arrived at Hawiku, a pueblo they believed to be one of the seven cities. But that community, like the others, lacked the riches that Coronado had believed existed there. The conquistador and some of his party pushed on to Tiguex, near modern Albuquerque, for the winter. By spring they marched eastward into the expansive grasslands of the American plains, across the panhandle of Texas and eventually northward in search of a city they called Quivira. They reached the homeland of the Quiviras, near modern Wichita, but found no great wealth. Coronado then headed back to Tiguex, where he spent the winter of 1541–1542 before journeying south back into Mexico.

On October 20, 1541, Coronado dictated a letter to Charles V. By that point he knew Cibola and its rumored wealth were not to be found, if they existed at all. But he claimed to have been busy "overseeing the subjugation and pacification of the natives" of Tiguex. While there, some Indigenous told him of wealthy towns where rulers ate out of golden dishes. But since he had gathered this information primarily through the exchange of signs, he could not be sure that he was getting the information right, which made his eyewitness report all the more valuable—yet another example of a European in the Western Hemisphere writing to a

36. "The Expedition of Fray Marcos de Niza, 1539," *NAW*, 1:343. Recognizing the utility of this information, Hakluyt translated letters relating to Coronado that had been published in Ramusio's *Terze Volume de Navigatione et Viaggi* (1556): see Richard Hakluyt, *The Principal Navigations, Voyages, Traffiques and Discoveries of the English Nation*, 3 vols. (London, 1598–1600), III:362–364.

37. Coronado to Mendoza, March 8, 1539, *NAW*, 1:343–344 (report from de Niza); Coronado to the Viceroy of New Spain, n.d., *NAW*, 1:345, 344.

powerful patron in Europe that he could be trusted because of the power of firsthand observation.[38]

The grasslands held none of the treasures Coronado thought he would find—no stone houses, no gold or jewels, and often little in the way of potable water or adequate food. Coronado instead came upon a region that resembled nothing he had ever seen before. "These [people] do not plant [crops]," he despaired, but instead ate the meat and drank the blood of bison. They relied on the skins to make clothing and "pavilion-like tents." They went wherever the bison traipsed, across grasslands "so extensive," he wrote, "that whenever I traveled on them I did not find their end," even though he rode across 300 leagues (almost 800 miles). The one constant was the bison, which lived in herds so large that they were never out of his sight. Only when he reached Quivira, where the Natives tended maize, plums, grapes, mulberries, and walnuts, did he claim to find a group that did not rely on bison—perhaps, as he wrote, because they had the best soil he had ever seen "for growing all the [crops] of Spain."[39]

Although he came to appreciate what could be extracted from a bison, Coronado concluded that these expansive grasslands held little promise. Tiguex, where he spent the winter before and after his expedition, was too far from either the Atlantic or the Pacific for regular communication. Quivira was, he estimated, 950 leagues (or about 2,500 miles) from Tenochtitlán. Besides, it was also too cold for Spaniards "because here is no firewood or clothing with which the men could protect themselves from the cold, except hides with which the natives clothe themselves and some cotton *mantas* [which are] in short supply." Spaniards, he believed, would die without the support of Indigenous. He obtained a copper necklace but nothing else of value on grassy "plains so without landmarks that it was if we were in the middle of the sea." Years later he sought restitution for his investments.[40]

Coronado believed that he was a pioneer who shared the first news from a remote world. But long before his letter reached the king, Indigenous across the broad Southwest had already met or heard of Spaniards. In 1540, the viceroy sent Hernando Alarcón on an *entrada* that

38. Coronado to the Holy Catholic Imperial Majesty, October 20, 1641, in Richard Flint and Shirley Cushing Flint, eds., *Documents of the Coronado Expedition, 1539–1542* (hereafter *Coronado Documents*) (Albuquerque: University of New Mexico Press, 2005), 317, 319.

39. *Coronado Documents*, 319–321. Spanish travelers at the time used different distances for a league, but by one modern estimate Coronado would have traveled over 1,000 miles. For the conversion, see Roland Chardon, "The Elusive Spanish League: A Problem of Measurement in Sixteenth-Century New Spain," *HAHR* 60 (1980), 294–302.

40. *Coronado Documents*, 320–321 (copper), 319 (no landmarks), 581–585.

brought him into contact with multiple Indigenous groups.[41] When coastal Chumash met Spanish traveler Juan Cabrillo in 1542 in present-day California, they told him about Coronado and the "armed and mounted men" who a year earlier had paraded across much of the plains. Information about the *entrada* lingered in the Colorado basin too, spread among Natives who likely wondered whether the Spanish would be purveyors of unknown trade goods or menacing invaders who needed to be killed.[42]

Indigenous peoples across the southern tier of the modern United States did not all speak the same language, which put them at a disadvantage in terms of finding common cause in the face of invaders who could talk to each other as they rode along. But Natives who often traveled far to engage in trade did find ways to communicate with each other about news—and perhaps nothing was as newsworthy as the appearance of armed men on horses making demands in every village they entered. Spaniards had long utilized print to share their views, including about America. But as the newcomers to North America learned, Natives without books also spread information far and wide. They did so through oral networks that proved efficient for telling others about newcomers on the way and the dangers they might pose.

Taken together, these Spanish *entradas* had three effects. First, the encounters provided Indigenous Americans with information about Europeans, which led to growing antagonism toward newcomers. Second, it is possible that these encounters from the late 1520s to the early 1540s facilitated the spread of Old World diseases, which were just then beginning to devastate communities north of Mexico, but the surviving documentation makes it impossible to know precisely when these deadly maladies arrived.[43] Third, these expeditions shaped Spanish plans for new colonies. Imperial officials hoped to expand the model they had created

41. "The relation of the navigation and discovery [of] Captaine Fernando Alarchon," in Hakluyt, *Principal Navigations* (1598–1600), III:425–439. The original manuscript is lost, but Ramusio obtained and published an Italian version of Alarcon's letter, and Hakluyt then included an English-language translation of Ramusio's version in 1600; see Albert B. Elasser, "Explorations of Hernando Alarcon in the Lower Colorado River Region, 1540," *Journal of California and Great Basin Anthropology* 1 (1979), 8–37.
42. Natale Zappia, *Traders and Raiders: The Indigenous World of the Colorado Basin, 1540–1859* (Chapel Hill: University of North Carolina Press, 2014), 49.
43. See Henry F. Dobyns, *Their Number Become Thinned: Native American Depopulation Dynamics in Eastern North America* (Knoxville: University of Tennessee Press, 1983), 250–274.

in the West Indies and south of the Rio Grande but soon learned that colonization to the north would be much more difficult.

In the early decades of the sixteenth century, Spanish monarchs looked at paper maps and claimed that they had an undisputed right to the human and natural resources to be found from the Atlantic to the Pacific north of New Spain. They did so by applying the same principles that Columbus had put in place in the West Indies. If there was no proof of the territory being claimed by another Christian state or monarchy, then the land was available to be claimed. For Spain, the claims for La Florida also fell within the lands that the Vatican had allocated to the Spanish in 1493 and 1494. Further, after 1512, Spaniards relied on the Requerimiento (requirement or notification), a statement first drawn up by jurist Juan López de Palacios Rubios, likely soon after 1509 in the wake of the initial Spanish conquests in the Caribbean. Via this text, Spaniards asserted a claim to Indigenous lands and offered the protections of their monarch to those who would accept him (or her), but refusal would constitute an act of hostility that would be met with violence. According to protocols it established, colonizers read it to Native peoples in Spanish even if those listening to the newcomers did not know the language.[44]

Armed with this legal device that they believed entitled them to Indigenous lands and property, Spanish explorers on the ground in North America proved eager to catalog information about the resources and peoples of territory they were in the process of claiming. Their efforts went beyond fleshing out an imperial vision. They needed to grasp local practices lest they create a situation in which the Indigenous, who far outnumbered the visitors during these decades, turn against them. To succeed, they needed a strategy beyond that employed by Ponce de León, who had only limited encounters with small groups when he meandered along the coastlines of Florida. He just barely understood that those he met had mastered an estuarial ecozone where local residents thrived despite the fact that they had not been swept up in the maize revolution that had spawned the spectacular growth of Mexican cities and later spread outward from the Mississippi Valley.[45]

The explorers who came in the next wave and marched across the continent entered very different kinds of social and economic systems, defined by larger groups of Native peoples than those Ponce de León

44. See Patricia Seed, *Ceremonies of Possession in Europe's Conquest of the New World, 1492–1650* (Cambridge: Cambridge University Press, 1995), 69–99.

45. See Clark S. Larsen, "Colonialism and Decline in the American Southeast: The Remarkable Record of La Florida," in Catherine M. Cameron, Paul Kelton, and Alan C. Swedlund, eds., *Beyond Germs: Native Depopulation in North America* (Tucson: University of Arizona Press, 2015), 74–98.

encountered. The spread of corn, squash, and beans had altered subsistence patterns, allowing those in regions where these crops could grow to rely on regular, substantial food supplies. Earlier, the Caddos of modern east Texas and western Louisiana had trade ties to Cahokia, where they sent some of their distinctive pottery and, likely in exchange, brought back clay figurines and copper. But the Caddos did not live like the Mississippians of Cahokia. Rather than inhabit a centralized state, Caddo families maintained their own supplies of grain and made offerings to the *caddí*, whom they recognized as their leader, rather than waiting on him to provide food to them.[46]

Europeans often did not realize it when they marched long distances through the lands of the Caddos, Tejas, Apaches, and Puebloan peoples but they strode across boundaries between the homelands of disparate peoples. They likely were unaware of any customary borders because they never encountered anything like the stone walls that had protected the Tlaxcalans or the various physical defenses around Tenochtitlán.[47] Nonetheless, these Spanish travelers ventured through lands that bore the signs of long-term human occupancy and histories as complex as those of similarly sized locales in Europe, including the rise and fall of regional dynasties, enduring expressions of religious sensibilities, and private and public architecture that reflected evolving ideas about power and reputation.[48] Coming from a continent where the idea of shared use of resources was by then anathema—even animals roaming in forests tended to be the customary property of elites—Europeans missed the unspoken clues that Americans knew well. Ignorant of local distinctions and cultures, the Spaniards on their *entradas* got lost in tangled forests, trudged through murky swamplands, and could make no sense of the extensive grasslands

46. Juliana Barr, "There's No Such Thing as 'Prehistory': What the Longue Durée of Caddo and Pueblo History Tells Us About Colonial America," *WMQ*, 3rd Ser., 74 (2017), 207–217.
47. Barr, "No Such Thing as 'Prehistory,'" 213; Juliana Barr, "Geographies of Power: Mapping Indian Borders in the 'Borderlands' of the Early Southwest," *WMQ*, 3rd Ser., 68 (2011), 5–46.
48. See, e.g., William K. Hartmann and Richard Flint, "Migrations in Late Anasazi Prehistory: 'Eyewitness' Testimony," *Kiva* 66 (2001), 375–385; James F. Brooks, "Women, Men, and Cycles of Evangelism in the Southwest Borderlands, AD 750–1750," *AHR* 118 (2013), 739–764; Barr, "No Such Thing as 'Prehistory,'" 223–229; Stephen H. Lekson and Catherine M. Cameron, "The Abandonment of Chaco Canyon, the Mesa Verde Migrations, and the Reorganization of the Pueblo World," *Journal of Anthropological Archaeology* 14 (1995), 184–202; Catherine M. Cameron and Andrew I. Duff, "History and Process in Village Formation: Context and Contrasts from the Northern Southwest," *American Antiquity* 73 (2008), 29–57.

they encountered. They were ill-suited conquerors for the lands they claimed for their monarchs.

When the Spanish had first heard about La Florida they presumed that it would soon yield its riches following the model that Cortés had established in Mexico: an era of exploration would give way quickly to commerce and then colonization, even if local Native populations the Spaniards encountered were much larger than the relatively small number of men and horses who arrived by ship. The cost would likely be high for the Indigenous, as it had been for the Tainos of Hispaniola and the Bahamas, who had been captured, sold, enslaved, starved, and worked to death in horrifying numbers. But the invaders also believed that they would provide a path to salvation for Native peoples, thereby justifying to themselves what they all knew would be enormous loss of Indigenous lives.

The Iberians soon awoke from their feverish fantasies. Those on Narváez's expedition either drowned on makeshift rafts or died in violent encounters. De Soto, who perhaps bought into the myth that he was the son of the sun and could reduce the peoples he met to civilization, sank to the bottom of the Mississippi River so that Natives would not desecrate the corpse of a man whose soldiers had brutalized so many Indigenous. Coronado survived his *entrada*, but the plains baffled him.

Unlike the conquests of the West Indies, Mexico, and Peru, the Spanish, at least into the early 1540s, had not learned how to reckon with the Native peoples of La Florida or how to create colonies in landscapes where so many had prospered for generations before they arrived. Even when they rode along well-worn paths, as de Soto and Coronado did, they failed to link such paths or the Natives' understanding of particular landscapes to ongoing settlements.[49] They saw signs of long-distance trade, expertise about natural resources, and political systems durable enough to survive when newcomers arrived.[50] Some Indigenous traveled enormous distances across the South as well, though at times—as with a woman taken as a slave by Coronado's men who escaped and found herself then in possession of de Soto's followers in what must be the unluckiest

49. Robbie Ethridge, "Navigating the Mississippian World: Infrastructure in the Sixteenth-Century Native South," in Gregory A. Waselkov and Martin T. Smith, eds., *Forging Southeastern Identities: Social Archaeology, Ethnohistory and Folklore of the Mississippian to Early Historic South* (Tuscaloosa: University of Alabama Press, 2017), 67–69.

50. *Coronado Documents*, 319; Barr, "Geographies of Power."

migration in the region's history—they did so in response to challenges posed by Europeans.[51] Unable to grasp how Americans utilized local resources, the members of these *entradas* failed despite the fact that they marched through thriving communities. Virtually all of La Florida, from the pueblos through the panhandle to the Atlantic, had yet to suffer permanent losses from European colonizers. Other Indigenous were not as lucky.

51. Juliana Barr, "How Do You Get from Jamestown to Santa Fe? A Colonial Sun Belt," *Journal of Southern History* LXXIII (2007), 553–566.

6

The Destruction of the Indies

In the middle of the sixteenth century, chroniclers on both sides of the Atlantic took stock of the first two generations of European exploration, trade, conquest, and colonization in the Western Hemisphere. Crucially, following Columbus's experience, the Europeans among them often rushed their accounts into publishers' hands. In an age when modern notions of copyright did not yet exist, scholars quickly translated these works, making them available far beyond the audience of a reporter's own nation.

The first encounters had been moments of mutual discovery and often led to opportunities for trade. But newcomers became greedy quickly, believing that they had moral as well as political rationales for taking what they wanted, even if that meant enslaving Indigenous. The legacy of the papal decrees of the 1490s remained strong even into the mid-sixteenth century, when Europeans lurched into what became a century of religious warfare between Rome and its Protestant enemies. Undaunted by papal dicta decrying slavery, Spaniards displaced and enslaved thousands in the West Indies. On the mainland, invaders defeated and plundered the Aztec and Incan empires and created labor systems in central Mexico and Bolivia based on tribute or compulsory service. Their Portuguese rivals engaged in similar practices in Brazil, though on a smaller scale. But no European nation could defeat the Indigenous peoples in the north or in La Florida. The Norse had been to Newfoundland and retreated. The English had claimed territory based on Cabot's discovery—and then concentrated their labor on fishing cod. French claimants to the St. Lawrence Valley went home with reports of the grandeur of Hochelaga and Stadacona but had almost nothing to show for their efforts. From the Gulf of California to the northern and eastern shores of the Gulf of Mexico, Natives had rebuffed foreigners who sought their territory. But along the shorelines, at least, Indigenous residents and Europeans on fishing fleets often engaged in trade, an early sign of a consumer revolution that would eventually transform Indian Country.

Despite Native victories to the north, none could deny the impact of the Spanish in the Caribbean, Mexico, Central America, and northern South America. Two generations into the era of conquest, thoughtful observers penned reports about what they had seen, especially in the territories where the Spanish had undermined Indigenous peoples. They wrote histories of the previous half-century with the hope that they might redirect what happened next. The most influential European version came from the Spanish Dominican Bartolomé de Las Casas, who detailed the barbarous actions of conquistadores following orders to displace, defeat, and enslave Indigenous. His searing reports generated a potent response at home and led to a culture-shaping debate in mid-century with Córdoban theologian Juan Ginés de Sepúlveda, who was Charles V's chaplain as well as the court's official historian. Sepúlveda, who had never crossed the Atlantic, had provided a moral justification in the 1540s for Spanish actions toward Americans. The two churchmen squared off in front of Charles V in 1550 at Valladolid in a dispute that revealed that the battle for the Western Hemisphere would forever shape the Old World as well as what Europeans, following Vespucci's lead, were already calling the New World.[1]

Europeans were not alone in assessing what had happened since 1492. Indigenous chroniclers also weighed in, including a well-traveled Andean named Guaman Poma and Mexicas who worked with a Spanish priest to record, in remarkable detail, their view of what had transpired since the creation of New Spain. They testified to similar events through images as well as words. But unlike Las Casas's account, which reached an audience across Europe when printers rushed to publish editions of it, Indigenous accounts almost disappeared from view.

In 1493, a Seville merchant, Pedro de Las Casas, traveled to Hispaniola on the second voyage of Columbus. After returning to Spain, he sailed back to the island with his son, eighteen-year-old Bartolomé, arriving in Santo Domingo on April 15, 1502. They traveled on the expedition led by Nicolás de Ovando, one of the conquistadores who gained a commission

1. European authors had begun to include content about the Western Hemisphere soon after the publication of Columbus's first letter in 1493, often referring to discoveries by Spain. The term "new world" (also sometimes "new found world" or "newly discovered world") became popular after the initial publication by Vespucci as *Mundus novus* (Venice, 1504). Vespucci's own writings, like Columbus's earlier, could be found in translations across the continent quickly, and others adopted the term too; see, e.g., Fracanzano da Montalbaddo, *Paesi novamente retrovati* (Milan, 1512); Fracanzano da Montalbaddo, *Le Nouveau monde et navigacions faites per Emeric de Vespuce* (Paris, [1516]).

in the aftermath of Columbus's first expeditions. As soon as they landed, the young man heard of a looming war with the Tainos and that the Spanish planned to capture and enslave Indigenous Americans. Bartolomé soon became the owner of an encomienda and had the right to own slaves, which he set out to do immediately. That much might have been expected, but his next move was perhaps not. He became a priest.[2]

A week before Christmas 1511, Antonio Montesino, a Dominican who had just landed on the island, delivered a sermon that changed the course of Bartolomé's life. His text was John 1:22–23, the passage where John summons the prophet Isaiah, answering the Pharisees' inquiry about who he was. "I am the voice of one calling in the desert," Montesino read, " 'Make straight the way for the Lord.' " Montesino wanted to halt what he saw as the most sinful aspect of the conquest: the vicious treatment of the Tainos. "With what right and with what justice do you keep these poor Indians in such cruel and horrible servitude?" he asked those assembled in the main church in Santo Domingo. Who, the friar continued, had given the right to enslave people who committed no crimes against the Spanish? "Are these not men?" he continued. "Do they not have rational souls? Are you obliged to love them as yourselves?" An apparently unchastened Columbus was among those in attendance. Unlike with the famed explorer, the last of those questions began to deeply agitate Las Casas's conscience.[3]

Soon after Montesino's sermon, a group of Dominican brothers arrived in Cuba. As they settled in to establish their mission, they decided that it was sinful to own slaves and, as a result, they would deny confession to any slaveholder. At that point, Las Casas was not quite ready to embrace the social justice agenda of the newcomers. Instead, he took up a position as a minister during the conquest of Cuba, joining the military expedition led by Pánfilo de Narváez and Diego Velázquez de Cuéllar in 1512. He accepted a second encomienda there in 1511 and held it until 1514.[4]

Stunned by the violence of that invasion, Las Casas quickly began to reassess the ways that Spaniards treated Tainos and other Americans. He became convinced that the time had come to abolish the encomienda

2. Nigel Griffin, ed., *Las Casas on Columbus: Background and the Second and Fourth Voyages*, Repertorium Columbianum VII (Turnhout, Belgium: Brepols, 1999), 3–4. There is no certainty to the date of his ordination, which could have been as early as 1507 in Seville; see Lawrence A. Clayton, *Bartolomé de las Casas: A Biography* (Cambridge: Cambridge University Press, 2012), 55–56.

3. Griffin, ed., *Las Casas on Columbus*, 4; for the context of the sermon and the emotions it stirred, see Clayton, *Las Casas*, 56–62.

4. Clayton, *Las Casas*, 46.

system. He departed for Spain in the fall of 1515, hoping to meet King Ferdinand. At the time the monarch was ill and recuperating in Plasencia. Las Casas arrived on Christmas Eve. While he waited to meet the king, he began to write an account of what he had seen. Over subsequent years he would continue to write, honing his argument about the way that the Spanish should treat Americans. He gave up his own encomienda. In 1521 he joined the Dominican order in Santo Domingo, where his youthful revulsion fueled his study of ethics and history.[5]

When Las Casas embraced the Dominican agenda, he followed a spiritual path that had attracted thousands before him. St. Dominic (1172–1221) had founded the Order of Preachers in the early thirteenth century in Toulouse. In 1217, after surmising that his and his brothers' situation was deteriorating in the town, Dominic decided that the time had come to disperse. He went to Rome along with a few of the other monks, while a small group went to Madrid and seven migrated to Paris. His mission, which stressed monastic poverty like that advocated by the Franciscans, launched by St. Francis of Assisi at approximately the same time, soon attracted adherents. Women and men across much of Europe joined communities, especially in cities with universities, including Poitiers, Orléans, Metz, Reims, Verona, Limoges, Palencia, Brescia, Faenza, Asti, and Barcelona. By the end of the century, 500 Dominican monasteries housed monks who prayed and preached across Europe and the Christian Holy Land. From the start, the group attracted praise for its erudite theological studies. The sons and daughters of wealthy families joined the order, including Thomas Aquinas, a brilliant master of ancient texts whose philosophical interests led him to Aristotle and whose commentaries on Scripture made him perhaps the leading Christian theologian of the thirteenth century, resulting in his canonization in 1323. Coming after a period of intense religious turmoil that had spawned the creation of orders such as the short-lived Waldensians and Humiliati, the Dominicans from the start had a reputation for being devoted to scholarship as well as poverty.[6]

In 1527, Las Casas began to write a history of the Spanish in the West Indies that he hoped would end crimes against innocents. Las Casas claimed authority for his account because he was an eyewitness to the events he described. That, he later reminded readers of his long treatise,

5. Clayton, *Las Casas*, 39.
6. See Lester K. Little, *Religious Poverty and the Profit Economy in Medieval Europe* (Ithaca, NY: Cornell University Press, 1978), 146–169.

was how Isidore of Seville had identified the role of the historian in his sixth-century CE *Etymology*: "We know those things which we have seen with our own eyes better than those which we know by hearsay."[7]

Before he completed his work, Las Casas returned to Spain. While there he tried to wrestle with what seemed to him the greatest challenge in the Indies: how could he dissuade Spaniards from enslaving Natives or working them to death on their encomiendas? He thought that the era of exploration and trade should evolve into one of colonization, in which Spaniards could still own plantations but the labor on them would be provided by servants who had accepted positions as laborers rather than individuals who were enslaved. Las Casas embraced this possibility because it aligned with his own experience. In late 1518 he had traveled through much of Castile and Aragon, often staying in small churches in towns suffering economic hardship. From what he saw around him he thought it reasonable that some of those with limited economic prospects might be better off in the Indies.[8]

While he hoped that free Spaniards would become the major component of the labor force in the islands, Las Casas also initially endorsed the importation of enslaved Africans. He had grown up in a world where he encountered African slaves daily. In Seville, the city he knew the best, about 10 percent of the population was enslaved in the early sixteenth century, and approximately 4,000 of the almost 5,300 inhabitants were identified in records as African or mulatto. Africans had become integrated into the daily life of the city, a group ensnared in a centuries-long tradition of slavery within Europe that dated back to antiquity. A few had shed their shackles and lived freely, while many of those bound to service participated in local religious and cultural institutions. Following laws codified in the thirteenth century, any child born to an enslaved woman was enslaved too even if the father was free (*partus sequitur ventrem*).[9]

In 1517, before he left Hispaniola for Spain, Las Casas suggested to a local official that African slaves might be a better labor source than Tainos.[10] Almost two decades later, having apparently embraced (for a time) the idea that was common among the Spanish and Portuguese that being a slave in a Christian household was preferable to a life in Africa without what they believed was the one true faith, Las Casas supported

7. Griffin, ed., *Las Casas on Columbus*, 15.

8. Clayton, *Las Casas*, 146–149.

9. *Las Siete Partidas*, trans. Samuel Parsons Scott and ed. Robert I. Burns, 5 vols. (Philadelphia: University of Pennsylvania Press, 2001), IV: 977; Clayton, *Las Casas*, 138–139.

10. Clayton, *Las Casas*, 135–136.

sending enslaved Africans to the West Indies. By then, the African slave trade had already ballooned, with enslavers sending approximately 8,900 bound Africans to Spanish American destinations between 1501 and 1525.[11] For his part, Columbus believed that the Indies could transport 4,000 American slaves to Europe each year, anticipating that they would be purchased because "they use many slaves in Castile, Portugal, Aragón, Italy, Sicily and the islands of Portugal and Aragón and the Canaries." Las Casas knew Columbus's thoughts because he had transcribed them.[12]

In his own work, Las Casas repudiated the idea of selling captured Americans. He instead believed that Columbus had "learned and retained that blindness and corruption" about slavery from the Portuguese, whose slave trade Las Casas judged a "most execrable tyranny in Guinea." Las Casas, who eventually concluded that enslavement of Africans also could not be justified, maintained his steadfast opposition to enslaving Americans based on his observations. He had seen how capture and enslavement had devastated Tainos because of the psychological upheaval of the separation from family and homeland, inadequate provisions, and being placed, as he put it, "in the power of inhumane and cruel people (as they believed the Christians to be, and with good reason)." He wrote about Isabella's aversion to enslavement and wondered how she would have wrestled with the eventual enslavement of, by his count, 6 million Americans.[13]

Las Casas was not the only European theologian to condemn enslavement. In 1537, Pope Paul III issued *Sublimis deus*, an encyclical designed to remind those sailing to the Western Hemisphere that Jesus Christ had declared, in Paul's words, that "all are capable of receiving the doctrines of the faith." That message had become lost in the rush to profit in the Americas. But the encyclical reminded them that the Indigenous peoples there "are by no means to be deprived of their liberty or the possession of their property" even if they were "outside the faith of Jesus Christ." Nor, the text declared, "should they be in any way enslaved."[14]

On November 20, 1542, in response to reports about the abuse of Indigenous Americans, Charles V proclaimed the New Laws (Leyes

11. Lawrence Clayton, "Bartolomé de las Casas and the African Slave Trade," *History Compass* 7, no. 6 (2009), 1526–1541; David Eltis and David Richardson, *Atlas of the Transatlantic Slave Trade* (New Haven, CT: Yale University Press, 2010), 197, 202.
12. Geoffrey Symcox, ed., *Las Casas on Columbus: The Third Voyage*, Repertorium Columbianum XI (Turnhout, Belgium: Brepols, 2002), 83.
13. Symcox, ed., *Las Casas on Columbus*, 84 (Portuguese), 91 (Tainos), 121–122 (Isabella).
14. "Sublimis Deus: On the Enslavement and Evangelization of Indians (1537)," Papal Encyclicals Online.

Nuevas) to halt ongoing persecution of peoples who he claimed, since the time of Columbus's arrival, as his subjects. His logic followed that of Isabella in her quest to end the enslavement of Indigenous peoples. Less than two years after the promulgation of the New Laws, Las Casas became the bishop of Chiapas (in modern Mexico). In 1545, he wrote a pastoral letter decreeing that the church would withhold absolution to those who did not make provisions for the emancipation of their slaves by the time they died, an act that enraged local holders of encomiendas. He also threatened to excommunicate anyone who abused Natives within his diocese. Protest against the New Laws led the king to modify them in October 1545. Las Casas left Chiapas on January 12, 1546, bound for a meeting in Mexico City, where he confronted others upset by his ideas. Realizing that he could not prevail, he chose to return to Spain, where he transformed his theoretical advocacy against enslavement into practical use by appearing in several court cases to argue for the release of Indigenous Americans caught up among the enslaved.[15]

Before he left, Las Casas wrote *Confesionario para los confesores* (Confessionary for confessors), which dictated that priests who would hear confessions demand that those who sought the sacrament promise to make restitution to Indigenous people they had harmed. This policy would have barred those who kept slaves from making confession unless they promised to right that wrong. But the hostility he faced in Mexico remained. In 1548, the king ordered the burning of all copies of Las Casas's *Confesionario*. Intellectual currents against Las Casas within Spain had also grown, evident in Sepúlveda's 1545 tract *Demócrates segundo*, which justified wars of conquest in the Americas. In 1550, Sepúlveda argued that it was just to wage war to subjugate those who, he wrote, were "barbarous and inhuman peoples abhorring all civil life, customs and virtue." He contended as well that weaker Native groups needed to be protected from the more powerful. Over time, he reasoned, Indigenous would eschew their most lethal practices, like cannibalism, and embrace Spanish culture.[16] His views no doubt delighted the supporters of slavery and the encomienda

15. Rolena Adorno, *The Polemics of Possession in Spanish American Narrative* (New Haven, CT: Yale University Press, 2007), 104–105; Nancy Van Deusen, *Global Indios: The Indigenous Struggle for Justice in Sixteenth Century Spain* (Durham, NC: Duke University Press, 2015), xi–xiii.

16. David Thomas Orique, *To Heaven or to Hell: Bartolomé de Las Casas's Confesionario* (University Park: Pennsylvania State University Press, 2018), 1–3; Juan Gines de Sepúlveda, *Apologia . . . pro libro de justis bellis causis* (Rome, 1550); Adorno, *Polemics of Possession*, 115–118; Anthony Pagden, *The Fall of Natural Man: The American Indian and the Origins of Comparative Ethnology* (Cambridge: Cambridge University Press, 1982), 114–118, quotation at 116.

system as well as some in Spain who believed that Las Casas's assault on the institution of slavery could be perceived as treasonous since the monarch was entitled to one-fifth of all slaves captured in the Americas.

Shortly after publishing his book, Sepúlveda faced off against Las Casas in the ornate halls of the Colegio de San Gregorio in Valladolid. Though other scholars had offered opinions about the proper tactics Europeans should employ in their effort to control or coexist with Indigenous Americans, it was Las Casas, whose work had inspired the New Laws, and Sepúlveda, with his defense of legitimate wars of conquest against non-Christians, who had emerged as the most influential voices in what had become a fevered cultural debate.

Sepúlveda and Las Casas each began with the same premise: it was the responsibility of Christians to bring enlightenment to Native Americans. Their debate, then, was not about the ultimate goal but instead pivoted on what should be legal during the conquest, including the amount of force that Spaniards could employ to achieve their goals. Sepúlveda, anxious to root out idolatry and cannibalism, believed that conversion would come only after military conquest. Las Casas took the opposite position: the newcomers should work to evangelize the Indigenous and resort to force only if it became necessary. As he reminded Sepúlveda, God did not endorse the murder of people whose only crime was to worship idols. He offered examples from Scripture, notably from Deuteronomy, to prove that divinely sanctioned war could occur only for reasons other than idolatry. The Canaanites had occupied the land promised to the Jews and so had to be vanquished because of their refusal to leave, not because they were idolatrous. Las Casas accepted that "the Church is obliged to preach the gospel," a point made by the evangels Mark and Matthew, but that did not mean that they could "force unbelievers to hear the gospel."[17]

After each man had presented his views, the council debated who had prevailed. After the court rendered an ambiguous judgment in 1551, each of the disputants continued to press his claim. No doubt sensing that the result would be disastrous for Americans, Las Casas in 1552 published four books, including *A Short Relation of the Destruction of the Indies*. It would soon become the most influential European published work about the Western Hemisphere since the 1493 publication of Columbus's first report—and the foundational text for what would become known as the

17. Bartolomé de Las Casas, *In Defense of the Indians*, trans. Stafford Poole (DeKalb: Northern Illinois University Press, 1992), 104–106, 176–177; Adorno, *Polemics of Possession*, 120–124.

"Black Legend," the propaganda employed especially by Protestants to castigate Spanish actions in the Americas.[18]

For Las Casas, the "marvelous discovery of the Americas" overshadowed "all the deeds of famous men of the past, no matter how heroic, and to silence all talk of other wonders of the world." But he intended no paean to the grandeur of Columbus and the conquistadores. Instead, he offered a tragic tale of "the massacres of innocent peoples, the atrocities committed against them and, among other horrific excesses, the ways in which towns, provinces, and whole kingdoms have been entirely cleared of their native inhabitants." He had given the king his eyewitness report but realized that news of the horrors he had seen was not widespread. He feared that some of those whose crimes would fill his pages had "become so anaesthetized to human suffering by their own greed and ambition they had ceased to be men in any meaningful sense of the term." They were "degenerate" and many an individual had "a reprobate mind," a phrase he borrowed from Romans 1:28. These Spaniards had "honed to perfection the art of cruelty in order to wipe human beings from a large part of the globe." Worse still, they were unrepentant and intended to continue their wanton destruction. Fearing the worst, Las Casas told his readers, he believed "it would constitute a criminal neglect of my duty to remain silent about the enormous loss of life as well as the infinite number of human souls dispatched to Hell in the course of such 'conquests.'"[19]

The Dominican argued that the king needed to pay attention to eyewitness testimony. While he dithered, criminals worked. These despoilers, Las Casas declared, thought it "as nothing to drench the Americas in human blood and to dispossess the people who are the natural masters and dwellers in those vast and marvelous kingdoms, killing a thousand million of them, and stealing treasure beyond compare, grow by the day, and, masquerading under false colors, they do everything within their power to obtain further license to continue their conquests." Las Casas believed that the monarch needed to stop the depredations. God

18. Printers issued other editions of his book as well as his debate with Sepúlveda and a treatise on the legitimacy of Spain's American claims; see *Aqui se contiene una disputa . . . entre el Obispo . . . Bartholome de las Casas . . . y el doctor Gines de Sepulveda* (Seville, 1552); *Aquí se contienen treynta proposiciones muy juridicas* (Seville, 1552); Griffin, ed., *Las Casas on Columbus*, 6–7. Las Casas did not publish his *Defense of the Indians*, which he had perhaps written before the debate; see Las Casas, *In Defense of the Indians*, xx. For a listing of his works in 1552, see *EA*, 1:69–70.

19. Bartolomé de Las Casas, *A Short Account of the Destruction of the Indies*, trans. Nigel Griffin (London: Penguin, 1992), 3–4, 6.

was watching and would not bless Spain again if these despicable acts continued.[20]

To Las Casas, writing a history was a form of bearing witness. Following this logic, the only historical accounts that could be accepted as true were those composed by individuals who had seen events unfold with their own eyes. This idea existed in Europe well before 1492. But in the aftermath of Columbus's voyages, with news about the Western Hemisphere spreading ever more quickly in printed books and told from one person to another in a chain that stretched from a dock where a returning ship unloaded its crew and wares to an elite patron who purchased a book that promised the freshest account of developments thousands of miles away, the premium on being the eyewitness grew. There had been an epistemological shift, which drew inspiration from leading philosophers like Lucretius (whose most important book had circulated in Europe in the fourteenth century) and theologians like Aquinas, away from reliance on ancient fables and toward assessments based on witnesses. In dispelling the idea that monsters roamed the Western Hemisphere, Columbus himself had helped propel the move away from the fantastic claims of a Mandeville to the more sober reporting of a Cartier.[21]

Las Casas knew that he had two audiences for his book: a king who, by the Dominican's own telling, was too busy or lazy to read his magisterial history, and an audience of unknown size acquiring new works about the Western Hemisphere as they rolled off presses across Europe, including in Seville, where by 1552 printers had produced over forty books that included content about the Western Hemisphere.[22] Las Casas's background played a direct role in the ways that he wrote. In particular, following the traditions of Dominican (and, more generally, scholastic) practice, he drew on four kinds of sources known to Europeans to support his accounts of the Indies: law (both canon and Roman civil), scripture, Aristotle, and the writings of earlier theologians.[23] Las Casas's personal peregrinations back and forth across the Atlantic, with time spent at Hispaniola, Puerto Rico, Cuba, Venezuela, and Guatemala, gave him the bona fides to tell about much of New Spain and the Indies.

Throughout his account, Las Casas betrayed both of his affiliations—as a man loyal to the Crown and a Dominican friar who viewed the world

20. Las Casas, *Short Account*, 6–8.

21. On the shift, see Stephen Greenblatt, *The Swerve: How the World Became Modern* (New York: W. W. Norton, 2011) and Lorraine Daston and Katherine Park, *Wonders and the Order of Nature, 1150–1750* (New York: Zone Books, 1998).

22. See the list of printers and imprints in *EA*, 1:323–325. The number of imprints from printers in Seville not including Las Casas's own books from 1552 totaled forty-three.

23. Las Casas, *Defense of the Indians*, xxii.

through the lens of a missionary. He did not believe that the Spanish should leave the Western Hemisphere. Instead, they needed to understand that its original inhabitants were also the children of God who, not knowing better, should be loyal to both their caciques and the conquerors "in whose service they now find themselves," a reference to the fact that the invaders had enslaved most of the residents of Hispaniola. Treating Natives harshly was not fair to people who had more in common with the Desert Fathers of Christian lore than with contemporary Iberians. Like those ancient wanderers, the Americans could embrace Christianity because they had "fewer impediments" to religious conversion "than any other people on earth" and were eager to embrace the friars' agenda.[24]

The trope of the innocent Native formed one of the keys to Las Casas's logic. If the Tainos had been fierce—if they struck fear in the hearts of the arriving Spanish in the ways that the Island Caribs once did—then it might make sense to treat them with force. But he believed that aggressive invaders attacked "like ravening wolves upon the fold, or like tigers and savage lions who have not eaten meat for days." The violence the Spanish visited on the Natives recurred time and again for the next fifty years. The Spaniards "still do nothing save tear the natives to shreds, murder them and inflict upon them untold misery, suffering and distress, tormenting, harrying and persecuting them mercilessly." That last accusation was the most damning: the countrymen of Columbus lacked the necessary mercy that their God intended for those who were innocent. The cost of Iberian barbarism could be seen in the population of the islands. The Taino population of Hispaniola, by Las Casas's reckoning, had been reduced from 3 million Tainos in 1492 to only 200. Cuba, as wide as the distance from Valladolid to Rome, "is now to all intents and purposes uninhabited." Puerto Rico and Jamaica had suffered a similar fate. The Bahamas no longer had any Indigenous occupants, a fact supported, though Las Casas might not have known it, by the failure of enslavers looking for human quarry to provide labor for Ayllón's proposed colony. Spaniards had transported enslaved Bahamians to replace the Tainos they had already worked to death. Las Casas knew this to be true, he informed his audience, because he had seen with "his own eyes" the last eleven Indigenous in the Bahamas. The mainland, by which he likely had in mind the Valley of Mexico, "once teeming with human beings, is now deserted" over a distance as long as a round-trip journey from Seville to Jerusalem.[25]

Las Casas claimed that the invaders had killed between 12 million and 15 million men, women, and children in the first forty years of colonization.

24. Las Casas, *Short Account*, 10–11.
25. Las Casas, *Short Account*, 11–12.

While he overestimated the loss of life on Hispaniola, he may have underestimated the demographic catastrophe across New Spain, since the death toll from smallpox alone during the conquest of Mexico may have reached 8 million, a horrifying total that was likely eclipsed by the loss of 15 million more in an epidemic of hemorrhagic fevers that began in 1545 and was caused by *cocoliztli*, a disease that spread from rodent hosts to the human population.[26] Las Casas emphasized the violence of the conquest, not the impact of infections. In his assessment, conquistadores unleashed waves of violence, first in wars against any who opposed them, mostly adult men, and then in campaigns to murder those who escaped their initial assault. Worse still, the Iberians "have had as little concern for their souls as for their bodies, all the millions that have perished having gone to their deaths with no knowledge of God and without the benefit of the Sacraments." "Even the tyrannical murderers themselves acknowledge the truth of it," Las Casas commented. "The indigenous peoples never did the Europeans any harm whatever." The conquistadores' actions undermined any hope of convincing Natives that the newcomers' faith should be emulated.[27]

Las Casas dwelled at length on the conquest of Hispaniola, "the first to suffer the wholesale slaughter of its people and the devastation and depopulation of the land." The horrors began with the invaders first taking women and children to be their sex slaves and servants. Then the newcomers took local food supplies. If the Tainos resisted, the Christians beat and flogged them. When many Tainos rose in response to a European commander raping the wife of the most powerful chief on the island, Spaniards on horseback used superior weapons to quell the uprising.[28] With defenders vanquished, the invaders entered Taino towns,

> slaughtering everyone they found there, including small children, old men, pregnant women, and even women who had just given birth. They hacked them to pieces, slicing open their bellies with their swords as though they were so many sheep herded into a pen. They even laid wagers on whether they could manage to slice a man in two at a stroke, or cut an individual's head from his body, or disembowel him with a single blow of their axes. They grabbed suckling infants by the feet and, ripping them from their mothers' breasts, dashed them headlong against the rocks. Others, laughing and joking all the while, threw them over their shoulders into a river, shouting: "Wriggle, you little perisher." They slaughtered anyone and everyone in their path, on occasion running through a mother and her baby with a single thrust of their swords.

26. John L. Brooke, *Climate Change and the Course of Global History: A Rough Journey* (Cambridge: Cambridge University Press, 2014), 432.
27. Las Casas, *Short Account*, 12–13.
28. Las Casas, *Short Account*, 14–15.

> They spared no one, erecting especially wide gibbets on which they could string their victims up with their feet just off the ground and then burn them alive thirteen at a time, in honor of our Savior and the twelve Apostles, or tie dry straw to their bodies and set fire to it.

Las Casas reported that conquistadores sometimes chopped off victims' hands and sent the victims home as a warning to others. He claimed that they roasted leaders "over a slow fire, with the result that they howled in agony and despair as they died a lingering death." When the Tainos screamed in agony, an executioner rammed wooden sticks down their throats. Perhaps sensing that his readers might not believe him, he added: "I saw all these things for myself and many others besides." Conquistadores set ravenous dogs on Tainos and avenged every death of an invader by killing 100 Indigenous. Las Casas reported that he had seen individuals who escaped to the mountains but there died of despair, "a direct result of the despotism and slavery to which they were subjected." The Spaniards killed regional leaders regardless of their sex, at times luring them into houses, setting the structures on fire, and then using lances and swords to murder those who tried to escape the flames. With the social structure in tatters and the resident communities almost erased, the Spanish took over the best lands and set up sugar plantations. They enslaved surviving men to work in mines and women in their fields. He gave up counting the ways that conquistadores tortured, abused, and killed.[29]

Hard as it is to imagine, Las Casas believed the situation deteriorated even further after the death of Isabella. Spaniards on the island had heard that she was opposed to the brutal treatment of her new subjects. But there was no similar legal or moral authority after her death in 1504. When conquistadores arrived at Puerto Rico and Jamaica in 1509 they perpetrated the same kinds of crimes as on Hispaniola. Las Casas conveyed horrific stories from other clerics, who told him of the atrocities they had witnessed, adding to the catalog of cruelty the Dominican had already compiled. Las Casas reckoned that from 1514 to 1521—from their arrival on the mainland through Cortés's victory in Tenochtitlán—Spaniards killed at least 800,000 in Mexico, Panama, Guatemala, and Honduras. He laced his narrative with searing accounts of a mother killing her son and herself before Spanish dogs mauled them, would-be captors lopping off a boy's ears and nose, a conquistador killing a child and cutting him into pieces to feed to his hungry dogs, and a group of thirty soon-to-be converts finding enslavement, not Heaven, at the hands of the invaders. He included reports of horrors visited on Natives in Colombia, Trinidad, Peru, and Venezuela. Desperate for gain, conquistadores also

29. Las Casas, *Short Account*, 15–23.

killed missionaries and pearl divers. In New Grenada, he claimed, some operated "a kind of human abattoir or flesh market, where a dog-owner can casually ask, not for a quarter of pork or mutton, but for 'a quarter of one of those likely lads over there for my dog.'" Widespread murder and enslavement produced a "heart-rending spectacle" on Cuba, which had been transformed "into one vast, barren wasteland."[30]

Las Casas knew less about La Florida, but he gathered that the Spaniards had acted in the same way there. He knew this in part because those who went there, notably Ponce de León and Pánfilo de Narváez, already had well-deserved reputations as men who had "clawed their way up to their present commands not on merit but over the dead bodies of their fellow-men." He never met De Soto, though Las Casas knew that he too planned a similar assault, "for he is a notoriously ruthless and seasoned campaigner." Even after his death, according to Las Casas, De Soto's followers tortured and murdered Americans "who lived in well-ordered and structured societies."[31]

Las Casas's book contained inaccuracies about the size of Indigenous populations and exaggerations about the cruelties inflicted by conquistadores. But at a time when relatively few literate Europeans produced firsthand reports about the Western Hemisphere, his caught the attention of a rapt public. That interest only grew over time, which meant that Las Casas's short history became a crucial ideological weapon in the hands of other Europeans, especially Protestants, who furthered the Hispanophobia among Europeans that Las Casas's book had unleashed.[32]

Las Casas had hoped that his book constituted sufficient evidence that Charles V would initiate policies that would stem the excesses of the conquistadores who had flocked to the Western Hemisphere in the early decades of the sixteenth century. Although he thought his words had made some inroads when he first completed the manuscript in 1542, he realized that the same kinds of wanton criminality continued just as they had for years. The conquistadores had "sheathed their swords and no longer murder the natives on sight," but instead worked them to death through forced labor despite the Vatican's condemnation of enslavement.

30. Las Casas, *Short Account*, 23–25 (Isabella), 26 (Puerto Rico), 32–43 (800,000), 72–77 (acts of torture), 81–83 (Colombia), 87–88 (Trinidad), 100–114 (Peru), 96 and 101 (Venezuela), 88–90 (missionaries), 93–94 (pearl divers), 125 (New Grenada), 29–30 (Cuba).

31. Las Casas, *Short Account*, 102–104.

32. Benjamin Keen, "The Black Legend Revisited: Assumptions and Realities," *HAHR* 49 (1969), 703–719; David J. Weber, "The Spanish Legacy in North America and the Historical Imagination," *Western Historical Quarterly* 23 (1992), 4–24.

The workshop of Flemish engraver Theodor de Bry produced the earliest illustrated version of Las Casas's account of Spanish depredations in the Americas. In this work, which appeared in 1599, the illustrators translated the Spaniard's searing words into graphic illustrations, helping to solidify the idea of the "Black Legend" of the conquest. Courtesy of the John Carter Brown Library.

He despaired that change could ever come since "everyone, young and old alike, who journeys to the New World is either openly or in secret a fortune-hunter," with some worse than others, "and all such fortunes are made at the expense of the local people." Their actions dishonored their monarch and the Christian God, but they continued.[33]

After drafting the *Short Account*, Las Casas began work on a long manuscript. Like his *Historia*, this document was not published during his lifetime. Known thereafter as *In Defense of the Indians*, this manuscript exposed Las Casas's training, with its Latin betraying three distinct forms of the language, reflecting classical, medieval, and Renaissance practice.[34] He had quite likely begun the book before the debate of 1550 with

33. Las Casas, *Short Account*, 127–130.
34. Las Casas, *Defense of the Indians*, xxv–xxvi.

Sepúlveda but returned to it to follow up the points he made in his historical accounts.[35] The text contains numerous examples drawn from scripture, earlier philosophers, and historians, all brought together to undermine what he saw as the immoral and dangerous deceptions at the heart of Sepúlveda's argument.[36]

Most of the *Defense* consisted of the methodical application of widely accepted ideas to the particular situation pondered by the council: was it legitimate to enslave and launch a just war against Americans? No serious commentator doubted that Indigenous in the Western Hemisphere were humans; even Sepúlveda presumed their humanity, reserving his scorn for their culture but still believing that they could, under the right circumstances, convert to Christianity.[37] In some ways, Las Casas echoed Sepúlveda, though with more sympathy for Americans' mores. He defined "Indians" as people who lacked an understanding of Christianity, since they had never been exposed to it before, but who lived in orderly societies. Even if one accepted the notion that they were "barbarians," he added,

> it does not necessarily follow that they are incapable of government and have to be ruled by others, except to be taught about the Catholic faith and to be admitted to the holy sacraments. They are not ignorant, inhuman, or bestial. Rather, long before they had heard the word Spaniard they had properly organized states, wisely ordered by excellent laws, religion, and custom. They cultivated friendship and, bound together in common fellowship, lived in populous cities in which they wisely administered the affairs of both peace and war justly and equitably, truly governed by laws that at very many points surpass ours, and could have won the admiration of the sages of Athens.

To Las Casas, Americans did not fit the categories that would make them eligible to be conquered in a so-called just war, as defined by Augustine of Hippo more than a millennium earlier, nor did they deserve the torture they had suffered at the hands of conquistadores any more than the ancient inhabitants of Spain would have deserved such a fate

35. Las Casas, *Defense of the Indians*, xx. The text circulated in manuscript long before it was printed. Only the first part of the earliest manuscript is in Las Casas's hand, and paleographical evidence reveals that four other scholars worked on the text; see Las Casas, *Defense of the Indians*, xxii. What survives is a Latin copy of a Latin copy of a long work (253 folios) likely written originally in Spanish, which then migrated to a Benedictine monastery in Paris between 1677 and 1740 and now resides in the Bibliothèque Nationale in Paris. The history of the manuscript can be found in Las Casas, *Defense of the Indians*, xx–xxii, which mentions that the manuscript did not appear in a catalog of St. Germain dePrès in 1677 but was listed in the 1744 catalog.
36. Las Casas, *Defense of the Indians*, 3, 5.
37. See, e.g., Las Casas's summary of Sepúlveda's views in *Defense of the Indians*, 11–16.

after the Roman conquest.[38] The Spanish could condemn the Americans for engaging in human sacrifice, but the widespread practice of it in the ancient world, which Las Casas knew of from his reading of Eusebius, Lactantius, Plutarch, and Herodotus, suggested that prevailing custom, no matter how inerrant, could not be used to justify widespread slaughter. Nor did Alexander VI in the *Inter caetera* justify holy war against the Americans, a point that Sepúlveda had also made. How, Las Casas asked, could the pontiff "permit something that conflicts with Christ's precept and instruction and produces hatred of the name of Christ in the hearts of unbelievers, and is utterly irreligious?" Per church teachings, "it is unlawful to force the Indians to the faith by war." Queen Isabella, "the ornament of her century" to Las Casas, also demanded that the Americans, as her subjects, should "be treated well and justly." The Spanish had an obligation to redress any harm they had experienced as a result of the conquest.[39]

Experience had taught Las Casas that the best way forward was to preach the word, not to wield the sword. Those who had already converted demonstrated enviable piety. They were, he wrote, "docile and clever, and in their diligence and gifts of nature, they excel most peoples of the known world." He hoped that the latter part of his *Defense* would silence the voices of the "wicked plunderers" who had already done so much to harm the Americans.[40]

Las Casas had the personal experience and the professional and scholarly contacts to gather the materials to make an effective case. But he was not the only witness to the human costs of the conquest.

Even as the scholars debated at Valladolid, Spaniards continued to expand their territory in the Western Hemisphere, first in the lands extending outward from Tenochtitlán and then in the Andes as a result of Pizarro's ruthless conquest of the Incans. While Indigenous resistance continued in some areas, including in the Andes, conquistadores mastered techniques that allowed an invading army to defeat large Native populations, providing a lesson that could be employed, Spanish officials hoped, in other promising areas, such as North America. Each colonial arena, then, offered resources to be harvested (if the invaders could command a sufficient workforce) as well as new additions to the playbook of

38. Las Casas, *Defense of the Indians*, 42–43.
39. Las Casas, *Defense of the Indians*, 221–225 (sacrifice), 349–350 (holy war), 356–357 (Isabella).
40. Las Casas, *Defense of the Indians*, 361–362.

American conquest that might be of use in areas where the newcomers found silver.

Across the Caribbean and parts of the continent, Spaniards enslaved Americans to work on their encomiendas, in communities of pearl divers, and eventually, starting in 1545, in the silver mines of Potosí in modern Bolivia. From the start, these mines devoured the Andeans who worked there, another example of Spanish administrators' ability to manipulate an existing labor system—in this case, the Incan *mita*—for their own ends. Before the arrival of Pizarro, Incan elites had lured residents of far-flung communities to work in the service of the empire. But these labor demands had limits, consuming only a limited amount of time. As a result, inhabitants of Incan communities could have the benefits of a growing state while still enjoying their traditional practices, including control over where they worked.[41]

After Pizarro's conquest, Spanish bureaucrats eager to extract silver from Potosí placed new demands on small communities and cities alike. At first, some Andeans migrated to the region voluntarily, often with their families in tow, though it was not long before the conditions in the mines would have dissuaded anyone who toiled there. Still, the silver boom fed the creation of a new town at the mountain's base, with people and horses traveling back and forth between the city and coastal ports. The transportation network, which allowed Spaniards to export silver, also facilitated the movement of infectious diseases.[42] Local mining techniques, notably the use of mercury, could be lethal as well, with mercury intoxication contributing to deaths within the mines and in nearby towns.[43] Many Andeans, wary of the mines and their dangerous fumes, chose to abandon their homes and customary rights to become *forasteros* (outsiders)—beyond the reach of the *mita* but also poorer as a result of what they had to surrender.[44] Most could not escape. By the 1570s, Spanish

41. Jeremy Mikecz, "Beyond Cajamarca: A Spatial Narrative Reimagining of the Encounter in Peru, 1532–1533," *HAHR* 100 (2020), 195–232.
42. On the shift in perception about the desirability of Potosí as a place to work, see Kris Lane, "Potosí Mines," in *Oxford Research Encyclopedia: Latin American History*, May 2015; for the disease routes, see Noble David Cook, *Born to Die: Disease and New World Conquest, 1492–1650* (Cambridge: Cambridge University Press, 1998), 125, 127, 169, 187.
43. Nicholas A. Robins and Nicole A. Hagan, "Mercury Production and Use in Colonial Andean Silver Production: Emissions and Health Implications," *Environmental Health Perspectives* 120 (2012), 627–631.
44. Ward Stavig, "Continuing the Bleeding of These Pueblos Will Shortly Make Them Cadavers: The Potosi Mita, Cultural Identity, and Communal Survival in Colonial Peru," *The Americas* 56 (2000), 529–562.

officials imposed labor requirements that demanded that upward of 17,000 Andeans worked in the mines each year.[45]

The Spanish used the silver extracted from Potosí to enrich their bourgeoning empire. Contemporary observers understood that the mines there produced staggering amounts of silver, even if the effort took an extraordinary toll in this world of darkness, extreme cold, and, as observer José de Acosta reported in his natural history first printed in 1590, a "very heavy atmosphere unfit for man's nature." The conditions in the mines reminded Acosta of what Pliny had written about similar ancient practices: " 'We penetrate the inner parts of the earth and seek riches even in the place of the damned.' "[46] Spaniards who had not seen the deleterious consequences of mining silver in South America could be more sanguine. The great profits coming from Potosí were as well known as the riches of Venice, as renowned writer Miguel de Cervantes observed in *Don Quixote*.[47]

The loss of Indigenous lives at Potosí, like those on countless encomiendas, replicated the labor problems that Spanish administrators had recognized since the death of most of the Tainos early in the century. Rather than abandon wealth-generating overseas communities, the Spanish instead looked for a new and seemingly larger pool of laborers—Africans who had been captured in war and sold into slavery. From 1526 to 1550, the Spanish imported almost 36,000 enslaved Africans. During the next twenty-five years they purchased over 40,000 more, and another 85,000 before the end of the century.[48]

At roughly the same time that Las Casas was gathering materials that would later inform his historical and moral treatises, Indigenous scholars also wrote accounts of the military invasion they witnessed. The most detailed was produced by a team of Mexica scribes working with the Franciscan missionary Bernardino de Sahagún. Beginning in 1545, they together created an illustrated manuscript called *The General History of the Things of New Spain*. Now known as the Florentine Codex, their work included an account of the conquest of Mexico that was in many ways as harrowing as Las Casas's chronicle.

45. See Melissa Dell, "The Persistent Effects of Peru's Mining 'Mita,'" *Econometrica* 78 (2010), 1863–1903, esp. 1867.

46. José de Acosta, *Natural and Moral History of the Indies*, ed. Jane E. Mangan (Durham, NC: Duke University Press, 2002), 180–181; see also Pedro Cieza de León, *The Discovery and Conquest of Peru*, trans. Alexandra Parma Cook and Noble David Cook (Durham, NC: Duke University Press, 1998), 39.

47. Cervantes, *Don Quixote*, book 2, chapter 71: "el tesoro de Venecia, las minas del Potosí."

48. Eltis and Richardson, *Atlas*, 202.

The scribes and Sahagún used pictures and words (in both Nahuatl and Spanish) to describe many aspects of their world, including detailed accounts of the assault on Tenochtitlán, the captivity and death of Moctezuma, the pillaging of temples, and the slaughter of innocents. Their descriptions seethe with contempt for the invaders, who were motivated by greed, not glory. Invaders stole Moctezuma's most precious objects, including valuable golden jewelry adorned with sacred feathers. They took "the turquoise diadem, the attribute of the ruler." They plundered "goods without number. They took it all. They possessed themselves of all, they appropriate all to themselves, they took all to themselves as their lot." They destroyed icons and stripped gold off shields, melting it into bars, a theft made more horrific in its assault on the material objects of their faith. "Very high rose the flames, the tongues of fire," when the Spaniards set a temple on fire. "It was as if the flames continually crackled and continually flared up." Images of the slaughter during the Feast of Uitzilopochtli depict sword-wielding conquistadores slicing off hands, legs, and heads of celebrants.[49]

Nearly a century later, in 1616, an Andean native named Felipe Guaman Poma de Ayala, who had been born in Santiago de Chipao at roughly the same time that Pizarro was completing his conquest of the Incans, wrote a long and extraordinary letter to King Philip III of Spain. Unlike most such accounts, Guaman Poma's included 399 pen-and-ink illustrations along with a detailed narrative of his travels across New Spain. The book, *El primer nueva corónica y buen gobierno*, likely did not circulate far at the time, yet it became the most perceptive Indigenous critique of its era of the European expansion in the Western Hemisphere.[50]

Born into an elite family, Guaman Poma understood all that he and others had lost with the expansion of Spanish power across the Andes

49. Bernardino de Sahagún, *General History of the Things of New Spain: Florentine Codex*, 2nd ed., trans. and ed. Arthur J. O. Anderson and Charles E. Dibble, School of American Research Monograph Series (Salt Lake City: University of Utah Press, 1981), quotations at 12:49 (plunder) and 107 (temple).

50. The book was not printed during its author's life, but by the middle of the century it had become part of the collection of the Royal Library in Copenhagen, where it remains. For the context of the narrative and the manuscript, see Rolena Adorno, *Guaman Poma and His Illustrated Chronicle from Colonial Peru: From a Century of Scholarship to a New Era of Reading* (Copenhagen: Museum Tusculanum Press, 2001); Rolena Adorno and Ivan Boserup, *New Studies of the Autograph Manuscript of Felipe Guáman Pomo de Ayala's* Nueva corónica y buen gobierno (Copenhagen: Museum Tusculanum Press, 2002), 19–20.

The Florentine Codex, created after the conquest of Mexico, contains the most extensive Indigenous commentary on the event that transformed control of Tenochtitlán and the Valley of Mexico. Illustrations created by Native Mexica artists depicted assaults including the slaughter at the Feast of Uitzilopochtli. Courtesy of the Biblioteca Medicea Laurenziana, Florence, and by permission of MiBACT.

and beyond. Personal reasons likely added to the motivation for his extraordinary effort, but his chronicle nonetheless remains a document that is almost unique in the annals of the Americas for the sixteenth and seventeenth centuries: a testimony of a world that had once existed and then collapsed. Like Las Casas, Guaman Poma hoped to shape the administration of imperial authority in the years to follow. For this reason, he needed to write to the king to instruct him about "all that I have seen as well as that which I have learned from very old lords" of Peru,

> who had full accounts and reports of everything about their ancestors, so that their memory might endure throughout the ages of their world and so that things so great and memorable might not be lost on account of the lack of writing, and so that Your Majesty's historians may have fuller understanding than that which I understand them to have been able to have until this time.

Putting the report together had been difficult and expensive for him, he added, but he understood, as a Christian and loyal subject of the crown, that the investment was necessary for the good of the realm. He also expected, as he told the king, that the monarch would fulfill the promise he had made to the chronicler about having the work printed.[51]

Throughout his book, Guaman Poma wrote with a sense of the tragedy that had unfolded over the course of his own life, including the time he was on the road and away from home. "The author returns from the world," he wrote of his arrival "in the middle" of the new kingdom of Peru, specifically at the towns of San Cristóbal de Suntuntu and Santiago Chipao. Soon "he saw the town and the province in ruin and taken over [by outsiders] and destroyed." He had worked for the Spanish king for thirty years, enough time for the landscape he once knew well to disappear. He "found everything tumbled to the ground and his houses and cultivated fields and pastures invaded." Before he had left, he had dressed in silk and fine woolens and thought of himself "as a lord and prince, being the grandson of the tenth king." Guaman Poma had left when he was, by his reckoning, about fifty years old. At age eighty he was back, with "all white hair and thin and naked and barefoot." He had aged. His family had fallen into poverty and were paying tribute like others who

51. Felipe Guaman Poma de Ayala, "El primer nueva corónica y buen gobierno," Copenhagen, Royal Library, GkS 2232, 4to., 11. All quotations from the text are from the translation by Rolena Adorno, José Cárdenas Bunsen, Jan Szeminski, and John Charles, found at the Guaman Poma website of the Royal Library of Denmark, https://www.kb.dk/en/find-materials/collections/manuscript-collection/chronicle-guaman-poma.

lacked political and economic authority. Others had taken over his house and his ancestral holdings.[52]

Wherever he traveled he saw that the conquerors had created a regime that upended the once stable culture of the Andes. In San Cristóbal he heard that priests had launched a campaign against the local Uachos and Yauyos. They had demanded individuals to be sold into slavery and single women to work as weavers. They also accused them of being witches. With that calumny in the air, the priest "began to hang the old men and women and children one by one and torment them until they gave false confessions." To escape the torture, they showed the priest objects of devotion known as *huacas*. In response, he ordered a hundred of them imprisoned, whipped, and deprived of food. The priest also robbed them of their silver jewelry and clothing as well as "animal horns, feathers, and red-dyed wool, with which in their feasts they sing and dance and frolic." He melted their silver to make a new silver service for his own use and turned their cloth into his own bedcovers. His selfishness came at a high cost for those he had imprisoned: eighty of them soon died.[53] The *corregidor*, the official who represented the state in each jurisdiction, made matters worse by ordering the flogging of some of the locals, hanging some, and exiling some of the women to other cities.[54] At Oropesa of Guancabilca, a once-prosperous town, he walked into the plaza and was shocked to see the beating of local lords even though they had accepted the conquerors' faith. It seemed, he wrote, "that all the demons of hell had come forth in order to trouble the poor of Jesus Christ." The local *corregidor* there forced a hundred to leave their fields, where they performed their *mita*, to haul his wine.[55]

Guaman Poma hoped to show the king that the administration of justice always favored the Spanish at the expense of Natives. To make his point he recounted the story about the death of a Spaniard named Juan Apo Alanya, who had been traveling and tried to rob a group of Yauyos near Córdoua. He pulled his sword and stabbed three of them. In "defending themselves," as Guaman Poma wrote, they killed him. Before there was "any investigation or judicial inquiry, the law officers hanged the said ten Yauyos Indians." This, he added, was how "the said Spaniards receive justice and the said Indians get none in this kingdom, nor is there anyone who advocates for them."[56]

52. Guaman Poma, "Nueva corónica," 1094, 1097 [1104, 1107].
53. Guaman Poma, "Nueva corónica," 1101 [1111].
54. Guaman Poma, "Nueva corónica," 1102 [1112].
55. Guaman Poma, "Nueva corónica," 1113–1114 [1123–1124].
56. Guaman Poma, "Nueva corónica," 1118 [1128].

Eventually, Guaman Poma reached Lima, the city of Incan kings. He arrived as a poor man, yet none would give him any aid. He found, he wrote, a city "full of Indians who had abandoned their communities and African slaves who had escaped from their masters and become servants, even officials, although they were laborers, low born and tribute-paying Indians, who put on fine clothing, and dressed like Spaniards and donned swords." Some of the Natives cut their hair, perhaps in an effort to pass as non-Natives, so that they could escape being forced to make tribute payments or being sent into the mines. There were, he thought, no Natives left to work in the mines, but many local women had come to the city and become prostitutes, "loaded down with mestizo and mulatto children." Their actions, he claimed, meant that other Natives would not marry them. Lima's poorest neighborhoods "are full of Indians, and there is no remedy for it." The locals who had gone there did not have children, he wrote. "See here," he exclaimed, "the world upside down!"[57]

No written Indigenous accounts detailing the earliest encounters with Europeans north of New Spain survive. But the Indigenous scribes who contributed to the Florentine Codex and the long travel report of Guaman Poma, each devoted to chronicling the invasion and its aftermath, confirm the brutality of the conquest in words similar to those of Las Casas.[58]

Even though it did not circulate widely at the time, Guaman Poma's book was part of an effort to redefine the historical and spiritual legacy of the conquest, a memorial to a world not just upended but destroyed. Las Casas was right: there would be no return to a land of the stable communities that Spaniards had destroyed in the years of the conquest. This part of the globe would forever bear the mark of the half-century of economic, social, demographic, and political change that stretched from the arrival of Columbus in 1492 to the discovery of silver and the creation of the mining economy at Potosí. Just as significant, the Spanish learned lessons that they could apply in other regions where they hoped to extract American resources and where, they believed, they would again be able to conquer Indigenous peoples and establish colonies.[59]

Las Casas failed to eradicate the worst aspects of Spanish colonial policies in the Americas. But in the long run his book, by motivating

57. Guaman Poma, "Nueva corónica," 1128 [1138].
58. Kevin Terraciano, "Competing Memories of the Conquest of Mexico," in Ilona Katzew, ed., *Contested Visions in the Spanish Colonial World* (New Haven, CT: Yale University Press, 2011), 55–77.
59. See Rolena Adorno, *Guáman Poma: Writing and Resistance in Colonial Peru*, 2nd ed. (Austin: Institute of Latin American Studies and University of Texas Press, 2000), 3.

Protestant northern Europeans, notably the English, helped to establish a northern boundary for Spanish expansion—not through pulling back in light of his reporting but instead by inspiring European foes. He imagined a contest for the Western Hemisphere between Spaniards and Indigenous. Little could he have known that he contributed to a new strategic reality at the same time that his countrymen hoped to expand their influence north and east of New Spain.

7

Florida

Despite the failure at Chicora, Spaniards remained eager to establish a colony north of New Spain. Perhaps, imperial dreamers may have thought, they could create a northern viceroyalty as successful as what they had built in Peru. In many ways, they had advantages that Pizzaro had lacked, notably knowledge that had been gained by De Soto, Cabeza de Vaca, and Coronado. Philip II, who rose to the Spanish throne in 1556, wanted to succeed where his predecessors had failed. He had cartographic proof to support his claims, including Diego Gutiérrez's 1562 large, printed wall map of the Americas that demarcated "Terra Florida." Such maps, like books, reminded those who wanted to lay claim to parts of the Western Hemisphere that publication could advance their cause.[1] Gutiérrez's two-dimensional representation of American territory in the sixteenth century fell far short of capturing the reality on the ground. As Philip learned, Guales of the Carolina coastline and Timucuans who controlled modern northeast Florida possessed political and military might along the southeastern coast.

Europeans' dreams turned into nightmares in Florida. Unwilling or unable to make a major investment in ships, soldiers, or settlers, neither the French nor the Spanish stood much of a chance. That much could have been predictable. But less obvious to the Europeans were the ways that Native peoples paid close attention to them. By the early 1570s, Indigenous residents across the Southeast had established mental boundary lines to demarcate the limited zones where they would allow Europeans to live and the far larger territory where they could not. Europeans who pushed too far paid a high price for their inability to understand local peoples and cultures.

The fiery Protestant Reformation and the fevered Catholic response to it divided Europeans—at home and abroad. Although there were

1. Diego Gutiérrez, "Americae sive quartae orbis partis nova et exactissima descriptio" (Antwerp, 1562), Library of Congress, https://www.loc.gov/item/map49000970/.

This detail from Diego Gutiérrez's 1562 "Americae sive quartae orbis partis nova" provided visual evidence of Spanish claims to Terra Florida, an area far more extensive than the boundaries of the current state. Library of Congress, Geography and Map Division, map49000970.

confessional differences between French Huguenots and Catholic Spaniards in Florida, their feud pivoted on rival claims between the Spanish house of Habsburg and the French Valois. As the French saw it, the voyages of Verrazzano, Cartier, and Roberval had given them the clear right to much of the East Coast of North America. By contrast, the Spanish believed that these lands were theirs per the terms of the *Inter caetera* of 1493 and the Treaty of Tordesillas of 1494. In the absence of clear boundaries between these European claimants to lands that remained in the hands of Indigenous Americans, Europeans concluded that a victory in this dispute between two royal houses would mean control of coastal waters, possibly with inviting harbors (few of which had been found yet), as well as interiors, which could be reached via the network of rivers that Europeans had already learned reached into the continent. The situation had become so fraught that in 1562 Philip II informed Pedro Menéndez de Avilés, then captain-general of the Spanish fleet in the region, that the French (as well as Scots and English) posed a threat to already worked-out agreements and hence were "a disservice to God and Lord." He defined the French as "peace-breakers and robbers and violators of the orders of their own lords and rulers." He gave Menéndez the authority to dispatch them without hesitation.[2] It was among the early efforts to control Florida through force, but not the last.

When Philip asked Menéndez to solidify Spain's claim to the North American coast, he was perhaps not aware of the difficulty such a mission might entail. In the late 1540s, a Spanish colonial mission suffered the death of a Dominican missionary near modern Tampa.[3] Writing after the fact, Spanish historian Francisco López de Gómera claimed that the Natives had come down to the shore, clubbed Spaniards, "and ate them and so they died, martyred for preaching the faith of Christ."[4] If they were to succeed in Florida, Spaniards needed someone who could prevail in the adversity that was sure to come. Menéndez seemed perfect for the moment—a man with demonstrated animosity toward the French and the other European claimants to Florida, as well as a willingness to kill to advance his monarch's agenda.

Before he arrived, Menéndez was an experienced privateer who had a history of taking French ships—including three in 1550 off the coast of La Rochelle. Legalized piracy was a dangerous business, as he learned in 1552 when a French privateer captured him. After raising funds to purchase his release, he remained in the Caribbean, appearing before the Audiencia in Santo Domingo before his return home. In 1563, officials of the Casa de Contratación, which Isabella had established in 1503 as a trading house in Seville to oversee (and eventually help manage) her realm's expanding Atlantic interests, charged him with smuggling and imprisoned him. He

2. Eugene Lyon, "The Captives of Florida," *Florida Historical Quarterly* 50 (1971), 1–3.
3. Eugene Lyon, *The Enterprise of Florida: Pedro Menéndez de Avilés and the Spanish Conquest of 1565–1568* (Gainesville: University Press of Florida, 1974), 7; Woodbury Lowery, *The Spanish Settlements Within the Present Limits of the United States, 1513–1561* (New York, 1901–1905), 1:411–427, 474–478; Michael V. Gannon, *The Cross in the Sand: The Early Catholic Church in Florida, 1513–1870* (Gainesville: University Press of Florida, 1965), 9–14.
4. *NAW*, 2:189–190; see also Philip, Prince of Spain to the treasury of New Spain, December 18, 1553, in *NAW*, 2:197–198.

eventually surfaced in Madrid, where he was again imprisoned. In the end, the Council of the Indies reduced the charges and Menéndez departed Spain in the spring of 1565, armed not only to conquer the French but also with an *asiento* or contract that would enable him to rule over an extensive new Spanish colony in La Florida.[5]

By the time Menéndez had the resources to launch his Florida venture, the French had already arrived. In mid-February 1562, French explorer Jean Ribault, eager to explore the American coast but wary of Spanish threats to his two-ship expedition, sailed directly across the Atlantic rather than follow the then well-known route that would have taken him south toward the African coast, westward across to the Caribbean, and then northward. Ribault had both experience and knowledge of possible routes, having worked with Sebastian Cabot in England on plans to find water routes to the South Sea. Others had avoided this route for fear that they would lose the wind in the middle of the ocean and would drift until they exhausted their supplies and perished. But Ribault managed to find a way. On April 30, he arrived on the coast at modern Florida's St. Johns River, which the newcomers called the River of May. The next day he had his men erect a stone column, possibly made of marble, which had been carved in advance and bore the sign of the arms of King Charles IX. It was one of five columns that Ribault had brought with him across the ocean, each intended to mark territory for the realm. The column remained in the land of the Timucuans, who soon showed it to other French explorers who arrived.[6]

The French next sailed approximately 200 miles to the north and erected a second column on modern Parris Island on the Carolina coast. The following month Ribault, per his agreement with his sponsors, made plans to return home. Before he left, he told his men of the ways that history would record the feats of those who remained to become "the first to live in this strange land."[7]

Left on their own, the French who remained behind built an outpost they called Charlesfort and established positive relations with the local Guales. They participated in a feast, gave and received gifts, and relied on the Natives to provide them with food since they always needed more. Their ability to communicate with signs improved, or they managed to

5. Lyon, *Enterprise of Florida*, 11 (La Rochelle), 12 (Audiencia), 14–18 (privateer), 25–29 (smuggling), 29–30 (son), 34–37 and 41 (legal case resolved), 47–51 (*asiento* and title).

6. For the five columns, see René Laudonnière, *Three Voyages*, ed. Charles E. Bennett (Tuscaloosa: University of Alabama Press, 2001), 219n36; for Ribault, see John T. McGrath, "Admiral Coligny, Jean Ribault, and the East Coast of North America," *French Colonial History* 1 (2002), 63–76.

7. Laudonnière, *Three Voyages*, 31–38.

learn some of the local language. They visited the homes of the Guales, including that of the leader, who lived in a house that featured finely embroidered coverlets and tapestries fashioned from colored feathers—a sight that dazzled the visitors. The Guales tolerated the newcomers' presence. They even kept the French alive after their supply shed burned to the ground.[8]

Despite positive signs from the Guales, the French survivors decided it was time to abandon the colony. That meant building a boat, something that none of them had ever done before. They sawed planks from local trees, harvested resin from pines, and employed a local moss for caulking. The Guales brought them ropes. The French fashioned sails out of their own bedclothes. With the task completed, they set off. But soon they were becalmed in the middle of the ocean. They rationed their food to the equivalent of twelve peas each day. With no more fresh water, they resorted to salt water and urine. When the food ran out, they ate their shoes and jerkins (sleeveless jackets). In their desperation, they killed one of their own and ate him. The cannibalism kept them alive until they encountered an English ship. The English sailors agreed to take the French survivors to their homeland, promising some of them could meet Queen Elizabeth.[9]

Despite the abandonment of Charlesfort, Ribault, Laudonnière, and others in France remained committed to establishing a permanent French settlement in the Southeast. Their destination was the St. Johns River, the first territory that Ribault had explored in 1562. Laudonnière set sail in 1564 and Ribault the following year. They knew that they would perish if they could not enlist Timucuan allies.[10]

When the French approached the place where they first landed, they met Timucuans who spoke some French. More surprising, the Natives took the newcomers to the stone column that the explorers had left there two years earlier. They found it, Laudonnière wrote, "crowned with magnolia garlands and at its foot there were little baskets of corn. They kissed the stone on their arrival with great reverence and asked us to do the same." The French agreed, fearing that they could not go against the wishes of their hosts.[11]

8. Laudonnière, *Three Voyages*, 38–46.
9. Laudonnière, *Three Voyages*, 48–51.
10. Laudonnière, *Three Voyages*, 53–59.
11. Laudonnière, *Three Voyages*, 60–61.

Over the next few months, the French remained as guests in a town led by the Timucuan headman Satouriona. After most of the ships set off on their return journey to France in late July, Laudonnière witnessed Satouriona preparing for war with an unnamed foe. He called together 500 Natives for the ritual and prayed to the sun for victory. He declared that he hoped to sprinkle the blood of his enemies as easily as he had sprinkled water during the ritual. The combatants returned with scalps as well as twenty-four prisoners. Satouriona distributed the captives among the Timucuans and put the scalps on display over the entrance to his abode, crowning each with magnolia. Here was a regional leader with real power, unlike the Europeans who had arrived with grand yet unrealistic dreams.[12]

The long summer months took a toll on Laudonnière, who grew wary of what he perceived as Satouriona's growing displeasure. As the weeks went by, he realized that this Native world contained multiple rivalries that had nothing to do with the newcomers. Just as worrisome, some of his own men rebelled, which prompted him to execute four of them. The French strung the corpses on a scaffold at the mouth of the river, mimicking the actions of European leaders who had long suspended the bodies or heads of pirates along waterways to deter similar actions.[13]

During the summer two Spanish captives, naked and with hair down to their waists, arrived in town. They reported that they had been held prisoner by a local headman. Laudonnière took them in and ordered their hair cut. The Spaniards asked to keep their shorn locks "as evidence of the misery they had experienced in the Indies." The French discovered that one of them had tucked bits of gold into his hair, which the captive gave to Laudonnière. The commander learned that the men had been wrecked fifteen years earlier off the coast of south Florida when their ship, catching the prevailing winds in the Florida Straits, ran aground in the territory of the king of Calos. The headman had kept four women, who married into the community, and had his people gather the riches from the ships. The town had accumulated a great deal of gold through such naval disasters and also through trade, enabling the headman to become the most powerful man in south Florida. The former prisoners reported that he sacrificed one Spanish captive each year.[14]

Laudonnière, sensing that matters would not improve anytime soon, decided once again to return to France with the other French who had stayed. Before he set off, an English expedition, led by the slave trader

12. Laudonnière, *Three Voyages*, 62 (cloak), 67 (contest), 82–86 (battle and aftermath).
13. Laudonnière, *Three Voyages*, 88–89 (Satouriona), 100–106 (rebellion among French).
14. Laudonnière, *Three Voyages*, 109–111.

John Hawkins, arrived at Fort Caroline. Among his crew was a man from Dieppe named Martin Atinas, who had been on Ribault's 1562 expedition with Laudonnière and was now in the service of the English. Hawkins offered to take Laudonnière home, but the Frenchman feared that he would take them to England. Instead, they traded the cannon from the fort—since they were leaving, they had no more need of it—for one of Hawkins's ships, which they could sail on their own. As they were about to depart, Laudonnière thought it would make sense to entice some of the Timucuans to join them "so that if a return voyage were to be made, they could tell their kings of the grandeur of our king, the excellence of our princes, the abundance in our country, and the fashions of life in France." He also planned to teach them to speak French so they could act as translators.[15] He had a more sanguine view of the locals than the English, one of whom reported that the "people of the cape of Florida, are of more savage and fierce nature, and more valiant than any of the rest."[16]

On August 28, as Laudonnière was about to leave, one of the lookouts saw sails on the horizon—the first sign of Ribault, who had returned with orders to assume the governorship from Laudonnière. Soon a group of local Native kings arrived, some of whom recognized Ribault from his previous sojourn on the coast, perhaps because of his prominent beard. One promised to take the French to a mine where they could find red copper, a metal that Ribault's assayer believed to be gold. Laudonnière, battling an illness, gave over command to Ribault and continued his preparation for his departure on the ship he had purchased from Hawkins.[17]

On September 4, a convoy of six Spanish ships appeared offshore. A storm prevented them from getting close enough to mount an attack, so they sailed southward. Almost immediately Ribault decided that he would pursue them because he had learned from Emola, one of the local headmen, that "the Spaniards had gone ashore in great numbers and seized the houses of Selow and used them for their Negroes, whom they had brought to do labor." Ribault soon set off, with thirty-eight of Laudonnière's men under his command.[18]

15. Laudonnière, *Three Voyages*, 139–147.
16. John Sparke the Younger, "The Voyage made by the worshipful M. John Hawkins . . . to the coast of Guinea, and the Indies of Nova Spania, being in Affrica, and America," in Richard Hakluyt, *The Principall Navigations, Voiages and Discoveries of the English Nation* (London, 1589), 523–543, quotation at 538.
17. Laudonnière, *Three Voyages*, 149–157.
18. Laudonnière, *Three Voyages*, 159, 161.

Early autumn, as Natives of coastal Florida long knew and every European sailor came to learn, brought hurricanes.[19] Having been in a safe harbor when the storm hit, Ribault might have been forgiven if he thought that conditions were fine for him to set out on a chase. But this turned out to be a particularly ferocious storm season. On September 10 another storm roared in. Laudonnière reported that "the Indians assured me that it was the worst that had ever come to that coast." He and others on the shore, fearing that their ships were gone and knowing that their fort was in need of repair, set about to fix the damage. The next storm arrived on the night of the nineteenth. It provided cover for a group of Spanish soldiers who struck Fort Caroline when the French had let down their guard. Facing little opposition, the Spaniards planted their flag on the fort's ramparts, a signal that they had taken the fort. Laudonnière and a small number of others managed to escape. They made their way to the water, where they awaited rescue.[20]

Though Laudonnière had to abandon the boat he had purchased from Hawkins, he and the other survivors found spots on a different French vessel. They departed on September 25, arrived at the Azores a month later, and in mid-November landed in Wales, an unexpected destination. In Swansea, Laudonnière encountered a group of merchants from Saint-Malo, Cartier's hometown. They lent him money for new clothes and food for those on board. From there he made his way to Bristol and then to London. Ultimately he booked passage across the English Channel to Calais. Soon enough he was in Paris, where he set off to meet the king.[21]

Laudonnière's luck proved better than Ribault's, whose ship had wrecked in the hurricane. The survivors who made it back to the land were unaware that Menéndez's spies had caught sight of them. Menéndez, draping himself in French clothing, approached them on his own. The French saw him and asked for help. The Spaniard dropped the disguise. He told the French that they had built the fort on Spanish land without their monarch's permission and, worse still, they were propagating Protestant ideas. Following directions from Madrid that the Spanish were to bring the Roman faith to the Natives of Florida, Menéndez ordered his men to kill the French.[22]

Menéndez soon executed Ribault and his companions. It was good that this French man was dead, he wrote to the king, because Ribault had had

19. See Stuart B. Schwartz, *Sea of Storms: A History of Hurricanes in the Greater Caribbean from Columbus to Katrina* (Princeton, NJ: Princeton University Press, 2015).
20. Laudonnière, *Three Voyages*, 161 (Ribault's departure), 164–165 (Spanish seizing fort).
21. Laudonnière, *Three Voyages*, 167–169.
22. Laudonnière, *Three Voyages*, 169–170; Lowery, *Spanish Settlements*, 2:191.

long experience as a sailor in the Indies and along the coasts of Florida, which had been treacherous waters for many Spaniards. Had he continued to live, the French could have established themselves in lands Menéndez thought the Spanish should colonize.[23]

Menéndez was unapologetic about his actions. He informed Philip II that he had to rid Florida of "this wicked sect," a reference to the fact that these French were Huguenots, and hence make it possible for the Spanish "to plant the Gospel in these parts and to enlighten the natives, and bring them to allegiance" to the king. He estimated that it could take fifty years to accomplish both goals, "but a good beginning gives hope of a good ending." Besides, by killing the French, Menéndez thought that the Spanish would "gain much reputation with the Indians, and shall be feared by them, although we also make them gifts." Such alliances would be necessary since more French likely remained in North America. Menéndez was confident that if he had additional soldiers, ships, and funds, by the spring of 1566 Philip would be "master of this coast of Florida."[24] Other Spaniards, including the king, agreed that the captain had acted appropriately.[25] For his part, Laudonnière offered a less than sympathetic assessment, stating matter-of-factly that Ribault had walked directly into the arms of Menéndez and the Spanish.[26]

News of Menéndez's murder of Ribault and his crew sparked outrage against the Spanish. One French witness who had managed to escape claimed that the Spanish had taken the French women and children to Puerto Rico and that perhaps seventeen or eighteen men, the last survivors of Ribault's crew, were imprisoned in Havana.[27] The first published French account of the debacle appeared in 1566 when historian Nicolas Le Challeux dwelled on the perfidy of Menéndez and the Iberians, who, he wrote, ignored pleas to spare the lives of the French. A surviving witness reported that the Spanish cut off Ribault's beard and shipped it to Seville. Then, "as a trophy of their victory," the Spaniards "dismembered the body of that good and faithful servant of the King and cut the head into quarters which they placed on four pikes planted in the four corners of the fort." That year, printer Henry Denham published an

23. Lowery, *Spanish Settlements*, 2:200–201.
24. Menéndez to Philip II, October 15, 1565, in *NAW*, 2:395–404, quotations at 398 (killing of French), and 404 ("master of this coast").
25. Lowery, *Spanish Settlements*, 2:204, 206.
26. Laudonnière, *Three Voyages*, 169–170.
27. Deposition of Jean Memyn, October 16, 1566, in *NAW*, 2:380–381.

English translation in London, emphasizing the "monstrous crueltie" of the Spanish, adding fuel, as if it were needed, to the "black legend."[28]

Despite Laudonnière's exodus and Ribault's death, seventy to eighty French remained in La Florida and started to construct a new fort at Cape Cañaveral. They also built a new boat to send word back to France about the developments along the Florida coast. Before they finished, the Spanish burned the almost complete fort and boat. Menéndez then proceeded to round up as many of the French survivors as he could find. But taking captives did not mean the French threat had passed. When Menéndez landed in Havana, he learned about the preparations for the possible arrival of a large French fleet, possibly to assault the new Spanish settlement at St. Augustine, which was then only two years old. He returned to St. Augustine, ready to do his part—especially if the king could send him the troops, supplies, and resources that he still needed to secure the coastline.[29]

Menéndez believed that the French intended to create two outposts on the coast, one at the natural harbor at Santa Elena (modern Parris Island South Carolina) and another at Chesapeake Bay, which the Spanish called the Bay of Santa María. The latter destination was especially worrisome to Menéndez since he believed that the French could sail across the Atlantic to Newfoundland in as little as three weeks and from there sail south to the bay. More distressing to Menéndez was his belief that the Chesapeake was connected to an extensive inland network of waterways, which would allow the French to reach both the silver mines at Zacatecas and a passageway to the Pacific. He gathered his geographical knowledge in part from the testimony of someone he called "the Indian Velasco," a reference to a native of the Chesapeake Bay region named Paquiquino whom Spanish captors had taken in 1561 to Spain, where he converted and was baptized as Don Luis de Velasco. At the time, Don Luis was living in New Spain, though he would sail to Spain the following year.[30]

28. Nicolas Le Challeux, *Discours de l'historie de la Floride* (Dieppe, 1566), trans. in *NAW*, 2:370–379; *A True and Perfect Description of the Last Voyage or Navigation attempted by Captaine Rybaut . . . into Terra Florida* (London, 1566); sig. [Dvii^{v}–Dviii^{v}], quotation at [Dviii^{v}].

29. Menéndez to Philip II, December 5, 1565, in *NAW*, 2:405–413.

30. Menéndez to Philip II, December 12, 1565, *NAW*, 2:414–417, quotations at 415–416; Menéndez to Philip II, December 16, 1565, *NAW*, 2:418; L. A. Vigneras, "A Spanish Discovery of North Carolina in 1566," *North Carolina Historical Review* 46 (1969), 402, 405–407; James Horn, *A Brave and Cunning Prince: The Great Chief Opechancanough and the War for America* (New York: Basic Books, 2021), 5–12; Anna Brickhouse, *The Unsettlement of America: Translation, Interpretation, and the Story of Don Luis de Velasco, 1560–1945* (New York: Oxford University Press, 2015), 46–53.

Menéndez justified his actions by setting them into the context of a potential rivalry between the Spanish crown and French Huguenots. By acting in this way, he downplayed the complicated politics of the moment. After all, Philip II was married to Elizabeth of France, the daughter of Henri II and Catherine de' Medici, the queen mother of France who stepped in to govern when her son, Charles IX, was ill. Menéndez might not have realized how much the death of Ribault had meant to the French court. In a series of back-and-forth communiqués between monarchs and their ambassadors and representatives in foreign courts, Philip, Charles, and Catherine aired views that revealed deep fissures in the idea of a united Catholic Europe or the non-Iberians' acceptance of the terms of the Treaty of Tordesillas two generations earlier.[31]

Menéndez, no doubt more aware of this high-level diplomatic tension after his return to Spain in 1567, issued a statement, apparently at the urging of Philip II, to be sent to the French court. He told them the French he had met were pirates who could not be trusted to sail off, if he provided them with a new ship, or be left on land, even if they lacked weapons. After all, they outnumbered the small contingent of Spaniards that Menéndez knew to be setting up at St. Augustine. Under the circumstances, the murders his men committed stemmed not from his cruel nature but instead from his desire to serve Philip II.[32]

The return to Spain must have stung Menéndez. Two years earlier, on March 20, 1565, he and Phillip II had agreed that a colony should be established in the heart of the Timucuan homeland. To advance their goal, the king would provide Menéndez with a fleet sufficient to take 500 Spaniards with him—"people of pure descent and not those who are prohibited," a reference to Muslims and Jews, groups driven out of Spain by the Reconquista and prohibited from Spain's offshore communities. Menéndez promised to transport Old World livestock, missionaries, and 500 enslaved Africans within three years. The king imagined that these bound laborers would plant sugar cane and build and work in sugar mills—essentially, a replication of the economic model that the Spanish had first employed in Madeira and then across the Caribbean. To ensure a future supply of bound labor without needing to capture or purchase new workers,

31. The most relevant letters are Philip IX's complaint of November 1565; Charles IX to the Spanish ambassador, November 28, 1565; M. de Fourquevaux to Charles IX, February 18, 1566; and Catherine de Médici to M. de Fourquevaux, March 17, 1566, all in *NAW*, 2:465–471.

32. The statement, likely from July 1567, is in *NAW*, 2:472.

one-third of the enslaved had to be female. In exchange for his efforts, Menéndez would assume enormous political and economic power as *adelantado*, a title that he could pass on to his family, which would hold it in perpetuity. He also had the authority to grant *repartimientos*, licenses to extract forced labor from local Indigenous residents that were intended to encourage Spanish-style development of the region. His own land would amount to twenty-five square leagues, or about sixty-five square miles. After his ship dropped anchor on September 8, Menéndez claimed the territory for his king. Following Columbus's precedent for renaming Indigenous places, he called it St. Augustine.[33]

Yet while the Spaniard could name a place with great hope, creating a colony turned out to be far harder. He wanted continuous financial support from the king, especially for soldiers. But Philip II would not pay for more than 150, too few to maintain a durable fort, let alone to police a large territory that was to have not only Menéndez's own plantation but encomiendas as well. He was never able to organize the importation of slaves or to find the right places for them to work, so he sent many to Havana and distributed some to work in the households of soldiers at the garrison. Menéndez could not even get his own hacienda established. The failure to establish a viable agrarian or mining economy led Menéndez to shift efforts away from harvesting goods for export to Spain, a crucial component of a successful colony, and instead to supply the treasure ships sailing the Bahama Channel. Spaniards plied this route from New Spain to take advantage of the circulation of winds. But the channel's swirling currents and the ever-lurking presence of French and English corsairs meant danger on every voyage.[34]

Menéndez also failed to launch any viable missions. In October 1566 he wrote to a Jesuit resident in Cádiz to share his disappointment. The king had sent 1,500 soldiers, Menéndez wrote, but had not provided enough missionaries from the Society of Jesus. "I was delighted to see how well Our Lord and King helped us," he wrote, "and on the other I felt upset and thwarted to see that nobody of the Company was coming, nor even a learned man of religion." Menéndez claimed that he had had conversations with local Natives who seemed eager to convert to Christianity. It would take only six religious, he estimated, to advance the church in the region.[35]

33. Lyon, *Enterprise of Florida*, 47–51 (*asiento* and title), 115–116 (St. Augustine).
34. See *NAW*, 2:476–477; see also Gonzalo Solís de Merás, "Memorial . . . of all the voyages and deeds of the Adelantado Pedro Menéndez de Avilés his brother-in-law and of the conquest of Florida and the justice he worked on Juan Ribao and other frenchmen," in *NAW*, 2:424–436.
35. Menéndez to an unnamed Jesuit, October 15, 1566, *NAW*, 2:536.

Menéndez's frustration stemmed from his assessment of the potential to convert Timucuans. These Natives possessed religious beliefs already, which pivoted, he believed, on worship of the sun and moon. They engaged in regular ceremonies. Some were so devout that they fasted for three days—no food, no drink, no sleep—as a sign of their commitment. They were, to him, believers who happened to believe in the wrong deities but were ready to change their ways. "They ask me to make them Christians as we are," he wrote. But success depended on the migration of religious who could master Indigenous languages and hence guide Timucuans to the proper god. Menéndez claimed that he had already given them crosses, at their request, and sent soldiers and boys to teach them doctrine, a strategy that he knew would fail. To be sure, one Jesuit had arrived a month earlier and the "Indians who are enemies" had killed him. Perhaps Menéndez added that detail because he knew that Jesuits did not shy from possible death since they understood that martyrdom could be as important as conversion. Still, sensing that news of the death of the missionary might be a disincentive to other religious, Menéndez promised to protect them just as he would the king himself.[36]

In early June 1567, Menéndez returned to Spain. He went in part to serve Philip II but also to press his case that he had fulfilled the requirements of his contract in Florida. He boasted to the Council of the Indies about destroying the French at Fort Caroline and killing Ribault. He took credit for establishing Spanish towns and forts and organizing explorations of the region. In response to these claims, Philip II appointed him governor and captain-general of Cuba on October 24, 1567, allowing him to hold that post while still maintaining his holdings and titles in Florida. Soon the king named him captain-general of a fleet of twelve ships to defend Spanish American territory. He also named him *comendador* of Santa Cruz de la Zarza, near Castile, which would provide income for his other ventures and, the king hoped, become a base to organize migration to Florida. With these resources at hand, Menéndez again sailed across the Atlantic. This time he laid plans for a Jesuit college in Havana where the children of Florida's Native elites could learn Catholic doctrine and Spanish, thereby advancing the civilizing mission. On January 1, 1568, Menéndez presided over the baptism of five Florida Native captives. Four months later, the party set sail for Florida, arriving in St. Augustine on June 19.[37]

This sojourn proved no more successful for Menéndez than his prior effort. The killing of Ribault had not eradicated the French threat, as the

36. Menéndez to an unnamed Jesuit, 537–538.
37. Lyon, *Enterprise of Florida*, 187–197.

Spanish learned when a French force enhanced by an alliance with Timucuans, who had become disenchanted with the Spanish, routed a small garrison at San Mateo. The invaders left the bodies of eight Spaniards hanging from trees, a signal that the French sought to avenge the deaths of Ribault and the destruction of Fort Caroline. Soon after, Juan Pardo, who had been exploring the interior of La Florida on an *entrada* that took him past the southern end of the Appalachian Mountains and as far as modern Alabama, traveled through ruined Spanish camps, bearing witness to Indigenous hostility toward soldiers. With his plans crumbling, Menéndez once again returned to Spain.[38]

In 1570, Menéndez ordered a group of Jesuits to Chesapeake Bay. A party consisting of two priests, five other members of the order, Don Luis de Velasco (né Paquiquineo), and two others—including a boy from Santa Elena—arrived in the bay on September 10, 1570. The sketchy documentary record suggests that Don Luis, renowned for his linguistic skills and seeming alliance with the Spanish, advised them to travel up one of the broad rivers that fed the bay. They set up a post—the exact location has never been identified—and settled in for the winter. If they could survive the cold, springtime gatherings of Indigenous would provide an ideal opportunity to spread the word. The missionaries thought Don Luis could act as an intermediary, showing other Native residents that the newcomers wanted commerce, not conflict.[39]

The missionaries' reliance on Don Luis proved a fatal error. Rather than act as a go-between, he instead seems to have encouraged local Indigenous to murder the Jesuits. They also sacked the mission, killing everyone except the boy, Alonso de Olmos. News of the debacle reached a Spanish resupply ship that arrived later in 1571. Those on board fought with some Natives and took a captive who told them what had transpired. The next year Menéndez, enraged by news of the assault, sailed into Chesapeake Bay bent on revenge or, he likely hoped, to discover that the story was just a rumor and that perhaps the missionaries were still alive. Hostilities broke out again. The Spanish captured a man who was the uncle of Don Luis. They also managed to find and rescue Alonso de Olmos. Menéndez ordered his men to kill those they deemed responsible

38. Lyon, *Enterprise of Florida*, 197–201, 204–205; Charles Hudson, *The Juan Pardo Expeditions: Exploration of the Carolinas and Tennessee, 1566–1568*, rev. ed. (Tuscaloosa: University of Alabama Press, 2005), 18.

39. Luis de Quirós and Juan Baptista de Segura to Juan de Hinistrosa, September 12, 1570, in *NAW*, 2:557–559.

for the murder of the missionaries. Menéndez avoided the fate of De Soto, but like that explorer he realized that the Spanish could not succeed in the region, as the Spaniards lacked the numbers to displace local Natives. They abandoned hope of establishing a Spanish presence along the Chesapeake.[40]

By 1572, news about the inability to colonize Florida reached Spain. Santa Elena boasted few colonists, at least some of whom lived in derelict shacks trying to solve the problem of the island flooding every time there was a full moon. They had cleared some of the woods, but they could not harvest much maize because they did not know how to keep ravenous crows, moles, thrushes, and foxes at bay. They had no livestock either, though there were plenty of fish to be caught. St. Augustine had not fared much better. Spaniards first tried to build a settlement on an island, but frequent flooding led them to try again on the mainland, though they set up on a spit of land that also flooded. The soil around the settlement was too poor to be planted, though Menéndez, who owned most of it, still had soldiers work the land for him. The Spanish put livestock on the island they abandoned, but the population did not grow because of insufficient food. All told, there were thirteen married men, a few married soldiers, and some single soldiers at the outpost. By any measure, one official wrote, Menéndez had failed to live up to the terms of the *asiento*. He had not imported any slaves, and he had planted an outpost "in a place that can be neither settled nor inhabited, where cattle can neither feed nor raise young." The migrants he had lured complained about the governor's failure "because he took them to a place where they can neither cultivate nor even feed themselves." Given their setting, the official suggested that these "forts called Santa Elena and [St. Augustine], and the people who are in them, do not seem to be worth supporting by His Majesty at such a cost, nor at any cost." In the contest for royal resources to promote conquest and colonization in the Western Hemisphere, Florida stood little chance.[41]

Menéndez understood that his achievements were meager, but he laid the blame on Indigenous who resisted Spanish encroachments on their territory. He reminded Philip that he had arrived in Florida with peaceful intentions and had done all he could to support missionaries while they

40. *NAW*, 2:556; for the violent end of the Spanish effort, see Seth Mallios, *The Deadly Politics of Giving: Exchange and Violence at Ajacan, Roanoke, and Jamestown* (Tuscaloosa: University of Alabama Press, 2006), 37–57.

41. *NAW*, 2:580–588, quotations at 581–583.

tended to the spiritual needs that would bring the Natives to Catholicism and European-style civilization. But this plan failed because, he complained, Natives had killed Spaniards who had gotten lost, murdered twenty Spanish soldiers at Tocobaga, killed eight Spanish survivors of a shipwreck at Los Mártires, broken their promises about supporting Europeans who survived an ocean crossing, and assaulted a Spanish contingent walking to St. Augustine after their ship went down on its way from Mexico to Hispaniola, murdering some and enslaving others, though Menéndez claimed he had managed to ransom those kept alive.

Menéndez hoped that the enumeration of such details would convince imperial officials in Spain to accept his word because he knew firsthand the kinds of violence that Iberians suffered in Florida. He even had personal experience to back up his assessment of other debacles, having watched an Ays cacique order the murder of nineteen survivors of a shipwreck in the Bahama Channel. He believed that Indigenous groups in the interior captured and enslaved colonists, at times severing the heads of their captives to use in ceremonies and ballgames. Inland caciques seemed to accept the claims of the coastal headmen that they were "the masters of the Christians and hold them as slaves." In the face of such challenges, Menéndez proposed launching a raid to claim the region around St. Augustine. He informed the king in 1572 that Spaniards should capture Ays, Tocobagas, and Indigenous residents of the Keys and the Florida Strait—"infamous peoples, Sodomites, sacrificers to the devil of many souls"—and then exile them. It would serve the interest of both the crown and the church, he added, if these dangerous people could "be sold or given as slaves" in Puerto Rico, Cuba, and Hispaniola.[42]

The following year he urged the king to understand that the Spanish needed to control the Bahama Channel, which he saw as "the key to all the Indies" since the treasure ships passed through these dangerous waters. Without the income from the mines of New Spain, the Spanish would not be able to sustain their expenditure. Besides, he added, Protestants had made allies among the Natives, opening yet another front against the realm. Menéndez, then serving the king in Flanders, wanted to be absolved from all responsibility if "the Indies of Florida will be depopulated of the Spaniards who are settled there."[43]

42. Menéndez to R.C.M. [Royal Caesarian Majesty], c. 1572, in J. T. Connor, ed., *Colonial Records of Spanish Florida* 1 (Deland: Florida Historical Society, 1925), 78–81, quotation at 81; see also *NAW*, 2:588–589. The incident referring to the English might have been related to an English assault on St. Augustine in December 1571; for details on that episode, see *NAW*, 2:575–576.

43. Menéndez to Royal Caesarian Majesty, [1573], *NAW*, 2:589–590.

Menéndez returned to St. Augustine in the autumn of 1572 but sailed for Havana on December 20. He was back in Spain at some point in 1573, never again to see the lands he claimed in North America. The next year Philip II, having grown weary of disappointment, quashed Menéndez's newest plan to expand the boundaries of Terra Florida westward.[44]

At the time Menéndez fled, St. Augustine was barely surviving. The small number of soldiers and farming families never figured out how to turn the island's sandy soils into fields, nor could they manage the seasonal deluges of April and May even when they moved to the mainland. Their crops failed. Vermin feasted off stored seeds. The colonists' cattle devoured the meager corn they managed to coax out of the ground. Still not getting enough nutrition to survive, the cows and sheep died. Local Natives killed their pigs. Unable to create a European-style agricultural economy, the migrants subsisted on seafood, greenbrier roots, and acorns. They never found profitable mines or any other resource that might draw potential migrants. Spaniards who chose to leave their homeland for the Western Hemisphere certainly had more inviting places to go, and they often wound up in Spain's western colonies by following other family members who had sailed earlier. The only things of value these Spanish migrants to Florida ever found were sassafras, then believed by many in Europe to be a wonder drug, and nut grass, which they used to make rosaries as well as a powder that could improve one's skin and aid indigestion.[45]

On November 8, 1574, Menéndez wrote to his nephew from Santander. He hoped that the king would allow him to sail back to Florida. If this happened, he promised, he would never leave it again, "for that is the sum of my longings and happiness." Nine days later he was dead, never learning that St. Augustine, against all odds, would become the longest-lasting Spanish settlement north of the Rio Grande, though little of what the first migrants had built survived even until 1600.[46]

44. The decree, dated June 1, 1574, is in *NAW*, 2:592.

45. Lowery, *Spanish Settlements* 2:376–381; on the migrants' diet, see Kathleen A. Deagan, "The Historical Archaeology of Sixteenth-Century La Florida," *Florida Historical Quarterly* 91 (2013), 349–374, esp. 361; on family migration patterns as well as various destinations for emigrants, see Ida Altman, "A New World in the Old: Local Society and Spanish Emigration to the Indies," in Ida Altman and James P. P. Horn, eds., "*To Make America*": *European Emigration in the Early Modern Period* (Berkeley: University of California Press, 1991), 30–58.

46. Lowery, *Spanish Settlements*, 2:383; Susan R. Parker, "St. Augustine in the Seventeenth-Century: Capital of La Florida," *Florida Historical Quarterly* 92 (2014), 554–556.

Menéndez's failed quest came at a moment when Spanish officials had again begun to debate policies about how to treat Native Americans in the Americas. In the aftermath of the publication of Las Casas's work and the dispute about the humanity of Native Americans, reports about Spaniards' mistreatment of Indigenous continued to circulate in Spain. In response, royal authorities promulgated a new policy to govern relations with Natives. "Cruel and unjust wars," the returned Spaniard Luís Sanchez wrote to authorities in Madrid in 1566, "which the Spaniards have waged and are waging against the Indians, killing, robbing, attacking them, and driving them from their lands," were in direct violation of the "very Christian orders and instructions" that these invaders had received from the realm's kings. Just as bad was the enslavement of Indigenous, which further threatened the lives and communities of those who survived the wars of the conquerors.[47] As it turned out, the circulation of such views occurred just when the expansion of Spanish silver mining in the ore-rich mountains in modern Chihuahua drew migrants eager to make a quick profit, many of whom soon heard tales of potential profits that lay to the north, in the lands Coronado had visited during his *entrada*.[48]

Fearing that profit-seekers might continue the earlier practices that Las Casas and Sanchez had described, King Philip II in 1573 issued his "Orders for New Discoveries." The monarch declared that anyone who went into "pacified" lands without proper permission risked confiscation of property and even a death sentence. Priests, not conquistadores, were to organize any efforts to establish a Spanish presence in New Mexico, a policy that ignored the warning of Sanchez that clerics, alongside judges and soldiers, had played a prominent role in earlier atrocities.[49] "If, after many different attempts have been made to gain their consent, the natives still withhold it," Philip II decreed, "then the settlers are to proceed to establish their town but are not to take any of the personal belongings of the Indians or do to them more hurt than what may be necessary in order to protect the settlers and enable them to build without interference." The king added that Natives should be kept away from the town while Spaniards built it so that when they saw the finished city "they will be

47. "Memorial presented by the Bachiller Luís Sanchez . . . to President Espinosa in Madrid, August 26, 1566," in Charles W. Hackett, ed., *Historical Documents Relating to New Mexico, Nueva Vizcaya, and Approaches Thereto, to 1773*, 2 vols. (Washington, DC: Carnegie Institution, 1923), 1:156–165, quotation at 159.

48. See David J. Weber, *The Spanish Frontier in North America* (New Haven, CT: Yale University Press, 1992), 78.

49. Weber, *Spanish Frontier*, 78; "Memorial presented by the Bachiller Luís Sanchez," 163–165.

filled with wonder and will realize that the Spaniards are settling there permanently and not temporarily."[50]

In 1596, two decades after Menéndez's death, a dozen Franciscan missionaries arrived at St. Augustine. They did so with the support of imperial officials, including Domingo Martínez de Avendaño, who as governor had entertained a number of Guales and Ays in St. Augustine and managed to secure their agreement for a renewed Spanish presence. This agreement, the so-called *amistades* (friendships) of 1596, promised mutual defense between Natives and colonizers, which allowed the Spanish to secure the region for trade. The Indigenous accepted the idea that they would be obedient to the king through his designated governor. They also agreed to allow missionaries to work in the region to instruct them about Christianity.[51] Most of the friars did not remain long in the small outpost. Instead, they went out into the territory of the Timucuans and the Guales. There, according to the head of the mission, the friars busied themselves learning the local languages, "and thus the natives are coming to like them, and gladly come to the mission and ask for Holy Baptism." While their flesh was willing, these priests lacked the missals, bells, and sacramental manuals they needed to spread the faith.[52]

Still, Christianity might take hold, one friar believed, but it would not be easy. That, at least, fitted the Franciscans' agenda when they set off into the mission field. The religious were likely unaware that by then some of the Natives had concluded that the Franciscans and the other Spaniards who had invaded their territory were the cause of many of their misfortunes. In September 1597, the Guales who inhabited modern St. Catherine Island off the Georgia coast decided that the time had come to rid their homeland of those trying to spread Christianity.[53]

50. Zelia Nuttall, trans., "Royal Ordinances Concerning the Laying Out of New Towns," *HAHR* 5 (1922), 249–254, quotations at 253–254.
51. Amy Turner Bushnell, "'These People Are Not Conquered Like Those of New Spain': Florida's Reciprocal Colonial Compact," *Florida Historical Quarterly* 92 (2014), 530.
52. Fray Francisco de Marrón to Philip II, January 23, 1596, in *NAW*, 5:54.
53. The story of what happened remained told from one priest to another, and one Native oral historian to another, for over a century before a Franciscan named A. G. de Barcia told about the war in his history of Florida, which was published in Madrid in 1723: A. G. de Barcia, *Ensayo cronológico de la Florida* (Madrid, 1723), translated and excerpted in J. R. Swanton, *The Early History of the Creek Indians*, Smithsonian Institution Bureau of American Ethnology Bulletin 73 (Washington, DC: GPO, 1922), 85–88.

The rebellion began when the son of the preeminent Guale headman Don Francisco objected to criticisms he had received from the Franciscan Pedro de Corpa. Don Francisco's son, Don Juan (or Juanillo), became enraged when Friar Corpa claimed that these converted Christians did not live up to the teachings he had offered. Juanillo gathered some allies and broke into Corpa's house in the middle of the night. They found the missionary on his knees praying and used an axe to kill him. "Although the friar is dead he would not have been if he had not prevented us from living as before we were Christians," Juanillo declared, adding: "Let us return to our ancient customs, and let us prepare to defend ourselves" against the reprisal they were certain the Spanish governor would launch.[54]

Juanillo outlined the cause for the rebellion. He complained that the missionaries had taken women from the community and left "only one and that in perpetuity," perhaps a reference to the Virgin Mary. The other complaints were less ambiguous. "They obstruct our dances, banquets, feasts, celebrations, fires, and wars," he continued,

> so that by failing to use them we lose the ancient valor and dexterity inherited from our ancestors: they persecute our old people calling them witches; even our labor disturbs them, since they want to command us to avoid it on some days, and be prepared to execute all that they say, although they are not satisfied; they always reprimand us, injure us, oppress us, preach to us, call us bad Christians, and deprive us of all happiness, which our ancestors enjoyed, with the hope that they will give us heaven.

The result of such practices, he reasoned, would be to turn the Guales into slaves of the Spanish. The only way to avoid such a fate was to kill the invaders. If they succeeded, he believed, the governor would be forced to "treat us well," a result that the Guales would welcome. But before that happened, the Guales decapitated Corpa's body, drove a lance into the severed head, and displayed it on the portal of his house as a trophy. They dragged his body into the woods. No one ever found it.[55]

Once convinced that the son of the Guale headman was correct, like-minded Natives marched to the abodes of other Franciscans. Friar Blas Rodríguez in Topiqui asked those who came to his house if he could say Mass first. They allowed him to do so, then killed him, likely with axes, and threw his body outside to be eaten by carrion-hungry animals and

54. *NAW*, 5:69–70; J. Michael Francis and Kathleen M. Kole, *Murder and Martyrdom in Spanish Florida: Don Juan and the Guale Uprising of 1597*, American Museum of Natural History Anthropological Papers 95 (New York: American Museum of Natural History, 2011), 13.

55. *NAW*, 5:70.

birds, though an elderly convert came and buried the corpse. When they got to Assopo they entered the abode of the missionaries Miguel de Añón and Antonio de Badajoz, who had heard about what happened and, believing their end was near, began to pray. The Natives clubbed them to death, leaving their bodies behind. Converted Indigenous buried both at the foot of a high cross that Añón had erected. Then the rebels hunted for a monk named Francisco de Veráscola. They beat him to death when he disembarked from his canoe near Asao. Next they marched to Ospo, the mission run by Francisco Dávila. There they shot three arrows into his shoulders and would have killed him except that an Indigenous, presumably one of the Guales, intervened to take the friar's clothing, sparing his life in the process. The others then took the missionary to a town where there were no converts and left him to be a slave. Residents there planned to burn him alive but instead released him to Spanish authorities in exchange for one resident's son.[56]

Violence spread across the landscape. When Spanish soldiers seeking to avenge the assault on the religious could not find perpetrators they burned Guales' fields, which precipitated a famine in a drought year.[57] In an effort to calm frayed nerves, the Natives agreed to surrender a priest they had captured. But to ensure this was not a trap, the soldiers of Governor Gonzálo Méndez de Canzo took seven Natives hostage.[58] Still not satisfied, the armed Spaniards sailed along the coast, attacking towns where the miscreants might have lived, killing scores of Natives and capturing others, men and women, whom they took as slaves. The soldiers, one witness reported, "burned and destroyed everything."[59] In the aftermath the governor, eager to expand Spanish control across the southeastern coast, listened to spies' reports about the region, including resources to be found in the land of the Tamas (in modern Georgia) and a fear that the English had been exporting large supplies of pearls from Jacan (likely Ajacan), the Spanish name for Chesapeake Bay.[60] He told Philip III, who had acceded to the Spanish throne after the death of his father in 1598, that a Native woman named Doña María, the female chief of the Indigenous town of Nombre de Dios, adjacent to St. Augustine, had embraced Christianity, as had her family.[61] But his sanguine opinions had little purchase when other Spanish witnesses reported that St. Augustine remained a sorry outpost. A missionary named Báltasar López thought it "one of the

56. *NAW*, 5:70–71.
57. *NAW*, 5:71–72.
58. Gonzálo Méndez de Canzo to Philip II, July 1, 1598, in *NAW*, 5:86–88.
59. *NAW*, 5:69, 83–88, quotation at 85.
60. See the reports of Gaspar de Salas and David Glavan in *NAW*, 5:93–96.
61. *NAW*, 5:102–103.

worst" ports on the coast, "surrounded by saltwater marshes" and other land that he deemed useless. A September 1599 hurricane flattened many of the houses and fruit trees. Even a mild storm could flood the town. López explained the governor's more optimistic scenario as the result of greed motivated by fear that he would soon be recalled to Spain and wanted to go home with some tangible rewards.[62] For his part, the king and his officials demanded that the governor free those he had taken captive.

Despite widespread suspicion about the Spanish, in mid-May 1600 a group of Indigenous visited St. Augustine to reestablish positive relations. Méndez de Canzo accepted what he saw as their act of contrition. There were no representatives at the meeting from Tolomato, the source of the original violence. Still, the governor managed to convince imperial bureaucrats that Spaniards should remain in the region.[63] To advance their goals, local Franciscans taught the catechism in Timucuan (later published in Mexico) and instructed neophytes to read and write. One friar claimed there were soon 2,000 Christians in the area, an assertion that might have seemed plausible given that Indigenous converts in New Spain earlier in the century provided labor to build churches and monasteries even in the aftermath of devastating epidemics.[64] Still, rumors persisted that the English planned to establish a major town on the East Coast. Spanish authorities concluded that Florida was not going to be invaded, but they recognized that a threat remained.[65] St. Augustine received just enough support from Spain to survive as a hedge against possible English or Native invasions, though its imbalanced sex ratio prevented the town from prospering.[66]

The near-total failure of the Spanish to establish durable communities along the coast even after they had vanquished the French reflected

62. Báltasar López to Philip III, December 12, 1599, in *NAW*, 5:98–100, quotations at 99.

63. Mary Ross, "The Restoration of the Spanish Missions in Georgia, 1598–1606," *Georgia Historical Quarterly* 10 (1926), 171–199, quotation at 174; Jerald T. Milanich, *The Timucua* (Oxford: Blackwell, 1996), 100–101.

64. *NAW*, 5:103–106; for the larger context, see George A. Broadwell and Alejandra Dubcovsky, "Chief Manuel's 1651 Timucua Letter: The Oldest Letter in a Native Language of the United States," *Proceedings of the American Philosophical Society* 164 (2023), 226–229; for New Spain, see Ryan D. Crewe, *The Mexican Mission: Indigenous Reconstruction and Mendicant Enterprise in New Spain, 1521–1600* (Cambridge: Cambridge University Press, 2019), 156–196.

65. *NAW*, 5:106–107.

66. Weber, *Spanish Frontier*, 90.

decisions made thousands of miles away. It had been more than fifty years since Ponce de León had traveled around the peninsula. Explorers like De Soto and chroniclers of doomed missions like Cabeza de Vaca at times thought they had the upper hand in negotiations with various Indigenous peoples. Although Natives found some utility in allowing Cabeza de Vaca and his few traveling companions to live, none of the Spanish (or the French, for that matter) ever sent reports to Europe testifying to the natural resources that could be harvested to great profit in the region. They found no large supplies of tempting spices, like those whose scents wafted through the air when Columbus arrived in Hispaniola. They unearthed no great caches of gold, silver, or jewels, like those found by Cortés. It had taken Pizarro less than two years to realize the extractive potential of the enormous region lying to the south of New Spain. Seeing no similar resources after sixty years of start-and-stop exploratory expeditions convinced the Spanish that there was no point in making large investments in Florida. They saw no lure for potential soldiers seeking a new fortune or farmers eager for an encomienda—nothing, in short, that would attract Spaniards who preferred the islands and New Spain. Absent sustained investment, St. Augustine struggled, though its residents fared better than the Jesuits who strayed beyond an acceptable line in Chesapeake Bay.

For his part, Don Luis remained near the Chesapeake, biding his time while his anger at uninvited visitors grew. Unlike the vast majority of Indigenous Americans, he had seen Europe with his own eyes and had spent a great deal of time with clerics. The sack of the Jesuit mission was no nihilistic assault but sprang from his fears about what a growing European presence could mean in mainland North America. Eventually he would play a decisive role in relations between the English and the Powhatan confederacy. By then he called himself Opechancanough.[67]

67. Horn, *A Brave and Cunning Prince.*

In the era before its population dispersed due to climate change, Cahokia's residents had built a series of mounds, including Monk's Mound, which rose almost 100 feet from the near-flat floor of the regional flood plain. Its residents included artisans who made intricate fishhooks, arrowheads, and a distinctive style of pottery that had wide influence across the Mississippi Valley and beyond.

Monk's Mound. Courtesy of Cahokia Mounds State Historic Site.

Arrowheads and fishhooks. Courtesy of Cahokia Mounds State Historic Site.

Cahokia pottery. Courtesy of Cahokia Mounds State Historic Site.

Spaniards who arrived in Hispaniola recognized unique local architectural styles and the ubiquity of carved effigies of zemi figures, which observers noted could be found in every house.

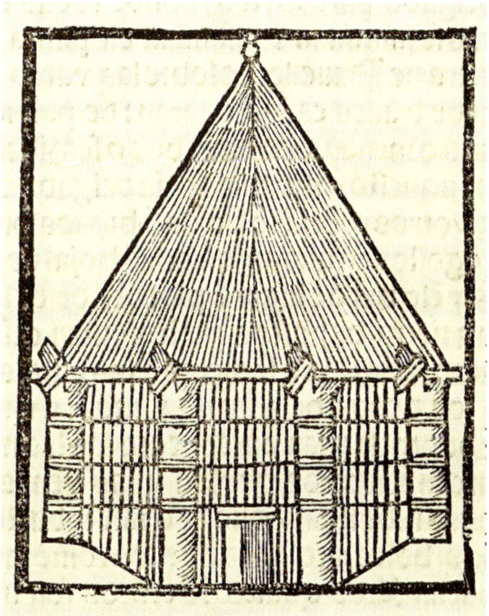

Taino house. From Gonzalo Fernández de Oviedo y Valdés, *La historia general delas Indias: con priuilegio imperial* (1540). Courtesy of the John Carter Brown Library.

Zemi. Courtesy of the Metropolitan Museum of Art, New York.

Indigenous architectural styles reflected local climates, building supplies, and economies, evident in the town of Patuxet (which the English would later name New Plymouth), with its fields near houses; in a community likely of Wichitas, whose ancestors created a Cahokia-style agricultural economy but without large public works; and at Pu'ukoholā Heiau National Historic Site on the Big Island of Hawaii, situated on the shoreline and used for religious rituals.

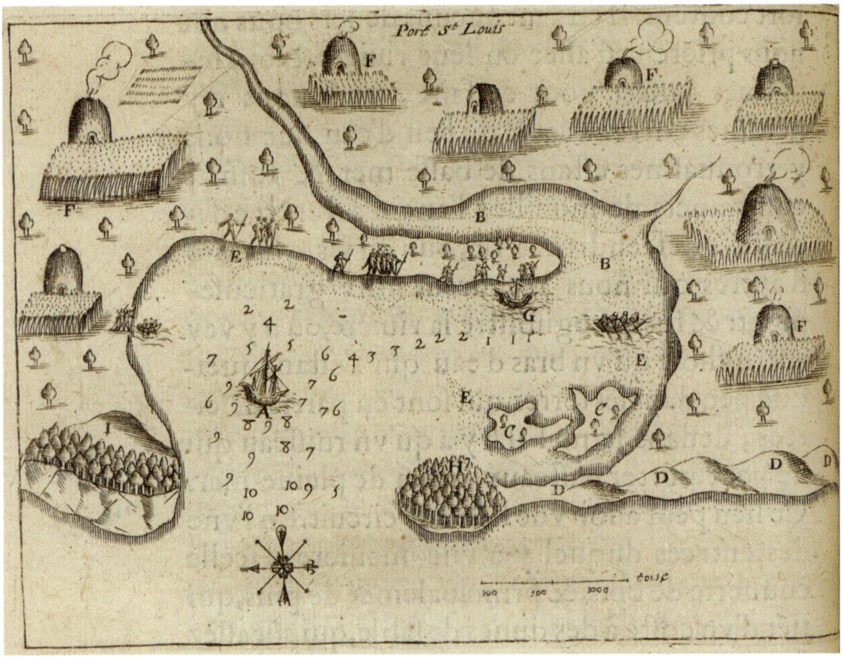

Patuxet. From Samuel de Champlain, *Voyages* (1613). Courtesy of the Huntington Library, San Marino, California.

Wichita village. Courtesy of the Western History Collections, Special Research Collections, University of Oklahoma Libraries, Fitch Collection 87.

Puʻukoholā Heiau. Courtesy of National Park Service.

These nineteenth-century Irish watercolors capture the enduring presence of distinctive architectural styles imposed by invaders from across the Irish Sea. The Anglo-Normans who invaded in the twelfth century and after erected formidable tower blocks, like imposing Trim Castle in Co. Westmeath. During the sixteenth century, Elizabethan invaders felt confident enough to build large houses, like Portumna Castle in Co. Galway, but still maintained slits in the walls to shoot arrows and openings over the front door to pour hot oil on invaders.

Trim Castle. Reproduced courtesy of the National Library of Ireland.

Portumna Castle. Reproduced courtesy of the National Library of Ireland.

Ever since Columbus first described the environment of the West Indies, Europeans hoped to garner profits from exporting natural products. Among the most enticing plants were tobacco, described at length by Seville-based physician Nicolas Monardes in a widely read book. Within two decades, an unknown observer in the greater Caribbean filled a small book with watercolors detailing the healing properties of tobacco, the ways that local residents caught parrots and dove for pearls, and the ferocious hordes of mosquitoes that were too small to see but powerful enough to torture their victims.

Tobacco. From Monardes, *Joyfull Newes from the Newfound World* (1577). Courtesy of the John Carter Brown Library.

Tobacco for healing. From *Histoire Naturelle des Indes*. Courtesy of the Morgan Library and Museum.

Parrots. From *Histoire Naturelle des Indes.* Courtesy of the Morgan Library and Museum.

Pearl diving. From *Histoire Naturelle des Indes.* Courtesy of the Morgan Library and Museum.

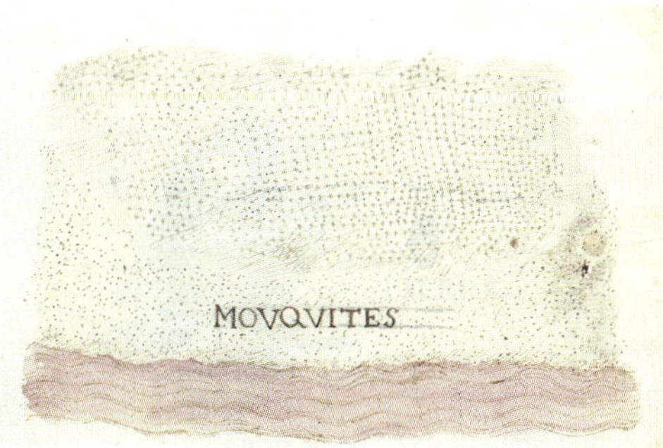

Mosquitoes. From *Histoire Naturelle des Indes.* Courtesy of the Morgan Library and Museum.

Meetings between Indigenous Americans and European explorers ranged from peaceful interaction, evident in Jacques Le Moyne de Morgues's representation of René Laudonnière's meeting with Timucuans in Florida in 1564, to violent encounters, captured in this image, possibly by John White, of the deadly clash of Inuit and sailors on Frobisher's 1577 expedition.

René Goulaine de Laudonnière and American Natives in Florida, 1564. Courtesy of the Miriam and Ira D. Wallach Division of Art, Prints and Photographs: Print Collection, The New York Public Library.

Skirmish at Bloody Point. © The Trustees of the British Museum.

John White's watercolors of the Outer Banks in 1585 represented Carolina as he saw it with his own eyes. Yet the printed versions produced in Flemish engraver Theodor de Bry's workshop in Frankfurt am Main for Thomas Harriot's *Briefe and True Report of the Newfound Land of Virginia* reveal substantial changes from the eyewitness account to the published page. In each instance, engravers added details not evident in White's original, fleshing out scenes for European readers eager to learn about North America. The images of Carolina Algonquians fishing and of the town of Secota reveal the kinds of alterations that the printers made in their versions of the original watercolors.

© The Trustees of the British Museum.

Fishing, as depicted by White and de Bry. Courtesy of the Huntington Library, San Marino, California.

Secota, as depicted by White and de Bry. ©The Trustees of the British Museum.

Courtesy of the John Carter Brown Library.

In addition to his watercolors of individuals and their economy, White also drew this map of what the English, like Thomas Harriot, then called "Virginia," the modern coast of North Carolina, which indicated the location of Algonquian towns and the arrival of European ships.

8

Elizabethans and Americans

The voyages of the Cabots gave the English what they saw as a right to claim much of the land on the far northwestern shores of the Atlantic. But in the decades that followed, the realm sponsored few voyages despite prodding by promoters like Robert Thorne, whose book and map remained available for those who wanted to promote English exploration, resource extraction, and possible colonization of the territory north of Florida.[1]

Upon the accession of Elizabeth I in 1558, English men and women who had been eager to capitalize on new information about Atlantic opportunities saw an opening. With the notable exception of a campaign on the coast of France, Henry VIII had concentrated his efforts within Britain, where he and his advisors looked for ways to eradicate any vestiges of the Catholic church. Mary Tudor, who took the throne following the death of her father in 1553, focused on restoring the authority of Rome and persecuting Protestants. After Mary passed in 1558, Elizabeth I embraced her father's disdain for the Catholic Church. She came to see world affairs as a struggle between the antiquated and wrongheaded practices of Rome against the right-thinking theological beliefs associated with Martin Luther and John Calvin. She embraced Henry's effort to eliminate Catholicism, especially in Ireland, a battlefield where the forces of proper faith would, she believed, triumph over those of ignorance and darkness.

With what seemed like success in hand in Ireland, Elizabeth awakened to what opportunities across the Atlantic could mean for the nation's honor, security, and finances. She believed that expansion could lead to the spread of Protestant religion and the possible emigration of her subjects, especially younger men, in search of work. These various strands—political, economic, religious, and social—together encouraged her and those around her to be more receptive than her predecessors had been to proposals to sail to North America. The time had come, she

1. For Thorne's writings, see Richard Hakluyt, *Divers Voyages touching on the Discoverie of America, and the Ilands adjacent* (London, 1582), sig. B^{r}–[D3^{r}].

concluded, to find the Northwest Passage and capitalize on the enormous advantages that would accrue to the European nation that could control access to and through the waterway.

From the mid-1570s to the mid-1580s, four English explorers—Martin Frobisher, Francis Drake, Humphrey Gilbert, and John Davis—led expeditions to territory that Europeans knew little about. All of them went in search of the Northwest Passage, which European cartographers had mapped even without visual evidence that these routes could be traversed. But they took different paths, which led them to encounters with Indigenous peoples including Inuit, the masters of the Arctic, and likely the Coast Miwok of the mid-California coast. In the end, these encounters did not produce immediate economic returns for either Indigenous peoples or the visitors, nor did they result in the spread of English-style Protestant practice in the Western Hemisphere. Still, these expeditions signaled a new direction for the English: the time had come to establish colonies in the Western Hemisphere if they could figure out how to succeed on the western shores of the Atlantic, a calculation that pivoted on establishing enduring relations with Native Americans.

Henry VIII, a visionary monarch who reshaped religious practice in England and initiated policies that reoriented his nation's economy, initially had little interest in North America, though he was no doubt aware that Spanish, Portuguese, and French rivals had sent explorers, soldiers, and colonizers to the Western Hemisphere. To be sure, the king had an interest in foreign affairs, launching a brutal campaign to reclaim the port city of Boulogne in northern France, which he believed belonged to the English.[2] But he put his energies into reforming Britain in the years after the Reformation.

Henry was a man of voracious tastes who applied the spiritual energy of Protestantism to solve his own problems. Only seventeen when he took the throne, he soon married Catherine of Aragon, his dead brother's widow. But they were unable to produce a son, which set the king on a course to change history. His emissaries reached out to Rome asking for an annulment. When Pope Clement VIII refused, Henry set loose a team of English theologians to find a way out. In an argument that drew on ancient texts, they reported to him that England was an "empire"; as its ruler, he was the ultimate authority and so could do as he chose.[3]

2. See Neil Murphy, *The Tudor Occupation of Boulogne: Conquest, Colonisation and Imperial Monarchy, 1544–1550* (Cambridge: Cambridge University Press, 2019), esp. 18–65.

3. Unless otherwise noted, the material on the Reformation in England can be found in Peter Marshall, *Heretics and Believers: A History of the English Reformation* (New Haven,

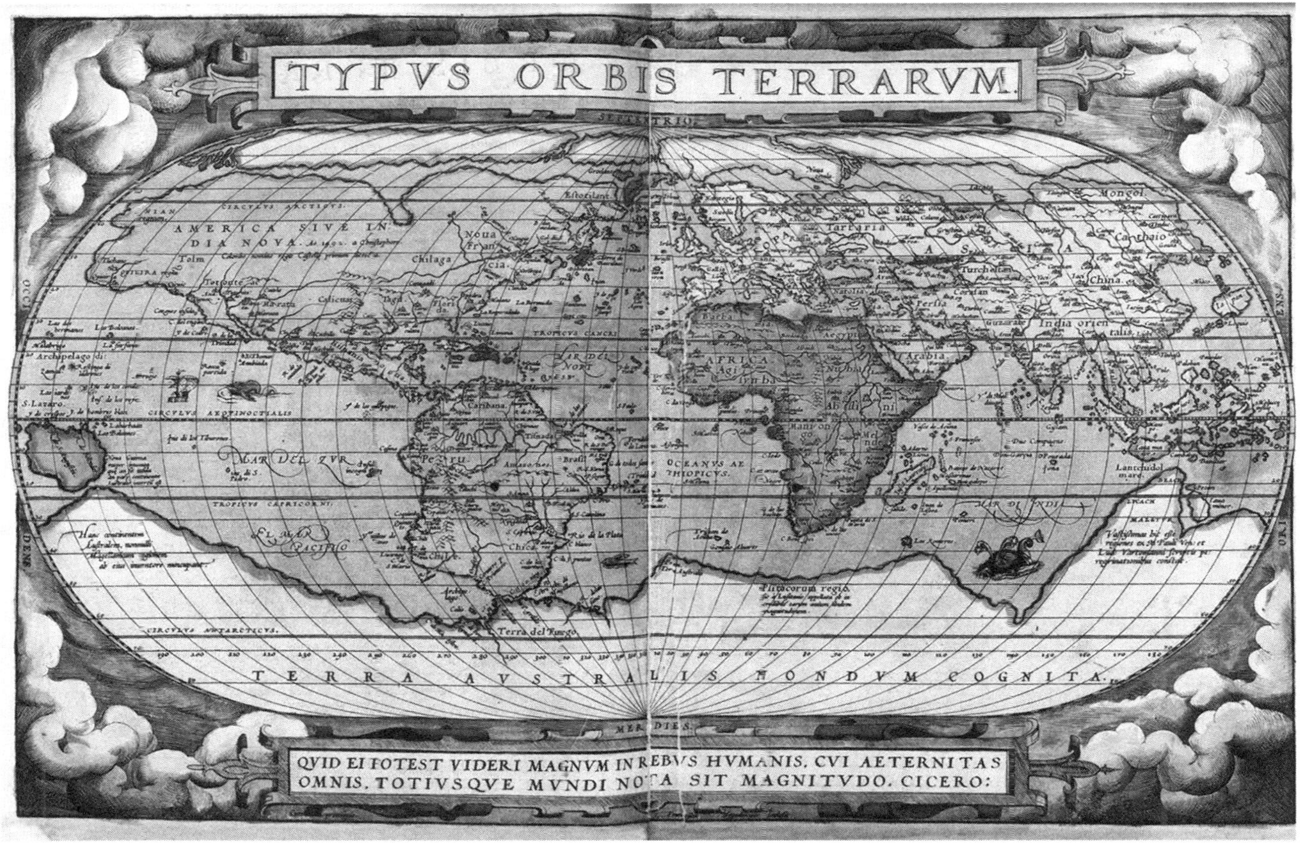

Abraham Ortelius's 1570 world map served as visual proof that the Northwest and Northeast Passages existed even though no European had ever sailed through either one. Courtesy of the Huntington Library, San Marino, California.

Acting on this newfound discovery of his status, Henry endorsed the Supremacy Act of 1534, which made him the head of the national church as well as of the state. He quickly divorced Catherine and married Anne Boleyn, a thirty-two-year-old familiar at the court whose renowned beauty had attracted the king. Although she gave birth to their daughter Elizabeth about eight months after their marriage, tragic stillbirths followed. Impatient, the king took a lover, which infuriated Boleyn. In response, he (likely falsely) accused her of adultery and treason and ordered her execution in May 1536. Within days he married Jane Seymour, a twenty-eight-year-old who had been lady-in-waiting to both Catherine and Anne Boleyn. She quickly became pregnant and delivered a son, Edward VI. But she died of postpartum complications, leaving Henry without a spouse. In the years that followed he agreed to an arranged marriage with Anne of Cleves, whom he divorced in six months; Catherine Howard, a teenage (no more than nineteen) lady-in-waiting to Anne of Cleves, whom Henry ordered executed after hearing stories of her infidelity; and Catherine Parr, who outlived him.

Henry's relentless pursuit of wives reflected his underlying drive to reshape the world to satisfy his needs. That same passion animated his political actions too. In 1536 he and his allies began to dissolve English monasteries, a program that Henry expanded in 1537 after the Irish Supremacy Act extended his clerical authority across the Irish Sea. From 1536 to 1541, English officials dissolved approximately 900 religious houses, executed clerics who refused to embrace the Church of England, and waged an iconoclastic campaign to destroy or deface thousands of religious statues.[4]

Despite his efforts to minimize the influence of Rome across Britain and the parts of Ireland under English control, thousands of Roman Catholics or Vatican sympathizers still lived in England at the time of his death in 1547. Among them was Mary I, the daughter of Henry and Catherine of Aragon, who became queen after the death of her brother Edward, who succumbed in July 1553 at age fifteen. Soon after taking the throne, Mary launched a campaign against prominent Protestants. By the time of her death in 1558, 283 had been executed, many of them burned at the stake, another sign of the ferocity of religious fervor at the

CT: Yale University Press, 2017), and Diarmaid MacCullough, *The Reformation: A History* (New York: Viking Penguin, 2004), 198–204.

4. Eamon Duffy, *The Stripping of the Altars: Traditional Religion in England, 1400–1580* (New Haven, CT: Yale University Press, 1992), 379–447; James G. Clark, *The Dissolution of the Monasteries: A New History* (New Haven, CT: Yale University Press, 2021); Marshall, *Heretics and Believers*, 261–264.

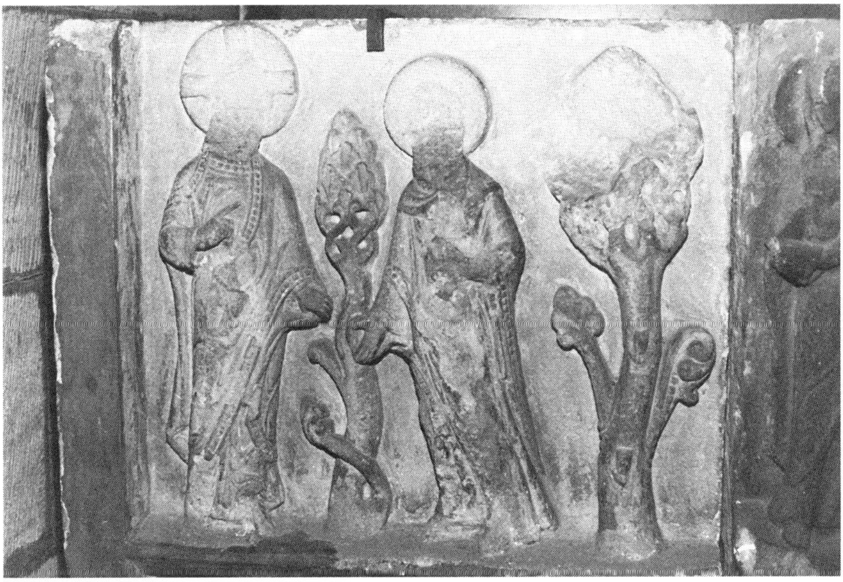

The effacement of statues on English churches, such as this one at Durham Cathedral, mirrored the iconoclasm already evident across much of northern and western Europe. Image courtesy of the Conway Library, The Courtauld,

moment. Protestant printers churned out books reveling in the horrors, none more dramatic (or more frequently reprinted) than John Foxe's *Book of Martyrs*.

In 1554, the new thirty-seven-year-old queen married Philip of Spain, the son of King Charles V. The alliance sent shock waves through Britain, where Protestants feared that a royal alliance with Spain would open a path for the hated Inquisition to launch systematic persecution in the realm. But Mary proved unable to produce an heir. Knowing that her death would mean the accession of her Protestant sister Elizabeth, Mary attempted to change the laws of succession. But she failed, and Elizabeth took the throne in 1558, marking the return of the monarchy to Henry's creed. Unlike her father, whose embrace of the Protestant cause enabled his own passions, Elizabeth's faith was often all-consuming—and more sincerely held.

During these years of tumult, perhaps few in England grasped that Henry's dissolution of the monasteries was a dress rehearsal for how the English could act in other circumstances. If the monarch's allies could dispossess his own subjects, there were in theory no limits to what another king or queen could do in territory that they claimed. Among those who learned that lesson was his daughter Elizabeth.

In the mid-1560s, Elizabeth I and her commanders launched a campaign to bring Ireland under English control once and for all. For a decade, English soldiers devastated parts of the island with merciless attacks on Catholic communities followed by efforts to reshape the landscape. Earlier Anglo-Norman conquerors had built formidable towers with few windows and surrounded their keeps with tall stone walls, an unsubtle show of force. Now, English architects designed buildings better suited for victors in battle: large houses with rose gardens and easier access—but still with arrow slits in upper chambers to repel angry locals and an opening above a main doorway to douse the unwelcome with burning oil.

English propagandists celebrated barbaric acts of the realm's commanders who terrorized Irish Catholics by burning their fields and houses and desecrating the remains of their dead.[5] On April 27, 1570, Pope Pius V, believing that the queen had "embraced the errors of the heretics"

Artist John Derrick's image of English soldiers parading with the heads of decapitated Irish men provided a visual complement to the written texts that celebrated the exploits of the brutal commander Sir Humphrey Gilbert—and a sign of the brutal tactics that Britons were willing to use to claim new territory. John Derricke, *The Image of Ireland*. Wikimedia Commons.

5. Nicholas Canny, "The Ideology of English Colonization: From Ireland to America," *WMQ* 30 (1973), 575–598; Nicholas Canny, "Reflections on the Golden Jubilee of the Publication of 'The Ideology of English Colonization: From Ireland to America,'" *WMQ* 80 (2023), 485–492.

like her father in her efforts to oppress "the followers of the Catholic faith," excommunicated her.[6]

The Elizabethan campaign in Ireland had effects well beyond the blood-spattered fields her soldiers left behind. Her father's efforts to take Boulogne had involved violent assaults against non-combatants too, a strategy that the queen's officers embraced in Ireland. In 1575, her military, which included a young Francis Drake, killed entire families, including up to 500 women, children, and men who had fled an assault on Raithlin Island, which lies between Northern Ireland and Scotland. English writers glorified the perpetrators of such actions.[7]

Among those who embraced her cause was Sir Thomas Smith, a Tudor courtier and diplomat who had served as ambassador to France from 1562 to 1566. In 1571, he received a royal grant for land in Ulster. From 1572 to 1575, he launched three expeditions to erect a colony in the region. During the first year he dispatched his son with 100 soldiers to subdue native Irish. At the time, the queen limited the extent of her investment to the pay of soldiers, with the idea that after a successful campaign they would receive title to land in the conquered areas instead of any further monetary compensation. Smith understood that in his lands he would assume the powers of a colonel, which would give him control of soldiers, and he would also be able to set up feudal courts. Like some of his contemporaries, he believed that overpopulation in Britain created an opportunity, though his preferred migrant was the younger son of a gentry family rather than an unemployed youth. These younger sons would have an incentive to develop parcels of land, thereby giving them a way to escape the limits imposed by primogeniture within Britain. They would become Smith's allies, joining him in his efforts to transform the "wastes" or undeveloped lands of Ireland into profitable settlements. In his mind, these migrants would employ local Irish through persuasion rather than coercion.

Smith, though well read in classical authorities and Thomas More's *Utopia*, underestimated the challenges he faced. He believed that the English would reap substantial economic profits by modernizing the northern Irish economy, which until that point had been based on local elites maintaining their wealth in creaghts, herds of sheep they could move across the landscape. This economic system had worked for generations,

6. "Pope Pius's Bull Against Elizabeth" (1570), https://tudorhistory.org/primary/papalbull.html. Pius did not make reference to the ongoing conflict in Ireland, but the actions Elizabeth endorsed there mirrored the accusations he made in his denunciation of her.

7. Murphy, *Tudor Occupation*; David Heffernan, *Walter Devereux, First Earl of Essex and the Colonization of North-East Ulster, c. 1573–6* (Dublin: Four Courts Press, 2018), 137–140 (Raithlin Island); Thomas Churchyard, *A generall rehearsal of warres* (London, 1579).

enabling native Irish to take advantage of ecological variation. Like other English, Smith believed that the land could be more profitable if used to farm barley and wheat, which could be exported to Britain and the continent. He thought too that there were great profits to be made from rich fisheries and dense forests. Investors in London supported colonization with the idea that they could profit from new business even if they allowed local lords like Smith to run their fiefs with the ancient rules of feudalism.

The crucial change would be the spread of agriculture. "Nothing doth more people the country with men," Smith wrote, "maketh men more civil nor bringeth more commodities to the sustenance of man than the plough." An English-style economy transplanted to this foreign soil would do more than produce gain. It would also discourage migrants from emulating the experience of Old English, the descendants of migrants who had crossed the Irish Sea in the twelfth century when King Henry II laid claim to Ireland with the authority of Pope Adrian IV, the only Englishman to ever hold the title.[8] That generation of would-be English conquerors married into Irish families and their heirs adopted ancient Irish customs. By the sixteenth century Smith and others saw them as degenerates unable to resist a Gaelic culture based, at least in part, on moving their sheep herds rather than living in one place all year round, the farming style the English preferred.

Despite his careful plans and his ability to understand the opportunities of Elizabeth's policies, Smith's venture failed. An ally of a local Irish leader killed Smith's son on October 20, 1573, and the soldiers his father had dispatched there soon abandoned their cause. The would-be proprietor's next two missions foundered before they made any progress. Despite Smith's personal losses and what could be seen as the failure of a colonial model based on subduing and then employing the local population rather than displacing them with migrants from the homeland, his plan suggested, in theory at least, the benefits of merging private investment with state support. He publicized his ideas in correspondence and in a pamphlet published in 1572, when his dreams had yet to be punctured by local reality in Ulster. There he revealed that he had been influenced not only by More's *Utopia*, which he quoted directly, but also by classical sources and a 1563 proposal from promoter Thomas Stukeley for an English colony in Florida.[9]

8. "Bull of Pope Adrian IV Empowering Henry II to Conquer Ireland, A.D. 1155," Avalon.
9. Hiram Morgan, "The Colonial Venture of Sir Thomas Smith in Ulster, 1571–1575," *Historical Journal* 28 (1985), 261–278; Jonathan DeCoster, "'Have You Not Heard of Florida?': Jean Ribault, Thomas Stukeley, and the Dream of England's First Overseas Colony," *Itinerario* 43 (2019), 397–422; [Thomas Smyth], *A letter sent by I.B. . . . wherein is conteined a large discourse of the peopling & inhabiting the cuntrie called the Ardes, and other adjacent in the north of Ireland* (London, 1572); Nicholas Canny, *Making Ireland British, 1580–1650* (Oxford: Oxford University Press, 2001), 48–49.

Smith's torturous ordeal reminded anyone who heard his story that expanding the realm into foreign territory could devastate those on such ventures. But sad tales could also motivate others to try their hand in service to the queen—even if it meant embarking on journeys more geographically distant than any could have earlier imagined. Personal sacrifices like Smith's aside, Ireland became a model for how many, including the queen, thought about American territory. But first the English would need to know more about what could be found across the Atlantic.

In 1576 English explorer Martin Frobisher sailed through the North Atlantic, coasting Greenland before he entered modern Hudson Strait in search of the Northwest Passage. The captain and most of his crew traveled homeward in the waning days of summer, arriving in London in early October, but without five men who had been out exploring and could not be found when it was time for the English to leave. Frobisher believed his men faced two possible deaths—from an unforgiving climate or at the hands of people whom the English believed to be "barbarians," "savages," and "cannibals."[10]

By the time Frobisher set sail, the English knew that Breton, Norman, Basque, and Portuguese fishing crews had long trolled the cod banks of the northwestern Atlantic.[11] These European travelers were engaged in

10. Richard Willes, "For. M. Cap. Furbyshers Passage by the Northwest," in Richard Eden, comp., *The History of Travayle in the West and East Indies* (London, 1577), 230^{r}–236^{r}, quotation at 230^{v}; Thomas Churchyard, *A Prayse, and Reporte of Maister Martyne Forboishers Voyage to META INCOGNITA* (London, [1578]), sig. B1^{v}–B2^{r} ("brutishe," "dissemblyng), sig. [B6^{v}, B7^{r}, B7^{v}] ("Caniballes"); Thomas Churchyard, "A welcome home to Master Martin Frobusher," in Churchyard, *A Discourse of the Queenes Majesties entertainement in Suffolk and Norffolk* (London, 1578), sig. L^{r}–[L4^{v}]; William Camden, *The Historie of the Most Renowned and Victorious Princesse Elizabeth* (London, 1630), sig. Kk4^{r} ("barbarians"); "Notes framed by M. Richard Hakluit of the middle Temple Esquire, given to certaine Gentlemen that went with M. Frobisher in his Northwest discoverie," in Richard Hakluyt, *Principall Navigations Voiages and Discoveries of the English Nation* (London, 1589), 636 ("savages"); [George Best], *A True Discourse of the late voyages of discoverie, for the finding of a passage to Cathaya, by the Northweast, under the conduct of Martin Frobisher Generall* (London, 1578), sig. M^{r} ("cannibals"), D3^{v} ("sweete meate"); Thomas Ellis, *A true report of the third and last voyage into Meta incognita: atchieved by the worthie Capteine M. Martine Frobisher* (London, [1578]), sig. [B6^{r}] ("barbourous and uncivill"); Joan. Tho. Freigium, *De Martini Forbisseri Angli Navigatione in Regiones Occidentis et Septentrionis Narratio historica* (Noribergae, 1580), sig. [D6^{v}] ("barbari"); Peter C. Mancall, "The Raw and the Cold: Five English Sailors in Sixteenth-Century Nunavut," *WMQ*, 3rd Ser., 70 (2013), 3–40.

11. W. Jeffrey Bolster, "Putting the Ocean in Atlantic History: Maritime Communities and Marine Ecology in the Northwest Atlantic, 1500–1800," *AHR* 113 (2008), 19–47;

resource extraction, not exploration or colonization. Like Frobisher, they understood that they had to time their voyages to avoid the worst of winter. Anyone who remained in northerly coastlands after the autumn faced enormous risks. Sailors also grasped that the dangers were even greater for individuals who strayed far from the marginally warmer winds of the Atlantic and traveled into the interior along waterways connected with the Arctic Ocean.

Confronting cold and danger was part of the bargain for Frobisher, who knew that fame and fortune would smile on the one who found the passage. Like all English explorers and promoters interested in the Western Hemisphere, Frobisher would have known Sir Humphrey Gilbert's *A Discourse of a Discoverie for a New Passage to Cataia*, which appeared in London in 1576.[12] Gilbert showed more forcefully than any earlier promoter how the English, by transiting the fabled Northwest Passage, could enhance the prospects of the realm and simultaneously solve domestic problems related to overpopulation and underemployment, crises that shipping and colonization could ease. Two surviving manuscript maps reveal that English explorers, embracing the pursuit of the Northwest Passage, had amassed considerable geographical knowledge about the region by the early 1580s. Knowing what discovery of the route would mean for their own and their benefactors' glory, they did their best to keep this information secret.[13]

The Arctic posed problems for Europeans, but not for its Indigenous residents. While later developments threatened Native cultures, no one

Peter Pope, *Fish into Wine: The Newfoundland Plantation in the Seventeenth Century* (Chapel Hill: University of North Carolina Press for the Omohundro Institute of Early American History and Culture, 2004), 15–20; David B. Quinn, *North America from Earliest Discovery to First Settlements: The Norse Voyages to 1612* (New York: Harper and Row, 1977), 347–368; Daviken Studnicki-Gizbert, *A Nation upon the Sea: Portugal's Atlantic Diaspora and the Crisis of the Spanish Empire, 1492–1640* (Oxford: Oxford University Press, 2007), 20; James Axtell, "At the Water's Edge: Trading in the Sixteenth Century," in *After Columbus: Essays in the Ethnohistory of Colonial North America* (New York: Oxford University Press, 1988), 144–181.

12. See David Beers Quinn, ed., *The Voyages and Colonising Enterprises of Sir Humphrey Gilbert*, Hak. Soc., 2nd Ser., 83–84 (London: Hakluyt Society, 1940), I:8. The book circulated quickly enough for Willes to praise it in his report on Frobisher, published the next year; see Willes, "For. M. Cp. Furbyshers Passage," 231^{r}. Richard Hakluyt gave the small pamphlet additional circulation when he reprinted it: see Hakluyt, *Principall Navigations*, 597–610.

13. John Dee's map of the Northern Hemisphere, 1580, Cotton Augustus I.1.i, British Library; map purportedly by Dee and Humphrey Gilbert, 1582, Elkins Americana 42, Free Library of Philadelphia. For a discussion, see Ken MacMillan, *Sovereignty and Possession in the English New World: The Legal Foundations of Empire, 1576–1640* (Cambridge: Cambridge University Press, 2006), 151–161.

understood the American north in the 1570s better than the Inuit.[14] Their poems and songs expressed hard-won knowledge about how to live in the Arctic.[15] Linguistic traits reveal sophisticated assessments of natural resources. Given the importance of hunting and fishing for these northern peoples, it is perhaps not surprising that Inuit groups possessed multiple ways to discuss meteorological concepts that Europeans tended to render more simply, including eleven different words for wind and eleven others for snow depending on its consistency (*aniuk* or *anio* for snow that melted in water) or when it fell (*apingaut*, the first snowfall).[16]

Since the Arctic growing season was too brief for regular crops, food came from other sources: caribou, migratory birds, fish, whales, walrus, and seals. Gathering provisions could be difficult even for knowledgeable Natives when the ice sheet covered vast stretches of water for up to six months of the year. One needed to understand how to fashion effective bows, arrows, and spears using bone and sinew; how to make and use kayaks to hunt large sea mammals; how to create shelters to fend off the cold; and how to prepare food when fuel and fire were not to be had.[17] Inuit created economics and domestic architecture best suited to prevailing conditions.[18] They built durable kayaks out of skin pulled tight over frames of bones and driftwood. These craft were so light that a single Inuk could haul several at a time, yet they could navigate where heavier and bulkier European sailing vessels could not. Inuit moved swiftly through water as they hurled spears into the tough hides of seals.

14. Renée Fossett, *In Order to Live Untroubled: Inuit of the Central Arctic, 1550–1940* (Winnipeg: University of Manitoba Press, 2001), 9–32; Barnett Richling, "Labrador's 'Communal House Phase' Reconsidered," *Arctic Anthropology* 30 (1993), 67–78; James M. Woollett, "Living in the Narrows: Subsistence Economy and Culture Change in Labrador Inuit Society During the Contact Period," *World Archaeology* 30, no. 3 (1999), 370–387; James M. Woollett, "Labrador Inuit Subsistence in the Context of Environmental Change: An Initial Landscape History Perspective," *American Anthropologist* 109 (2007), 69–84; Dorothy Harley Eber, *When the Whalers Were Up North: Inuit Memories from the Eastern Arctic* (Norman: University of Oklahoma Press, 1996).
15. *Eskimo Poems from Canada and Greenland, from Material Originally Collected by Knud Rasmussen*, trans. Tom Lowenstein (Pittsburgh: University of Pittsburgh Press, 1973), xv–xvi, xxiii, 25.
16. See Arthur Thibert, *Eskimo (Inuktitut) Dictionary*, rev. ed. (New York: Hippocrene Books, 2004), 64, 52; see also Donald Webster and Wilfried Zibell, *Iñupiat Eskimo Dictionary* (Fairbanks: Alaska Rural School Project, University of Alaska, 1970), 104–109; Ludger Müller-Wille, ed., *Franz Boas Among the Inuit of Baffin Island, 1883–1884: Journals and Letters*, trans. William Barr (Toronto: University of Toronto Press, 1998), 273–276.
17. See Marc Stevenson, *Inuit, Whalers, and Cultural Persistence: Structure in Cumberland Sound and Central Inuit Social Organization* (Toronto: Oxford University Press, 1997), 32–71.
18. See Lisa Rankin, "Native Peoples from the Ice Age to the Extinction of the Beothuk (c. 9,000 Years Ago to AD 1829)," in *A Short History of Newfoundland and Labrador* (Portugal Cove–St. Philip's: Newfoundland Historical Society, 2013), 1–19.

Lacking timber, they used whalebone covered with sealskins to protect themselves from inclement weather.[19] They understood the seasons and invariably looked forward each spring to the arrival of enormous flocks of migrating birds. Sub-Arctic Crees, who inhabited territory around the southern edges of Hudson Bay, had 200 names for birds, some of which revealed detailed knowledge of avian behavior.[20] Inuit mapping practices similarly emphasized specific aspects of particular places, including verbal descriptions of locales that guided individuals on journeys.[21]

Europeans who met Americans in the sixteenth century believed that Indigenous needed to be converted to Christianity because they dwelled in spiritual ignorance. But there was no lack of religious belief in the Arctic (or anywhere else). Inuit quite likely used whalebone to make harpoons to hunt at sea but employed caribou bones to make arrowheads for hunting on land, suggesting a conceptual linkage between the pursuit of quarry and beliefs about protocols for killing the hunted.[22] Local tales confirmed the close ties between humans, the sea, and the spirit world. Among the Inuit of Baffin Island, the goddess Nerrivik (or Sedna) controlled the movement of living sea mammals and thus determined whether a hunt was successful. Humans who violated long-standing taboos offended the souls of mammals killed in the hunt, and their indifference or ignorance led Sedna to make Inuit ill, deprive them of animals in the future, or send inclement weather.[23]

19. [Best], *True Discourse*, sig. C^{v}–$C2^{r}$; James M. Savelle and Junko Habu, "A Processual Investigation of a Thule Whale Bone House, Somerset Island, Arctic Canada," *Arctic Anthropology* 41 (2004), 204–221.

20. Stuart Houston, Mary Houston, and Arok Wolvengrey, "Cree Names for Natural History Species," in Stuart Houston et al., eds., *Eighteenth-Century Naturalists of Hudson Bay* (Montreal: McGill-Queen's University Press, 2003), 210–234.

21. Renée Fossett, "Mapping Inuktut: Inuit Views of the Real World," in Jennifer S. H. Brown and Elizabeth Vibert, eds., *Reading Beyond Words: Contexts for Native History*, 2nd ed. (Toronto: University of Toronto Press, 2009), 118–126; Gail Whiteman and William H. Cooper, "Ecological Embeddedness," *Academy of Management Journal* 43 (2000), 1265–1282.

22. See Robert McGhee, "Ivory for the Sea Woman: The Symbolic Attributes of a Prehistoric Technology," in Susan Pierce, ed., *Interpreting Objects and Collections* (London: Routledge, 1994), 59–66.

23. Knud Rasmussen, *Eskimo Folk-Tales*, ed. W. Worster (London, 1921), 20, 38; [Jean-Frédéric Bernard], *Cérémonies et coutumes religieuses de tous les peuples du monde* (Amsterdam, 1723–1743), 3:77–79. These ideas did not disappear with the arrival of Europeans; see Kristen Borré, "Seal Blood, Inuit Blood, and Diet: A Biocultural Model of Physiology and Cultural Identity," *Medical Anthropology Quarterly*, n.s., 5 (1991), 48–62, esp. 53–55; Charles Francis Hall, *Arctic Researches and Life Among the Esquimaux: Being the Narrative of an Expedition in Search of Sir John Franklin, in the Years 1860, 1861, and 1862* (New York, 1865), 544; Charles Francis Hall, *Life with the Esquimaux* 2 vols. (London, 1864), II:271.

Even though Inuit had never ceded any of their territory and could survive there far better than Europeans, Frobisher and his companions in 1576 believed that the English had a claim to Nunavut because of the earlier expeditions of the Cabots. They concluded that those earlier explorers sponsored by Henry VII had, in the words of chronicler George Best, "brought home sundry of the people, and manye other things of that Countrey," which gave the English "token of possession, beeing (I say) the firste Christians that ever there sette foote on land."[24] To Frobisher, kidnapping legitimized a claim to Arctic lands even though the English had not returned there for decades.[25]

At first Frobisher was more interested in finding the passage than in laying claim to territory. He believed that the water route to the Pacific existed since it appeared on the most recent maps issued by Europe's leading geographical authorities such as Abraham Ortelius and Gerard Mercator.[26] The English were particularly keen to find the passage so that they could undermine Portuguese domination of commerce around the Pacific's southwestern shores. If they succeeded in finding the shortcut to East Asia and the bountiful Spice Islands of the Southwest Pacific, they would win profits for English merchants, business for English marine firms, the freshest possible supplies of spices for English grocers and herbalists, and glory for the English queen.[27] But geographers and scientists in England thought that such a passage could exist only when the summer sun was intense enough to warm the Arctic, melt the ice blocking the seaways, and open up a northern polar sea. The trick was to find the entrance to the sea and get through it before the advance of the next year's ice.[28]

24. [Best], *True Discourse*, 16.
25. See Pope, *Fish into Wine*, 15–16.
26. See, e.g., Abraham Ortelius, *Theatrum Orbis Terrarum* (Antwerp, 1570); Gerardus Mercator, "Nova et orbis terræ descriptio" (Duisburg, 1569), in Marcel Watelet, ed., *The Mercator Atlas of Europe* (Pleasant Hill, OR: Walking Tree Press, 1998), 80–81.
27. The English obsession with finding the passage would continue for decades, with economic ambition linked to geopolitical rivalry and religious competition. See Richard Hakluyt, *A Particuler Discourse concerning the greate necessittie and manifold commodyties that are like to growe to this realme of England by the western discoveries lately attempted known as Discourse of Western Planting* [1584], ed. David B. Quinn and Alison M. Quinn, Hak. Soc., Extra Ser., 45 (London: Hakluyt Society, 1993), 76, and John Davis, *Worldes Hydrographical Discription* (London, 1599), sig. A2^{v}.
28. William Bourne, *A Regiment for the Sea* (London, 1574), sig. 35^{v}; William Bourne, *A Regiment for the Sea* (London, 1590), f. 77; Thomas Blundeville, *A briefe description of universal mappes and cardes* (London, 1589), sig. C2^{v}–3^{r}; and "Hondius his Map of the Arctike Pole, or Northerne World," in Samuel Purchas, *Hakluytus Posthumus, or*

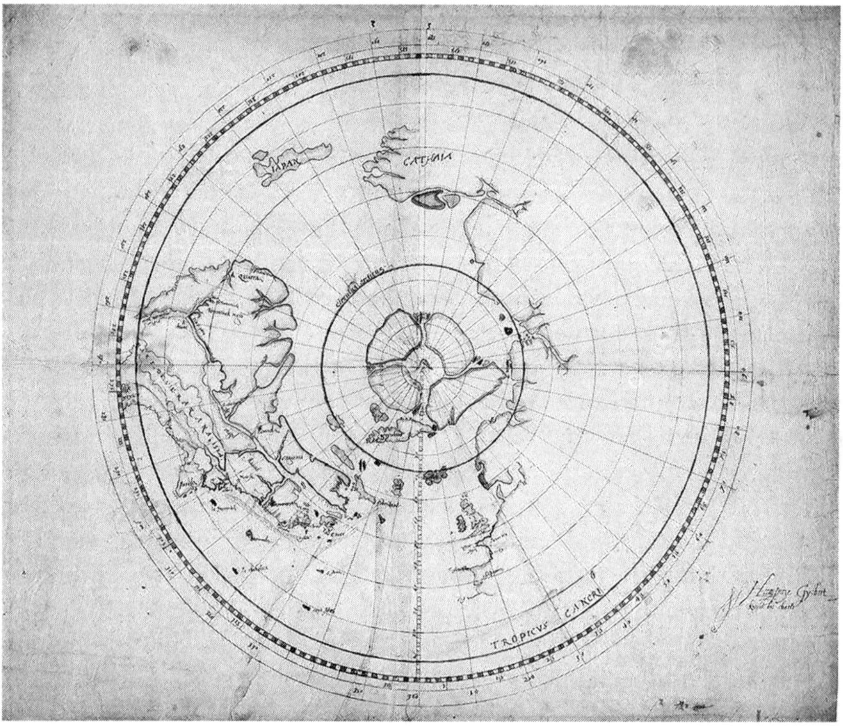

English polymath John Dee's 1582 map of the Arctic revealed passages across the polar region that European scholars believed could be accessed during summer months when the sun melted the icecaps. Free Library of Philadelphia, Rare Book Department.

Gaining knowledge of the region was only the first part of the challenge. To succeed, explorers needed the support and advice of local residents. "Nothing is more to be indeavoured with the Inland people then familiaritie," the elder Richard Hakluyt, a trained lawyer with a passion for overseas discoveries, had advised Frobisher. "For so may you best discover all the natural commodities of their country, and also all their wants, all their strengths, all their weakenesse, and with whome they are in warre, and with whome confederate in peace and amitie, &c. which knowen you make work many great effects of greatest consequence."[29] Frobisher apparently took such guidance seriously. Through improvised sign language, the explorer learned that the Inuit were interested in trade. Frobisher might not have realized it at the time, but it is likely that some

Purchas his Pilgrimes, 4 vols. (London, 1625), 3:625; see also John K. Wright, "The Open Polar Sea," *Geographical Review* 43 (1953), 338–365.

29. "Notes framed by M. Richard Hakluit," 636.

Inuit had met Europeans a decade or so earlier, as evidenced by an engraving of Inuit from the hand of an unknown artist in Nuremberg, allegedly based on firsthand reports.[30] During their stay in Nunavut, the English wrote down some Inuit words, a sign that they planned to return.[31]

The fate of the missing five men weighed heavily on Frobisher when he headed northwest again in the spring of 1577. He knew that he would never find them if he could not communicate with Nunavut's residents. While some Inuit proved eager to trade, the English chose violence, capturing an Inuk man with such force that they broke a rib that would later cause a fatal infection, as an autopsy in England revealed.[32] The kidnapped man fascinated his captors. Chronicler George Best reported that he placed five small sticks in a circle and laid a bone in the middle, an action that the English thought might be an attempt at sorcery. But then the English came to surmise that the sticks signified the five missing men taken the year earlier and that the bone represented their prisoner. The English then showed the Inuk a "picture of his Countreyma[n], which ye last yeare was brought into England (whose counterfeit we had drawne, with boate, & other furniture, both as he was in his own, & also in english

30. For the engraving, see *Warhafftige Contrafey einer wilden Frawen . . . Novaterra gennant* (Nuremberg, 1566). (See p. 81, above.)

31. Christopher Hall, "The first Voyage of M, Martine Frobisher, to the Northwest for the search of the straight or passage to China," in Hakluyt, *Principall Navigations*, 621. Hall, "First Voyage," 621–622; "East India by the Northwestw[ard]," in Richard Collinson, ed., *The Three Voyages of Martin Frobisher*, Hak. Soc., 1st Ser., 38 (London: Hakluyt Society, 1867), 83–85; Thomas Wood to Richard Bagot, October 10, 1576, shelf mark L.a. 987, Folger Library (the text is reprinted in Rachel Doggett, ed., *New World of Wonders: European Images of the Americas, 1492–1700* [Seattle: University of Washington Press, 1992], 39); Dionyse Settle, *A true report of the laste voyage into the West and Northwest regions, & c. 1577, worthily atchieved by Capteine Frobisher* (London, 1577), sig. [B9v]; [Best], *True Discourse*, sig. 1r-v (death of the captive), sig. Ciir (portrait made of him); Neil Cheshire et al., "Frobisher's Eskimos in England," *Archivaria* 10 (1980), 23–50. The painting by Lucas de Heere, entitled "Homme sauvage amené des païs Septeentrionaux par M. Furbysher L an 1576," is in the collection of the Universiteitsbibliotheek Gent; it is reproduced in Thomas H. B. Symons, ed., *Meta Incognita: A Discourse of Discovery: Martin Frobisher's Arctic Expeditions, 1576–1578* (Hull, Quebec: Canadian Museum of Civilization, 1999), 1:plate 10. The image was part of a series created by de Heere, a manuscript book entitled *Theatre De Touse les Peuples et nations de la terre avec leurs habits, et ornements divers, tant ancients que modernes diligemment depeints au natural Par Luc Dheere, Peintre et Scuplteur Gantois*; for the larger context, see Sir James Watt and Ann Savours, "The Captured 'Countrey People': Their Depiction and Medical History," in Symons, ed., *Meta Incognita*, 2:553–554. Also, Richard Hakluyt, *Particuler Discourse*, 76; Willes, "For. M. Cap. Furbyshers Passage," 231r.

32. Settle, *True reporte*, sig. [B6v–B7r]; for the autopsy conducted by Edward Dodding, see Cheshire et al., "Frobisher's Eskimos in England," 38–42; see also Watt and Savours, "The Captured 'Countrey People,'" 2:553–562.

aparell)." The English thought that perhaps they would be able to speak with him at that moment, but the Inuk grew silent, perhaps out of fear. As Best put it, he presumably knew that the English "coulde make menne live or die at oure pleasure."[33]

Several days later Frobisher found a safe harbor for his ship and allowed his men to go ashore.[34] Soon after, the explorer met with a group of Inuit. One English chronicler believed that the Natives made signs to suggest that three of the five were still alive; he thought they wanted ink, pen, and paper and would return in a few days with survivors. The English encountered the same group of Inuit four days later, probably sometime in early August, but gained no additional information about the missing men, though they did spy some of their possessions in an Inuit camp.[35]

Rather than waiting for the Inuit to take the writing implements to the captives (if they were still alive), the sailors went exploring. They were especially eager to find gold. Soon enough they encountered a larger group of Inuit who began shooting arrows at the visitors. The English returned fire. The scene would later capture the attention of an English artist.[36] As the skirmish wound down, English sailors captured two Inuit women, one with a newborn child and the other elderly, at a place they later labeled Bloody Point. They thought, chronicler Dionyse Settle wrote, that the older one might be a witch or demon, so they pulled off her buskins "to see if she were cloven footed." After establishing that she was in fact human, they released her.[37] There was no other sign of the missing English men, but once again Frobisher left behind paper, ink, and pen. He also ordered his men to lay goods on the ground, thereby adapting to what they believed was the local practice. "It seemeth they have bene used to this trade or traffique, with some other people adjoining," Settle added, "or not farre distant from their Countrie"—possibly a reference to Labrador, a site of extensive European fishing activity since early in the sixteenth century.[38] They found the clothes of the men left behind the year before, prompting Frobisher to tell the Inuit he met that if they did

33. [Best], *True Discourse*, sig. Cii^{r-v}.
34. Settle, *True reporte*, sig. [Bix^{v}].
35. Settle, *True reporte*, sig. Cii^{v}–Ciiii^{r}.
36. The artist could have been John White, who would later become well known for his depictions of American *naturalia* as well as the outer banks of Carolina around Roanoke. See Kim Sloan, *A New World: England's First View of America* (Chapel Hill: University of North Carolina Press, 2007), 164–165.
37. Settle, *True reporte*, sig. C^{r-v}.
38. Settle, *True reporte*, sig. Ciii^{r-v}.

not deliver the captives the English would kill everyone they saw. He offered to trade one of his three captives for any new information.[39]

When they returned to England without the missing men, the voyage's chroniclers provided detailed accounts of Inuit material culture. They wrote too that the Inuit were cannibals.[40] Frobisher's crew put the three Inuit captives on display. The captors believed that Kalicho, the man, was the partner of Arnaq, the mother of the infant, Nutaaq. That soothing view was wrong but did not stop artists from capturing likenesses of the Inuit. In one resulting image, engravers placed the three into a fictitious background, with the wounded Kalicho, restored to health, fishing from a kayak. Among those excited by the captives was Queen Elizabeth. She was eager to meet them, but they died before that happened. Besides the Inuit, Frobisher also brought home ore that he believed contained flecks of gold. Though an assayer soon agreed, magnifying Frobisher's reputation and enabling him to organize a much larger expedition for 1578, there was no gold in the rocks.

When Frobisher set sail again in 1578, his party included fifteen ships and almost 400 men, a sign that his goal had evolved from seeking the passage to establishing a mining colony. The flotilla was the most substantial English investment in North America in the sixteenth century.[41] Frobisher and his allies had hoped to establish alliances with Inuit, but he found their settlements abandoned.[42] Undaunted, the English hauled over 1,000 tons of glistening ore home at the end of the summer. Unfortunately for Frobisher and his supporters, a new assay revealed that the ore was iron pyrite or fool's gold. The English used the rocks to make walls and pave roads. The disappointing find ended plans to create a mining colony with 2,000 English laborers. It also brought ruin to the company that had financed his expedition.[43]

39. [Best], *True Discourse*, sig. D^v.
40. Settle, *True reporte*, sig. Cv^r–D^r.
41. See Joyce E. Chaplin, *Subject Matter: Technology, The Body, and Science on the Anglo-American Frontier, 1500–1676* (Cambridge, MA: Harvard University Press, 2001), 47–48, 56–57; Walter Kenyon, ed., "The Canadian Arctic Journal of Capt. Edward Fenton, 1578," *Archivaria* 11 (1980–1981), 171–203.
42. Ellis, *True Report*, sig. [Bvi^v]; Michael Lok, "Doynges of Captayne Furbusher," f. 2^v, reprinted in James McDermott, ed., *The Third Voyage of Martin Frobisher to Baffin Island, 1578*, Hak. Soc., 3rd Ser., 6 (London: Hakluyt Society, 2001), 75–76; Kenyon, "The Canadian Arctic Journal," 185, 186, 188–189.
43. "Thaccount gyven by Michael Lok of the third voiage of Martin Furbusher for the discourye of Cathaj &c by the Northwest parties" [1578], HM 715, Huntington Library; James McDermott, *Martin Frobisher: Elizabethan Privateer* (New Haven, CT: Yale University Press, 2001), 245–256. Only in the 1860s did the English even find the

This 1578 engraving of the Inuit captives Kalicho, Arnaq, and Nutaaq, imagined by an unknown artist on an English coastline, circulated widely in printed books, including texts in French and German. *La Navigation du capitaine Martin Forbisher* [*sic*] (La Rochelle, 1578). Courtesy of the Huntington Library, San Marino, California.

Frobisher's three summers of Arctic exploration led to no material gains. Perhaps more damning, the disappearance of the five men solidified

likely location of Frobisher's planned colony; see William W. Fitzhugh and Dosia Laeyendecker, "Exploration History of Frobisher Bay," in William W. Fitzhugh and Jacqueline S. Olin, eds., *Archaeology of the Frobisher Voyages* (Washington, DC: Smithsonian Institution Press, 1993), 11–25; William W. Fitzhugh, "Archaeology of Kodlunarn Island," in Fitzhugh and Olin, eds., *Archaeology of the Frobisher Voyages*, 59–98. For an analysis of the items that Hall found, see Eric Klingelhofer, "Three Lost Ceramic Artifacts from Frobisher's Colony, 1578," *Historical Archaeology* 10 (1976), 131–134. For the fate of the ore that survived the journey, see Robert McGhee, *Arctic Voyages of Martin Frobisher: An Elizabethan Adventure* (Seattle: University of Washington Press, 2001), 139–147. The original plan had been for English miners to remain on Baffin Island and send an additional 2,000 tons of ore after 1578, but the English abandoned the effort; on the plan, see McDermott, *Martin Frobisher*, 208–209. Though the English explorers never found them, there are gold reserves in Nunavut; see Patrick Mercier-Langevin, "Gold Deposits of Nunavut," *Exploration Minière* 2 (2022).

English views of Inuit savagery. They never learned that, in all likelihood, Inuit in Nunavut tried to help the mariners and even sang to the spirits to protect them before they embarked on what became a doomed mission homeward.[44]

Despite their disappointment, the English did not abandon their claim to the Arctic. Perhaps the seizure of the Inuit man, woman, and child was Frobisher's way to mimic Sebastian Cabot's actions a century earlier: by taking and displaying captives, he too asserted an English claim to the region. But those claims did not erase the oft-told tale of the missing men. The Inuit continued to tell the story as a cautionary tale: learn about the environment and appease the gods to survive in the Arctic. But the English had heard enough. Although they continued to seek a water route to the Pacific, they recognized that the realm's prospects would be better served by limiting their investments in Arctic explorations, which would never again be as extensive as the fleet Frobisher assembled in 1578. Unlike other parts of eastern North America, Nunavut remained free of an enduring European presence.

While Frobisher never made it to the Pacific nor found precious gold veins, the geographical knowledge he conveyed circulated and motivated others, including Francis Drake. In 1577, with London investors and scholars still buzzing about Frobisher's initial achievements, Drake left London on a mission to find the Pacific opening to the Northwest Passage. He returned three years later as the most famous navigator of his age.

Born in humble circumstances on a tenant farm in the small Devon town of Tavistock around 1540, Drake spent the 1560s working for John Hawkins, a mariner eager to enrich England by stealing enslaved Africans from imperial rivals, which pleased Queen Elizabeth I. By 1568 Hawkins trusted Drake with the command one of his ships during an expedition to sell enslaved Africans to Spanish colonists in the Caribbean. While the two had a falling-out when Drake failed to come to Hawkins's rescue

44. Details about this Inuit intervention emerged much later in an oral history collected by an American whaling captain in the nineteenth century. See Susan Rowley, "Frobisher Miksanut: Inuit Accounts of the Frobisher Voyages," in Fitzhugh and Olin, eds., *Archaeology of the Frobisher Voyages*, 37–40; Chaplin, *Subject Matter*, 58; William W. Fitzhugh, "Questions Remain," in Fitzhugh and Olin, eds., *Archaeology of the Frobisher Voyages*, 231–232; Karen Ordahl Kupperman, *The Jamestown Project* (Cambridge, MA: Harvard University Press, 2007), 94–95. Hall recorded the story twice; see *Life with the Esquimaux*, II:93–94, 101, 282–284, and *Arctic Researches*, 543–544. See the questions posed by Hall and the answers of some his informants in Hall's journal for October 2, 1861, in Charles Francis Hall Collection, 1858–1871, Box 2, .021, Archives Center, National Museum of American History, Smithsonian Institution.

during a Spanish raid on English ships, Drake escaped the debacle with his reputation intact. In 1575 he commanded a ship that provided naval support to the campaign to take Raithlin Island. Drake's ship quite possibly bombarded an Irish fort, driving its residents to seek shelter.[45]

Two years later, Elizabeth commissioned Drake to lead a flotilla through the Straits of Magellan and northward along the Pacific coast in search of the western opening to the Northwest Passage. After forty-five days they reached Brazil on April 26, 1578. By August they had managed to get through the Strait of Magellan and then headed north, eager to find the opening to the passage Frobisher had promised.[46]

On April 16, 1579, Drake led the *Golden Hinde* and a small, stolen Spanish ship out of the port of Huatulco. Over the next forty-eight days they headed toward what they called the Strait of Anian, which they believed would be the western opening to the Northwest Passage. Before he set off, Drake learned about wind patterns from two kidnapped Spanish pilots who sailed with the silver galleons linking Acapulco to Manila. That knowledge convinced him that rather than sail more or less north, he should instead follow the trade winds, which would take him far out into the Pacific but then enable him, likely around 30°, to track north and east. By the time he reached the North American coastline near modern Vancouver Island on June 3, he had sailed about 5,000 miles while avoiding winds that might have otherwise hindered his progress.[47]

Drake and his crew spent months exploring the coastline, repeating the kind of behavior that other European explorers had engaged in earlier. Like Frobisher, Drake had no doubt about the existence of the passage. But in the absence of other Europeans having mapped it earlier, these English needed to read the local coastline, taking soundings of depths. Like their predecessors, they also met Indigenous, virtually all of whom seemed to know about their imminent arrival before the English sailed in. Often, they set fires at the spots they thought the English would likely see. Impressed, Drake called one part of the coastline the Bay of Fires. Time

45. Heffernan, *Walter Devereux*, 137–139.
46. Harry Kelsey, *Sir Francis Drake: The Queen's Pirate* (New Haven, CT: Yale University Press, 1998), 93–204; Samuel Bawlf, *The Secret Voyage of Sir Francis Drake, 1577–1580* (New York: Walker, 2003), 11–12; E. G. R. Taylor, "The Missing Draft Project of Drake's Voyage of 1577–80," *Geographical Journal* 75 (1930), 46–47; William Camden, *Annales rerum Anglicarum et Hibernicarum regnante Elizabetha* (London, [1625]), 2:420–426.
47. Bawlf, *Secret Voyage of Sir Francis Drake*, 275–277.

and again Drake and others would sail into a promising opening, only to discover that it became too shallow to be the Strait of Anian.

After spending time along the coast, Drake and a group of his men traveled inland. His exact location remains something of a mystery, confounded not only by ambiguity in the written texts but also by later historians' efforts to claim that he must have been around present-day Drake's Bay, California—though he may have been in southern Oregon. Either way, less mysterious was the English response to the Natives they met, who were likely Coast Miwoks (if at the California location) or a Chinook- or Coos-speaking population (if farther north).[48] According to the voyage's chronicler, the English believed it crucial to cover Indigenous naked bodies, so they gave them clothing, which the Natives accepted and for which they then gave gifts in return. The sailors believed that the Indigenous thought the visitors were gods and that the offering of presents signaled some kind of devotional act. Soon after, the English encountered a large group who perched at the top of a hill. One of them made a long speech. The men then laid down their bows, a peaceful gesture, and walked down to greet the visitors, offering tobacco along with feathers. But the women stayed behind, "tearing their flesh from their cheekes," an English chronicler observed, "whereby we perceived that they were about a sacrifice." Drake and his companions responded with their own religious rite: he read Scripture out loud. The English believed the act calmed the Indigenous.[49]

In the days that followed, Drake learned that news of the ship's arrival had spread far among the Natives, many of whom came to see the visitors. The locals had allowed Drake and his companions to set up a small camp, providing physical distance between them and the growing number of Natives. Like other Indigenous who met unexpected Europeans, these Natives tried to communicate with sign language and gifts, practices that the English soon mimicked. The Indigenous had dressed for a ceremonial meeting, having painted their faces white or black. Their leader, whom the English identified as their king, wore muskrat furs and elaborate necklaces, and his attendants carried what the English identified as a mace and two intricate feather crowns. Drake and the others seemed to believe that they controlled the local situation. The separate camp they

48. See Melissa Darby, *Thunder Go North: The Hunt for Sir Francis Drake's Fair and Good Bay* (Salt Lake City: University of Utah Press, 2019), 192–229.

49. "The course which Sir Francis Drake held from the haven of Guatulco in the South sea on the backe side of Nueva Espanna, to the Northwest of California," in Richard Hakluyt, *The Principal Navigations, Voyages, Traffiques, and Discoveries of the English Nation* (London, 1598–1660), III:440–441.

had erected was theirs to control, so it was up to Drake to decide to let the king in. This, at least, is how the English understood what became the most pivotal moment of their time on the Pacific coast.

Once in Drake's camp, the headman made signs that the English believed meant that they would give Drake, according to the chronicler, "their right and title of the whole land, and become his subjects." He then placed one of the crowns on Drake's head, draped chains around his neck, offered up other goods, and then honored him "by the name of Hioh, adding thereunto as it seemed a signe of triumph." Drake claimed to hesitate to accept what he believed was a grant of new territory, but he thought it might have strategic advantages for the queen's realm. Confident that he was acting for his god and his sovereign, Drake took the scepter and crown and said that he wished he could find a way to transport "the riches & treasure" of this land to England. Soon after, Native men and women began to lacerate their own flesh. Blood poured from their faces in a sign the English interpreted as an act of devotion "to the living God, whome onely they ought to worshippe." Before leaving, Drake took a tour of this region he believed was now part of Elizabeth's realm. Large herds of deer caught his attention, as did the local muskrat population, another American animal that Europeans could only describe by comparing these mammals' bodies with rodents known at home.

Drake named the territory Nova Albion in honor of local white cliffs that faced the sea like Dover's and because he believed the territory looked like England. The chronicler added that the English believed they might find gold and silver there. To protect the claim, Drake and his men took a plate decorated with Elizabeth's image, engraved the date on it, and nailed it to a post. They then added a sixpence that had her image and her arms on it. The marker, according to the chronicler, noted that this memorial commemorated "the free giving up of the Province and people into her Majesties hands." Following the logic of the European doctrine of discovery, the explorers believed no one could challenge Elizabeth's possession of Nova Albion.[50]

On August 29, the *Golden Hinde* departed. Though contemporary documentation has long since disappeared, early seventeenth-century observers believed that Drake headed out into the Pacific hoping to catch winds to take him back to the western opening of the alleged Strait of Anian or Northwest Passage. Like other English explorers of the age, he reckoned that the summer heat would have thawed the ice that choked it during winter. Instead, the ship likely encountered ice again, this time floes that had detached in the warmer weather. Unable to determine a way forward,

50. "The course which Sir Francis Drake held," 441–442.

Drake weighed his two options: a return through the Strait of Magellan, which seemed impossible given the prevailing currents and winds, or a journey toward the more profitable and perhaps safer waters of the Southwest Pacific. He chose the latter.[51]

The English reached the Moluccas in November 1579. From there they sailed to Java, then through the Indian Ocean to the east coast of Africa, then south around the Cape until they landed at Plymouth on November 9, 1580.[52] Along the way he and his men had raided Spanish ships and terrorized those on board, including (according to the Spanish ambassador to London) chopping the hands off some Spaniards. The Council of the Indies, aware of Drake's movement across the Atlantic, kept Philip II apprised, raising the monarch's ire.[53]

Drake, a tormenter of the Spanish, returned home a hero. He had overcome monumental problems: enemy attacks, dangerous storms, ill sailors. His arrival thrilled the queen, who had his ship hauled onto land and then hosted a feast on its main deck, where she knighted him on April 4, 1581. English writers celebrated the achievement in poetry and prose.[54] Scholars delighted in the knowledge that Drake had acquired, including about the workings of mariners' instruments at sea as well as valuable plants such as cacao and coconut.[55] One enterprising engraver created an image of Drake's ship being guided around the circumference of the globe by the hand of God.[56]

Drake's return inspired other Elizabethans to expand the realm through expeditions across the Atlantic. Among them was Sir Humphrey Gilbert, a half brother of Sir Walter Ralegh, who saw the utility of linking the

51. Bawlf, *Secret Voyage*, 322–326.
52. Bawlf, *Secret Voyage*, 322–326.
53. Don Antonio de Padilla to Philip II, August 6, 7, 11, 16, 23, 31, and September 5, 1570, in Zelia Nuttall, trans. and ed., *New Light on Drake: A Collection of Documents Relating to His Voyage of Circumnavigation, 1577–1580*, Hak. Soc., 2nd Ser., 34 (London: Hakluyt Society, 1914), 400–405; "The Answer of the Spanish Ambassador," October 29, 1580, *Calendar of State Papers, Foreign Series, of the Reign of Elizabeth*, ed. Joseph Stevenson et al. (London: Her Majesty's Public Record Office, 1863–1850), 14:463–464.
54. David B. Quinn, *Sir Francis Drake as Seen by His Contemporaries* (Providence, RI: John Carter Brown Library, 1996); Nicholas Breton, *A discourse in commendation of the valiant gentleman, maister Frauncis Draek, with a rejoysing of his happy adventures* (London, 1582).
55. W[illiam] B[urrough], *A Discours of the variation of the Cumpas, or Magneticall Needle* ([London], 1581); [Charles D'Ecluse], *Caroli Clusii Atreb. Aliquot Notæ in Garciæ Aromatum Historiam* (Antwerp, 1582), 28–30 (cacao), 9–10 (coconut).
56. Geffrey Whitney, *A Choice of Emblemes, and Other Devises* (Leiden, 1586).

An emblem commemorating Sir Francis Drake, famous well beyond England for having led—and survived—a circumnavigation of the Earth. Courtesy of the Huntington Library, San Marino, California.

acquisition of territory abroad with solving domestic problems. Extracting resources, as Frobisher and Drake had promised, would be important, but the gains from transporting English migrants might be higher. In 1566, he had written an extensive argument linking exploration and colonization. Published in 1576 as *A Discourse of a Discoverie for a New Passage to Cataia*, Gilbert connected the existence of the Northwest Passage, the desirability of establishing English outposts in the northwest reaches of the Atlantic basin, and the profits to be had if the English could establish regular trade with Americans. In addition to his speculations about geography, Gilbert argued that the state should not execute the growing number of people who faced capital punishment. Instead, authorities should release these young men and deport them on colonizing missions. A cynical reading of his idea might suggest that he was trying to export a social problem rather than treat it and did so with the lives of men who were going to die if they remained in England. Although Gilbert had demonstrated a cavalier attitude toward those whom he deemed inferior, his plan nonetheless presented a way forward.[57]

Gilbert's first experience abroad was in Munster in southwest Ireland, not North America. He arrived as one of the military commanders Elizabeth had dispatched in her effort to vanquish indigenous Irish and their Roman faith. According to one of his contemporaries, Gilbert understood that ultimate victory relied on more than winning on the battlefield. He wanted to find a way to demoralize the native Irish population so they would abandon their ancestral ties to Gaelic lords as well as to Rome, two impediments that prevented them from becoming as civilized as the English. To achieve his ends, Gilbert ordered his men to go out onto the battlefield at the end of a day and decapitate dead Irish soldiers. They were then to bring the heads back to Gilbert, who had them arranged on either side of the path leading to his tent, the route that surviving family members walked to plead their case to the commander. Gilbert used the heads "*ad terrorem*," chronicler Thomas Churchyard reported, to convince survivors of battles to surrender. His tactics advanced his political career and earned him a knighthood in January 1570. The following year he was elected to represent Plymouth in Parliament.[58]

Gilbert gained additional military experience in 1572 when he led an English mission to support the Dutch against the Spanish during the early years of what would become known as the Eighty Years' War (1568–1648). Back in England, with his reputation as an eager promoter of English expansion growing after the publication of his book, he gathered with others planning journeys to the American north. After his first attempt to establish an English settlement in North America collapsed in 1579, he met with the elder Hakluyt, the polymath John Dee, and the queen's secretary Sir Francis Walsingham, each of them well versed in knowledge and theories about establishing colonies to benefit the English state.[59]

In 1583, in the aftermath of the celebration of Drake for his circumnavigation, Gilbert led three ships to Newfoundland. The younger Hakluyt had considered going along, but he gave up his spot to a close friend he had known at Oxford, a Hungarian poet named Stephen Parmenius.[60]

57. Humphrey Gilbert, *A Discourse of a Discoverie for a new Passage to Cataia* (London, 1576).

58. Thomas Churchyard, *A general rehersall of warres, called Churchyardes Choise* (London, 1579), sig. Di^r–$Diii^r$; for the context, see Canny, "The Ideology of English Colonization."

59. David B. Quinn, "Sir Humphrey Gilbert and Newfoundland," in *Explorers and Colonies: America, 1500–1625* (London: Hambledon Press, 1990), 207–223.

60. Before Gilbert left, Parmenius had published two poems, one to his patron and the other, *De Navigatione*, about Gilbert; for the text of the latter poem and details about

Unlike his predecessors, Gilbert was more interested in colonization than the extraction of resources, though he knew that profits would come from exports if he could create English settlements abroad. He imagined establishing a feudal state in the Western Hemisphere where he would have control over the land (via a grant from Elizabeth) and would be able to establish manorial courts, thereby augmenting his control over the region. But his dreams, like so many others, failed. On the return, two of the three ships sank, including Gilbert's. The third made it back to England, carrying news of the disaster and also, as it happened, a report by Parmenius about the resources to be found in Newfoundland. The poet, who had been traveling on one of the lost ships, had written in Latin hoping that his report would expand European knowledge about Canada in the lingua franca of European scholars.[61]

Gilbert's loss shocked many in England. The last report on him, from a survivor on the one ship that returned safely, had him sitting on the deck possibly reading the copy of Sir Thomas More's *Utopia* that he had taken with him, one of many who turned to that text in their efforts to make sense of the intellectual challenges following 1492.[62] A fawning observer declared that "in service upon the enimie" Gilbert was "as valiant and courageous as no man more." He shared the story of Gilbert and only a dozen others taking the redoubtable Irish castle at Kilkenny when it had 1,000 defending it, part of a campaign in which his 5,000 soldiers subdued the entire province of Munster. Yet for all his fortitude, he was gone. The younger Hakluyt saw the tragedy as well, which he described using testimony from a survivor of the only ship that returned, who reported that the mission's flagship had been "devoured and swallowed uppe of the sea." Gilbert, brutal on the killing fields of Munster, did not survive the kind of storm that threatened every explorer.[63]

his life, see David B. Quinn and Neil M. Cheshire, eds., *The New Found Land of Stephen Parmenius: The Life and Writings of a Hungarian Poet, Drowned on a Voyage from Newfoundland, 1583* (Toronto: University of Toronto Press, 1972), esp. 140–155.

61. Parmenius to Hakluyt, 1583, in E. G. R. Taylor, ed., *The Original Writings and Correspondence of the Two Richard Hakluyts*, Hak. Soc., 2nd Ser., 76–77 (London: Hakluyt Society, 1935), 1:198–202.
62. Quinn, "Sir Humphrey Gilbert and Newfoundland," 221–222; J. Martin Evans, *America: The View from Europe* (New York: W. W. Norton, 1976), 4–19.
63. Raphael Holinshed, *Chronicles* (London, 1587), 2:132–133, quotation at 132; Edward Hayes, "A report of the voyage and successe thereof, attempted in . . . 1583 by Sir Humphrey Gilbert," in Hakluyt, *Principall Navigations* (1589), 679–697, quotation at 695.

Despite the loss of both Gilbert and Parmenius, news about Newfoundland soon reached the English from George Peckham, a member of a group of English Catholics who had been looking for American territory to establish their own settlement where they could practice their religion without the persecution many experienced in England. In 1582, Peckham and his associates purchased a section of Newfoundland from Gilbert. They did not set out to explore their new land. Instead, they wanted to hear about the region from Gilbert after his return in 1583. Though Gilbert was gone, Peckham and others met with Edward Hayes, the captain of the ship that survived the mission. Soon after, Peckham produced his own book, printed in London in late 1583, yet another "true reporte" of a European expedition across the Atlantic.[64]

Newfoundland, to Peckham, was an ideal place for English colonization. Emigrants would be far from home but still under English law, customs, and practices. Anyone who acted against the interests of the queen or spoke ill of her would be punished. They would be considered traitors, have their goods confiscated, and have their ears chopped off. Abiding by English practice was a small price to pay since those who ventured there would soon make a profit from their trade with Natives. While it would take time for Indigenous and English to learn to speak with each other, sign language was sufficient for the moment since the Natives of Newfoundland were already familiar with Europeans. To make sure that trade could be set up quickly, the English needed to provide gifts to their hosts: mirrors, beads, bells, glass, bracelets. Such things, "though to us of small value," meant much more to the Natives and would soon "induce theyr Barbarous natures to a likeing and mutuall society with us." Peckham believed that Elizabeth's claim to the land had been established through the discovery of the region by the Welsh sailor Madoc in 1170, an ancient story that had begun to circulate again in an era when the English sought legitimacy for their claims to North America. Confident in the legal basis for owning this distant territory, he saw no reason to delay establishing trade. There was too much at stake to let the opportunity go, especially given the extent of profitable exports: fur-bearing animals (beaver, marten, fox, leopard), silkworms, fish, trees, naval stores, and valuable stones and minerals such as gold, silver, copper, lead, tin, rubies, pearls, and marble.[65]

64. George Peckham, *A true reporte of the late discoveries and possession, taken in the right of the Crown of Englande, of the Newfound Landes: by . . . Sir Humphrey Gilberte* (London, 1583).

65. *NAW*, 3:40 (punishments), (gifts), 48 (Madoc), 51–52 (commodities).

In Peckham's mind, or at least in his rhetoric, these material gains were secondary to the benefits of establishing a colony in Newfoundland. Launching an outpost would allow the English to provide "the most happy and gladsome tydings" of the Gospel, which would encourage Indigenous to move "from falsehood to truth, from darknes to light, from the hieweay of death, to the path of life, from superstitious idolatry, to sincere Christianity, from the devill to Christ, from hell to Heaven."[66] He also embraced Gilbert's idea that North America could be a destination for unemployed English whose numbers had become so large because God had spared England the most horrible wars and plagues. Peckham argued that getting to the northwestern Atlantic was easy because the English could avoid the tropics, where their water and food often spoiled. Besides, colonists could find space aplenty on English fishing vessels that sailed to the cod banks with almost-empty ships since all they needed was salt and a few soldiers to guard them. God, he told his readers, had provided these blessings to the English, but they had resisted the offer. Once they had been bolder, when Richard fitz Gilbert de Clare, known as Strongbow, conquered much of Leinster in 1170 with limited forces. But more recent English temerity had enabled the Spanish to "conquer, possesse and enjoy" West Indian islands and expansive territory on the mainland, much of it "beautiful and full of treasure." Other Spaniards, with limited resources, had claimed even more: Balboa had only 70 with him when he claimed Panama; Cortés, with fewer than 500 soldiers, conquered the Aztecs; Pizarro, with only 210 under his command, captured and ransomed Atahualpa and brought back to Spain what Peckham claimed was 132,425 pounds (in weight, not sterling) of gold and silver. The Portuguese had similarly made extensive gains in Brazil, Africa, and South Asia.[67]

Peckham laid out a formulation that would soon come to dominate English thinking about the colonization of North America. If the newcomers could get the Natives to accept Christianity, other benefits would follow. With their spiritual practices in line with those of the English, Indigenous would be open to incorporating English-style agricultural practices. They would abandon their riotous ways of living and support a well-governed colony. The English would then be able to teach them the arts of civilization and, because they would be living side by side, the immigrants could defend the locals from "their tyrannicall and blood sucking neighbors, the Caniballes." Colonists would also eliminate sacrificial rituals that had taken "many of their poore innocent children." It

66. *NAW*, 3:53.
67. *NAW*, 3:55–57.

did not matter to Peckham that he claimed the presence of social ills in much of North America that did not exist. Like those who wondered about the five men Frobisher had abandoned in northern waters, the English presumed the worst.[68]

Gilbert promised that investors in the venture would receive land in direct proportion to their contribution. Each person who put in £100 would hold 16,000 acres in perpetuity. The investor or designee would also have the power to create feudal courts to handle criminal issues within a lord's manor as well as civil disputes like the enforcement of a contract. Stakeholders would pay a modest tax to Gilbert and promise one-fifth of any gold, silver, and pearls to him, with another fifth going to the queen. Those who invested less owned less—8,000 acres for those who put in £50, 4,000 for those who spent £25—but all of them had "free libertie to trade and trafique" in the newly claimed land.[69]

In Peckham's hands, Gilbert's plan survived longer than its creator. His pamphlet provided a template for other English ventures: identify a place along the expansive arc of Elizabeth's American claims, find a way to reach accommodation with the local residents, determine the commodities that could be extracted, export the labor necessary to bring desired goods to ships, and then entice investment even if that meant, as was to have been the case in Newfoundland, giving those who went there legal, economic, and political power they could never achieve at home.

In 1585, English sea captain John Davis went in search of the Northwest Passage, which he believed could be entered west of Greenland, a watery route that Frobisher had ignored. During his first journey he encountered Natives, presumably Inuit, and howled into the air in imitative response to the locals' cries. He had his musicians play instruments on board while other men danced and made "many signes of friendship." When the locals paddled out, the English mimicked one gesture—pounding the chest and pointing toward the Sun—which they understood as a sign of greeting. Soon enough, the Natives offered to trade with visitors. "They are very tractable people," the chronicler of the journey wrote, "void of craft or double dealing, and easie to be brought to any civility or good order," even though they seemed "to be idolaters and to worship the Sunne."[70] When Davis

68. *NAW*, 3:54.
69. *NAW*, 3:59–60.
70. John Janes, "The first voyage of M. John Davis . . . for the discoverie of the Northwest Passage," in Hakluyt, *Principal Navigations* (1598–1600), III:100–101.

returned the following year, some of the locals recognized him and his sailors and immediately offered their greeting. When Davis went ashore, he gave them eighteen knives. The next day a flotilla of perhaps a hundred kayaks came to see the English, bringing the visitors the skins of seals and stags, seal meat, the fur from white hares, salmon, cod, and other fish. Over time, the English began, as Frobisher's men had earlier, to collect a preliminary vocabulary of the Natives' dialect, including words for trade goods (oar, knife, iron, needle, coat, seal, bracelet) as well as commands necessary for commerce: *yliaoute* ("I meane no harme"); *unuicke* ("give it"); *canyglow* ("kisse me"), *maconmet* ("Wil[l] you have this?"); *nugo* ("no"); *quoysah* ("give it to me").[71]

Yet the English never shook their suspicion of the Inuit, whom they saw as idol-worshippers who tried to use witchcraft to advance their goals. Some of the Inuit were so eager to get iron and cloth that they ransacked English ships. Davis ordered his men to shoot into a crowd to frighten them with the noise, but the Inuit came back the next day. The situation did not surprise the chronicler, who saw their thievery as a predictable component of a savage culture based on consuming raw flesh, drinking salt water, and surviving by harvesting ocean resources only. Though Davis was furious that the Indigenous had stolen an anchor from one of his ships during the second voyage, he returned the following year and began to trade once again. [72] At times the deals seemed to Davis too good to be true, especially when the Inuit offered to give a boat or a coat in exchange for a single bracelet (which the natives called *ponigmah*, a word the English learned quickly). In the end the English managed to get twenty skins from the Inuit, who promised more if the visitors would accompany them ashore. The offer was apparently too frightening for Davis, who declined.[73] Like Frobisher, he decided to capture an Inuit man who, like Frobisher's victim, apparently died before he reached England.[74]

71. "The second voyage attempted by M. John Davis with others, for the discovery of the Northwest passage," in Hakluyt, *Principal Navigations* (1598–1600), III:103–105.
72. "The second voyage attempted by M. John Davis," 104–106.
73. John Janes, "The third voyage Northwestward, made by M. John Davis . . . for the discovery of a passage to the Isles of the Moluccas, or the coast of China, in the yeere 1587," in Hakluyt, *Principal Navigations* (1598–1600), III:112.
74. Michael Harbsmeier, "Bodies and Voices from Ultima Thule: Inuit Explorations of the Kablunat from Christian IV to Knud Rasmussen," in Michael Bravo and Sverker Sőrlin, eds., *Narrating the Arctic: A Cultural History of Nordic Scientific Practices* (Canton, MA: Science History Publications, 2002), 38.

When those who recorded Davis's futile efforts to find the passage included phrases employed by Inuit, they demonstrated that the English had learned much in the decade since Frobisher's voyages. Though there was no quick water route to the Pacific, the English read a great deal about American resources and how to get to various parts of the Western Hemisphere. Modern-day California would appear on English maps as belonging to the realm, but only someone with the navigational mastery of a Drake would be able to get there, at least for the foreseeable future.

The northwestern Atlantic was a different matter. Getting across the ocean, while dangerous, was feasible. That meant that transporting migrants became a viable possibility, especially if entrepreneurs made investments in ventures, thereby reducing the financial burden on the queen. But absent a major military invasion, which Elizabeth had no intention of launching in North America, the success of any colony still hinged on establishing positive relations with Indigenous. The English could tell each other that the Anglican Church, fealty to the monarch, and their culture were aspects of a civilization superior to that of the Indigenous. But such claims rang hollow when Inuit and others time and again proved their control of the north. If the English were to succeed in establishing colonies, they would need to set their sights on territory that resembled Britain, thereby making possible migration more attractive to potential colonists.

It had been almost a century since Columbus and the Cabots brought news of a previously unknown world to Europe. The Elizabethans' conquest of Ireland had revealed the violence the English would employ to control new territory. But it had taken a decade of exploration on the high seas and rumination within book-lined libraries and the halls of court policymakers to convince the English that the time had come to shift their energies from mounting voyages of discovery to provisioning ships bearing migrants eager to establish colonies.

9

The Algonquian Moment

On March 25, 1584, Elizabeth I granted Sir Walter Ralegh a patent "to discover search finde out and view such remote, heathen and barbarous lands, countries and territories, not actually possessed of any Christian Prince, nor inhabited by Christian People."[1] The charter reflected emerging opinion for the monarch and her court. Despite the violence unleashed by her soldiers during the previous decade, much of Ireland remained under the control of ancient chiefs as well as unreformed priests whose loyalty belonged to Rome, not Westminster. Even still, the knowledge generated by English explorers in North America contributed to a shift in Tudor sentiments, especially when reports of long-distance ventures fell into the hands of Richard Hakluyt the Younger, an ambitious and devoted promoter of the idea that the English should become more involved in overseas exploration, pursue new economic opportunities, and seek locales for possible English colonies well beyond Ireland. The intellectual ground for colonization evolved too because the queen and her advisors had grown increasingly concerned with Iberian, and especially Spanish, gains in the Western Hemisphere.

The Frobisher and Gilbert expeditions reminded the queen that the Western Hemisphere posed challenges that did not exist in Europe. The native Irish might be stubborn and formidable foes, but they shared a similar climate, offered comparable environmental possibilities, and, until Henry VIII, were in theory fellow members of the same confessional tradition. The issue following the return of Frobisher and the loss of Gilbert pivoted on a new question: could the English launch successful colonies in a region similar to Britain? During the 1580s, the English wanted to establish a colony on the Outer Banks of modern Carolina. This land, as far as they knew, remained free of other European claimants at the time, a belief that rested on the notion that French claims ended far to the north and the boundary of La Florida lay to the south.

1. Charter to Sir Walter Ralegh, 1584, Avalon.

But if the logic of colonizing this region made sense to some English and if Elizabeth eventually came to accept it as a pressing matter for her realm, they would need to find a way to either live with or conquer the Algonquian-speaking peoples of Carolina who controlled the Outer Banks and coastal Carolina. The English, who had confronted this same dilemma in Ireland, quickly learned that the Algonquians had a vibrant culture and a durable political system. This Native population would resist conquest and invasion just like Inuit, Crees, Guales, and others who had up to that point staved off European incursions along the Atlantic coast. More worrying perhaps was the fact that getting soldiers across the Atlantic would be far more expensive than sending them across the Irish Sea, which meant that would-be colonizers would have access to less military might than they had deployed in Ireland.

In the 1580s, the encounter of Elizabethans and Algonquians became pivotal in the history of eastern North America. At this moment, some English committed to the idea of colonization. But they still needed to convince others among their countrymen of the logic of making substantial investments in the wakes of so many exploratory disappointments.

Elizabeth's court stood at a crossroads. Explorers had brought back enticing reports, but there were as yet no English colonists beyond Ireland. Further, the Irish experience had suggested both the durability of others' cultures and the failure of the idea that non-English people would speedily embrace English ways. Once they became disillusioned by reality, colonial authorities shifted from campaigns based on cooperation to those based on coercion. Colonial administrator and landholder Sir William Herbert, drawing on personal experience in Munster and his knowledge of texts from antiquity, justified the harsh treatment of a native population. "Colonies degenerate assuredly when the colonists imitate and embrace the habits, customs, and practices of the natives," he wrote in the early 1590s about his time in Ireland. "There is," he added, "no better way to remedy this evil than to do away with and destroy completely the habits and practices of the natives." Only by threatening to eradicate existing cultures could the colonizers convince an indigenous population to embrace the newcomers' ways. "It will then come about that," he wrote, "once you have removed those things which can alienate hearts and minds, they will both become united, first in habits, then in mind."[2]

2. Sir William Herbert, *Croftus Sive de Hibernia Liber*, ed. Arthur Keaveny and John A. Madden (Dublin: Irish Manuscripts Commission, 1992), 81.

The new strategy necessitated the migration of women as well as men, in part to create new families to build a new social order and in part to keep wayward men from having children with Indigenous women. English political theorists of the time, some of them anxious that traditional sex roles might fracture, emphasized that married men and women who bore children created the foundations for a durable patriarchal society in which the authority of the father mirrored the power of the monarch. "A Householde is as it were a little commonwealth," puritan writers Robert Cleaver and John Dod explained in the early seventeenth century, "by the good Government whereof, Gods glorie may be advanced, the Commonwealth which standeth of several families, benefited, and all that live in that familie receive much comfort and commodity." If English colonies were to succeed in North America, creating the conditions for family formation was a paramount concern. No one in Elizabeth's or any other European monarch's court could know if such a plan would work nor how long it would take. The first century of European expansion into the Atlantic had been dominated by men on ships. Would the next generation of colony builders recognize they would fail without women? The Spanish, for their part, had quickly formed sexual unions with Indigenous women and began to create new families from the West Indies to Peru, but they did so at least in part because so few Spanish women migrated across the Atlantic. The English, with the lessons of Ireland firmly in mind, eschewed that model.[3]

Even before Elizabeth's ascent, printers took the lead in spreading information that might encourage wider English interest in the possibilities available across the Atlantic basin. The publication in 1551 of an English translation of Peter Martyr's *Decades*, which chronicled the era of Columbian conquests, suggested interest about other Europeans' expansionary plans. Other writers and editors soon added yet more titles. Merchants and members of guilds became more active in long-distance

3. Robert Cleaver and John Dod, *A Godlie Forme of Householde Government* (London, 1610), quotation at 13; Alexandra Shepard, "From Anxious Patriarchs to Refined Gentlemen? Manhood in Britain, Circa 1500–1700," *Journal of British Studies* 44 (2005), 281–295; Lawrence Stone, *The Family, Sex, and Marriage in England, 1500–1800*, abridged ed. (New York: Harper and Row, 1977), 109–127; Nicolás Sánchez-Albornoz, "The First Transatlantic Transfer: Spanish Migration to the New World, 1493–1810," in Nicholas Canny, ed., *Europeans on the Move: Studies on European Migration, 1500–1800* (Oxford: Oxford University Press, 1994), 26–36. The central importance of families and how they should be ordered and maintained remained central to English writers' views of their domestic and colonial lives in the seventeenth century; see Mary Beth Norton, *Founding Mothers and Fathers: Gendered Power and the Forming of American Society* (New York: Alfred A. Knopf, 1996), 3–137.

trade. The Royal Exchange, built by investors eager to make London a hub for merchants across western Europe and to take business away from Antwerp, opened in 1571. As Sir Thomas Smith's experience in Ulster revealed, investors supported new corporations, proving that they were willing to finance colonization schemes if they saw the potential for opening new markets.[4]

The expanding Elizabethan mental horizons commanded the attention of the younger Richard Hakluyt, who had become obsessed with learning about the world after he studied books and maps in the Middle Temple rooms of his cousin the elder Richard Hakluyt, a lawyer. By 1580, that interest drove him to edit a series of travel accounts to demonstrate England's authority to establish colonies in the Western Hemisphere. He became the most eager proponent of English overseas expansion, in America and elsewhere. The growing number of printed works of cosmography and geography provided additional information for those keen to expand their intellectual horizons—or perhaps even contemplate migration.[5]

Despite the proliferation of printing presses in London and elsewhere, details about travels abroad, like other information, continued to circulate via manuscripts passed from hand to hand as well as in daily conversation. Those who wanted to promote colonization needed to establish and maintain political connections, enabling them to share the information they received with those at the institutions that would shape English

4. See Edward Arber, ed., *The First Three English Books on America* (Birmingham, 1885); Stephen Alford, *London's Triumph: Merchants, Adventurers, and Money in Shakespeare's City* (New York: Bloomsbury, 2017); Philip J. Stern, *Empire, Incorporated: The Corporations That Built British Colonialism* (Cambridge, MA: Harvard University Press, 2023), 16–48. The phenomenon was not limited to England; in 1556, a Venetian civil servant published a large volume of travel accounts about the Western Hemisphere translated into Italian, one of three expansive volumes of travel accounts; see Giovanni Battista Ramusio, *Navigationi et Viaggi*, 3 vols. (Venice, 1554–1559).

5. Richard Hakluyt, *The Principall Navigations, Voiages, and Discoveries of the English Nation* (London, 1589), sig. *2[r]; Leslie B. Cormack, *Charting an Empire: Geography at the English Universities, 1580–1620* (Chicago: University of Chicago Press, 1997); Mary Fuller, *Lines Drawn Across the Globe: Reading Richard Hakluyt's Principal Navigations* (Montreal: McGill-Queen's University Press, 2023); Sebastian Münster, *Cosmographia Universalis Liver VI* (Basel, 1552); Sebastian Münster, *La Cosmographie Universelle* (Paris, 1552); Elizabeth L. Eisenstein, *The Printing Press as an Agent of Change: Communications and Cultural Transformations in Early-Modern Europe*, rev ed. (Cambridge: Cambridge University Press, 1980), 109; [Andrew Borde], *The first boke of the Introduction of knowledge* [London, 1562], sig. B1[r] (on the importance of London); William Cunningham, *The Cosmographicall Glasse . . .* (London, 1559); Rodney W. Shirley, *The Mapping of the World: Early Printed World Maps, 1472–1700* (London: Holland Press, 1983), 28–31, 113–137; Peter C. Mancall, *Hakluyt's Promise: An Elizabethan's Obsession for an English America* (New Haven, CT: Yale University Press, 2007), 19–24.

policy—with the queen and her advisors, in the legal offices of the Inns of Court, and among the growing number of merchants in London, as well as in Bristol, Plymouth, and other ports where profits could be made from the shipping trades.[6]

The economic benefits that could accrue to the English seemed obvious enough. After all, the riches that the Spanish had extracted had enabled them to establish a global commercial network that took silver and gold from Mexico to the Philippines in exchange for silks, spices, and other East Asian goods, which Spanish fleets then hauled back to Acapulco for eventual transit to the Gulf of Mexico. There, East Asian goods filled crates next to gold, silver, and feathers that the Spanish shipped, via the Florida Strait, to Seville and from there across the realm. Philip II, a master at displaying the power that such material gains made possible, was for a time the wealthiest monarch in Europe and—as far as Europeans were concerned—in the world.[7]

English writers argued that creating colonies could solve domestic problems as well, especially what they perceived as a population that had expanded too quickly after the demographic collapse brought by the Black Death in the late 1340s. Like the climate change that had led to the dispersal of Cahokia's residents, this fourteenth-century calamity had expanded possibilities for survivors. In England, the plague had killed thousands—perhaps up to 45 percent in some areas.[8] But in the decades that followed, England's population reached 3.25 million by 1570 and was increasing thereafter by perhaps over 20,000 each year.[9]

Population recovery created problems as well as opportunities. By the middle of the sixteenth century, writers argued that the realm was becoming too crowded. Fortunately, as they saw things, wealthy landowners had begun to reorganize their holdings, embracing the idea that it was time to evict long-term tenants from small farms to create larger fields, a process known as enclosure. The shift constituted nothing less than a revolution

6. On the continuation of manuscripts, see Harold Love, *Scribal Publication in Seventeenth-Century England* (Oxford: Oxford University Press, 1993); on trade and merchants, see Alford, *London's Triumph* and David Harris Sacks, *The Widening Gate: Bristol and the Atlantic Economy, 1450–1700* (Berkeley: University of California Press, 1991).
7. See Henry Kamen, *Philip of Spain* (New Haven, CT: Yale University Press, 1997), esp. 178–210.
8. For estimates of the population at the time see Andrew Hinde, *England's Population: A History Since the Domesday Survey* (London: Hodder Arnold, 2003), 38–52; John Hatcher, *Plague, Population and the English Economy, 1348–1530* (London: Macmillan for the Economic History Society, 1977), 21–30.
9. By the turn of the seventeenth century the realm's population reached 4.07 million; see E. A. Wrigley and R. S. Schofield, *The Population History of England, 1541–1871* (Cambridge, MA: Harvard University Press, 1981), 531–532.

in land use. For centuries, the majority of rural families across much of Europe had tended relatively small farms, with about enough land to provide them with much of the food they consumed. Most kept some livestock and gained cash by selling the surplus—eggs from their chickens, perhaps, or more likely wool from their sheep and the meat of their pigs. But the post-plague population explosion encouraged many landlords to raise rents, driving off families living at the economic margin. Many of those families migrated to small towns, where they looked for work. Those unable to make a living moved to larger, regional cities. If their search for employment still did not produce enough revenue for their families, they turned to still larger cities, especially to London. The capital's population boomed in the last decades of the century, crowding against and beyond the walls of the medieval city. The landowners, for their part, then reorganized the lands, concentrating especially on raising sheep for the woolens industry—a business that, because of the growth of population and the larger number of connections between English merchants and consumers, increased dramatically during Elizabeth's reign.[10]

The domestic migration of families was not a new phenomenon for the English or for other Europeans since young people had been moving from village to village for decades.[11] But English observers believed that they were witnessing a dangerous increase in the number of young, unattached men who lacked the social ties that would restrain them from doing harm. Some writers recorded stories of young men roving in gangs, assaulting innocent bystanders, and engaging in impermissible sexual behavior. Social critics, voicing their concerns in fast-produced and inexpensive

10. On medieval and European rural economies, see Marc Bloch, *French Rural History*, trans. Janet Sondheimer (Berkeley: University of California Press, 1970); and Joan P. Thirsk, "Enclosing and Engrossing," in Joan P. Thirsk, ed., *The Agrarian History of England and Wales* (Cambridge: Cambridge University Press, 1967), IV:200–255; for internal migration within Britain, see James P. P. Horn, "Servant Emigration to the Chesapeake in the Seventeenth Century," in Thad Tate and David Ammerman, eds., *The Chesapeake in the Seventeenth Century* (Chapel Hill: University of North Carolina Press for the Institute of Early American History and Culture, 1979), 51–95; for the shift in economic attitudes, see Joyce Appleby, *Economic Thought and Ideology in Seventeenth-Century England* (Princeton, NJ: Princeton University Press, 1978), 28, 54–55, 59; for the effects of enclosure, see Robert C. Allen, *Enclosure and the Yeoman: The Agricultural Development of the South Midlands, 1450–1850* (Oxford: Oxford University Press, 1992), esp. 24–55.

11. See George Fertig, "Transatlantic Migration from the German-Speaking Parts of Central Europe, 1600–1800: Proportions, Structures and Explanations," in Canny, ed., *Europeans on the Move*, 192–235; and Nicholas Canny, "In Search of a Better Home? European Overseas Migration, 1500–1800," in Canny, ed., *Europeans on the Move*, 263–283.

pamphlets, believed that some of these able-bodied young men might have fallen under the sway of demonic forces. The rising public criticism signaled a shift from medieval times, when beggars who accepted charity served a vital public service by allowing those with greater resources to demonstrate their beneficence and hence their character. But that idea had been embedded in an idea of Christian charity associated with Rome. After Henry VIII dissolved monasteries across England, many poor families, which had earlier relied on the support of religious institutions, became wandering vagrants, kept alive by charitable institutions but no longer socially valuable. Few starved to death in Tudor England, but the growing visibility of the poor sent warning signals to those concerned with the future of the realm.[12]

The problem was most acute in London, the primary magnet for the displaced as well as home to the largest number of printers and social critics. In 1550, the city had 120,000 residents. From then until the end of the century, its numbers grew by an average of 1,600 annually, reaching 168,000 in 1580. From 1550 to 1600 the number of people who needed at least some relief tripled. Desperate for solutions and fearing that poverty could encourage criminal behavior, courts meted out severe punishments to send a message about the need to protect property. The result was a dramatic expansion of individuals sentenced to death, many for crimes as minor as petty theft. The great majority eluded execution, but they crowded the jails, which were inadequate to handle what was in essence a problem of population growth outstripping the capacity of the economy to absorb new workers.[13]

Domestic social changes at home provided an opening for those eager to increase England's power on a global stage. Among the most avid of these promoters were the two Richard Hakluyts, who understood both the growing complexity of the realm's emerging ambitions and the desirability of co-existing with rather than conquering Indigenous Americans. The elder Hakluyt believed that the English needed to colonize North America to advance three simple goals. "The ends of this voyage are these," he wrote:

12. A. L. Beier, *Masterless Men: The Vagrancy Problem in England, 1560–1640* (London: Methuen, 1985), 4–8, 40, 56, 69, 73, 85; Joyce Youings, *Sixteenth-Century England* (Harmondsworth, UK: Penguin, 1984), 254–259.

13. Rates of growth here are an average based on the increase in the city's population from 120,000 in 1550 to 200,000 in 1600. Beier, *Masterless Men*, 40, 164–169; Paul Slack, *Poverty and Policy in Tudor and Stuart England* (London: Longman, 1988), 69–71.

1. To plant Christian religion.
2. To trafficke
3. To conquer.

Or, to doe all three.[14]

He clung to the hope that relations with Native Americans might be mutually beneficial as well as peaceful. That belief prompted him to urge restraint in the inevitable clashes that were always part of colonization. "If seeking revenge on every injurie of the Salvages we seeke blood & raise war," he suggested, "our Vines, our Olives, our Figge trees, our Sugar-canes, our Orenges and Limons, Corne, Cattell, & c. will be destroyed, and trade of merchandise in all things overthrowen." If this were to happen, "the English nation there planted and to be planted, shalbe rooted out with sword and hunger."[15]

English promoters with the model of Ireland in mind would have known that the queen might be willing to offer patents to land but so far had eschewed the chance to make direct investment in overseas exploration or possible settlement. This strategy, which differentiated her from monarchs on the continent who had proved more willing to make personal or state investments in such ventures, meant that those who wanted to establish colonies needed to raise capital for ships and supplies. They had to recruit artisans to build new towns and ships and prepare American resources for European consumers. Most of all, they needed to convince others that the rewards justified risks that could include financial failure, lost revenue, possible capture, and death. The queen's aversion to making a direct investment beyond allowing her subjects to colonize lands she believed she owned under the doctrine of discovery led would-be colonizers to create joint-stock companies. Investors looking much farther afield launched companies to support shipping into territory where English men and women had commercial if not, at first, territorial ambitions.[16]

In this moment of royal hesitation, the younger Hakluyt saw his chance. He had emerged on the public scene in 1580 when he had parts of Jacques Cartier's narratives, earlier published by Ramusio, translated into English by Oxford-based linguist John Florio. Two years later he produced a small book entitled *Divers Voyages Touching the Discovery of America and the Ilands Adjacent*, which brought together an eclectic blend of accounts of the Western Hemisphere that Hakluyt believed laid out an English claim for

14. *NAW*, 3:64–66.
15. *NAW*, 3:66, 68.
16. See Philip J. Stern, *Empire, Incorporated: The Corporations That Built British Colonialism* (Cambridge, MA: Harvard University Press, 2023), 29–48.

owning parts of the American coast.[17] That book came to the attention of Sir Francis Walsingham, one of Elizabeth's closest advisors, who quickly dispatched Hakluyt to Paris as a spy to gather more information about the Western Hemisphere. Hakluyt accepted, even though it meant turning down the chance to join an expedition across the Atlantic. While in Paris, Hakluyt spoke to people who had knowledge about Europeans who had traveled abroad, including at least one merchant in Rouen who was involved in the fur trade. Hakluyt informed Walsingham that the French were planning "to send out certayne ships to inhabite some place for the north part of America." On board were to be missionaries, though Hakluyt thought their migration was not imminent.[18]

In 1584, he made his pitch directly to the queen. In a long manuscript known now as the *Discourse of Western Planting*, he expanded—and made more poignant—the arguments he had learned from his cousin. He emphasized the religious benefits of such an investment, arguing that English settlements would add substantial territory for expanding reformed Christendom, thereby enhancing Elizabeth's reputation as the Protestant European monarch most devoted to the cause. Success in the missionary field would limit the spread of Catholicism, one of the primary goals of Spanish, French, and Portuguese monarchs. Hakluyt pointed out that English travelers who had ventured into territories claimed by Philip II had been forced "to flinge their Bible and prayer Bokes into the sea, and to forsweare and renownce their religion and conscience and consequently theyr obedience" to the queen. Politics and religion could not be separated here. The Spanish conquest had generated wealth that enhanced the prominence of first Charles and then Philip II, "the great Antechriste of Rome" who used the haul of American gold and silver to fund ever-greater threats to the English realm. Building and keeping English ships in the Western Hemisphere would provide a way to raid Spanish ships, perhaps up to 200 vessels fishing in the waters off Newfoundland alone. By

17. John Florio, *A Shorte and briefe narration of the two Navigations and Discoveries to the Northweast partes called Newe France* (London, 1580), a translation from Ramusio, *Navigationi et Viaggi* 3:435–553; David B. Quinn, *Richard Hakluyt, Editor* (Amsterdam: Theatrum Orbis Terrarum, 1967), 7; Richard Hakluyt, *Divers Voyages* (London, 1582).

18. Hakluyt to Walsingham, January 7, 1584, in E. G. R. Taylor, ed., *The Original Writings and Correspondence of the Two Richard Hakluyts*, Hak. Soc., 2nd Ser., 76–77 (London: Hakluyt Society, 1935), 1:207; for Hakluyt in Paris and declining his chance to join a 1583 expedition to Newfoundland, see Mancall, *Hakluyt's Promise*, 102–127.

robbing Spanish ships, the English could help bring down Phillip II "from his high Throne, and make him equal to the Princes his neighbours."[19]

In case the religious and economic arguments proved insufficient, Hakluyt urged Elizabeth to recognize that the cause of justice demanded English intervention. Someone, he wrote, needed to recognize that "the Spaniardes have executed most outrageous and more th[a]n Turkishe cruelties in all the west Indies." As a result, they have become "odious" to peoples across the Caribbean "whoe would joyne with us or any other moste willingly to shake of[f] their moste intolerable yoke." There was also glory to be had since establishing English settlements in the Western Hemisphere would presumably assist any new efforts to find the Northwest Passage, which Hakluyt and others remained convinced could still be found. If the English could create outposts on American shores, especially in places with easy access to naval stores to replace broken masts, torn sails, or leaky hulls, ships that might otherwise be in danger of becoming lost would have recourse to friendly harbors. They could also restock their supplies, thereby avoiding the problems that frequently beset travelers on long-distance journeys where mold and rats both put food in a hold at risk.[20]

In the final analysis, Hakluyt pressed legal and practical arguments. Her title, he wrote, was "more lawfull and righte then the Spaniardes or any other Christian Princes." He dismissed the significance of Alexander VI's 1493 Bull of the Donation (*Inter caetera*), noting that Alexander was a Spaniard and hence never had the interests of other Europeans in mind, a situation that would have been more exasperating after the Reformation splintered European Christendom. To further entice her, he detailed the natural resources to be extracted from American forests, identified the geographical advantages that the English possessed because of their location in northwest Europe, and explained how mines or woolen factories would be ideal workplaces for the unemployed who threatened domestic peace and crowded prisons awaiting execution. He even provided details about what English men and women would need when they crossed the ocean, including chickens, pigs, rabbits, mastiffs, and bloodhounds. Artisans would ensure that the migrants could create communities quickly, and physicians, surgeons, and pharmacists would keep them healthy. Ships should transport books too, including travel narratives to explain what

19. Richard Hakluyt, *A Particuler Discourse concerninge the Greate Necessitie and Manifolde Commodyties that are like to growe to this realme of Englande by the Westerne Discoveries lately attempted, known as Discourse of Western Planting*, ed. David B. Quinn and Alison M. Quinn, Hak. Soc., Extra Ser., 45 (London: Hakluyt Society, 1993) (henceforth *Discourse of Western Planting*), quotation at 4, 67–71 (economic argument).

20. Hakluyt, *Discourse of Western Planting*, 52 ("Turkishe cruelties"), 80–87 (Northwest Passage).

migrants would face and legal testimonies detailing the rights of discovery. Once on the ground, leaders should compose legal codes, an effort to govern loyal subjects 3,000 miles from domestic law enforcement authorities.[21]

While his argument to the queen was private, the younger Hakluyt also made a bold public move when he arranged for translator James Aliggrodo to craft an English-language edition of Las Casas's searing book alleging Iberian atrocities. Hakluyt had it published as *The Spanish Colonie*, sending the unsubtle message that brutality was inherent in Iberian culture, another sign that Luther, Calvin, Henry VIII, and Elizabeth were right in their condemnation of Rome.[22]

The Carolina Algonquians had likely first encountered Europeans when Ayallón tried to establish his settlement in 1526. There is a good chance that they could have encountered the Spanish Jesuits who hoped to set up a mission at Ajacan. But in 1584, the year Ralegh received his patent, these Natives had not yet experienced sustained contact with Europeans. Infectious disease had not yet taken a toll; no European manufactured goods had been incorporated into the local economy other than perhaps some nails scavenged from shipwrecks; no knowledge of Christian doctrine existed; no demands had been issued for their land so that immigrants could establish homesteads; no Old World livestock or plants had arrived. Their world was not a *tabula rosa*, but when the English disembarked, these Algonquians had not yet felt the seismic disruptions that the arrival of Europeans had inflicted elsewhere in the hemisphere. The Carolina Algonquians, like the Inuit and Coast Miwoks, controlled the first encounters.

These Algonquians had deep understanding of local flora and its importance. Silkgrass grew to two and a half feet tall without any effort, and the English newcomers thought they could make a silk-like fabric from it. Plus the area had silkworms as large as a walnut, which the English thought could help them rival silk producers in Turkey, Italy, Persia, and Spain. Hemp, useful to the newcomers for linen and cordage, also sprouted on its own. The region also boasted natural supplies of alum as well as trees that could be used to produce rosin, tar, turpentine, and pitch. The

21. Hakluyt, *Discourse of Western Planting*, 88–112 (the queen's claim and refutation of the 1493 bull); 115–120 (gains of colonization), 120–124 (what to take along).

22. M.M.S. [James Aliggrodo], trans., *The Spanish Colonie, or Briefe Chronicle of the Acts and gestes of the Spaniardes in the West Indies, called the newe World* (London, 1583). For Hakluyt's own use of Las Casas's writings, see his *Discourse of Western Planting*, 52–60.

forests had an ample supply of oak, willow, walnut, fir, beech, ash, and elm, along with maple, which the Algonquians used to make bows.[23] They cultivated the medicinal plant *winauk* (sassafras), as well as *wasewówr*, *cháppacor*, and *tangomóckonomindge*, useful for dyeing clothes, hair, human flesh, mantles made from deerskins, and rushes woven into baskets. They cultivated maize, *okindgier* (beans), *wickonzówr* (peas), *macócqwer* (pumpkins or melons), and marigolds, which they used to make soup and bread. Their fields were so fertile that they never used manure but instead planted crops by poking holes in the ground and raking away the dried remains of previous harvests. They also harvested a variety of root crops and fruits. They tended *tsinaw*, similar to the China root that the English imported from the East Indies, which the Algonquians used to make bread and a tasty jelly. They grew *cofcúshaw*, which resembled West Indian cassava, for bread, understanding that the juice of the root was poisonous, so the plant needed to be processed with care. And they produced *uppówac* or tobacco, pulverizing the dried leaves to make a powder to be smoked in clay pipes. This plant cleared bodily obstructions and eliminated disease-causing phlegm. Like other Indigenous in the Western Hemisphere, the Algonquians employed tobacco in rituals to propitiate their deities.[24]

Algonquians' knowledge of animals and minerals reflected their long experience in the region. They caught otters, civets, and enormous numbers of deer; deerskins were the primary material for their clothing and an object they traded. Their forests had over thirty mammal species. They had names for at least eighty-six birds in addition to the twenty-eight the English recognized. To supplement their harvest, they ate a variety of shellfish, tortoises, and fish—including herrings, porpoises, sturgeons, and rays—many of them trapped in elaborate weirs. Coastal Algonquians had a horde of 5,000 pearls when the English arrived, with some so exceptional that the visitors fashioned a necklace for their queen from them. The strand reportedly disappeared during an ocean crossing.[25]

The Algonquians shaped the physical world to meet their economic and political needs. Town sizes varied, but most had at least ten longhouses in them and some up to twenty, with each of these housing between four and twenty individuals. Members of nearby communities could speak to each other, but linguistic differences became more apparent the

23. Thomas Harriot, *A briefe and true report of the new found land of Virginia* (Frankfurt am Main, 1590), 7–16, 22–23.

24. Harriot, *Briefe and true report*, 16–19 (*tsinaw* and *cofcúshaw*; fruits; tobacco).

25. Harriot, *Briefe and true report*, 9–11, 20–21; David B. Quinn, *Set Fair for Roanoke: Voyages and Colonies, 1584–1606* (Chapel Hill: University of North Carolina Press, 1985), 110, 138.

farther one traveled. Werowances and priests took leading roles in preserving the social order and punishing those who deviated from accepted norms. Male members of a family line maintained a community's records orally.[26]

The Carolina Algonquians' spiritual world, which included practices for handling human illness, was as well formed and as complex as their living arrangements. They believed that there were many deities, all in human shape. They paid respects to them by creating icons of these gods, who were known as *kewasowok* (sing. *kewás*). They prayed, sang, worshipped, and made offerings to the idols in temples known as *mathicómuck*. The Algonquians, like the English, believed that the soul was immortal and that after death it left the body and traveled to "the habitacle of gods, there to enjoy perpetuall blisse and happinesse, or els to a great pitte or hole." That less desirable place could be found far to the west, somewhere beyond where the sun set. They called this place Popogusso.[27]

In every respect, these Algonquians' world was in balance and stable. They had little need for European products, religion, or colonists. They also had no way to stop large ships from arriving on their shores.

On April 27, 1584, English ship captains Arthur Barlowe and Philip Amadas, sailing on vessels paid for by Ralegh, departed from England to explore lands between New France and Florida. When they returned in September, they provided Ralegh with a report, which soon circulated among learned chroniclers in London, including Hakluyt.[28] The voyage had been brief but notable, one chronicler reported, because the English returned with "two savage men of that countrie," a reference to the Algonquians Manteo and Wanchese.[29]

The crossing had been difficult, but by July 2 they entered an environment with air so fresh that Barlowe wrote that it reminded him of being in "the midst of some delicate garden, abounding with all kind of odoriferous flowers." They claimed possession of the modern Outer Banks "in the right of the Queenes most excellent Majestie, as rightfull Queene, and Princesse of the same." They followed with the conveyance of the queen's

26. Harriot, *Briefe and true report*, 24–26.
27. Harriot, *Briefe and true report*, 26.
28. "First voyage made to the coastes of America," in Hakluyt, *Principall Navigations*, 728–732.
29. David B. Quinn, ed., *The Roanoke Voyages, 1584–1590*, Hak. Soc., 2nd Ser., 104–105 (London: Hakluyt Society, 1955), 1:90–91.

grant "and letters patents, under her Hignes great Seale." They had done so according to what Barlowe called "the ceremonies used in such enterprises," which might have meant affixing the text and seal on a tree or post as a marker of English possession.[30] There were grapes aplenty and towering cedar trees finer than any known in the Old World. They spotted large flocks of cranes, herds of deer, and innumerable rabbits and birds. "I think in all the world the like aboundance is not to be founde," Barlowe wrote.[31]

On the third day three Algonquians came paddling out of a nearby stream. Two remained with their canoe while the third approached the English and spoke to them, but they could not understand what he said. Still, the visitors invited him onto their ship, gave him a hat and shirt, and offered him meat and wine. The man inspected the two ocean-going vessels and then returned to his canoe. Soon the English watched him haul in so many fish that they filled the canoe. He returned to the English, divided the fish into two piles, and offered half to the visitors. Then he paddled away.[32]

The next day a large party of Algonquians arrived including Granganimeo, the brother of Wingina, the king of the country. Granganimeo made what the English interpreted as friendly signs and spoke at length even though the visitors had no idea what he was saying. When he stopped speaking, they offered him presents, which pleased him. Within two days the English began to trade with the Algonquians, acquiring deer, rabbits, fish, fruit, cucumbers, pumpkins, nuts, peas, maize, and possibly bison skins in exchange for hatchets, copper kettles, knives, axes, and a tin dish. Granganimeo drilled a hole into the tin plate and threaded it through a string so that it would hang around his neck, "making signes, that it would defende him against his enemies arrowes," a reference to hostile neighbors. As Granganimeo became more familiar with the visitors he spent more time with them on their ships, where he consumed their meat, wine, and bread. Eventually he brought along his wife, daughter, and other small children, along with an entourage of fifty attendants. Granganimeo and his spouse both wore jewelry bedecked with pearls the size of English peas. Other women wore copper pendants and earrings.[33]

Over the course of the summer months, the English explored much of the region. Eventually they traveled to Roanoke Island, where they found

30. Quinn, ed., *Roanoke Voyages*, 1:91–94. Drake in 1579 and Gilbert in 1583 had engaged in similar acts; see Quinn, ed, *Roanoke Voyages*, 1:94n5.

31. Quinn, ed., *Roanoke Voyages*, 1:95–96.

32. Quinn, ed., *Roanoke Voyages*, 1:98.

33. Quinn, ed., *Roanoke Voyages*, 1:101–106.

nine cedar houses surrounded by a wall made of sharpened logs to repel enemies. Granganimeo's wife invited them in for a meal. While there, some of her attendants removed and washed the socks of the English and bathed their feet in warm water. They sat down to a feast of venison, boiled and roasted fish, pumpkins, and various fruits. The Algonquians mostly drank water but added ginger, black cinnamon, sassafras, and other medicinal plants. An inner room apparently housed a religious effigy. During the weeks that followed, the English learned even more about the many towns in the region, the impressive sound that separated the barrier islands from the mainland, and rivalries between communities that at times erupted into violence. After about six weeks the English, their task of claiming and assessing the territory accomplished, sailed for home. On board were two Carolina Algonquians: Manteo, a member of an elite Croatoan family near modern Cape Hatteras who voluntarily joined the expedition, and Wanchese, a subject of Wingina, who may have been kidnapped by the English.[34]

Back in England, Barlowe extolled the region and its residents. "We were entertained with all love, and kindnes," he wrote, and given everything they needed. "We found the people the most gentle, loving, and faithfull, void of all guile, and treason, and such as lived after the manner of the golden age," he added. "The earth bringeth foorth all things in aboundance, as in the first creation, without toile or labour."[35] This was a place that offered the English better prospects than any American destination they had already visited.

On April 9, 1585, a small fleet under the command of Sir Richard Grenville (a relative of Ralegh's) set sail on an expedition to plant the new colony of Virginia. Among those who sailed were Manteo and Wanchese, the Algonquians who had spent the winter in England, as well as Thomas Harriot and artist John White. Also on the expedition was Colonel Ralph Lane, who had been serving as a military commander in Ireland, another sign of the links between two lands the English hoped to control. Grenville sailed on the flagship, the *Tiger*, along with Simon Fernandes, who acted as the chief pilot and who had previous experience exploring the Caribbean. Amadas was there too, eager to take up the position of admiral of the new colony. The ship had recently been refitted, which improved its capacity to sail across the ocean—though, as the English would eventually

34. Quinn, ed., *Roanoke Voyages*, 1:107–109 (feast), 113–114 (geographic knowledge), 115–116 and 116n (return home); Quinn, *Set Fair for Roanoke*, 39, 235.

35. Quinn, ed., *Roanoke Voyages*, 1:108.

learn, at a cost. In making the ship sturdier, shipmasters had made it so large that it could not navigate the shallow waters off Carolina. They were joined by the *Roebuck*, captained by John Clarke, another veteran of transatlantic exploration. The *Elizabeth* was under the command of Thomas Cavendish, who served as the commanding legal authority of the group. Ralegh sent the *Dorothy*, which might have been commanded by Barlowe. Each of the vessels carried weapons the English hoped would be sufficient to get them past any Spanish warships. Two smaller pinnaces, unnamed in the record but likely sailing alongside the larger vessels, completed the group. These six ships carried 600 men and boys, 300 of whom would remain to create the outpost when most of the ships returned to England to gather additional migrants and supplies. As the Algonquians soon observed, these ships had no women aboard, a sign that this was an advance guard preparing a settlement that would later attract women.[36]

Like many expeditions, this one started off well and then ran into trouble. All the ships made it unscathed from their departure at Bristol through the English Channel and the Bay of Biscay. But then a gale blew them apart off the Portuguese coast. Separated from the others, the *Tiger* made it to Dominica and then sailed to Puerto Rico. While they waited for the other English ships to arrive, the men at Guayanilla Bay set up a forge and began to cut lumber they would take to Virginia. They also built a new pinnace to replace one lost in the storm. Eight days later, the *Elizabeth* sailed in as well. None of the other ships arrived in the bay.[37]

In the weeks that followed, the English prepared to launch their colony. Grenville, the seasoned military commander, captured two small Spanish ships between Hispaniola and Puerto Rico and brought them back to the bay. Lane took one of the other ships to Salinas Bay and stole salt that the Spanish had stored there. On the twenty-ninth of the month the five ships—the *Tiger*, the *Elizabeth*, the new pinnace, and the two taken from the Spanish—set sail heading northwest, bound for Isabela. There they traded with the locals, who seemed to have no animosity toward the newcomers. Some of the English went into the fields to gather pineapples, plantains, and sugar cane. While they were there artist John White created his first images of American nature, creating pictures of crabs, scorpions, fireflies, an alligator and an iguana, and various kinds of local fruit. In the weeks that followed he would paint or sketch much of the coastal habitat he encountered, including the shoreline of the mainland.[38]

36. Quinn, *Set Fair for Roanoke*, 55–56.
37. Quinn, *Set Fair for Roanoke*, 57–60.
38. Quinn, *Set Fair for Roanoke*, 60–63; Paul Hulton and David B. Quinn, eds., *The American Drawings of John White* (Chapel Hill: University of North Carolina Press, 1964), II:plates 4 (crab), 6 (fireflies), 7 (scorpion), 9 (alligator), 8 (iguana), 10–13 (fruit).

After gathering what they could, the English set off for their planned settlement, skirting close to the Florida coast.[39] By the fourth week of June they had reached the Outer Banks. Disaster almost struck again when the *Tiger* became wedged on a sandbar, but a high tide lifted it after two hours. The hull was intact, much to the amazement of those on board, but the water had ruined some of their food.[40] In early July they reached Port Ferdinando, an inlet on Hatteras Island named for the pilot Fernandes, and discovered that two of the missing convoy, the *Dorothy* and the *Roebuck*, had already arrived. The English explored the area and soon heard that Wingina knew of their arrival. By the end of the month there were approximately 500 English men in the area. Though Grenville had hoped to leave about half of those available, he surmised that the stores would be inadequate to keep even 200 alive for long. By July 11, he concluded that the settlement would need to proceed with 100 men, who would be left on Roanoke Island. The English explored the local waters, made extensive contact with the Algonquians, and prepared what they hoped would be a sturdy settlement to protect those who remained behind. Grenville left on August 25, reaching Plymouth two months later.[41]

At the time Grenville departed, he surmised that the English had left enough men on Roanoke Island to maintain a new settlement. He was either indifferent to the complexities of the Algonquian world he and his men had encountered or so arrogant that he thought that these English, thousands of miles from home, in an unfamiliar place, would be able to withstand a deterioration in relations with the Natives. He could scarcely imagine what might have been obvious if he had just paid attention: they never had a chance.

After Harriot returned to London in 1585, he set about producing an account of the region the English now regularly called Virginia. He was probably in contact with Manteo, who had returned to England in June 1586 and become a crucial intellectual partner to the young mathematician embarking on his ethnography of the Outer Banks. Manteo sailed back to Carolina in 1587 and was baptized on Roanoke Island, a sign of his apparent spiritual conversion. In 1588, Harriot published his report about the 1585 journey in a small pamphlet, primarily to correct the historical record of English efforts in Carolina. There had been, he wrote, English expeditions to Virginia since 1584. But only the Grenville expedition

39. Quinn, *Set Fair for Roanoke*, 63; Quinn, ed., *Roanoke Voyages*, 2:744–751.
40. Quinn, *Set Fair for Roanoke*, 63.
41. Quinn, *Set Fair for Roanoke*, 63–82.

mattered because the journey the previous year had been too brief for the English to learn much about the place. Harriot believed that the subsequent journeys of 1586 and 1587 should be considered as efforts to resupply the colonists who remained behind, which included the first English women in the Western Hemisphere. He feared that the reports that had come back from those later visits had spread disinformation about Virginia. English travelers missed their regular food and soft beds, Harriot surmised, and as a result they found America "miserable."[42]

Harriot's task, as he saw it, was to provide a "true report." Toward that end, he broke his account into three parts: an enumeration of what he labeled "marchantable commodities" that enterprising English colonists might bring to market; a section on the natural resources of the region that could sustain communities; and a longer part that included his assessment of the "nature and manners of the people of the countrey."[43] He then offered the English reading public a more detailed assessment of an Indigenous community in the Western Hemisphere than any European had provided to date.

Having learned to speak the language from Manteo and Wanchese, Harriot was in a better position than any English man to that point to grasp subtleties of the local economy as well as elements of the local belief system. "There are many other strange trees whose names I knowe not but in the *Virginian* language," he admitted, a recognition of Indigenous natural knowledge. He admired their bodies, observing that the Algonquians "are notably preserved in health, & know not many greevous diseases wherewithal wee in England are oftentimes afflicted." The Algonquians had told him about two different men who rose from their graves to instruct the living to follow community mores. Harriot dismissed the stories as nonsense, but he recognized their social utility. The werowances and priests might have tricked their communities, he suggested, but their words helped preserve the social order. Those who still violated norms faced either corporal punishment, having their possessions confiscated, or execution if the crime was serious enough.[44]

Harriot used his understanding of Indigenous beliefs to argue that the English might be able to steer the Algonquians in a new direction by appealing to their religious sensibilities. He revealed that his strategy was based on having "special familiarity with some of their priestes," a benefit of knowing the local dialect. Harriot believed that these holy men wanted

42. Quinn, *Set Fair for Roanoke*, 232–235 (Manteo); Harriot, *Briefe and true report*, 5–6.

43. Harriot, *Briefe and true report*, quotations at 7 and 22.

44. Harriot, *Briefe and true report*, 22–23 (plant knowledge), 16 (health), 26 (religious beliefs).

to learn what they could from the visitors. The way forward for newcomers who wanted to establish a colony in the region was not through violence but instead through facilitating easier communication and sharing knowledge about the material objects that the English had with them: "Mathematicall instruments, sea compasses, the vertue of the loadstone in drawing yron, a perspective glasse whereby was shewed manie strange sightes, burning glasses, wildefire woorkes, gunnes, books, writing and reading, spring clocks that seem to go of themselves." These physical items had been unknown to the Algonquians, who Harriot believed saw them as "rather the works of god th[a]n of men, or at the leastwise they had bin given and taught us of the gods." This was the crucial opening. If the English possessed objects that had been given to them by their god, then that must mean this all-powerful deity must possess some special love for the visitors.[45]

Adopting a strategy that European missionaries had used earlier in efforts to convince non-Christians to embrace the newcomers' faith, Harriot believed he could use the Algonquians' fascination with English technology to introduce them to the teachings of Christian Scripture. He told those he met that the contents of the Bible contained the teachings of "the true and only God" and that salvation was possible if the Algonquians studied European scripture. Although he emphasized that the physical Bible was not crucial, the Algonquians craved contact with the book itself. Many, he wrote, would "be glad to touch it, to embrace it, to kisse it, to hold it to their brests and heads, and stroke all over their bodie with it." Twice, Harriot claimed, Wingina asked the English to pray for him when he became deathly ill. Others also prayed for their health and to protect their maize in a drought. Harriot took such comments as a sign that the Algonquians, having learned about Christianity through discussions with the English, might convert.[46]

Yet the Algonquians' apparent awe of the English visitors' god proved double-edged in the summer of 1585 when an unknown epidemic spread quickly among them. As Harriot wrote, "within a few dayes after our departure from everie such towne, the people began to die very fast, and many in short space." Some communities lost 20, but in others up to 60 and in one case 120 succumbed, a staggering rate of mortality given the size of their communities. This phenomenon took place only in towns that the English visited. The fact that Harriot did not recognize the symptoms suggests that this disease was likely not smallpox, which all English travelers would have known about since that virus was endemic in Europe;

45. Harriot, *Briefe and true report*, 27.
46. Harriot, *Briefe and true report*, 27–28.

scholars knew that it had struck in New Spain earlier, and many individuals bore lifelong scars from childhood episodes. The absence of recorded symptoms in the written record makes posthumous diagnosis impossible.[47]

The Algonquians believed that the English visitors must have been the agent for the spread of this death-dealing contagion. Some believed the disease "was the worke of our God through our meanes," Harriot reported, and that the newcomers would kill the locals without even approaching them. Such thinking supported a notion that spread among the Algonquians that the English were not human but in fact some other kind of entity. Their explanation for this theory rested on two indisputable facts. First, the only English to have arrived by the time Harriot wrote his report were men, suggesting that these travelers from across the ocean "were not borne of women, and therefore not mortall," but instead "were men of an old generation many yeeres past then risen againe to immortalitie," a notion not too far off their claims that some Natives had in the past risen from the ground. This idea made even more sense given the Algonquians' impression that, according to Harriot, the English visitors lacked interest in Algonquian women. Second—and just as revealing about the possible non-human nature of the visitors—none of the English became ill when the disease spread.[48]

With no effective treatment, the Algonquians determined that the English might not be as friendly as they suggested. Those who believed the English were not human saw the visitors as an advance guard, with more of an ancient generation of non-human men set to follow and complete the work that the first visitors had started. Some claimed that there were unseen English in the air who shot "invisible bullets" into them, a claim that fit Indigenous etiologies that disease sprang from matter inserted into a body. Local healers embraced this theory, which Harriot believed they used to cover up their failure to cure the disease.[49] Some of the Algonquians believed that the mortality had to have been caused by the English god "for our sakes," as Harriot reported, adding that the English thought this a reasonable explanation too. The signs of divine disfavor had appeared even before the ships sailed to the Outer Banks. There had been an eclipse of the sun, visible to the English during their voyage across the ocean, which Harriot reported had upset the Algonquians. There was also a comet that had appeared in the skies shortly before the illness began

47. Harriot, *Briefe and true report*, 28; Alfred W. Crosby, *Ecological Imperialism: The Biological Expansion of Europe, 900–1900* (Cambridge: Cambridge University Press, 1986), 199–200; John L. Brooke, *Climate Change and the Course of Global History: A Rough Journey* (Cambridge: Cambridge University Press, 2014), 343, 360, 432.

48. Harriot, *Briefe and true report*, 28–29.

49. Harriot, *Briefe and true report*, 29.

to spread. Since many English scholars believed that celestial disturbances could cause epidemics, a phenomenon that had been reported in Europe, the notion that the eclipse and comet prompted the epidemic made more sense at that time than it might otherwise appear now. In an age when no one understood how viruses and bacteria traveled, this explanation at least satisfied Harriot, who could rely on it to describe the course of the deadly disease without taking any kind of responsibility for it.[50]

The epidemic of 1585 took a toll, to be sure, but even Harriot recognized that the Algonquians remained in firm control of their territory. Rather than mock them for what others might consider such ridiculous notions as an army of invisible English men accompanying the travelers, he instead emphasized that they possessed a coherent set of religious beliefs that provided guidance. "Some religion they have alreadie," he wrote, "which although it be farre from the truth, yet bying as it is, there is hope it may bee the easier and sooner reformed." The Algonquians might be unlettered in an English sense in that they did not possess a written language. But the language they did possess was sufficiently complex that Harriot had to admit he could not record all their beliefs because his knowledge of the dialect was too primitive. The Algonquians were inquisitive, not sealed off. They wanted "to learne more than we had meanes for want of perfect utterance in their language to expresse."[51]

If the English could communicate more effectively and thoroughly with them, Harriot believed, the queen's subjects might be able to establish an overseas community that could survive. He believed that Natives and newcomers could coexist once the Algonquians learned "to honour, obey, feare and love us," a statement prompted by knowledge that English travelers had killed some of the Algonquians over issues that Harriot deemed minor. Even if some of the Natives deserved such harsh treatment, he was all too aware of the impact that violence could produce.[52]

Harriot understood that the rewards for the English would be enormous if the queen's subjects could find a way to conquer and then cohabit with the Algonquians. After all, those on the 1585 journey had arrived with only twenty days' worth of supplies, yet they lived for months on the fresh water and abundant food of the region, harvesting what they needed by adopting the tactics of the Algonquians. The air was perhaps healthier

50. Harriot, *Briefe and true report*, 29; Aubrey on Harriot (undated) in Quinn, ed., *Roanoke Voyages*, 1:388; T[homas] B[rasbridge], *The Poor mans Jewell, that is to say, a treatise of the Pestilence* (London, 1578). For contemporary English understanding of disease and contagion, see Joyce Chaplin, *Subject Matter: Technology, the Body, and Science on the Anglo-American Frontier, 1500–1676* (Cambridge, MA: Harvard University Press, 2001), 160–175.

51. Harriot, *Briefe and true report*, 25, 27.

52. Harriot, *Briefe and true report*, 29.

than that to be found at home, an argument that Harriot made based on the demographic observation that 108 English men had arrived and by summer's end only four had succumbed, and three of them had been so "feeble, weake, and sickly" that it was incredible they lived as long as they did. The English could make the round-trip voyage three times a year, further proof that this could be the place where, almost a century after hearing about Columbus's explorations, the English could at last create a viable community in North America.[53]

From early autumn 1585 until midway through the following spring, the English who remained in Carolina acquired pearls and fished for mussels. Some of the residents of Wingina's town helped the English set up weirs to catch fish, and at least some of the Natives also provided enough corn for the English to bring in a good harvest in April 1586.[54]

The English survived that winter, but they needed more supplies from England, which they expected to arrive in the next sailing season. But relationships the colonists hoped to maintain with local Algonquians fractured. One leader, Granganimeo, who had initially welcomed the English, died that winter. In late April Ensenore, another ally for the English among the Roanokes, also succumbed. After Granganimeo died, his brother Wingina changed his name to Pemispan. The colonists came to believe that he was organizing a military assault to oust them. To avoid military catastrophe, the English launched an attack against the Roanokes at the end of May. They pursued Pemispan and his followers, who had never wanted the colonists around, but also Manteo and his allies, who had seen an advantage in the newcomers' presence. During an assault on Dasemunkepeuc, the Roanokes' primary settlement, the English commander Ralph Lane (who believed the Natives had planned to execute him) claimed that he was trying to save Manteo's friends, but other English killed indiscriminately, believing "that none of the [Algonquians] should escape." English soldiers shot Pemispan, who managed to flee into nearby woods. An Irish servant named Edward Nugent found the wounded leader and decapitated him. The English impaled his head on a post.[55]

Conflicting reports about the Outer Banks circulated that season. Spanish observers, who had been watching English ships passing through

53. Harriot, *Briefe and true report*, 31–33.

54. Harriot wrote an account and White created a map of local communities, but both manuscripts have disappeared; see Quinn, *Set Fair for Roanoke*, 99–104, 123.

55. [Ralph Lane], "The second part touching the conspiracy of Pemispan," in Hakluyt, *Principall Navigations*, 742–747, quotation at 746; Michael L. Oberg, *The Head in Edward Nugent's Hand: Roanoke's Forgotten Indians* (Philadelphia: University of Pennsylvania Press, 2008), esp. 81–100; Karen Ordahl Kupperman, *Roanoke: The Abandoned Colony* (Lanham, MD: Rowman & Littlefield, 1984), 66–87.

the Florida Straits, believed that the English had likely established an outpost on or near the site of the former French effort at St. Helena, a sea island off the coast of mainland South Carolina. The *adelantado* Pedro Menéndez Marqués sent an exploratory ship to Cape Fear. The sailors returned without news, leading Menéndez Marqués to conclude that the English, who by then were engaged in a growing war with Philip II, must have landed in Chesapeake Bay, a location the Spanish knew about from their destroyed mission of 1570. The truth was less complicated: By June 1586, in the aftermath of the killing of Pemispan, the English colonists at Roanoke packed up to leave.[56]

While the English on the Outer Banks prepared to depart, they had an unexpected visitor. Sir Francis Drake had left England with forty-three English ships to attack St. Augustine. Believing that the Spanish were plotting to eliminate the English in Carolina, he launched an assault on the Florida fort on May 28, 1586. Pedro Menéndez Marqués, the commander, reported that Drake sent 2,500 men ashore and hauled four heavy cannons onto the dunes and aimed them at the fort. Menéndez Marqués, seeing no other options, abandoned the fort, which the English soon overran. "The enemy took and sacked the town and burned the church with its images and crosses," the Spaniard informed the Casa de Contratación, "and cut down the fruit trees, which were numerous and good." Drake and his men hauled off the weapons and food the Spanish had stockpiled in the fort.[57] "Everybody was left naked," the Spanish regional accountant Pedro de Valdés testified in August, "stripped of everything, in the open country, and without recourse."[58] The English also captured about 100 enslaved Africans. Their actions enraged Philip II, who ordered Menéndez Marqués to find the English colony, which he had heard was located on a river that ran through the interior of the continent to the Pacific. The king feared English pirates finding the route, which they could then use to their advantage.[59] The Spanish thought that Drake might return to cause

56. Quinn, *Set Fair for Roanoke*, 130–131.

57. Menéndez Marqués to the President of the Casa de Contratación, June 17, 1586, in *NAW*, 5:40. See the letter from local officials to the crown, June 17, 1586, and the deposition of a twenty-four-year-old illiterate sailor named Juan de Lepe, taken on June 30 at Havana, in *NAW*, 5:41. Also see the depositions of Bartólome Cordoriel and Francisco Hernández, taken at Havana on June 30, in *NAW*, 5:42.

58. The testimony is in *NAW*, 5:47–49, quotation at 49.

59. Philip II to Menéndez Marqués, November 27, 1586, in *NAW*, 5:57; for the number of enslaved, see Quinn, ed., *Roanoke Voyages*, 1:254.

even more damage, but he never did.[60] Despite their efforts, the Spanish never discovered the English.[61]

On June 8, 1586, Drake appeared off the Carolina coast, bearing plunder from St. Augustine that included windows, locks, and doors that the English believed would be of use in Roanoke, along with the formerly enslaved Africans. But a major storm, possibly an early-season hurricane, blew in on June 13, forcing the ships into deeper water so that they would not be grounded on the shoals and sands. One of the ships, the *Francis*, never returned.[62]

By June 17, Drake and Ralph Lane, the outpost's commander, agreed that the best course was to abandon Roanoke and load the surviving colonists onto Drake's ships. Limited space forced the English to leave some of their possessions behind, including notes and drawings made by Harriot and White, which some of Drake's men reportedly tossed into the water to make room for more survivors. Lane lost a rare string of black pearls that the werowance of Choanoak had given him. One of those who boarded the ship was Manteo, who decided to return to England, this time in the company of an Algonquian man named Towaye. On the eighteenth they set sail. Some of the ships headed north to gather fish off Newfoundland. Others sailed directly across the ocean. The *Elizabeth Bonaventura*, which had both White and Lane on board, arrived in Portsmouth on July 28.[63] There is no record of what happened to the enslaved men, though Drake likely left them free in Carolina, perhaps his way of atoning for his earlier participation in Hawkins's slave raids.

Lane learned later that in April of that year Ralegh had sent a ship with new supplies and additional colonists under the command of Sir Richard Grenville. They arrived at Hatteras after the other English had evacuated. Grenville's crew searched for survivors. But three who had remained behind had likely gone inland and did not hear of the arrival of the resupply ship. Unable to find any other English people, Grenville soon headed home.[64]

Before he set off, Grenville left fifteen men behind at the then-abandoned English fort at Roanoke. They did not last long. When the next English expedition arrived in the summer of 1587, they found the

60. See the letter from the Casa de Contratación to Philip II, September 5, 1586, in *NAW*, 5:52.

61. See the narratives of Vincent González and Juan Menéndez Marqués in *NAW*, 5:60–64, 66–68.

62. Quinn, *Set Fair for Roanoke*, 132–133 (Drake's assault on Spanish), 137 (storm).

63. Quinn, ed., *Roanoke Voyages* 1:301–303 (Drake), 308 (*Primrose*), 261 (loss of pearls); Quinn, *Set Fair for Roanoke*, 137–139.

64. Quinn, *Set Fair for Roanoke*, 140–141, 147.

post abandoned. White, who returned that year, learned from Manteo and others that Algonquians in the region, including those who lived at Dasemunkepeuc, Aquascogoc, and Secota, had decided to eliminate the English. The Natives tricked the first two English men they found, murdering one and allowing the other to run to tell his comrades that they were in danger. The Algonquians followed and killed several others, leaving nine survivors who managed to find their way to the beach, where they paddled their small boat into the sound. They picked up four other English travelers, who had missed the battle because they had been out gathering oysters. The thirteen soon vanished in the sea.[65]

Those who arrived in 1587, unable to find the fifteen left behind earlier, set about establishing yet another English outpost. They were by then all too aware of the risks of trying to create a durable settlement on Roanoke Island, but remained committed to the task. White, who was to be the governor of the community, believed that any colony needed women and perhaps children in addition to men. He imagined a transplanted English community that would become self-reliant and locally governed. White had thought that he could entice 150 possible colonizers to join him, though in the end he managed to lure only about 100. They set off for Carolina on May 8, when the winds were the most favorable for a safe crossing, even though leaving then meant that they would arrive too late to get their first maize crop in the ground. Among the travelers were Manteo and Towaye, returning again from England.[66]

Despite the first steps toward creating a lasting community, the situation on the ground in Roanoke remained tense. Some of the Algonquians shot sixteen arrows into an English leader named George Howe who had been in the shallows spearing crabs. To avenge his death, White led an assault on Dasemunkepeuc, the Algonquian town on Roanoke Sound, not knowing that it had been abandoned by its residents after the murder. When the English arrived, they attacked a group of Algonquians, only eventually realizing that they were Croatoans, who had previously had peaceful relations with the newcomers. The English halted their actions when they realized their mistake, but by then word of their actions had spread. Manteo, who was becoming more loyal to the English than to his own community, blamed the victims, who he thought should not have been there. Soon after, the English christened him the lord of Dasemunkepeuc "in reward for his faithfull service." He had risen farther in the English hierarchy than Wingina or any of the other Algonquians. White hoped that he would become the eventual leader of the entire island when the

65. Quinn, *Set Fair for Roanoke*, 150–153.

66. Quinn, *Set Fair for Roanoke*, 241, 267–269, 273, 279–280; Kupperman, *Roanoke*, 107.

English set sail for the Chesapeake, a better place to hide privateers fresh from raiding Spanish ships. Soon after, White's daughter Eleanor and her husband, Ananias Dare, celebrated the birth of their daughter, the first English child born in the Western Hemisphere, though one of the other women had arrived nursing a newborn. She was christened on August 24 as Virginia because, as White wrote, "this child was the first Christian born in Virginia."[67]

By then, most of the English had concluded that their precarious outpost could survive only if they received more people and goods from England. After an internal debate, they convinced White to make their case in London. They even presented him with an official record so that he could prove that he had not abandoned the others but instead returned at their insistence. His return was rough, but he eventually reached London, where he hoped to finish his task.[68]

Unfortunately for White, and for those in Carolina, tensions between the English and Spanish had exploded by late 1587. Philip II of Spain (who had also become Philip I of Portugal in 1580), enraged by Elizabeth's decision to execute Mary Queen of Scots that February and Drake's raids on his ships, decided that the time had come to invade Britain. He aimed to reestablish the authority of the Roman church and halt the English from harassing the Spanish and their claims in the Netherlands, Portugal, and the West Indies. In early July 1588 the Spanish Armada departed for England, entering the English Channel at the end of the month. But English commanders, through acts of trickery and skill, routed one Spanish flotilla off Flanders, and unfavorable winds forced many others out into the ocean or onto the Irish coast, where locals assaulted and murdered survivors. Though 130 ships had taken to the seas to vanquish the English, fewer than 60 returned home, some heavily damaged. The Spanish lost 15,000 sailors and soldiers, half of those they had dispatched on the mission. One observer wrote that the debacle, "one of the most notable disasters ever to have happened," produced "tears and lamentations throughout Spain."[69] In the years that followed, other Spaniards feared that the loss marked a period of imperial decline, an idea that seemed especially powerful to Spaniards who had likened their previous greatness to the glory days of Rome.[70]

67. Quinn, *Set Fair for Roanoke*, 282–287.
68. Kupperman, *Roanoke*, 122–123; Quinn, *Set Fair for Roanoke*, 288–294.
69. Henry Kamen, *Philip of Spain* (New Haven, CT: Yale University Press, 1997), 269–276.
70. See J. H. Elliott, "Art and Decline in Seventeenth-Century Spain," in *Spain and Its World, 1500–1700* (New Haven, CT: Yale University Press, 1989), 264. See Colin Martin and Geoffrey Parker, *Armada: The Spanish Enterprise and England's Deliverance in 1588* (New Haven, CT: Yale University Press, 2022), 16–17 (size of fleet), 553–559 (timeline of events).

On December 4, Queen Elizabeth went to St. Paul's Cathedral to offer thanks for the deliverance of the nation.[71] Ecstatic with the results of this "miraculous year," she had her portrait painted with her fleet depicted over her shoulder routing Spanish ships. Her hand grips a globe, with her fingers stretching across North America, a visual sign of her expansive claims.

While the actual warfare had gone better than English courtiers might have imagined, the threat that the Spanish Armada posed to England pushed aside any efforts to resupply the colonists on the Outer Banks. Unable to find a way to send provisions and new colonists to Virginia, White did what he could to fulfill the goals of the mission. He offered sketches of American insects to naturalist Thomas Penny, who was then creating a catalog of bugs. He gave herbalist John Gerard milkweed and smilax that he had brought from Carolina. He met with Hakluyt, who in 1589 brought attention to White's actions. He had become integrated into London's community of scholars and promoters, the group most likely to appreciate the watercolors White had produced in 1585. Eventually he found and stocked a resupply ship, but his vessel soon battled a French crew. Twenty-three of those on White's ship died. Unable to carry on, the ship returned home.[72]

White managed to return to Roanoke in mid-August 1590. But there were no colonists to be found, just an abandoned settlement. Someone had carved "CRO" onto a tree in one place and, near the destroyed former houses, "CROATOAN" on a second. Neither bore the mark of the Maltese cross, which White had instructed them to carve if they were in distress. A search revealed that someone had broken into White's three chests, tossing his precious items out to be ruined by the rain. White returned home with the news that the colonists could not be found. Despite intensive searching, no one has ever determined their fate.[73]

Before the destiny of the colonists could have been known, the younger Hakluyt had established a relationship with Flemish engraver Theodor de Bry, who was based in Frankfurt am Main. A conversation had likely

71. Martin and Parker, *Armada*, 440–442.

72. Quinn, *Set Fair for Roanoke*, 300–310; John White, "The first voyage intended for the supply of the Colonie planted in Virginia," in Hakluyt, *Principall Navigations*, 771–773.

73. David Stick, *Roanoke Island: The Beginnings of North America* (Chapel Hill: University of North Carolina Press, 1983), 204–246; Quinn, *Set Fair for Roanoke*, 327–412; Kupperman, *Roanoke*, 130–132.

taken place in London, where Hakluyt had returned after his years in Paris. By then, Hakluyt had emerged as the most active promoter of English colonization abroad. In 1589 he published an enormous compendium offering reports of English efforts to sail the seas of the world. The third part of that work, which focused on the Western Hemisphere, included thirty-three primary texts and another forty-three supporting documents and reports. Among the texts was a complete version of the account Harriot had published as a small book in 1588.[74]

The discussion in London led to an unprecedented partnership: Hakluyt shepherded White's surviving paintings to the de Bry workshop, where engravers appended a series of twenty-three plates based on the watercolors (or sketches) to the text of Harriot's *Briefe and True Report*. De Bry and his team also added an engraved title page that drew on some of the same visual elements as the watercolors, an engraving of Adam and Eve as their Eden began to collapse, and five images of the ancient inhabitants of Britain. Because neither Harriot's 1588 version nor Hakluyt's of 1589 included any images, the printing shop also added captions, possibly written by Hakluyt. When the engravings were done, the printers produced editions in four different languages—English, Latin, French, and German—which enabled them to reach an international audience of scholars (hence the Latin), others who would advance Elizabeth's agenda (the English version), other Protestants in the German-speaking territories, and French Huguenots. This was the first instance of any single printer producing works about America in four languages simultaneously. The text and images circulated far, including into the hands of other artists who created new versions of them as far away as India, where one painter crafted a version drawing on Mughal visual tropes.[75]

Besides the invented captions, which at times expanded on comments that Harriot had made in his original published report, the engravers took extraordinary liberties with the portraits. White had painted his subjects as if they were standing in a portrait studio with a plain white backing. The engravers magnified some of the musculature on the figures, especially the men, added images of what a subject looked like from the back as well as the front (even when there was only a surviving image of the front), and

74. For a list of the texts, see Hakluyt, *Principall Navigations*, sig. [*7^v–8^v].

75. Harriot, *Briefe and true report*, [35]; Michiel van Groesen, *The Representations of the Overseas World in the de Bry Collection of Voyages (1590–1634)* (Leiden: Brill, 2008), 112–116; Ute Kuhlemann, "Between Reproduction, Invention and Propaganda: Theodor De Bry's Engravings After John White's Watercolours," in Kim Sloan, ed., *A New World: England's First View of America* (Chapel Hill: University of North Carolina Press, 2007), 79–92; Mancall, *Hakluyt's Promise*, 195–196; "A Hunter and his Wife" (gouache, 1620–1630?), 2008,6014,0.1, British Museum, https://www.britishmuseum.org/collection/object/W_2008-6014-0-1.

"One of the Religeous men in the towne of Secota," according to this 1590 engraving by the de Bry workshop for Harriot's *Briefe and True Report of the Newfound Land of Virginia*, can be identified by his distinctive hairstyle and apparel. Courtesy of the John Carter Brown Library.

posed the subjects like figures who had walked out of a Renaissance atelier. The engravers enhanced the classical elements in the poses, making these Americans look even more like models from antiquity, another sign of the way that Europeans who had not yet seen any Indigenous Americans thought of them using ancient attitudes. More dramatically, they invented backdrops that did not exist in the originals. The "weroan or great Lorde of Virginia," for which the watercolor survives, stands on a hill overlooking a deer hunt. "One of the chief Ladyes of Secota" observes Algonquians spear-fishing from her perch at the water's edge. A priest from Secota, with his distinctive clothing and hair modeled on the watercolor, stands in front of Algonquians hunting ducks from a canoe.[76]

76. For analysis of the watercolors and engravings, see John Bakeless, *The Eyes of Discovery: America as Seen by Its First Explorers* (orig. pub. 1950; New York: Dover, 1989), 176–196; Mary Fuller, *Voyages in Print: English Travels to America, 1576–1624* (Cambridge: Cambridge University Press, 1995); Michael Gaudio, *Engraving the Savage: The New World and*

Because of the hurried preparations for the departure of White and Harriot, with men jostling for space on the rescue ships in the summer of 1586, some of the original materials disappeared. This meant that the engravers in Frankfurt either worked from sketches or watercolors that no longer survive or created images based on the descriptions that Harriot had provided. One of these invented images depicted two Algonquian men burning out a canoe in the foreground while others tend fires behind them, suggesting that additional canoes were to be created too. The image suggests careful planning: the tree being turned into a canoe lies perched on low racks, not lying on the ground; the men carving it out hold specific tools, including a small fan to control the fire as it worked its way through the wood. But even when the original watercolor existed, the engravers still modified the image, usually enhancing background details. The engravers also created a page that displayed the back of a tattooed man and a series of images that identified specific tattoos with particular places. With this image in hand, a visitor to Virginia would be able to identify those they met, a sign even before they began to speak about whether the local werowance would be friendly or hostile to the English.[77]

De Bry and the others understood that an image could serve as more than an illustration. Properly combined with a caption that described the action being depicted, the engraved image became yet another piece of evidence in an argument about the suitability of this part of the American coastline for European colonization. A bird's-eye view of the town of Secota presented an idealized rural village. The Algonquians could be seen feasting and celebrating, which could be read as signs of how far they still needed to travel to embrace English-style living. But the fields were fertile and locals had built nearby houses to sort their grain. The Algonquians even had figured out efficient ways to keep crows from stealing their corn. Nearby Pomeiooc had a wall around it and a cluster of buildings with specific functions.[78]

The explicit political function of the illustrated edition emerged in a series of engravings that the workshop appended to the Virginia materials. An unsigned note informed the reader that she or he was about to see pictures of Picts, the ancient Britons who had met the Romans centuries earlier, created from an old English chronicle. These pictures revealed "how that the Inhabitants of the great Bretannie have bin in times past as

Techniques of Civilization (Minneapolis: University of Minnesota Press, 2008); Hugh Honour, *The New Golden Land: European Images of America from the Discoveries to the Present* (New York, 1975); Hulton and Quinn, eds., *American Drawings of John White*; Sloan, ed., *A New World*; Harriot, *Briefe and true report*, sig. A^v–A2^v.

77. Harriot, *Briefe and true report*, sig. [B4^r] (canoe), [B4^v–B5^v], [D3^v] (tattoos).

78. Harriot, *Briefe and true report*, image XX (sig. [B3^v–C4^r]).

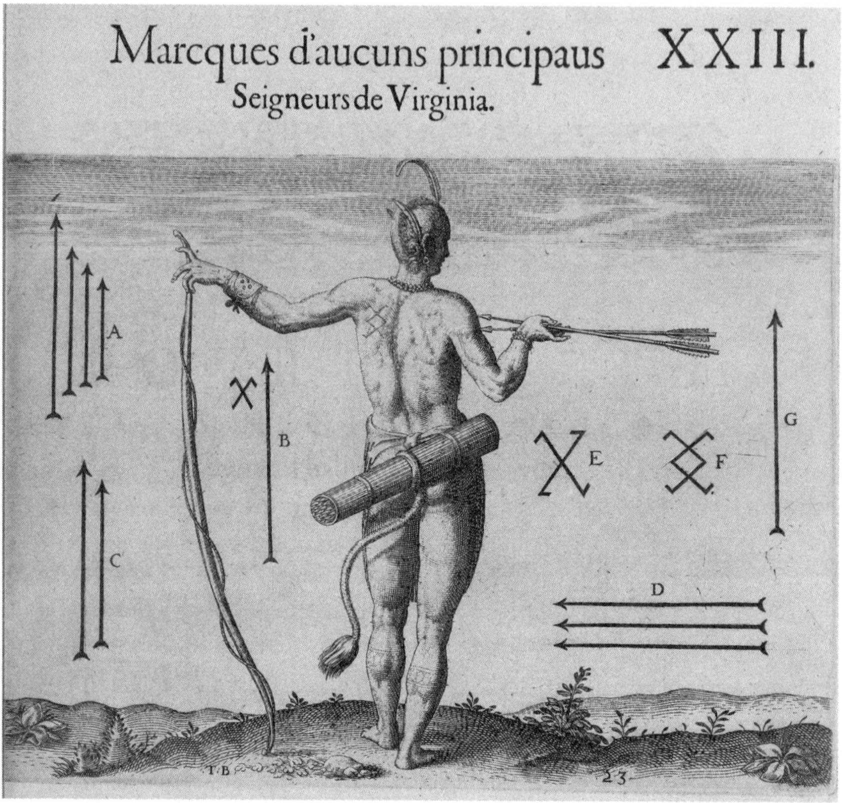

According to the caption for this engraving from the de Bry workshop, tattoos were common among Carolina Algonquians, usually marking "what Princes subjects they bee, or of what place they have their originall." Courtesy of the Huntington Library, San Marino, California.

sauvage as those of Virginia." That was a bit of understatement. The first image depicted a Pict man holding a head still dripping blood and another head lying at his feet. The next presented a Pict woman, who held three spears and had a broadsword attached to an unseen belt at her waist. Both are naked—unlike the Algonquians, who wore at least some clothing in every image—and both have more tattoos than any of the Americans. A third presented a young woman, who differed from the older model because she carried only one spear (though she still had a sword) and her tattoos were of flowers, suggesting a kind of savage innocence that would no doubt mutate into the more elaborate symbols of the adults.[79]

79. Harriot, *Briefe and true report*, sig. E^{r}–[E5^{r}].

The palisaded town of Poomiooc, inhabited only by "the kinge and his nobles," had a building (marked A) for religious rituals and a pond (marked C) dug to provide a local water supply. Courtesy of the John Carter Brown Library.

The images in the engraved version of Harriot's *Briefe and True Report* illuminated Indigenous culture on and near the Outer Banks. The depiction of the palisaded town of Pomeiooc identified the location of the religious house where residents kept their most powerful idol. An engraving of an Algonquian ossuary included ten naked male corpses, lying on a

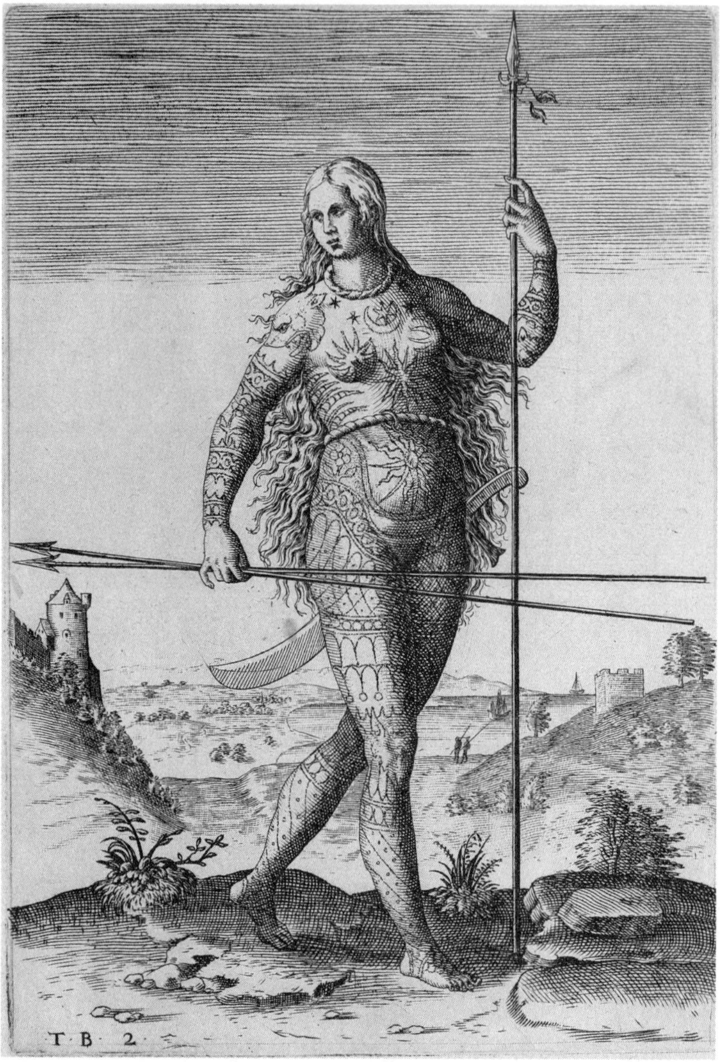

This "true picture of a women Picte" was one of five illustrations appended to Harriot's text to provide visual support for the claim that the native peoples of Britain, by which the engraver might have meant modern Scotland, had been savages too in ancient times. Courtesy of the John Carter Brown Library.

tall scaffold with an icon of Kiwasa attending them. Below them a priest tended a fire, which burned perpetually. He slept there as well, on two skins underneath the bodies. Kiwasa guarded these revered members of the community. One caption claimed that the Algonquians were so eager to learn the secrets of European Scripture that they grasped a Bible and ran it along their bodies, then gave the book back.[80] Eventually, Harriot promised his English readers, the Algonquians would embrace the cause of reformed Christianity. But not yet.

The English who had gone to Carolina after the first glowing report of Barlowe and Amadas had expected to do what no one from the realm had managed earlier: establish a surviving outpost on the coast of North America. But until they could figure out a way to live in the Western Hemisphere, the English would never be able to secure the territory they believed they owned as a result of the Cabot voyages almost a century earlier. The purported legitimacy of their claim had led the queen to carve out territory to award to her favorites Gilbert and Ralegh. The news of Drake's return from his circumnavigation proved to even the most skeptical that the English remained masters of ocean exploration, a point that Hakluyt argued too. The natural fertility of the soil and the water along the Carolina coast, the presence of pearls and copper (if not silver and gold), thick stands of tall trees, and abundant herds of fur-bearing animals all suggested that economic success could come soon to those willing to board a ship bound for America. Harriot's text minimized the sense of risk that had stood as a barrier to English efforts and promised spiritual as well as material gain, an issue of enormous interest to a queen whose military commanders had used terror to subdue Catholic Irish. From the encounters of the mid-1580s, Harriot seemed convinced that it would be possible for the English to achieve on the Outer Banks what they could not in Ireland. Since coexistence seemed possible, evident in Manteo's baptism and the knowledge he had provided to Harriot, perhaps there was no need for military conquest.

Harriot's text and de Bry's engravings represented a break from a set of ideas that had taken shape a century earlier. The reports from the age of the Cabots had been vague, lacking detail about everyday life as well as potentially marketable commodities. Harriot's visit and his discussions with Manteo (and perhaps Wanchese or two other Algonquians who also visited England) elevated English (and wider European) analysis of the potential of eastern North America, both as a source of a wide range of extractable materials and a population that seemed likely to embrace Christianity. Tales from the age of Henry VII lingered in hazy memories. Harriot offered reports grounded in scientific observation.[81]

80. Harriot, *Briefe and true report*, images XIX and XXII.

81. For the other visitors, Towaye (who had sailed to England in 1586 and returned to the Outer Banks the next year) and a man known as Rawley who died in England in 1587, see Quinn, *Set Fair for Roanoke*, 236.

As even the most determined English promoter realized, in 1590 this hoped-for world remained in the future. For the moment, it was the Algonquians who set the terms of the encounter. They suffered at times from the arrival of the English, but this remained their territory. The disappearance of the colonists left behind in 1587 served as a powerful reminder that neither the English nor any other European nation had managed to wrest control of the mid-Atlantic coast from those who possessed it.

10

After Roanoke

The disappearance of the colonists left at the Outer Banks troubled those in England paying attention to long-distance affairs. But their loss did not put a substantial dent in the plans of those who were still eager to propel England from a nation of explorers eager to learn more about the world to one of colonizers who would expand the realm, which seemed especially imperative given the fevered rivalry with Spain. The Spanish Armada might no longer pose a threat, but only a deluded English observer would conclude that the danger had passed forever, especially given ongoing conflicts within Europe pitting Catholics against Protestants. The path to a secure English future in the Western Hemisphere lay, as the Hakluyts had argued, through the establishment of colonies, the surest way to wealth and power for Europeans in the sixteenth century.

At this moment, the fact that the colonists had gone missing did not mean that the English should abandon potential settlement schemes. Harriot intended the publication of the engraved version of Harriot's *Briefe and True Report* to encourage others to take up the challenge of creating outposts of Britain on the western shores of the Atlantic. Still, that book did not resolve an open question: where was the best place to try again? Absent any clear indication of why the Roanoke settlers had disappeared or any way to know in the short run if other migrants to Carolina might suffer a similar fate, supporters of colonial plans sponsored initiatives to other Atlantic destinations, including the northeast shores of South America and the coast of modern Maine. These ventures included many of the individuals who had the most knowledge about the voyages to Carolina in the 1580s, including Sir Walter Ralegh, who retained the patent for the Outer Banks.

By the turn of the new century, those who wanted to establish colonies began to embrace new schemes for funding potential overseas communities in North America. The queen, they knew, was still unwilling to make personal or state investments in such ventures, which meant that her subjects who wanted to establish colonies needed to raise capital for ships and supplies. They had to recruit artisans to build new towns and ships and prepare American resources for European consumers. Most of all, they needed to convince others that the rewards justified risks that could still include financial failure, lost revenue, possible capture, and death. They turned their attention to the growing popularity of joint-stock companies, corporations that encouraged projects by distributing costs and risks among a pool of investors. Corporations had some legal benefits, including the ability to bring lawsuits and to exist in perpetuity. These schemes had the added advantage of concentrating capital for overseas investments. In the years when the fate of the Roanoke missing remained unknown, companies composed of individual investors who bought shares of stock to be managed by small groups of directors took the lead in England's efforts to compete against other European claimants for territory, resources, and possibly new homesites for those looking for work.

On February 6, 1595, Ralegh sailed out of Plymouth's harbor bound for Guiana. It had been five years since news reached London about the vanished colonists on the Outer Banks. He followed what was then the well-known route for ships departing from England bound for South America—past Grand Canary and Tenerife and then west to Trinidad, where he arrived six weeks later. There had been three ships in the small convoy, but Ralegh reported that by the time they reached Trinidad one was no longer in sight. He had high hopes for a profitable journey. His goals epitomized those of the Elizabethans who believed their realm should extend to the Western Hemisphere. But in this case, there was an added personal incentive since Ralegh's lands in Virginia had as yet produced no profit, added no honor, and proved sufficiently difficult that the English left in Roanoke had disappeared, either after abandoning their small settlement or perhaps when the Carolina Algonquians drove them away. Perhaps Guiana would be better for the first permanent English colony in the Western Hemisphere.[1]

The Orinoco River and the American territories near it dazzled and impressed Ralegh when he arrived at the island of Trinidad. While he awaited his comrades, he marveled at the natural bounty and began to trade with Natives even though he understood that the Spanish had already established outposts there.[2] Soon some Spaniards came on

1. Sir Walter Ralegh, *The Discovery of the Large, Rich, and Beautiful Empire of Guiana*, ed. Robert H. Schomburgk, Hak. Soc., 1st Ser., III (London, 1848), 135–140; Sir Walter Ralegh, *Discoverie of the Large, Rich, and Bewtiful Empyre of Guiana* (London, 1596), 1.
2. Ralegh, *Discoverie*, 2–3; Neil L. Whitehead, ed., *The Discoverie of the Large, Rich, and Bewtiful Empyre of Guiana by Sir Walter Ralegh* (Norman: University of Oklahoma

board his ship to purchase linen. Sensing that they might view an English ship with suspicion, he told them that he planned only a brief stopover on Trinidad on his way to refresh the English in Virginia, whom the Spaniards had likely known about but perhaps not realized their fate. While on the island Ralegh also met with some Acarewanas, who told him that Anthonio de Berreo, the local *adelantado*, threatened to kill any Indigenous who boarded an English ship. Ralegh's men, no doubt under their commander's orders, captured Berreo. Ralegh, echoing the rhetoric of Las Casas, thought he was a sadistic tyrant who kept Indigenous "in chains, & dripped their naked bodies with burning bacon, & such other torments." Ralegh claimed he saw five caciques chained together starving.[3] Despite the horrific crimes he believed the Spaniard had perpetrated, Ralegh treated his prisoner well since the *adelantado* was a pedigreed gentleman who had served his monarch valiantly in Naples, Milan, and the Netherlands. The English adventurer, more interested in gathering intelligence about the Orinoco, soon let Berreo go. Perhaps in thanks, the *adelentado* divulged that the heart of a great Indigenous empire lay 600 miles upriver. Ralegh, apparently undaunted by the challenge of reaching such a destination, kept this information from his countrymen since he feared many might refuse to go if they knew how far they had to travel.

After the delayed English ship arrived, Ralegh prepared to head to the mainland. Before leaving he had his interpreter, who had been living in England, explain to the Acarewanas that he was "the servant of a Queene, who was the great *Casique* of the north, and a virgin, and had more *Casiqui* under her th[a]n there were trees in their Iland." He told them that she fought against the tyranny of the Castilians, had liberated the northern parts of the world from their grip, and would soon free them. He then pulled out a likeness of Elizabeth I, later claiming they "admired and honored" the image so much that he thought they might venerate it as an idol.[4]

The information that Ralegh gathered in Trinidad, along with what he had learned from reading older reports by Spanish chroniclers Pedro Cieza de Léon and Francisco López de Gómara, convinced him that the empire of Guiana lay due east of Peru, just south of the equator. He expected to find more gold than the Spanish had discovered in Peru,

Press, 1997), 132n17. In his book Ralegh referred specifically to Thevet's *Les singularitez de la France Antarctique, autrement nommée Amerique* (Paris, 1557), which had been translated into English by Thomas Hacket and published as *The New Found Worlde, or Antarctiche, wherein is contained wonderful and strange things, as well of humaine creatures, as beastes, fishes, foules, and serpents, trees, plants, mines of gold and silver . . .* (London, 1568).

3. Ralegh, *Discoverie*, 4–6.

4. Ralegh, *Discoverie*, 7.

housed in magnificent cities more impressive than the Incans'. He believed that Manoa, its reputed capital, was without equal. Spaniards called it El Dorado and believed it was the richest city in the world. Soon enough, Ralegh entered the Orinoco, dreaming of the wealth and glory he could bring to his queen.[5]

The Orinoco drains a vast territory—most of present-day Venezuela as well as parts of Colombia. From its headwaters it meanders for almost 1,700 miles, with water levels rising and falling based on proximity to mountain runoff. Temperature varies only slightly throughout the year, though rainy and dry seasons alternate and give the impression of seasonal change. The indigenous Warao gave the river its name, which meant "a place to paddle." Those who navigated their canoes or other shallow-drafting boats in its waters could witness natural creatures of stunning beauty, such as the scarlet ibis and flamingo among the 1,000 species of birds that reside there, as well as a pink river dolphin. Danger lurked too, especially in the water, where electric eels, piranhas, and caimans that could grow to twenty feet preyed on the unfortunate. The river and its myriad tributaries ran through steep mountain ranges, wide plains, and dense forests. Thick stands housed jaguars, tapirs, anteaters, armadillos, and capybaras.

Europeans called the region Guiana, derived from the local word meaning either "land of water" or, more specifically, the coastal lowlands of the frequently flooded plains. To those looking at maps from the other side of the Atlantic, water was as important as land in their calculations. A European sailing ship from the east would follow the Atlantic winds to the south and west, heading into the Caribbean. From there most would eventually, by the later decades of the sixteenth century at least, head toward Central or North America. But they knew about the Orinoco since Columbus had sailed along the northeastern coastline of South America during his third journey in 1498. He believed he had located an "earthly paradise" that might have been a newfound Eden. Printers continued to share tales told by Vespucci, who had described fantastic creatures roaming dense forests and immense supplies of gold to be found in the interior. Europeans, taking these reports together, thought of Guiana as Edenic, with or without the religious associations Columbus had offered.[6]

5. Ralegh, *Discoverie*, 8–10.

6. Benjamin Schmidt, ed., *The Discovery of Guiana by Sir Walter Ralegh* (Boston: Bedford, 2008), 20–21; *Mundus Novus: Letter to Lorenzo Pietro di Medici*, trans. George Tylor Northup (Princeton, NJ: Princeton University Press, 1916), 8–9; Valerie Flint, *The Imaginative Landscape of Christopher Columbus* (Princeton, NJ: Princeton University Press, 1992).

By the time he arrived at the mouth of the Orinoco, Ralegh had already become a renowned expert on European travel to the region.[7] From the outset, politics drove his motivation. Eager to further his prominence in the queen's court, he knew that establishing an English presence between New Spain and Brazil—which at that point was also a Spanish territory, since Philip II had seized the Portuguese throne in 1580—would please Elizabeth. A base at the mouth of the Orinoco could be an ideal haven for English privateers who wanted to raid Spanish treasure ships as well as a port to organize the shipment of gold and other valuables from Guiana to England.[8]

Ralegh, like the younger Hakluyt, understood the intricate political web within the Elizabethan court. Aware that knowledge was power, he created a detailed report of Guiana.[9] To him, the colonization of Guiana was the quickest way to achieve a number of the queen's goals. If the English could get there before the Spanish, then Protestants would rescue heathens from idolatry, ignorance, and sacrifice by showing them the path to "worshipping of the true God." Just as important, conversion to English-style Christianity would strike a blow at the efforts of "Romish Catholickes" eager to spread false practices. Myriad economic benefits would follow as well, resulting from the gold, silver, pearls, and precious stones the English would gather. This treasure would enrich the queen and the realm and at the same time deprive Philip II of the kind of wealth that Pizarro had stolen earlier.[10]

Likely with his experience of Carolina on his mind, Ralegh understood that the queen and the realm's merchants, who had to underwrite colonial schemes since Elizabeth refused, needed assurance that the investment of wealth and human subjects would succeed. He claimed, improbably, that English would thrive in the semi-tropical lowlands of Guiana that he had observed on his journey. Like other promoters, he enumerated local resources to be extracted: "corne, beasts, fowle, fish, and fruit for victuals, and steele and copper for the making of armor and ordinance." The English could even purchase horses from the Caraccas and Amapagotos,

7. Ralegh's book was so popular that publishers produced three editions in London just in 1596, and it soon appeared in Dutch as *Waerachtighe ende grondighe beschryvinge van . . . Guiana* (Amsterdam, 1598).

8. Schmidt, ed., *Discovery of Guiana*, 22–27.

9. Ralegh circulated the report when he returned; it later became the basis of a book. Unless otherwise noted, the material here is from Ralegh's "Of the Voyage for Guiana," Sloane MSS 1133, reprinted in Ralegh, *The Discovery of the Large, Rich, and Beautiful Empire of Guiana*, ed. Schomburgk, 135–153.

10. Ralegh, "Of the Voyage for Guiana," 135–136.

which meant that they did not need to crowd their ships with colts and mares.[11]

The most compelling argument that he made focused on imperial rivalry. Because Pizarro and the Spanish had alienated but not destroyed the Incans, Ralegh, despite knowing how much trouble the English had faced in Ireland, believed that Indigenous would rush to support the English effort. Even the mythical army of female Amazons would side with them.[12] He wrote of the "barbarous and exquisite massacres" perpetrated by Spaniards, who he believed murdered millions of Natives in the Andes. Ralegh, whose depictions of Spanish barbarity paralleled Las Casas's "booke of the Spanish crueltyes," understood the careful intersection of psychology and religion, claiming that Incan religious figures prophesied that "the just God in judgment will one day horribly chasten and peradventure wholy subvert and root out the Spanish nation from the world." Ralegh sensed a rare ecumenical moment where the religious sensibilities of a European aligned with those of an Indigenous American nation. The time had come to free these people from the yoke of their unjust persecutors.[13]

With the logic for an English colony in Guiana secure, Ralegh still needed a plan that would work. Understanding that alienating Indigenous would undermine his larger political vision, Ralegh thought that the English should start by establishing trade with the residents of Guiana and support them while the Incans prepared to reclaim Peru. They should avoid military conflict too: "No Christians may lawfully invade with hostility any heathenish people nor under their allegiance, to kill, spoile, and conquer them, only upon pretence of their fidelity."[14] He supported his argument with biblical exegesis drawn from the books of Genesis, Jeremiah, Daniel, Judges, and Luke, which led him to conclude that expanding Christendom was insufficient motivation for colonization. Following from that logic, he questioned the power of the pope or any other religious figure to claim the lands from any original possessors on religious grounds alone. By this reasoning, he believed that "all sound Christians" saw the monarchs of Castile and Portugal as unjust usurpers in Africa and America. Protestants should send missionaries to work among the infidels, he agreed, but resistance to a religious program was insufficient justification for conquering their territory. He drew some of his inspiration for this argument from his understanding of the debate between Las Casas and Sepulveda, another sign that Ralegh had immersed himself in

11. Ralegh, "Of the Voyage for Guiana," 137.
12. Ralegh, "Of the Voyage for Guiana," 136–138.
13. Ralegh, "Of the Voyage for Guiana," 138–139, 141–143 (Las Casas).
14. Ralegh, "Of the Voyage for Guiana," 139–141.

the most pertinent issues before he set sail for South America.[15] He suggested that the English create an illustrated edition of Las Casas's book to present to the residents of Manoa to prove through pictures the kinds of cruelties the Spanish had unleashed elsewhere. Once convinced of the danger the Iberians posed, Ralegh believed, the Indigenous would dismiss the authority of the pope, that infamous "troubler of the world," who had (in Ralegh's view) encouraged his followers to destroy the spiritual practices of those they invaded.[16]

Unlike others from the realm who had preceded him, Ralegh understood that the English needed to encourage Natives to embrace them. Juggling the politics of court with those along the Orinoco, he hoped that visitors could describe Elizabeth's beneficence and the role that she had played in battling Spaniards. In his mind, the queen would need to provide gifts to local caciques to demonstrate her debt to them. Just as he had recommended getting an illustrated edition of Las Casas's book, he again believed that visual images would help the newcomers make their case. In this sense, he saw the printed book as an additional tool for conquerors. He thought that the Guineans would respond to maps in Giovanni Baptista Boazio's recently published account of Drake's voyage to the West Indies, which revealed the places where Elizabeth was willing to send her forces to benefit those held by the Spanish. He also thought they should bring maps of London, which would reveal the magnificence of her realm. The representations of the physical world she governed became an accessible way to understand her grand and generous policies. Unlike the Iberians' practices, hers were based on "truth, justice, and faythfulnes, prohibiting all murders, treasons, adulteries, thefts" and anything else that interfered with creating a realm governed by "equity and reason."[17]

In exchange, Ralegh argued that the residents of Guiana needed to renounce "Idolatry" and accept monotheism. Further, the ruler of Manoa would need to engage in a ritual where he surrendered the caciques and others working for him to the English queen. Although they would be her agents, they would still follow the ruler's orders, a variant of the Tudor surrender and regrant policy employed earlier in Ireland. The deal would be sealed with two gifts: an annual tribute of gold, silver, pearls, precious stones, and Indigenous captives, "speciall hostages" who would travel to England to become civilized. With the conditions met, the queen would ceremonially arrive not as "Cortez, Pisarro, or the other conquerors

15. Ralegh, "Of the Voyage for Guiana," 141–143.
16. Ralegh, "Of the Voyage for Guiana," 144.
17. Ralegh, "Of the Voyage for Guiana," 144–145; Giovanni Baptista Boazio, *The famous West Indian voyadge made by the Englishe fleete* ([London (?)], [1589 (?)]).

against a naked unarmed people" but as their benefactor and partner. Ralegh believed that an English assault on Spanish territory in Peru, Hispaniola, or Florida would likely attract Guineans to join them in a coordinated effort to reduce Philip II's hold in the Western Hemisphere.[18]

When he returned home Ralegh, like Vespucci before him, spread tales of what he had seen along the Orinoco. While his boasts might have been driven by bravado, telling these stories was itself part of the process of advancing his political agenda. Like the younger Hakluyt, Ralegh understood that it would take more than a compelling argument to prompt the English to launch colonies in the Americas. He began by circulating a manuscript account of his report, hoping to secure support at court.

Since his vision rested on the idea that the English should export men and women, Ralegh revised his text before having it published. Here he fell back on the strategies of others who had written travel narratives with political aims. He testified to the accomplishments of others who had already been there and returned home, provided ethnographic details about the Natives of Guiana that portrayed them as capable of English-style civilization after they renounced their former ways, gushed about the hospitality that newcomers received, and boasted of the gold to be extracted. Like other travelers, he wove in details so that readers might understand a world they had never seen. Since antiquity, Europeans believed that Amazons lived beyond the boundaries of the known world. Rather than dismissing claims that they existed, Ralegh instead emphasized that these arrow-wielding warrior women could be allies. He knew that some would likely greet such news with skepticism. But describing even threatening elements of Guiana gave his report more power because it seemed he had nothing to hide. An armadillo might seem strange and even monstrous. Yet the English had learned from the Guineans that the bones on its back could be ground up and used to treat deafness.[19] Blemmyes, mythical headless beings with their facial features on their chest, might live in the woods, he acknowledged, but they were rare and non-threatening. Ralegh reported hearing about them but never seeing one. The searing detail of the existence of the monstrous fit popular conceptions and captured the public's attention, as one enterprising printer knew when he commissioned an engraving of blemmyes and Amazons for the cover of a book based on Ralegh's account.[20]

18. Ralegh, "Of the Voyage for Guiana," 146–153, quotations at 146 ("renounce their idolatry," "hostages"), 149 ("Cortez").

19. Ralegh, *Discoverie*, 22–24, 13 (geography), 61 (armadillo), 27 (gold).

20. Levinus Hulsius, *Brevis & Admirando descriptio Regni Guianæ* (Nuremberg, 1599); Ralegh, *Discoverie*, 69–71.

Brevis & admiranda deſcriptio
REGNI GVIANÆ, AVRI
ABVNDANTISSIMI, IN AMERICA,
SEV NOVO ORBE, SVB LINEA ÆQVINOCTILIA
ſiti: Quod nuper admodum, Annis nimirum
1564. 1595 & 1596.
Per Generoſum Dominum,
Dn. GVALTHERVM RALEGH EQVI-
tem Anglum detectum eſt: paulò poſt juſſu ejus
duobus libellis comprehenſa:
Ex quibus
IODOCVS HONDIVS TABVLAM GEO-
graphicam adornavit, addita explicatione
Belgico ſermone ſcripta:
Nunc verò in Latinum ſermonem tranſlata, & ex variis
authoribus hinc inde declarata.

NORIBERGAE,
Impenſis LEVINI HULSII, D, M, XCIX.

Despite the fact that Sir Walter Ralegh admitted that he had never seen monsters with his own eyes, the printer of this Dutch version of his account of traveling up the Orinoco still put blemmyes and an Amazon on the cover, suggesting that these creatures did exist in the Americas. From Levinus Hulsius, *Brevis & Admirando*, 1599. Courtesy of the Huntington Library, San Marino, California.

Ralegh embodied the quintessential traits of a Renaissance gentleman: learning, bravery, and loyalty.[21] He employed sexual metaphors to make his points about the need for the English to penetrate this "Country that hath yet her Maydenhead, never sackt, turned, nor wrought." Here was a pristine place, a prelapsarian paradise where even the ancient graves remained undisturbed, unlike the countless gutted tombs of Mexico and Peru that had fallen victim to treasure-hungry Spaniards. Guiana was to him an obvious place for an English colony.[22] The younger Hakluyt agreed. Four years after Ralegh's book appeared, he included all of it in an expanded version of his *Principal Navigations.* For this edition, Hakluyt dropped a Latin version of Mandeville's travels, with its fantastical elements. He also removed the dubious account of an English traveler named David Ingram, who had allegedly walked from Florida to Canada. The elision of the improbable reinforced the impression that Hakluyt believed in the veracity of Ralegh's claims.[23]

At the turn of the century, any English woman or man interested in the Western Hemisphere could turn to a quickly growing library of travel accounts. The widespread publication and distribution of these texts reveal a revival of English interest in the efforts of the Cabots and increasing knowledge of the cod fisheries off Newfoundland, where English fishing crews had been hauling in ever-greater numbers after the mid-1570s.[24] English readers could learn too about Frobisher's expeditions, which had become the source of extensive commentary, as well as about the tragedy that befell the Gilbert expedition of 1583.[25] Chronicles from all of these voyages and others circulated in England in the latter years of Elizabeth's

21. See Benjamin Schmidt, "Introduction: Ralegh's Courteous Conquest," in *The Discovery of Guiana by Sir Walter Ralegh,* ed. Schmidt, 1–44, esp. 3–11; cf. David B. Quinn, *Raleigh and the British Empire*, new ed. (London: English Universities Press, [1962]).
22. Ralegh, *Discoverie*, 99–101.
23. On the changes to Hakluyt's compilations from the first to second editions, see Peter C. Mancall, *Hakluyt's Promise: An Elizabethan's Obsession for an English America* (New Haven, CT: Yale University Press, 2007), 232–233; for Ingram, see also Dean Snow, *The Extraordinary Journey of David Ingram: An Elizabethan Sailor in Native North America* (New York: Oxford University Press, 2023).
24. Peter E. Pope, *Fish into Wine: The Newfoundland Plantation in the Seventeenth Century* (Chapel Hill: University of North Carolina Press for the Omohundro Institute of Early American History and Culture, 2004), 15–20.
25. See Alden T. Vaughan, *Transatlantic Encounters: American Indians in Britain, 1500–1776* (Cambridge: Cambridge University Press, 2006), 1–20; Peter C. Mancall, "The Raw and the Cold: Five English Sailors in Sixteenth-Century Nunavut," *WMQ*, 3rd Ser., 70 (2013), 3–40; Mancall, *Hakluyt's Promise*, 102–127.

reign, notably in the massive volumes edited by the younger Hakluyt.[26] Though he did not publish another large collection of travel accounts after 1600, Hakluyt continued to gather materials that he hoped would spur others to engage in long-distance trade and settlement schemes.[27]

With this record of accomplishment available, others hoped to expand the realm's achievements. On May 14, 1602, an expedition led by an English lawyer named Bartholomew Gosnold arrived in modern New England after a six-and-a-half-week crossing. John Brereton, a gentleman on the voyage, praised the abundant sources of fresh water and the richness of the soil, suggesting that "the most fertil part of England" was "barren" by comparison. He and his companions planted barley, oats, peas, and wheat on a small shoal they named Elizabeth's Island; within two weeks the seedlings were allegedly already nine inches tall. Brereton's narrative also included a list of trees, birds, animals, minerals, and plants (including many kinds of berries) available at the site. He singled out the abundance of copper he saw in the region, which the locals used to make jewelry, cups, and arrowheads. The travelers, Brereton wrote, "were much fatter and in better health than when we went out of England." With that observation Brereton introduced what became a notable theme in English travel accounts of the region. This was, as a later observer put it, a "medicinable climate." Most notable, perhaps, were the region's abundant aquatic resources, which exceeded those in Newfoundland.[28]

Brereton praised the appearance, generosity, and economy of the local Algonquians, with whom he communicated in sign language. This proved sufficient to facilitate trade and learn about local practices, such as widespread tobacco use. He taught some English words to one Indigenous man

26. Richard Hakluyt, *The Principall Navigations, Voiages and Discoveries of the English Nation* (London, 1589), 506–825; Hakluyt, *The Principal Navigations, Voiages, Traffiques and Discoveries of the English Nation* (London, 1598–1600), III, passim.

27. Hakluyt remained interested in North America after the turn of the century and authored a pamphlet to support the struggling Virginia Company in 1609, but he had wider interests as well, including in the Southwest Pacific. He passed on his new manuscripts to the minister Samuel Purchas, who incorporated Hakluyt's unpublished papers in an even larger four-volume collection in 1625. On Hakluyt's later years, see Mancall, *Hakluyt's Promise*, 195–235; for what Purchas got from Hakluyt, John Parker, "Contents and Sources of *Purchas his Pilgrimes*," in L. E. Pennington, ed., *The Purchas Handbook*, Hak. Soc., 2nd Ser., 185–186 (London: Hakluyt Society, 1997), 2:383–464.

28. John Brereton, *A Briefe and true Relation of the Discoverie of the North part of Virginia* (London, 1602), 12–13 (list of commodities), 7 (fertility of the land), 6 (quickly sprouting plants), 9–10 (copper), 11 (health of the English), 5 (ease of fishing); William Wood, *New England's Prospect*, ed. Alden T. Vaughan (orig. pub. 1634; Amherst: University of Massachusetts Press, 1977), 32–33, quotation at 32.

who, Brereton reported, "suddenly spake so plaine and distinctly, as if he had beene a long scholar in the language." By mid-June Brereton and the other English set off for home, bringing back the first detailed information of a region they labeled Cape Cod in honor of the plentiful supply of the fish there.[29]

Among the avid readers of travel accounts like Brereton's were investors in joint-stock companies, the corporations that had begun to take shape in response to an economic downturn in the mid-1580s.[30] They knew as well as anyone that England faced a series of challenges in the 1590s and beyond. Despite their victory in 1588, the costs of battling the Spanish Armada had fueled an economic depression. To make matters worse, plague struck in 1592. From late March through the end of the year a total of 11,503 died in London alone, about 40 percent of the almost 26,000 residents of the city who died that year. By contrast, there were only 5,827 baptisms, a sign that infection either took a heavy toll among those of child-bearing age or depressed the incentive to reproduce. Plague returned in 1593, taking the lives of 10,662 of the 17,844 souls who passed in London that year. Again, the mortality likely discouraged pregnancy; there were just over 4,000 baptisms that year. Poor harvests from 1594 to 1597 exacerbated the crisis, evident in the rising cost of basic foods including wheat. Rents had increased during the boom years, but the decline made it difficult for many rural residents to afford them anymore. Losses on the seas at the end of the decade—including the seizure of ships owned by both the Russia and Levant companies—distilled the troubles into moments of national humiliation and financial loss.[31]

On December 31, 1600, Elizabeth put her seal on the charter for a corporation called the Governor and Company of Merchants of London, Trading into the East-Indies (known as the East India Company or the EIC). Its first governor was London alderman Thomas Smythe (or Smith).

29. Brereton, *Briefe and true Relation*, 10–11 (appearance of the Natives), 9 (sign language), 6 (tobacco), 11 (conversation).

30. William R. Scott, *The Constitution and Finance of English, Scottish and Irish Joint-Stock Companies to 1720* (Cambridge: Cambridge University Press, 1912), 1:64–65, 72–73.

31. Scott, *Joint-Stock Companies*, 1:97–104, 129 (1603 plague); *London's Lord have mercy upon us: A true Relation of Seven modern Plagues or Visitations in London* [broadside] (1665); John Graunt, *Natural and Political Observations mentioned in a following Index made upon the Bills of Mortality*, 3rd ed. (London, 1665), 65; Dale Ingram, *An Historical Account of the Several Plagues that have appeared in the World since the Year 1346* (London, 1745), sig. B3^{v}. According to Ingram, plague killed 11,503 in London in 1592 and 10,662 in 1593, then returned in 1603 and took 35,417 lives.

He and other investors gained the authority to open shipping to the East Indies and to govern those who fell within the company's broad ambit. Eventually the company gained legal authority over the expanding English colonial presence in Asia, evolving into the all-but-sovereign entity that would rule the Indian subcontinent for generations.[32]

According to its charter, the EIC could "freely traffick and use the Trade of Merchandize, by Seas" for fifteen years along routes that were already known and others that might be discovered. The charter defined the East Indies broadly as "Parts of Asia and Africa, and into and from all the Islands, Ports, Havens, Cities, Creeks, Towns and Places of Asia and Africa, and America, or any of them, beyond the Cape of Bona Esperanza [the modern Cape of Good Hope] to the Straights of Magellan." In other words, EIC ships could sail without limitation across the Southern Hemisphere as long as they did not initiate trade with what the charter termed lands "already in the lawful and actual Possession of any such Christian Prince or State" that stood in opposition to the realm or to commerce with the EIC.[33]

Elizabeth and her agents knew they had to establish certain rules and to provide enticements for investors. Among the challenges that all European colonizers faced was how to control the behavior of a monarch's subjects when they were thousands of miles from home. The EIC charter granted the governor and his assistants the authority of a court, including the ability to imprison anyone who violated the orders of the governor and company as long as the punishment fit standards at home. Per the terms of its charter, the EIC could have twelve armed ships and 500 sailors, with the understanding that the navy could, in times of war, recall both the ships and the men into the nation's service. But absent a national call to arms, the company's directors understood that they controlled, in essence, their own private military force.

Yet directors of companies understood that having the powers of a state—the ability to establish courts in distant locales and to back up their decisions with armed men and ships with cannon—meant little if they could not attract migrants to their distant outposts. Fortunately for them, as the century neared its end, Hakluyt reappeared on the public stage with a new edition of his collection of travel narratives. The first

32. See Philip J. Stern, *The Company-State: Corporate Sovereignty and the Early Modern Foundations of the British Empire in India* (New York: Oxford University Press, 2011), esp. 19–40.

33. Charter granted by Queen Elizabeth to the East India Company, December 31, 1600, in *Charters Relating to the East India Company from 1600 to 1761*, ed. John Shaw (Madras: Government Press, 1887), 1–15.

edition had appeared in 1589, in those heady months after the defeat of the Armada. But Hakluyt spent the 1590s gathering other stories—collecting manuscripts and printed books, winnowing down a growing pile of accounts. By the time he was done he had gathered far too much for a single volume. He could have jettisoned content to offer his readers an updated but mostly similar compilation, a strategy that other editors of travel accounts routinely used.[34] But Hakluyt realized that the volume of stories was, in fact, the story. He used printed travel narratives to show a still-reluctant English public how many earlier explorers had benefited the realm through overseas travel. Some died in distant places; others had gone into debt. But all had done their part for England, just as if they were loyal soldiers who had died on a battlefield. The sacrifices they made when they left family and friends behind for uncertain journeys needed to be remembered, just as countless memorials in churches across the realm testified to the virtues of those who had come and gone in the past. No marble epitaphs survived for most of these travelers. Their immortality, Hakluyt knew, would come in his pages. Cataloguing recent exploits by Davis, Drake, and Ralegh gave an immediacy to his book—and a new goad to those in the queen's court who saw new opportunities on the horizon.

Elizabeth I, who had reigned since 1558, had been in excellent health for most of her life. Antiquarian William Camden attributed her vitality to a "temperate" diet and avoiding alcohol. But in January 1603, the sixty-nine-year-old matriarch had begun to slip. Her attendants took her from Westminster, where she had been a stalwart head of state, to her rural palace at Richmond. She was likely suffering from blood poisoning that led to septicemia and sepsis, a fatal condition. If this was the case, she might have spent her last days suffering from high fever, chills, increased heart rate, confusion, an inability to urinate, shock, and, eventually, organ failure. Observers noted her swollen gums and lack of appetite. Soon she sank into a depression. With her suffering increasing, she chose to abstain from medicine, prompting one observer to note that she was perhaps becoming confused, with her brain "somewhat distempered." Her hands swelled, including the finger on which she wore the same ring she had since her coronation forty-five years earlier. The pain was so great that she ordered her courtiers to cut off the ring. Camden saw a metaphor.

34. See, e.g., Samuel Purchas, *Purchas his Pilgrimage, Or Relations of the World* (London, 1613); Samuel Purchas, *Purchas his Pilgrimage, Or Relations of the World* (London, 1614); Samuel Purchas, *Purchas his Pilgrimage, Or Relations of the World* (London, 1617).

Removing the jewelry "portended that the marriage with her Kingdome contracted by the Ring, would be dissolved." Her attendants got her into her bed for a final time on March 21. She died three days later.[35]

Elizabeth's death brought London to a stop. The news raced across the realm soon after word of her passing reached Whitehall. Mourners quickly marched to the city's walls, where they met London's alderman and lord mayor at Ludgate. From there the party traveled to the high cross in Cheapside to proclaim King James VI of Scotland as King James I of England. Public orations followed across the city. Within days her funeral cortege marched slowly through London. A surviving sketch, purportedly by Camden, testified to its length and grandeur, an ornate parade attended by seemingly every important person in London. Elizabeth's principal advisor, William Cecil, walked alone ahead of the palanquin. Sir Walter Ralegh, too, walked unattended, trailing near the end. "There was such a general sighing, groning, and weeping," one annalist later wrote, "as the like hath not beene seene or knowne in the memory of man." The queen was laid to rest in the chapel of Henry VII in Westminster, where grand monuments still mark her tomb. There she lay for eternity with her grandfather, her sister, Mary (her political rival), and Mary Queen of Scots, whom Elizabeth had had executed. In life, confessional differences had mattered. In death, royal blood bound them together.[36]

The queen's death came at a challenging moment for those invested in overseas colonization, which continued to pivot on the idea that English settlements far from home could solve domestic overpopulation. But as Elizabeth faded, plague returned. Five residents of the city died of it in the two weeks leading up to Elizabeth's passing, an ominous start to a catastrophic epidemic. During the last two weeks of June a total of

35. William Camden, *Annals, or, The Historie of the most renowned and victorious princesse Elizabeth, late Queene of England* (London, 1635), 584–585; John Chamberlain to Dudley Carleton, [March 30, 1603], in *The Letters of John Chamberlain*, ed. Norman E. McClure (Philadelphia: American Philosophical Society, 1939), 1:188–190; Edmund Howes, *Annales, or A Generall Chronicle of England* (London, 1631), 812.

36. William Camden (?), *The Funeral Procession of Queen Elizabeth* (London, 1791 [?]), HEH 601835; Howes, *Annales*, 812–815; Camden, *Annales*, 586; Chamberlain to Carleton, [March 30, 1603], in *Letters of John Chamberlain*, 1:189; [William Camden], *Reges, Reginæ, Nobiles, Et alij in Ecclesia Collegata B. Petri Westmonasterij sepulti* (London, 1606), 25; Johann Jacob Grasser, "Notes on England, Circa 1606," in William B. Rye, ed., *England as Seen by Foreigners in the Days of Elizabeth and James the First* (London, 1865), 127. James VI and I arranged commemorations of Mary Queen of Scots, his mother, and Elizabeth in the same chapel as the others. In the nineteenth century, historian Thomas Babington Macaulay wrote that the presence of their bodies helped the abbey become "a temple of reconciliation." See Richard Jenkyns, *Westminster Abbey* (Cambridge, MA: Harvard University Press, 2004), 60–61.

230 more succumbed to plague, with 263 more dead by July 7, another 424 the following week, followed by 917 during the week that ended on July 21. As summer moved on, the pace of death increased. Surviving mortality bills reveal that the weekly death toll topped 1,300 the last week of July, a sign of a lethal summer: 1,925 dead by August 4, 1,743 the next week, 2,719 the following week, and 2,535 from August 18 to 25. The last week of the month was the worst of the year: 3,024 residents dead from plague. The numbers remained above 1,000 each week through October 13. By year's end, plague had killed 30,583 residents of the city, over three-fourths of that year's total mortality of 38,250. The last victims of this epidemic passed during the last week of the year. There would be no similar calamity in the city until 1625, another wave of epidemic disease that coincided with the death of the realm's monarch.[37]

Despite domestic tragedies that could have undermined one of the major arguments for establishing colonies, some continued to see the establishment of settlements in North America as central to the future of the realm. Among them was Devon native George Waymouth, who reconnoitered the shores of modern Maine in 1605. Upon the expedition's return James Rosier produced a report entitled, in the familiar breathless prose of the age, *A True Relation of the Most Prosperous Voyage made this present year, 1605, by Captain George Waymouth, in the discovery of the land of Virginia, where he discovered, sixty miles up, a most excellent river, together with a most fertile land.* The narrative focused on the modern George River, which feeds into Casco Bay.[38]

Rosier focused on subjects sure to be on the minds of his readers, including seemingly endless schools of fish, shallow waters crowded with lobsters and other shellfish, and its fertile lands.[39] Present-day Monhegan Island, where Waymouth first landed in mid-May, was covered with oak, beech, fir, and birch. Wild peas, rosebushes, gooseberries, and strawberries grew along the forest's edge. The travelers saw birds' nests amid the rocks and along the shoreline. Rosier claimed that it took almost no effort to catch cod and haddock, which could be dried on the ubiquitous rocks along the shore. They gathered oysters, collected pearls, and found an American fir tree that exuded a gum that smelled like frankincense, useful for making pitch and tar.[40]

37. *London's Lord have mercy upon us*; John Graunt, in *Natural and Political Observations . . . made upon the Bills of Mortality*, 5th ed. (London, 1676), 46, notes that the 1603 epidemic killed 30,561 out of the 37,294 who died in the capital that year.
38. *Rosier's Narrative of Waymouth's Voyage to the Coast of Maine, in 1605, with Remarks by George Prince* (Bath, ME, 1860), 4–14.
39. *Rosier's Narrative*, quotation at 15.
40. *Rosier's Narrative*, 18, 30, 21–22.

Like other travelers, Rosier described Indigenous residents in detail. Unable to speak with them, he too relied on an improvised sign language.[41] He wrote about the trade that the English conducted along the shoreline, noting the Algonquian-speakers' fascination with manufactured goods such as combs and mirrors. The noise of guns terrified them, he claimed; they all fell to the ground when they heard a shot. The English expected little from these Natives, but they impressed him nonetheless, especially the technical prowess he saw in their canoes and the way they welcomed newcomers. The English felt joy when they encountered "the kind civility we found in a people, where we little expected any spark of humanity." They were "a people of exceeding good invention," he noted, "quick understanding and ready capacity." The English hoped that establishing trade would have advantages beyond the ability to collect furs and deerskins. Commerce, as Rosier suggested, could "bring them to an understanding of exchange" so that the locals "might conceive the intent of our coming to them to be for no other end." Rather than conquering them, the English sought to establish good relations based on Indigenous respect for the newcomers' technological superiority. On one occasion the visitors used a lodestone to move an iron sword. "This we did to cause them to imagine some great power in us," Rosier wrote, "and for that to love and fear us," using phrasing that Harriot had employed earlier.[42] To advance this plan the English decided it would be best to capture a handful of Natives as a defensive measure to prevent an assault, an action they found consistent with their efforts to establish peaceful relations.[43]

After a successful summer, the explorers set off for home in possession of new information about a place that promised valuable natural resources and friendly inhabitants—the kinds of discovery that might draw the interest of prospective investors. Hopes for an English colony abroad survived the death of the monarch who had moved the idea from drawing board to reality.

The ventures of Ralegh and Rosier came at a crucial moment for the English realm. Rather than abandon efforts to establish communities in North America after the debacle on the Outer Banks, policymakers instead looked for new ways forward, in terms of both destinations for

41. On earlier English efforts at sign language in North America, see Samuel Purchas, *Hakluytus Posthumus, or Purchas his Pilgrimes* (London, 1625), 3:606.

42. *Rosier's Narrative*, 23–25; Thomas Harriot, *Briefe and True Report of the New Found Land of Virginia* (Frankfurt am Main, 1590), 29.

43. *Rosier's Narrative*, 29 (captives).

possible colonies and financial instruments to make colonization possible. The rise of the joint-stock company provided a funding vehicle to support long-distance exploration and colonization when corporations could provide the kind of financial support that monarchs would not. Though Elizabeth had not made investments in North America as she had in Ireland, where she drew on the state to finance a military invasion, her willingness to grant patents to encourage exploration that might lead to colonization proved a crucial step in creating opportunities in the aftermath of the Roanoke disaster. In the years immediately following her death, no one in England could have known whether the future of the realm would be found along the banks of the Orinoco, near the shores of Casco Bay, or perhaps in a return to Carolina. But as James VI and I, as well as other European monarchs, understood, a successful European invasion of North America was no foregone conclusion—nor, as the English king would learn, was Ralegh's planned conquest of the Orinoco.

11

Acoma and Santa Fe

La Florida had remained of interest to Spanish imperial bureaucrats because it seemed a place where colonization could succeed. Even a cursory glance at a map would suggest that the southeastern portion of the mainland was within relatively easy reach of Spanish outposts in the West Indies, and ship captains had already learned about prevailing winds and currents. In addition, reports since the time of Ayallon's attempted settlement had routinely indicated the resources to be found there. Although the Guales had turned on the Franciscans, the community of friars had managed to make some spiritual inroads. Philip III, who inherited the throne in 1598, initially had misgivings about Florida. But missionaries there convinced him to subsidize the colony for the sake of Natives who had converted.[1]

Across the still largely unreconnoitered continent, expansion into New Mexico raised other issues. Reports from Coronado's *entrada* had revealed the difficulty of survival in arid lands dotted by mesas and on windswept prairies. Rather than inspiring additional colonizing efforts, his expedition produced little in the years that followed. Virtually no Spaniards traveled into the region after 1543. The 1573 Orders for New Discoveries, which demanded humane treatment of Indigenous, proved an additional disincentive to potential migrants. Visitors would also have had difficulty understanding a region where Indigenous peoples spoke multiple, often mutually unintelligible, languages.[2]

Yet by century's end, imperial officials believed that the time had come to try again in New Mexico. Success in northern New Spain had convinced them that the right leaders could produce the desired results. They knew more, too, about ancient paths that had stretched from the Valley of Mexico into New Mexico, which they re-created as the *camino real de tierra adentro*—the "royal road of the interior." It had once borne

1. David J. Weber, *The Spanish Frontier in North America* (New Haven, CT: Yale University Press, 1992), 88–89.
2. Weber, *Spanish Frontier*, 17–19.

Indigenous traders carrying obsidian, feathers, and maize. It would become an avenue for a new generation of conquistadores armed with guns and machetes.[3] They were ready to cut a bloody swath through ancient pueblos to clear the way for priests bearing Bibles and colonial farmers seeking protection for their families.

In 1567, Spaniards had established a presence in the Chichimeca homeland at Santa Bárbara, in the modern Mexican state of Chihuahua. Having learned that there was silver in the region, the Spanish decided it was worth the investment even though their community was over 200 miles from the nearest Spanish town. The mining community did not fare well at first, which prompted Viceroy Don Luis de Velasco to appoint a military veteran named Don Juan de Oñate to be the governor and "carry out the discovery, pacification, and conquest of the provinces of New Mexico." On September 21, 1595, at a ceremony in Mexico City, Oñate accepted the contract. He believed he was the right man for the task since he had spent the previous two decades, as he put it, "fighting and pacifying the Chichimecas and Guachichiles Indians and other nations in the kingdoms of New Galicia and New Vizcaya." In his mind, he followed in the path of his father, Cristóbal, the captain general of New Galicia, who had "conquered, pacified, and settled" much of the region "at his own cost."[4]

Oñate knew the obstacles he faced. To succeed, he told Velasco, he required 200 men along with their families. They would haul extensive amounts of maize and corn flour, seeds to grow wheat, 1,000 cattle, 3,000 sheep, 1,000 rams, 100 black cattle, 20 oxen with carts, and 150 colts and an equal number of mares. This did not count his own personal possessions, which were to include another twenty-five horses, along with mules, saddles, lances, harquebuses, swords, and daggers. In addition, the new community would need bellows to set up a blacksmith shop, medicine, iron agricultural tools, and a supply of gifts for local Natives. The viceroy approved the mission, adding six Franciscans along with the trappings they would need to conduct their sacral duties. That meant, as Oñate detailed, vestments, books, bells, and "some trumpets or musical instruments for the churches." He specified too that his secular jurisdiction

3. Tatiana Seijas, "The Royal Road of the Interior in New Spain: Indigenous Commerce and Political Action," in Danna A. Levin Rojo and Cynthia Radding, eds., *The Oxford Handbook of Borderlands and the Iberian World* (New York: Oxford University Press, 2019), 294–313; *NAW*, 5:365–366; Lyle McAlister, *Spain and Portugal in the New World* (Minneapolis: University of Minnesota Press, 1984), 237–238.

4. George P. Hammond and Agapito Rey, *Don Juan de Oñate: Colonizer of New Mexico, 1595–1628*, 2 vols (Albuquerque: University of New Mexico Press, 1953), 1:42–43.

would include wherever these friars went "so that there may be no obstacle to the conversion and pacification of the natives." Oñate also asked to take captives who had come from that region, including one woman who he believed could act as an interpreter. He insisted as well on the authority to divide lands among potential colonists, to appoint others to serve his administration (who would be named *adelantado*), and to be able to demand tribute from conquered Natives for his own use in addition to any funds to be sent to the viceroy. With his terms met, Oñate promised to govern all those in his jurisdiction "with the greatest Christian generosity."[5]

Before he set off, Velasco insisted that Oñate had to follow the guidelines of the laws of 1573, which contained "the royal ordinances for new colonizations and pacifications in new discoveries in the Indies." The new governor needed to preserve order among the soldiers and the nonmilitary Spanish settlers. That meant that Oñate had to keep these migrants from disrespecting the friars, since the Natives could not see anything that might undermine the friars' spiritual authority. Oñate should recruit interpreters whenever he could and allow any Indigenous converts to live with Spanish colonists. The governor should also encourage local residents to learn new trades. This was a well-peopled region, Velasco reminded him. Attracting the Natives to service would be ideal, but they could not be compelled to work for the Spanish. Velasco wanted Natives to live with Spanish colonizers, a model that he believed worked in New Spain. Under no circumstances were the Spanish to force the Natives to work in their mines since they would run away, which Spanish officials had observed from their efforts to force Indigenous slaves into the mines of Potosí. Despite getting Oñate's assent, the mission did not set off until 1598.[6]

On his journey northward, Oñate was to have one of his party read the Requerimiento to any Native groups they met. Spaniards in the field, including Oñate and his subordinates, believed that the earlier papal grant of authority to Iberian monarchs extended to New Mexico. According to the terms of the document they proclaimed, members of the "barbarous nations" who accepted Spanish rulers would find a path to Christian salvation. They could also remain in their own homes as long as they paid tribute, converted to Christianity, and promised perpetual allegiance to the crown. But resistance, a more likely event in New Mexico than it was on Hispaniola at the time of the creation of the Requerimiento, would lead to the capture and enslavement of Native women and children, theft

5. Hammond and Ray, *Oñate*, 44–57, quotations at 46 (friars), 47 ("Christian generosity").
6. Hammond and Ray, *Oñate*, 65–68.

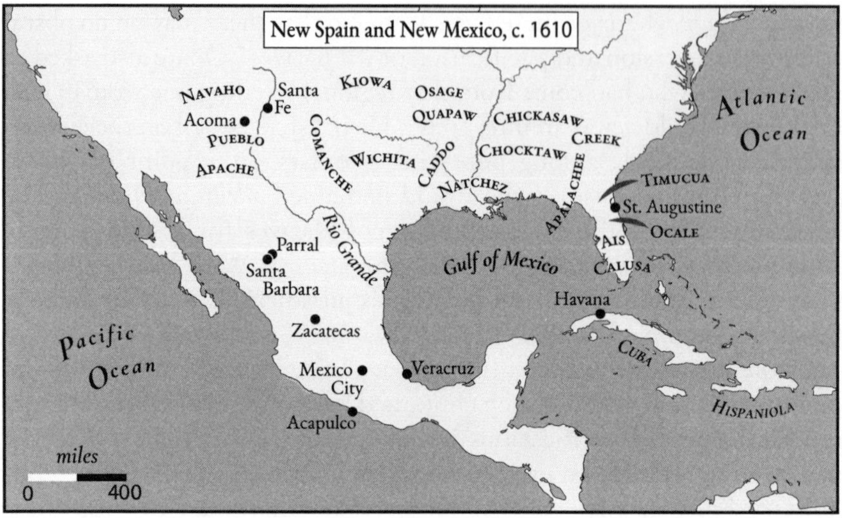

of Indigenous property, and war against any who stood in their way. The defiant ones would be subjected to "the yoke and obedience of the Church" as well as monarchs. This two-headed militant state, with power from divine and secular authorities, insulated those who promulgated it. "The deaths and losses" that were sure to come were, the agents told Indigenous, "your fault, and not that of our highnesses, or ours, or of the soldiers who come with us." Oñate's agents read this permission to commit atrocities in Spanish, a language likely unknown by the vast majority of Natives who heard it.[7]

On his migration northward Oñate first settled in Tegua territory at San Juan in northern New Mexico. He subsequently joined a delegation in search of the Gulf of California (the so-called Sea of Cortés). The Spaniards visited multiple pueblos, inspected local salt mines, and mapped the location of springs. Eventually they reached Acoma, which he estimated contained 500 houses. As was the case in other locations during his journey, the residents of the pueblo treated the visitors well, providing water, corn, and fowl, and, the governor claimed, offered "obedience" to Philip III. That was good news to Oñate, who recognized that this pueblo, which rose atop a formidable mesa, was "practically impregnable, because

7. Weber, *Spanish Frontier*, 15–16, 79–80; S. Lyman Tyler, ed., *The Indian Cause in the Spanish Laws of the Indies*, American West Center Occasional Papers 16 (Salt Lake City: University of Utah, 1980), xxxv–xxxvii.

there is no way to ascend it except by climbing up some holes that they had made in the rock itself."[8]

After a day's rest the party continued, trudging through heavy snow while some of their horses ran off, never to be recovered. They arrived in Zuñi territory, where the inhabitants also offered hospitality. As he looked across the landscape, Oñate recognized that there were crosses in all the pueblos, probably remnants of Coronado's *entrada*. "The Indians show great devotion for them and often offer them what they offer their idols," the *adelantado* reported, "such as flour, sticks painted in various colors, and feathers of native fowls." The visitors were able to speak a bit to the locals because Coronado had left behind two Natives he had once captured. Both were now gone, but the son of one survived and he spoke some Spanish. The traveling party studied the region's resources, convinced that they could establish profitable silver mines there. They left the Zuñi on December 12, bound for San Juan. En route, they heard a rebellion against the Spanish had erupted at Acoma.[9]

According to the earliest written report, a group of Spaniards had gone to Acoma while Oñate was on his expedition to find the sea. At first the Acoma residents had treated the Spaniards with customary hospitality. But the visitors stayed longer than their hosts expected, and while they were there a soldier stole two turkeys. The inhabitants killed him almost immediately, shooting down from one of the town's many terraces. At that moment, other residents of the city joined the fray, killing eleven of the invaders.[10]

In the aftermath of the killing, Oñate and his subordinates gathered testimony from other Spanish soldiers who had witnessed the assault. They described a premeditated attack launched during a dispute about the provision of flour and corn that led to women and men hurling rocks, shooting arrows, and swinging clubs at the Spaniards. Witnesses recommended swift and brutal retaliation. Unless Acoma was "destroyed and made permanently uninhabitable and the Indians severely punished for their treachery," Captain Gaspar López Tabora declared, "no one will be able to live securely anywhere in New Mexico." A mestizo named Alonso González, who had traveled to New Mexico from Mexico City, concurred that the attack had to have been premeditated. In all, Oñate heard sworn

8. Hammond and Ray, *Oñate*, 393–394.
9. Hammond and Ray, *Oñate*, 396–397.
10. Alonso Sanchez to Rodrigo del Rio, February 28, 1599, in Hammond and Ray, *Oñate*, 425–427.

testimony from almost thirty witnesses and also solicited opinions from the friars and other Spanish colonizers. He agreed that his soldiers needed to send a signal. "If these Indians were not punished this time," he informed others, "they would form a league, rebel, and destroy us easily." The married Spanish colonists, who were supposed to be protected in the territory, told him that if the soldiers did not act soon, they would return to New Spain with their families.[11]

On January 11, 1599, Oñate informed Vicente de Zaldívar, the lieutenant governor, that the deaths of the soldiers had "resulted in disrupting the general peace of the land, which is now in serious danger of revolting if the offenders are not properly punished, as their vileness would be emulated by other savages whenever they wished." Absent such a response, Spaniards in the region risked death or enslavement. But Oñate grasped that long-term success depended on psychology: the Spaniards needed to understand what peoples whose words he did not comprehend thought about the newcomers who had declared themselves the rulers of the land and who had demanded tribute and religious change. Fear of the Spaniards had kept Natives in check, the governor believed. The soldiers had to make Indigenous tremble again. He raged against the ways that those in Acoma had gone against their agreement to accept Spanish governance. But he thought, too, that perhaps their actions could be caused by intellectual defects or brutality (*brutalidad*), so he instructed Zaldívar that he could offer clemency if it was warranted. Even in that instance, the town still needed to be destroyed. "Burn it to the ground," he instructed, "and leave no stone on stone, so that the Indians may never be able again to inhabit it as an impregnable fortress."[12]

Despite fierce resistance, Spanish soldiers took Acoma. Zaldívar ordered his men to burn the town. His soldiers captured 500 of the residents and marched them to face Oñate in Santo Domingo pueblo. On February 9, 1599, Oñate listened to the testimony of the captives, each of whom offered brief details about what had led to the initial assault and its aftermath. The next day Captain Alonso Gómez Montesinos, who had acted as an attorney for the Natives in the trial, sought to have them freed on the grounds that his clients had claimed either that they were not there when the violence broke out or that they were unaware of what happened. He pled for Oñate to "show clemency to the Indians in view of the fact that they are uncivilized (*bárbaros*)."[13]

11. Hammond and Ray, *Oñate*, 431 (assurance of protection), 439 (Tabora testimony), 448–449 (González testimony), 456 (fear of further consequences).
12. Hammond and Ray, *Oñate*, 456–460.
13. Hammond and Ray, *Oñate*, 462 (capture), 463–468 (Native testimony), 469.

On February 12, Oñate pronounced sentences. All men over age twenty-five were to have one of their feet severed and then be enslaved for 20 years. Males aged twelve to twenty-five kept their feet but were sentenced to twenty years of slavery, the same sentence he gave to all women over age twelve. He singled out two men from Moqui who had been at Acoma and fought with the locals against the Spaniards. Each was to lose his right hand and then be released so that "they may convey to their land the news of this punishment." Girls under age twelve went into the care of Friar Alonso Martínez, who had the authority to "distribute them in this kingdom or elsewhere in monasteries of other places where he thinks they may attain the knowledge of God and the salvation of their souls." The boys were to go to Zaldívar, with the same idea. He banished the elderly to Querechos and forbade them from ever leaving the pueblos there.[14]

Oñate's soldiers killed hundreds of men (and likely women too) in Acoma and then destroyed the physical town. They left a small army of angry men missing a foot and doomed scores of people to lives of slavery. On one level, Oñate acted as he did to punish those who opposed Spanish rule. But on a deeper level he ordered the violence to send a message. Unlike Coronado, who had traveled through the region as an explorer, Oñate was bent on creating conditions for colonization. He believed that the only way for the Spanish to survive in this desert environment was to reduce or eliminate any threats to the colonists he led into the region or those who would follow. He knew that if potential migrants became scared, they could ride back to New Spain, thereby undermining his effort to establish a colony. Resistance to earlier explorers had been one thing, Oñate grasped, but if Spaniards were to create durable colonies, they needed to be willing to become even more violent. He recognized that friars working in dispersed pueblos needed protection too, though he perhaps underestimated their willingness to die as martyrs in the mission field. There were commodities to be extracted from New Mexico, notably silver (he hoped) and salt. But any venture would fail if he lacked the soldiers to protect communities and roads, miners to work in the ground, and farming families who might be able to turn a profit from the herds they marched northward from New Spain. The only way to keep them in place in this land was to make them feel secure, and the only way to achieve that goal was to send a clear signal to those who did not perish at Acoma. Heed the word of the invaders and pay your tribute, his actions stated, or face dire consequences.

14. Hammond and Ray, *Oñate*, 477–479.

That, at least, was his hope, though if he had had access to a map that marked the many existing Indigenous settlements across New Mexico he would have known that the Spanish could survive in this world only if they formed alliances with at least some Native peoples. Far from New Spain, far from the coast, the Spaniards who remained were demographically insignificant, fragile islands of Iberian Catholics and soldiers who believed they controlled hundreds of square miles. In reality, they were as isolated as Coronado had been when he made his *entrada* in the 1540s.

In the decade after Oñate's arrival in New Mexico in 1598 and his insistence that Indigenous accept the legitimacy of the Spanish monarch and the Catholic Church, Spaniards had mostly managed to alienate the Native peoples they met. Oñate apparently believed that the punishment his soldiers had exacted on the people of Acoma in 1598 signaled the end of any challenges. The crosses he erected across New Mexico testified to his sense that this was marked as Spanish territory. He hoped to administer it from San Gabriel, a Tewa pueblo known to its residents as Yúngé. By 1608 he and his soldiers had convinced many of the Tewa to move to Ohke, on the opposite side of the Rio Grande, where the Spanish had first hoped to establish their presence but eventually came to believe that the Indigenous dwellings they seized had become too crowded since the Tewa would not leave.[15]

Spanish officials who tried to expand their authority northward knew that in some isolated locales it would be possible to extract profits and convert souls. One model they would have known was Zacatecas, a satellite city 350 miles from Mexico City that had become home to the richest silver mines north of Potosí. By 1550, its population had boomed—not only with colonial creoles but also with enslaved workers, at least some of them African, and with free Indigenous drawn to the opportunities in the city, including Native merchants who lived close together and at least some of whom went to a church that attended to the spiritual needs of those who had converted. The settlement also had Indigenous "sheriffs" who apparently helped recruit workers for the Spaniards.[16]

In Zacatecas, Spanish colonizers abandoned the *repartimiento* (forced labor) and tribute systems that they had employed closer to Mexico City, recognizing that the development of the silver mining complex created opportunities that drew Indigenous workers from a wide area. But even the people attracted to the area could not satisfy the extraordinary

15. Weber, *Spanish Frontier*, 77–78.
16. Federico Sescosse, "Zacatecas in 1600," *Artes de Mexico* 194–195 (1978), 114–118.

labor demands in the mines. As a result, those who commanded the most resources in the community turned to enslaved labor. Cristóbal de Oñate, a Basque immigrant who led the group of explorers who discovered silver in Zacatecas, became the wealthiest person in the new city. He owned thirteen smelters and stamp mills as well as 101 houses for enslaved people. He also had a church built to tend to their spiritual needs. He was not the only slaveholder. One needed 24 houses for the enslaved workers he owned, another had 12, and still another 10. In all, Zacatecas had at least 268 houses just for the enslaved, enumerated in a census that referred to one slaveholder who had a house "for his negroes" and another who owned four dwellings "for himself and his workers."[17]

No such economic engine emerged in New Mexico, which meant that Spanish administrators needed different strategies to create a viable colony. But Don Juan de Oñate failed to understand the *realpolitik* of the Puebloan homeland. Rather than convince the Tewas and others to accept the king and the cross, his actions stirred resentment. In 1599, within a year of the assault at Acoma, Jumanos rose up against the Spanish. The colonizers raised fewer than 100 soldiers, an insufficient number to suppress the insurrection. Spaniards hoped to develop San Gabriel, but the colonists, surrounded by Pueblos, fled back to Mexico. By the time Oñate eventually returned in 1605 after a journey that had taken him to the Gulf of California, San Gabriel's prospects seemed so dim that Viceroy Juan de Mendoza y Luna, marquis of Montesclaros of Mexico, who had authority over the Spanish in New Mexico, ordered the venture abandoned. Oñate, as crown investigators eventually determined, had undermined Spanish chances to create another mining outpost. Colonial officials took him to court, where magistrates found him guilty of adultery and abuse of both the Spaniards under his authority and the Puebloan peoples he had persecuted. Mexican authorities fined him and banished the onetime governor from New Mexico. He sailed to Spain having failed to attain glory in the eyes of Spanish bureaucrats or clerics, though still sufficiently well connected to earn back the wealth he once possessed, endow religious institutions, advise King Philip IV on mining issues, and become a knight in the Order of Santiago.[18]

17. Dana Velasco Murillo, "The Creation of Indigenous Leadership in a Spanish Town: Zacatecas, Mexico, 1609–1752," *Ethnohistory* 56 (2009), 669–698; Sescosse, "Zacatecas in 1600," 115–116.

18. Weber, *Spanish Frontier*, 86–87; James Ivey, "An Uncertain Founding: Santa Fe," *Commonplace* 3, no. 4 (2003), http://commonplace.online/article/uncertain-founding-santa-fe/; Eric Beerman, "Death of an Old Conquistador: New Light on Juan de Oñate," *New Mexico Historical Review* 54 (1979), 305–319.

In 1608, after Oñate sailed to Spain, royal authorities encouraged Franciscans to return to New Mexico, with the crown bearing the cost. They would be aided by a new governor, Pedro de Peralta, and would inhabit a new capital near the Santa de Cristo Mountains called Villa Real de Santa Fe. Imperial policymakers also reconceptualized the colony. Oñate had gone there as *adelantado*, a privately funded leader. The Spanish decided that New Mexico should instead become a royal colony, even though that meant it might become a constant drain on the finances of the realm. Still, the investment seemed worth it once Philip III had heard from the viceroy that the Franciscans claimed to have converted 7,000 Puebloans since 1598, an extraordinary and likely exaggerated boast. Velasco added that the Spanish "could not abandon the land without great offense to God and great risk of losing what had been gained."[19]

On March 30, 1609, the viceroy issued detailed instructions to Peralta. He was to leave as soon as possible and take a group of twelve, which included both soldiers and Franciscans. Crucially, Peralta had to ensure that the soldiers caused no harm to any Native peoples along the journey. Beyond that, he needed to make sure that the livestock were healthy when they arrived since the newcomers would put them to work as soon as possible. When he got to Santa Fe, Peralta also had to make sure the site was suitable for the others who would follow so that they could live, as the viceroy put it, "with some cleanliness and stability."[20] The viceroy dictated that Peralta or his lieutenant would have jurisdiction over the Natives. To lure colonists, Santa Fe would provide plots for immigrants sufficient for their houses, gardens, and vineyards, as well as claims to water transported by any irrigation system. In response, each of those who accepted such property needed to remain in place for at least ten years. Peralta was to lay out a central square "for the purpose of erecting Royal Buildings and other public buildings." Legislation would come from the king to New Mexico via Mexico City, but the city's daily affairs would be governed by a locally elected council.[21]

Royal officials' overriding concerns focused on minimizing tensions with local Native peoples in order to launch what the Spanish anticipated would be an agrarian society. There were no provisions in the original instructions about looking for or operating mines, another sign that the

19. Weber, *Spanish Frontier*, 89–90; David J. Weber, "Santa Fe," in James C. Kelly and Barbara Clark Smith, eds., *Jamestown, Québec, Santa Fe: Three North American Beginnings* (Washington, DC: Smithsonian Institution Press, 2007), 136–141.
20. "Ynstruccion a Peralta por Vi-Rey," transcribed by Lansing B. Bloom and translated by Ireneo L. Chaves as "Instructions to Peralta by Vice-Roy," *New Mexico Historical Review* 4 (1929), 179.
21. "Ynstruccion a Peralta," 181.

crown assumed that this colony would cost more than it would bring to royal coffers. Instead, Peralta had to find ways to rein in any potential aggression from Spanish soldiers so that they would not provide an excuse for Indigenous to attack the thinly populated enclave the colonizers planned to erect close to groups of Apaches, many of whom had been harboring resentments toward the Spanish since the days when colonial soldiers captured and enslaved community members for mining work. To facilitate intercultural communication, which he believed foundational to the Franciscans' efforts to convert Indigenous, Peralta encouraged teaching Spanish to Native children.[22] Spanish authorities were not opposed to Peralta waging campaigns against Indigenous, but they insisted that the Franciscans play a leading role in local politics. The priests in the field occupied a winning position: they would either preside over flocks of those they had "reduced" to Christianity or suffer a violent death, which would lead to martyrdom and spiritual reward.[23]

The viceroy wanted Peralta to reach Santa Fe by the end of 1609, but that target proved optimistic. First, the new governor had to organize those who would join him, including nine Franciscan friars who, as it turned out, did not get their necessary breviaries, robes, and mules until May. It took until June for Peralta's associates to purchase the supplies they would need to build houses and plant vineyards in Santa Fe. The entourage marched first to Zacatecas, where Peralta purchased 210 oxen, 25 carts, 500 head of cattle, 30 mares, 100 sheep, and 130 steers. While in Zacatecas he also acquired six enslaved Natives and hired an unknown number of others. By the time he departed for Santa Fe, his traveling party included nine friars riding mules, nineteen soldiers on horseback, over 1,000 domesticated animals, and, according to one estimate, a minimum of 100 Natives, all of them presumably walking. The march likely took three to four months to cover the approximately 1,100 miles from Zacatecas, through territory with no roads suitable for ox-driven carts, which no doubt bogged down in rain and snow. It seems likely that they reached the location of the new capital sometime in early 1610.[24]

By the time Spaniards established a small community at Santa Fe it had been ninety years since the conquest of Mexico. In the decades following the death of Moctezuma, Spanish claims extended through Central

22. "Ynstruccion a Peralta," 183–185.
23. "Ynstruccion a Peralta," 187.
24. Lansing B. Bloom, "When Was Santa Fe Founded?," *New Mexico Historical Review* 4 (1929), 188–194.

America, across northern South America, and along the Pacific to the southern reaches of the continent. But territory lying to the north remained of only marginal interest, a situation like St. Augustine's. In Santa Fe, Spanish imperial officials saw the possibility of establishing the capital of a profitable colony, though the region had not produced much wealth for them other than the small number of souls the Franciscans had brought into Christendom. Just like they had in Florida, imperial officials concluded by the last decades of the sixteenth century that the time had come to fulfill the goals of the doctrine of "new discoveries" in places that Spaniards had visited previously. Time would tell whether this new round of activity would produce lasting results given the hesitancy of Spanish men, and especially Spanish women, to become colonizers in these far reaches of New Spain. In the meantime, the Spaniards most likely to appear in these possible colonies were Franciscans and soldiers, each essential to the king's twinned secular and spiritual goals but not sufficient to create durable communities.[25]

The modest launch of Santa Fe, an isolated outpost of Spanish dreams of North American conquest, came at a moment when other Europeans also decided to make a more substantial effort to create durable communities on the continent. Just like those who started to build Santa Fe, the architects of a small French settlement at Québec and an English village at Jamestown would soon learn that surviving in North America was going to be much more difficult than any could have imagined.

25. According to one estimate, during the seventeenth century—not to mention the sixteenth—the total Spanish population in New Mexico and La Florida combined never exceeded 5,000. Weber, *Spanish Frontier*, 90.

12

Promise and Peril Along the St. Lawrence

When Jacques Cartier and Jean-François Roberval sailed home in the early 1540s, they turned their backs on a region that boasted everything colonizing Europeans sought: a temperate climate suitable for European-style agriculture, forests roamed by large numbers of fur-bearing mammals, waterways teeming with fish and shellfish, and a substantial number of Indigenous residents who, by French visitors' accounts, were eager to engage in trade. The St. Lawrence was the ideal venue for territorial expansion, a place to extract material profits and spread Christianity. The claims about the conversion of St. Lawrence Iroquoian captives to Christianity in Saint-Malo provided more proof, if any was needed, of the seeming cultural malleability of Native peoples in this region. Economic and social problems in France had produced a domestic population primed to embrace the possibility of migration to achieve stability. What better place to find colonists than in a country where famine, dearth, and social upheaval undermined daily life for countless inhabitants?[1]

And yet the St. Lawrence, almost alone among sites where Europeans had hoped to create their future, had failed for everyone. The arrival of Europeans led to the collapse and dispersal of the St. Lawrence Iroquoians. But such circumstances on the ground, if they were known across the Atlantic, were insufficient to dispel notions that French women and men held about Canada. Geography may not be destiny, but the lure and the danger of the northwestern Atlantic and the nearby mainland could be seen in the exemplary case of Sable Island, an offshore pile of sand that became a metaphor for French efforts to establish North American settlements at the turn of the seventeenth century. Sable Island was a site of failed starts, unfortunate but by no means tragic. A worse fate enveloped the Indigenous of the St. Lawrence Valley. Their two booming cities disappeared in the years following the initial arrival of French explorers.

1. See Peter N. Moogk, "Reluctant Exiles: Emigrants from France in Canada Before 1769," *WMQ*, 3rd Ser., 46 (1989), 463–505.

The people now known as St. Lawrence Iroquoians had inhabited the valley for centuries—perhaps more than a millennium—before Cartier arrived. Like many other Indigenous peoples across North America, they sustained vibrant communities by maximizing their use of local resources. Cartier's descriptions of maize agriculture at Stadacona (modern Quebec) and Hochelaga (on the island where Montreal is found) fit the physical record of their earlier occupation, which shows signs of corn growing at least a thousand years ago. During difficult times of the year such as winter's end, when the supplies of fresh food ran low and forest animals grew skinny, residents of these towns traveled to the shoreline to take advantage of local populations of harbor seals, beluga whales, and yellow perch. They knew too about the abundance of harp seals, which migrated into local estuaries from January into April, and they feasted on these animals' layers of fat. Seasonal migrations brought hunters into contact on the shoreline with Montagnais (Innu) and, when they traveled inland, with Wendats (also known as Hurons) as well as Haudenosaunee. The rhythms of their life, developed over centuries, were stable and sustainable.[2]

So what happened to them after Cartier's visits? It is possible that infectious diseases could have traveled from one group to another from the Atlantic coastline, where European fishing crews arrived every year to harvest cod. Or perhaps some kind of political rivalries within villages, maybe triggered by the disappearance of community leaders who sailed to Saint-Malo with Cartier, exploded in ways that undermined the stability of these communities. The deepening cold of the Little Ice Age likely had little impact since other Native nations in the region—to the north (Cree and Inuit), south and west (Haudenosaunee and Wendat), and southeast (Montagnais)—remained dominant in their own territories. Whatever caused the apparent dispersal of the two large population centers did not lead to the disappearance of the individuals who once lived there. When a Recollect missionary put together a dictionary of the Wendat language as part of a growing arsenal of intellectual tools to facilitate the conversion of Indigenous residents, he included St. Lawrence Iroquoian words and pronunciations, a sign that the descendants of those Cartier had met probably had become integrated into other Native communities.[3] Émigrés

2. Christian Gates St-Pierre, "Iroquoians in the St. Lawrence River Valley Before European Contact," *Ontario Archaeology* 96 (2016), 47–64.

3. John Steckley, "St. Lawrence Iroquoians Among the Wendat: Linguistic Evidence," *Ontario Archaeology* 96 (2016), 17–25; Jennifer Birch, "Geopolitics and Dimensions of Social Complexity in Ancestral Wendake, c. A.D. 1450–1600," *Ontario Archaeology* 96 (2016), 35–46; Peter Ramsden, "Becoming Wendat: Negotiating a New Identity Around Balsam Lake in the Late Sixteenth Century," *Ontario Archaeology* 96 (2016), 121–132; Gary Warrick and Louis Lesage, "The Huron-Wendat and the St. Lawrence

from the valley may also have joined Haudenosaunee towns.[4] Despite their survival, more changes were sure to come to the valley as well as the territories nearby if the French could figure out how to launch colonies, a task that continued to befuddle them—even though the St. Lawrence Iroquoians had provided detailed information about how to succeed there.

On January 12, 1598, King Henry IV granted the marquis de la Roche, then planning an expedition to Canada, the right to condemn criminals from France and take them along on the journey. Less than eight weeks later, Henry de Bourbon, the governor of Normandy, "having recognized how useful the conquest of the Islands of Canada" could be for the realm, granted the marquis the right to gather soldiers to accompany him on his mission. On May 20, Normandy's parliament authorized a "trumpet proclamation" to encourage "each and every one of the strong tramps and beggars" of Rouen to gather, with the idea that the town would provide the marquis 200 men and 50 women to take to Canada. Once selected, civic authorities would provide them with bread to keep them alive. Any who strayed into their old habits would be whipped. Local police rounded up 800 possible candidates so that the organizers of the venture could choose "the strongest and healthiest" from among them. La Roche identified one criminal he wanted to add to the cohort, but authorities, deeming his crime of raping a girl too severe, instead had him executed.[5]

La Roche had in mind establishing a colony on modern Sable Island, which he called the Île de Bourbon. This might have been the place called Fagunda by Portuguese explorer João Álvares Fagundes, who had set off from the Portuguese fishing center of Vianna in 1520 on a journey to the cod fishing banks that took him to the coast of Newfoundland and Nova Scotia. He named many places, including a series of offshore islands. He had secured a patent to develop a colony there, but apparently he had become too saddled with debts to pursue them. The debts remained to be paid by his estate. Any claim to land he found faded quickly.[6]

Iroquoians: New Findings of a Close Relationship," *Ontario Archaeology* 96 (2016), 133–143.

4. See Susan Dermarkar et al., "St. Lawrence Iroquoians and Pan-Iroquoian Social Network Analysis," *Ontario Archaeology* 96 (2016), 87–103.
5. *NAW*, 4:308–310.
6. H. P. Biggar, ed., *The Precursors of Jacques Cartier, 1497–1534* (Ottawa: Government Printing Bureau, 1911), xxii–xxv.

The island is little more than a narrow spit of land, about 130 miles southeast of modern Halifax.[7] It has never had a sustained human presence, though from time to time people did try to live there until they realized they could not survive.[8] European livestock fared better than humans who traveled across the ocean. The French found the descendants of cows and bulls deposited there in the mid-sixteenth century. There was enough grass to sustain them, along with black foxes, which the French hunted for their skins. French colonizers who remained long enough for their clothes to tatter began to dress themselves using the hides of seals. Despite their initial ability to survive, long-term prospects looked bleak. The would-be conquerors soon left on a French fishing ship that had been nearby harvesting cod.[9] Their departure marked La Roche's failure. Unable to make a profit, he became a victim of shifting political winds in France that reduced his authority and emboldened those who opposed him. In 1606, when he realized his efforts had produced no results, La Roche wrote that the island had little chance of doing much to advance the efforts of the French king.[10]

A generation earlier, such discouraging news about an American venture might have elicited little interest in France. In some sense things had not changed. Henry IV did not develop a keen notion to send other beggars, however stout of body, to Sable Island. Although Cartier, Roberval, and Laudonnière had crossed the Atlantic and created plans to stay that went nowhere, this new venture made little sense. The only advantage that Sable Island could have had for Europeans was as a way station for ships plying the rich cod banks. Archaeological evidence of shipwrecks suggests that ships likely did try to moor near Sable Island, presumably to restock their supplies. But the sunken spars of European hulls reveal that Sable Island took its place among the growing number of American locations where European dreams of colonization crashed into reality.[11]

7. Edmund F. Slafter, "Memoir of Samuel de Champlain," in Samuel de Champlain, *Voyages of Samuel de Champlain*, trans. Charles P. Otis (Boston: Prince Society, 1880) [hereafter Champlain, *Voyages*], 1:31.
8. See Marq de Villiers and Sheila Hirtle, *Sable Island: The Strange Origins and Curious History of a Dune Adrift in the Atlantic* (New York: Walker, 2004), 11–22; J. Terasmae and R. J. Mott, "Postglacial History and Palynology of Sable Island, Nova Scotia," *Geoscience and Man* 3, no. 1 (1971), 17–28. The island's inhospitable reputation remained for centuries; see Philip Booth, "Sable Island," *Kenyon Review* 23, no. 2 (1961), 255–257.
9. Champlain, *Voyages*, 1:235–236.
10. *NAW*, 4:310–311.
11. de Villiers and Hirtle, *Sable Island*, 41–51.

La Roche's effort reflected changed circumstances in France. During the early decades of the sixteenth century, monarchs who had supported the idea of American colonization, including François I, Henri II, and Catherine de' Medici, had not separated the idea of establishing distant outposts from the goal of spreading Catholicism to those in the Western Hemisphere whom they saw as heathens. As a result, when Cartier and Roberval explored the St. Lawrence in the 1530s and 1540s, they did so with the idea that their efforts would support, as Roberval put it, "the augmentation and increase of our holy Christian faith and holy mother Catholic church."[12] Others had different motivations: those who supported the establishments of Huguenots at Fort Caroline (with Laudonniére) and on the coast of Brazil (with the missionary Jean de Léry) saw the Western Hemisphere as a place for Protestants to escape from Catholic persecution. In each of these cases, state authorities did not see the promotion of one faith or another as crucial. French Catholics who went to Canada or Protestants in Brazil all served the interests of the state. Surviving on American shores legitimized European claims based on discovery alone. Extracting resources—furs from the St. Lawrence or brazilwood from South America—would pay benefits for French furriers and dye makers.

That philosophy broke down during the religious wars, when most French women and men focused on threats they faced at home. Emigration to New France, which had never amounted to much, came to a halt. At century's end, the signing of the Edict of Nantes, which allowed toleration for Protestants within the realm, meant that the French could once again expend resources on establishing colonies. At the moment when La Roche pitched the colonization of Sable Island, the monarchical approach had not changed: colonies could be self-governing along whatever confessional lines their governors wanted as long as they recruited migrants and paid for their move, erected their own defenses (so they would not need to rely on royal soldiers), and eventually sent resources home.[13] Soon enough, however, the situation shifted. The French administration became more keen to promote the planting of Catholicism abroad and hence less ecumenical in its approach to who would make suitable colonizers, one of many domestic shifts that favored Rome to the disadvantage of Huguenots.[14]

12. Marcel Trudel, *Histoire de la Nouvelle-France*, 8 vols., (Montreal: Fides, 1963–1983), quotation at 1:131.
13. Leslie Choquette, "Recruitment of French Emigrants to Canada, 1600–1760," in Ida Altman and James Horn, eds., *"To Make America": European Emigration in the Early Modern Period* (Berkeley: University of California Press, 1991), 133–134.
14. On the shifting fortunes and pressures on French Huguenots, see Philip Benedict, "The Huguenot Population of France, 1600–1685: The Demographic Fate and Customs of a Religious Minority," *Transactions of the American Philosophical Society* 81, no. 5 (1991), i–164.

While the French might not have realized it, the Indigenous residents of the St. Lawrence Valley and their neighbors who lived along nearby Atlantic coastlines had already changed their lives in response to the arrival on their shores of French fishing crews fetching up with some frequency after the middle of the century. Natives had seen these newcomers as the source of useful goods they could not produce. To get metal tools, they brought beaver skins and oil from whales, walrus, and seals to the shoreline. Basque sailors had begun plying this trade as early as 1527. By the middle of the century Tadoussac, an Indigenous town with its own small harbor at the juncture of the St. Lawrence and Saguenay Rivers, had become an annual destination for French traders. The fact of trade at this exposed beach was no surprise since this had been a location for human activity for centuries.[15] Trade between Europeans and Natives faded from about 1550 to 1580, but then resumed. One French ship sailed up the river in 1581, a larger one the following year, and three arrived in 1583. Traders on these expeditions gathered the furs that Hakluyt saw in Paris in 1584 when he was working as a spy for Queen Elizabeth. Cartier's nephew Jacques Noël, who had found his uncle's plans among his papers, made it as far as Mont Royal in 1585. By decade's end, a growing number of French ships competed for furs and oil. In 1599, an explorer named François Gravé du Pont recorded place-names that appeared on a map of New France in 1601, redefining the cartography of a region earlier and imperfectly mapped by Cartier.[16] For the French, the fur trade, once an adjunct to the cod fishery, became an enterprise in its own right.

The St. Lawrence Iroquoians also adapted to the changed circumstances in less obvious ways. In previous times, as abundant archaeological and oral evidence reveals, the Indigenous residents of the St. Lawrence Valley created and sustained an economy based on harvesting maritime resources. But French traders who wanted beaver encouraged some of them to spend more time each year away from the shoreline to hunt for fur-bearing animals. Their diet began to change, with increased use of

15. G. R. Lowther, "Archaeology of the Tadoussac Area, Province of Quebec," *Anthropologica*, n.s., 7, no. 1 (1965), 27–37.

16. Bruce G. Trigger, *The Children of Aataentsic: A History of the Huron People to 1660*, 2 vols., (Montreal: McGill-Queen's University Press, 1976), 1:208–211; Hakluyt to Sir Francis Walsingham, January 7, 1584, in E. G. R. Taylor, ed., *The Original Writings and Correspondence of the Two Richard Hakluyts*, Hak. Soc., 2nd Ser., 56–57 (London: Hakluyt Society, 1935), 1:205–207.

dried biscuits obtained from French traders. Such preserved food had advantages for those who might spend weeks in woods far from their traditional supplies of nutrients.

This commerce had one other unexpected consequence: it apparently encouraged residents of the St. Lawrence to trade with Native peoples farther south, perhaps as far as modern Massachusetts, who had a long-established, seasonal agricultural economy but less access to skins and furs, or at least preferred having others handle such hunts. To obtain food, the St. Lawrence Iroquoians at times traded European manufactured goods to these more southern peoples who, at that point, had little sustained access to Europeans since those who crossed the ocean concentrated their time in the fisheries and the St. Lawrence.

Trade along the St. Lawrence also led to the development of a new commercial language built on Indigenous and European phrases. The French had hoped that Native peoples they had taken to France would learn French and become interpreters. But lingering hostility from the time that Cartier kidnapped ten left such linguistic dreams unfulfilled. It is possible that three St. Lawrence Iroquoians traveled to Saint-Malo around 1584. They were likely voluntary travelers, not kidnap victims, whom the French had hoped would help them broker terms along the river upon their return. Whatever their role, the economic transformation had taken hold. Furs traded at Tadoussac arrived from as far afield as Hudson Bay, along Indigenous trade routes that took European goods deep into the continent's interior, passing from hand to hand.[17]

The lust for European trade goods possibly contributed to the dispersal of the St. Lawrence Iroquoians by 1603. Scholars who have combed the archaeological and oral records have not agreed on why this occurred. Perhaps they were driven out of the region by the Haudenosaunee. Maybe the Mi'kmaqs, who had gained iron weapons from Europeans, used their newfound technological advantage to drive off the Stadacoans, who had annually traveled to the Gaspé Peninsula to fish and hunt. It is possible the colder temperatures of the Little Ice Age shortened the growing season for maize and reduced the food supply that could reach Natives of the valley. Whatever the cause, at the dawn of the seventeenth century, the French faced no resistance from the peoples who had controlled the valley since well before the time of Cartier and Roberval.[18]

17. Trigger, *Children of Aataentsic*, 1:208–209 (economic change), 212–213 (trade language), 213–214 (extent of trade).

18. Trigger, *Children of Aataentsic*, 1:214–224.

In 1603 Henri IV, having lost faith in La Roche, entertained an inquiry from Pierre Du Gua, sieur de Monts, a Huguenot who recognized that the conflict in France had come to an end but that the underlying religiously fueled tensions had not been resolved. Looking for a brighter future, he traveled to the St. Lawrence in 1603 and then returned home with a bold appeal. On November 6, he asked Henri IV for permission to establish French settlements in Acadia. He wanted the king to name him viceroy and captain general on land and sea and asked for the "power to make war and alliances, grant pardons and privileges as well to those of the country as to persons who shall go to settle there, to distribute lands, and to assign titles and seigneuries." He sought land that stretched from 40° to 46° north latitude. Like La Roche, he wanted permission to recruit migrants from among the population of "sturdy beggars" who then roamed the streets of France's towns and farmland. He also wanted permission to build forts, have French courts recognize his claims, and monopolize the fur trade in what he called the Bay of St. Clair—possibly a reference to the Gulf of St. Lawrence—and the River of Canada, presumably the St. Lawrence. To show his commitment, he promised to transport French artisans to handle the tasks migrants would need done.

The king acceded to most of his requests. To support the venture, he ordered judges to convert sentences of banishment to a period of service in the new villages of Acadia. The king authorized a minor tax, "a sol for a livre," for those who invested in the colony. The monarch and the colonizers agreed that Rouen, a city that had once had extensive connections to the Huguenot efforts to convert Tupinambás to Christianity in Brazil and embraced the brazilwood trade, would be the logical place to organize the French administration of the colony. In practical terms, that meant that all pelts sent to France would arrive there, presumably where they would be tallied and taxed.[19] Henri emphasized that Du Gua should work to convert Native Americans to Roman Catholicism. He also expected that the Frenchman would establish commerce peacefully. Only with amicable economic relations could religious conversion proceed.[20]

19. *NAW*, 4:321–323; Choquette, "Recruitment of French Emigrants," 134; Amy J. Buono, "Representing the Tupinambá and the Brazilwood Trade in Sixteenth-Century Rouen," in Regina R. Féliz and Scott D. Juall, eds., *Cultural Exchanges Between Brazil and France* (West Lafayette, IN: Purdue University Press, 2016), 19–34; see also Michael Wintroub, *A Savage Mirror: Power, Identity, and Knowledge in Early Modern France* (Stanford, CA: Stanford University Press, 2006).

20. "The Patent of the French King . . . for the inhabiting of the Countries of La Cadia Canada, and other places in New France," in Samuel Purchas, *Hakluytus Posthumus, or Purchas his Pilgrimes* (London, 1625), IV:1619–1620.

Two ships, one with Du Gua on board, departed from the small Normandy port of Honfleur on March 15, 1604. The origin made sense given the fact that fishing crews had regularly departed from the port, usually after those on board visited the local church seeking divine support. There were 120 migrants on the voyage, including Samuel de Champlain, who acted as one of the pilots and also recounted the history of this effort in his first major work, *Les Voyages*, published in Paris in 1613.[21] Also on board were two unnamed Natives from the St. Lawrence Valley who had been living in France.[22] Those on the journey faced routine risks—unfavorable winds, storms, a close encounter with an iceberg—but by mid-May they had reached Anticosti Island, opposite the mouth of the St. Lawrence. On May 21 they sighted Gachepé, now known as Gaspé, a place that had gotten its name from an Abenaki word signifying that there was an offshore rock known for the violence of the waves crashing into it. On May 26, they sailed into the harbor at Tadoussac.[23]

As soon as they landed a delegation went to visit Anadabijou, the sagamore (chief or headman). At that time those in the town were attending a *tabagie* or banquet. Following what Champlain recorded as the "custom of the country"—a phrase that Europeans across North America would routinely use to describe their initial dealings with Indigenous peoples—Anadabijou invited the visitors to join them. At that point, one of the unnamed Indigenous travelers who had returned with the French began to speak. He told the assembled that he had met the king of France and that he and his unnamed companions had been treated well during their visit. He added, according to Champlain, that the king "wished them well, and desired to people their country, and to make peace with their enemies (who are the Iroquois) or send forces to vanquish them." Champlain reported that he "also told them of the fine castles, palaces, and houses, and peoples they had seen, and of our manner of living."[24]

When he was done Anadabijou offered tobacco to Champlain, Gravé du Pont, and some sagamores who were sitting near him. "After smoking some time," as the Frenchman reported, Anadabijou addressed the gathering. Champlain believed that he said that the Natives were pleased to have Henri as an ally. Those in the chamber responded "*Ho, ho, ho*, which is to say *yes, yes*." Champlain wrote that the sagamore said

21. *Les Voyages du Sieur de Champlain . . . ou, Journal Tres-Fidele des Observations faites és descouvertures de la Nouvelle France* (Paris, 1613).

22. *Des Sauvages, ou Voyage de Samuel Champlain, de Brouage, fait en la France nouvelle* [1603], trans. H. H. Langton, in H. P. Biggar, ed., *The Works of Samuel de Champlain* (Toronto: Champlain Society, 1922–1936), 1:98.

23. *Des Sauvages*, 95–96.

24. *Des Sauvages*, 99–100.

"he was well content that His said Majesty should people their country, and make war on their enemies, and that there was no nation in the world to which they wished more good than to the French." When he finished, the assembled continued with the *tabagie*, consuming large quantities of bear, seal, elk, and beaver. After they ate, they started to dance. Champlain reported that the gathering was not to mark the arrival of the French, whose appearance the St. Lawrence Iroquoians appreciated, but instead to celebrate a victory over the Iroquois, "of whom they had slain about a hundred, whose scalps they cut off, and had with them for the ceremony." He wrote that the Haudenosaunees had been vanquished by 1,000 fighters, whom he identified as Etchemins, Innu (Montagnais), and Algonquins. They had won because they surprised their enemies because otherwise, as Champlain reported, "they would be afraid, and too much in dread of the said Iroquois," who outnumbered the three groups combined.[25]

While the French remained anchored in the harbor, Anadabijou came down to the shoreline and told his community that the time had come to paddle to Tadoussac to meet their new allies. Almost at once the men and women who were there struck camp, loaded their possessions into 200 birchbark canoes, and paddled out. Champlain, like other Europeans, marveled at the dexterity of the paddlers and the ease with which the canoes sliced through the water.[26]

In his published report on what he saw, which included praise for local economic practices, Champlain included details he hoped would demystify Native Americans for his French readers—even when he described practices that might have seemed shocking. Perhaps for that reason, he emphasized aspects of Indigenous life that seemed the most sensational, including a ritual in which an Algonquin sagamore named Besouat commanded women and men to disrobe and then dance in front of their French, Etchemin, and Montagnais visitors. The women were nude other than for "beads and braided cords made of porcupine quills," but the men wore brief loincloths. In Champlain's hands, the ritual was titillating but not explicitly sexual. Instead, when the dance came to an end those who participated gathered gifts, some of which must have come from the French since they included kettles, swords, and hatchets along with the elk and seal meat, and then retired to their houses.[27] Champlain also reported that he had a long theological debate with a sagamore, presumably Anadabijou. They disagreed about much, including the origins of the world, but each believed that there was a single almighty deity and that

25. *Des Sauvages*, 100–103.
26. *Des Sauvages*, 104–105.
27. *Des Sauvages*, 107–109.

human souls were immortal. The French explorer used that knowledge to encourage colonization as a way to gain new souls for Christendom. Indigenous and French differed, but areas of agreement suggested they had already started to learn how to coexist, an idea that Champlain memorialized on a map indicating the proximity of where Native travelers stayed in the area to the house of a French fur factor named Pierre Chauvin.[28]

After its departure, the French expedition paddled up the Saguenay River. Along the way, Algonquins told the French that about ten or so days' journey from Tadoussac there was a large lake. On the banks of the local rivers "are many lodges," Champlain reported, where other tribes come from the north, to barter beaver and martin skins with the [Innu] for other merchandise, which the French ships bring to the said [Innu]." Those who lived in these northern regions claimed that they lived "in sight of a sea which is salt." They were likely telling him about James Bay or perhaps even Hudson Bay, places that no European had yet seen.[29] Somewhere between Coudres Island and Tadoussac the party spoke with a young Algonquin man who claimed to have wide experience of regional geography. A group of Algonquins near Tadoussac told him about lakes to be found 400 leagues away. "Without doubt," Champlain wrote, "from their account, this can be nothing else than the South Sea, the sun setting where they say it does."[30]

Champlain and his men spent the rest of the summer exploring the region. When they reached Trois Rivières he thought he found an ideal place for a defensible settlement.[31] The local woods housed deer, beaver, and otter, which could bring profits. Native inhabitants drew a sketch of the region, which Champlain took with him to guide the visitors. The Algonquins had obtained copper bracelets from Wendats, an observation that whetted Champlain's appetite with the thought that mines could not be too far distant.[32] After they left Tadoussac the French reached Île Percée, where they found a merchant named Sieur Prévert who had come from Saint-Malo. He had gathered information about the region from the residents, including details about the location of a copper mine and

28. *Des Sauvages*, 111–117; Derek Hayes, *Historical Atlas of Canada* (Seattle: University of Washington Press, 2002), 49.

29. *Des Sauvages*, 121–124.

30. *Des Sauvages*, 164–165.

31. *Des Sauvages*, 135–137.

32. *Des Sauvages*, 144–146 (resources), 153 and 159 (sketch), 164 (copper).

the possibility that there might be silver to be extracted from rocks in the area.[33]

As they were about to board for their journey homeward, a Montagnais sagamore named Bechourat asked Gravé du Pont, so Champlain attested, to take his son to France. The French then asked if they could also take along a Haudenosaunee hostage, whom they believed the residents of Tadoussac were about to eat. The locals agreed. Prévert, the Saint-Malo merchant, took four more Indigenous—a man from the coast of Acadia and three Innu, a woman and two boys. With their captives or guests on the ship, the French set off. On August 24 they rounded the Gaspé Peninsula. They reached the cod fishing banks on September 5. Fifteen days later they sailed into Havre de Grace.[34]

In 1605, Champlain returned to North America. That year the French explorers sailed farther south, coasting modern New England. On July 8 they passed Casco Bay. A few days later they were in Saco Bay. Champlain produced a detailed map, which included the location of an Abenaki fortress as well as the houses the Natives had erected amid their maize fields. They also grew beans, pumpkins, squash, and tobacco. His map identified dwellings right along the coast where they gathered after setting their crops as well as the marshes, just inland from the sand, where birds congregated. On July 18, he arrived at the Wampanoag town of Patuxet in modern Plymouth harbor. Just offshore, he observed "a great many cabins and gardens." That day the winds were against his crew, so they decided to anchor in the bay as they waited for better conditions, a typical tactic used by European explorers along the Atlantic coast at the time. While they waited for the winds to freshen, they were not alone. "Two or three canoes" of Wampanoag residents approached the French after fishing for cod and other marine creatures, "which are plentiful thereabouts."[35]

Champlain understood that locals harvested fish and shellfish from these waters, planted maize near the coast, embraced trade, and were generous to visitors. As was his custom, he drew a map of the region, which included Native dwellings and noted that these were the cabins where Indigenous residents tilled the ground ("labourent la terre"). The wording

33. *Des Sauvages*, 181–185.

34. *Des Sauvages*, 188–189.

35. *Les Voyages du Sieur de Champlain*, 70; Otis, ed., *Les Voyages*, 61–69; see also David Hackett Fischer, *Champlain's Dream: The European Founding of North America* (New York: Simon & Schuster, 2008), 182–192.

mattered, as did his description of the ways that Wampanoags used what he thought was hemp to bait their hooks. These Indigenous residents of North America, like countless others whom the French had labeled *sauvage*, cultivated their fields and understood the utility of particular plants. By no stretch were they "savages." Despite the fact that the visitors knew the land had occupants, the French christened it Port du Cap St. Louis, applying their name in an act of securing possession. The next day, July 19, Champlain and his crew sailed off.[36]

Champlain's maps and journal entries provide the surest evidence about the St. Lawrence Valley in the early years of the century. While the St. Lawrence Iroquoians might have dispersed at some point after the early 1540s, the territory remained altered by their earlier efforts. As Champlain knew, local Indigenous communities reshaped the physical environment, primarily to grow crops. Just as important, they had created maps. Like many other Native peoples in North America, the Indigenous maps of the St. Lawrence Valley likely existed in memory, not on paper. Specific oral knowledge passed from one generation to the next. Rather than provide a visual rendering of a coastline with soundings for

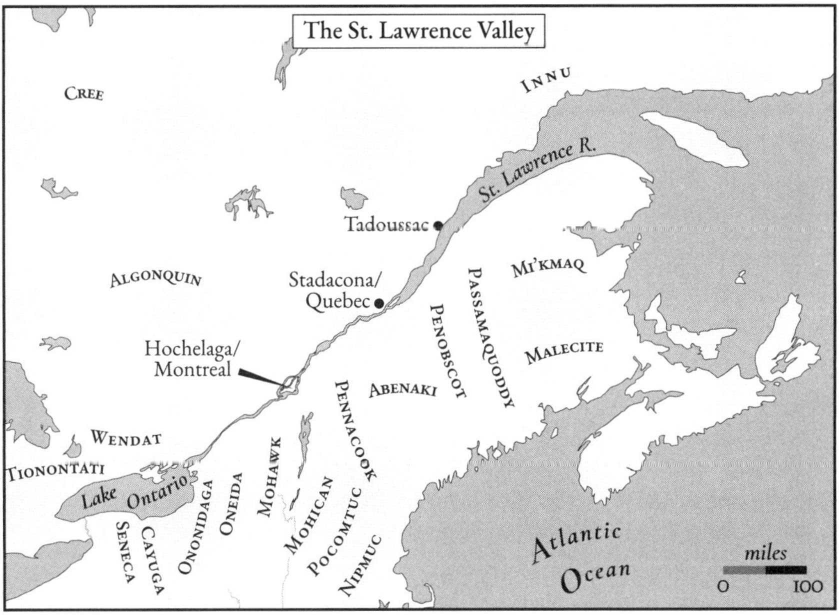

36. *Les Voyages du Sieur de Champlain*, 78–81.

ships, which Europeans would have no doubt preferred given their practice of measuring the depth of waters wherever they sailed, Native maps instead charted the locations of resources, which they then also marked with place-names.[37]

Learning more about Canada encouraged French explorers to take the formal steps of claiming land, practices transatlantic travelers had employed since the age of Columbus: erecting a cross and a flag in any territory that lacked the signs of occupation by a Christian prince and his followers. Sometimes Europeans in the north blew trumpets. At other times they mimicked Drake by erecting a post and nailing some metal monument of their monarch to it. Whatever the strategy, the gestures often proved as ephemeral as the presence of a sailor.

The Indigenous knowledge that Europeans obtained was far more important than ephemeral rituals, especially if the French were to ever convince other subjects of their king that they should migrate to the St. Lawrence. Champlain translated into print (including maps) what he saw, such as well-populated coastlines near modern Portland, Maine, and Plymouth, Massachusetts, which had more residents in Champlain's (or his cartographer's) renderings than interior communities. But his published maps of 1613, which contained up-to-date information about America's interior, provided viewers with details about the valley too.[38]

Time and again, Champlain used similar phrasing to indicate that the residents of communities in the St. Lawrence Valley shaped the lands they inhabited. The maps provide clues to resources that could be found in certain places, information likely gleaned from Indigenous informants. Soundings in the water allowed potential explorers or the migrants they brought along to assess the viability of ascending the deep river, including at the broad expanse facing Quebec.[39] Indigenous peoples traveled these waters in canoes, which Champlain's maps illustrated, but Europeans could sail a three-masted vessel around barrier islands and toward vibrant

37. See Renée Fossett, "Mapping Inuktitut: Inuit Views of the Real World," in Jennifer S. H. Brown and Elizabeth Vibert, eds., *Reading Beyond Words: Contexts for Native History*, 3rd ed. (Toronto: University of Toronto Press, 2009), 111–131.

38. Champlain's "Carte geographic de la Novelle France" in his 1613 book included both the location of Sable Island and modern James Bay with a note that this was the place where Hudson had spent the winter (of 1610–1611), a geographic detail that had appeared only the year before. Champlain's map is in *Les Voyages du Sieur de Champlain* at 161; for the earlier map marking the location of Hudson's demise, see *Descriptio ac delineation Geographica Detectionis Freti* (Amsterdam, 1612), plate between sig A2^{v} and A3^{r}.

39. *Les Voyages du Sieur de Champlain*, 232.

Native communities.[40] He did not intend to reveal a peaceful and vacant paradise for potential migrants. Details of conflicts, including one in which Champlain and his allies battled Haudenosaunee warriors, attest to the dangers that still existed in certain places.[41] Opportunity nonetheless beckoned, evident in the plan for a colonial settlement on the island of St. Croix, which featured the location of future gardens as well as the location where migrants should install their cannons. Maps warned of places where the region's mighty tides covered marshes regularly and where natural resources could be found.[42]

Champlain sailed back to France in 1607. During that winter, French officials, who had contemplated making a sustained investment in Acadia, decided that their best prospects lay along the St. Lawrence. Champlain returned to the valley, seeking a homesite for himself and a foothold for his realm. "I looked for a place suitable for our settlement," he wrote in his journal on a long summer day in 1608, "but I could not find any more suitable or better than the point of Québec, so called by the natives, which was covered by nut trees." He quickly dispatched workers to clear some of the forest and to erect a fortified town, which included building his own substantial house. He informed the French king that he would use the village as a base for further explorations in search of the Northwest Passage and to process what he imagined as a bountiful trade in salmon, sturgeon, eels, and timber. He knew the importance of maintaining a permanent presence to protect French interests in the northwestern Atlantic cod trade. Champlain dreamed of a great city that would soon arise there, perched on the water's edge with openings in the walls for cannon—a fantasy metropolis that he never saw come into existence.[43]

The maps in Champlain's *Voyages* encouraged viewers to look back into the past and forward to a possible, but not yet clear, future. Indigenous peoples had planted maize in the fields that spread outward from the St. Lawrence. They had mapped the region's abundant natural resources. They had built towns. They demonstrated that it was possible to move goods across hundreds of miles of an interior still mostly unknown to Europeans other than the watery corridors that would take Hudson to his

40. *Les Voyages du Sieur de Champlain* (1613), at p. 119.
41. *Les Voyages du Sieur de Champlain* (1613), at p. 137 and at p. 232.
42. *Les Voyages du Sieur de Champlain* (1613), at p. 34 (St. Croix), at p. 23 (tidal marshes).
43. Biggar, ed., *Works of Samuel de Champlain*, 2:331; Hayes, *Historical Atlas of Canada*, 50–52; Brett Rushforth, "The Establishment of a French Empire in North America," in Stephan Gervais et al., eds., *Quebec Questions: Quebec Studies for the Twenty-first Century*, 2nd ed. (Oxford: Oxford University Press, 2016), 3–17.

eponymous bay and Cartier to Stadacona and Hochelaga. Europeans too contributed to the growing volume of information about the region, most evident in the soundings that guided their large ships to safer waters and away from shoals and sandbars that could turn dreams of profit into nightmares. But the visitors knew all too well that this region, even without its two great cities, needed to be explained to them by Indigenous observers.

13

The Coldest Years

The first years of the seventeenth century brought bitter cold across North America and the North Atlantic. Temperatures had begun to drop around the turn of the fourteenth century, but the decline accelerated sometime after 1550, reaching its nadir around the time of the death of Queen Elizabeth I. While temperatures began to moderate within the next two decades, the Little Ice Age shaped encounters between Indigenous Americans and Europeans eager to explore and colonize North America.

The cold did not respect national boundaries or expansionary dreams. Sailors struggling to cross the ocean and others who observed from the shoreline noted extraordinary formations of sea ice around Iceland in 1602, 1604, 1605, 1608, and 1610. Famine took the lives of perhaps 9,000 Norse settlers in Iceland, the descendants of those who had crossed the ocean with high hopes half a millennium earlier. King Christian IV of Denmark believed that Danish communities along the shores of Greenland might still survive, but three efforts to find them failed. The extant narratives mention icebergs as high as mountains. Under such conditions, the Danish explorers informed the king, there was no chance that any transplanted European community could have lasted. That observation hid a crucial fact: the Danes met Inuit on each of their missions, a reminder that the north was inhabitable, but not yet by Europeans.[1]

At his accession, James became king of England, via Elizabeth, and Ireland, a title he assumed from his direct line to Henry VII. His ascent accelerated English attention to the broad swath of the Atlantic coast between the northern boundaries of La Florida and the lands Cartier had claimed two generations earlier. Although the monarch claimed the land, James, following Elizabeth's earlier policy, had little interest in spending his own money on it. As a result, in the early years of his reign, different

1. Sam White, *A Cold Welcome: The Little Ice Age and Europe's Encounter with North America* (Cambridge, MA: Harvard University Press, 2017), 1–4; Eli Kintisch, "Why Did Greenland's Vikings Disappear?," *Science* 354 (2016), 696–701.

groups of investors in London, Bristol, and Plymouth invested in joint-stock companies at a time when environmental conditions posed the greatest threat since the drought and mega-storm that destroyed Cahokia and the contagion of the Black Death across Europe several hundred years earlier.

Cold challenged English colonizers perhaps more than any could have imagined. But at a moment when eager explorers and putative colonizers wanted to prove their worth, journeys across the Atlantic beckoned more powerfully than at any moment since the disappearance of their community at Roanoke two decades earlier.

When the Devon native George Waymouth returned home from the coast of modern Maine in 1605, he and James Rossier brought back more than the details of what could be found there. These explorers also returned with five captive Eastern Abenakis. Waymouth left three of them—Maneddo, Skicowaros, and Sassocomoit—in the charge of Ferdinando Gorges, a thirty-seven-year-old military veteran whose martial prowess had earned him a knighthood despite his fleeting role in a plot to kill Elizabeth.[2]

In 1606, a year or so after the three Indigenous men moved in with Gorges, James supported the formation of two colonies in coastal North America. Following established European ideas, the English needed to avoid lands that might be peopled by French or Spanish migrants. Occupation by Native peoples mattered less in this legal calculus. Per his grants, each colony could claim forty miles along the coast. The southern colony would need to be established between 34° and 40° north latitudes, and the northern between 38° and 45°. The council for the first colony would be based in London, and the group organizing the second would be housed in or around Plymouth. The king's patent specified that each of

2. These Natives were also called Manida and Skidwarres/Skidwares/Skettwarroes; see Alden T. Vaughan, *Transatlantic Encounters: American Indians in Britain, 1500–1776* (New York: Cambridge University Press, 2006), 57–60. As Vaughan noted, one named Tahanedo went to the house of Sir John Popham, one of Gorges's allies, and Amoret went to John Slany, who was the Newfoundland Company's treasurer; see *Transatlantic Encounters*, 61. For Gorges, see James Phinney Baxter, ed., *Sir Fernando Gorges and His Province of Maine* (Boston, 1890), 1:1–198, esp. 67–68 (captives), 14–16 (military experience), and 188–196 (plot against the queen and regaining his position at Plymouth). For additional details, see C. M. Macinnes, *Fernando Gorges and New England* (Bristol, UK: Bristol Branch of the Historical Association, 1965), 2 (knighted by Essex), and John Latimer, *Annals of Bristol in the Seventeenth Century* (Bristol, UK: William George's Sons, 1900), 27, 126–127.

these companies could govern land extending 50 miles inland as well as any islands that lay no more than 100 miles from the shoreline. The second colony could not be founded until the first had established its claim, a crucial point since there needed to be a 100-mile buffer between the two.[3]

Gorges, working with the newly formed Council for New England, concentrated his efforts on the colony the English referred to as Northern Virginia.[4] Living with the Abenaki captives solidified his plan to fuse religious conversion with territorial expansion. Planting the flag of the English king in North America would, he believed, repulse the "infernall spirits, which have so long kept those poore distressed creatures (the inhabitants of those parts) in bondage."[5] He and others associated with the potential colony hoped to learn the local language from the captives, as well as gather information about their communities. The council financed two more trips to the Maine coast to gather intelligence, but both failed, leaving Gorges and others with less information than they needed to create a plan for a successful colony.[6]

Despite English hopes that they would monopolize local opportunities, other Europeans, notably Champlain, continued to sail along the northeast coast. In 1607, undaunted by any news they picked up about other Europeans' travels, English supporters of colonization sent two more ships with 100 men westward. They sailed under the leadership of George Popham, the son of Sir John Popham, the lord chief justice of England, who had been one of the investors in an ill-fated exploratory journey of 1606. George Popham worked alongside Rawley Gilbert, the brother of the president of the Council for New England. They also took along Skicowaros, one of the three men who had been living with Gorges. Carrying provisions and ordnance, the English built a small fort at Sagadahoc and also a thirty-ton pinnace, which they christened the

3. Samuel Bemiss, ed., *The Three Charters of the Virginia Company of London with Seven Related Documents, 1606–1621*, Jamestown 350th Anniversary Historical Booklet 4 (Williamsburg, VA: Jamestown 350th Anniversary Celebration Corporation, 1957), 1–12.
4. See Latimer, *The Annals of Bristol in the Seventeenth Century*, 27–28.
5. *A briefe Relation of the Discovery and Plantation of New England* (London, 1622), sig. A3^{v}–[A4^{v}], quotation at [A4^{r}]. Gorges's name does not appear as the author of the pamphlet, but the dedication is signed "The President and Concell of New-England" when Gorges was its president. Three years later the text appeared again in Samuel Purchas's massive collection, *Hakluytus Posthumus, or Purchas his Pilgrimes* (London, 1625), 4:1827–1832.
6. Ferdinando Gorges, "A Briefe Narration of the Originall Undertakings of the Advancement of Plantations into the Parts of America," in *America Painted to the Life* (London, 1658), 4–5; *A briefe Relation*, sig. B^{v}; "The Voyage of M. Henry Challons intended for the North Plantation of Virginia, 1606," in Purchas, *Purchas his Pilgrimes*, 4:1832–1837.

Virginia. Although they managed to obtain both furs and a large supply of sarsaparilla, they were unable to locate any ore, necessary to forge weapons they would need, or determine if they would ever be able to grow crops. Travelers on a resupply ship soon learned that their stores could not rescue the struggling community. Rather than take additional chances, survivors boarded the *Virginia* and sailed for home, ending hopes for a colony on the Kennebec.[7]

English observers documented the travails the would-be colonizers faced, but they left out that the travelers had also lost a battle with local Natives. "They drove the savages away without ceremony," the French Jesuit Pierre Biard wrote in 1612 about an incident that precipitated the English defeat, and then "beat, maltreated and misused them outrageously and without restraint." In response, Indigenous launched an attack on three English fishing vessels, taking eleven lives. That action prompted the English to flee, leaving the coast open for the French to build forts and establish links with local Indigenous. It took the English two years to reclaim the region, but by then the colony at Sagadahoc was becoming a memory, not a place to be colonized.[8]

Gorges saw the strategic and financial advantages that colonizing Sagadahoc would have brought. The English could have likely prevailed in a contest with local Natives. But winter posed seemingly insurmountable challenges for any migrants who dreamed of establishing a colony near the Kennebec. "All our former hopes," he wrote years later, "were frozen to death."[9]

On April 23, 1607, Henry Hudson, about forty years old, captained the *Hopewell* out of London on a journey to the South Sea. An associate of Captain John Smith, Hudson was well connected to investors, including Thomas Smythe (Smith), whose interests extended across the realm and

7. William Strachey, *The Historie of Travell into Virginia Britania*, ed. Louis B. Wright and Virginia Freund, Hak. Soc., 2nd Ser., 103 (orig. 1612; London: Hakluyt Society, 1953), 173.

8. Pierre Biard, "Relation for 1612," in *JR*, 2:45–47; Alfred A. Cave, "Why Was the Sagahadoc Colony Abandoned? An Evaluation of the Evidence," *New England Quarterly* 68 (1995), 625–640; *A briefe Relation*, sig. B2^{r}–^{v}; Seymour V. Connor, "Sir Samuel Argall: A Biographical Sketch," *VMHB* 59 (1951), 162–175, esp. 168–169.

9. Gorges to Cecil, [February 7, 1608], quoted in James P. Baxter, "Memoir of Sir Ferdinando Gorges," in Baxter, ed., *Sir Ferdinando Gorges and His Province of Maine*, 83–84; Letter of the Council of the Virginia Company to Gorges, February 17, 1608, in Corporation Archives of Plymouth, in Baxter, "Memoir," 91; quotation ("frozen") in Baxter, "Memoir," 90.

its far-flung claims. Hudson planned to sail due north, following a then-prevalent geographical theory that the sun melted the Arctic icecap during the summer. The theory made sense on paper, and contemporary maps provided visual evidence that a large polar sea emerged from the ice floes sometime around the summer solstice. There was no question that this was true, geographers believed. But the journey still posed substantial risks. If the Arctic Ocean melted quickly in summer, it meant that it also froze quickly once the sun began to shine fewer hours each day. Every navigator knew that any ship that entered the open sea lanes would need to emerge into the South Sea before the winter freeze came. No one was certain when that would occur, so it made sense to speed through the water as quickly as possible. Hudson, seeking all the help he could, prayed with some of his crew at St. Ethelburga's Church on Bishops Gate Street in London four days before he embarked. Not known for his religious views, Hudson, like other sailors of the age, figured he had better have some allies looking out for them. He likely took his fourteen-year-old son John with him. The boy would sail with his father on every one of his transatlantic voyages.[10]

Despite careful planning, the expedition encountered difficulties by mid-June: frozen sails and shrouds, cold rain turning to snow, strong winds threatening to blow them onto rocky coastlines, frequent fogs so thick that they could not navigate. Hudson recorded the challenges in a dispiriting series of entries in his journal. On June 20, the sun reappeared for the first time in eighteen days, enabling them to see land, likely modern Kap Perry in Greenland. The *Hopewell* reached 78° north at the end of June but could go no farther in waters clogged with icebergs. Hudson knew that he had sailed farther north than anyone else from England. (As it turned out, no other English ships would reach the same latitude again until the nineteenth century.) While he could savor his achievement, he realized that he had to turn for home because there was no sign of an

10. For then-current geographical thinking about the presumed lack of ice during the Arctic summer, see William Bourne, *A Regiment for the Sea* (London, 1574), sig. 35^{v}; William Bourne, *A Regiment for the Sea* (London, 1590), f. 77; Thomas Blundeville, *A briefe description of universal mappes and cardes* (London, 1589), sig. C2^{r}–3^{r}; "Hondius his Map of the Arctike Pole, or Northerne World," in Samuel Purchas, *Purchas his Pilgrimes*, 3:625; Helen Wallis, "England's Search for the Northern Passages in the Sixteenth and Early Seventeenth Centuries," *Arctic* 37 (1964), 453–472; and John K. Wright, "The Open Polar Sea," *Geographical Review* 43 (1953), 338–365. The theory persisted for centuries; see William Scoresby, *An Account of the Arctic Regions, with a History and Description of the Northern Whale-Fishery* (Edinburgh, 1820), 1:46–49. For Hudson's departure, see Peter C. Mancall, *Fatal Journey: The Final Expedition of Henry Hudson—A Tale of Mutiny and Murder in the Arctic* (New York: Basic Books, 2009), 45.

opening to the South Sea. Hudson and his crew mapped a route that took them to the Faroe Islands in mid-August and reached London a month later. While he failed to get to the Pacific, they had charted waters that no European sailor had seen before, found the locations of abundant maritime resources such as seals and whales, and named lands that, to their knowledge, had no inhabitants and were not yet on any map. Perhaps most important, they brought the *Hopewell* and its entire crew home safely.[11]

The next spring, Hudson took command of the *Hopewell* again, sailing out of London on April 22, accompanied by fourteen others. This time they headed toward the Northeast Passage, the water route that geographers promised existed north of the Russian landmass. The Muscovy Company had sent ships into these waters earlier, but they returned without reaching their destination. Other Europeans had gone in search of it before, most notably Dutch explorer Willem Barentsz, who in the mid-1590s had led three expeditions in search of the passage, the last a catastrophe. Some of the crew survived, but not Barentsz, who died in 1597. The explorer became a legend among the Dutch, his story told time and again among the maritime community and within the tight-knit world of European geographers. The trials that the Dutch faced on these voyages became part of the lore of the Northeast Passage—information devoured by Hudson as he prepared to go into the same waters.[12] But the English explorer, who reached 74° north latitude by early June, could not make it through then either—though he returned with reports of polar bears and a possible mermaid sighting, a somewhat common claim by European sailors in little-known seas where claims of the monstrous and the magical could coexist with the mundane.[13] He was home again by early August, with all his men alive. Hudson told others about what he had seen, including the forbidding frozen seas they had encountered. Among others, he met with the younger Hakluyt, who regularly talked to captains and chroniclers after their time at sea.[14]

11. Mancall, *Fatal Journey*, 45–54.
12. Mary Fuller, *Lines Drawn Across the Globe: Reading Richard Hakluyt's "Principal Navigations"* (Montreal: McGill-Queen's University Press, 2023), 82–89; J. Braat, "Dutch Activities in the North and the Arctic During the Sixteenth and Seventeenth Centuries," *Arctic* 37 (1984), 473–480; Gerrit de Veer, *The Three Voyages of William Barents to the Arctic Regions*, trans. William Phillip, ed. Koolemans Beynen, 2nd ed., Hak. Soc., 1st Ser., 54 (London: Hakluyt Society, 1876). For Hudson's knowledge of Barentsz, see Purchas, *Purchas his Pilgrimes*, 3:579.
13. Purchas, *Purchas his Pilgrimes,* 3:575–578; Karl Banse, "Mermaids—Their Biology, Culture, and Demise," *Limnology and Oceanography* 35 (1990), 148–153.
14. Purchas, *Purchas his Pilgrimes*, 3:580–581.

In the spring of 1609, Hudson set off yet again for the Northeast Passage. This time he sailed with a mixed Dutch and English crew and with financial support not from English investors but instead from the Vereenigde Oostindische Compagnie or United East India Company. The VOC, as it was known, was a rival to the English East India Company, a joint-stock enterprise founded in 1600. The company fitted out the *Halve Maen* (*Half Moon*) for an expedition into the Northeast Passage, a waterway that had still captured Dutch imaginations. The ship departed on April 6. While the English and the Dutch were then commercial rivals, Hudson's employment by the VOC fitted both the needs of a company seeking a skilled commander and the politics of the moment. London and Amsterdam had emerged as commercial centers, with merchants from one aware of schemes in the other. Architects and artists, lured by patrons and the promise of fat contracts, had given each the distinctive look of a prosperous community, leaning into new opportunities while celebrating links to their storied histories. Goods from distant places appeared in local shops. Artists and scientists peered at the plants that had survived long journeys, eager to draw living specimens and ascertain their medical or culinary benefits. Printers produced illustrated tracts, testifying to the importance of long-distance trade to the Western Hemisphere and the Southwest Pacific.[15]

Despite the enthusiasm and the planning, the captain, as a contemporary put it, had "found the sea as full of ice as he had found it the preceding year, so that they lost all hope of effecting anything during the season." Hudson, sharing information with his crew that he had received from Captain John Smith that there might be a way into the Northwest Passage along a river somewhere north of Chesapeake Bay, convinced the men to turn the *Halve Maen* to the west. On the other side of the Atlantic they might find a more temperate climate if they did not sail too far northward.[16] A month later, the ship reached the cod-rich edge of the Atlantic shelf near Newfoundland, where they spotted that season's cluster of European fishing crews. They even spoke to the sailors on one of the

15. See Stephen Alford, *London's Triumph: Merchants, Adventurers, and Money in Shakespeare's City* (New York: Bloomsbury, 2017); Simon Schama, *The Embarrassment of Riches: An Interpretation of Dutch Culture in the Golden Age* (New York: Knopf, 1997); Anne Goldgar, *Tulipmania: Money, Honor, and Knowledge in the Dutch Golden Age* (Chicago: University of Chicago Press, 2008); Benjamin Schmidt, *Innocence Abroad: The Dutch Imagination and the New World, 1570–1670* (Cambridge: Cambridge University Press, 2001).
16. Emanuel van Meteren, "On Hudson's Voyage," in J. Franklin Jameson, ed., *Narratives of New Netherland, 1609–1664* (New York: Charles Scribner's Sons,1909), 6–7; Purchas, *Purchas his Pilgrimes*, 3:581–582.

French ships. On July 8 they hauled in 130 large cod. Soon they supplemented their diet with halibut and lobster.[17]

During the month of July, Hudson and his men began to encounter Indigenous for the first time, possibly Mi'kmaqs from Nova Scotia. When the *Halve Maen* dropped anchor some of these Natives paddled out to the ship. According to the first mate, Robert Juet, the English offered "trifles" to the Natives and welcomed them to join the crew for a meal. Since none of the English or Dutch on board could speak the local language, the Natives and the newcomers presumably tried to communicate in sign language. The English came away from the encounter with the idea that gold, silver, and copper mines were close. More important, the English and Dutch on the ship witnessed the Natives bringing furs to a nearby French ship, watching them trade for metal kettles, knives, axes, beads, and red cloth. They realized too that some of the locals had picked up some French, facilitating trade. Yet the English, though seeing the French gains, concluded that the Natives wanted to steal from them. In response, some of the sailors raided a local settlement. Soon after, the *Halve Maen* pressed on, its occupants apparently not having learned the skills that would enable them to succeed as traders along this part of the coast.[18]

By early August the ship reached the outer banks of Cape Cod. Again, the sailors met locals, likely Narragansetts or Pokanokets. Once again, Indigenous paddled out to the ship and the crew traded with them, this time offering some glass buttons in exchange for fresh meat and tobacco.[19] On August 18 they reached the mouth of Chesapeake Bay, which Hudson had heard from Smith did not lead to the passage. Six days later they reached the Outer Banks of Carolina, another place that the crew would have known, from reading Harriot's book, offered no entrance to the passage. The English turned north, reaching the modern boundary between New York and New Jersey by the start of September.[20]

The crew had arrived on the shores of Lenapehoking, the homeland of the Munsees, who constituted a large proportion of the Lenni Lenape, later known to the English as the Delawares. The Lenapes offered tobacco, and the crew responded with knives and beads. In the days that followed, some of the sailors went ashore, providing details about the Natives' fields and the natural wealth of the region's forests, and some of the Lenapes

17. Purchas, *Purchas his Pilgrimes*, 3:585–586.
18. Purchas, *Purchas his Pilgrimes*, 3:585.
19. Purchas, *Purchas his Pilgrimes*, 3:587.
20. Purchas, *Purchas his Pilgrimes*, 3:587, 589–592; Thomas Holland to the Earl of Salisbury, October 30, 1609, in *Calendar of the Cecil Papers in Hatfield House*, vol. 21, 1609–1612, ed. G. Dynfallt Owen (London, 1970), in *British History Online*, https://www.british-history.ac.uk/cal-cecil-papers/vol21/pp137-154.

boarded the *Halve Maen*. Despite the positive start, relations soon deteriorated. On September 6, just as some sailors returned from a fishing expedition, twenty-six Munsee men in two large canoes launched an attack. Their arrows hit three of the crew, killing one hit in the throat. The English believed the assault was unprovoked, though it is more likely that the visitors, ignorant of some of the nuances of proper dealings in the region, had instead violated local mores. Rather than trying to drive off their English and Dutch visitors, the Munsees were likely sending a specific message: remain and trade, but do not overstep your welcome or venture into places deemed off-limits. After several tense days, the *Halve Maen* began its ascent up the large river in whose mouth they had anchored. Later, after the ship's return, Europeans would name it after Hudson.[21]

During its journey into the interior, the sailors entered the homeland of the Mahicans and the Catskills, who traded beaver and otter pelts for metal hatchets, knives, and glass beads. Once again there was no access to the Northwest Passage. The proof came in late September, when some of the crew paddled twenty-five miles upstream, north of the confluence with the Mohawk. There the river was only seven feet deep. On the twenty-third the *Halve Maen* turned around. Those on board identified places they thought might be good for later colonial towns, a reflection of the growing interest in applying the reports of explorers to plans for establishing communities.[22]

On October 1, during a trading session, one Native man leapt onto the rudder of the *Halve Maen* and climbed into Juet's room. A sailor shot him in the chest, killing him instantly. Other Indigenous on board leapt into the sea, but the crew gave chase on a shallop. One Native man grabbed the small boat, prompting the ship's cook to slice off his hand. While the others in the water swam to safety, this man drowned. Over the next three days, as the ship tried to escape the river for the relative safety of the open sea, members of communities that had had positive relations with the

21. Purchas, *Purchas his Pilgrimes*, 3:592. On the likely reasons for the Munsees' actions and how they likely viewed the newcomers, see Charles T. Gehring and William A. Starna, "Dutch and Indians in the Hudson Valley: The Early Period," *Hudson Valley Regional Review* 9 (1992), 1–25; Anne-Marie Cantwell and Diana diZerega Wall, *Unearthing Gotham: The Archaeology of New York City* (New Haven, CT: Yale University Press, 2001), 119–124; Paul Otto, "Common Practices and Mutual Misunderstandings: Henry Hudson, Native Americans, and the Birth of New Netherland," *De Halve Maen* 72 (1999), 75–83; Paul Otto, "The Origins of New Netherland: Interpreting Native American Responses to Henry Hudson's Visit," *Itinerario* 13 (1994), 22–39; Evan Haefeli, "On First Contact and Apotheosis: Manitou and Men," *Ethnohistory* 54 (2007), 407–443; Robert S. Grumet, *The Munsee Indians: A History* (Norman: University of Oklahoma Press, 2009), 3–41.

22. Purchas, *Purchas his Pilgrimes*, 3:593–594.

crew of the *Halve Maen* on its ascent launched attacks from the shorelines and canoes. The English and Dutch learned that news could spread rapidly along the shoreline, from one riverine community to the next. The assaults killed eight to ten Natives but inflicted no additional fatalities among the visitors. After a debate at sea about whether they should overwinter or return home, Hudson and the crew sailed east, arriving in Dartmouth on November 7. Hudson confided to a friend that he would soon continue the search for the Northwest Passage.[23]

Hudson's journeys represented the continuation of the European, and especially the English, desire to sail through the Northwest Passage. Similar dreams had long inspired the community of merchants and propagandists eager to expand the realm. Others in that cluster of investors, all of them aware of the two Hakluyts' published and private articulations of the gains to be had from expansion, thought it best to focus their resources on establishing a colony in the mainland, in territory that would be safer than the frigid coast of Maine.

By late 1606, the directors of the Virginia Company had plans in hand for establishing the southern of the two colonies they envisioned. They believed it would serve five distinct functions. First, the English could encourage, as they had earlier, underemployed or unemployed men, most of them young, to move across the ocean. If they could survive there, then others would likely follow, perhaps easing the incipient tensions that the presence of the chronically underemployed produced at home. Second, survivors would become colonists. That is, they would satisfy the desire of policymakers to follow the Roman model of the *colonia*, the scheme that had, centuries earlier, led to the transformation of the English countryside. In the early seventeenth century, the remains of Roman villas remained ubiquitous across much of southern England, physical monuments to earlier colonial schemes. Third, colonists could produce valuable commodities for the home market as well as become consumers of English goods. Fourth, company directors believed that English heading to the Chesapeake would help convert Indigenous without proper notions of economy into Protestants occupying English-style towns. Finally, investors believed that the residents of the new community would soon start to build ships, enabling English colonists to raid Spanish vessels, which

23. Purchas, *Purchas his Pilgrimes*, 3:595; Emanuel van Meteren, "On Hudson's Voyage," 7–8; Holland to Salisbury, October 30, 1609.

typically sailed northward along the Atlantic coast to catch the most favorable currents home.[24] Success seemed like a foregone conclusion.

If they were to raid Spanish ships, the English would need to establish a post at the right location along an interior river. A sharp turn in the James seemed ideal because it was out of sight from the bay and in a position that would enable colonists on shore to hit any enemy vessels that managed to reach them with cannon fire. Their strategy stemmed from intelligence flowing through Europe, including from Spanish spies transmitting English plans to Madrid. Pedro de Zúñiga, the Spanish ambassador in London, informed Philip III in early January 1607 that the English planned to send four ships each month—two from London and two from Plymouth—bound for Virginia until the population there reached 2,000. He understood that the English planned to obtain American resources, cut off Spanish shipping, and find a water route to the Pacific. Seven months later he sent another report, suggesting that the anticipated migration was much smaller than he had first thought, but that the reports from Virginia testified both to the utility of its forests to produce masts and naval stores and to the belief that the existence of wild grapevines meant the English might soon create profitable vineyards.[25]

Over the course of the summer and into the autumn of 1607, Zúñiga continued to gather intelligence about English plans for Virginia, including plans to launch privateering raids. Zúñiga was convinced that James was ignoring a 1604 agreement between England and Spain in which the English, according to the ambassador's recollection, agreed not to settle in the Indies. In exchange for that promise, English ships could sail without fear of being seized. But Zúñiga believed that English scheme to establish a base in Virginia violated the agreement. He was also convinced that the English had no real intention of establishing a colony. "It is thoroughly evident that it is not their desire to people [the land], but rather to practice piracy," he informed Philip shortly before he gained an audience with James, "for they take no women, only men." After he confronted James in London in early October, the monarch claimed no detailed

24. Edmund S. Morgan, *American Slavery, American Freedom: The Ordeal of Colonial Virginia* (New York: W. W. Norton, 1975), 44–48; on the renewed importance of Roman remains, see William Camden, *Britain, or, A chorographicall description of the most flourishing kingdomes, England, Scotland, and Ireland, and the ilands adioyning, out of the depth of antiquitie* (London, 1610); John Cramsie, *British Travellers and the Encounter with Britain, 1450–1700* (London: Boydell and Brewer, 2015), 325–356.

25. For the spying, see the letters of Pedro de Zúñiga to Philip III dated January 24, 1607, August 22, 1607, and September [12, old style] 22, 1607, in Philip L. Barbour, ed., *The Jamestown Voyages Under the First Charter, 1606–1609*, Hak. Soc., 2nd Ser., 136–137 (Cambridge: Cambridge University Press, 1969), 1:69–71, 77–78.

knowledge of what his subjects might be doing in Virginia, using the fact that he did not fund colonial efforts as a way to claim ignorance of the joint-stock company's affairs. At the same time, James denied any Spanish right to the territory. Zúñiga, who claimed to have a spy within the Virginia Company, continued to monitor developments along the Chesapeake, but Philip took no immediate action.[26]

By the time Zúñiga's concerns reached Madrid, the English had already acted. On December 20, 1606, 144 English men and boys set sail for Virginia. The timing seemed auspicious. The launch of the East India Company had fueled the dreams of the investors in the Virginia Company who had read about earlier English voyages to the American mid-Atlantic coast. They no doubt believed that, with the right guidance from home, they would be able to avoid Roanoke's fate.

On board was George Percy, the eighth son of the eighth Earl of Northumberland. Percy might have seemed an unlikely participant in this migration. In 1572, eight years before he was born, Queen Elizabeth I had ordered the execution of his uncle (the seventh earl) for his part in trying to arrange the release of Mary Queen of Scots. When the young Percy was only five years old his father (the eighth earl) died in 1585 while imprisoned in the Tower of London. (A coroner ruled his death a suicide.) Despite the family trauma, Percy received the kind of elite education available to only the most privileged: Eton, Oxford, and training for the law at Middle Temple. Even that course of study did not guarantee success, so Percy, as was common for wealthy younger sons, sought opportunities abroad. In 1602 he traveled to the West Indies, perhaps seeking a warmer climate to help what one petition on his behalf termed his "grievous and tedious sicknesse." George, who also suffered from epilepsy, soon returned to England and was likely there when his older brother Henry (the ninth earl) was implicated in the Gunpowder Plot to blow up the Houses of Parliament in 1605. Soon after, Henry, who counted Ralegh and Harriot among his associates during his fifteen years in the Tower of London, likely concluded that it was time for George to return to the Western Hemisphere.[27]

26. Zúñiga to Philip III, September [12] 22, 1607, October 5 [September 25], 1607, October 8 [September 28], 1607, October [6] 16, 1607, and Philip III to Zúñiga, October [18] 28, 1607, in Barbour, ed., *Jamestown Voyages*, 1:114–123, quotations at 114–115, 117, and 118.

27. "Inquisition of a Jury of the City of London before the Coroner. . . [on] the Death of the Earl of Northumberland . . . 27 ELIZ. A.D. 1585," in T. B. Howell, comp., *A Complete Collection of State Trials and Proceedings for High Treason and Other Crimes and Misdemeanors . . . to the Year 1783* (London, 1816), no. 61; George Percy, "A Discourse of

The journey seemed endless to Percy. The ships faced multiple storms during their passage but managed to keep to the already known route that took them to Mattanenio (likely Martinique), Guadeloupe, Domenica, Nevis, the Virgin Islands, and Mona Island. They dropped anchor with regularity to refresh their supplies and trade with locals. Like many travelers, they marveled at the natural resources of the islands. Percy understood that, despite his efforts to characterize local residents as cannibals or savages, those he met had already begun to integrate European goods into their economies and understood both the rituals necessary for trade and the skills needed to harvest desired objects from shipwrecks, including cloth from Rouen that had been seized from a Spanish wreck off Domenica. His fascination with cannibalism, which he believed could be found from the islands to Brazil, was not unique; perhaps his family library contained a copy of the de Bry workshop's 1592 version of Hans Stade's account with its six lurid images of Tupinambá cannibalism.

Still, the Atlantic islands had obvious appeal to a younger son of the gentry on the make. On Nevis, the crew wandered into "a most pleasant Garden," remarkable for the tall trees that surrounded it and the presence of guaiacum and cottonwood, two trees with economic utility that could be harvested from a forest so thick that it seemed to the English as if it "had beene set by Art, which made us marvell very much to see it." Given his own family's properties at Alnwick Castle in Northumberland and Syon House (in modern west London), he likely used the word "garden" with some care.[28] All went well until a gentleman named Edward Brookes collapsed from the intense heat on Mona Island. His "fat melted within him," Percy reported. It was the first death of the expedition. After four months, they arrived in Tsenacommacah, territory dominated by the Powhatans of Chesapeake Bay.[29]

the Plantation of the Southern Colonie in Virginia," in *NAW*, 5:266–274; Mark Nicholls, "George Percy's 'Trewe Relacyon': A Primary Source for the Jamestown Settlement," *VMHB* 113 (2005), 214–215; Mark Nicholls, "'As Happy a Fortune as I Desire': The Pursuit of Financial Security by the Younger Brothers of Henry Percy, 9th Earl of Northumberland," *Historical Research* 65 (1992), 296–314.

28. The current gardens at both properties date from their re-creation in the eighteenth century by the famed landscape gardener Capability Brown and then other extensive work since; see Laura Mayer, "Landscape as Legacy: Elizabeth Percy, 1st Duchess of Northumberland and the Gothick Garden Buildings of Alnwick, Northumberland," *Garden History* 39, no. 1 (summer 2011), 34–50.

29. "George Percy's Discourse, 1608 [?]," in Barbour, ed., *Jamestown Voyages*, 1:129–133, quotations at 131–132.

The machinations of European monarchs likely held little interest for Wahunsonacock, werowance of the Powhatans, a confederacy of perhaps thirty-four distinct communities. By 1607, he had built a political alliance that encompassed most of the communities scattered across the Chesapeake. A large skin cloak, known as Powhatan's Mantle, might have been a visual record of this constellation of towns.

Wahunsonacock knew that the way to power was to gain resources and then redistribute them, a classic example of patron-client politics. Based in Werowocomoco, he understood the close relationship between kin and politics. As his authority grew, so too did his family. One colonist claimed that he had 100 wives. While that number might be exaggerated, his polygamous relationships allowed him to place children across the Powhatan landscape. Living in communities along Chesapeake Bay's tributaries, his children became his political agents, solidifying his control over the movement of resources. His pre-1607 experience shaped his approach to the English. He saw the newcomers not as conquerors but as the representatives of a new client state.[30]

Wahunsonacock did not have allies in every Chesapeake town, but the extent of the confederacy meant that he knew about any major developments. His prior experience with Europeans in the region, quite possibly including the short-lived Spanish Jesuit colony, did not suggest that he or his allies were at any risk on April 26, 1607, when three English ships arrived at the mouth of the bay. That day marked a collision of cultures that would have long-lasting implications for Powhatans and English alike.

The proposed colonization of Virginia started inauspiciously for the English. On April 26, the first ship arrived at the mouth of the bay. That night, a group of Chesapeakes menaced the newcomers as they landed, injuring two of them. The English retreated to their ship. They soon returned under the direction of Captain Christopher Newport, a renowned privateer whose exploits had brought him fame after leading devastating raids against Spaniards in the West Indies in 1591 and 1592—the kind of

30. Daniel K. Richter, "Tsenacommacah and the Atlantic World," in Peter C. Mancall, ed., *The Atlantic World and Virginia, 1550–1624* (Chapel Hill: University of North Carolina Press for the Omohundro Institute of Early American History and Culture, 2007), 29–65; Strachey, *Historie of Travell*, 61–62; Kathleen M. Brown, *Good Wives, Nasty Wenches, and Anxious Patriarchs: Gender, Race, and Power in Colonial Virginia* (Chapel Hill: University of North Carolina Press for the Institute of Early American History and Culture, 1996), 45–53; Ralphe Hamor, *A True Discourse of the present estate of Virginia* (London, 1615), 41; Frederic W. Gleach, *Powhatan's World and Colonial Virginia* (Lincoln: University of Nebraska Press, 1997), 135.

This mantle made of four deerskins stitched together and embellished with shell beadwork possibly refers to the towns of the Powhatan confederacy, with the figure at the center perhaps a representation of Wahunsonacock. The cloak, possibly a gift from the Powhatan werowance to King James I, was first recorded as being in London in 1638. Image © Ashmolean Museum, University of Oxford.

military experience that the Virginia Company valued. On April 29, confident that they had found the place to settle, they erected a cross and named that place Cape Henry; the next day they docked at a place they christened Cape Comfort. Soon afterward, five Powhatans approached the English, making signs that the English interpreted as an invitation. The newcomers, with local guides, paddled their shallops toward Kecoughtan, a principal home of Washunsonacock.[31]

The Powhatans welcomed the English with a ritual greeting and gave their guests cornbread and tobacco. Then they danced for half an hour. In the days that followed the English visited other towns, including the village of the Pasapeghs and that of the Rapahannas, where the local werowance had painted his body crimson and his face blue, donned, according to Percy, a "Crown of Deares hair colloured red," and wore a "great Plate of Copper" on his head; he also wore a string of beads (likely made of shells), hoop-shaped pearl earrings, and in each ear the claw of a bird held with copper or gold wire. Percy described this headman's abode as a "Palace" situated along well-worn paths that traversed the finest maize fields he had ever seen. Fresh springs provided clean drinking water, though none of the English then realized how important such resources would be for their survival. As they headed back downstream, the English studied the landscape before identifying a spot along the river, in Pasapegh territory, where they could moor in water six fathoms deep.[32]

Newport ordered the English to erect a large cross bearing the name of King James, following the familiar European strategy of claiming land for God and country simultaneously. The migrants were so confident that they had established control that they began to plant corn even before they unpacked their weapons. They soon learned that Newport's gesture did not have its intended effect. Only three days later men under Wahunsonacock's direction attacked the foundations of the fort the English had hoped to erect. Soldiers firing from the ship managed, for the time, to drive them away.[33]

31. John Twitt, "A true report of a voyage undertaken for the West Indies by M. Christopher Newport," in Richard Hakluyt, *The Principal Navigations, Voyages, Traffiques and Discovers of the English Nation* (London, 1598–1600), 3:567–569; "George Percy's 'Discourse,'" 135; "Chronology of Events in Jamestown, 1606–1608," in Philip L. Barbour, ed., *The Complete Works of Captain John Smith* (Chapel Hill: University of North Carolina Press for the Institute of Early American History and Culture, 1986), 1:17.

32. "George Percy's 'Discourse,'" 136–137.

33. Morgan, *American Slavery, American Freedom*, 71–72; [Gabriel Archer (?)],"A relation . . . written . . . by a gent. of y[e] Colony," in Barbour ed., *Jamestown Voyages* 1:80–95.

Almost immediately, the English began to build a fort, with openings for cannon pointing toward the river, an indication that they perceived their primary threat as an attack by a Spanish ship, not an attack by Powhatans. Percy and others explored the local area, discovering excellent forests, including trees that produced balsam, abundant honeysuckle and strawberries, and a landscape so colorful with flowers that, Percy wrote, it looked "as though it has beene in any Garden or Orchard in England." The newcomers believed that the river ran for 160 miles, with dense forests along its banks for its entire length filled with oak, cedar, beech, and cypress, with as much sassafras, walnuts, raspberries, mulberries, and vines as the English had ever seen. The finest sturgeon in the world swam in its waters and enormous flocks of deer browsed along the edges separating the dense forests from the fertile and vast fields. On May 24, the English erected another cross, this time at the mouth of the river where, Percy wrote, "we proclaimed James King of England to have the most right unto it." In the monarch's honor they called the place Jamestown. Percy never mentioned whether the English had done anything to purchase the land from Wahunsonacock or any other Indigenous leader.[34]

The English finished their fort in mid-June. A week later Newport set sail for England. The colonists believed themselves secure at Jamestown, in a "Country being so fruitfull," Percy wrote in his diary, that "it would be as great a profit to the Realme of England, as the Indies to the King of Spaine."[35] They remained wary of the Powhatans, but the real threat came neither from Indigenous nor from Spaniards.

Building Jamestown beyond that turn in the river, which made sense from a strategic perspective, turned out to be disastrous. Lacking detailed understanding of the ways that water levels in the James varied over the course of the year, they had no way of knowing that the fresh water they found on their arrival during the spring would soon become brackish when the water level dropped in the summer heat. This was not a problem for the Powhatans, who knew where to find fresh water in springs. But it proved more vexing for the English, who continued to draw drinking water from the James, risking salt poisoning. To make matters worse, the newcomers also dumped their waste in the river. The excrement and the

34. "George Percy's 'Discourse,'" 138–141, quotations at 139 (garden) and 141 (the king's right).
35. "George Percy's 'Discourse,'" 142–143.

salt created a toxic stew ideal for the circulation of the bacteria that could cause typhoid fever and dysentery.[36]

During the summer, colonists suffered from high fever, acute abdominal pains, constipation, nausea, chills, fatigue, and watery or bloody diarrhea. Percy observed all too well the misery that spread among them. The first to die was John Asbie, who succumbed to what the English called "the bloudie Flixe," likely amoebiasis. Three days later a man named George Flowre succumbed to "the swelling," a symptom likely caused by dysentery but possibly exacerbated by salt poisoning. On August 10, William Bruster, one of the gentlemen, died, not from a disease but after being attacked by one of the Powhatans. Four days later two others died, one from a wound and another who collapsed from no known cause. The pace of death accelerated: two more dead on August 15, and a gentleman named Thomas Gower the next day, followed on August 17 by Thomas Mounslic and on the eighteenth by two more. August 19 brought the end of a gentleman named Drue Piggase. On the twenty-second, Bartholomew Gosnold, a member of the council with long experience in overseas expeditions, died of unspecified causes. Five others died in August and two more during the first week of September.[37]

The deaths prompted introspection and anxiety, as well as a search for causes. "Our men were destroyed with cruell diseases as Swelling, Flixes, Burning Fevers, and by warres, and some departed suddenly," Percy confided in his journal, "but for the most part they died of meere famine." Percy's link between malnutrition and contagious disease was likely correct. "There were never Englishmen left in a forreigne Countrey in such miserie as wee were in this new discovered Virginia," he added, blaming the catastrophe as much on the planning of the colony as on local conditions. But it was their daily routines that likely proved fatal. As Percy reported, the men drank "cold water taken out of the River," which was salty at high tide and "full of slime and filth" at low tide. This, he believed, "was the destruction of many of our men." The only good news was that the Powhatans never launched a serious attack. Had they done so, they would have found the inhabitants of the fort ailing, weakened, and moaning in each nook. Up to four English perished on some nights. Each morning the survivors would drag the corpses "out of their Cabines like Dogges to be buried," Percy observed. "In this sort did I see the mortalitie of

36. Carville V. Earle, "Environment, Disease, and Mortality in Early Virginia," in Thad W. Tate and David L. Ammerman, eds., *The Chesapeake in the Seventeenth Century: Essays on Anglo-American Society* (Chapel Hill: University of North Carolina Press for the Institute of Early American History and Culture, 1979), 96–125.

37. "George Percy's 'Discourse,'" 143–144.

divers of our people." The situation could have been even worse had the Powhatans, perhaps cultivating loyalty among a new client community, left them alone. Instead, the Natives gave them "Bread, Corne, Fish, and Flesh in great plentie," as Percy wrote, which kept the colonists alive during those months when they tried to figure out how to survive.[38]

In 1608 Captain John Smith, a son of a yeoman who lacked the elite background of some of the nascent colony's initial leaders, took charge in Jamestown—more by the force of personality than the unfolding of a company-approved plan. Though the investors in London had sent a message that Smith should be among the leaders of the settlement, his rise owed more to the fact that he provided guidance for immigrants who had little idea about how to build a new town in an unfamiliar territory. To achieve his goals, Smith drew on his prior military experience. He was also a great self-promoter, a fabulist who bragged about slaying Turkish fighters but claimed to have relied on being rescued by a young girl when he was a captive. After the English gathered their first harvest in the autumn of 1608, history repeated itself when a group of Powhatans captured Smith while he was on a reconnaissance mission. He won his freedom, so he later maintained, through the intervention of Wahunsonacock's daughter, known to the English as Pocahontas. She was then probably around ten years old.[39]

Once freed, Smith remained in command in Jamestown until boarding a ship bound for London in autumn 1609. During that time, he ordered the English to work in the fields or face two unappealing options: starve or be exiled. As he put it in his 1612 history of early Virginia, colonists had to "obay this for a law, that he that will not work shall not eate." He made an exception for any who were too ill to farm. As might have been predicted, his style of leadership exacerbated growing tensions within the colony and between the Powhatans and the English.[40]

Even before news about the rapid deterioration of the colony in 1609 could get to England, reports about the Chesapeake reached policymakers and potential investors. They knew all too well the risks of trying to

38. "George Percy's 'Discourse,'" 144–145.

39. In his first accounts about Virginia, Smith did not mention the alleged rescue by Pocahontas, a story that he added seventeen years after the event. See Camilla Townsend, *Pocahontas and the Powhatan Dilemma* (New York: Hill and Wang, 2004), 51–60; Morgan, *American Slavery, American Freedom*, 75–76.

40. Captaine [John] Smith, *A Map of Virginia, with a Description of the Countrey, the Commodities, People, Government and Religion* (London, 1612), reprinted in Barbour, ed., *Jamestown Voyages*, 2:327–464, quotation at 441.

colonize the North American landscape. Rather than abandon the venture, the company and its allies persuaded investors to sustain the colony. An anonymous treatise from early 1608, intended to raise funds necessary for colonization, acknowledged the problems that company members understood would threaten the colony. Its author, well-versed in contemporary politics, emphasized how a colony in Virginia would benefit England because an island nation could flourish only through mastery of the oceans. That meant it needed more ships than it possessed as well as greater supplies of tar, pitch, rosin, cordage, and tall trees for masts. If England could not produce more ships, skilled mariners and shipwrights might seek employment in France, Spain, Italy, or elsewhere, another possible economic problem. Just as important, establishing a permanent presence on "strange Coasts" would protect the claims that the realm had made earlier through acts of discovery. Europeans' law of nations allowed a country to make a claim to territory not known to Europeans before, but any title would be forfeited unless colonists remained. The author noted that the Danish king had become increasingly interested in finding the Northwest Passage and rumors swirled about a possible French claim to Virginia.

The time had come to make the kind of commitment that the English had been unable or unwilling to make. Going forward, colonizing groups needed to set up something akin to insurance so that inevitable accidents would not prove ruinous or become a reason to abandon the task. Crucially, funds could not come from "the swe[a]t of the poore, or industries of the husbandman, Artificer, or trad[e]sman." The author believed that the king should be one of the contributors to the scheme, in exchange for some of the profits. Such royal action would prompt the younger sons of the landed gentry to risk their lives for the cause.[41]

On May 23, 1609, James appended his seal to a new charter for the Virginia Company. There were many new investors, including nine earls, fourteen lords (including the lord mayor of London), over ninety knights, and fifty individuals holding the rank of captain, including John Smith and Christopher Newport. Among that group was John Ratcliffe (a.k.a. Sicklemore), who had commanded one of the first three ships to Jamestown in 1607, became president of the colony that year, lost his position and returned to England in 1608, and then sailed back to Jamestown by August 1609. More remarkable were the scores of others: merchants, fishmongers, haberdashers, drapers, grocers, shoemakers, vintners, innkeepers, brewers, ministers, coopers. Fifty-five companies also purchased

41. Landsdowne ms. 160, ff. 356–357, British Library; on the continuing need for wood, see Keith Pluymers, *No Wood, No Kingdom: Political Ecology in the English Atlantic* (Philadelphia: University of Pennsylvania Press, 2021).

shares, including the guilds for pewterers, cutlers, butchers, masons, poulterers, weavers, scriveners, embroiderers, basket makers, and musicians. The charter emphasized that the colony's primary goal was "the conversion and reduccion of the people in those partes unto the true worship of God and Christian religion," a statement of religious sincerity reflecting the politics of post-Reformation England as much as the spiritual inclinations of its king. Sentiments about Catholics formed during Elizabeth's reign had not changed. Toward that end, the company prohibited the migration of any Roman Catholics, an act that paralleled earlier Spanish policies banning migration of Muslims and Jews to the Western Hemisphere. Only those who would swear the oath of supremacy, and thus accept the legitimacy of the monarch as the head of the church, would be able to go to Virginia.[42]

The company's directors understood that the Chesapeake could be dangerous. It would need forts to prevent unwelcome Europeans arriving by ship, but by 1609 the promoters recognized that the Powhatans and other Indigenous also posed a growing threat to their plans. This dual recognition—of needing to convert Natives and simultaneously guarding against possible attacks by them—led the organizers to instruct Sir Thomas Gates, the new governor, to capture Indigenous children and separate them from the authority of their "Priestes." Officials also needed to separate girls and boys from colonial prisoners who would be "so wrapped up in the fogge and miserie of their iniquity and so tirrified with their continuall tirrany" that they would retard the children's progress toward enlightenment. Better, the promoters believed, to execute English miscreants than allow them to pollute the minds of Natives.[43]

Even though the Powhatans had provided food to enable the first colonists to survive, the English likened their own efforts to a military invasion. The council reminded Gates that the Powhatans could burn down the colonists' houses, kill their livestock, steal their possessions, and attack those who roamed the countryside in small groups or even remained on ships. All the local inhabitants needed to do was "destroy but one harvest or burne your townes in the night," and any survivors would be prone to both malnutrition and exposure. Survival meant constant vigilance, which included overseeing the young men who arrived as servants. Officials were to mark work times by banging on a bell, indoctrinating

42. "The Second Charter," in Bemiss, ed., *Three Charters*, 28–42, 54; see Karoline P. Cook, *Forbidden Passages: Muslims and Moriscos in Colonial Spanish America* (Philadelphia: University of Pennsylvania Press, 2016), 55–62.

43. Virginia Council, "Instruccions Orders and Constitutions . . . to Sir Thomas Gates," in Bemiss, ed., *Three Charters*, 56–61.

migrants into proper labor regimes. The directors believed that capturing Wahunsonacock would be ideal, but if that failed, perhaps they could at least get him to acknowledge the supremacy of James I and pay tribute to the English monarch. They advised Gates to pry the locals away "from the tirrany of Powhatan," which would allow them to extract tribute. The colonists should determine the size of each werowance's territory and the number of men who lived there, and then use those numbers to calculate how many deerskins, baskets of dye, measures of maize, or days of work would constitute the proper payment. All trade, they advised the governor, should be conducted within the walls of the fort. Ever fearful of insubordination among the migrants, Gates had orders to send the council regular updates in a sealed box, extending the idea that a colony could be governed by a board situated across the ocean.[44]

After he was back in England, Smith portrayed his experience in heroic terms in a series of self-aggrandizing narratives. He did not dwell on the circumstances of how his first effort to command Virginia came to an end. Percy, an apt storyteller, did so in a withering 1612 report that he wrote to his brother, the ninth earl. The English, he recognized, were not the first European colonizers to suffer in North America: Laudonnière's Florida settlement, short of food, fell into self-immolating mutinies; the Spanish on the Rio de la Plata and in the Straits of Magellan also lacked necessary food, which drove some to rebel; Spaniards in one instance ate the bodies of their countrymen who had been executed for launching an insurrection, while others in Cartagena sated their hunger by eating snakes, toads, and "venomous wormes."[45]

The English thought that they would earn the trust of Powhatans and other Indigenous inhabitants nearby, but in a series of escalating raids and counterraids, Natives and newcomers repeatedly assaulted each other. On one occasion, the English wanted to purchase an island near Nansemond. Powhatans murdered the two emissaries the colonizers had sent. Percy "understood from the Indyans themselves" that "they weare sacrifysed and thatt their Braynes weare Cutt and skraped outt of their heads w[i]th Mussell shelles." In response, the English set fire to the residents' houses, ransacked what they believed were religious buildings, and stole copper, pearls, and bracelets that had been laid in the graves of past rulers. Violence also fed arguments among the English—and personal

44. Virginia Council, "Instruccions Orders and Constitutions," 61–65, 68 (black boxes), 66 (letters to England).

45. Nicholls, "George Percy's 'Trewe Relacyon,'" 242–243.

tragedy. When Smith was paddling back to Jamestown, a match lit gunpowder on his lap. Most likely it was an attempt on his life organized by those who vied to lead the colony. His clothes afire, Smith dove into the river, but the explosion had burned nine or ten square inches of his thighs. In agony, Smith reached Jamestown only to learn that leading members of the governor's council had concluded that he was an "ambityous unworthy and vayneglorious fellowe" unsuitable to lead. The councilors shipped him back to England and put Percy in charge.[46]

Two weeks later, the new governor dispatched Ratcliffe to supervise the construction of a new fort at Point Comfort. But seventeen colonists who attended him fled to Kegoughtan, mostly because they were starving. Percy heard that the Natives killed them all "w[i]th their mowthes stopped full of Breade," a sign that the locals treated these English with scorn. Once again, Indigenous inhabitants had access to what they needed while the English remained under threat—not only from the Powhatans but also from their inability, two years after they had arrived at Jamestown, to provide enough food to feed their own community. Hoping to end the violence, Percy dispatched Ratcliffe to meet with Wahunsonacock. According to one colonial witness, the werowance ordered the English leader captured and stripped. The Powhatans lit a fire in front of the captive before local women scraped the flesh off his body with mussel shells and tossed his skin into the fire.[47]

The death of Ratcliffe was only the most notable loss for the English during their horrific winter of 1609–1610. That autumn, before the troubles, the community's population had reached 500. By the time spring finally came, only 60 were still alive. Smith believed the fault lay not in the natural resources, which were abundant, but instead in the "want of providence, industrie, and governement" among the English. Had "we beene in Paradice it self" with the same leadership, he lamented, "it would not have been much better with us." If left in the hands of those on the banks of the river, Jamestown would become another Roanoke.[48]

On April 17, 1610, with news of English travails along the Chesapeake circulating in England, Henry Hudson decided it was time to launch yet

46. Nicholls, "George Percy's 'Trewe Relacyon,'" 244–246; James Horn, *A Land as God Made It: Jamestown and the Birth of America* (New York: Basic Books, 2005), 169–170.
47. Nicholls, "George Percy's 'Trewe Relacyon,'" 246–247.
48. W.S., *The Proceedings of the English Colonie in Virginia since their first beginning from England* (Oxford, 1612), reprinted in Barbour, ed., *Complete Works*, 1:275–276; Morgan, *American Slavery, American Freedom*, 73.

another expedition to find the Northwest Passage. With the financial support of twenty-four merchants, he set off across the North Atlantic on *Discovery*. Ten weeks into the journey, while sailing through modern Hudson Strait, the captain believed that some of the crew seemed to be reaching a psychological breaking point. Still, they pushed onward, observing polar bears and local fauna and flora that included fast-growing Arctic grasses, which sailors could eat to ward off scurvy. Amid this landscape of jagged coastlines and icebergs, the crew came upon a cone-shaped house filled with birds hanging by the neck, preserved by the cold, so they could still be eaten. The sailors were not as alone as they had thought. By then it was late September, and the ship was deep into what would soon be called Hudson Bay. The long Arctic days had begun to grow short, a signal that the crew needed to find the passage, turn for home, or find a way to survive the brutal winter they all knew would soon arrive. After a debate, Hudson ordered *Discovery* southward, into modern James Bay. By the time they set up camp for the winter, they had, according to Abucuk Pricket, a chronicler of the voyage, spent "three months in a Labyrinth without end."[49]

The winter crushed the sailors' souls. They had suffered storms and hunger and, having reached Hudson Bay, believed that they might have found the Pacific and would soon be bound for the Spice Islands and temperate climates. Instead, they disembarked, built a ramshackle house, and no doubt prayed they would not freeze to death. One day, they saw a human footprint in the snow, another sign, like the dead birds in the stone enclosure, that they were not alone. But *Discovery*, anchored off the shore to preserve its hull, remained encased in ice for months and its occupants had no Native visitors. Tensions soon rose, with some of the crew and Hudson screaming at each other over the proper distribution of their dwindling food supplies.[50]

For seven months they waited for James Bay to thaw. From the shore, they likely heard the sound of the moving ice, which a later explorer likened to thunder. They would have huddled in the house around a fire, its smoke condensing and freezing along the interior walls. Anyone who ventured outside ran the risk of falling into snowdrifts that could have been thirty feet deep and winds that froze uncovered human flesh in minutes. Yet virtually all of them survived the winter, subsisting on white partridges and fish they gathered before the worst of the winter came. These sources of protein got them to the spring, when seemingly endless flocks of migratory teal, geese, ducks, and swans stopped by on their way to

49. Purchas, *Purchas his Pilgrimes*, 3:596–601, quotation at 601; Mancall, *Fatal Journey*, 77–117.

50. Purchas, *Purchas his Pilgrimes*, 3:601.

their breeding grounds. When the supply of birds ran short, they ate moss and frogs.[51]

Around late May or early June the crew encountered a lone man, likely Cree. Hudson gave him a knife, some buttons, and a mirror and tried to communicate through signs. The man returned with a sled bearing two beaver skins and two deer. The English thought they had achieved a breakthrough. But the man soon left, never to return. The disappointment added to the anger felt by crew members who resented the captain's decision to ration food among all the men, even those who were so ill or injured that they might not survive.[52]

Discovery escaped the ice on June 17. On the twenty-first, five men launched a mutiny. They seized Hudson along with his teenage son, then aged seventeen or eighteen; the ship's carpenter (a loyal ally of Hudson's); and a half-dozen of the infirm. They lowered them onto a shallop and cut the rope. *Discovery* sailed off. Hudson and the other eight were never seen again, at least not by anyone who left a record of their appearance.[53]

Yet the ill will among those on board remained. All of them knew they might face charges of having killed Hudson and the others. Given the prominence of some of the mission's supporters, there was sure to be an inquiry to find out if they had become pirates. Perhaps some remembered the bodies of nineteen pirates King James had ordered hanged and displayed at the docks at Wapping.[54]

Despite what awaited them, the men on *Discovery* managed to find their way into Hudson Strait, likely surviving on fish and thick-billed murres,

51. Purchas, *Purchas his Pilgrimes*, 3:601–602; on the sound of the ice, see Fridjtof Nansen, *Farthest North* (orig. pub. 1897; New York: Modern Library, 1999), 116; on the effects of cold in this region, see Thomas James, *The Strange and Dangerous Voyage of Captaine Thomas James* (London, 1633), esp. 57–63.
52. Purchas, *Purchas his Pilgrimes*, 3:602.
53. This re-creation of the mutiny comes from Pricket's testimony in Purchas, *Purchas his Pilgrimes*, 3:603–605; for the unfurling of the sail, see Edward Wilson to the High Court of Admiralty, 1612, in Thomas A. Janvier, *Henry Hudson: A Brief Statement of His Aims and Achievements* (New York: Harper and Bros., 1909), 135–139.
54. Purchas, *Purchas his Pilgrimes*, 3:605; Peter Earle, *The Pirate Wars* (London: Methuen, 2003), 55–58; David D. Hebb, *Piracy and the English Government, 1616–1642* (Brookfield, VT: Ashgate, [1994]), 7–10; *Clinton, Purser & Arnold, to their Countreymen wheresoever* (London, [1583]); Thomas Haywood and William Rowley, *Fortune by Land and Sea: A Tragi-Comedy*, orig. pub. 1605 (London, 1655), 43–44; see also Claire Jowitt, "Rogue Traders: National Identity, Empire and Piracy, 1580–1640," in Thomas Betteridge, ed., *Borders and Travellers in Early Modern Europe* (Burlington, VT: Ashgate, 2007), 53–70, and Claire Jowitt, "Scaffold Performances: The Politics of Pirate Execution," in Jowitt, ed., *Pirates? The Politics of Plunder, 1550–1650* (Houndmills, Basingstoke: Palgrave Macmillan, 2007), 151–168.

auks that bred in vast numbers there. In late July, the crew encountered a group of Inuit approaching on seven kayaks. The Natives and visitors exchanged signs and goods, teaching each other how to hunt birds. A second meeting turned violent, with the Inuit mortally wounding four of the mutineers. Two of them bled to death on the deck of *Discovery*.[55]

In the days that followed the ten survivors on *Discovery* piloted the ship into Hudson Strait. Once again, food supplies ran low. Robert Juet, Hudson's first mate in 1609 turned key member of the mutiny, starved to death during the return. On September 6, the last nine encountered a fishing crew out of Fowey, in Cornwall, which helped them get home. The ship's pilot and at least one other survivor remained on board for the journey to London to meet with the investor Smythe. The long journey of *Discovery* ended sixteen months after it had begun. Those who returned had survived extreme temperatures, icebergs that could pierce a hull, Inuit bearing arms, starvation-level rations, and, of course, mutineers who could have left them behind in James Bay. But as they would soon discover, a bloodstained ship arriving at home without its captain or most of the original crew raised questions that would someday need to be answered.[56]

Hudson's demise was the most visible sign that the English had yet to find a way to succeed in North America. Over the previous generation, English expeditions had failed in Nunavut, failed to find the Northwest Passage, failed on the Orinoco, failed on the Outer Banks, and failed on the coast of Maine. The mutiny that doomed Hudson proved that even men hardy enough to join an expedition into Arctic waters could become so despondent that they risked near-certain execution for turning against their captain. The long, cold winters of the Little Ice Age only made matters worse. The fact that English struggled in Tsenacommacah could have been predicted. The real surprise lay not in the looming failure of Jamestown but instead in decisions made in London, Plymouth, and Bristol that the English should continue to advance their goals in North America. Little could investors and planners imagine that their prospects could grow worse.

55. Purchas, *Purchas his Pilgrimes*, 3:605–607; for the estimate of the number of murres, see Barry Lopez, *Arctic Dreams: Imagination and Desire in a Northern Landscape* (New York: Scribner, 1986), 156–157.

56. Purchas, *Purchas his Pilgrimes*, 3:608; for those killed, those left behind, and those who survived the passage to London, see Trinity House Transactions, vol. 1 (1609–1625), Guildhall Library, ms. 30045/1, f. 11v.

Part II

Colonies

14

Rescues

Two years after the Virginia Company had sent 144 men and boys to the Chesapeake, Jamestown looked more like Roanoke than the prosperous Powhatan communities that ringed it. The staggering death toll made it impossible for even the most skilled leaders to guide the community forward. The situation had become so bleak that colonists came to the only logical conclusion: the time had come to abandon their settlement and return home before still more died from diseases that shredded their intestines or from violent attacks by Indigenous neighbors.

But in a twist of fate that seemed unimaginable to the survivors even as they boarded ships to sail to England, rescuers appeared with new supplies and the promise of yet more to come. Unlike those who had waited on the Outer Banks for resupply ships that never arrived, salvation arrived just in time. Or so it seemed to those who had survived the first two years in Jamestown.

In 1609, with new funds in hand from the sale of more stock, the Virginia Company dispatched nine vessels to the Chesapeake. The flotilla was led by the 300-ton *Sea Venture*, which sailed with six other sizable ships and two pinnaces, smaller vessels useful for carrying people and news from one large ship to another. According to the London-based Spanish diplomat Zúñiga, ministers in England had been delivering sermons to "stress the importance of filling the world with their religion." He reported that the company had gathered 500 men and 100 women for the expedition, with hundreds more to follow once organizers at home received word of the safe landing of their ships. The gender breakdown was crucial to Zúñiga, who had earlier written that the voyage of 1607 must have been to set up a pirate nest since the English took no women with them, a reasonable conclusion by a sophisticated Spanish observer given the tendencies of unattached young men on Atlantic crossings to dream of the wealth they might make from such ventures. The enterprise was to be guided by Sir Thomas Gates, named to the position of deputy governor of the colony, and Sir George Somers, an admiral who had command of the ships. The ships left to great fanfare from London, though Somers skipped the festivities and boarded the *Sea Venture* in Plymouth, which left port on June 2. The two leaders sailed with Captain Christopher Newport, who had returned after his first expedition to Jamestown. Unlike those who plotted earlier voyages to the Chesapeake, who understood how Atlantic winds worked and hence sailed far south into the ocean to catch the northerly winds that would take them to the Americas, the leaders of this expedition decided to sail almost due west as soon as they hit the tropics. The plan was for the ships to remain within eyesight. If they lost track of each other, they would all steer for the Caribbean island of Barbuda for a planned rendezvous.[1]

The new route worked for the first fifty-one days, during which the ships sailed almost 3,000 miles. Newport reckoned that they were perhaps only a week or so away from Virginia. But a fierce storm blew in on July 24, terrifying the voyagers. According to William Strachey, who kept the most detailed account of the expedition, it felt "like an hell of darkness, turned black upon us, so much the more fuller of horror." One of the pinnaces disappeared. Five feet of water filled the underdecks of the *Sea Venture*, the strongest of the ships. Every man on the ship joined in bailing out 100 tons of water every eight hours, or a total of 2,000 tons by the time the storm subsided.[2] The relentless pounding of the waves and drenching rains kept the travelers awake for four days without fresh water or food. Stories of the storm may have inspired William Shakespeare when he was writing *The Tempest*.[3]

1. Zúñiga to Philip III, April [2] 12, 1609, [February 23] March 15, 1609, [September 25] October 5, 1607, and [February 23] March 15, 1609, in Philip L. Barbour, ed., *The Jamestown Voyages Under the First Charter, 1606–1609*, Hak. Soc., 2nd Ser., 136–137 (Cambridge: Cambridge University Press, 1969), 2:259–260 (ministers), 254–256 (large migration), 116–117 (no women earlier); William Strachey, "A True Reportory of the Wreck and Redemption of Sir Thomas Gates, Knight, upon and from the Islands of Bermudas," in Louis B. Wright, ed., *A Voyage to Virginia: Two Narratives*, 2nd ed. (orig. pub. 1964; Charlottesville: University of Virginia Press, 2013), 3–4; Virginia Bernhard, *A Tale of Two Colonies: What Really Happened in Virginia and Bermuda?* (Columbia: University of Missouri Press, 2011), 17–21; Mark G. Hanna, *Pirate Nests and the Rise of the British Empire, 1570–1740* (Chapel Hill: University of North Carolina Press for the Omohundro Institute for Early American History and Culture, 2015), 86–88.
2. Strachey, "True Reportory," 4–14; Silvester Jourdain, *A Discovery of the Bermudas, Otherwise Called the Isle of Devils* (London, 1610), in Louis B. Wright, ed., *A Voyage to Virginia in 1609*, 2nd ed. (Charlottesville: University of Virginia Press, 2013), 106; Bernhard, *Tale of Two Colonies*, 24–28.
3. Strachey, "True Reportory," 7 (water like rivers), 10 (garment), 11 (net), 12–14; Bernhard, *Tale of Two Colonies*, 29–31. The timing of Shakespeare's writing of the play and the circulation of the reports of the storm make it possible that he worked the theme into

When the skies finally cleared, the sailors caught sight of Bermuda, an archipelago known to European sailors for the frightful, hull-rending shoals and reefs that surrounded it. Strachey knew of the feared place from his reading of Spanish travel narratives and natural histories by Peter Martyr and Gonzalo Fernández de Oviedo y Valdes, each of them by then translated into English. Whatever risks they faced landing there paled to those that confronted them at the moment on the leaking flagship. The *Sea Venture*, battered by a hurricane and impossibly beached between two great rocks, never sailed again. Parts of it remained underwater until 1958.[4]

Bermuda had never been occupied, likely because it lay too far from prevailing winds for Indigenous peoples of the Caribbean to have paddled there.[5] Europeans knew to "avoid them as Scylla and Charybdis, or as they would shun the Devil himself," in the words of Silvester Jourdain, another chronicler of the English debacle. Although Bermuda had been, he added, "accounted the most dangerous, infortunate, and most forlorn place of the world," the reality did not match the myth since this was "in truth the richest, healthfullest, and pleasing land (the quantity and bigness thereof considered) and merely natural, as ever man set foot upon."[6]

The Somers (or Summers) Islands, as the English soon called Bermuda in honor of the admiral, were unpopulated but not uninhabitable. The archipelago boasted cedars that were better than those in Virginia and palmetto trees with broad leaves to thatch a cottage. Salmon, bonito, angelfish, stingrays, cod, mullet, swordfish, whales, and rockfish, as well as crayfish as large as an English lobster and pearl-bearing oysters, could be found off its shores. Giant flocks of birds nested there, as did tortoises. The English also found wild boars, likely the descendants of swine Spanish sailors had left behind years earlier.[7]

the play; see Charles Frea, "The Tempest and the New World," *Shakespeare Quarterly* 30 (1979), 29–41.

4. Strachey, "True Reportory," 18–19, 19n27; Jourdain, *Discovery*, 107; Bernard, *Tale of Two Colonies*, 32–33.
5. On Indigenous canoe routes and their relationship to currents, see Scott M. Fitzpatrick, "Seafaring Capabilities in the Pre-Columbian Caribbean," *Journal of Maritime Archaeology* 8 (2013), 101–138.
6. Jourdain, *Discovery*, 108–109.
7. Strachey, "True Reportory," 24–25 (trees), 27–29 (fish and sea mammals), 30–31 (birds), 32–33 (hogs); see also Jourdain, *Discovery*, 110–112; Martin Thomas, *The Natural History of Bermuda* (Bermuda: Bermuda Zoological Society, 2004), 42–45; and Keith D. Pluymers, "Environmental Knowledge, Expertise, and the Development of Slavery in Bermuda," in Thomas B. Earle and D. Andrew Johnson, eds., *Atlantic Environments and the American South* (Athens: University of Georgia Press, 2020).

Despite an environment that the English could master, tensions divided those who landed. Bermuda, as some among the travelers concluded, occupied an ambiguous legal position. Gates was to become the governor once the travelers arrived in Virginia. Until then, Somers was in command when everyone was on board a ship. But what to do with the passengers of the *Sea Venture* when they disembarked? Each of the leaders believed that he should be in control, but their division split the survivors. Some went to live with Gates and some with Somers. Despite the animosity, the English built two new boats, which together had the capacity to carry the 135 survivors toward Jamestown. Notwithstanding the problems posed by encircling reefs, the English managed their escape.[8]

Before they set off, the survivors erected a cross fashioned out of timber salvaged from the *Sea Venture* and local cedar. Gates attached a silver coin bearing the likeness of James I. He added an inscription, in both English and Latin, engraved in copper. The text rehearsed the core details of the visit—the departure of the seven ships, the wreck of the *Sea Venture*, and the identities of Gates, Somers, and Newport. On May 10, 1610, Gates left aboard a new pinnace named *Deliverance*, and then Somers departed on *Patience*. Eleven days later they approached Point Comfort.[9]

The survivors of the *Sea Venture* sailed into woe along the Chesapeake. The colonists' buildings were in disarray and the storehouse lay near empty. The English from Bermuda had brought provisions with them, but not enough to feed those who remained at Jamestown. The men they found seemed either incapable or indifferent to the tasks necessary for their own survival, such as planting corn or herbs. The Powhatans had made escape impossible. The English within Jamestown had made continued survival unlikely. It was, as Strachey put it, a site of "desolation and misery."[10]

Jamestown still had the resources that had drawn the English in 1607, yet it struggled. The violence with Powhatans that had begun when John Smith was present continued, less a war than spasmodic attacks, chronically destabilizing the English. Colonists had survived earlier through trade with the Powhatans, but Wahunsonacock and his allies cut them off. Absent a strong hand, Strachey believed, the "death and starving" would continue. To make matters worse, the English could not even manage to harvest any fish out of the river, which meant that they had to live on an "unsavory broth" produced from scrounged herbs and mushrooms.

8. Strachey, "True Reportory," 38–58; Bernhard, *Tale of Two Colonies*, 68, 92, 86–90.
9. Strachey, "True Reportory," 56–62.
10. Strachey, "True Reportory," 61–67.

By June 7, Gates, Somers, and Newport, in consultation with the remaining commanders of the fort, concluded that the time had come to abandon Jamestown. The English crowded together on two surviving pinnaces still at Jamestown, the *Discovery* and the *Virginia*, along with the makeshift *Patience* and *Deliverance* from Bermuda. They planned to sail north up the coast until they reached Newfoundland, where they hoped to find English fishing crews that could help them cross the Atlantic.[11]

Almost as soon as they started downriver, well before reaching open sea, the departing colonists spotted the advance skiff of Thomas West, Lord De La Warr, who had been sent by the Virginia Company in the spring of 1610 to take command of Jamestown. The fleeing ships turned around, returning to Jamestown on June 10.[12]

De La Warr arrived with the same confidence as earlier English commanders dispatched to carry on the business of the Virginia Company. His directions dictated that he dispatch ships for London quickly, freighted with the best natural produce found in Virginia. Company directors also repeated the advice they had given to Gates: it might be a good idea to capture Powhatans and send them to England to encourage them to convert abroad. Confident that the colony was going to succeed, they instructed him to have men explore the interior, especially inland waterways—presumably to find out if there was a passage to the Pacific.[13]

The new governor settled into the town with abundant finery. He went to church attended by a fifty-man livery adorned in "fair red cloaks." Once in the building, he sat in the choir on a "green velvet chair," with velvet cushions spread nearby for those moments in the service when he needed to kneel. The English understood the symbolic power of luxury goods.[14]

In the weeks and months that followed De La Warr's arrival, the English tried again to create a stable community. To do so, they combined English architectural ideas with Powhatan material culture. They decorated their interiors with a "delicate wrought fine kind of mat the Indians make," understanding that such items made their drab interiors more livable.

11. Strachey, "True Reportory," 71–76.
12. Strachey, "True Reportory," 76–79; Lorri Glover and Daniel B. Smith, *The Shipwreck That Saved Jamestown: The Sea Venture Castaways and the Fate of America* (New York: Henry Holt, 2008).
13. Virginia Council, "Instructions, Orders and Constitutions . . . to Lord La Warr," 1609–1610 (?), in Samuel Bemiss, ed., *The Three Charters of the Virginia Company of London with Seven Related Documents, 1606–1621*, Jamestown 350th Anniversary Historical Booklet 4 (Williamsburg, VA: Jamestown 350th Anniversary Celebration Corporation, 1957), 70–74.
14. Strachey, "True Reportory," 80–81.

The colonists covered their English-style houses with the bark of local trees, again borrowing a strategy from the Powhatans. This enabled the English to keep their interiors cool during the scorching days of summer while keeping away the worst winter storms.[15]

Nonetheless, the problems of Jamestown remained. Since they decided to remain on the original peninsula, the colonists could not escape the annual drop in the level of the river and the swamps left when the fresh water ebbed. They had still not managed to find any springs and continued to take their water from the James, a practice Strachey recognized likely produced the diseases that continued to wrack English bodies. The arrival of De La Warr's flotilla had increased the number of English at Jamestown to 400, in addition to another 100 who took up residence among the Nansemonds to the south. No English at that settlement got sick, but 100 became ill at Jamestown and half of them died.[16]

De La Warr understood that the survival of Jamestown depended on finding sufficient food to keep the colonists alive and establishing some kind of rapprochement with Wahunsonacock. He moved on the first need by accepting Somers's offer to dispatch a ship to Bermuda to gather live hogs. Relations with the Powhatans proved more vexing. The governor hoped to convince the werowance that the 1608 ceremony between Newport and Wahunsonacock meant that the headman had, as Strachey framed the issue, "formerly vowed not only friendship but homage, receiving from His Majesty therefor many gifts and upon his knees a crown and scepter, with other ornaments, the symbols of civil state and Christian sovereignty, thereby obliging himself to office of duty to His Majesty." In exchange for these gifts, Wahunsonacock had given Newport, James's delegate in Virginia, some shoes and a mantle—possibly the large shell-adorned cloak.[17]

Wahunsonacock quite likely saw the ceremony of 1608 as a rite in which the monarch of another nation offered up gifts in an act of obeisance,

15. Strachey, "True Reportory," 81–82.
16. Strachey, "True Reportory," 82–83.
17. Strachey, "True Reportory," 84–88, 90–92; W.S., *The Proceedings of the English Colonie in Virginia since their first beginning from England* (Oxford, 1612), in Philip L. Barbour, ed., *The Complete Works of Captain John Smith* (Chapel Hill: University of North Carolina Press for the Institute of Early American History and Culture, 1986), 1:237. The earliest, and likely first, catalog of what became the Ashmolean Museum notes that the collection included "*Powhatan*, King of *Virginia*'s habit all embroidered with shells, or Roanoke," along with three other coats from Virginia, one made from bearskin, a second from raccoon, and a third of feathers and deerskin. The museum also acquired a coat from the Indigenous people of Greenland made of fish entrails. See John Tradescant, *Museum Tradescantianum: Or, A Collection of Rarities preserved at South-Lambeth neer London* (London, [1656]), 47.

allowing the headman to symbolically adopt the English as one of his dependent communities. He told the English that he was a king too and the colonizers should tell James that he "is to come to me, not I to him." Wahunsonacock had repeated that action on a small scale when he spared Smith's life. From his vantage point, the English were no different from the other thirty or so communities that he had come to control. Perhaps he felt sorry for them, since these newcomers proved so incapable of handling the basic tasks for staying alive in the region.[18]

The clashing political sensibilities exploded in 1609, launching what later became known as the first Anglo-Powhatan War. Believing he had the upper hand, De La Warr sent a delegation to tell Wahunsonacock that if the Powhatans did not accept the English presence, the newcomers would attack. The Natives needed to return the English they held as captives too. If they did so, the governor promised, they would "enter friendship with him, as a friend to King James and his subjects," as Strachey put it. Instead of shifting course, Wahunsonacock replied that the English "should depart this country or confine ourselves to Jamestown only, without searching further up into his land or rivers." If the English overstepped these boundaries, the Powhatans would kill them. He also told them not to come back unless they "brought him a coach and three horses, for he had understood by the Indians which were in England, how such was the state of great werowances and lords in England, to ride and visit other great men." Such a request must have appalled De La Warr, who believed that arriving in this far outpost of the monarch's realm with his velvet cloaks and cushions testified that he, not Wahunsonacock, deserved signs of power.[19]

Over subsequent days, Wahunsonacock's spies reported on the progress the English made in building their new fort at Jamestown and assessing the health of the residents of the small village. Farther away, Powhatans lay well armed, murdering any English who strayed beyond the territory their werowance allowed the visitors to inhabit. But the English caught two of these attackers, both residents of Pasapegh, Wahunsonacock's hometown. De La Warr had them manacled and paraded in front of the colony's governing council. The assembled decided that they should chop off the right hand of each of these men, "sending them away withal with

18. W.S., *Proceedings of the English Colonie*, 1:236; see Frederic W. Gleach, *Powhatan's World and Colonial Virginia: A Clash of Cultures* (Lincoln: University of Nebraska Press, 1997), esp. 106–122.
19. Strachey, "True Reportory," 89–92.

a message to Powhatan [Wahunsonacock]," as Strachey wrote, "that unless he would yet return such Englishmen as he detained." If Wahunsonacock did not accept the terms, the English promised to kill every one of his people they found and burn every village and cornfield. Soon after, Gates sailed for England, eager to quell the rumors at home about the troubles in Virginia. On board was Kainta, the kidnapped son of Sasenticum, the werowance of Warrascoyack, as well as valuable stores of black walnut, cedar, and iron ore.[20]

Rising tensions around the bay often mystified the English but were not surprising given the power of the Powhatans. Wahunsonacock and his allies understood the moment better than the newcomers. Among those who recognized their mastery was a boy named Henry Spelman, who had arrived in Jamestown in 1609 when he was fourteen years old. Smith had "sold" the boy to Wahunsonacock. Smith soon departed for England, and the Powhatans agreed to let the boy go. Upon learning that the English had little food on hand, Spelman offered to return to the Powhatans to try to broker a deal. Once in the werowance's town, Spelman offered Wahunsonacock a hatchet and some copper. Three weeks later the werowance instructed Spelman to go back to Jamestown and tell the English that if they sent him more copper, he would provide the maize they needed. Only later did Spelman realize that the werowance had set a trap for the English, whom he intended to kill. Fortunately for the newcomers, the Powhatans' arrows could not pierce the sides of their ship. The English returned to Jamestown, hungry and more suspicious than ever about the intentions of their neighbors. Soon after, Spelman sailed for England, spared from the ongoing war in the bay.[21]

Like Harriot's *Briefe and True Report*, Spelman's "relation" provided details about the region and its occupants at a moment of heightened anxiety. He wrote about the Powhatans' religious practice, which he saw as a kind of devil worship involving icons. He described their coming-of-age rituals, courting and marriage rules, the ways they named their infants, their healing customs, and their mortuary practices. He claimed that while among the Patwomecks he had witnessed the execution of five individuals, a sign of how they handled serious infractions such as infanticide, murder, and theft. He described their architecture too, noting that

20. Strachey, "True Reportory," 93–94.

21. Henry Spelman, *Relation of Virginia: A Boy's Memoir of Life with Powhatans and Patawomecks*, ed. Karen Ordahl Kupperman (New York: New York University Press, 2019), 1–7, 13–21.

Wahunsonacock's house was grander than others. Towns consisted of twenty to thirty houses, with maize planted nearby. The men of a community would hunt together, setting fires in the grass to drive deer into an enclosed area where it would be easier to slaughter them for their skins, which the Powhatans valued more than venison. He also described Powhatan maize culture and weaponry.[22]

Spelman's depiction of Powhatan culture added to the English stock of knowledge about the practices of peoples who lived far from Europe's shores. The adolescent shared his firsthand views with others involved in colonization schemes. Anyone who saw Spelman's report, which circulated in manuscript, would have understood that no one had yet effectively challenged Wahunsonacock or his confederacy.[23]

Recognizing that Virginia might founder, the company decided to respond to the rumors of despair and death with a small pamphlet titled *A True Declaration of the Estate of the Colonies in Virginia, with a Confutation of Such Scandalous Reports as Have Tended to the Disgrace of So Worthy an Enterprise*. In many ways it was a typical promotional pamphlet intended to generate interest and counter the negative stories. Except that this one candidly noted that one Englishman had murdered his wife and then chopped up and salted her remains to ease his hunger. For his part, Percy claimed that colonists dug up corpses and "Licked upp the Bloode w[hi]ch hathe fallen from their weake fellowes." He told of a starving man named Hugh Pryse who began to rave and blaspheme before he ran out of the fort only to be murdered. By the time his comrades arrived, wolves or some other animals had ripped his corpse to shreds. While it is possible that these tales were untrue, archaeological evidence at Jamestown suggests that residents ate at least part of a young woman and then dumped her bones in the cellar of a kitchen, likely a sign that they knew they had committed a crime—and recognized their own descent into barbarism.[24]

22. Spelman, *Relation*, 22 (worship), 24 (coming of age), 28–32 (marriage), 32–35 (illness and death), 36–38 (executions), 26 (architecture and deer hunt), 38–41 (maize), 44–46 (weaponry).

23. His command of such details made Spelman attractive to both William Strachey, another traveler and would-be colonizer, and the minister Samuel Purchas, each of whom spoke with Spelman or read his report. See Spelman, *Relation*, 81–85.

24. *A True Declaration of the Estate of the Colonies in Virginia, with a Confutation of Such Scandalous Reports as Have tended to the Disgrace of So Worthy an Enterprise* (London, 1610); James Horn et al., *Jane: Starvation, Cannibalism, and Endurance at Jamestown* (Williamsburg: Colonial Williamsburg Foundation and Preservation Virginia, 2013); Mark Nicholls, "George Percy's 'Trewe Relacyon': A Primary Source for the Jamestown Settlement," *VMHB* 113 (2005), 251; Rachel B. Herrmann, "The 'Tragicall Historie': Cannibalism and Abundance in Colonial Jamestown," *WMQ*, 3rd. Ser., 68 (2011), 47–74. Cannibalism driven by famine existed within Europe too, as the Huguenot

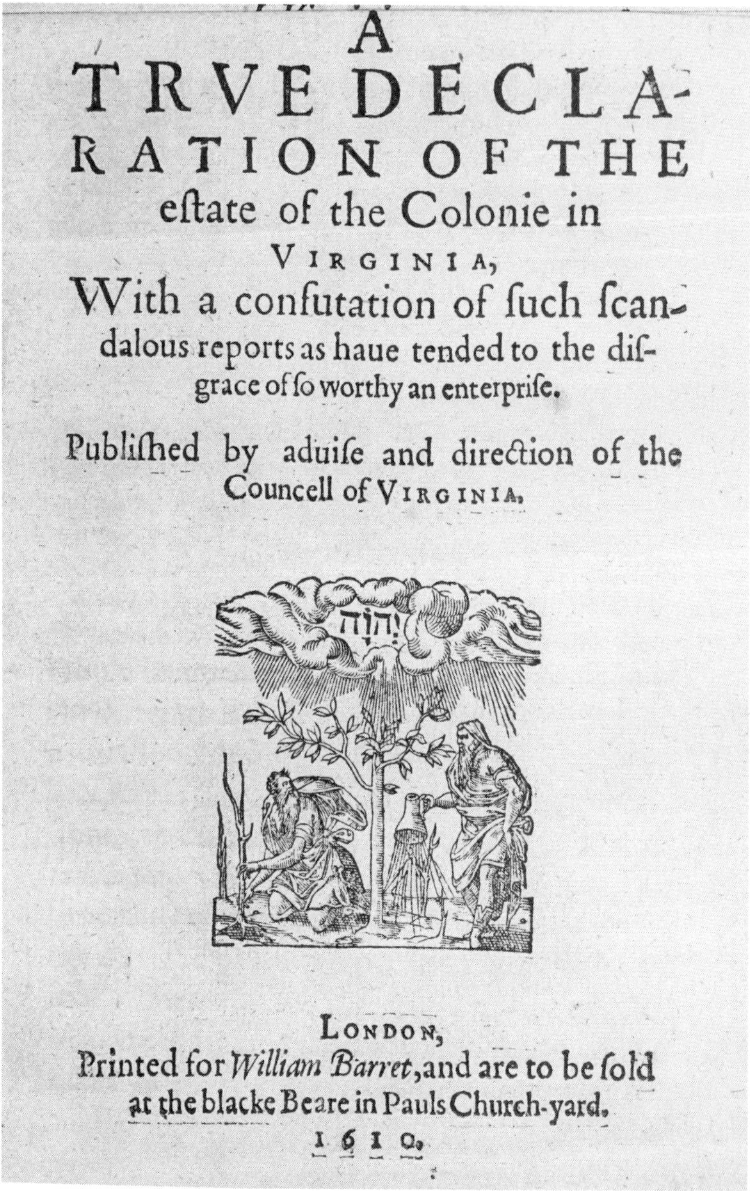

A
TRVE DECLA-
RATION OF THE
eſtate of the Colonie in
VIRGINIA,
With a confutation of ſuch ſcan-
dalous reports as haue tended to the diſ-
grace of ſo worthy an enterpriſe.

Publiſhed by aduiſe and direction of the
Councell of VIRGINIA.

LONDON,
Printed for *William Barret*, and are to be ſold
at the blacke Beare in Pauls Church-yard.
1610.

Like other Europeans trying to generate support for a colonial venture, the Virginia Company turned to printers to spread what it saw as reliable information about English migrants. In the annals of such promotional literature, *The True Declaration . . . of the Colonie in Virginia* stood out for its admission that some colonists had eaten the bodies of others. Courtesy of the Huntington Library, San Marino, California.

The English at Jamestown had been rescued by the arrival of supplies from Bermuda, but whatever solace they enjoyed proved fleeting. The war that had begun in 1609 had not abated by 1612, when John Smith's name appeared on the title page of a book published in Oxford entitled *A Map of Virginia, with a Description of the Countrey, The Commodities, People, Government and Religion*. He described territory in the broad region that the English called Virginia, which Smith claimed ran from 34° to 44°

Captain John Smith's 1612 map of Virginia included the names of many Powhatan towns as well as a depiction of the inside of Wahunsonacock's house at the time Smith was a prisoner. Courtesy of the Huntington Library, San Marino, California.

writer Jean de Léry reported in his history of the siege of the Protestant redoubt of Sancerre in the midst of France's religious wars. Léry published his account the year after his return from Brazil, a voyage that led him to write his well-known and often republished travel account. The situation in Sancerre at times reminded him of the travails of the Huguenots who had gone to Brazil. See Jean de Léry, *Histoire Memorable de la ville de Sancerre*, ed. Frank Lestringant (orig. pub. 1574; Paris: Librairie Générale Française, 2024), 149–174, esp. 161–163, and Janet Whately, "Food and the Limits of Civility: The Testimony of Jean de Léry," *Sixteenth Century Journal* 15 (1984), 387–400.

north latitude: "On the South lyeth *Florida*: on the North *nova Francia*." Despite having close-up views of a region dominated by Indigenous Americans, including the Powhatans who had taken him prisoner and could have murdered him, Smith, like many other Europeans, believed that these Christ-bearing travelers had legitimate title to the continent.[25]

Despite the claims of English possession, Smith's book revealed that the territory around the Chesapeake remained in the hands of its Native occupants. Smith made this clear with two devices: a three-page list of words used by the Powhatans and a two-page map.[26] An insert in the upper left corner depicted Wahunsonacock on a raised dais, in command of Cape Charles, Cape Henry, Point Comfort, and Jamestown. But most of the text referred to Powhatan communities. Smith, eager to show his mastery of this region he had briefly governed, managed to create (or endorse) a map that testified to Powhatan dominance.

Smith's map was typical of an age when virtually all of North America remained Indian Country. European maps of other places, such as Champlain's sketches of Algonquian-speaking peoples along the northeast coast and the Miguel map of Etzanoa, similarly revealed extensive Native presence and minimal intrusion by Europeans. Spanish explorer Antonio de Herrera's map of North America made a related point. Published in 1601 to illustrate a massive history of Spanish exploration, it revealed a blank continent, with no places north of Florida even mentioned. The map, labeled "Descripcion de las Yndias del Norte," ignored information that the Spanish possessed, perhaps in a bid to hide details from imperial rivals. Whatever this cartographer's goal, the effect was to show that the Europeans still had not established even the merest foothold in the area north of the Rio Grande.[27]

If the maps that Europeans passed around revealed the marginal impression that newcomers had made on the land, books and rumors circulated information suggesting that European explorers and migrants had begun to establish a durable presence. Printers met this increasing demand for news about North America with a stream of new books. Such texts, and the oral versions of them that circulated when a reader told another what she or he had seen on the page, testified that European fascination far outpaced European colonial activity. This growing interest played into the hands of monarchs eager to extend their rule or investors

25. [John] Smith, *A Map of Virginia, with a Description of the Countrey, The Commodities, People, Government and Religion* (Oxford, 1612), quotation at sig. A^{r}.

26. Smith, *Map of Virginia*, sig. *3^{r}–[*4^{r}].

27. David J. Weber, *The Spanish Frontier in North America* (New Haven, CT: Yale University Press, 1992), 56.

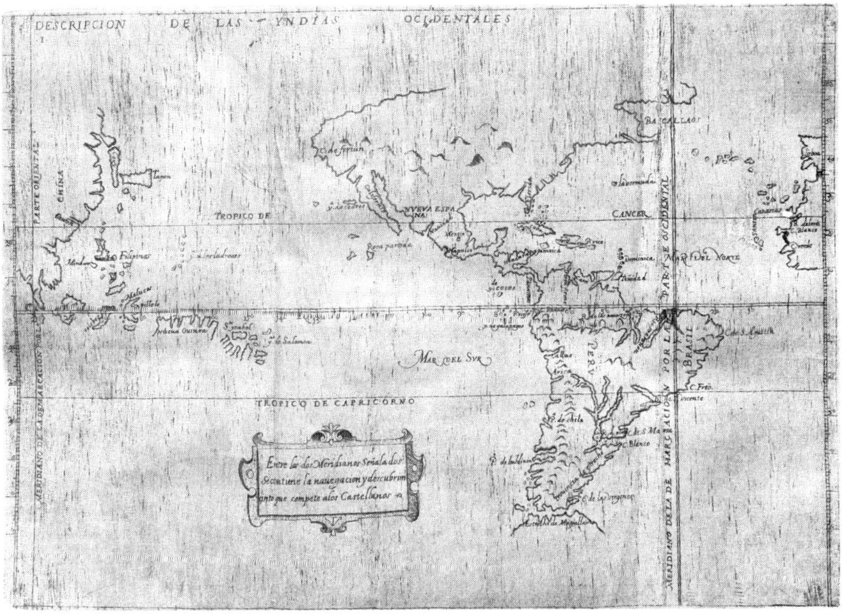

Antonio de Herrera's 1601 map illustrated New Spain but left North America almost entirely blank, perhaps for strategic purposes. Wikimedia Commons.

keen to get men and women onto the lands they claimed to possess. All knew that any legitimate claim to territory required physical occupation of the land, even if only by small numbers of underemployed boys and young men, limited numbers of poorly armed soldiers, or friars in medieval robes bearing the name of their savior into lands where they might soon be martyred.

Far from England and the tales that Smith spun, colonists struggled to survive in Virginia. Percy sent reports home offering excruciating details about the horrors visited upon the English at the hands of the Powhatans, whom Percy despised and mistrusted. The violence only begat more violence.[28] A deepening sense of victimhood drove Percy and the English to attack the Pasapeghs and Chickahominies. His men captured a woman he identified as the queen of one town and her children. The English threw her children off their boat and shot "owtt their Braynes in the water." Their bloodlust still not sated, the English then pillaged the town, stealing maize and desecrating temples and idols. The soldiers implored Percy

28. Nicholls, "George Percy's 'Trewe Relacyon,'" 244–248.

to burn the queen alive. He decided instead to have two soldiers paddle her to shore and then kill her with their swords.[29]

The stories that Percy told would make it difficult to convince any sane English woman or man to join an expedition to Virginia. Rather than lure possible migrants, he painted a verbal picture of the town as little more than a fetid heap where formerly civilized English men and women had descended into cannibalism. Fortunately for the Virginia Company, William Strachey, the former secretary of the colony, had returned to London. In 1612, he published a short book that included laws likely created first by Gates under orders from the Virginia Company and then supplemented by the martial law enacted by Sir Thomas Dale, a military commander who assumed command of the colony within three days of his arrival in May 1611. Dale's taking charge pleased Percy, who saw him providing the firm direction the migrants needed, especially when he put all of them to work. Strachey believed that the Virginia Company needed to engineer a Protestant version of the Reconquista, but this time with the English playing the part of the saviors of civilization.[30]

Publication of the laws was a crucial step for both investors and potential migrants, who each needed to believe that the English could maintain order in Virginia. With the laws printed, delinquents might be less likely to book passage.[31] Half of the forty laws threatened execution for a first offense for murder, sodomy, adultery, rape (of an English or Native woman), treason against the king, robbing a storehouse or church, bearing false witness, unauthorized trade with or running away to the Powhatans, or taking a ship out of the James River without proper permission. Brutal corporal punishment awaited those who committed blasphemy (tongue pierced for a second offense and death for a third), missing church service (six months' confinement for a third offense), fornication (whipping), slander or insubordination (three years in the galley for a second offense and death for a third), or killing livestock without permission (hands burned and ears lopped off). Statutes aimed to punish sailors as well as migrants. Publicizing these punishments did not mean these transgressions were common, though authorities did execute an English Catholic who they believed, according to an Irish witness, was going to tell the king of Spain "what goes on in that land."[32] Instead, the publication of the

29. Nicholls, "George Percy's 'Trewe Relacyon,'" 253–255.

30. [William Strachey], *For the Colony in Virginea Britannia: Lawes Divine, Morall and Martiall, etc.*, ed. David H. Flaherty (Charlottesville: University of Virginia Press for the Association for the Preservation of Virginia Antiquities, 1969), xx–xxiii, 2.

31. [Strachey], *For the Colony*, 3, 5–6.

32. [Strachey], *For the Colony*, 17–19, 24–25; "Francis Mangel's Relation of the First Voyage and the Beginnings of the Jamestown Colony, July 1, 1610," in Barbour, ed., *Jamestown Voyages* 1:151–157, quotation at 156.

laws was designed to send the message that the descent into incivility in the colony would be tolerated no longer. Virginia's laws fit early Stuart conceptions of the relationship between legal codes and the preservation of order. At the time, about fifty domestic laws specified execution, most of them for some kind of property crime.[33]

The new approach seemed to work, at least in terms of encouraging migration. In the years that followed the publication of the laws, servant emigration from Britain increased. Men far outnumbered women among the emigrating servants in the 1610s, but at least the possibility of colonial families near the bay began to seem plausible.[34]

In 1614, the war ended. It had been a devastating contest, for colonists and Powhatans alike, driven as much by the Powhatans' experience with the use of violence to build their polity as by the English belief that the land was theirs. Virginia's secretary Ralphe Hamor observed that the five years of "intestine warre with the revengefull implacable Indians" had been replaced by "a firm peace (not again easily to be broken)." Part of the newcomers' success rested on overtures to Indigenous residents who refused to accept Wahunsonacock as their sovereign, including Chickahominies who lived about seven miles from Jamestown. Members of this community promised to return any wayward cattle, which posed a threat to their maize fields, and to join the English if the Spanish should ever attack. In exchange, they received annual gifts of iron hatchets, beads, and copper. The English believed that the Chickahominies had become subjects of James I, an alliance they would reaffirm in annual rituals. The timing was auspicious: in addition to tobacco, the English believed that they had finally figured out how to establish a silk industry.[35]

Even as they formed alliances with Wahunsonacock's domestic foes, the Powhatan headman held the key to peace along the Chesapeake. After

33. [Strachey], *For the Colony*, 18–19; Leon Radzinowicz, *A History of English Criminal Law and its Administration from 1750*, 5 vols., (New York: Macmillan, 1948–1986), 1:4.

34. James Horn, "Servant Emigration to the Chesapeake in the Seventeenth Century," in Thad W. Tate and David L. Ammerman, eds., *The Chesapeake in the Seventeenth Century: Essays on Anglo-American Society* (Chapel Hill: University of North Carolina Press for the Institute of Early American History and Culture, 1979), 51–95, esp. 62–65.

35. Raphe Hamor, *A True Discourse of the Present Estate of Virginia, and the successe of the affaires there till the 18 of June 1614* (London, 1615), 13–15 (declining hostility), 35 (silk and silkworms); J. Frederick Fausz, "An 'Abundance of Blood Shed on Both Sides': England's First Indian War, 1609–1614," *VMHB* 98 (1990), 3–56; James D. Rice, "War and Politics: Powhatan Expansionism and the Problem of Native American Warfare," *WMQ*, 3rd. Ser., 77 (2020), 3–32.

one treaty session, Wahunsonacock told Hamor that he expected the English to bring him copper, a knife, two bone combs, and 100 fishhooks, as well as a dog and a cat, the next time they met. If the English provided these goods, the Powhatans would reciprocate with skins. The secretary replied by rehearsing the list, but Wahunsonacock, Hamor wrote, "bade me write them downe in such a Table book as he shewed me, which was a very fair one." Hamor believed that the book was of no use to the Powhatan, "but he tolde me, it did him much good to shew it to strangers which came unto him." Hamor agreed and wrote down the list in the book, and the two parted.[36]

While there were many causes for the truce, the most important was the unexpected union of Wahusonacock's daughter Pocahontas with the colonist John Rolfe. Colonial soldiers kidnapped her in 1613 believing that it would force her father to end the war. During the year she remained among her captors, Pocahontas came to know and, so colonists claimed, fall in love with Rolfe. The English speculated that a marriage between them would have myriad salutary benefits. Hamor, the secretary, believed that it was "merely for the good and honour of the Plantation." Dale, the governor, took credit for the young woman's religious conversion and public renunciation, as he claimed, of her idolatry. Alexander Whitaker, a prominent local minister, saw the marriage as analogous to a union of royal European houses—an important signal of peace between the English and Powhatans. Hamor suspected that some would look at the relationship between a widowed English man and a Powhatan teenager with suspicion, which perhaps explains why Rolfe made his views public. He saw the marriage as his "godly labor," another contribution to the colonists' efforts to convert Indigenous to Protestant Christianity and hence part of the migrants' obligation to embrace "so holy a worke."[37]

These aggrandizing claims ignored the fact that the marriage could hardly have been predicted when they abducted her. Fortunately for the newcomers, Wahunsonacock saw the advantage of this daughter's partnership with a prominent colonist. He even sent two of his sons to witness the ceremony.[38] To him, the marriage fit a long-standing pattern of his children marrying others to expand his influence.[39]

36. Hamor, *True Discourse*, 45.

37. Hamor, *True Discourse*, 2, 24, 55, 59–60; Hamor to Dale, undated, in Hamor, *True Discourse*, 63–68; James Horn, *A Land as God Made It: Jamestown and the Birth of America* (New York: Basic Books, 2005), 211–216.

38. Hamor, *True Discourse*, 8, 11.

39. Gleach, *Powhatan's World*, 134–136; Kathleen M. Brown, *Good Wives, Nasty Wenches, and Anxious Patriarchs: Gender, Race, and Power in Colonial Virginia* (Chapel Hill:

Soon after their union, Pocahontas and Rolfe sailed to London, where she became an instant celebrity.[40] King James and Queen Anne hosted her for a masque, a theatrical performance featuring masked or costumed actors and dancers, created by renowned playwright Ben Jonson for the celebration. Prominent members of the Virginia Company lavished praise on her. Minister and writer Samuel Purchas reported that she carried herself with civility "as the Daughter of a King." Members of the council of the Virginia Company hoped that the marriage and her conversion would "advance Christianitie." Even London's lord bishop attended her with an air of formal ceremony.[41] She sat for a portrait, which became the basis in 1616 for an engraving by Simon Van de Passe. This picture was more than a portrait of the daughter of Wahunsonacock or even the bride of the man most responsible for advancing the English tobacco trade. Here was visual proof of the promise made by Harriot and White a generation earlier. Despite the bloodshed in Virginia and colonists' willingness to destroy Native communities only a few years earlier, the idea that cultural conversion could occur continued to circulate among those who wanted to find a peaceful way toward coexistence in America. To these observers, the power of English culture could transform an Indigenous American into an English woman or man. Further, under the right guidance, cultural change could progress quickly. Pocahontas, after her christening, became Rebecca Rolfe. Her husband believed that Virginia provided an opportunity for colonizers to encourage the Powhatans "to abandon their old superstitions and idolatries, wherein they bene nursed and trayned from their infancies." He saw his marriage to her as a fitting task of an enlightened man bringing civilization to the wilderness.[42]

Back in England, John Rolfe became an ardent champion of the Virginia project. He shared his views with the king; William Herbert, Earl of Pembroke, a crucial patron of the Virginia Company; Robert Rich, son of the first Earl of Warwick, who was involved in the East India, Bermuda,

University of North Carolina Press for the Institute of Early American History and Culture, 1996), 52.

40. Hamor claimed she traveled in England with "the title of Nonparella of Virginia"; Hamor, *True Discourse*, 4.

41. James Horn and Paul Musselwhite, "Introduction," in Paul Musselwhite, Peter C. Mancall, and James Horn, eds., *Virginia 1619: Slavery and Freedom in the Making of English America* (Chapel Hill: University of North Carolina Press for the Omohundro Institute of Early American History and Culture, 2019), 4–5; Samuel Purchas, *Hakluytus Posthumus, or Purchas his Pilgrimes* (London, 1625), 4:1774.

42. John Rolfe, *A True Relation of the State of Virginia Lefte by Sir Thomas Dale, Knight, in May Last 1616* (New Haven, CT: Yale University Press, 1951), 40.

Simon van de Passe's 1616 portrait of Pocahontas after her marriage to John Rolfe and conversion to Christianity sent a clear cultural message: Native Americans could be transformed into English women and men. The portrait would help solidify her status as the most famous Indigenous person from North America to have yet visited England. Courtesy of the Huntington Library, San Marino, California.

and Virginia companies; and Purchas, who was already assuming Hakluyt's role as a prominent chronicler of English overseas ventures. Rolfe believed that the colonists had mastered the ecological challenges that had kept their numbers so low. At that point 81 colonial farmers and 201 other English men survived, along with 65 women and children. He argued that Virginia could become home to thousands of migrants and thus fulfill its role as a destination for the domestic destitute. Local conditions promised a future for growing flax and hemp as good as any in Europe, supposedly ideal conditions for silkworms, and perhaps the best tobacco to be found.[43]

Tobacco, despite its widely praised medicinal properties and the enjoyment it brought its European users, posed unique problems for the Virginia Company. James I had argued in his 1604 *Counter-blaste to Tobacco* that tobacco was a "custome loathsome to the eye, hatefull to the Nose, harmefull to the braine, daungerous to the Lungs, and in the black stinking fume therof, nearest resembled the horrible Stygian smoke of the pit that is bottomlesse." His slender book was his first published work after becoming king of England, so it represented not just his personal animus but also his adoption of the notion that it was "the Kings part (as the proper Phisician of his Politicke-body) to purge" the public of bodily afflictions, "sluggish delicacy," and "prodigiality."[44] In the years to come, those who wanted access to the plant would need to find a way around royal opposition and the lingering notion among Europeans that tobacco, employed by Indigenous peoples in rituals across the Western Hemisphere, might undermine Christian cultures.

Opponents of tobacco emphasized the risks, not only with the plant itself but also its association with known users—including those convicted in the Gunpowder Plot of 1605 who "tooke Tabacco out of measure, with a seeming carelessnesse of their crime."[45] That popular image—of the indelible link between taking tobacco and frivolity or heedlessness—became a fixture in English popular culture. A masque performed in Whitehall in 1613 included two characters dressed like "*Floridians*" and another wearing "Tobacco-colour stuffe cut like Tobacco leaves" while holding "an *Indian* Bow and Arrowes."[46]

Rolfe, a master at understanding the politics of colonization, saw the tobacco trade as one part of a larger set of emerging commercial relations.

43. Rolfe, *True Relation*, 22–23 (recipients of the report), 33–36 (commodities), 38–39 (colonial population).

44. [James I/VI], *Counter-blaste to Tobacco* (London, 1604), quotations at sigs. D^{v}–[D2^{r}] (loathsome results) and A3^{v}–A4^{v} (physician to the people).

45. *The Arraignment and execution of the late Traytors* (London, 1606), sig. B2^{v}–B3^{r}.

46. *The Maske of Flowers* (London, 1614), sig. B3^{r}.

He believed that Natives on whom colonists once depended for survival had become their clients, which was more important than any profits to be made from this crop. This crucial cultural and economic shift facilitated calls to the English in Virginia to implement a system that would ensure an adequate food supply even if it meant that colonists would devote less of their acreage to cultivating tobacco.[47]

Despite its many problems, Jamestown fared better than other European colonial efforts in the waning years of the Little Ice Age. There was no substantial population of Spaniards or Spanish creoles north of the mining complex at Zacatecas. The French population at the newly launched Québec was possibly less than thirty, or about as many would fit in an average Iroquoian longhouse, of which there were many at Stadacona alone, not far from Québec.[48] Perhaps as few as three English survived in Bermuda, though Somers's resupply voyage in the summer of 1610 temporarily boosted the population before they all abandoned it once again. By contrast, the population of Jamestown, with the infusion of new colonists who arrived in 1610, stood at more than 500, though death still could take half of that number in any given year. If the English were to maintain a colony in Virginia, they would need to find a rationale that justified the ongoing loss of the king's subjects as well as the company's investment.

In the meantime, the blank spaces on European maps hid the truth. Those unmarked regions were not empty. As the various European colonies struggled, the Indigenous population of the continent north of the Rio Grande stood at approximately 1.8 million,[49] including long-lasting and still thriving communities in the places Europeans hoped to claim: the shores of Hudson and James Bays, the many tributaries of Chesapeake Bay, across the land of the Pueblos from the mesa of Acoma to the foothills of the Sangre de Cristo mountains, and along the coasts of Maine and Florida.

Europeans relied on help coming from across the Atlantic. Indigenous Americans needed no one to rescue them.

47. Rolfe, *True Relation*, 26–29, 33–38.
48. The colonial population in the region reached 60 in 1620, the highest number it had achieved to that point; see Marcel Trudel, *The Beginnings of New France, 1524–1663*, trans. Patricia Claxton (Toronto: McClelland and Steward, 1973), 129; Louise Dechène, in *Habitants and Merchants in Seventeenth-Century Montreal*, trans. Liana Vardi (Montreal: McGill-Queen's University Press, 1992), 16, notes that over its first ten years only 150 French colonists arrived on the island where Montreal was located.
49. Douglas H. Ubelaker, "North American Indian Population Size Changing Perspectives," in John W. Verano and Douglas H. Ubelaker, eds., *Disease and Demography in the Americas* (Washington: Smithsonian Institution Press, 1992), table 3 (173).

Smallpox, with its distinctive effects on the human body, was among the most destructive diseases Europeans unwittingly transported across the Atlantic Ocean. This image in the hand of a Mexica artist who contributed to the Florentine Codex, depicts the spread of the disease during the time of the conquest of Tenochtitlan.

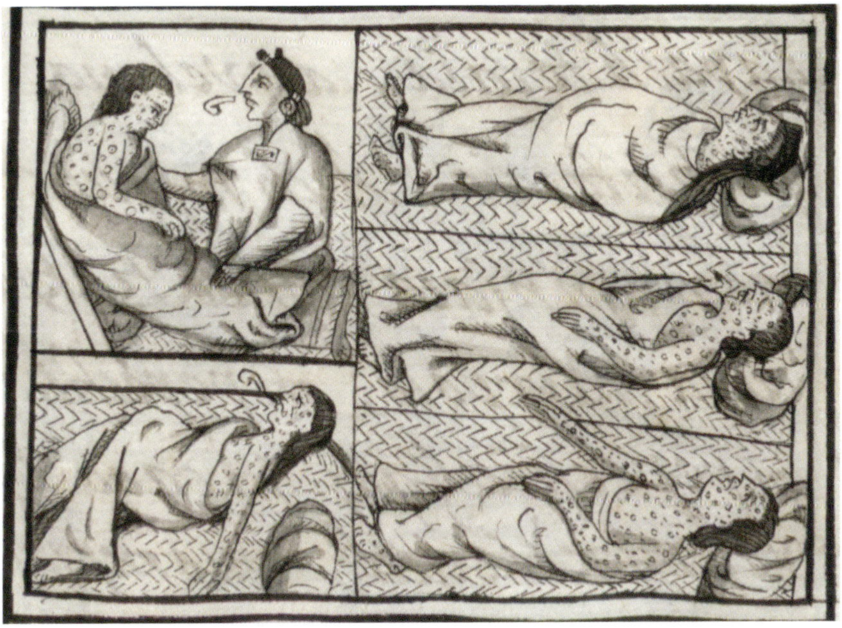

From *General History of the Things of New Spain by Fray Bernardino de Sahagún: The Florentine Codex. Book XII: The Conquest of Mexico*. Courtesy of the World Digital Library: Biblioteca Medicea Laurenziana, Florence. Library of Congress, 2021667857.

When Samuel de Champlain imagined his future in the St. Lawrence Valley, he designed a grand house fitting what he saw as his stature as the governor of New France. Yet he soon learned that claims on paper mattered little if he could not triumph over local adversaries, including Haudenosaunee warriors he met in battle.

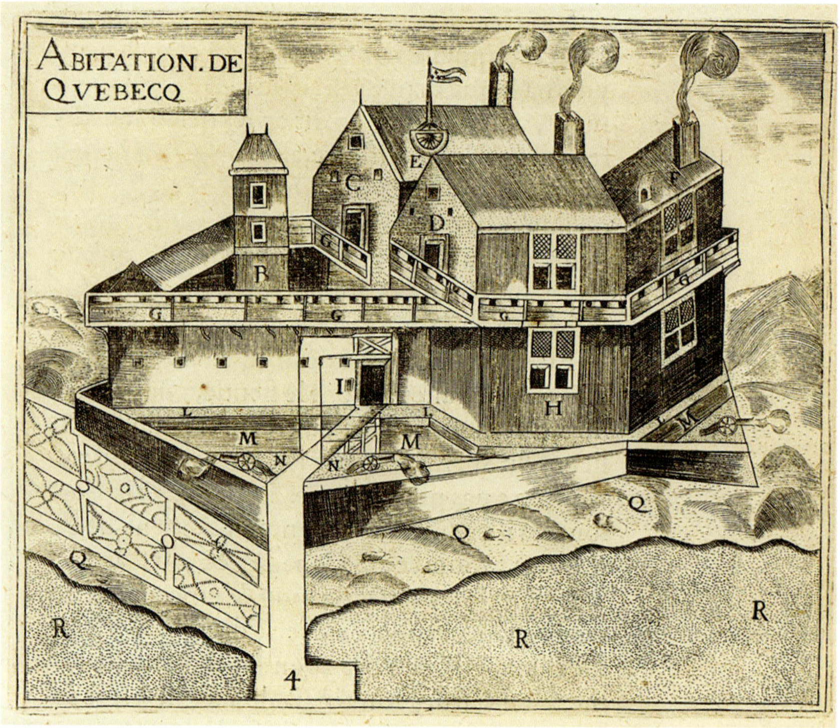

From *Les voyages du sieur de Champlain Xaintongeois* (Paris, 1613).
Courtesy of the Huntington Library, San Marino, California.

From *Les voyages du sieur de Champlain Xaintongeois* (Paris, 1613).
Courtesy of the John Carter Brown Library.

The unknown artist who painted this scene of New France in the early years of the sixteenth century likely had not seen Canada but instead rendered the map from written reports. Still the image captures crucial details, including Native peoples wearing fur, the presence of European nuns among the immigrants, and a fort with cannon pointing towards Indigenous communities and not towards the sea, a recognition that the most dangerous enemies might be Indigenous rather than other Europeans.

Vallard atlas, c. 1547. Courtesy of the Huntington Library, San Marino, California.

By the late sixteenth century, Europeans believed that tobacco had healing properties and was also enjoyable to smoke. But those who promoted the plant's use faced formidable opposition because of tobacco's association with Indigenous religious rituals, depicted by the engraver Theodor de Bry's workshop to illustrate a travel account about Brazil, and the fact that it was so pleasurable that it might lead to addiction and the squandering of one's money. This idea was championed by King James VI of Scotland in the *Counterblaste to Tobacco* (1604), the first book he published after becoming King James I of England. Merchants eager to profit from the plant, especially after the realization of the high-quality tobacco being exported from Virginia, fought back with an argument that Europeans could break the link between tobacco and pagan ritual if they changed the apparatus for smoking.

Tupinamba smoking ritual. From Theodor de Bry, *America Tertia Pars* (1592). Courtesy of the Huntington Library, San Marino, California.

An English man smoking tobacco. From Anthony Chute, *Tobacco* (1595). Courtesy of the Huntington Library, San Marino, California.

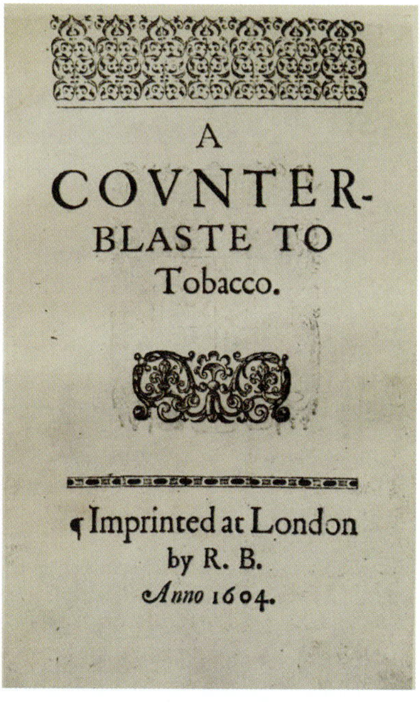

A
COVNTER-
BLASTE TO
Tobacco.

¶ Imprinted at London
by R. B.
Anno 1604.

Title page for James I, *Counterblaste to Tobacco*.
Courtesy of the Huntington Library, San Marino, California.

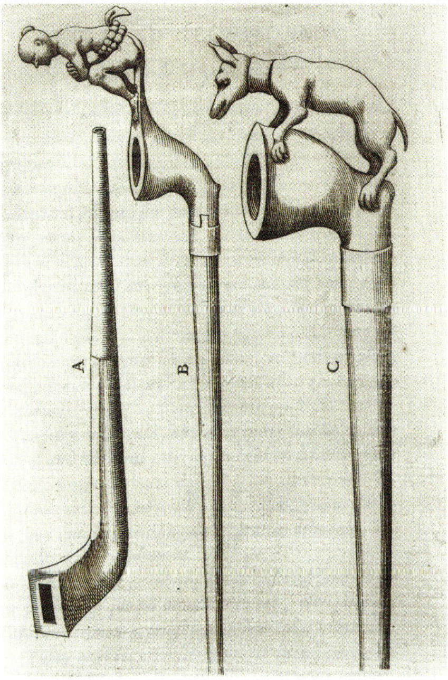

Native pipes. From Johann Neander, *Tabacologia* (1622). Courtesy of the Huntington Library, San Marino, California.

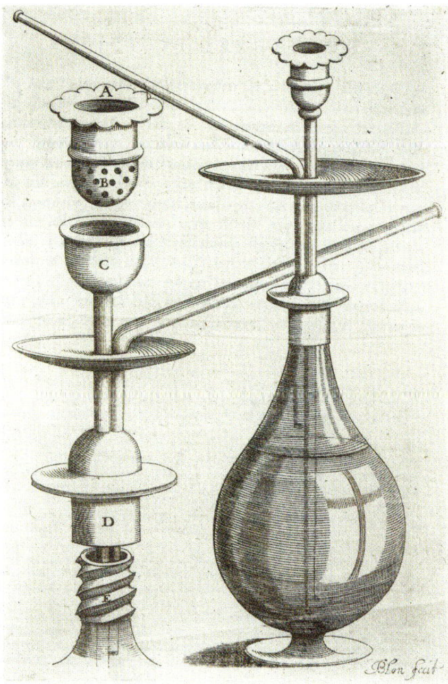

European pipes. From Johann Neander, *Tabacologia* (1622). Courtesy of the Huntington Library, San Marino, California.

Sugar production developed quickly in the Western Hemisphere in the early years of the seventeenth century, with planters studying the most effective ways to transform cane into molasses, used for distilling rum and brandy, and also refined sugar. The *ingenio* or water mill, depicted here in 1657, attracted great attention for those, like the planter Thomas Middleton, who cleared trees on his Barbadian plantation to expand acreage for the cultivation of cane by enslaved laborers.

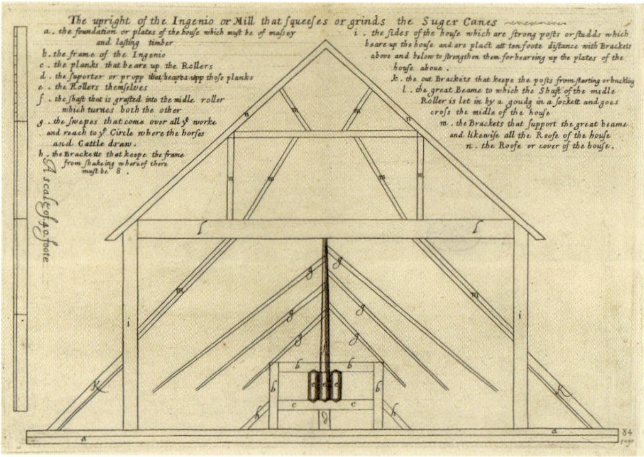

Ingenio. Courtesy of the John Carter Brown Library.

Middleton plantation. Courtesy of the John Carter Brown Library.

15

Gathering Storms

For most of the 1610s, Wahunsonacock remained the most consequential political figure along the mid-Atlantic coast. He maintained power by controlling the flow of prestige goods across the Powhatan confederacy, a system that predated the arrival of the English in 1607 but which he adapted to incorporate the rare, imported goods they brought. Unlike Europeans, the Powhatans, like many Indigenous Americans, lived in communities where property flowed through maternal lines, a system that gave Native women more power than European women typically experienced. Although matriarchy determined the movement of property from one generation to the next, Wahunsonacock retained control of the confederacy based on local military authority and the extension of his own kin ties, both real (through marriage to perhaps a hundred women in local communities) and fictive. Wahunsonacock's confederates possessed more military might, economic prowess, and ecological knowledge than the English could muster. But even the paramount chief faced limits. Some Native communities near the bay did not accept his rule, which meant they could form an alliance with the newcomers. He understood that he needed to calibrate his actions to maximize the Powhatans' power—even if that meant participating in the ancient practice, known in Europe as well as in North America, of blending his own family with a potential enemy's. For Wahunsonacock, the political and the personal could not be separated. The same held true for Pocahontas, who relied on Powhatan ideas about reciprocal obligations to navigate her marriage to the English colonist John Rolfe and manage the embassy to London that brought her side by side with the king and queen.[1]

1. See Daniel K. Richter, "Tsenacommacah and the Atlantic World," in Peter C. Mancall, ed., *The Atlantic World and Virginia, 1550–1624* (Chapel Hill: University of North Carolina Press for the Omohundro Institute of Early American History and Culture, 2007), 29–65; Kathleen M. Brown, *Good Wives, Nasty Wenches, and Anxious Patriarchs: Gender, Race, and Power in Colonial Virginia* (Chapel Hill: University of North Carolina Press for the Omohundro Institute of Early American History and Culture, 1996), esp. 50–53 (Wahunsonacock's wives), 72 (mutual obligations).

But while developments in Tsenacommacah garnered attention on both sides of the Atlantic, few could have anticipated how four seemingly unrelated developments would shift the political calculus within and beyond eastern North America: the realization by the English that they could produce a desirable strand of tobacco near the Chesapeake; a devastating epidemic in the Northeast; a new system of colonial government in Virginia; and the arrival of approximately twenty enslaved Africans, seized from a Portuguese ship, at Point Comfort.

The Africans who were forcibly brought to Point Comfort were not the first enslaved people in North America nor in British America. Enslavement of Indigenous captives had happened before and after European contact; the Spanish had brought captives to their territories much earlier; Drake had released enslaved Africans on the Outer Banks; and Bermuda, not Jamestown, was the destination of the earliest enslaved population in English America. But the Angolans' arrival in Jamestown signaled a shift: the tension between slavery and freedom, each with its unique political roots and rationales, would become a defining mark of English America.

By the time those Angolan captives set foot on the mainland in 1619, the world that Wahunsonacock had kept under his control had become less predictable than it had been for a generation. With growing confidence that they would be able to establish a colony on the shores of the Chesapeake, the English had by then expanded their horizons, paying renewed attention to Bermuda and the Atlantic coast of South America, where ambitious English colonizers hoped, again, to establish a community in territory that Spaniards had claimed but never settled.

At the dawn of the decade, prospects for success in North America looked bleak for the English. The underlying economic and political arguments for planting overseas colonies remained, notably chronic underemployment in England, the need to find new markets for manufactured goods, the belief that the English had a claim to the Chesapeake by right of discovery, and the desire to import valuable commodities, which had the additional benefit of creating more incentives to build ships and put young men to work. But the news trickling back to England from Virginia was horrific.[2] To make matters worse, English authorities responsible for overseas shipping, the masters of Trinity House (who supervised ships using the Thames River) and the High Court of Admiralty (which had legal jurisdiction over British ships at sea), had only begun to sort out what

2. See Mark Nicholls, "George Percy's 'Trewe Relacyon': A Primary Source for the Jamestown Settlement," *VMHB* 113 (2005), 215, 226, 238.

had happened to Hudson and the *Discovery*. The tattered ship's arrival in London with marks of the violence on board served as a visual reminder of what could happen when order broke down far from the metropolis.[3] On subsequent voyages, including five led by the master mariner William Baffin, and a 1612 royal charter to the Company of Merchants Discoverers of the North-West Passage, explorers still could not find the Northwest Passage.[4]

Still, fears over problems in the Arctic and near the Chesapeake did not diminish the enthusiasm that English investors and promoters of overseas expansion had for other colonial ventures, notably in Bermuda and South America. Some of those looking for new targets were already involved in colonization, including the directors of the Virginia Company. Its third charter (of March 1612) specified continued control over an area that extended 400 miles along the coast, with "Cape [or] Pointe Comfort" located at its center, and stretched from the Atlantic to the South Sea, along with an expansion of its claims to Atlantic islands, including "divers islandes lying desolate and uninhabited, some of which are already

3. Samuel Purchas, *Hakluytus Posthumus, or Purchas his Pilgrimes* (London, 1625), 3:608; Trinity House Transactions, vol. 1 (1609–1625), Guildhall Library, ms. 300451, ff. 11v–13r; Alwyn A. Ruddock, "The Trinity House at Deptford in the Sixteenth Century," *English Historical Review* 65 (1950), 460–462; G. G. Harris, *The Trinity House of Deptford, 1514–1660* (London: Athlone, 1969), 19–20; G. G. Harris, ed., *Trinity House of Deptford Transactions, 1609–35*, Publications of the London Record Society 19 (London: London Record Society, 1983), ix.
4. For the ships that departed in April 1612, see John Gatonbe, "A Voyage into the Northwest Passage, Undertaken in the Year 1612," in Awnsham Churchill and John Churchill, comps., *A Collection of Voyages and Travels* (London, 1732), 6:245–256; for the voyages that began in May, see Luke Foxe, *North-West Fox, Or, Fox from the North-west passage* (London, 1635), 117–137; Jonas Poole, "A briefe Declaration of this my Voyage of discovery to Greeneland, and towards the West of it," in Purchas, *Purchas his Pilgrimes*, 3:711–713; "A Relation written by Jonas Poole of a Voyage to Greenland, in the year 1612," in Purchas, *Purchas his Pilgrimes*, 3:713–715; William Baffin, "A Journall of the Voyage made to Grenland with sixe English Ships and a Pinasse," in Purchas, *Purchas his Pilgrimes*, 3:716–720; "A Short Discourse of a Voyage made in the yeare of our Lord 1613," in Purchas, *Purchas his Pilgrimes*, 3:300–303; Ro[bert] Frotherby, "A Voyage of Discovery to Greenland, & c. Anno 1614," in Purchas, *Purchas his Pilgrimes*, 3:728–731; William Baffin, "A true Relation of such things as happened in the fourth Voyage for the Discoverie of the North-west passage, performed in the year 1615," in Purchas, *Purchas his Pilgrimes*, 3:836–842; William Baffin, "The Voyage of Robert Bilot . . . 1615," in Fox, *North-West Fox*, 173; "A briefe and true Relation of Journall, contayning such accidents as happened in the fifth voyage, for the discoverie of a passage to the North-West....1616," in Purchas, *Purchase his Pilgrimes*, 3:844–848; Baffin to John Wolstenholme, in Purchas, *Purchas his Pilgrimes*, 3:843–844. For the charter: Noel Sainsbury, ed., *Calendar of State Papers Colonial, East Indies, China and Japan* (London, 1864), 1:238–241.

made knowne and discovered by the industry, travel, and expences of the said Company"—a direct reference to Bermuda. The first charter had also given the company the ability to govern inland 100 miles from the coastline, another presumption of ownership regardless of possible habitation by a Native population. The new charter extended the range of the company to 300 leagues—approximately 900 miles—into the ocean and authorized investors to "populate and plant" any islands "not already actually possessed or inhabited by anie other Christian prince or estate." That distinction was crucial since the English understood that the first European to land in Bermuda was Juan Bermúdez in 1503, whose name remained on European maps. But the Spanish never followed through with actual settlements, providing the English, as they saw the situation, with an opportunity to claim the archipelago without any legitimate competitor: to Europeans, continued occupation remained the only guarantor of sovereignty.[5]

In 1612, Richard Moore became Bermuda's first English governor. That spring he set off with fifty settlers, including women, men, and entire families. After their arrival they planted pumpkins, corn, and tobacco. Moore shipped to England a large deposit of ambergris, the sperm whale secretion then valued in Europe for its utility for medicines and perfumes. It brought in £8,000 to £10,000 for the company, erasing the costs associated with Moore's venture.[6] Promoters of investment, aware that news of the debacle of 1609 might dissuade potential migrants or new revenues, redefined the archipelago for English audiences. Bermuda was not, the eyewitness Silvester Jourdain wrote, "a habitation of Divells" but instead "a safe, secure, temperate, rich, sweet, and healthfull habitation for Man, and especially for English bodies." Migrants could find abundant fish, turtles, fruit, pepper, olives, palmetto trees, and hogs. Unlike Virginia, Bermuda needed no provisions or supplies other than men and women to bring its wonders to market. English colonial dreams could come true in a mid-Atlantic outpost where residents would pledge their allegiance to Protestant Christianity and the commonwealth.[7]

5. Samuel M. Bemiss, ed., *The Three Charters of the Virginia Company of London with Seven Related Documents, 1606–1621*, Jamestown 350th Anniversary Historical Booklet 4 (Williamsburg, VA: Jamestown 350th Anniversary Celebration Corporation, 1957), 3 (1606 charter), 77–78 (third charter).

6. Michael J. Jarvis, "Bermuda and the Beginnings of Black Anglo-America," in Paul Musselwhite, Peter C. Mancall, and James Horn, eds., *Virginia 1619: Slavery and Freedom in the Making of English America* (Chapel Hill: University of North Carolina Press for the Omohundro Institute of Early American History and Culture, 2019), 109–110.

7. [Silvester Jourdain], *A Plaine Description of the Barmudas, Now called Sommer Ilands* (London, 1613), sig. [B4^{r}]–[C4^{v}], quotation at sig. A3^{r}.

In 1614, the English received even more welcome news: a sea captain named Daniel Elfrith captured and towed a Spanish frigate to Bermuda, encouraging other potential English privateers to dream about Bermuda as a welcome haven for their booty rather than a treacherous pile of rocks. By 1615, over 600 colonists had arrived. They cleared fields, exported tobacco, erected a fort formidable enough to ward off a potential Spanish raid, and built a church. After Moore returned to London the councilors of the Virginia Company launched the Somers Island (or Bermuda) Company and appointed Thomas Smythe as governor, another project in his expanding dossier. Smythe weighed three possible futures: a self-contained colony, tobacco-exporting settlement, a privateering station. Some in England also saw it as a potential refuge for religious dissenters. On June 29, 1615, James I approved the royal charter for the Somers Island Company. Some 117 speculators purchased shares. Smythe, still the treasurer of the Virginia Company, selected Daniel Tucker, who had lived in Virginia, as governor.[8]

Contrary to its alleged promise, which prompted another 100 to migrate there in 1616, chaos reigned among the colonists. Tucker tried to suppress the disorder by declaring martial law. What followed was a reign of localized terror. Tucker confiscated private gardens, imposed a harsh daily work regime, and beat indentured servants who displeased him. He ordered the execution of one colonist for objecting to the loss of his own garden and another for stealing cheese.[9] While economic opportunity still beckoned, especially after English in Bermuda established trade contacts with the Virgin Islands, Hispaniola, and Venezuela, the opportunities paled in comparison to the problems, notably ecological devastation caused by European rats that had stowed away on English ships. To battle the vermin, the English imported cats, to no avail. They laid poison, which also did little. They lit fires, an act that reduced the number of valuable cedars they might otherwise have shipped home. Eventually the humans prevailed. But the disappearance of the rats led fat feral cats to seek food among colonists, and they only slowly returned to their domestic, tamer ways. Late in 1618 Tucker sailed for England, leaving behind a legacy of ill will and suspicion.[10]

8. Jarvis, "Bermuda and the Beginnings of Black Anglo-America," 111–113, 116.

9. [Nathaniel Butler], *The Historye of the Bermudaes or Summer Islands*, ed. J. Henry Lefroy, Hak. Soc., LXV (London: Hakluyt Society, 1882), 69–73; Jarvis, "Bermuda and the Beginnings of Black Anglo-America," 113.

10. [Butler], *Historye of the Bermudaes or Summer Islands*, 78, 84–87, 94–98; Jarvis, "Bermuda and the Beginnings of Black Anglo-America," 116–117, 91–92. For the rise and fall of Tucker, see Michael J. Jarvis, *Isle of Devils, Isle of Saints: An Atlantic History of Bermuda, 1609–1684* (Baltimore: Johns Hopkins University Press, 2022), 49–71.

English efforts to expand an American presence reached farther south in March 1610 when Sir Thomas Roe left the port at Dartmouth, in Devon, bound for the Amazon. He had attracted substantial investments, including from Ralegh and the Earl of Southampton.[11] Five weeks after departing, the ships reached the river and began an ascent that took them 200 miles into the interior before they shifted to a smaller boat to sail another 100 miles upriver, and then to an Indigenous canoe. Roe believed that he saw more of the Amazon than "any Englishman now alive," he wrote to one of his patrons.[12] But he was hardly the only European in coastal South America. Dutch, English, Spanish, and French ships were all crowding Port of Spain in Trinidad loading tobacco for European consumers. The Spanish were also building a new port city there, which they planned to use to claim the Orinoco.[13]

In January 1614 the London-based *Lions Clawe* arrived at Portsmouth carrying large quantities of brazilwood and sugar. Five months later the ship departed for the Amazon, hauling goods to Roe: thirty dozen axes and hatchets as well as quantities of glass beads and butchers' knives, presumably the goods Roe needed to trade with his unidentified commercial partners.[14] By then, English readers could have learned about the venture in a book by Robert Harcourt. Harcourt's brother Michael had earlier taken possession of the territory called Wiapoco (now Oyapock), which forms the modern boundary between Brazil and French Guiana, in the name of James I "by turf and twig," an ancient English ceremony to lay claim to land. Harcourt performed the ceremony because, by his reckoning, it had until that point not been "actually possessed, and inhabited by any other Christian Prince or State." Michael Harcourt established a community of twenty migrants, who started to create plantations and engage in local expeditions. Despite the king's interest, this gathering of English collapsed. Michael returned home in 1612.[15]

Just as the English tried and failed along the Amazon, Sir Walter Ralegh tried to revive interest in the Orinoco. Queen Elizabeth's onetime

11. Extract from the commonplace book of Sir Stephen Powle, [February 24] March 6, 1610, in Joyce Lorimer, ed., *English and Irish Settlement on the River Amazon, 1550–1646*, Hak. Soc., 2nd Ser., 171 (London: Hakluyt Society, 1989), 151–152.
12. Edward Howe's account of Sir Thomas Roe's voyage, in Lorimer, ed., *English and Irish Settlement*, 152–153; Roe to the Earl of Salisbury, [February 28] March 10, 1611, in Lorimer, ed., *English and Irish Settlement*, 153.
13. Roe to Salisbury, [February 28] March 10, in Lorimer, ed., *English and Irish Settlement*, 153–155.
14. Lorimer, ed., *English and Irish Settlement*, 155–156.
15. Harcourt's account in Lorimer, ed., *English and Irish Settlement*, 161–162, 39.

favorite had in 1607 sought support from the Earl of Salisbury, the lord treasurer, for a trip that ostensibly would be headed to Virginia but was actually a formal pretext for a voyage to Guiana.[16] In late 1609 or early 1610 he wrote to Queen Anne, whom he counted as a friend despite her husband's intense opposition to his plans, offering his services to advance the colonization of Virginia, territory he had once controlled through a patent from Elizabeth I. Echoing (perhaps unintentionally) an idea that Hakluyt had first articulated in 1589, Ralegh suggested that the English did not want to repeat Henry VII's missing the opportunity to support Christopher Columbus's voyages. Further, he implicitly linked Spanish support for those early voyages to the subsequent enrichment of their realm and the results of that newfound wealth, which "endangered all the states of Europa." James needed to trust in those willing to sacrifice their lives to locate and claim mines before the Spanish discovered them.[17]

Ralegh had spent much of the sixteen years since his expedition had hacked its way through the jungles of Guiana in the Tower of London, where he had been held because of his alleged participation in a plot to prevent the king's 1603 accession. While he was confined, his mind roamed the world. He had access to approximately 515 books and manuscripts in English, Latin, French, Italian, and Spanish, including multiple volumes produced by the de Bry workshop. Ralegh used this library to write a history of the world. He published the first part in 1611 and three years later had the remainder printed as well—but James had them confiscated.[18] Nonetheless, Ralegh hoped the king would release him from the Tower to "the imprisonment of a longe navigation." As he saw it, his goal and the nation's were the same.[19] He believed that the realm's greatest opportunity lay along the twisty bends of the Orinoco, a river that would transport riches from local mines back to England.[20]

After James relented in March 1616, Ralegh immediately prepared for a voyage he believed would yield 1,000 pounds of gold. If he failed, he would cover the expense of the journey, though that would impoverish his entire family.[21] He knew the venture would be expensive, so he tried

16. Ralegh to Salisbury, [c. July] 1607, in *The Letters of Sir Walter Ralegh*, ed. Agnes Latham and Joyce Youings (Exeter, UK: Exeter University Press, 1999) [hereafter Ralegh, *Letters*], 297–299.

17. Ralegh to Salisbury, [1611], in Ralegh, *Letters*, 322–325.

18. Nicholas Popper, *Walter Ralegh's History of the World and the Historical Culture of the Late Renaissance* (Chicago: University of Chicago Press, 2012), 29–33; Walter Oakeshott, "Sir Walter Ralegh's Library," *The Library*, 5th Ser., XXIII (1968), 285–327.

19. Ralegh to King James [after July 1611], in Ralegh, *Letters*, 330–331.

20. Ralegh to Sir Ralph Winwood, July 1615, in Ralegh, *Letters*, 333–335.

21. Ralegh to Salisbury, [before July] 1611, in Ralegh, *Letters*, 325–327.

to recover money he had lent to others and sought funding from Dutch and French investors.[22] After he departed, the crown profited from the sale of the confiscated copies of Ralegh's *History* along with another printing of the book.[23]

Ralegh was partnered with Lawrence Keymis, one of his closest supporters, who had sailed with him on the earlier expedition to the Orinoco. They reached Trinidad late in 1617 after a difficult passage, though one made marginally better by an English countess in the Canary Islands who provided oranges, lemons, pomegranates, and limes.[24] Still, he could not ameliorate the ravages of ocean travel in warm climates. By November he had been laid low by "the moste violent calenture," a tropical disease known to European sailors. The illness killed forty-two of those on board, including Richard Moore, the former governor of Bermuda. Fortunately, Ralegh wrote to his wife, Bess, their son Wat was still healthy. Although he could barely rise from his bed, Ralegh told her that he would be welcomed and nourished by the "kinge of the I[ndyans]."[25]

Ralegh's dream that he might preside over a boisterous and profitable gold-mining colony came to a screeching halt while he was bedridden for six weeks. Keymis, exploring the Orinoco, took fire from Spaniards who had tried to establish their own mines. They might have accomplished the task, Ralegh believed, had Charles V sanctioned the use of Indigenous labor in 1542 and had they brought enslaved Africans with them. On the ground, as Ralegh saw it, the English had an opportunity. But his plan hinged on a major invasion. Much to Ralegh's anguish, the Spanish fleet divided the English expedition, separating Keymis and those on the mainland from Ralegh and the others on Trinidad. Wat and other English commanders, outmanned, managed to sack San Tomé but died doing so. When Keymis met with Ralegh and told him about the failure along the river, Ralegh rejected his counsel and insulted him. Keymis retired to his cabin, took out a pistol, and shot himself in the chest. Miraculously, the bullet cracked a rib but did not go deeper. He then pulled out a knife and stabbed himself, finishing the job. Ralegh was only slightly less despondent.[26] He confided to Bess that "my braines are broken."

22. Ralegh to Sir George Villiers, March 17, [1606], in Ralegh, *Letters*, 337–336 (support of friends); Ralegh to Peter Van Lore, July 1, 1616, in Ralegh, *Letters*, 338–339 (seeking Dutch support); Ralegh to Monsieur de Bisseaux, May 14, [1617], in Ralegh, *Letters*, 341–341 (seeking French financing).
23. Popper, *Ralegh's History of the World*, 18–19.
24. On the delay, see Ralegh to Sir Richard Boyle, June 28, 1617, in Ralegh, *Letters*, 343.
25. Ralegh to Lady Ralegh, November 14, 1617, in Ralegh, *Letters*, 345–346.
26. Ralegh to Sir Ralph Winwood, March 21, 1618, in Ralegh, *Letters*, 347–352.

He felt betrayed by Keymis, mourned the loss of his son, and needed to use funds he had robbed from Spaniards to fix his ship.[27]

Back in Plymouth by June 1616, Ralegh, knowing he would be interrogated for the mission's failure and the assault on San Tomé, appealed to the king's sense of fairness. During a pre-trial confinement in Devon, he rehearsed his losses—the death of his son, his illness, his fortune, his reputation—and denied rumors that he had ever intended to become a pirate. He had miscalculated the mission's possible success, but he was not disloyal.[28] By late July he had been remanded again to the Tower. The king ordered a private trial in mid-October to tamp down any sympathy the public might have had for him. Ralegh denied all charges when he appeared before the Privy Council, but they paid little heed.[29] After the hearing concluded, he shared the treasures of his library with an associate, including a yard-wide manuscript atlas of all the countries of the world so impressive that a friend later told the king that it should be used to determine matters of state.[30] But it was all to no avail. Though he had been convicted of treason in 1603 for his alleged role in a plot against James I and then spent fourteen years in the Tower as punishment, the monarch decided that his recent efforts along the Orinoco endangered a fragile peace with Spain and hence justified his execution. On October 29, with the death warrant signed by the king, London sheriffs took Ralegh to a scaffold in Westminster. Ralegh defended himself one last time in a long speech before the executioner's axe fell. One witness praised his performance, noting that his protestations of "so High and so Religius a Resolution" sounded like a Christian being executed by a Roman for his beliefs.[31]

In March, less than six months after Ralegh's execution, the privy councilors once again contemplated northeastern South America—specifically the future of the small English settlement along the Amazon. They vacated the charter possessed by Robert Harcourt, who had not

27. Ralegh to Lady Ralegh, March 22, 1618, in Ralegh, *Letters*, 353–356.

28. Ralegh to Carew, c. June [11?], 1618, in Ralegh, *Letters*, 358–360; Ralegh to King James, June 16, 1618, in Ralegh, *Letters*, 362–363. He wrote another version six weeks later; see Ralegh to [Lord Carew (?), late July/early August 1619 (?)], in Ralegh, *Letters*, 364–367.

29. Vincent T. Harlow, *Ralegh's Last Voyage* (London: Argonaut Press, 1932), 255–260 (depositions), 260–284; Commissioners to the king, October 18, 1618 and the king's response (not dated), in Harlow, *Ralegh's Last Voyage*, 295–297; see Ralegh to the Marquess of Buckingham, August 12, 1618 (plea), Ralegh to Lady Ralegh, September 18, 1618 (health), and Ralegh to Queen Anne, [late?] October 1618, all in Ralegh, *Letters*, 368–370, 376–377.

30. Oakeshott, "Ralegh's Library," 326.

31. Harlow, *Ralegh's Last Voyage*, 297–311.

fulfilled his commitment to make a sustained effort to maintain a colony there. Soon investors promised to back the new Amazon Company, whose organizers planned to extract spices, tobacco, nutmeg, cotton wool, and dyestuffs. They would also hew to James's policy that all colonial ventures propagate "religion, and Christianitye amonge those barborous nations."[32]

James I had hoped that the execution of Ralegh would tamp down tension between his court and Phillip III's. But Ralegh's death did not diminish the passion of some English to establish a South American colony. In their mind, the Wild Coast, the northeast coast of South America stretching from the mouth of the Orinoco to the Amazon delta, remained available and attainable if they launched their operations south and east of the Orinoco basin. The Orinoco was Spanish territory, proponents of the newly forming Amazon Company argued, but the vast arc stretching toward and including the Amazon was not. Among those who approved the venture was Sir Edward Coke, the preeminent interpreter of the common law who had recently resumed his position on the company's council.[33]

The persistent English interest in the Amazon enraged Iberian courtiers, who informed James about their views.[34] How could the king of Spain be offended, the English king's agents asked in response, if the English wanted an area populated only by "various Irishmen" and people of other nations? While officials in London tried to slow the Amazon Company's plans, Captain Roger North was already at sea, hoping to establish the company's claims. Though he promised never to employ anyone who had been a pirate, an acknowledgment of the fluid boundary that divided the legal from the lawless on the seas, the king nonetheless condemned the operation in a public proclamation.[35] James had two

32. Lorimer, ed., *English and Irish Settlement*, 190–191 (discussions and action at the Privy Council), 192–195 (preamble to the Amazon Company charter, quotations at 192 and 193). For the identification of the plants, see Lorimer, ed., *English and Irish Settlement*, 192n3, and Carl O. Sauer, "Cultivated Plants of South and Central America," in Julian H. Seward, ed., *Handbook of South American Indians*, Smithsonian Institution Bureau of American Ethnography Bulletin 143 (Washington, DC: Government Printing Office, 1950), VI:535–538.
33. Lorimer, ed., *English and Irish Settlement*, 191.
34. Sanchez de Ulloa to James I, February 29, 1620, in Lorimer, ed., *English and Irish Settlement*, 198–199.
35. Calvert to Sanchez de Ulloa, [March 1], 1620, in Lorimer, ed., *English and Irish Settlement*, 199–201; Calvert to Sanchez de Ulloa, [March 10] 20, 1620 (which includes an appeal by North), in Lorimer, ed., *English and Irish Settlement*, 201–203; *Proclamation*

audiences: his domestic subjects, whom he wanted to discourage from joining unauthorized colonial schemes, and the Spanish court. The king apologized to Philip III and promised to confiscate any goods that the expedition brought back.[36] Within a month of the king's proclamation, the Amazon Company directors surrendered their charter.[37]

North's expedition returned to London in late 1620. By early January, the Privy Council ordered the captain arrested and sent to the Tower. The king's ministers informed the Spanish ambassador, Don Diego Sarmiento de Acuña, the *conde* de Gondomar, who delightedly told Philip that the Amazon Company's patent had been torn "to pieces."[38] Although the venture was over, it had raised issues about what territory could be claimed in the Atlantic, especially since the appeal to Spain had recognized the legitimacy of the 1493 division of the basin. If the English agreed that the Amazon belonged to Spain, then what about Virginia and Bermuda? How, English authorities wondered, could any European nation maintain ownership "of a desolate Countrie whereof noe bodye is in Possession"?[39]

In July 1621, James ordered North released from the Tower, with the understanding that the adventurer never return to the Amazon.[40] But what, exactly, had he done that differed from other English efforts to establish American colonies? Could the Spanish, by virtue of a long-dead pope's division of the world, lay a claim to all territory west of the line drawn in 1493? The cagey Gondomar grasped the implications of the situation. He suggested to Phillip III in mid-February 1621 that perhaps the Spanish should send an expedition to the Amazon because he had heard that the Irish there might make an alliance with the Dutch. They were not, he warned, the only potential interlopers: "The English thieves' dens

declaring his Majesties pleasure concerning Captain Roger North, May 15, 1620 (London, 1620), in Sel. B. 231 (229), QCL; Mark G. Hanna, *Pirate Nests and the Rise of the British Empire, 1570–1740* (Chapel Hill: University of North Carolina Press for the Omohundro Institute of Early American History and Culture, 2015), 53–58.

36. Gondomar to Philip III, May 30, 1620, in Lorimer, *English and Irish Settlement*, 203–213.
37. Measures taken by the Privy Council against the Amazon Company, May [7] 17, 1620, to [May 23] June 2, 1620, in Lorimer, ed., *English and Irish Settlement*, 213–216.
38. Privy Council order of January [6] 16, 1621, Buckingham to Gondomar, January [6] 16, 1621, and Gondomar to Philip III, January 17 and February 16, 1621, in Lorimer, ed., *English and Irish Settlement*, 216–219.
39. Lorimer, ed., *English and Irish Settlement*, 219–227, quotation at 221.
40. Lorimer, ed., *English and Irish Settlement*, 223–231.

in Virginia and Bermuda constitute a matter which requires a very considered and effective remedy."[41]

Promises of wealth to be found and souls to be harvested in South America must have sounded good to any of James's subjects who heard stories about the war that was raging along the Chesapeake. More promising still was news coming from Virginia even before the war reached a formal conclusion in 1614. In 1612, John Rolfe, who had spent ten months in Bermuda before joining the expedition to Jamestown, experimented with West Indian tobacco seeds to produce a plant more desirable to English consumers than the existing Chesapeake strain. In 1614, Rolfe's shipment to London elicited rave reviews. The public's enthusiasm produced what the Virginia Company needed the most: an economic reason to keep its Chesapeake experiment going despite the hardship that had characterized Jamestown's earliest years. With tensions between the English and the Powhatans easing, in part because of Pocahontas and Rolfe's marriage, the timing could not have been more auspicious.[42]

The arrival of the more desirable Virginia tobacco rekindled the debate about whether consumption of the plant was safe. Tobacco enthusiasts turned to printers to help them make a case about the plant's curative powers. One emphasized it was "one of the best & surest remedies in the world against Paralisie, epilepsie or apoplexie, that is, the falling ill, & *Vergito Idiopathica*, the passion of dizziness in the head by wind that ever was found out." Tobacco consumption cured diseases of the brain and was safe if "used physically and with discretion."[43] Another claimed that tobacco was a universal cure "for all maladies incident to mans bodie."[44] Tobias Venner, a Bath-based physician, feared that it could be habit-forming, but he believed that users could control their intake and even provided ten precepts for how to do so.[45]

41. Gondomar to Phillip III, February 16, 162[1], in Lorimer, ed., *English and Irish Settlement*, 219.
42. Raphe Hamor, *A True Discourse of the Present Estate of Virginia, and the successe of the affaires there till the 18 of June 1614* (London, 1615), 24; Lorena S. Walsh, *Motives of Honor, Pleasure, and Profit: Plantation Management in the Colonial Chesapeake, 1607–1763* (Chapel Hill: University of North Carolina Press for the Omohundro Institute, 2010), 35–38.
43. William Barclay, *Nepenthes, Or The Vertues of Tabacco* (London, 1614), quotations at sig. [A6^{r}], B$^{r–v}$.
44. [Richard Brathwaite], *The Smoaking Age, or The Man in the mist: with The Life and death of Tobacco* (London, 1617), quotation at 92.
45. Tobias Venner, *A Briefe and Accurate Treatise, concerning The taking of the fume of Tobacco, which very many, in these dayes, doe too licentiously use* (London, 1621).

The debate also reflected the political economy of the moment. In 1615, one author identified only as C.T. claimed that the amount of money spent on tobacco in England and Ireland amounted to £200,000 per year. Before the rise of Virginia, English purveyors had been buying it in Trinidad and along the Orinoco, giving "Gold, Silver, Coine, and plate" to Spanish merchants. While the commerce had spillover economic benefits, such as adding to the demand for ships to be built and crews to sail them, the long-term prospects were grim. Unscrupulous charlatans, knowing the public preference for tobacco to be as dark as possible, poured molasses, pepper, and the dregs of wine casks onto inferior plants and then rolled them with lighter leaves. Worse still, some Spaniards had been known to pour onto their crop "dissolved sublimate," a known poison that was extremely dangerous when inhaled. English consumers needed to understand that the best tobacco was a dark yellow and that the only honest brokers were Natives trading it from the shores of Guiana and on St. Lucia, Dominica, Santo Domingo, and St. Vincent.[46] Since it was often impossible to know the source of a plant grown in the Western Hemisphere, C.T. provided instructions for how to grow tobacco at home.[47] In the process, those who produced it would contribute to the larger effort to cure human afflictions.[48]

The anti-tobacconists failed. In 1614, 7,000 merchants reportedly sold tobacco among other wares at their shops in London—a number that seems improbable but not impossible in a city whose population had surpassed 200,000 at the turn of the century.[49] In 1616, English merchants imported 1,250 pounds of the plant. The following year, the volume reached close to 10,000 pounds, and nearly 25,000 pounds arrived in 1620.[50] Even with the king on their side, those who hoped to halt tobacco's encroachment into daily life could not surmount the combined pressure of tobacco purveyors and the physiological effect among smokers, including

46. C.T., *An Advice How to Plant Tobacco in England and How to bring it to colour and perfection, to whom it may be profitable, and to whom harmfull . . . with The Danger of the Spanish Tobacco* (London, 1615), sig. A3^{r}–B^{r}; for the larger context of English adaptation of others' agricultural techniques, see Charles Stevens and John Liebault, *Maison Rustique, or The country farme* (London, 1606).
47. C.T., *An Advice How to Plant Tobacco in England*, sig. A4^{r} sig. B^{v}–[B4^{r}].
48. C.T., *An Advice How to Plant Tobacco in England*, sig. C^{r}–[C4^{v}]; see also E[dmund] G[ardiner], *The Triall of Tabacco* (London, 1610), 24^{v}–30^{r}, 33^{r-v}, 35^{v}–38^{v}, 43^{v}–49^{v}.
49. Barnabe Rich, *The Honestie of This Age* (London, 1614), 26; see also Sandra J. Bell, "'Precious Stinke': James I's *A Counterblaste to Tobacco*," in *Royal Subjects: Essays on the Writings of James VI and I*, ed. Daniel Fischlin and Mark Fortier (Detroit: Wayne State University Press, 2002), 323; Roger Finlay, *Population and Metropolis: The Demography of London, 1580–1650* (Cambridge: Cambridge University Press, 1981), 51–69.
50. Bernard Bailyn, *The Barbarous Years: The Conflict of Civilizations, 1600–1675* (New York: Alfred A. Knopf, 2012), 79.

what were probably the first signs of addiction.[51] Further, at least some investors in the Virginia Company had started to grow their own tobacco at home.[52]

Pocahontas and Rolfe celebrated the birth of their son, Thomas, in London in January 1615, when she was probably eighteen years old. Two years later they set sail for Virginia. But she became ill by the time their ship reached Gravesend, where she died, perhaps of pneumonia. She was buried at St. George's Church on March 21, 1617. Rolfe still planned to take Thomas with him to Virginia. But the boy took ill soon after his mother, before the ship reached Plymouth, prompting Rolfe to leave him behind in his half-brother's care. They never saw each other again.[53]

Pocahontas's death robbed the English and Powhatans of a crucial go-between. For a brief moment, residents of the Tidewater lived in peace. Wahunsonacock had, through deft manipulation and the strategic employment of force, brought the English to the table and even made them record the gifts he was to receive moving forward. They remained his clients. Dale, for his part, soon left Virginia believing that his implementation of martial law had convinced otherwise young rowdy English men to behave with a common purpose. With tobacco exports likely to rise and the colonial population growing, at least incrementally, he thought the English had gained the upper hand.[54]

The fragile stability that rested on the strong will of Wahunsonacock was threatened when he died within a year of Pocahontas's passing. The English learned about his death in April 1618, at the same time they heard about the growing authority of Opechancanough, who was the paramount sachem's brother or cousin and also the war chief for Itoyatin, one of Wahunsonacock's brothers who had become werowance. Opechancanough had formerly been known first as Paquiquino and then as Don Luis de Velasco—he was the Algonquian boy taken captive to Spain who then returned to lead the ambush of the Jesuits not far from Chesapeake Bay in 1570.[55]

51. See David Harley, "The Beginnings of the Tobacco Controversy: Puritanism, James I, and the Royal Physicians," *Bulletin of the History of Medicine* 67 (1993), 28–50.
52. Nicholas Farrar, "Account of our Tobacco garden," February 16, 1618/1619, FP 101.
53. Jane Carson, "The Will of John Rolfe," *VHMB* 58 (1950), 58–65. A Mattaponi oral history recounts a belief that she was murdered; see Linwood "Little Bear" Custalow and Angela L. Daniel "Silver Star," *The True Story of Pocahontas: The Other Side of History* (Wheat Ridge, CO: Fulcrum, 2007), 83–88.
54. See Bailyn, *Barbarous Years*, 76–77.
55. James Horn, *A Brave and Cunning Prince: The Great Chief Opechancanough and the War for America* (New York: Basic Books, 2021), 235–240; David J. Weber, The *Spanish*

The deaths of Pocahontas and Wahunsonacock altered relations along the Chesapeake. He had held the reins of power for a half-century, made most of the Indigenous communities around the bay accept his rule by conquering or cajoling them, and defined the first decade of Powhatan-Anglo relations. He demonstrated his skills at key moments—his sparing of Smith, likely an act of ritual adoption of a new subordinate; his approval of the marriage of Pocahontas and Rolfe; his blessing of the voyage of her and her entourage across the ocean, where their celebrity only enhanced his reputation; his demand that Hamor record the tribute the English needed to pay in a book that Wahunsonacock would keep in his home, a sign not only of his status as the patron to his English clients but also of his grasp of the tools of statecraft. Wahunsonacock likely did not know how to read English, but he gained authority by demonstrating to visitors that he possessed an instrument of would-be empire-builders. The object of the lesson that Hamor recorded was not for the English delegate to remember what to send back. The point was to debase Hamor, reminding him that he was the subordinate recorder of an action dictated by the man who remained in power.

Pocahontas's death registered in a different idiom. She, too, understood politics and her role in the evolving culture along the Chesapeake and the Thames. The visual rendering of her conversion became an instant icon of the potential for the English vision of coexistence through cultural conversion. She had met the king and queen, married a far older man to solidify an alliance, and given birth to her only child thousands of miles from the community of women who would have guided her through the challenges of raising her firstborn. Her death revealed the precarious state of that political project.

Father and daughter alike had deployed their immense sophistication and mastery of cultural tools to expand and consolidate the Powhatan confederacy—even to the point of welcoming the English as dependent subordinates who needed to pay tribute to him whenever he entertained them. He kept his enemies, domestic and foreign, at bay, even when some, like the Chickahominies, became "English men" and cast their lot with the newcomers. She inspired hope for peace and cultural conversion. The English would soon learn why the loss of Wahunsonacock and Pocahontas mattered.

During the mid-1610s, European projects on the continent multiplied and intensified. On March 27, 1614, the Assembly of the Lords States-General, the

Frontier in North America (New Haven, CT: Yale University Press, 1992), 71–72; Hamor, *True Discourse*, 54.

governing body of the United Netherlands, began to encourage exploration and investment in territory that the Dutch believed they controlled between New France and Virginia based on Henry Hudson's VOC-funded explorations of 1609. Assembly members heard that the French were eagerly attempting to establish the community of Québec and that the English were exporting better-quality tobacco from the Chesapeake. The governors of the States-General publicized their plans, an effort to counter rumors that they were acting in secret.[56] On October 11, 1614, the governors granted exclusive rights to a group of Dutch merchants and their agents to conduct business in a place they labeled New Netherland.[57] In taking their actions, the governors of the States-General hoped to advance the cause of American colonization from theory to practice. Their confidence rested on an unassailable fact: in previous generations, Dutch merchants had made their republic the envy of Europe, its actions watched closely by rivals in Paris, London, Lisbon, and Madrid.

This incipient Dutch action did not dissuade English colonizers from trying to expand their own influence along the mid-Atlantic coast. In late 2014, Captain John Smith led two ships to North America to explore the territory between Penobscot Bay and Cape Cod. Hoping to locate whales and identify mines—he failed at both—his crew hauled in about 47,000 fish. They then traded with Algonquians for the pelts of 1,100 beaver, 100 martens, and approximately 100 otters. Smith returned to England in October with one ship loaded with salted fish, oil drained from cod livers, and furs. The other ship headed to Spain to sell dried fish. Smith claimed the American wares found ready purchasers.[58] But the cargo unloaded from those English ships was less significant than the most important commodity Smith brought home—information about a coastline (he compared it to Devonshire), its peoples, and the commodities of a region not yet settled by any European nation. Smith promptly dispersed his views in *A Description of New England*, coining a term that has stuck ever since.

Any reader of Smith's book would have easily concluded that this was territory that the English could colonize more easily than the Chesapeake.

56. "General Charter for Those who Discovery Any New Passages, Havens, Countries, or Places," March 27, 1614, Avalon.
57. "Grant of Exclusive Trade to New Netherland by the States-General of the United Netherlands," October 11, 1614, Avalon.
58. John Smith, *A Description of New England* (London, 1616), 1–2, 7–10; for what Smith believed was the range of the Massachusetts' settlements, see Philip L. Barbour, ed., *The Complete Works of Captain John Smith (1580–1631)* (Chapel Hill: University of North Carolina Press for the Institute of Early American History and Culture, 1986), 1:329n.

Smith compared the potential gains to be had there to the riches generated by the Venetians and the Dutch, European powers that had built great wealth through long-distance trade.[59] In New England, he argued, a mere 300 colonists could launch a successful colony by planting crops that flourished at the same latitudes in Europe. Local Indigenous peoples welcomed trade. If any objected, thirty to forty soldiers could subdue them. The colony would attract families to its cod-rich waters; boys already knew how to fish, and girls could spin cordage for nets.[60] As Smith or the book's compositor noted in the margins: "Imployment for poore people and fatherlesse children." This was no random observation but a specific response to the concerns of policymakers since Elizabethan times.[61] Smith held out enormous praise for the "Countrie of the Massachusetts," which he called "the Paradise of all those parts." But the entire region held promise, a fertile field not just for commodities but also for souls to be rescued from the possible influence of Spaniards. The future lay in exploring and planting "these North parts of America."[62]

Shifting attention to the north meant resolving the lingering ambiguity of Hudson's last voyage. That, at least, was the opinion of the members of the High Court of Admiralty (HCA). They had first taken testimony in 1612 after the conclusion of the study by the masters of Trinity House. News of the Dutch advance prompted the jurists to interrogate survivors.[63] They met in a time of growing concern about an alarming rise in pirate attacks on English ships near Tangiers and Tunis, where the Muscovy Company and the East India Company each had suffered recent losses. Pirates' thievery had impoverished sailors, who then lacked the resources to support their families back home. Some of those in London who became desperate went to the house of Sir Thomas Smythe seeking assistance. With anxiety permeating the king's court, the Privy Council asked Smythe to collect opinions from nine trading companies, with the understanding that he would then make recommendations to the king, whose

59. Smith, *Description of New England*, 10–12.
60. Smith, *Description of New England*, 16–17.
61. Smith, *Description of New England*, 17–18, 40; Peter C. Mancall, *Hakluyt's Promise: An Elizabethan's Obsession for an English America* (New Haven, CT: Yale University Press, 2007), 128–155; A. L. Beier, *Masterless Men: The Vagrancy Problem in England, 1560–1640* (London: Methuen, 1985).
62. Smith, *Description of New England*, 26 ("Paradise"), 43–45 ("North parts").
63. See Thomas A. Janvier, *Henry Hudson: A Brief Statement of His Aims and His Achievements, to which is added a newly-discovered partial record of the trial of the mutineers by whom he and others were abandoned to their death* (New York: Harper and Bros., 1909), 135–139.

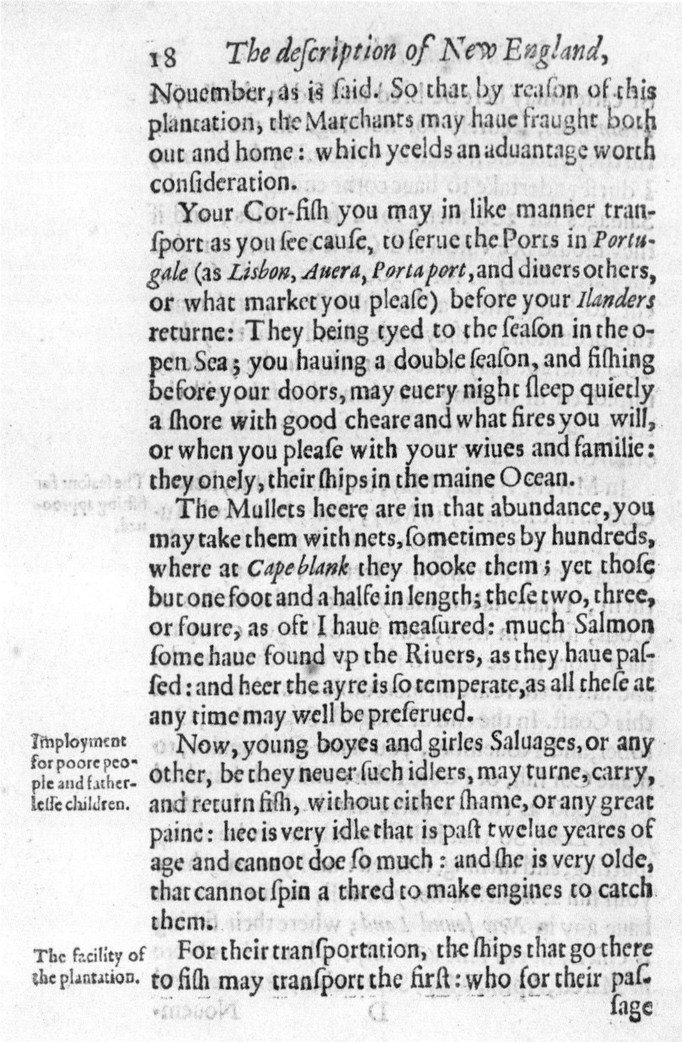

18 *The deſcription of New England,*

Nouember, as is ſaid. So that by reaſon of this plantation, the Marchants may haue fraught both out and home: which yeelds an aduantage worth conſideration.

Your Cor-fiſh you may in like manner tranſport as you ſee cauſe, to ſerue the Ports in *Portugale* (as *Lisbon, Auera, Porta port*, and diuers others, or what market you pleaſe) before your *Ilanders* returne: They being tyed to the ſeaſon in the open Sea; you hauing a double ſeaſon, and fiſhing before your doors, may euery night ſleep quietly a ſhore with good cheare and what fires you will, or when you pleaſe with your wiues and familie: they onely, their ſhips in the maine Ocean.

The Mullets heere are in that abundance, you may take them with nets, ſometimes by hundreds, where at *Cape blank* they hooke them; yet thoſe but one foot and a halfe in length; theſe two, three, or foure, as oft I haue meaſured: much Salmon ſome haue found vp the Riuers, as they haue paſſed: and heer the ayre is ſo temperate, as all theſe at any time may well be preſerued.

Imployment for poore people and fatherleſſe children.

Now, young boyes and girles Saluages, or any other, be they neuer ſuch idlers, may turne, carry, and return fiſh, without either ſhame, or any great paine: hee is very idle that is paſt twelue yeares of age and cannot doe ſo much: and ſhe is very olde, that cannot ſpin a thred to make engines to catch them.

The facility of the plantation.

For their tranſportation, the ſhips that go there to fiſh may tranſport the firſt: who for their paſſage

English policymakers drawing up plans to colonize eastern North America had the assistance of printers, who sometimes added marginal notes to promotional tracts to draw a reader's attention to a specific passage—in this case, a paragraph in John Smith's 1616 *Description of New England* that might be of interest to those needing work. Courtesy of the Huntington Library, San Marino, California.

long-standing and public opposition to pirates had once led him to declare that he himself would help to hang anyone convicted of the crime.[64]

64. Privy Council to Sir Thomas Smith, March 9, 1617, in *Acts of the Privy Council of England, 1616–1617* (London, 1890–1964), 35:181–182; *Calendar of State Papers . . . Venice* (London, 1864–1947), 10:100; David D. Hebb, *Piracy and the English Government, 1616–1642* (Aldershot, UK: Scolar Press, 1994), 9–10.

On February 7, 1617, the HCA deposed Abacuck Pricket, who had produced the most substantial written account of Hudson's last voyage. He arrived ready to explain that the bloodstains on the ship were the result of the mortal wounds the Inuit had inflicted on the four rebels who had led the mutiny in 1611. Members of the HCA had a different concern: had the shipboard uprising been caused by some of the men becoming pirates? Yes, Pricket responded. At least some of them had spoken about becoming pirates, but their murder at the hands of the Inuit prevented that from happening.[65] Other survivors brought into the court told similar stories.[66] On July 24, 1618, the court charged four of the survivors with the murder of Henry Hudson through the act of exposure. Unlike other unfortunates summoned that day, the court acquitted the four survivors from the *Discovery*. No explanation survives, though it seems likely that the court could not come to a resolution given the absence of evidence.[67]

The trial of the four survivors pointed to a problem that the English, and other would-be European colonizers, would face time and again when the population of migrants across the Atlantic grew. English and other Europeans who went abroad never had the license to govern themselves entirely. Even those who would participate in local self-government owed fealty to the sovereign who granted them the right to explore or settle territory far from home (or her or his heirs). The thousands of miles that separated migrants from those who remained behind made it impossible for courts in London or elsewhere to know precisely what happened in North America. No court wanted to acquit an individual who came home to face justice because of a lack of evidence. But their options were limited. It would be best, officials in each colonizing society came to conclude, to get explorers or colonizers to swear they would not violate the laws of their realm and then hope that the actions they took on the ground—including their contests with Indigenous peoples and other Europeans—reflected the laws of their homeland and loyalty to their sovereign. This issue would remain unresolved for generations.

65. Pricket's testimony is in High Court of Admiralty 1/48, f. 118^{r}–120^{r}.
66. Testimony of Bennet Matthews, HCA 1/48, f. 127^{r-v}; see also the testimony from Francis Clemens, HCA 1/48, f. 130^{r-v}; for Robert Bylot, HCA 1/48, f. 120^{r}–121^{v}; for Wilson, HCA 1/48, f. 135^{r}–136^{r}.
67. The surviving manuscript is incomplete and fragile, listing the not-guilty verdicts for three of the four but not Mathews, though he was presumably acquitted as well. See HCA 1/6, f. 133 (the indictment), ff. 88–90. The documents are reprinted in Llewelyn Powys, *Henry Hudson* (London: John Lane, 1927), 190–198; for other details of the trial and the setting, see Peter C. Mancall, *Fatal Journey: The Final Voyage of Henry Hudson—A Tale of Mutiny and Murder in the Arctic* (New York: Basic Books, 2009), 185–210.

The rising pace of European intrusions also vexed Native communities. During the mid-1610s, the Algonquian-speaking peoples of the northeastern Atlantic coast—including Mi'kmaqs, Eastern Abenakis, Massachusetts, Wampanoags, and the many communities of Lenapehoking—began to encounter Europeans with regularity. These meetings were not like those that had taken place earlier when Indigenous Americans met Europeans on summer fishing expeditions or encountered the occasional explorer like Smith. These Europeans intended to stay.

Québec, the European town established near Stadacona, remained a small outpost. But by maintaining a presence, the French signaled that they saw opportunities to be exploited—and in the process prompted Dutch and English to follow up on their earlier efforts. With the worst years of the Little Ice Age passing, a slightly warming climate made colonization more likely. The newcomers would soon learn that Indigenous knowledge circuits worked efficiently, spreading information about Europeans, their wares, and the ways to acquire copper kettles and metal knives in exchange for old beaver skins. For their part, Natives soon found that the greatest threat Europeans posed was not their claims to Indigenous territory but their role in transporting disease-bearing rats.

At some point in 1617, a European fishing ship of unknown origin landed along the coast of New England. There is no record of what its occupants and the Algonquian-speaking peoples of the coast thought about each other, though they probably engaged in trade.[68] One thing is likely: Old World rats jumped ship and swam to shore. They were the most dangerous European migrants to have appeared north of the Rio Grande yet.

Some of these rats invariably carried the bacteria that caused leptospirosis, a devastating illness in humans. While there is no definitive proof that this was the ailment that came ashore, it seems the most likely since the scanty historical record reveals that the victims suffered from nosebleeds, headaches, fever, and lesions on their skin—telltale signs of leptospirosis, according to modern medical historians. Once the bacteria arrived in New England, Natives could have become exposed either through rodent feces on the ground, which could enter a body through cracks on their feet, or via rat urine in bodies of water frequented by Algonquian-speaking peoples. In either scenario, Indigenous residents were more likely to be exposed and then succumb than any Europeans, who were unlikely to spend much time where the bacteria would have thrived. Once begun, the epidemic raged, quite possibly spread when Natives spent a large amount of time with deceased relatives or friends, engaging in practices intended to smooth the transition from worldly

68. See James Axtell, "At the Water's Edge: Trading in the Sixteenth Century," in *After Columbus: Essays in the Ethnohistory of Colonial North America* (New York: Oxford University Press, 1988), 144–181.

existence into the realm of the spirits. Such care for the dying likely provided more frequent chances for opportunistic bacteria to find new hosts.[69]

The pace of death was terrifying. Most epidemics, even of highly contagious diseases like plague, typically left large numbers of survivors.[70] But this series of infections apparently killed entire communities. The high death toll meant crops went unplanted, game unhunted, fish uncaught. Food shortages weakened the Algonquian-speaking peoples of southern New England, known collectively as Ninnimissinuok, physically and made individuals even more likely to succumb to bacterial infection.[71]

The devastation altered both the demography and psychology of the region. English observers writing a few years after the calamity believed that the epidemic had killed up to 95 percent of coastal Algonquian-speaking peoples. Stories circulated that death came so quickly and to so many that long-established mortuary customs collapsed, leaving bodies on the ground without burial.[72] Catastrophic losses among the Indigenous provided an opening for Europeans.

69. Retrospective clinical diagnosis is often imprecise, in part because of the ways that observers recorded symptoms. For this epidemic, see John S. Marr and John T. Cathey, "New Hypothesis for Cause of Epidemic Among Native Americans, New England, 1616–1619," *Emerging Infectious Diseases* 16 (2010), 281–286. For mortuary practices that might have facilitated transmission, see James W. Bradley, "European Contact and the Continuity of Mortuary Ceremonialism on Cape Cod: An Update from the Corn Hill Site, Truro, MA," *Archaeology of Eastern North America* 26 (1998), 189–199. On the possibility of smallpox, see David Silverman, *This Land Is Their Land: The Wampanoag Indians, Plymouth Colony, and the Troubled History of Thanksgiving* (New York: Bloomsbury, 2020), 104–109.

70. Historians estimate that the bubonic plague that arced across Europe from 1347 to 1349 likely killed about one-third of the population, though the death rate could have climbed to two-thirds in regions where food shortages, perhaps produced by an inability to bring in crops or tend livestock, followed pestilence. See Alfred W. Crosby, *Ecological Imperialism: The Biological Expansion of Europe, 900–1900* (Cambridge: Cambridge University Press, 1986), 52–53. Such death rates reshaped the culture and society of the survivors, often in unexpected ways, as the experience of plague in fourteenth-century Europe demonstrated; see David W. Herlihy, *The Black Death and the Transformation of the West* (Cambridge, MA: Harvard University Press, 1997).

71. On the relationship between malnutrition and morbidity, see David S. Jones, "Virgin Soils Reconsidered," *WMQ*, 3rd Ser., 60 (2003), 703–742.

72. "Cushman's Discourse," in John Masefield, *Chronicles of the Pilgrim Fathers* (London: J. M. Dent, 1910), 229–230; Emmanuel Altham to Sir Edward Altham, September 1623, in Sydney V. James Jr., *Three Visitors to Early Plymouth* ([Plymouth, MA]: Plimoth Plantation, 1963), 29; Thomas Morton, *New English Canaan* (Amsterdam, 1637), 23; see also Cristobal Silva, *Miraculous Plagues: An Epidemiology of Early New England Narrative* (New York: Oxford University Press, 2016).

On November 18, 1618, the council of the Virginia Company appointed George Yeardley to be the new governor of the colony, ordering him to recruit migrants who would "lay a foundation" for "a flourishing state." To make this venture work, the company needed to establish a system that approached self-government for the distant population. Drawing on the existing charter, the councilors planned to establish "a laudable form of government" that would provide the necessary legal administration "for the happy guiding and governing of our people there inhabiting." Yeardley was to establish a new government on a 3,000-acre allotment that included Jamestown as well as "the lands formerly conquered or purchased" from the Pasapeghs, one of the communities in Powhatan's confederacy. They gave him detailed directions about how he was to organize four "cities or burroughs" to be called Jamestown, Henrico, Charles City, and Kiccowtan, the last presumably the English-conquered community of Kecoughtan. They ordered him to set aside sufficient land for cattle, which would be "the public stock and store" of the company. Once on the ground, he was to erect a college for instructing Native children, keep records of the colony's actions, and provide from time to time "the number, names, ages, sex, trades and conditions of every such person so transported or shipped" to Virginia.[73] Migrants mattered, but so did the conversion of Natives, as ministers in London had declared in sermons about the future of the colony. Of course, if Indigenous resisted, as the cleric Robert Gray had noted in 1609, "a Christian King may lawfullie make warre upon barbarous and Savage people" who fought conversion.[74]

On November 29, Yeardley met with King James at Newmarket. After attending a church service, the pair proceeded to dine together. They spoke about matters in Virginia for an hour and a half. James told the incoming governor that he was concerned about the number of cattle, which he saw as a public trust crucial to the future of the colony. He emphasized that the planters need "to deal gently & favourably w[i]th the Indians, and by faire meanes and good example of life to induce them to christianity" and "not to tyrannize over them like the Spannyards," a point suggesting he was aware of the 1583 English translation of Las Casas's book. Nor did he want the English to pit one Native group against another, a tactic Las Casas had described. The conversion of Indigenous to proper Christianity remained a high priority for him, likely a reflection of earlier failures to bring many Natives into the Church of England and the growing anxiety James had about religious dissenters at home. He

73. Bemiss, ed., *Three Charters*, 95–104, 105–107.

74. R[obert] G[ray], *A Good Speed to Virginia* (London, 1609), sig. C2v–[C4v], quotation at [C4r]; Lauren Working, "'The Savages of Virginia Our Project': The Powhatans in Jacobean Political Thought," in Musselwhite et al., eds., *Virginia 1619*, 42–59.

wanted churches to look like those in England so that the new built environment of the sacred would reflect accepted values just as surely as those who spoke within them. The king instructed Yeardley to establish a college as a seminar for "Indian children, to bee sent abroad afterwards as laborers into gods harvest, to converte those of there owne nation to the Christian faith." He also offered specific economic directions: import mulberry trees for silk, cultivate silkgrass for ropes and linen, harvest the forests for masts and pitch, and set up ironworks.[75] While he retained his "natural antipathy" to tobacco, which "hee hateth as much as any mortall man," he saw its value. Yet since "Man liveth not by smoke alone," as the company's secretary Richard Ferrar recorded, the colonists needed to plant maize too—enough, perhaps, so that they might in due time abandon tobacco.[76]

At the meal's conclusion the king offered his hand to Yeardley, who kissed it. James left with a final statement of his blessing for the venture. After his audience with the king was over, the incoming governor made the rounds of London gathering more advice—and additional resources. He met with the Archbishop of Canterbury, who promised Yeardley the church would recruit the ministers the colony needed. The Earl of Lincoln told him he would send over some of his finest horses and help to set up a racecourse in Virginia. The chancellor of the exchequer confided that he had been working to convince the king to invest directly in the company. Viscount Doncaster, one of James's close advisors, promised that he would continue to implore the king to support the colony with arms as well as funds.

Ferrar, intimate with the works of the company, told Yeardley that martial law was to be suspended and authority over colonists should be held by the governor and his council, all of whom would "conform themselves to our lawes & customes here in England." The council would be formed from representatives, to be known as burgesses, who would be elected from each town and plantation. The system would be organized by Edwin Sandys, "our Solon & Licurgus." Sandys, previously part of the administration of the East India Company, became the Virginia Company's treasurer in 1619, replacing Thomas Smythe. These new laws, Ferrar wrote, were not to be "chested or hidden like a candle under a bushel" but instead were to be "published to the whole colony" in the form of "a Magna Charta," a publicly recognized charter that specified

75. For the economic context, see Keith Pluymers, "Atlantic Iron: Wood Scarcity and the Political Ecology of Early English Expansion," *WMQ* 73 (2016), 389–426.

76. R[ichard?] F[errar?] to an unnamed member of the Berkeley Hundred syndicate, December 5, 1618, FP 93. The identity of Ferrar is not certain because the author signed only with initials, but I follow the logic of David Ransome, the editor of the online version of the Ferrar Papers, who suggested this identification.

rights and privileges. The governor would have the authority to impose martial law only in an emergency.

The following year Ferrar's brother Nicholas enumerated the number of residents at each outpost. At James City there were 84 men, 24 women, and 9 "Younge persons," for a total of 117. Charles Hundred had 184 residents. There were 45 men at West and Shorley Hundred, who lived there without any women or children. A second enumeration, based on evidence gathered in March 1619 by Tristam Conyam, counted 670 men, 119 women, 39 teens, and 57 children. In addition to these 885 individuals, Conyam also enumerated "Others not Christians in the Service of the English." This category included 4 Indigenous, whose gender was not recorded, and 32 "Negros in the service of sev[er]all planters," including 15 men and 17 women. After some fine-tuning following the last muster, he estimated a total population of 928, which included the teenage Thomas Savage, one of the three English boys who had lived for a time among the Powhatans to learn their language. Livestock numbered 336 cattle, 10 horses, 233 goats, and 308 domesticated swine, but he did not include feral swine that, by definition, belonged to the public. He also noted the English had 284 complete sets of armor, 516 swords, and 686 guns other than (uncounted) pistols. The residents inhabited a total of 222 buildings, not including storehouses or barns, and possessed 39 "Boats and Shallops," a number that excluded any oceangoing vessels. They had on hand at that time 400 bushels of maize recently acquired at Rappahannock, with more being sought at Accomac and Acohanak. There was, the account noted, "now Corne enough in the Collony if it be well p[re]served on all hands" to feed 500 people or more until the following harvest. Neither Ferrar nor Conyam dwelled on the non-Christian members of the community.[77]

In August 1619, the *White Lion*, a privateer commanded by John Colny Cope, arrived at Point Comfort. Cope had been sailing with a letter of marque from the Dutch government, which gave him the authority to raid other nations' ships and then make a case that he should be able to own whatever he seized. When he arrived, Cope reported that he and Elfrith, captain of *Treasurer* and the privateer whose capture of a Spanish ship in 1614 had brought him praise, had confronted the Portuguese *São João Bautista*, bound for Veracruz, in the middle of July in the Bay of Campeche and stolen sixty enslaved Africans. These five dozen men and women had been part of an original total of 350 enslaved Angolans forced

77. "The Number of People in Virginia," n.d., FP 139. The section in Conyam's hand is dated "the beginninge of March 1619." A "hundred" was in England a subdivision of a shire or county that had its own court.

onto the ship in Luanda. Cope, low on provisions, sold what Rolfe later called "20. And odd Negroes" to the English. Several days later, Elfrith arrived with other captives on board *Treasurer*. But his letter of marque had expired, meaning that he no longer had the legal authority to sell those whose bodies he had claimed. Still, he left two or three of the captives at Point Comfort and then set sail for Bermuda, perhaps believing that he would be able to sell the rest there.[78]

The documentary record does not reveal if these Angolans were enslaved, but the enumeration of them in a separate category in the census suggests that the English assigned them a special kind of status. More telling was the fact that there is no evidence that they were ever to be released from bondage. In his will Yeardley separated out eight of this group from other servants, suggesting that he believed he owned the eight for the rest of their lives. A decade later, his son Argoll still had two of them in his possession; in 1653 he sold ten-year-old Doll and her twelve-year-old sister Denise, the children of two of the original enslaved group. The sale suggested that the progeny of enslaved Africans also became the property of a planter, following the idea of *partus sequitur ventrem*, which likely existed from the start. These Africans, like the English, struggled to survive in Virginia. Of the thirty-two enumerated at first, only twenty-two were alive in 1625. Virginia planters did not quickly embrace the idea of importing many other Africans, though they did not prevent additional enslavement. Even if the numbers remained modest, enslavement of Africans and the slave trade, already known in North America and across much of the Atlantic basin, had taken root in the Chesapeake.[79]

In 1610, stable polities existed across most of North America, enabling Indigenous Americans and Europeans to find ways to coexist, at least where there was a will to do so. That stability cracked near the end of the decade, brought down by the accession of Opechancanough and the pandemic in coastal New England. Political tension destabilized European polities too, including England, where some of the rising number of religious dissenters had begun to think that their future lay beyond their homeland—perhaps in Leyden with like minded nonconformists, perhaps

78. Philip D. Morgan, "Virginia Slavery in Atlantic Context," in Musselwhite et al., eds., *Virginia 1619*, 85; Engel Sluiter, "New Light on the '20. and Odd Negroes' Arriving in Virginia, August 1619," *WMQ*, 3rd Ser., LIV (1997), 395–398, and John Thornton, "The African Experience of the '20. and Odd Negroes' Arriving in Virginia in 1619," *WMQ*, 3rd Ser., LV (1998), 421–434.

79. Morgan, "Virginia Slavery," 85–107; Michael Guasco, *Slaves and Englishmen: Human Bondage in the Early Modern Atlantic World* (Philadelphia: University of Pennsylvania Press, 2014), 1–3.

across the Atlantic in lands that now had far fewer inhabitants. Various actors who had played a leading role in colonial affairs left the stage: Hudson in 1611, Hakluyt in 1616, Pocahontas in 1617, Wahunsonacock and Ralegh in 1618. Each of them had shifted others' sensibilities in ways that long survived them.

The novel stratagems of the late 1610s began to take hold. Tucker left Bermuda disgraced, but his efforts had led to greater economic security for English immigrants. Nine hundred traveled there by 1621, raising the population to about 1,800, though many resented the ways that the colony's governors had treated them.[80] Colonists in Virginia could maintain their own government as long as they did not violate the laws of their realm.[81] The first groups of enslaved Africans had arrived in English colonies, though their presence meant less on the mainland than in Bermuda, where colonial leaders saw the benefits of their labor despite, as an act of the assembly put it, they were wary of their "insolencies."[82] Spanish, French, and English spies still tried to glean the truth about their rivals' intentions amidst the noise and rumors.

The expansion of opportunity for Europeans migrating to the mainland came at a high cost for some Indigenous peoples and enslaved Africans. Greater security for Europeans in some places also represented a narrowing of their geographic focus. Virginia seemed more ensured, but the High Court of Admiralty's final resolution about the survivors from the *Discovery* debacle of 1611 limited investment in the Arctic. The execution and repudiation of Ralegh narrowed the horizons of the Stuart court. The northeast coast of South America also came to seem beyond bounds for the English, though the granting of the new charter suggested hope for future endeavors. In South America and in the Arctic, the English had so far failed to expand their grasp in territories they had believed held extraordinary promise. In both places, Indigenous peoples prevailed. Inuit and Crees would continue to dominate the Arctic. The Amazon remained Tupinambá country, and the Warao still controlled the Orinoco delta. Most of the continent's vast expanse remained in the control of Native peoples, but Europeans, spurred by imperial rivalries, greed, and conscience, ever more lustily dreamed about expanding their holdings in North America.

80. "Grievances of the People in Bermuda, ca October 1622," in Vernon A. Ives, ed., *The Rich Papers: Letters from Bermuda, 1615–1646* (Toronto: University of Toronto Press for the Bermuda National Trust, 1984), 237–239; Jarvis, "Bermuda and the Origins of Black Anglo-America," 117–122.

81. See Jack P. Greene, "From John Smith to Adam Smith: Virginia and the Founding Conventions of English Long-Distance Settler Colonization," in Musselwhite et al., eds., *Virginia 1619*, 282–307.

82. Ives, ed., *Rich Papers*, 229, 240.

16

The Battle for Tsenacommacah

With the tobacco economy established, English colonizers felt more sanguine about the Chesapeake region's potential. Immigrants began to lay out plans for new colonial towns. Migrant men, women, and children, most of them indentured servants, hoped to expand tobacco production, their economic dreams perhaps clouding local leaders' understanding of the fragile nature of Powhatan-English relations.

Colonial expansion in the Chesapeake mattered to the English. It also mattered to Spanish officials, who feared the impact that a stable English presence would have on their realm's ships. But by 1622, the group most concerned with those expanding tobacco fields was the Powhatans, who saw in the growing number of migrants a threat they could no longer tolerate.

In 1619, the Privy Council again turned its attention to the Chesapeake. These English advisors to the king appreciated that Jamestown and its nearby environs seemed more stable with an enlarged population. But there were still not enough migrants there to create real stability. A durable colony would need women as well as men, especially given prevailing ideas about the foundational role of the family in the creation of a stable society. At the time, an English household often contained more than individuals related to each other by blood. Living alongside family members were servants, many of them children or adolescents who also resided under the direction of the father.[1] This residential pattern and set of expectations may have contributed to an emerging idea among colonial planners: could the state compel indigent children to be indentured servants in the colony? In a society where stealing food could land a poor child in prison, the issue seemed ripe for exploitation by those more con-

1. See Peter Laslett, *The World We Have Lost: England Before the Industrial Age*, 3rd ed. (New York: Charles Scribner's Sons, 1984), 1–8; Lawrence Stone, *The Family, Sex, and Marriage in England, 1500–1800*, abridged ed. (New York: Harper and Row, 1979), 28–29.

cerned with making profits with tobacco than with the best interests of unfortunate girls and boys.

The matter gained attention when authorities learned that children condemned to transportation might have been poor, but they did not lack a voice. Some of them protested their sentence, an act that raised questions about the limits of the state's authority over minors in England. Sir Edwin Sandys, the Virginia Company's new treasurer, argued that these children had no place in England and were "fitter for any remote place than for this cittie." At home they would cause trouble, but "in Virginia," he wrote, "under severe masters they may be brought to goodnes." The councilors agreed. On January 31, 1620, they ordered that these children could be shipped across the Atlantic despite their protests. Company members, for their part, welcomed the decision, but understood that they also accepted responsibility for educating their new wards. Boys and girls had to serve until age twenty-one, though a girl could be freed from her term if she got married sooner, a likely scenario given the preponderance of men among the migrant population. Those who survived would get a house with some clothes and furnishings, fifty acres of land, some tools, weapons for self-defense, a cow, enough maize to last them a year, and, after seven years, their own indentured servants. The City of London approved indentures for children as young as eight.[2]

The binding of children constituted only one part of the Virginia Company's plans to provide labor for nascent tobacco plantations. By the spring of 1620, some of its supporters argued that marshals should scour

2. "Conditions of the Children sent by the Citty," February 2, 1619/1620, FP 153; Misha Ewen, "'Poore Soules': Migration, Labor, and Visions for Commonwealth in Virginia," in Paul Musselwhite, Peter C. Mancall, and James Horn, eds., *Virginia 1619: Slavery and Freedom in the Making of English America* (Chapel Hill: University of North Carolina Press for the Omohundro Institute of Early American History and Culture, 2019), 141–143; Misha Ewen, *The Virginia Venture: American Colonization and English Society, 1580–1660* (Philadelphia: University of Pennsylvania Press, 2022), 102–116; Steven Hindle, *On the Parish? The Micro-Politics of Poor Relief in Rural England, c. 1550–1750* (Oxford: Oxford University Press, 2004), 171–226; Pamela Sharpe, "Poor Children as Apprentices in Colyton, 1598–1830," *Continuity and Change* VI (1991), 253–270, esp. 253–254; Simon Newman, *A New World of Labor: The Development of Plantation Slavery in the British Atlantic* (Philadelphia: University of Pennsylvania Press, 2013), 31–32; Christopher Tomlins, *Freedom Bound: Law, Labor, and Civic Identity in Colonizing English America, 1580–1865* (Cambridge: Cambridge University Press, 2010), 78–82. The high death rate among migrants fueled familial instability but at the same time provided opportunities for young women who were willing to remarry if they could be convinced that the property they had amassed in a prior marriage would be protected for their children. See Lois Green Carr and Lorena S. Walsh, "The Planter's Wife: The Experience of White Women in Seventeenth-Century Maryland," *WMQ*, 3rd Ser., 34 (1977), 542–571.

the countryside and arrest miscreants, forcing them into terms of service that would be "more severe and proportioned in terme & severity according to the Quallity of their offences." Such a system, argued the Parliament member Sir John Danvers, "would incourage thousands of increase towards the Peopling of that large territory."[3] Sandys, aware that Commons had been debating a new bill about how to handle the large numbers of indigent, argued that the realm should export those who could not find work. "Never," he argued, "was ther a fairer gate opened to a nation to disburden it selfe nor better meanes by reason of the abundance of people to advance such a plantation" than in Virginia.[4]

In 1621, George Yeardley's term as the governor of Virginia expired. He had presided over what in retrospect amounted to wide-ranging changes in the structure and politics of the longest-lasting English colony west of Ireland. By surviving on the ground, the colonists had shifted the structure of politics across the Atlantic Ocean. Until the cessation of active hostility between the Powhatans and English in 1614, there was every reason for the English to abandon the James River. Hundreds of potential colonists had died and those who remained depended largely on the Powhatans, who still could have eliminated them. But the English persisted, demonstrating an acceptance of the risks inherent in any overseas colonization. Their ability to stay, though they might not have said or known it, also sprang from the reality that their presence fit Wahunsonacock's strategic vision for his confederacy.

After Yeardley's departure, the directors of the Virginia Company took an opportunity to restructure the governance of the colony to allow colonists greater opportunity to rule their own affairs, the direct result of changes they had implemented in 1619. On July 24, 1621, the company's council determined that the governor would be advised by two councils: one "appointed in London, the other in Virginia, with the latter including two burgesses from "every towne, [hundred] and other particular plantacion." It would be known as the General Assembly.[5] The company's directors reminded those in Virginia that they were to pay attention to

3. "Project by S[i]r John Da[u]vers for advancing ye Plantation of Virginia, April 1620 (endorsed by Sandys)," FP 166.

4. Ewen, "Migration, Labor, and Visions for Commonwealth," 145; Wallace Notestein et al, eds., *Commons Debates 1621* (New Haven, CT: Yale University Press, 1935), April 30, 1621, at 4:274–275 and 5:113–114; Theodore Rabb, *Jacobean Gentleman: Sir Edwin Sandys, 1561–1629* (Princeton, NJ: Princeton University Press, 1998), 227–236.

5. "Treasurer and Company, An Ordinance and Constitution for Council and Assembly in Virginia, July 24, 1621," in Samuel M. Bemiss, ed., The *Three Charters of the Virginia*

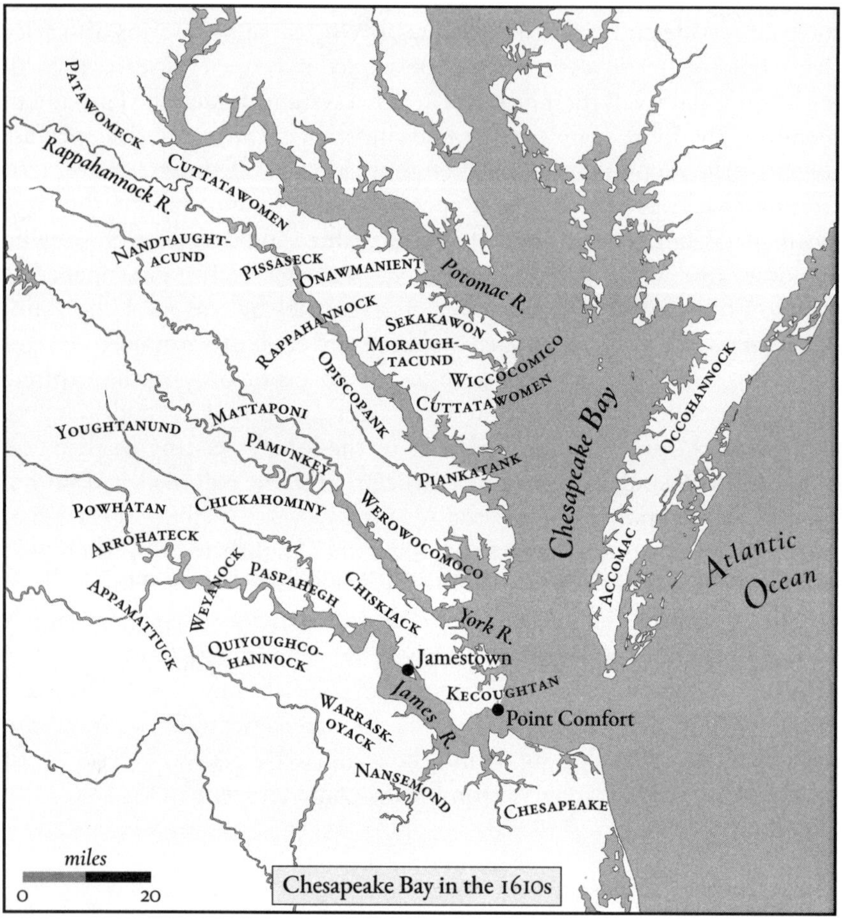

Chesapeake Bay in the 1610s

the conversion of Natives, not stray from the Church of England's teachings, and reaffirm their loyalty to the king. Those in London worried about possible attacks from the Powhatans, though that did not stop them from directing that colonists "obtaine" Indigenous children, including boys who they believed would receive formal education once the colony launched its college. They also directed the governor to punish any colonists who threatened the social order through idleness, drunkenness, or wearing gold, silver, or silk. Such laws reflected sumptuary codes at home, which prohibited those of lesser status from imitating social superiors by displaying valuable clothing. And, as always, colonists needed to

Company of London, Jamestown 350th Anniversary Historical Booklet 4 (Williamsburg, VA: Jamestown 350th Anniversary Celebration Corporation, 1957), 126–128.

look to the east as well as the west, remaining ever vigilant in the perpetual battle against European pirates. Colonial officials would be rewarded with land grants.[6]

Confident of their prospects, the company tried to orchestrate an American economy from London. Each of the new towns needed to keep the governor apprised about the number of births, marriages, deaths, and cattle at each household, and all had a responsibility to erect and maintain fences to keep their cows, swine, and poultry from denuding nearby fields. While existing and arriving colonists had the flexibility to determine how they lived and set up their households, the king's condemnation of tobacco limited its production. Seeking economic diversification, company directors hoped to encourage exports of pitch, tar, salt, and walnut oil. They wanted more valuable commodities too, even though it meant tapping the knowledge of non-English experts. The company sent over French farmers skilled at growing mulberry trees, vital for the silk industry some company directors believed would become the most important export-oriented venture. Others believed that vignerons sent to tend vines, Italians dispatched to build a glass furnace, and Dutch recruited to build mills would put the colony on a faster path toward re-creating a European-style landscape and built environment. To encourage agricultural expansion, the council sent the surveyor William Claiborne (Cleyburne) to create a new map that would lay out the colony's future. They also sent word that they had heard the Dutch were creating a lucrative fur trade in the territory Hudson had explored in 1609.[7]

War and disease had dominated the colonists' first seven years along the James. Since 1614, the cautious peace had reduced the fears of violence, and dispersed tobacco farms minimized some of the ecological dangers that the earlier immigrants had suffered when, following the company's orders, they clustered near Jamestown, even during its deadly summer months. Virginia, once a home for bloody flux and cannibalism, began to take on the trappings of a series of small English villages. The rumors of its horrors diminished in London, which made it a more tempting locale for poor English men and women, most of them young. Even with the changes, men continued to far outnumber women among those accepting contracts to become indentured servants with the promise of a payout should they survive their term of bondage.

6. Virginia Company, "Instructions to the Governor and Council of State in Virginia," July 24, 1621 [hereafter Virginia Company Instructions, 1621], in Bemiss, ed., *Three Charters*, 109–113.

7. Virginia Company Instructions, 1621, 114–124.

With the psychological battle perhaps turning in their favor, the London-based councilors of the Virginia Company turned to the next stage of creating a new England—the redefinition of the look of the land. On one level, recasting the land was a logical and perhaps not even conscious result of the emergence of a settled agricultural regime similar to the English countryside. But that world of small villages had come into existence hundreds of years earlier, so long ago that few would have given much thought to the fact that stones retrieved from fields because they might dent or break a plough and stacked up along its edge came to constitute a permanent marker on the landscape. To this day, aerial photographs reveal the permanence of these lines even when farmers and town builders have long since removed the stones.[8]

But hedgerows and stone walls signaled more than where one farmer's land ended and another's began. Land enclosed in walls was owned by someone. That would have been obvious to the councilors of the Virginia Company and the colonizers it sent westward. But it represented a fundamental shift in attitudes toward land near the Chesapeake. The Algonquian-speaking peoples of the Tidewater, including the Powhatans, Susquehannocks, and other Iroquoian-speakers beyond the fall line that marked the boundary between the coastal plain and the piedmont, owned what they produced and had rights to travel to places where they had customarily gone—to spring planting grounds for maize, to forests to hunt game in newly fallen snow, to the marginal edge grounds between grassland and trees where deer congregated. They had farmed the region for centuries and did not lack a claim to land even though they never fenced their fields.[9]

8. The definitive text here is William Camden's *Britannia*, which he first published in Latin in 1586 and then, in 1610, in an English translation. He was moved to write his exhaustive survey of the landscape by the Dutch geographer Abraham Ortelius, who had, as Camden wrote, implored him to "restore antiquity to Britaine, and Britain to his antiquity." See Camden, *Britain, or A Chorographicall Description of the Most flourishing Kingdomes, England, Scotland, and Ireland, and the Ilands adjoining, out of the depth of Antiquitie* (London, 1610), trans. Philemon Holland, quotation in the "Author to the Reader" note following the title page. For a more recent effort to trace the shifts in the landscape, see Francis Pryor, *The Making of the British Landscape* (London: Allen Lane, 2010).
9. Helen C. Rountree, *Pocahontas's People: The Powhatan Indians of Virginia Through Four Centuries* (Norman: University of Oklahoma Press, 1990), 5–6; Stephen R. Potter, *Commoners, Tribute, and Chiefs: The Development of Algonquian Culture in the Potomac Valley* (Charlottesville: University of Virginia Press, 1993), 32–43; Martin Gallivan, *The Powhatan Landscape: An Archaeological History of the Algonquian Chesapeake* (Gainesville: University Press of Florida, 2018), 68–98; Timothy Silver, *A New Face on the Countryside: Indians, Colonists, and Slaves in South Atlantic Forests, 1500–1800* (Cambridge: Cambridge University Press, 1990), 37–38, 46–52; James D. Rice, *Nature and History in the Potomac Country: From Hunter-Gatherers to the Age of Jefferson* (Baltimore: Johns Hopkins University Press, 2009), 26–42.

The twenty-one-year-old Claiborne, who had attended Cambridge University's Pembroke College, arrived in Virginia to address colonial tobacco planters' need to establish boundaries on the land. The tools he brought to demarcate which English party owned what piece of land were as important as the compass and sextants that had enabled navigators to get ships back and forth across the ocean. The difference was that Claiborne's marks on the ground could be seen by all who passed. Once he and others who followed him laid down lines and identified the places for roads and bridges, migrants could feel more secure in taking the risk to establish their stake. Claiborne's work might have been motivated by the fact that the Earl of Pembroke had decided to purchase 30,000 acres in Virginia. Surely he would need to know which lands were his. Pleasing such investors would be crucial for the next stage of the colonial process.[10]

The councilors wanted to re-create an English landscape. They had started the process earlier when they had launched what was essentially a dual aural and temporal revolution—the transportation of bells to signal church services and drums and drummers to beat out the time to go to work. New orders to construct fences along the edges of private and public land kept livestock close to owners and from destroying fields. Earlier, colonial officials had done little to rein in voracious cows and pigs, figuring that they did not have the supply of laborers necessary to chop trees and prepare fences. The English at times enraged Powhatans because of their unwillingness or inability to keep their animals from ruining Indigenous fields. By 1621, hungry swine and cattle threatened colonists' fields as well as those of the Powhatans. Neither scenario could be accepted any longer: cattle destroying colonists' maize undermined the agricultural economy that pleased James I, while unrestrained browsing on Indigenous fields risked retaliation and a return to the fears of 1609–1614. Eventually, the colonial landscape would come to seem natural and even timeless, the rhythms of quarterly court meeting times and ship arrivals constituting as much of a revolution in sensibilities as European livestock eating imported grasses along a meandering tributary of a river the English called the James. But this creation of a new landscape necessitated an erasure of the Powhatans'.[11]

10. Virginia Company Instructions, 1621, 120 (Claiborne), 124 (Pembroke); Clayton Torrence, "The English Ancestry of William Claiborne of Virginia: Part II: The English Connection," *VMHB* 56 (1948), 431–460.
11. See Virginia DeJohn Anderson, *Creatures of Empire: How Domestic Animals Transformed Early America* (Oxford: Oxford University Press, 2004), 107–140; Rhys Isaac, *The Transformation of Virginia, 1740–1790* (Chapel Hill: University of North Carolina Press for the Institute for Early American History and Culture, 1982), part one.

Virginia colonists' increasing desire to expand tobacco plantations also aroused the ire of James I. By the late 1610s, he had begun to take an increasingly active role in the administration of the colonies, with a particular interest in regulating economic behavior. On March 29, 1619, he issued a proclamation intended to prevent incursions into the monopoly on the logwood trade that he had bestowed on a favorite. Europeans used the blood-red heart of the tree, which had been indigenous to Belize, to produce crimson and black dyes.[12] Less than two months later, he declared that the Muscovy Company, which included Greenland in its orbit, had a monopoly on the importation of whale fins.[13] On November 10, after hearing reports of tobacco being sold "ungarbled" (that is, the desirable parts remained mixed with detritus) and thus dangerous to users, James ordered the inspection of any premises where tobacco changed hands.[14]

The link between economics and public health continued to attract his attention. About six weeks after his message of November, the king issued another order proclaiming that tobacco was corrupting bodies and morals. To make matters worse, the growing of tobacco at home meant it had "begun to be taken in every meane Village even amongst the basest people." This English tobacco, the king believed, was "more crude, poysonous and dangerous for the bodies and healths" of his subjects than the tobacco exported from hot climates. Domestic production also undermined the economies of Bermuda and Virginia, thereby weakening the stability of these still-new colonies, and deprived the treasury of any customs fees applied to imports. To prevent such harm, the king forbade the planting of tobacco in England and Wales after February 2, 1620. Anyone in possession of domestic tobacco needed to destroy it, and violators would be arrested, tried, and punished.[15] In a related move, he struck out against those who made tobacco pipes without permission, depriving some poorer subjects a chance to improve their finances.[16] In March 1620, James prohibited the Virginia Company from using lotteries to raise funds, claiming that those

12. *A Proclamation for prevention and restraint of the abuses and inconveniences, occasioned by dying with Logwood*, March 29, 1619 (London, 1619) in Sel b. 231 (226), QCL.
13. *A Proclamation inhibiting the Importation of Whale Finnes . . . by any, but the Muscovy Company*, (London, 1619), Sel b. 231 (216), QCL.
14. *A Proclamation concerning the viewing and distinguishing of Tobacco* (London, 1619), Sel b. 231 (220), QCL. At the time, "garble" meant to remove refuse or dust from plant matter meant for human consumption, so "ungarbled" tobacco leaves had not been properly cleaned.
15. *A Proclamation to restraine the planting of Tobacco in England and Wales* (London, 1619), in Sel b. 231 (224), QCL.
16. *A Proclamation commanding Conformity to his Majesties pleasure, expressed in his late Charter to the Tobacco-pipe-makers*, May 27, 1620 (London, 1620), in Sel b. 231 (379?), QCL.

under its direction had failed to expand the realm, increase trade, or convert Natives to Christianity.[17] By June, his distaste for tobacco led him to once again try to restrain the distribution and sale of the plant.[18] Tobacco might have been the economic salvation for the Virginia Company, but for him it remained an unsuitable and dangerous foreign commodity.

Despite the king's reservations, colonists continued to seek new lands for their farms. Through 1621, the Powhatans tolerated the migrants' agricultural expansion. Opechancanough and George Thorpe, the colony's new governor, even agreed that some Powhatans could live among the English and some English among the Powhatans, including a small number of boys from both groups.[19] By the spring of 1622, colonial communities, most of them consisting of fewer than twenty people, reached closer to the fall line, with houses ever farther from existing forts, which the English constructed near the broad stretches of the James where Spanish ships or pirates might attempt a bold attack. Why waste human and material resources building blockhouses in areas so safe that Powhatans and colonists walked unarmed into each other's towns and often ate together?[20] Colonists even dismissed a rumor in 1621 that Opechancanough might attack them. He denied the truth of the tale, and the English took him at his word.[21]

Whatever hopes the English had for continued good relations vanished in March 1622. Sometime around the middle of the month, an ally of Opechancanough named Nemmattanow (or Jack o' the Feather) got into an argument with a colonist. By the time it ended, the Powhatan and the immigrant were both dead. The incident concerned the colonial governor, but Opechancanough promised that he was still committed to "peace so firme that the sky should fall ere he dissolved it."[22]

17. *By the King* (London, 1620), in Sel b. 231 (240), QCL.
18. *A Proclamation for restraint of the disordered trading for Tobacco* (London, 1620), Sel b. 231 (231), QCL.
19. Thorpe to Sir Edwin Sandys, May 15 and 16, 1621, and Wyatt and the Virginia Council to the Virginia Company of London, January 1621/1622, both in *RVC*, III:446–447, 584; Edmund S. Morgan, *American Slavery, American Freedom: The Ordeal of Colonial Virginia* (New York: W. W. Norton, 1975), 98; Karen Ordahl Kupperman, *Pocahontas and the English Boys: Caught Between Cultures in Early Virginia* (New York: New York University Press, 2019).
20. On the spread of colonial communities, see James Horn, *A Land as God Made It: Jamestown and the Birth of America* (New York: Basic Books, 2005) 256.
21. William S. Powell, "Aftermath of the Massacre: The First Indian War, 1622–1632," *VMHB* 66 (1958), 44–45.
22. Powell, "Aftermath of the Massacre," 45.

About a week later, on March 22, 1622, that peace disappeared when Powhatans attacked English colonists, primarily those living on dispersed tobacco farms away from Jamestown. By day's end, the Powhatans had killed 347, amounting to one-fourth of the colonial population.[23] The colonial administration almost immediately launched a counterattack, escalating the stakes. "Our first worke," according to Sir Francis Wyatt, the colony's newly arrived governor, "is expulsion of the Salvages to gaine a free range of the countrey." He understood that it was "infinitely better to have no heathen among us, who at best were but as thornes in our sides, th[a]n to be at peace and league with them." Over the next few months, the English attacked eight Indigenous groups, including the Powhatans and the Pamunkeys. They sailed or paddled up the James, shooting into towns. When occupants fled, colonists stole maize and set fire to whatever was left. For their part, the Powhatans continued to attack, though in small bursts of violence followed by quick retreat into cover. The colonists, despite Wyatt's plea for quick revenge, lacked the might to defeat the Powhatans.[24]

News about the disaster reached England quickly. "There is also this week ill newes come from Virginia (which every man reports that comes from London)," the Reverend Joseph Mead wrote from Cambridge. Between 300 and 329 "of our colonie there massacred by the Indians at the instigation, as should seeme, of their wicked God Ochee." The calamity would have been worse had a converted boy not shared his knowledge about the plot. Even so, as Mead understood, the Powhatans attacked the colonists, "& beat out their braines scarce any escaping." The uprising had religious roots, at least to Mead. "It seemes this God of theirs is something of kind to him that manages the massacres now in France," he added, "& other parts of Christendome. But our God, the God of Gods, confound them quickly."[25]

English on both sides of the Atlantic prepared for a brutal war. Meeting in London on July 29, 1622, the Privy Council accepted the Virginia Company council's plea for arms stored in the Tower; though they were old and "altogether unfit, and of no use for moderne Service," they "might neverthles be serviceable against that naked people." Soon after, Crown officials authorized the shipment of 1,000 halberds, 300 harquebuses, 300

23. Horn, *A Land as God Made It*, 260; Robert C. Johnson, ed., "The Indian Massacre of 1622: Some Correspondence of the Reverend Joseph Mead," *VMHB* 71 (1963), 408; Morgan, *American Slavery, American Freedom*, 98–99.

24. Horn, *A Land as God Made It*, 267–268, quotations at 267; Powell, "Aftermath of the Massacre," 45–46.

25. Mead to Sir Martin Stuteville, July 13, 1622, in Johnson, ed., "Indian Massacre," 408–409.

short pistols, 700 calivers, 400 bows, 2,000 helmets, and 40 armored coats. Although the arms were on their way, soldiers were not. The company's promise to send 400 never materialized. A scheme to send 100 young men (presumably primarily as laborers, though likely they could be counted on to bear arms if needed) went nowhere when officials in England realized that there was not enough food for them in Virginia. They sailed for Bermuda instead.[26]

Even before they had heard about the shipment, Wyatt and the council in Jamestown issued commissions as early as April 13, giving military veterans who were then in Virginia enormous power to organize forces and attack their enemies. By June, the council in Virginia sent a message to the company informing them that colonists had attacked Natives, "slaine divers, burnte their Townes, destoyde their Wears [weirs] & Corne." They bragged that they had "slayne more of them this yeere, then hath been slayne before since the begininge of ye Colonie." They attacked Weyanokes, Warraskoyacks, Pamunkeys, Potomacs, Chickahominies, and Rappahannocks. Still, the Council members did not expect a swift conclusion, since the Powhatans knew the territory better than the English and proved much faster at navigating the landscape. Victory would require starving them and using whatever means the English could devise to "pursue their extirpatione."[27]

Even without the military forces they wanted, the colonists embraced the company's call for vengeance. "We conceave it a Sinne against the dead, to abandon the enterprize, till we have fully settled the possession for which so many of our Brethren have lost theire lives," the council wrote to the governor. "This is the first thing due from us and you; and the next, which will likewise much further the other, is a sharp revenge uppon the bloody miscreante[s], even to the measure that they intended against us, the rooting them out from being longer a people uppon the face of the Earth."[28]

In Tsenacommacah, combatants fought on the ground, but across the Atlantic the conflict became a contest about the nature of colonization. Was it ever going to be possible, some came to argue, to convert Powhatans

26. Powell, "Aftermath of the Massacre," 49–54; *Acts of the Privy Council of England: Colonial Series* (London, 1908–1912), I:54 for the quotation; Horn, *A Land as God Made It*, 262–263; *RVC*, III:665–667, 676, and 683, and IV:9.

27. Council in Virginia to the Virginia Company of London, January 20, 1622/1623, *RVC*, IV:9–17, quotations at 9 and 10.

28. Edwin Sandys to the Governor and the Council in Virginia, October 7, 1622, *RVC*, III:683–690, quotation at 683; Powell, "Aftermath of the Massacre," 50–51.

and their neighbors to English-style culture when the actions near the James had revealed the true nature of an enemy bent on deceiving the bearers of civilization? That sense of betrayal permeated a pamphlet published in London that year: Edward Waterhouse's *A Declaration of the State of the Colony and Affairs in Virginia, with A Relation of the Barbarous Massacre in the time of peace and League, treacherously executed by the Native Infidels upon the English.* On the title page, Waterhouse promised a list of all the victims so that their heirs "may take order *for the inheriting of their lands and estates in Virginia.*" From its opening words, a reader would conclude that the colonization project would continue, its lands passing from the deceased to the living just as if a similar disaster had taken place in England.[29]

In the pamphlet, which would eventually be illustrated and translated into German and Latin, Waterhouse painted a view of depraved Natives battling against civilized English. This was a history fused with promotion: Waterhouse included a two-page insert reminding readers of the headright system that gave any English migrant to Virginia by midsummer 1625 fifty acres for themselves and another fifty acres for every other person whose voyage they paid for, with the amount to be doubled in any additional division of the company's holdings.[30]

Still, offering a new paean to Virginia's natural bounties and its industrious colonists was not why Waterhouse wrote. Instead, he emphasized the violence and duplicity of the Natives' assault, which represented a departure from earlier good relations. In his opinion, the situation had shifted when the Powhatans launched their rebellion. That day, colonists thought Powhatans had come to trade, so they invited some to join them for breakfast. But then the visitors attacked, seizing the colonists' own weapons and tools. Armed, "they basely and barbarously murthered," Waterhouse wrote, "not sparing eyther age or sexe, man, woman or childe; so sodaine in their cruell execution, that few or none discerned the weapon or blow that brought them to destruction." He claimed that the Powhatans murdered colonists in their houses and out in the fields, some while they were planting tobacco and maize, others while they made bricks, sawed wood, or constructed new buildings. The death toll was high because, again in Waterhouse's view, the previous experience of close relations had provided the Powhatans with detailed information about where they could find colonists and how best to surprise them.[31]

29. [Edward Waterhouse], *A Declaration of the State of the Colony and Affaires in Virginia* (London, 1622).

30. [Waterhouse], *Declaration*, sig. A3^{r-v}, 1–10, 13, quotations at A3^{v} and 5; the list of goods follows the enumeration of the errata at sig. [A4^{v}].

31. [Waterhouse], *Declaration*, 12–14.

The result horrified colonists and their English supporters. Sneaking up on their victims "that fatall Friday morning," Waterhouse reported, "there fell under the bloudy and barbarous hands of that perfidious and inhumane people, contrary to all lawes of God and men, of Nature & Nation, three hundred forty seven men, women, and children, most by their own weapons." Even worse, the attackers, "not being content with taking away life alone," desecrated the bodies of their victims—"a fresh murder, defacing, dragging, and mangling the dead carcasses into many pieces, and carrying some parts away in derision, with base and bruitish triumph."[32] The dead included "Gentlemen of birth, vertue, and industry, and of the Council."[33] Echoing Waterhouse, Anthony Chester, who had arrived in Virginia only two years earlier, wrote that since "simply killing our people did not satisfy their inhuman nature, they dragged the dead bodies all over the country, tearing them limb from limb, and carrying the pieces in triumph around."[34]

Waterhouse, knowing that he was writing for an audience eager for details, dwelled on one murder in particular: the assault on George Thorpe, the man who was to be in charge of the college for Natives, someone dedicated to their "conversion, and [who] was so tender" to his charges that he would punish any colonists who mistreated a Powhatan. Thorpe had spoken frequently with Opechancanough, believing that the headman had accepted the idea that "our God was a good God, and better much th[a]n theirs." Until the fateful day, the Powhatans had demonstrated nothing but affection for Thorpe, professing "outward love and respect unto him." But on that Friday, they killed him and desecrated his remains. The victim became, in Waterhouse's opinion, "a glorious Martyr."[35] Fortunately for the English, the Powhatans did not march on Jamestown, and Opechancanough's soldiers lacked the means to assault ships on the river. Waterhouse declared that the death toll, which included cattle as well as the 347 humans, would have been higher still had Opechancanough managed to get a stock of poison from a sachem on the Eastern Shore. Fortunately for the English, that Indigenous leader rebuffed the Powhatans' overture.[36]

In previous years, colonial calamity in North America, whether caused by nature (such as extreme cold) or humans, had prompted retreat to England.

32. [Waterhouse], *Declaration*, 14.
33. [Waterhouse], *Declaration*, 20.
34. Chester's account appeared in 1707 in a Dutch version of Waterhouse's pamphlet by the acclaimed printer Peter van der Aa, and was translated later in "Two Tragical Events," *WMQ*, 1st Ser., 9 (1901), 203–214, quotation at 209.
35. [Waterhouse], *Declaration*, 15–17.
36. [Waterhouse], *Declaration*, 18–22, quotation at 22.

In the early 1620s, misfortune inspired a shift in strategy, away from coexistence and toward a plan, as Waterhouse put it, "to destroy them who sought to destroy us." Adding to this new bloodlust was the economic reality that if the English could push Indigenous residents away, the colonists could claim the Powhatans' fields, which occupied the best lands in the region.[37]

The violence changed the underlying logic of the English approach to colonization along the Chesapeake. Previously, James had insisted that religious conversion be the prime reason for expanding his realm in the region, with economic gain (such as the expansion of trade or relieving the realm of underemployed and dangerous men) a secondary benefit. But by the late 1610s, with the English having made little notable progress converting Indigenous other than Pocahontas and the boy who warned colonists about the 1622 attack, the underlying commercial logic of colonization came to dominate public discussion—even when that meant abandoning what some had once claimed was the highest goal for Christians in the Americas. As Waterhouse recognized, "the way of conquering them is much more easie th[a]n of civilizing them by faire meanes, for they are a rude, barbarous, and naked people, scattered in small companies, which are helps to Victorie, but hinderances to Civilitie." With impediments to action removed, the English were free to launch surprise attacks, create famine by burning Indigenous fields, destroy the Natives' economy by wrecking their canoes and houses, interrupt their winter hunts by riding through them with horses and hounds, and set mastiffs "to teare them," an act that English believed produced the greatest fear among Natives. Such tactics would bring quick victory, speeding the timetable to the establishment of a successful colony built not with Indigenous residents but instead on top of their erased landscape. Earlier English promoters had castigated Spaniards for engaging in such brutality. After the spring assault, at least some of James's subjects seemed ready to emulate the policies they believed had been central in the Iberian conquest.[38]

Waterhouse used history to goad the English forward. In particular, he hoped that colonists would imitate the ways that the Spanish in Mexico and Peru and the Romans in ancient times had found ways to pit existing rivals against each other. "In VIRGINIA," Waterhouse wrote, "the many divers Princes and people there are at this day opposed in infinite factions one unto another, and many of them beare a mortall hatred to these our barbarous Savages."[39] Waterhouse had read Oviedo's account of Columbus's actions and believed it apposite for redefining the future of

37. [Waterhouse], *Declaration*, 22–23.
38. [Waterhouse], *Declaration*, 24.
39. [Waterhouse], *Declaration*, 24–25.

what was then the most durable English Colony in North America. Columbus, learning of the deaths of men he had left behind in the Indies and the Natives' treachery toward them, turned on the Tainos and others. Waterhouse knew this to be true because he had read it in Oviedo's history, which the English writer claimed had described the reduction of the Indigenous population of Hispaniola from 1 million to 500 within forty years. This was a model that would work for the English since "the Natives in VIRGINIA are nothing populous, but thin and scattered Nations, as it knowne to all." Destruction of the Powhatans would also enrich the English, again an echo of the Spanish experience to the south.[40]

Waterhouse linked vengeance with enslavement of Powhatans, who could be put to work digging mines. Any bound Powhatan not put to service in Virginia could be sent to Bermuda. Waterhouse understood that a crisis in the short run presented opportunities for the future. "*Virginia* is most abundantly fruitfull," he concluded, and it was vital that "this Massacre must rather be beneficiall to the Plantation th[a]n impaire it."[41]

Waterhouse's tract bore vivid witness to the horrors the colonists had experienced. The names of every woman, man, and child killed on March 22, 1622, filled nine full pages of Waterhouse's account, a heartbreaking record of lives snuffed out, almost all of them in small communities sprinkled across the Tidewater.[42] Their loss represented a betrayal to the many generous supporters who from 1619 to 1621 had donated funds for the education of Natives. Yet in the same pamphlet readers could study the newest theory about getting through the Northwest Passage based on local observations that the rivers running from the Piedmont to the Chesapeake must originate in the same sea that fed Hudson Bay. Indigenous reporters from Florida and Canada as well as Virginia all testified that the passage existed. The fact that the pamphlet contained new information about a passage that maritime experts had largely concluded could not be found testifies to the obsession that the English still had for finding a trade route through North America—though, in this instance, that strategic quest could be linked to actual colonization.[43]

Waterhouse's near-instantaneous pamphlet became the public face of the Virginia Company's response to the attack. Others jumped in, claiming

40. [Waterhouse], *Declaration*, 26–33, quotation at 30 ("thin and scattered").
41. [Waterhouse], *Declaration*, 25–26 (enslavement), 33–34 ("beneficiall").
42. Horn, *A Land as God Made It*, 255–258.
43. [Waterhouse], *Declaration*, 35–43 (list of the dead), 45–50 (Northwest Passage), 51–54 (charity).

that the situation was even worse than Waterhouse had realized. The most fertile parts of the area lay deserted, one claimed; the only commodity being produced was tobacco, and no public works survived.[44] A French horticultural promoter named John Bonoeil, who wrote a pamphlet for the Virginia Company extolling the benefits of the silk industry, decried the base nature of the Powhatans. These Natives had "no industry, no Arts, no culture, nor no good use of this blessed Country here, but are mere ignorance, sloth, and brutishnesse, and an unprofitable burthern onely of the earth." Gone was the chance to live as neighbors or even the dream of converting Indigenous into English. A generation after the illustrated version of Harriot's account had touted the possibilities of reducing Natives to English ways and only four years after Pocahontas had become Rebecca Rolfe, the colonizers justified forced acquiescence on unremitting enemies.[45]

Privately, council members could not quite grasp how the colonists could have been so duped by Opechancanough and his allies. On August 1, having heard about the "great Massacre," they asked Wyatt how the English colonists could "fall by the hands of men so contemptible." Hadn't those on the ground realized that the threat of Powhatan violence had never diminished? Why had they ignored the 1621 rumor, which the councilors understood had been a warning? Missing the signs of the plot, colonial leaders like Wyatt were "made in parte instruments of contriving it, and almost guiltie of the destruccon by blindfold and stupid entertaining it." The realization of their credulity, they told him, "do add much to o[u]r sorrow." Colonists' poor moral calculus, evident in skipping religious services and excessive drinking, came to explain the situation as much as Opechancanough's cunning.[46]

Reports arriving in London by February 1623 acknowledged that the English had killed many of the Powhatans, but the counterassault did not eradicate the threat. In February 1623, the Powhatans attacked again, killing twenty-four men and burning a pinnace.[47] That incident furthered the sense of despair that had settled over the colony. "I thinke the last massacre killed all our Countrie," a planter named William Capps wrote

44. "An Answere to a Declarac[i]on of the Present State of Virginia," in *RVC*, IV:130–151, quotations at 138 and 151.
45. John Bonoeil, *His Majesties Gracious Letter to the Earl of South-Hampton* (London, 1622), 58–86; Alden Vaughan, "'Expulsion of the Savages': English Policy and the Virginia Massacre of 1622," *WMQ*, 3rd Ser., 35 (1978), 79–80.
46. Horn, *A Land as God Made It*, 261–262.
47. Unknown author to Mead, February 28, 1622/1623, and Mead to Stuteville, July 13, 1622, in Johnson, ed., "Indian Massacre," 409–410.

in the spring of 1623. In addition to the lives lost, the Powhatans "burst the heart of all the rest."[48]

The passion for revenge could not make up for the fact that the English in Virginia found themselves, yet again, short of food. An indentured servant named Richard Frethorne, living at Martin's Hundred, wrote to his parents in March 1623 that he was destitute and starving, his only coat stolen by another servant who apparently traded it for food. "I yo[u]r Child am in a most heavie Case by reason of the nature of the Country," he despaired, explaining the danger he faced from "scurvie and the bloody flix, and divers other diseases, which maketh the bodie very poore and Weake."[49] Supplies began to arrive from England by August, with 3,000 bushels of corn landing in January. Despite the imports, the colonists suffered through the winter of 1622–1623. Sandys believed the death toll that winter was twice the number of colonists lost in the initial attack. The colonists also lost most of their cattle. Food shortages drove prices up, making conditions even worse.[50] The diseases Frethorne described weakened English bodies yet again. One observer claimed that there were not enough healthy people to bury the dead. The year starting with the uprising in March 1622 was the costliest in Virginia's colonial history, with 1,000 or more colonists dead and the survivors barely able to carry on.[51]

Rather than subsiding, the violence escalated in the spring of 1623. In late March, a group of Patawomecks, angered by a raid led by Captain Isaac Maddison the previous year that had led to the deaths of thirty to forty of their community, attacked a contingent led by Captain Henry Spelman, who had returned to Virginia as an adult, that was then sailing the Potomac River. The Natives killed most of the colonists, including Spelman. In addition to the human toll, the event represented the first time that an Indigenous group had managed to destroy an English pinnace.[52]

48. William Capps to Dr. Thomas Wynston, March or April 1623, in *RVC*, IV:38; J. Frederick Fausz and Jon Kukla, "A Letter of Advice to the Governor of Virginia, 1624," *WMQ*, 3rd Ser., 34 (1977), 104–129, quotation at 104; Capps to John Ferrar, March 31, 1623, in *RVC*, IV:76.
49. Frethorne to his parents, March 20, April 2 and 3, 1623, in *RVC*, IV:58–62, quotation at 58; see also Emily Rose, "The Politics of Pathos: Richard Frethorne's Letters Home," in Robert Appelbaum and John Wood Sweet, eds., *Envisioning an English Empire: Jamestown and the Making of the North Atlantic World* (Philadelphia: University of Pennsylvania Press, 2005), 92–108.
50. Powell, "Aftermath of the Massacre," 55 (supplies), 58 (winter), 60–61.
51. Horn, *A Land as God Made It*, 274.
52. Horn, *A Land as God Made It*, 268.

On May 12, 1623, the English captain William Tucker led a contingent to the Pamunkey River to meet with Opitchapam, Opechancanough's brother. The English, believing that Opechancanough was present as well, came pretending to seek peace, an opening they made by offering their hosts some fortified wine. The Natives were suspicious, so they waited until the English had the first drink. Seeing no harm, they then indulged, missing the fact that the colonists drank from a different sack. The English, as one observed, had poisoned 200 Powhatans. Tucker also ordered his men to shoot among their hosts, killing fifty. The colonists came home bearing "parte of ther heades."[53]

The report of the poisoning alarmed those who heard it, as colonists anticipated. Some immediately claimed that they had no knowledge of the incident, trying to appease a king who remained annoyed that the colonists were still spending so much energy trying to produce tobacco.[54] None were more defensive than Governor Wyatt and his council in Virginia. In April 1624 they wrote a formal denial of the charge that their soldiers had ever used poison. Reeling at the time from a report arriving in London that castigated the local government for its incompetence and the sorry state of the colony, the governor and his allies strove to disarm those who used rumor and innuendo to ruin the reputation of the colony in James's eyes.[55] They first claimed that Opechancanough, "the prime plotter and actor of the late inhuman massacre," should not be considered a Powhatan "king," the term that some colonists had employed without recognizing it was an affront to the English monarch. They argued that the English could not have had a parley with the Powhatans because they lacked an interpreter, thereby undermining the claim that the English had somehow tricked the Powhatans amid a negotiation. Besides, Wyatt and the councilors argued, the accusation was preposterous, "two hundred being said to be destroied by poyson at a feast when there was neither feast made nor any man poyson'd." Also, the English did not shoot fifty men "to death, when there were but nine," though if the soldiers had killed more, they added, their actions would have been justified.

After denying that they had committed the crime, the governor and councilors then added that such an act would have been legitimate given the fact, already reported by Waterhouse, that Opechancanough had planned to use poison against the English earlier and then launched the

53. Horn, *A Land as God Made It*, 268–270; Powell, "Aftermath of the Massacre," 61–66.
54. Draft of letter of John Ferrar, likely to Francis Wyatt, April 1624, FP 539.
55. The most thorough and alarming to the Virginia Company's directors was the report by Captain Nathaniel Butler, which the company refuted point by point on February 16, 1623/1624; see FP 527.

raid in March 1622. They acknowledged that they had sent a commander and twelve soldiers up the Pamunkey River to rescue hostages and, if possible, "surprise or kill" Opechancanough. But the contingent had been unable to fulfill that mission, which led to them shooting "nine of the Salvages, and [bringing] away their heades." They claimed that Opechancanough was so dangerous that it made sense for these armed men to take poison with them on the raid, which they would use only if they could not otherwise extract the captives, but "whither it were [used] or no we know not, but this we are assured of, that none died by itt." Such an action might be worthy of sanction in London, they understood, but those on the ground who had seen the suffering perpetrated by the Powhatans would find it acceptable to save "so many captivated Christians." Under the circumstances, they hoped the king would disregard the false information he had been fed by rumor-mongers.[56]

The king was unmoved by such claims of innocence. "I have sent back to Mr. [John] Pory w[th] the Commission desiring you to put out Mr Pottes," the Earl of Warwick wrote to Secretary Edward Conway in August 1624 about Virginia's apothecary, likely the producer of what Tucker had offered the Powhatans. "[H]is Ma[jes]tie knows the reason, w[ch] was the Poysoner of the Savages th[ere] and therefore it is very unfit he should be imployed by the State in any business."[57]

Despite the fact that the English had by 1623 killed hundreds of Powhatans, reports from Chesapeake Bay revealed that colonists were approaching a psychological breaking point, evident in the fact that, at least in the opinion of their own king, some of them had used poison against their enemies, an action that the English had never taken before and that Europeans would have likely seen as a war crime, a concept that was only then beginning to be defined in international law.[58] Other disquieting signs could be seen too. Margrett Lady Wyatt, wife of the governor, wrote to her mother that months after the rebellion the price of food was still too high. "Here hath ben a generall death of men and Cattle," she

56. "The Answers of the Govern[ou]r and Councell in Virginia to the false informac[i]ons concerning the poysoning of the Indians," likely April 1624, FP 556.

57. Warwick to Conway, August 9, 1624, Bancroft Papers, Virginia 2:521, New York Public Library.

58. Alberico Gentili, *De Iure Libri Tres*, trans. John C. Rolfe, 2 vols. (Oxford: Clarendon Press, 1933), II:155–161. As the Dutch legal theorist Hugo Grotius wrote in 1625, "By the Law of Nations it is forbidden to kill any by Poison." See Hugo Grotius, *The Rights of War and Peace*, 3 vols., ed. Richard Tuck (Indianapolis, IN: Liberty Fund, 2005), III:1290–1291.

noted, "but now I thanke god it is ceased."[59] She told her sister that the ship she had taken to Virginia was so infested with disease that there were few other survivors, an exaggerated claim but one that fit the moment of despair.[60] The governor himself informed his father that misery was widespread among the colonists.[61] A colonist named Thomas Niccols dwelled on the horrors suffered by English women who died "miserablie through nastines & many dep[ar]te the World in their owne dung for want of help in their sicknes." He noted an equally terrible development: Opechancanough was holding nineteen English "in great slavery."[62] One after another testified to pervasive dearth. Edward Hill wrote to his brother that the English lived "*in the fearefullest age that ever Christians lyved in*."[63] It was all too much for Phoebus Canner: "[W]e have had *the sword, Famine and great mortalitye. I beseech god to give me life & health that I may this yeare end this troublesome voyage*."[64] Governor Wyatt and his council informed the company in January 1624 that it was difficult to convince colonists to embrace "a war where nothinge is to be gained."[65]

By early March 1624, members of the General Assembly, mindful of the criticism about their prior tactics, concluded that they needed to sever relationships with the Indigenous in order to launch an offensive against them. "The terms betwixt us and them are irreconcilable," they wrote in response to commissioners charged by the company with investigating the situation. The colonists would be better off if they could drive the Powhatans away. Since the initial attack in March 1622, they had suffered from a series of ambushes that weakened colonial communities. "We have not the safe range of the Country for the increase of Cattle, Swyne, etc. nor the game and fowle which the Country affords in great plentye," they informed the investigators. At the same time, they could not let down

59. Wyatt's letter was summarized by Sir Nathaniel Rich and included in "Notes taken from letters which came from Virginia in the 'Abigail,'" *RVC*, IV:228–229; for her full name, see John C. Hotten, *The Original Lists of Persons of Quality . . . Who Went from Great Britain to the American Plantations, 1600–1700* (London: Hotten, 1874), 173.

60. Wyatt to her sister, April 4, 1623, in "Notes taken from letters which came from Virginia in the 'Abigail,'" *RVC*, IV:232–233.

61. In "Notes taken from letters which came from Virginia in the 'Abigail,'" *RVC*, IV:229.

62. Summary of the letter from Thomas Niccolls to Sir Jo. Worsenholme [Wolstenholme?], April 2, 1623, in "Notes taken from letters which came from Virginia in the 'Abigail,'" *RVC*, IV:231–232.

63. Edward Hill to his brother Jo., April 14, 1623, in "Notes taken from letters which came from Virginia in the 'Abigail,'" *RVC*, IV:234.

64. Phoebus Can[n]er to Lawrence Ley, n.d., in "Notes taken from letters which came from Virginia in the 'Abigail,'" *RVC*, IV:235.

65. Francis Wyatt et al. to the Virginia Company of London, January 30, 1623/1624, in *RVC*, IV:450–455, quotation at 451.

their guard, necessitating the employment of colonists to guard others rather than all of them tending to their farms.[66]

The colonists initiated what they hoped would be their final assault in the summer of 1624. They claimed to have taken many victims, lost not a single life, and also destroyed corn fields said to be so extensive that they could have fed 4,000 people for a year.[67] George Wyatt, the father of the governor and a classically educated justice of the peace in Kent, believed that the history of ancient Greece and Rome provided clues to the current despair. Rather than dismiss the vengeance as an act of savages who just needed to be suppressed, the elder Wyatt wanted his son to learn from the experience. "The first Military precept your Barbarians have tought [taught] you now," he wrote. "Not to trust a faithles trust."[68]

The uprising renewed tensions within the company and led to an investigation of the situation in the colony. Captain Nathaniel Butler, who spent the winter of 1622–1623 in Virginia after completing his term as governor of Bermuda, told the company's councilors in April 1623 about the poor physical shape of the colony, including migrants living near salt marshes "full of infectious Boggs and muddy Creeks and Lakes," which opened the English to "all those Inconvenyences and diseases, w[hi]ch are so com[mon]ly found in the most unsound and most unhealthie partes of England." He observed that colonists lived along watercourses too shallow for oceangoing ships to dock, lacked even rudimentary shelters for newcomers, suffered from shortages of food that drove up prices, and lived in houses as miserable as the worst to be found in England. They had not yet built enough forts. He found the ironworks abandoned and its workers dead, and the residents committed only to tobacco production to the detriment of all other activity. Henrico and Charles City had been "lefte to ye spoyle of the Indians" who burned houses and stole livestock. Butler claimed that 10,000 English had gone to Virginia since 1607, but there were no more than 2,000 still there, many ill and desperate. "Instead of a Planta[ti]on," he concluded, Virginia "will shortly get ye name of a slaughter house and soe justly becom both odious to our selves &

66. Powell, "Aftermath of the Massacre," 65–66.

67. Powell, "Aftermath of the Massacre," 67–68; Council in Virginia to the Earl of Southampton and the Company in London, December 2, 1624, *RVC*, IV:507–508.

68. J. Frederick Fausz and John Kukla, "A Letter of Advice to the Governor of Virginia, 1624," *WMQ*, 3rd Ser., 34 (1977), 104–129, quotation at 118.

contemptible to all the world."[69] Some previous residents of the colony disputed Butler's points, but the damage had been done. Butler's report, among others, led the king to appoint a commission to investigate the situation along the Chesapeake.[70] Even before its results could be known, Governor Wyatt reminded anyone who would listen that these migrants still suffered from summer fevers, "the flixe or dropsy and where many are sick together, is infectious." Wyatt believed that the English needed to drive off the Powhatans if the colonists were to gain the lands necessary for their farms and herds. Disputes among colonists over specific parcels magnified the uncertainty.[71]

The commissioners reaffirmed the veracity of Butler's report: Virginia suffered because it was poorly led. If the king took no action, the colony might collapse. In response, James authorized his attorney general to recover the charter through a writ of *quo warranto* filed with the Court of the King's Bench. This legal device had come into practice in England in the thirteenth century. A *quo warranto*—technically, information in the form of a *quo warranto*—posed a question: by what authority does a chartered entity have the right to do something? It had arisen as a way to regulate relations between monarchs and corporations. When used by a king, it came to mean that a chartered body had exceeded its mandate. If the Court of King's Bench ruled for the monarch, the corporation had to give back the original parchment version of its charter, which bore the signature and seal of the king or queen who had authorized it. In an age when many could not read, the seal symbolized the approval of a monarch.[72] Sometime before November 4, 1623, the council received a formal order of a *quo warranto* demanding that the council address "by what warrant they claime to have the liberties priviledges and franchises" that they asserted.[73]

69. RVC, II:374–376; Horn, *A Land as God Made It*, 276–277.
70. Powell, "Aftermath of the Massacre," 69; Discourse of the Old Company, April (?) 1625, in *RVC*, IV:519–551.
71. "Letter of Sir Francis Wyatt, Governor of Virginia, 1621–1626," *WMQ*, 1st Ser., 6 (1926), 114–121, quotations at 117 and 118.
72. See M. T. Clanchy, *From Memory to Written Record: England, 1066–1307*, 3rd ed. (Oxford: Wiley-Blackwell, 2013), 31–45, 309–328; Paul D. Halliday, *Dismembering the Body Politic: Partisan Politics in England's Towns, 1650–1730* (Cambridge: Cambridge University Press, 1998), 26–27, 162–164; and Catherine F. Patterson, "Quo Warranto and Borough Corporations in Early Stuart England: Royal Prerogative and Local Privileges in the Central Courts," *English Historical Review* 120 (2005), 879–906.
73. Copy of Quo Warranto [November 4, 1623], FP 515; Court of King's Bench, "Record of Proceedings upon Information of Quo Warranto," November 4, 1623, to May 24, 1624, in *RVC*, IV:295–398.

After six months of hearings, the company lost its charter on May 24, 1624.[74] Within a year, Virginia became the first English royal colony in North America.[75] The move represented a decisive shift, a sign that overseas colonies would be consolidated into what historians have labeled a "composite monarchy" under which disparate places might still have their own governments but would be subject to the ultimate authority of the king. The practice, already common in parts of Europe, would eventually come to shape relations across English possessions stretching from Canada to the Caribbean.[76]

The surrender of the charter did not represent the end of the colony but instead opened new opportunities for those in a position to take advantage of them.[77] But the attack of 1622 signaled a major inflection point both in terms of official policy and in terms of the behavior of colonists. Earlier, English writers like Rolfe had acted on their belief that cultural conversion could work. The events of March 22, 1622, and the English interpretation of them evident in Waterhouse's tract, flipped the script. Conquest replaced coexistence as the dominant impulse among colonists in Virginia. Even Captain John Smith, who early in his experience had seen the utility of alliance with Powhatans as a way toward building a colony where English and Natives could live near each other, abandoned whatever sense of optimism he once had. Keen to cast aspersions on other colonists for the debacle, he blamed the catastrophe on poor management, alleging that the colonists might have withstood the 1622 assault if they had remained in concentrated communities near forts to seek refuge if necessary. But his proposed solution was to embrace violence. He volunteered to return to Virginia, leading a crew of a hundred soldiers and thirty sailors into battle with Opechancanough and his confederates. The company's council declined his invitation, which the always heroic (in his own prose) Smith attributed not to any defect in his plan but instead to divisions within the company.[78]

74. Vaughan, "'Expulsion of the Savages,'" 81, Horn, *A Land as God Made It*, 277
75. "A Proclamation for Setling the Plantation of Virginia," in Clarence S. Brigham, ed., *British Royal Proclamations Relating to America, 1603–1783* (orig. pub. 1911; New York: Burt Franklin, 1964), 52–55, quotation at 53.
76. J. H. Elliott, *Empires of the Atlantic World: Britain and Spain in America, 1492–1830* (New Haven, CT: Yale University Press, 2006), 117–118; J. H. Elliot, "A Europe of Composite Monarchies," *Past and Present* 137 (1992), 48–71.
77. See, e.g., "Discourse of the Old Company," April [?] 1625, in *RVC*, IV:519–551.
78. John Smith, *The Generall Historie of Virginia, New-England and the Summer Isles* (London, 1624), in Philip L. Barbour, ed., *The Complete Works of Captain John Smith*

The shift in English attitudes can be seen in the work of Samuel Purchas, the heir to Hakluyt's project of promoting English expansion by publishing accounts of the realm's subjects abroad. In 1625 he included a series of texts relating to Virginia in his massive, four-volume work entitled *Hakluytus Posthumus, or Purchas his Pilgrimes in Five Bookes*.[79] A trained minister, Purchas described events in Virginia from a scripturally inflected perspective. He embraced what had been until 1622 the core idea of English colonization in the Chesapeake—"not to make Savages and wild degenerate men of Christians, but Christians of those Savage, wild, degenerate men." The Indigenous might have once had a right to land, but he thought it "ungodly, and inhumane also to deny the world to men, or like Manger-dogges (neither to eat hay themselves, nor to suffer the hungry Oxe) to prohibite that for others habitation, whereof themselves can make no use."[80]

In drawing on scripture and legal precedent, Purchas captured the mood of the moment. The Powhatans, he argued, had violated the laws of nature and hence given up any claim to being considered as a nation. "And if they bee not worthy of the name of a Nation, being wilde and Savage," Purchas surmised, "yet as Slaves, bordering rebells, excommunicates and out-lawes are lyable to the punishments of Law, and not to the priviledges; So it is with these Barbarians, Borderers and Out-lawes of Humanity." The English claim to Virginia was to him unassailable and recognizable through specific, distinct moments: "first discovery, first actuall possession, prescription, gift, cession, and livery of seisin [the "by turf and twig" ceremony used to claim land], sale for price" as well as "the naturall Inheritance of the English their naturally borne, and the unnaturall outcries of so many unnaturally murthered, for just vengeance of rooting out the authors and actors of so prodigious injustice." He then rehearsed the historical moments that preceded this one: the actions of Cabot (verified by Ramusio, "the Map with his picture in the Privy Gallery hath 1497"); possession of Virginia by Queen Elizabeth in 1584; Ralegh's planting of a colony; other Europeans' failure to establish a settlement in the region; and various transactions with the Powhatans, including Wahunsonacock accepting a copper crown indicating that he

(Chapel Hill: University of North Carolina Press for the Institute of Early American History and Culture, 1986), 2:301–307.

79. "Virginias Verger: Or a Discourse shewing the benefits which may grow to this Kingdome from American English Plantations, and specifically those of Virginia and the Summer Islands," in Samuel Purchas, *Purchas his Pilgrims* (London, 1625), 4:1809–1826.

80. "Virginias Verger," 1811.

was "Vassall to His Majesty." Among the evidence confirming English ownership was "the fatal possession taken by so many murthered English." The bodies of English martyrs sanctified the Chesapeake as English land.[81]

Policies hatched in London did not dictate reality along the James. Opechancanough and his followers did not respond to rules created by the Virginia Company or the newly launched colonial assembly. He led a rebellion in 1622 because he understood the existential threat facing the Powhatans. Put simply, the violence he and his allies unleashed in March 1622 was an Indigenous effort to halt the expansion of unwelcome neighbors. Opechancanough understood the risk that colonial settlements produced. Years of small-scale bickering and occasional bloodshed convinced him that the time had come to halt further encroachments. The English were still outnumbered, but the Powhatans recognized that the newcomers possessed better weapons—guns that had more lethal force than a bow, armor that could repel Native arrows, ships that arrived bearing cannon capable of ripping through Indigenous houses. The uprising of 1622 did not, as the English believed, demonstrate failings on the part of the uncivilized. Instead, the rebellion was the purest manifestation of loyalty to an Indigenous vision. What remained uncertain was the fate of the 1,200 or so English still living in Tsenacommacah who had cast off any pretense about coexistence and had adopted a policy of outright elimination of any potentially dangerous Indigenous community.

The contest for the Chesapeake represented a decisive shift in relations between Indigenous and English colonizers in the region. But was it a harbinger of wider changes in North America? Opechancanough's rebellion and its brutal suppression fit specific local circumstances: English and European demand for tobacco; colonists' greater ability to survive in the Tidewater; Indigenous power in the hands of a man more inclined to see the risk of coexistence than the potential for partnership. Close observers like Purchas saw the shift playing out. Different Europeans, in other venues, still needed time to learn that there was likely no going back to a moment when the highest calling of the colonizer was to convert Native peoples. But from Oñate at Acoma to the poisoners of the Powhatans, a growing number of colonizers proved willing to eliminate Native peoples in the pursuit of profit.

81. "Virginias Verger," 1826.

17

Pilgrims

In the 1620s, representatives of three very different groups of European migrants—English Protestant dissenters from the Church of England, Spanish Franciscans, and French Jesuits—sought to spread Christianity across North America. Each hoped to spearhead efforts that emphasized faith more than economics. They employed different methods, none more dramatic than the Franciscans who hauled the contents of an entire church from Mexico City to Santa Fe. They also at times relied on miracles, including, in the Southwest, the spectral appearance of Maria Agreda, a bi-locating Spanish nun whose body never left her Spanish convent but whose presence, so Christian believers claimed, helped to bring Natives to the joys of baptism.

While the desire to spread Christianity was widespread among European monarchs and governments, the French and Spanish expected that the major burden would fall on professional religious, especially Catholic missionaries who had taken vows of poverty and celibacy. Royal subjects in Spain and France, Catholic nations riven by religious disputes, saw the Western Hemisphere as a new field for converts who would be transformed by those who had made the expansion of Roman Catholicism the central purpose of their lives. Dominicans and other Catholic missionaries had been working among Indigenous Americans since Columbus dispatched Fray Ramón Pané, of the Order of St. Jerome, to Hispaniola to convert Tainos. Religious missions to the west, like other Catholic missions to the east, aimed to bring those ignorant of Christian scripture into the faith. Jesuits and Recollets (or Recollects) embraced the same goal, though persistent religious tension within France and the undesirability of the St. Lawrence Valley to potential colonists hampered their efforts.[1]

1. Ramón Pané, *An Account of the Antiquities of the Indians*, trans. Susan C. Griswold (Durham, NC: Duke University Press, 1999), xiii–xiv; Christian Le Clercq, *First Establishment of the Faith in New France*, trans. John G. Shea, 2 vols. (New York, 1881); Jonathan D. Spence, *The Memory Palace of Matteo Ricci* (New York: Viking Penguin, 1984); Liam M. Brockey, *Journey to the East: The Jesuit Mission to China, 1570–1724* (Cambridge, MA: Harvard University Press, 2008).

To advance what they saw as their god's work, they worked alongside European soldiers and colonists. They saw themselves as the spiritual heirs of medieval Crusaders who had gone to war to advance the cross.

By contrast, English dissenters crossed the Atlantic with a competing, but just as fierce, agenda. They claimed they were eager to convert Indigenous to their avowedly anti-Rome Protestant interpretation of Scripture. But they saw themselves as a religious minority persecuted by the Church of England. As a result, their quest differed from that of Catholic missionaries adhering to the idea that the ruler's faith demanded strict allegiance (*cuius regio, eius religio*).

In sending emissaries abroad, the Protestant dissenters known as puritans and the Leiden emigrants, often called "Pilgrims" after a reference by Governor William Bradford,[2] had a three-part mission: to halt the spread of Roman-style practice in North America; to spread what they saw as proper religious ideas to Indigenous Americans; and, in the process, to show the world—including English women and men who never emigrated—how the entire body of Christ could live godly lives, which the dissenters believed was no longer possible within the Church of England. These migrants saw Roman Catholics as in thrall to a clerical hierarchy that promised salvation for those who would follow steps laid out by a priest. By contrast, these intellectual heirs of theologians like Martin Luther and John Calvin eschewed the idea of a divinely chosen elite able to provide guidance. Instead, they turned to books, including many that dwelled on the question of predestination. They spent countless hours interrogating themselves and others about possible signs of salvation.

For all their differences, European Catholics and Protestants in the Western Hemisphere had two things in common. Both were beneficiaries of epidemics that had devastated Indigenous communities. And both took steps to sacralize a landscape they saw as godless, using the rhetoric of pilgrimage to justify their conquest and enhance their nations' struggles against other Europeans.

In 1619, James I's council, following precedent for the Chesapeake, issued a patent for a territory the English then called Northern Virginia.[3]

2. William Bradford, *Of Plimoth Plantation*, ed. Kenneth P. Minkema et al. (Boston: Colonial Society of Massachusetts, 2020), 3n.

3. "Warrant to Prepare a Patent for the Northern Company of Virginia," in John Poor, *A Vindication of the Claims of Sir Ferdinando Gorges as the Father of English Colonization in America* (New York, 1862), 108–109. Since the time of Henry VIII, the term "letter patent" (often shortened to "patent") and "charter" had become interchangeable in the conveyance of permission to lay claim to territory.

The next year about forty investors based in Plymouth, including Ferdinando Gorges, who had been involved with the earlier English effort to establish a colony on the Maine coast, launched plans to create a colony to be called New England in America. It was to stretch from 40° to 48° north latitude from the Atlantic across the continent, a shift in strategy from the earlier patent that had defined a westward limit for Virginia. The English drew on the existing European doctrine of discovery, which allowed Europeans to claim lands not occupied by any Christian nation. The group, which contended that its primary goal was to convert Indigenous "unto the true worship: of god & Christian Religion," proved far more eager to create its own government and divide the land as it saw fit.[4] The company's directors promised that all migrants would sign the oath of supremacy recognizing the king as the head of the church, a plan that would prevent Catholics or religious dissenters from joining the venture. The company also wanted to prevent any expansion of the land controlled by the Virginia Company. They got their permission to launch a colony just after the epidemic in coastal New England that had left, as one put it, "those large and goodly Territoryes, deserted as it were by their natural Inhabitants" and hence available for the king's subjects.[5]

The English saw the epidemic as divine intervention. Captain John Smith wrote that "God had laid this Country open for us, and slaine the most part of the inhabitants by cruell warres and a mortal disease; for where I had seene 100 or 200 people, there is scarce ten to be found." He claimed that there were fewer than twenty Natives in the area between Penobscot Bay and Casco Bay, another thirty between there and Cape Ann, and only about forty from Salem Harbor to the Charles River. He added that none of the English became ill, but that one Frenchman had

4. The patent, dated November 3, 1620, is in CO 5/902, 1–28, esp. 2 (Gorges's role), 3 (name of the proposed colony), and 26 (conversion). See also Charles E. Clark, *The Eastern Frontier: The Settlement of Northern New England, 1610–1763* (New York: Knopf, 1970), 1617; Charles M. Andrews, *The Colonial Period of American History*, 4 vols. (New Haven, CT: Yale University Press, 1934), 1:320–326. The expansive claim was even broader than that understood by Smith, who thought that New England should run from 41° to 45° north latitude; see Smith, "Letter to Francis Bacon," in Philip L. Barbour, ed., *The Complete Works of Captain John Smith* (Chapel Hill: University of North Carolina Press for the Institute of Early American History and Culture, 1986), I:378.

5. CO 1/1, no. 47, March 3, 1620; John Latimer, *The Annals of Bristol in the Seventeenth Century* (Bristol: William George's Sons, 1900), 73; *Acts of the Privy Council of England* (London, 1967–), vol. 38 (1932), 51; "A Letr to Thomas Coventrie," November 3, [1620], in Poor, *Vindication,* 109–119, quotation at 110.

succumbed to the disease.[6] The illness altered both the demography and psychology of the region. One English traveler reported that the epidemic combined with internecine warfare reduced the Indigenous population by 95 percent.[7] In 1623, one visitor to Cape Cod claimed that there had been 2,000 Natives in Patuxet a few years earlier, but "not one living now."[8] English lawyer Thomas Morton later wrote that the "hand of God fell heavily" on the Ninnimissinuok "with such a mortall stroake that they died on heapes as they lay in their houses and the living," taking so many lives that they were unable to bury the dead. "Crowes, Kites and vermin" feasted on the corpses.[9]

English observers believed that the epidemic increased chances for a colony's survival in this territory, not far from where the 1607 colony had surrendered in the face of relentless cold on the Maine coast. They also hoped that surviving Native residents of the epidemic-scarred territory would accept the proselytizing plans of newcomers.[10] As Gorges recognized, the decline in the number of Indigenous and relentless propaganda about the resources along America's East Coast provided an opportunity for success, not a guarantee that the migrants' plans would succeed. Colonization remained available to those who would seek chances, just as it had seemed in the 1570s and again in 1607 at Sagadahoc and Jamestown. The trick was to figure out when possibilities remained open. In that effort, few were as well positioned as Gorges, an adventurer who knew—and learned from—the three Eastern Abenakis who had lived with him in 1607. He also knew how to use his clout to support a new colony.[11]

6. John Smith, *New Englands Trials*, 2nd ed. (London, 1622), sig. [B4^r]. For the modern place-names, see Barbour, ed., *Complete Works of Captain John Smith*, I:428n. Smith likely knew of the epidemic by 1619 but did not mention it in the first edition of *New Englands Trials* (London, 1620).
7. "Cushman's Discourse," in John Masefield, ed., *Chronicles of the Pilgrim Fathers* (London: J. M. Dent and Sons, 1910), 229–230.
8. Emmanuel Altham to Sir Edward Altham, September 1623, in Sydney V. James Jr., ed., *Three Visitors to Early Plymouth* (Plymouth, MA: Plimoth Plantation, 1963), 29.
9. Thomas Morton, *New English Canaan* (Amsterdam, 1637), 23.
10. See Robert E. Moody, ed., *The Letters of Thomas Gorges, Deputy Governor of the Province of Maine, 1640–1643* (Portland: Maine Historical Society, 1978); Ferdinando Gorges, *A briefe Relation of the Discovery and Plantation of New England* (London, 1622), sig. B^r; Ferdinando Gorges, "A Briefe Narration of the Originall Undertakings of the Advancement of Plantations into the Parts of America," in *America Painted to the Life* (London, 1658), 11.
11. CO 1/1, March 3, 1620; CO 1/2, no. 14, December 30, 1622; *Records of the Council for New England* (Cambridge, MA, 1867), 59–60, 63; Peter C. Mancall, *The Trials of Thomas Morton: An Anglican Lawyer, His Puritan Foes, and the Battle for a New England* (New Haven, CT: Yale University Press, 2019), 91–95.

Over the next two years, the Council for New England created elaborate plans for colonizing the coastal territory that had already been described by both Champlain and Smith. They negotiated with sea captains to transport cows, swine, poultry, goats, fishing equipment, and salt. They discussed recruiting 100 children from the streets of London, presumably to act as servants, and laid out rules prohibiting the abuse of any Indigenous. Members of the gentry, including the Lord Duke of Richmond as well as the earls of Arundel and Surrey, Middlesex, Warwick, Holderness, and Carlisle, signed on to the venture.[12]

Three years after receiving the original patent, the council dispatched Ferdinando Gorges's son Robert to the region bearing the title of governor-general of New England, a moniker that suggested more authority than he had.[13] They sent him west knowing that he would encounter other English migrants who had gotten there first.

In the waning summer days of 1620, English dissenters living in Leiden decided to cross the Atlantic. They had first gone east to the Netherlands to flee persecution from the Church of England, but at least 100 of them, and likely more of the total community of about 400, concluded that their chances for religious freedom would be greater in New England. They pooled resources and borrowed funds to pay for two ships. Shortly before sailing across the open ocean, they realized that one of the two vessels was unlikely to survive the journey. On September 6, 1620, about 100 members of the congregation, along with assorted non-Pilgrims, departed from Plymouth on the *Mayflower*. After a long and difficult journey, they reached Cape Cod on November 9. William Bradford, the prime chronicler of the community's history, wrote that the view of the shore "much comforted us, especially, seeing so goodly a Land, and wooded to the brinke of the sea, it caused us to rejoice together, and praise God that had given us once again to see land." The travelers stayed near modern Provincetown for five weeks, then sailed to the Wampanoag town of Patuxet, which the migrants called New Plymouth.[14]

12. CO 1/2, no. 14, December 30, 1622; *Records of the Council for New England*, 67, 73–79, 85, 89, 96.
13. Bradford, *Of Plimouth Plantation*, 248–250; Gorges, "Briefe Narration"; see also "Records of the Council for New England," *Proceedings of the American Antiquarian Society*, 1857, 59; Andrews, *Colonial Period*, 1:338–343; and Henry S. Burrage, *Beginnings of Colonial Maine, 1602–1658* (Portland, ME: State of Maine, 1914), 156–157.
14. William Bradford, *A Relation or Journall of the Beginning and Proceedings of the English Plantation Setled at Plimoth in New England* (London, 1622), [1]; George D. Langdon Jr.,

While anchored in November, many of those on board agreed to certain principles for self-government, which became known as the Mayflower Compact. Signatories to the pact asserted that they had sailed across the ocean for "the glory of God, and advancement of the Christian Faith and honour of our King and Countrey." They had arrived to "plant the first Colony in the Northerne parts of VIRGINIA." With their signatures they agreed, in the eyes of the almighty and one another, to form into "a civill body politicke" for their common good and that they would follow all laws passed there. They chose John Carver, who had previously been a merchant in London but had migrated to Leiden in 1610, to be their first governor. But in April 1621, Carver became ill when working in a field on a hot day. After complaining of a splitting headache, he lay down and, as Bradford wrote, "within a few hours his senses failed." He died just days later. Bradford became both the colony's political leader and its ablest historian.[15]

The Leiden migrants were a subset of the larger group of dissenters known as puritans. The differences between the two groups hinged on close reading of scripture and religious commentaries, particularly relating to whether it was acceptable to become Separatists or whether such an act constituted a schism, which was unacceptable (the view of the other puritans as well as of the Church of England). The Leiden congregation avoided that problem by arguing that the Church of England was not a legitimate church—in part because it mandated that everyone be a member, which these dissenters believed violated the notion that a church should be a gathering together of the individuals their god had chosen for salvation. Since such membership policies stood as a holy affront to those who believed in predestination (and, hence, whose ultimate fate could not be changed through good acts or prescribed rituals), it was permissible to become Separatists. In contrast, religious dissidents who chose to remain in England criticized the Anglican establishment but still believed that, despite the corruption they saw around them, a legitimate church could be rescued.[16]

Pilgrim Colony: A History of New Plymouth, 1620–1691 (New Haven, CT: Yale University Press, 1966), 12–14.

15. Bradford, *Relation or Journall*, 3; Bradford, *Of Plimouth Plantation*, 190.
16. As Michael P. Winship put it, the puritans believed that they saw about them a legitimate church that could still be rescued because "within the bloated, corrupt, putrefying body of episcopacy there were the ghostly breathings of real churches." See Michael P. Winship, *Godly Republicanism: Puritans, Pilgrims, and a City on a Hill* (Cambridge, MA: Harvard University Press, 2012), esp. 60–64 (quotation at 63); Edmund Morgan, *Visible Saints: The History of a Puritan Idea* (orig. pub. 1963; Ithaca, NY: Cornell University Press, 1965), 17–32.

Once they landed, Bradford realized the magnitude of the challenge they faced. When he settled down to describe the experience some years later, he drew on his deep knowledge of Scripture. "Being thus passed the vast ocean, and a sea of troubles before in their preparation"—a reference to the community's prior difficulties in Europe as well as perhaps to chapter 10 of the book of Zechariah—he proclaimed that the migrants "had now no friends to welcome them nor inns to entertain or refresh their weatherbeaten bodies; no houses or much less towns to repair to, to seek for succor." Using a common strategy among writers with a religious bent, he employed biblical analogies. He turned to Acts 28, which taught that it was "a mercy to the apostle and his shipwrecked company, that the barbarians showed them no small kindness in refreshing them." He then adapted that notion to his new circumstances. "These savage barbarians," he wrote in reference to the Ninnimissinuok, "were readier to fill their sides full of arrows than otherwise," a description driven by his fears rather than an accurate assessment of any threat they faced.[17]

The dissenters arrived late in the year, with winter upon them, "and they that know the winters of that country, know them to be sharp and violent," Bradford recalled, and "subject to cruel and fierce storms, dangerous to travel to known places, much more to search an unknown coast." Despite the devastations of the recent epidemic, which he acknowledged in his history of the colony, he found New England "a hideous and desolate wilderness, full of wild beasts and wild men—and what multitudes there might be of them they knew not." The new migrants could not, Bradford wrote, "go up to the top of Pisgah to view from this wilderness a more goodly country to feed their hopes"—a reference drawn from Deuteronomy 34:1–5. Unlike Moses, who could look down onto the promised land but not descend to enjoy it, the migrants saw only menace, "for which way soever they turned their eyes (save upward to the heavens) they could have little solace or content in respect of any outward objects."[18]

The moment held little promise, Bradford lamented, "for summer being done, all things stand upon them with a weather-beaten face, and the whole country, full of woods and thickets, represented a wild and savage hue." Bradford intended the reader of his book to grasp the unique sense of foreboding that comes from being lost in a dense wood. If the migrants "looked behind them," he continued, "there was the mighty Ocean which they had passed and was now as a main bar and gulf to separate them from all the Civil parts of the world." They were no longer adrift, but they were more alone than any of them had been before. But, Bradford wrote, drawing on Psalm 107, there was one sure way forward.

17. Bradford, *Of Plimouth Plantation*, 179.
18. Bradford, *Of Plimouth Plantation*, 179.

"What could now sustain them," he asked rhetorically, "but the spirit of God and his grace?"[19]

Bradford's take on the initial moments of colonization revealed the terror felt by some of the migrants. As they would soon learn, they had arrived in an ideal place to create a colony. Fields once cleared by local Indigenous farmers had not yet become overgrown with forest. There was clean water, which gave these English an advantage over those who had gone to Jamestown or remained in crowded towns and cities at home. And there were abundant fur-bearing mammals to be captured, their pelts sent home to pay off the debts that the Pilgrims had accrued to finance their migration.[20] Bradford would have dismissed such a naturalistic explanation. As he saw it, his community survived despite the dangers only because a forgiving god had planned for this to happen, just as that beneficent deity had designed all events to unfold. From that premise, Bradford knew, moving forward demanded obeisance to their god.

Despite their suspicions and fears, the English kept to their plans. In late December they staked out ground for a new town, even though many of them were suffering from ailments exacerbated by the cold. Bradford was among those who thought he might die, but he recovered. They organized for their own defense, appointing Miles Standish as their captain. In late February they hauled some of their cannon from the ship, preparing for assaults they were sure would occur. They also surveyed the nearby territory, finding abandoned houses and fields. Some of them robbed Indigenous graves and uninhabited houses. Time and again they took stored corn, planning to use it for seed when the time approached. "This was our first discovery," an observer known as G. Mourt wrote. They took it as a sign from their god, "for else we know not how we should have done, for we knew not how we should find or meet with any Indians, except it be to do us mischief."[21] The dissenters' greatest fear seemed to be realized during their first winter, when half of the migrants perished.[22]

19. Bradford, *Of Plimouth Plantation*, 179–180.

20. See William Cronon, *Changes in the Land: Indians, Colonists, and the Ecology of New England* (New York: Hill and Wang, 1983), 19–33.

21. Dwight B. Heath, ed., *Mourt's Relation: A Journal of the Pilgrims at Plymouth* (Cambridge, MA: Applewood Books, 1986), 42–43 (cold and recovery), 49 (Standish), 50 (assaults), 20–26 (planting), 24 ("discovery"), 26 ("mischief"), 34. The author of the report was likely Edward Winslow, perhaps at Bradford's urging. The manuscript reached England with Robert Cushman, who had been a deacon at the Pilgrims' church in Leiden; he returned to London in late 1621, and the book appeared in print the next year; see Heath, ed., *Mourt's Relation*, xi–xiii.

22. Langdon, *Pilgrim Colony*, 12–14.

On March 16, 1621, the Eastern Abenaki headman Samoset approached the newcomers. "He saluted us in English, and bade us welcome," Mourt reported, "for he had learned some broken English among the Englishmen that came to fish at Monchiggon," probably a reference to Monhegan Island. He claimed to be a sagamore or headman from that region who had spent the previous months nearby. "He told us the place where we now lived is called Patuxet," the Englishman wrote, "and that about four years ago all the inhabitants died of an extraordinary plague, and there is neither man, woman, nor child remaining." The English took the absence of occupants as a signal that "there is none to hinder our possession, or to lay claim unto it."[23]

The next day Samoset led the English to Massasoit, the sachem of the Wampanoags. (Massasoit, the name by which the English knew him, was actually his title; his name was Ousamaquin.) Before they arrived, he explained that there were tensions between the Wampanoags and the Nausets. He emphasized that many Indigenous in the region bore ill will toward the English because of the actions of a man named Thomas Hunt, "a master of a ship, who deceived the people, and got them under color of trucking with them." Hunt had captured twenty of the residents of Patuxet and seven Nausets, "and carried them away, and sold them for slaves."[24]

In the days that followed, these English visitors learned a great deal about the Indigenous peoples of this part of the shoreline, from Samoset and Tisquantum (also known as Squanto), the last known survivor of Patuxet and one of the Natives who had been enslaved by Hunt. Tisquantum had, in the years since his capture, spent time in England, an experience that enabled him to be a translator when the Pilgrims met Massasoit. Mourt reported that the Wampanoags and the English agreed to coexist. The two groups would return stolen tools, provide military support if the other was attacked, and leave their weapons behind when they met each other.[25]

Over the course of the summer of 1621, Tisquantum earned the trust of the English, accompanying them on expeditions to other towns. He went with them to visit the Nausets to help them negotiate the return of an English boy who had been taken captive. The English went to Nemasket on behalf of Massasoit, in part to avenge what they believed had been the

23. Heath, ed., *Mourt's Relation*, 51.
24. Heath, ed., *Mourt's Relation*, 52.
25. Heath, ed., *Mourt's Relation*, 55–58, quotation at 57; Andrew Lipman, *Squanto: A Native Odyssey* (New Haven, CT: Yale University Press, 204), 101–111.

murder of Tisquantum, a rumor that turned out to be false.[26] That spring, the English planted twenty acres of maize and six acres of peas and barley, using herring as manure "according to the manner of the Indians." At some point in that season Massasoit and ninety of his men visited the English. They remained together for three days, feasting on fowl the English had taken and venison brought by the Wampanoags. The event would later become celebrated as the first Thanksgiving. Colonist Edward Winslow reported that Indigenous and English lived in peace.[27] "I make no question," Winslow emphasized, "but men might live as contented here as in any part of the world." From his perspective, all that was missing were "industrious men to employ," a perfect solution to the problem of an overcrowded England and an underpopulated New England.[28]

These migrants had little trouble justifying taking Wampanoag land. Even still, sensing there might be opposition, Robert Cushman, one of the leaders of the Leiden community and an architect of the migration to New England, offered a defense against possible arguments about the seizing of Indigenous territory. Drawing on Genesis 12:1–2 and 35:1, he believed that Scripture provided explicit guidance about their god's intent in such situations. "But some will say," as Mourt reported his argument, "what right have I to go live in the heathens' country?" Setting aside what he saw as the undisputed English claim to land that stretched "from the Cape of Florida unto the Bay of Canada," Cushman's argument pivoted on the larger goal of converting local Algonquian-speakers. Genesis 13:6, 11, 12; 34:21; and 41:20 instructed that people had the right to move from crowded places to those that were "more roomy, where the land lay idle and waste, and none used it, though there dwelt inhabitants by them." By this reasoning, "so is it lawful now to take a land which none useth, and make use of it." To him, New England "is a common land or unused, and undressed country." He also claimed that Massasoit, who controlled territory probably larger than England and Scotland combined, "acknowledged the King's Majesty of England to be his master and commander." He added that sagamores in other communities, including among the Nausets, Narragansetts, and Nemaskets as well as those who lived along the waters of Massachusetts and Patuxet, had also voluntarily accepted James as their sovereign. Cushman believed New England was "a vast and

26. Heath, ed., *Mourt's Relation*, 69–72 (English boy), 73–79 (Tisquantum).
27. Heath, ed., *Mourt's Relation*, 82–83.
28. Heath, ed., *Mourt's Relation*, 81–85, quotation at 84.

empty chaos" that was theirs to occupy since James I had given them a charter.[29]

The argument for why the English claimed a right to establish colonies in an already settled part of the world rested on notions that many of the migrants knew to be false. Part of their claim lay in the belief that most of New England was *vacuum domicilium* or vacant land. But other than the loss of population in the recent epidemic, there was no evidence that the region lacked inhabitants. Surviving Ninnimissinuok taught the English the best ways to grow maize, provided seed, showed how to store surplus corn, understood the seasons for harvesting aquatic resources, and knew how to catch fur-bearing animals that Europeans prized. They had changed the landscape to meet their needs, and those alterations—such as clearing forests for fields—survived longer in some instances than the human communities that created them. The epidemic reduced the population, but it did not create chaos.[30]

But the thinning of the population did create an opportunity for the English. Cushman's claim that Massasoit controlled territory more expansive than that of James I was not a boast about Indigenous power. Instead, he made the point to expand the authority of the English since, by the reckoning of these migrants in New Plymouth, James I controlled all territory of his subordinates. Cushman and other writers emphasized Massasoit's subjectship to James because it enabled the English to claim a far larger section of the American continent than the relatively small number of actual migrants could control. The author of *Mourt's Relation* sought to convince hesitant English to cross the Atlantic. New England, a reader would learn, was not another Jamestown, where the presence of local Indigenous peoples posed a continual threat.

Despite the newcomers' claims about Natives' acceptance of their presence, growing tension between the New Plymouth colonists and the Massachusetts soon led to bloodshed. In 1623, Standish led a raid into the land of these Algonquian-speakers, killing six or seven. The soldiers brought home the head of the Massachusett leader and set it atop their fort. Instead of a flag, they flew a piece of linen stained with the blood of the headman.[31] Despite the raid, Bradford feared that relations with the Narragansetts might be deteriorating quickly. He attributed rising tension

29. Heath, ed., *Mourt's Relation*, 89, 91–92, 95.
30. See Cronon, *Changes in the Land*, 19–53, 56–57.
31. Emmanuel Altham to Sir Edward Altham, September 1623, and March 1623/1624, in James, ed., *Three Visitors*, 23–41.

to Tisquantum spreading rumors—including that the colonists "kept the plague buried in the ground, and could send it amongst whom they would." The fears of hostile neighbors coexisted with the return in 1623 of food shortages, reminding Bradford of depictions of dearth in the time of Jacob: "Go buy us food," he wrote in his history, drawing from Genesis 42:2 and 43:1, "that we may live and not die."[32]

By 1623, the residents of New Plymouth had erected a fort as well as a blockhouse. They were less successful recruiting ministers, which likely explained why there were only fifty members of the church after that first terrible winter.[33] In 1623 ninety new colonists arrived from Europe, thirty of them from the congregation at Leiden. Among the others were ten known as "particulars," who, having paid their own way, were not part of the company or members of the church at Plymouth.[34] Some of these non-Pilgrims had dreams of becoming "great men and rich all of a sudden," as Bradford sneered, but they agreed to leave the fur trade alone, at least until the community decided it could move away from its initial corporate mode of settlement, known as the "communality."[35] One small group of colonists followed a London ironmonger to set up a small outpost they called Wessagusset at a place the dissenters would later call Mount Wollaston after a man known only as Captain Wollaston, who soon departed for Virginia. Bradford was delighted when this community collapsed, which he attributed to the fact that some cavorted with local Native women, while "others (so base were they) became servants to the Indians." These English migrants tried to survive by selling off their possessions, but "they came to that misery that some starved and died with cold and hunger," Bradford reported, adding that one man out gathering shellfish had died stuck in the mud, while others had become so desperate that they combed the ground for nuts.[36]

32. Bradford, *Of Plimouth Plantation*, 214–215, 245.
33. The church in Plymouth did not have many members for decades; there were only forty-seven in the late 1660s. Bradford, *Of Plimouth Plantation*, 111; John Pory to the Earl of Southampton, January 13, 1622/1623, and later, and Emmanuel Altham to Sir Edward Altham, September 1623, in James, ed., *Three Visitors*, 11, 24; Mark A. Peterson, "The Plymouth Church and the Evolution of Puritan Religious Culture," *NEQ* 66 (1993), 570–593. For those early tensions, see Phineas Pratt, *A Declaration of the Affairs of the English People That First Inhabited New England*, ed. Richard Frothingham (Boston, 1858). Pratt offered a detailed retrospective of the early years of Plymouth in a manuscript he wrote in 1662, which Increase Mather later used in 1677.
34. Winship, *Godly Republicanism*, 119–123; Langdon, *Pilgrim Colony*, 17–20.
35. Bradford, *Of Plimouth Plantation*, 247; Langdon, *Pilgrim Colony*, 17–20.
36. Bradford, *Of Plimouth Plantation*, 231–234, quotation at 231.

When they began their migration from Leiden in 1620, the dissenters knew that they would face myriad challenges. After news of the events along the James had circulated by the middle of 1622, those already in New England and others yet to depart had new reason to wonder about their Native as well as colonizing European neighbors. A growing Dutch presence along the Hudson, which became more evident by 1626, added to the list of potential external threats. If, as Bradford had written in his history, the migrants believed that the Atlantic served to block their access to Europe in a rhetorical if not realistic sense, the residents of New Plymouth needed to pay close attention to the actions of individuals like Tisquantum, Samoset, and Massasoit lest they turn on the newcomers like other Indigenous had on the English who arrived at Sagadahoc.

Given the small number of migrants to New Plymouth, it would not take many individuals to create problems that could undermine the entire venture. Bradford and others in the community understood that potential threats existed even among the English, some of whom aired complaints about the failures of the new colony, including the fact that these expatriates had yet to secure a permanent minister and lacked the ability to learn either the catechism or how to read. They even complained about local mosquitoes, though Bradford believed that annoyance would dissipate since "the more the land is tilled, and the woods cut down, the fewer there will be, and in the end scarce any at all." While he was wrong on that last prediction, his understanding of local ecology was precise: a decrease in wetlands, a by-product of the extension of European-style farming, would have lessened the number of mosquitoes in the area, though this deforestation had far-reaching consequences for the regional climate.[37]

While many migrants feared Indigenous residents, the greatest threat to New Plymouth came from colonists in their own ranks. Bradford, who understood the precarious nature of the little town, reacted strongly to two non-Pilgrim migrants, John Oldham and a minister named John Lyford, who Bradford believed had been undermining the settlement. He likened Lyford to a villain from the Book of Jeremiah who "went out weeping and met them that were coming to offer incense in the house of the Lord, saying 'Come to Gedaliah' when he meant to slay them."[38] Bradford knew about their plans to seduce others into their "fool's paradise" because he intercepted a series of long letters they had dispatched to London on the eastward-bound *Charity* in 1624. Bradford found Lyford's

37. Bradford, *Of Plimouth Plantation*, 260–262, quotation at 262. On the decline of wetlands and the long-term impact, see Cronon, *Changes in the Land*, 122–126.
38. Bradford, *Of Plimouth Plantation*, 269–270, with scriptural references to Psalm 10:10 and Jeremiah 41:6.

messages, "large and full of slanders and false accusations," to be aimed at the "ruin and utter subversion" of the colony. Bradford's allies copied the letters and sent the copies to England, holding on to the originals so that they could more effectively prosecute the authors. These men, the governor concluded, "intended a reformation in church and commonwealth, and as soon as the ship was gone, they intended to join together and have the sacraments, etc." Soon they even called their own meeting on a Sunday, a sign that they had decided "now publicly to act, what privately they had been long plotting"—namely, the establishment of the Church of England in New Plymouth.[39]

With the letters in hand, Bradford hauled Lyford and Oldham into court in the summer of 1624 and confronted them with the evidence against them. At first the defendants demurred and then countered that they were the victims and that the authorities had plotted to deprive them of their right to live peacefully. In the end, those in court heard the letters. Lyford confessed; the court exiled him. Oldham, whose crime was a bit murkier since his handwriting was too poor for anyone to know exactly what he had in mind, was allowed to stay for another six months before he too had to leave. Although they were gone, some of their associates remained, splintering off New Plymouth to establish their own small outposts along the shore.[40]

With the threat averted, the dissenters had time, as Bradford put it, to enjoy "peace and health and contented minds." They produced surplus corn in 1624, which they sent up the Kennebec to obtain furs. The traders returned bearing 700 pounds of beaver and other furs, proof that these religious migrants could, if unburdened by other claimants, secure trade with Algonquian-speakers along the shores. They soon expanded their

39. Bradford, *Of Plimouth Plantation*, 271–273.

40. Bradford, *Of Plimouth Plantation*, 273–288. Bradford did not provide the date of the trial, but noted that Lyford wrote a letter on August 22, 1624, "a month or two" after its conclusion; see Bradford, *Of Plimouth Plantation*, 280–282, quotation at 280. After the court's sentence Lyford, having been discovered to be a serial adulterer by his wife, moved to Virginia, where he took up a ministerial post at Martin's Hundred; Oldham, for his part, after trying to return to the Plymouth area, also went to Virginia before heading back north, where a dispute led to his death at the hands of Indigenous, perhaps Pequots since Bradford claimed this was one of the causes of the war of 1637. See William Bradford, *Of Plymouth Plantation*, ed. Samuel Eliot Morison (New York: Alfred A. Knopf, 1952), 169–170n; "Minutes of the Council and General Court, 1622–1629," *VMHB* 31 (1923), 214; Eric Klingelhofer and William Henry, "Excavations at Martin's Hundred Church, James City Country, Virginia: Techniques for Testing a 17th Century Church Site," *Historical Archaeology* 19 (1985), 98; Ivor Noël Hume, *Martin's Hundred* (Charlottesville: University Press of Virginia, 1991), 64–65; Winship, *Godly Republicanism*, 122–133.

contacts with Dutch at New Amsterdam, and three of the colony's leaders—Bradford, the colony's military commander, Myles Standish, and Bradford's assistant, Isaac Allerton—formed into a company. They assumed all the remaining debts the colony still had in exchange for access to a pinnace recently constructed at Manomet, a shallop, some trade goods, and exclusive control of the fur trade for six years. The group enlisted more partners in London and received a patent for land on the Kennebec, where they soon set up a trading house.[41]

Their discussions with the Dutch also opened the wampum trade. Before 1628, the English of Plymouth knew little about these strings of polished quahog shells, which could be found only in Narragansett Bay and Long Island Sound. Before the arrival of colonists, Indigenous used wampum in various rituals, such as the condolence rites that preceded formal meetings. Strings could also communicate specific messages, though colonists did not know how to read them. The abundance of quahog shells along the shores of the bay and sound is difficult to fathom. By the eighteenth century some colonial merchants had gathered millions of the small shells. Other enterprising colonists, who similarly saw the importance of the strings, imported glass beads from Europe, often in colors other than the natural white, black, and purple of the shells.[42] The English recognized that, as Bradford wrote, the Pequots and Narragansetts had grown "rich, & potent" by the commerce, adding that "it may prove a drug in time." The Narragansetts in particular embraced the business, producing wampum and selling it to the English, who then used it in the fur trade. The Natives used wampum to purchase guns, initially from Dutch and French traders as well as some English. Soon enough King Charles forbade the English from trading arms to the

41. Bradford, *Of Plimouth Plantation*, 300–301 (quotation at 301), 319–327; "Plymouth Company Accounts" for 1628, signed by Sherley, in *Collections of the Massachusetts Historical Society* 1(1825), 199–201. In his first history of the colony, which he wrote before what became known as *Of Plimouth Plantation*, Bradford reported that the colonists went to visit the Massachusetts "partly to make Peace with them, and partly to procure their trucke." Bradford, *Relation or Journall*, 57.

42. On the merchants' collection of wampum, see Paul Otto, "'This Is That Which . . . They Call Wampum': Europeans Coming to Terms with Native Shell Beads," *Early American Studies* 15 (2017), 1–36; see also Marc Shell, *Wampum and the Origins of American Money* (Urbana: University of Illinois Press, 2013); on the far-reaching impact of colonizers recognizing the utility of wampum, see Neal Salisbury, *Manitou and Providence: Indians, Europeans, and the Making of New England, 1500–1643* (New York: Oxford University Press, 1982), 148–152, and Christopher L. Miller and George R. Hamell, "A New Perspective on Indian-White Contact: Cultural Symbols and Colonial Trade," *JAH* 73 (1986), 311–328.

Natives, though by then the region's Indigenous inhabitants already had guns in their possession.[43]

The dissenters' increased economic success did not allay their leaders' fears that their religious mission faced threats from the other English migrants who migrated to New England. For Bradford, the greatest danger came from the nearby community at Wessagusset. By 1624 or 1625, Captain Wollaston had come and gone, and the small outpost fell under the control of Thomas Morton, an Anglican lawyer and adventurer who had made a quick round-trip journey to New England, probably in 1622, and had returned in 1627 or 1628 to take over Wollaston's homestead, which he soon called Mare Mount because it overlooked the bay.

In late 1628, Morton and a small band of merry followers became an irritant to the dissenters and a direct challenge to their view of a new Christian community. "They fell to great licentiousness, and led a dissolute life," Bradford wrote, "pouring out themselves into all profaneness." Bradford claimed that Morton and his followers engaged in one noxious behavior after another. They gained wealth by trading with the Ninnimissinuok and, as a result, threatened the agreement that Bradford and his partners had signed with the residents of the nascent colony. They erected an eighty-foot maypole, aping pagan rituals that had infuriated dissenters in Britain earlier, and cavorted with the locals, "drinking and dancing about it many days together, Inviting the Indian women for their consorts, dancing and frisking together (Like so many fairies, or furies rather), and worse practices." To Bradford, it looked like the second coming of "the Roman Goddess Flora; or the beas[t]ly practices of the mad Bacchanalians." Morton compounded his crimes by writing salacious poems and attaching them to the maypole as well as singing a bawdy song. Bradford believed that the name of the new settlement was "Merrymount, as if this jollity would have lasted for ever." In this lair of sinfulness, Morton himself reigned as the "Lord of misrule and maintained (as it were) a school of Atheism."[44]

43. Bradford, *Of Plimouth Plantation*, 327–329, quotations at 329.

44. Bradford, *Of Plimouth Plantation*, 329–332, quotations at 332; song verses in Charles Francis Adams, ed., *The New English Canaan of Thomas Morton* (Boston: Prince Society, 1883), 277–280, 279–280; for the height of the pole and the renaming, see Charles Francis Adams, *Three Episodes of Massachusetts History* (Boston, 1896), I:175–177, and Adams, ed., *New English Canaan*, 277. On the debate over maypoles in Britain, see Emma Griffin, *England's Revelry: A History of Popular Sports and Pastimes, 1660–1830* (Oxford: Oxford University Press, 2005), 26; Frederick J. Furnivall, ed., *Phillip Stubbes's Anatomy of the Abuses of England in Shakespeare's Youth, AD. 1583* (London:

Morton's challenge to the dissenters went further than his contempt for their religious practice. By providing guns to the Natives in exchange for furs, he cut into their economic plans and armed their potential enemies. Bradford claimed that once the Ninnimissinuok realized the power of guns, they did not want to use bows and arrows, even though their traditional weapons were likely more accurate. Morton, confronted by Pilgrim authorities, refused to halt such transactions. At the time, he had the law on his side. Only later did the sale by colonists of guns to Natives become a crime in the colony.[45]

Soon enough, the dissenters in and around New Plymouth concluded that Morton and his followers needed to be removed. If they were not, Mare Mount would soon attract, as Bradford put it, "all the scum of the country." To Bradford, the English faced as a great threat from "this wicked, & debased Crew as from the savages themselves." Other colonists agreed. English immigrants in small towns at Piscataqua (New Hampshire), Nantasket, and Naumkeag (Salem), among other locales, sent funds to New Plymouth to organize an action and wrote directly to Morton to change his ways since he was violating a proclamation the king had made in 1622 to crack down on illegal trade with Indigenous. He refused their request and told them that he was prepared to defend the settlement if the others came after him.[46]

New Shakespeare Society, 1877–1879), I:146–150; L. A. Govett, *The King's Book of Sports* (London: E. Stock, 1890), 52–54.

45. Bradford, *Of Plimouth Plantation*, 333–334; on the accuracy of guns of this era, see Joyce E. Chaplin, *Subject Matter: Technology, The Body, and Science on the Anglo-American Frontier, 1500–1676* (Cambridge, MA: Harvard University Press, 2001), 80–81; *Governor William Bradford's Letter Book* (Bedford, MA: Applewood, 2001), 41. King James I, responding to reports of the sale of firearms to Natives in New England, banned what he called "disorderly trading" there in 1622, but the earliest law regulating Native use of guns in Plymouth took effect in 1644, when the colony fined any colonist who repaired "any guns or armes for the Indians," suggesting that at least some already possessed such weapons. In 1651 the colony banned colonists from allowing any Native servants to possess a gun, but it was not until 1676, in a period of widespread war in New England, that providing arms to Natives became a capital crime. See "A Proclamation Prohibiting Interloping and Disorderly Trading to New England in America," November 6, 1622, *Stuart Royal Proclamations, Vol. 1: Royal Proclamations of King James I, 1603–1625*, Oxford Scholarly Editions Online (accessed May 18, 2016); William Brigham, ed., *The Compact and Charter and Laws of the Colony of New Plymouth* (Boston, 1836), 76 (1644), 94 (1651), 178 (1676). Despite any existing laws, Natives acquired firearms soon after Europeans arrived; see Angela R. Riley, "Indians and Guns," *Georgetown Law Journal* 100 (2012), 1675–1745, esp. 1685–1693.

46. Bradford, *Of Plimouth Plantation*, 334–335, quotations at 334; *Bradford's Letter Book*, 41; "A Proclamation Prohibiting Interloping."

Despite the threat, the leaders of New Plymouth organized a small force under Standish and marched on Mare Mount, which then had only seven men in residence, all of whom were inebriated when the Pilgrim soldiers arrived. The arrest took place without incident, except, as Bradford wrote, "one was so drunk, that he ran his own nose, upon the point of a sword that one held before him, as he entered the house; but he lost but a little of his hot blood."[47]

The authorities arrested Morton and deposited him on the Isle of Shoals off modern Portsmouth, New Hampshire, where he presumably survived with the support of Natives and fishing its rich waters. After Morton had been offshore for a month, an English ship picked him up. Bradford sent along a letter to the Council for New England, informing them about Morton's actions at Mare Mount, including the community's fear that Morton's alliance with local Natives increased the threat of attack on New Plymouth. John Endecott, who had just arrived with the seal of the Massachusetts Bay colony and would later be a founder of Salem as well as governor, went to Mare Mount and ordered the maypole cut down. The New Plymouth authorities asked that Morton be prosecuted in England, presumably for violating the king's order about giving arms to the Natives. The whole episode depressed Bradford, even years later. "I have been too long about so unworthy a person," he wrote years later, "and bad a cause."[48]

Morton played a major role in Bradford's history for many reasons, including economic rivalry. But to the governor and other dissenters, his greatest threat was religious. By living apart from the strict confines and structures of a scripturally defined community where residents believed they had embarked on a world-changing quest, Morton demonstrated a different path to colonizing New England. The Pilgrims, aware that other non-puritans continued to cross the ocean, saw themselves in competition for the women and men they needed to bolster their meager population. Migrants going to Mare Mount instead of New Plymouth would do more than enhance the authority of an economic competitor. Such a possible migration struck at the heart of the Pilgrims' understanding of their relationship with the Christian god. If a drunken, obnoxious, and blasphemous man could attract English as well as Indigenous partners, what did that mean for the dissenters' cause? Since the colonists who governed

47. Bradford, *Of Plimouth Plantation*, 335–336, quotation at 336.

48. [Samuel Maverick], *A Briefe Discription of New England and the Several Townes Therein* (Boston, 1885), 10 (this edition is based on Maverick's manuscript of 1660); Bradford, *Of Plimouth Plantation*, 332, 336 (quotation); Morton, *New English Canaan*, 70; *Bradford's Letter Book*, 41–42.

New England looked for scriptural precedents for their actions, behavior that fell outside biblical models necessitated punishments that would have worked for the ancients.[49]

Morton embodied the world that the separatists scorned. To prove the truth of their pilgrimage and convince themselves that they were saints predestined for salvation, Morton had to be eradicated.

During the 1620s, the dissenting Protestants in New Plymouth were not the only Europeans trying to adapt their religious mission to life in North America. Across the continent, similar struggles lay at the heart of the Franciscans' struggle to bring their form of Christian practice northward from New Spain. Unlike the English, these religiously driven migrants had a rich American experience to draw on, including the proliferation of Catholic churches stretching from modern Mexico into Peru.[50] Could that experience, missionaries wondered, be replicated in the territory that had repulsed Coronado and other Spaniards decades earlier?

On January 24, 1626, the Franciscan Alonso de Benavides headed a delegation from Mexico City to Santa Fe, where he was to take up residence as *custodio* of New Mexico. Born in the Azores, Benavides first appeared in the public record as the *alguacil mayor* (sheriff) of the Inquisition in Hispaniola sometime around the turn of the new century. Within three years he had migrated to Mexico City, where he took his vows in the Convent of Nuestro Padre San Francisco. By 1608 he was resident in Veracruz. There he took a direct hand in suppressing idolatry among enslaved Africans, part of what he saw as his job as the Franciscan in charge of reducing non-Christians to the faith. Over subsequent years he took a position in Cuernavaca, perhaps as part of the Inquisition. By 1621 he was in charge of the Convent of San Juan Temamatlac. In 1623, with a

49. In a notorious case from 1642, an indentured servant named Thomas Granger who admitted to bestiality with "a mare, a Cow, two goats, five sheep, 2 calves and a turkey" received the death penalty—but Plymouth's authorities also killed the animals since, according to Leviticus 20:15, they had become inedible. After they threw the dead animals into a pit, they then killed Granger, who was sixteen or seventeen years old. See Bradford, *Of Plimouth Plantation*, 496–497.

50. Churches had appeared on maps of New Mexico from shortly after Cortés's conquest, including maps that blended Mexica and Spanish cartographic traditions; see Jennifer Saracino, "Indigenous Stylistic and Conceptual Innovation in the Uppsala Map of Mexico City (c. 1540)," *Artl@s Bulletin* 7, no. 2 (2018), art. 2, and Mary E. Miller and Barbara E. Mundy, eds., *Painting a Map of Sixteenth-Century Mexico City: Land, Writing, and Native Rule* (New Haven, CT: Yale University Press, 2012), 18, 57.

new commission in hand, this itinerant religious of the Atlantic world set out into New Mexico toward what he hoped was a garden full of converts, but he knew it was more likely a desert of non-believers.[51]

Like the 1609 expedition that launched Santa Fe, the transportation of Benavides's crew to the town became an occasion to restock the outpost. Sixteen wagons headed northward, bearing material objects to create a simulacrum of a Spanish town. In addition to food and building supplies (including 23,000 nails), the bearers hauled materials reflecting Spanish participation in a global economy, including medicines sent from Mexico City the previous year to the Philippines, Castile vinegar, and spices likely from the Southwest Pacific. Each of the twelve Franciscans would get his own lockbox and his own writing case. They dispatched religious items too, including eleven breviaries, eleven Chinese damask frontals "lined with Anjou linen," and eleven chasubles with fringe lined with Castile buckram. They carried valuable religious goods including gold-plated patens and chalices and gilded wooden and brass candleholders along with bassoons, flageolets, and trumpets. Two boxes contained "the pictures, canvasses, and some processional candle holders," likely a reference to the visual aids that priests used to teach catechumens about Catholicism. There were five expensive oil paintings and two wooden crucifixes, each one and a half yards tall. Among the most expensive items was 2,600 yards of sackcloth to make the brothers' robes. There was also an icon of the Virgin.[52]

The parcels testified to the Franciscans' belief that their transportable religion could be reconstituted in a new desert, its cultural values shared through the kinds of material objects to be found in any Catholic church. The missionaries planned to employ images and music along with sermons and rosaries to convey the mysteries of the faith to the unconverted. They did so by aggregating material objects from across the Spanish mercantile world—Rouen and Anjou linen, Flemish locks, Turkish carpets, Chinese damask, Mexican silk and blankets, Michoacán friezes, silver likely from American mines, and gold from melted Aztec icons.

51. *Fray Alonso de Benavides' Revised Memorial of 1634*, trans. and ed. Frederick W. Hodge, George P. Hammond and Agapito Rey (Albuquerque: University of New Mexico Press, 1945), 1–2, and see 4n15 for use of the word "convent" in this context. Benavides wrote two memorials, one in 1630 and a revised version in 1634, addressed to Pope Urban VIII. Unless otherwise noted, all material here comes from the revised, 1634 version.

52. *Benavides' Revised Memorial of 1634*, 109–124. For the use of visual aids to teach the unbaptized, see Daniela Bleichmar, *Visual Voyages: Images of Latin American Nature from Columbus to Darwin* (New Haven, CT: Yale University Press, 2017), 80.

On the stormy evening of January 24, 1626, Benavides and his entourage arrived in Santa Fe. They immediately set to work planning the next day's events: the public reading of the "edicts of our holy Catholic faith," as Fray Pedro de Hortega, a notary who would play a supporting role in the drama, put it. The governor and other officials walked Benavides to his monastic cell, and then paraded through the streets announcing that the next day "the edicts of our holy Catholic faith would be read and published in the parish church of the city." With each announcement they blew bugles and soldiers fired their guns. The next morning, Benavides followed a procession into the church, the assemblage mixing the religious, the civil, and the military.[53]

Benavides understood that the Franciscans and their military allies stood at a decisive point. Oñate had claimed the region a generation earlier, and there had been a colonial presence in Santa Fe for fifteen years. But the town remained the physical embodiment of the colonial predicament—a small village boasting a parish church surrounded by Indigenous Americans. These pilgrims, acolytes of the faith adorned in the fineries of Roman religion, hoped to build their religious edifice hundreds of miles from any sizable non-Indigenous population. There were few soldiers to guard them should relations with local residents sour. New Mexico, despite its name on Spanish maps, remained Indian Country. Spanish authorities like Oñate believed that they had conquered in the name of their state and their religion, with emblems of both displayed on their standards.[54] But no display of flags, sounding of bugles, reading of sermons, notarial signatures, or enacting of rituals had yet made this region resemble the more densely colonized parts of New Spain and Peru.

The Franciscans quickly began to impose their version of the sacral on top of the still-sacred Indigenous landscape. By 1629, the friars had supervised the construction of fifty friaries or churches across New Mexico, where women built the walls and men did the necessary carpentry.[55] Benevides enumerated the numbers of the baptized in one Indigenous nation after another: 7,000 Tiowas, 4,000 Queres, 10,000 of the Tompira,

53. *Benavides' Revised Memorial of 1634*, 127–129. In the twentieth century, one Franciscan's report emphasized that Benavides had made the celebration of an icon of the Virgin known as "La Conquistadora" central to his performance, but Benavides does not mention such an act; see Fray Angelico Chavez, *La Conquistadora: The Autobiography of an Ancient Statue*, revised ed. (Santa Fe, NM: Sunstone Press, 1983), 21–27.
54. Juliana Barr, "There's No Such Thing as 'Prehistory': What the *Longue Duree* of Caddo and Pueblo History Tells Us About Colonial America," *WMQ*, 3d Ser., 74 (2017), 233–234.
55. David J. Weber, The *Spanish Frontier in North America* (New Haven, CT: Yale University Press, 1992), 96–97; *Benavides' Revised Memorial of 1634*, 56–61.

4,000 among the Tanos, 2,000 Pecos, 6,000 among the Tewa, 2,500 at Taos. Wandering into the pueblo the Spaniards had renamed Sevilleta, Benavides found the locals scattered across the hillside, the survivors of a raid from unnamed Indigenous enemies. "I refounded several pueblos which had been burned down during their wars," he wrote. "Thus with their own labor, my efforts and those of my companions, and divine assistance, I succeeded in congregating them, and thus their conversion was facilitated."[56]

After he returned to Spain in 1630, Benavides informed Pope Urban VIII that the Franciscans had spread the faith in the region where the brothers represented a tiny fraction of the population, most of them living by themselves or perhaps with one other religious in churches dispersed throughout the region dominated by Puebloan and Apachean peoples. Following in the spiritual path established by the "seraphic Francis," Benavides wrote, the missionaries "have worked in such a way" during Urban's tenure that "more than 500,000 souls of barbarous Indians have been converted to our holy Catholic faith." He claimed too that multiple histories of the region proved that the religious had "baptized more than fifteen million Indians" in New Mexico alone. The victories had come at a high personal cost to some of the Franciscans, who had become martyrs to the cause, but not before they had saved Natives' lives, defeated the "sorcerer priests" of the Zuni nation, and brought sight to a blind Hopi boy. In the aftermath of this "great miracle," one chronicler recalled, "conversion rose like foam." But local priests poisoned the brother, another martyr.[57] Benavides believed that the long-sought religious conquest of New Mexico had been achieved, with thirty-three churches and convents in the main pueblos and another 150 scattered across the land. As he saw it, "the whole land is dotted with churches, convents, and crosses along the roads."[58]

Benavides exaggerated the success of the church. However energetic and committed to the cause, there were not enough Catholic religious in New Mexico to reach into every pueblo. But just as the building of churches across Spanish America had helped to promote conversion of Mexicas, Incans, and others in the sixteenth century, so too did circulations of the stories of miracles. The most famous was of the Virgin of

56. *Benavides' Revised Memorial of 1634*, 64–67, quotation at 64, 68 (Tewa), 71 (Taos).

57. *Benavides' Revised Memorial of 1634*, 35–36 (500,000 souls), 45, 47, 72–77, quotation at 73; Weber, *Spanish Frontier*, 98–99.

58. *Benavides' Revised Memorial of 1634*, 80–92, quotation at 80.

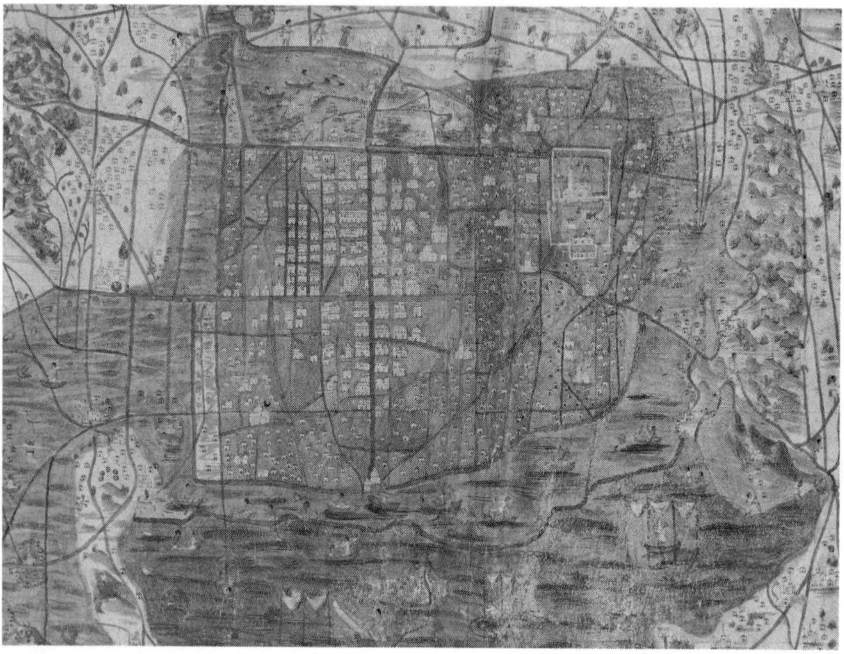

As this detail from the so-called Uppsala map of c. 1540 reveals, Spanish colonizers had erected many churches in Tenochtitlán, a visible sign of what they saw as their successful efforts to expand the boundaries of Christendom into New Spain. Uppsala University Library, World Digital Library.

Guadalupe, who appeared four times to a Nahuatl-speaking Chichimec named Juan Diego near Tenochtitlán in December 1531. Within three weeks of the first sighting, the story of Juan Diego's vision, enhanced by the Virgin's alleged cure of his uncle and the seeming miracle of her appearance on a cloak that the Chichimec man wore to an audience with the archbishop of Mexico City, had begun to spread across New Spain. Opportunistic Catholic religious, once they convinced themselves of the reality of the vision, incorporated the story into their efforts to spread the faith. Given the long acceptance of the miraculous in Roman Catholic practice and the role of marvelous apparitions in the toolkit of evangelicals spreading Christianity across the planet, it did not take long for religious working in the Western Hemisphere to recognize the utility of Marian visions. They soon learned that this Virgin could be of use when trying to teach the miracles of the Bible to peoples whose own religious beliefs included communication with supernatural entities.[59]

59. See Amy G. Remensnyder, *La Conquistadora: The Virgin Mary at War and Peace in the Old and New Worlds* (New York: Oxford University Press, 2014), 330–334; Stafford Poole,

The Roman Catholic miraculous also included the acceptance—after serious interrogation by clerical authorities—of the notion of bi-location. That prior history helped shape the reception of divine assistance in the apparition of a nun named María de Jesús de la Concepción, a Poor Clare from Agreda in Burgos province, about 150 miles north of Madrid in the former kingdom of Castile and León. María de Agreda or Sor María never left her home in Spain, but that did not prevent her spectral arrival in New Mexico. Benavides had heard about her actions when he was living in Santa Fe. In 1629, as he later reported, he welcomed a group of thirty Franciscans who had just been sent to New Mexico from Mexico City. Having had no contact with clerical authorities for four years, he was eager to hear what they had to say. They reported that it was "common news" that Sor María "was miraculously transported to New Mexico to preach our holy Catholic faith to those savage Indians." The Franciscans who met with Benavides were part of an official delegation to investigate the case in 1628, a standard practice following miracles or Marian visions.

Before the delegation's arrival, Benavides had never heard of Sor María, but he began to think carefully about some of his interactions with Indigenous. He understood that a group of Xumana (Jumanos) who lived east of New Mexico, and hence beyond the reach of any of the Franciscans, had arrived in Santa Fé a few days before the Franciscans and asked to be baptized. Benavides asked how they knew to make the request. "Gazing at a portrait of Mother Luisa in the convent," he reported, "they said: 'A woman in similar garb wanders among us over there, always preaching, but her face is not old like this, but young.' " The Franciscans asked them why they had not mentioned her earlier. " 'Because you did not ask us,' " they replied, " 'and we thought she was around here, too." Benavides immediately dispatched the Franciscans to the Xumana nation, where they met locals carrying flowers and a large cross. How, the clerics wondered, did the Natives know to welcome the religious in this way? Because, they replied, Sor María "had instructed them as to how they should come out in procession to receive them, and she had helped them to decorate the cross." Franciscans seized the opening to baptize as many as possible, believing that they were receptive because she had visited them first. Benavides sent additional friars back into the field with them, to build

Our Lady of Guadalupe: The Origins and Sources of a Mexican National Symbol, 1531–1797 (Tucson: University of Arizona Press, 1995), 26–68; Timothy Matovina, *Guadalupe and Her Faithful: Latino Catholics in San Antonio, from Colonial Origins to the Present* (Baltimore: Johns Hopkins University Press, 2005), 1–12; William B. Taylor, "The Virgin of Guadalupe in New Spain: An Inquiry into the Social History of Marian Devotion," *American Ethnologist* 14 (1987), 9–33.

churches and gather the new flock. All the Franciscans believed the woman was María de Jesús.[60]

When he returned to Spain, the minister-general of the Franciscans permitted Benavides to go to Agreda to meet her. She was, he later wrote, not yet twenty-nine years old, with "a beautiful face, very white, although rosy, with large black eyes." Like the other women in her convent, she wore robes like the brothers, though her cloak was blue. When she was a girl, so he reported, a divine revelation had encouraged her to bring enlightenment to the unconverted. Committed to the cause, she "has preached in person our holy Catholic faith in every nation, particularly in New Mexico," borne there with wings from St. Francis and St. Michael. She went to North America for the first time in 1620, when she would have been about eighteen years old, and returned often, sometimes "three and four times in less than twenty-four hours." When asked why she never appeared to the brothers, she replied that there was nothing she could offer them. Only the Indigenous needed to see her, and the angels arranged her visits. "She convinced me absolutely by describing to me all the things in New Mexico as I have seen them myself," he told the pope, "as well as by other details which I shall keep within my soul." In mid-May 1631, Sor María confirmed that angels had taken her to New Mexico. Benavides informed the Franciscans in New Mexico that she reported that all they were doing "was very pleasing to our Lord, as it was all directed to the aim of the conversions, which is the greatest charity." Anxious to document as much as he could about her miraculous feats, Benavides met with others who were also investigating the case. They all believed that she had bilocated across a vast expanse, visiting Xumana, Japies, Quivera, Navaho, Zuñi, and Moqui communities.[61]

Near the end of her life, Sor María testified to another Franciscan that she did not understand how she managed to appear in New Mexico other than through divine intervention. She claimed that she preached in Spanish, which the Natives understood, and was able to catechize them. Others who heard the tale concluded that "she was transported bodily."[62]

60. *Benavides' Revised Memorial of 1634*, 92–95; for the identification of the Jumanos, see Nancy P. Hickerson, "The Visits of the 'Lady in Blue': An Episode in the History of the South Plains, 1629," *Journal of Anthropological Research* 46 (1990), 67–90.

61. *Benavides' Revised Memorial of 1634*, 135–142, 143–146 (letter from Sor Maria), 146–149 (letter from Benavides to the New Mexican Franciscans), 96, quotations at 140, 143, 146, and 96; see also Weber, *Spanish Frontier*, 99–100.

62. The text and context are in Hickerson, "Visits of the 'Lady in Blue,'" 75–76, who noted that the information the Jumanos and other Natives of the southern plains possessed when they met the Franciscans could also be explained by their prior contact with Spanish priests who had been in attendance for the *entradas* of both Cortés

Her story eventually reached King Philip IV. On the verge of being overcome by political strife in the 1640s, he turned to her to serve as an intermediary, urging her to "fulfill your promise of crying out to heaven on my behalf." The nun and the king exchanged 600 letters between 1643 and 1665. She became a spiritual advisor to him, and he kept her letters in a private desk, treating them as if they were holy relics.[63]

Sor María's reputation lasted for generations in North America. An eighteenth-century painting in a Franciscan monastery, now the parish church in Ozumba, Mexico, depicted her writing her epic *Mystical City of God* perched under the left arm of St. Francis.[64] This "Lady in Blue," as she came to be known, remained an inspiration for converts and her story useful for later missionaries, notably Junípero Serra when he launched his church-building campaign in California in 1769.[65]

Benavides's report on what he had seen in New Mexico circulated widely in print. The first edition appeared in Spanish in Madrid in 1630. In 1631, a French translation was published in Brussels and a Dutch edition was printed in Antwerp. The first Latin edition came out in 1634;

and Cabeza de Vaca and then the survival of these ideas within the communities for generations. The Jumanos also, she notes, might have seen the Spanish, particularly the Franciscans, as individuals who might provide protection from attacks from Apache bands, another aspect of life on the southern plains that earlier Spanish chroniclers had described. See Hickerson, "Visits of the 'Lady in Blue,'" 84–85.

63. In 1637, after her alleged visits to New Mexico, she began to write *Mística ciudad de Dios . . . Vida de la Virgen* or *Mystical City of God: A Life of the Virgin*; first published posthumously in 1670, the book has been subsequently published in over 250 editions in multiple languages. The book almost did not survive. Sor María destroyed her own copy when she was being interrogated by the Inquisition, but she had sent a copy to the king, who held it, allowing for its subsequent publication. See Luis R. Corteguera and Sherry Velasco, "Authority in the Margin: Re-Examining the Autograph Letters of Sor Maria de Agreda and Philip IV of Spain," in Jennifer L. Eich et al., eds., *Women's Voices and the Politics of the Spanish Empire: From Convent Cell to Imperial Court* (New Orleans: University Press of the South, 2008), 235–262, quotation at 241.

64. The painting pairs her with Duns Scotus (c. 1266–1308), a Scots theologian who also had an enduring influence among the Franciscans. See Cristina Cruz González, "Our Lady of El Pueblito: A Marian Devotion on the Northern Frontier," *Catholic Southwest: A Journal of History and Culture* 23 (2012), 3–21, esp. 6–7.

65. Anna M. Nogar, "Junípero Serra's Mission Muse: Sor María de Jesús de Ágreda and Her Writings," in Steven W. Hackel, ed., *The Worlds of Juniper Serra: Historical Contexts and Cultural Representations* (Berkeley: University of California Press, 2018), 69–86; Anna M. Nogar, *Quill and Cross in the Borderlands: Sor Maria de Ágreda and the Lady in Blue, 1628—the Present* (South Bend, IN: University of Notre Dame Press, 2018), 206–212; William H. Donahue, "Mary of Agreda and the Southwest United States," *The Americas* 9 (1953), 291–314; Weber, *Spanish Frontier*, 99–100.

Antonio de Castro's 1730 rendering of María de Jesús de Ágreda depicts her, long after her death, as preaching to "Chichimecos," a onetime Nahuatl term that Spaniards had appropriated and used to refer to Indigenous peoples of New Mexico as "uncivilized." Courtesy of the John Carter Brown Library.

others in Brussels and an undated German translation, printed in Salzburg, probably appeared that year too.[66] These printings brought New Mexico into an elite trans-European discussion about the prospects for Catholicism north of Mexico. Among the most eager promoters of her

66. *Benavides' Revised Memorial of 1634*, 18–28.

legend was Benevides, who tried to convince the Vatican to establish a bishopric for New Mexico.

Like Las Casas, Benevides believed that conversion would succeed only if the Spanish stopped abusing Native Americans by forcing them to work. He knew the fragility of the Franciscans' achievement. Their triumphs on the mission field would be short-lived until colonizers stopped kidnapping "Indian boys and girls from the pueblos on the pretext that they are orphans" to make them "serve permanently in the houses of the Spaniards where they remain as slaves." He also wanted to halt the practice of sending Natives captured in wars outside of New Mexico into lives of slavery. Instead, orphans should be allowed to live with their relatives and war captives deposited into convents or "in houses of Spaniards or Indians of exemplary conduct" where they could be converted. He warned against Spanish governors mistreating local leaders and the practice of making secret land grants to colonists who deprived Natives of their land and cattle without any prior notice or approval. While his comments were cloaked in a sincere language of beneficence toward Indigenous, Benavides hoped to change the behavior of secular governors, whom he saw as power-hungry and indifferent to royal proclamations intended to protect all of the king's subjects, including the Indigenous and less prosperous colonists. He hoped to return to New Mexico, but he instead became the auxiliary bishop in Goa, where he likely died. After his death, Franciscans oversaw the construction of San Estévan del Rey in Acoma. The church, begun in 1629 and completed in 1642, stands to this day.[67]

Benavides and Sor María arrived in New Mexico by different routes, but with the same purpose. He trekked heavily, burdened by the expectations and armature of a church establishment that considered him an emissary of the divine, capable of the sacred act of baptism. She traveled more lightly, unable to baptize because of her gender, but capable of flying on the wings of angels.

Franciscans who wanted to spread Roman practice to New Mexico had the advantage of using imperial resources in New Spain to launch their efforts. Jesuits eager to establish missions in the St. Lawrence Valley had more difficulty since they lacked any colonial community to support them. When Champlain was first establishing Québec in 1608, he planned to take religious with him since a central goal of creating a colony was to spread Christianity. Despite an early promise of support by Pierre Coton,

67. *Benavides' Revised Memorial of 1634*, 12–17, 168–190, 199 (departure for Goa); Ward A. Minge, *Ácoma: Pueblo in the Sky* (Albuquerque: University of New Mexico Press, 1991), 20–21.

The church of San Estévan del Rey in Acoma, seen here in a late nineteenth-century photograph, is the oldest Catholic building in New Mexico. Courtesy of the Huntington Library, San Marino, California.

the king's Jesuit confessor, and financial resources from a rich patron, no missionaries arrived in the new town at first. In 1610, the Jesuits Pierre Biard and Énemond Massé agreed to sail from Dieppe, but local Huguenot merchants refused to outfit the ship. In response, Madame de Guercheville, a wealthy supporter, purchased the vessel, which allowed the two brothers to sail to modern Mount Desert Island. But their plans did not survive an assault from the English under the command of Samuel Argall, who arrived in Acadia from Virginia in 1613 to destroy their nascent mission during a raid that also led to the burning of a small French outpost and assaults on French fishing crews.[68]

The early disappointment did not deter Champlain, who continued to believe that the French had three goals in North America: to find the Northwest Passage, to extract resources, and to spread the faith "among an infinite number of souls." But he continued to face severe obstacles

68. David Hackett Fischer, *Champlain's Dream* (New York: Simon and Schuster, 2008), 239–240, 290, 355; *JR*, 3:5–7; Order in Council against Argall, January 2, 1613, in *DRCHNY*, 3:1–2; Seymour V. Connor, "Sir Samuel Argall: A Biographical Sketch," *VMHB* 59 (1951), 162–175, esp. 168.

given the unwillingness of many French to sail to Canada. When he called a meeting of all residents of Québec in August 1621, his invitation went to the approximately sixty men who lived there, and even some from this paltry number refused to show up. The assassination of Henri IV, a Huguenot, at the hands of a Catholic zealot in 1610 had opened an opportunity for Jesuits since the king's successors, Louis XIII and Marie de' Medici, promoted the spread of Catholicism despite their purported tolerance of Protestants, a plank of the 1598 Edict of Nantes intended to end the nation's religious wars. Champlain embraced the cause too, evident when he ordered the burning in Québec of a tract that defamed the ideas of the Jesuit Pierre Coton. The book alleged that the Jesuits and Coton were responsible for Henri IV's murder, a calumny that Champlain could not tolerate.[69]

Despite the intendant's enthusiasm for the Church and the Jesuits, Champlain had little luck in the earliest years recruiting more missionaries. The situation frustrated him since he believed that conversion would help create durable ties with local Indigenous communities. Innu (Montagnais) who controlled the Saguenay Valley (where Champlain hoped to establish colonial farms) opposed his efforts to prevent non-French ships from ascending the St. Lawrence. Understanding how markets worked, the Innu threatened to kill the small number of French colonists. "I will say," Champlain wrote in an account of his voyage of 1620, "that we have no worse enemies than these savages; for they say that, if they were to kill off our men, other vessels would come, the owners of which would be greatly pleased," and the Natives "would themselves be much better off than they are, owing to getting goods more cheaply from the Rochellais or the Basques." By 1622, understanding that he could not simply push Innu out of the way, Champlain made an alliance with a headman named Miristou (also known as Mahigan Aticq), offering French support in exchange for 100 beaver skins. To solidify the new alliance, the intendant presented a lavish feast for the Innu.[70]

While Champlain slowly learned strategies for securing French settlements from Indigenous assault, he made little progress in his goal to

69. H. P. Biggar, ed., *The Works of Samuel de Champlain* (Toronto: Champlain Society, 1922–1936), 2:339–332; Fischer, *Champlain's Dream*, 377 (assembly of residents), 380 (Coton); *Lettre du Pere Charles L'Allemant . . . Envoyee au Pere Hierosme l'Allemant son frere* [Letter from Father Charles L'Allemant . . . Sent to Father Jerome L'Allemant, his brother] (Paris, 1627), in *JR*, 4:209–211; *Anti-Cotton: Or, A Refutation of Cotton's Letter Declaratory; Lately directed to the Queen Regent of France; and Apologizing for the Jesuits touching the Doctrine of Killing KINGS* (London, 1689).

70. Biggar, ed., *Works of Samuel de Champlain*, 5:124–125, 80–81; Fischer, *Champlain's Dream*, 381–382.

spread the faith. Only in the 1630s did an infrastructure exist to transport missionaries to New France and enable them to enter Indigenous communities. Nonetheless, Catholic religious made almost no progress in their efforts to reshape the landscape with churches. Decades later, when French missionaries finally managed to found a chapel in the Mohawk community of Kahnawake in the mid-1670s, a lightning strike demolished it within five years.[71]

In 1629, shortly before he was to join the mainstream migration of Protestant dissenters to New England, John Winthrop wrote a treatise to convince others who shared his religious views to sail across the Atlantic. By then, many English women and men who came to embrace the puritans' cause were living in towns and cities and often involved in clothing trades, an industry that had suffered hard economic times.[72] Facing regular threats from Anglican authorities, and vividly remembering the previous century's religious strife across Europe, Winthrop believed that the time seemed right to take a chance on building new communities abroad. News coming from New Plymouth indicated that English could survive in coastal New England, even if it meant dealing with the occasional miscreant like Thomas Morton.

Winthrop was born for this moment. In 1544, his grandfather Adam Winthrop had purchased the manor of Groton in Bury St. Edmunds in Suffolk. The house had been part of the property the king had confiscated in 1539 while he tried to rid England of the vestiges of Roman Catholicism. Before the Reformation, the town had been a holy ground, the last resting place of the physical remains of St. Edmund, a martyred East Anglian king whose followers had translated his relics there in 903 CE. In 1020, the Benedictines built a magnificent abbey. Pilgrims flocked there for decades, eager to seek divine grace near the "body of the most Christian king Edmund," as the antiquarian William Camden put it. The Reformation altered the situation even at the thriving church of Bury St. Edmunds, where local residents worked with monks to try to preserve the establishment. Within two decades of the initial seizure, the abbey could not be sustained and eventually fell into ruin, a visual symbol of the era of

71. See Gauvin A. Bailey, *Architecture and Urbanism in the French Atlantic Empire: State, Church, and Society, 1604–1830* (Montreal: McGill-Queen's University Press, 2018), 42–46.

72. See Virginia DeJohn Anderson, "Migrants and Motives: Religion and the Settlement of New England, 1630–1640," *NEQ* 58 (1985), 339–383, esp. 364–367.

dissolution and the rise of Protestantism in England. It was a fitting place to nurture intense discussion of religious issues.[73]

Like promoters of Virginia and New Plymouth, Winthrop emphasized that the English needed to spread Protestant faith among Indigenous Americans in part for their own good but also "to rayse a Bulworke against the kingdome of Ante-Christ," a reference to the feared expansion of Catholicism in the Western Hemisphere—an expansion that would have been known to literate elites aware of the circulation of tracts touting (however incorrectly) Catholic gains in the mission field.[74] His prose evoked long-standing anti-Spanish feeling among many in England, a sentiment likely growing given English awareness of French efforts to develop Québec. Even though aspects of his argument mirrored views held widely in England, his was a dissenter's cause, not that of the clerical establishment. Winthrop believed that the true church in England was collapsing, with "noe place lefte to flie into but the wildernesse," another parallel to biblical precedent. Domestic problems kept increasing in England, with the number of the poor growing too quickly for their needs to be accommodated. Disorder was rampant. The present was desperate, he argued, with English at the "height of Intemperance in all excesse of Riott," and the future nightmarish. "The Fountains of Learning & Religion are so corrupted," he warned, that children could not be properly educated while surrounded by poor role models and tainted by an educational elite more concerned with small doctrinal differences than major issues—the embodiment of Matthew 23:24: "men straine at knatts [gnats] & swallow Camells." The Earth, according to Genesis 1:28, was to be cultivated along divinely sanctioned lines. But England was too overcrowded, while "a whole Continent, as fruitfull and convenient for the use of man [lies] waste without any improvement."[75]

73. William Camden, *Britannia* (London, 1587), 294–295; James G. Clark, "Reformation and Reaction at St. Albans Abbey, 1530–58," *English Historical Review* 115 (2000), 297–328; Francis J. Bremer, *John Winthrop: America's Forgotten Founding Father* (New York: Oxford University Press, 2003), 23–38.

74. See, e.g., [Marc Lescabot], *La conversion des sauvages qui ont esté baptizes en la Nouvelle France, cette annee 1610* (Paris, [1610]), [M. Bertrand], *Lettre Missive, touchant la conversion et Baptesme du grant Sagamos de la nouvelle France* (Paris, 1610).

75. John Winthrop, "Reasons to Be Considered, and Objections with Answers," Winthrop Family Papers, vol. 2, MHS, https://www.masshist.org/publications/winthrop/index.php/view/PWF02d079 (accessed January 15, 2025); printed as Winthrop, "Reasons to be Considered for Justifying the Undertakers of the Intended Plantation in New England and for Encouraging Such Whose Hearts God Shall Move to Join with Them in It," *Proceedings of the Massachusetts Historical Society* 8 (1864–1865), 420–425. On Winthrop and the origins of the Massachusetts Bay colony, see Mark A. Peterson, *The City-State of Boston: The Rise and Fall of an Atlantic Power, 1630–1865*

Circumstances in England revealed to Winthrop that migration was a logical choice, but he understood that colonization was the product of organized efforts by companies, not a spontaneous movement of individuals who may have heard about the wonders of a new world and rushed to book passage there. Indeed, it was in his capacity as someone centrally involved with the Massachusetts Bay Company that he laid out his argument with the understanding that they needed to convince others to join their cause. Was the American Atlantic coast too dangerous for the English given what had happened near the shores of the Chesapeake? Winthrop argued that those who had gone to Virginia suffered because they were too lazy to defend themselves. What about the fact that the migration of the "visible saints," those who seemed most likely to achieve salvation, would weaken the cause in England? Winthrop saw the migration as strengthening the dissenters' campaign. He reminded skeptics that "since Christes [Christ's] tyme the Church is to be considered as universall without distinction of Countries, so as he that doeth good in any one place serves the Church in all places." He reminded his readers that the start of a new colony might pose difficulties but, invoking the writings of Paul (from Philippians 4:11–12), he believed that the "difference in quality may a little displease us," he added, "but it cannot hurt us."

Winthrop confronted an issue that had vexed thoughtful Europeans since the times of Columbus: how could newcomers claim land "soe long possessed by others"? He answered that question in a way that applied not just to New England but to all colonies. "That which lies common, and hath never beene replenished or subdued is free to any that will possesse and improve it," he wrote, "For God hath given to the sonnes of men a double right to the earth." He called the first a "natural" right and the second a "civil" right. When, in ancient times, "men held the earth in common every man sowing, and feeding where he pleased," everyone possessed a natural right. But the increase in people "and theire Cattle" demanded the fencing of certain parcels of land. New England's Indigenous residents had no fences nor any "tame Cattle to improve the Land by." They maintained a natural right to their land, but not a civil right. Following this logic, the English could occupy already peopled land as long as they left enough "for their use." He understood that the epidemic of 1616–1619 had reduced the Native population, leading him to argue that there was plenty of land for survivors and newcomers. The disease

(Princeton, NJ: Princeton University Press, 2019), 16–17, 27, and Richard Dunn, ed., *The Journal of John Winthrop, 1630–1649* (Cambridge, MA.: Harvard University Press, 1996), xvi–xxxiii.

was the proof: "God hath consumed the Natives with a great Plag[u]e in those partes soe as there be few Inhabitants lefte."

A decade after the Leiden migrants arrived on Cape Cod, Winthrop understood that the dissenters' mission would succeed only if the Massachusetts Bay Company could attract migrants. Economic want and religious persecution provided the motivation for what he needed: a new generation of Pilgrims to advance their holy script in a fresh arena.

On March 4, 1629, Charles I affixed his seal to the charter for the Massachusetts Bay Company, granting it the right to settle the territory between the Merrimack River to the north and a line to be drawn three miles south of the Charles River to the south, which would become the border between Massachusetts and New Plymouth. Following the practice established in Virginia in 1619, the governor (or his deputy) had the authority to organize a general assembly that would convene four times each year. All migrants and their children would possess the same rights as subjects of the realm who lived in England. The local council would have the authority to enact legislation as long as it did not violate English law. The king hoped that the colonists would serve as models of peaceful, civil, and religious individuals whose behavior would "incite the Natives of the Country, to the Knowledg and Obedience" of the Christian faith, which "is the principall Ende of this Plantacion." The company chose for its image a Native man carrying an arrow stating "Come Over and Help Us," a line derived from Acts 16:9. The colonists took the parchment charter with them, a break from precedent unnoticed at the time.[76]

In 1629, Winthrop drafted a lay sermon now known as "A Modell of Christian Charity." There is little indication that he delivered his words to dissenters before they left, and even if he did, he was not alone in attaching the religious enthusiasm of the moment to the English colonization of New England. John Cotton, one of the leading ministers involved in the creation of the colony, published two sermons intended for the migrants, including *God's Promise to His Plantations*, which he preached in Southampton before Winthrop and his fellow travelers departed. Yet Winthrop's words, which betrayed his legal training in much the same way that his justification for taking lands from Indigenous people had the year before, came to have a powerful place in American culture.[77]

76. Charter of Massachusetts Bay, 1629, Avalon.

77. John Cotton, *Gods Promise to His Plantation* (London, 1630); Bremer, *John Winthrop*, 174–184; Peterson, *City-State of Boston*, 8–10; Alan Heimert and Andrew Delbanco,

In depicting an Indigenous (perhaps Wampanoag) man uttering a line from Scripture in its original seal, the directors of the Massachusetts Bay Company provided a visual complement to the verbal arguments of Winthrop and other leaders: dissenters should establish colonies in New England because the Natives wanted their spiritual guidance. Wikimedia Commons.

Winthrop's words reflected his understanding of core ideas of the Reformation and how it had progressed in England. As he saw things, God had determined that "some must be rich, some poor, some high and eminent in power and dignity, others mean and in subjection." Following from that premise, certain ideas seemed clear. First, their god chose to have the word spread from "man by man" rather than through "his own immediate hands," a notion that reflected the Protestant idea that the ways of the divine could be known through intensive study and not, as followers of Rome believed, passed only from a priest to the laity. Further, anyone in a godly society should accept the existing distribution of wealth and power: "the rich and mighty should not eat up the poor, nor the poor and despised rise up against their superiors and shake off their yoke." The elites were to embody the core virtues of mercy and temperance, and "the poor and inferior sort" would provide models of obedience, faith, and patience. There would be no leveling in New England, where people

eds., *The Puritans in America: A Narrative Anthology* (Cambridge, MA: Harvard University Press, 1985), 81–82.

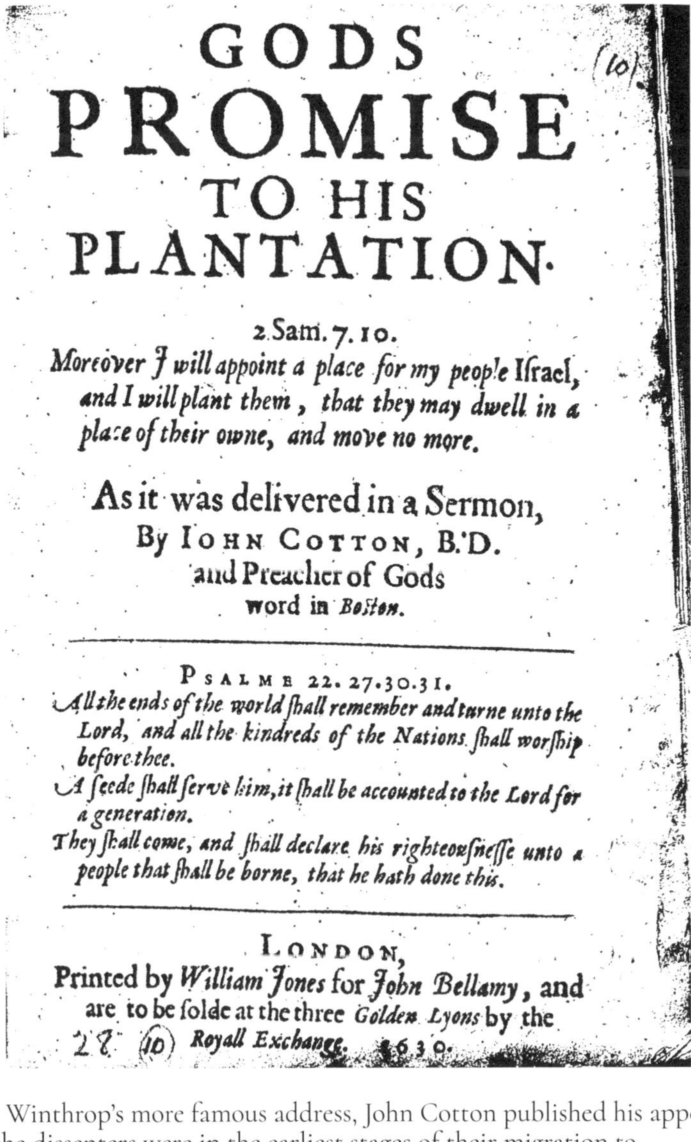

GODS
PROMISE
TO HIS
PLANTATION.

2 Sam. 7. 10.
Moreover I will appoint a place for my people Iſrael, and I will plant them, that they may dwell in a place of their owne, and move no more.

As it was delivered in a Sermon,
By IOHN COTTON, B.D.
and Preacher of Gods
word in *Boſton*.

PSALME 22. 27. 30. 31.
All the ends of the world ſhall remember and turne unto the Lord, and all the kindreds of the Nations ſhall worſhip before thee.
A ſeede ſhall ſerve him, it ſhall be accounted to the Lord for a generation.
They ſhall come, and ſhall declare his righteouſneſſe unto a people that ſhall be borne, that he hath done this.

LONDON,
Printed by *William Jones* for *John Bellamy*, and are to be ſolde at the three *Golden Lyons* by the *Royall Exchange*. 1630.

Unlike Winthrop's more famous address, John Cotton published his appeal while the dissenters were in the earliest stages of their migration to Massachusetts Bay. This version, which is relatively brief, is one of many examples of English Protestant clergy using printing presses to advance the legitimacy of their missions. Wikimedia Commons.

across the economic scale would keep communities intact through "Brotherly affection."[78]

78. John Winthrop, "A Model of Christian Charity," in Heimert and Delbanco, eds., *Puritans*, 82–83.

Traveling across the ocean did not sever the bonds with co-religionists at home because the migrants needed, as Winthrop put it, to profess "ourselves fellow members of Christ, in which respect only though we were absent from each other many miles, and had our imployments as far distant, yet we ought to account ourselves knit together by this bond of love, and live in the exercise of it." Following from that premise, and relating directly to the act of migrating, Winthrop added that it was "by a mutual consent and through a special overvaluing providence" that the puritans should "seek out a place of cohabitation and consortship under a due form of government both civil and ecclesiastical." Laying a foundation for his expectations of what would transpire when the religiously imbued set to the hard work of creating an actual community, he warned that "the care of the public must oversway all private respects." Civility and conscience needed to coexist. Too much concern with one's own prospects would bring the "ruin of the public."[79]

These dissenters planned to enlarge the number of those who thought and prayed like them. They had in mind creating a sanctuary from what Winthrop called "the common corruptions of the world." This meant understanding their contractual relationship with the divine. Here, as Winthrop put it, "stands the cause between God and us. We are entered into a covenant with him for this work." The almighty expected that the puritans would hold up their end. The stakes were high. If the migrants "shall fall to embrace this present world and prosecute our carnal intentions, seeking great things for ourselves and our posterity," Winthrop warned, "the Lord will surely break out in wrath against us, be revenged of such a perjured people, and make us know the price of the breach of such a covenant." The only way to avoid looming disaster would be to follow the lead of Micah: "to do justly, to love mercy, to walk humbly with our God" and be "knit together in this work as one man." They should celebrate together in good times, console each other in sad moments, and never lose sight that their mission had divine origins.[80]

Winthrop understood that their god was all-knowing because their lord had established the course for humanity, determining in advance who would find salvation and setting clues for finding out how to sort out the elect who needed to be gathered together apart from the world. These individuals were to create a new church, free of the polluted ideas promulgated by an overzealous archbishop and a Roman-tolerating monarch. Everything they did would be visible. This led Winthrop, drawing on Matthew 5:14, to pen the most memorable passage he ever wrote:

79. Winthrop, "Model of Christian Charity," 89.
80. Winthrop, "Model of Christian Charity," 89–91.

> We shall find that the God of Israel is among us, when ten of us shall be able to resist a thousand of our enemies; when he shall make us a praise and glory that men shall say of succeeding plantations, "the Lord make it like that of New England." For we must consider that we shall be as a city upon a hill. The eyes of all people are upon us.

Winthrop did not presume that these dissenters would succeed in creating their godly republics where the interests of the material and divine worlds coexisted. As he put it, "if we shall deal falsely with our God in this work we have undertaken," and as a result prompt him to withdraw his favor, "we shall be made a story and a by-word through the world. We shall open the mouths of enemies to speak evil of the ways of God, and all professors for God's sake."[81]

Winthrop's sermon, taken together with his commentary a year earlier justifying English occupation of land in New England, established an ideological foundation for a certain kind of colony-making. Because the dissenters planned to use land as their god instructed, they believed they were creating a dual right to territory in the Western Hemisphere. But their plans would work only if they hewed to the core principles of godly republicanism, an interwoven and inextricable system in which success followed only if they did right by each other. In England, these ideas could exist in theological discussions among the critics of the Church of England. On the western side of the Atlantic, the dissenters would need to find a way to put their ideas into practice. Though the emigration from Leiden had suggested the possibility of creating communities of the godly, the fact that relatively few English (or other Europeans) moved to New Plymouth sent a signal that just getting to New England was not enough. If the Massachusetts Bay Colony was to prosper, it would need to figure out how to encourage women and men to take a chance on a new life in an area that, according to all the existing evidence, had great potential but not many other English people.

In 1630, English and French eyed each other warily along the northern arc of the northwestern Atlantic, with a dwindling number of Beothuks in Newfoundland and Iroquoian-speakers along the St. Lawrence who must have wondered how many more Europeans would arrive and what their migration might mean for those who were already there. Over 7,000 English men and women, most of them young and poor, had gone to the Chesapeake since 1607, but twenty-three years later their total population stood at only 2,600, and many still perished annually from dysentery and

81. Winthrop, "Model of Christian Charity," 91.

typhoid fever, their symptoms exacerbated by shortages of food.[82] New Plymouth, having survived the catastrophic demographic collapse of its first year, had recovered, but its population still stood at under 500. In each of these locales, the violent times seemed to be coming to an end, with an anxious peace spreading across the continent.

Within that context, Winthrop's articulation of what constituted dual rights epitomized a moment of European pilgrimage and plunder. Still outnumbered by Indigenous across North America, English, Spanish, and French became increasingly confident that they would control the Western Hemisphere and remake its landscapes to fit their interests. They believed that their god, working as a lady shrouded in a humble blue cloak in New Mexico or an inscrutable judge of whether a dissenter was destined for salvation, would sanction their conquest. Just as important, promoters of colonization in each of these nations believed that these missions would further their own political and religious interests. North America was to be the next arena for intra-European rivalry, fought over by secular and spiritual foes alike. For all their differences, these Europeans shared an overriding notion: in their minds, the spread of Christendom justified the dispossession of Native Americans who refused conversion.

82. Edmund S. Morgan, *American Slavery, American Freedom: The Ordeal of Colonial Virginia* (New York: W. W. Norton, 1975), 402–405; John J. McCusker and Russell R. Menard, *The Economy of British North America, 1607–1789* (Chapel Hill: University of North Carolina Press for the Institute of Early American History and Culture, 1985), 136.

18

The Arc of European Opportunity

On March 27, 1625, James I, debilitated by kidney stones, gout, arthritis, a stroke, and dysentery, died at Theobalds, his hunting retreat in Hertfordshire. His closest confidants had believed the fresh air in the countryside might alleviate some of his suffering, but he succumbed to his chronic illnesses. Rumors swirled that his political rivals had poisoned him, launching generations of speculation about possible regicide.[1] Since his firstborn son, Henry, the Prince of Wales, had died seven years earlier, Charles, James's twenty-five-year-old second son, inherited the throne. Given the central role that James had played in the dissolution of the Virginia Company and the creation on the North American mainland of the first royal English colony, the transition mattered. Less than three weeks after his father's death, Charles created a commission, possibly inspired by the Spanish Casa de Contratación (founded in Seville in 1503), to report to him and the Privy Council on developments far from home. The commission began to meet by early 1626. Among the first issues it handled was a complaint from Ferdinando Gorges about his American claims, a sign that the king and his agents had every intention of establishing as much control as possible over colonization as well as trade.[2]

The creation of the English commission came at a time when promoters of American projects began to muster energy across western Europe. Proposals for new investments sprang from divergent sources, reflecting less a particular economic sector for development and more the sense that opportunities had gone unpursued. Those pushing for colonial projects

1. See Thomas Cogswell, "The Politics of Propaganda: Charles I and the People in the 1620s," *Journal of British Studies* 29 (1990), 187–215, esp. 192; Alastair Bellany and Thomas Cogswell, *The Murder of James I* (New Haven, CT: Yale University Press, 2015).
2. Charles M. Andrews, "British Committees, Commissions, and Councils of Trade and Plantations, 1622–1675," *Johns Hopkins University Studies in History and Political Science* XXVI (1908), 12–13; Richard S. Dunn, *Sugar and Slaves: The Rise of the Planter Class in the English West Indies* (Chapel Hill: University of North Carolina Press for the Institute of Early American History and Culture, 1972), 29; William Saunders, ed., *Colonial Records of North Carolina*, 10 vols., (Raleigh, NC: P. M. Hale, 1886–1890), I:5–13.

no doubt understood that European enthusiasm had flagged across much of North America. In 1625, most of the continent still looked as it had for centuries, at least on the surface. Colonizers in New Mexico, Florida, Québec, Newfoundland, Bermuda, the Chesapeake, and New Plymouth had managed to establish communities, but their numbers remained low. There were then likely fewer than a hundred English in Newfoundland, about the same number as the English and Irish who lived somewhere on the Wild Coast in South America. The Spanish and creole population of Florida probably numbered no more than 300, with the largest number in St. Augustine. As late as 1630, Québec had only eighty-five migrants from France, fewer than twenty-five of whom intended to stay—an improvement over 1623, when the émigré population of Port-Royal had not reached twenty men and there were no French women to be found.[3] The population of Acoma was likely far more substantial than that of Santa Fe.

Although their populations remained small, Europeans had learned how to build communities and extract profits in some regions, two processes necessary for a colony's survival. Even the biblically minded religious dissenters of New Plymouth depended on the extraction and export of natural resources to pay off the debts they had accrued establishing their colony. Europeans also recognized the importance of circulating news of their actions. Virginia's experience was telling. Despite the horrors of the second Anglo-Powhatan war and the collapse of the Virginia Company, scores of migrants continued to sail there each year, making it the most populous European colony north of the Rio Grande. Even the most devastating account of the colony's troubles—Waterhouse's vivid description of the events of March 1622—included sections designed to encourage migration. Young women and men responded to such appeals, booking passage (often as indentured servants) in numbers just as large as before the war. Many died relatively soon, unable to adjust to the region's environment. But the decrease in the numbers of Powhatans allowed those who survived the first brutal years to establish farms in places that did not suffer the periodic ailments still common in Jamestown, thereby boosting the non-Indigenous population to just under 5,000 by the mid-1630s.[4]

3. Leslie Choquette, "Proprietorships in French North America," in L. H. Roper and B. Van Ruymbeke, eds., *Constructing Early Modern Empires: Proprietary Ventures in the Atlantic World, 1500–1700* (Leiden: Brill, 2007), 119–120.

4. Edward Waterhouse, *A Declaration of the State of the Colony and Affaires in Virginia, with A Relation of the Barbarous Massacre* (London, 1622), 45–50; See Carville V. Earle, "Environment, Disease, and Mortality in Early Virginia," in Thad W. Tate and David L. Ammerman, eds., *The Chesapeake in the Seventeenth Century* (Chapel Hill: University of North Carolina Press for the Institute for Early American History and Culture, 1973), 120–121.

Before the mid-1620s, the most active Europeans in the area north and east of Mexico had been Spaniards and Spanish creoles. Cuba, Puerto Rico, and Hispaniola vied with Zacatecas as profit-making centers, with Caribbean sugar competing with southwestern silver as the most lucrative commodities to be exported. Demography followed economics. The decline in Indigenous peoples, first evident among the Tainos in Hispaniola, continued in areas frequented by Spanish colonizers, some of them the unwitting bearers of infectious disease. The drive for profits led Spanish officials to seek new workers for their two most lucrative labor-intensive industries: mining and sugar production.

After the death of James I, a fresh spirit of opportunism spread throughout much of England and parts of western Europe. The psychological burdens and financial costs of long-distance travel seemed less onerous given the economic, political, and religious gains to be made. Responding to reports about the lure of American wealth or the chance to escape religious persecution, the number of Europeans increased in the territory stretching from modern New England to Carolina. By the decade's end, migrants had managed to create self-sustaining colonies in New Netherland, Massachusetts Bay, Maryland, and Barbados. Still, failure lurked, as a new generation of explorers seeking the Northwest Passage discovered at almost the same time as a group of Protestant dissenters gave up their efforts to create a colony in Providencia (Providence Island), an island off the Nicaragua coast. Other Europeans struggled too, including Swedes who had hoped to create a colony along the Delaware.

Such disappointments mattered to the English but did not diminish their interest in maintaining American colonies. From those vantage points, they could witness developments that altered life in the Western Hemisphere—including the dramatic expansion of the slave trade shipping bound African bodies to American plantations, a practice that the English had to that point only occasionally embraced. Europeans had for generations written and spoken about their desire to convert Indigenous to Christianity as the highest goal they could achieve in the Western Hemisphere. But in one colonial arena after another, the drive for profit came to overwhelm the desire for conversion. The primary gains they sought were to fill their coffers, not their churches.

Soon after King James's death, English policymakers and would-be promoters reopened the debate about the future of its then sparsely populated claims in Guiana (the Orinoco), the Wild Coast (the Amazon), and Newfoundland. In 1626, Robert Harcourt continued his efforts to justify an English colony in Guiana, emphasizing that success there would allow the English to convert Indigenous to Protestant Christianity, expand the territory of the realm, and gain wealth from the extraction of the region's sugar cane, silkgrass, balsam, amber, honey, wax, nutmeg, mace, sweet gums, cotton wool, "rich" woods, feathers, jasper, porphyry, sapphires, topaz, and dyestuffs. The previous effort had failed because of the intervention of the Spanish ambassador Gondomar, who had a powerful influence over James. But the Spaniard died in 1626, clearing the path to restart the colonial project, especially if the English could forge alliances with Indigenous. The Spanish could not prevail, Harcourt boasted, "whilest the Natives remayne so adverse and irreconcilable unto them, and so firme and Constant unto us."[5] Other promoters argued that the best opportunities lay along the Wild Coast, where a small English outpost remained from earlier voyages. In May 1627, Charles I issued a patent to the Guiana Company. The king appointed George Villiers, first Duke of Buckingham, to be its first governor, with the understanding that a council would help determine the colony's policies—including, if necessary, the authority to impose martial law. But after an assassin felled Buckingham in August 1628, the company lost its primary advocate in court.[6]

While the plans for an English presence in coastal South America did not progress beyond a small circle of advocates, Newfoundland attracted far more attention. In many respects, this northern island seemed to offer much, just as Peckham and Parmenius had promised in the 1580s (Hakluyt circulated their reports) and other promoters had argued in the years since. Though English migrants, who had been arriving in small numbers

5. Robert Harcourt, *The Relation of a Voyage to Guiana . . . Now newly reviewed & enlarged, by addition of some necessary Notes* (London, 1626), sig. A2^r–A3^v, 41–42 (sugar), 80–83, quotations at 41 and 83.

6. "A Summary Relation concerning the Pattent for the River of Amazones & the Countrie & Coast Adjoyning" [1625], in Joyce Lorimer, ed., *English and Irish Settlement on the River Amazon, 1550–1646*, Hak. Soc., 2nd Ser., 171 (London: Hakluyt Society, 1989), 276–277; Charles I to the Attorney General, [January/February] 1626, in Lorimer, ed., *English and Irish Settlement*, 277–278; Roger North's Prospectus for the Guiana Company, c. March 1626, in Lorimer, ed., *English and Irish Settlement*, 282–285. (That month, in a separate document, North emphasized Charles I's support; see Lorimer, ed., *English and Irish Settlement*, 285–286.) North's petition of February [11] 21, 1627, is in Lorimer, ed., *English and Irish Settlement*, 287–288; an extract from the patent is in Lorimer, ed., *English and Irish Settlement*, 288–297, with the return of the previous patents noted at 289–290, the appointment of Buckingham at 296, and the authority to impose martial law at 297.

since the 1610s, had struggled with the local climate, their small émigré community remained intact—a contrast to the quick collapse of the colonizing effort in Sagadahoc, the other cold-weather English colony in the Northeast. Fortunately for the English, the climate probably moderated a bit by the 1620s. While earlier colonists had mentioned the cold, an English observer in 1622 noted that "All our Corne and Seedes have prospered well, and are already growne almost to perfect maturitie, &c."[7] Like other prospective ventures, Newfoundland had its propagandists, who published books extolling its natural virtues and its strategic importance. English writer John Mason noted that the colony was closer to England than any other possible American destination, with sailing times that ranged from twelve to thirty days. Further, the cod-rich waters were already supporting 3,000 English employed on fishing vessels, and their efforts supported a total of 20,000 at home. With few Natives in the northern parts of Newfoundland and, as far as the English could tell, none in its southern reaches, colonists would need only to defend themselves from an invasion by sea.[8]

In the 1620s, hope for an English colony fell to George Calvert, who had become lord of the manor of Baile an Ti Mhóir (Baltimore) in County Longford in 1623. Likely raised as a Catholic, Calvert committed to the faith in 1624 after he had completed years as a servant in James's court and in Parliament. James, less fervent in his anti-Roman tendencies than Elizabeth had been, was sufficiently tolerant of Catholics that many in England suspected his motivations, but his attitudes comforted those once persecuted by the Church of England. Calvert thought that perhaps Newfoundland, where he had first acquired land in 1622, could be a refuge for like-minded believers. In 1625, he appointed Sir Arthur Aston, another Catholic, to be the new governor and helped to arrange transportation for fifteen others to join the nascent colony at Avalon. An Irish Carmelite priest named Simon Stock believed that Newfoundland would become a crucial link in a global Catholic missionary effort.[9]

7. N.H. to W.P., August 18, 1622, in Samuel Purchas, *Hakluytus Posthumus, or Purchas his Pilgrimes*, 4 vols., (London, 1625), 4:1890–1891.
8. See John Mason, *A Briefe Discourse of New-found-land* (Edinburgh, 1620); Orpheus Junior [William Vaughan], *The Golden Fleece* (London, 1626); William Alexander, *An Encouragement to Colonies* (London, 1624); Gillian T. Cell, ed., *Newfoundland Discovered: English Attempts at Colonisation, 1610–1630*, Hak. Soc., 2nd Ser., 160 (London: Hakluyt Society, 1982), 31–39, 103.
9. Cell, ed., *Newfoundland Discovered*, 18–19, 44–56; Ronald Hoffman, *Princes of Ireland, Planters of Maryland: A Carroll Saga, 1500–1782* (Chapel Hill: University of North Carolina Press for the Omohundro Institute of Early American History and Culture, 2000), 20–21.

Despite these Catholics' best efforts, their plans fizzled—but not the support they had from the king. On November 22, 1629, Charles praised Calvert for how he had earlier worked with James to do what was best for the nation. Since Newfoundland seemed to be failing, Charles thought Calvert should pursue another American option. Calvert, who stood to lose £20,000 to £30,000 he had invested in Newfoundland, abandoned the project, concluding that the future of English colonization in coastal North America lay farther south. When he died in 1632, his dreams for an American refuge for Catholics were still unrealized.[10]

While English observers promoted Newfoundland, the lower Hudson gained far more attention among Protestants in western Europe. On June 3, 1621, the Dutch Republic granted a charter to the West India Company (WIC) with the specific goal of establishing an outpost in lands explored by Hudson during his third voyage in 1609. Organizational difficulties prevented the company from sending migrants until March 1624, as did ongoing English claims that the lower Hudson Valley and Manhattan belonged to James's realm. The Dutch countered that such assertions were meaningless unless colonists inhabited the territory. To solidify their hold, they sent more migrants, along with cows and horses, in September. These efforts to hold the territory barely registered on the minds of English observers other than Sir Dudley Carleton, the ambassador in The Hague, who was well aware of the significance of these migrations and concerned too with WIC ships heading to Virginia for trade. In London, James and his courtiers believed that England owned this territory by right of first occupation (*jure primae occupationis*), calling it North Virginia. But they did little to advance their cause other than informing the States General that the king had "expressly forbidden" the renaming of territory and the migration of colonists there. For its part, the Virginia Company initially seemed open to allowing Dutch migrants to settle some portion of their territory.[11]

10. Charles I to Lord Baltimore, November 22, 1629, in Cell, ed., *Newfoundland Discovered*, 296–297; Peter E. Pope, *Fish into Wine: The Newfoundland Plantation in the Seventeenth Century* (Chapel Hill: University of North Carolina Press for the Omohundro Institute for Early American History and Culture, 2004), 45–56.

11. Jaap Jacobs, *The Colony of New Netherland: A Dutch Settlement in Seventeenth-Century America* (Ithaca, NY: Cornell University Press, 2009), 27–31; resolutions of the States General for September 15, September 24, and September 21, 1621, and its resolution in response to Carleton's concerns, March 16 and April 27, 1622, all in *DRCHNY*, 1:26–28; Privy Council to Carleton, December 15, 1621, Carleton to the Lords of the Council, February 5, [1622?], Carleton's memorial to the States General, February 9,

Soon enough, English visitors to North America recognized the growing threat the Dutch posed. Emmanuel Altham, an agent for the Council for New England who also visited New Plymouth in the fall of 1623, argued that the Dutch were already trying to monopolize the fur trade, though he believed that the English would eventually make a greater profit from exporting fish. The following year John Pory, a younger son of a Norfolk gentry family who had attended Cambridge, became one of the commissioners sent by the Privy Council to investigate the situation in Virginia. On his return, he stopped at New Plymouth and concluded that the WIC posed a substantial threat to English claims. Pory believed that the Dutch intended to claim the shoreline between 40° and 44°.[12]

In 1626, the Dutch acquired the rights to create a settlement on Manhattan Island from a group of Munsees, who remained nearby along with other Indigenous, all of them potential trade partners for the newcomers. That year the colonists built Fort Amsterdam along the North (now Hudson) River, an ideal location for the exchange of furs, wampum, and manufactured goods. The next year, the *Bruynisch* arrived with the colony's first enslaved Africans. From its origins, New Amsterdam had a more mixed population than much of the rest of eastern North America. But even here the dominant population—by Dutch design—remained Indigenous even though the newcomers immediately began to impose a new order and imported architectural styles on the land.[13]

Within a few years, Dutch ships began to regularly sail to the community, which occupied the southern reaches of Manhattan. Soon enough, colonists—likely drawing on the labor of enslaved Africans—began to build both stone and wooden structures, thereby sending a message to anyone who sailed nearby that the Dutch intended to add New Amsterdam to its list of far-flung holdings. They used their position there to launch other colonizing projects along the shores of the Hudson River,

1622, Petition of Walloons and French to Carleton, [February 5], 1622, and Calvert to Carleton, February 7, [1622?], all in *DRCHNY*, 3:6–11.

12. Pory to Southampton, January 13, 1622/1623, Pory to Wyatt, autumn 1622, Emmanuel Altham to Sir Edward Altham, September 1623 and March 1623/1624, and Altham to James Sherly, May 1624, all in Sydney V. James, ed., *Three Visitors to Early Plymouth* (Bedford, MA: Applewood Books, 1997), 5–11, 14–18, 23–41, 44, 49.

13. Jacobs, *Colony of New Netherland*, 30–31; Paul Otto, *The Dutch-Munsee Encounter in America: The Struggle for Sovereignty in the Hudson Valley* (New York: Berghahn, 2006), 81–86; Paul Otto, "The Dutch, Munsees, and the Purchase of Manhattan," *New York State Bar Association Journal* 87, no. 1 (2015), 10–17; Nicole S. Maskiell, *Bound by Bondage: Slavery and the Creation of a Northern Gentry* (Ithaca, NY: Cornell University Press, 2022), 2–3.

thereby expanding their connections to the Indigenous communities in Lenapehoking as well as toward the homelands of the Mohawks, the easternmost of the five Haudenosaunee nations.[14]

The English desire to colonize the Orinoco and Amazon deltas testified to the willingness to set aside their long-standing and reasonable fear of hot climates in the pursuit of material and spiritual gain. When those mainland efforts waned, some turned their attention to more promising venues in the Caribbean. On May 14, 1625, an English ship called the *Olive Blossom* arrived at Barbados. Its sailors, unaware that their king had recently died, laid claim to it in the name of James I. The island had once been dominated by Kalinagos (sometimes called Island Caribs) who had migrated there from the Guianas in the middle of the thirteenth century and displaced the Lokono, an earlier group that had migrated from the same region around 800 CE. The Kalinago economy had focused on the production of fish, maize, cassava, cotton, and pottery. But in the early decades of the sixteenth century, Spaniards had likely captured, enslaved, and deported all of them. When a Portuguese explorer named Pedro a Campos arrived in Barbados in 1536, he found it unoccupied. There is no evidence that any sizable or durable community replaced the Kalinagos before the arrival of the English, who believed the island uninhabited even though they found material remains revealing that Barbados once did have residents. (Most evidence of prior habitation disappeared in a climate not conducive to the preservation of objects made from plants, cloth, or wood.) The absence of a Native population that might resist the creation of colonial communities provided the English an advantage there that they lacked on St. Kitts, where they had trouble developing a settlement after arriving in 1624 because of resistance from Kalinagos.[15]

14. See Anne-Marie Cantwell and Diana diZerega Wall, *Unearthing Gotham: The Archaeology of New York City* (New Haven, CT: Yale University Press, 2001), 149–187; Sung Bok Kim, *Landlord and Tenant in Colonial New York, 1664–1775* (Chapel Hill: University of North Carolina Press for the Institute for Early American History and Culture, 1978), 3–7.
15. Karen Ordahl Kupperman, "Fear of Hot Climates in the Anglo-American Colonial Experience," *WMQ*, 3rd Ser., 41 (1984), 213–240; George Gmelch and Sharon Bohn Gmelch, "Barbados's Amerindian Past," *Anthropology Today* 12 (1996), 11–15; Hilary McD. Beckles, *A History of Barbados: From Amerindian Settlement to Caribbean Single Market*, 2nd ed. (Cambridge: Cambridge University Press, 2006), 3–8; Tessa Murphy, *The Creole Archipelago: Race and Borders in the Colonial Caribbean* (Philadelphia: University of Pennsylvania Press, 2021), 25–27.

The first English migrants arrived at Barbados in April 1627, establishing a small encampment under the authority of Sir Peter Courteen and Sir William Courteen, who had obtained a patent and raised funds in London to establish a colony. Soon after, the English sea captain Henry Powell, who had previously landed on the Guiana coast, arrived in the company of mainland Indigenous, Arawaks who may have canoed regularly to the island to capture pigs (the progeny of stock left behind by earlier European visitors). Powell enticed them with the promise of land and Christianity. Soon after they arrived, he enslaved three dozen of them. Disputes over who should govern flared in London, leading to a succession of would-be governors—including Henry Hawley, who arrived in the late 1620s and had his predecessor, William Tufton, executed for sedition when he refused to step down.[16]

The internal divisions among the English colonists in Barbados signaled that the order that James had hoped to establish in his colonies had not yet solidified in the earliest years of the reign of Charles I. Efforts to claim Barbados also revealed pent-up English demand for establishing new profitable American colonies, though no group had yet emerged to dominate the new king's overseas policies.

By 1629, Charles had decided to draw on an old model for establishing colonies. Unlike the charters English monarchs had granted before—to the companies that organized the attempted or realized colonization of Virginia, Newfoundland, Sagadahoc, Bermuda, Massachusetts Bay, Guiana, and the Amazon—Charles relied on an ancient idea of establishing proprietary colonies. The precedent could be found not abroad but in northern England, in the palatinate of Durham, a once-powerful northern kingdom that had possessed separate privileges since before the Norman Conquest. Any visitor to that city far from London would have been awed by its towering cathedral, its interior supported by perhaps the largest stone columns ever constructed in the realm. The massive edifice made visible the extraordinary authority possessed by the bishop of Durham, which had originated in the vast holdings and power of St. Cuthbert in the seventh century. Within that palatinate, residents had freedom from royal taxes but needed to pay whatever the bishop decreed, a situation that led

16. Beckles, *Barbados*, 9–12; Gmelch and Gmelch, "Barbados's Amerindian Past," 15; Jerome Handler, "The Amerindian Slave Population of Barbados in the Seventeenth and Early Eighteenth Centuries," *Caribbean Studies* 8 (1969), 38–64; Jerome Handler, "Amerindians and Their Contribution to Barbadian Life," *Journal of the Barbados Museum and Historical Society* 35 (1977), 189–210.

to inhabitants complaining to the king about their grievances. It was an enviable perch for the proprietor, if not for residents.[17]

On October 30, 1629, Charles granted a proprietary patent to Sir Robert Heath allocating territory lying south of Virginia and north of Florida, specified in the patent as between 31° and 36° north latitudes, including the Bahamas. The patent referred to the islands as Carolarns and the mainland as both Carolina and New Carolana. The patent to Heath made explicit reference to the palatinate of Durham. Like other grants establishing a new colony, the monarch defined the boundaries of the new territory and reminded its organizers that those who lived there would be expected to follow English law just like every other subject of the realm. The decision to establish a proprietor reflected Charles I's understanding, following his father's, that governing affairs relating to colonization and transatlantic trade fell under the monarch's jurisdiction, not Parliament's. Heath had been a close associate of Buckingham and, through him, of the king. While the assassination of his patron in 1628 destabilized Heath's position, the patent suggested he continued to enjoy the loyalty of the king.[18] At the time, as far as anyone in Europe knew, the Bahamas had no residents, though both Spanish and French court officials believed that they had a claim. The fact that the islands were unoccupied was enough for the English to assert ownership following their understanding that discovery led to permanent possession only if the colonizing power maintained a resident population.[19]

Getting a patent did not mean that one could launch a successful colony, as Heath's experience revealed. He had hoped to attract 20,000 Huguenots who might be desperate to leave France after Louis XIII, stung by a combined Dutch and Protestant victory at Rochelle, laid siege to

17. See Jean Scammell, "The Origin and Limitations of the Liberty of Durham," *English Historical Review* 81 (1966), 449–473.
18. W. Hubert Miller, "The Colonization of the Bahamas, 1647–1670," *WMQ*, 3rd Ser., 2 (1945), 33; Paul E. Kopperman, *Sir Robert Heath, 1574–1649: Window on an Age*, Royal Historical Society Studies in History 56 (Woodbridge, Suffolk: Boydell Press, 1989).
19. The islands once had a thriving population, though scholars debate whether the Taino-Lucayan people, who colonized the islands centuries before Columbus's arrival, came from Hispaniola or Cuba; see Mary Jane Berman and Perry L. Gnivecki, "The Colonization of the Bahama Archipelago: A Reappraisal," *World Archaeology* 26 (1995), 421–441; William H. Sears and Shaun O. Sullivan, "Bahamas Prehistory," *American Antiquity* 43 (1978), 3–25; Michael Craton and Gail Saunders, *Islanders in the Stream: A History of the Bahamian Peoples*, 2 vols., (Athens: University of Georgia Press, 1992–1998), 1:8–9; W. Hubert Miller, "The Colonization of the Bahamas," *WMQ*, 3rd Ser., 2 (1945), 33. For the deeper history, see David W. Steadman et al., "Holocene Vertebrates from a Dry Cave on Eleuthera Island, Commonwealth of the Bahamas," *The Holocene* 28 (2018), 806–813.

that city. Despite his plans, the colony never materialized. Heath solicited Huguenots to sail there, but the potential colonizers stopped in Virginia and never reached Carolina.[20] Another Huguenot refugee sent a petition to the king, proposing that the English send a fifty-ship fleet to the Caribbean to harass the Spanish, but nothing came of that proposal either.[21]

Heath pressed his case, but by 1633 it became clear to him and his allies that, regardless of their plans, which included building a large fort, there would be no Huguenot colony along the Atlantic coast of North America. Heath then appealed to the king with the idea that the colony could be peopled only by those who were members of the Church of England. Despite the change, neither he nor any other of Charles's subjects could generate the necessary financing or enthusiasm to launch the colony. Even those who expressed some interest spent more of their time and attention on developing possibilities in the Caribbean. By the middle of the decade, Carolana was already on its way to joining the list of other failed English colonial projects.[22] The Bahamas would remain without residents. The mainland region remained in the possession of Occaneechees, Pedees, Wacamawas, Santees, Sewees, and other Indigenous residents of coastal Carolina and the adjacent piedmont.[23]

Charles turned his attention elsewhere. On June 20, 1632, he issued a patent to Cecil Calvert, the second Lord Baltimore and the son of Charles's associate George Calvert, for a new colony to be located adjacent to Virginia. The shift improved the chances for success. Potential colonists would not suffer from the northern winter, and the region was then well known because of the scores of ships that had sailed to Virginia. For Charles I, the elder Calvert's commitment to the twinned cause of colonization and Christianization was worthy of emulation. As he put

20. W. Noel Sainsbury, "The First Settlement of French Protestants in America," *The Antiquary* 3 (1881), 101–103.

21. See Paul E. Kopperman, "Ambivalent Allies: Anglo-Dutch Relations and the Struggle Against the Spanish Empire in the Caribbean, 1621–1641," *Journal of Caribbean History* 21 (1987), 58; Paul E. Kopperman, "Profile of Failure: The Carolana Project, 1629–1640," *North Carolina Historical Review* 59 (1982), 2–7.

22. Kopperman, "Profile of Failure," 14–23; William S. Powell, "Carolana and the Incomparable Roanoke: Explorations and Attempted Settlements, 1620–1633," *North Carolina Historical Review* 51 (1974), 1–21, esp. 3–8.

23. See James H. Merrell, *The Indians' New World: Catawbas and Their Neighbors from European Contact Through the Era of Removal* (Chapel Hill: University of North Carolina Press for the Institute of Early American History and Culture, 1989), 4.

it, Cecil Calvert, "treading in the steps of his Father, being animated with a laudable, and pious Zeal for extending the Christian religion, and also the Territories of our Empire," merited a chance to establish a colony in a region "hitherto uncultivated, in the Parts of America, and partly occupied by Savages, having no knowledge of the Divine Being." The king affirmed that he alone had the authority to bestow this territory.[24]

The charter granted Calvert the eastern shore of Chesapeake Bay for a colony to be known as Maryland. Calvert and his descendants would be "the true and absolute Lords and Proprietaries of the region," owing allegiance only to the monarch. The proprietor had "free, full, and absolute Power" to make and enforce laws to the benefit of his own family or other private individuals, but Calvert should do so only in consultation with delegates chosen by the freemen of the colony and only if the laws conformed to England's. He could also establish manors within the province, each of which could have its own court-baron and "have and . . . Keep View of Frank-Pledge," a reference to a feudal system that had already faded away in England. The proprietor had the responsibility to organize, build, and consecrate churches, another power derived from the palatinate of Durham.

Under the terms of its founding agreement, Calvert and his family had the authority to erect forts and recruit soldiers to protect the colony from "the Incursions of Savages, or of other Enemies, Pirates, and Ravagers." The monarch granted the proprietor the explicit permission to pursue enemies even beyond the colony's borders, to root out evildoers "infesting those Parts by Land and by Sea, and (if God shall grant it) to vanquish and captivate them, and the Captive put to Death." Such powers normally resided with military leaders. Charles bestowed them on the proprietor, along with the ability to suppress insurrections.[25] Under the terms of the agreement, the proprietor of Maryland had authority over all residents within the bounds of the province—even those who had earlier traveled to the region thinking that they were taking up residence in Virginia.[26]

Charles I included much in the charter, but he only alluded to an issue that he knew was of paramount concern to the Calvert family: creating a refuge for English Catholics. The elder Calvert had declared his sympathies for Rome in 1625, an affirmation that did not bother the new king.

24. Charter of Maryland of 1632, clause 1, Avalon.

25. Charter of Maryland of 1632, clauses 2–3 (boundaries), 6 (legal system), 19 (courts-baron), 4 (powers equivalent to Durham), 9, 12, and 13 (protection and pursuing enemies).

26. Charter of Maryland of 1632, clause 21 (migrants to Virginia).

In Maryland, the family would have the authority to preside over the construction of churches and, presumably, the recruitment of a resident clergy. Charles knew full well that the family had in mind bringing Catholic priests to the region. As long as religious practice fell under the broad and not clearly defined boundaries of Christianity, the monarch had no objections, a stunning contrast to the views of Elizabeth and her advisors, whose actions had triggered the creation of English colonies in eastern North America.[27]

During the early 1630s, English explorers once again went in search of the Northwest Passage, though they looked for the opening to it in very different places. In 1631, almost fifteen years after the High Court of Admiralty in London had exonerated the survivors of the *Discovery* debacle, some English merchants decided that the time had come to return to the Arctic. A group of Bristol merchants sponsored a mission toward the passage led by Thomas James, which departed on May 3. Two days later, Luke Foxe of Hull, with the financial backing of London's merchant community and Charles I, left from Deptford.[28]

The party led by James sailed into the bay where Hudson's *Discovery* had been frozen over in the brutal winter of 1610–1611. He and his men found two stakes driven into the ground on Danby Island, as well as the remains of an ancient fire. James pulled up the stakes to examine them. They were, he reported, about the width of his arm, with a pointed end that seemed like it had been chopped by an iron tool, perhaps a hatchet, and then driven into the ground. James admitted that he could not determine why someone would drive stakes into the ground close to the water unless it was to serve as some kind of marker for boats—something that an Englishman might make but that would have been useless for Inuit or Crees who hauled their kayaks onto

27. See Edward G. Gray, *Mason-Dixon: Crucible of the Nation* (Cambridge, MA: Harvard University Press, 2023), 23–33; Susan Juster, *A Common Grave: Being Catholic in the Early English Atlantic* (Chapel Hill: University of North Carolina Press for the Omohundro Institute of Early American History and Culture, 2025), 76–81.

28. Luke Foxe, *North-West Fox, Or, Fox from the North-west passage* (London, 1635), 171–172 (preparations), 173–174 (oath), 181, 183–184, 268–270; Thomas James, *Strange and Dangerous Voyage of Captain Thomas James* (London, 1633), 112–116.

the shore. Finding the stakes made James eager to speak with some of the Crees, "for without doubt," he wrote, "they could have given notice of some Christians, with whom they had some commerce." James's find convinced him that some Europeans had to have been there earlier, either to cut the stakes or to trade the tools to make them. Perhaps James had found evidence of Hudson's presence, another marker of the specter haunting English efforts to search for the passage.[29]

The crews on both expeditions suffered through the winter, trying in vain to find an opening to the Pacific. When they returned, English printers quickly offered the public new firsthand accounts of the Arctic. Each offered details about the climate, especially the bitterness of the frigid winters they suffered.[30] James, like others who explored territory peopled by Indigenous, named the bay where Hudson died after himself. That name aside, these explorers came home bringing yet additional proof that there was no access to the passage via Hudson Bay.

Two years after news spread of the failure to find an Arctic opening to the passage, a fifty-four-year-old English captain named Thomas Yong (or Young) took a more southerly route. He believed that the opening could be found via modern Delaware Bay. He began his ascent upriver on July 20, 1634, and spent late summer and much of the autumn exploring the territory and establishing relations with its Indigenous occupants.[31] He was the first English explorer to describe this territory, though it overlapped with Baltimore's planned Maryland.[32] The explorer met Lenapes already familiar with trade protocols from their earlier commerce with other visitors. He learned from them about their enmity with the Susquehannocks (Minquaos), the dominant group whose territory then covered the lower Susquehanna Valley and the northern reaches of

29. James, *Strange and Dangerous Voyage*, 90–91. Two hundred fifty years later, one scholar suggested that the *Discovery*'s carpenter must have chopped those stakes; see Miller Christy, ed., *The Voyages of Captain Luke Foxe of Hull and Captain Thomas James of Bristol, in Search of a north-west passage, in 1631–1632*, Hak. Soc., 1st Ser., 88–89 (London, 1894), 2:568–569n.

30. The journals from these expeditions were so vivid that the natural philosopher Robert Boyle drew on them to define the concept of "cold." See Robert Boyle, *New Experiments and Observations touching Cold, or an Experimental History of Cold* (London, 1665), 522–524, 532, 535–537.

31. "Relation of Captain Thomas Yong, 1634," in Albert C. Myers, ed., *Narratives of Early Pennsylvania, West New Jersey and Delaware, 1630–1707* (New York: Scribner's, 1912), 33–34. In his nephew Robert Evelin's account, this explorer bears the name "Young." See *A Direction for Adventurers with small stock to get two for one, and good land freely . . . Together with a Letter from Master Robert Evelin* (London, 1641), sig. A2[v].

32. See Edward C. Carter 2nd and Clifford Lewis 3rd, "Sir Edmund Plowden and the New Albion Charter, 1632–1785," *PMHB* 83 (1959), 150–179.

Chesapeake Bay. The Englishman and the Lenapes forged an alliance: the English would become partners to these Natives and they would pledge their loyalty to Charles I. Yong had managed, in his own mind, to create new subjects for the English king, a new client state in distant territory that would soon become part of what seemed an ever-expanding arc of English colonies along the mid-Atlantic coast.[33]

By late August, a Native guide led Yong's ship toward the falls of the Delaware. The English realized then that this could not be the passage through the continent or, if it was, it was too shallow for oceangoing vessels. On September 1, some Dutch explorers arrived, having heard that the English were reconnoitering the region. Yong rejected their claim of authority, noting that the king of England owned this territory through the doctrine of discovery. He let the Dutch examine the commission he carried, but when they asked to make a copy, he refused. The Dutch eventually accepted Yong's claim and departed. The English soon concluded their original mission, though they gathered intelligence from the brother of a Mohegan king that indicated a possible route to the Pacific—if only they could get their ships past the falls upriver that blocked passage.[34]

Although the passage remained elusive, the English gained knowledge about territory that none had ever known about before. Yong claimed the climate was like Italy's, with extensive meadows "and full of Beaver and Otter." The fish were abundant, especially during summer sturgeon runs, and the birds so plentiful that the English once took forty-eight partridges in a single hunt. The climate and soil were perfect for hops, which already grew in abundance, and the water was "the most healthfull, fruitefull and commodious River in all the North of America, to be planted"—a stark contrast to the James, as Yong would have learned from his time in Virginia. He was confident too that the Dutch would respect the English claim to the region.[35] Seven years later, his nephew Robert Evelyn published a short account of the journey and the region. He was so confident of English success that he enumerated the supplies a potential colonist would need to bring along—another failed exploration transformed into a plea for colonization.[36]

On August 22, 1631, Art Hopton, the agent of the English court in Madrid, wrote to Lord Dorchester about what he perceived as a threat to

33. "Relation of Captain Thomas Yong," 43.
34. "Relation of Captain Thomas Yong," 43–47.
35. "Relation of Captain Thomas Yong," 47–49.
36. *A Direction for Adventurers*, [sig. A3^{v}–A4^{r}].

Charles I's North American claims. Hopton heard that Franciscan missionaries had "discovered in America that land which lies northward of New Spain and westward of Florida," which the Spanish called New Mexico. Recently he had learned that two of them had arrived on a ship from New Spain. Though he did not name them, he was referring to Benavides, who had returned to Madrid with a report on the progress of mission work in New Mexico. These newly returned emissaries came "to demand a supply of Religious Men, and an increase of maintenance." That might have seemed trivial, but to Hopton the request suggested the emergence of danger. Apparently the visitors had informed the Spanish council that New Mexico "must at length come to the westward of Virginia" and that "it will be necessary to the safety of the Plantation, and to them to pass to it by the nearest way, to root out the English from that continent." Hopton, whose writing suggested that he was among the growing number of English subjects to realize that the rivalry between Spain and England would play out on a continental scale, believed that the Council of the Indies agreed that Spaniards should drive English out of North America. He did not know if they would launch their campaign from home or from "the Indies," which in this case could have referred either to the West Indies, where the Spanish remained the dominant military power, or to the Philippines.[37]

Hopton's warning to London, arriving at a moment of mounting English desire to control larger portions of North America, may have magnified English concerns about New Mexico. But he misunderstood the nature of the Spanish colonial project at that time. Farther south and east, in Mexico, Peru, and Hispaniola, Spanish colonial authorities had created outposts of an empire enriching itself by seizing American natural resources (silver) or creating export-oriented sugar plantations, which were increasingly worked by enslaved Africans. Further, a demographic transition was well underway in New Spain. In 1570, Mexico City had 18,000 occupants; over the next seventy-five years it grew threefold. The decline in the Indigenous population also meant that the city was increasingly dominated by colonists (some of them American-born creoles) and their families. The Spanish colonial population was smaller in the Viceroyalty of Peru, but the gains to be had there remained remarkable, especially from the rich silver mines at Potosí.[38] Transforming cities from

37. Hopton to Dorchester, August 22, 1631, in *Fray Alonso de Benavides' Revised Memorial of 1634*, trans. and ed. Frederick W. Hodge, George P. Hammond, and Agapito Rey (Albuquerque: University of New Mexico Press, 1945), 149–150.

38. See Kris Lane, *Potosi: The Silver City That Changed the World* (Berkeley: University of California Press, 2019); P. J. Bakewell, *Miners of the Red Mountain* (Albuquerque: University of New Mexico Press, 1984); Mary E. Miller and Barbara Mundy, eds.,

Indigenous to colonial control enabled authorities to convince Spanish women, many of them from Seville or other urban regions, to migrate to the Western Hemisphere, either alongside their husbands or to follow those who had gone ahead. As early as the middle decades of the sixteenth century, the sex ratios of Spanish colonial cities, though still uneven, had begun to move toward balance.[39]

Any security felt in Madrid about Mexico and Peru did not apply to New Mexico. Rather than brag about his efforts, Benavides warned about dangers to the Franciscans' achievements, fearing "that from Virginia and the islands of North America, through the navigation of the English and Dutch, heresy might be introduced into New Mexico, which borders on those places." To counteract their potential influence, he recommended establishing "a mission of Irish fathers who know the English language." Such an effort would have multiple benefits. The Irish missionaries "may not only convert the heathen of those places to the Catholic faith," he continued, "but also the heretics who have come from England and Holland and have increased in large numbers, taking Indians for wives, and together might convert the heathen already perverted, and hinder the propagation of heresy in New Mexico, and finally help the Spaniards who have been made slaves in wars with the said English and Dutch, and also the negroes, whom the Portuguese bring to New Spain and sell."[40]

By the early 1630s, fearing that some Native communities in New Mexico posed more risk than others, officials in New Spain sent delegates to secure their empire's control to the north. Twenty soldiers and a local governor traveled with the two missionaries who went to the Apachean communities of Manasas and Quinía. Soon afterward, a larger expedition, which included 30 armed soldiers along with 400 cavalry on horseback, traveled to Acoma. Franciscans among the Zuñi traveled to Hawikuh, a place they reached having passed through ten leagues of a vivid and desolate landscape, a plateau where local lore had it that the red of the rocks was the stain from the blood of an ancient giant.[41]

These emissaries of Spain entered a world where Indigenous faith and practices remained intact. "All the people of this colony cling closely to

Painting a Map of Sixteenth-Century Mexico City: Land, Writing, and Native Rule (New Haven, CT: Yale University Press, 2012). For the population of Mexico City, see Richard Boyer, "Mexico in the Seventeenth Century: Transition of a Colonial Society," *HAHR* 57 (1977), 455–478, esp. 469–470.

39. Peter Boyd-Bowman, "Patterns of Spanish Emigration to the Indies until 1600," *HAHR* 56 (1976), 580–604, esp. 596–601.

40. *Fray Alonso de Benavides' Revised Memorial*, 197–198.

41. *Fray Alonso de Benavides' Revised Memorial*, 210–214, 213n7 (Zuñi myth), 214n8 (Hawikuh identified).

their superstitious idolatry," the Franciscan Estéban de Perea wrote about the Zuñis. "They have their temples with idols of stone and wood." None but the priests could enter the brightly painted holy places, and the only entrance was through a trap door on the roof. These kivas contained the earthly form of gods that protected fields, rivers, forests, and houses. Bountiful fields of beans, corn, and calabashes provided food, along with abundant local game and fowl.[42]

The clerics faced steep odds among the Zuñis at Hawikuh and the Moquis at San Bernardo de Awátobi. The devil was powerful in both places, Perea wrote. Rumors swirled that the Spanish had intended to assault the Indigenous. One apostate reached the Moqui pueblo before the Spaniards, warning that soldiers would "burn their pueblos, steal their property, and behead their children" and that monks were "impostors and that they should not allow them to sprinkle water on their heads because they would be certain to die from it." Similar stories circulated among the Zuñis at Hawikuh, though some Indigenous leaders, so Perea claimed, asked for forgiveness and baptism once they had cast off the words of their own religious. Seizing the moment, another Franciscan orchestrated the construction of an altar in the plaza at Hawikuh. He also renamed the most prominent cacique, who from that day forward bore the name Don Agustín. Once baptized, the cacique, again in Perea's report, urged his community to accept the sacrament too, telling the others that he "felt such great rejoicing and courage in his heart that he considered himself to be much braver than before." The missionaries achieved enough success among the Apaches that the latter entrusted the Franciscans with twelve adults of their own, along with a boy "who was to learn the Spanish language and teach them his own." The Franciscans and the Apaches returned to Santa Fe, where they were "received with general rejoicing due to the success of their heroic enterprises." Driven by spiritual gains, the Franciscans realized the other rewards that could be obtained among the Apaches, including cattle and silver.[43]

The possibility of gaining material wealth would have pleased the clerics and brought particular delight to secular officials eager to make good on what they saw as the promise of the region that Coronado had visited almost a century earlier. But for the moment, Spaniards barely made any substantial gains. This European arc of opportunism did not transform the Southwest.

42. *Fray Alonso de Benavides' Revised Memorial*, 213–216, quotation at 214.

43. *Fray Alonso Benavides' Revised Memorial*, 216–221, quotations at 217 ("burn their pueblos"), 220–221 (Apaches, baptism, resources).

Even though the population of Europeans in eastern North America grew slowly if at all in most colonial arenas, the number of reports about the opportunities along the Atlantic coast continued to increase. In 1625 alone, over 150 authors published books that included content about the Americas. Ten years later, another 100 or so authors offered books. That year saw the publication of Luke Foxe's account of the Arctic, the Jesuit missionary Paul Le Jeune's relation of what was happening in the St. Lawrence Valley, and an account of the newly launched colony of Maryland.[44]

Not surprisingly, enticing accounts attracted attention across the continent. On June 15, 1636, Peter Minuit, a onetime director of the New Netherland colony then residing in Amsterdam, believed it was time for the Swedish government, which had gathered extensive knowledge about international affairs during its ongoing colonization of the Saami and its military involvement in the Thirty Years' War, to support launching a colony on the banks of the Delaware River. The territory had been claimed by the English after Yong's exploration in 1632 but had not had a steady European presence. It remained, like most of North America, Indian Country. In this case the place was crucial to the economy and societies of both the Susquehannocks and the Lenapes.[45] Since the Dutch, French, and English were among the "many kingdoms and countries" that "prosper by means of navigation" in the Americas, Minuit believed that the Swedes should make an investment too. He estimated he would need one armed oceangoing ship in the 150-to-225-ton range and a small bark to reach trade opportunities closer to shore. He hoped that the initial migration would include individuals who could tend tobacco fields, which Minuit believed would fare well in the area. Such farmers could also be pressed into military duty if necessary. Minuit knew the seasonal practices of Native hunters, knowledge that allowed him to suggest the Swedes could harvest 4,500 to 6,000 beaver pelts each year. He, like other colonial promoters, was self-interested—he thought his new company should be exempt from paying any taxes for a decade—but he attracted almost immediate interest from the Swedish royal family.[46]

Queen Christina—or her regent, since she was still not quite eleven years old—supported the creation of a new colony along the Delaware

44. *EA*, 2:239–258, 352–361; Foxe, *North-West Fox*; Paul Le Jeune, *Relation de ce qui s'est passé en la Nouvelle France en l'anee 1634* (Paris, 1635); *A Relation of Maryland* ([London], 1635).
45. "Letter of Peter Minuit Proposing the Founding of the Colony of New Sweden," trans. G. B. Keen, *PMHB* 6 (1882), 458.
46. "Letter of Peter Minuit," 458–460; C. T. Odhner, "The Founding of New Sweden, 1637–1642," trans. G. B. Keen, *PMHB* 3 (1979), 269–284.

and put up half the funds needed for the Södre Compagniet (South Company or New Sweden Company), with the rest coming from Dutch merchants. The queen and her supporters accepted the argument that creating a colony would bring the same trifecta of rewards evident in other European mid-Atlantic outposts: enhancement of shipping opportunities, a substantial increase in revenue like those the Spanish and Dutch had gained, and the chance to spread their version of Christianity among the Natives.[47]

In the autumn of 1637 Minuit set off with the armed *Kalmare Nyckel* (*Key of Calmar)* and the smaller *Fågel Grip* (*The Griffin*). They ascended the Delaware in March or early April, halting well south of the reach of the Dutch. (The English had not yet followed up on Yong's effort to claim the Delaware Valley.) The newcomers landed along what they called the River of New Sweden, claimed that they immediately purchased land from local Natives (presumably Lenape), hammered stakes in the ground to mark the boundaries of their new possession, and employed a Swedish surveyor to map the territory. Minuit orchestrated the construction of Fort Christina on the west side of the river at the Lenape community of Hopokahacking, an area that would later become Wilmington, Delaware. They built adjacent to Minquas Kill, where the Susquehannocks had traditionally brought furs to trade with Europeans, a commerce that predated the new colonial project. A party of Swedes also set up at the confluence of the Delaware and the Schuylkill, which would later become the origins of Philadelphia. There had been two Dutch forts along the Delaware earlier, but according to the Reverend Israel Acrelius, an eighteenth-century Swedish theologian and historian, "both of these were entirely destroyed by the Americans, and their people driven away." Despite their absence, the Dutch thought the territory was still theirs. In May 1638, Willem Kieft, the new director-general of New Netherland, informed Minuit that the Dutch had a claim to this region, which they called the South River. He threatened to use force to displace the newcomers, a promise of yet more bloodshed in an area that had already seen plenty.[48]

The Native peoples of the valley saw the newcomers as neighbors to be tolerated as long as they were useful, but they quickly surmised that the Swedes were overstepping their bounds. For their part, the Swedes

47. Gunlög Fur, *Colonialism in the Margins: Cultural Encounters in New Sweden and Lapland* (Leiden: Brill, 2005), 88–90.

48. Israel Acrelius, "Account of the Swedish Churches in New Sweden, 1759," in Myers, ed., *Narratives of Early Pennsylvania*, 59–64; Odhner, "Founding of New Sweden," 278–279 (Minuit's arrival).

believed they had purchased land at a negotiated and fair price, unable to understand that sachems in this area behaved like Europeans who bestowed titles and lands on their favorites and expected loyalty and service in exchange. The cultural gap along the Delaware fed feelings of resentment among Europeans, especially since the Swedes had signed deeds. They believed that the written record provided their good intentions to pay an honest price for land and become neighbors of Indigenous, all the better to advance the other main goals of the colony—making a profit from the fur trade and spreading Reformed Christianity.[49]

In 1638, four of the sailors from the *Key of Calmar* visited a notary after the ship returned to Amsterdam. There they attested to the transfer of the land, providing unusual detail for an initial land transaction in eastern North America. Seeing that the Lenapes could not understand what the Swedes hoped to accomplish, they testified, a man named Andress Lucassen stepped forward to act as a translator, having learned the local language from having "lived long in the country." According to the sailors, the Swedes had looked for other Europeans and found none, and they sought the Susquehannocks too but found none of them. Having made their presence known by firing cannons, Minuit and his allies eventually managed to gather a group of Natives, including five sachems who claimed to have the support of other Indigenous peoples, including the Susquehannocks and Mantes (the latter probably the Lenapes who lived across from Tinicum Island). The entire group went into the captain's cabin and in front of witnesses they "ceded, transported, and transferred all the land, as many days' journeys on all places and parts of the river as [the Swedes] requested." Minuit took possession of the land in the name of the "most mighty Princess and Virgin Christina, elected Queen of the Swedes, Goths and Wends." After the signing the Swedes erected Queen Christina's arms, fired cannons again, and participated in rituals in front of the sachems. Once witnessed, the notary agreed to give the text to Peter Spiring, Minuit's original partner.[50]

It seems that at first the Swedes, perhaps annoyed that Natives kept coming back with the expectation of receiving gifts, believed that the Lenapes understood the transaction in European terms. Although the Indigenous allowed the Swedes to build their fort, they never disappeared. Instead, they returned regularly to trade. They normally arrived in June, after they had planted their maize for the year. They remained along the river's edge for much of the summer gathering wild peas, which

49. Acrelius, "Account of the Swedish Churches," 73.
50. "Affidavit of Four Men from the *Key of Calmar*, 1638," in Myers, ed., *Narratives of Early Pennsylvania*, 85–89.

they dried in the sun. The Swedes thought of them as visitors. The Lenapes thought that they retained customary rights. Just like they expected gifts, so too they demanded access to their traditional fishing, hunting, and pea-gathering areas, maintaining their economy as it had existed long before any Europeans arrived. They came in June because they had to wait until the last frost had passed, which they marked, like the Haudenosaunee did, with the appearance of the Pleiades in one part of the spring sky. The Swedes hoped to create a new world here. The Lenapes remained content with the one that they still inhabited.[51]

Despite these Europeans' high hopes, New Sweden did not become an immediate draw for migrants. Part of the problem lay in the homeland, where the population, which was not nearly as large as that of other European nations interested in colonizing North America, had been depleted by years of war on the continent. With that conflict having ended, the Swedish government took advantage of peacetime to create what amounted to a migration draft. The central government ordered the local leaders in Elfsborg and Värmland, two of the country's western provinces, to round up the families of men who had dodged military service or committed some other infraction. According to the plan, these men, along with their spouses and children, would go to New Sweden and spend at least two years there before they could seek return. Måns Kling, who had gone on Minuit's voyage and soon returned, hoped to find recruitable migrants from among the *drift-finnar*, individuals of Finnish descent living in Swedish forests. While at home, these Finns had practiced slash-and-burn agriculture, a technique that minimized the labor of a farming family but came at a high environmental cost. By the early decades of the seventeenth century, the value of wood had increased, which heightened the desire of Swedish officials to remove the *drift-finnar*. Much better, officials argued, to put them to work developing the colony than have them continue to spoil a valuable natural resource.[52]

Even these modest plans produced marginal results. A mission of 1641 carried just thirty-five individuals, including eight—four boys and four young men—sentenced to servitude. There was a tailor who set sail with his wife and three children, hoping to start a farm. Married couples tended to be rare, and the sex ratio skewed heavily male. In its first seventeen years, Swedish ships brought a total of only 650 individuals to the Delaware.[53]

51. Acrelius, "Account of the Swedish Churches," 73. Acrelius noted that the Lenapes kept at their seasonal rounds until the turn of the next century.
52. Fur, *Colonialism in the Margins*, 94–95.
53. Fur, *Colonialism in the Margins*, 95–96.

Minuit departed for Sweden in June 1638, sailing aboard the *Kalmar Nyckel* to St. Christopher, where he traded what he had acquired along the Delaware for tobacco. He dispatched a vessel to the West Indies, where its crew spent time in Havana and then returned to the Delaware. In mid-April 1639, the ship sailed for Sweden, making the journey to Gothenburg in five weeks. Minuit was less fortunate. Shortly before he planned to sail for home, he was aboard a Dutch ship called *Het vliegende hert* (*The Flying Deer*) when a massive hurricane blew in. Twenty European ships scattered in the storm. Minuit apparently drowned when *The Flying Deer* sank.[54]

English travelers' reports, like those from Yong, Foxe, and James, spread in a realm increasingly gripped by crisis. London, still recovering from bouts of plague, had become a scene of political turmoil. Charles I's belief in the idea of personal rule led him to keep Parliament in abeyance and often suspended. Signs of growing religious discontent became ever more pronounced, exacerbated by an ongoing depression in the cloth trades and the idea that the world teetered on the edge of a precipice. Ministers warned their readers about the looming catastrophe. A moralist named William Gouge in 1631 summarized the fraught moment. "Now are the times," Gouge warned, "wherin the clouds of God[']s anger have obscured the bright skie of the Church." The English suffered from disease, conflict, and hunger. The barbarians of St. Augustine's time posed less of a threat than "*Jesuites*, *Monks*, *Priests*, *Friers*, and the rest of that rabble," the agents of "the Popish Clergy." Wars spread across Europe and grain prices rose. "Is it not now time," Gouge rhetorically asked, "for *Plaisters* to be made *for the plague*, *Provision* to be procured against *Dearth*, and *Protection* provided against the *Sword*?"[55]

54. Odhner, "Founding of New Sweden," 282–284; see also C. W. Weslager, *New Sweden on the Delaware, 1638–1655* (Wilmington, DE: Middle Atlantic Press, 1988), 51–55.
55. William Gouge, *Gods Three Arrowes: Plague, Famine, Sword* (London, 1631), quotations at sig. [A6^{r}–^{v}]; for the context, see "The Life and Death of Dr. Gouge who dyed *anno Christi* 1653," in Sa. Clark, *A Collection of Lives of Ten Eminent Divines* (London, 1662), 95–125. For the king's governing philosophy, see Kevin Sharpe, *The Personal Rule of Charles I* (New Haven, CT: Yale University Press, 1992). By the early 1630s, Gouge was already a well-known observer of English society with a keen interest, as he demonstrated in a 1622 sermon, in the use of corporal punishment for children; see Kathryn Sather, "Sixteenth and Seventeenth Century Child-Rearing: A Matter of Discipline," *Journal of Social History* 22 (1989), 735–743.

At this moment of high tension at home and the circulation of reports about new opportunities abroad, a group of religious dissenters focused their attention on Providencia, a small island off the coast of Nicaragua already known to Dutch and English privateers. They were aware of the region from news reports and policy debates within England that focused on the booming business of privateers, whose raids on Spanish ships lined the pockets of officials like Buckingham (as lord admiral), provided infusions of wealth, and discouraged their continental rivals.[56] These dissenters, learning that Charles I and Philip IV had agreed to a truce, decided to act by founding the Providence Island Company in 1629. Their seal, derived from Isaiah 42:4, reads "Legem eius insulae expectabunt" (the isles shall wait for his law), a reference to the centrality of the missionary impulse to the launching of the colony.[57]

Almost all the investors in the Providence Island Company had been involved in earlier overseas ventures. Thirteen of them sat in Parliament, including Robert Rich, the second Earl of Warwick, who had prior involvement in the Africa, Guiana, East India, New England, Massachusetts Bay, Somers Island, and Virginia companies. Daniel Elfrith, the captain of one of the first ships to explore the island, was a major landholder and the father-in-law of the governor of Bermuda, where he stopped on his voyage home to report on the island's potential. Coral reefs, he knew, posed a threat to ships trying to land there, but that was less of a risk than the fact that Providence Island lay "in the heart of the Indies & the mouth of the Spaniards." Charles I granted local leaders the ability to govern themselves, adding that anyone born there would be free, as would the rest of the inhabitants.[58]

A contingent of fewer than 100 men and boys departed for the island in February 1631. They went as "tenants at halves," which meant that they would pay half of whatever they grew to the proprietors and keep the rest for themselves. The migrants were free to recruit servants, who would

56. Karen Ordahl Kupperman, *Providence Island, 1630–1641: The Other Puritan Colony* (Cambridge: Cambridge University Press, 1993), 14–17; Mark G. Hanna, *Pirate Nests and the Rise of the British Empire, 1570–1740* (Chapel Hill: University of North Carolina Press for the Omohundro Institute of Early American History and Culture, 2015), 67–70; and John A. C. Conybeare and Todd Sandler, "State-Sponsored Violence as a Tragedy of the Commons: England's Privateering Wars with France and Spain, 1625–1630," *Public Choice* 77 (1993), 879–897.

57. "Silver Seal-Die of the Providence Island Company," Friends of the Nations' Libraries, https://grants.fnl.org.uk/silver-seal-die-providence-island-company (accessed July 29, 2023).

58. Kupperman, *Providence Island*, 357–360 (investors), 24–26 (Elfrith); patent dated December 4, 1620, *Calendar of State Papers: Colonial Series, America and West Indies* (London, 1860–), 1:123–124.

serve for two or three years and then be entitled to land, an appealing prospect on Providence Island just as it had been in Virginia. Few of the earliest migrants died, a dramatic and welcome difference from the experience of the English in other colonies. Success came through experimentation, specifically an effort to identify salable commodities, a pursuit that was common among Europeans crossing the Atlantic.[59]

Despite so many things in their favor, the Providence Island Company and its colonists did not live up to initial hopes. As early as the spring of 1632, disagreements threatened to end the scheme almost as soon as it began. The colonists bristled at the terms of their initial agreement to share half of their profits with the investors. They complained about the absence of women, a common situation in new English colonies outside of New England; the presence of soldiers, who posed potential threats to the fragile order that the planters were trying to create; and the fact that company investors controlled the sale of their tobacco and could demand whatever prices they wanted for goods shipped from England. At home, similarly distressed people sometimes rioted, as they did twice in the Essex port town of Maldon in 1629. In spite of the tensions, perhaps 150 new migrants from southeastern England sailed there in 1632. Two years later, the company supported the formation of local self-government. But anxiety remained, driven by the long distance between the colonists and the wealthy investors in England who remained, in many ways, their employers rather than their partners.[60] More distressing was the disappointment that followed efforts to make substantial profits from palma Christi (the castor bean), which produced an oil that could be added to soap in the English textile industry, as well as rhubarb, mechoacan (popularized among Europeans by the Seville physician Nicholas Monardes in the 1570s), silkgrass, guacum, libnum vitae, wax, honey, and logwood trees. Hoped-for trade with the Moskito Indians on the

59. Kupperman, *Providence Island*, 24–31, 32–34; minutes of meetings of the Company of Adventurers for Providence Island, November 22, 1630, and February 7, 1631, in *Calendar of State Papers: Colonial* 1:121–123, 125–128; Karl Offen, "Puritan Bioprospecting in Central America and the West Indies," *Intinerario* 35 (2011), 15–47; Londa Schiebinger, "Prospecting for Drugs: European Naturalists in the West Indies," in Londa Scheibinger and Claudia Swan, eds., *Colonial Botany: Science, Commerce, and Politics in the Early Modern World* (Philadelphia: University of Pennsylvania Press, 2005), 119–133.

60. Kupperman, *Providence Island*, 34–39, 41–44, 46–48, 50–57; John Walter, "Grain Riots and Popular Attitudes to the Law: Maldon and the Crisis of 1629," in John Brewer and John Styles, eds., *An Ungovernable People: The English and Their Law in the Seventeenth and Eighteenth Centuries* (London: Hutchinson, 1980), 66–84.

Nicaraguan coastline 150 miles to the west generated little return from colonists' search for contrayerva (an antidote for poison) and the rumored health-promoting properties to be extracted from the bodies of manatees and alligators.[61]

By 1635, the transformation of Providence Island from a tropical paradise into a profitable colony stalled. Some English observers thought that the island would best be used as a base for privateers, reviving an idea that had been central to the location of Jamestown in 1607. But the small number of privateers based on Providence Island had strained relations with local planters. More threatening was the ongoing labor shortage. Efforts to ameliorate the gender imbalance attracted some English women, but not nearly enough, which meant that there were no realistic prospects of creating a creole labor force. Five years into the operation, only 500 or so English migrants lived there. They seemed incapable of establishing good relations with the Moskitos, whom some colonists likely would have tried to enslave but the company prohibited such an action. By the middle of the decade, the company's directors decided that they could fulfill their economic demands only by importing enslaved Africans.[62]

In the 1630s, no European nation embraced the prospect of emigration to North America more than England, which sent 80,000 to 90,000 across the Atlantic during the decade. In 1635 alone, fifty-three ships carrying a total of 7,507 men and women left London's ports. Almost 5,000 of them were migrants bound for English territory, including small communities hugging the North American shoreline as well as Barbados, Providence Island, and Bermuda. Another 1,000 sailed for the European continent, and approximately 1,500 were soldiers on missions. Those who left the city that year equaled 2.1 to 2.5 percent of London's population. This figure does not include the passengers on ships that set sail from Dover, Harwich, Ipswich, Plymouth, Sandwich, Southampton, and Weymouth. To be sure, some of the travelers, especially soldiers, did not remain in American possessions permanently. Nonetheless, this stream of migrants did fuel population growth. There were 9,500 colonists in English American communities in 1630. In 1640, that number stood at 53,700, an

61. Kupperman, *Providence Island*, 84–91; Offen, "Puritan Bioprospecting," 15; [Nicholas Monardes], *Joyfull Newes out of the newfound world*, trans. John Frampton (London, 1580), ff. 23^{v}–30^{v}.

62. Kupperman, *Providence Island*, 93–98 (Moskitos), 102–105 (privateers), 159–160 (migrants), 165–167; Offen, "Puritan Bioprospecting," 21 (population in 1635).

increase of over 500 percent.[63] Still, however impressive the gain, the number of migrants to English colonies in the mainland was far less than the 180,000 who went to Ireland from 1600 to 1640 or the 190,000 who would migrate to the West Indies by 1660.[64]

But those numbers of free migrants mask the larger story that was unfolding across the Atlantic basin in the early decades of the seventeenth century. The vast majority of Europeans went west eager to make a profit. But the greatest gains lay in labor-intensive industries, notably the production of sugar. To achieve profits from the crop that changed European tastes, many invested in the slave trade to bring workers to regions where northern Europeans had succumbed to dysentery and scurvy. By the 1630s, ships bearing enslaved Africans became increasingly common on the seas.[65]

Before 1580, the Spanish had captured or purchased 45,000 enslaved Africans, most of them bound for the Caribbean, given the limited need for labor in either New Spain or Peru, where the conquerors could exploit Indigenous, through enslavement, forced tribute, or the expansion of encomienda. The Portuguese acquired another 13,000. All but about 1,000 of the enslaved arrived on ships owned by one or the other Iberian nation, with the remainder transported on English ships. But after 1580, with rapidly expanding sugar plantations and the perception that owners could not attract enough European workers or conscript Indigenous laborers, the transatlantic slave trade exploded. From 1580 to 1640, 289,000 enslaved Africans arrived in Spanish American territory, and another 204,000 went to Portuguese holdings, primarily Brazil. For the first time, substantial numbers of enslaved Africans went to Dutch and English American colonies, including the new English colony in Barbados and the parts of Brazil captured by the Dutch. By 1640, the total number of the enslaved brought to these outposts of northern European Protestant nations totaled about 12,000. Hardly any of these Africans arrived in the Chesapeake, where the population of the enslaved was likely not more than 500 as late as 1645. Sugar, not specie or tobacco, drove the slave

63. Alison Games, *Migration and the Origins of the English Atlantic World* (Cambridge, MA: Harvard University Press, 1999), 1–4.
64. Nicholas Canny, "English Migration into and Across the Atlantic During the Seventeenth and Eighteenth Centuries," in Nicholas Canny, ed., *Europeans on the Move: Studies on European Migration, 1500–1800* (Oxford: Oxford University Press, 1994), 64.
65. See J. R. McNeill, *Mosquito Empires: Ecology and War in the Greater Caribbean, 1620–1914* (New York: Cambridge University Press, 2010), 92–94.

trade, evident in the fact that the number of enslaved in Barbados expanded when planters shifted their fields from tobacco to sugar.[66]

The increase in the number of the enslaved bore little relation to the Iberian demand for gold and silver. By the late sixteenth century, mining had come to dominate the economy in specific places, including Potosí and Zacatecas. But to neither place did the Spanish import many enslaved bodies. Instead, those who worked the silver mines in Potosí were wage-earning Natives. About 50 percent of those in the silver mountain were *mingas*, paid the going rate, or *mitayos*, who earned even less. The workers here and in New Spain were coerced but not enslaved. By the early seventeenth century, there were probably not more than 10,000 Natives working in mines in New Spain, and perhaps 20,000 in Potosí. If Europeans believed that mining was the only important industry in the Western Hemisphere, there would have been limited demand for African bodies.[67]

But the potential for producing sugar in Brazil and the West Indies changed Europeans' calculations. Production of cane was notoriously grueling, with backbreaking work in the fields, the threat of losing a hand or arm in grinding mills, and the possibility of dying when boilers exploded. The profits either blinded Europeans to its horrors or were enough to calm any latent squeamishness. Portuguese and Dutch planters expanded their operations in Brazil to take advantage of dark clay soil (known as *massapé*) and to erect mills (*ingenios*), shipping processed sugar to the coast for transportation across the Atlantic. As early as 1623, one Dutch observer reported to the WIC that there were 137 *ingenios* operating in Pernambuco, Paríba, and Itamaracá, each capable of processing seventy tons of sugar annually. From 1631 to 1651, the Dutch exported 1,200 tons each year, even though increased production drove the price of sugar down. Dutch colonists soon followed sugar planters. "Every mill [has] a chapel, a schoolhouse, a priest, a barber, a smith, a shoemaker, a

66. David Eltis, *The Rise of African Slavery in the Americas* (Cambridge: Cambridge University Press, 2000), 9 (number of enslaved); Edmund S. Morgan, *American Slavery, American Freedom: The Ordeal of Colonial Virginia* (New York: W. W. Norton, 1975), 298; Dunn, *Sugar and Slaves*, 49–54, 67–69. Enslaved Africans had been present earlier in Barbados, but their numbers increased dramatically with the growth in sugar exports; see John J. McCusker and Russell R. Menard, "The Sugar Industry in the Seventeenth Century: A New Perspective on the Barbadian 'Sugar Revolution,'" in Stuart B. Schwartz., ed. *Tropical Babylons: Sugar and the Making of the Atlantic World, 1450–1680* (Chapel Hill: University of North Carolina Press, 2004), 289–330, and see also Russell R. Menard, *Sweet Negotiations: Sugar, Slavery, and Plantation Agriculture in Early Barbados* (Charlottesville: University of Virginia Press, 2006).

67. Eltis, *The Rise of African Slavery in the Americas*, 24–25.

carpenter, a joiner, a potter, a tailor, and all other artificers necessary," one English visitor wrote.[68]

By the end of the 1630s, enslavement, already present in the expansion of European communities in the Western Hemisphere, had become central to colonization. There were still free migrants who could choose to sell their labor for a set number of years as part of a long-term plan to improve their lives. But a growing number of transatlantic migrants had no choice. Opportunity for Europeans became inextricable from enslavement for Africans.

68. Stuart B. Schwartz, "A Commonwealth Within Itself: The Early Brazilian Sugar Industry, 1550–1670," in Schwartz, ed., *Tropical Babylons*, 158–170, quotation at 158. The Portuguese term for *ingenio* was *engenho*.

Part III

Fractures

19

"From East to West"

In the spring of 1634, smallpox spread across southern New England, the suffering it produced most evident in Native communities. It began, William Bradford reported, near a trading house that New Plymouth maintained. The afflicted, he wrote, "died most miserably; for a sorer disease cannot befall them, they fear it more than the plague." The characteristic symptom was the eruption of small lesions on the skin. Bradford observed that those who had the pox "have them in abundance; and for want of bedding & linen, and other helps, they fall into a lamentable condition, as they lie on their hard mats, the pox breaking and mattering, and running one into another; their skin cleaving (by reason thereof) to the mats they lie on." He claimed that just by rolling over a victim might lose all of the skin on one side of their body. "And then being very sore," he added, "what with cold, and other distempers, they die like rotten sheep." Normally, as colonists recognized, Indigenous communities had individuals who stepped in to heal the ill. Europeans might have doubted the efficacy of Indigenous cures that the immigrants saw as the signs of heathen devotions to dark forces. But even in their skepticism they knew that members of a Native town tended to rally around to cure someone who was sick.[1]

But in 1634, the normal practices fractured. There were not enough healthy Indigenous people available to bring water to the sick, maintain fires, or bury the dead. Unable to gather new firewood, Bradford wrote that Native peoples would eventually "burn the wooden trays, & dishes they ate their meat in, and their very bows, & arrows." Some were so weak that they could not make it back to their houses after having crawled out to find water. Bradford claimed that the colonists, after getting over their initial fear, "seeing their woeful, and sad Condition, and hearing their pitiful cries, and lamentations," felt enough compassion that they brought firewood, food, and water, and buried the dead. Even still, a local sachem

1. William Bradford, *Of Plimoth Plantation*, ed. Kenneth Minkema et al. (Boston: Colonial Society of Massachusetts, 2020), 418.

and almost everyone in the town died. "But by the marvelous goodness, & providence of God," Bradford wrote, employing the characteristic rhetoric of dissenters who believed in predestination, "not one of the English, was so much as sick, or in the least measure tainted with this disease," even though they visited the Indigenous daily.[2]

During the 1630s, infectious diseases killed thousands in North America, territory that, with the notable exception of the epidemic in coastal New England from 1616 to 1619, had been spared the kinds of catastrophic epidemics of hemorrhagic fevers that had taken the lives of millions in New Spain the previous century. But no more. The increased volume of shipping across the Atlantic amplified the chances that contagious individuals might land in North America, enhancing the possibility of Old World diseases killing individuals whose bodies may have already been weakened by stress induced by physical displacement and relentless attacks on their culture and beliefs.[3]

At the same time that imported diseases scarred and destroyed Indigenous bodies, the number of colonists increased dramatically, especially in territory claimed by the Massachusetts Bay Company. The opposite demographic profiles of shrinking Native towns and growing immigrant communities contributed to rising tensions in eastern New England. The tensions erupted in the cataclysmic Anglo-Pequot War of 1637. Even after its bloody conclusion, anxieties continued. Authorities in English colonial towns believed that they could solve some of their problems by expelling malefactors. Native leaders were more circumspect. Narragansetts who sided with English to reduce the authority of the Pequots, the once-dominant population in modern southeastern New England, came to realize that relentless, westward-moving colonists would destroy them unless they found a way to keep their communities safe.

To John Winthrop and his allies, the arrival of Protestants in Massachusetts signaled a decisive moment. Separatist dissenters had established New Plymouth a decade earlier, but they had never managed to attract many others to their outpost. Those who organized the colonization of Massachusetts Bay believed they would reap more success than the Pilgrims if they welcomed non-Separatists, individuals and families whose religious views set them apart from the Church of England but whose theological impulses did not lead them to conclude that the established church of their homeland was no longer legitimate. These traveling

2. Bradford, *Of Plimouth Plantation*, 418–419.

3. See David S. Jones, "Virgin Soils Revisited," *WMQ*, 3rd Ser., 60 (2003), 703–742.

dissenters saw their migration to New England as a way to demonstrate that the Church of England could be reformed if there existed a place where only their god's elect would be full members of a church. They wanted to cleanse the national church of everything that made it, to them, an affront in the eyes of their almighty.[4] Among those who embraced the dissenters' cause was John Cotton, who had studied at Trinity and Emmanuel Colleges in Cambridge and taken up his first ministerial position at St. Botolph's in Boston, Lincolnshire, in 1612. By the late 1620s, fearing that his unorthodox views of Anglican priests might lead to punishment, he and other prominent critics of the national church joined the Massachusetts Bay Company migration to the new Boston across the Atlantic.[5]

Even before he left England, Cotton had heard that two ministers, Francis Higginson and Samuel Skelton, had gone to the north shore of Massachusetts Bay in 1629 and established a small church in Salem. Word had reached England that the ministers had denied sacraments to other English immigrants, including Winthrop and three other "godly & faithfull Servants of Christ," as Cotton wrote to Skelton, as well as baptism for an infant born on the passage across the ocean. Cotton told Skelton that he believed the Salem church's policies had "sprung from new-Plimmoth-men" who based their practices on flawed readings of theological texts relating to who could receive the sacraments. Cotton and his allies battled against these separatist tendencies, relying on printers to spread their views among the community of English dissenters. Separatism or church policies that resembled it prevailed in New Plymouth, these clerics knew, but the colonists eager to launch Massachusetts believed that it needed to be quashed in their new communities. After all, they had a high calling because colonies, as the minister John White put it then, "have their warrant from Gods direction and command." The colonizers needed to take as many "empty Lands" as they could because "the taking in of large Countreys presents a naturall remedy against covetousnesse, fraud, and violence; when every man may enjoy enough without wrong or injury to his neighbour." Rather than separate from the Church of England, Winthrop and other leaders instead saw common cause with those who were like-minded but who remained back in England. "Wee are not of those that dreame of perfection in this world," they wrote from *Arbella* on April 7, 1630, when it was docked at Yarmouth. "Yet we desire you would

4. Edmund S. Morgan, *Visible Saints: The History of a Puritan Idea* (Ithaca, NY: Cornell University Press, 1963), 17–26.
5. John Cotton, "Letter from New England," in Alan Heimert and Andrew Delbanco, eds., *Puritans in America* (Cambridge, MA: Harvard University Press, 1985), 93.

be pleased to take notice of the principals, and body of our company, as those who esteeme it our honour, to call the *Church* of *England*, from whence wee rise, our deare Mother."[6]

By 1633, Roger Williams, who had arrived in Massachusetts in 1631, had replaced Salem's first two ministers, but he held to their interpretations while he remained in that pulpit. On October 9, 1635, Massachusetts authorities asked all the ministers of the colony to consider letters that Williams had written, including one to his flock at Salem in which, as Winthrop described it, he hoped "to persuade them to renounce Communion with all the Churches in the Baye, as full of Antichristian pollution." Williams declined to back down. The general court ordered him to leave the colony within six weeks. Williams traveled back to Salem, where his congregation "refused Communion with his owne Churche, who openly disclaimed his errors." In January 1636 the court met again after hearing rumors that Williams had still neither renounced his position nor left the colony. They ordered Captain John Underhill to arrest him and bring him back to Boston, from which they would then send him to England. The desperate measure fit a moment of urgency among the rulers of the colony, who had heard that Williams had convinced about twenty others to join him on a migration to Narragansett Bay. Underhill failed to find him.[7] But the rift between Cotton and Williams continued. Even on their own in a territory that had few Indigenous, dissenting English waged spiritual battle against each other.[8]

Dissenting clerics who battled over theological principles on the ground in New England soon learned that the establishment of puritan colonies in Massachusetts Bay, along with New Plymouth, angered the

6. John Cotton to Samuel Skelton, October 2, 1630, in Sargent Bush Jr., ed., *The Correspondence of John Cotton* (Chapel Hill: University of North Carolina Press for the Omohundro Institute of Early American History and Culture, 2001), 141–149; John Cotton, *Gods Promise to His Plantation* (London, 1630); Cotton, "Letter from New England," 93–94; Morgan, *Visible Saints*, 85–88, 101–104; David D. Hall, *The Puritans: A Transatlantic History* (Princeton, NJ: Princeton University Press, 2019), 225–226; [John White], *The Planters Plea, Or the Grounds of Plantations examined, and usual Objections answered. Together with a manifestation of the causes mooving such as have lately undertaken a Plantation in New-England* (London, 1630), quotations at 1 and 4–5; [John Winthrop et al.], *The Humble Request of his Majesties loyall subjects . . . to the rest of their Brethren in and of the Church of England* (London, 1630), quotation at 3.
7. John Winthrop, *The Journal of John Winthrop, 1630–1649*, ed. Richard S. Dunn et al. (Cambridge, MA: Harvard University Press, 1996), 158, 163–164.
8. Cotton to Williams, early 1636, in Bush, ed., *Correspondence of John Cotton*, 211–225, quotations at 213–214.

councilors of the Council for New England. By late 1631, military commander Ferdinando Gorges, an early investor in this Plymouth, England–based Council, took a lead in an effort to derail the Massachusetts Bay colony.[9] To them, the dissenters in New England were trespassers setting up communities on land owned by the members of the council. On November 6, 1632, the president and council laid out a detailed plan for how the region should be colonized. They wanted the king to issue a new patent for the region and demand that all prior patents be returned. All economic activity, including decisions about who could emigrate to New England, was to be controlled by the council.[10] In 1633, members of the council understood that Charles I approved of the dissenters' early efforts.[11] Two years later, in the face of what they saw as an existential threat to their patent, they sued. In November 1635, with the twice-exiled Thomas Morton as their lawyer, the council brought a *quo warranto* suit to the King's Bench, arguing that the Massachusetts Bay Company and the colonists it supported did not have the authority to establish a colony in the region.[12]

Gorges, Morton, and their allies won in court. The judgment declared that the rights assigned in the charter "should be seized into the King's hands." The colonists in Massachusetts needed to return their charter. Once they did so, Gorges would become the governor of the region. He alone, according to one of the king's proclamations, would have the authority to decide who could take up residence there.[13]

Yet while the Privy Council, the King's Bench, and even Charles I could demand that the colonists in Massachusetts return the charter, putting the revocation into action proved more difficult. Immediately the colonists voiced vigorous opposition. Edward Winslow went to London to battle the plan. He learned that the Gorges group had the support of the archbishop of Canterbury, who, Winslow feared, wanted to vacate the

9. The document, is CO 1/6, November 4, 1631 to November 1, 1638 (hereafter Minutes of the Council of New England); the material from 1631 to 1638 was printed as *Records of the Council for New England* (Cambridge, MA, 1867), 97–131.

10. Minutes of the Council for New England, ff. 59, 61, and 65.

11. *Acts of the Privy Council of England, Colonial Series* (London, 1908–1912), 1:184–185.

12. The two entries are for November 23 and 24, 1635, in KB 21/12, f. 11r–11v, TNA.

13. Egerton Ms. 2395, British Library; [Thomas Hutchinson], A *Collection of Original Papers Relative to the History of the Colony of Massachusetts Bay* (Boston, 1769), 101–103; G. D. Scull, "The 'Quo Warranto' of 1635," *New-England Historical and Genealogical Register* XXXVIII (1884), 209–216; Order of the Privy Council, May 3, 1637, CO 1/9, no. 49; minutes of the Court of King's Bench, 1637, CO 1/9, no. 50; the king's manifesto for the government in New England, July 23, 1637, CO 1/9, no. 60; *Records of the Council for New England*, 7–80.

New England patents and bring the dissenters' churches under his control.[14] Massachusetts authorities contested the court's finding for years, arguing that revocation of their charter would have disastrous consequences for the king's subjects living in the province.[15]

In the end, they did not need their elaborate arguments. In 1635, Gorges and his allies built a great ship, which they planned to use to transport 1,000 soldiers to New England to support his new government. Although their god "had carried so many weak and crazy ships" across the ocean, one contemporary reported, it seemed like divine intervention when "this strong new-built ship in the very launching fell all in pieces." After the ship's demise Gorges never commissioned another, perhaps concluding that a military invasion was too expensive to mount.[16] In the aftermath of the disaster, he came to the realization that he was too old, and his financial resources stretched too thin, to make the journey across the ocean to take matters in hand. Instead of putting the king's order into action, he remained in England, where he continued his legal battle. In 1636 he sent his nephew William to govern a settlement to be called New Somersetshire, which Winthrop claimed would extend from "Cape Elizabeth to the Sagadahoc." The younger Gorges soon began the process of establishing a community near modern Saco, Maine.[17]

Members of the Council of New England realized that events within England made their complaints seem trivial. Charles became distracted by the violent Scots reaction to the introduction of a prayer book that he and William Laud, the archbishop of Canterbury, introduced to minimize Presbyterian practices in the north. A riot broke out in St. Giles

14. *Plymouth Church Records, 1620–1859* (New York, 1920), I:89–91.

15. Winthrop, *Journal*, 262; Winthrop journal, HM 39724, HEH, 25–26. The back-and-forth can be found in William Hubbard, *A General History of New England from the Discovery to MDCLXXX*, 2nd ed. (orig. completed 1680; [Boston, 1898]), 263–272; the petition is reprinted in Ebenezer Hazard, ed., *Historical Collections* (Philadelphia, 1792–1794), I:435–436.

16. James O. Halliwell, ed., *The Autobiography and Correspondence of Sir Simonds D'Ewes* (London, 1845), 2:117–118; James P. Baxter, ed., *Sir Ferdinando Gorges and His Province of Maine* (Boston: Prince Society, 1890), 171–173; for D'Ewes as a chronicler, see Wallace Notestein, ed., *The Journal of Sir Simonds D'Ewes* (New Haven, CT: Yale University Press, 1923), vii–xvii.

17. Baxter, *Gorges and His Province of Maine*, 173–174; Charles M. Andrews, *The Colonial Period of American History*, 4 vols. (New Haven, CT: Yale University Press, 1935–1938), 1:421–422; Winthrop, *Journal*, 224; Henry S. Burrage, *The Beginnings of Colonial Maine, 1602–1658* (Portland, ME: State of Maine, 1914), 233–234.

Cathedral in Edinburgh on July 23, 1637, the first instance of open rebellion against what many Scots saw as an effort by Charles I and Laud to impose a Roman-style liturgy. By the next year the English and Scots were deep into the so-called Bishops' Wars, an event that occupied the monarch's time and drained the state's finances. Though no one could have known it at the time, the ensuing crisis helped trigger the rise of puritan power in England and, eventually, the Civil War.[18]

By the 1630s, European ships sailed with increasing frequency back and forth across the Atlantic and along the coasts. These journeys increased the knowledge that Europeans had about the Americas, especially when attentive captains or navigators published detailed accounts of distances between colonies or what particular islands looked like when viewed from the sea.[19] Increased knowledge eased merchants' ability to organize shipments of sugar, tobacco, lumber, and fish. But the movement of ships—many of them crowded with people, along with livestock, rodents, and shallow puddles—also provided ideal pathways for pathogens to cross the ocean. There was nothing new about the diseases themselves, but the toll that they took came to the attention of those trying to build colonies, especially when germs killed recent immigrants or reduced Indigenous communities. A particularly devastating epidemic, like the one that ripped through the Native population of New England from 1617 to 1619, could provide unexpected benefits for European monarchs, merchants, and planters eager to turn the empty claims on their maps into real gains on the ground. Further, the expansion of the slave trade by the 1630s meant pathogens could travel across the basin from Europe to the Americas, between Europe and Africa, and between Africa and tropical environments in the Americas, primarily the West Indies and South America.[20] Pernambuco suffered a devastating smallpox epidemic from 1621 to 1623, years that witnessed an increase in the number of ships bearing enslaved Africans to the Brazilian coast. Other epidemics struck that region or Bahia in 1626, 1630, and 1637.[21]

18. See David Como, *Radical Parliamentarians and the English Civil War* (Oxford: Oxford University Press, 2018), 23–49; Conrad Russell, *The Fall of the British Monarchies, 1637–1642* (Oxford: Oxford University Press, 1991), 27–146.
19. See, e.g., Stanley Pargellis and Ruth Lapham Butler, "Daniell Ellffryth's Guide to the Caribbean, 1631," *WMQ*, 1st Ser., 1 (1944), 273–316.
20. Philip D. Curtin, "Disease Exchange Across the Tropical Atlantic," *History and Philosophy of the Life Sciences* 15 (1993), 329–356.
21. Noble David Cook, *Born to Die: Disease and New World Conquest, 1492–1650* (Cambridge: Cambridge University Press, 1998), 190–192.

Among the diseases that spiked in the early 1630s was typhus, which produced an epidemic in Mesoamerica less than a decade after smallpox had already ravaged much of the vast region. "All that country was generally infected with a kind of contagious sickness, almost as infectious as the plague, which they call tabardillo," the English traveler Thomas Gage wrote in his account of his journey to the West Indies in the early 1630s, "and was a fever in the very inward parts and bowels, which scarce continued to the seventh day but commonly took them away from the world to a grave on the third or fifth day." Gage reported the horrid symptoms of the afflicted. "The filthy smell and stench which came from them which lay sick of this disease," he added, "was enough to infect the rest of the house, and all that came to see them. It rotted their mouths and tongues, and made them as black as coal before they died." Like certain other diseases, the Indigenous suffered far more than the Spanish, quite likely because the Spanish had been exposed to the bacteria *Rickettsia prowazekii* as children. The bacteria likely migrated across the Atlantic in the gut of body lice, which excretes it; the pathogen can live for days even in desiccated feces. The bacteria can enter the body through scratches and then incubate for up to two weeks. The symptoms of a louse biting a human, as Gage reported, included intense headaches, fever, loss of appetite, and a rash covering the chest, so prominent that some observers believed it resembled a coat without arms. Children normally survived, with mortality rates of perhaps one in twenty. But half of older sufferers could succumb in an epidemic. The 1630s contagion raged from New Spain southward, reaching pandemic levels. The death rate approached one-fourth of the population. This epidemic, terrible as it was, never spread north of Mexico.[22]

Other diseases marched westward across North America from the Atlantic shoreline with devastating efficiency. Smallpox, measles, and typhus spread in northwestern New Spain and beyond. "The people that may be counted today in these settlements will total 40,000, or a little less," Father Juan de Prada wrote in 1638 about New Mexico, "for, although there must have been more than sixty thousand baptized, to-day those conversions are diminished to that extent on account of the very

22. Thomas Gage, *The English-American his Travail by Sea and Land: Or, A New Survey of the West-Indias* (London, 1648), 164; Cook, *Born to Die*, 166–178; Didier Raoult and Véronique Roux, "The Body Louse as a Vector of Reemerging Human Disease," *Clinical Infectious Diseases* 29 (1999), 888–911. Gage had traveled to the West Indies as a Dominican but had embraced the Church of England by the time he wrote *The English-American*.

active prevalence of smallpox and the sickness which the Mexicans called *cocolitzli*."[23]

In September 1636, a fever-producing virus, likely influenza that originated in Europe and spread from person to person across the Atlantic and into the interior of the continent, arrived in the Wendat communities north and west of Lake Ontario. Among its first victims were European missionaries, though they survived their week-long illness, their only medical intervention consisting of being bled by other Jesuits. A local Native healer visited the ill brothers, offering to help cure them if they paid him. They refused his services, but he did tell them about two local roots and how to apply them, information that the Jesuits welcomed since they tended to be open to information about unfamiliar environments. Soon the missionaries' condition improved, which they attributed less to Indigenous intervention and more to the power of their god, whose goodwill they invoked through prayer. But the contagion remained. "Your Reverend will hear only sickness mentioned, from now on," as the missionary François Le Mercier put it in his annual report.[24]

As the illness spread among Natives, some of them turned to the Jesuits for help. As was their custom, the brothers offered to baptize the afflicted, an effort to ensure the salvation of their souls even if it did little for their bodies. Some of the Indigenous looked askance at the joining of healing and conversion. When asked by one Jesuit if a man would rather go to Heaven or Hell if he died, the patient retorted that such a question was inappropriate. "We people do not ask such questions," he replied, "for we always hope that they will not die, and that they will recover their health." According to Le Mercier, "Another one said, 'For my part, I have no desire to go heaven; I have no acquaintances there, and the French who are there would not care to give me anything to eat.' " The missionary attributed the response to what he saw as a typical Native concern because "they think of nothing but their stomachs, and of means for prolonging this miserable life."[25]

23. "Petition [of Father Juan de Prada, September 26, 1638]," in Charles W. Hackett, ed. and trans., *Historical Documents Relating to New Mexico, Nueva Vizcaya and Approaches Thereto, to 1773*, 3 vols. (Washington, DC: Carnegie Institution, 1923–1937), 3:108; Ann F. Ramenofsky, *Vectors of Death: The Archaeology of European Contact* (Albuquerque: University of New Mexico Press, 1987), 132–133; Cook, *Born to Die*, 192–193. *Cocolitzli* was the Nahuatl word for pestilence, often used for hemorrhagic fevers; see Rodolfo Acuna-Soto et al., "Megadrought and Megadeath in 16th Century Mexico," *Emerging Infectious Diseases* 4 (2002), 360–362.

24. *JR*, 13:93–105, quotation at 93. Le Jeune's relation for 1637 consisted mostly of François Le Mercier's journal of his time among the Hurons for 1637; see *JR*, 13:1–5.

25. *JR*, 13:127.

Le Mercier's annual report revealed the frustrations that he and his fellows were experiencing. Rather than accept baptism as the solution to their daily problems, the Natives he met instead kept listening to local healers, including the one who had told the Jesuits about the roots. Even when they baptized some who seemed about to perish, they got little in return. "It is a source of grief to us that, as we have not yet any wholly converted Villages," he lamented, "we afterwards get from these new Christians, whom we baptized only in the last hour, nothing but fine words." Should they recover, he added, "the torrent of old customs and common superstitions [bears] them away."[26]

The spreading contagion prompted an existential crisis, and not only for afflicted Indigenous. By early December, the number of those ill in Ossossané (renamed as La Rochelle by the Jesuits) prompted the brothers to take decisive action, at times on their own. If the brothers gained access to cabins where ill adults had fallen into a stupor, they used the opportunity to try to baptize them shortly before they succumbed. "I will even add that some little innocents were baptized in their last moments," Le Mercier confessed, "unknown to, and against the wishes of their relatives." The father superior of this small order told the residents of the town that following baptism they should live like Christians, which meant abandoning the Wendat belief in the power of dreams, embracing lifelong monogamy, having sex only for procreation, and eschewing cannibalism and feasts where people ate until they vomited. If they survived through the winter, he promised, he would have a chapel built there. Hearing these words, a Wendat headman named Onaconchiaronk told the friars that their requests would go unheeded. Worse still, he told them that residents of another town who had accepted baptism the year before had done so only to get tobacco. "We have our own ways of doing things," he explained, "and you yours, and all the nations. When you speak to us about obeying and acknowledging as our master him whom you say made Heaven and earth, I imagine you are talking of overthrowing the country." Rather than accept the Jesuits' offer of assistance and baptism as the clerics intended, Onaconchiaronk instead saw the visitors as part of a long line of those who never intended to do good. "Your ancestors assembled in earlier times, and held a council, where they resolved to take as their God him whom you honor," he declared, "and ordained all the ceremonies that you observe; as for us, we have learned others from our own fathers."[27]

26. *JR*, 13:127–133, quotations at 133.

27. *JR*, 13:161–173, quotations at 167 (baptism), 171 ("our own ways"), and 171–173 ("our own fathers").

By January, the dispute between the residents and the Jesuits flared into open ideological warfare. With influenza still spreading in Ossossané, other Jesuits arrived to assist the effort to baptize Wendats before they died. But they confronted a local physician who continued to have the support of the community. "The whole company listened to him with unparalleled manifestations of approval," one brother recorded, adding that the "little sorcerer" threw tobacco on heated stones while "addressing the devil." The man spoke about the promise of an even more powerful healer who told them that if they followed traditional routines, including putting on a three-day feast, then the illness would dissipate. He went into cabins bearing what Le Mercier termed "a kettle filled with a mysterious water" as well as the wing of a turkey. He offered drink to the ill and then fanned them with the wing. The Wendats danced and sang throughout the nights of the feast, their actions annoying the Jesuits, who saw such rituals as impeding their efforts to baptize as many as they could. Traditional practices proved powerless in the face of the epidemic, which raged for weeks. Among the victims was the healer himself, who gave deathbed instructions that "they should put him in the ground, in order that, as he was a demon, he might return to the place when he had come."[28]

During their travels from one town to another, the Jesuits studied the local language in order to become more efficient at spreading the gospel. "The Father Superior had already composed some discourses for us," Le Mercier reported, "which had accustomed us, in great measure, to the instruction of the Savages." They drew on translated catechisms to teach "the mystery of the life, death, and passion" of Jesus. They contributed to a bilingual dictionary, one of several that religious in New France would compose to advance their mission. "After our devotional exercises, we have no greater consolation than to devote ourselves to this study," he added; "it is our most common subject of conversation, and we gather up all the words from the mouths of the Savages as so many precious stones, that we may use them afterwards to display before their eyes the beauty of our holy mysteries." They learned that the trick to Algonquian languages lay in the conjugation of verbs. Their linguistic quest paralleled their physical journey. "However far we advance," Le Mercier observed, "we shall still continue to discover new lands."[29]

The last of the influenza faded by summer, but by then many Wendats had turned against the Jesuits. Some had been in touch with an Algonquin

28. *JR*, 13:201–249, quotations at 203 ("manifestations of approval"), 241 (ritual), 245 (death).

29. *JR*, 14:9–11.

leader who had, Le Mercier reported, "given our [Wendats] to understand that they were mistaken in thinking that the devils caused them to die, that they should blame only the French for this." The Algonquin identified the most likely sorcerer as the sister of a Jesuit who had died in a Wendat town five years earlier. Bent on revenge, she opined that the Jesuits "meddle with sorcery; that we use for that purpose the images of our saints," a devastating critique for Roman Catholic missionaries who relied on pictures of their canonized dead to help spread the faith. Le Mercier reported that she told others that when the Jesuits brought out icons, "certain tainted influences issue therefrom" and enter the chests of Natives—an explanation for why they succumbed to pulmonary infections. He added that he thought local leaders were skeptical about the theory, but it was possible that matters could spiral out of control. The Jesuits were not that concerned, he claimed, because they understood the honor that would come to them should they be martyred for the cause.[30]

Two years later smallpox, which had become the most dreaded disease across North America, spread into Wendake, the Wendats' traditional homeland. The Jesuits blamed the arrival of the epidemic on a Huron who had consorted with Algonquins, whom the clerics believed had to have been ill. While that was one possible route for infection, it was just as likely that Wendats who had recently traveled to Québec picked up the disease there. Whatever its origins, the results proved catastrophic, with mortality likely higher than that caused by influenza. Many Wendats believed that the missionaries must be responsible for the epidemic, arguing, as the missionary Jérôme Lalemant put it, that "we had a secret understanding of the disease (for they believe that it is a demon)" since the Jesuits remained healthy while Indigenous perished. "No doubt we carried the trouble with us," he reported hearing, "since, wherever we set foot, either death or disease followed us." These swirling rumors turned Wendats against the Jesuits. "Many held us in abomination," Lalemant balefully wrote. "They expelled us from their cabins, and did not allow us to approach their sick, and especially the children: not even to lay eyes on them. In a word, we were dreaded as the greatest sorcerers on earth."[31]

After his exile by the Massachusetts General Court in 1635, Roger Williams went to New Plymouth, where he believed that his views about who could be in a church would fit in a small community that had always embraced the idea of Separatism. But there too he became embroiled in a

30. *JR*, 14:53–55.
31. *JR*, 19:91–93.

theological controversy relating to membership in the church. Williams, unconcerned about the personal consequences of his actions, questioned whether the church members in New Plymouth had in fact separated themselves enough from churches in England. If not, by the logic he had already articulated in Salem, then they too had sanctioned the formation of a church that might be an affront to the Christian god. Soon after his arrival, he left, bound again for Salem. He began to preach there again but soon left. He headed for the northern shores of Narragansett Bay, where he planned to build a new community supported, he hoped, by Indigenous converts. He had already spent time among the Ninnimissinuok and had begun to study their language. He went back, though by no known English authority since he migrated to an area not yet covered by an English patent. The Wampanoag sachem Massasoit (Ousamaquin) welcomed him. By the end of the summer of 1636, Williams had led a small group of like-minded English colonists, including his wife and two children, to the confluence of the Woonasquatucket and Moshassuck Rivers. He called his town "New Providence." Eventually, it would become the principal city in Rhode Island.[32]

By the autumn of 1636, relations between the Ninnimissinuok and English had deteriorated. In September, John Winthrop wrote in his journal that he had heard that the Narragansetts had made a truce with the Pequots, who had been telling the Narragansetts that the colonists planned to kill all Natives.[33] When the Narragansett headman Canonicus sent a message to the puritans that Pequots had killed some colonists at Saybrook (and possibly also on Block Island), Winthrop sent for the Narragansett sachem Miantonomi, who arrived in Roxbury around noon on October 21. Twenty armed guards escorted the headman to Boston, where the governor had already assembled most of the colony's ministers and magistrates to help find a way forward to prevent further troubles.[34]

After dinner that evening in Boston, Miantonomi tried to reassure the colonists of the Narragansetts' loyalty. He claimed, Winthrop reported, that they "had always loved the English, and desired firm peace with us," and that they stood ready to oppose the Pequots. The next morning the two sides signed an agreement, whose terms Winthrop summarized in his journal. The allies hoped to preserve trade and promised that neither would agree to terms with the Pequots unless the other approved. To minimize tensions, the Narragansetts agreed not to approach colonial

32. Patricia E. Rubertone, *Grave Undertakings: An Archaeology of Roger Williams and the Narragansett Indians* (Washington, DC: Smithsonian Institution Press, 2001), 5–13.
33. Winthrop, *Journal*, 187.
34. Winthrop, *Journal*, 189–191.

settlements during time of war with the Pequots "without some Englishman or known Indian." The Natives also agreed to return runaway servants who had come to live with them.[35]

Hopes for peace soon faded. In late January 1637, Winthrop wrote in his journal that Lion Gardiner of Saybrook, a military veteran who had traveled to New England in 1635 to help defend English settlements, had been out with nine armed colonists near the mouth of the Connecticut River when they came up on three Ninnimissinuok, who fled. The colonists gave chase—right into what Winthrop saw as an ambush by fifty Natives. Soon enough, four of the English lay dead.[36] A month later, the churches in Massachusetts Bay participated in a general fast, a communal day of prayer to seek their god's protection. Much was on their mind. The English in Massachusetts heard story after story of the persecution that dissenters kept experiencing at the hands of the Church of England. They worried too about a downturn in their own economic prospects. Colonists in Connecticut and Massachusetts faced dissension within their own congregations, in part because of intense religious debates relating to the doctrines of justification and sanctification.[37] As Winthrop saw the situation, "it began to be as common here to distinguish between men, by being under a covenant of grace or a covenant of works, as in other countries between Protestants and Papists."[38]

Just as they feared divisions among their own relating to doctrine and practice, so the dissenters grew ever more nervous about their Indigenous neighbors. In March Miantonomi, trying to retain positive relations, sent forty fathoms of wampum to the English. (A fathom was a string of shells about six feet long, which was worth nine to ten shillings in Massachusetts at the time.) The Natives also sent the hand of a Pequot. The colonists sent gifts back, presumably pleased to see that tensions divided one group of

35. Winthrop, *Journal*, 191–192. Winthrop had Williams in mind since the minister had lived in both Plymouth and Massachusetts; though he became unwelcome in both, he still maintained the respect of colonists for his abilities with the Natives, including the Wampanoags who tended to him in the winter of 1635–1636 when he was banished from Massachusetts. By early 1636 he had begun a new settlement along the shores of Narragansett Bay that would become the colony of Rhode Island. Bradford, who had earlier been happy to see Williams leave Plymouth (as he wrote in 1633), valued his intervention in a tense moment after a colonist murdered a Narragansett in 1638; see Bradford, *Of Plimouth Plantation*, 398–399, 457–458.

36. Winthrop, *Journal*, 207.

37. Winthrop, *Journal*, 207–208. Justification, as Edmund Morgan explained, was "the imputation of Christ's righteousness to man" and sanctification "the gradual improvement of a man's behavior in obedience to God." Morgan, *Visible Saints*, 67.

38. Winthrop, *Journal*, 208–210; Morgan, *Visible Saints*, 64–138.

Ninnimissinuok from another.[39] But the newcomers' fear of the Pequots grew during the spring, with colonists convinced that Indigenous could soon overwhelm their small towns.[40] Stories of Pequot attacks on English spread through the colonies. Plymouth and Massachusetts formed an alliance for their mutual protection.[41]

In mid-May, Winthrop was reelected governor, in an election marked by "fierce speeches" and "great danger of tumult" due to doctrinal disputes.[42] Rumors swirled within colonial towns about local Natives blaming colonists for spreading disease among them.[43] Colonists heard reports that the Pequots had sent away women and children "to an island for their safety." Sensing rising danger, the puritans dispatched forty men to the Narragansetts. Miantonomi augmented that force with sixteen of his own men. Then the colonists decided to enlist another 160 men "to prosecute the war." Soon afterward, armed English killed eight Pequots along the Connecticut River and captured seven women with the idea that they would trade them for two young English women whom the Pequots had recently taken.[44]

In the autumn of 1637, a combined force from Massachusetts and Plymouth, along with Narragansett allies, set a Pequot town on the banks of the Mystic River on fire, consuming houses that contained women and children. By the time the fighting ceased, the English had killed or captured 400 to 700 of the Pequots and suffered only sixteen casualties.[45] One English chronicler justified the slaughter of women and children who cried out for mercy by arguing that the colonists could not provide it since "some of the Souldiers think the Devil was in" the Pequots.[46] The raid's military commander, John Underhill, knew that his tactics would elicit criticism. "Why should you be so furious (as some have said)," he

39. Winthrop, *Journal*, 211; Mary S. Herman, "Wampum as a Money in Northeastern North America," *Ethnohistory* 3 (1956), 21–33.
40. Winslow to Winthrop, April 17, 1637, in *The Winthrop Papers*, 6 vols. (Boston: Massachusetts Historical Society, 1863–1892), 3:391–392.
41. Winthrop, *Journal*, 212–214; Winthrop to Bradford, [May 20], 1637, in *Winthrop Papers*, 3:17–419, quotation at 418–419, and also in Bradford, *Of Plimouth Plantation*, 394–396.
42. Winthrop, *Journal*, 214–217; see also *Winthrop Papers*, 3:422–426.
43. Williams to the governor of Massachusetts, May 13, 1637, and Williams to Sir Henry Vane and Winthrop, [May 15, 1637], *Winthrop Papers*, 3:410–414.
44. Winthrop, *Journal*, 218; Winslow to Winthrop, May 22, 1637, *Winthrop Papers*, 3:419–420, quotation at 420.
45. P. Philip Vincent [P. Vincentius], "A True Relation of the Late Battell fought in New England, between the English, and the Salvages: With the present state of things there (1637)," ed. Paul Royster, *Electronic Texts in American Studies*, paper 35 (accessed April 28, 2016), 8–12, 15–19, quotation at 15.
46. [Edward Johnson], A *History of New-England* (London, 1653[?]), 114–115.

asked, "should not Christians have more mercy and compassion?" He told them to consider David's war, likely a reference to 1 Samuel 30, when an enemy's arrogance and errant ways demanded "the most terriblest death that may be." This death of innocents was unfortunate, but "sometimes the Scripture declareth women and children must perish with their parents." The time had passed to challenge what had happened. "We had," he concluded, "sufficient light from the word of God for our proceedings."[47] Underhill included a diagram depicting the assault on the Pequots living

John Underhill's rendering of the mass murder of Pequots near the Mystic River appeared soon after the attack. The artist's bloodless depiction made it seem like any other battlefield sketch, ignoring the fact that such nighttime violence against a town might have seemed to many to repudiate the dissenters' earlier claims that they had migrated to help bring Indigenous into Christendom. John Underhill, *Newes from America* (London, 1638). Courtesy of the Huntington Library, San Marino, California.

47. John Underhill, *Newes from America; Or, A New and Experimentall Discoverie of New England; containing, A True Relation of Their War-like proceedings these two yeares last past, with a figure of the Indian fort, or Palizado* (London, 1638), 2–3, 6–16, 32–36. All page numbers refer to the electronic version edited by Paul Royster, *Electronic Texts in American Studies*, paper 37 (accessed April 30, 2016). For the biblical David's war as it

at Mystic. "The figure of the Indians fort or Palizado in New England," the caption read, "And the maner of the destroying it by Captayne Underhill and Captayne Mason." The image depicted an orderly slaughter.

Underhill claimed that the colonists killed 1,500 Pequots in two months "so as their Countrey is fully subdued and fallen into the hands of the English."[48] On June 15, Winthrop reported that the colonists had "a day of thanksgiving" in their churches to honor their victory over the Pequots.[49] But the war was not yet over. Roger Williams heard a rumor that surviving Pequots would have attacked Narragansetts if they had the chance—a mist prevented them—and used the incident to warn Winthrop that colonial officials should treat any remaining Pequots "kindly" so they would not "turne wilde Irish," a reference to the long-standing resistance that the English invaders had encountered in Ireland.[50] Rumors swirled from summer into autumn about alleged Pequot threats.[51] Such fears motivated the murder in late June of twenty-two Pequot men by the colonist Israel Staughton and his men, though the soldiers spared two of the men and the eighty-one women and children with them.[52]

The war's end brought two related developments. In southern New England, colonial officials authorized the sale of Pequot captives into slavery—some to Providence Island in the Caribbean, where one local record referred to them as "the Cannibal Negroes brought from New England."[53] Two decades earlier some of the founders of New England had rebuked Thomas Hunt for his slave-trading activities, and stories of his heinous actions resonated within the Algonquian-speaking community,

was understood in seventeenth-century England, see Obadiah Sedgwick, *The Parable of the Prodigal* (London, 1666), 81.

48. Underhill, *Newes from America*, 1–2.

49. Daniel Patrick to the governor and Council of War in Massachusetts, June 19, 1637, *Winthrop Papers*, 3:430–431; Winthrop, *Journal*, 222.

50. Williams to Winthrop, c. June 21, 1637, *Winthrop Papers*, 3:433–434, quotations at 434.

51. See Israel Staughton to the governor and Council of Massachusetts, [August 14, 1637], *Winthrop Papers*, 3:481–483; Richard Davenport to Winthrop, [c. August 23, 1637], *Winthrop Papers*, 3:490–491; Roger Williams to Winthrop, [September 9, 1637], *Winthrop Papers*, 3:494–496; Williams to Winthrop, [c. October 26, 1637], *Winthrop Papers*, 3:500–501. Davenport claimed that other Natives would "bee glad to make women of all the Pecots now," but in the margin wrote the word "slaves." See *Winthrop Papers*, 3:491, 491n.

52. Michael L. Fickes, "'They Could Not Endure That Yoke': The Captivity of Pequot Women and Children After the War of 1637," *NEQ* 73 (2000), 59–60.

53. Karen Ordahl Kupperman, *Providence Island, 1630–1641: The Other Puritan Colony* (Cambridge: Cambridge University Press, 1993), 172, 178, 335, quotation at 178.

passed down generation after generation.[54] By the summer of 1637 colonial officials thought that the Pequots had surrendered any right to be free.[55] This did not represent a condemnation of all Natives. In August 1638, Massachusetts authorities heard about the murder of an Algonquian-speaking man in Providence by four runaway English servants from Plymouth. The officials prosecuted and executed the three colonists they could find.[56]

The other legacy could be found in dissenters' writings. In his account, Bradford collapsed much of the violence of the war into the assault on the fort, which he described in brief but searing detail. "It was conceived they thus destroyed about 400 at this time," he wrote. "It was a fearful sight, to see them thus frying in the fire, and the streams of blood quenching the same," he continued, "and horrible was the stink & scent thereof, but the victory seemed a sweet Sacrifice"—a line he borrowed from Leviticus—"and they gave the praise thereof to God, who had wrought so wonderfully for them; thus to Enclose their enemies in their hands; and give them so speedy a victory over so proud, & insulting an enemy."[57] Other dissenters and English observers joined the chorus, blaming prideful Pequots for bringing on their own destruction.[58]

On the banks of the Mystic River, the dissenters enacted a ritual bloodletting echoing the unconventional tactics that colonial soldiers had unleashed against the Powhatans from 1622 to 1624. These colonists organized the assault on the Pequots because they perceived that it was these Natives, not the immigrants themselves, who were the trespassers, the people who threatened to undermine the colonists' society, the violators of the sacred bonds that kept English communities together. Though migrants were still crossing the ocean, the dissenters did not see their colony as new or themselves as invaders. This was, in their minds, their homeland, as ancient as England, with rules just as venerable. From this vantage point, the Pequots were the aggressors, and the puritans the noble warriors in defense of their godly republic. Violence that would have been

54. William Apess, *Eulogy on King Philip, as Pronounced at the Odeon, in Federal Street, Boston* (Boston, 1837), 8; "Eulogy on King Philip," in Barry O'Connell, ed., *On Our Own Ground: The Complete Writings of William Apess, a Pequot* (Amherst: University of Massachusetts Press, 1992), 279n, which clarifies that Apess confused Hunt with another enslaver, Henry Harley.
55. For the context, see Wendy Warren, *New England Bound: Slavery and Colonization in Early America* (New York: Liveright, 2016), 25–36.
56. Winthrop, *Journal*, 260–261.
57. Bradford, *Of Plimouth Plantation*, 448–451, quotation at 450.
58. John Mason, *A Brief History of the Pequot War*, ed. Thomas Prince (Boston, 1736), 4, 8–10.

difficult for any people to justify under normal circumstances became heroic action to be celebrated in one text after another. The dissenters did not try to hide the brutal assault. They boasted about their achievements because they saw themselves as the preservers of the proper social and political order.[59]

Winthrop and his allies did not have much time to savor their savage victory before another kind of challenge undermined social relations within the Massachusetts Bay colony. In 1634, thirty-year-old Anne Hutchinson had arrived in Boston. A native of Lincolnshire and a devotee of the minister John Cotton, Hutchinson sailed across the ocean with her husband to follow her spiritual mentor, who had emigrated the previous year. By all accounts, Hutchinson was an intelligent interpreter of Scripture, with a rapier wit that allowed her to parry with the best weapons in an intellectual armory—rapid and precise biblical references. However brilliant, she could not hold a pulpit in Massachusetts because she was a woman among colonists eager to impose a rigid separation between the public worlds of husbands and the private domains of their spouses. Limited in possible public venues, Hutchinson nonetheless paid rapt attention to the details of ministers' debates. Within two years of her arrival, she had begun to share her views in what Winthrop called her "table talk," meetings primarily of women in her own house. Worried leaders of the community, including the governor, believed these gatherings to discuss the meaning of "sanctification" and "justification," among other topics, represented a threat to the colonial enterprise as serious as the rumors of Pequots allying with Narragansetts to send the English into the sea. Sensing that the issue needed to be handled publicly to send a message to others, Massachusetts authorities put Hutchinson on trial in November, only weeks after the slaughter of the Pequots.[60]

The issues that brought Hutchinson in front of the colony's political establishment had a long pedigree within the Protestant canon. Ever since the time of Calvin, those who dissented from the Roman church

59. This justification of brutality as caused by the victim was not unique to this incident; see Lauren Benton, *They Called It Peace: Worlds of Imperial Violence* (Princeton, NJ: Princeton University Press, 2024), 27–60, esp. 50–56.

60. Ann Fairfax Withington and Jack Schwartz, "The Political Trial of Anne Hutchinson," *NEQ* 51 (1978), 226–227; "The Examination of Mrs. Anne Hutchinson" (hereafter "Examination of Hutchinson"), in Heimert and Delbanco, eds., *Puritans in America*, 157; Mary Beth Norton, *Founding Mothers and Fathers: Gendered Power and the Forming of American Society* (New York: Knopf, 1996), 27–95 (gendered roles), 360–367 (Hutchinson).

had believed that their god determined who would achieve salvation and that an individual's fate was set by the time they were born. Most adherents of the Roman tradition believed that any individual could achieve salvation through good works, a message they received from priests who themselves had received divine signs of their special role as intercessors between their god and humans. But the idea that priests had a divine calling became unacceptable among Protestants, who instead relied on individuals to study Scripture and determine how to live an honorable life. In Europe, including England, that shift had led to greater educational opportunities for Protestants, who became literate in higher numbers than Catholics. But once a parish priest could no longer make an authoritative statement about who was to be saved, the decision about whom to allow to become a full member of a church, worthy of baptism and communion, became the topic of intense debate. Among those focused on the question was Cotton, who quickly set up his own church in Boston after he arrived.[61]

Cotton's teaching represented a challenge to a core aspect of orthodoxy in Massachusetts Bay. If, as he preached, justification hinged on predestination alone and could not be achieved, then the improvement in how one lived, known to the dissenters as "sanctification," could not be the result of honorable living but was instead a sign of salvation. How was one to know if they were among the elect, and who could make this determination? These theoretical questions mattered less in England, where everyone, under statutes of the Church of England, needed to be a member of a church and each household paid a tax to support the clerical establishment. But in Massachusetts, where the number of migrants dwarfed the relative few who had gone to New Plymouth, the question of who could be a member of a church demanded constant attention. Even Cotton had to apply for membership when he arrived in Boston. If a church was to be a gathering of the elect—or the "saints," as the puritans employed the term—how could anyone know the ultimate fate of any

61. Morgan, *Visible Saints*, 96–98. Within England, illiteracy remained high in the 1640s; only in London could a majority of men sign their name, with the inability to write likely signaling an inability to read. See David Cressy, *Literacy and the Social Order: Reading and Writing in Tudor and Stuart England* (Cambridge: Cambridge University Press, 1980), esp. 72–76. The first generation of English colonists in Massachusetts and Connecticut, recognizing the importance of literacy, enacted statutes between 1642 and 1650 that required the teaching of both reading and writing to free boys and girls; see Carole Shammas, "The Extent and Duration of Primary Schooling in Eighteenth-Century America," *History of Education Quarterly* 63 (2023), 313–335, esp. 316–319. In New England in 1660, 60 percent of men signed their own wills, though the number increased moving forward; see Kenneth A. Lockridge, *Literacy in Colonial New England: An Enquiry into the Social Context of Literacy in the Early Modern West* (New York: Norton, 1974), 13–19.

individual when it was, according to dissenters' writings, impossible to know the will of an inscrutable divine? And unless any could argue that their god intended only men to be in a position to sort out who was entitled to the sacraments, why would someone expert in the delicate act of scriptural exegesis be excluded from the debate on the basis of sex? Before the creation of dissenting communities in New England, no congregation engaged in the kind of spiritual trial that would determine who could be a member. Even in Massachusetts, creating the rules for admission took years to work out.[62]

Hutchinson, for her part, was not inclined to wait for ministers and lay leaders to answer the most pressing questions of the day. Nor was she an outspoken radical. The colony's leaders worried that her opinions might be seen as reasonable alternatives to the establishment. By the start of 1637, she could count Henry Vane, then governor, among her followers.[63]

In November, Hutchinson appeared before a synod of the colony's ministers in Newtown (modern Cambridge). Winthrop, who had been reelected as governor, informed her that she had been summoned to appear before them because she was "one of those that have troubled the peace of the commonwealth and the churches here." To him the evidence was beyond dispute: she had been meeting with others in her house, a practice "that hath been condemned by the general assembly as a thing not tolerable nor comely in the sight of God nor fitting for your sex." They had told her to halt the gatherings. She had refused. It had reached the point where the magistrates "thought good to send for you to understand how things are, that if you be in an erroneous way we may reduce you that so you may become a profitable member here among us." If she remained "obstinate," then the court would banish her.[64] Perhaps without knowing it, Winthrop had echoed the language that English colonizers had employed for years when discussing their goals for Indigenous Americans: to reduce them to civilization. Having just lived through what happened when reducing a foe did not work peacefully, Winthrop understood well the meaning of his words.

Hutchinson, after watching a back-and-forth between Cotton and the ministers who led the synod, told the court how she had come to find "what I know to be true." In a short speech that touched on Catholics,

62. Morgan, *Visible Saints*, 96–97 (Cotton's arrival), 76 (no prior tests). Morgan, reading back across texts from the early decades of the century, argued that the puritans came to see various stages in an individual's dawning recognition of potential saving grace, a process he aptly termed the "morphology of conversion"; see *Visible Saints*, 67–74.

63. Heimert and Delbanco, eds., *Puritans in America*, 155.

64. Heimert and Delbanco, eds., *Puritans in America*, 156.

Turks, and passages from John (2:18) and Hebrews (9:16), she declared that she had come to trust what her conscience told her. "How do you know that that was the spirit?" one of her accusers asked. "How did Abraham know that it was God that bid him offer his son," she replied, "being a breach of the sixth commandment?"

"By an immediate voice," the deputy governor replied.

"So to me by an immediate revelation," she responded.

"How! an immediate revelation," the official retorted.

"By the voice of his own spirit to my soul," she replied, and then launched into a speech that drew on Jeremiah 46:27–28, Isaiah 30:20, and Daniel 6:4–5. The trial records suggest that this was the decisive moment and settled the case, though not before the men conducting the proceeding interrogated Cotton again.[65]

Hutchinson's trial had begun with an effort on the part of Massachusetts Bay's leaders to determine if she had privately preached that the colony's ministers had been teaching the notion, which puritans deemed false, that good works could lead to salvation. In the course of the argument, she had claimed that she had experienced a direct revelation, an act that her accusers believed impossible. Those who claimed such a revelation, even if they could cite scriptural precedent (as Hutchinson did), committed the crime of antinomianism. The court determined her insistence a threat to the public good and banished her. She and her family, along with others who subscribed to her beliefs, departed for Rhode Island.[66]

Why would someone as smart and subtle in her thinking as Hutchinson burst out with a statement that she knew would lead to her banishment? Perhaps she understood that the debate in front of the synod was not about religious belief but was instead a show trial, a public event put on by an insecure colonial administration eager to make a point that dissent from orthodoxy was unacceptable. As she told Winthrop near the beginning, she did not even understand what charges were being laid against her. Her goal had not been to destroy the godly republic. Instead, she claimed to live according to the dictates of her conscience. Unable to have her own church because she was a woman, Hutchinson refused to stifle her thoughts. As would occur time and again in New England, an individual's dissenting views did not accord with others' opinions. The sentence had nothing to do with the original charges. She threatened colonial authorities. They sent her away.[67]

65. Heimert and Delbanco, eds., *Puritans in America*, 156–161.

66. Morgan, *Visible Saints*, 109–110; Norton, *Founding Mothers and Fathers*, 374–394.

67. Withington and Schwartz, "Political Trial," 226–240.

By the late 1630s, the English had increased their presence across coastal North America. Barbados, unpopulated when the English arrived, had 6,000 residents. Among them were 200 enslaved Africans, the rest of the population dominated by English and Irish indentured servants who saw better economic prospects on a small, low-lying island 4,000 miles from their homelands. Most of these inhabitants produced either cotton or tobacco on the island's western coast.[68] Ships traveled between English mainland colonies, hauling corn, fish, and cattle.[69] The growth of the colonial population in Massachusetts prompted colonists to migrate inland toward the Connecticut River. While some in Massachusetts thought the migration inadvisable because of persistent threats from Natives and Dutch, by late 1635, the first English had arrived on the banks of the interior river and begun to develop Connecticut, another new colony.[70]

A remarkably detailed port register from London from 1635 suggests both the vitality and the extent of westward-facing transatlantic migration at that moment. Port officials recorded details for 7,507 emigrants that year. Of that total, 1,035 went east to the continent—158 to Rotterdam, 111 to Amsterdam, 107 to Dunkirk, and then lesser numbers to cities scattered across northwestern Europe. Fewer than fifteen went to major metropolises, including Paris, Antwerp, Constantinople, Brussels, and Bruges. The vast majority emigrating from London that year crossed the Atlantic: 2,009 went to Virginia, a sign of the continuing need for demand to farm tobacco, and 1,169 traveled to New England, part of the so-called Great Migration of approximately 21,200 dissenters who went there from 1630 to 1642. The other major destinations were islands: 983 to Barbados, 423 to St. Kitts, 218 to Bermuda, and just 76 to Providence Island, a sign of the company's continuing inability to lure workers from the homeland. The composition of these migrant groups varied. The dissenting communities in Providence and New England attracted relatively more women—between 37 and 39 percent—than the others. These destinations also had the largest shares of migrants over age twenty-five and under age four, a

68. J. Harry Bennett, "Peter Hay, Proprietary Agent in Barbados, 1636–1641," *Jamaican Historical Review* 5 (1965), 10–11; Edward B. Rugemer, "The Development of Mastery and Race in the Comprehensive Slave Codes of the Greater Caribbean During the Seventeenth Century," *WMQ*, 3rd Ser., 70 (2013), 433–434; Larry D. Gragg, *Englishmen Transplanted: The English Colonization of Barbados, 1627–1715* (Oxford: Oxford University Press, 2003), 113–131; and see Russell R. Menard, *Sweet Negotiations: Sugar, Slavery, and Plantation Agriculture in Early Barbados* (Charlottesville: University of Virginia Press, 2006), 30–32.

69. Winthrop, *Journal*, 125.

70. Winthrop, *Journal*, 126–128, 161–164.

sign that dissenters often traveled in family groups. Of the travelers to Virginia, 86 percent were male, and 68 percent of them were between fifteen and twenty-four years old, the prime group for labor-seeking planters. The sex and age ratios of the migrants to Barbados were even more skewed. There 90 percent of the travelers were men, only 2 percent were under age fourteen (none were under four), and almost 70 percent were aged fifteen to twenty-four. Such migration patterns demonstrate not only where the need for labor was most intense but also the success promoters enjoyed by spreading effective messages within England, especially among the great armies of unemployed who had made their way to London looking for work. Many—over three-quarters on one ship bound for Virginia—opted to become indentured servants rather than remain at home.[71]

Despite the increase in free migrants heading west, for every European success there seemed to be a corresponding failure. Barbados moved forward as colonists hoped, but Providence Island, launched with aspirations of a profit-making dissenters' colony, stagnated. Enslaved Pequots and Africans added to its labor force, but to little good. In 1641, the English colony there succumbed to Spanish attack.[72] Baltimore launched Maryland, but Carolina withered. There were other colonial disappointments too. Cardinal Richelieu, hoping to establish a French colony on four Bahamian islands in 1633, had offered a grant to Guillaume de Caen, who was from that point forward to be known as the baron des Bahames. But de Caen, a Protestant, was not allowed to transport others of his faith to the islands, and the colony dissipated, a lonely echo of the French inability to establish a colony earlier on Sable Island.[73] The Northwest

71. Alison Games, *Migration and the Origins of the English Atlantic World* (Cambridge, MA: Harvard University Press, 1999), 42–51; James Horn, "Servant Emigration to the Chesapeake in the Seventeenth Century," in Thad W. Tate and David L. Ammerman, eds., *The Chesapeake in the Seventeenth Century: Essays on Anglo-American Society* (Chapel Hill: University of North Carolina Press for the Institute of Early American History and Culture, 1979), 51–95; Virginia DeJohn Anderson, "Migrants and Motives: Religion and the Settlement of New England, 1630–1640," *NEQ* 58 (1985), 339–383.
72. See Alison Games, "'The Sanctuarye of Our Rebell Negroes': The Atlantic Context of Local Resistance on Providence Island, 1630–1641," *Slavery and Abolition* 19 (1998), 1–21; Kupperman, *Providence Island*, 288–294.
73. Michael Craton and Gail Saunders, *Islanders in the Stream: A History of the Bahamian People*, 2 vols. (Athens: University of Georgia Press, 1992–1998), 1:65.

Passage remained elusive despite the two competing English expeditionary parties that had searched for it recently.

Still, in spite of some Europeans' disappointments, the decade had witnessed a demographic transition. In Virginia, an early generation of colonizers had drawn heavily on elites, including younger sons of landed families. But few of these individuals or their families could cope with local diseases. Instead, the colony's leadership fell to migrants who survived the so-called seasoning process of adjustment, many of whom had arrived as indentured servants.[74] Among them was Maurice Thomson, born in Hertfordshire in 1600. By the time he was seventeen he had moved to Virginia, though soon after he had become a ship captain. In 1625 he had at least ten servants, making him among the elite in the colony. Thomson returned to England no later than 1626, where he joined an ambitious cohort of English merchants who concluded that opportunities for transatlantic commerce would be their path to success.[75] By the 1630s, he had invested in a project to transform Kent Island, become a provisioner for the English colony on Providence Island, and gained a monopoly over the sale of tobacco in London. His rise provided opportunities for relatives to play leading roles in the launch of English colonies on Montserrat and the shipment of tobacco from St. Kitts and Barbados. Starting from humble means in the Chesapeake, Thomson had become an economic dynamo.[76]

On their maps, Europeans trumpeted their successes—their ability to create lasting colonial communities on lands that until recently had hardly any European presence. In some places, especially Massachusetts,

74. See Bernard Bailyn, "Politics and Social Structure in Virginia," in James M. Smith, ed., *Seventeenth-Century America: Essays in Colonial History* (Chapel Hill: University of North Carolina Press for the Institute of Early American History and Culture, 1959), 90–115.

75 Robert Brenner, *Merchants and Revolution: Commercial Change, Political Conflict, and London's Overseas Traders, 1550–1653* (London: Verso, 2003), 118–120; see also Paul G. E. Clemens, "The World of Maurice Thomson," *Reviews in American History* 21 (1993), 575–583.

76. Brenner, *Merchants and Revolution*, 120–129. Thomson's Kent Island venture ended in more litigation than profits; see "Claiborne vs Clobbery et als. in the High Court of Admiralty," *Maryland Historical Magazine* XXVI (1931[?]), 381–404; XXVII (1932), 17–28, 99–114, 191–214, 337–352, XXVIII (1933), 26–43, 172–195, and 257–265.

those claims made sense: from 1630 to 1642, over 21,000 English migrants had arrived in the Bay colony and Boston had begun its rise as the dominant community in the region.[77] That said, these increasingly secure colonists had presided over developments that none had planned. The Anglo-Pequot War encouraged colonists to commit mass murder and sell captive Indigenous, developments they neither expected nor, beyond the bloodthirsty aftermath of the slaughter in Mystic, celebrated. Internal tensions within New England—with Hutchinson, Williams, Gorges, and Morton, among others—meant that they could still face threats as severe as those of Spaniards in New Mexico and Jesuits near the Great Lakes.

Indigenous communities faced far graver dangers. The English present at the signing of the Treaty of Hartford, which brought a formal end to the Anglo-Pequot War on September 21, 1638, had sought to broker a peace between the Narragansetts and the Mohegans within territory that the colonists believed was theirs. The treaty authorized these other Natives to capture or decapitate Pequots known to have fought in the war, with the remainder to be absorbed by the two Indigenous nations. After the "Peaquots shall be divided," the treaty declared, they "shall no more be called Peaquots but Narragansetts and Mohegans," nor would the English allow them "to live in the country that was formerly theirs but is now the Englishes by conquest," which meant that the other Native communities also could not "possess any part of ye Peaquot country without leave from the English."[78]

Such a statement of colonial authority had little meaning. Apart from those killed and sold into slavery, perhaps 2,000 Pequots survived. Some dispersed into Narragansett and Mohegan communities. Others remained in place, and at times became victims of aggressive colonial soldiers. Colonists in New Haven captured Nepaupuck and decapitated him, attaching his head to a pole on their town common. Many Pequots fled westward, perhaps seeking refuge among the Mohawks, though that proved disastrous when members of this easternmost of the Haudenosaunee (or Iroquois) confederacy attacked and killed refugees, at times sending their

77. See Virginia DeJohn Anderson, *New England's Generation: The Great Migration and the Formation of Society and Culture in the Seventeenth Century* (Cambridge: Cambridge University Press, 1991), 89–130; Mark Peterson, *The City-State of Boston: The Rise and Fall of an Atlantic Power, 1630–1865* (Princeton, NJ: Princeton University Press, 2019), 27–84.

78. "Articles between ye Inglish in Connecticut and the Indian Sachems," *Collections of the Rhode-Island Historical Society* 3 (1835), 177–178.

heads and hands to the English as a sign of their commitment to a possible alliance.[79]

Narragansett sachem Miantonomi understood the threats that faced his and other Indigenous communities. He had been a primary architect of the alliance between his people and colonists in the battle against the Pequots, and a beneficiary of the distribution of his foes' land and bodies. He knew that Natives still outnumbered colonists—probably by a factor of ten around the shores of Narragansett Bay. Even still, within five years of the fatal assault along the Mystic River, he foresaw an existential crisis—and he went in search of allies for the next conflict.[80]

In 1642 Miantonomi, likely trailed by colonial spies, traveled from one Indigenous town to another on Long Island, gathering commitments for a war he believed Natives needed to launch. While there, he offered a radical vision of the circumstances that had led to this charged moment. To do so, he put aside tribal differences. "For so we are all Indians as the English are, and say brother to one another," he declared to a group of Montauks that summer, expressing a new kind of ethnic consciousness, "so must we be one, as they are." Circumstances had changed, he warned, and if Natives did not join together "we shall all be gone shortly." He based this assessment on the changes that he had seen in his own lifetime. "Our fathers had plenty of deer and skins," he continued, "our plains were full of deer, as also our woods, and of turkies, and our coves full of fish and fowl. But these English having gotten our land, they with scythes cut down the grass, and with axes fell the trees; their cows and horses eat the grass, and their hogs spoil our clam banks." The result of this trend was obvious: "We shall all be starved." While the times were dire, he had not abandoned hope. The way forward from this recognition of colonial-inspired environmental degradation was a new war. That idea motivated Miantonomi to tell the Montauks that they should "do as we, for we are all Sachems from east to west, both Moquakes and Mohauks joining with us, and we are all resolved to fall upon them all, at one appointed day."

79. Winthrop published an account where he acknowledged that the Narragansetts had taken in refugee Pequots, and Williams had written to Winthrop to warn that the Pequots still in the area had begun to reform their communities after the war; see [Jo. Winthrop], *A Declaration of Former Passages and Proceedings betwixt the English and the Narrowganset* (Boston, 1645), 1; Katherine A. Grandjean, "The Long Wake of the Pequot War," *Early American Studies* 9 (2011), 379–411, esp. 391–394, 396–398.

80. Neal Salisbury, *Manitou and Providence: Indians, Europeans, and the Making of New England, 1500–1643* (New York: Oxford University Press, 1982), 228.

Once news of his plans leaked, colonial authorities recognized that they needed to halt his campaign.[81]

Miantonomi never saw a day when the Narragansetts or any other Indigenous nation in eastern North America could halt the spread of European colonists. But in telling the Montauks that Native communities from east to west needed to come together for their mutual defense, he revealed that it was not just infectious diseases that spread inland from the coast. So too had the resentments caused by colonial expansion.

81. Lion Gardiner, "Lieft Lion Gardiner His Relation of the Pequot Warres," *Collections of the Massachusetts Historical Society*, 3rd Ser., 3 (1833), 154; Michael L. Oberg, "'We Are All the Sachems from East to West': A New Look at Miantonomi's Campaign of Resistance," *NEQ* 77 (2004), 478–499; Salisbury, *Manitou and Providence*, 13–14, 228–235.

20

Uncivil Wars

Sending captive Pequots to Providence Island after the slaughter on the Mystic was the opening salvo in what became a decade of unprecedented warfare in North America. To the English, the Pequots had become enemies whose insolence and threats, in the eyes of the victors, transformed them from proper subjects for conversion to suitable candidates for murder, capture, and enslavement. The passage to Providence Island took survivors to a place where the English needed labor to produce exports—and presumably beyond any efforts to entice them into Christendom. In the long run, the plan failed when the English ceded control of the island to Spain in 1641, but not before revealing that religious dissenters who had migrated across the ocean seeking religious tolerance were eager to grow rich from American lands.

At the end of the Anglo-Pequot War, no one could have predicted how widely scattered conflicts would soon shape daily life in much of North America. After all, the descent of the English into civil war, which was followed by the execution of Charles I, and the rise of new hostilities between the English and the Dutch took place far from American shores. Those conflicts altered the structure of politics in the entire Atlantic basin, which had a direct impact on those living in eastern North America. So too did hostilities inside territory that the English claimed—in southern New England, along the shores of the Chesapeake and its tributaries, and most brutally in Lenapehoking in territory claimed by the Dutch for New Netherland. European colonists and soldiers were eager participants in battles against Indigenous, but they were not the only combatants on the field. To the west of Dutch and English claims, Haudenosaunee forces assaulted Wendat communities clustered near the Great Lakes. Their motivation was to gain authority over a longtime rival and more control over the fur trade with colonists, another sign of the unpredictable expansion of colonialism.

By the late 1640s, eastern North America and islands across the Caribbean had become integrated into what was fast becoming an English empire built not on the persuasiveness of English ideas but instead on the

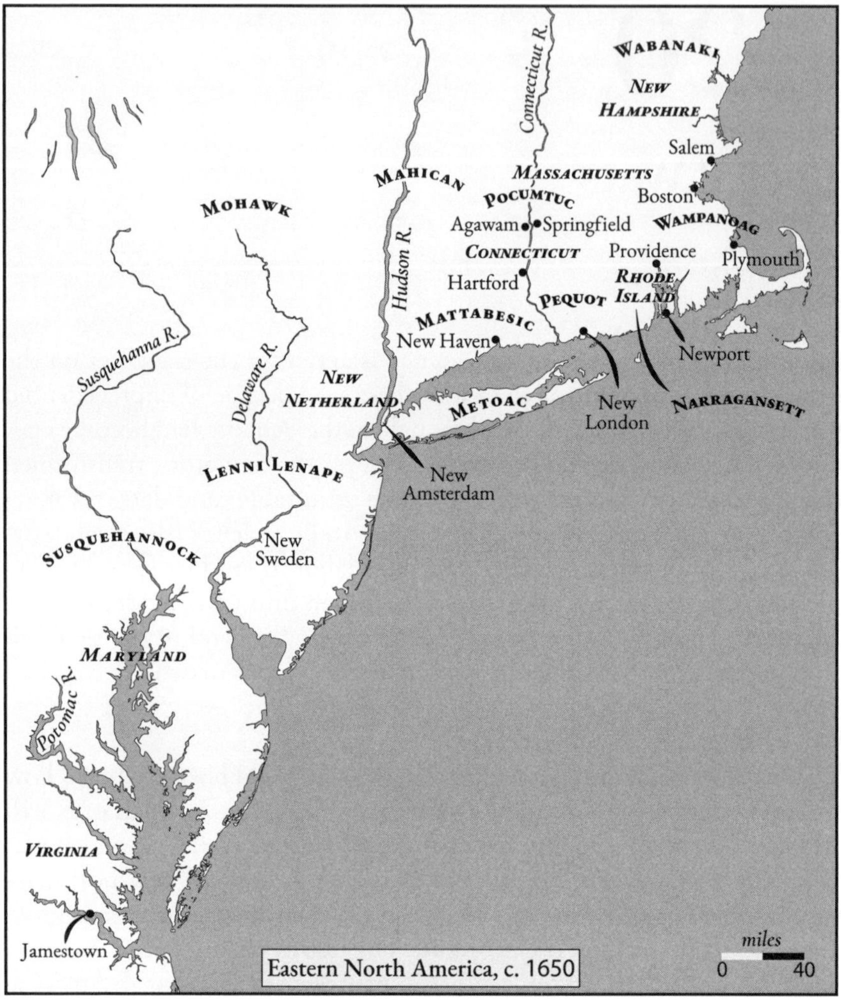

Eastern North America, c. 1650

brutality of its soldiers, a repeat of the late Tudor and early Stuart conquest of Ireland. But before the architects of that empire could establish how it would function, colonizers first had to survive an era of very uncivil warfare.

In 1637, Charles I found himself embroiled in a domestic crisis. Aided by William Laud, the archbishop of Canterbury, and others in the clerical hierarchy and encouraged by his Catholic spouse, Henrietta Maria, the king decided that the time had come to rein in dissenting religious voices. To do so, he ordered that the Book of Common Prayer be used across the realm, including in Scotland, where many churches had begun to use a Presbyterian liturgy that differed in substantial ways from the practices of the Church of England. From the perspective of London, such a strategy posed few legal problems since Charles was the king of Scotland and Ireland as well as England. But the riot in Edinburgh in 1637 had initiated the so-called Bishops' Wars, with the Scots serving notice that they would not tolerate Anglican religious practice. In the Pacification of Berwick, a June 1639 agreement, the king backed off, bringing an uneasy peace before anyone fired a shot.[1]

The conflict between England and Scotland subsided, but anxieties spurred by confessional differences steadily deepened. In October 1641, Catholics across Ulster revolted against the Protestants who had sailed to Ireland as part of the plantation scheme that had reshaped the landscapes of Munster and Ulster. Simmering tensions that had remained across Ireland since the bloody conquest launched by Elizabeth almost seventy years earlier exploded. Native Irish agitated for an acceptance of Roman Catholicism, a position rejected by the English state and the Church of Ireland, a Protestant redoubt. Within weeks, some Irish rebels laid claim to the fortresses that loomed over the colonial landscape. Built to mark the authority of Anglo-Norman and then Elizabethan conquerors, the ancient forts and newer fortified houses served the interests of radicals with wide popular support. After violence broke out, stories of atrocities swirled, including reports of mass drownings of fifty Protestants in County Monaghan and another thirty to fifty in County Cavan. By the end of October, a rebellion that its leaders had hoped would be orderly had descended into anarchy.[2]

Local variations in Ireland disappeared in English public discussion of the uprising. Almost immediately, one English commentator after another issued declarations of the horrors being perpetrated by Catholics, including murder, sexual assault, infanticide, and the display of bodies on public streets.[3] One pamphleteer reported that rebels burst into the house of a Protestant and "then they layd hold of his wife being big with

1. See Conrad Russell, *The Fall of the British Monarchies, 1637–1642* (Oxford: Clarendon Press, 1991), 27–146; Kevin Sharpe, *The Personal Rule of Charles I* (New Haven, CT: Yale University Press, 1992), 769–824.
2. Nicholas Canny, *Making Ireland British, 1580–1650* (Oxford: Oxford University Press, 2001), 469–471, 431–432; Tim Harris, *Rebellion: Britain's First Stuart Kings* (Oxford: Oxford University Press, 2014), 431–432; see also Micheál Ó. Siochrú, "Atrocity, Codes of Conduct and the Irish in the British Civil Wars 1641–1653," *Past and Present* 195 (2007), 59–62.
3. *Bloudy Newes from Ireland, or The barbarous Crueltie by the Papists used in that Kingdome* (London, 1641), title page and sig. [A3^v].

child, & ravisht her, then ript open her wome, and like so many *Neroes* undantedly viewed nature's bed of Conception, [and] afterward tooke her and her infant and sacrifiz'd in fire their wounded bodies."[4] Texts poured out of English printers' shops—thirty-two before the end of 1641. Despite the exaggerations and outright lies, many English Protestants saw the pamphlets as confirmation of their deep anxieties about Catholics in general and their fears of a rising international Catholic conspiracy—a dread fed by news that Henrietta Maria had been trying to convince the Vatican to provide Charles with enormous financial support if he would expand freedom for Catholics to practice freely in Ireland and Scotland.[5]

What might have appeared to English readers as a unified effort to expand Rome's power was far less coherent. There was no single rebellion in Ireland and little documentary evidence to support allegations of the most heinous atrocities. Protestant pamphleteers described unrestrained bloodlust, but many of the attacks against the British government focused on symbolic targets, such as the trees that English had planted. In County Mayo rebels put English cows on trial, killing any beasts unable to read a book.[6]

When the rebellion exploded in Ireland, Charles I was in Scotland, attending Presbyterian services and agreeing to a Scots parliamentary act that dictated that "all idolatrous images, crucifixes, pictures of Christ, and all other idolatrous pictures" in every chapel, church, and college needed to be destroyed. On November 25, with the bells of each of London's 121 parish churches ringing, he made a triumphal return to the city, promising to support Protestant practice.[7]

By then, religious dissenters and their supporters had gained control of the House of Commons. Less than three weeks after his return, Parliament sent the king a list of their grievances, which they published as *A Remonstrance of the State of the Kingdom*, known as the Grand Remonstrance.

4. Ethan H. Shagan, "Constructing Discord: Ideology, Propaganda, and English Responses to the Irish Rebellion of 1641," *Journal of British Studies* 36 (1997), 4–34; *A Bloody Battell: or the Rebels Overthrow, and Protestants Victorie* (London, 1641), sig. A3^{v} ("so many *Neroes*"); *Worse and Worse News from Ireland* (London, 1641).
5. The queen sought 150,000 pounds from the pontiff; see Harris, *Rebellion*, 437–444 (pamphlets), 426 (Henrietta Maria).
6. Canny, *Making Ireland British*, 534–535; Harris, *Rebellion*, 435–437; Keith D. Pluymers, "Cow Trials, Climate Change, and the Causes of Violence," *Environmental History* 25 (2020), 287–309.
7. Harris, *Rebellion*, 427–428 (actions in Scotland), 446–447 (return to London).

The authors believed that the realm was spiraling into a crisis but that there remained time to recover if the monarch would act quickly. Specifically, he had to find a way to eliminate Jesuit priests, "who hate the Laws" and worked for the "Subversion of Religion"; bishops and "the corrupt part of the Clergie, who cherish formality, and superstition," and promoted "their own Ecclesiasticall Tyranny, and Usurpation"; and the king's courtiers and councilors who had promoted the interests of foreign princes to the detriment of Charles's subjects.[8] They feared that he might use the Irish rebellion as an excuse to raise an army that he would then deploy against domestic foes. To prevent such an action, they enumerated his many concerning acts, which included expanding the size of royal forests against the 1217 doctrine of the Charta de Foresta, which limited his subjects' access to wood and fields for their livestock.[9] He tolerated the destruction of the Forest of Dean, selling the wood to Catholics and hence undermining the supply of wood needed to maintain the realm's ships. He and his agents engrossed all gunpowder and moved it to the Tower of London at the same time they disarmed well-trained militia units.[10] Judgments from the Star Chamber had inflicted excessive punishments even for minor infractions.[11] They identified signs of corruption across his court. Just as worrying, they feared that he was undermining the realm's American colonies and providing an opening for Spaniards to seize British territory.[12]

While the king denied the accusations and claimed he still supported Parliament, his efforts proved fruitless. Recognizing that he had lost the support of many in London, Charles left on January 10, first for Hampton Court and then for Windsor Castle. Sensing worse to come, Charles and troops loyal to him fled to York, where they arrived on March 18.[13]

By the time he reached the north, Henrietta Maria, one of the king's closest political confidants, had sailed for the Netherlands.[14] She traveled

8. *A Remonstrance of the State of the Kingdom* (London, 1641), sig. A2[v], B[r]–B2[r], A2[r]; see Harris, *Rebellion*, 448–451.
9. *Remonstrance of the State of the Kingdom*, sig. B2[v].
10. *Remonstrance of the State of the Kingdom*, sig. B2[v]–B3[r]; see also Keith Pluymers, *No Wood, No Kingdom: Political Ecology in the English Atlantic* (Philadelphia: University of Pennsylvania Press, 2021).
11. *Remonstrance of the State of the Kingdom*, sig. B3[r]–[B4[r]]; see David Cressy, "Saltpetre, State Security and Vexation in Early Modern England," *Past and Present* 212 (2011), 73–111.
12. *Remonstrance of the State of the Kingdom*, sig. [B4[v]], C[r]–C2[r], B[v], [D4[v]].
13. [John Rushworth], *Historical Collections from April 1641, to Decemb. 1642* (London, 1708), 452–453; Harris, *Rebellion*, 454–455.
14. William J. Bulman, "The Practice of Politics: The English Civil War and the 'Resolution' of Henrietta Maria and Charles I," *Past and Present* 206 (2010), 43–79.

with her ten-year-old daughter Mary, the wife of William (Willem) I, the young Prince of Orange, whom Mary had married when she was nine and he was fifteen. The queen claimed they sailed to go to a spa for their health, but that was a cover story. As Charles knew, she planned to pawn the crown jewels to pay for weapons for the king's army.[15] To hide their actions, they smuggled out jewels sewn into dresses, though one of the two ships that conveyed the pair sank off Texel, an island off the coast of North Holland in the Netherlands. On July 15, 1641, members of Commons informed the king that they had "received information of great Quantities of Treasure, in Jewels, Plate, and ready Money, packed up, to be conveyed away with the Queen" and destined to be taken along with other goods "beyond the Seas; which will not only impoverish the State" but which might also disturb the public peace.[16] As it happened, other English monarchs had pawned the crown jewels too to meet short-term financial demands. But they had done so in calmer times, not when rumors swirled about a king using his wife and daughter to advance his nefarious political schemes.[17] While the queen faced some difficulties, she managed to get enough to fill six shipments of arms in the latter half of 1642.[18]

15. Jack David Sargeant, "Parliament and the Crown Jewels in the English Revolution, 1641–1644," *Historical Journal* 63 (2020), 811–835; *Calendar of State Papers and Manuscripts, relating to English affairs existing in the archives of Venice, and in other libraries of Northern Italy* (London, 1864–), 25:186–187.
16. David Humphrey, "To Sell England's Jewels: Queen Henrietta Maria's Visits to the Continent, 1642 and 1644," *E-rea: Revue électronique d'études sur le monde anglophone* 11, no. 2 (2014), https://doi.org/10.4000/erea.3715,
17. Robert Cotton, *An Abstract out of the Records of the Tower, touching The Kings Revenue: And how they have supported themselves* (London, 1642), *Strange and Terrible Newes from the Queene in Holland shewing Plainely the intelligence of the King of His intention to raise Armes* (London, 1642), quotation at sig. A3^r; Elizabeth Stuart to Sir Thomas Row, February 3, 1642, SP 16/488, no. 85 (ff. 154–155), TNA, in Nadine Akkerman, ed., *The Correspondence of Elizabeth Stuart, Queen of Bohemia, 1632–1642* (Oxford: Oxford University Press, 2011), accessed via Oxford Scholarly Editions online; Humphrey, "To Sell England's Jewels," para. 9; Henrietta Maria to Charles I, March 1643, and the following undated letter in Mary Anne Everett Green, ed., *Letters of Queen Henrietta Maria* (London, 1857), 49–63, Harris, *Rebellion*, 454–455; *The Queenes Resolution Discovered by Some Letters read in the House of Commons* (London, 1642), 7; Edmund Ludlow, *Memoirs of Lieutenant Ludlow, the Third and Last Part* (Vivay, Bern, Switzerland, 1699), 319–320, 369, Gordon Darroch, "400-Year-Old Dress Found in Shipwreck Sheds Light on Plot to Pawn Crown Jewels," *The Guardian*, April 21, 2016; Elizabeth Hines, "How to Pawn the Crown Jewels," *The Court Historian*, 30 (2025), 196–213.
18. *The Queens Majesties Message and Letter from the Hague in Holland, directed to the Kings most excellent Majesty* (London, 1642), 3; Humphrey, "To Sell England's Jewels," para. 22.

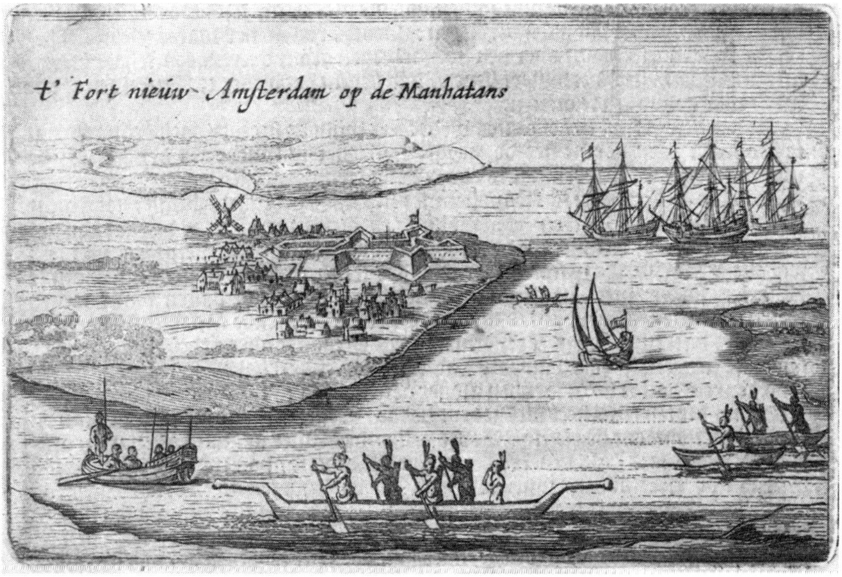

At midcentury, Adriaen Van der Donck included this view of lower Manhattan in his book recounting what the Dutch had accomplished in New Netherland. The fort dominates the picture, but nearby houses and a windmill reveal how the earliest colonists had already begun to impose Dutch architectural ideas on the island. There are no Indigenous buildings to be seen, though the central role of Munsees and other residents of Lenapehoking can be seen in the prominent place of Native canoes in the harbor. From Van der Donck, *Beschryvinge van Nieuw-Nederland (Ghelijck het tegenwoordigh in Staet is)* [Description of New Netherland (as it is today)] (Madrid, 1655). Library of Congress, 2021666733.

In June, Parliament sent the king a petition demanding the enforcement of laws against Catholics, accepting parliamentary control over the militia, and vacating charges against those targeted for their views. He refused. Convinced that his political foes had gone over the line from legitimate opposition to treason, Charles I prepared for the unimaginable.[19]

During the era when Charles's ability to govern fizzled, some Europeans in North America, not all of them English, began to question whether they could live alongside Native communities. Among them was Willem Kieft. He had been forty-one years old in 1638, when the council of the WIC appointed him director-general of New Netherland, and had little useful experience at a time when the WIC evolved from a commercial venture toward being an actual colonial government. The shift altered

19. Harris, *Rebellion*, 455–456.

Kieft's position from a manager to something like a governor, a task for which he was even less prepared. On September 15, 1639, Kieft and his associates passed a resolution to protect New Amsterdam from its Indigenous neighbors. Kieft and the council demanded payments in maize, wampum, or fur from local Natives who, until that point, the Dutch had wanted to protect from their enemies.[20] Kieft's action met with a predictable response from Munsees and others. Rather than paying, they questioned the utility of having Europeans in the area.

Tensions in the area exploded during the winter of 1639–1640 when 400 Mohawks attacked Lenapes living near Fort Orange with guns they had purchased from the Europeans. The Lenapes, unwilling to pay tribute, sought the protection of the Dutch.[21] Whatever amity drove some Indigenous to Kieft's administration proved short-lived. In the spring of 1640, a group of religious dissenters from Lynn, Massachusetts, purchased land on the eastern end of Long Island from local Natives. The move displeased the Dutch. As soon as they heard, John Winthrop, then governor of Massachusetts, reported that the Dutch "sent men to take possession of the place, and set up the arms of the Prince of Orange upon a tree," a tactic that the English and other Europeans had also used to mark their territory, often in advance of an actual effort to build a community. The English from Lynn took down the standard and began to set up their houses. "The Dutch took this in high displeasure," Winthrop observed, sending soldiers to imprison the English. They held them captive for a few days and then released them.[22]

Anxiety mounted into the new year. In early 1640, a group of Raritans killed colonists' swine foraging on Staten Island. On July 16, 1640, Cornelius van Theinhoven, who had previously been the bookkeeper of the community before being promoted to secretary of New Netherland, led 100 men into Raritan territory seeking satisfaction. The Dutch official, whose pigs had been killed, lacked the authority to attack the Raritans. Rebuffed by them, he turned for home, but left some soldiers behind. Some of them then killed an unknown number of Raritans and took the headman's brother as a captive. "Whereupon the Indians," as colonist David de Vries later wrote, "killed four of my men, burned my house" and another's "in revenge." The violence began to spiral. De Vries

20. Jaap Jacobs, *The Colony of New Netherland: A Dutch Settlement in Seventeenth-Century America* (Ithaca, NY: Cornell University Press, 2009), 44, 76.
21. "Journal of New Netherland, 1647," in J. Franklin Jameson, ed., *Narratives of New Netherland, 1609–1664* (New York: Scribner's, 1909), 271–274.
22. John Winthrop, *The Journal of John Winthrop, 1630–1649*, ed. Richard S. Dunn et al. (Cambridge, MA: Harvard University Press, 1996), 327.

noted that the soldiers lashed a captive to a mast and assaulted him "in his private parts with a piece of split wood."[23]

The heightened tensions produced by the arrival of more colonists encouraged those in disputes to see their individual problems as emblematic of larger anger. This was the context that turned a criminal act in 1642 into a predicate for a massive response. That year, a Native from Wecquaeseck, never identified in the surviving documents, went to trade furs with Claes Cornelisz Swits (also known as Rademaker), who lived near a Dutch fort erected near modern Turtle Bay on the East River. According to the Wecquaeseck's testimony, Swits went to pay the man by taking things out of a locked chest. With the chest open and the colonist leaning down, the Native struck him on the neck with an axe, killing him instantly. He then took everything from the chest. According to de Vries, the murderer admitted to the crime, which he committed not because of anything that Swits had done but because when he was a child he had traveled to New Amsterdam "while the fort was being built" along with his uncle to trade beaver, and while they were there a group of Dutch murdered his uncle and stole his furs. "He was then a small boy," de Vries wrote, "and resolved that, when he should grow up, he would revenge that deed upon the Dutch, and since then had seen no better chance to do so than with this Claes Rademaker." Kieft immediately hoped to avenge the murder. Other Dutch warned him that their cattle were browsing and would no doubt be stolen or killed if the colonists sought justice at that moment, possibly triggering yet more violence when the Dutch lacked the might to protect themselves. Wait until we are more like the English, they said. "It is a pleasant and charming country," as De Vries put it, noting that the region could produce everything that grew in England, France, and Holland, "if only it were well peopled by our nation." De Vries added that crustaceans that migrated there in the summer had orange, white, and blue claws like the flag of the Dutch prince, "so that the crabs show sufficiently that we ought to people the country, and that it belongs to us."[24]

Neither de Vries nor Kieft grasped that the residents of Lenapehoking had no intention of accepting colonists who tried to expand onto lands that the Natives were not yet ready to sell. Unlike the Haudenosaunee,

23. David de Vries, *Korte Historiael, ende Journaels Aenteyckeninge van verscheyden Voyagiens in de vier deelen des Wereldts-Ronde* . . . (1655), translated as "Short Historical and Journal-Notes of various Voyages performed in the Four Quarters of the Globe . . ." (hereafter de Vries, "Short Historical Notes"), in Jameson, ed., *Narratives of New Netherland*, 208–209.

24. De Vries, "Short Historical Notes," 213–223, quotations at 213 (revenge), 219 "pleasant and charming country," 223 (crabs); Jacobs, *Colony of New Netherland*, 77.

who had designed an Indigenous alliance to the north and west centuries before the arrival of Europeans, the Lenapes had not formed a confederacy. To be sure, they spoke mutually intelligible Algonquian dialects, which facilitated trade and communication, and shared certain economic and cultural practices, notably the central importance of maize agriculture and harvesting freshwater and saltwater fish and shellfish. But they were not organized into a political unit. Among those inhabiting Lenapehoking was a group that lived near Manhattan Island and spoke Munsee, which led various Europeans to lump different communities together under that name. Lenapehoking stretched north up the Hudson to include the Esopus and Wappinger communities, who lived near modern Albany; the Hackensacks, who lived on the western banks of the Hudson River; the Canarsee, who inhabited western Long Island, distinct from the Rockaways, Massapequas, and Martinecocks, who inhabited the central part of that island; the Raritans, who lived opposite Staten Island; the Siwanoys and Wiechquaeskecks, who lived just north of the Dutch on Manhattan Island; and many other communities scattered from the Tulpehocken, whose territory lay between the Delaware River and Blue Mountains, to the more than twenty groups that controlled the territory covering most of modern New Jersey and along both banks of the Delaware River and Bay.[25] The Jesuit Isaac Jogues, who traveled in the region in 1643 and 1644, commented that there were "many nations between the two Dutch settlements," a recognition that Europeans understood they were dealing not with a unified Indigenous nation but instead with a cluster of communities across the region.[26]

In May 1642, John Underhill, an English commander during the slaughter on the Mystic River in 1637, moved to New Netherland. His migration made sense from Kieft's perspective. Here was a man who had a Dutch wife, could speak Dutch, and could provide tactical assistance should relations with local Natives reach a dangerous point. Underhill was not the only émigré from Massachusetts to travel to New Netherland. Anne

25. On the territory and shared cultural practices of the inhabitants of Lenapehoking, see Anne-Marie Cantwell and Diana diZerega Wall, *Unearthing Gotham: The Archaeology of New York City* (New Haven, CT: Yale University Press, 2001), esp. 119–122; Jean R. Soderlund, *Lenape Country: Delaware Valley Society Before William Penn* (Philadelphia: University of Pennsylvania Press, 2015), 12–34; Robert S. Grumet, The *Munsee Indians: A History* (Norman: University of Oklahoma Press, 2009), 3–41. For the Haudenosaunee experience, see Matthew Dennis, *Cultivating a Landscape of Peace: Iroquois-European Encounters in Seventeenth-Century America* (Ithaca, NY: Cornell University Press, 1993), 43–115.

26. Isaac Jogues, "Novum Belgium," in Jameson, ed., *Narratives of New Netherland*, 262.

Hutchinson, who had gone first to Roger Williams's new community along Narragansett Bay after her banishment, had moved with her family in 1624 to modern Pelham Bay Park in the Bronx, which became known as Anne's Hoeck (Anne's Neck).[27]

Kieft recruited Underhill knowing that danger loomed. His fears were well founded. On February 22, 1643, conflict broke out among some of the Indigenous. Winthrop heard that the incident began when a group of Mohawks living near the Hudson, having suffered at the hands of the Dutch, went for revenge and came upon a group of other Natives living near New Amsterdam. The Mohawks killed approximately thirty of them. De Vries claimed that 400 to 500 came rushing to his property to avoid the Mayekanders (perhaps Mohawks?) who were pursuing the Tappans and Wecquaesgeeks for tribute. De Vries decided that the only way to defuse the situation was to find Kieft. The fastest way to the fort was via a canoe, which he paddled between the ice floes since his own boat was held fast by the winter ice. Over a meal on the twenty-fourth, the governor told De Vries that "he had a mind to *wipe the mouths* of the savages." De Vries reminded the director that "on account of trifling with the Indians we had lost our colony in the South River at Swanendael, in the Hoere-kil, with thirty-two men, who were murdered in the year 1630." He added that, a decade later, a relatively minor incident had led to violence on Staten Island.[28]

When the meal ended, the governor took De Vries into a large hall that he had just added to his fortified house. There, De Vries reported, "stood all his soldiers ready to cross the river to Pavonia to commit the murder." De Vries heard screaming around midnight. He leapt to the ramparts and stared across at Pavonia. He later wrote that he "saw nothing but firing, and heard the shrieks of the savages murdered in their sleep."[29] Kieft's soldiers had killed eighty Natives, De Vries observed, "considering they had done a deed of Roman valor, in murdering so many in their sleep,"[30]

27. Winthrop, *Journal*, 388; Cantwell and diZerega Wall, *Unearthing Gotham*, 127.

28. De Vries, "Short Historical Notes," 227; Winthrop, *Journal*, 427.

29. De Vries, "Short Historical Notes," 228.

30. Jameson, ed., *Narratives of New Netherland*, 228. As Jameson noted, De Vries lifted his description of the violence from an anonymous anti-Stuyvesant pamphlet entitled *Breeden Raedt aen de Vereenighde Nederlandsche Provintien* [Broad advice to the United Dutch Provinces], published in Antwerp in 1649; see *Extracts from a work called Breeden Raedt aen de Vereenighde*, trans. Mr. C. (Amsterdam, 1850), https://archive.org/details/extractsfromworkoomely/page/n5/mode/2up; Henry C. Murphy, trans., "Broad Advice to the United Netherland Provinces," in *Collections of the New-York Historical Society*, 2nd Ser., III (1857), 237–284, esp. 249–256. Murphy identified the

Winthrop confirmed that the Dutch killed seventy to eighty "men, women and children."[31]

The story, as De Vries told it, was chilling. Dutch soldiers had, he claimed, entered Munsees' houses "where infants were torn from their mother's breasts, and hacked to pieces in the presence of the parents, and the pieces thrown into the fire and in the water, and other sucklings, being bound to small boards, were cut, stuck, and pierced, and miserably massacred in a manner to move a heart of stone." He claimed that the soldiers had thrown children into the river, but when their parents tried to save them, the Dutch would not let them on shore. Five- and six-year-olds, along with some elderly, drowned. Some escaped the onslaught and hid in the bushes. When they believed the fighting was over, they emerged from their refuges and begged for food and a chance to get warm by the fire. But they, he wrote, "were murdered in cold blood and tossed into the fire or the water." Survivors limped from the carnage, some having lost arms or legs or "holding their entrails in their arms." In addition to the massacre at Pavonia, other colonial soldiers, led by Underhill, killed forty sleeping Indigenous near another patroon's plantation, raising the death toll to 120 during a single night.[32]

Just as de Vries had predicted, the surviving Natives in the region soon launched a series of raids on Dutch farms, destroying the colonists' possessions and killing the men, though they spared children and women.[33] Anne Hutchinson was not so fortunate. A Munsee named Wampage claimed that he led a raid to Anne's Hoeck, killing her and her family.[34] Soon after, the Dutch sent 130 armed soldiers via three yachts to Greenwich, where they had heard there was a large cluster of Indigenous enemies. Under the glare of a full moon illuminating the wintry landscape, the Dutch and English soldiers first battled with swords and then, following precedent that Underhill boasted about earlier, set the village on fire and prevented anyone from escaping. "According to the report of the Indians themselves," an unknown Dutch observer wrote, "the number

author as Cornelis Melyn, who owned a patroon on Staten Island and was the chairman of the Eight Men, the governing body that protested Kieft's actions to the Dutch parliament. For Melyn, see "Cornelis Melyn," Historical Society of the New York Courts, https://history.nycourts.gov/figure/cornelis-melyn/ (accessed January 20, 2025).

31. Winthrop, *Journal*, 427.

32. De Vries, "Short Historical Notes," 228–229; "Journal of New Netherland, 1647," 281–282; Winthrop, *Journal*, 427–428; Jacobs, *Colony of New Netherland*, 77–78; Cantwell and diZerega Wall, *Unearthing Gotham*, 126–127.

33. De Vries, "Short Historical Notes," 229.

34. Cantwell and diZerega Wall, *Unearthing Gotham*, 127.

then destroyed exceeded five hundred. Some say, full seven hundred." After the carnage, the forces marched eastward for two days until they reached the English community at Stamford. "The English received our people in a very friendly manner, affording them every comfort," the anonymous observer noted. He added that "a thanksgiving was proclaimed on their arrival."[35]

Kieft's War came to a formal end on August 30, 1645. Missionary Isaac Jogues estimated the death toll was 1,600 after just one burst of carnage, though perhaps he meant that was the total for the conflict.[36] Despite the high number of casualties, the war had not destroyed the residents of Lenapehoking, as Kieft had hoped. Nor did his vicious strategy end his rule.[37] Kieft remained in charge in New Amsterdam until early 1648, when news of disputes and dangerous conditions in the colony reached the WIC, which decided to replace him. He never made it home. The 400-ton *Prinses Amelia* he and 100 others boarded sailed into Bristol Channel by mistake and ran aground off south Wales. The governor and eighty of the others died there. The event was unfortunate, as Winthrop noted, but it also demonstrated to the English that they "had Intelligence of an observable hand of God [upon] the dutche at New Netherlandes, which thoughe it were sadly to be lamented in regarde of the Calamytye, yet there appeared in it so muche of God in favor [of] his poore people heere, & displeasure towardes suche as have opposed & injured them."[38]

Kieft's War also shaped the struggling colony of New Sweden. Under the directorship of Johan Printz, a native of Bottnaryd in the southern Swedish province of Småland then living on modern Tinicum Island, colonists there farmed tobacco and purchased furs to export. Printz thought that success lay in creating an economic system that linked the Delaware to the Caribbean, a Swedish triangle trade that would result in profits for investors in Stockholm. But he had heard about the bloodshed to his north, including a rumor that the Dutch had lost 1,000 men in New Netherland, and he continued to fear nearby Lenapes, who periodically attacked isolated farmsteads. By 1646, New Sweden's population stood at 183, including children. Despite their small numbers, the colonists

35. "Journal of New Netherland, 1647," 282–284.

36. Jogues, "Novum Belgium," 263; see also Cantwell and diZerega Wall, *Unearthing Gotham*, 128.

37. See Alan Trelease, *Indian Affairs in Colonial New York: The Seventeenth Century* (Ithaca, NY: Cornell University Press, 1960), 82–84. Trelease estimated that 1,000 Natives perished in the conflict.

38. Jacobs, *Colony of New Netherland*, 152; Winthrop, *Journal*, 698. The wreck also apparently destroyed Kieft's own records of his time in New Netherland; see Jameson, ed., *Narratives of New Netherland*, 267.

dispatched 2,000 beaver pelts, obtained primarily with imported copper kettles, and 20,000 pounds of tobacco packaged into seventy-seven hogsheads.[39] But warning signs remained. There were too few women to sustain population growth, and the Dutch sale of weapons to Natives kept the Swedes and a small number of Finns who lived among them on edge.[40] The community survived but never thrived, reaching a population of merely 368 in 1654.[41]

New Sweden's stunted growth reflected widespread midcentury turbulence. European colonists hoped that success in battle would end Indigenous resistance. But Natives, even with their numbers declining across the coastal arc from the Chesapeake to southern New England, remained formidable, forging alliances that kept Europeans wary. In 1642, before the horrors unleashed by Kieft and Underhill, Miantonomi and 100 allies traveled through the Native communities within New Netherland, "soliciting them to a general war against both the English and the Dutch," according to one anonymous observer.[42] The following spring, representatives from Massachusetts, New Haven, New Plymouth, and Connecticut, concerned about the threats that Indigenous posed, formulated plans for what they called the United Colonies of New England.[43]

In 1643, Massachusetts and Connecticut officials summoned Miantonomi and the Mohegan sachem Uncas to Hartford, hoping they could broker a deal between two hostile neighboring nations. Although the signs were all around them, they missed the fact that these Indigenous leaders had their own agendas. Like other Natives whom Europeans believed stood in the way of colonial expansion, Uncas and Miantonomi had less concern for the newcomers than for maximizing the prospects of their own

39. "Report of Governor Johan Printz, 1644," 93–99, 102–107, 110–116 (census), and "Report of Governor Johan Printz, 1647," both in Albert C. Myers, ed., *Narratives of Early Pennsylvania, West New Jersey and Delaware, 1630–1707* (New York: Scribner's, 1912), 120–126; Visa Immonen, "Farming and Brass Kettles as Forms of Colonial Encounter: New Sweden from an Archaeological Perspective," *Scandinavian Studies* 83 (2011), 365–386, esp. 375–378.
40. "Report of Governor Johan Printz, 1647," 123–125.
41. Gunlög M. Fur, *Colonialism in the Margins: Cultural Encounters in New Sweden and Lapland* (Leiden: Brill, 2006), 96; Sten Carlsson, "The New Sweden Colonists, 1638–1656," in Carol E. Hoffecker et al., eds., *New Sweden in America* (Newark: University of Delaware Press, 1995), 171–187.
42. "Journal of New Netherland, 1647," 276.
43. Mark Peterson, *The City-State of Boston: The Rise and Fall of an Atlantic Power, 1630–1865* (Princeton, NJ: Princeton University Press, 2019), 67–70.

communities. As the English realized, the Narragansetts, their nominal ally in 1637 because of their deep-seated enmity against the Pequots, quickly absorbed those they believed had been assailants into their own communities. Yes, Winthrop wrote later in a short tract published on the orders of the commissioners for the United Colonies in 1645, the English had managed to subdue the Pequots, who had grown "to an excesse of violence and outrage, and proudly turned aside from all wayes of justice & peace" before the war. But in its aftermath, the Narragansetts, especially the community of Niantics, not only had "many of the Pequot nation, but such of them [who] have had their hands in the blood & murder of the English" but also laid claim to former Pequot territory "which by right of conquest justly appertaines to the English." Worse still, the English had heard rumors about "Miantonimo's ambitious designes"—namely, that he had traveled among other Indigenous in the region, offering gifts and promises in an effort "to make himself their universall Sagamore or Governor, perswading and ingaging them, at once to cut off the whole body of the English in these parts." This was the same nightmarish scenario that Winthrop and Bradford had feared earlier, which prompted them to launch their war against the Pequots. When confronted in New Haven, Miantonomi, as Winthrop put it, "threatened to cut off any Indians head that should lay such a charge upon his face." The colonists once again feared assault and stood armed in their communities. Uncas took a more deliberate approach: he captured Miantonomi and brought him to Hartford for interrogation.[44]

During the investigation, the colonial commissioners in the area learned details about a treaty between the Narragansetts and Massachusetts in 1637. At that time Miantonomi had promised he would not launch attacks on other Natives, and specifically not against Uncas. Despite those promises, the investigation revealed that the Narragansett sachem had plotted to assassinate Uncas. Other attempts to kill Uncas came to light too, including efforts to use poison and sorcery to kill him and a second assault by bow and arrow by an ally of Miantonomi's. Uncas testified too that a group of 900 to 1,000 Narragansetts had approached a Mohegan community that then had perhaps half as many people to defend themselves. Uncas sued for peace; Miantonomi launched an attack but the Mohegans prevailed. Uncas managed to capture Miantonomi, perhaps because he was weighed down by borrowed English armor. After the capture, they sought the advice of the English, who failed to broker a lasting peace between the Mohegans and Narragansetts. The message from

44. [John Winthrop], *A Declaration of Former Passages and Proceedings betwixt the English and the Narowgansetts* (Boston, 1645), 1–2.

Miantonomi was explicit: the Narragansetts would accept peace only after they received Uncas's head.[45] Winthrop and other English colonial leaders concluded that "the Country would suddenly be all on fyre." The Narragansetts had replaced the Pequots as their great menace. If they managed to kill Uncas and subdue the Mohegans, then the English would be next. In this scenario, the colonists would need to appeal to the Narragansetts "for their future safety." If that were to happen, "the English may not trust an Indian in the whole Country. The premises being duly weighed, it clearly appears that God calls the Colonies to a warr." From that moment forward, Miantonomi had become the most feared Native in the region, his every movement a potential effort to raise an army to vanquish not only the Mohegans but the English as well.[46]

The English believed that the Narragansett had committed a series of crimes that justified his execution. They instructed Uncas to bring Miantonomi out of Hartford and to kill him once they reached Mohegan territory. If the Mohegan sachem refused, the colonists offered to bring the condemned man to Boston via a pinnace until they sorted out what to do with him. In the end there was no need for such a contingency. While leading Miantonomi away from Hartford, Uncas's brother walked up behind him and smashed his head with an axe. To send a message of unity between the English and the Mohegans, the colonists authorized an armed guard of twelve to fourteen to escort Uncas to his home. "We were now also freed," Winthrop confided in his journal in October 1644, "from as great a fear of war with the Naragansetts."[47]

Miantonomi's murder cheered colonial authorities across New England. But it did not signal an end to the kind of resentment that the Narragansett leader had articulated in his speech to the Montauks. Soon enough, colonial officials would recognize that the Narragansetts were not the only Indigenous nation eager to halt the spread of English settlements in eastern North America.

In the spring of 1644, Opechancanough once again led an army against English colonists in Virginia. By then, an emerging planter aristocracy had begun to take shape along the lower reaches of the James and the shores near the Chesapeake, lands with ideal soil for growing tobacco and

45. [Winthrop], *A Declaration of Former Passages*, 2–6, quotation at 6; Winthrop, *Journal*, 471–472; John A. Sainsbury, "Miantonomo's Death and New England Politics, 1630–1645," *Rhode Island History* 30 (1971), 111–124, esp. 117–118.

46. [Winthrop], *A Declaration of Former Passages*, 6–7.

47. Winthrop, *Journal*, 472–473, 547; Sainsbury, "Miantonomo's Death," 118–120.

unrestricted access to the waterways they could use to move their crop to market. Newer migrants, who arrived in a region where bacteria still regularly killed English before the end of their initial period of servitude, realized that the only place they could afford was farther out. Their residential practices mirrored those the English had put in place since 1607: the newly arrived needed to go into territory that was more Indian Country than Virginia colony, no matter what their maps told them. As in other areas where newcomers had limited supplies of labor, they tended to fence in their fields and let their livestock browse freely, presumably on Natives' fields.[48] In 1644, these colonists bore the brunt of the Powhatans' attack. On April 18, Opechancanough and his allies killed 500 English, a larger death toll than that produced by the 1622 rebellion, which the English had publicly called a "massacre." Surviving colonists in the outlying area fled to a somewhat decrepit fort that spanned the short peninsula between the James and the York. Rather than continue the assault, Opechancanough and the Powhatans went home.[49]

On June 1, Governor William Berkeley and the colonial assembly met at Jamestown to plot a strategy. Those there knew well that the conflict that had begun in 1622 did not really come to an end until Opechancanough signed a treaty in 1632, which they believed had resolved tensions between Powhatans and colonists. They had to determine how to respond. The constant arrival of migrants, most of them indentured servants, had increased the colonial population to about 8,000 in 1644, despite continued early deaths of young adults. It is possible that by 1644 there were more colonists in Virginia than Powhatans in Tsenacommacah. If this was the case, colonists did not need to mount the same kind of response as they had from 1622 to 1624, especially since there were relatively few Powhatans living in the prime colonial region bounded by the two rivers. But even if the newcomers held the upper hand in the Tidewater, they still needed to protect colonists in outlying areas and, just as important, send a message to prospective immigrants who could choose other locales including Maryland, southern New England, or Barbados.

48. For imported livestock: Virginia DeJohn Anderson, *Creatures of Empire: How Domestic Animals Transformed Early America* (New York: Oxford University Press, 2006); for shifts in the landscape, see James D. Rice, *Nature and History in the Potomac Country: From Hunter-Gatherers to the Age of Jefferson* (Baltimore: Johns Hopkins University Press, 2009), and Timothy Silver, *A New Face on the Countryside: Indians, Colonists, and Slaves in South Atlantic Forests, 1500–1800* (Cambridge: Cambridge University Press, 1990).

49. William L. Shea, "Virginia at War, 1644–1646," *Military Affairs* 41 (1977), 142–147, esp. 124; James Horn, *A Brave and Cunning Prince: The Great War Chief Opechancanough and the War for America* (New York: Basic Books, 2021), 222–224.

Despite the lower risk, the English mimicked what they had done two decades earlier. In the records of the General Assembly next to a marginal note reading "Perpetuall Warre w[i]th ye Indians," the governing body declared its intentions. "Whereas the Indians have justly made themselves our Irreconcileable enemyes by the late Bloody Massacre" in which they killed almost 400 colonists, the body resolved that it would "for ever abandon all formes of peace and familiarity w[i]th the whole Nation and will to the uttmost of our power pursue and root out those w[hi]ch have any way had their hands in the shedding of our blood and Massacring our People." They resolved to spend the summer destroying the Natives' corn and pursuing the Powhatans until they ran out of ammunition.[50]

At the end of June Captain William Claiborne led 300 soldiers into battle with the Pamunkeys, whose territory was Opechancanough's homeland. Each man was to bring his own powder, bullets, rifle, helmet, sword or cutlass, and three weeks' of food. The counties would be responsible for providing pinnaces or shallops to ferry them to the front. On July 8, the assembly ordered the residents of Upper Northumberland County to raise a crew to attack the Nansemonds, Seacocks, Warisquoyacks, Chawanoke, and "any other neare unto them." Residents of the other outlying counties, Charles City and Henrico, should attack their neighbors, the Tancks and Weyanokes, on July 15 to distract them from helping the Pamunkeys. Given the pressing need for bullets, the assembly ordered lieutenants to go house to house and confiscate any lead items, leaving only leaded windows behind.[51] The assembly soon dispatched Berkeley to London to gather more weapons and sent an agent to New England, New Netherland, and New Sweden seeking other assistance.[52] Over the next several months the legislature raised funds by taxing counties. To prevent shirking, the assembly ordered that "all negro men and women, and all other men from the age of 16 to 60 shall be adjudged tithable," a sign that Africans already possessed a unique status under the law. They also authorized the construction of Fort Royal, to rise on the former site of Pamunkey; Fort Charles, to be built at the falls of the James; and Fort James, to be constructed on the Chickahominy.[53]

Berkeley returned from England in June 1645, but with nothing to help the cause since during the English Civil War there were no arms to be spared to support Virginia. By then there was little need since colonial

50. "Acts, Orders and Resolutions of the General Assembly of Virginia," *VMHB* 23 (1915), 229–230.
51. "Acts, Orders and Resolutions of the General Assembly of Virginia," 230–237.
52. "Acts, Orders and Resolutions of the General Assembly of Virginia," 238–239.
53. Hening, *Statutes*, 292–293; Shea, "Virginia at War," 142–144.

soldiers had by laid waste to much of Tsenacommacah. To forestall a new starving time, the assembly declared in November 1645 that colonists could purchase corn from "any Nation being in peace and Amity."[54] Nonetheless, the threat of war dissipated among colonists. One unidentified observer, in a report to the *Mercurius Civicus*, a London newspaper, wrote about the new defense measures the colony put in place, but added that "we are at peace among our selves and have beene so ever since the massacre."[55] Opechancanough's alliance began to fracture, with some groups defecting even though moving closer to colonists often put them at increased risk.[56]

In 1646, Virginia authorities ordered the construction of Fort Henry, to be raised at the falls of the Appomattox River and house forty-five soldiers to defend colonists who lived on the south side of the James. They ordered, too, that the residents of Upper and Lower Northumberland Counties destroy the Nansemond cornfields and perform "any act or acts of hostility against them."[57] They also realized that they had been chasing Opechancanough for two years at considerable expense and there was little else to be accomplished since their remaining foes had left their towns. It would be best to bring the war to a close.[58]

The war took a toll on Opechancanough. He was then perhaps 100 years old and his allies needed to carry him around. "His Flesh was all macerated," Robert Beverley wrote in his history of the colony, "his Sinews slacken'd, and his Eye-lids became so heavy, that he could not see" unless they "were lifted up by his Servants." Given the Native leader's weakened state, Berkeley and his allies managed to capture him. The governor had hoped to ship Opechancanough to England to prove to his supporters that Natives could live very long lives and remained able to field many more soldiers than the poorly equipped colony.[59] But less than two weeks after Berkeley's forces captured Opechancanough, a soldier, as Beverley put it, "resenting the Calamaties the Colony had suffer'd by this Prince's Means, basely shot him thro' the Back." Mortally wounded, the

54. "Acts, Orders and Resolutions of the General Assembly of Virginia," 239.
55. See Joseph Frank, "News from Virginny, 1644," *VMHB* 65 (1957), 84–87.
56. Lars C. Adams, "'The Battle of Weyanoke Creek': A Story of the Third Anglo-Powhatan War in Early Carolina," *Native South* 6 (2013), 171–195. For evidence of the Weyanokes in the region, see [Edward Bland], "The Discovery of New Brittaine, 1650," in Alexander S. Salley, ed., *Narratives of Early Carolina, 1650–1708* (New York: Scribner's, 1911), 9–10.
57. Hening, *Statutes* (for March 1645/1646), 315.
58. Hening, *Statutes at Large* (for March 1645/1646), 317–318; Robert Beverley, *The History and Present State of Virginia, in Four Parts* (London, 1705), 50–51.
59. Beverley, *History and Present State of Virginia*, 52.

most powerful Powhatan war chief the English had ever encountered did not succumb quickly. As he lay dying, he heard a commotion and looked around him to see a crowd that had gathered. Opechancanough demanded to see Berkeley, who came to visit. The Pamunkey told him if the situation had been reversed—if the Powhatans had captured Berkeley—he "should not meanly have exposed him as a Show to the People."[60]

After Opechancanough's death, the English colony and the Powhatans, represented by Necotowance, agreed to a treaty. From that point on, the York River would become a boundary line. Indigenous could live and hunt to its north, but the area between the York and the James "from the falls of both rivers to Kequotan" was open for colonists. While the Natives' territory would be off-limits for colonial farms, colonists could still fell trees and cut sedge on Indigenous lands, and colonists had until the following March to capture any cattle or hogs on the north side of the York. Powhatans who wanted to travel through the colony needed to obtain a badge. In an echo from an earlier time, colonial officials permitted Native children up to twelve years old to live in English households.[61]

Despite the losses during the conflict, especially on its first day, colonists were able to continue their transformation of the piedmont and Tidewater into tobacco farms.[62] One traveler estimated that there were 15,000 English living in Virginia in the late 1640s, along with 300 Africans. The colonists had 20,000 cattle, oxen, or calves, along with growing numbers of horses (then 200) and sheep (3,000, all producing fine wool), 5,000 goats, and a seemingly infinite number of swine and poultry. Each year the colonists cleared more ground and produced excellent wheat. The natural resources that had once attracted visitors' attention remained too, including abundant populations of birds, fish, and deer. The area still boasted the finest tobacco to be found, and had begun to produce larger amounts of indigo, flax, and hemp; the colonists had established productive ironworks run by skilled migrants from England. Some 700 to 800 sailors arrived each year on the thirty ships that connected the colony to the homeland and beyond. On Christmas day 1647 there were seven ships from New England, two from Bristol, ten from London, and a dozen Dutch vessels. Some of the captains kept residences there, a sign of the regularity of transatlantic traffic. Plantations dotted the riverbanks, and hundreds of pinnaces and small boats facilitated commerce, including in an expanding silk industry that employed women and children as well as men. Perhaps most reassuring was that the colonists seemed so healthy,

60. Beverley, *History and Present State of Virginia*, 52–53.
61. Hening, ed., *Statutes*, 1:323–326.
62. Shea, "Virginia at War," 146–147; Rice, *Nature and History in the Potomac Country*, 118.

with fewer dying each year than in comparable communities in England. Carpenters, shoemakers, tanners, tailors, potters, and turners flocked to the area. The colony faced greater risks from possible encroachments by Dutch or Swedes than from Powhatans.[63]

In retrospect, colonists came to believe that Opechancanough struck in 1644 when he heard that "all was under the Sword in England" and that the tumult had spilled across the Atlantic, producing divisions among the colonists. He surmised, one observer concluded, that "now was his time, or never, to roote out all the English." Believing that the colonists would receive no aid from England, he had ordered not only the killing of inhabitants but also the destruction of their cattle and cornfields, trying to bring on another famine. But despite the success of their initial assault, they "had not the heart" to follow Opechancanough's advice. Rather than continue their march into the more densely colonized regions of the peninsula, Powhatans instead, for reasons that the English never understood, retreated into their homelands. That retreat gave the colonial government enough time to muster troops and bring in surviving cattle, preparing the way for the two-year campaign that followed. With Opechancanough captured, the rest capitulated.[64]

No surviving testimony from the 100-year-old revealed his motivations for the attack, nor was there any from Necotowance explaining his capitulation to the onerous terms of the treaty of 1646.[65] But the surviving evidence from the war suggests that the situation in Tsenacommacah resembled that in Lenapehoking and the extended territory that Miantonomi hoped to control. In each instance, Indigenous leaders studied colonists, found weak points, and tried to take advantage of the situation. The fact that Europeans prevailed revealed not the inevitable conquest of eastern North America but instead the advantages newcomers had come to possess over Natives in three similar locales. They could just as easily have failed, as the 500 graves of English in Virginia suggested.

The shifting views of Miantonomi, from ally of the English to their foe, reflected the insidious and dynamic nature of European colonial expansion in eastern North America. The arrival of larger numbers of migrants triggered disputes in southern New England and Virginia. But the spread

63. *A Perfect Description of Virginia: Being, A full and true Relation of the present State of the Plantation, their Health, Peace, and Plenty* (London, 1649), 1–6, 8–9, 12, 15.
64. *A Perfect Description of Virginia*, 10–11.
65. See Horn, *A Brave and Cunning Prince*, 230–232.

of the fur trade produced its own destabilizations, often far away from colonial communities. Even before this moment of scattered wars, the desire for manufactured items had already taken a toll on regional beaver populations. Unlike other fur-bearing animals that needed to be tracked, beaver could be easily located because they always lived near their lodges, which could typically be found in ponds created when the creatures had dammed streams. Before Europeans arrived, Indigenous hunters had taken only as many beaver as they needed in a given year. But the appearance of European traders bearing otherwise unobtainable items prompted Native hunters to kill more beaver. By the 1630s, the population in southern New England and across Iroquoia had already become thin, an early sign of the environmental costs of conquest and colonization.

The Haudenosaunee, eager to maintain a steady supply of imported goods, in the 1640s recognized that they needed more territory to find beaver. But they felt hemmed in. The Susquehannocks claimed territory along the lower Susquehanna, the route to the Chesapeake. The Mahicans and River Indians separated the Mohawks, the easternmost tribe in the confederacy, from the Dutch. Innu, Algonquins, and Wendats all claimed territory leading toward the St. Lawrence Valley and the beaver-rich lands beyond Lake Ontario. Members of Haudenosaunee communities also recognized that their numbers were dwindling, in large part because of the spread of smallpox. There were perhaps 10,000 in the confederacy at the start of the 1640s, half the number from 1600.[66]

After assessing their options, the Haudenosaunee decided to launch an invasion of Wendake, the Wendats' territory, which stretched west and north of the ancestral homeland of the Senecas, the keepers of the western gate to Iroquoia. Gaining control over the fur-bearers there had multiple advantages for the Haudenosaunee. Ever since they started to trade with Europeans, many of them had developed a fondness for copper kettles, glass beads, metal scissors, mirrors, and mouth organs. Like other Indigenous in eastern North America, some also developed a taste for brandy and rum, a different kind of commodity that would come to pose its own issues for those who liked to drink—just as alcohol had in every other society where it was present. In the mid-seventeenth century, Europeans distilled rum and brandy from Caribbean sugar.[67]

66. Daniel K. Richter, *The Ordeal of the Longhouse: The Peoples of the Iroquois League in the Era of European Colonization* (Chapel Hill: University of North Carolina Press for the Institute for Early American History and Culture, 1992), 50–60, with population estimates at 58–59.

67. See Peter C. Mancall, *Deadly Medicine: Indians and Alcohol in Early America* (Ithaca, NY: Cornell University Press, 1995), 29–61.

Wendats and Haudenosaunee had been attacking each other for years, long before the arrival of Europeans bearing desirable goods. During earlier bouts of aggression, neither strove to destroy the other. Instead, they engaged in a more limited kind of warfare in which the goal was not to eradicate a foe. Arguments and disagreements that ended in violence tended to be small-scale, in large part because killing many of one's enemy would only feed desire for revenge and thus fuel an endless cycle of murders that could stretch on for years and weaken every community. Across Iroquoia and in regions where Haudenosaunee launched attacks, the aggressor sought some kind of advantage, but it was less territory than humans—captives to be taken home and put through a ritual adoption process. Long-standing cultural practices often included a captive running through a gauntlet while a town's rulers, usually the matriarch of a clan who had lost one of its members in a prior battle, decided the captive's fate. These women tended to be more likely to accept a younger child or a woman, each of them deemed more pliable and hence suitable for adoption than an adult man. "They will seldom kill women and children in the heat of the attack and never afterward," Dutch jurist and colonial traveler Adriaen van der Donck wrote in the early 1650s about Indigenous practices in the areas abutting New Netherland. "Instead they take away with them as many as they can capture. The women they treat as their own, and the children are brought up as though born among them in order to strengthen the nation."[68]

In the early 1640s, the Haudenosaunee abandoned the concept, at least as far as it applied to the members of the Wendat confederacy. In 1642, a group of Senecas attacked the Wendat community of Arendaronon. The Jesuit Isaac Jogues reported that "the scourge of war" was so vast "that one may say that this country is but one scene of massacre." That year the Haudenosaunee killed women, men, and children "and destroyed all by fire, except a score of persons" who fled. From then until 1647, the Senecas and other Haudenosaunee allies had annual battles with the Wendats. Jogues believed that the Five Nations intended to capture every Wendat, "put the chiefs and a great part of the nation to death," and then absorb the remainder "to form one nation and one country." He was especially upset because many of the victims had either converted to Christianity or seemed disposed to doing so. Nonetheless, the violence escalated. In 1649, a 1,000-strong Haudenosaunee force attacked the Ataronchronon

68. Daniel K. Richter, "War and Culture: The Iroquois Experience," *WMQ* 40 (1983), 528–559; Adriean van der Donck, *A Description of New Netherland*, trans. Diederick Willem Goedhuys, ed. Charles T. Gehring and William A. Starna (Lincoln: University of Nebraska Press, 2008), 101.

community of Saint-Louis, the Attingneenongnahac town recently named Saint-Ignace by Jesuits, and the Jesuit mission town of Sainte-Marie. The Haudenosaunee might have lost one-third of their men, but they dealt such a blow to these communities that the survivors fled deeper into Huronia. One missionary believed that the assaults had led to the destruction of fifteen towns. In 1650, the Haudenosaunee turned on the Petun nation, which lay north and west of Lake Ontario. The following year their victims were the Neutrals, who lived on the lake's southwest shores.[69]

Despite their losses, the victims of the Haudenosaunee did not vanish. Instead, by 1652, survivors joined with Ottawas, Nipissing, Ojibwas, Petuns, and Susquehannocks in a confederacy that stretched around the core of Iroquoia. These Native nations found themselves allied with Christian religious, especially Jesuits who had gone into the continent's interior to save Indians' souls, an effort that the Europeans believed would lead to a revolution in daily life, family practices, and gender norms along with spiritual beliefs. Periodic Haudenosaunee murders of Jesuits, including of Gabriel Lalemant and Jean de Brébeuf in 1649, only served to stiffen clerical responses. The murdered became martyrs to the cause, fulfilling a destiny that had motivated some if not all of them. Survivors listened to Marie de L'Incarnation, who had traveled to New France after having a vision of St. Teresa of Ávila. She embraced the possibility of her own martyrdom but also endorsed a militaristic approach, applauding the efforts of the Jesuit Paul Le Jeune soliciting martial assistance from the king of France. "If we do not humiliate these barbarians," she wrote to her son in early November 1660, "they will destroy the country and drive us all away by their warlike and carnivorous nature."[70]

Missionaries believed that they had been targeted for special punishment, an idea circulated widely in mid-century in lurid illustrated accounts of torture and martyrdom, echoing the violent engravings of earlier European books. But the Haudenosaunee did not seek to root out the Jesuits, Ursulines, or other orders. Instead, they recognized the utility of missionary villages in their larger effort to control the beaver trade. The volume of that business, according to the traveler van der Donck, had reached

69. *JR*, 26:75; Jogues to the Chevalier de Montmagny, June 30, 1643, in Felix Martin, *The Life of Father Isaac Jogues*, trans. John G. Shea (New York, 1885), 134; Richter, *Ordeal*, 60–62.

70. Marie de L'Incarnation to her son, November 2, 1660, in Joyce Marshall, ed., *Word from New France: The Selected Letters of Marie de L'Incarnation* (Toronto: Oxford University Press, 1967), 255; Natalie Zemon Davis, *Women on the Margins: Three Seventeenth-Century Lives* (Cambridge, MA: Harvard University Press, 1995), 63–139; Richter, *Ordeal of the Longhouse*, 62–64.

80,000 beaver a year, in addition to the pelts from otters and bears and the skins of deer and elk. While elements of traditional Haudenosaunee culture remained intact, including seasonal migrations between familiar planting, fishing, and hunting regions and the construction of longhouses that could hold 100 to 150 individuals, the fur trade eroded traditional restraints on warfare. European observers often described what they saw as the brutality of Native life. Had they taken a step back, they might have realized that imported consumer goods were driving changes within Indian Country.[71]

Well-informed colonists no doubt knew that Charles I and Parliament had been unable to find a way out of the ideological morass they had created. Parliamentarians blamed the king, goaded by Laud, for pursuing a religious agenda that struck them as additional efforts to suppress dissenters' practice. They criticized him for the events that fueled the Irish Rebellion and his opportunistic response to it. He had avoided crisis in 1641 by postponing Parliament. But in 1642 he waited too long, and by current law he needed Parliament's assent to halt its term. When the members refused, staying in place for what became known as the Long Parliament, he saw his options limited. He soon fled London and began to amass an army of loyalists. By April, Royalists and Parliamentarians had begun to fight each other. On August 22, the king launched a war against those he deemed engaged in treason.[72]

On October 23, forces loyal to the king and those summoned by Parliament faced off at Edgehill in Warwickshire, the Royalists keen to retake London and the Parliamentarians desperate to halt the king's return. Charles's forces totaled 14,000 to 18,000 soldiers, up to 10,000 of them infantry. The Parliamentarians, under the command of the Earl of Essex, had 11,000 infantry and 8,000 on horseback, including dragoons who rode into battle but then dismounted to fight. Few on either side had ever fought before, which might explain why they stopped fighting when night fell after a day that had given neither much of a strategic advantage. However futile the battle was for both, the casualties were high. One

71. Van der Donck, *Description of New Netherland*, 99 (beaver trade), 83–83 (social practices); Ned Blackhawk, *The Rediscovery of America: Native Peoples and the Unmaking of U.S. History* (New Haven, CT: Yale University Press, 2023), 100. One hundred fifty-three French religious died at the hands of Haudenosaunee from the founding of Quebec until 1666; see Richter, *Ordeal of the Longhouse*, 64.

72. Charles Carlton, *This Seat of Mars: War and the British Isles, 1485–1746* (New Haven, CT: Yale University Press, 2013), 121; Ann Hughes, *The Causes of the English Civil War*, 2nd ed. (New York: St. Martin's, 1998), 149–173.

contemporary believed that at least 1,200 died that day, and perhaps over 2,000, though neither side prevailed. "The slain of both sides the number is uncertain," a Royalist sympathizer observed, claiming that the king's forces "kill'd five for one" killed by the rebels.[73] Still, in the telling of the story, Charles I lost the day, an account that would echo for generations among the English. "Tell your neighbors and your children that this is holy ground," John Adams, the second president, wrote after visiting the battlefield in 1786, adding that "all England should come in pilgrimage to this hill once a year."[74]

Charles decided to continue his efforts to regain London, but despite considerable violence his forces could not prevail. He retreated to Oxford, which he made his capital. The war that he had never intended to fight seemed well beyond his control.[75] Conflict raged into the following summer. On June 14, Oliver Cromwell led a massive assault against the king's forces, led by Prince Rupert, at Marston Moor. By evening, the Parliamentary forces, which lost 1,500 men, had killed 3,000 to 4,000 of the king's. The battle propelled Cromwell's career forward.[76] Among the dead were an elderly woman and Prince Rupert's dog Boy, each of whom became an object of fascination, especially among the Parliamentarians, who believed that she was a witch and that the dog possessed supernatural powers, all proof that the Royalists had hoped to draw on dark forces in their effort to quash legitimate dissent.[77] In a single day, the conflict in England took two to three times the total number of casualties who had fallen in the wars for the East Coast of North America from 1642 to 1646.

73. G. Ross, "The Battle of Edgehill," *English Historical Review* 2 (1887), 533–543; Carlton, *This Seat of Mars*, 121–124; Nathaniel Fiennes, *A most True and Exact Relation of Both Battels fought by his Excellency and his Forces against the bloudy Cavelliers* (London, 1642), 8; *A Relation of the Battaile lately fought between Keynton and Edghill by His Majesties Army and that of the Rebells* (Oxford, 1642), 4–5, quotation at 4.

74. ["Notes on a Tour of English Country Seats, & c., with Thomas Jefferson, 4–10? April 1786], from the Diary of John Adams, *Founders Online,* National Archives, https://founders.archives.gov/documents/Adams/01-03-02-0005-0002; Carlton, *This Seat of Mars*, 111.

75. Carlton, *This Seat of Mars*, 124–125; on Charles's motivations and inability to avoid conflict given his staunch positions, see Conrad Russell, *The Causes of the English Civil War* (Oxford: Oxford University Press, 1990), 185–211; cf. Clive Holmes, *Why Was Charles I Executed* (London: Hambledon Continuum, 2007), 55–69.

76. Carlton, *This Seat of Mars*, 126–128; Christopher Hill, *God's Englishman: Oliver Cromwell and the English Revolution* (New York: Penguin, 1990), 54–55; C. H. Firth, "Marston Moor," *Transactions of the Royal Historical Society* 12 (1989), 17–79; C. H. Firth, "Two Accounts of the Battle of Marston Moor," *English Historical Review* 5 (1890), 345–352, "Mr. Ogden's Narrative," in Firth, "Marston Moor," 71–72.

77. See Mark Stoyle, *The Black Legend of Prince Rupert's Dog: Witchcraft and Propaganda During the English Civil War* (Exeter: University of Exeter Press, 2011), 116–141.

Despite the loss, Charles's forces regrouped while he sought an alliance with the Dutch, taking a meeting with the ambassador at Oxford. During their discussions, the diplomat offered to return the jewels that Henrietta Maria had pawned in 1642 in exchange for the herring fisheries along the English coast. Charles apparently declined, perhaps because he felt he had sufficient resources to prevail in the conflict.[78] For a time that seemed a smart calculation, until Cromwell's soldiers defeated Charles and his soldiers at Newberry on October 27, 1644.[79] By then Henrietta Maria, who had given birth to a girl named Henriette on June 16, had departed for France, again trying to pawn jewels. She made a small profit for what became an enduring loss: she would never see her husband again.[80]

Grievances and hostility grew by the week, with stories of battlefield crimes piling up in the collective imagination. In December 1643, a Royalist contingent trapped twenty Parliamentary men from Barthomley in Cheshire in the local church. With nowhere to escape, the men pled for mercy, which the Royalist commander promised. "But when they had them in their Power," as one witness reported, "they stript them all naked, & then most barbarously murthered 12 of them, contrary to the Laws of Arms, Nature, & Nations." They slit the throat of the minister, who was among those trapped in the church. In March 1644 the Royalist army forced a Parliamentary contingent holed up in Hopton Castle in Herefordshire to surrender, but the king's soldiers drove the captives into an unfinished cellar, clubbed many to death, and set fire to the building above them. "This inhuman and barbarous act," one witness reported, "wherein the laws of God, of man, of nature, of nations and of arms are violated, cries to the great Justice of heaven to revenge." Parliamentarians too resorted to horrific acts, including the summary execution of prisoners, a tactic that drew wide attention in the waning days of the war, when commanders ordered such murders in what had become a settled affair.[81] Civilians who escaped the violence of conflict often found that soldiers had pillaged their homes.[82]

78. Humphrey, "To Sell England's Jewels," paras. 25–26.
79. Carlton, *This Seat of Mars*, 128–129.
80. Humphrey, "To Sell England's Jewels," paras. 27–29.
81. Barbara Donagan, "Atrocity, War Crime, and Treason in the English Civil War," *AHR* 99 (1994), 1137–1166, esp. 1152–1158, quotations at 1153 (Barthomley) and 1152 (Hopton); see also Barbara Donagan, *War in England, 1642–1649* (Oxford: Oxford University Press, 2008).
82. See Barbara Donagan, "War, Property and the Bonds of Society: England's 'Unnatural' Civil Wars," in Erica Charters, Eve Rosenhaft, and Hannah Smith, eds., *Civilians and War in Europe, 1618–1815* (Liverpool: Liverpool University Press, 2012), 52–67.

In April 1645 Parliament created the New Model Army, which took the field in the small village of Naseby on June 14. They killed 500 of the king's troops and captured another 4,000, imprisoning almost 700 of them in Lambeth Palace, and confined the others on Tothill Fields. Fighting continued across the realm for another year, with the Parliamentarians laying siege to Oxford in April 1646. But after Naseby there was no path forward for Charles. He surrendered to Scots forces in Newark, Scotland. Charles arrived in London in January 1647, a prisoner in the city where only five years earlier his command had been so extensive that he could disband Parliament.[83]

The war had come to an end, but not the conflict. The set pieces of the war inspired some authors to write about the details of battles. But tracts focused on the death of an elderly woman accused of witchcraft or the prince's beloved dog serve as a stark reminder that this was a domestic war, with soldiers rampaging through territory that could have been one village over. Political identity, often based on confessional difference, drove English men and women apart. Many could understand the need to use extreme measures in Ireland, such as attacking non-combatants or destroying crops, which after all were but a return to strategies that military commanders like Sir Humphrey Gilbert had boasted about seventy years earlier. Across the Irish Sea, many English believed, uncivilized Irish Catholics needed to be destroyed, whatever the cost. Within England, though, despite deep differences about religious practice, even the most resolute Roundhead or Royalist must have wondered if destroying an opponent was needed.

Commanders and political officials wanted to win, but to do so without inspiring *lex talionis* and years of reprisals. As a result, they wanted to launch restrained, limited warfare so that peace could come swiftly in a new political alignment. They knew too well the violence that war had unleashed across the continent when the conflict now known as the Thirty Years' War began in 1618. As dissenting minister William Gouge had written in 1631, "Warre is a kind of execution of publique justice; and a means of maintaining right." Those guiding such conflicts needed to find the "just and right use of warre." They learned about atrocities on the continent through books such as Philip Vincent's *The Lamentations of Germany*, printed in London in 1638, which included graphic engravings and told of sexual assaults in churches, captives forced to eat excrement or burned alive, men castrated in front of their families, a tormenter slicing off the skin of an enemy bound to a post, and cannibalism including an allegation that women had to eat their own children. Such visceral

83. Carlton, *This Seat of Mars*, 129–131.

images reminded them that they needed to fight in a way that limited possible domestic atrocities. But they were unable to do so.[84]

The war drew to a close by late 1646. Charles I made a brief escape in July 1647, even managing to get to the Isle of Wight. But his enemies recaptured him. The last Royalist forces surrendered on August 25, 1648. In the aftermath, the Parliamentarians put the king on trial, declaring him a "tyrant, traitor, murderer and public enemy." The fifty-nine commissioners found him guilty of high treason. On January 30, 1649, an executioner decapitated him at Whitehall.

On May 14, 1649, three and a half months after the beheading of his father, Charles II sent word to the Virginia House of Burgesses that he would maintain authority over the colony, continuing the same policies as Charles I. Legislators in the royal colonies of Barbados, Antigua, and Bermuda issued declarations that they were loyal to the new king. In response, Parliament in October 1650 declared the four colonies to be in rebellion against the Commonwealth. The act banned trade to these colonies unless the participants obtained a special license, and it authorized the seizure of ships going to or coming from them. That same year Parliament also banned trade with Scotland for similar reasons. Immediately some of London's most prominent investors in Atlantic commerce protested that they had lost access to valuable markets. Among them was Maurice Thomson, the same merchant who had been involved with the English slave trade since 1626, when he arranged for ships to carry sixty enslaved Africans to St. Kitts, subsequently obtained 1,000 acres on the island, participated actively in the fur trade in Canada, and in 1632 had tried to corner the Virginia tobacco market. In the 1640s, Thomson developed a large sugar plantation in Barbados, an investment he wanted to protect. He believed that the English should also establish colonies on Assada, an island off Madagascar, and on Pulo Run in the Spice Islands. Neither came to fruition. Indigenous on Madagascar killed English who

84. William Gouge, *The Churches Conquest over the Sword* (London, 1631), in Gouge, *Gods Three Arrowes: Plague, Famine, Sword, in Three Treatises* (London, 1631), quotation at 214; [Philip] Vincent, *The Lamentations of Germany* (London, 1638), 16–19 (sexual assaults), 8–14 (torture), 44 (women eating their own children), sig. [A9^v] (image of cannibalism); Donagan, "Atrocity, War Crime, and Treason," 1141–1149. For the larger conflict, see, among many sources, Peter H. Wilson, *Europe's Tragedy: A History of the Thirty Years War* (London: Allen Lane, 2009) and Geoffrey Parker, ed., *The Thirty Years' War*, 2nd ed. (London: Routledge, 1997).

tried to set up their works there, and the Dutch stymied English efforts in the Southwest Pacific.[85]

To enforce its order, the Commonwealth ordered a flotilla of fifteen ships to suppress the rebels and persuade them to accept the new order. They sailed to Barbados, where the show of force quickly produced results. Then they set sail for Virginia, following the well-known winds and currents. But a hurricane sank eleven of the ships. The last four made it to Jamestown. Sensing the threat, the House of Burgesses disavowed its link to Charles II. Commerce—in their case, the need to import indentured servants and export tobacco—triumphed over any sense of loyalty to the Stuart regime.

Yet demanding loyalty to the Commonwealth did not solve the realm's problems, which by 1651 centered largely on rapidly deteriorating conditions with the Dutch. Before 1650, Cromwell's government had hoped that when smallpox took the life of the Prince of Orange on November 6, 1650, his passing would remove the last stumbling block to peaceful relations between England and the Low Countries. Even Dutch pamphleteers believed that the moment cemented ties between the two Protestant republics and improved chances to defeat the Catholic Church.[86]

Hopes for a close union soon flickered away. Within months of the Stadtholder's death, English and Dutch politicians, each side goaded by tireless writers who published pamphlets and newsletters insulting the other, found their relations deteriorating. On October 9, 1651, Parliament passed an act "for increase of Shipping, and Encouragement of the Navigation of this Nation," recognizing both that long-distance commerce was crucial to the realm and that trade with the colonies had established a new foundation for wealth. As of December 1, commodities produced in "Asia, Africa, or America," including nearby islands or any other territory identified as English on existing maps, had to be shipped

85. An Act to prohibit all Commerce and Traffique between England and Scotland, [August 2, 1650], and An Act for prohibiting Trade with the Barbadoes, Virginia, Bermuda and Antigua, [October 3, 1650], in C. H. Firth and R. S. Rait, eds., *Acts and Ordinances of the Interregnum, 1642–1660* (London, 1911), 2:406–409, 425–429; Robert Brenner, *Merchants and Revolution: Commercial Change, Political Conflict, and London's Overseas Traders, 1550–1653* (London: Verso, 2003), 168–181; Carla G. Pestana, *The English Atlantic in an Age of Revolution, 1640–1661* (Cambridge, MA: Harvard University Press, 2004), 86–122; J. E. Farnell, "The Navigation Act of 1651, The First Dutch War, and the London Merchant Community," *Economic History Review*, n.s., 16 (1964), 439–454, esp. 443–444.

86. Steven C. A. Pincus, *Protestantism and Patriotism: Ideologies and the Making of English Foreign Policy, 1650–1668* (Cambridge: Cambridge University Press, 1996), 17–23.

to England, Ireland, or any other English territory on English ships. The law also applied to salted cod, herring, pilchard, whalebone, and ling.[87]

War between England and the Netherlands broke out in May 1652. In its desire to destroy the Dutch at sea, the English Parliament seized large merchant ships from both the East India Company and the Levant Company. Press gangs kidnapped able-bodied men and rushed them into service for the nation, including many who had previously been working to better the realm's economic prospects by working on the two companies' vessels. In less than two years, the combatants recognized that peace served their respective interests more than war. On April 5, 1654, both sides accepted terms in the Treaty of Westminster. They remained commercial rivals, but the English could at least claim that, as one Spanish merchant put it, "the seas will be open" once again.[88] For the moment, New Netherland remained in Dutch hands, but growing tensions with both Lenapes and English threatened to undermine its hard-won, but still precarious, stability.

By mid-century, the WIC had built four North American forts: on the southern tip of Manhattan Island; at New Amsterdam, the confluence of the East and North (Hudson) Rivers; at Orange, modern Albany; and at Fort Nassau, on the South (Delaware) River at modern Gloucester City, New Jersey. They had chosen the locations to demarcate the extent of their territory. But growing English communities at Stamford and New Haven, already evident by the late 1640s, signaled problems that the New Netherland's leaders could not avoid for long given the reluctance of Dutch women and men to migrate there. Van der Donck believed that 5,000 English were "capable of bearing arms" in the region. New Haven alone had 1,300 families, a fast start to a place that had been in Indigenous hands before Kieft's War. The Dutch feared a similar path forward along the Delaware, where Edward Plowden continued to press his claim that he had been appointed by James I to be the Earl Palatine of New Albion.[89]

In 1642, Miantonomi, Opechancanough, and Charles I ruled over large territories. By the end of the decade, each had been taken captive and

87. "October 1651: An Act for increase of Shipping, and Encouragement of the Navigation of this Nation," in Firth and Rait, eds., *Acts and Ordinances of the Interregnum*, 559–562.

88. Pincus, *Protestantism and Patriotism*, 97–191, quotation at 179.

89. *Remonstrance of New Netherland*, trans. E. B. O'Callaghan (Albany, NY, 1856), 15–23, 34–35, 49; [Beauchamp Plantagenet], *A Description of the Province of New Albion* (London, 1648); Edward C. Carter 2nd and Clifford Lewis 3rd, "Sir Edmund Plowden and the New Albion Charter, 1632–1785," *PMHB* 83 (1959), 150–179.

executed. Miantonomi and Charles at least had trials, although in both instances their fates seem predetermined. Opechancanough never had a chance to defend himself. Unlike the others, who swiftly died with the blow of an axe, he got the last word, mocking Berkeley for his lack of decorum and civility.

Taking place at almost the same time, Kieft's War, the third Anglo-Powhatan War, and the English Civil War all wrought terrible consequences for participants. The disputes between and within European societies paralleled those between Indigenous nations, which had become exacerbated by the growing presence of European colonists, traders, and soldiers in North America. However horrific the war crimes in the British Isles, they paled in comparison to the atrocities in North America. No troops ever set an entire English, Scots, or Irish village alight and then shot at defenseless individuals trying to survive. The English, aware of the horrors that unrestrained war had caused for civilians across the continent, had no desire to replicate the same carnage in their own country, especially since both Royalists and Parliamentarians hoped to achieve a lasting peace when their conflict abated. Rumors of soldiers' depredations would have slowed any move toward domestic amity.

Yet the moral and political calculus that inhibited English soldiers at home dissipated in the Western Hemisphere. The English and other Europeans had always claimed that they wanted to reduce Native Americans to civilization through peaceful means. Those claims seemed empty at mid-century. A decade of trauma had produced a North America more on edge than ever before. Soon enough, Europeans would expand the other conflict they had already begun: a war on Africans' bodies.

21

Enslavement

Forced labor took many forms in mid-seventeenth-century North America. Along the Chesapeake, indentured servants, most of them young men from England, had done most of the work clearing fields and planting tobacco in the Tidewater after colonists laid claim to Powhatan territory. They attended to the plant's specific growing and harvesting needs, packed the cured plant into hogsheads, hauled their crop by small boat or horse cart to port, and then left it in the hands of other young men, many from similar social backgrounds, who had signed on to similarly arduous work, to transport the processed plants across the Atlantic. Artists who engraved images of tobacco use typically left these workers out of their pictures. Instead, gentlemen sit on fine chairs, long pipe in hand, smoking tobacco in comfortable seating rooms. The work to produce the pungent smells and exhilarating rush of nicotine had become invisible to the consumer.

By the 1640s, some colonial tobacco planters in Virginia and Maryland had begun to purchase enslaved Africans, but most of those in the fields remained English indentured servants. By contrast, sugar planters, starting on the coast of Brazil and then from one island in the West Indies to another, eagerly embraced the trade in enslaved bodies earlier and on a much larger scale than Chesapeake planters. They added a Caribbean dimension to a system of enslaved labor that was already flourishing in mining communities across Spanish America. Eventually, English planters on the mainland also began to purchase enslaved laborers, though the direct association between origins (Africa or America) and status (free or enslaved) remained muddled even when the number of enslaved Africans began to increase on Chesapeake farms by the 1660s. Earlier experience in New England had suggested the English colonial acceptance of enslaved Africans. As Emmanuel Downing, a lawyer who had married John Winthrop's sister Lucy in 1622 and later migrated to Salem, observed in August 1645, if the colonists could capture Narragansetts in a "Just warre," they could "exchange them for Moores, which wilbe more gaynefull pilladge for us th[a]n wee conceive"—as it cost less to keep twenty enslaved "Moores" than a single English servant.[1]

The experience of captivity, shackling, being crowded onto boats built for purposes other than transporting humans, physical abuse, poor food and sanitation, and the desperation of watching one's family ripped apart either before the Middle Passage or in the Americas cruelly scarred everyone who experienced it. Enslavers cared about profits and losses, which they measured in their ledgers in calculations that transformed people into commodities. The degradations fueled psychological as well as physical crises for those caught up in their dehumanization.[2]

In Barbados, which became the model for English profiting from forced labor, enslavement emerged slowly in the mid-seventeenth century. Unlike what the English had found along the banks of the Chesapeake, Barbados was carpeted with dense forests composed of fiddlewood, cedar, mastic, locust, and mangroves, with the forest canopy reaching 100 feet. To make a profit there meant organizing laborers to hack down trees and clear fields. The effort made sense if they could find profitable exports to send home. At first, English adventurers thought that tobacco would be ideal, so they concentrated their energies on its production. When their tobacco could not compete with Virginia's, the Barbadians turned to cotton. They failed here too. By the mid-1640s, planters started to reap substantial profits when they turned their energies briefly to indigo, valued in Europe for the rich blue dye it produced, and then eventually to sugar. The change came quickly. In 1639, tobacco constituted 57 percent of exports, with cotton the next most popular crop. In 1644, sugar still only amounted to 8 percent of their crop. It doubled the next year, reached 27 percent by 1646, and reached 60 percent in 1648. By 1652, planters and merchants listed only sugar in their transactions.[3]

1. Mark Peterson, *The City-State of Boston: The Rise and Fall of an Atlantic Power, 1630–1865* (Princeton, NJ: Princeton University Press, 2019), 62–66, quotation at 64; for Downing, who sailed back and forth across the Atlantic before reemigrating to England in 1654, see Susan Hardman Moore, *Abandoning America: Life-Stories from Early New England* (Woodbridge, Suffolk: Boydell Press, 2013), 91–93.
2. As Stephanie E. Smallwood put it, during the ocean crossing "the practices of commodification most effectively muted the agency of the African subject and thereby produced their desired object: an African body fully alienated and available for exploitation in the American marketplace." Stephanie E. Smallwood, *Saltwater Slavery: A Middle Passage from Africa to American Diaspora* (Cambridge, MA: Harvard University Press, 2007), 33–152, quotation at 122.
3. Richard S. Dunn, *Sugar and Slaves: The Rise of the Planter Class in the English West Indies, 1624–1713* (Chapel Hill: University of North Carolina Press for the Institute of Early

Many English planters had gone to Barbados in the 1630s because they were the younger sons of gentry families, sometimes the younger sons of younger sons. They might be educated, and they likely had far more wealth than the desperate who signed away years of their lives to be indentured servants. While they lacked the land or the deep accounts that would allow them to live well in England, they had enough to sail to Barbados and other colonies and had sufficient resources to pay for the transportation of servants.

In 1630, 900 English and 100 Africans lived in Barbados. Ten years later, the number of Europeans there, most of them English, reached 13,500, with an additional 500 Africans. Soon the shift to sugar production altered the landscape, physical as well as human. By 1650, 30,000 Europeans dwelled on the island—mostly English, but substantial numbers of Irish prisoners of war and Dutch (including Jews) who had come from Brazil. That year the population of enslaved Africans reached 12,800.[4]

In 1647, Richard Ligon, a younger son of a younger son who did not stand to inherit much wealth if he remained in England, sailed to the island. He stayed for three years and then returned to London. Ligon was not an ordinary minor member of the gentry. Ferdinando Gorges was one of his cousins, which linked the Ligon family to the Council of New England. Among his close associates was John Coprario, court composer for Charles I when he was still the Prince of Wales.[5]

When Ligon arrived, Barbados was in the midst of environmental, labor, and economic revolutions. Thousands of workers converted land into cane fields.[6] The spread of sugar plantations swelled the population. "The Island is divided into three sorts of men, *viz.*, Masters, Servants, and

American History and Culture, 1972), 46–83; John J. McCusker and Russell R. Menard, "The Sugar Industry in the Seventeenth Century: A New Perspective on the Barbadian 'Sugar Revolution,'" in Stuart B. Schwartz, ed., *Tropical Babylons: Sugar and the Making of the Atlantic World, 1450–1680* (Chapel Hill: University of North Carolina Press, 2004), 289–330, esp. table 9.1 (292).

4. McCusker and Menard, "Sugar Industry," table 9.2 (293).
5. Richard Ligon, *A True and Exact History of the Island of Barbados*, ed. Karen Ordahl Kupperman (Indianapolis, IN: Hackett, 2011), 1–7.
6. This reshaping of Barbados paralleled the transformation of parts of England, a series of ecological changes promoted by people known as "projectors" who at times incurred the wrath of those who hoped to prevent wide-scale change of their domestic landscape. See Eric H. Ash, *The Draining of the Fens: Projectors, Popular Politics, and State Building in Early Modern England* (Baltimore: Johns Hopkins University Press, 2017); Joan Thirsk, "The Farming Regions of England" and "Enclosing and Engrossing," in Joan Thirsk, ed., *The Agrarian History of England and Wales, vol. 4, 1500–1640* (Cambridge: Cambridge University Press, 1967), 38–40, 200–255; Mark E. Kennedy, "Charles I and Local Government: The Draining of the East and West Fens," *Albion* 15 (1983), 19–31.

Slaves," Ligon observed. "The slaves and their posterity, being subject to their Masters for ever, are kept and preserved with greater care than the servants, who are theirs but for five years, according to the law of the Island." He summarized the plight of the servants by saying they "have the worser lives, for they are put to very hard labor, ill lodging, and their diet very slight." Ligon contrasted their lot with that of "Negroes," a word that in his mind already meant people who were enslaved.[7]

Ligon's remarks reflected far-reaching changes in the legal codes of the Anglo Atlantic basin. The English had been purchasing enslaved Africans since the mid-1610s in Bermuda and soon after in Virginia. But laws at home and in overseas possessions lagged behind the emergence of a labor regime built on the premise that some humans could be purchased and never released, while the laws insisted on the emancipation of those who had arrived as servants, even if, as was the case in Barbados, many of those servants had been prisoners of war, captured in the English suppression of the Irish uprising of 1641 or in raids on the mainland, which accounted for Native slaves whom Ligon also saw on Barbados. English planters claimed to loathe Irish servants, but they nonetheless imported them. Their agents at times shipped over kidnapped teens, giving rise to the phrase that they had been "barbadosed." The English also captured Indigenous from the mainland. "As for the *Indians*, we have few, and those fetched from other Countries," Ligon reported, "some from the neighboring Islands, some from the Main, which we make slaves."[8]

Ligon described the degrading sale of Africans on ships docking at Barbados. "When they are brought to us, the Planters buy them out of the Ship, where they find them stark naked, and therefore cannot be deceived in any outward infirmity." He likened the process to a livestock auction. "They choose them as they do Horses in a market," Ligon wrote about the practices of English planters, "the strongest, youthfullest, and most beautiful, yield the greatest prices." He claimed that planters purchased the same number of each sex, hoping that a balanced sex ratio would reduce possible tension among the enslaved and hence minimize potential rebellion.[9]

Colonial officials took other steps to reduce their risks too. According to Ligon, no African was allowed to handle a weapon. The planters, fearing an insurrection, deliberately purchased enslaved who came from different parts of West Africa, some "are fetched from Guinny and Binny,

7. Ligon, *True and Exact History*, 92.
8. Ligon, *True and Exact History*, 92 (three groups), 106 (Native slaves); Dunn, *Sugar and Slaves*, 69.
9. Ligon, *True and Exact History*, 97.

some from Cutchew, some from Angola, and some from the River of Gambia." Long exposure to African nations along the coast had taught Europeans that these populations spoke different and often mutually unintelligible languages. But no scheme could be foolproof. Ligon reported that there was an uprising, and it might have destroyed the island's economy had word of it not leaked to one of the planters. Upon hearing the news, planters determined that eighteen men had indeed planned to rebel. They hanged them all as an example to the hundreds of others on the island, hoping to discourage another rebellion.[10]

Perhaps the anxieties of planters reflected the sense that their own lives, while often lavish, could also be precarious. Clearing land for sugar did not in itself reduce the populations of the mosquitoes that transmitted yellow fever and malaria to immigrants.[11] Further, these English younger sons' lifestyle—excessive eating and drinking, wearing heavy clothing, and building houses with glass windows instead of slatted shutters—contributed to shorter lifespans. Such problems paled in comparison to the sufferings inflicted on enslaved children, women, and men, who could succumb to brutal work regimes, inadequate medical attention, poor diet, and accidents in mills (*ingenios*).[12]

During the 1640s, the tall forests that had dominated the skyline began to disappear, the wood used to construct buildings, fences, and sugar works. Barbados had once been Eden-like in its ecological diversity. By the middle of the seventeenth century, it was fast becoming a monocultural desert. No landscape in the Americas had undergone such a rapid transition or one with more wide-ranging impact. Inhabitants continued to grow and harvest cassava, sweet potatoes, plantains, guava, and citrus fruits including pineapples, often relying on techniques planters had learned from the three dozen Arawaks whom Powell had captured and enslaved in 1627. While fruit trees remained, sugar came to dominate the landscape. The waters around the island still boasted the great schools of fish that the first European observers had seen, but the rise of sugar cultivation diminished planters' desire to allow their servants and enslaved

10. Ligon, *True and Exact History*, 96–97.
11. On migration of servants, see Alison Games, "Opportunity and Mobility in Early Barbados," in Robert Paquette and Stanley Engerman, eds., *The Lesser Antilles in the Age of European Expansion* (Gainesville: University Press of Florida, 1996), 165–181; for local diseases, see John McNeill, *Mosquito Empires: Ecology and War in the Greater Caribbean, 1620–1914* (Cambridge: Cambridge University Press, 2010), 32–68.
12. See Dunn, *Sugar and Slaves*, 281–286 (clothing), 290–291 (planters' housing), 300–334 (mortality); "A German Indentured Servant in Barbados in 1652: The Account of Heinrich Von Uchteritz," ed. and trans. Alexander Gunkel and Jerome S. Handler, *Journal of the Barbados Museum Historical Society* 33 (1970), 93.

workers to spend time catching fish. By mid-century, planters were importing dried fish from New England. A German war prisoner on the island claimed that "one hears no birds."[13]

From the early colonial period until 1650, Spaniards transported 250,000 to 300,000 enslaved Africans to the Americas, most of them to Mexico and Peru. In 1646, the number of enslaved Africans reached 35,000 in Mexico, less than 2 percent of the colony's population. Peru, with its extensive mining industry, had an enslaved African population of almost 100,000 then, about 10 to 15 percent of its total population. Many of these enslaved people arrived between 1625 and 1650, a time when Spanish mine and plantation owners embraced the shipment of bound Africans; 93,850 enslaved children, men, and women arrived in Spanish America during that period, while the Portuguese exported approximately 50,000 to Brazil. Meanwhile, plantation owners in the English West Indies purchased 20,700 enslaved Africans in this same quarter-century, with the French importing another 2,500 to their Caribbean islands.[14]

By 1650, Spanish colonial officials began to rethink their commitment to labor forces made up of enslaved Africans. As they already knew, importing someone across an ocean was far more expensive than recruiting a local laborer. That did not stop them from importing captured people from Southeast Asia and the South Asian subcontinent, though those victims of the Manila slave trade tended to serve far south of New Mexico and often in households as opposed to in mines or on plantations.[15] Elsewhere, starting in the sixteenth century, embracing the African slave trade made sense to Spanish imperial bureaucrats when the Indigenous population of the Caribbean basin shrank rapidly in the decades after Columbus's arrival, primarily due to forced relocation, excruciating and almost homicidal work regimes, and the arrival of infectious Old World diseases. A century later, with the encomienda system in place and the rise of an Indigenous labor force drawn from modern Bolivia and Peru to

13. Ligon, *True and Exact History*, 99; Larry Gragg, *Englishmen Transplanted: The English Colonization of Barbados, 1627–1660* (Oxford: Oxford University Press, 2003), 16–24; Richard H. Grove, *Green Imperialism: Colonial Expansion, Tropical Island Edens, and the Origins of Environmentalism, 1600–1860* (Cambridge: Cambridge University Press, 1995), 24–32, 67–71; Dunn, *Sugar and Slaves*, 276–281; "German Indentured Servant in Barbados," quotation at 93.
14. Herbert Klein, "The Atlantic Slave Trade to 1650," in Schwartz, ed., *Tropical Babylons*, 207–208, 230–231.
15. See Tatiana Seijas, *Asian Slaves in Colonial Mexico: From Chinos to Indians* (Cambridge: Cambridge University Press, 2014).

extract silver at Potosí, enslaved Africans no longer seemed to be worth the expense.

The shift in Spanish attitudes could be seen at Parral, in modern Chihuahua, about 330 miles south of Ciudad Juárez. In 1631 a Spanish soldier named Juan Rangel de Biesma had discovered silver at a place he named La Negrita, a locale with distinctive black and gray rock that he correctly surmised must contain silver. As it turned out, the vein was so rich that other Spaniards flocked there. Within six months this recently near-deserted land had a population of 400 colonists and 800 "people of service." By 1640, the local population reached 8,500. Newcomers rapidly built houses and a church, which faced onto a plaza, the characteristic urban mark of all Spanish communities. There, near the church, colonists auctioned off captives, almost all of them Indigenous, though among them were the largest number of enslaved Africans in northern New Spain.[16]

When Rangel de Biesma arrived, finding silver was easy. Within twenty years, the quick wealth to be had by digging at the surface had faded. As had been the case at Potosí, the profits that remained lay deeper in the ground. To achieve the treasure that had lured them to Parral, colonists dug deep shafts, one of them reaching 420 feet below the ground. Those consigned to digging the pits had to haul rocks via rickety ladders, carrying bags holding up to 350 pounds of rock by means of a strap across the forehead since they needed their hands to climb. While underground they inhaled dust containing silica, which scarred their lungs and led to silicosis, a painful wasting disease that could kill those who had worked under the ground. Workers died when ladders collapsed or fell into deep holes. Those working above ground processing the rock hardly escaped the risks. One popular way to extract silver from the ore was to pulverize it and pour mercury and water on top, which enabled the heavier silver to ooze from the crushed rock. Finishing the process entailed heating the sludge, which turned the mercury into vapor. Absorbed through cracks in skin when workers walked across the pile before the heating or into the lungs during heating, mercury, like silica, debilitated human bodies. A once-healthy worker who never went into a mine might be dead within two or three years just from absorbing mercury.[17]

To mine owners and local merchants who profited from the town's swelling population, the human toll to extract silver at Parral mattered less than the cost of obtaining labor. In 1640, 1,000 of the 8,500 residents

16. Andrés Reséndez, *The Other Slavery: The Uncovered Story of Indian Enslavement in America* (Boston: Houghton Mifflin Harcourt, 2016), 104–107.

17. Reséndez, *Other Slavery*, 107–109.

were either enslaved American-born creoles or African-born, from Angola, Mozambique, the Congo, and other major slave markets. African workers cost much more than Indigenous, either because they possessed mining skills or because mine owners believed they were less likely to flee to a nearby Native community. But the costs associated with transporting enslaved Africans to a silver mining town in the interior of northern New Spain remained sufficiently high that only the wealthy could afford to purchase them.[18]

Under these circumstances, investors looking for cheaper sources of labor set their sights on Indigenous, as had earlier residents of New Spain. As early as 1640, there were 5,500 Natives in Parral, accounting for almost two-thirds of the resident population. Many, possibly 2,000, had gone there voluntarily, seeking high wages they hoped mine owners would pay. In turn, mine owners allowed these free individuals to pick up rocks at the end of the day, a practice that became so widely known that it bore its own name: *pepena*, the picking-through or picking-up system. Some workers saw an advantage, but many who traveled to Parral on their own soon found themselves in debt since they had to pay their own housing and food costs. To escape debt, they needed to work even more. They were free under the law, yet impoverished and trapped by the circumstances of daily life. Silver had lured them. Then it threatened to bury them.[19]

Other Native workers arrived in Parral through the obligations created by the encomienda and *repartimiento* systems. From start to finish, these Spanish-imposed institutions produced new animosity when mine owners asked colonial officials for workers. Those officials then turned to Indigenous towns demanding certain numbers of laborers, who were to serve for a set time to meet the town's obligations under the colonial system the Spanish had created in the sixteenth century. In the 1640s, during its boom years, many of the 3,000 workers in Parral, most of them male, came from surrounding towns. This system created economic problems at home when workers could not tend fields or livestock, worsening the conditions for their families. The sense of resentment grew year by year until many of these Natives joined uprisings against the mine owners, who feared that the easiest silver was long gone and extracting additional silver meant more-demanding work—the exact daily conditions that fed resentment. The demographic consequences of these local rebels' actions shook the town's rulers, who saw the population dip from 8,500 to 5,000 in the 1650s.[20]

18. Reséndez, *Other Slavery*, 110–112.
19. Reséndez, *Other Slavery*, 112–113.
20. Reséndez, *Other Slavery*, 114–115.

Fearing that their source of wealth would disappear, the mine owners and merchants of Parral turned toward enslaved Natives. As early as 1637, New Mexico governor Luis de Rosas had begun to take Apaches and Utes captive and force them to work. By 1640, about 500 bound Indigenous lived in Parral, though many of them were not permanently enslaved.[21] Colonial courts dispatched them to Parral as *esclavos temporales*, temporary slaves whose labor could be controlled for fifteen years as part of a criminal sentence but who would then, in theory, be freed. One colonial official after another believed that Apaches should be captured and enslaved, a fitting punishment for those the Spanish saw as ungrateful thieves and troublemakers who refused the entreaties of missionaries. Adult male Apaches garnered high prices in Parral, bringing greater profits to those involved in this interior slave trade. By the late 1640s, Spanish officials, having turned against the use of Indigenous and Asian slaves across New Spain, issued orders emancipating enslaved Apaches in Parral. But the repetition of such orders through the 1670s suggests that many Apaches living in Parral—there were at least 400 Apache baptisms and 300 Apache funerals in the town in these decades—had little choice but to remain in bondage. The majority of the enslaved Apaches in the town were children or women, who tended to work within colonial households or cultivating nearby fields.[22]

Among those who profited from the sale of bound bodies were New Mexico's provincial governors. Luis de Rosas, who served as governor from 1637 to 1641, launched attacks against Ute and Apache communities with the explicit goal of capturing individuals who, because of their status as prisoners, could be treated as if enslaved. His actions spurred counterattacks, which gave him yet additional opportunities to justify taking captives, at least as long as the Spanish possessed the upper hand in military conflicts. The situation got worse for Indigenous when twenty-eight-year-old Juan Manso, who had never worked in the colonial administration but had recently married Petronila Ponce de León, daughter of a wealthy Mexico City family, became governor in 1656. Three years earlier he had commanded a wagon train that transported six enslaved Apaches from New Mexico to Parral, an early signal of his support of the commerce in bound bodies. Once in power, he declared war on Apaches and "others of the same ilk." He offered certificates to colonists allowing them to hold

21. Reséndez, *Other Slavery*, 115.
22. Rick Hendricks and Gerald Mandell, "The Apache Slave Trade in Parral, 1637–1679," *Journal of Big Bend Studies* 16 (2004), 59–81, esp. 63–65; Paul Conrad, *The Apache Diaspora: Four Centuries of Displacement and Survival* (Philadelphia: University of Pennsylvania Press, 2021), 47–78, esp. 47–51, 60–65.

Apaches "in deposit," a legal device that produced a larger enslaved population without calling the kidnapped Natives slaves. In October 1658 he issued a certificate to hold a seven-year-old boy, who was to be kept until he was twelve and then for another fifteen years. According to the document, his crime was simply that the "Apaches have been irreducible enemies of our Catholic faith and of all Christians" of the kingdom of New Mexico. His fate sealed, his captors took the child to Parral. Provincial governors across northern New Spain, in Nueva Vizcaya as well as New Mexico, understood that this slave trade was illegal. But they knew too that they were far from the center of authority in New Spain and believed, with good evidence, that they could make a substantial profit from the slave trade well before its illegality would cause them any problems. Unfettered by the laws, they presided over a system that enslaved Wichitas and Pawnees, who lived as far away as modern Kansas, as well as Utes from southern Colorado and Indigenous prisoners held in Pueblo communities.[23]

News of rampant illegality reached the Audiencia of Guadalajara in 1659. Judges there rejected the claims of provincial governors that Apaches and others could be held indefinitely because they were unconverted enemies. But when word of the decision reached Parral, those who possessed the contracts for enslaved Indigenous did not free those they held. Instead, they sued the individuals who had sold them Apaches, a legal strategy that hardly clarified the status of the enslaved. Complicating the situation was a provision in the audencia's decision that Apaches could not travel to New Mexico. Manumitted from slavery, many of the Indigenous of Parral remained in the city. They had some greater control over their lives—no one could keep them for fifteen years anymore—but they faced limited economic opportunities. Many remained, finding low-paid work on local farms or in silver-processing operations.[24]

In 1654, Oliver Cromwell and his allies, having defeated Charles I, turned their attention across the Atlantic. As the Protector saw it, the Parliamentarians' victory in England was a necessary but not final step in

23. Reséndez, *Other Slavery*, 120–121; Hendricks and Mandell, "Apache Slave Trade," 66–69; Rick Hendricks and Gerald J. Mandell, "Juan Manso, Frontier Entrepreneur," *New Mexico Historical Review* 75 (2000), 339–367. The enslavement of Apaches continued for generations, often with the active complicity of missionaries who played a central role in a system that sent many as far as Cuba; see H. Henrietta Stockel, *Salvation Through Slavery: Chiricahua Apaches and Priests on the Spanish Colonial Frontier* (Albuquerque: University of New Mexico Press, 2008), esp. 111–127.

24. Hendricks and Mandell, "Apache Slave Trade," 68–69.

the larger destruction of Catholicism. Eager to weaken Spain, he took advice from religious dissenters who had been involved in the effort to colonize Providence Island, which by the time of the civil war seemed an abject failure despite the shipment of enslaved Pequots there. Instead of a profitable plantation economy, the island represented capitulation to Spain. Before his ascent, Cromwell had close associates and relatives invested in both the Providence Island and Virginia companies. He also reached out to New England's leaders, including John Cotton, who in July 1651 told Cromwell that he was God's chosen servant. Cotton suggested that Cromwell meditate on Revelation 17:14, a verse that testified that the lamb would overcome all who warred with him, "for he is Lord of lords, and King of kings; and they that are with him are called, and chosen, and faithful." In his self-deprecating reply, Cromwell signaled his pleasure at Cotton's praise. Cotton was not seeking special privileges from the Protector. Rather, he was a true believer in Cromwell's cause who found ample scriptural support for the act of regicide. In a Thanksgiving speech in 1651, Cotton celebrated the death of the king as a necessary step toward victory for "the people of god & churches" over "popery over the Catholique visible churche & over the marke of the Beast." Other New England colonists, including Roger Williams and John Winthrop Jr., agreed that Cromwell's efforts to protect the true church rested on unimpeachable biblical authority. Cromwell's plans, such talk confirmed, combined biblical exegesis with a cool-eyed assessment of Spanish military weakness. Cromwell understood that Spain no longer had the dominant power it once wielded, and an invasion of its Caribbean possessions with an overwhelming force—unlike the rather meager resources sent to Providencia in 1630—might prove decisive.[25]

To advance the cause, Cromwell and his supporters sent a fleet consisting of thirty-eight ships and 9,000 armed men to take Hispaniola. The English recruited half of the men at home, some of them battle-tested veterans and others rumored to be felons who would otherwise have been imprisoned at Newgate, London's most notorious prison. The rest

25. Karen Ordahl Kupperman, "Errand to the Indies: Puritan Colonization from Providence Island Through the Western Design," *WMQ*, 3rd Ser., 45 (1988), 70–99, esp. 88–94; Christopher Hill, *God's Englishman: Oliver Cromwell and the English Revolution* (New York: Penguin, 1990), 20, 27–28 (companies); Cotton to Cromwell, July 28, 1651, and Cromwell to Cotton, October 2, 1651, in Sargent Bush Jr., ed., *The Correspondence of John Cotton* (Chapel Hill: University of North Carolina Press for the Omohundro Institute of Early American History and Culture, 2001), 458–464 (quotation at 460), 468–470; Francis J. Bremer, "In Defense of Regicide: John Cotton on the Execution of Charles I," *WMQ*, 3rd Ser., 37 (1980), 103–124, quotation at 116.

consisted of men picked up in the Leeward Islands, most of them indentured servants looking to better their lot in life. The fleet arrived in Barbados at the end of January. In early April, Admiral William Penn and Robert Venables, his second-in-command, led the ships to Santo Domingo. With the Spanish still reeling from defeat in the Thirty Years' War, which included substantial loss of ships to the English, the time seemed auspicious.[26]

In May 1655, Penn and Venables unleashed their forces in Jamaica. The invaders far outnumbered the Spanish, who then had only about 2,500 men in arms on the island. While the victory was swift, the aftermath proved to be deadly. The English hoped to make Jamaica a launching point for other raids. But insect-borne diseases, most likely falciparum malaria, struck hard, either killing victims outright or making them more susceptible to dysentery and typhoid. Illness spread rapidly among the invaders, sickening 3,000 in only three weeks. By year's end, the English forces had dropped from 9,000 to 3,720, and the majority of the survivors were so ill that they could not help the cause. In less than one year, 5,000 of the English on Jamaica had perished. Hoping to keep the newly acquired colony viable, Cromwell's agents recruited 1,500 migrants from Nevis to feed the army. These newcomers arrived in December 1656. Only one-third remained alive by March. Venables and Penn, each blaming the other for the calamity, sailed for home. Cromwell, enraged at the news about the debacles on Hispaniola and Jamaica, had both arrested and imprisoned in the Tower of London, though he soon ordered their release.[27]

In Jamaica, with the English commanders and virtually all the ships departed, Spanish soldiers, some of whom had remained on the island in the face of the evacuation order and others who had sailed there from Cuba, engaged in a long-running guerilla war with the English. They enlisted maroons, who had escaped enslavement, as their allies. These individuals were less motivated by any alliance to the Spanish crown than by the fear that English control over the island would lead to reenslavement. Still, their efforts were not enough. Military losses in 1657 at Ochos Rios and 1658 at Rio Nuevo doomed whatever hopes the Spanish maintained for regaining the island. While the Spanish crown did not relinquish formal control until 1670 as part of a general agreement between

26. McNeill, *Mosquito Empires*, 97–99.

27. McNeill, *Mosquito Empires*, 98–104; Hill, *God's Englishman*, 129–132; Carla G. Pestana, *The English Conquest of Jamaica: Oliver Cromwell's Bid for Empire* (Cambridge, MA: Harvard University Press, 2017), 117–138.

England and Spain, Jamaica had by then become part of the English realm's claims in the Caribbean.[28]

Jamaica was not then particularly profitable or heavily populated, and the English hoping to create sugar plantations barely outnumbered the maroons who had created their own communities in the mountainous interior. Still, Cromwell had managed to succeed in the tropics where Charles I and an earlier generation had failed at Providence Island. Jamaica belonged to the English, at least on their maps. In 1662, according to a surviving census, its total population was only 4,207, of whom 87 percent (3,653 individuals) were English and the other 13 percent (554) were of African origin. Among the English, men outnumbered women by four to one, hardly a ratio that held much promise for natural increase, especially given immigrants' continued inability to withstand local diseases. If Jamaica was to become valuable as anything more than a resupply depot for English ships, those who controlled it would need to solve its labor shortage.[29]

Hoping to solve two problems at once, Cromwell planned to export Catholic Irish who continued to resist the conquest of their homeland to work Jamaican fields. Ever since the uprising of 1641, the English had tried to manipulate domestic public opinion by publishing accounts of alleged Irish atrocities, providing Cromwell and his associates with justification for horrific treatment by the New Model Army. To be sure, the Irish response to English invasion had been bloody. The Irish had killed one-seventh of the English on the island, making their rebellion the most damaging to date of any the realm faced in the Atlantic basin. In 1649

28. "Treaty between Great Britain and Spain, for Settling Peace in America, July 8/18. 1670," in *A Collection of All the Treaties of Peace, Alliance, and Commerce, between Great-Britain and Other Powers* (London, 1765), 1:197–198.

29. Edward B. Rugemer, "The Development of Mastery and Race in the Comprehensive Slave Codes of the Greater Caribbean During the Seventeenth Century," *WMQ*, 3rd Ser., 70 (2013), 443; Trevor Burnard, "European Migration to Jamaica, 1655–1780," *WMQ*, 3rd Ser., 53 (1996), 769–796, esp. table 1 (772); cf. Hilary McD. Beckles, "A 'Riotous and Unruly Lot': Irish Indentured Servants and Freemen in the English West Indies, 1644–1713," *WMQ* 47 (1990), 505. Jamaica would, in the eighteenth century, become the most profitable English colony in the Western Hemisphere, primarily from its sugar planters' active participation in the slave trade, but no one could have anticipated such success based on the fate of the expeditionary forces in the 1650s and the relatively low number of English, Irish, and Africans living there in the early 1660s. For its later history, see T. G. Burnard, "'Prodigious Riches': The Wealth of Jamaica Before the American Revolution," *Economic History Review* 54 (2001), 506–524, and Trevor Burnard and Kenneth Morgan, "The Dynamics of the Slave Market and Slave Purchasing Patterns in Jamaica, 1655–1788," *WMQ*, 3rd Ser., 58 (2001), 205–228.

Cromwell's troops, which had been occupied by battles in England until the execution of Charles I, unleashed a reign of terror across much of Ireland that lasted until 1652. At Drogheda alone they killed 2,000. Parliament passed the Act of Settlement in 1652, dictating that Catholic Irish migrate west of the Shannon and that English colonists take up their property.

Seeking ideological and intellectual justification, Cromwell and his allies argued that the migration of Catholic Irish would be to their benefit since in the Caribbean, free of the stultifying hold of the Irish church and clan-based traditions, these migrants might convert to Protestant practice. The plan, echoing English expectations during the Elizabethan conquest, was one component of Cromwell's overarching vision of attracting Protestants, or would-be converts, to territory newly under English control. The same impulse would lead English authorities to recruit Dutch and Huguenot refugees to the West Indies and a small number of Massachusetts colonists to Ireland. The New Englanders resisted that overture, though during the era of the Protectorate perhaps 3,000 returned to England to join the cause against Royalist remnants and the Church of England. Behind these plans lay brute force: under Cromwell's leadership the English army grew from scattered militia units to a professional force numbering 30,000 and the navy from 4,000 to near 20,000.[30]

In the wake of Cromwell's conquest, hundreds of poor Irish looking for work migrated to the West Indies in the 1650s and 1660s, especially to Barbados.[31] But the troubles they had hoped to escape followed them into the tropics. From 1654 to 1659 English officials in Barbados launched a series of efforts to discourage Irish remaining there. They pursued rumors of Irish men who seemed to lack regular employment and feared collusion between "Irish Servants and Negroes out in Rebellion." The governor and council paid close attention to an Irish migrant named Cornelius Bryan, whom others had heard employing "Mutinous Language." Bryan, according to witnesses, "did say as he was eating Meat in a Tray, that if there was

30. Alison Games, *The Web of Empire: English Cosmopolitans in an Age of Expansion, 1560–1660* (New York: Oxford University Press, 2008), 255–287; for individual reasons for returning to England, see Moore, *Abandoning America*; for more willing Irish migrants to the West Indies, see L. M. Cullen, "The Irish Diaspora of the Seventeenth and Eighteenth Centuries," in Nicholas Canny, ed., *Europeans on the Move* (Oxford: Clarendon Press, 1994), 113–149, esp. 126–127; Nicholas Canny, "English Migration into and Across the Atlantic During the Seventeenth and Eighteenth Centuries," in Canny, ed., *Europeans on the Move*, 39–75, esp. 59–60; for similarities to the sixteenth century, see Nicholas Canny, "The Ideology of English Colonization: From Ireland to America," *WMQ*, 3rd. Ser., 30 (1973), 575–598.

31. Cullen, "The Irish Diaspora"; Canny, "English Migration."

so much English Blood in the Tray as there was Meat, he would eat it." For his insolence, the council sentenced him to receive twenty-one lashes from the town's hangman. Officials also found Bryan, or someone with the same name, guilty of trying to cause an insurrection. For that crime he was to leave the island within a month. If he remained longer, they would prosecute him for mutiny, though when he petitioned, they extended his time there by two months. The council exiled three Catholic priests, ordering them to leave within fifteen days "to any place" outside of English territory. The council sentenced two servants in one household, convicted of acting "Rebelliously and Mutinously" toward the husband and wife who owned their contracts, to thirty-one lashes each followed by an unspecified prison term.[32]

In his report on Barbados, Ligon had scorned the way planters treated their servants, claiming that overseers beat them for insignificant infractions. "Truly," Ligon wrote, "I have seen such cruelty there done to Servants, as I did not think one Christian could have done to another." He believed that this behavior had prompted some to launch a conspiracy against the planters. The servants planned to cut the masters' throats and "make themselves [not] only freemen," Ligon observed, "but Masters of the Island." At the last minute, one servant confessed the plan to a planter, who spread word to suppress the insurrection. The planters executed the leaders, the only solution they imagined since they feared another insurrection. The enslaved likely would have risen up as well, Ligon surmised, but the planters—knowing the risk of importing so many Africans that they would be outnumbered—deliberately separated bound laborers when they arrived, minimizing the chances for the enslaved to mount a rebellion.[33]

The harsh government treatment of these Irish migrants sprang from the recognition that English colonial society in Barbados remained fragile through the 1650s. In 1655, the council heard that renegade Irish servants had joined forces with runaway Africans and were then "in rebellion." Governor Daniel Searle and his allies ordered a local officer to raise a company to hunt down the miscreants. The officials hoped to capture all of them and return them to service. But if they would not surrender, then the commander had orders to eliminate them.[34]

Two years later, with the situation still unsettled, Searle issued a proclamation targeted at capturing and controlling Irish men and women

32. Aubrey Gwynn, "Documents Relating to the Irish in the West Indies," *Analecta Hibernica* 4 (1932), 233–236.
33. Ligon, *True and Exact History*, 94–97.
34. Gwynn, "Documents Relating to the Irish in the West Indies," 233–234.

who had "no certain place of residence," some of whom had been found wandering "up and down from Plantation to Plantation, as vagabonds, refusing to labour, to put themselves into any service." Instead, they led "dissolute, lewd, and slothful" lives, resorting to robbery, theft, and other felonies to survive. Their rudeness toward the planters made their continued freedom more problematic. The governor had heard that these menacing Irish had tried to arm themselves. Some traveled from one plantation to another bearing forged documents claiming that they were free women and men. The most dangerous among them had tried to purchase guns. They were unwilling to surrender, and "it appears," Searle wrote, that if they gained "a condition of power, or had opportunity, they would soon put some wicked and malicious design in execution." Fearful of possible insurrection, the governor ordered "all Masters and Mistresses of Families, Overseers of Plantations" and anyone else to report the appearance of any suspicious Irish to local constables. Those arrested would be tried. If found guilty, they would be whipped and then sentenced to an additional year of servitude. Fears of Irish insurrection thousands of miles from home prompted Cromwell to inform Searle that every Irish man or woman, along with "such others as are of the Romish Religion," could no longer bear any arms. English regiments were to hunt them down and seize their "Swords, Rapier, Cutlasses, Daggers, Sheaves, Pikes, half-pikes, Lances, Powder, Bullett, Shot or Match."[35]

While Cromwell's Caribbean officials were implementing his anti-Catholic policies in Barbados, Cromwell himself became ill, possibly with malaria. He resisted the known treatment with quinine reportedly because it had been discovered by Jesuits.[36] Other infections and pneumonia followed, leading to his death on September 3, 1658. His supporters laid his body to rest in Westminster Abbey in a funeral reputed to be as grand as that of any monarch. Richard Cromwell inherited his father's position but lacked Oliver's passionate military support. He resigned in 1659. Leaders of the New Model Army, which had propelled his rise, abandoned the cause of constitutional reform, clearing the way for the restoration of the monarchy. Two years after the Protector's death, crowds exhumed his body and hanged it at Tyburn.[37]

35. Gwynn, "Documents Relating to the Irish in the West Indies," 236–238.
36. Natalie Harrison, "In Celebration of the Jesuit's Powder: A History of Malaria Treatment," *Lancet: Infectious Diseases* 15, no. 10 (2015), P1143.
37. Hill, *God's Englishman*, 121–158.

On May 23, 1660, Charles II departed The Hague, where he had taken refuge, bound for London. He traveled with his two brothers, James, Duke of York, and Henry, Duke of Gloucester. As the ships set off, enormous crowds crammed the nearby beach and the hills above it, more people in one place than had ever convened before in Holland, according to one bystander. The king was so delighted that his court commissioned a German-born artist named Johannes Lingelbach to re-create the scene on canvas for the royal collection. Peter van Abeele, a renowned Dutch artist, fashioned a medal to mark the occasion: an angel flying above the English fleet blaring out *Soli deo gloria*, "To God alone be the glory."[38] Courtiers, pamphleteers, and members of the public celebrated his return. On May 29, his thirtieth birthday, Charles traveled the five miles from the Tower to Westminster Palace for his coronation. He paraded through crowded streets, with local militia companies lining the sidewalk and women packed together on balconies to get the best view. The blaring of trumpets and the steady beat of kettledrums could be heard far and wide, an aural counterpoint to military officials wearing green coats and the lord mayor's entourage bearing plush scarlet cloaks. Fountains across the city poured out claret instead of water. Poets dashed off verses: "And now I sing / That Prince our King / The cure of all our wounds is He," one anonymous observer declared; "Guns, every Bell, And Bone-fires tell / His safe return, our island round / Nothing but Charles, King Charles refound. A joyful sight to see." The king had returned, a bold leader for a church and a nation looking to put Cromwell's misdeeds in the past and build on his successes.[39] Among those he sought to eliminate were the fifty-nine men who had signed his father's death warrant, including two who had escaped to New England and others who had fled to the continent. After he made public arguments justifying their actions, English courts ordered some of them drawn and quartered and others to be hanged. The new king had no hesitation about using the ultimate power of the state to further his agenda.[40]

38. Rufus Bird and Martin Clayton, ed., *Charles II: Art and Power* (London: Royal Collection Trust, [2017]), 50–52.
39. *A True Relation of the Reception of His Majestie and Conducting Him through the City of London* (London, 1660); *The chearfull Acclamation of the City of Edinburgh, For the happy Return of his Sacred Majesty, Charles the Second* (Edinburgh [?], c. 1660); *An Ode upon the Happy Return of King Charles II. To his Languishing Nations, May 29. 1660* (London, 1660), quotation at sig. A3[r]; Olivia Fryman, "Coronation & Ceremony," in Bird and Clayton, eds., *Charles II*, 54–57.
40. Matthew Jenkinson, *Charles I's Killers in America: The Lives and Afterlives of Edward Whalley and William Goffe* (Oxford: Oxford University Press, 2019), 20–70; Gaby

Before the end of his first year back home, Charles became aware that previous efforts to recruit Irish, Scots, and English to Barbados and the other sugar islands had not met the planters' need for labor. He decided to formalize the shipment of enslaved Africans. Using his newly acquired authority and believing that he and his relatives should profit from the business, the king established the Company of Royal Adventurers Trading to Africa. For the first time, an English monarch decided to profit from the sale of humans to produce American commodities.

Charles II was not the first English monarch to believe that there was great profit to be made through the buying and selling of African bodies, though his predecessors stretching back to Elizabeth had provided little more than encouragement for a business that by mid-century had not yet come to rival that of the Portuguese. Charles believed that such a company could have three primary benefits. First, creating a monopoly on the shipment of enslaved Africans to the Caribbean would generate profits to the crown at a time of remaining political instability. Second, such a venture might provide strategic advantages in the ongoing conflict with the Dutch, who also had increased their participation in the slave trade. (It was too soon for anyone in England to know that Spanish enthusiasm for the slave trade had already begun to slacken, though planters in Spanish American colonies still proved eager to purchase enslaved Africans who had been transported to the Western Hemisphere by other Europeans.) Third, and most important, the new company would address what had emerged as a substantial economic problem: the need for labor to produce sugar in the West Indies. By 1660, the English had concluded that they could not attract sufficient indentured labor across Britain. The most reliable source of labor, the king believed, was captive Africans, primarily from the central western coast.[41] The recent conquest of Jamaica, he knew, could encourage the movement of enslaved bodies from one English overseas possession to another, especially supporting Barbados, which had emerged as the most profitable English American colony, its generation of wealth dependent only on the constant arrival of bound bodies to harvest sugar on the then-cleared island.[42]

Mahlberg, "*Les Juges Jugez, ses Justifians* (1663) and Edmund Ludlow's Protestant Network in Seventeenth-Century Switzerland," *Historical Journal* 57 (2014), 369–396.

41. See William A. Pettigrew, *Freedom's Debt: The Royal African Company and the Politics of the Atlantic Slave Trade, 1672–1752* (Chapel Hill: University of North Carolina Press for the Omohundro Institute of Early American History and Culture, 2013), 22–23.
42. The number of enslaved Africans arriving in Spanish American colonies from 1640 to 1700 was less than 50 percent of the number who had been sent there from 1580 to 1640, and the number of enslaved who arrived on Spanish ships declined from 100,000 during those six decades to 10,000 between 1640 and 1700; see David Eltis,

The charter for the Company of Royal Adventurers of England trading into Africa identified James, the Duke of York, as the director of the venture, though the enterprise would profit other members of the royal family and other gentry, including some who were already involved in the transatlantic colonial scheme. At the time, the English conducted trade across the West African coast, from the Senegal River in the north to New Calabar. It claimed monopoly rights to ivory, redwood, wax, grains, gums, and "negro slaves." The king imagined that the English would soon create a series of distinct colonies, with the company's owners possessing all authority to establish local government, appoint officials to command them, and ensure not only the enforcement of monopoly rights to the enslaved but also half of any gold discovered by colonists. In his bid to incentivize adherence to his scheme, Charles II offered a 50 percent share of all seized slave ships to the company, reserving the rest for himself.[43]

The charter of the new company suggested that the English had decided to follow a path established by the Dutch, who had emerged as their primary rival not only on the North American mainland but also throughout much of the Caribbean. During its early years, the Company of Royal Adventurers did not manage to transform the racial balance as quickly as its promoters anticipated, including in Barbados. In 1667 one observer commented that most of the poor whites in Barbados were Irish, "derided by the Negroes, and branded w[i]th the Epithite of white slaves." That year William Willoughby, who had recently become governor, complained to the king about Barbados's populace, which he described as "a strange composition of people what w[i]th Blacks Irish & servants." His views received a sympathetic hearing in London, where officials feared that the employment of English and Scots in a recent effort to defend the Leeward Islands had left Barbados "in an ill Condition" given that Irish and Africans constituted a substantial majority of the population.[44]

The Rise of African Slavery in the Americas (Cambridge: Cambridge University Press, 2000), 9, 27.

43. Charter for the Company of Royal Adventurers into Africa, December 18, 1660, in Cecil T. Carr, ed., *Select Charters of Trading Companies, A.D. 1530–1707* (London, 1913), 172–177. For the geographic range of English activity, see P. E. H. Hair and Robin Law, "The English in West Africa to 1700," in Nicholas Canny, ed., *The Origins of Empire* (Oxford: Oxford University Press, 1998), 241–263.

44. Simon P. Newman, *A New World of Labor: The Development of Plantation Slavery in the British Atlantic* (Philadelphia: University of Pennsylvania Press, 2013), 81–88; "Some Observations on the Island Barbados (a. 1667)," Willoughby to the king, September 16, 1667, and "Report of the Committee for Reimbursement to the Barbados, March 12, 1668," all in Gwynn, "Documents Relating to the Irish in the West Indies," 250, 266, 267.

During the 1660s, 46,000 enslaved Africans arrived in Barbados, Jamaica, and Nevis. There was no need for a court to rule that a runaway of African origin would serve the remainder of her or his life if caught. Having arrived naked and in chains, cut off from those who spoke the same language, put into brutal work by overseers, and provided only minimal shelter, insufficient food, and inadequate medical treatment when they became injured or ill, these bound workers faced the social death of enslavement before the physical death that came too early and often suddenly. This was the enterprise that Charles II and his brother saw as the future of what was then the most profitable corner of the English Atlantic world.[45]

The dramatic increase in forced migration was no accident. During a period of rapid expansion in the numbers of enslaved Africans, the council in Barbados had ruled that "*Negroes* and *Indians*, that came here to be sold, should serve for Life, unless a Contract was before made to the contrary."[46] The motivation for the act had less to do with defining life sentences for Africans than differentiating their legal status from the thousands of Irish prisoners captured by Cromwell's forces and sent to the island. These "Barbadozz'd" prisoners of war rose up in rebellion in the mid-1650s, which prompted authorities to ban them from having weapons. Actual rebellions and fears of more motivated legislators to act. Earlier laws designed to regulate servants and the enslaved came together in the island's legal code in 1652.[47]

In 1661, the Barbadian assembly enacted a statute "for the better ordering and governing of Negroes." Its authors intended to write a law that would not contradict those of England but admitted that they had "no track" to follow since English law to that point had not provided specific guidelines on "how to govern such Slaves." The law, and another about the regulation of servants, differentiated between "Christians," on the one hand, and "Negroes," on the other. The authors claimed they wanted to protect the enslaved so they would not be at the whim of "the cruel, and

45. See Orlando Patterson, *Slavery and Social Death: A Comparative* Study, 2nd ed. (Cambridge, MA.: Harvard University Press, 2018); Vince Brown, *The Reaper's Garden: Death and Power in the World of Atlantic Slavery* (Cambridge, MA: Harvard University Press, 2010); Dunn, *Sugar and Slavery*; Richard B. Sheridan, *Sugar and Slavery: An Economic History of the British West Indies, 1623–1775* (Kingston, Jamaica: University Press of the West Indies, 2000); Trevor Burnard and John Garrigus, *The Plantation Machine: Atlantic Capitalism and French Saint-Domingue and British Jamaica* (Philadelphia: University of Pennsylvania Press, 2016), 25–49.

46. *Memoirs of the First Settlement of the Island of Barbados, and Other the Carribee Islands* (London, 1743), 20.

47. Rugemer, "Development of Mastery and Race," esp. 433–436; Beckles, "A 'Riotous and Unruly Lot,'" 502–522; [*Acts and Statutes*] *of the Island of Barbados* (London, [1654]).

The Transatlantic Slave Trade, c. 1450–1650

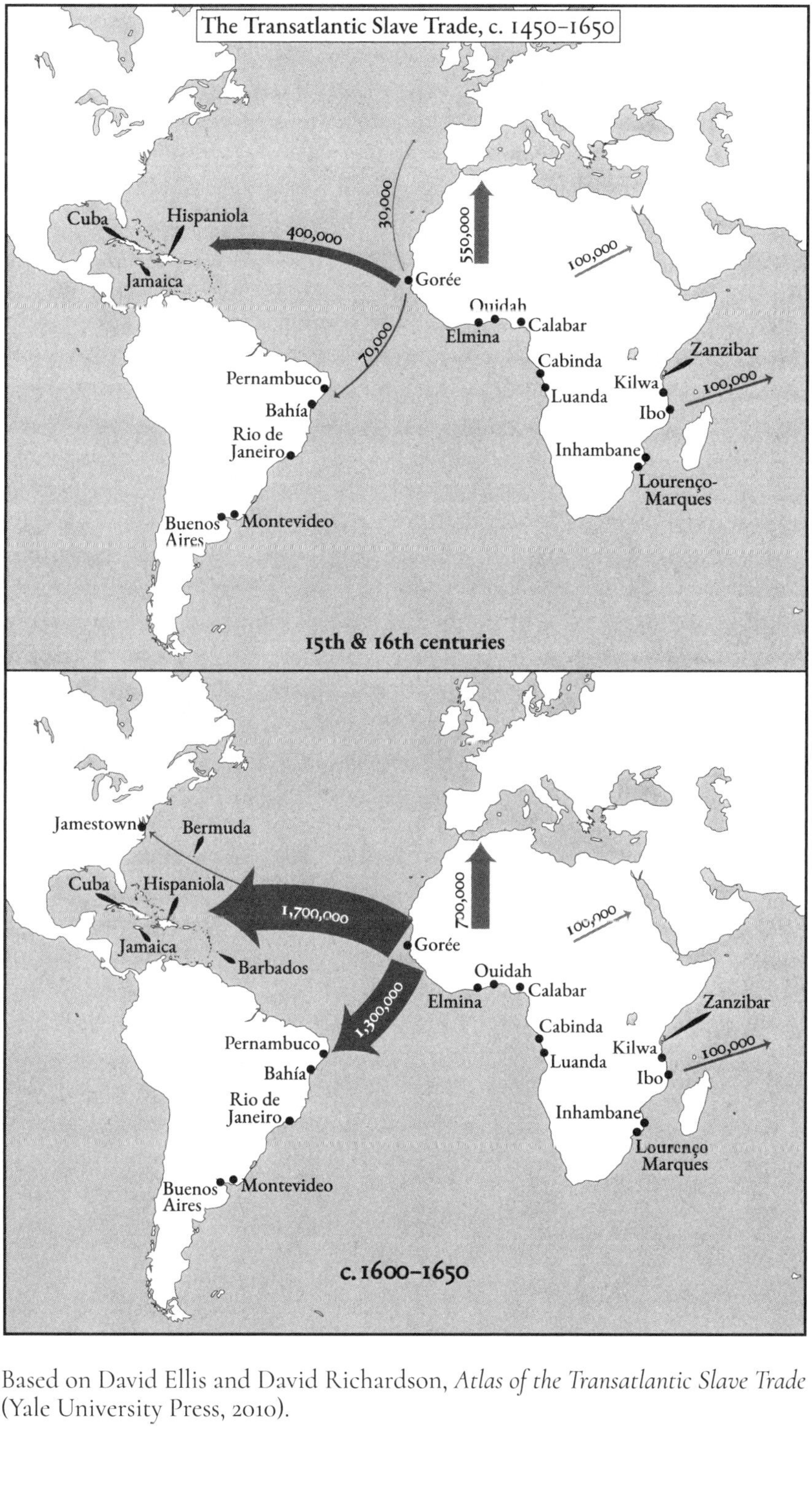

Based on David Ellis and David Richardson, *Atlas of the Transatlantic Slave Trade* (Yale University Press, 2010).

outrageous wills of every evil disposed person." Many servants, the assembly recognized, had arrived in Barbados as convicts with a specific criminal past—serious actions, to be sure, but not enough to condemn them to a life of perpetual service. Africans, on the other hand, differed in fundamental ways. The statute described them as a "heathenish brutish and an uncertain dangerous pride of people." This population, the new code specified, needed to be treated with "punishary Laws" that would protect non-Africans on the island. Indentured servants who committed crimes had their cases tried before juries. Enslaved Africans, defined in the code as "brutish Slaves," faced summary judgment at the hands of slave courts consisting of three freemen and two justices of the peace. The twinned law codes reduced punishments for indentured servants who committed crimes but increased them for the enslaved. A first conviction of a "Negro" hitting a "Christian" brought whipping; a second resulted in having one's nose slit and being branded on the face; a third demanded "greater Corporal punishment," likely including execution.

The code reflected planters' anxieties about the changing demography of Barbados. Fearing rebellion and dangers posed by runaways, the assembly limited the movement of Africans on the island, banned them from possessing any weapons, ordered any planter to import at least one "Christian" for every twenty acres they owned, and took steps to crack down on maroon communities. The bill did, in theory, protect Africans from death at the hand of planters motivated by "cruel intention" by forcing any who killed an enslaved African to pay into the public treasury, though that section was perhaps less important to planters than a clause that specified rewards for capturing runaways "either alive or dead."[48] Three years later, Sir Thomas Modyford brought a copy to Jamaica, where it became the law on that island too. Africans in Barbados, and then in Jamaica, lacked the protections retained by white servants there or enslaved Africans in Portuguese Brazil or across Spanish America.[49]

These codes crystallized the legal boundaries of enslavement at a time when the population of bound Africans soared, with approximately 5,000 coming off European vessels each year in Barbados alone in the mid-1660s. By then, the sugar industry was booming, providing economic justification for planters who may have felt any qualms about the ways that they treated enslaved Africans. In 1665–1666, planters exported over 12,000 metric tons of sugar (mostly muscovado or unrefined) along with over

48. "An act for the better ordering and governing of Negroes," CO 30/2/16-26, reprinted in Stanley Engerman, Seymour Drescher, and Robert Paquette, eds., *Slavery* (Oxford: Oxford University Press, 2001), 105–113.

49. Rugemer, "Development of Mastery and Race," 442–444.

567,000 liters of rum and 529,000 liters of molasses, with a value of over £259,000—or likely close to 2 percent of the income of England and Wales, an astonishing output for an island of only 166 square miles.[50]

In 1667, the island's leaders, still fearful of what they called "their Negroes, an heathenish, brutish, and an uncertaine dangerous kind of people," believed it necessary to protect them and "many other goods and Chattels" from "the arbitrary, cruel and outrageous wills of every evil disposed person." Recognizing, again, the possible danger that enslaved people posed, the government forbade any from leaving their plantations even on Sunday or holy days without a ticket from their "Master, Mistress, Commander, or Overseer's hand." Owners of enslaved Africans who traveled without such a pass had to "punish them by a moderate whipping" or else forfeit 500 pounds of sugar.[51]

Barbadian legislators wanted to intimidate enslaved Africans and hence discourage them from rebelling. But in 1675, the planters learned that even draconian laws could not suppress widespread desire to be free of the shackles of enslavement. That year, a group of enslaved who had originated on the Gold Coast crafted a plot to kill the island's white population. They were the followers of an enslaved man named Cuffee (or Coffee), who planned to make himself the king of the island. When Fortuna (or Anna), who toiled in the household of a local captain named Giles Hall, heard about the plot, she revealed what she had learned. Planters mustered a militia to hunt down the plotters. They initially captured seventeen, ordering that six be burned alive and the others hanged. Right before they set flames to kill him, an enslaved man named Tony (or Toney) refused to tell his inquisitors what they wanted to hear. "If you Roast me today," he declared in words captured in a pamphlet describing the abortive uprising, "you cannot Roast me tomorrow." By the time the planters' soldiers took control, local authorities had executed a total of thirty-five and five others had committed suicide, perhaps believing that in death they would return home. But not Fortuna, whom Hall released from her bondage.[52]

50. By comparison, Wales alone is over 8,000 square miles and England over 50,000. For the estimates see David Eltis, "The Total Product of Barbados, 1664–1701," *Journal of Economic History* 55 (1995), 321–338, migration estimate at 333; David Eltis, "Estimates of Exports from Barbados and Jamaica, 1655–1701," *WMQ*, 3rd Ser., 52 (1995), 631–648, table 1 (638) and table 3 (642).

51. "An act for the better ordering and governing of Negroes."

52. *Great Newes from the Barbadoes. Or, a True and Faithful Account of the Grand Conspiracy of the Negroes against the English* (London, 1675), 9–14, quotation at 12; Dunn, *Sugar and Slaves*, 256–258.

Unlike the mainland, the first English who arrived in Barbados, like those who went to Bermuda, came upon a place that had no resident population. They went through a period of economic experimentation with cotton and tobacco before finally realizing that the greatest profits to be had would be in sugar production. They then set about to reshape the island's topography and demography. At first, those in control believed, like their counterparts along the Chesapeake, that importing indentured servants would be the best way to develop the island. Finding themselves unable to get enough labor from Britain, and unhappy with and afraid of the servants coming from Ireland, they shifted toward an enslaved labor force. Doing so meant creating a military force to quell possible insurrections, which governors recognized could cross racial lines. Such a situation posed risks for the English who had come to Barbados to build profitable establishments.

Among those who managed to succeed was James Drax, who had arrived as a twenty-five-year-old English would-be planter in 1627. Over the course of the next two decades, he took advantage of every opportunity he saw. After clearing forty acres within a year, presumably with laborers he hired with the 300 pounds he invested in the venture, he began to produce tobacco. With the profits he hired forty white servants. When tobacco prices fell, he turned to cotton. In 1640 he sailed to Pernambuco to observe Dutch sugar plantations. While there he made contacts that enabled him to go into business with merchants, Dutch and Sephardic, living in Amsterdam. In 1644, he decided to expand his labor force by purchasing enslaved Africans. That year he built the island's first windmill. By the end of the decade, he realized that even in the tropics he could not escape the politics of an England engulfed by civil war. He became an ally of Cromwell's and rode the politics of the Protectorate to profitable office in Barbados. Drax was wealthy enough to go back to England in 1654 but chose to return to the island. When he went back to London four years later, Cromwell knighted him. By then he had married into a prosperous family and built the most famous mansion on Barbados, entertaining visitors in style, an unsurprising achievement for the planter later English celebrated for pioneering advanced sugar-production techniques in Barbados.[53]

53. Michael Craton, "Reluctant Creoles: The Planters' World in the British West Indies," in Bernard Bailyn and Philip D. Morgan, eds., *Strangers Within the Realm: Cultural Margins of the First British Empire* (Chapel Hill: University of North Carolina Press for the Institute of Early American History and Culture, 1991), 314–362, esp. 331–332; *Memoirs of the First Settlement of the Island of Barbados,* appendix, 1.

Ligon visited Drax when he was hosting a "*Regalio*" for his fellow planters: fourteen different beef dishes, followed by elaborate servings of pork, chicken, a pasty made from young goat, mutton shoulder, ducklings, turtledoves, turkey, rabbits, oysters, anchovies, caviar, olives, plantains, guavas, bananas, and cheesecake. His staff seasoned this grand meal with nutmeg, possibly from the Spice Islands, and served puffs and bread made from flour imported from England, "for the Cassava will not serve for this kind of Cookery." The guests drank copious amounts of alcohol, including brandy, mauby (a local concoction made of sugar and tree bark), Kill-Devil (made from fermented sugar), claret, white wine, sherry, Canary, red sack, and "all Spirits that come from *England*." In his last years, Drax sailed regularly to London, joining a community of Caribbean planters who met at the Jamaica Coffee House near the Royal Exchange. Like others who would follow, he had become the model of a successful colonial planter, his wealth generated on the backs of bound laborers, his opportunities expanded by an ever more sophisticated transatlantic economy, and his personal life the envy of observers.[54]

Drax was the wealthiest planter in the interior of the island, but that exuberant party he threw, while perhaps a bit more extravagant than others', was hardly unique. Ligon also visited Colonel Walrond, a planter whose lands stretched to the coast, who offered grand feasts featuring parrotfish, mullet, snapper, crab, lobster, and mackerel, among other seafood. Walrond stocked his house from the 100 or so ships that docked in Bridgetown each year. Ease of transport facilitated Walrond's desire to stuff his cellars with, as Ligon put it, "all rarities that are brought to the Island, from any part of the world." He could offer guests imported wines and olive oil, English peas, and meat dried and brought to market in Hispaniola and then transported to Barbados. His wine cellar was far better than that of even a wealthy planter like Drax because the road network was still too primitive to haul expensive bottles into the interior. Despite the travails some planters faced when seeking to gather every luxury item imaginable, the integration of Barbados into the Atlantic economy meant that those with means on the island could purchase dried beef and pork from the Netherlands, England, New England, Russia, and Virginia. More important, ship captains brought cows and horses, the tools for processing sugar, and artisans to build houses, docks, and stores. Ligon complained that some of the goods unloaded on the island were of poor quality, including overcooked and oversalted sturgeon from New England. But that mattered less than the periodic arrival of dry goods: shoes, hats, gloves, knives, swords, locks and keys, linen, and woolen

54. Ligon, *True and Exact History*, 87.

cloth. The unloading of these imports enabled planters to create an economy based almost entirely on the production of sugar. Economic specialization had never reached such an extent elsewhere in North America.[55]

Manual workers, probably both indentured servants and enslaved Africans, cleared roads and constructed houses that would be considered "well built" in England, as one traveler put it, noting that "Shops and Store-houses are well furnish'd with all sorts of Commodities." The English had divided the island into parishes and erected churches in them. "The most considerable of the Inhabitants think themselves so well," French natural historian Charles de Rochefort wrote, "that it is seldom seen they ever remove thence."[56]

Such a system inflated planters' profits through maximizing efficiencies. But its success, like that of the silver mines in Parral, hinged on controlling the labor supply. In Barbados, the gap between planters could be seen in the kind and amount of food available. Drax, Walrond, and their friends ate lavishly. Indentured servants and the enslaved fared far worse. Ligon wrote that African men each were given two mackerels a week and women one. They received their ration of fish on Saturday evening, along with a single bunch of large plantains or two small bunches. If a cow died, servants could eat the meat. The enslaved could then eat the remaining head, entrails, and skin. Servants drank mauby, while the enslaved had only water. If Barbados was, as some observers claimed at the time, the jewel in the English crown, it owed its wealth to the most noxious labor regime yet developed in the Atlantic world.[57]

Barbadian planters created a world built on the premise of an enslaved and dependent workforce. They exercised their power at every possible stage. When ships bearing the chained bodies of the enslaved arrived, planters understood that it would be best to purchase humans from different places. "They are fetched from several parts of Africa," Ligon observed, "who speak several languages, and by that means, one of them understands not another." Those sold on Barbados had been captured in Guinea, Benin, Angola, the valley around the Gambia River, and the Portuguese port of Catcheo.[58] The naturalist Rochefort, describing the commerce in bodies across the Caribbean, put it bluntly: "They are bought and sold after the same manner as Cattle in other places." There was no possible improvement in their condition. "[T]heir service being perpetual,"

55. Ligon, *True and Exact History of Barbados*, 85–89.
56. Charles de Rochefort, *The History of the Caribby-Islands*, trans John Davies (London, 1666), I:9.
57. Ligon, *True and Exact History*, 86, 93,
58. Ligon, *True and Exact History*, 97.

he added, "their number increases from time to time by the Children that are born of them, which have no other Inheritance than that of the slavery and subjection of their Parents."[59]

Ligon described the scene in the racist tropes of the era but from time to time provided his readers with a glimpse of the horrors of the islands. The enslaved, he wrote, believed in "a God" and the resurrection of the soul, which explained why some committed suicide rather than face the enduring torture meted out by planters and overseers. In death they would "go into their own Country again, and have their youth renewed."[60]

Ligon returned to England in 1650. Seven years later, he published his study of Barbados. Cromwell died the next year. When Charles II installed his brother James as the director of the Royal African Company, and when London merchants put their capital into a venture that would facilitate the transportation of enslaved men and women to Barbados and other revenue-producing parts of the realm, they all knew exactly what their actions meant.

In 1661, the Virginia House of Burgesses, following Barbadian precedent, made the enslavement of Africans legal, a first in the English mainland colonies. In some sense, the statute formalized an unspoken code that had differentiated Africans from Europeans (and Natives) since the arrival in 1619 of the twenty or so Angolans who were taken captive, sold, bundled onto a ship for transportation to the Western Hemisphere, captured again, and then deposited in Jamestown. These laws represented a new development in the Chesapeake colonies at a time when there were far fewer residents of African than European descent. As late as 1660, the Black population of the Chesapeake colonies, which had stood at approximately 700 a decade earlier, was only 1,700 at a time when the total immigrant population exceeded 35,000. That year, enslaved constituted approximately one-fourth of those bound to service in the region.[61]

59. Rochefort, *History of the Caribby-Islands*, II:200, 203.

60. Ligon, *True and Exact History*, 97–98, 102.

61. Christopher Tomlins, *Freedom Bound: Law, Labor, and Civic Identity in Colonizing English America, 1580–1865* (Cambridge: Cambridge University Press, 2010), 40–42. In 1658, the Black population of four well-documented counties on the Eastern Shore of Maryland amounted to 3 percent of the total non-Indigenous population; see Russell R. Menard, "The Maryland Slave Population, 1658 to 1730: A Demographic Profile of Blacks in Four Counties," *WMQ* 32 (1975), 29–54, esp. 30–31. Bermuda had a similar experience, with the presumption of enslavement before the appearance of actual laws; see Vernon A. Ives, ed., *The Rich Papers: Letters from Bermuda, 1615–1646* (Toronto: University of Toronto Press for the Bermuda National Trust, 1984), 240.

Earlier practice had suggested that many Africans were already enslaved in the Chesapeake. In 1640, three of the planter Hugh Gwyn's servants ran away. The court added years to the contracts for the two white servants. But the court treated the other differently: "The third being a negro named John Punch shall serve his said master or his assigns for the time of his natural life there or else where." The court saw Punch as Gwyn's property, no matter where Gwyn might take him or if he sold him to another enslaver. Around mid-century, Chesapeake courts rendered similar rulings in other cases.[62]

Before the 1660s, transplanted Africans or American-born creoles might be free or enslaved. No statute in Virginia or Maryland defined the status of all persons of African origin. Instead, local circumstances mattered. Some men and women of African origin, who likely had arrived as enslaved on the eastern shore of Virginia from either the West Indies or New Amsterdam, managed to purchase their freedom. They bought property, appeared in court to give testimony, made claims that they were owed land because they had paid for the transportation of workers, wrote wills that enumerated their possessions, and created extensive kin groups. Anthony Johnson had an estate of 250 acres along Pungoteague Creek in Northampton County, with his family owning land nearby. After a devastating fire in 1653 threatened the family's livelihood, Johnson appealed to local magistrates to ease his tax burden to enable him to rebuild his estate. The local court accepted his argument. While the records of the case reveal that colonial authorities recognized that he was a "Negro," the term that they put next to the names of only some members of the community, that fact had no obvious bearing on the decision to lighten his economic burden. Nor did being of African origin prevent him from owning the labor of John Casar, who had complained that Johnson had held him for seven years beyond the length of his original indenture. The court found for Johnson, ordering Casar back into service.[63] The ability to own property and exercise legal rights existed beyond the Eastern Shore. On October 25, 1657, Anne Barnhouse, a resident of Martin's Hundred, freed Mihill Gowen "from any service" and specified that no one who came to control her estate could change his status. She added that Gowen's

62. H. R. McIlwane, ed., *Minutes of the Council and General Court of Colonial Virginia, 1622–1632, 1670–1676, with Notes and Excerpts from Original Council and General Court Records, into 1683, Now Lost* (Richmond: Library of Virginia, 1924), 466; Tomlins, *Freedom Bound*, 454–455; Oscar Handlin and Mary F. Handlin, "Origins of the Southern Labor System," *WMQ*, 3rd Ser., 7 (1950), 199–222.

63. T. H. Breen and Stephen Innes, *"Myne Owne Ground": Race and Freedom on Virginia's Eastern Shore, 1640–1676* (New York: Oxford University Press, 1980), 7–18.

son William, "of the body of my negro Rosa," would never owe service, though Martin did not specify what would happen to Rosa. In 1673, a man of African origin named Francis Paine bequeathed his entire estate to his wife, Agnes, a sign that they had control over their property.[64]

Only gradually did laws begin to capture a shift in the status of Africans on the mainland, and often lawmakers had in mind clarifying existing practices rather than making a definitive statement about slavery and freedom. In 1661, Virginia legislators passed an act to punish runaway white servants. The law noted that these escaped servants merited a different fate than "any Negroes who are incapable of makeing satisfaction by addition of time," a reference to the fact that at least some were already being held for the duration of their lives. The following year, Virginia's assembly passed a second bill that further cemented the link between race and the possibility of enslavement when it dictated that an individual's ability to be "slave or free" depended on "the condition of the mother." In instances where a colonist impregnated a woman bound to the service of another, the offender would pay twice the existing fine for fornication.[65]

Despite the clarification in the laws, not a single slave ship arrived in Virginia or Maryland from 1661 to 1670.[66] Instead, these colonies still lured free migrants from England—19,700 during this decade alone. These individuals had contracts that set the terms of their indenture. They signed up perhaps even knowing that the conditions they would face after their indenture, should they live long enough, were no longer as attractive as they had been earlier. By the early 1660s, the duties freed servants received for fulfilling their contract would be enough only to purchase less fertile upland, farther from the tobacco markets, on lands that put them closer to Indigenous people who remained, in the minds of the English, just over the next hillside. The economic opportunity indentured servants once dreamed about had become harder to grasp, and each passing year diminished these limited opportunities.[67] Soon, emigrants from territory claimed by England (including Ireland) would turn to other

64. Warren Billings, ed., *The Old Dominion in the Seventeenth Century*, rev. ed. (Chapel Hill: University of North Carolina Press for the Omohundro Institute of Early American History and Culture, 2007), 180–181 (Johnson), 194 (Gowen), 181–182 (Paine).
65. Hening, *Statutes*, 2:26 (1661) and 2:170 (1662).
66. Eltis, *Rise of African Slavery*, table 2.1 (48); David Eltis, "The Volume and African Origins of the British Slave Trade Before 1714," *Cahiers d'Études Africaines* 35 (1995), 617–627.
67. Russell R. Menard, "From Servant to Freeholder: Status Mobility and Property Accumulation in Seventeenth-Century Maryland," *WMQ*, 30 (1973), 37–64.

destinations, a response to the dramatic increase in Africans exported to English American colonies in the latter decades of the century.[68]

Modyford's role in the formalization of enslavement in Jamaica set the stage for his next and more dramatic action. In 1660, he partnered with John Colleton, another prosperous English planter and Barbadian enslaver, to petition Charles II for territory in Carolina. The English had claimed the region much earlier, but the king agreed with the pair that insufficient effort to maintain a colony had rendered the earlier titles meaningless. He also understood that establishing a viable English colony on the coast, just north of Florida, might undermine Spanish communities on the mainland. On March 20, 1663, the king granted the territory between 31° and 36° north latitude to Colleton, Modyford, and six other men, making them the proprietors of land that many others, Indigenous and Spanish as well as English, had long realized had enormous potential, its woods thick with whitetail deer, its coastline and adjacent interior boasting rich soils from periodic flooding. A clever promotional campaign soon lured 200 investors, from Barbados and England, who could purchase 500 acres for 1,000 pounds of sugar. The first emigrants arrived under the auspices of the Corporation of Barbados Adventurers, a signal that the mainland colony would follow the path of the island.[69]

Modfyford and Colleton understood that making a profit in hot climates entailed recruiting laborers to produce exportable commodities. Carolina had what Barbados by mid-century lacked: land that, once acquired from its Indigenous owners, could be turned into plantations. The proprietors also had the advantage of knowing the history not only of the island economies but also that of Virginia and Maryland. Success along the Chesapeake, the proprietors surmised, had come when the English devised the headright system. They reasoned that the same logic could succeed in Carolina. Unlike the early English migrants to Virginia, those who planned to establish a new colony in Carolina from the start

68. From 1580 to 1640, English slave traders exported approximately 4,000 Africans to their colonies; from 1640 to 1670, that number increased to 371,000. See James Horn and Philip D. Morgan, "Settlers and Slaves: European and African Migrations to Early Modern British America," in Elizabeth Mancke and Carole Shammas, eds., *The Creation of the British Atlantic World* (Baltimore: Johns Hopkins University Press, 2005), 19–44, esp. 20–27.

69. Peter H. Wood, *Black Majority: Negroes in Colonial South Carolina from 1670 Through the Stono Rebellion* (New York: Knopf, 1975), 13–15; William Hilton, "A Relation of a Discovery" (1664), in Alexander S. Salley, ed., *Narratives of Early Carolina* (New York: Scribner's, 1911), 53–54.

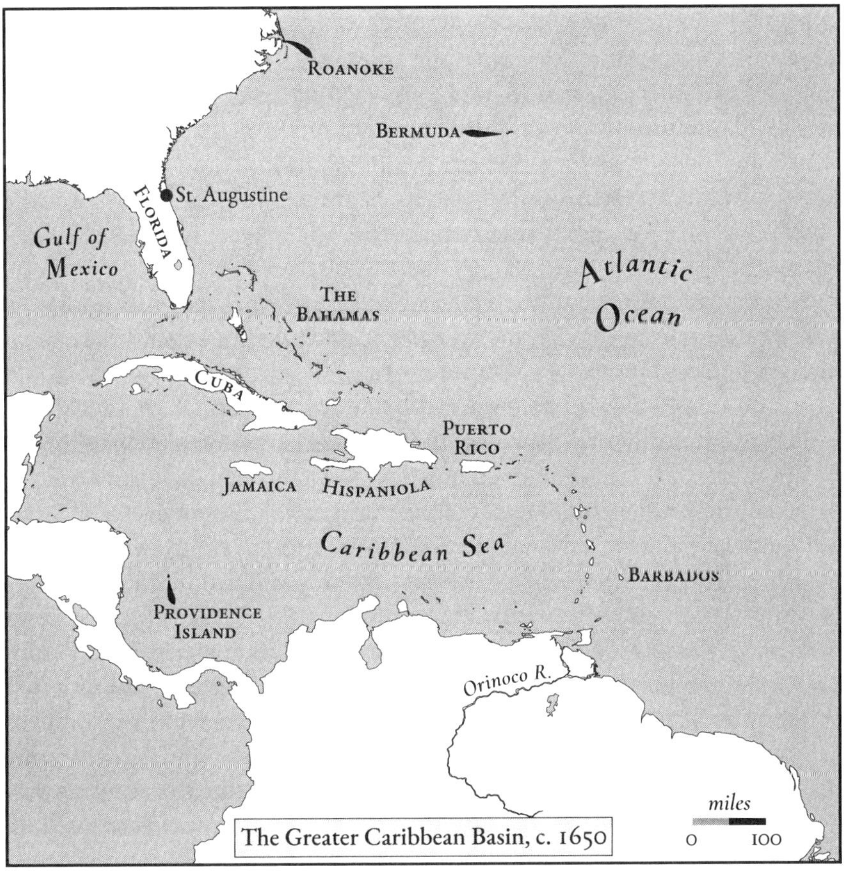

The Greater Caribbean Basin, c. 1650

recognized that enslaved laborers had enormous value. But success was not a given, something that many realized when the first English efforts to establish a community to be called Charles Town failed.[70]

In 1663, English ship captain William Hilton sailed from Barbados to Cape Fear. While there, he took note of the fact that other Europeans had tried and failed to establish a colony there, including a group from New England that had departed recently but left behind their cattle. They met and rescued some English shipwreck victims and had fairly extensive connections with local Indigenous. The next year, a London printer published

70. See "A declaration and proposals to all that will plant in Carolina" (headright) and "An answer to certine demands and proposealls made by several gentlemen and persons of good quality in the island of Barbados to the Lord Propreytors of the province of Carrolina" (awareness of other colonies), in William L. Saunders, ed., *Colonial Records of North Carolina*, 10 vols. (Raleigh, NC: P. M. Hale, 1886–1890), 1:43–46, 57–59.

Hilton's pamphlet, which he sent to the press to encourage potential migrants. Opportunity beckoned, he implored others, evident in prodigious Native maize, pumpkin, and watermelon harvests. Abundant desirable birds, animals, and fish could be found, and the climate was so salubrious that even the shipwreck victims, despite landing in a season that had felled so many in Virginia, "had their perfect healths all the time." A substantial population of elderly Indigenous proved the healthfulness of the area. On the area's sandy soils Natives also tended cattle and swine that the New Englanders had left behind, surprising visitors who never anticipated that local Indigenous could keep them thriving in such conditions.[71]

Hilton's pamphlet became the public announcement of the plans that Colleton and Molyford had used in their petition. Investors could reap substantial profits if they moved quickly either through purchases funded by sugar or through paying the transportation of colonists, a strategy echoing the plan that had fueled servant migration to Virginia earlier. The organizers, eager to launch a self-sustaining colony, promised forty acres to any free female over age twelve or a free male at least fourteen years old. Each parish church would receive 100 acres, eliminating risk for ministers who might have feared for their livelihoods. Free men would enjoy political liberty, including the right to choose a local assembly capable of passing its own laws. The freeholders also had freedom to trade and "Liberty of Conscience." Carolina's proprietors built the first English colony where those transporting enslaved Africans would receive free land. There was no ambiguity about the status of Africans in the new colony.[72]

Despite careful planning, the colony almost collapsed before it began, as Colleton died in 1666 and Molyford became so ill he had to withdraw. By the end of the decade, Carolina's fate seemed closer to the Amazon Company's than Barbados's. But reorganization in London had brought Anthony Ashley Cooper (Baron Ashley), whom Charles II had named the first Earl of Shaftesbury in 1672, to a position to encourage the other proprietors to make a more personal investment than they had planned. In 1666, Ashley had gone in search of healing waters to cure an inflamed liver. On his way to Astrop he stopped at Oxford and met John Locke. Though only thirty-seven, Locke had shifted his primary interest from political philosophy to medicine and he happened to have bottles of water from Astrop. The next year, Locke moved into Ashley's house as his personal physician. By 1669, Ashley had rewarded Locke with the position of tutor to his children and secretary to both the Council for Trade

71. Hilton, "Relation of a Discovery," 44–45, 52–53.
72. Hilton, "Relation of a Discovery," 57–61.

and Plantations and the proprietors of Carolina. In that latter capacity, Locke was quite likely the guiding force behind the Fundamental Constitutions of Carolina, a plan that solidified his standing among the realm's most influential political theorists.[73]

The Fundamental Constitutions laid out plans to create a landed English aristocracy to be dominated by eight proprietors and their heirs. Each would have the authority to parcel out lands within their claims as well as the ability to create and preside over their own courts. Yet as much as the text reflected the lingering allure of establishing an American feudalism reminiscent of Gilbert and Gorges, Locke and Ashley also included incentives for free migrants: the ability to become naturalized, a guarantee of trial by jury, freedom from double jeopardy, and the ability to sit in local parliaments, which would convene at regular times, if they owned at least 500 acres. All residents, including Indigenous and others who were not members of the Church of England, could worship freely as long as they made a public profession of their belief in a god. Even enslaved could be members of a church, though that would not alter their status, as the text clarified: "Every freeman of Carolina shall have absolute power and authority over his negro slaves, of what opinion or religion soever."[74]

Despite the high hopes of Locke and Ashley, the English did not manage to create an American feudal reign. But that did not stop colonists and their English supporters from creating the first mainland colony in North America where the enslaved, who arrived with free migrants from Barbados, would fall under the draconian strictures of laws first formulated on the island. From the perspective of the planters, the model worked: by 1708, enslaved Africans outnumbered free colonists. Some of these African migrants brought knowledge about how to cultivate rice, the crop that would dominate low-country plantations for much of the eighteenth century. By doing so, they mimicked earlier generations of enslaved who had cultivated rice in South America as early as the 1530s, transferring West African ecological knowledge about water and land management to create durable fields. But before plantation owners brutalized enslaved workers in rice swamps, Carolina's demographic model

73. M. Eugene Sirmans, *Colonial South Carolina: A Political History, 1663–1763* (Chapel Hill: University of North Carolina Press for the Institute of Early American History and Culture, 1966), 6–8.

74. The Fundamental Constitutions of Carolina, March 1, 1669, Avalon, articles 1 and 2 (proprietors), 118 (naturalization), 69 (jury trial), 64 (double jeopardy), 71–73 (local parliament), 95 to 100 (belief in god), 110 (enslavement).

remained Barbados, where enslaved Africans amounted to two-thirds of the island population by the middle of the 1670s.[75]

English colonial planters and local legislators understood the increasing importance of enslaved African workers to the English overseas economy, especially in Barbados. While geographically small, Barbados had an impact beyond providing a model for mainland colonists eager to produce tobacco or rice. The immense profits that sugar generated for the planter class fueled economic development elsewhere, especially in England, where the family fortunes of island planters soared. Eventually that wealth contributed to the origins of the Industrial Revolution. In the short run, the accumulation of capital from the backs of some but not all laborers revealed that the English, no matter how powerful some of their anti-enslavement pronouncements had sounded earlier, felt few qualms about enslaving Africans. Economics drove the rise of the slave trade and the creation of rigid laws from Barbados to the Chesapeake and Carolina. When those who enacted the legislation did so, they were codifying European views toward Africans and blackness that had existed for generations. Barbados was the laboratory that offered examples of the knowledge English had sought since the Elizabethan period about how to increase their wealth without exacerbating domestic social problems.[76]

75. Wood, *Black Majority*, 18–28, 144 (1708); Judith A. Carney, *Black Rice: The African Origins of Rice Cultivation in the Americas* (Cambridge, MA: Harvard University Press, 2001), esp. 73–85; Linford D. Fisher, "'Dangerous Designes': The 1676 Barbados Act to Prohibit New England Indian Slave Importation," *WMQ* 71 (2014), 104; Richard S. Dunn, "The Barbados Census of 1680: Profile of the Richest Colony in English America," *WMQ* 26 (1969), 3–30.

76. For the central importance of Barbados and the question of whether racism or economics drove the growth of the slave trade, see, among many sources, Trevor Burnard, "Capitalism and Modernity in the British Caribbean Plantation System," in Ewout Frankema and Tirthankar Roy, eds., *The Routledge Handbook of the Economic History of Colonialism* (London: Routledge, 2025); Patterson, *Slavery and Social Death*, esp. 176–181; David Brion Davis, *Inhuman Bondage: The Rise and Fall of Slavery in the New World* (Oxford: Oxford University Press, 2006), esp. 48–76; Tomlins, *Freedom Bound*, esp. 428–431; Eltis, *Rise of African Slavery*, esp. 57–84; John S. Harpham, *The Intellectual Origins of American Slavery: English Ideas in the Early Modern Atlantic World* (Cambridge, MA: Harvard University Press, 2025).

The English colonization of Virginia produced moments of intense drama, including Pocahontas's alleged saving of Captain John Smith, vicious battles between Powhatans and English, and a revolt led by Opechancanough against the English captured in a 1628 engraving from the workshop of Theodor de Bry, which continued to produce illustrations well after the death of the engraver himself in 1599. James Reeve, who engraved a full page for Smith's 1624 *Generall Historie of Virginia*, drew on the de Bry workshop's earlier illustrations for Thomas Harriot's *Briefe and True Report of the Newfound Land of Virginia* even though, by the time of Smith's book, English colonists knew that Harriot was describing the Outer Banks and adjacent territory of the Carolina Algonquians and Smith wrote about the Powhatans and Chesapeake Bay. By the time Smith's book appeared, Opechancanough, depicted in Reeve's illustration in the top right, had led the surprise attack that devastated much of the English colony in 1622.

Smith facing off against Opechancanough (upper right corner) and other scenes from Smith, *Generall Historie of Virginia* (London, 1624). Courtesy of the Huntington Library, San Marino, California.

Pocahontas saving Smith. From Smith, *Generall Historie of Virginia* (London, 1624). Courtesy of the Huntington Library, San Marino, California.

In 1628, six years after the rebellion led by Opechancanough in Virginia, the de Bry workshop printed this engraving by Matthäus Merian. The image emphasized what Europeans saw as the brutality of the moment. In *Dreyzehender Theil Americae*. Courtesy of the John Carter Brown Library.

In the decades when the Dutch laid a claim to Manhattan Island and the surrounding territory, colonists saw the fur trade as so central to their economic livelihood that they proposed a coat of arms with two beavers on it, though in the end they replaced them with lions. They also remade the island's landscape, as this mid-century view depicts.

Dutch proposed coat of arms. Courtesy of the New-York Historical.

New Netherland. By permission of the Rijksmuseum, Amsterdam.

By the middle decades of the seventeenth century, Europeans' eagerness to expand sugar cultivation in the Americas led them to increase the number of enslaved Africans they transported against their will to the tropics. Hostility against the conditions of their life prompted enslaved in Barbados to plot a rebellion in 1675. The colony's leaders suppressed that insurrection. The ferocity of the trade began even before bound women, children, and men arrived in the Caribbean when their captors hauled them into notorious prisons, like the one on Elmina, to await the dreaded and often deadly Middle Passage.

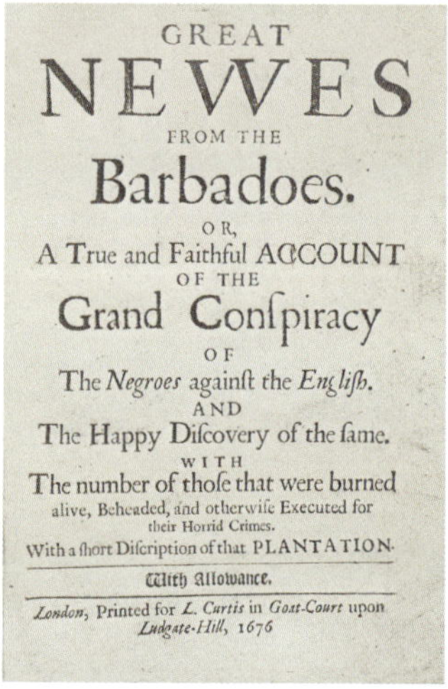

GREAT
NEWES
FROM THE
Barbadoes.
OR,
A True and Faithful ACCOUNT
OF THE
Grand Conſpiracy
OF
The *Negroes* againſt the *Engliſh*.
AND
The Happy Diſcovery of the ſame.
WITH
The number of thoſe that were burned alive, Beheaded, and otherwiſe Executed for their Horrid Crimes.
With a ſhort Diſcription of that PLANTATION.

With Allowance.

London, Printed for *L. Curtis* in *Goat-Court* upon *Ludgate-Hill*, 1676

Courtesy of the Huntington Library, San Marino, California.

Elmina prison. By permission of Österreichische Nationalbibliothek.

Long after Las Casas's account of the destruction of the Indies riveted European readers, enterprising printers continued to circulate the text, adding illustrations that drew attention to some of the most graphic accounts in the book. This page from *The Teares of the Indians*, a 1656 English-language book, kept the idea of the "black legend" alive for new generations of readers. Courtesy of the Huntington Library, San Marino, California.

News of the rebellions that led to widespread loss of property and lives in the 1670s, especially across New England, immediately caught the public's attention. John Seller, a mapmaker who was the English royal hydrographer, included a detail about a battle between Indigenous and colonial soldiers on his contemporary map. The war's memory lingered long after the last fires had gone out. Metacom, a figure reviled by English colonists in the 1670s, became an object of fascination during the era of the American Revolution, evident in Paul Revere's portrait for Thomas Holmes's *The Entertaining History of King Philip's War* (1772). Bacon's Rebellion remained a fixture in the study of the nation, as this image of a still-smoldering Jamestown from David B. Scott's 1879 *A School History of the United States, from the Discovery of America to the Year 1878* suggests.

Seller map. Courtesy of Yale Digital Collections.

Paul Revere created his portrait of Metacom, or King Philip as he called him, almost a century after the war that claimed hundreds of lives across New England. Courtesy of Yale University Art Gallery, Mabel Brady Garvan Collection.

Bacon's Rebellion. From Scott's *A School History of the United States*. Library of Congress Prints and Photographs Division, 02005162.

The enduring power of the images first created by John White in 1585 and then engraved by the de Bry workshop in 1590 can be seen in this 1675 painting by James Woolridge that depicts the palisaded town of Pomiooc as well as Carolina Algonquians burning out the inside of a canoe, sitting down at a feast, and gathered around a fire in a ritual—all scenes that had appeared in the 1590 book. The painting reveals the power of images more than a commitment to accuracy. Reprinted by permission of the Crystal Bridges Museum of American Art.

The Pueblo Revolt drove Spaniards out of New Mexico for twelve years and destroyed many aspects of the colony's earliest history. This seven-foot tall pink marble statue of Po'pay by the sculptor Cliff Fragua, from Jemez Pueblo, can be found in Emancipation Hall in the U.S. Capitol Visitor Center. In the front, Po'pay holds the knotted cords that the Pueblos used to coordinate their assault on Spanish colonizers. The reverse of the statue depicts scars on his back, a vivid reminder of the physical suffering that Po'pay endured in 1675, an experience that shaped the views that led to his actions in 1680. Courtesy of Architect of the Capitol.

22

An Empire for Extraction

In 1650, an English engraver named Edward Williams produced "A mapp of Virginia discovered to ye Falls." Most of the map, which was oriented with north to the viewer's right, presented details about the East Coast, from Cape Cod to Cape Fear, place-names that exemplified English attitudes about one locale famed for its economic utility and another for shallow waters that could doom a voyage. The typography on the map reflected politics. Williams included Maryland in lettering smaller than Virginia, and Carolana as an inland locale reached by a bay starting at Roanoke Island and then splitting into two rivers bearing Indigenous names. He included the locations of the Virginia villages of Elizabeth City, Jamestown, Charles City, and Henrico City. He marked the northern side of the Delaware as New Albion and recognized a Swedish claim on the south. The Dutch controlled the Hudson Valley, with a large beaver stretched out between the two rivers, a visible marker of the most valuable animal to be hunted. The thin sliver between the crest of the Appalachians and the Pacific offered few details, other than noting that Drake had arrived on the West Coast in 1577 at 37° north latitude. Williams believed the English could get to the Pacific in a mere ten days' march from the head of the James. He added a western opening to a bay that fed into "A Mighty great Lake," which joined the Hudson just south of New France. Seventy-five years after Frobisher's efforts, the English would finally control the Northwest Passage—at least on a map.[1]

Williams's map cast political fictions across North America. Like many other European maps, it obscured as much as it revealed. By 1660, Europeans had managed only to create fragile frameworks for colonies in five corners of North America: the Southwest, claimed by Spaniards; the St. Lawrence Valley and the Great Lakes, which the French hoped to

1. [Edward Williams], "A mapp of Virginia discovered to ye Falls, ([London], 1651), John Carter Brown Library, 30653-1.

This "mapp of Virginia" depicted the mid-Atlantic coast, from modern North Carolina to the Hudson River, as territory where rivers reached deep into the interior, a visual encouragement to those who may have contemplated colonization or wondered about continued investments there. While cartographer Edward Williams identified the presence of both Swedes and Dutch, there is little here to suggest that the region remained dominated by Native peoples. In that sense, it was more an encouragement for investment than an accurate rendering of the peoples who lived there at the time. [Edward Williams], "A mapp of Virgina discovered to the Hills . . ." Courtesy of the John Carter Brown Library, 30653-1.

dominate; the Atlantic coast from Maine to Carolina, where English and, to a lesser extent, Dutch believed they had founded durable communities; Florida and a thin band around the northern edge of the Gulf of Mexico, where Spaniards had turned over most of their colonizing energy to priests; and the Caribbean, where Europeans, reliant on indentured and enslaved laborers, had transformed bucolic, ecologically complex islands into wealth-generating sugar plantations. The rest of North America remained in Indigenous control, despite boundary lines drawn by Europeans like Edward Williams.

During the 1660s and 1670s, English policymakers hoped to expand their North American territory and their access to exportable commodities. They now faced new challenges. Few migrants headed toward New England, likely aware of the fact that there was no need for their labor given the natural population growth that had followed the so-called Great Migration of 1630 to 1642. Some looking for work did head toward the Chesapeake, but their numbers had ebbed, perhaps a reflection of diminished opportunity for those who survived their indentures as well as of new opportunities in England.

The decline in emigration to North America was not a problem unique to the English. New Netherland had failed to attract many Dutch immigrants even before the English claimed it in 1664.[2] New Sweden, never as vibrant or attractive as New Netherland, became an afterthought. Tales of woe emanating from the Caribbean, especially from disillusioned Irish migrants, depressed possible European migration to the islands, where planters had already made the fateful decision to import enslaved Africans to produce sugar. Virtually no one in France wanted to go to Canada. The combined non-English colonial population in the Americas—including Florida, New Mexico, and the St. Lawrence Valley—likely never exceeded 10,000. Across North America, colonizers found themselves in a position analogous to European slavers in West Africa: they could bring goods that they could sell, but beyond limited territory near the coast or major inland waterways, they needed to attract customers for their wares. The success of their ventures depended on positive relations with powerful Native nations.[3]

Although their situation was not unique, it was in this moment that English politicians, flush with the enthusiasm of political rebirth at home and more eager to pursue opportunities in North America than their European rivals, saw an opening. Starting in 1660, they created a new political structure, embodied in a series of navigation acts, to control the flow of goods across the basin. The politics of empire extended beyond the desire for material wealth, of course, evident in yet more violence between European competitors. But underlying English efforts to reorganize politics at the moment of royal restoration was a newfound commitment to garner profits from the western shores of the Atlantic.

Europeans had recognized the potential of the Western Hemisphere since the publication of Columbus's first report in 1493. In restructuring their relations with overseas possessions, the English put themselves into a position to transform the aspirational claims on maps like Williams's into reality. Unconcerned about evidence of the environmental consequences of an unfettered pursuit of profit, the architects of an emerging

2. Oliver A. Rink, "The People of New Netherland: Note on Non-English Immigration to New York in the Seventeenth Century," *New York History* 62 (1981), 4–42.

3. See Sean M. Kelley, *American Slavers: Merchants, Mariners, and the Transatlantic Commerce in Captives, 1644–1865* (New Haven, CT: Yale University Press, 2023), 23–47.

empire created the legal apparatus to make even greater profits from their economy of extraction. Unlike the Elizabethan notion of exporting workers to produce goods valued at home, investors came to rely ever more on the labor of non-Europeans, seizing opportunities regardless of their human costs. It was, many thought, time to get what they always wanted: more.

Soon after the Restoration, Charles II, secure in power, wanted to generate more revenue at home by increasing exports from English working on ships or abroad. On September 13, 1660, he authorized a new navigation act, which would take effect on December 1. A decade earlier, those who wanted to participate in trade had to ship their goods on English-owned ships. Now the king decided to limit participation in such business to his own subjects, which included those born in colonies, as well as any who had been naturalized or become a free denizen. The authors of the 1660 act also tightened the provisions of existing regulation by enumerating certain commodities that would be subject to particular fees. Anyone who produced sugar, tobacco, dyestuffs, and ginger in an English colony in Africa, America, or Asia had to ship those goods directly to English territory. Under the terms of the act, the king's customs officials would receive 2 pence per pound, a fee based on weight that guaranteed revenue regardless of the price of a commodity.[4] Three years later the king authorized another act that demanded that ships participating in trade between England and its colonies be "laden and shipped" only from England, Wales, or Berwick upon Tweed in Northumberland County on the border of Scotland.[5]

With the legal foundation for the movement of commodities set, the crown expanded its territory with the acquisition of Tangier and Bombay (via the king's 1661 marriage to Catherine of Braganza of Portugal), which he proclaimed would be free ports where merchants could buy and sell without paying duties, though they had to use English ships and sailors for any goods going to England and Ireland. He also imposed new rules on English colonists in North America. Royal officials began with a charter for Connecticut in 1662. The new colony, whose non-Indigenous residents

4. The Navigation Act of 1660 (12 Chas. II, c. 18), https://www.british-history.ac.uk/statutes-realm/vol5/pp246-250 (accessed January 24, 2025). Freight rates for English colonies remained constant at £3 per ton; see Lawrence A. Harper, *The English Navigation Laws: A Seventeenth-Century Experiment in Social Engineering* (New York: Columbia University Press, 1939), 268n121.

5. The Navigation Act of 1663 (15 Chas. II, c. 7), https://www.british-history.ac.uk/statutes-realm/vol5/pp449-452 (accessed January 24, 2025). The bill made an exception for salt needed for fishing crews and wines produced in the Azores and Madeira.

had come from Massachusetts, was to stretch from Narragansett Bay in the east, with a southern border along Long Island Sound, and west to the Pacific Ocean. Anyone born in the colony would be a subject of the king and enjoy the benefits that entailed, including the right "upon just Causes to invade and destroy the Natives, or other Enemies of the said Colony." Its first governor was to be John Winthrop Jr., the son of the Massachusetts governor who had died in 1649.[6] New Haven colony, which never had its own royally approved charter, soon joined Connecticut.[7] Rhode Island's new charter resembled Connecticut's, but it included a clause that its government should not attack Natives within its bounds without first informing other colonies in New England, none of whom could act against Indigenous in Rhode Island without prior notice. The clauses, unusual in governing documents for the period, suggested awareness in London that the war of 1637 had perhaps produced more of an appearance of long-term peace than actual comity on the ground. Charles accepted Rhode Island's tradition of religious toleration and clarified that its members owed no allegiance to the Church of England.[8]

Organizing new mainland American colonies constituted only a part of the king's desire to expand English authority in the Atlantic basin to maximize profits. Toward that end, he brought renewed attention to fisheries. English monarchs since Edward III in the fourteenth century had proclaimed the realm's ownership of seas adjoining its coastline. That did not halt Dutch fishing crews, which had begun to trawl the waters around Lewes in 1594. When local English captains complained to James I, he realized that the fisheries and the fortunes of each nation were inseparable.[9] In the years that followed, other monarchs also sought ways to support

6. Charles II, "A Proclamation Declaring His Majesties Pleasure to Settle and Establish a Free Port at His City of Tanger in Africa," November 16, 1662, University of Michigan Digital Collections, https://quod.lib.umich.edu/e/eebo/A32397.0001.001?rgn=main;view=fulltext; Tristan Stein, "Tangier in the Restoration Empire," *Historical Journal* 54 (2011), 985–1011; Charter of Connecticut, 1662, Avalon; *The Life of Edward Earl of Clarendon* (Oxford, 1660–1661), 1:333–335.
7. On June 4, 1639, residents of the towns in the region signed on to the Fundamental Agreement, or Original Constitution of the Colony of New Haven, but this was a local document never recognized by any English king or even Cromwell, who had hoped to entice its colonists to migrate to Ireland, Hispaniola, Mexico, and Jamaica after he seized those places. The Fundamental Agreement is in Avalon; for the failure of Cromwell's idea and the town-by-town capitulation to Connecticut, see Charles M. Andrews, *The Colonial Period of American History*, 4 vols. (New Haven, CT: Yale University Press, 1934–1938), II:173–174 (Cromwell's plan), 187–194 (surrender).
8. Charter of Rhode Island and Providence Plantations, July 15, 1663, Avalon.
9. John R. Elder, *The Royal Fishery Companies of the Seventeenth Century* (Glasgow: James Maclehose and Sons, 1912), 1–14.

the fisheries. Because salt was used to preserve the catch, Charles I granted monopolies to two salt companies, which would pay fees to the treasury, but their workers would be exempt from military service. He subsequently created the Society of Saltmakers, located in Durham and Northumberland, and imposed orders fixing the price of the commodity.[10]

On June 12, 1661, Charles II authorized an act to promote fisheries in Scotland. Over the following months, a number of fishing companies launched their efforts, all of which benefited from favorable terms, including the suspension of duties during their early years.[11] On August 22, 1661, the king appointed his brother James, the Duke of York, and other members of the gentry to be the Council of the Royal Fishing of Great Britain and Ireland, a body with the authority to adjudicate any disputes relating to fishing. On February 6, 1662, he forbade the sale of meat on each Wednesday, Friday, and Sunday during Lent, driving up demand for fish and hence supporting poor fishing families. On March 12, 1664, the king formalized the initiative in a new corporation, with James as its governor. A lottery would raise funds, and the company would provide work for "many of the lazy and idle people," an echo of the promotional dreams of the Elizabethans. The company hired Samuel Pepys, an avid diarist and naval official, to be one of its assistants.[12] He and others bore witness to the emergence of an empire at a moment when a small group of politically connected, wealthy investors poured capital into multiple companies engaged in far-flung commerce and colonization.[13]

On May 15, 1664, four English ships bound for North America set off from Portsmouth under the command of Richard Nicolls. Rough seas dispersed the convoy, but they reconvened off Nantucket. On July 29, the

10. Cecil T. Carr, ed., *Select Charters of Trading Companies, A.D. 1530–1707*, Publications of the Selden Society 28 (London: B. Quaritch, 1913), 142–160, 167–172.

11. "Charles II—Volume 40: August 1661," in *Calendar of State Papers Domestic: Charles II, 1661–2*, ed. Mary Anne Everett Green (London, 1861), 54–79, *British History Online*, http://www.british-history.ac.uk/cal-state-papers/domestic/chas2/1661-2/pp54-79; Elder, *Royal Fishery Companies*, 90–92, 97–98.

12. Elder, *Royal Fishery Companies*, 90–92, 97–101; Carr, ed., *Select Charters of Trading Companies*, civ–cvi, 182–186, quotation at 182. For Pepys's involvement, see his diary for March 4, July 7, and September 5, 1664, at https://www.pepysdiary.com.

13. See, e.g., Thomas Mun, *England's Treasure by Foreign Trade, Or, The Balance of our Forraign Trade is The Rule of our Treasure* (London, 1664), sig. A3^{r-v}, B^{r-v}; Barry M. Gough, "The 'Adventurers of England Trading into Hudson's Bay': A Study of the Founding Members of the Hudson's Bay Company, 1665–1670," *Albion* 2 (1970), 35–47. Mun died before the book reached print, but his son John had it published in 1664.

flotilla set sail for Manhattan. On August 18, they picked up soldiers from the English Long Island militia. Word spread quickly to Peter Stuyvesant, who had become the director of the colony of New Netherland in 1647 after Kieft's War. Knowing that he lacked the military might to halt the invasion, which formed an early part of the broader second Anglo-Dutch War, which would begin in 1665, Stuyvesant dispatched messengers up the Hudson and down to the Delaware in a failed effort to rally support.[14]

With an armed invasion imminent, Stuyvesant welcomed Governor John Winthrop Jr. from Connecticut, who had stepped forward to act as an intermediary between Nicolls and the Dutch. The two leaders met in a tavern, where the English official gave Stuyvesant a letter from Nicolls detailing a promise that the English would concede certain terms to the Dutch in exchange for the director's surrender. As soon as the governor left, Stuyvesant ripped up the offer, but not before other Dutch had heard about the contents. Facing a rebellion from his own colonists, Stuyvesant pieced the ripped paper together. Once they heard the contents, ninety-three local officials wrote to Stuyvesant, detailing their diminished prospects and urging an end to the standoff. The director conceded, knowing that what mattered most to him at that moment—that Dutch troops could leave the fort under their own flag and that the English would allow any Dutch who wanted to sail eastward to travel without risk—had been achieved.[15]

On August 27, English and Dutch representatives met at Stuyvesant's house to settle the final details. The timing was auspicious for Nicolls, who understood that he might soon lose militiamen eager to get home for the harvest and that two of the naval ships had to set off for home. The agreement offered much to Dutch colonists who chose to remain, including the freedom to practice their religion as they wanted, continued use of the port for the WIC for another six months, permission for local officials to stay in place until the next election, and preservation of colonists' property rights. With the agreement signed, Stuyvesant and his soldiers marched under their own flag to the port, boarded the *Gideon,* and sailed for Amsterdam. With Manhattan secured, Nicolls dispatched ships to bring the peripheries of the former colony under control.[16]

Even back home, Stuyvesant's ordeal was not yet over. Summoned to the States General, he explained that resistance would have been futile

14. Robert C. Ritchie, *The Duke's Province: A Study of New York Politics and Society, 1664–1691* (Chapel Hill: University of North Carolina Press, 1977), 20–21.
15. Ritchie, *Duke's Province*, 21–22.
16. Ritchie, *Duke's Province*, 20–24.

since the Dutch were so outnumbered by nearby English. Worse, wars with Indigenous had prompted many Dutch to leave earlier, and many who stayed had taken shelter in Fort Amsterdam, a place he found "more a molehill than a fortress, without gates, the walls and bastions trodden under foot by men and cattle." The situation had not improved since, leaving the colony exposed to the maritime invasion of late August, shortly before a harvest likely would have put the Dutch into a stronger position.[17]

On the ground, the shift in governance of Manhattan and nearby territory mattered less than many Dutch colonists probably feared. Wealthy patroons with vast estates along the lower Hudson maintained their properties, and merchants around Manhattan continued to conduct business as before, just under an English flag instead of a Dutch one. In the years to come, the early coexistence of Dutch and English colonists provided a model for what was soon known as New York City, which boasted the most diverse population to be found in North America.

By the middle of the 1660s, slivers of North America had begun to look like parts of Europe, especially in Boston and Manhattan. Church spires, rare across the continent at the dawn of the century, rose in scattered locales—several in New Mexico, a few along the St. Lawrence, and more regularly in an arc from Boston to the Chesapeake, including churches in Dutch-turned-English territory. Ships traversed the Atlantic more regularly, hauling cod from Georges Bank to northwest Europe and enslaved Africans to the West Indies and northeastern South America. Among those who made the journey westward were poorer English men and women. Even after the enslavement of Africans had begun to take hold, some still signed up as indentured servants, perhaps lured by promoters' published tracts.[18]

Even the most avid English promoters soon learned that their fortunes teetered on unseen forces: disease-bearing microbes, wars within Europe,

17. Letter of the Town Council of New Amsterdam, September 16, 1664, and Stuyvesant's testimony to the States General, October 16, 1665, in J. Franklin Jameson, ed., *Narratives of New Netherland, 1609–1664* (New York: Scribner's, 1909), 452–453, 458–466, quotation at 459. Stuyvesant made accusations about the failure of Dutch intelligence, based on a report he had received on April 21, 1664, which he presented to the States General as proof that he was not the only one to miss the English king's actual intent at the time; see 461–462.

18. See, e.g., *A Brief Description of the Province of Carolina on the Coasts of Florida* (London, 1666), 1–3, 9–10.

Indigenous American resistance, and the all-too-human motivations of resentment, envy, and anger. Crises on the eastern shores of the Atlantic could undermine Europeans on the western edges, as the English learned when London, the most important destination for American goods and the point of export for young women and men looking for work, suffered through two of the greatest calamities in its history, erasing the good feelings that had blossomed after a major naval victory over the Dutch at Lowescroft in June 1665.[19]

In the summer of 1665, plague returned to England, which had been spared a major epidemic since 1603. Warning signs such as primroses and violets blooming out of season, meteor trails in the night sky, and wells drying up sent fears across the realm. But no one anticipated the ferocity of this strain of the disease, which took the lives of 920 in Cambridge alone—about 12 percent of the town's entire population. Three of every four who became sick in the university town perished.[20]

Plague had hit London with some regularity in the previous two generations, but never to this degree. Official counts calculated from bills of mortality identify 68,596 who died in 1665 and 1666, or about 15 percent of the city's population. The real death toll was likely higher, quite possibly over 100,000. Wealthy residents fled, including Charles II, who went first to Hampton Court and then to Oxford. In the capital, novelist Daniel Defoe later reported, workers dug a pit forty feet long, fifteen feet wide, and twenty feet deep for a mass grave. Poor women, men, and children, barely making a living in the city before the epidemic, died far more frequently than those with means. Urban crowding and rat-inviting piles of garbage in the streets made the city an ideal locale for plague-bearing fleas. Efforts to ward off plague through perfuming the air, drinking vinegar infused with wormwood, and boiling off swellings with homemade concoctions failed. Authorities closed down every theater, concert, and pub, turning the once-vibrant city into a ghost town. Mourners could not pray near their deceased relatives. "Thus this month ends with great sadness upon the publick," diarist Samuel Pepys wrote on August 31. The plague killed 6,102 that week alone, out of a total loss of life of 7,496. "But it is feared that the true number of the dead, this week is near 10,000," he

19. Steven C. A. Pincus, *Protestantism and Patriotism: Ideologies and the Making of English Foreign Policy, 1650–1668* (Cambridge: Cambridge University Press, 1996), 276–286; J[ohn] Dolben, *A Sermon Preached before the King . . . June 20th. 1665, Being the Day of Solemn Thanksgiving for the late Victory at Sea* (London, 1665).

20. Evelyn Lord, *The Great Plague: When Death Came to Cambridge in 1665* (New Haven, CT: Yale University Press, 2014), 128.

continued, "partly from the poor that cannot be taken notice of, through the greatness of the number, and partly from the Quakers and others that will not have any bell ring for them." The toll abated during the cold months, but the deaths began again in the spring, often striking neighborhoods it had spared earlier.[21]

Pestilence devastated families across much of England. None knew how the disease that took victims across the society spread. Church officials, who believed that plague emanated from miasma and could be detected through noxious smells, dispatched workers to clear out a ditch in Cambridge cluttered with dead rats. John How, one of the men charged with the task, died soon after working there, as did one of his children. Smoking tobacco, believed to ward off the scourge, offered no help. Refugees from other plague-infested locales fled to London, exacerbating the local situation.[22]

On September 2, 1666, with plague still spreading in and around London, fire broke out on Pudding Lane. The flames spread quickly, destroying the houses on nearby streets as well as the Church of St. Magnus the Martyr, and panic soon followed. Acrid smoke filled the air; warehouses stocked with brandy and wine went up in flames. Hour after hour, fearful residents tried to preserve their possessions. Embers flew through the darkening sky, setting roofs alight, "and, as it grew darker," Pepys recalled, "appeared more and more, and in corners and upon steeples, and between churches and houses, as far as we could see up the hill of the City, in a most horrid malicious bloody flame." He wept when the arc of the fire spanned the river. "The churches, houses, and all on fire and flaming at once," Pepys despaired, "and a horrid noise the flames made, and the cracking of houses at their ruins."[23] The flames burned for days. The roof of St. Paul's collapsed. Landlords stood to lose £600,000 a year. Rumors swirled that French agents had set the capital alight, but Londoners were too busy trying to preserve their remaining property to

21. *London's Lord have mercy upon us* ([London, 1665]); *Orders Conceived and Published by the Lord Mayor and Aldermen of the City of London, concerning the Infection of the Plague* (London, [1665]); Donald J. McGraw, "Etiology of the 1664–1665 Black Plague in London," *Bios* 41 (1970), 109–113; Pepys online diary for August 31, September 14, December 31, 1665, and April 5 and 23 and August 6, 1666. A 2013 archaeological analysis of a mass grave in Farringdon revealed the remains of perhaps 50,000 victims; see Gwyn Topham, "Builders Unearth Medieval Plague Victims in City of London Square," *The Guardian*, March 15, 2013.
22. Lord, *The Great Plague*, 27 (tobacco), 49 (portents), 96 (How).
23. Pepys diary, September 2, 1666.

pay much attention.[24] By the time residents had brought the conflagration under control, much of medieval London was gone. Engravers soon produced images that captured both the extent of the flames and the height of the fire, which illuminated the night sky and struck terror into any who saw it.[25]

The fire consumed eighty-four churches, at least 13,000 dwellings, and some of the city's most famous buildings, including the Guildhall, the prisons at Newgate and Ludgate, and even the gates to the city. Somewhat surprisingly, it took relatively few lives, possibly because the sound of the flames racing through narrow streets produced extraordinary noise from crackling wood, exploding houses, and neighbors' shrieks. Access to the Thames helped too, as individuals rushed to its banks to preserve their lives and whatever property they could grab. The extraordinary mortality from the plague reduced the potential loss of life in the fire since there were fewer poor crowded into ramshackle houses.

A parliamentary commission investigating possible causes placed blame on French and Irish Catholics.[26] To those caught up in the politics of the war with the Dutch, the flames owed their origin to malevolent enemies who lurked in the city's shadows. For the monarch's political foes, the fire signaled divine displeasure with the Restoration.[27] Clerics linked the fire to the plague, two signs of their god's displeasure at public arrogance and licentious behavior.[28] Unusual weather likely contributed too, notably a shift in prevailing winds. Normally, London's residents lived with cool and damp air, a result of prevailing westerly winds. That season, the winds came from the east—drier than normal and hence lacking the natural fire suppression that breezes normally brought. The combination of extraordinary fuel and unseasonal winds explains why the fire, hardly the first in the city, so quickly raced ahead of any human

24. Pepys diary, September 5, 6, 15, and 7.

25. Simon Turner, "A Print of the Great Fire of London," *Print Quarterly* 26 (2009), 18–27.

26. *London's Flames: Being an Exact and Impartial Account of Divers Informations Given in to the Committee of Parliament* (London, 1679), 1, 4–5, 8.

27. Pincus, *Protestantism and Patriotism*, 347–348.

28. Edward Stillingfleet, *A Sermon Preached before the Honourable House of Commons, At St Margarets Westminster* (London, 1666); *Londons Lamentations: Or, Some affectionate breathings forth on London's late Ruines by FIRE, Begun Septemb. 2, 1666* (London, 1665 [actually 1666]), sig. A2r; *A Short and Serious Narrative of Londons Fatal Fire* (London, 1667), sig. A2r; J.A., *Upon the late Lamentable Fire in London* (London, 1667), verse XII (sig. B2v); William Sancroft, *Lex Ignea: Or The School of Righteousness* (London, 1666), quotations at 19–20 (Dutch and French), 46–47 ("Grimaces of Sorrow"); and, for the context, see Jack Gilpin, "God's Terrible Voice: Liturgical Response to the Great Fire of London," *Anglican and Episcopal History* 82 (2013), 318–334.

efforts to suppress it.[29] Psychology mattered too: rather than fight the fire, many fled in panic.[30]

The crises of 1665 and 1666 revealed the close connections between England and its North American colonies. On the ground at home, the blaze demonstrated the structural problems of cities built without due attention to the larger environment, a situation that would eventually change when scientific expertise—including about how cities should be engineered—gained social value that it had never possessed earlier.[31] But in the short run, the catastrophes created new opportunities. The leading architects of the day, including Christopher Wren, suddenly had a broad canvas on which to imagine more capacious works as well as the relationship of buildings to each other, rather than having to squeeze new creations into an urban landscape that had evolved willy-nilly for centuries.[32]

Put simply, constructing a post-medieval city provided jobs for legions of young unemployed and underemployed from across the king's realm. Before 1665, many of them saw little opportunity in their villages, in port towns, or even in London, and their migration to the capital put many at risk in overcrowded wooden houses that stood no chance against the flames. These mobile women and men often booked passage for lives in North America. By the start of 1667, the employment situation in England looked more promising than it had since at least the mid-sixteenth century. Any who might have been tempted earlier to sell their labor for seven years' service on a tobacco plantation or to sign on at the docks to haul goods across an unfamiliar ocean had other options. Almost immediately, ship captains and plantation owners saw a drop in the number of those signing contracts to work in the Western Hemisphere. Bristol, a traditional source of such migrants, witnessed a steep decline in servants booking passage for America. The decline began in 1664 and bottomed

29. The London fire, in this sense, was like other well-known urban conflagrations; see Stephen J. Pyne, *Fire: A Brief History* (Seattle: University of Washington Press, 2001), 102–118, esp. 107–109.
30. *A True and Exact Relation of the Most Dreadful and Remarkable Fires . . . In the Cities of London and Westminster and other Parts of England* (London, 1666).
31. Jacques Heyman, "The Crossing Space and the Emergence of the Modern Professional Architect and Engineer," *Construction History* 31 (2016), 25–60.
32. The rebuilding reflected new opportunity as well as the retention of some traditional ideas; see Kathleen James-Chakraborty, *Architecture Since 1400* (Minneapolis: University of Minnesota Press, 2014), 174–179; Emily Mann, "In Defence of the City: The Gates of London and Temple Bar in the Seventeenth Century," *Architectural History* 49 (2006), 75–99, esp. 81–82.

out in 1665 and 1666. After the drop in the number of those willing to sail to the West Indies, the figures never recovered. By 1680, the number departing from Bristol for the islands had fallen to almost nothing.[33] The pattern repeated across the English-speaking Atlantic. The substantial migration streams that had sent 200,000 to either the West Indies or the Chesapeake during the seventeenth century dried up.[34] London, which had always absorbed newcomers, many of whom suffered in poverty, continued its demographic ascent, sparking economic growth across the realm.[35] When he oversaw the reconstruction of St. Paul's, Wren recognized the utility of gathering stone and marble from many locations, which produced quarrying and hauling work across Britain, including teams to carry large blocks from the Thames to the site.[36]

Had he been concerned only with the homeland, Charles II would have likely celebrated the decline in unemployment produced by the increased need for labor. But ever since he married Catherine of Braganza in 1661, the king had embraced opportunities to expand the economic reach of his realm. In 1663 he had reorganized the Royal African Company (RAC) and installed his brother James as its primary director, thereby embracing the realm's wider commercial horizons regardless of the moral stain it might produce. To the king, the RAC provided a mechanism for fulfilling the labor needs on English American plantations. Further, shipping enslaved Africans would generate additional payments to the royal treasury and might minimize Dutch power across the Atlantic.[37]

In 1667, the English concluded their war with the Dutch with an imperial trade of distant territories: Pulau Run (in the Spice Islands of the Southwest Pacific) and Surinam (in northeastern South America) to the

33. See James Horn, "Servant Emigration to the Chesapeake in the Seventeenth Century," in Thad W. Tate and David L. Ammerman, eds., *The Chesapeake in the Seventeenth Century: Essays on Anglo-American Society* (Chapel Hill: University of North Carolina Press for the Institute of Early American History and Culture, 1979), fig. 4 (85).

34. Nicholas Canny, "English Migration into and Across the Atlantic During the Seventeenth and Eighteenth Centuries," in Nicholas Canny, ed., *Europeans on the Move. Studies on European Migration, 1500–1800* (Oxford. Oxford University Press, 1994), table 4.1 (64). Note that the table mislabels the majority who went to the Chesapeake as mostly post-1660 when it should have been pre-1660.

35. See E. A. Wrigley, "A Simple Model of London's Importance in Changing English Society and Economy, 1650–1750," *Past and Present* 37 (1967), 44–70.

36. James W. P. Campbell, "The Supply of Stone for the Rebuilding of St. Paul's Cathedral, 1675–1710," *Construction History* 28, no. 2 (2013), 23–49.

37. See William A. Pettigrew, *Freedom's Debt: The Royal African Company and the Politics of the Atlantic Slave Trade, 1672–1752* (Chapel Hill: University of North Carolina Press for the Omohundro Institute of Early American History and Culture, 2013), 22–23.

Dutch, New Netherlands (already under English control) and the Gold Coast outpost of Cape Corso to the English.[38]

With those issues settled, Charles and his court turned more attention to Africa. In 1672, the king rechartered the RAC. The new charter clarified that, in the minds of the company's organizers, African bodies were the equivalent of gold and silver: each could be extracted and sold as the company saw fit. The company specified four destinations and costs for enslaved men or women between the ages of twelve and forty: £15 for those headed for Barbados, £16 for Nevis, £17 for Jamaica, and £18 for Virginia, the cost going up in proportion to the length of the voyage.[39] The company had a monopoly on the English slave trade, supported by courts set up at "forts[,] plantations[,] or factories" on the West African coast that had the authority to seize assets from any ship that violated the terms of the charter. As long as it existed, the monopoly allowed the less wealthy to purchase enslaved bodies, thereby extending the practice to a wider share of the colonial population.[40]

Once reorganized, the company directed its ships toward three primary markets in the West Indies: Barbados, Jamaica, and Nevis. In 1673, the number of enslaved arriving in Barbados on company ships was 200, but the next year a total of 1,945 enslaved Africans survived the harrowing journey to the Caribbean—1,066 to Barbados, 410 to Jamaica, and 469 to Nevis. By 1676, the total reached almost 3,600, with over half (1,836) arriving in Barbados alone. In 1680, the company transported more than 4,300 enslaved to the islands: 1,673 to Barbados, 1,623 to Jamaica, and 819 to Nevis. In all, from 1673 to 1680, 22,170 enslaved Africans arrived in the Caribbean on the company's ships, primarily to Barbados (10,315), Jamaica (7,100), and Nevis (3,978), with 777 going to Antigua, St. Christopher, and Montserrat (in 1679 and 1680). These numbers do not include the thousands who did not survive the journey nor take account of the deadly conditions that remained in the islands.[41]

38. *A Perpetual League of Mutual Defence and Allyance between His Majesty, and the Estates General of the United Provinces of the Low-Countries* (London, 1668); Pincus, *Protestantism and Patriotism*, 387–392; Herbert H. Rowen, *John de Witt, Grand Pensionary of Holland, 1625–1672* (Princeton, NJ: Princeton University Press, 1978), 611–633.

39. *Calendar of State Papers Domestic, 1669–1674*, no. 985 (444); K. G. Davies, *The Royal African Company* (New York: Atheneum, 1970), 294–295.

40. "African Company," in Carr, ed., *Select Charters of Trading Companies*, 186–192; Trevor Burnard, "'A Pack of Knaves': The Royal African Company, the Development of the Jamaican Plantation Economy and the Benefits of Monopoly, 1672–1708," *Journal of Colonialism and Colonial History* 21 (2020); Maxine Berg and Pat Hudson, *Slavery, Capitalism and the Industrial Revolution* (Cambridge: Polity, 2023), 17–18.

41. K. G. Davies, *The Royal African Company* (London: Longmans, 1957), appendix III (361–364).

On May 2, 1670, Charles II approved a charter for the Governor and Company of Adventurers of England Trading into Hudson's Bay, known as the Hudson Bay Company (HBC). Like other grants from the time, the boundaries were expansive in direct proportion to European geographic ignorance about the American north. The company gained access to the "North-west Part of America," specifically the lands surrounding all the rivers that drained into Hudson Bay and Hudson Strait. As a result, the company claimed land surrounding Hudson Bay, the largest inland sea in the world, and reaching into any territory not already claimed by a Christian prince. The land stretched from the Atlantic to the Rocky Mountains, and in places from the Arctic to the northern plains of the modern United States. Its 1.5 million square miles was five times larger than France. In effect, the company gained ownership of all trade and territory stretching from modern northern Labrador and Quebec and including most or all of modern Saskatchewan, Alberta, and Manitoba, along with large sections of Nunavut, the Northwest Territories, and western Ontario, plus a small part of the northern plains of the United States. On their maps, the English called this territory Rupert's Land. When the Canadian government later purchased the land from the company, it encompassed one-third of the modern nation.[42]

The king's charter recognized that this territory had Native inhabitants but made no provision for how they were to fall under the company's jurisdiction. Since the English at the time still believed that the land was unsuitable for anything other than producing natural resources such as furs or, they still hoped, minerals, its managers spent little time devising plans for how to live alongside Indigenous. Unlike colonies where English hoped to profit from agriculture, which demanded a labor force to produce exportable crops, the company directors instead planned for Native hunters to perform the necessary labor. Rupert's Land, unlike other territory that the English claimed, would be a colony without colonists.

The HBC, like the RAC, reflected an English preoccupation with material gain. In this sense, policymakers departed from earlier imperial bureaucrats who dreamed of establishing Christianity as the dominant faith in parts of North America that as yet had few European colonizers. HBC organizers harbored no such illusions of grandeur. Instead, the

42. *The Royal Charter for Incorporating the Hudson's Bay Company* (London, 1865), quotation at 5; Ann M. Carlos and Frank D. Lewis, *Commerce by a Frozen Sea: Native Americans and the European Fur Trade* (Philadelphia: University of Pennsylvania Press, 2010), 4–5, 38–39.

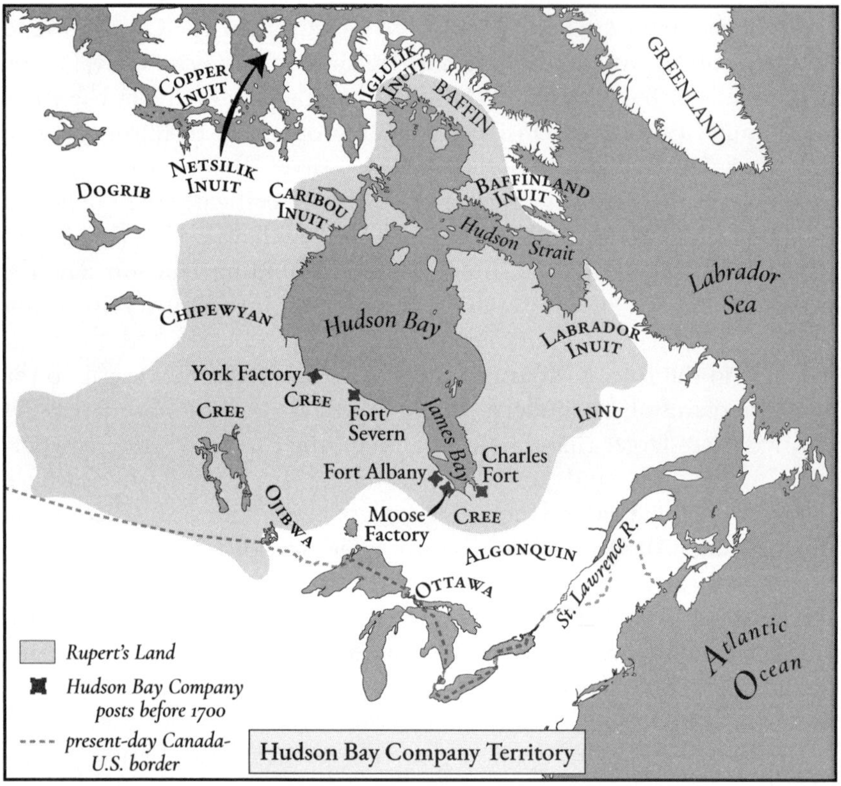

directors in London saw the venture in economic terms, a chance to capture a valuable market with no competitors. With the Dutch removed as imperial rivals from the Hudson Valley and the French still concentrating their energies in the St. Lawrence Valley, the English were the only ones sailing oceangoing ships toward Hudson Bay. It was a sensible calculation. When French officials complained almost twenty years after the HBC secured its charter, English officials used the European doctrine of discovery to rebut the attempt, reinforcing their claim to the area by asserting a right derived from the voyages of Cabot and Hudson.[43]

Yet a secure title, or at least one recognized by other European nations, meant little on the ground in northern North America. The success the HBC achieved depended on establishing positive relations with Inuit, Cree, Assiniboine, and other northern plains nations. Over time, that calculation—and a realization that Europeans needed to understand the

43. CO 1/62, no. 49; CO 135/2, 18–28; CO 135/2, 34–48; CO 1/49, no. 92; see also Hudson's Bay Company to the Lords Commissioners, March 4, 1699, CO 134/3, no. 8.

desires of Indigenous consumers—proved wise, as the growing coffers of the HBC revealed by the early decades of the eighteenth century.[44]

In 1644, the colonial population of Virginia stood at 8,000. By the early 1660s, it topped 25,000, and in 1674, it approached 32,000 despite the fact that London's twinned disasters reduced immigration. The population expanded because colonists born and raised in Virginia never experienced "seasoning," the kind of systemic physiological shock that felled so many migrants. It helped that by the 1660s servants tended to arrive in autumn instead of summer, a shift that allowed ship owners to reduce risk from worms that ate through hulls in summer.[45] While parental death was still common, families tended to remain intact, in large part because there were so many more men than women (in the first decades) that any woman who wanted to marry and have a family could do so, and any man who lost his wife (for example, in childbirth) often became a tempting potential mate for a young woman looking for someone who already had an established household.[46] Psychological trauma was common, but household economics tended to be stable, at least among the non-servant colonial population. Colonists also planted orchards, which improved their diets and enabled them to produce cider, which reduced the frequency of drinking possibly contaminated water. The growing number of colonists in Maryland, where the population of newcomers mushroomed from approximately 8,300 in the mid-1640s to almost 34,000 two decades later, provided additional demographic stability for the English.[47]

The increase in population benefited those who wanted to sell tobacco in England and on the continent and encouraged those who saw the importance of domestic consumers purchasing products made by English colonists abroad, but it was an economic setback for recently liberated

44. See Carlos and Lewis, *Commerce by a Frozen Sea*, 96–105.

45. Edmund S. Morgan, *American Slavery, American Freedom: The Ordeal of Colonial Virginia* (New York: W. W. Norton, 1975), 184 and table 1 (404).

46. Lorena S. Walsh, "'Till Death Us Do Part': Marriage and Family in Seventeenth-Century Maryland," in Tate and Ammerman, eds., *Chesapeake in the Seventeenth Century*, 126–152; Darrett B. Rutman and Anita H. Rutman, "'Now-Wives and Sons-in-Law': Parental Death in a Seventeenth-Century Virginia County," in Tate and Ammerman, eds., *Chesapeake in the Seventeenth Century*, 153–182.

47. Darrett B. Rutman and Anita H. Rutman, *A Place in Time: Middlesex County, Virginia, 1650–1750* (New York: W. W. Norton, 1984); Morgan, *American Slavery, American Freedom*, 183; Lorena S. Walsh, *Motives of Honor, Pleasure, and Profit: Plantation Management in the Colonial Chesapeake, 1607–1763* (Chapel Hill: University of North Carolina Press for the Omohundro Institute of Early American History and Culture, 2010), 131.

servants. Earlier, tobacco had generated high profits because the plant was scarce and the price high. Those boom times had ended in the 1620s, a time when colonists in Virginia exported 500,000 pounds of tobacco each year. The price began to fall by mid-century and remained low because the supply kept increasing, with planters increasing production by a factor of ten from 1640 to about 1670. By 1663, customs houses in London registered the arrival of more than 7 million pounds of tobacco; six years later the volume reached 9 million pounds, and by 1672 it topped 10.5 million pounds. Prices for tobacco remained in a trough.[48]

Because the crown profited from the volume of tobacco shipped to England under the terms of the Navigation Act, the price of the plant was of no concern to the monarch. But for young farming families who understood that tobacco was the only crop they could plant that could generate the cash they needed to build a house, purchase seed and livestock, and clothe (let alone educate) their growing families, not producing tobacco meant isolation from the market, a situation that few found desirable. They found themselves caught in an unvirtuous cycle. The Tidewater land that produced the best tobacco was out of their reach, as was the supply of potential labor necessary to produce a labor-intensive crop. Looking for opportunity, they moved to marginal lands, where they then had to find a way to transport what they had to market and haul goods back to their houses, many of them so flimsy that they could blow over in a strong wind. The rich built with bricks, but the rest used and reused wood, creating impermanent houses, barns, and curing sheds.[49] Each additional harvest only added to an oversupplied market.

The decline in price was less important to royal officials in London than the continued duties to be extracted from the shipment of tobacco. In the 1660s, tobacco duties alone might have constituted one-fourth of the realm's total customs revenue. The only way to raise the price would be to limit production. Since tobacco was being grown by colonists in Maryland and Carolina as well as Virginia, any of the three colonial administrations could undermine an effort to fix the price by not participating in an agreement. In 1667, Lord Baltimore vetoed the Maryland assembly's agreement to limit production, ending whatever scenario existed for inter-colonial cooperation. For their part, the wealthiest

48. Morgan, *American Slavery, American Freedom*, 185, 203–204; Russell R. Menard, "Farm Prices of Maryland Tobacco, 1659–1710," *Maryland Historical Magazine* LXVIII (1973), 80–85; Walsh, *Motives of Honor*, 101–102, 131; Allan Kulikoff, *Tobacco and Slaves: The Development of Southern Cultures in the Chesapeake, 1680–1800* (Chapel Hill: University of North Carolina Press for the Institute of Early American History and Culture, 1986), 78–82.

49. Morgan, *American Slavery, American Freedom*, 185.

planters continued to produce as much as they could. Members of the Virginia House of Burgesses, who were themselves prosperous planters or merchants, tried to magnify their gains by seeking ways to have servants stay longer on their farms. By the mid-1660s, that meant supporting a system that encouraged their English agents to send them adolescents who had to serve until they were twenty-four. In two counties, the median age of servants from 1662 to 1680 was fifteen to sixteen. Servants who broke the law—by running away (most commonly), getting pregnant, or slaughtering a hog they found in the woods—had extra years added to their contracts.[50]

With their prospects hemmed in by the fall in tobacco prices and the unavailability of good, affordable land, many onetime servants decided to become tenants instead of freeholders, exchanging a meager chance to own land to gain a semblance of security—a calculation that made sense for most people who wanted to start a family. Often they agreed to plant an orchard, build a house, and pay rent in tobacco. The alternative to tenancy was to become a hired hand, once again using their labor to fatten the coffers of wealthier members of their community. Their efforts made landowners' investments more valuable but did little for the long-term economic prospects of young women and men. For their part, planters used hired workers to create integrated businesses: their workers cleared fields, planted seeds, dried mature plants, packed tobacco in hogsheads built on the premises, and hauled the barrels to a dock where the owner might maintain a storefront as well. Landlords who traveled to London might have complained about the low cost for their tobacco, but they retained control over the goods they brought back, charging whatever prices they could to workers who had few economic options.[51]

Despite promising demographic signs, the Chesapeake colonies suffered a series of setbacks starting in 1667, a year in which a fierce April hailstorm destroyed newly planted tobacco and corn fields and killed livestock. In June, during the ongoing Anglo-Dutch War, five Dutch ships arrived at the mouth of the Chesapeake. They switched their own flags out for English flags, and colonists fell for the ruse. Within ten days they had destroyed the H.M.S. *Elizabeth*, a massive forty-six-gun frigate that was only thinly defended when it was being repaired, burned at least five ships hauling tobacco from Maryland and Virginia, and stole twelve other vessels.[52] During the summer, the skies unleashed a biblical forty days of

50. Morgan, *American Slavery, American Freedom*, 193–194, 216–217.

51. Morgan, *American Slavery, American Freedom*, 221–224.

52. Donald G. Shomette and Robert D. Haslach, *Raid on America: The Dutch Naval Campaign of 1672–1674* (Columbia: University of South Carolina Press, 1988), 126–128.

rain, which devastated the tobacco crop that survived the hail. A hurricane struck on August 27, ripping down lesser wooden houses as well as fences, enabling cows and pigs to trample whatever fields might still have crops in them. Six years later, despite knowing that another Dutch attack could come, Virginia had still not managed to rebuild its defenses. Aware that they faced risks from the Dutch at sea, planters in Virginia and Maryland agreed to postpone the tobacco ships until mid-July 1673. The delay gave time for Dutch warriors, eager to avenge the loss of New Netherland, to arrive at the Chesapeake. The invaders destroyed at least 3,000 hogsheads of tobacco; captured seven ships, including one based in London that was hauling 1,050 hogsheads; and destroyed another ten vessels. To make matters worse for the Virginia colonists, an epizootic took the lives of 50,000 head of cattle that year, further weakening their economy.[53]

The range of problems that unfolded during the 1660s and 1670s would have tested any colonial administrator's ability to maintain order when the underlying material conditions posed one challenge after another to a growing population of native-born free women and men who had limited economic horizons. In Virginia, the challenge fell to William Berkeley, who had been governor of the colony under Charles I from 1642 to 1652, when he resigned after Cromwell's victory, but regained his position with the Restoration and the sudden death in January 1660 of another governor. In 1661, he sailed for London, hoping to assure Charles II of his loyalty and gain support for a plan to reorient Virginia away from its reliance on tobacco and toward what he saw as a more durable, diversified economy. In 1663, the Oxford-educated Berkeley, who had been a playwright in his thirties, wrote a short tract laying out his plans for what Virginia could become once it broke its addiction to the "vicious ruinous plant." Despite the colony's overreliance on tobacco, Berkeley believed that Virginia's natural assets would "make it the Fortresse, Mart and Magazin of all the *West Indies*." Finding a way to limit the crop's production and bringing in new migrants would bring prosperity.[54]

Berkeley's public appeal fell on deaf ears in England, where continued tobacco imports generated profits, and among the emerging landed aristocracy of the colony. His scheme also did nothing for struggling former servants. Wage labor and farm tenancy became more common options than owning a freehold. Still, his ideas did elicit a response from the assembly, which established bounties to encourage shipbuilding and the

53. Shomette and Haslach, *Raid on America*, 130–133, 137–138, 148–161; Morgan, *American Slavery, American Freedom*, 242–243.

54. [William Berkeley], *A Discourse and View of Virginia* ([London, 1663]), 2, 4.

production of linen, wool, and silk. The landscape of Virginia, remade once with the expansion of tobacco across Indigenous fields in the tidewater, began to diversify. Jamestown started to look like a proper capital to the governor and his allies. Eager to show the powerful that his plans could work, Berkeley boasted about the corn he exported to Barbados in 1667, and the next year he sent the king 300 pounds of silk. Challenges remained, of course, primarily related to the tension that had always existed for English in the Chesapeake: how to gain and then allocate land in ways that minimized social friction, and how to find the labor needed to produce tobacco. As Berkeley would soon learn, even a master politician could be challenged in unexpected ways.[55]

English policymakers' commitment to North America becomes clear when considered in comparison to England's two major European competitors, Spain and France. From a demographic perspective, Florida was a backwater. Its colonial population, a century and a half after Ponce de León had explored its coasts, could be numbered in the hundreds, most of them farmers trying to eke out a living around St. Augustine and a small number of Catholic missionaries who had moved into Indigenous communities across the panhandle. Resentment within Indigenous communities fueled violent rebellions in Guale in 1645, Appalachee in 1647, Timucua in 1656, and Apalachicola in 1675. Missionaries thought that they could establish firm footholds, but they often miscalculated.[56] A similar situation existed in New Mexico. Other than the small community at Santa Fe, Franciscans, colonial farmers, and imperial soldiers were inadequate to overcome threats posed by Natives, as the immigrants would learn to their horror in 1680. By century's end, Florida's colonial population stood at no more than 1,500 and New Mexico at about 3,000.[57]

A Franciscan effort to establish a mission in the modern panhandle of Florida revealed the uneasy dynamic in the parts of North America claimed by Spain.[58] The Apalachee town of Anhaica had attracted Spaniards from the time of their first *entradas* in the 1520s and 1530s. Those encounters had proved deadly for Apalachees, especially when de Soto used their home as the basis for his soldiers during the winter of 1539–1540.

55. Morgan, *American Slavery, American Freedom*, 186–192.
56. David J. Weber, *The Spanish Frontier in North America* (New Haven, CT: Yale University Press, 1992), 122, 133, 141.
57. Weber, *Spanish Frontier*, 89–91.
58. Details here from Bonnie G. McEwan, "Colonialism on the Spanish Florida Frontier: Mission San Luis, 1656–1704," *Florida Historical Quarterly* 92 (2014), 591–625.

Franciscans arrived toward the end of the first decade of the seventeenth century, though they lacked permission from the regional governor to establish a mission until 1633. In the intervening years, the spread of Old World diseases and forced labor from the introduction of the *repartimiento* system had reduced the population of Timucuas, Mocamas, and Guales who lived along the Atlantic coast. By contrast, the Apalachee farmers of Anhaica, separated by almost 200 miles from St. Augustine, rebounded from their earlier loss, which made their town more inviting to missionaries.

The first resident Franciscans moved to Anhaica in 1633. Within five years, Spanish authorities stationed soldiers there and a frigate arrived from St. Augustine, a journey that took only thirteen days. The growing presence of the newcomers could be seen when the Franciscans arranged for the building of eight churches across Apalachee lands. Spanish colonizers' increasing control over the region produced tensions that erupted in 1647 when many Apalachees, perhaps aided by other Indigenous in the region, burned seven of the churches and killed three priests and at least one colonial family. There was division among the Apalachees about what to do. Several of their leaders guided five surviving priests into Timucuan territory. When the Timucuans rose in rebellion in 1656, Spanish authorities turned toward the Apalachees again, not only as allies but also because the Indigenous population of modern northern Florida had dropped precipitously. In its aftermath, Governor Diego de Rebolledo y Suárez de Aponte, who had taken office in 1654, tried to fortify a *camino real* that would run from St. Augustine to Anhaica, known to Spaniards as Mission San Luis. In response, Indigenous leaders moved the center of their activities to a new site, which the Spanish would call San Luis de Talimali. An uneasy truce settled over the region, but in the long run it did not benefit the Apalachees, whose numbers continued to drop.

The colonial presence took a severe toll even among those who had converted to Christianity. By century's end, two local caciques—Don Patricio (of Ivitachuco) and Don Andrés (of San Luis)—complained to the Spanish king about being forced to build a garrison for Spanish soldiers. The job took a toll on local forests and discouraged at least some members of their communities from attending Mass for fear that they would be pressed into additional service. To make matters worse, famine and smallpox together struck Florida in mid-century, with devastating results: 10,000 Natives died between 1655 and 1662. The population of the Apalachees dropped from 16,000 in 1638 to approximately 5,000 forty years later.[59] Indigenous decline did not trigger a new wave of Spanish

59. Robert A. Matter, "Mission Life in Seventeenth-Century Florida," *Catholic Historical Review* 67 (1981), 401–420, esp. 412.

emigration. New Mexico was essentially a colony of New Spain and never perceived as a place that was crucial to the Spanish imperial vision. Souls could be harvested there, but local silver deposits amounted to little compared to those from Potosí. Few Spanish or creole families wanted to take a chance in the arid Southwest.

To the north, New France beckoned weakly. During the seventeenth century no more than 300 migrants took the six-to-nine-week journey from France to the St. Lawrence each year, even though devastating famines from 1660 to 1662 and 1675 to 1679 forced many people to wander France looking for work. A plan by the king to subsidize migration from 1662 to 1671 collapsed. From 1663 to 1673 royal officials subsidized the migration of 774 women known as *filles du roi*, who accepted free passage with the understanding that there were ample unmarried men in New France eager to marry. Yet attempts to convince larger numbers of potential migrants failed, perhaps because even advocates for colonial development admitted to pervasive problems: cold winters, rattlesnakes, mosquitoes, and threatening Indigenous peoples. Even lowering the service term for male indentured servants to three years proved insufficient. Canada's poor reputation in France was so pervasive that many who might otherwise have gone in search of opportunity refused to board ships, opting instead for a life of uncertainty and likely poverty.[60] A census taken in 1663 identified French colonists in three communities, none of them especially populous. The region around Trois-Rivières probably had around 600 non-Indigenous residents. Montreal was marginally larger, but it numbered only 760. Québec, the site of Champlain's greatest efforts, was the largest, but there were still under 3,000 colonizers there.[61]

While the numbers remained low—the Canadian total of just over 4,000 *habitants* amounted to less than one-eighth of the non-Native population of Maryland—the census revealed continuing commitment to spreading Roman Catholicism and an early indication of family formation, a crucial sign for a colonial region that had never attracted many migrants from the home country. Québec alone had forty-three priests, fifteen of whom were Jesuits. They had come from various parts of France, with the largest number—nineteen in all—emigrating from Normandy, the origin point for Champlain a half-century earlier. But the village

60. Peter N. Moogk, "Reluctant Exiles: Emigrants from France in Canada Before 1760," *WMQ* 46 (1989), 463–505; Pierre Boucher, *Histoire Véritable et Naturelle des Moeurs & Productions du Pays de la Nouvelle France* (Paris, 1664), esp. 135–163.

61. Marcel Trudel, *La Population du Canada en 1663: Recensement Reconstitué* (Sillery, QC: Éditions du Septentrion, 1995), 67.

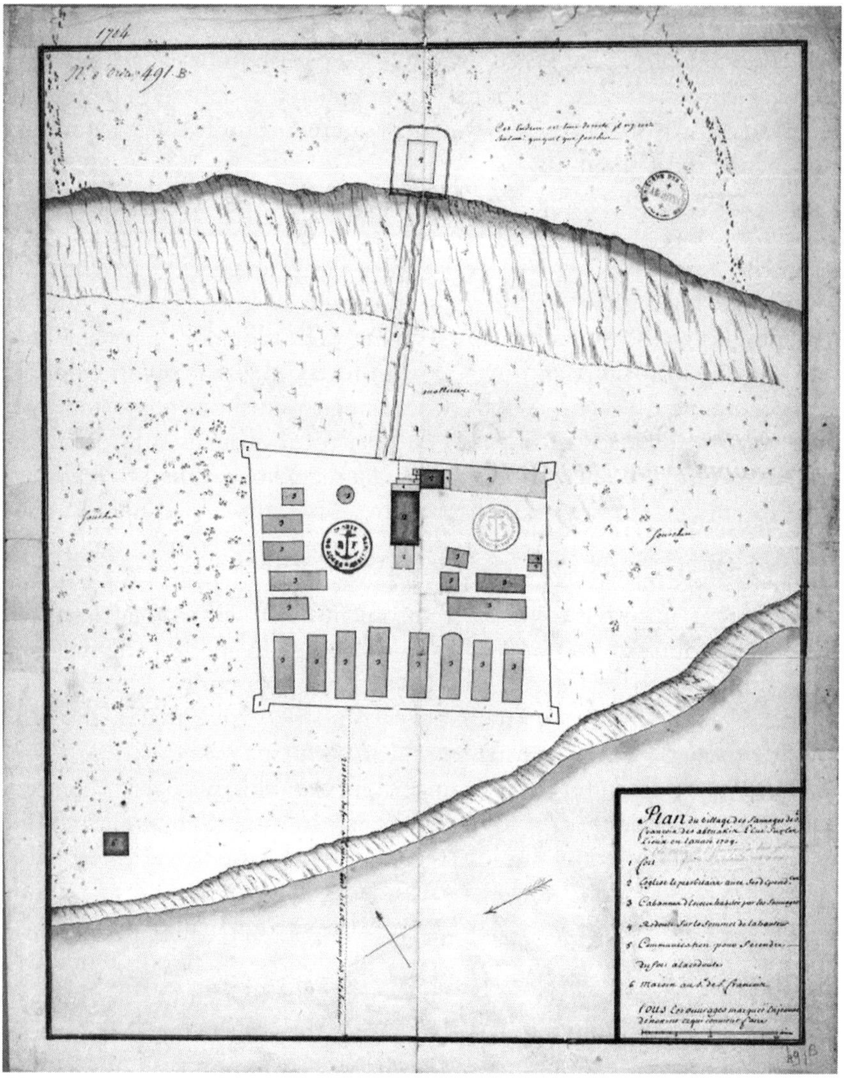

Jacques Levasseur de Néré's 1704 "Plan of the Native village of St. Francois des Abenakis" depicts a church and a fort in the midst of approximately twenty Native houses, a visual sign of how French colonizers remained greatly outnumbered long after France had laid a claim to the St. Lawrence Valley. Archives Nationales d'Outre-Mer, Aix-en-Provence, 03 DFC 491B.

attracted women religious too, primarily Ursulines (eighteen) and Hospitalières (seventeen). As with the male religious, the largest number (thirteen) came from Normandy. Beyond these celibate communities, an emerging balance in the sex ratio had led to some natural increase. Mathieu and Marie Amiot Dit Villeneuve, he (age thirty-six) born in

Picardie and she (age thirty-three) in Saintonge, had nine children in their household when the census taker made his enumeration. The number of their children was exceptional, but other women and men had begun to have children there as well. Other communities attracted religious too, though not as many as Québec: there were three Jesuits and one nun in Trois-Rivières and four Sulpicien brothers and eight religious women in Montreal. Among Montreal's families was the Ailleboust des Muceaux household, with a father aged thirty-nine born in Champagne, his twenty-eight-year-old wife from Normandy, three children born in Québec, and another three born in Montreal. Each of these communities had also begun to experience economic diversification. While many of the *habitants* were presumably farmers or laborers (*travaillants*), there were also merchants as well as those who offered the skills of a barber-surgeon, mason, weaver, baker, butcher, carpenter, cabinetmaker, gardener, nail-maker, wheelwright, gunsmith, and soldier.[62]

Not surprisingly, French colonists tended to erect buildings that fit their long-standing architectural ideas. While perhaps hoping to express through architecture that it would be possible to build a new France, the small size of the immigrant population (even with their growing families) suggested the limits of their interest. The St. Lawrence Iroquoians may have dispersed, but into the eighteenth century French cartographers nonetheless depicted Wendat and Haudenonsaunee longhouses outnumbering houses built—or in the planning stage—for *habitants*.[63]

When European colonial dreamers gazed upon maps of the world beyond their borders, they imagined the great profits that would come to their realms if they could find ways to claim and occupy distant lands. For the English, developing North American colonies was supposed to address domestic problems relating to perceptions of overpopulation. All the sugar and tobacco in the world would mean nothing if unemployed and underemployed residents destroyed the social order.

English-claimed eastern North America became the arena in which to assess whether an empire built on extraction could work. As it turned out, it could, at least if measured in population gains. The non-Indigenous

62. Trudel, *Population du Canada*, 74–78 (religious), 80 (Québec family), 236 (Trois-Rivières), 274–275 (Montreal); see also Louise Dechêne, *Habitants and Merchants in Seventeenth Century Montreal*, trans. Liana Vardi (Montreal: McGill-Queen's University Press, 1992), 42–62.

63. Gauvin Bailey, *Architecture and Urbanism in the French Atlantic Empire: State, Church, and Society, 1604–1830* (Montreal: McGill-Queen's University Press, 2018), 55–78 and passim.

population of New England grew from about 33,000 in 1660, including 600 African or African American residents, to almost 52,000 by 1670, of whom 400 were of African origin, and to about 69,300 in 1680, with a Black population of 500. Virtually all the growth in the region's population came from natural increase among colonists.[64] The non-Indigenous population of New York, along with small numbers in modern Delaware and New Jersey, reached about 7,400 in 1670, including 800 of African origin, and almost 15,000 by 1680, including about 800 Africans or African Americans.[65] In 1660, Virginia and Maryland together had a combined population of approximately 25,000, of whom 900 were of African origin. Ten years later, the European colonial population stood at about 38,500 and the African and African American population had grown to 2,500. By 1680, the African and African American population had grown by about 80 percent (to 4,300) while the European colonial population increased by about one-third (to approximately 55,600). In Carolina, the minuscule non-Native population of 1660 (1,000 people of European origin) grew to 4,000 by 1670 (including 200 of African origin) and to 6,600 in 1680 (of whom likely 400 were enslaved Africans). In 1660 there were 47,000 individuals of English, Irish, or Scots descent in the English Caribbean along with 34,000 of African origin. Ten years later, the non-African population had decreased to 44,000 as the African population reached 52,000. This demographic trend continued until 1680, when there were 42,000 non-Africans in the Caribbean and 76,000 Africans, virtually all of them enslaved. Barbados alone had over half (65,400) of the total population (118,000) in English-controlled islands. These immigrants, their numbers enhanced by enslaved Africans, continued the physical transformation of the land that earlier colonizers had initiated.[66]

By century's end, over half a million English women, men, and children had left home for Atlantic destinations. The largest number, approximately 190,000, traveled to the West Indies, most before 1660. Another 180,000 sailed across the Irish Sea, the shortest migration. From this perspective, the renewed English attention to the North American mainland

64. John J. McCusker and Russell R. Menard, *The Economy of British America, 1607–1789* (Chapel Hill: University of North Carolina Press for the Institute of Early American History and Culture, 1985), 101–103.

65. Rink, "The People of New Netherland"; Sung Bok Kim, *Landlord and Tenant in Colonial New York: Manorial Society, 1664–1775* (Chapel Hill: University of North Carolina Press for the Institute of Early American History and Culture, 1978), 4–5; McCusker and Menard, *Economy of British America*, 203; Bernard Bailyn, *The Peopling of British North America: An Introduction* (New York: Knopf, 1986), 20–43.

66. McCusker and Menard, *Economy of British America*, 135–139 (Chesapeake), 169–172 (Carolina), 149–155 (Caribbean).

might seem insignificant. But the navigation acts and the increase in the slave trade testified to the realm's desire to garner wealth from the Western Hemisphere.[67] So did the increase in the volume of American-made goods arriving in England and Wales.[68]

The emergence of this transatlantic commercial system proved to be a revolution just as powerful as the spread of maize centuries earlier. The first had led to population growth and created optimal conditions for Europeans looking to expand their colonies. The latter made permanent the export of American resources to serve European customers, regardless of the cost for enslaved Africans and displaced Indigenous and the reduction of ecological diversity. The economics of extraction worked for Europeans seeking material gain.

67. At the end of the century, the white population of British America, which then included New York, East and West Jersey, and Pennsylvania, totaled 272,400, from a total migration (including the West Indies) of 530,500. See Canny, "English Migration," 39–75, esp. table 4.1 (64); McCusker and Menard, *Economy of British America*, 103, 136, 153, 172, 203 (white population in 1700); Bailyn, *Peopling of British North America*, 20–43.

68. Elizabeth Boody Schumpeter, *English Overseas Trade Statistics, 1697–1808* (Oxford: Clarendon Press, 1960), tables XV (value of imports to England and Wales), VI (source of imports), XVI (quantity of imports), and XXXIII (beaver hats).

23

A New England

New England, perhaps more than any other part of North America, reflected the opportunities and costs of European colonization. From the time of the epidemic of 1616–1619, the region had witnessed the greatest loss of Indigenous life anywhere north of New Spain. Further, its clean water and temperate climate provided immigrants with a healthy climate as well as an ideal setting to create communities free of the problems of Europe. An arc running from modern-day Down East Maine along the coast to Long Island Sound and inland as far as the Connecticut Valley became a laboratory for what Europeans, especially English, hoped to create in this emerging new world.

By the third quarter of the seventeenth century, the colonial population of New England was similar to the Chesapeake's in size. Almost all its growth had come from migrants who had arrived between 1630 and 1642, testimony to the benefits to be had when environmental and demographic conditions proved ideal for creating new communities. On the ground, clustered in small towns along the shores or on rivers that ran to the sea, these American-born colonists were more concerned with affairs in Boston, fast becoming the region's commercial and political hub, than with those in London.[1] Less connected to producing wares for long-distance trade than planters in the Chesapeake or Barbados, many colonial women and men in New England had the economic independence to advance the goals that had propelled their parents across the ocean. But as its colonial residents realized, ongoing threats—from demons, Quakers, and Indigenous, among others—needed to be contained, an effort that led to the execution of some English migrants and the quest for a way to coexist with Ninnimissinuok, the Algonquian-speaking peoples who still dominated much of the region.

1. See Mark Peterson, *The City-State of Boston: The Rise and Fall of an Atlantic Power, 1630–1865* (Princeton, NJ: Princeton University Press, 2019), 27–84.

The so-called Great Migration that funneled English migrants to New England came to an end when domestic politics in Britain convinced religious dissenters to stay home to advance their cultural agenda. But the migratory pattern had enormous long-term implications. Before 1642, adult migrants had often crossed the Atlantic with children, with each family hoping to inhabit a "little commonwealth" where the father took on the role of beneficent ruler, modeling proper decorum to provide the moral guidance to sustain church-oriented communities. Clean water and a relative lack of infectious diseases led to a drastic increase in population, with families often having up to ten children, the vast majority surviving the perilous early years that felled so many in Europe. This population growth encouraged colonists to create new towns. With houses clustered around a central green and local church, the English divided up lands based on how much wealth each family had when they had all arrived. The richest families gained the most, making it possible for them to settle their grown children nearby. But as early as mid-century, some of the children of less prosperous migrants recognized that they would need to leave their home communities if they were going to establish households that could provide enough for the next generation, some of whom were already born by 1650. They understood that from the start those with greater assets gained access to more land in these emerging towns. Some villages even had absentee owners, a substantial departure from the idea of self-contained towns embedded in the logic of religious dissenters.[2]

Andover, Massachusetts, founded by a group of eighteen English families in 1646, exemplified attitudes toward land use and the ways that English town planners divided up the spoils of the conquest. Most who moved there had come from three counties: Hampshire and Wiltshire from southern England and Lincolnshire along the central east coast. The group first secured a grant from the Massachusetts General Court for a parcel totaling sixty square miles located about twenty miles north of Boston and fifteen miles from the ocean. The amount that each received was, according to a conversation at a town meeting on January 18, 1663, in proportion to the "estate" of each at the time of the community's founding. Those with more property got larger lots. In the initial division, the wealthiest were Simon Bradstreet and John Osgood, each of whom received a plot estimated to be twenty acres. By contrast, the majority of

2. See Virginia DeJohn Anderson, *New England's Generation: The Great Migration and the Formation of Society and Culture in the Seventeenth Century* (Cambridge: Cambridge University Press, 1991) and John F. Martin, *Profits in the Wilderness: Entrepreneurship and the Founding of New England Towns in the Seventeenth Century* (Chapel Hill: University of North Carolina Press for the Omohundro Institute of Early American History and Culture, 1991).

free householders received plots that ranged from four to eight acres. For many this represented an enormous upward economic leap from their situation before they crossed the Atlantic, especially when the householders, who eventually numbered forty by 1660, subsequently decided to allocate the rest of their initial grant.[3]

From 1646 to 1662, Andover's freemen distributed land seven times—four divisions for land suitable for planting, two for meadows, and one for the "swamp," a term colonists used to describe land so thickly wooded that the forest floor rarely dried out. Forested land had great value for immigrants who had come from areas where wood was often in short supply, a topic of popular discussion in the early decades of the seventeenth century. Woods represented the possibilities for economic gain: raw materials for housing and fuel and, in some places, an export to supply masts and other materials for ships. Many in England feared growing deforestation.[4] Although colonists had no similar qualms in New England at the time, the fear of wasting wood contributed to an enduring feature of the New England landscape: stone walls. In the parts of England where migrants had originated there were typically ancient hedgerows that separated fields. In southern New England, rocks, left behind by the retreat of the last glacier ten millennia earlier, littered the ground. In the small satellite communities that colonists created in the areas around Boston and other ports, farming families would haul rocks out of their fields to the edge, piling one on top of another. Doing so allowed them to keep their livestock in, though animals escaped constantly, and reduced the need for them to build wooden fences.[5]

When the patriarchs of Andover began to divide up their original grant, they were little concerned with preventing an unequal distribution of property. As a result, Bradstreet and Osgood received proportionally more in each successive division. Those at the lower end, who had initial grants of four-acre town lots, received 104 acres of upland, 10 acres of meadow, and 4 acres of swamp, for a total of 122 acres, more than enough to satisfy the needs of even a large family. By contrast, Bradstreet and Osgood received 520 acres of upland, 50 acres of meadow, and 20 acres of swamp, totaling 610 acres. What had once been a relatively narrow gap in

3. Philip J. Greven Jr., *Four Generations: Population, Land, and Family in Colonial Andover, Massachusetts* (Ithaca, NY: Cornell University Press, 1970), 41–60.
4. Keith Pluymers, *No Wood, No Kingdom: Political Ecology in the English Atlantic* (Philadelphia: University of Pennsylvania Press, 2021), esp. 1–58.
5. William Cronon, *Changes in the Land: Indians, Colonists, and the Ecology of New England* (New York: Hill and Wang, 1983), 127–156.

holdings between those having four acres and those having twenty had opened into a chasm.[6]

A twenty-acre parcel was still large enough to take care of a family's needs, but it would not be enough to divide evenly for the next generation. By the time the third generation—the grandchildren of the adult migrants—came of age after 1660, many believed better opportunity lay elsewhere. Rather than remaining in the same community one generation after the next, these women and men pushed on, often into territory still controlled by Indigenous peoples, many of whom had no plan to surrender or sell their traditional homelands to newcomers.[7]

Healthy bodies and a balanced sex ratio, another demographic characteristic that separated English migrants in southern New England from those near the Chesapeake or Barbados, Jamaica, or (earlier) Providence Island, meant ample opportunities for young women and men to produce children. In seventeenth-century Plymouth, for example, immigrant parents tended to have on average 7.8 children, with 7 of them surviving to adulthood. Their children were in turn even more prolific: they had 8.6 children on average, and about 7.5 survived to age twenty-one. Reaching age twenty-one was more than a statistical accomplishment. Women who reached that age in New England typically lived to 62.4 years, while men survived until they were 69 years old. Those who reached age sixty, which was most of the first and second generation, typically survived until their mid-seventies.[8]

By 1650, English colonists had imposed a new economy on territory from Boston to the Connecticut River Valley, a region that still had a sizable Indigenous presence. The majority of newcomers, judging from the locations they chose and the towns they established, had in mind new versions of the first colonial towns near the shoreline. A smaller number pushed farther away from the coast, not because they sought isolation for religious introspection but because they thought there might be greater profits to be found, especially if they could establish durable ties with Native hunters for the region's diminishing supply of beaver.

Colonial farmers in inland communities produced crops for sale, notably rye, maize, and wheat, which they hauled first to local millers and then to coastal towns. There they exchanged what they had for imported

6. Greven, *Four Generations*, 58.
7. Greven, *Four Generations*, 55–68.
8. John Demos, *A Little Commonwealth: Family Life in Plymouth Colony* (New York: Oxford University Press, 1970), tables 1 and 2 (192).

goods from England, mainland Europe, and other colonies: tobacco, salt, iron nails, knives, paper. Often these transactions occurred without any money changing hands. Instead, farmers brought in goods that merchants valued in their ledgers, and then the merchants sold farmers goods that also had specific monetary value. Such exchanges constituted a formal layer of economic behavior but did not capture the economy in its entirety because each individual and family became embedded in a web of commercial relationships that existed beyond the reach of account books. Raising a barn or building a church took the labor of a community, so neighbors participated in such common tasks, knowing very well that their neighbors would provide labor when they needed it as well. Owners of cows and sheep branded animals with distinctive marks so that those who found them could return them, typically after the owner paid for any damages their roaming four-legged companions had caused. Women's household labor might also appear invisible, cloaked by informal exchanges only rarely written down. Some historians have described the spread of the colonial economy as an emergent market-driven one. But this new economy, like the one it replaced, also rested on a web of reciprocal relationships.[9]

Judged by prevailing English measures, the colonial economy of New England was a success, at least for most immigrants and their children. Colonists added on to their houses to accommodate the large number of surviving children in each family. The range of goods to purchase at stores increased too, though many items remained relatively expensive. Merchants sold imported cloth, but women across the region likely produced most of the clothing worn in their households. Eventually, wearing homespun would be a marker of a political position, especially during the Revolution, when colonists enraged with Britain eschewed purchasing imported goods. But in the mid-seventeenth century, homespun was widespread because there were few other options. Wheat, pork, and apples could be traded for guns, powder, and rum, but free colonial families manufactured whatever they could. Tall trees might have been of use for building, but English shipbuilders eyed them too for masts.[10]

9. Greven, *Four Generations*, 67–68. See also James P. Henretta, "Families and Farms: *Mentalité* in Pre-Industrial America," *WMQ* 35 (1978), 3–32; Winifred B. Rothenberg, "The Emergence of a Capital Market in Rural Massachusetts," *Journal of Economic History* 45 (1985), 781–808; Laurel Thatcher Ulrich, *Good Wives: Image and Reality in the Lives of Women in Northern New England, 1650–1750* (New York: Knopf, 1982), 13–34; Brian Donahue, *The Great Meadow: Farmers and the Land in Colonial Concord* (New Haven, CT: Yale University Press, 2004).

10. William R. Carlton, "New England Masts and the King's Navy," *NEQ* 12 (1939), 4–18.

Colonial population growth, especially in Boston and its surrounding countryside, fueled the transformation of the landscape. Small wharves along the shoreline became the location of market stalls. Fishing crews hauled cod and lobster to the mainland, where individuals furnished their households with the profits from a catch. The first fields colonists planted had quite likely been previously cleared and planted by Native farmers, which reduced the newcomers' labor needs in the short run and enabled them to quickly plant household gardens. Colonial leaders, immersed in European ideas about how to create the most efficient and sensible cities, imposed a series of rectangular grids onto their maps, laying out proto-urban communities inspired by ideas about mercantile efficiency, notions of town planning drawn by the ancient Roman architect Vitruvius, and in some instances (such as New Haven) idealized cities from Scripture. Artisans, bricklayers, masons, and glaziers constructed warehouses and churches, part of the reshaping of the built landscape that changed the look of Salem, Boston, Newport, New Haven, and Strawberry Banke (modern Portsmouth, New Hampshire), starting at the shoreline and working inland. Developers of these towns, as well as ship captains eager to bring in cod or whales for export, often relied on bound or indebted colonists and Indigenous workers to perform vital tasks.[11]

In their best times, colonial families prospered and kept tensions within the walls of their household, obeying strictures that demanded that women be subordinate to their husbands, children loyal to their parents, and servants obedient to their employer. Everyone had responsibilities. Mothers and daughters typically maintained the house and household garden, prepared food, milked cows, wove fabric and sewed clothing, and perhaps gathered wild herbs or dug for clams; fathers and sons cleared fields, sowed seeds, brought in the harvest, chopped wood, and slaughtered livestock. If any member of a household truckled at their lack of freedom, fathers had the ultimate responsibility to keep them in line. The responsibilities of the household did not end at the edge of its property. All, whether freeholder or servant, were to be loyal to local authorities. Each household was to contribute to the maintenance of their town's minister and provide labor for tasks that benefited the community, such as clearing roads (and keeping them free of hindrances) and

11. John Archer, "Puritan Town Planning in New Haven," *Journal of the Society of Architectural Historians* 34 (1975), 140–149; Daniel Vickers, *Farmers and Fishermen: Two Centuries of Work in Essex County, Massachusetts, 1630–1830* (Chapel Hill: University of North Carolina Press for the Omohundro Institute of Early American History and Culture, 1994), 41–64. See also John R. Stilgoe, *Common Landscape of America, 1580 to 1845* (New Haven, CT: Yale University Press, 1982), 43–58, and Daniel Vickers, "The First Whalemen of Nantucket," *WMQ*, 3rd Ser., 40 (1983), 560–583.

maintaining fences or walls to keep their livestock from trampling their neighbors' fields. Townsfolk gathered periodically in town meeting halls, which the first generation of colonists typically built near the church and facing the town green. During those sessions men would discuss common problems and find solutions, with the will of the majority prevailing. Disputants who lost their arguments normally accepted the result if they had had a chance to air their views. The system, which excluded women (and children) from playing a public governing role, prevailed for decades. If all worked well, there would be little need for local constabularies and little deviance or criminality.[12]

When religious dissenters had sailed across the ocean before 1642, they wrote about creating a society where individuals would put the interests of the community ahead of those of an individual. That meant grappling with the daunting responsibility of making their churches accept only those who seemed likely for salvation, the "saints." The first colonial generation, still alive at mid-century, had created rules to promote the godly enterprise, notably through establishing elaborate processes for becoming full church members. But what happened when those communities became so crowded that children of the migrants needed to move away to gain land for their large families? What happened when colonists argued with each other?

By mid-century, some colonists began to experience anxiety about emerging psychological pressures, sometimes tied directly to profitable economic actions. If someone grew rich as a result of his or her activities, was that proof of God's favor or a sign of selfishness? In the spiritual world of the migrants, it seemed impossible to ignore the tensions that built up and often turned one neighbor against another.[13] Even the most market-oriented puritan merchant felt pangs of guilt, while the seemingly most godly must have wondered why divine providence had not led them to worldly success. Economic anxieties played out in public venues, evident in the very different careers of William Pynchon, who came to dominate a small town on the Connecticut River, and Robert Keayne, a Boston merchant.

12. See Demos, *Little Commonwealth*; Mary Beth Norton, *Founding Mothers and Fathers: Gendered Power and the Forming of American Society* (New York: Knopf, 1996); Ulrich, *Good Wives*, 13–50; Michael Zuckerman, "The Social Context of Democracy in Massachusetts," *WMQ*, 3rd Ser., 25 (1968), 523–544.

13. See Helena Wall, *Fierce Communion: Family and Community in Early America* (Cambridge, MA: Harvard University Press, 1990), esp. 30–48.

Pynchon, born in 1590 in Writtle, a village in southeastern Essex, grew up in a wealthy family. When his father, John, died in 1609, the nineteen-year-old William gained control of the family's possessions and ten years later became a churchwarden. In 1618 he married Anne Andrew. They had four children together before they became increasingly immersed in the cause of religious dissenters and decided by 1629 to sail to North America. They landed in Salem and soon established a household near modern Dorchester, Massachusetts. Anne died soon after they got established, and William then married a widow from Dorchester named Frances Sandford, resuming the kind of family life that he and his associates believed foundational to creating stable communities. They moved to Roxbury and helped to establish its church. By then, William had begun to play a leading role at the Court of Assistants in Boston, a body concerned with the colony's defense and day-to-day management. He also established a fur-trading partnership with John Winthrop.[14] By 1634, he decided to move to the Connecticut Valley to pursue the fur trade, extending his commercial connections, which now stretched from Agawam, the town that would become Springfield, to London. By the next year, Pynchon's crew was shipping ten times more beaver pelts to England than any other colonist in the Massachusetts Bay colony.[15]

In the summer of 1636, with the assistance of John Winthrop Jr., Pynchon purchased much of Agawam from its owners, also known as Agawams.[16] The agreement reflected Pynchon's understanding of local traditions, including recognition that women as well as men played a role in the transfer of property. The transaction represented a radical shift in local concepts of land. Earlier, Indigenous communities across the region believed that individuals and families could lay claim to what they produced and to hunt or fish in regions where other Native peoples might also extract resources. Pynchon recognized that for his business to move forward, he needed to convince the Agawams that they owned the land itself. By in effect making them owners of something that earlier could not be owned, he made it possible to purchase land from them, which enabled him to establish permanent residency. The Agawams agreed to allow Pynchon to conduct business and settle on specific *muckeosquittaj*

14. Malcolm Gaskill, *The Ruin of All Witches: Life and Death in the New World* (New York: Penguin Random House, 2021), 12–18; Ruth A. McIntyre, *William Pynchon: Merchant and Colonizer, 1590–1662* (Springfield, MA: Connecticut Valley Historical Museum, 1961), 5–9; Stephen Innes, *Labor in a New Land: Economy and Society in Seventeenth-Century Springfield* (Princeton, NJ: Princeton University Press, 1983), 3–4.
15. Innes, *Labor in a New Land*, 4–5.
16. William Pynchon to John Winthrop Jr., June 2, 1636, in *Proceedings of the Massachusetts Historical Society* XLVIII (1914–1915), 38–39.

(meadows), but he had no rights to their *cotinackeesh* (cultivated fields). The agreement specified that the Natives could still harvest all their fields and would retain the freedom to gather acorns, walnuts, and *saschiminesh* (peas), and could continue to fish in the river and hunt deer in the woods.[17]

In 1641, Pynchon purchased more land and began to recruit colonists to work it.[18] By 1646 the town had about 100 residents, who all shopped at the Pynchon store. When they fell into debt, the Pynchon family became their bank as well as their employer. By 1650, Pynchon had come to live like the lord of an English manor. He even adjudicated disputes as the local magistrate, including contests between Natives and newcomers. In 1641, in the midst of a dispute with Connecticut authorities, Pynchon successfully petitioned the Massachusetts General Court to transfer Springfield to the Massachusetts Bay colony's jurisdiction. Nothing seemed beyond his grasp. William returned to England in 1652 and turned over operations to his son John. From 1652 to 1657, John sent almost 14,000 pounds of beaver pelts to market, along with the skins and fur of hundreds of moose, mink, muskrat, and otter. During those five years he netted £5,520 16s, an amount that would have enabled him to purchase, if he so chose, over 850 horses or 1,000 cows.[19]

While it is tempting to see in Pynchon a prototype of an individualist seeking profits in all instances, he was also absorbed by the kind of religious fervor that characterized many of those who had sailed west in the 1630s. He had paid close attention to dissenting theology before he left England and knew that those who strayed from an orthodox line might pay for their heresy, even with their lives. Like others imbued with the eschatological frenzy of the moment, Pynchon thought that the end days had arrived. As he wrote to Governor John Winthrop in 1644, "Now is the day of Antichrist's great overthrow at Armageddon."[20] Five years later he sent a theological manuscript to London, published the next year as *The Meritorious Price of Our Redemption, Justification, &c Cleering it from some*

17. Harry A. Wright, ed., *Indian Deeds of Hampden County* (Springfield, MA, 1905), 11–12; Gaskill, *Ruin of All Witches*, 19–21; David M. Powers, "William Pynchon, the Agawam Indians, and the 1636 Deed for Springfield," *Historical Journal of Massachusetts* 45 (2017), 150–158.
18. Land purchase, April 20, 1641, in *Proceedings of the Massachusetts Historical Society* XLVIII (1914–1915), 51–54.
19. Innes, *Labor in a New Land*, 8–12; Bernard Bailyn, *The New England Merchants in the Seventeenth Century* (Cambridge, MA: Harvard University Press, 1955), 53–55. For the monetary conversion, see "Currency Converter: 1270–2017," TNA, https://www.nationalarchives.gov.uk/currency-converter/#currency-result (accessed July 31, 2025).
20. Michael P. Winship, "Contesting Control of Orthodoxy Among the Godly: William Pynchon Reexamined," *WMQ*, 3rd Ser., 54 (1997), 795–822, esp. 796 (possible execution) and 807 (Armageddon).

common Errors. The book aroused criticism among the colony's leaders, but Pynchon went back to England before he ever appeared before them to answer for his possible deviation from their orthodoxy.[21]

Keayne ran into different problems. Born in 1595 in Windsor in Berkshire County, he spent his adolescence, from age ten to eighteen, as an apprentice in the Cornhill district of London, a commercial center. In 1615, at age twenty, he became a member of the Worshipful Company of Merchant Taylors, which had been founded in 1327. At twenty-two, he married a woman named Anne Mansfield. By 1625 she had given birth to four children, though only one survived. By then he had become a member of the Honourable Artillery Company of London. He also became an early investor in New Plymouth, though he sold his interest in 1626. Like other religious dissenters entering into a life of commerce, he paid attention to spiritual affairs as well. The notes he took on sermons later filled three volumes. On July 17, 1635, he, Anne, and their son Benjamin sailed to Boston on the *Defence*. He quickly set up a house and shop near the center of the nascent town. In March 1636 he became a full member of the First Church. He had fulfilled the goal that drove many English dissenters across the ocean: material success and spiritual liberty. He was an exemplar of the core ideology of this colonial enterprise.[22]

In 1636, Keayne joined a committee of the Boston Town Meeting whose purpose was to handle the colony's business, including keeping track of town lots. Yet within three years, others had begun to wonder about his own business practices. In November 1639 one colonist charged him with marking up the price of certain goods beyond what was acceptable. The sums were trifling, but he was accused of violating the unspoken rules of fair trading

21. William Pynchon, *The Meritorious Price of Our Redemption, Justification, &c Cleering it from some common Errors* (London, 1650); Winship, "Contesting Control of Orthodoxy," 809–815; Philip F. Gura, "'The Contagion of Corrupt Opinions' in Puritan Massachusetts: The Case of William Pynchon," *WMQ*, 3rd Ser., 39 (1982), 469–491; Philip F. Gura, *A Glimpse of Sion's Glory: Puritan Radicalism in New England, 1620–1660* (Middletown, CT: Wesleyan University Press, 1984), 304–322. As Winship noted, Pynchon's text is so complex that modern observers have concluded that he was not guilty of Arminianism (whose adherents believed in free will), Antinomianism (the idea that the elect could be free from moral laws), or Socinianism (a doctrine that denied the sanctity of the Trinity). His critics believed it crucial to exile him because of his departure from their views, even if they did not view his argument as falling into otherwise identified heretical beliefs.

22. Bernard Bailyn, "The Apologia of Robert Keayne," *WMQ*, 3rd Ser., 7 (1950), 568–572; Bernard Bailyn, ed., *The Apologia of Robert Keayne . . . The Self-Portrait of a Puritan Merchant* (New York: Harper Torchbooks, 1965), vii–xii; Mark A. Peterson, *The Price of Redemption: The Spiritual Economy of Puritan New England* (Stanford, CA: Stanford University Press, 1997), 1–5.

that had long governed commerce in England. The General Court announced a fine of £200, an extraordinary sum, but later lowered it to £80—still an amount far out of proportion for the fairly small profits he allegedly took. The church elders weighed in too, arguing that he had caused a public scandal and dishonored their god's name. Keayne claimed that their judgment "was the griefe of my soule." He believed the church records contained lies, reflecting libelous assaults on his character rather than a clear-eyed appraisal of his trading practices.

As Keayne explained it, he had sold a bag of nails that cost him six pence a pound for eight pence. The purchaser found them too small, brought them back, and instead bought larger nails. Keayne charged him ten pence, a price that included a two-pence markup from the eight-pence cost of the larger nails. He changed the amount in his register to ten pence, but the consumer, whom he never named, never paid. The matter ended in court, with the purchaser claiming that Keayne had overcharged him for the smaller nails. Others heard about the legal affair and came forward with additional instances of Keayne purportedly overcharging them for a bridle, buttons, and thread. Within four years of his arrival, Keayne had seen his reputation tarnished, his business practices smeared, and his soul interrogated. Soon enough he found himself being questioned about an allegedly stolen sow and charged with engaging in usury. Boston selectmen accused him of arriving late to their meetings and of being publicly inebriated. They smeared him by association with his daughter-in-law, Sarah Dudley, who had come to the attention of the church for "Irregular prophycying" and having an affair with a man named Nicholas Hart, who had been excommunicated from the church in nearby Taunton. Keayne, who had kept track of every slight and accusation, poured out his anger in a 51,000-word will, a testament to his community's inability to understand commerce and their hard-hearted dealings with a once-respected member of the community. He quantified every perceived infraction, likening his actions to Jesus's practice of keeping "in memory and records the unkind usage of many Citties and Townes and the injuryes that he received of his unthankfull countrymen." He died three years later.[23]

23. Bailyn, "Apologia of Robert Keayne," 572–585, quotation at 581, and 575–577; Arthur P. Rugg, "A Famous Colonial Litigation: The Case Between Richard Sherman and Capt. Robert Keayne, 1642," *Proceedings of the American Antiquarian Society* 30, no. 2 (1920), 217–250.

The turmoil that Pynchon and Keayne felt came as a direct result of Massachusetts authorities' unwillingness to see their actions as within the bounds of acceptable behavior. On a deeper level, their travails at the hands of authorities signaled a wider psychological crisis evident in three unrelated developments: a raft of witchcraft accusations, the growing awareness that the children of the original migrants were not coming forward to undergo the vigorous spiritual testimony and cross-examination that would allow them to become full church members, and the arrival of English Quakers in Massachusetts.

Fear of demonic possession was common across the Atlantic basin, embedded in European, Indigenous, and African communities long before 1492. Authorities in many societies accused others of witchcraft. In the age of the Protestant Reformation, English courts found thousands of witches guilty and sentenced them to death. Such verdicts were common in France, German- and Dutch-speaking principalities, and the Iberian monarchies—all locales that had witnessed large numbers of emigrants bound for the Western Hemisphere. Much of the anxiety sprang from a widely held belief, articulated frequently by theologians, that the end of the world was near. One writer after another invoked Revelation 12:12: "Woe to the inhabitants of the earth, and of the sea," in the Geneva Bible translation of 1599, "for the devil is come down unto you, which hath great wrath, knowing that he hath but a short time." In the *Malleus Malificarum*, a widely circulated treatise on demonic reasoning first published around 1510, Heinrich Krämer and Jakob Sprenger had warned that sin had become ubiquitous, charitable donations had declined, and witches' demonic actions appeared with shocking regularity. No place was too small for the devil to do his work. A possessed nun in France in 1610 voiced the thoughts of the devil that had invaded her: the time for the Last Judgment had arrived. In the hamlet of Thoiry in the Pays de Vaud, a Huguenot missionary argued in 1653 that the demon had become more violent because he knew that the end was at hand.[24]

The logic and language of witchcraft traveled to English colonial communities during their earliest years, with ample literature explaining when the devil decided to take up residence. Fears of the demonic flowed in the writings of religious writers, whose books traveled along with the devout. Eschatological reasoning and the desire to find and punish witches

24. Stuart Clark, *Thinking with Demons: The Idea of Witchcraft in Early Modern Europe* (Oxford: Oxford University Press, 1997), 321–323.

became inseparable elements in New England dissenters' pursuit of godly commonwealths for decades.[25]

Although fears of demonic possession had been common well before the first English landed in New England, there were only four accusations of witchcraft levied before 1647. One was against Anne Hutchinson, which fizzled out. Only Jane Hawkins, who lived in Boston in 1638, was ever indicted, and there is no record of any verdict or punishment. But in 1647, Alice Young in Windsor, Connecticut, and Elizabeth Kendall in Cambridge went to trial. Both were convicted and executed. Two more women had the same experience the next year; the husband of one was also indicted, though that indictment led to no known trial or verdict. By 1651, trials for witchcraft had become more common: nine in 1651, all of them in Massachusetts except for the wife and husband Jane and John Carrington of Wethersfield, Connecticut, who were among the four executed that year; two cases in 1652; seven in 1653; two more in 1654; and another four the following year. From 1650 to 1659, there were forty cases in all, at times clustered together in small groups: four cases in Springfield in 1651, the same number in Gloucester in 1653, and five in New Haven in 1653 and 1654. When there was more than a single case in a town it often involved accusations launched against members of the same family. Hugh and Mary Parsons from Springfield faced charges in 1651. The court exonerated her but convicted him, though the verdict was subsequently overturned. There were thirty-eight more accusations in the 1660s, but no executions. Arguments between individuals in these towns took on added weight since, per the dominant theological doctrine, every action and thought had been predetermined by their god. In this mental universe, a quarrel over a debt could lead to accusations that threatened to ruin reputations and entire households.[26]

Across mid-century English America, those most likely to be accused and convicted of witchcraft were women, especially those whose behavior

25. Clark, *Thinking with Demons*, 325; William Perkins, *A Discourse of the Damned Art of Witchcraft* ([Cambridge], 1610); Nathaniel Homes, *Daemonologie and Theologie* (London, 1650); Cotton Mather, *Late Memorable Providences, Relating to Witchcrafts and Possessions* (Boston, 1689); Cotton Mather, *The Wonders of the Invisible World: being an account of the tryals of several witches lately executed in New-England* (Boston, 1693).

26. John Demos, *Entertaining Satan: Witchcraft and the Culture of Early New England* (New York: Oxford University Press, 1982), 401–406; see also David D. Hall, ed., *Witch-Hunting in Seventeenth-Century New England*, 2nd ed. (Boston: Northeastern University Press, 1999), 19–259; Samuel Drake, *Annals of Witchcraft in New England* (Boston, 1869), 71, 233, 222–223; Joseph H. Smith, ed., *Colonial Justice in Western Massachusetts (1639–1702): The Pynchon Court Record* (Cambridge, MA: Harvard University Press, 1961), 23–25; Gaskill, *The Ruin of All Witches*; Winship, "Contesting Control of Orthodoxy," 818–820.

challenged what dissenters believed to be proper behavior. Accusers turned against their neighbors far from New England. In Bermuda, there had been no accusations of witchcraft until 1651, but by the end of the next decade there were fifteen trials. Most of the accused were acquitted. However, the courts convicted four of those who pled not guilty, along with one man who confessed to being possessed.[27]

No area saw more cases than New England. While accusations of demonic invasion were phrased in religious rhetoric, community leaders often invoked such accusations as a form of social control, specifically to police and punish those the majority deemed deviant. Anne Hutchinson preached and needed to be exiled. Margaret Jones healed others and was hanged. Mary Parsons never confessed to being a witch but did confess to the tragic killing of her child; she died in prison. Yet the spouses in each of these cases escaped the censure that fell upon their wives. Upstanding dissenters who were full members of churches spent a great deal of time trying to figure out who among them should celebrate the Mass, a task that posed myriad logistical challenges since, as they understood, none could know their god's will. Yet while they engaged in a literal soul-searching of their neighbors, they often fell back on the misogyny that had fueled witchcraft accusations in Europe for centuries, from the time of Joan of Arc to more recent decades when witch-hunters murdered thousands of female victims. Much had changed for Europeans when they crossed the ocean, but certain patterns of thought remained durable.[28]

Equally durable was the dissenters' hostility toward Quakers, notably those who refused to accept limits on their speech and actions. On July 11, 1656, Ann Austin and Mary Fisher, two English women who had embraced the teachings of theologian George Fox and espoused the doctrine of the Religious Society of Friends, arrived in Boston after a long journey that had taken them from London to Barbados. They brought along a trunk filled with pamphlets touting the ideology of the new religion, whose

27. John Henry LeFroy, *Memorials of the Discovery and Early Settlement of the Bermudas or Somer Islands, 1515–1685* (1879), 2:602–632 (Cole's reprieve is at 630); Virginia Bernhard, "Religion, Politics, and Witchcraft in Bermuda, 1651–55," *WMQ*, 3rd Ser., 67 (2010), 677–708; Heather M. Kopelson, "Sinning Property and the Legal Transformation of Abominable Sex in Early Bermuda," *WMQ*, 3rd Ser., 70 (2013), 459–496; Michael J. Jarvis, *Isle of Devils, Isle of Saints: An Atlantic History of Bermuda, 1609–1684* (Baltimore: Johns Hopkins University Press, 2022), 230–240.

28. Demos, *Entertaining Satan*; Carol F. Karlsen, *The Devil in the Shape of a Woman: Witchcraft in Colonial New England* (New York: W. W. Norton, 1987); Tracy Borman, *Witches: James I and the English Witch-Hunts* (London: Jonathan Cape, 2013), 39–42; Malcolm Gaskill, *Witchfinders: A Seventeenth-Century English Tragedy* (Cambridge, MA: Harvard University Press, 2005).

earliest devotees had been known to shake when they believed the light of their lord filled their bodies, a tendency that led them to be called Quakers. Boston authorities seized Austin and Fisher as soon as they arrived. They strip-searched them, part of a ritual humiliation intended to convince them to leave, and then put them in prison. They also confiscated their belongings and set fire to their pamphlets, an act they conducted publicly to send a message to anyone who had considered deviating from orthodox Puritan teachings. Within days, eight more Quakers arrived. Boston's theocratic rulers treated them just as harshly, ordering them to be beaten and jailed as well. While the women were still in jail, authorities passed an act promising to levy a fine of £500 on any ship captain who transported Quakers to the city. Austin and Fisher departed the town, unwilling emigrants from a land they never saw beyond public humiliation and the inside of a jail cell.[29]

In 1657, in the face of the General Court specifying the brutal punishments to be meted out to Quakers and penalties for any resident who harbored such "blasphemous hereticks," Mary Dyer, William Robinson, and Marmaduke Stephenson arrived in Boston. Dyer, a close friend of Anne Hutchinson, already knew firsthand about the costs of exile. Authorities arrested and banished them and threatened to execute them following a new law of October 1658. Recognizing the threat that the Quakers' printed materials (in addition to their speech) might draw colonists of "weake capacities," they ordered the circulation of written refutations of these dissenters' ideas. On October 19, the General Court ordered the banishment of six Quakers, warning them that execution awaited them if they returned. A year later the court recaptured Mary Dyer, William Robinson, and Marmaduke Stephenson. Dyer had earlier traveled to visit friends in Rhode Island, where Roger Williams's brand of religious tolerance had made it acceptable for Quakers to live. Robinson and Stephenson, more defiant, were imprisoned; when they were released, they refused to leave the colony, and returned to jail. Dyer, who had visited them and also went back to jail, left the colony again but then returned once more. Her arrival and the men's continuing defiance prompted Boston's officials to order the hanging of the three of them on

29. Rufus M. Jones, *The Quakers in the American Colonies* (London: Macmillan, 1911), 65–67. After leaving New England, Fisher gained prominence among Quakers for going to Adrianople (modern-day Edirne) to spread her faith to the Great Turk; see George Bishop, *New England Judged* (London, 1661), sig. C2^{r}–[4^{v}]. Moving between colonial outposts, a strategy that fit Quakers' pursuit of their religious ideas, added to the hostility that authorities expressed against them; see Carla G. Pestana, "Atlantic Mobilities and the Deviance of the Early Quakers," *Journal of Early Modern History* 28 (2024), 187–208.

October 27, 1659. Expecting that the action might elicit condemnation, the members of the General Court offered a lengthy justification for their actions, which included condemnation of the accused for their biblical errors, an assertion that their defiance meant that they felt subject to no laws at all, the fact that "Christians should obey magistrates," and that the court had a duty to protect the community from "defilement of the mind," a contagion as deadly as an infectious disease. The executioner hanged the men before Dyer's eyes and threatened to hang her too. While she was on the scaffold word came that local authorities had changed their mind and banished her instead.[30]

Dyer spent the winter of 1659–1660 traveling between Rhode Island and Long Island, planning her next move. On May 21, she traveled back to Boston again. This time she was not so lucky: authorities hanged her on June 1. Six months later, the General Court again asserted that it had not wanted to order any executions but that the return of Quakers after banishment could not be accepted. "Such was their daingerous, impetuous, & desperate turbulency, both to religion & the state civil & ecclesiastical," that they brought their deaths on themselves. By the end of 1661, they had also executed William Leddra, who had sailed there from Barbados. That same year, authorities ordered that two other Quaker men be removed from prison, stripped from the waist up, and whipped twenty times in Boston—and then given ten more lashes in Roxbury and another ten in Dedham, after which they were deported. Soon afterward the General Court, in response to a letter from the king imploring them to stop such harsh treatment, again reaffirmed the need to prosecute Quakers for their "restless intrusions & impetuous disturbance."[31]

The executions of the Quakers in Boston exemplified a specific moment in the lives of New England's orthodox community. By 1660 the first

30. *Records of the Governor and Company of the Massachusetts Bay in New England* (Boston: W. White, 1853–1854), IV, part I, 308–309 ("hereticks"), 345–346, 349, 383–390, quotations at 387 ("obey magistrates") and 389 ("defilement"); Bishop, *New England Judged*, sig. N^{r}–[O3^{v}]; on Dyer and Hutchinson, see Francis J. Bremer, *First Founders: American Puritans and Puritanism in an Atlantic World* (Durham, NH: University of New Hampshire Press, 2012), 66–69.

31. *Records of the Governor and Company of the Massachusetts Bay*, IV, part I, 419 (Dyer), 451 (defense of their action), and IV, part II, 19–20, 34 (quotation), 59; *An Appendix to the Book, Entituled, New England Judged . . . With a Short Relation of the Tryal, Sentence, and Execution of William Leddra* (London, 1661), sig. [Bb3^{v}]–[Cc4^{v}]; Carla G. Pestana, "The Quaker Executions as Myth and History," *JAH* 80 (1993), 441–469; Francis J. Bremer, *The Puritan Experiment: New England Society from Bradford to Edwards*, rev. ed. (Hanover, NH: University Press of New England, 1995), 154–158.

generation of migrants had aged and were beginning to die with some regularity.[32] Their life expectancies were remarkable by any measure, and so too was the size of their families. But physical health did not translate into achieving the spiritual goals the migrants had set for themselves. Consumed by the sense that most of them were among their god's elect, the migrants presumed that their children would follow in their path. For many communities, that might have meant young adults attending the same congregations as their parents, hearing the same sermons each week, and seeing the same people at the communion table. But the membership policies that those ambitious migrants had set when they launched their churches came back to haunt them. One set of parents after another realized that their own children, including many born in England who had sailed across the Atlantic, did not offer themselves up for full membership. Some issues the General Court could resolve, such as Christmas revelries, which were banned and became subject to a fine in 1659.[33] But what should be done about the apparent spiritual shortcomings of law-abiding dissenters and their children?

In 1662, ministers gathered in Cambridge for a synod, an unexpected development for a religious group that prided itself on each congregation setting its own spiritual agenda and membership practices. They wrestled with a problem that would determine their future: could churches offer the sacrament of baptism to the third generation of children, the grandchildren of the migrants, whose own parents had never come forward and put themselves through the psychologically excruciating process of proving that they deserved to be among the presumptively elect? The synod's members understood that denying baptism to an infant whom their god had selected for salvation would prevent that individual from achieving salvation—a terrible tragedy for the individual, but a moral problem for those whose actions put them between the fate of an individual child and the inclinations of an inscrutable deity. They solved the problem by creating what later became known as the "half-way covenant." Under this doctrine, the ministers decreed that the children of members would remain under the "Watch, Discipline and Government" of their parents' church but would not be entitled to all of the benefits of the church unless and until they offered themselves up to be full members. After all, the minister Thomas Shephard wrote in a pamphlet analyzing the issue, children needed access to the rite because "*baptisme* seales up our *first entrance* into

32. William Bradford, *Of Plimoth Plantation*, ed. Kenneth P. Minkema et al. (Boston: Colonial Society of Massachusetts, 2020), 441–448.

33. Stephen Nissenbaum, *The Battle for Christmas: A Cultural History of America's Most Cherished Holiday* (New York: Knopf, 1996), 3–16.

the Covenant." Baptism did not guarantee church membership for adults. As New Haven minister John Davenport clarified, if these baptized individuals "when they are Adult" do not, "holding forth Faith and Repentance, joyn into the Church, that then they cannot retain their Membership, which had in minority." The burden at the moment fell on parents: as long as these adults could understand and publicly profess their commitment to "the Doctrine of Faith," and as long as they avoided scandal, their children could be baptized. The crisis of the third generation—the grandchildren of the adult migrants—could be solved, so the ministers believed, without abandoning the strict policies they had set for admission to full membership. Soon after they made their decision, prominent ministers, including Increase Mather and Thomas Shepard, distributed their views in pamphlets printed in Cambridge. These dissenters, often unbending on religious issues, found a reason to soften one of their most cherished hopes—that the churches in a world that they created would gather together only the elect.[34]

In 1637, an Indigenous man from Long Island named Cockenoe had the misfortune to be traveling among the Pequots. He escaped the flames on the Mystic, but the English took him captive and forced him to work as a servant for a Dorchester resident named Richard Calicott. At the time, Massachusetts Bay had no statute that allowed a colonist to keep a Native as enslaved, the likely status of Cockenoe. Unlike servants who had traveled with free migrants from England, this Algonquian-speaking man had no contract, no promise that he would be taught a particular skill like an apprentice, and no end to his period of service.[35]

34. Thomas Shepard, *The Church Membership of Children, and their Right to Baptisme* (Cambridge, MA, 1663), quotation at 16; John Davenport, *Another Essay for Investigation of the Truth, in answer to two questions* (Cambridge, MA, 1663), quotation at sig. a^{v}–a2^{r}; Edmund Morgan, *Visible Saints: The History of a Puritan Idea* (orig. pub. 1963; Ithaca, NY: Cornell University Press, 1965), 129–136. Increase Mather, who had opposed infant baptism during the synod of 1662, eventually came to embrace the practice, though he believed that those who never achieved saving grace would be worse off in the end; see Increase Mather, *Pray for the Rising Generation, or a Sermon wherein Godly Parents are Encouraged, to Pray and Believe for their Children* (Cambridge, MA, 1678) and David D. Hall, ed., *Puritans in the New World: A Critical Anthology* (Princeton, NJ: Princeton University Press, 2004), 97.
35. Four years later, in the so-called Body of Liberties of 1641 (which the Massachusetts General Court adopted in 1648), the colony banned "bond slaverie" with the exception of "lawfull Captives taken in just warres, and such strangers who willingly selle themselves or are sold to us." See "The Body of Liberties, 1641," in William Henry Whitmore, *A Bibliographical Sketch of the Laws of Massachusetts Colony from 1630 to 1686,*

Sometime in the early 1640s, Cockenoe met minister John Eliot, who had arrived in Boston in 1631 and took up the pulpit at Roxbury. The cleric, unlike many other migrants, believed that the dissenting Protestants could make great advances among the Ninnimissinuok.[36] By the late 1630s, Eliot had established his religious bona fides as an interrogator of Anne Hutchinson and as one of the banishers of Roger Williams, and in 1640 he was part of the team that published the Bay Psalm Book, the first book printed in an English American colony.[37] In the early 1640s, he found his purpose: he would bring the word of Christ to the Algonquian-speaking peoples of southern New England.

At some point after 1637, Cockenoe and Eliot began to work together as partners in what became the most significant effort to convert Native peoples in English North America: a translation of the Bible into the Massachusett language, now known as Wampanoak. Eliot taught Cockenoe to read and write English. Cockenoe's linguistic dexterity impressed the missionary. He was, Eliot wrote in 1666, "a pregnant witted young man," who "pretty well understood our Language, better than he could speak it, and well understood his own Language, and hath a clear pronunciation; Him I made my Interpreter." Cockenoe helped Eliot translate the Ten Commandments, the Lord's Prayer, and at least some of the Bible. "I compiled both exhortations and prayers by his help," Eliot added, noting that he "diligently marked the difference of their grammar from ours; when I found the way of them, I would pursue a Word, a Noun, a Verb, through all the variations I could think of." He was, the English missionary believed, an actual godsend, sent to Eliot "by Gods wise providence," a sure sign that the puritan mission to convert Indigenous was part of an unseen plan.[38]

By the 1640s, Eliot believed many Algonquian-speaking peoples wanted to live near colonists. That explained why, as he saw it, they often invited "the English unto fit places for Townes, because of the benefit they receive

in which are included The Body of Liberties of 1641 (Boston: Rockwell and Churchill, 1890), part 91; Wendy Warren, *New England Bound: Slavery and Colonization in Early America* (New York: Liveright, 2016), 34–35; Christopher Tomlins, *Freedom Bound: Law, Labor, and Civic Identity in Colonizing English America, 1580–1865* (Cambridge: Cambridge University Press, 2010), 250–256.

36. Eliot to Simonds D'Ewes, September 18, 1633, in Everett Emerson, ed., *Letters from New England: The Massachusetts Bay Colony, 1629–1638* (Amherst: University of Massachusetts Press, 1976), 104–108.

37. Richard W. Cogley, *John Eliot's Mission to the Indians Before King Philip's War* (Cambridge, MA: Harvard University Press, 1999), 47–49.

38. William W. Tucker, *John Eliot's First Indian Teacher and Interpreter: Cockenoe-De-Long Island* (New York: Francis P. Harper, 1896), quotations at 13; Michael P. Clark, ed., The Eliot Tracts (Westport, CT; Praeger, 2003), 10.

by our neighbourhood." This was, for Eliot, the necessary step that would allow missionaries to spread the gospel among them. Cockenoe provided the second step, enabling Eliot and other missionaries to "write and imprint no nother but Scripture principles in the *abrasa tabula scraped board* of these naked people." With proper instruction, they would fulfill their own destiny and join the puritans as their god's chosen.[39]

In 1646, the Massachusetts General Court, echoing an aspiration of the founders of the Massachusetts Bay Company, enacted a law to support the "propagation of the gospel" among Indigenous peoples. On October 28, Eliot, drawing on what he had learned from Cockenoe, traveled to Nonantum and preached in Wampanoak in the house of Waban, the first known convert to the English faith in the region. In November, the General Court encouraged Eliot and his associates to establish a community of Christian Natives, often referred to as "praying Indians" by colonists, near Boston. The government would cover the initial monetary costs, but those who lived there would need to abide by a specific set of social practices, living in a way that was closer to what the puritans thought was proper. This new code of conduct dictated that Indigenous men should spend more time working in the fields, a task that had previously been performed by women in communities in the region. Native men were to abjure extramarital relations, women would be fined if they walked around topless, and all were to style their hair like the English. Soon, some of the residents of Neponset, where Eliot had begun to preach in 1647, also opted to convert.[40]

By decade's end, the English missionaries had begun to make inroads into Massachusett communities. Indigenous leaders including Waban and Wamporas, seeing the benefits of English-style literacy, sent their children to colonial communities to learn to read and write. In 1647, some Pawtuckets, impressed by what they had observed in nearby Massachusett towns, decided that they, too, wanted to reform their communities to make them more like those of the colonists. The residents of Musketaquid asked Waban and a Concord resident named Simon Willard to create a civil and legal code similar to Nonantum's. Here the local rules went further. Drunkenness, lying, gambling, sabbath-breaking, fornication, and

39. "The learned Conjectures of Reverend Mr. John Eliot touching the Americans, of new and notable consideration, written to Mr. Thorowgood," in Tho[mas] Thorowgood, *Jews in America, Or Probabilities, that those Indians are Judaical* (London, 1660), sig. A^{r}–D2^{v}, quotations at sig. D^{r} (land titles) and D2^{r} ("*abrasa tabula*"). Thorowgood had produced an edition of his book in 1650, and at an unknown date Eliot in response sent him his "Conjectures," which Thorowgood then incorporated into the 1660 edition.

40. Cogley, *Eliot's Mission to the Indians*, 50–55.

entering colonists' homes without permission all brought penalties. The code also altered traditional practices, such as menstrual seclusion and polygamy. Any who committed murder, bestiality, or adultery would face capital punishment. Other Natives heard about Eliot's work and reported that they might be interested in conversion too, including Nipmucks, who lived in the interior, including at Natick.[41]

Eliot regularly visited Nonantum and Neponset, but his individual commitment was less crucial to missionary success than Indigenous converts were. Eliot gave them credit: "The most effectual and general way of spreading the Gospel will be by themselves," he wrote in 1651. Other missionaries agreed. "God is wont ordinarily to convert Nations and peoples by some of their owne countrymen who are nearest to them, and can best speak," wrote the anonymous author of *The Day-Breaking, if not the Sun-Rising of the Gospell with the Indians in New-England* in 1647, understanding that these Native converts did the real work at hand.[42]

Eliot understood that the Protestants needed the Natives "to read our Bible, the book of God," as the scribe behind *The Day-Breaking* put it, so that "therein they should see most cleerly what Jesus Christ was." From that principle they could advance to others: to think about what the Christian god could teach them, and how imported conceptions of prayer and repentance would allow them to learn of the deity's wonders and confess their sins, two necessary steps to take their place among the faithful. When an unconverted Native told one of the converts that they prayed in vain because Jesus did not speak their language, the missionaries realized that they had an opening. Such a conjecture was false, they taught the converts, because "Jesus Christ and God by him made all things, and makes all men, not onely *English* but *Indian* men, and if hee made them both," then the almighty knew all that was within humans. "If he made *Indian* men," the text proclaimed, "then hee knowes all *Indian* prayers also." Natives needed to learn to read so they could have the direct encounter with Scripture necessary to understand the possibility of salvation, but it did not matter if a holy text was written in English or Wampanoak. Jesus spoke them all.[43]

41. Cogley, *Eliot's Mission to the Indians*, 55–60.
42. Cogley, *Eliot's Mission to the Indians*, 61–62; [Thomas Shepard?], *The day-breaking, if not the sun-rising of the Gospell with the Indians in New-England* (London, 1647), quotation at 16.
43. [Shepard?], *The Day-Breaking*, quotations at 3 and 4; see also Sarah Rivett, *Unscripted America: Indigenous Languages and the Origins of a Literary Nation* (Oxford: Oxford University Press, 2017), 22–54. For the identification of Shepard as the possible author, see Cogley, *Eliot's Mission to the Indians*, 278n1.

In 1649, Parliament founded the Company (or Society) for the Propagation of the Gospel in New England and Parts Adjacent in America (SPG). English supporters raised £12,000. The next year, Eliot petitioned the General Court to establish a town for converted Indigenous at Natick. The colony's authorities agreed that having such a settlement close to Boston would make sense for both the Natives and the colonists. In 1662, Eliot acknowledged that it was perhaps less the will of his god than the determination of some of the Indigenous, who reminded others that Natives had farmed some of this land "even beyond the memory of the oldest man alive." The General Court carved out a 2,000-acre parcel that lay within the boundaries of lands it had previously granted to Dedham in 1635. In 1651, the residents of the town accepted the plan: they would not challenge the Natives' claim to 2,000 acres as long as the Indigenous "lay downe all claimes in that toune elsewhere, and sett no trapps in unenclosed ground." Later, when the colonists thought the Natives had taken some of what was theirs, the General Court awarded them 8,000 new acres—and added 6,000 acres to the Natick community. The converted Natives soon reorganized the landscape, mimicking the strategy of their colonial neighbors, even building a meeting house and starting work on a sawmill.[44] Missionaries working on Martha's Vineyard also reported success. "On that Island, there is not onely a *Form*," missionary Matthew Mayhew wrote later, "but in some measure the *Power of Godliness*."[45]

Eliot understood that the only way Natives would embrace the dissenters' faith and practice would be to accept aspects of their life, offer strategies to meet emerging opportunities in a colonizing landscape, and,

44. Jean M. O'Brien, *Dispossession by Degrees: Indian Land and Identity in Natick, Massachusetts, 1650–1790* (Cambridge: Cambridge University Press, 1997), 31–39.

45. John Elliot [*sic*], *A Brief Narrative of the Progress of the Gospel amongst the Indians in New-England in the Year 1670* (London, 1671), 4; Matthew Mayhew, *Conquests and Triumphs of Grace: Being A Brief Narrative of the Success which the Gospel hath had among the INDIANS of Martha's Vineyard (and the Places adjacent) in New-England* (London, 1695), quotation at 37; Thomas Mayhew Sr. to John Winthrop Jr., December 7, 1675, *Collections of the Massachusetts Historical Society*, 4th Ser., 7 (1865), 43; David J. Silverman, "Indians, Missionaries, and Religious Translation: Creating Wampanoag Christianity in Seventeenth-Century Martha's Vineyard," *WMQ*, 3rd. Ser., 62 (2005), 141–174; David J. Silverman, *Faith and Boundaries: Colonists, Christianity, and Community Among the Wampanoag Indians of Martha's Vineyard, 1600–1871* (Cambridge: Cambridge University Press, 2005). Missionaries claimed progress on Nantucket as well Martha's Vineyard; see Thomas Mayhew to Daniel Gookin, September 1, 1674, in Daniel Gookin, "Historical Collections of the Indians in New England," *Collections of the Massachusetts Historical Society for the Year 1792*, vol. 1 (orig. pub. 1792; Boston, 1806), 204–205.

crucially, find a way to speak to them directly. He knew that he and other missionaries needed Algonquian-speakers to read as well as recite Scripture because the principle of *sola scriptura* (by Scripture alone) guided ministers' approach to conversion just as surely as they recognized its importance for English migrants. In 1663 Eliot and Cockenoe completed the translation of the Bible into Wampanoak and had it printed in Cambridge.[46]

In 1651, Harvard College, having opened in 1636 across the Charles River from Boston as an American institution to train Protestant ministers, launched its Indian College. The college's president and fellows likely knew that Virginia's planned Henrico College had never amounted to much. In a more suitable location like Cambridge, the dissenters believed, they would provide the world with proof that they could create civilized, profitable, godly communities among Indigenous. Despite their high hopes, the college closed in 1698, having taught only a small number of students, some of whom became accomplished Latinists. Among those who worked in the building was Wawaus (or Wowaus), later known as James Printer, a Nipmuck from the town of Hassanamesit (modern Grafton, Massachusetts), who had learned English as a child. Wawaus became an apprentice at the printing press in Cambridge, which was located in Harvard's Indian College, and he helped set the type for the Bible translated by Cockenoe and Eliot.[47]

The publication of the Bible in Wampanoak, the founding of Natick, the printing of narratives of Indigenous converts on Martha's Vineyard, and the establishment of Harvard's Indian College all suggested that the hostilities that had exploded in 1637 would not be repeated. Instead, as the SPG's supporters in England argued, capital would be better spent teaching Algonquian-speakers to read Scripture in their own language than preparing for reprisals from them. The past had been violent. The future, to Eliot and others who saw the world like him, belonged to the Christian god, even if few English who promulgated this plan ever articulated that its potential success lay less with devout colonial missionaries than with individuals like Cockenoe, Wawaus, and Waban. If southern New England was to witness the fulfillment of the dissenters' impulse to

46. Rivett, *Unscripted America*, 65–74.

47. Lisa Brooks, *Our Beloved Kin: A New History of King Philip's War* (New Haven, CT: Yale University Press, 2018), 4–5, 90–92; Thomas Keeline and Stuart M. McManus, "Benjamin Larnell, the Last Latin Poet at Harvard Indian College," *Harvard Studies in Classical Philology* 108 (2015), 621–642; Samuel Eliot Morison, *Harvard College in the Seventeenth Century*, 2 vols. (Cambridge, MA: Harvard University Press, 1936), 1:340–344.

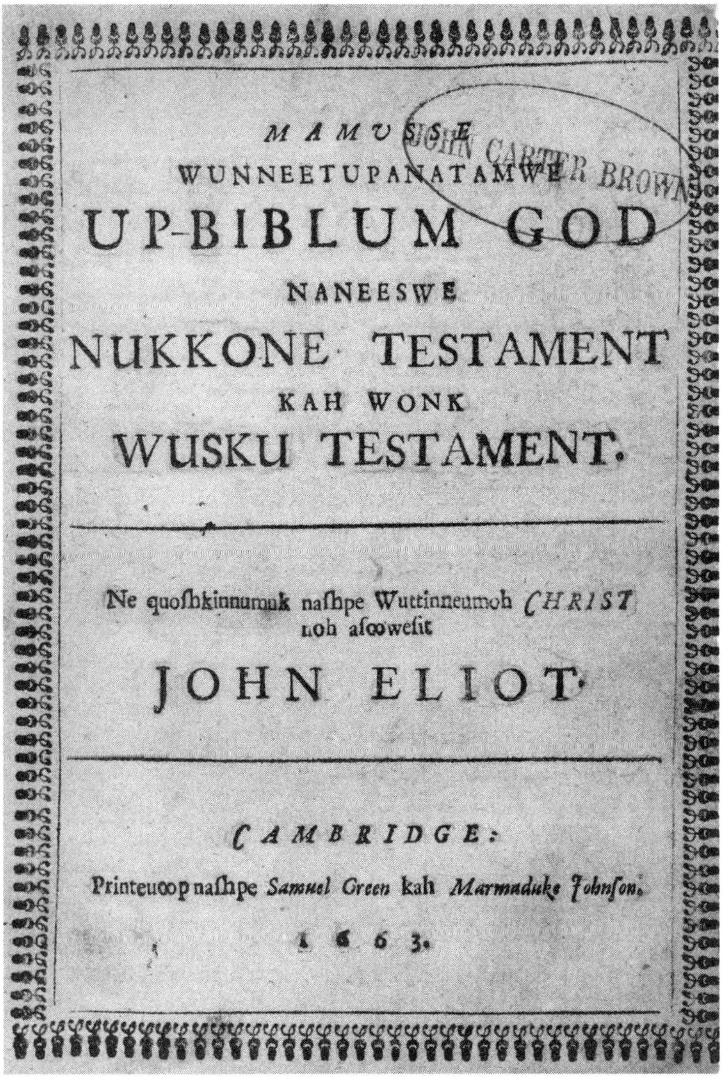

MAMUSSE
WUNNEETUPANATAMWE
UP-BIBLUM GOD
NANEESWE
NUKKONE TESTAMENT
KAH WONK
WUSKU TESTAMENT.

Ne quoshkinnumuk nashpe Wuttinneumoh *CHRIST*
noh asoowesit

JOHN ELIOT.

CAMBRIDGE:
Printeuoop nashpe *Samuel Green* kah *Marmaduke Johnson.*
1663.

Missionary John Eliot was so proud of his efforts translating Scripture into Wampanoak that he put his name on the title page of the 1663 work *Mamusse Wunneetupanatamwe Up-Biblum God.* Yet, as he was aware, he could have never achieved such a literary feat without the assistance of local Natives, especially Cockenoe. Courtesy of the John Carter Brown Library.

convert Indigenous, it would come only from partnership, not continued brutality.

At the colonies' origins, the dissenting Protestant migrants to New England saw themselves on a mission to better the world. In some ways they succeeded. They reshaped the landscape to make much of it look like rural England, which included the importation of cows, sheep, horses, and pigs. They established local polities to control local affairs, typically giving adult men a voice in a town's politics, a strategy that encouraged individuals to go along with collective decisions even when there was no constabulary or other agent to force compliance. They created a system embracing current English ideas about proper gender relations, within a household and in the world beyond its doors. They enhanced the growth of transatlantic commerce through local shipbuilding, fishing, and lumber industries. Boston's merchants, as Keayne's experience revealed, facilitated the distribution of manufactured goods across the countryside. And they created rules for who had power within local congregations, a status necessary to have political authority in a region where there was no separation between church and state.[48]

Having a vision of an idealized society proved far different from creating one in the land of Algonquian-speaking peoples of coastal New England. Even the rather mundane issue of keeping one's livestock out of the crops of Indigenous communities became a problem when colonists made the initial decision to protect their own fields by fencing them in and allowing their animals to browse freely beyond. Trespassing sheep and cows could denude a field. Imported pigs had jaws strong enough to destroy a clamshell. An individual violation might not have meant much on a given day. But the accumulated invasions of Indigenous lands and property had the cumulative effect that prompted Miantonomi's declaration about doom for Native peoples on the horizon. The accretion of small injuries contributed to the periodic violence that rocked the land. English migrants wanted to avoid strategies Catholic Spaniards had employed in their conquest of New Spain. But in allowing their animals to feed in Native fields they unconsciously mimicked a strategy that had fueled famine in Mexico and contributed to demographic catastrophe.[49]

48. For landscape, see Cronon, *Changes in the Land*; for gender, see Norton, *Founding Mothers and Fathers*, 28–56.

49. See Virginia DeJohn Anderson, *Creatures of Empire: How Domestic Animals Transformed Early America* (New York: Oxford University Press, 2004), 230–237; Elinor Melville, *A*

Tensions festered in New England for decades. One early sign emerged in what may seem an unlikely and insignificant venue: an argument that began over the proper behavior of the wife of the governor of the New Haven colony in 1646. It was an improbable place to experience trouble, at least in the opinion of its leading colonists. "God hath here bestowed upon us the greatest outward priviledge," the minister John Davenport, one of New Haven's wealthiest residents, observed in 1639, "and hath promised that in every place where he shall so sett his name, he will come unto his people and blesse them."[50]

Among those who might have at first agreed that New Haven possessed divine favor was Ann Yale, a widowed mother of three who married Theophilus Eaton, a widower with his own children. The blended family sailed to Boston in 1637 and then migrated to New Haven the following year. Soon after, he became the governor. They drew on the wealth she had inherited from her first husband to build a mansion large enough to contain seventeen fireplaces. Even that spacious abode was not large enough to prevent Ann Eaton from arguing with her mother-in-law, her stepchildren, and even some of the servants who lived with them.

While disputes within a household would normally have been contained within its walls, Ann Eaton's case was anything but normal. Elected to full church membership after the cross-examination that every would-be church member suffered in front of the congregation, she knew well what Scripture taught and also about those who had already dissented from the orthodoxy, including Anne Hutchinson and Roger Williams. She knew too that New Haven, unlike the Massachusetts Bay colony, did not have a charter, which raised questions about the extent of the colony's leadership. Aware that they needed a governing authority, New Haven's leaders dispatched a mission to London in 1646 aboard the *Great Shippe*, but it sank before reaching Britain, an incident that to some may have signaled divine displeasure at the entire enterprise. For her part, Ann Eaton corresponded with Lady Deborah Moody, who moved to Long Island (and eventually to modern Brooklyn) after being excommunicated

Plague of Sheep: Environmental Consequences of the Conquest of Mexico (Cambridge: Cambridge University Press, 1994).

50. Here and below, unless otherwise indicated, details of the New Haven case can be found in Lilian Handlin, "Dissent in a Small Community," *NEQ* 58 (1985), 193–220; quotation in John Davenport to Mary, Lady Vere, 28th day, 7th month, 1639, in Isabel M. Calder, ed., *Letters of John Davenport, Puritan Divine* (New Haven, CT: Yale University Press for the First Church of Christ in New Haven, 1937), 76.

from the church in Salem for her alleged deviance from orthodox practice.[51]

In response to reports of her behavior, church authorities examined Ann Eaton. After finding that she had violated religious rules—they concluded she disrespected her husband, slandered others, borne false witness, and mistreated those who lived in her house—they excommunicated her in 1645. By then, her case had drawn the attention of others in New Haven, including three women who rallied to her side because they thought she was living a godly life and her accusers were not. In a case that in its outlines paralleled Hutchinson's a decade earlier, church authorities inveighed against these women's participation in a theological dispute and eventually punished them too—though, like Ann Eaton, they remained in New Haven.[52]

While the banishing of those who held heterodox beliefs was not unusual in early New England, the allegations against Ann Eaton went beyond arguing with her husband or her onetime ally Davenport. On one occasion she assaulted her stepdaughter Mary, knocking "her head against the dresser, which made her nose bleed much," according to the clerics who investigated the case. They added: "Besides others who were present, this was done before four Indians, who were then in the Kitchen."[53]

The investigation as a whole and this detail epitomized the psychological crises that at times beset New England's dissenting community. It was bad enough that they had erred in admitting her to the church. Worse still was the fact that she had engaged in such un-Christian behavior in front of four Indigenous. If Native peoples saw the wife of the governor and a wealthy inhabitant of one of the town's two largest houses behave this way toward her own family, what did that mean about colonists' commitment to creating a godly community? Formal arguments about theology could be addressed in various ways—by summoning a William Pynchon to testify about his writings, barring a Robert Keayne from being a selectman, banishing an Anne Hutchinson or a Lady Moody, or questioning whether accusations of witchcraft might be true or instead slanders hurled in a dispute. Those issues all could be resolved within the (metaphorical) house of the church members. But when issues crossed the cultural divide from those who needed to embody biblical purity toward

51. For Moody, see Thomas J. Campanella, *Brooklyn: The Once and Future City* (Princeton, NJ: Princeton University Press, 2019), 39–57.

52. Details of the accusations can be found in Newman Smyth, "Mrs. Eaton's Trial (in 1644) as it appears upon the records of the First Church of New Haven," *Papers of the New Haven Colony Historical Society* 5 (1894), 133–148.

53. Smyth, "Mrs. Eaton's Trial," quotations at 138–139.

those whom the dissenters wanted to bring into Christendom, the fragility of the entire religious operation burst out into the open. Even in divinely blessed New Haven the English struggled to create communities that matched their rhetoric.

New England's colonists were perhaps the most literate of any Europeans who had crossed the Atlantic in the seventeenth century. They contributed to a flourishing print culture, often sharing ideas about religious practice. Yet as the cases of individuals such as Pynchon, Keayne, Hutchinson, and Eaton suggest, living up to publicly expressed standards could be difficult. Time would tell what this meant across their region and beyond.

24

From the Headwaters

By the 1670s, Europeans who had arrived in North America had created complex relations with Indigenous peoples, sought ways to extract natural resources, and mapped ocean routes facilitating the transportation of free colonists and enslaved Africans to the coastline. Following from logic that dated to the late fifteenth century, they took as truth the doctrine of discovery: anyone from a Christian land who arrived in territory where there were no existing Christian princes could lay claim to it—not only the coastline but also the interior. While they recognized that such claims had little meaning if they did not people territory with inhabitants (as opposed to explorers, who were always just passing through on their way to the next destination), cartographers wasted no time dividing up North America into European zones. The French had the St. Lawrence Valley. The English laid claim to Hudson Bay as well as coastline from modern-day Maine to Georgia. The Spanish owned La Florida and New Mexico, as well as the territory along the Gulf of Mexico. European America extended into the Caribbean, where colonial emissaries representing England, France, Spain, Portugal, and the Netherlands all laid claim to their own sugar-producing islands, territories that by the latter decades of the century tended to have more enslaved Africans than free or indentured Europeans living on them.

Yet by their own logic as well as reality, no Europeans had a legitimate claim to the interior of the continent. To be sure, in certain areas European exports, notably guns, diseases, and horses, had reshaped how Native peoples lived. But in the expanse of the continent's interior, Indigenous peoples continued to live as they had for generations—not in permanent religious ignorance, as missionaries claimed, nor as economic primitives without any conception of property, as putative empire-builders may have concluded. Some European diseases had likely penetrated the interior, carried by Native peoples engaged in trade with one another after being exposed to a pathogen-bearing colonist or disease-bearing rat. Still, as yet there had been no demographic collapse, nor even widespread depopulation across the continent despite the ferocity of localized epidemics.

Yet while the number of Indigenous remained healthy, the impact of Europeans' arrival in North America could be seen in shifting attitudes toward some commodities and what some groups were willing to do to get them. Specifically, the assaults of Haudenosaunee against Indigenous communities across Wendake, homeland of the Wendats, forced some Native peoples to travel farther west seeking security. In the process, they came into greater contact with Indigenous communities inhabiting the territory west of Lake Michigan and south and southwest of Lake Superior. To protect themselves and to pursue beaver, Native peoples across the region hoped to establish ongoing and secure ties to French traders who had taken up residence around the Great Lakes. Like residents of Indigenous communities farther east, the peoples of the Mississippi Valley had become eager participants in a consumer revolution. Wanting guns, iron tools, and copper kettles, Native hunters took an increasing number of beaver from the woods. By the middle decades of the century, some of those hunters also wanted alcohol, another good new to them, and one that traders believed crucial to the fur trade.

Europeans interested in North America needed to cross the Atlantic to access the resources and peoples of the Western Hemisphere. But the ocean mattered much less, if at all, in the interior. The Colorado and the rivers flowing into it remained the prime avenue for the movement of goods and people across much of the West and the Southwest. The Mississippi and its tributaries, which included the Missouri draining from the northwest and the Ohio from the northeast, mattered in the center of the continent: it facilitated trade, war, and family formation, and it was the route through which Indigenous knowledge traveled far, just as it had centuries earlier when the bearers of maize ascended to Cahokia.

The reality of a continent dominated by Indigenous nations was apparent to missionaries who traveled through it on exploratory journeys—including the Jesuit Jacques Marquette, who traveled hundreds of miles from Lake Huron to near modern-day Memphis in 1673, almost two centuries after Columbus first told Europeans about the Western Hemisphere. He paddled downstream, with occasional portages, in a party of seven Frenchmen, including explorer Louis Jolliet, who had spent time around the Great Lakes and learned the language of the Odowas. The missionary kept a detailed record of a journey that took him into what he saw as godforsaken (or god-ignored) territory, knowing all the while that at any moment he could die at the hands of Native antagonists. Like other missionaries, he had no fear of death. "I believed," he wrote in his journal, "there was no greater happiness than that of losing my life for the glory of Him who has made all." The Jesuit father could only succeed: either he survived and brought home information about the ways that Natives lived, which would have made it easier to figure out strategies for their conversion to Christianity and integration into French commercial networks, or he died and would, he hoped, become a saint, an achievement even more important to him.[1]

When the journey began on May 17, 1673, at Michilimackinac, an Indigenous trade hub where the Jesuits had established a mission, Marquette knew that the mission's fate hinged on the French travelers' ability to learn from their Native guides. Descending into what the French saw as "*paÿs Inconnus*" (unknown countries), Marquette and his companions "obtained all the information we could from the Indians who had frequented those regions, and we even traced out from their reports a map of the whole of that new country." Learning where the major rivers went, especially the Mississippi, was crucial for these French, who tried to figure out if "the great river" turned westward toward New Mexico and the Pacific or continued southward to the Gulf. Either way would mean an encounter with Spanish, a group that terrified these French more than the Indigenous they knew they would meet along the way. They also hoped to verify the existence of two treasure-filled towns, Theguaio and Quivera.[2]

They never found hoards of gold and silver. Instead, they discovered thriving Indigenous communities. The Menominees, whom Marquette labeled the "Wild Rice" nation, developed and maintained an elaborate economy based to a large extent on the production and consumption of wild rice. The travelers arrived shortly before the plant broke the water's surface from its muddy roots. The grain it produced, twice as long as European-style oats, was the mainstay of the local diet. The Menominees paddled into the flooded fields in September, shaking the plants so that the rice fell easily into their canoes. Women put the grain onto drying racks over a slow-burning, smoke-producing fire. Once the grains were dry, women dropped them into a pouch, buried it in the ground, and walked on it, an act that separated the grain from the remaining husk.

1. Jacques Marquette, "Le premier Voyage qu'a fait le P. Marquette vers le nouveau Mexique & Comment s'en est formé le defsein," *JR*, 59:89 (on Jolliet), 123 (martyrdom). Their willingness to suffer death for their beliefs was not unique in Christendom at the time; see Brad S. Gregory, *Salvation at Stake: Christian Martyrdom in Early Modern Europe* (Cambridge, MA: Harvard University Press, 1999).
2. Marquette, "Premier Voyage," 87–91; "État Présent des Missions des Pères de la Compagnie de Jésus en la Nouvelle-France" (1675), *JR*, 59:217–219 (mission at Michilimackinac).

They then ground some of it into flour and cooked with the rest, seasoning it with fat. "Cooked in this fashion," the Jesuit remarked, the wild rice had "almost as delicate a taste as real rice has when no better seasoning is added." Beyond learning about the vitality of the local industry, Marquette also spoke to the Menominees about the next stages of his journey downriver. They warned him that there were cannibalistic monsters and warring Indigenous nations that would attack with no warning. Marquette told them he would continue nonetheless "because the salvation of souls was at stake, for which I would be delighted to give my life."[3]

Farther downstream, the French entered Maskoutens, a town shared by Miamis, Kickapoos, and Maskoutens. One of the travelers, eager as always to gather Indigenous knowledge, learned about local healing waters and a plant that was a cure for poison, including snakebite. Inhabitants of the town grew maize and gathered grapes and plums. There was limited wood in the area to make houses, so local residents built theirs using rushes for their roofs and walls. That proved less than ideal when it rained, but as Marquette understood, their dwellings could be taken down and carried off when hunting season approached. Awaiting the corn harvest that was soon to begin, "a great crowd" was available to send the travelers off as they paddled down the Wisconsin River toward the Mississippi.[4]

As the party reached the edge of the grasslands, the woodlands thinned and the terrain became flatter. They had come into country dominated not by humans but by *pisikious*, bison, whose appearance dazzled Europeans who had never seen such creatures, twice as wide as the cattle they knew at home, covered with thick curly hair that resembled that of a sheep except it was, Marquette observed, "stronger and thicker." The peoples they encountered had multiple uses for bison, including using hides to make robes, often painted. The creatures roamed their territory in large herds, capable of defending themselves against most aggressors.[5]

When they reached the Illinois country, Marquette and Jolliet split off from their party, following a path that led from the river into a nearby town. The local Illinois welcomed the pair with the ritual of smoking the sun, raising their calumets in careful patterns. They offered the pipes to the visitors, a necessary step before inviting them into their town. The missionary saw that some of them were "Clad in Cloth," which indicated

3. Marquette, "Premier Voyage," 93–97, quotations at 95 (rice) and 97 (life); Allan Greer, ed., *The Jesuit Relations: Natives and Missionaries in Seventeenth-Century North America* (Boston: Bedford Books/St. Martin's Press, 2000), 190–191.
4. Marquette, "Premier Voyage," 101–105, quotation at 105.
5. Marquette, "Premier Voyage," 110–113, quotation at 111.

to him that they were allies of the French. Time and again, residents offered their calumets, a signal that these Illinois maintained long-standing practices for welcoming strangers. Marquette referred to their hospitality as the "usual civility of the country," practiced even among groups in which few, so he believed, had ever seen Frenchmen before. One local leader gave the visitors his son, a continuation of long-standing rituals relating to enslavement and hospitality, and the community put on a feast for the travelers.[6]

Marquette and Jolliet understood that, contrary to the missionary's own claim that these Indigenous lived in spiritual darkness, the Illinois inhabited a bustling town with its rituals and economy intact. There were 300 houses in the city. When the visitors paddled onward, 600 people came to witness their departure, a crowd substantially larger than any these Frenchmen had seen in the Western Hemisphere. Like others inhabiting the prairies, the Illinois hunted with bows and arrows but also had begun, in a very limited way, to integrate guns into their arsenal, though they primarily used them to terrify other Natives with their smoke and noise. They staged periodic missions to procure captives, whom they enslaved and sold to other nations. Their daily sustenance came both from hunting and from farming melons and beans as well as maize. The calumet dance, the most important of their rituals, was so carefully choreographed that Marquette observed that "it might pass for a very fine opening of a ballet in France."[7]

Across the Mississippi Valley there was little sign of European activity. Instead, this landscape reflected the consistent efforts of Indigenous communities. Paddling downriver from the Illinois community, Marquette observed two large monsters painted on rocks overlooking the river. The travelers believed that they were intended to warn Natives not to proceed any farther. What struck Marquette was the artistic skill of the painters. "Good painters in [F]rance would find it difficult to paint so well," he wrote, "and, besides, they are so high up on the rock that it is difficult to reach that place Conveniently to paint them."[8]

Day after day, the French visited thriving communities seemingly little scarred by any spread of infectious diseases or colonial invaders. At the confluence of the Ohio and the Mississippi they discovered large "districts" of Shawnees. One contained twenty-three separate villages and the other had fifteen. Just as significant, there was no obvious diminution in Indigenous knowledge, which often surpassed that of traveling Europeans.

6. Marquette, "Premier Voyage," 115–123.
7. Marquette, "Premier Voyage," 123–137, quotation at 135–137.
8. Marquette, "Premier Voyage," 139–141.

Marquette marveled at the architectural ingenuity of the residents of one unnamed community who built their houses specifically to minimize mosquito attacks. Rather than sleep on the ground on rushes, they instead built a scaffold, keeping smoky fires burning underneath and erecting roofs from bark to keep off the rain and the burning heat of the summer sun. These houses allowed in breezes, cooling the inhabitants. "With the same object," the missionary reported, "we were compelled to erect a sort of cabin on the water, with our sails as protection against the mosquitoes and the rays of the sun."[9]

The party sailed down the river, reaching the Quapaw town of Kappa, located along the Mississippi about twenty-five miles north of its confluence with the Arkansas River. They had reached 33° 40′ north latitude and, by their reckoning, they could have made it to the shores of the Gulf in only a few more days, though the Quapaws suggested that the journey could take another five to ten days. These Indigenous residents provided the travelers with fish and *sagamité* (hominy), following the common hospitality customs of the country. A young man who spoke Illinois became a translator at what became a decisive moment for Marquette and his companions since they had unknowingly reached a dangerous place. The Quapaws warned the travelers that they themselves never went that far because their enemies, bolstered by guns they had acquired from Europeans, might kill them. They convinced the French to paddle northward rather than finishing their journey.

Had the French been better able to speak with the Quapaws, and had their hosts been more forthcoming about themselves, the travelers would have learned that these Indigenous had themselves only recently moved into the region. They had previously lived farther east, but an unidentified Iroquoian-speaking group, armed with weapons they had gotten from Dutch traders, forced them and others westward across the Mississippi. There they needed to establish communities while keenly understanding that the region's existing residents—Caddoan-speakers to the west and Koroas, Tunicas, and Yazoos to the south—resented the newcomers' arrival. What the Quapaws wanted was access to European trade goods so that they could rival the power of their enemies. Marquette and Jolliet arrived at just the right time: if the Quapaws could convince these visitors that they were worthy allies, perhaps French traders far to the north would establish relations with them, exchanging weapons for the bison that Marquette saw as crucial to the local economy. The Quapaws succeeded. The French scurried homeward convinced of the Quapaws' friendship and thankful that their new allies had warned them about the

9. Marquette, "Premier Voyage," 145–147, quotation at 147.

enemies who would have confronted and likely captured them had they continued downriver. The Quapaws saved the lives of the French and, as Marquette recorded in his journal, prevented them from "losing the results of this voyage."[10]

After they turned around, the French expedition returned with Marquette's report, which included information they had gathered from Indigenous residents they had met. A map of their journey from 1681 identifies the location of portages and the names of many of the towns they visited. It also bears two captions. Near the northern edge, in territory west of Lake Michigan, it identifies "*Terres inhabités*"—occupied lands. To the far south, just north of the Gulf of Mexico, is a single word: "Europeans."[11] Few images ever captured the marginal nature of colonial expansion so effortlessly.

Marquette and Jolliet had paddled down the Mississippi on a voyage of exploration. Jolliet, who would later propose the construction of a canal in the Illinois country and become a professor of hydrography at a college established by the Jesuits in Québec, was especially interested in geography. Marquette, like other Jesuits of his era, was keen to find the best ways to convert Natives. He returned to the Illinois country but died there in 1675. One of the younger Jesuits who attended his death soon fell ill. After saying a prayer, he grabbed some of the earth covering Marquette's body and held it to his chest. According to an unknown observer, he recovered instantly. Perhaps Marquette was indeed destined for sainthood, and this would be but the first of his miracles.[12]

Marquette and Jolliet, the first of their nation to make a sustained visit to the region, had gone in search of geographical wisdom and to find new souls for Christ. What they discovered was an Indigenous world where Europeans hardly mattered.

10. Marquette, "Premier Voyage," 153–155, 159–161; Kathleen DuVal, *The Native Ground: Indians and Colonists in the Heart of the Continent* (Philadelphia: University of Pennsylvania Press, 2006), 1–3.

11. "Carte de la découverte faite l'an 1673 dans l'Amérique septentrionale" (1681?), Library of Congress Geography and Map Division, 2003627092.

12. On Jolliet: Greer, ed., *Jesuit Relations*, 186–188; Robert M. Morrissey, *Empire by Collaboration: Indians, Colonists, and Governments in Colonial Illinois Country* (Philadelphia: University of Pennsylvania Press, 2015), 42–43. On the death of Marquette: "Recit du second voyage et de la mort du P. Jacques Marquette," *JR*, 59:195–201.

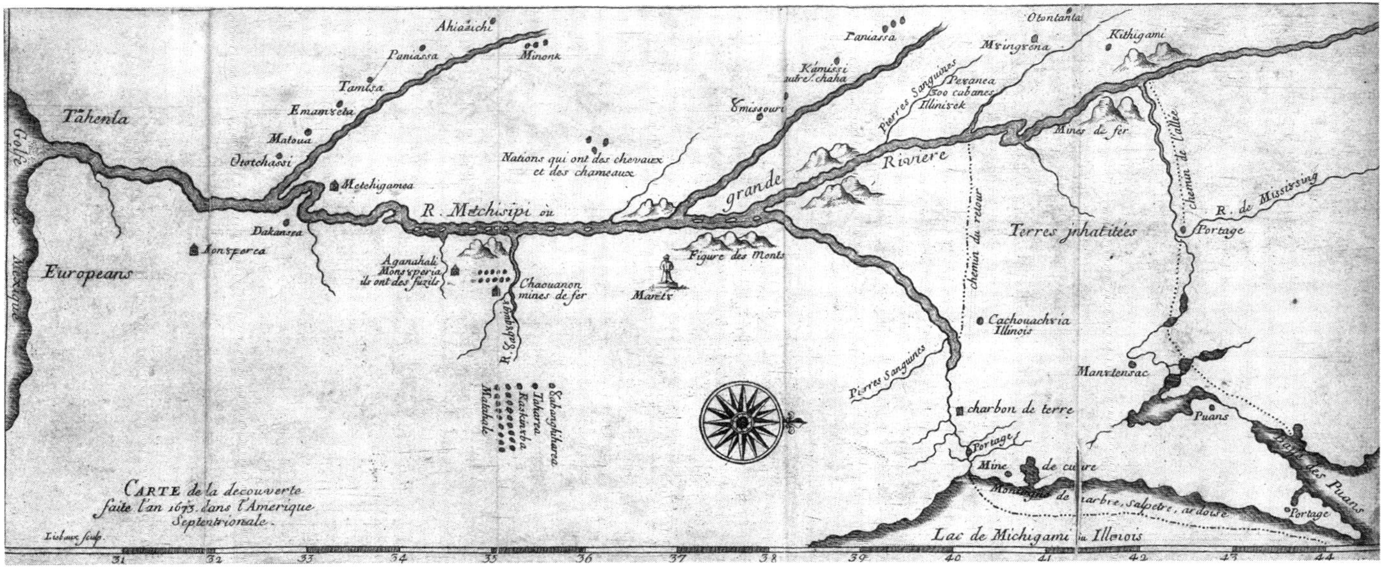

This 1673 map, oriented with north to the right, reveals a truth that every European who traveled west of the Appalachian Mountains understood: the Mississippi Valley remained in Indigenous territory, as the names of Native towns reveal. "Carte de la découverte faite l'an 1673 dans l'Amérique septentrionale." Library of Congress, Geography and Map Division, 2003627092.

From the arrival of Europeans in North America in the early sixteenth century until the 1670s, the number of Native people had changed only marginally in the territory that stretched from the crest of the Appalachian Mountains to the Pacific Ocean. There had of course been localized catastrophic epidemics, such as the leptospirosis that ravaged coastal England in the late 1610s, the smallpox or influenza epidemics that spread through Wendake (or Huronia) in 1637 and 1639, and various epidemics that spread in the Southeast near Spanish *entradas* and missions. But these scourges had far less of an impact on the overall number of Native people than the hemorrhagic fevers that had taken millions of lives in Mexico in 1545 and 1576, and it is likely that the contagions that spread close to the Atlantic had no substantial demographic impact in the Mississippi Valley or farther west.[13]

Population stability across much of North America through the late seventeenth century was not mysterious. The epidemics that ravaged coastal areas relied on four elements. First, some vector had to spread an infectious virus (like smallpox) or bacteria (leptospirosis) from a host (which could be a rat or monkey as well as a human) to a human whose body lacked immunity to it. Second, humans tend to develop at least some (if not total) immunity to a disease if exposed to it in childhood, when the body is better able to recover. Smallpox remained alive in major European cities because there was always a possible new host for the virus. In the American heartland, where large clusters of people were rare, new contagious diseases might take a horrendous toll on adults and have spillover social and economic consequences, but they would likely flare out quickly. Third, diseases often led to mortality when humans were undergoing stress, which could have been caused by a variety of factors including reduced food consumption, dispossession and forced relocation, and even psychological forces. Across the interior, food supplies remained constant, no colonial group had the capacity to displace Indigenous communities, and there was only the transitory emotional stress that one

13. Lalemant in *JR*, 19:89–95; John L. Brooke, *Climate Change and the Course of Global History: A Rough Journey* (Cambridge: Cambridge University Press, 2014), 432; Paul Kelton, *Epidemics and Enslavement: Biological Catastrophe in the Native Southeast, 1492–1715* (Lincoln: University of Nebraska Press, 2007), 48–87. Douglas Ubelaker noted steep reductions in the Northeast (from approximately 346,000 in 1500 to 149,000 from 1600 to 1700) and the Southeast (from 157,400 to 105,000 during the same century), but no change in the Indigenous population of the Great Basin, Plateau, or the Plains before 1700; see Douglas L. Ubelaker, "North American Indian Population Size," in John S. Verano and Douglas H. Ubelaker, eds., *Disease and Demography in the Americas* (Washington, DC: Smithsonian Institution Press, 1992), table 3 (173).

might experience when being told, for example, that their traditional belief system should be replaced by Christianity. Fourth, epidemics often followed repeated contact with disease-bearers. Marquette and Jolliet were among the first Europeans to travel through the Mississippi Valley, and their party of seven was too small for them to sustain any infection very long.

Demographic steadiness across the interior did not mean an absence of violence. The Haudenosaunee raids that had begun in the 1640s, prompted by the urge to claim a larger share of the continent's shrinking beaver population, continued to reshape Indigenous communities, with residents lost through deaths in battle, taken as captives, or forced into exile. But even though many Native communities held to notions of avenging the death of those taken in conflict, Indigenous warfare tended more toward the kidnapping of potential slaves than the kinds of wholesale slaughter that had at times characterized battles between Natives and Europeans. Apart from the western thrusts of Haudenosaunee, violence within the Ohio and Mississippi Valleys remained limited in so-called mourning wars, in which the goal of conflict was not to destroy another community but instead to limit violence by killing the same number of an enemy that the enemy had killed. This kind of warfare had deep personal consequences and threatened families, which often adopted captives through elaborate rituals to replace the deceased. But it had little impact on overall populations across the interior.[14]

Europeans who traveled to the Great Lakes region and then descended into the Mississippi Valley were all too aware that any efforts to alter the economies and religious practices of Indigenous had amounted to little even by the last decades of the seventeenth century. At times, their failure to change Natives' lives proved advantageous, as French explorer Henri de Tonty learned when his traveling party entered an Illinois village in late December 1679. The inhabitants were away on their annual winter hunt. But that did not stop the Europeans, who were starving, from stealing forty bushels of stored maize. The travelers were suffering dearth because of recent fires in the prairies, an event that had no apparent impact on local Natives, who still maintained an economy based on farming maize, gathering local fruits, and hunting bison. Their diet no doubt

14. See Ned Blackhawk, *The Rediscovery of America: Native Peoples and the Unmaking of U.S. History* (New Haven, CT: Yale University Press, 2023), 95–103; Eric Hinderaker, *Elusive Empires: Constructing Colonialism in the Ohio Valley, 1673–1800* (Cambridge: Cambridge University Press, 1997), 12–13; Daniel K. Richter, "War and Culture: The Iroquois Experience," *WMQ*, 3rd. Ser., 40 (1983), 528–559.

contributed to their health, with de Tonty remarking that they were the fastest runners in America.[15]

Decades after would-be colonizers created what they believed were viable notions of trade that they hoped would transform Indigenous economic practices—primarily by enticing hunters to bring them beaver pelts or bison hides in exchange for European manufactured goods—they discovered an enormous gulf between Native and newcomer notions of material objects. Rather than become market-oriented individuals who would value the accumulation of new goods, Indigenous across the interior continued to behave in the ways that Europeans had criticized near the coast. The persistence of local religious and economic attitudes found no greater expression than in rituals known as the feast of the dead. Some communities practiced such events every twelve or so years, though there is insufficient documentation to know if that pattern repeated across the interior. Whether a community held a feast according to a set calendar is less crucial than the fact that European efforts to colonize the continent had had as of yet had only a minor impact on these rituals.

During a feast of the dead, a ritual observed by Europeans among the Wendats in 1636 and the Anishinaabeg as late as 1660, communities gathered to memorialize their recently deceased. These ceremonies were not limited to a specific town. In 1660, the Anishinaabeg hosted a three-day feast that brought together members of their communities as well as Athinuwick and Dakota. Over 1,000 attended the event that year, watching the sacred handling of the dead and the exchange of goods with other communities. The goal in that instance was to create Anishinaabewaki, a homeland for the Anishinaabeg that incorporated others, transforming foreigners (*meyaagizid*) into relatives (*inawemaagen*). Indigenous incorporated European goods into their rituals, interring them with the bodies of their former enemies in an effort to reduce tensions by creating symbolic alliances.[16]

The logic of the ceremony baffled European observers. The point of commerce, in their mind, was the accumulation of wealth. Those who witnessed the interring of trade goods with the dead could not grasp why

15. Henri de Tonti, *Relation of Henri de Tonty Concerning the Explorations of La Salle from 1678 to 1683*, trans. Melville B. Anderson (Chicago: Caxton Club, 1898), 27–29; Robert M. Morrissey, *People of the Ecotone: Environment and Indigenous Power at the Center of Early America* (Seattle: University of Washington Press, 2022), 64.

16. Greer, ed., *Jesuit Relations*, 61–69 (1636); Michael Witgen, *An Infinity of Nations: How the Native New World Shaped Early North America* (Philadelphia: University of Pennsylvania Press, 2012), 59–64.

anyone would engage in such an act, which flew in the face of the market-oriented logic that had contributed to Europeans' thirst for the resources of the Western Hemisphere. French trader Nicolas Perrot, a native of Burgundy who had traveled from Montreal to the western shores of Lake Michigan in 1665 and joined an expedition that sailed from the western edge of Lake Superior back to Montreal five years later, witnessed a feast of the dead among Algonquians. He and Jesuit observers had already watched while Indigenous mourners buried deceased relatives and friends with what he saw as valuable goods, including weapons and wampum—the very goods that Native hunters had obtained for pelts. He then watched them disinter many of these goods along with human remains in the ritual, only to rebury them again in a permanent grave. In doing so, he wrote, "they reduce themselves to such an extreme of poverty that they do not reserve for themselves a single hatchet or knife." Some held on to copper kettles. But they buried other goods with the deceased. They had traded for these valuable objects earlier not for their utility, he believed, but so "they may render the souls of the departed more happy and more highly respected in the country of the dead." This puzzled Europeans, who had long observed that community leaders obtained trade goods to distribute them to others, thereby solidifying their communities and their role as guardians of their community's welfare. They missed the point that rituals, most notably the feast of the dead, had the same intent. It was only "lavish spending," Perrot commented, that "can fully secure rest for the departed souls." By burying valuable worldly goods in the ground to please the spirits of the dead, leaders reinforced a sense of community that extended into the past, thereby facilitating supportive ties among the living.[17]

Long-standing practices also continued to shape landscapes to maximize their utility. Missionary Louis Nicolas, whose detailed natural history of the Great Lakes region provided vivid evidence of a thriving economy, was struck by the way that local peoples tended to chestnut trees. "The natives have not found a better way of gathering this fruit than to set fire to the woods," he observed. But his criticism immediately faded into praise. "When all the leaves and some of the undergrowth is burned,

17. Nicholas Perrot, *Memoire sur les moeurs, coustumes et religion des sauvages de l'Amerique septentrionale* (Paris, 1864), translated as "Memoir on the Manners, Customs, and Religion of the Savages of North America," in Emma H. Blair, *The Indian Tribes of the Upper Mississippi Valley and Region of the Great Lakes* (orig. pub. 1911; Lincoln: University of Nebraska Press, 1996), 1:86–88, quotations at 88; Richard White, *The Middle Ground: Indians, Empires, and Republics in the Great Lakes Region, 1650–1815* (Cambridge: Cambridge University Press, 1991), 99–104; Witgen, *Infinity of Nations*, 63.

the chestnuts are easy to see and gather." He also reported that Indigenous had "carved or made indecent figures" on some of these trees and worshipped them, an act he believed revealed their "deplorable blindness." Still, he had to admit that the chestnuts were "as good as those of French trees."[18]

The persistence of cultural traditions did not reflect an unchanging continent. While there are precious few extant firsthand accounts from the latter decades of the seventeenth century, abundant evidence reveals a dynamic Indigenous world where relations between nations were often in flux even far away from the ocean, reflecting what may best be understood as second-order effects: European-driven change among Indigenous along the Atlantic coast or in northern New Spain could have an impact unwitnessed by colonizers. Spanish officials laid claim to a vast territory they labeled New Mexico, but those assertions of ownership meant little across the Great Basin, the territory stretching from modern eastern California to Colorado and the southern border between modern Arizona and California north into Wyoming, Idaho, and Oregon. These were the homelands of the Northern Paiute, Southern Paiute, Northern Shoshone, Eastern Shoshone, Western Shoshone, and Washoe, as well as the Owens Valley Paiute. The arrival of Spanish traders did open the possibility of forming enduring alliances with the colonizers. Jostling for trade goods facilitated new alliances, including between Utes and Comanches, which only enhanced the territorial authority of some Native peoples.[19]

During the middle and last decades of the century the availability of horses began to create yet more new relations across regions dominated by Indigenous. There had been horses in North America earlier, but they became extinct approximately 12,000 years ago, likely because of climate change and human hunting. Horses did not return to areas north of New Spain in any substantial numbers until the 1640s. At that point, Indigenous in the Southwest began to learn about horses, and some communities began to integrate them into their economies. Nations that adopted horses understood that they could be used to facilitate the long-distance movement of people as well as goods and, eventually, to redefine bison hunting, which had been done in earlier times by people on foot but became increasingly the specialty of Natives with equestrian skills. By

18. François-Marc Gagnon, ed., *The Codex Canadensis with the Writings of Louis Nicolas*, trans. Nancy Senior (Tulsa, OK: Gilcrease Museum, 2011), 295–296.
19. Ned Blackhawk, *Violence over the Land: Indians and Empires in the Early American West* (Cambridge, MA: Harvard University Press, 2006), 35–54.

the latter decades of the seventeenth century, Apaches, Comanches, and possibly Utes had adopted horses, with the Comanches eventually able to take most advantage of them.[20]

The changes in the interior can be understood by following the experiences of Siouan-speaking peoples, who inhabited territory southwest of Lake Superior. They constituted not a single nation but instead a cluster of communities in which towns shared membership in the Očhéthi Šakówin—the Seven Council Fires. Four groups together made up the Dakotas, who lived near Mde Wakan (also known as Mille Lacs): Mdewakantons, Sissetons, Wahpekutes, and Wahpetons. The Yanktons and Yanktonais lived in the Mississippi Valley, and the Lakotas settled in the Minnesota Valley. They lived on lands where forests, which dominated the landscape to the east, and prairie met. Their location gave them access to a wide range of resources, including bison, elk, wild rice, muskellunge, plums, berries, nuts, maple trees (which could be tapped for their syrup), and *mdo*, a plant similar to a potato. Though residents in the three clusters spoke local dialects, they had enough in common to understand each other, which facilitated large meetings—including at communal bison hunts, described in winter counts on hides that predated the arrival of horses in the region. Community members traveled to maximize their access to resources in particular seasons, with women in canoes harvesting rice and men taking the lead in trade and political meetings. Winter hunts dominated the colder months, and then fishing took over when the temperature climbed.[21]

Whatever stability these nations had achieved by mid-century came under pressure from events that began farther east, especially the smallpox epidemic that erupted from the Atlantic inward in 1633. Among its victims were the Haudenosaunee, whose combined numbers dropped by approximately half, from 20,000 to 10,000, during the scourge. In their efforts to repopulate their homeland, Haudenosaunee, who had already mastered creating trade relationships with Europeans, sent raiding parties westward, marching into the lands of Kickapoos, Mascoutens, and Potawatomis, which prompted survivors of the epidemics from those nations to move westward too. Eventually, these new refugees, who were fleeing the Haudenosaunee, not Europeans, took up residence to the east

20. Peter Mitchell, *Horse Nations: The Worldwide Impact of the Horse on Indigenous Societies Post-1492* (Oxford: Oxford University Press, 2015), 65–68 (extinction of original horse), 76–83 (return of horses); Pekka Hämäläinen, *The Comanche Empire* (New Haven, CT: Yale University Press, 2008), 18–67.

21. Pekka Hämäläinen, *Lakota America: A New History of Indigenous Power* (New Haven, CT: Yale University Press, 2019), 15–21; Morrissey, *People of the Ecotone*, 20–41.

of the Seven Council Fires of the Sioux. Their arrival brought opportunity and threat to the eastern edges of the alliance.[22]

The danger arrived first. Indigenous peoples around the Great Lakes, notably the Odawas, Sauteurs, and Wyandots, established alliances with French fur traders, who provided Native hunters with guns. With access to eastern territories closed off by Haudenosaunee, these Indigenous partners turned their sights toward the rich beaver-hunting lands to their west. Soon after mid-century, Crees and Sauteurs, enticed by the same rewards as Odawas (who had become the prime threat to the peoples clustered around Mde Wakan), also invaded the lands of the Očhéthi Šakówi. The historic isolation of the Sioux from regular contact with Europeans (and their Indigenous allies) had meant that they never suffered the kind of severe population losses that had afflicted so many others. In the shifting alliances of the era, French traders sent overtures to the Sioux, sensing that they would become ideal partners in the fur trade.[23]

It was not European ingenuity that altered relations in this territory that few Europeans had ever even seen. Instead, some of the Sioux accepted an overture from the Sauteurs to bring home the bones of those who had fallen in battle between the Sioux and the Sauteurs and Crees. The Sauters, that is, had invited their enemies eastward to participate in a feast of the dead. Men and women who spent several days walking to the event understood that through this reburying of the dead they could make their enemies into their fictive kin, thereby reducing (or even eliminating) any future threats to the Sioux from these onetime antagonists. French traders present for the event knew that women accompanying men guaranteed that their acceptance of the invitation would lead to peace, not further hostilities. More revealing still, French observers realized that Sioux men took advice from their partners (the newcomers believed that each man had two wives), another ongoing difference between American gender norms and those of Europeans. The Sioux also engaged in ritual acts to greet French traders Pierre-Esprit Radisson and Médard Chouart Des Groseilliers, including offering them a calumet, the universal signifier of peaceful intent. Their act of piety gave the traders the chance to welcome the Sioux as new adopted children of Onontio, an Indigenous name for the governor of New France, whose

22. Hämäläinen, *Lakota America*, 20–23.
23. Hämäläinen, *Lakota America*, 24–28.

authority, derived from the king of France, made him the symbolic father of the French family around the Great Lakes.

The Europeans left the ritual convinced that they alone had brokered peace between the Sioux and the Sauteurs and, they hoped, the Crees. If so, it gave them greater access to the presumably substantial population of beaver to be found to the west, access that meant even more given the near disappearance of beaver across New England. For the Sioux, the arrangement meant that they would have access to guns and other European trade goods. To help seal the deal, Sioux representatives let the French traders know that Native women might be open to intermarriage, an appealing prospect to emigrant men living on a continent with few single European women.[24]

As much as the French hoped that there would be peace to their west, which would facilitate the capture and hauling of beaver to the Great Lakes and then up the St. Lawrence, relations among Indigenous at times remained tense. The Sioux had established an alliance with Crees and Sauteurs by 1660, but they had no ongoing ties to Natives who lived farther east. During the 1660s and 1670s, tensions occasionally flared, at times pitting Natives from the Great Lakes, such as the Wyandots, against groups of Sioux. French observers reported in horror the ways that captors sometimes cooked and cannibalized their Native captives. Avenging the death of one traveling party consumed by Wyandots, the Sioux captured their leader, Sinagos. They kept him alive, at least according to a French observer, slicing off parts of his thighs to feed to him, to symbolically represent his role in the deaths of their own. Even such horrific violence did not rekindle permanent warfare. Sioux and Sauter leaders reestablished peace in 1679.[25]

The rapprochement fit economic dreams as far as Paris. Earlier, in 1663, Jean-Baptiste Colbert, the French finance minister, had dispatched soldiers to Iroquoia to establish a claim by right of conquest to that region. Those troops burned four Mohawk towns along with their stored food. By 1669, Colbert and the king understood the importance of free trade ("*liberté du commerce*") in the interior and encouraged its expansion. The finance minister hoped that the movement of goods, beyond its economic value at home, would encourage French migration westward.

24. Hämäläinen, *Lakota America*, 28–31; White, *Middle Ground*, 21–23 (calumet), 39–40 (Onontio); William Cronon, *Changes in the Land: Indians, Colonists, and the Ecology of New England* (New York: Hill and Wang, 1983), 97–99 (New England).

25. Hämäläinen, *Lakota America*, 33–38.

But he knew as well as others that the *pays d'en haut* would long remain under Natives' control.[26]

While politics shifted over time, the effects of the Indigenous market revolution remained constant, especially evident in the sale of distilled beverages—rum in territories where English and Dutch were able to ply their trade and brandy among the French. For Europeans, this new market had enormous benefits, including providing a new justification for the use of enslaved laborers to produce sugar. More sugar meant more rum and brandy, which could be sold for beaver and other furs. Europeans knew that the consumption of alcohol could cause social problems. To reduce danger, colonial governments had created multiple laws banning its sale to Indigenous. Even though its sale was illegal, Europeans around the Great Lakes and the Mississippi Valley knew all too well that alcohol was the perfect trade good. It posed less of a risk to the sellers than guns. Bearers of liquor into the interior could also increase their profits by watering down the contents of their kegs. Eventually many Indigenous peoples protested the trade, but its damage was too recent to have encouraged widespread Native temperance movements before 1680.[27]

Even in the early years of the trade, clerics often objected to alcohol's use in commerce. François Xavier de Laval de Montigny, the bishop of Québec, saw the problems by 1660. That year, he ordered the excommunication of any French trader who sold brandy to Indigenous. He followed through with two who violated his will, and he threatened still others. In his mind, the liquor trade had the power to undermine the

26. Colbert, who held Indigenous Americans in low regard and wanted to find ways to convert them to French ways, thought that expanded trade would, as he put it, "convieront un nombre considérable de François d'y passer tous les ans; en sorte que ce pays se peuplera et s'augmentera sans aucune peine" (invite a considerable number of French to pass through every year; as a result, this country will be populated and increased without any difficulty). Colbert to the governor-general of Canada, May 15, 1669, in Jean-Baptiste Colbert, *Lettres, Instructions, et Mémoires*, ed. Pierre Clément, 8 vols. (Paris, 1861–1862), 3:449–451; W. J. Eccles, *The Canadian Frontier, 1534–1760* (New York: Holt, Rinehart, and Winston, 1969), 62–64; Frank E. Ross, "The Fur Trade of the Western Great Lakes Region," *Minnesota History* 19 (1938), 271–307, esp. 274–277; Gilles Havard, *Histoire de coureurs de bois: Amérique du Nord, 1600–1840* (Paris: Les Indes Savantes, 2016), 61–112; Alisa Petrovich, "Perception and Reality: Colbert's Native American Policy," *Louisiana History* 39 (1998), 73–83.

27. See Peter C. Mancall, *Deadly Medicine: Indians and Alcohol in Early America* (Ithaca, NY: Cornell University Press, 1995), 39–61 (trade), 103–110 (colonial legislation), 101–129 (temperance efforts).

gains that Jesuits and other religious had been making in the St. Lawrence Valley and around the Great Lakes. Jesuits and the Indigenous who worked with them celebrated the bishop's actions. They believed that the scourge of alcohol abuse might disappear. However personally committed the bishop was to the cause—the famed Ursuline Marie de L'Incarnation thought the campaign took a severe toll on Laval—civil authorities demanded the revocation of the original order and another that followed it. Despite praise that he received in Paris from theologians at the Sorbonne, he could do no more than assert that those who traded brandy to Natives were committing a mortal sin, not breaking a provincial law.[28]

Fear of damnation had little impact on those who saw the profits to be made, even when they risked being flogged for these sales. "The evil continued its rapid progress," the Jesuit Pierre François Xavier de Charlevoix lamented in the early 1660s, afflicting Indigenous "who are not able to refrain from it when offered, and in whom the least effect of this drink is the suspension of their reason, plunged into scandals which cost many tears to those who had at such cost begotten them to Christ." Alcohol-fueled violence grew over the course of the 1660s. Some Native communities abstained, as did Indigenous individuals across North America. But the superior of the Sulpician order in Montreal, François Dollier de Casson, who saw entire towns abstaining, claimed that Haudenosaunee and Algonquins drank whenever they could, making "the same use as the madman makes of his sword." Clerical admonitions had little power in the face of the economic logic of the fur trade. If French *coureurs de bois* (traders) did not bring brandy to trading sessions, Indigenous who wanted alcohol would get it from other Europeans, most likely Dutch entrepreneurs. The fear of losing commerce overrode French missionaries' concern for Native bodies. One Algonquin chief who was also a convert told the Sulpician that the colonial governor was "killing us by permitting people to give us liquors." One Jesuit after another, sensitized to the spiritual dangers of alcohol abuse, claimed that excessive drinking led to poverty, violence, the sale of Native children to purchase brandy, and young men using alcohol to have sex with young women. Liquor, as one put it in the characteristic language of these religious, was "a demon that robs [Indigenous] of their reason" and prompted them to sell an entire year's

28. *Mandements, lettres pastorales et circulaires des éveques de Québec* (Quebec, 1887–1888), 1:14–15, 30–32, 42–43, 94; *JR*, 46:105, 46:187; Marie de L'Incarnation to her son, August 10, 1662, in Joyce Marshall, trans. and ed., *Word from New France: The Selected Letters of Marie de L'Incarnation* (Toronto: Oxford University Press, 1967), 274; Jean Delanglez, *Frontenac and the Jesuits* (Chicago: Institute of Jesuit History, 1939), 96–97n.

hunt to obtain brandy, which forced them "to pass the winter in nakedness, famine, and all sorts of deprivation."[29]

In the face of such claims, Frontenac summoned interested colonial parties to a meeting to discuss the brandy trade in 1678. He invited no Indigenous men or women. At the meeting, some colonists again invoked the specter of losing furs to Dutch or even English traders, which meant not only a loss of revenue but also greater exposure to Protestants and their hopes to convert Indigenous to an anti–Roman Catholic Christianity. One went so far as to argue that Natives needed access to alcohol if they were to adopt European ways since negotiations among Europeans often included drinking. If Europeans denied them "the freedom to live as we do, they will never become Christians." Explorer La Salle offered what he saw as definitive proof of the need for traders to offer brandy. According to his estimates, French traders hauled in 60,000 to 80,000 beaver skins each year, using liquor to lubricate sales with perhaps 20,000 Natives. Others at the meeting agreed that limiting the sale of alcohol would harm the trade. Still, one suggested that reducing the trade would prompt French colonists to turn their attention to farming, which he saw as a more likely avenue to economic success in the province. His was a minority voice. The final word came from the king of France, who in 1679 issued a proclamation that the sale of brandy to Natives could continue, but only in colonial communities and not in Indigenous towns.[30]

North and west of any territory French could claim, English merchants supplying the newly launched Hudson Bay Company also came to the conclusion that providing distilled spirits to Indigenous hunters could facilitate the fur trade. They embraced the same logic as other fur-trading Europeans: if bearers could get kegs of rum or brandy to interior posts,

29. *JR*, 46:187 (flogging), 53:247, 251, 257 (violence), 51:123, 53:241, 55:85, 57:81 (fear of Dutch influence), 44:99, 46:103–105 (social ills), 53:191–193, 55:85, 58:77, 193 (sober Natives); [François] Dollier de Casson, *A History of Montreal, 1640–1672*, trans. and ed. Ralph Flenley (New York: Dutton, 1928), 339–341; Pierre François Xavier de Charlevoix, *History and General Description of New France*, trans. John G. Shea (New York, 1866–1862), 3:54–55; Marie de L'Incarnation to her son, August 10, 1662, 274.

30. "Délibération sur le cas reserve du commerce de l'eau-de-vie avec les sauvages, 1678," in Pierre Margry, ed., *Découvertes et établissements des français dans l'ouest et dans le sud de l'Amérique septentrionale (1614–1754)* (Paris, 1875–1886), 1:407–419; G. B. Munro, "The Brandy Parliament of 1678," *Canadian Historical Review* 2 (1921), 172–189; Delanglez, *Frontenac and the Jesuits*, 122–124; W. J. Eccles, *Frontenac, the Courtier Governor* (Toronto: McClelland and Stewart, [1959]), 61–68; George F. G. Stanley, "The Indians and the Brandy Trade During the Ancien Régime," *Revue d'Histoire de l'Amérique Française* 6 (1953), 489–505.

those selling it would reap a handsome profit in pelts, though it took decades before alcohol constituted a substantial portion of HBC sales.[31]

In 1700, Hudson Bay Company traders working in Fort Albany, one of their two factories facing James Bay—the same bay where Hudson's crew had left him to die—created a price list for goods. All items were to be valued in comparison to one whole beaver skin, known as "made beaver." The fur of a marten was worth one-quarter of a made beaver, while a red fox was worth half, a bear was worth two, and a moose skin was worth six. Native traders with skins could purchase goods at an established price. A gun cost seven made beaver, a blanket cost five, a kettle cost one, a hatchet cost one-half, one pound of powder cost two-thirds, and one pound of shot cost one-fifth. Prices for non-durable goods were equally specific: a pound of tobacco cost one made beaver, while a pound of vermillion, the most expensive item available for purchase at the factory, cost ten. By creating this hierarchy, Indigenous and English traders accepted a new system of values, set in a local currency (made beaver), for goods that had traveled often hundreds of miles to reach James Bay. In the last years of the seventeenth century there were relatively few HBC agents working the shores of Hudson and James bays. Whatever success the trade had relied on the willingness of Crees, Anishinaabeg, Assiniboines, and other Native hunters to haul beaver skins to the factories to obtain both everyday durable goods like knives along with what Europeans saw as luxury goods: mirrors, rings, glass beads from China and Venice, and vermillion, an expensive pigment to make red paint that Europeans traded to Anishinaabe women at least as early as the 1650s.[32]

Those traders learned the same lessons that Jesuit missionaries had learned earlier. Success in the interior meant living in a world where Indigenous rules dictated behavior. Among the European religious, the Jesuits had the greatest success in the mission field, possibly because Native peoples accepted the presence of their small numbers in Indigenous communities. The Jesuits in New France traveled more lightly than the Franciscans who journeyed northward from Mexico loaded down by large bells and liturgical hardware. They also studied Native languages across the St. Lawrence Valley to produce dictionaries to facilitate dialogue with those they hoped to convert.

31. Ann M. Carlos and Frank D. Lewis, *Commerce by a Frozen Sea: Native Americans and the European Fur Trade* (Philadelphia: University of Pennsylvania Press, 2010), 89–94.

32. Carlos and Lewis, *Commerce by a Frozen Sea*, 52 (price of goods in made beaver), 168 (Native traders and non-durable goods), 217n68 (volume of luxury goods); Bruce M. White, "The Woman Who Married a Beaver: Trade Patterns and Gender Roles in the Ojibwa Fur Trade," *Ethnohistory* 46 (1999), 109–147, esp. 118.

Among those enticed by the Jesuits' message was a young Mohawk woman named Tekakwitha, who had survived smallpox as a child. Inspired by the teachings of the newcomers, she moved to Kahnawake (known as Sault St. Louis to the missionaries), where she came to the attention of Claude Chauchetière, a Jesuit from Poitiers who had lived in the St. Lawrence Valley for three years—enough time to learn how to speak a local language. Like other women in the community, Tekakwitha, known to the missionaries as Catherine, embraced abstinence, fasting, and self-flagellation. Only twenty-four when she died in the spring of 1680, her devotion to Christ was so admirable that in 2012 Pope Benedict XVI called her "the Protectress of Canada and the first native American saint" when he canonized her.[33]

Although some Native individuals converted to Christianity in each colonial setting, the changes across the interior were more commonly evident in the adoption of European goods. An Indigenous consumer revolution drove the success of the fur trade near Hudson Bay, across the Great Lakes region, and into New England. The arrival of European horses transformed some communities in the southern plains. One tragic outcome of this continent-wide shift in buying tastes was the increase in meetings between Native peoples and European traders who likely carried infectious diseases into the interior. The extraction of natural wealth for Europeans almost always meant increased risk of illness and death in Indigenous to avoid red communities.

New political alliances emerging in parts of the Mississippi Valley signaled that the impact of European conquest and colonization could be felt even when there were hardly any Europeans in the vicinity. Even though many Indigenous wanted goods that had become more available since the middle of the century, few wholly reoriented their lives and cultures to obtain them. Instead, guns, horses, iron tools, and even alcohol became objects of desire that encouraged some reorganization of traditional economic and cultural practices without undermining extant traditional cultures. The same could not be said of Christianity, an ineffable European product that demanded changes in how one lived. The frustrations that Jesuits felt along their journeys reflected the persistence of traditional mores, gender roles, and political organizations. As even the most optimistic missionary would have known, the American interior remained Indian Country.

33. Allan Greer, *Mohawk Saint: Catherine Tekakwitha and the Jesuits* (New York: Oxford University Press, 2005); Homily of His Holiness Pope Benedict XVI, October 21, 2012, https://www.vatican.va/content/benedict-xvi/en/homilies/2012/documents/hf_ben-xvi_hom_20121021_canonizzazioni.html.

25

Rebellions

On January 14, 1665, Fernando de Villaneuva became the governor of New Mexico. Born in San Sebastián in the Basque country, he enlisted in the Armada in 1630. In the years that followed, he fought in Catalonia and traveled with the Armada of the Indies to the Algarve, in southern Portugal, to suppress an uprising. By the mid-1640s, he had crossed the Atlantic and taken on a series of positions to support the Spanish imperial effort. His storied career led to his appointment in the north, landing him in a colonial world soon to collapse.[1]

Villaneuva understood the precarity of Spanish claims to New Mexico. He knew about and participated in transporting enslaved Indigenous to Parral, a commerce that continued to enrage Apaches. Like every governor of the expansive territory, he would have also known the location of each mission church. He was extremely sensitive to the real possibility that a revolt could erase New Mexico from European maps, the only place where it had any meaning at the time. He grasped, too, that politics and religion could not be separated here. The cause of empire was the cause of Christendom, just as it remained for other Europeans eager to conquer and colonize North America.

Villanueva had arrived at a dangerous time. He was an immigrant given authority over people in a territory that had been suffering from a drought and where tensions between Indigenous and Spaniards had already erupted when some Natives fled rather than pay tribute payments.[2] In 1665, Spanish soldiers had attacked Cacaxtles, who lived in modern south

1. Rick Hendricks, "Fernando de Villaneuva y Armendaris," unpublished manuscript in author's possession. Jack D. Forbes, *Apache, Navajo, and Spaniard* (Norman: University of Oklahoma Press, 1960), 160–161.
2. Colin Calloway, *One Vast Winter Count: The Native American West Before Lewis and Clark* (Lincoln: University of Nebraska Press, 2003), 167; William C. Foster, ed., *Texas and Northeastern Mexico, 1630–1690 by Juan Bautista Chapa*, trans. Ned F. Brierley (Austin: University of Texas Press, 1997), 53–66.

Texas and along the Rio Grande, murdering 100 of them. The Natives plundered colonists' households and killed any who confronted them. A priest who witnessed the violence believed that if soldiers could not suppress the rebels, then "all this has served for nothing more than to have many Spaniards die far from their homelands at the hands of those Indians for whom they have worked." Spanish soldiers suppressed an anti-clerical insurrection along the lower Rio Grande in 1667, but another threatened among the Mansos near El Paso, where the local Spanish captain subdued the rebels and murdered two of their leaders. Puebloans and Athapascans plotted a larger rebellion. In Piros (or Piru), some rebels with Apache allies killed five Spaniards, including the *alcalde mayor* in Sierra de la Magdalena. Villaneuva identified the leaders of an incipient rebellion in a community of Piru called Senecú (or Tze-no-que or Tzen-o-cue), accusing them of the twinned crimes of treason and sorcery. The governor ordered them hanged and burned in the town.[3]

The governor's action only served to fuel rebellious sentiment. Soon after the murders at Senecú, a Tompiro Pueblo leader known in Spanish as Don Esteban Clemente organized a wide uprising. As one witness later claimed, "the whole kingdom secretly obeyed him" and the conspiracy he launched spread far. Those involved planned to steal or drive out all the Spaniards' horses. But word of their plans escaped. Spanish officials captured Clemente and hanged him—yet another martyr to a nascent Indigenous independence movement.[4]

Villaneuva encountered episodic spasms of anti-colonial violence in New Spain. Within a decade, other Indigenous, and even some colonists, concluded that brute force had become a necessity. This era of violence began in New Spain in the mid-1660s, but soon spread elsewhere, erupting along the Atlantic coast a decade later, and reached its apogee in the

3. Forbes, *Apache, Navajo, and Spaniard*, 162–163. An unidentified lieutenant general of the cavalry, deposed on December 20, 1681, testified that "the common people of this kingdom have always been punished as idolators," and that under Villaneuva's administration "some were hanged and burned in the pueblo of Senecú as traitors and sorcerers." On December 21, 1681, another deponent testified that in the years before the Pueblo revolt Spanish authorities had punished "sorcery and idolatry," but he did not specify the context. See Charles W. Hackett, ed., *Revolt of the Pueblo Indians of New Mexico and Otermin's Attempted Reconquest, 1680–1682*, 2 vols. (Albuquerque: University of New Mexico Press, 1942), 2:266, 278–279.

4. Declaration of the lieutenant general of cavalry, [December 20, 1681], in Hackett, ed., *Revolt*, 2:266; [Juan Dominguez de Mendoza to Antonio de Otermin, December 10, 1681], in Hackett, ed., *Revolt*, 2:225–227; [Declaration of Diego López, December 22, 1681], in Hackett, ed., *Revolt*, 2:292–303 (quotation at 299); [Opinion of Fray Francisco de Ayeta, December 23, 1681], in Hackett, ed., *Revolt*, 2:309; Forbes, *Apache, Navajo, and Spaniard*, 163.

Pueblo Revolt of 1680, the largest Indigenous uprising in the history of North America.

Sometime around 1660, annual rainfall across the Southwest decreased and remained below normal for years. "Many Indians perished of hunger," Fray Juan Bernal later wrote to the Inquisition from Santo Domingo, "lying dead along the roads, in the ravines, and in their huts."[5] The dry conditions altered relations between Native peoples. For centuries, agrarian Pueblos had traded with Athapaskan-speaking peoples at Pecos, where Faraón Apaches traveled; Taos, a friendly site for Jucarillas; Jemez, a market for Navajos; and Zuñi, a destination for Salinero Apaches.[6] But drought diminished the amount of food that farmers could store, as did Spanish slave raids, which reduced the number of laborers capable of producing crops. Problems for the Pueblos increased when Apachean peoples, desperate for food, began to steal from them.[7] In 1671, pestilence killed cattle and people, weakening precarious communities. By the mid-1670s, Puebloan communities on the most marginal lands could no longer survive. Residents abandoned Abó and migrated toward the Rio Grande. They had better chances to survive there, but their presence put greater strain on existing resources, especially since food stores had been dwindling in the dry years.[8]

Despite worsening conditions, Spanish authorities maintained their commitment to both spreading Christianity and enslaving Apaches and other Athapaskans. Had sufficient rain fallen to provide enough food for all, the tensions might merely have lingered with occasional flare-ups. But the drought raised the stakes of every decision. In 1668, 450 died in Humanas. By December, warfare spread across the region. "The whole land," the missionary Bernal wrote in April 1669, "is at war with the widespread heathen nation of the Apache Indians." On June 24, 1671, a group of Apaches assaulted the wagon train of the incoming governor, Juan de Miranda, killing four and stealing their mules. Miranda saw the Indigenous

5. Juan Bernal to the Tribunal, April 1, 1669, in Charles W. Hackett, ed., *Historical Documents Relating to New Mexico, Nueva Vizcaya, and Approaches Thereto, to 1773*, 3 vols. (Washington, DC: Carnegie Institution, 1923), 3:272.
6. Calloway, *One Vast Winter Count*, 168–169.
7. See Forbes, *Apache, Navajo, and Spaniard*, 147.
8. Petition [of Father Fray Francisco de Ayeta], May 10, 1679, in Hackett, ed., *Historical Documents*, 3:302; David J. Weber, *The Spanish Frontier in North America* (New Haven, CT: Yale University Press, 1992), 134; Calloway, *One Vast Winter Count*, 169; James E. Ivey, "'The Greatest Misfortune of All': Famine in the Province of New Mexico, 1667–1672," *Journal of the Southwest* 36 (1994), 76–100.

as "the common enemy of our Holy Catholic Faith." In 1672, according to Fray Francisco de Ayeta, Apaches "rebelled and rose up, and the said province was totally sacked and robbed." The raiders stole the residents' sheep and cows, the basis for their economy.[9]

By the mid-1670s, Spanish authorities recognized that they would be able to subdue only parts of the expansive territory they believed was part of the kingdom. In some places, their targeted raids worked, but those successes revealed a larger truth: unable to convince most Indigenous about the glories of Christ and incapable of escaping the taint of a slave trade that had sent hundreds to the mines in Parral and others to service in small hamlets, the Spaniards' only viable path to control New Mexico was through military force. The Spanish practice of desecrating Indigenous icons, rather than convincing the doubtful of a better way forward, only gave additional intellectual and spiritual ammunition to Indigenous who believed that the horrors of the present might dissipate or disappear if the invaders could be vanquished.

At almost the same moment, on the other side of the continent, Wassausmon, a bilingual Massachusett who had converted to Christianity through the tutelage of John Eliot and others, heard that some Narragansetts were poised to launch an attack against Plymouth. The assault of January 1675 was to be led by the Wampanoag sachem Metacom (or Metacomet, known to the English as King Philip). Wassausmon, called John Sassamon by colonists, learned English at an early age, spent a year at Harvard's Indian College, and in 1660 was among the converted Indigenous who formed the Christian Native town of Natick. Like many other Ninnimissinuok, he had mastered the art of moving back and forth between towns in southern New England. Warning Plymouth's governor, Josiah Winslow, of an impending attack seemed a reasonable choice for a man who still believed it possible for Natives and colonists to live near each other. This time he miscalculated. Winslow thought that Wassausmon was peddling falsehoods, so he sent him away. On his return, Wassausmon died under mysterious circumstances at Assawompset Pond. Soon after, an unnamed Native told a convert named William Nahauton that he had seen one of Metacom's allies, a man named Tobias, along with Tobias's son and an unnamed companion, knock Wassausmon on the head and

9. Bernal to the Inquisition, April 1, 1669, in Hackett, ed., *Historical Documents*, 3:271–272; Forbes, *Apache, Navajo, and Spaniard*, 161, 164, 166–167.

leave him on the ice to die. Plymouth authorities arrested, tried, and convicted the three. The colony executed them on June 4, 1675.[10]

Officials in Plymouth never questioned their own actions. Their laws mandated death for someone who committed murder, and they had earlier applied that code to colonists who had killed Natives. But news of the executions angered many Wampanoags, Narragansetts, and other Indigenous in coastal and southern New England. They believed that the English, once perceived as possible allies in contests with Native antagonists, needed to be put back in their place. Colonial authorities' decision to punish a crime committed by one or more Natives against another represented a particular threat, signaling provincial officials' presumption that their judicial rules should trump existing legal codes. The singular event, following years of colonists' transgressions, became an unacceptable encroachment against Indigenous sovereignty.

From January through the summer, Indigenous and colonial fighters battled each other, typically in small-scale skirmishes that only fueled anger on each side. By late summer, the governors of Connecticut, Massachusetts, and Rhode Island agreed that their communities faced an existential threat. Using authority embedded in their chartering documents, the governors organized a cross-colony militia. Joining their ranks were Pequots and Niantics, a sign that some Indigenous still believed that greater threat lay in an empowered Narragansett nation, which had become the most numerous in southern New England, rather than in towns dominated by colonists.[11]

On June 24, Plymouth held a day of prayer and fasting to beg for their god's assistance in what minister Increase Mather defined as a holy campaign against the Wampanoags for organizing the assassination of Wassausmon in part because "he was Christianized and baptiz'd" and had tried to spread his new faith among Natives. When colonists in Swansea walked home from that day of prayer, an unknown number of Metacom's allies attacked, killing nine. "Thus did the War begin," Mather intoned, "this being the first english blood which was spilt by the Indians in a hostile way."[12]

10. Yasuhide Kawashima, *Igniting King Philip's War: The John Sassomon Murder Trial* (Lawrence: University Press of Kansas, 2001).
11. William Bradford, *Of Plimoth Plantation*, ed. Kenneth P. Minkema et al. (Boston: Colonial Society of Massachusetts, 2020), 456–458; Daniel R. Mandell, *King Philip's War: Colonial Expansion, Native Resistance, and the End of Indian Sovereignty* (Baltimore: Johns Hopkins University Press, 2010), 44–46, 69.
12. Increase Mather, *A Brief History of the Warr with the Indians in New-England* (Boston, 1676), 2–3.

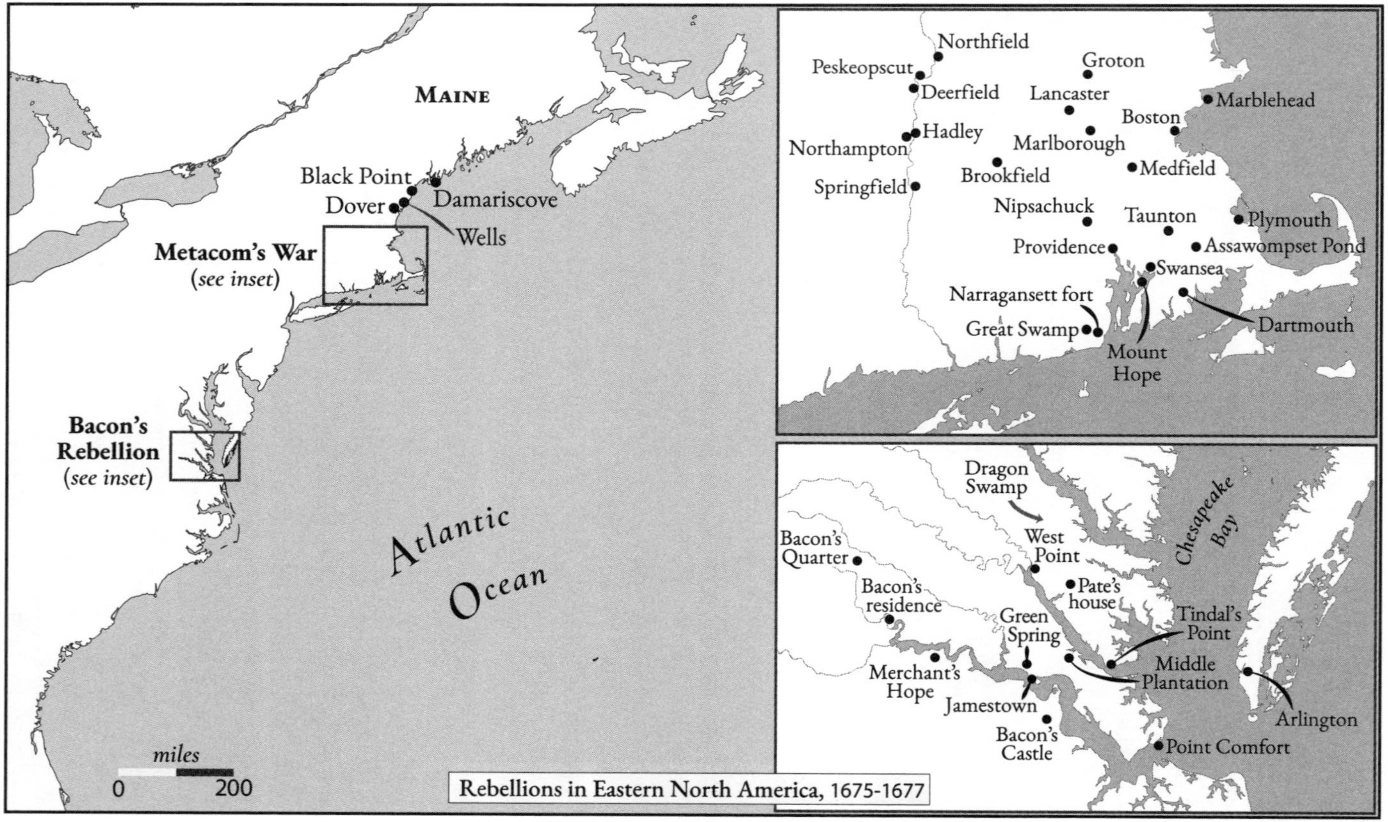

Maine
Black Point
Dover
Damariscove
Wells
Metacom's War
(see inset)
Bacon's
Rebellion
(see inset)
Atlantic
Ocean
miles
0
200
Northfield
Peskeopscut
Deerfield
Groton
Lancaster
Marblehead
Boston
Hadley
Northampton
Marlborough
Brookfield
Medfield
Springfield
Nipsachuck
Taunton
Plymouth
Providence
Assawompset Pond
Swansea
Narragansett fort
Great Swamp
Mount
Hope
Dartmouth
Dragon
Swamp
Chesapeake
Bay
West
Point
Bacon's
Quarter
Pate's
house
Bacon's
residence
Green
Spring
Tindal's
Point
Middle
Plantation
Merchant's
Hope
Jamestown
Arlington
Bacon's
Castle
Point Comfort
Rebellions in Eastern North America, 1675-1677

Mather did not mention that the colonists' decision to expand the war came at a propitious moment. In 1673, possibly as a result of fears spreading with the launch of yet a third Anglo-Dutch war, Boston merchant John Hull, who had been running the Massachusetts mint since 1652 and played a leading role in securing the colony's finances, had ordered 500 flintlock muskets from England. Early the next year he ordered another 100 to 120. In addition, the General Court placed an order for sixty cannons, presumably for use to defend the coastline from any invading Dutch ships. By August 1674, the colony had launched preparations to set up its own powder mill. Hull soon followed by placing orders for saltpeter, a necessary ingredient. By the time Plymouth officials decided to act against the Wampanoags, they were secure in their knowledge that colonial militia units would be well armed for whatever came next. That proved an accurate assessment. The Massachusetts government soon took the lead in providing soldiers and arms for an assault on the Wampanoags.[13]

Hearing of the deaths, Plymouth's authorities sent word to Boston seeking assistance. On June 26, as an eclipse covered the moon, colonial soldiers began to march into battle. Approaching Mount Hope, they discovered the bodies of freshly killed colonists. Soon the English found more bodies at Taunton lying near charred houses. The soldiers' grim march took them through Swansea, where half of the houses had been consumed by flames, and other charred dwellings in Dartmouth and Middlebury. Mather claimed the Natives had stripped men and women and then killed and scalped them, "leaving them in the open field as naked as in the day wherein they were born."[14]

On August 1, colonial soldiers with a group of Mohegan allies under the direction of Uncas, killed thirty Narragansetts, but Metacom escaped. At almost the same time, Captain Edward Hutchinson met a group of Nipmucs at Quahog. He thought he had gone to agree to a treaty, but he instead rode into an ambush. Unknown Indigenous allied with Metacom attacked Hutchinson and eight of his allies. The survivors fled the scene, leaving the bodies of their comrades lying on the ground "as meat for the Fowls of Heaven," as Mather wrote, "and their Flesh unto the Beasts of the Earth." The wounded Hutchinson and the other survivors rode to Quahog to discover the town burned and colonial bodies scattered on the ground. The soldiers believed that survivors of the initial assault had taken refuge

13. Mark Peterson, *The City-State of Boston: The Rise and Fall of an Atlantic Power, 1630–1865* (Princeton, NJ: Princeton University Press, 2019), 110–111 (mint), 122–126 (weapons, joint commitment to war).

14. Mather, *Brief History of the Warr*, 4–5.

in a single house, which the Natives possibly set alight. Hutchinson died from the wounds he sustained.[15]

In the following days, rumors swirled that the Wampanoag leader had traveled into the interior toward Northampton, Hadley, and Deerfield, the small colonial towns that defined the western reach of English colonists in Massachusetts Bay. Provincial authorities had formed alliances with Natives in the Connecticut Valley earlier, but apparently Metacom subsequently purchased these Indigenous communities' loyalty with wampum. Colonial soldiers fought against a group near Hadley. Mather did not know how many Indigenous died, but he reported that nine colonial men had fallen, each from a different town. "Now the *English* have a multitude of open Enemies more th[a]n when this trouble began," he observed, "so that greater desolations are now expected." Colonists feared that Indigenous across the region would rise against them if the provincial soldiers did not subdue them.[16] On September 1, Natives sacked Deerfield, killing one person and burning almost all of the houses. In early September, a witness claimed that Indigenous had decapitated some of the soldiers serving with Captain Richard Beers near Squakheag (modern Northfield) and mounted their heads on poles. On September 18, on the road between Hadley and Deerfield, colonists and Natives faced off in a gruesome contest that left ninety-five Indigenous and sixty colonists dead.[17]

The rising toll of war prompted the three colonial governors to raise an army of 1,000. Following guidelines set in 1672 when representatives of the three largest New England colonies formed a confederation for their mutual interest, Massachusetts contributed 527 soldiers, while Connecticut sent 315 and Plymouth mustered 158.[18] On October 4, John Pynchon, son of William and the scion of Springfield, led a contingent of colonial soldiers from the town in search of a group of hostile Natives. The day after he left, Indigenous warriors attacked Springfield. Pynchon returned to what he called a "Lamentable and & woefull site." Most of the buildings in the town lay in ashes, including his own corn mill and grist mill, along with an associate's library. He estimated economic devastation for forty families, all of them "utterly destitute of Subsistence" and unlikely to

15. Mather, *Brief History of the Warr*, 6.
16. Mather, *Brief History of the Warr*, 6–11, quotations at 7 ("greater desolations") and 11 ("to be feared").
17. Mather, *Brief History of the Warr*, 7 (Deerfield), 10–12 (casualties).
18. "Articles of Confederation" for the United Colonies, in *The Compact with the Charter and Law of the Colony of New Plymouth . . . and an appendix containing the Articles of Confederation of the United Colonies of New England* (Boston, 1836), 314–320; Peterson, *City-State of Boston*, 127.

survive the coming winter without assistance from the colony. Governor John Leverett responded with characteristic puritan logic: the tragedy revealed that the colonists' humiliation was so inadequate "that the Lord carries it as being angry with our prayers."[19]

As the toll of the conflict grew, colonists sharpened their cultural critique of Natives. Rather than seeing Indigenous fighting techniques as innovative—an assessment some would make later—colonists' views of their Native neighbors darkened just as the days grew shorter. Before the war, they had come to see Indigenous as profitable trade partners, a crucial step in the long-standing English colonial project to convert Natives to English ways. But the way that Wampanoags and Narragansetts fought undermined such assumptions. The Narragansetts, a colonist named William Harris wrote in August 1676, fought "in a secret sly, skulking way," making it impossible to find them. Nathaniel Saltonstall, who would later become a jurist, published a short pamphlet decrying what he saw as the atrocities of the colonists' "Cruel Wars." There he compared these "*Barbarous Enemies*" to "wolves and other beasts of prey, that commonly do their Mischiefs in the Night, or by stealth." Attackers would not come out of the woods but instead remained hidden, their knowledge of the landscape making it impossible for colonists to catch them. Colonial militia groups, convinced that the alienation of Indigenous from colonists was permanent, embraced an ethos not evident in New England since the assault on the Pequots' fort on the Mystic in 1637. Thomas Danforth, a member of the colony's Court of Assistants, which typically heard legal cases, believed that the time had come to annihilate their enemies "in all places & by all wayes & meanes." He ordered soldiers to "take, kill, & destroy the enemy without limitation of place or time."[20]

19. John Pynchon to [John Russell?], October 5, 1675, and Leverett to Russell, 9.8.75 [October 9, 1675], in "Three Letters Written by Gov. Leverett in 1675—Newly Brought to Light," *NEHGR* 48 (1894), 316–321, quotations at 317 (Springfield) and 321 (divine wrath); John Grenier, *The First Way of War: American War Making on the Frontier* (Cambridge: Cambridge University Press, 2005), 30–31.

20. Grenier, *First Way of War*, 32–34; "William Harris to Sir Joseph Williamson, August 12, 1676," *Rhode Island Historical Collections* 10 (1902), 162–179, quotation at 163; [Nathaniel Saltonstall], *A New and Further Narrative of the State of New-England* (London, 1676), quotations at 1 and 8; Thomas Danforth to Charles Frost, in "Indian War Papers," ed. Charles W. Parsons, *NEHGR* 3 (1849), 24. Members of the Court of Assistance included the governor and deputy governor along with others to hear appeals from lower courts as well as "all Causes of Divorce, all Capital and Criminal causes, extending to life, member or banishment." See John Noble and John F. Currin, eds., *Records of the Court of Assistants of the Colony of Massachusetts Bay, 1630–1692*, 3 vols. (Boston, 1901–1928), 1:vi.

By November, with violence spreading, leaders of the three United Colonies ordered impressments to add another 1,000 soldiers in the field. Hull, working from Boston, coordinated the logistics. He ordered bullet molds from London, created a system to pay soldiers, and worked with associates to keep careful track of any supplies or clothing sent to soldiers, costs that Hull and others would deduct from their wages. The General Court ordered Hull to keep track of the taxes that it assessed to towns to cover the costs of the conflict. Short of coin during the war, some colonists paid their dues with corn and cows.[21]

In November, at Winslow's urging, the thousand-strong colonial militia and its Indigenous allies gathered for an assault on the main Narragansett homeland in Rhode Island. Armed men torched Native houses and fields, often after their occupants had fled. On December 19, a colonial force massed outside the walls of a large Narragansett fort situated in a frozen lowland in modern South Kingstown to set the buildings on fire, burn food stored for winter, and shoot those who tried to flee. By morning, 300 of the fort's residents, many of them non-combatant children, women, and elderly, lay dead, many of them burned to death. Seventy of the invaders died that night too, and perhaps another 150 were wounded. The event played a central role in the ways that colonists and Indigenous understood a devastating moment in the region's history.[22]

Colonists, believing that this show of force would end the threat, once again miscalculated. Rather than stifle the Wampanoags, the battle in the swamp energized Indigenous, who now had more proof that the English intended their destruction. Metacom and a large group of Wampanoags headed west, hoping to recruit Mohawks into a wide campaign against the New England colonies. But the Mohawks had their own political agenda, defined by local circumstances. Well before Metacom arrived, they and other Haudenosaunee had received Sir Edmund Andros, who had arrived in November 1674 as the first governor of New York, eager to maintain the goodwill that the Dutch had established with the Five Nations. Rather than offer help to other Indigenous, the Mohawks, likely trying to preserve their access to guns and ammunition from the English colony, turned on the Wampanoags in February 1676. In a fierce battle, Metacom lost most of his followers. The Wampanoag headman headed east soon after.[23]

21. Peterson, *City-State of Boston*, 127–129.

22. Grenier, *First Way of War*, 32; Lisa Brooks, *Our Beloved Kin: A New History of King Philip's War* (New Haven, CT: Yale University Press, 2018), 240–245.

23. Daniel K. Richter, *The Ordeal of the Longhouse: The Peoples of the Iroquois League in the Era of European Colonization* (Chapel Hill: University of North Carolina Press for the

During the rest of the winter and into the early spring, Native groups took the war into Plymouth, Lancaster, Marlborough, Northampton, Medfield, Groton, Sudbury, and Warwick. They burned colonial towns along the entire western side of Narragansett Bay. On March 29 they torched Providence. Colonial officials responded in kind. William Turner, captain of a Massachusetts militia regiment, stormed a Native community at Peskeopscut, a fishing spot along the Connecticut River at modern Turners Falls, killing perhaps 200. John Seller, hydrographer to Charles II, memorialized the conflict in an inset of his contemporary map of New England. On their return, Turner and forty others died at the hands of Natives. On July 2, a colonial brigade surprised a group of 100 Narragansetts who had returned to Nipsachuck hoping to gather stored food. They were led by Quaiapen, a female sachem. But soon after arriving colonial forces swept in, killing her and many of her allies. The colonists numbered 300, though they had about 100 Pequot and Mohegan allies. The victors captured the survivors and sold them—adding to the numbers of enslaved Indigenous from New England.[24]

For their part, Native soldiers understood that winning the war meant undermining colonists' faith that they could survive. In the spring of 1676, after destroying Lancaster, Indigenous warriors assaulted Medfield. "Know by this paper, that the Indians that thou hast provoked to wrath and anger, will war this twenty one years if you will," wrote one anonymous observer in a note the raiders left behind. Its author was quite possibly Nipmuc scholar Wawaus (James Printer). During the war he had become a scribe for the Nashaway leader Monoco. "There are many Indians yet," his letter continued, "we come three hundred at this time. You must consider the Indians lost nothing but their life; you must lose your fair houses and cattle." Mather claimed that Wawaus surrendered to the English, "promising for the future to venture his life against the common Enemy."[25]

Institute of Early American History and Culture, 1992), 135–136 (Andros); Mandell, *King Philip's War*, 90–91.

24. John Seller, "A mapp of New England," in *Atlas maritimus, or The sea-atlas* (London, 1675); Mather, *Brief History of the Warr*, 26–30, 36–40; Brooks, *Our Beloved Kin*, 320–321; Wendy Warren, *New England Bound: Slavery and Colonization in Early America* (New York: Liveright, 2016), 96.

25. Daniel Gookin, "An Historical Account of the Doings and Sufferings of the Christian Indians in New England," *Transactions and Collections of the American Antiquarian Society* 2 (1836), 494; Mather, *Brief History of the Warr*, 39; on Printer and Monoco (the latter would later be executed by colonial authorities for his role in the war), see Brooks, *Our Beloved Kin*, 4–5, 257–261, 336–337.

Benjamin Church, born in Plymouth in 1639 and Governor Winslow's primary military aide, took a commanding position for desperate, war-weary colonists. In July, he and his soldiers found Metacom at Mount Hope (modern Bristol). On August 12, 1676, a colonial soldier shot Metacom. "This seasonable Prey was soon divided," a ship captain named Caleb More soon reported, "they cut off his head, and hands, and conveyed them to Rhode-Island, and quartered his body, and hung it upon four Trees." On August 28, the colonists captured a Pocasset headman named Annawan. They decapitated him too.[26] Colonial soldiers did not reserve such barbarity for Indigenous enemies. In January 1676 a court found James Tift (or Tefft) guilty of fighting against the colony. They hanged him for treason and then drew and quartered his remains.[27]

The violence spared no one, though it took very different forms depending on local circumstances. Four hundred Narragansetts, Nipmucs, and Wampanoags attacked Lancaster in February 1676, burning houses and killing colonists who could not escape. The raiders captured Mary Rowlandson, spouse of the local minister. Over the next three months, she moved with her captors at least twenty times, watched as her six-year-old daughter, injured in the initial attack nine days earlier, died in her arms, and witnessed what she saw as acts of both cruelty and compassion by those who held her. Among them was Weetamoo, one of the most powerful political figures in the region. A Pokanoket who had been married to Wamsutta, Metacom's older brother who had died under mysterious circumstances in 1662, Weetamoo commanded enormous respect and authority, a sign of women's political authority. She separated from her second husband after the war began, forming an alliance with the Narragansetts, including with a man named Quinnapin, whom she married. English observers believed her to be almost as powerful as Metacom—"as Potent a Prince as any round about her," in Nathaniel Saltsonstall's words—and that she had as much command over maize, men, and land as her former brother-in-law. Yet her power could not insulate her from the brutalities of the war. After she drowned in the Taunton River, colonists dredged up Weetamoo's body and decapitated her, putting her head on display in Taunton. Rowlandson, for her part, survived the war and wrote

26. R[ichard] H[utchinson], *The Warr in New-England Visibly Ended . . . Being a true and perfect account brought in by Caleb More* (London, 1677), 2; Colin G. Calloway, "Introduction: Surviving the Dark Ages," in Calloway, ed., *After King Philip's War: Presence and Persistence in Indian New England* (Hanover, NH: University Press of New England, 1997), 1; Mandell, *King Philip's War*, 127–128.

27. "The Examination and Relation of James Quannapaquait," January 24, 1676, in Mary Rowlandson, *The Sovereignty and Goodness of God* (1682), ed. Neal Salisbury (Boston: Bedford Books, 1997), 126n.

what became the era's most widely known captivity narrative, a text that emphasized her devotion to the Christian god and, in contrast to Wetamoo, her almost complete lack of political authority.[28]

In the aftermath of the summary killing of Metacom, the English rounded up and imprisoned captives, including Metacom's spouse, Wootonekanuske, and their nine-year-old son (whose name does not appear in any records). The boy's fate became the subject of a political and scriptural debate among colonial elites, who pondered different textual passages trying to determine if a son should suffer for the sins of his father. Deuteronomy 24:16 and 2 Chronicles 25:4 ruled out such consideration, but Increase Mather believed that 1 Kings 11:17 suggested that the child be either enslaved or executed, an opinion supported by those who saw similar justification in verses 7 and 8 of Psalm 137. Fragmentary surviving records of individuals taken captive at the time provide no clue about the fate of Wootonekanuske, but colonists apparently took her son out of the region to be sold into slavery.[29]

The argument over the boy's fate prefigured a much larger discussion among colonial leaders in Massachusetts, Connecticut, and Rhode Island. John Eliot opposed selling any of the captives into slavery. He feared that if Indigenous heard that colonists enslaved and sold captives, they would be more resolute in battle. Aside from such practical considerations, Eliot argued that the practice violated the core idea that English colonists were to bring heathens into Christendom, not exile them from their homelands. The original letters patent to the king, he reminded them, emphasized "the Indians conversion, not theire extirpation." Exiling captives and selling them abroad would place them in "a way of p[er]petual darknesse, to the eternal ruine of their soules," which would be an "act contrary to the mind of Christ." He did not object to killing those who "deserve to dy" because of heinous actions; they should be executed with proper penitential care. But, he added, "when Christ hath provided meanes of grace for them," then colonists should not destroy "their soules, when we are highly obliged to seeke theire conversion, & salvation, & have [opportunity] in our hands so to doe."[30]

28. Mary Rowlandson, *The Sovereignty and Goodness of God* (London, 1682); N[athaniel] S[altonstall], The *Present State of New-England with respect to the Indian War* (London, 1676), 3; Mather, *Brief History of the Warr*, 70–71; Mandell, *King Philip's War*, 123; Brooks, *Our Beloved Kin*, 324–326.
29. Jill Lepore, *The Name of War: King Philip's War and the Origins of American Identity* (New York: Alfred A. Knopf, 1998), 150–153.
30. John Eliot to the Massachusetts governor and council, August 13, 1675, in Nathaniel B. Shurtleff, et al., eds., *Records of the Colony of Plymouth in New England*, 12 vols. (Boston, 1855–1861), 10:451–453; Lepore, *The Name of War*, 158–160.

By September 1676, Eliot had lost the argument. That month Massachusetts governor John Leverett and Governor Josiah Winslow of Rhode Island, well aware of scores of Wampanoags being shipped abroad to lives as slaves, signed certificates explaining their actions. As they saw the situation, these Indigenous had rebelled not against the colonies but against their sovereign, Charles II. They had done so by accepting the protection of the realm, including in a 1671 agreement with Plymouth, and then violating their "League and Covenant" by perpetrating "many notorious barbarous and execrable murthers, villanies and outrages" against the king's subjects. Having been sentenced by local courts, these individuals were "condemned to perpetuall Servitude." Leverett sent his certificate to captain Thomas Smith of the *Sea-flower*, whose men had just loaded at least 180 Native captives under the ship's deck for passage to the West Indies. The enslaved included 70 captured in Massachusetts and another 110 captured in Plymouth.[31]

Under the laws of the three colonies, individuals who captured Indigenous rebels had the right to sell them. "I bought 9 the other day," wealthy Boston merchant Samuel Shrimpton boasted to his spouse in July 1676. He thought he would ship them all to Jamaica but then realized that it might be best to keep three and dispatch the others.[32] Hull sold captives to thirty-two different customers in Boston. Many of the enslaved were children. On August 24, he recorded the sales of fifteen "infants" or "small children" as well as forty-eight girls or women, fourteen boys, and one elderly man among the seventy-seven captives sold that day. Most sales involved one or two individuals, though on some days Hull recorded far larger purchases, including forty-one obtained by merchant and sea captain Thomas Smith on September 23. Daniel Gookin and Thomas Prentis, who in August 1676 oversaw the distribution of orphaned Indigenous children into servitude, benefited too: Gookin took an eight-year-old boy into his household and Prentis a thirteen-year-old.[33]

Natives who surrendered, including a group of 150 who turned themselves in at Plymouth, enjoyed no protection, especially those confined in the dismal conditions of Deer Island in Boston Harbor. Colonists sold them into slavery—all but one elderly man, whom they decapitated instead, rationalizing that this constituted more humane treatment than a life of bondage.[34] John Eliot and Daniel Gookin, fearing that Native

31. Lepore, *The Name of War*, 150–151, 162–164, quotation at 163.
32. Lepore, *The Name of War*, 154–155; see also Warren, *New England Bound*, 99.
33. Peterson, *City-State of Boston*, 131–132; "A Memorandum of Indian Children Put Forth into Service to the English," August 10, 1676, in Rowlandson, *The Sovereignty and Goodness of God*, ed. Salisbury, 141–144.
34. Lepore, *The Name of War*, 155; Warren, *New England Bound*, 96.

converts would be sold into slavery, led a group from Natick to Boston in October 1675. If left in their own town, Eliot worried, enraged colonists would massacre them. But their fate, as he soon learned, was little better. From the city they sailed to Deer Island, the scraggly outcrop in Boston Harbor owned by Shrimpton, where they spent a miserable winter under conditions so harsh that some died. Gookin, who believed that teaching Native children to "speak, read, and write, the English tongue" would be the best way to eradicate their "barbarous" practices, lamented that colonists had transported 500 Natives to the island in 1675, many if not most of them converts to Christianity.[35]

Colonists presumed that insatiable planters in the tropics would purchase captive Natives. Narragansetts and their allies feared the same result. "Young men [who are the Natives' principal soldiers]," reported James Quannapaquait, a Nipmuc who had been released from Deer Island to spy among the colonists' enemies, said that they saw no reason to end the war while this danger remained. "Why shall wee have peace to bee made slaves," he reported, "& either be kild or sent away to sea to Barbadoes & c." They decided it was best to "live as long wee can & die like men, & not to bee enslaved."[36]

While war raged in southern New England, the Barbadian government feared an insurrection of the enslaved on the island. They suppressed the conflict in early 1676 but decided that importing hundreds of Algonquian-speaking peoples who had just been rounded up, imprisoned, shackled, and sent across the ocean would pose a new security risk. Despite the constant need for labor to produce sugar, the Barbadians banned the importation of Natives captured in New England.[37] Planters on Jamaica apparently felt the same anxiety and also declined the opportunity. Nor could the New England enslavers find a market in Virginia and Maryland, where word about the devastations of the war had already poisoned the

35. Warren, *New England Bound*, 109–110; Daniel Gookin, *Historical Collections of the Indians in New England* (Boston, 1792), 79–84, quotation at 80; Daniel Gookin, "An Historical Account of the Doings and Sufferings of the Christian Indians in New England, in the years 1675, 1767, 1677," *Transactions and Collections of the American Antiquarian Society* 2 (1836), 485–487, 500. Gookin drew inspiration for his efforts to alter Algonquian ways from the failure of the English to eradicate the Irish language, which he believed had weakened efforts to maintain order there; see Gookin, *Historical Collections*, 81–82, and Jane Ohlmeyer, *Making Empire: Ireland, Imperialism, and the Early Modern World* (Oxford: Oxford University Press, 2023), 40–41.
36. "The Examination and Relation of James Quannapaquait," January 24, 1676, in Rowlandson, *The Sovereignty and Goodness of God*, ed. Salisbury, 124–125.
37. Linford D. Fisher, "'Dangerous Designes': The 1676 Barbados Act to Prohibit New England Indian Slave Importation," *WMQ* 71 (2014), 99–124.

minds of white planters against importing any captive Natives who, they feared, would also pose a risk to their own security. Lacking a market in American waters, colonial captains hauled captives eastward—to Madeira, the Azores, Portugal, and Spain.[38] At least some captive Wampanoags arrived in Tangier, a reverse slave trade that alarmed John Eliot. He wanted to find a way to repatriate them. His appeal fell on deaf ears.[39]

At the moment when prominent colonists in Massachusetts tried to sell their human wares, violence erupted on the coast of Maine, where a sagamore known as Squando led a series of assaults. An attack along the shores of Casco Bay claimed the lives of a colonial married couple, their married son and his wife, and two of their grandchildren. The Natives took three other children captive. In Falmouth, this same group of attackers burned five more houses, killed six adults and two children, and took three more children captive. Thirteen colonists died in Saco, where insurgents set houses on fire. Natives killed another nine at Black Point and burned twenty-two houses.[40]

Elsewhere, under the leadership of Mogg Hegon (Kennebec) and Madockawando (Penobscot), Indigenous peoples along the northern New England coastline led a series of campaigns from 1675 into 1677. Together, they seized colonists' fishing vessels to create a Wabanaki navy that might have numbered over forty ships. Natives stole boats as far south as Salem and launched repeated raids against the dispersed colonial communities on Damariscove (an island in modern Boothbay Harbor), Wells, and Black Point (modern Scarborough). During the summer and autumn of 1676 alone, Abenakis, Mi'kmaqs, and other Indigenous who had previously fought with Metacom had almost erased the colonial presence across sixty miles of coastline north and east of Casco Bay. Despite the circumstances, colonists remained capable of inflicting serious losses. In September, English major Richard Waldron tricked 400 Natives to attend a treaty negotiation at Dover, a small village on the banks of the Piscataqua River. Colonists attacked, capturing 200 they believed had been involved in assaults during the war. They sent several to Boston, where they were executed. Waldron then supervised the sale of others into slavery. Madoasquarbet, an Abenaki religious leader, complained to Boston authorities that Waldron had plied those in attendance with "drink & when [they] were drunk killed us" despite the fact that the Abenakis had not murdered any of the colonists they had captured.

38. Peterson, *City-State of Boston*, 131.
39. Lepore, *The Name of War*, 167–170.
40. Mather, *Brief History of the Warr*, 12–14.

The violence unleashed in the war reflected pent-up grievances so intense that it could fuel bloodlust. In July 1677, when the Sokokis and other Indigenous from Down East Maine laid plans to destroy Boston from the sea, small numbers of Native men captured approximately twenty ketches crewed by men from Marblehead. After a bloody fight, colonists managed to reclaim one vessel, then captured and bound two Indigenous men and sailed them home. Their plan had been to take the pair to Boston to face charges and, they hoped, get some compensation for their losses. But after arriving in Marblehead, rumors swirled that these two had played a role in the murderous attacks on colonial fishermen. A crowd of women leaving the Marblehead meeting house seized the prisoners and began to pelt them with stones and wooden planks. The women chased off the colonial soldiers, grabbed the captives by the hair, and killed them with their hands. "We were kept at such distance that we could not see them till they were dead," one of the men informed Boston authorities, "and then we found them with their heads off and gone, and their flesh in manner pulled from their bones." They would have killed others too, the women promised, even if doing so would have gotten them hanged. If word of the way the women "barbarously murdered" the captives reached Indigenous communities, cleric Increase Mather feared, "the captives among them will be served accordingly."[41]

On April 12, 1678, Madockawando met with representatives from New York, which at the time had jurisdiction over modern Maine, to bring the war in the north to a close. According to the terms of their agreement, English colonists could move back into the area, but each household needed to pay one peck (about eight quarts) of corn to the Abenakis, acknowledging the ancestral ownership of the land.[42]

41. James Axtell, "The Vengeful Women of Marblehead: Robert Roules's Deposition of 1677," *WMQ* 31 (1974), 647–652, quotation at 652; Mather quoted in [Thomas] Hutchinson, *The History of the Colony of Massachusetts-Bay, From . . . 1628 . . . [to] 1691* (Boston, 1764), 307n; Mandell, *King Philip's War*, 130–134; Brooks, *Our Beloved Kin*, 330–342, quotation from Madoasquarbet at 330–331; James D. Drake, *King Philip's War: Civil War in New England, 1675–1676* (Amherst: University of Massachusetts Press, 1999), 182–183. Historian and minister William Hubbard wrote that the women "literally tore them to pieces"; see William Hubbard, *The History of the Indian Wars in New England* (Roxbury, MA, 1865), 2:236–238, quotation at 238n. On Abenaki seapower, see Andrew Lipman, *The Saltwater Frontier: Indians and the Contest for the American Coast* (New Haven, CT: Yale University Press, 2015), 66–72, and Matthew R. Bahar, *Storm of the Sea: Indians and Empires in the Atlantic's Age of Sail* (New York: Oxford University Press, 2019), 88–97.

42. The treaty is summarized in Jeremy Belknap, *History of New-Hampshire* (Boston, [1784–1792]), 1:163–164.

The treaty ended the most destructive war that had taken place—or ever would again—across New England. It took the lives of approximately one-tenth of the regional population. Colonists lost 1,200 houses and much of the productive fishing industry, and were forced to recognize the precarious nature of the colonial project. Narragansetts, who had come to support the Wampanoags, paid an extraordinary price in lives, food, and houses. Colonial leaders authorized the sale of hundreds of Native captives into slavery. Most of them never came home again. Among those captured and sent abroad were Native converts, the so-called praying Indians whom missionaries like Eliot had once celebrated. Not since the Pequot War had English colonists gone on such an extended campaign to enslave and export Indigenous from the region. The memory of that noxious commerce, along with the physical scars of communities burned and burial sites across the region, haunted survivors. The time had come, as seventy-five-year-old Richard Hutchinson wrote in 1677, to repair "the Spoils made by our Barbarous Neighbours" who had been defeated, the survivors coming "in dayly with submission, and the rest withdrawn into places remote, hiding their weapons of War, and flying from Justice in small numbers." He had migrated to Salem in 1634, likely never anticipating what he had just witnessed. Four decades later he celebrated the killing and quartering of Metacom and looked forward with confidence that colonists would soon return "to their Old Habitations, and Mow down their Ground, and make hay, and do other occasions necessary for their re-setling."[43]

Despite the brutality of the conflict, the postwar era did not witness a permanent alienation of Indigenous from colonists. Notwithstanding his close association with Metacom, Wawaus returned to set type in Cambridge, reintegrating almost seamlessly into a province more dominated by colonists than ever before—as he knew well when he tried to help kin sentenced to death or enslavement.[44] Further, the war had been profitable, at least for some colonial merchants. Hull, organizer of armaments and recorder of human sales, found himself in a stronger economic position at the end of 1676 than at the start. In addition to the fees he had earned from the General Court, he also presided over a growing fur trade. By 1679, he was selling more beaver, along with other skins, than ever before.[45]

43. Lepore, *The Name of War*, 156–162; [Hutchinson], *The Warr in New-England Visibly Ended*, 1–2.

44. Brooks, *Our Beloved Kin*, 316–318.

45. Peterson, *City-State of Boston*, 133–134.

Minister William Hubbard saw the war as both a trial from his god and a necessary punishment for Indigenous. Although he wrote in a triumphant mode, he provided a litany of loss. The insurrection took a terrible toll in one colonial town after another: Mount Hope, Swansea, Middleborough, Dartmouth, Pocasset, Taunton, Mendam, Brookfield, Deerfield, Squakheag, Springfield, Hatfield, Northampton, Hadley, Westfield, Quonsigomog, Pettiqemscat, Warwick, Providence, Patuxet, Lancaster, Groton, Wickford, Medfield, Sudbury, Concord, Chelmsford, Andover, Woburn, Wells, Falmouth, Spurwink, Kennebec, the colonists scattered along Casco Bay and on its islands. Hubbard mentioned a few Native towns too, though mostly to identify the places where Metacom's forces and allies had organized their raids.[46]

Hubbard echoed Mather, who wrote while the war raged. Mather believed the descent into the nightmare had two primary causes. First, Natives had come to possess guns and ammunition, which gave them an enormous advantage over the bows and arrows they had used in earlier conflicts. The second cause was not about Indigenous ingenuity but instead about the colonists' shortcomings. English in the region had never suffered so much while the first generation of migrants was alive. They had crossed the ocean on a godly mission. Mather believed that the Christian god delivered "so dreadfull a judgment" because "another Generation [has] risen up which hath not so pursued, as ought to have been, the blessed design of their Fathers, in following the Lord into this Wilderness, whilst it was a land not sown." To him, the colonists deserved to suffer.[47] Others agreed. In an unconscious echo of Winthrop's evocative metaphor, minister Joseph Rowlandson, Mary's husband, believed that the dissenters had destroyed their chances. "If God be gone, our guard is gone," he lamented, "and we are as a Citty, in the midst of Enemies, whose walls are broken down."[48]

In 1674, Nathaniel and Elizabeth Bacon and perhaps their two daughters sailed from Britain to Virginia. Nathaniel, then twenty-seven years old, had been a student at St. Catherine's College, Cambridge, for two years, but dropped out when his father stopped paying his fees, finished his undergraduate training with a tutor with whom he had taken a tour

46. W[illiam] Hubbard, *A Narrative of the Troubles with the Indians in New-England* (Boston, 1677), sig T[r]–[T4[r]].
47. Mather, *Brief History of the Warr*, 1–2.
48. Joseph Rowlandson, *The Possibility of Gods forsaking a people, That have been visibly near & dear to him* (Cambridge, MA, 1682), 10.

of Europe, gained admission to Gray's Inn, one of London's Inns of Court, and returned to Cambridge, where he received an M.B. in 1667, a degree for those who intended to practice medicine. In 1670, Elizabeth, the daughter of Sir Edward Duke, married Nathaniel. Her displeased father disinherited her. Soon after, the couple became involved in a case of fraud surrounding a land deal. They left that problem behind when they embarked for Virginia, though the case lingered for years.[49]

Soon after they arrived, the Bacons negotiated with a colonist named Thomas Ballard for an 820-acre parcel in Henrico County and another tract near the falls of the James. Unlike most English migrants to Virginia, Bacon, related to Governor William Berkeley and to his wife, Frances Culpeper Stephens Berkeley, was also politically connected. Within eight months of his arrival, the governor had appointed the newcomer to the colony's council. Frances Berkeley and Elizabeth Bacon became friends, solidifying the connections between the two families.

After his first purchases, Bacon saw an early opportunity for gain through conducting business with Natives. He partnered with William Byrd, who had been born in London in 1652 but migrated with an uncle at some point in the 1660s. By the early 1670s, Byrd had set up a household with Mary Horsmanden Filmer, whom he married in 1672 or 1673. Like Bacon, the Byrds put down roots near the falls of the James. It was an ideal location for conducting business with Indigenous traders, most likely Susquehannocks, who visited the falls of the James regularly, knowing that they could find colonists who would purchase their furs and deerskins.[50]

The many transactions that linked Indigenous and colonists near the fall line testified to the continuing lure of commerce. Natives saw newcomers to the area as suppliers of goods they could not otherwise obtain. Immigrants like Bacon and Byrd, taking a page out of Berkeley's aspirations for a more diversified economy, knew that the skins and furs they bought could be taken easily down the James, then bundled and sent across the ocean. Everyone, in their minds, prospered as long as they could get along. But the violence of 1644–1646 cast a long shadow, darkening any rosy picture of the past and narrowing hopes of a golden future. Anxiety and fear lay beneath the veneer of cross-cultural exchange. To make matters more fraught, colonists in Virginia had complained that the winter of 1674–1675 had posed new challenges: masses of squirrels ate

49. Brent Tarter, "Nathaniel Bacon (1647–1676)," *Encyclopedia of Virginia* (accessed January 23, 2025).
50. Edmund S. Morgan, *American Slavery, American Freedom: The Ordeal of Colonial Virginia* (New York: W. W. Norton, 1975), 254.

their potatoes and maize, the crop the previous autumn had been subpar, and many of their cattle had recently died.[51]

In the spring of 1675, a group of Doegs, then residing along the northern reaches of the Chesapeake in territory that the English claimed as part of Maryland, took some hogs from a colonial farmer named Thomas Mathew who would not pay them what he owed. The Doegs went to settle an account. To colonists, the action constituted theft. Mathew and his servants, disputing the Doegs' claim, ran after them. In a skirmish, Mathew and his servants killed some of the Indigenous and beat others. In swift retaliation, another group of Doegs attacked Mathew's house and killed a servant. In response to what other colonists saw as a violation of the terms of the treaty of 1646, a quickly roused colonial militia rushed to seek vengeance. They split into two parties. One murdered eleven Doegs, including a headman. The other attacked a group of Susquehannocks. They killed fourteen, learning soon after that the Susquehannocks had played no role in the initial dispute but instead had only recently moved into a Piscattaway community after a brutal encounter with a group of Senecas.[52]

After the unprovoked assault, Susquehannocks, their numbers already depleted by European diseases and displacement from their traditional territory by Haudenosaunee, launched a series of reprisals against colonists in Virginia. In response to these attacks, a colonial militia consisting of approximately 1,000 armed men laid siege to the Piscattaway fort on September 26. Sensing that the end was approaching, five of the Indigenous left the walls to sue for peace. The colonists murdered them and then surrounded the fort. Eventually, the Susquehannocks managed to escape and launched attacks across northern Virginia. Fear gripped colonists' households, terrifying the young women and men who had chosen to take up lands too far from Jamestown to receive the adequate protection they felt the colonial government owed them.

By January, Berkeley understood that his administration had to take action to prevent what he saw as additional unjustifiable assaults on colonial farmers. He also wanted to restore goodwill with Indigenous before the still-localized violence spread. Having heard about the war that had

51. *Calendar of State Papers, Domestic Series, of the Reign of Charles II* (London, 1860–1939), 17:98.

52. Unless otherwise noted, the details about Bacon's rebellion can be found in Michael Leroy Oberg, ed., *Samuel Wiseman's Book of Record: The Official Account of Bacon's Rebellion in Virginia* (Lanham, MD: Lexington Books, 2005), 12–22; Morgan, *American Slavery, American Freedom*, 250–270; and Matthew Kruer, *Time of Anarchy: Indigenous Power and the Crisis of Colonialism in Early America* (Cambridge, MA: Harvard University Press, 2021), 50–77.

bloodied southern New England, he feared a similar deadly wave crashing over Virginia. While some colonists clamored for a retaliatory force to hunt down the Susquehannocks, the governor and assembly agreed that the best strategy would be to erect forts on each major river and then, following the precedent of the 1640s, require each county to station 500 men at each stronghold. Berkeley and his aides sent directions to the tributary communities that they were to support the colonists in any future actions.

Only a few years earlier, such a strategy would have garnered widespread support. But to colonists who had moved beyond the fall line, onto more marginal lands and farther from the comforts of larger communities and the goods to be found in Tidewater stores, this plan reeked of corruption. Rather than confront the problem head-on, these colonists believed, Berkeley and the assembly had created a system that would fuel profits to the wealthy investors who owned the lands where forts would be built. They feared, too, that the soldiers they needed to send would cost more than these Piedmont farming families might bring in for an entire year. Disgruntled and fearful colonists in isolated ramshackle cabins felt they remained at risk. In their minds, they had been victimized again—first by Natives and then by Berkeley and his cronies. Among the angered were Byrd and Bacon: Indigenous during these months of discontent had killed three of Byrd's servants and one of Bacon's employees.

Bacon and Berkeley still had much in common, including deep antipathy to Indigenous residents. But Berkeley understood that he had to respond to the local situation, not a more generalized fear. Bacon for a time seemed to side with Berkeley, and into the spring of 1676 he remained a member of the governor's council. Soon a group of disgruntled colonists formed a posse at a place called Jordan's Point in what had been Weyanoke territory. Hearing a rumor of their gathering, Bacon crossed the James from his home on the north side to meet the insurgents. Always able to read a crowd, Bacon surmised that the hostility of these people he called "volunteers" could be turned away from their possible target—the colonial elite—but only if the government would support an all-out war against Natives. Playing on their sentiments, Bacon soon became their leader, despite the fact that he was a member of the elite they hoped to destroy.

After taking on a commanding role among the protesters, Bacon reached out to Berkeley to suggest a devil's bargain. Rather than live by the terms of the 1646 treaty, under which the colonial administration had to protect tributary Native communities, Bacon urged the governor to transform the anger of the moment into a war against all Indigenous in Virginia. Berkeley demurred, but Bacon persisted. The newcomer saw himself in these months as an intermediary, a leader of an upstart rebellion who remained on friendly terms with the government. His sentiments shifted in response to the sense of grievance he heard from other colonists who felt victimized. He understood that Berkeley wanted to shield the Pamunkeys from the angry colonists, but his allies believed that these tribute-paying Natives were just spies for more powerful groups, notably the Susquehannocks. "The whole country is much alarmed with the feare of Generall Combinacion" of Indigenous, he wrote to Berkeley, "and I think not without reason." Bacon wanted Berkeley to give him a commission to lead this ragtag crew into a war. More suspicious of colonists whom the governor's allies saw as vulgar upstarts, Berkeley refused.[53]

Rather than retreat into the comforts of his prior life, Bacon instead sent a message to the governor labeled a "Humble Appeale of the Voluntiers to all well minded and Charitable People."[54] He implored the administration to see the uprising as a chance to defend the colony at their own risk and expense. He urged Berkeley to ignore the rumors that he intended to overthrow the government. Berkeley responded by removing Bacon from the council but offered to hold a new election, which would provide an opportunity for unhappy colonists to articulate their criticisms. Bacon would not wait. He soon enlisted Occaneechees to help the colonists capture Susquehannocks, whom he and his followers murdered. Then the colonists shot and killed the Occaneechees.

Berkeley found Bacon's action insolent but did not dispute that even Indigenous in tribute-paying communities had likely become allies of the Susquehannocks. The governor informed one of his commanders that the government's forces should "spare none that has the name of an Indian for they are now all our Enemies." Bacon pled again for a commission. Interpreting the resistance not as a policy difference but instead as an act of treason, Berkeley and his council proclaimed that Bacon and his followers were rebels. Rather than surrender, Bacon instead sought office in the election that Berkeley had authorized. He arrived in Jamestown on June 6 with fifty allies. Berkeley had him taken prisoner and paraded him in front of the assembly. Bacon, seeking his release, had to appear on his knees and write out a confession—using words supplied by Berkeley. The governor accepted the confession and pardoned Bacon on June 10.

With Bacon sidelined at least temporarily, Berkeley and his allies in the assembly put new restrictions on tribute-paying Natives. In the past, Indigenous in the area had had freedom of movement. Now, any who traveled without colonial permission were labeled enemies subject to the

53. Morgan, *American Slavery, American Freedom*, quotation at 258.
54. Morgan, *American Slavery, American Freedom*, quotations at 258–259.

seizure of their property. Colonists who captured them would be rewarded, which added new incentive for hostile actions against Natives. Sensing an opportunity to solve the colony's persistent labor shortage, the assembly ruled that "all Indians taken in warr be held and accounted slaved dureing life."[55]

Berkeley thought that he had survived the challenge to his administration. But when Bacon appeared back in Jamestown on June 22, this time with 500 followers, the governor realized his miscalculation and offered Bacon the military commission he had so eagerly sought. The governor's allies saw Bacon's followers as lowlife rabble, but as observers in the capital recognized, they were tax-paying freemen eager to escape onerous public charges, not indentured servants who signed on in some hope of becoming free. On June 25, word reached Jamestown that Natives had killed eight colonists in New Kent. When Bacon and his men went in pursuit, Berkeley voided his commission. Enraged by the news, Bacon and many of his followers abandoned the pursuit of Pamunkeys and instead marched on Middle Plantation (modern Williamsburg). There he presented a manifesto in formal language reflecting his Cambridge education. In this "Declaration of the People," Bacon defined Berkeley and his allies as traitors to the Crown because of their protection of the colony's "darling Indians," raising taxes without protecting colonists remote from Jamestown, and suspending military assaults that could have vanquished Indigenous foes. Their passions aroused, the rebels promised to destroy all commerce with Natives and to "to ruine and extirpate all Indians in general."[56] During their campaign they plundered the houses of Berkeley's wealthy allies and captured forty-five Pamunkeys in New Kent. To guarantee his success, he offered freedom to the servants and enslaved of Berkeley's allies, a proposition that attracted at least 100 to his cause. This army of the unfortunate then marched to Jamestown, where Bacon hoped to display the Pamunkey captives. Recognizing that he could not prevail, Berkeley boarded a ship and fled. Bacon's men torched the capital.

Over the following weeks, Bacon's men seized plunder wherever they could find it, an anarchic pillaging that some elite colonists saw as the sign of the end of their way of life. Then on October 26 Bacon died, a victim like so many before him of the "bloody flux," probably dysentery. With its opportunistic and charismatic leader gone, the ragtag rebellion

55. Morgan, *American Slavery, American Freedom*, quotation at 260 ("spare none"); Hening, *Statutes*, II:346.

56. Nathaniel Bacon, "Manifesto Concerning the Troubles in Virginia (1676)," in Merrill Jensen, ed., *English Historical Documents*, vol. IX, *American Colonial Documents to 1776* (Oxford: Oxford University Press, 1955), 581–584, quotations at 582. For details of the complaints from each county, see *Wiseman's Book of Record*, 207–256.

began to collapse. The end came when English warships sailed up the James and York Rivers, once again proving the advantage that those naturally deep channels had for soldiers to reach troubled areas. By January, Berkeley was back in power. His forces rounded up the eighty enslaved and twenty servants who held out until the end, sending them back to those who owned their labor.

On May 29, 1677, the queen of the Pamunkeys, her son John West, the queen of Waonoke, the king of the Nancymonds, and the king of the Nottoways met a colonial delegation at Middle Plantation. The war had come to an end, with Indigenous and Berkeley both eager to find a way toward peaceful coexistence. The colonial ambassadors promised to protect Native lands, with each town surrounded by a buffer of three miles that would be off-limits to any colonists. They also promised the Natives that they could travel onto colonists' lands to go oystering and fishing and to gather curtenemons, wild oats, tuckahoe, rushes, puckoone, and, as the colonists in attendance reported, "any thing else (for their natural support) not useful to the English," a sign of the continuing viability of Indigenous economic practices. The English also guaranteed that these Native queens and kings had full authority to govern their own people, with the queen of Pamunkey owed submission by unspecified Indigenous according to traditional practices. In exchange, the Natives had to return any children, servants, or horses they had taken from colonists during the war. The colonists promised to provide arms to Indigenous residents so that they could together repel any new threat. The peace treaty did not erase any existing contracts Natives had as servants as long as the terms of their service matched those for colonists, but it forbade them from being sold as slaves, another sign that the spread of enslavement in Virginia would ensnare Africans, not Indigenous. Above all, the English sought to clarify that these Natives would be subjects of the English king, a political affiliation they would reaffirm each year with payment of three arrowheads and twenty beaver skins. Once they had agreed to terms, the Native royalty in attendance knelt to sign the text, "kissing the Paper as they Transferred it from hand to hand to each other" in what the scribes saw as reverence to the king and "joyful acceptance" of the agreement.[57]

57. *Articles of Peace between Charles II . . . and Several Indian Kings and Queens* (London, 1677), https://anthologydev.lib.virginia.edu/work/Stuart/Stuart-Articles_of_Peace (accessed August 1, 2025), 7 (buffer), 9 (traditional gathering), 11–12 (Indigenous sovereignty), 15 (returning children), 11 (bearing arms), 12–13 (servitude and enslavement), 17 (signing ritual); and see Haylen Negrin, "Cockacoeske's Rebellion: Nathaniel Bacon, Indigenous Slavery, and Sovereignty in Early Virginia," *WMQ*, 3rd Ser., 80 (2023), 49–86.

Bacon's ill-fated rebellion had briefly threatened the hard-won gains made by colonists along the shores of the Chesapeake. Berkeley and his allies could have lost their homes and their positions. They got lucky. But they also knew that the way to guard against another uprising would be to find a way to preserve order in the hinterland, which explained the approach to Cockacoeske, the queen of Pamunkeys, and other Indigenous elites, as well as to mollify the grievances of poorer colonial farming families. Rather than improving these poorer colonists' material circumstances, colonial officials instead decided that the best way forward was to limit additional migration of indentured servants.

Virginia's elite did not need to look hard for a model for the transition in the labor force they imagined. Multiple connections between the mainland colonies and Barbados meant Tidewater planters understood that their island counterparts had imported an enslaved workforce once they determined that English or Irish servants were unwilling to perform the arduous work of producing and refining sugar. Virginians knew about this decision firsthand because one-time Barbadian servants sailed to the Chesapeake looking for land after the terms of their indentures ended. Barbados was simply too small to provide opportunities for any who lacked the financial resources of the island's planter class. Wealthy Anglo-Barbadians had launched Carolina as an offshoot of the island. The tropics became a model for the Chesapeake. By 1670, according to Berkeley, there were approximately 38,000 English colonists in Virginia, including 6,000 servants, as well as 2,000 "black slaves."[58]

In 1675, residents of Tewa pueblo began to recapture elements of their traditional religious practice, which Spanish soldiers had repressed decades earlier. During what they hoped would be a spiritual revival, local shamans bewitched some of the priests living in the area. Earlier, such actions had prompted bloody reprisals by Spanish troops, as had occurred when Major Jacinto García de Sepúlveda suppressed a rising of Hualahuis by hanging twenty-two prisoners. "These Indians were the ones who died on that occasion," missionary Juan Bautista Chapa later wrote, "and this punishment pacified the land for some time."[59]

58. Warren M. Billings, ed., *The Old Dominion in the Seventeenth Century: A Documentary History of Virginia, 1606–1700*, rev. ed. (Chapel Hill: University of North Carolina Press for the Omohundro Institute of Early American History and Culture, 2007), 133; Morgan, *American Slavery, American Freedom*, 298–299.

59. Juan Bautista Chapa, *Texas and Northeastern Mexico, 1630–1690*, trans. F. Brierley, ed. William C. Foster (Austin: University of Texas Press, 1997), 40–41; Forbes, *Apache, Navajo, and Spaniard*, 171,

The quick resolution of incidents convinced Spain's regional governors and their top commanders to crush any sign of religiously infused rebellion. They did so to bring areas under control and to send a message that this army of Christ was on a holy as well as a territorial mission. Resistance to the destruction of Indigenous icons signaled apostasy. Participation in traditional rituals insulted the Christian savior. Failure to pay tribute threatened the finances of the imperial state and weakened its ability to keep this territory under Spanish control. Those who stood against the two ascendant kings, Christ and Carlos II, needed to be punished: whipped, ears or limbs lopped off, hanged, sold into slavery. The drive for Christian spiritual perfection supported the ongoing desire to harvest silver and tend livestock. Brutal assaults on Indigenous peoples conducting traditional rites could work only in isolated communities since there were in the early 1670s 17,000 Pueblos inhabiting a territory where the Spanish had fewer than 200 soldiers.[60]

Within this mental universe, the actions at Tewa in 1675 loomed as yet another potential problem. This time, the situation went beyond insubordination, stealing colonists' property, and not attending mass. In Tewa, residents bewitched Spaniards. Between eight and twelve soon died, including at least five priests. A missionary at San Ildefonso thought he was bewitched. Idolatrous practices soon emerged into the open in Acoma, Taos, and Zuñi. In response, Governor Juan Francisco Treviño sent troops into these pueblos to find the culprits. His soldiers hanged three Tewas, and another captive committed suicide. The Spaniards captured and beat forty-three others, sentencing them to slavery. Soon after, a group of seventy Tewas arrived in Santa Fe and demanded that the governor release the prisoners. Treviño, seeing no other options, let them go. Among the released prisoners was the spiritual leader Po'pay (sometimes written Popé or Popah), a Tewa from Ohkay Owingeh who had earlier traveled to Taos and been captured along with others.[61]

From the moment he was released, Po'pay began to forge an alliance that would link politics to religion, a holy crusade drawing on the power of kachinas to wrest control of the region from Spanish soldiers and clerics and place it back in the hands of Native peoples. Indigenous captives later told the Spanish that Po'pay affiliated himself with Po'se yemu, a rain-providing Tewa culture hero. During the late 1670s, Po'pay burnished his religious credentials, gaining access to the innermost chambers of the

60. Forbes, *Apache, Navajo, and Spaniard*, 175.

61. Calloway, *One Vast Winter Count*, 172; Forbes, *Apache, Navajo, and Spaniard*, 171–172; John Kessell, *Spain in the Southwest* (Norman: University of Oklahoma Press, 2002), 118–119.

kiva at Taos. There, he told others, he visited with the kachinas and spread the word he received from Po'se yemu. His message resonated among multiple groups, including Tewas, Tiwa-speaking residents of Taos, Hopi, Keres, Towa, and Zuñi, all of whom had a figure similar to Po'se yemu among their spiritual protectors. Some long-standing ritual practices, which had survived alongside Christianity in New Mexico since the late sixteenth century, detailed how Po'se yemu waged a spiritual battle with Christ, including through authorizing secret kachina dances that Spaniards never witnessed. Po'pay taught others the lessons that Po'se yemu preached, including a rejection of European ritual practices.[62]

Initially unbeknownst to local Spaniards, Po'pay and his allies communicated regularly with each other. They were all too aware that the ongoing drought, which had likely begun around 1664, reduced food supplies, and periodic epidemics took a heavy toll on both humans and livestock. Declining resources also pitted Indigenous groups against each other, with Apache raiders taking captives and killing those who stood against them. To make matters worse, Treviño, who held his post from 1675 to 1677, tried to quash traditional religion by banning large gatherings in kivas and dances that many Pueblos believed would bring rain. Such official actions spurred deeper resentment among struggling residents. They shared stories about the invaders' depredations: theft, rape, destruction of sacred objects, beatings, torture, murder. These were not specious claims invented in feverish political moments. Spanish authorities knew about soldiers' and priests' violent treatment of Indigenous. Perhaps administrators calculated that punishing their own would be counter-productive since they remained so outnumbered by Indigenous. Whatever their logic, official inaction in the face of cleric-, colonist-, and soldier-caused humiliation only fed suspicion.[63]

Po'pay understood that the Spanish assault on the physical objects of Indigenous faith could be used as a symbol to unite those feeling dispossessed. In the heat of the desert summer in 1680, he convened a group of twenty-two war captains, men occupying a distinct niche in Pueblo communities, and shared the lessons of Po'se yemu. The group included individuals who were mestizos, *indios ladinos* (mission-educated, Spanish-speaking Indigenous), and *coyotes* (of mixed Native and African heritage). In a series of discussions, he and his allies plotted a path toward reclaiming their lands. The group dispersed in early August, with Po'pay's allies

62. Matthew Liebman, *Revolt: An Archaeological History of Pueblo Resistance and Revitalization in 17th-Century New Mexico* (Tucson: University of Arizona Press, 2012), 50–52.

63. See Liebman, *Revolt*, 44–45; Calloway, *One Vast Winter Count*, 170–173.

carrying a cord braided from maguey fiber or deerskin. Each string had thirteen knots in it. The individuals were to return to their communities, untying a knot each day. When there were no knots left, the Pueblos would launch attacks on every individual and structure affiliated with the Spaniards. Po'pay envisioned a mass uprising erupting on August 13 in the communities surrounding the Spanish colonial capital at Santa Fe. The insurgents were to first destroy local garrisons and churches, kill soldiers and clerics, murder colonists in their scattered estancias, and then march toward the Governor's Palace, the administrative heart of Spanish New Mexico. Some Indigenous resisted Po'pay's plan, including Nicolas Bua, his son-in-law, who was the local governor at Ohkay Owingeh. Survivors of the insurrection who gave testimony to Spanish officials later reported that Po'pay killed Bua. The action, if true, signaled a shift in Po'pay's thinking. Before this encounter, he had been a holy man and, as such, had access to the most sacred chambers of a kiva. According to Pueblo tradition, the shedding of another's blood meant losing such status. From then onward, Po'pay employed the language of religious war not as a prophet but instead as a warrior. Fearing that there might be other Natives who would leak the plot to the Spanish, Po'pay ordered that the message not be sent into certain communities, including in the southern administrative unit of Piro, along the Rio Grande.[64]

Try as they might, the rebels could not prevent their plan from leaking. When two of the messengers from the Tewa pueblo of Tesuque entered nearby Tano to share the plot, word reached three priests who warned Antonio de Otermín, the regional governor living in Santa Fe. Colonial soldiers captured the Pueblo messengers and brought them in front of the governor. Eventually, perhaps succumbing to torture tactics that Otermín had used in other examinations, they revealed the plot on August 9. Otermín learned that the rebels gathered together to cast aside any obedience to the Spanish king and abandon Christianity, and "they wish to kill the priestly ministers and all Spaniards, women and children, wiping out the people of this region." Especially alarming was news that the pueblos had formed an alliance with the "infidel Apaches," who would join the Pueblos to "execute their disobedience, deceit, treason and atrocities."

64. Liebman, *Revolt*, 54–57; Alfonso Ortiz, "Popay's Leadership: A Pueblo Perspective," *El Palacio* 86 (1980), 18–22. For deerskin, see "Santa Fe, August 9, 1680, First Report," in *Autos Tocantes al alsamiento de los yndios de la provinçia de la Nueba Mexico/Documents Concerning the Revolt of the Indians of the Province of New Mexico in 1680* [hereafter *Documents Concerning the Revolt of the Indians*], trans. and ed. Juan A. Sempere-Martínez and Damian Bacich (Berkeley: Cibola Project, n.d.), https://escholarship.org/content/qt5xvot5bq/qt5xvot5bq_noSplash_cc89b3368943b904edf25dd5621f14d2.pdf?t=otp4rr), 20.

The informants from Tesuque specified that the leader was "a lieutenant of Poheyemu" who was "very tall, black and had very large, yellow eyes, and all feared him greatly." The description fitted a traditional rendering of the deity.[65]

When word of the rope runners' capture reached Tesuque, local leaders launched the rebellion. On the night of the ninth they killed Cristóbal Herrera, a colonist with no knowledge of the uprising, when he arrived in the pueblo. The next day, an *indio ladino* killed the local priest, who had come to the church to recite his pre-dawn prayers. Later that day rebels at Kewa, home of the colony's Franciscan administration, murdered the five soldiers who guarded the clerical establishment and then killed the three priests. They piled the guards' corpses outside and put the bodies of the priests in a grave in front of the church altar. Rebels at Acoma rounded up three missionaries there, stripped them, and paraded them through the town. Eventually they stoned them to death in front of their church. Hopi insurgents at Shugopovi seized the local priest after he managed to stab one of the intruders with a sword. They suspended him from the beams of the church and burned him alive. At Atat'ovi other Hopis also burned the bodies of priests in the local church. By the end of the day, rebels had killed twenty-one Franciscans, about one-half of the order's entire population in New Mexico. In the eyes of the church, the dead missionaries became martyrs. To Po'pay and his allies, their deaths confirmed the righteousness of their cause and the power of Po'se yemu.[66]

Priests and soldiers represented one part of the Spanish colonial program. By August 1680, the rebels had also come to understand that they had to rid the land of all physical traces of Christianity, not just the friars. At Sandia they smashed the mission's bells, ripped off doors, chopped the arms off a wooden sculpture of Francis of Assisi, whipped the varnish and paint off a crucifix, stoned a depiction of the Immaculate Conception (including digging out the eyes of the Virgin), buried chalices in manure, rubbed human excrement on other statues, and set the church on fire. These would be the first, but hardly the last, efforts to erase signs of Christianity. Erasure, though devastating to Spaniards, was not uniform.

65. "Santa Fe, August 9, 1680," in *Documents Concerning the Revolt of the Indians*, 15–19, quotations at 18–19; Hackett, *Revolt*, 1:204–205; Andrew L. Knaut, *The Pueblo Revolt of 1680: Conquest and Resistance in Seventeenth-Century New Mexico* (Norman: University of Oklahoma Press, 1995), 3–4; Liebman, *Revolt*, 56–58.

66. Liebman, *Revolt*, 58–60; for the killing of the priest at Tesuque, see the statement of Pedro Hidalgo, August 10, 1680, in *Documents Concerning the Revolt of the Indians*, 23–24; for Sandia, see *Documents Concerning the Revolt of the Indians*, 57–58; for the killing of the soldiers and priests, see Writ of the March, August 24, 1680, in *Documents Concerning the Revolt of the Indians*, 50.

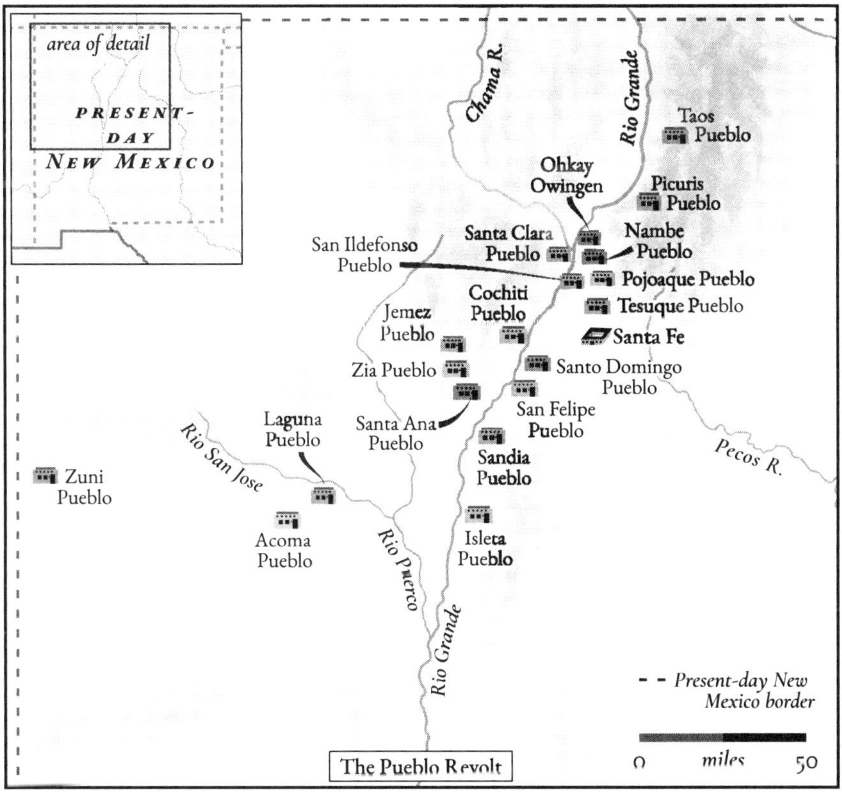

Residents of Nuestra Señora de la Asunción de Zia let the local priest survive, though they assaulted nearby farms. Zuñi oral tradition notes that Fray Juan Greyrobe survived the rebellion too, opting to repudiate the church and embrace an Indigenous lifestyle. He was lucky. By nightfall on August 10, rebels had killed 380 colonists, burned their houses, stolen livestock and grain, and murdered every soldier they could find. Often the warriors stripped their victims and left their bodies piled in houses or scattered along the side of a road. Within a day, news reached Otermín of casualties from Taos to Sandia and even in nearby missions in San Ildefonso and Galisteo. Almost immediately, about 1,000 surviving colonists, soldiers, and priests rushed to Santa Fe to shelter in the Governor's Palace. Otermín, understanding the risk, ordered local priests to take all religious paraphernalia from the local church of San Miguel into the administrative compound.[67]

67. Liebman, *Revolt*, 60–64; Writ of A. Otermin, August 10, 1680, in *Documents Concerning the Revolt of the Indians*, 25–26.

Cowering in fear and anger, Otermín and his allies schemed to find a way out. They could not stay in the palace forever, they knew. Each day brought reports of other assaults. One informant told him that the rebels were gathering to destroy the capital "and all the Spaniards, so that the whole kingdom might be theirs, and they might profit at the expense of the Spaniards and their haciendas." The rebels boasted that "now God and Santa Maria were dead, that they were the ones whom the Spaniards worshipped, and that their own God whom they obeyed never died." The governor, responding to an appeal to surrender, claimed that he wanted peace. Not grasping the magnitude of the threat, he even offered to pardon the rebels, a gesture that the Pueblos ignored.

Rather than accept his entreaties, the rebels marched ever closer to the center of Santa Fe. Insurgents joined from Pecos, Keres, and Tano, until their numbers reached 2,500 by August 16. That day the rebels dammed the irrigation canals, Santa Fe's lifeline. By the eighteenth, Spanish livestock began to perish from thirst. Cries of trapped colonists filled the air. On August 20, believing that he had run out of options, the governor ordered the seventy or so soldiers in the palace to attack. By day's end, Otermín would later report, the Spanish had killed 300 Pueblos and suffered only five casualties. They also took forty-seven prisoners. Those captives informed the Spanish that they had come to destroy Santa Fe under the orders of a "lieutenant of Pose'yemu." Otermín ordered them executed on the spot. The next day the Spanish evacuated. Pueblos watched the survivors of the nine-day siege leave, likely observing their trek all the way to El Paso del Norte, 300 miles south of Santa Fe.[68] Rebels soon pillaged the governor's palace, with one declaring that Natives were free to "live as we would like and we will settle in this township wherever we wish."[69]

The Spanish evacuated their regional capital in military formation, a gesture that masked their desperate state. Most of the refugees were women, children, and others the governor and aides deemed unable to bear arms. They retreated guarded by only 155 soldiers. While they walked, they heard reports that Pueblos and their allies, likely including Apaches, were en route to El Paso as well, though their primary target was Parral, the site where so many captured Indigenous had been kept enslaved. By

68. Liebman, *Revolt*, 64–67; Hackett, *Revolt*, 1:204–205, 214–217, quotation and estimate of Pueblo forces at 216; Knaut, *Pueblo Revolt*, 3–8, 11–12.

69. Declaration of an unnamed Indian, August 23, 1680, in *Documents Concerning the Revolt of the Indians*, 47–49, quotation at 48–49.

then, the Spanish had lost 380 colonists or soldiers as well as perhaps thirty-two of the forty Franciscans in the province.[70]

In the aftermath of the revolt, Spanish authorities gathered testimony about what had happened. Time and again, witnesses who had been among the Pueblos on August 10 and after told of how Natives "wearing war paint, with their bows, arrows, lances, and shields," killed priests, as soldier Pedro Hidalgo reported about Tesuque near the start of the uprising. The militants took no prisoners.[71] Insurrectionists from Los Jemez and Teguas raided Spanish houses, taking their cattle and committing "inequities, atrocities, and robberies" with impunity.[72] Spanish soldiers arrived in Santa Clara and Pojoaque after the Pueblos had killed at least thirty, with entire families missing and presumed dead.[73] Invaders at Santa Domingo murdered the three resident friars and four soldiers and then stole livestock and sacred objects.[74]

During their retreat from Santa Fe, the governor and his associates found pillaged churches, some with straw in them that no rebel had yet lit.[75] Each day they came upon similar scenes: horses and cattle gone, Spanish houses robbed and empty, evacuees hoping to escape mounted harquebus-wielding rebels, Spanish women and children left behind scrounging for their safety and survival.[76] Word of these losses eventually reached Parral. "The destruction of all the temples, sacred vessels, and vestments, shows the iniquity of those barbarians and the hatred which they feel for our holy faith," Governor Don Bartolomé de Estrada wrote to the viceroy. "These are sufficient reasons for war being waged against them without mercy, and for declaring all those who may be captured slaves for a period of ten years," following earlier precedent.[77]

70. Auto de Junta [El Paso, August 25, 1680], in Hackett, ed., *Pueblo Revolt*, 1:234 (estimate of priests killed); Knaut, *Pueblo Revolt*, 12–15.
71. Declaration of Pedro Hidalgo, [Santa Fe, August 10, 1680], in Hackett, ed., *Pueblo Revolt*, 1:208.
72. Judicial process and declaration, [Santa Fe, August 10, 1680], in Hackett, ed., *Pueblo Revolt*, 1:210.
73. Auto and declaration of Francisco Gómez, [Santa Fe, August 12, 1680], in Hackett, ed., *Pueblo Revolt*, 1:211.
74. Auto, [Santa Fe, August 13, 1680], in Hackett, ed., *Pueblo Revolt*, 1:213.
75. Departure for Sandia and arrival at Isleta, August 26, 1680, in *Documents Concerning the Revolt of the Indians*, 57.
76. [Continuation of Otermín's march, August 26, 1680], in Hackett, ed., *Pueblo Revolt*, 1:228–229; Auto de Junta [El Paso, August 25, 1680], in Hackett, ed., *Pueblo Revolt*, 1:232.
77. Bartolomé de Estradra [to the viceroy], July 22, 1680, in Hackett, ed., *Pueblo Revolt*, 1:247.

Spanish observers including Otermín depicted the year as a tragedy precipitated by the followers of icons and the ravings of delusional individuals who claimed to speak to the gods. Much of what had happened sprang from Spanish actions, however, and was not simply the result of laying claim to an area and then demanding tribute from its residents. The Spanish had prevailed in other arenas, from Hispaniola to Tenochtitlan and Cuzco, because they could destroy those who stood in their paths. Rather than see their victory as stemming from good luck (in the case of the diseases they unwittingly transported) or even martial advantage in places where their numbers and arms were strong, their success bred arrogance: if they prevailed elsewhere, then they would in the desert. That kind of confidence fed the Franciscan strategy to insist on prayers spoken in Spanish and little sustained effort to learn Indigenous languages. Indifferent to the need to learn local dialects, the Franciscans and the soldiers were deaf to the complaints that swirled in front of them and, more important, from one Native group to another. Unlike the colonizers, at least some of the local Indigenous had learned Spanish, giving them the ability to understand the plans of the governor and his subordinates and to share insights with others.[78] The bilingual among the Pueblos could explain that Indigenous had grown weary "of the work they had to do for the Spaniards and the religious, because they did not allow them to plant or do other things for their own needs."[79] The Apaches and Pueblos had once been mortal enemies. The Spanish, by abusing both through slave raiding and corporal punishment, transformed them into allies. Pueblos and Navajos had traded for generations but not been close allies before. The Spanish brought them together.

In the aftermath of the revolt, the rebels cleansed the landscape. Po'pay articulated a plan to make the world whole again. The Pueblos, he argued, needed to erase every sign of Christianity, from rosaries and icons to churches. They needed to build new kivas and perform ritual dances to consecrate them. Any Christian converts among them needed to plunge into the Rio Grande with a yucca root in hand to scrub off the stain of baptismal water. Po'pay banned the use of Christian names and the Spanish language, and he vacated clerical marriage customs to reintroduce serial monogamy, a traditional practice among the Pueblos. The rebels stole Catholic vestments they found in churches. Informants reported the burning of churches in eighteen pueblos as well as others scattered

78. See, e.g., Declaration of an Indian rebel, [Place of the Arroyo de San Marcos, August 23, 1680], in Hackett, ed., *Pueblo Revolt*, 1:221.

79. Declaration of Pedro García, [near the estancia of Christóbal de Anaya, August 25, 1680], in Hackett, ed., *Pueblo Revolt*, 1:225–226.

among the Zuñis and Hopis. Po'pay's followers dug up and destroyed Catholic objects that priests had buried. At Senecú, Indigenous scalped an icon of Jesus, then pulled apart a large cross and left it in a graveyard. At Nuestra Señora del Socorro they burned both a large cross and a statue of the Christian savior. After setting the church at Pecos alight, Indigenous returned to find the walls still standing after the roof collapsed. They systematically took it apart. At Taos they desecrated the bodily remains of five soldiers. Rebels fearing the possible return of Christian practice at Sevilleta destroyed the local church, reclaiming the physical materials to build a kiva. Across New Mexico, insurgents destroyed church bells, which many saw as a marker not only of Christian practice but also an effort by the colonizers to impose a European-style daily regimen, the sound of each peal a constant reminder of a differently sacralized land. Many survivors likely bore witness to the installation of bells, a Catholic ritual in which the objects had been baptized and even had godparents, treating a physical object like a disciple. These relics needed ritual death, which included drowning some bells, pulling others apart and burying them in cemeteries, and removing their clappers to render them mute.[80]

Imperial hubris explained how the Spanish thought they could control New Mexico despite being far outnumbered by Indigenous. Local administrators thought that enslaving Apaches would bring them under control while fattening Spanish coffers with silver at Parral and Zacatecas. Spanish officials believed that whipping, amputation, and executions would suppress Indigenous sorcery in Acoma and Senecú. Clerical authorities presumed that the miracle of transubstantiation would quiet and quell the kachinas. As the Pueblo Revolt ended, they learned they were wrong.

To the Spanish, 1680 had produced a landscape haunted by ghosts. For Pueblos, the rebellion brought the triumphant return of the kachinas, a landscape reborn through the power of faith.

80. Liebman, *Revolt*, 71–77.

26

Legacies

Around 1599, William Shakespeare wrote *The Life of Henry V*, a history play that culminated in a contest between the medieval English king and his French foes. After the climactic re-creation of a brutal battle in the fields of Agincourt, the bloodied ruler who had led his soldiers into battle did not know "if the day be ours or no." It was a question that many thousands of Indigenous and colonists in North America could have asked themselves then, at the dawn of the seventeenth century, and again eighty years later.

Like his historical protagonist, Shakespeare pondered the fate of the English realm, including the then-nascent efforts to conquer territory far from home. He channeled some of his interest into *The Tempest*, a 1611 play possibly based on his reading of pamphlets about the early English colonization of Bermuda. Many of those in the audience for performances of that play may also have wondered about affairs on the far shores of the Atlantic, their interest piqued by the flood of books appearing with greater frequency offering details about the Americas.

Many Europeans writing in the sixteenth and seventeenth centuries promised readers "true" reports about events in the Western Hemisphere. Cortés wrote about battles and exploitable resources in accounts that quickly reached a broad public. French readers learned about a mock battle between their nation's soldiers and a group of Tupinambás, captured in Brazil, staged to entertain King Henri II in Rouen in 1550.[1] Thomas Harriot, the younger Richard Hakluyt, and the Flemish engraver Theodor de Bry added alluring illustrations to published accounts. A series of Jesuit writers penned yearly reports recounting the progress of Christendom as well as the many setbacks that befell religious men and women in the Americas—more proof, as if any were needed, that expanding the realm

1. *C'est la deduction du Somptueux ordre, plaisantz spectacles et magnifiques theatres dresses et exhibes, par les citoiens de Rouen* (Rouen, 1551); Michael Wintroub, "Civilizing the Savage and Making a King: The Royal Entry Festival of Henri II (Rouen, 1550)," *Sixteenth-Century Journal* 29 (1998), 465–494.

of their lord required the kind of sacrifice that the earliest evangelists experienced. Dutch artists created delicate watercolors of New Netherland and painted plantation scenes in Brazil, works that reached even the illiterate. North America in 1680 remained an arduous journey's distance from Europe. But by then it had become closer as a place to imagine.

Four crucial developments had launched the struggle for North America. The expansion of maize into the well-watered fields of the Mississippi Valley allowed for Indigenous populations to grow far larger than in the arid lands west of the 100th meridian. The western expeditions of the Norse hinted at the profits—as well as the challenges—to be found in the Western Hemisphere. The development of the slave trade in the Azores and Madeira prefigured the later expansion of the noxious commerce into temperate and tropical American climates. And the evolution of an effective system to spread news of the Americas across Europe drove profit-seekers, religious believers, missionaries, and glory-hounds to turn their eyes westward. These developments set the stage for deep and enduring change. But nothing had yet determined who would prevail in the contest for the continent's abundant resources.

The Columbian Exchange mattered, but it did not settle the fate of the peoples who vied for North America. To be sure, some epidemics caused by Eurasian pathogens devastated certain Indigenous communities—smallpox in Tenochtitlán during the time of the Spanish conquest, hemorrhagic fever across the Valley of Mexico a generation later, leptospirosis in coastal portions of New England in the late 1610s, smallpox and influenza across Wendake in the 1630s. But it was another element of the exchange that likely mattered more: the eastward shipment of American resources, with each commodity-laden ship arriving in western Europe whetting the appetites of those who sought commercial profits. Ships bearing gold, pearls, sugar, tobacco, and furs also brought proof that Europeans could go back and forth across the Atlantic. Those who returned brought news and hope, including for those seeking religious refuge or new souls to harvest for the Christian god. No wonder that eager propagandists like English writers Richard Hakluyt and Samuel Purchas, following an intellectual path forged by witnesses to Columbus's exploits, devoted their time to publishing reports about territory that lay beyond the daily experience of almost every European. Once printers started spreading stories about the Western Hemisphere, they never stopped. The trickle of tracts that bore witness to the exploratory ventures of Columbus and Vespucci became a torrent. Authors of herbals incorporated American plants into the regimes they recommended to physicians and apothecaries for healing illnesses. The benefits of colonization went beyond fattening company accounts or allowing planters to build grand estates. The Americas contained possible cures for myriad human afflictions.[2]

Yet as the events of 1675 to 1680 demonstrated, Europeans had not yet conquered North America. The voluntary migration of Europeans and the forced movement of enslaved Africans had put pressure on Indigenous peoples near North American shorelines, many of whom found themselves facing the existential anxiety expressed so poignantly by the Narragansett leader Miantonomi when he warned that English men and women were destroying the natural resources that Natives needed to live. But the decline in English migration after the plague and London fire of the 1660s, the continued inability of French promoters to lure free men and women to the St. Lawrence Valley, and the near collapse of westward migration from other parts of Europe demonstrated that North America was something less than the irresistible lure that its eager promoters claimed. Colonists in Boston, New York, and Ciudad de México (Mexico City, formerly Tenochtitlán) had succeeded in developing commercial cultures that facilitated transoceanic commerce, including regional hubs for processing natural resources and arranging for distribution to consumers in Europe, the West Indies, and the American interior. Their economic success continued to feed imperial dreams—but did not guarantee long-term stability or prosperity across the territories Europeans claimed.

From 1521, after the Spanish conquest of the Mexica, until the mid-seventeenth-century contest between English and Spanish ships in the West Indies, most people arrived in the Western Hemisphere either as colonizing Europeans or, far more numerous, enslaved Africans. Rather than deploy legions of soldiers and architects to build large forts, European leaders persisted in believing that colonists would be able to establish towns and ports on their own. The result was often barbarously brutal warfare—along the shores of Chesapeake Bay from 1609 to 1614, again from 1622 to 1624, and yet again in 1644; in coastal New England in 1637; across Lenepahoking in 1643. Europeans had some military advantages, especially when they transported horses. But it was colonists, not troops, who drove the conquest of the territory that Europeans were able to control.

European elites hoped to profit through taxing their subordinates. In some ways, they paralleled Indigenous American models. Tribute payments had long flowed into Tenochtitlán, enabling the construction of a grand city funded by conquered peoples. Wahunsonacock established

2. See, e.g., the section on tobacco in Nicolás Monardes, *Joyfull Newes out of the Newfound World*, trans. John Frampton (London, 1580), ff. 33^{v}–41^{v}.

tributary relationships with approximately thirty communities around the Chesapeake, though he saw the strategic utility of redistributing goods to solidify his power rather than build a city. Europeans created different systems, though they too harvested American resources to support elites. The glittering ceilings of the basilica of Santa Maria Maggiore, in Rome, offered visual proof of the gold the Roman church received in exchange for its part in the conquest of New Spain. English policymakers hoped to enrich their own state by taxing, via the navigation acts, the westward movement of commodities.

Europeans were not reluctant to use force to grow richer. Their brutal treatment of enslaved Africans was an ongoing assault on the bodies and souls of their captive victims. By the early decades of the seventeenth century, Europeans had learned it was easier to buy captive Africans than to capture them, another example of funding economic expansion without relying on their own soldiers. To purchase labor for their American plantations, European merchants exported goods to West African rulers. That commerce grew dramatically in the seventeenth century. Slave traders forced approximately 315,000 captive Africans onto ships to the Western Hemisphere from 1626 to 1650, with the number growing to 488,000 between 1651 and 1675. Enslavers held captives in fortified African prisons before forcing them onto American-bound ships. In the long arc of time, those notorious warehouses for humans unsettled Europeans wracked by doubts about the slave trade. Many of those who survived the initial ordeal faced yet other forced movement in an intercolonial trade that developed at the same time.[3] But in 1680, few abolitionists were to be found across Europe or in American colonies. The Royal African Company was then eight years old. Those it employed apparently expressed few qualms about treating humans like livestock. The profits to be made from sugar trumped moral concerns. Even Quakers eager to bring enslaved Barbadians into Christendom emphasized that their concerns lay with the souls, not the bodies, of captive Africans. They reassured planters that conversion would not lead to rebellion or emancipation.[4]

The sugar trade threw into high relief the varied legacies of the contest for North America. With profits expanding in direct proportion to the

3. David Eltis and David Richardson, *Atlas of the Transatlantic Slave Trade* (New Haven, CT: Yale University Press, 2010), 23; Gregory E. O'Malley, *Final Passages: The Intercolonial Slave Trade of British America, 1619–1807* (Chapel Hill: University of North Carolina Press for the Omohundro Institute of Early American History and Culture, 2014), 114–150.

4. See John S. Harpham, *The Intellectual Origins of American Slavery: English Ideas in the Early Modern Atlantic World* (Cambridge, MA: Harvard University Press, 2025), 230–231.

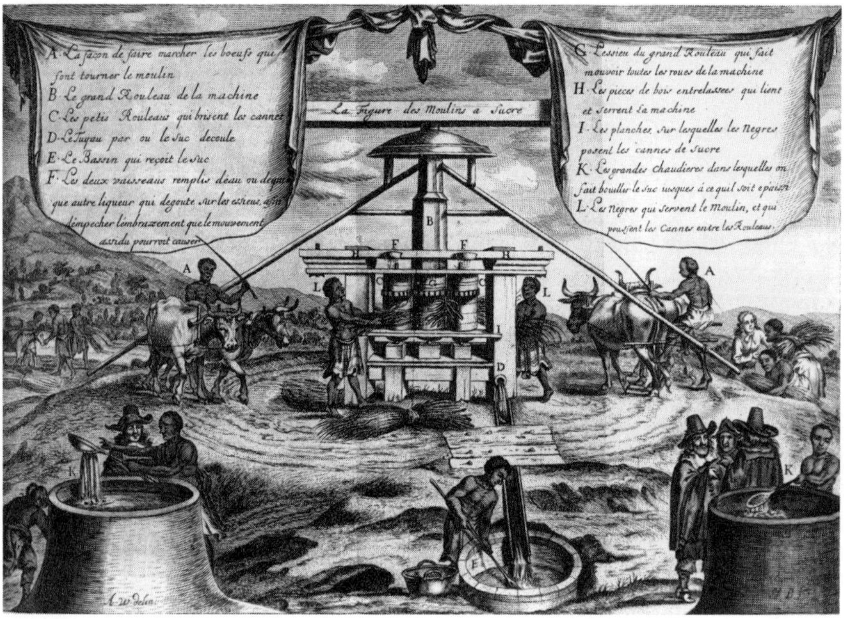

This 1681 image of enslaved Africans in a *moulin à sucre*—a sugar mill—masked the brutality of daily life on a Caribbean plantation. From [Charles de Rochefort], *Histoire naturelle et morale des îslè Antilles de l'Amérique*. Slavery Images.

amount of land under cultivation and the ability of planters to transform cane into molasses, brandy, and rum, few Europeans challenged the business with the kinds of logic that James I and VI had voiced about tobacco near the start of his reign. Clearing land in tropical climates was arduous and dangerous. So was working near vats of boiling cane, which could explode, or feeding stalks into grinders, a task that often severed fingers and arms. Such dangers did not dissuade planters and merchants who saw the slave trade as an inexhaustible source of laborers. Enslaved humans had become integrated into profit-making machines.

European extractive economies encouraged environmental destruction. Planters devastated the natural diversity of one-time ecological Edens in the West Indies. There were other environmental costs too, especially when mainland merchants integrated rum into the wares they sold to Native hunters in exchange for furs. Rum, the ideal trade good since those who consumed it did not know how to make it, became yet another commodity encouraging Indigenous to overhunt species, especially beaver. Beaver populations collapsed across North America, their dams falling apart since nature's most famous engineers, attuned to plugging any holes that developed, no longer lived there. Some farmers benefited when the dams broke since the impounded water had enriched the soil with nutrients. But that small economic victory for some came at a steep cost. Songbirds fell silent across treeless sections of Caribbean islands planted with sugar cane so that Europeans could use its products to purchase pelts.

Despite these alterations of their ancestral environments, Indigenous peoples—Puebloans, Haudenosaunee, Ojibwas, Comanches, Timucuans, Caddos, Crees, Inuit, and countless others—remained in control of most of North America. Spaniards made inroads into Indigenous territory lying north of Tenochtitlan, as the development of Parral revealed, but they struggled farther north. Even in Florida, colonists mostly clung to the coastline. Except for small numbers of religious, few French women or men lived far from the St. Lawrence Valley. English, Dutch, Swedish, and Finnish colonizers also tended to stay near the Atlantic, with the exception of the relatively few who established farms along waterways like the Hudson, Delaware, York, and James Rivers. The continent's largest watersheds—those of the modern-day Mississippi, Missouri, Ohio, and Colorado Rivers—remained in Indian Country.

Still, these centuries brought wide-ranging changes within many Native communities. Expanding commercial appetites led some Indigenous peoples into practices—most notoriously the fur trade—that threatened their own environments. For others, including those on mid-Atlantic coasts who saw no option but to sell their labor, the American commercial revolution brought onerous work to pay off debts. Indigenous peoples who had constant contact with arriving Europeans or Africans faced exposure to infectious disease. But individual stories of loss, however searing, did not signal dependency on European goods. Promoters of conquest and colonization had to learn what strategies to employ to consummate deals with Native commercial partners. When such negotiations collapsed, as was often the case, the wars that followed produced casualties on all sides.

The three broad stages in the centuries-long contest for North America, from the era of mutual discoveries through the creation of colonies and then the generation of fractures, established durable patterns. It was inconceivable, after the dissemination of news about a wondrous Western Hemisphere, that Europeans would ever forsake their quest for gain, as the Norse had done earlier. The trade in enslaved Africans proved too profitable for those who benefited from its horrors to abandon their practices. Only occasionally would Indigenous women and men make concerted efforts to end all commercial relations with colonists (though such ideas later permeated Native religious revivals). Colonists who had cleared land for fields and erected houses, churches, and stores were not going to abandon their communities even if some died defending land they believed was theirs. Christian religious at times perished when trying to spread the word of their god, but the Roman Catholic church and countless dissenting Protestant communities saw setbacks as disappointments, not as signals to end their efforts to expand Christ's earthly realm. European and colonial printers had a vested interest in generating reports about American exploits and resources, with each book rolling off their presses further feeding the imagination of readers.

In the decades from 1450 to 1680, the most substantial change in North America could be found in the ways that the peoples of the continent thought about the world around them. Before Europeans arrived, Native peoples who kept their traditions and histories orally conveyed their cultures from generation to generation, from one keeper of a nation's wisdom to the next. Those ways of transferring ideas survived, even as writing facilitated the spread of ideas and goods across the Atlantic basin. Writing and especially print accelerated and made more permanent knowledge about a new world coming into its own. Books whetted appetites about profits to be made. Letters transported on sailing ships relayed news of emerging partnerships and possibilities. Reports from the field inspired missionaries and their orders. Account books bore witness to the gains made by enslavers eager to bring sugar eastward. Imperial proclamations, including Pope Alexander VI's Bull of the Donation (*Inter caetera*) in 1493, offered justification for acts that many may have otherwise avoided. In the beginning was the Word, the Christian Bible announced. In North America, the written word solidified Europeans' worldly gains.

Yet even news of European triumphs did not mean unquestionable success. Po'pay was captured and suffered a severe beating in 1675. Five years later, after he abandoned the possibility of becoming a religious leader when he killed his son-in-law, he led a rebellion. So did Weetamoo, Metacom, and Bacon. These individuals followed a long line of others who tried, in their own ways, to change the course of history—Christopher Columbus and his sons; Hernán Cortés and Malinche; Cabeza de Vaca, Frobisher, Drake, and Hakluyt; Manteo and Wanchese; Wahunsonacock and Pocahontas; Guaman Poma; Henry Hudson and the unnamed Cree man he met; William Bradford, Thomas Morton, John Winthrop, Anne Hutchinson, and Roger Williams. They all possessed agency, the human capacity to take control over at least some aspects of one's life. So did the aggrieved colonial women of Marblehead who murdered two Indigenous captives in the waning weeks of Metacom's rebellion as well as the unnamed colonizers who shackled captive Africans for the westward passage. Fortuna and Cuffee, each enslaved, took opposite paths in Barbados in 1675. He died for his choice; she gained her freedom. Thousands of the enslaved resisted their fate too. Observers may not have recorded their names, but their actions mattered.

The body of the early Jamestown colonist whose remains, scarred by other colonists scraping her flesh for a meal, were found in a basement—no one knows her name, but archaeologists call her Jane—bears witness to the brutality of this era. Something, perhaps dysentery or typhoid fever, had felled her. Maybe she was murdered. Whatever happened, her body ended up underneath a kitchen. Countless thousands of humans, not abstract forces like capitalism or imperialism, struggled to survive in the new world that the era of Columbian voyages had pushed into existence—even if it meant eating their own to avoid starvation.

Almost two centuries passed between the voyages of Columbus and the wars that destroyed communities in New England, the Chesapeake, and New Mexico from 1675 to 1680. During those ten or so generations, Europeans time and again thought they had created a new world according to their own vision. In some ways they succeeded, though perhaps not as many had intended. The development of the transatlantic slave trade represented the tragic fulfillment of a drive for profit no matter what the costs, ripping off the fig leaf of some colonizers' claims that they were primarily bent on bringing new souls into Christendom. Thousands of Protestants and Catholics alike enslaved Africans. That is not to say that Europeans were hypocrites. For most, religious practice was inseparable from the rest of daily life. Yet in North America and across the Atlantic basin, Europeans found ways to adapt their faith traditions to justify their brutality. Governor Juan de Oñate ordered enslavement and mass amputations for those in Acoma who resisted the acceptance of his Christian monarch. Governor William Bradford attributed the burning bodies at Mystic to the unfolding of a divine plan. Enslavers tolerated missionaries proselytizing among their captives in Barbados as long as the expansion of the faith did not trigger rebellion.

Adherents of a religion premised on peace and love went to war on the bodies of the less powerful. Proponents of Old World denominations had in common that they wanted to spread Christianity among those they saw as living in ignorance. Most Indigenous peoples rejected the premise of the immigrants' argument, hardly surprising given the durability and dynamism of Native American cultures and faiths before and after the arrival of the cross bearers. As Po'pay and his allies demonstrated, Native religious views remained vibrant, as rooted in American soil as maize was.

The embers slowly burning in central Massachusetts, along the James, and in the scattered locations of one-time churches in New Mexico, as well as the incipient slave rebellion in Barbados, revealed the weakness of European visions. Colonizers had been the prime agents in the political, religious, and ecological transformations that had swept across parts—but not yet all—of North America. Colonial leaders often proved incapable of managing the myriad grievances that had festered during decades of expansion. If the eyes of the world were indeed on America, as John Winthrop once suggested, those looking in 1680 saw a troubled and contested land.

Epilogue

In 1683, English surveyor Thomas Holme produced his "Portraiture of the City of Philadelphia in the Province of Pennsylvania in America." He drew the area between the Delaware and Schuylkill rivers as a series of squares, a grid laid out across one section of Lenapehoking where nothing like it had ever existed earlier. Four years later he produced a plan for William Penn and his agents so that they could apply geometric logic to the territory they claimed as the proprietor's eponymous colony. A generation earlier, Penn's father had left Jamaica in shame and was briefly imprisoned in the Tower of London for his failure in the Caribbean. Holme confidently rendered the present and planned future of the son's capital city and its environs.

Holme's plan included an elaborate set of captions intended to provide directions for emigrants seeking a new home. To the English, this was undefined space free of any link to prior Indigenous use, a rare opportunity for Europeans at the time. Even Mexico City, by then in Spanish hands for almost 160 years, retained marks of its Aztec origins. Philadelphia, by contrast, represented a chance to create order in what many Europeans still imagined was an American wilderness.[1] The map's white spaces erased Indigenous occupation, rewriting the past of this slice of North America and offering a blank page to write its future. Holme's effort followed that of English artist James Woolridge, who in 1675 had relied on the late-sixteenth-century engravings by the De Bry workshop to paint Carolina Algonquians as if nothing had ever changed in their lives.[2]

1. Thomas Holme, "A Portraiture of the City of Philadelphia in the Province of Pennsylvania" (London, 1683); Thomas Holme, "A Map of the Improved Part of the Province of Pennsylvania in America" (London, 1687); Mary E. Miller and Barbara E. Mundy, eds., *Painting a Map of Sixteenth-Century Mexico City: Land, Writing, and Native Rule* (New Haven, CT: Yale University Press, 2012).
2. James Woolridge, "Indians of Virginia" (1675), Crystal Bridges Museum of American Art, https://commons.wikimedia.org/wiki/File:Indians_of_Virginia_by_James_Wooldridge,_c._1675.JPG.

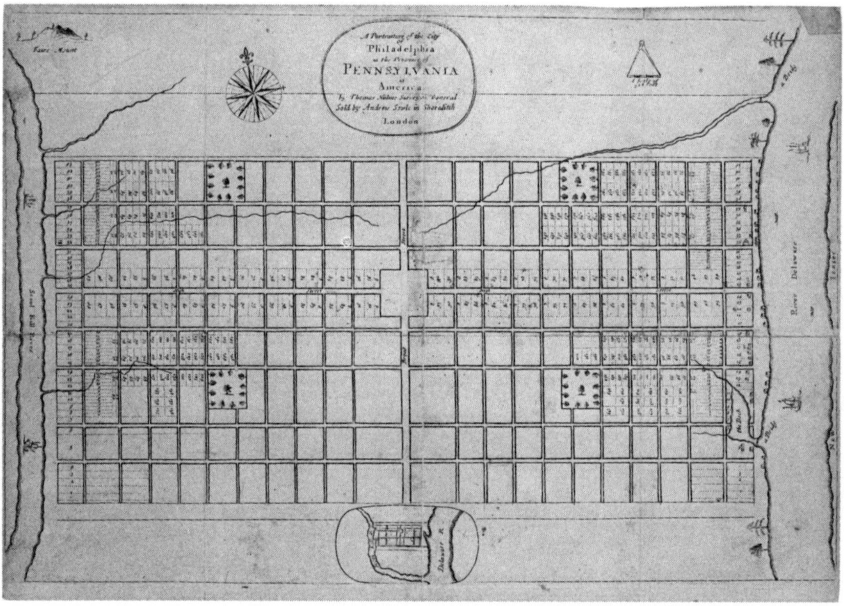

Thomas Holme, "A Portraiture of the City of Philadelphia" (1683). The Miriam and Ira D. Wallach Division of Art, Prints and Photographs: Print Collection, New York Public Library, 53908.

For William Penn, this imagined emptiness represented opportunity. Arriving in North America in 1682, he laid plans to launch his colony, loyal to his king, in a region with far more Indigenous than European residents. He landed on a continent that had just witnessed three near-simultaneous rebellions, each of them propelled by charismatic individuals including Metacom, Weetamoo, Bacon, and Po'pay. He no doubt knew of the recent suppression of the planned rebellion in Barbados. In the five years before his arrival, North America, including islands in the Caribbean, had endured a bloody baptism as significant as the arrival two centuries earlier of Columbus. The ferocity evident in the suppression of others—of Doegs, Susquehannocks, and poor English farmers near Chesapeake Bay; Narragansetts in southern New England; Puebloans in New Mexico; and enslaved Africans plotting a rebellion in Barbados—revealed psychological insecurity and deep-seated resentments. Desecrated churches in the Southwest, decapitated Indigenous in New England, burned bodies in Barbados: no one had fully anticipated a landscape littered with such a legacy of hatred and revenge.

Ever since the first maize farmers brought cobs to Cahokia, Indigenous peoples of the Western Hemisphere reshaped the continent. So too did enslaved Africans working on tobacco and sugar plantations. Fertile fields attracted Europeans, many seeking religious freedom, who then proceeded to engineer systems to extract wealth even though it meant upsetting long-evolved ecosystems. Indigenous peoples sometimes allied with colonists and often traded with them, though more frequently they felt the looming danger of an expanding European presence. Enslaved Africans understood that the forced bondage they endured became transferable to their children, a shift in notions of slavery that meant captives in North America suffered a different fate than those whose service in Africa did not pass to the next generation. Natives across the continent and migrants from West Africa and western Europe collectively created a new world like nothing that had ever existed before—a world that likely would have shocked the Carolina Algonquians Manteo and Wanchese had they lived long enough to see it. By 1680, peoples across the continent were shaping new identities forged in the unexpected course of events that had brought them together in the Western Hemisphere. Conquest and colonization created new frameworks for understanding their world. Natives and newcomers, Europeans and Africans, wealthy and poor had all become Americans.

Penn could not have known the history of North America before he arrived, though family experience taught him about the importance of the Caribbean to the English colonial project. Nor could he have anticipated that within a century, in the very city that his cartographers planned, the next major transformation of the continent would take place. A few short blocks west of his first landing, on streets the city's earliest planners laid out to be built in the future, other colonists would declare their America independent.

Bibliographical Essay

Most of the narrative in *Contested Continent* emerged from primary sources, but making sense of these strands of the past depends upon the guidance of countless scholars who have closely examined aspects of the seven-century period covered in these pages. The great majority of secondary works cited here appeared in the years after 1992, when the 500th anniversary of Columbus's first journey prompted new and vital reconsiderations of what earlier generations of historians had referred to as the "founding era" or the "age of discovery." *Contested Continent* stands as proof that those who lived in North America centuries ago inhabited what historian James Axtell identified as an age of "mutual discovery." The shift in emphasis is important. Earlier generations of historians in the United States (or writing about North America) saw Europeans as the discoverers of a "new world," and they often wrote as if only the actions of Europeans mattered. Nowadays, scholars recognize that, even if most of the written evidence emphasized Europeans' actions, Indigenous Americans and Africans, even those brutalized by enslavement, retained agency as well. Indigenous, Africans, and Europeans together created a new world.

This essay emphasizes works for the general reader, not necessarily specialists. I concentrate here primarily on the secondary literature since the notes throughout *Contested Continent* provide the sources for the primary materials that I used as well as many specialized texts. Because I have profited so much from all the material that I cite here, I have tried, like other authors in the *Oxford History of the United States* series, to minimize superlatives. I have for the most part listed sources within each section in alphabetical order. Given the expanse of the territory covered in the book, this essay is organized by thematic and chronological sections.

Unless otherwise specified in the notes, biographical details for many individuals can be found in the *Oxford Dictionary of National Biography*, the *Encyclopedia of Virginia*, the *Dictionary of American Biography*, and the *Dictionary of Canadian Biography*.

Overviews

Some historians with a keen eye for telling details have in recent years written studies of the colonial era with both narrative flair and immense learning. Among the best are Bernard

Bailyn, *The Barbarous Years: The Conflict of Civilizations, 1600–1675* (2012); Jack P. Greene, *Pursuits of Happiness: The Social Development of Early Modern British Colonies and the Formation of American Culture* (1988); Daniel K. Richter, *Before the Revolution: America's Ancient Pasts* (2001); Alan Taylor, *American Colonies* (2001); and the opening chapters of Jill Lepore's *These Truths* (2018). Greg Grandin in *America, América: A New History of the New World* (2025) makes the crucial point that the terms "America" and "Americans" have different meaning across the Western Hemisphere. For a brief introduction to the field, see Alan Taylor, *Colonial America: A Very Short Introduction* (2013).

Much of the primary evidence I used for *Contested Continent* can be found in accessible published versions. The most important are David B. Quinn, Alison Quinn, and Susan Hillier, eds., *New American World: A Documentary History of North America*, 5 vols. (1979); Merrill Jensen, ed., *English Historical Documents*, vol. IX, *American Colonial Documents to 1776* (1955); Rueben G. Thwaites, ed., *The Jesuit Relations and Allied Documents*, 73 vols. (1891–1901); and many of the volumes published by the Hakluyt Society, which has issued travel narratives since its first offering in 1847. For a listing of the Hakluyt Society's volumes during its first 150 or so years, see R. C. Bridges and P. E. H. Hair, eds., *Compassing the Vaste Globe of the Earth* (1996). There are digitized copies of almost every book published in England before 1700 in Early English Books Online (EEBO), which is available at many research libraries. For a selection of texts, see John Demos, *Remarkable Providences: Readings on Early American History*, rev. ed. (1991), and Peter C. Mancall, ed., *Envisioning America: English Plans for the Colonization of North America, 1580–1640*, 2nd ed. (2017).

While much of the history told in *Troubled Continent* describes the experience of Indigenous peoples in the Americas, and especially in North America, this is a book about encounters between peoples from the four continents ringing the Atlantic Ocean. Fortunately, those interested in Native-centered work can find abundant remarkable books focused on specific Indigenous communities, many of them cited in the notes, and overarching syntheses that have shaped the field. For exemplary studies that offer long perspectives on Native American history, see Ned Blackhawk, *The Rediscovery of America: Native Peoples and the Unmaking of U.S. History* (2023); Colin Calloway, *One Vast Winter Count: The Native American West Before Lewis and Clark* (2003), and his *New Worlds for All: Indians, Europeans, and the Remaking of Early America* (1997); Kathleen DuVal, *Native Nations: A Millennium in North America* (2024); Pekka Hämäläinen, *Indigenous Continent: The Epic Contest for North America* (2022); and the opening chapters of David Treuer, *The Heartbeat of Wounded Knee: Native America from 1890 to the Present* (2019). Readers may want to read Nichole Eustace's discerning analysis of major themes of such works in "An Expanding Vision of America," *New York Review of Books*, March 27, 2025. These studies follow important work that put encounters and conflicts between Indigenous at the center, not the periphery, of early American history. For pioneering and still vital work, see Karen Ordahl Kupperman, *Indians and English: Facing Off in Early America* (2000) and Daniel K. Richter, *Facing East from Indian Country: A Native History of Early America* (2001). For a remarkable example of the survival of a specific nation's history, see Josephine Waggoner, *Witness: A Húnkpapha Historian's Strong-Heart Song of the Lakotas* (2013). For analyses of the records that scholars have used to understand the Indigenous experience, see Calvin L. Martin, ed., *The American Indian and the Problem of History* (1987), especially the essay by Henrietta Whiteman entitled "White Buffalo Woman"; and Alyssa Mt. Pleasant, Caroline Wigginton, and Kelly Wisecup, eds., "Forum: Materials and Methods in Native American and Indigenous Studies," *William and Mary Quarterly*, 3rd Ser., 75 (April 2018).

The survival of hundreds of Native nations should not obscure what a generation of historians has revealed to be extraordinary violence, much of it directed by Europeans against Indigenous Americans in the centuries following 1492. That viciousness took many forms and differed from one region to another. Earlier historians, most notably Frederick Jackson Turner, saw clashes as inevitable stages in the progress of "civilization" from the Atlantic to the Pacific. But no serious historian echoes that view now. Instead, many more emphasize the central role of brutality in the conflicts between Indigenous and Europeans. Among the best of the works that recognize violence as a central feature of conquest and colonization rather than an ancillary development, see Ned Blackhawk, *Violence over the Land: Indians and Empires in the Early American West* (2006) and Benjamin Madley, "Reexamining the American Genocide Debate: Meaning, Historiography, and New Methods," *American Historical Review* 120, no. 1 (2015).

Many scholars of these centuries have focused their attention on particular areas, so much of what follows identifies sources for those regions. Works relating to the history of the book, gender, and economies elude geographic categorization, as does much of the work relating to enslavement and the slave trade.

Writing as well as printing played a major role in developments covered in *Contested Continent*. The most important source, which remains underutilized as a tool to understand the intersection between actions and news about them, is *European Americana: A Chronological Guide to Works Printed in Europe Relating to the Americas, 1493–1776*, a five-volume catalog edited by John Alden and others that was organized by the John Carter Brown Library and published from 1980 to 1998. The guide goes beyond listing books; it also provides details about each edition, including translations, as well as the location of original copies of each of the books mentioned. This catalog of thousands of individual imprints offers proof of the importance of the Americas to European writers, some motivated by the lure of gain and others seeking to expand their own knowledge. When combined with plants (like maize and tobacco), animals, and birds that ultimately could be seen in cabinets of curiosity, apothecary shops, menageries, and gardens, these books instructed Europeans about a world that was unknown to virtually all of them before 1492.

For studies of book and print culture relevant to these centuries see the American Antiquarian Society's five volume *A History of the Book in America*, especially vol. 1, Hugh Amory and David D. Hall, eds., *The Colonial Book in the Atlantic World* (2007). See also Elizabeth L. Eisenstein, *The Printing Press as an Agent of Change: Communications and Cultural Transformations in Early-Modern Europe*, 2 vols. (1979); Lucien Febvre and Henri-Jean Martin, *The Coming of the Book: The Impact of Printing, 1450–1800*, trans. David Gerard (1976); Mary Fuller, *Voyages in Print: English Travels to America, 1576–1624* (1995); Michael Gaudio, *Engraving the Savage: The New World and Techniques of Civilization* (2008); Adrian Johns, *The Nature of the Book: Print and Knowledge in the Making* (1998); Harold Love, *Scribal Publication in Seventeenth-Century England* (1993); and Nicholas Popper, *Walter Ralegh's History of the World and the Historical Culture of the Late Renaissance* (2012). The literature on the history of the book overlaps, as it must, with studies on literacy; see David Cressy, *Literacy and the Social Order: Reading and Writing in Tudor and Stuart England* (1980); Kenneth A. Lockridge, *Literacy in Colonial New England: An Enquiry into the Social Context of Literacy in the Early Modern West* (1974); and Carole Shammas, "The Extent and Duration of Primary Schooling in Eighteenth-Century America," *History of Education Quarterly* 63 (2023). Writing and print played central roles in multiple religious movements; see Stephanie Kirk and Sarah Rivett, eds., *Religious Transformations in the Early Modern Americas* (2014).

Most studies of gender issues in these centuries focus on particular areas and can be found in sections on those regions, but some works provide more general interpretations. The best starting point for English colonists and the social mores that they brought across the ocean is Mary Beth Norton, *Founding Mothers and Fathers: Gendered Power and the Forming of American Society* (1996). See also Natalie Zemon Davis, *Women on the Margins: Three Seventeenth-Century Lives* (1995); Jennifer Morgan, *Laboring Women: Reproduction and Gender in New World Slavery* (2004); Jennifer Morgan, *Reckoning with Slavery: Gender, Kinship, and Capitalism in the Early Black Atlantic* (2021); and Lawrence Stone, *The Family, Sex, and Marriage in England, 1500–1800*, abridged ed. (1977).

The sections on specific regions also include much about religion in early America, but some works transcend such boundaries. Among the best are Susan Juster, *A Common Grave: Being Catholic in the Early English Atlantic* (2025); William Pencak, *Jews and Gentiles in Early America, 1654–1800* (2005); and the Library of Congress digital exhibit "From Haven to Home: 350 Years of Jewish Life in America" (at https://www.loc.gov/exhibits/haventohome/haven-haven.html).

The starting point for any understanding of the Atlantic economy remains John J. McCusker and Russell R. Menard, *The Economy of British America, 1607–1780* (1985). Other suggestive works include James A. Henretta, "Families and Farms: *Mentalité* in Pre-Industrial America," *William and Mary Quarterly* 35, no. 1 (1978), and John J. McCusker, *Money and Exchange in Europe and America, 1600–1775: A Handbook* (1978), which facilitates making conversions between the myriad ways of recording monetary transactions in the early modern Atlantic basin. For the importance of corporations in the Atlantic basin and beyond, see Philip J. Stern, *Empire, Incorporated: The Corporations That Built British Colonialism* (2023), and his *The Company-State: Corporate Sovereignty and the Early Modern Foundations of the British Empire in India* (2011). For intercultural trade and its consequences, see James M. Crawford, *The Mobilian Trade Language* (1978); Peter C. Mancall, *Deadly Medicine: Indians and Alcohol in Early America* (1995); Sidney W. Mintz, *Sweetness and Power: The Place of Sugar in Modern History* (1985); Christopher L. Miller and George R. Hammell, "A New Perspective on Indian-White Contact: Cultural Symbols and Colonial Trade," *Journal of American History* 73 (1986); Stuart B. Schwartz, ed., *Tropical Babylons: Sugar and the Making of the Atlantic World, 1450–1680* (2004); and Molly A. Warsh, *American Baroque: Pearls and the Nature of Empire, 1492–1700* (2018).

Slavery and the Slave Trade

The enormous literature on enslavement and the slave trade stands on its own. The best starting point on the trade is the database SlaveVoyages.org, which includes four sections: the Trans-Atlantic Slave Trade Database, the Intra-American Slave Trade Database, the People of the Atlantic Slave Trade Database, and the extensive Image Galleries. Stanley Engerman, Seymour Drescher, and Robert Paquette's edited volume *Slavery* (2001) looks at the institution in a transnational context. David Eltis and David Richardson's *Atlas of the Transatlantic Slave Trade* (2010) distills much of the material about the sale of humans in a series of maps that provide a visual overview of the notorious traffic. For studies that analyze slavery across regions, see Alex Borucki, David Eltis, and David Wheat, eds., *From the Galleons to the Highlands: Slave Trade Routes to the Spanish Americas* (2020); Kevin Dawson, *Undercurrents of Power: Aquatic Culture in the African Diaspora* (2018); and David Eltis, *The Rise of African Slavery in the Americas* (2000) and his *Atlantic Cataclysm: Rethinking the Atlantic Slave Trades* (2025). See also Maxine

Berg and Pat Hudson, *Slavery, Capitalism and the Industrial Revolution* (2023); Ira Berlin, *Many Thousands Gone: The First Two Centuries of Slavery in North America* (1988) and his *Generations of Captivity: A History of African-American Slaves* (2003); Vincent Brown, *The Reaper's Garden: Death and Power in the World of Atlantic Slavery* (2010); Gad Heuman and Trevor Burnard, eds., *The Routledge History of Slavery* (2011); Sean M. Kelley, *American Slavers: Merchants, Mariners, and the Transatlantic Commerce in Captives, 1644–1865* (2023); Simon P. Newman, *A New World of Labor: The Development of Plantation Slavery in the British Atlantic* (2013); Gregory E. O'Malley, *Final Passages: The Intercolonial Slave Trade of British America, 1619–1807* (2014); Orlando Patterson, *Slavery and Social Death: A Comparative* Study, 2nd ed. (2018); Nicholas Radburn, *Traders in Men: Merchants and the Transformation of the Transatlantic Slave Trade* (2023); Paul Polgar, Marc H. Lerner, and Jesse Cromwell, eds., *Beyond 1619: The Atlantic Origins of American Slavery* (2023); Casey Schmitt, *The Predatory Sea: Human Trafficking and Captivity in the Seventeenth-Century Caribbean* (2025); Emily Berquist Soule, "From Africa to the Ocean Sea: Atlantic Slavery in the Origins of the Spanish Empire," *Atlantic Studies* 15 (2018); and Hugh Thomas, *The Slave Trade: The Story of the Atlantic Slave Trade, 1440–1870* (1997). Enslaved peoples also arrived in the Americas from the Pacific; see Tatiana Seijas, *Asian Slaves in Colonial Mexico: From Chinos to Indians* (2014). David Galenson's *White Servitude in Colonial America: An Economic Analysis* (1981) analyzes the other system of imported bound labor in North America.

Studies of the slave trade often focus on the numbers of peoples forced onto ships, the places where they began and ended their journeys, and how enslavers continued to move people to address emerging economic opportunities. Other works assess the impact of the trade on those who experienced it. For this literature see, among others, Saidiya Hartman, *Lose Your Mother: A Journey Along the Atlantic Slave Route* (2007) and Stephanie Smallwood, *Saltwater Slavery: A Middle Passage from Africa to American Diaspora* (2007).

For the origins of slavery in Europe and the emerging justifications for its existence, see Michael Guasco, *Slaves and Englishmen: Human Bondage in the Early Modern Atlantic World* (2014); John S. Harpham, *The Intellectual Origins of American Slavery* (2025); William A. Pettigrew, *Freedom's Debt: The Royal African Company and the Politics of the Atlantic Slave Trade, 1672–1752* (2013); and Christopher Tomlins, *Freedom Bound: Law, Labor, and Civic Identity in Colonizing English America, 1580–1865* (2010). For New England, see Gloria McCahon Whiting, *Belonging. An Intimate History of Slavery and Family in Early New England* (2024) and Wendy Warren, *New England Bound: Slavery and Colonization in Early America* (2016). For European predecessors, see Hannah Barker, *That Most Precious Merchandise: The Mediterranean Trade in Black Sea Slaves, 1260–1500* (2019) and Debra Blumenthal, *Enemies and Familiars: Slavery and Mastery in Fifteenth Century Valencia* (2009).

For crucial studies of Africa that touch directly on encounters that shaped the Atlantic basin see Herman L. Bennett, *African Kings and Black Slaves: Sovereignty and Dispossession in the Early Modern Atlantic* (2019); Judith A. Carney, *Black Rice: The African Origins of Rice Cultivation in the Americas* (2001); Howard W. French, *Born in Blackness: Africa, Africans, and the Making of the Modern World, 1471 to the Second World War* (2021); Cécile Fromont, *The Art of Conversion: Christian Visual Culture in the Kingdom of Kongo* (2014); Toby Green, *A Fistful of Shells: West Africa from the Rise of the Slave Trade to the Age of Revolution* (2019); David Northrup, *Africa's Discovery of Europe, 1450–1850* (2002); John Thornton, *Africa and Africans in the Making of the Atlantic World, 1400–1800*, 2nd ed. (1998); and Thornton and Linda M. Heywood, *Central Africans, Atlantic Creoles, and the Foundation of the Americas, 1585–1660* (2007).

For enslavement of Indigenous peoples, see James F. Brooks, *Captives and Cousins: Slavery, Kinship, and Community in the Southwest Borderlands* (2002); Alan Gallay, *The Indian Slave Trade: The Rise of the English Empire in the American South, 1670–1717* (2002); Andrés Reséndez, *The Other Slavery: The Uncovered Story of Indian Enslavement in America* (2016); Brett Rushforth, *Bonds of Alliance: Indigenous and Atlantic Slaveries in New France* (2012); and Christina Snyder, *Slavery in Indian Country: The Changing Face of Captivity in Early America* (2010).

For studies of enslavement relating to the Chesapeake, see T. H. Breen and Stephen Innes, *"Myne Owne Ground": Race and Freedom on Virginia's Eastern Shore, 1640–1676* (1980); Oscar Handlin and Mary F. Handlin, "Origins of the Southern Labor System," *William and Mary Quarterly*, 3rd Ser., 7 (1950); Russell R. Menard, "The Maryland Slave Population, 1658 to 1730: A Demographic Profile of Blacks in Four Counties," *William and Mary Quarterly* 32 (1975); Engel Sluiter, "New Light on the '20. and Odd Negroes' Arriving in Virginia, August 1619," *William and Mary Quarterly*, 3rd Ser., 54 (1997); and John Thornton, "The African Experience of the '20. and Odd Negroes' Arriving in Virginia in 1619," *William and Mary Quarterly*, 3rd Ser., 55 (1998).

For the greater Caribbean, see Trevor Burnard and John Garrrigus, *The Plantation Machine: Atlantic Capitalism in French Saint-Domingue and British Jamaica* (2016); Richard S. Dunn, *Sugar and Slaves: The Rise of the Planter Class in the English West Indies, 1624–1713* (1972), and his "The Barbados Census of 1680: Profile of the Richest Colony in English America," *William and Mary Quarterly*, 3rd Ser., 26 (1969); Linford D. Fisher, " 'Dangerous Designes': The 1676 Barbados Act to Prohibit New England Indian Slave Importation," *William and Mary Quarterly* 71 (2014); Larry Gragg, " 'To Procure Negroes': The English Slave Trade to Barbados, 1627–60," *Slavery and Abolition* 16 (1995); Russell R. Menard, *Sweet Negotiations: Sugar, Slavery, and Plantation Agriculture in Early Barbados* (2006); and Edward B. Rugemer, "The Development of Mastery and Race in the Comprehensive Slave Codes of the Greater Caribbean During the Seventeenth Century," *William and Mary Quarterly*, 3rd Ser., 70 (2013).

Indigenous Studies

The 500th anniversary of Columbus's first voyage opened a new era for scholarship on early America. In that literature, two regional studies have had an enormous impact on scholars: Richard White, *The Middle Ground: Indians, Empires, and Republics in the Great Lakes Region, 1650–1815* (1991), and David J. Weber, *The Spanish Frontier in North America* (1992). Since then other vital work considering multiple Native peoples has appeared, including Alejandra Dubcovsky, *Talking Back: Native Women and the Making of the Early South* (2023); Kathleen DuVal, *The Native Ground: Indians and Colonists in the Heart of the Continent* (2006); Elizabeth Ellis, *The Great Power of Small Nations: Indigenous Diplomacy in the Gulf South* (2022); Elizabeth Fenn, *Encounters at the Heart of the World: A History of the Mandan People* (2014); Allan Greer, *Property and Dispossession: Natives, Empires, and Land in Early Modern North America* (2018); Pekka Hämäläinen, *The Comanche Empire* (2008), and his *Lakota America: A New History of Indigenous Power* (2019); Gilles Havard, *Les Natchez: Une histoire coloniale de la violence* (2024); Eric Hinderaker, *Elusive Empires: Constructing Colonialism in the Ohio Valley, 1673–1800* (1997); Wayne E. Lee, *The Cutting-Off Way: Indigenous Warfare in Eastern North America, 1500–1800* (2023); Michael McDonnell, *Masters of Empire: Great Lakes Indians and the Making of America* (2015); Robert M. Morrissey, *Empire by Collaboration: Indians, Colonists, and Governments in Colonial Illinois Country* (2015); Sarah Rivett, *Unscripted America: Indigenous Languages and the*

Origins of a Literary Nation (2017); and Michael Witgen, *An Infinity of Nations: How the Native World Shaped Early North America* (2012).

As all these scholars have revealed in abundant detail, Indigenous Americans never suffered the fate that artist and observer George Catlin believed loomed in the near future when he rushed into the West in the late 1820s to paint peoples, primarily on the Plains, because he thought they would disappear. Catlin and photographer Edward Curtis, who titled his 1904 photograph of Natives on horseback "The Vanishing Race," dwelled on what they saw as the tragic legacy of colonial expansion rather than the evidence of Native adaptation and survival that was quite literally in front of their eyes. Modern scholars, often working with Indigenous communities, have recognized the hardships that Native peoples faced, and they have been engaged with unearthing unknown or lesser-known stories about the past. Among these efforts is the Stolen Relations project (StolenRelations.org), which focuses on enslavement and servitude as well as resilience. The existing volumes of the Smithsonian Institution's *Handbook of North American Indians*, which began under the general editorship of William Sturtevant in 1978, provide introductions to the histories and cultures of specific Indigenous peoples as well as issues that are transregional. James Axtell's deeply researched and suggestive essays remain readable and engaging; see the essays in *The European and the Indian* (1981), *After Columbus* (1988), *Beyond 1492* (1992), and *Natives and Newcomers: The Cultural Origins of North America* (2001), as well as *The Invasion Within: The Contest of Cultures in Colonial North America* (1985).

Adaptation to challenges in the Americas long predated the arrival of colonizing Europeans. The northern spread of maize led to substantial demographic, economic, and residential changes. For the rising importance of this plant, see Betty Fussell, *The Story of Corn* (1992). Maize production and distribution was only one dynamic element of pre-contact Native economies and societies. For an introduction into the range of possibilities, see Juliana Barr, "There's No Such Thing as 'Prehistory': What the Longue Durée of Caddo and Pueblo History Tells Us About Colonial America," *William and Mary Quarterly* 74 (2017); Ann M. Carlos, "The Country They Built: Dynamic and Complex Indigenous Economies in North America Before 1492," *Journal of Economic History* 83 (2023); Lynn Ceci, "Watchers of the Pleiades: Ethnoastronomy Among Native Cultivators in Northeastern North America," *Ethnohistory* 25 (1978); Alvin M. Josephy Jr., ed., *America in 1492: The World of the Indian Peoples Before the Arrival of Columbus* (1992); Neal Salisbury, "The Indians' Old World: Native Americans and the Coming of Europeans," *William and Mary Quarterly* 53 (1996); and Tatiana Seijas, "The Royal Road of the Interior in New Spain: Indigenous Commerce and Political Action," in Danna A. Levin Rojo and Cynthia Radding, eds., *The Oxford Handbook of Borderlands and the Iberian World* (2019).

Dramatic adaptations took place in the Mississippi Valley, evident in the rise of Cahokia, the largest city north of Mexico until its collapse in the thirteenth century. For its crucial history, see Thomas E. Anderson, *Cahokia and the Archaeology of Power* (1997); M. R. Balthus et al., "Diasporic Connections: Cahokia and the Greater Southeast," *Journal of Archaeological Method Theory* 27 (2020); and T. R. Pauketat, *Ancient Cahokia and the Mississippians* (2004). For the legacy of Cahokia, see Patricia Cleary, *Mound City: The Place of the Indigenous Past and Present in St. Louis* (2024); Patricia Galloway, *Choctaw Genesis, 1500–1700* (1998); and Gregory A. Waselkov and Marvin T. Smith, eds., *Forging Southeastern Identities: Social Archaeology, Ethnohistory, and Folklore of the Mississippian to Early Historic South* (2017).

In the Southwest, some ancient cities also rose and fell, their populations dispersing when confronted with unconquerable environmental challenges, most notably extended droughts. For the pre-contact Southwest, see Brian Fagan, *Chaco Canyon: Archaeologists Explore the Lives of an Ancient Society* (2005); Stephen H. Lekson and Catherine M. Cameron, "The Abandonment of Chaco Canyon, the Mesa Verde Migrations, and the Reorganization of the Pueblo World," *Journal of Anthropological Archaeology* 14 (1995); and Lynne Sebastian, *The Chaco Anasazi: Sociopolitical Evolution in the Prehistoric Southwest* (1992).

Failure and dispersal were not the only possible fates for peoples who created cities centuries ago. The longest continually settled city within the boundaries of the current United States is Acoma. For its history, see Edgar Proctor Hunt, *The Origin Myth of Acoma Pueblo*, ed. Peter Nabokov (2015); Ward A. Minge, *Acoma: Pueblo in the Sky* (1991); and Peter Nabokov, *How the World Moves: The Odyssey of an American Indian Family* (2015).

Once Spaniards arrived and laid a claim to New Mexico, Acoma became part of a complex Indigenous and colonial world. For the history of colonial New Mexico and nearby territory, see Jack D. Forbes, *Apache, Navaho, and Spaniard* (1960); George P. Hammond and Agapito Rey, *Don Juan de Oñate: Colonizer of New Mexico, 1595–1628*, 2 vols. (1953); John L. Kessell, *Spain in the Southwest: A Narrative History of Colonial New Mexico, Arizona, Texas, and California* (2002); Lyle McAlister, *Spain and Portugal in the New World* (1984); and Dana Velasco Murillo, "The Creation of Indigenous Leadership in a Spanish Town: Zacatecas, Mexico, 1609–1752," *Ethnohistory* 56 (2009).

Europe and the Americas

The records the Norse left of their time in the North Atlantic were scarce, but imaginative scholars have used sagas and physical remains dug by archaeologists to create a vivid portrait of the era. The history of the Norse expeditions across the North Atlantic and into the Maritime Provinces of Canada is the subject of numerous works, including Eleanor Barraclough, *Beyond the Northlands: Viking Voyages and the Old Norse Sagas* (2016) and her *Embers of the Hand: Hidden Histories of the Viking Age* (2024); Noel Broadbent, *Lapps and Labyrinths: Saami Prehistory, Colonization, and Cultural Resilience* (2010); William W. Fitzhugh and Elisabeth I. Ward, eds., *Vikings: The North Atlantic Saga* (2000); and Anders Winroth, *The Age of the Vikings* (2014). For gripping translations of the sagas and the marvelous stories they report, see *The Sagas of the Icelanders*, translated by Karina Attwood and others (2000), and the more accessible *The Vinland Sagas*, translated by Magnus Magnusson and Hermann Pálsson (1965).

Norse sagas are among the earliest records testifying to the prevalence of violence in these centuries, including within Europe. On this crucial point, see Natalie Zemon Davis, "The Rites of Violence: Religious Riot in Sixteenth-Century France," *Past and Present* 59 (1973). For the waves of violence that followed Martin Luther's posting of his critiques of the church, see Lyndal Roper's chilling *Summer of Fire and Blood: The German Peasants' War* (2025), which recreates in detail what happened in the early years of the conflict that ripped Christendom apart.

Tudor and Stuart England and the territories its rulers claimed also became scenes of violence, not only between combatants but also against civilians. Nicholas Canny and others have written powerful works about the horrors that English soldiers perpetrated in Ireland. For the works that reveal the foundational role of violence stretching forward from the time of Henry

VIII, see Nicholas Canny, "The Ideology of English Colonization: From Ireland to America," *William and Mary Quarterly*, 3rd Ser., 30, no. 4 (October 1973); Canny, *The Elizabethan Conquest of Ireland: A Pattern Established, 1565–76* (1976); Canny, *Making Ireland British, 1580–1650* (2001); Alison Games et al., "Nicholas Canny's 'The Ideology of English Colonization' at Fifty: A Reevaluation," *William and Mary Quarterly*, 3rd Ser., 80, no. 3 (July 2023); and Ciaran Brady and Raymond Gillespie, eds., *Natives and Newcomers: The Making of Irish Colonial Society, 1534–1641* (1986). The English also hoped to claim parts of France; see Neil Murphy, *The Tudor Occupation of Boulogne: Conquest, Colonisation, and Imperial Monarchy, 1544–1550* (2019). For the earlier efforts by Anglo-Normans, see R. R. Davies, *Domination and Conquest: The Experience of Ireland, Scotland and Wales, 1100–1300* (1990).

The English Reformation and the English Civil War transformed Britain into a stage for barbarity. For the Reformation era, see Eamon Duffy, *The Stripping of the Altars: Traditional Religion in England, 1400–1580* (1992); James G. Clark, *The Dissolution of the Monasteries: A New History* (2021); Christopher Hill, *God's Englishman: Oliver Cromwell and the English Revolution* (1970); Clive Holmes, *Why Was Charles I Executed?* (2006); Ann Hughes, *The Causes of the English Civil War*, 2nd ed. (1998); Clare Jackson, *Devil-Land: England Under Siege, 1588–1688* (2021); and Peter Marshall, *Heretics and Believers: A History of the English Reformation* (2017). For the Civil War, see Michael J. Braddick, *God's Fury, England's Fire: A New History of the English Civil Wars* (2008); Robert Brenner, *Merchants and Revolution: Commercial Change, Political Conflict, and London's Overseas Traders, 1550–1653* (1993); Charles Carlton, *This Seat of Mars: War and the British Isles, 1485–1746* (2013); David Cressy, *England on Edge: Crisis and Revolution, 1640–1642* (2006); Barbara Donagan, "Atrocity, War Crime, and Treason in the English Civil War," *American Historical Review* 99 (1994), and her *War in England, 1642–1649* (2008); and Matthew Jenkinson, *Charles I's Killers in America: The Lives and Afterlives of Edward Whalley and William Goffe* (2019).

For England and its emergent empire, see the essays in Nicholas Canny, ed., *The Origins of Empire*, which is vol. 1 of Wm. Roger Louis, ed. in chief, *The Oxford History of the British Empire*, 5 vols. (1998), and in Elizabeth Mancke and Carole Shammas, eds., *The Creation of the British Atlantic World* (2005); see also David Armitage, *The Ideological Origins of the British Empire* (2000); Heather Dalton, *Merchants and Explorers: Roger Barlow, Sebastian Cabot, and Networks of Atlantic Exchange, 1500–1560* (2016); Andrew Fitzmaurice, *Humanism and America: An Intellectual History of English Colonisation, 1500–1625* (2003); Alison Games, *The Web of Empire: English Cosmopolitans in an Age of Expansion, 1560–1660* (2008); Ken MacMillan, *Sovereignty and Possession in the English New World: The Legal Foundations of Empire, 1576–1640* (2006); Peter C. Mancall, *Hakluyt's Promise: An Elizabethan's Obsession for an English America* (2007); Jane Ohlmeyer, *Making Empire: Ireland, Imperialism, and the Early Modern World* (2023); Steven C. A. Pincus, *Protestantism and Patriotism: Ideologies and the Making of English Foreign Policy, 1650–1668* (1996); Abigail L. Swingen, *Competing Visions of Empire: Labor, Slavery, and the Origins of the British Atlantic Empire* (2015); and Lauren Working, *The Making of an Imperial Polity: Civility and America in the Jacobean Metropolis* (2020).

Still, what happened in North America was different from what happened in Europe, and the change was evident as soon as Christopher Columbus landed in October 1492. The literature on the era of the Columbian voyages and their consequences is enormous. That library of scholarship grew dramatically leading up to and following the 1992 quincentennial. For Columbus's thinking and actions, the best starting point is the documents and commentary in the monumental *Repertorium Columbianum*, 13 vols. (1993–2004). Studies of Columbus and his circle appear with regularity, but among those well worth reading are Felipe Fernández-Armesto, *Columbus* (1991), and his *Columbus on Himself* (2010); Oliver Dunn and James E. Kelley Jr., trans., *The Diario of Christopher Columbus's First Voyage to America, 1492–1493* (1989); Nicolás Wey Gómez, *The Tropics of Empire: Why Columbus Sailed South to the Indies* (2008); Maricio Obregón, *The Columbus Papers: The Barcelona Letter of 1493.the Landfall Controversy, and the Indian Guides* (1991); William D. Phillips Jr. and Carla Rahn Phillips, *The Worlds of Christopher Columbus* (1992); Edward Wilson-Lee, *The Catalogue of Shipwrecked Books: Christopher Columbus, His Son, and the Quest to Build the World's Greatest Library* (2019); and José María Pérez Fernández and Edward Wilson-Lee, *Hernando Colon's New World of Books: Toward a Cartography of Knowledge* (2021). For the visual record of the encounter and what followed, see Rachel Doggett, ed., *New World of Wonders: European Images of the Americas, 1492–1700* (1992) and Jay A. Levenson, ed., *Circa 1492: Art in the Age of Exploration* (1991). Charles Mann's *1491: New Revelations of the Americas Before Columbus* (2005) and his *1493: Uncovering the New World Columbus Created* (2011) provide a comprehensive overview of changes in the hemisphere. The "Histoire Naturelle des Indes," a beautifully illustrated manuscript in the Pierpont Morgan Library in New York City, can be found in a facsimile edition with translations as *The Drake Manuscript* (1996).

The scholarly literature on the impact of the Columbian voyages is vast. An excellent starting point is the work of J. H. Elliott, especially *The Old World and the New, 1492–1650* (1970); "A Europe of Composite Monarchies," *Past and Present* 137 (1992); *Empires of the Atlantic World: Britain and Spain in America, 1492–1830* (2006); and *Spain, Europe, and the Wider World, 1500–1800* (2009). The encounter and its impact have also been explored in a series of vibrant books that began to appear at the 500th anniversary and have continued since. Among the best are David Abulafia, *The Discovery of Mankind: Atlantic Encounters in the Age of Columbus* (2008); Rolena Adorno, *The Polemics of Possession in Spanish American Narrative* (2007); John Bakeless, *The Eyes of Discovery: America as Seen by Its First Explorers* (orig. pub. 1950; reprint, 1989); Samir Boumediene, *La colonisation du savoir: une histoire des plantes médicinales du nouveau monde (1492–1750)* (2016); Caroline Dodds Pennock, *On Savage Shores: How Indigenous Americans Discovered Europe* (2023); Valerie Flint, *The Imaginative Landscape of Christopher Columbus* (1992); Anthony Grafton, *New Worlds, Ancient Texts: The Power of Tradition and the Shock of Discovery* (1992); Stephen Greenblatt, *Marvelous Possessions: The Wonder of the New World* (1991); Christopher Hodson and Brett Rushforth, *Beyond the Ocean: France and the Atlantic World from the Crusades to the Age of Revolutions* (2026); Hugh Honour, *The New Golden Land: European Images of America from the Discoveries to the Present Time* (1975); Karen Ordahl Kupperman, ed., *America in European Consciousness, 1493–1750* (1995); Anthony Pagden, *The Fall of Natural Man: The American Indian and the Origins of Comparative Ethnology* (1982); Patricia Seed, *Ceremonies of Possession in Europe's Conquest of the New World, 1492–1640* (1992); and Kim Sloan, ed., *A New World: England's First View of America* (2007).

For the long-term cultural impact, see Daniela Bleichmar, *Visual Voyages: Images of Latin American Nature from Columbus to Darwin* (2017); Benjamin Schmidt, *Innocence Abroad: The Dutch Imagination and the New World, 1570–1670* (2001); and Michael Wintroub, *A Savage Mirror: Power, Identity, and Knowledge in Early Modern France* (2006). For Giovanni Battista Ramusio, see Andrea di Robilant, *This Earthly Globe: A Venetian Geographer and the Quest to Map the World* (2024). *William and Mary Quarterly*, 3rd Ser., 49, no. 2 (April 1992) is an entire issue devoted to the impact and legacy of the Columbian encounters and the world they helped usher into existence.

The announcement of what could be found and extracted from the Western Hemisphere motivated many thousands of Europeans to consider migration across the Atlantic Ocean. Yet as scholars have noted, this transoceanic experience needs to be seen in the context of Europeans already searching for new places to live, including within Europe. The ideal starting point for the larger context of such movements is Bernard Bailyn, *The Peopling of British North America: An Introduction* (1986) and Nicholas Canny, ed., *Europeans on the Move: Studies on European Migration, 1500–1800* (1994). Close analysis of the records of those who moved has revealed much about the factors pushing people away from their homes and towards new destinations. Few have mined such sources as well as Alison Games, *Migration and the Origins of the English Atlantic World* (2001); see also Ida Altman and James Horn, eds., *"To Make America": European Emigration in the Early Modern Period* (1991); Bernard Bailyn and Philip D. Morgan, eds., *Strangers Within the Realm: Cultural Margins of the First British Empire* (1991); Peter Boyd-Bowman, "Patterns of Spanish Emigration to the Indies until 1600," *Hispanic American Historical Review* 56 (1976); and Henry A. Gemery, "Emigration from the British Isles to the New World, 1630–1700: Inferences from Colonial Populations," *Research in Economic History* 5 (1980). The movement of peoples and goods also shaped legal cultures; see Lauren Benton and Nathan Perl-Rosenthal, eds., *A World at Sea: Maritime Practices and Global History* (2020).

Studies of migration tend to focus on free or indentured Europeans moving westward. During the period covered in *Contested Continent*, those studies need to be paired with the enormous literature on the slave trade, covered below, and also with the recognition that Indigenous peoples, like Manteo and Wanchese, often traveled eastward. For these migrants see Coll Thrush, *Indigenous London: Native Travelers at the Heart of Empire* (2016) and Alden T. Vaughan, *Transatlantic Encounters: American Indians in Britain, 1500–1776* (2006).

All migrants crossed an ocean filled with human and natural threats, ranging from pirates to hurricanes. For this context, see especially Mark G. Hanna, *Pirate Nests and the Rise of the British Empire, 1570–1740* (2015); Kenneth R. Andrews, *Elizabethan Privateering: English Privateering During the Spanish War, 1558–1603* (1964); J. H. Parry, *The Discovery of the Sea* (1974); and Stuart Schwartz, *Sea of Storms: A History of Hurricanes in the Greater Caribbean from Columbus to Katrina* (2015).

The Greater Caribbean and Spanish America

The arrival of Europeans had an immediate impact on the Indigenous peoples of the greater Caribbean basin. See Philip P. Boucher, *France and the American Tropics to 1700: Tropics of Discontent?* (2008); Kathleen Deagan and José María Cruxent, *Columbus's Outpost Among the Taínos: Spain and America at Las Isabela, 1493–1498* (2002); Pablo F. Gómez, *The Experiential Caribbean: Creating Knowledge and Healing in the Early Modern Atlantic* (2017); Massimo Livi-Bacci, "Return to Hispaniola: Reassessing a Demographic Catastrophe," *Hispanic American Historical Review* 83 (2003); Tessa Murphy, *The Creole Archipelago: Race and Borders in the Colonial Caribbean* (2021); Juan José Ponce Vázquez, *Islanders and Empire: Smuggling and Political Defiance in Hispaniola, 1580–1690* (2020); Irving Rouse, *The Tainos: Rise and Decline of the People Who Greeted Columbus* (1992); and Erin W. Stone, *Captives of Conquest: Slavery in the Early Modern Spanish Caribbean* (2021).

The Spanish conquest of territory they labeled New Spain, Peru, and New Mexico had different, but also far-reaching, consequences. Although Spaniards' arrival had a major impact, it is crucial to put it into chronological context, especially since the pre-contact history of relations between Mexica (Aztecs) and other Native peoples played such an important role in the Iberians' conquest. An excellent starting point is Camilla Townsend, *Fifth Sun: A New History of the Aztecs* (2019). There is a rich literature on what followed when Spaniards arrived, notably the remarkable bilingual and heavily illustrated book produced by Bernardino de Sahagún and his Nahua collaborators. The text is available online in the Digital Florentine Codex (https://florentinecodex.getty.edu) and in *Florentine Codex: General History of the Things of New Spain*, trans. Arthur J. O. Anderson and Charles E. Dibble, 12 vols. (2012). Other primary sources include Miguel León-Portilla, *The Broken Spears: The Aztec Account of the Conquest of Mexico* (1962) and Anthony Pagden, trans., *Hernán Cortés: Letters from Mexico* (1986).

For additional enlightening studies about New Spain and its place in both Atlantic and Pacific contexts, see Luis R. Corteguera, *Death by Effigy: A Case from the Mexican Inquisition* (2012); Ryan D. Crewe, *The Mexican Mission: Indigenous Reconstruction and Mendicant Enterprise in New Spain, 1521–1600* (2019); Diego Javier Luis, *The First Asians in the Americas: A Transpacific History* (2024); Matthew Restall, *When Montezuma Met Cortés: The True Story of the Meeting That Changed History* (2018); Camilla Townsend, *Malintzin's Choices: An Indian Woman in the Conquest of Mexico* (2006); Ilona Katzew, ed., *Contested Visions in the Spanish Colonial World* (2011); Mary E. Miller and Barbara E. Mundy, eds., *Painting a Map of Sixteenth-Century Mexico City: Land, Writing, and Native Rule* (2012); Andrés Reséndez, *Conquering the Pacific: An Unknown Mariner and the Final Great Voyage of the Age of Discovery* (2021); Daviken Studnick-Gizbert, *A Nation upon the Ocean Sea: Portugal's Atlantic Diaspora and the Crisis of the Spanish Empire, 1492–1640* (2007); Nancy Van Deusen, *Global Indios: The Indigenous Struggle for Justice in Sixteenth Century Spain* (2015); and Juliet B. Wiersema, *The History of a Periphery: Spanish Colonial Cartography from Columbia's Pacific Lowlands* (2023).

Few observers of life in the Americas in the sixteenth century had as much impact as Bartolomé de Las Casas, both for his own observations and for the way that other Europeans deployed them to create an anti-Spanish canon. See Bartolomé de Las Casas, *A Short Account of the Destruction of the Indies*, trans. Nigel Griffin (1992); Bartolomé de Las Casas, *In Defense of the Indians*, trans. and ed. Stafford Poole (1992); Lawrence A. Clayton, *Bartolomé de las Casas: A Biography* (2012); Benjamin Keen, "The Black Legend Revisited: Assumptions and Realities," *Hispanic American Historical Review* 49 (1969); and David J. Weber, "The Spanish Legacy in North America and the Historical Imagination," *Western Historical Quarterly* 23 (1992).

The impact of the arrival of Spaniards in Peru and across South America was documented over time in the writings of European travelers, who often offered discerning appraisals of local resources, the challenge to Incan rule, and the reshaping of parts of the landscape to serve the newcomers' goals. For firsthand accounts, see José de Acosta, *Natural and Moral History of the Indies*, ed. Jane E. Mangan (2002), and Pedro Cieza de León, *The Discovery and Conquest of Peru*, trans. Alexandra Parma Cook and Noble David Cook (1998). These works need to be read alongside the remarkable writings and drawings of Felipe Guaman Poma de Ayala in his astonishing *El primer nueva corónica y buen gobierno*, which is in the Royal Library in Copenhagen. Fortunately, a new translation by Rolena Adorno, José Cárdenas Bunsen, Jan Szeminski, and John Charles can be found at the Guaman Poma website of the Royal Library of Denmark (https://www.kb.dk/en/find-materials/collections/manuscript-collection/chronicle-guaman-poma). For other studies of his significance, see Rolena Adorno, *Guaman Poma and His Illustrated Chronicle from Colonial Peru: From a Century of Scholarship to a New Era of Reading* (2001), and Rolena Adorno and Ivan Boserup, *New Studies of the Autograph Manuscript of Felipe Guáman Pomo de Ayala's* Nueva corónica y buen gobierno (2002). For other studies of the continent, see P. J. Bakewell, *Miners of the Red Mountain* (1984); Karoline P. Cook, *Forbidden Passages: Muslims and Moriscos in Colonial Spanish America* (2016); Kris Lane, *Potosi: The Silver City That Changed the World* (2019); and Jeremy Mikecz, "Beyond Cajamarca: A Spatial Narrative Reimagining of the Encounter in Peru, 1532–1533," *Hispanic American Historical Review* 100 (2020).

The *entradas* of Spanish explorers have garnered substantial attention, and the primary texts are available in readable and engaging translations: Rolena Adorno and Patrick Charles Pautz, eds. and trans., *The Narrative of Cabeza de Vaca* (1999); Lawrence A. Clayton, Vernon J. Knight Jr., and Edward C. Moore, eds., *The De Soto Chronicles: The Expedition of Hernando de Soto to North America in 1539–1543*, 2 vols. (1993); David E. Duncan, *Hernando de Soto: A Savage Quest in the Americas* (1995); Richard Flint and Shirley Cushing Flint, eds., *Documents of the Coronado Expedition, 1539–1542* (2005); Paul E. Hoffman, *A New Andalucia and a Way to the Orient: The American Southeast During the Sixteenth Century* (1990); Charles Hudson, *Knights of Spain, Warriors of the Sun: Hernando de Soto and the South's Ancient Chiefdoms* (1997); and Andrés Reséndez, *A Land So Strange: The Epic Journey of Cabeza de Vaca—The Extraordinary Tale of a Shipwrecked Spaniard Who Walked Across America in the Sixteenth Century* (2009).

Spanish conquest and colonization across the modern Southwest has attracted substantial attention; see Juliana Barr, *Peace Came in the Form of a Woman: Indians and Spaniards in the Texas Borderlands* (2007); James F. Brooks, *Captives and Cousins: Slavery, Kinship, and Community in the Southwest Borderlands* (2002); Paul Conrad, *The Apache Diaspora: Four Centuries of Displacement and Survival* (2021); William H. Donahue, "Mary of Agreda and the Southwest United States," *The Americas* 9 (1953); Ramón Gutiérrez, *When Jesus Came the Corn Mothers Went Away: Marriage, Sexuality, and Power in New Mexico, 1500–1846* (1991); Jack D. Forbes, *Apache, Navaho and Spaniard* (1960); Steven W. Hackel, ed., *The Worlds of Juniper Serra: Historical Contexts and Cultural Representations* (2018); Anna M. Nogar, *Quill and Cross in the Borderlands: Sor Maria de Ágreda and the Lady in Blue, 1628–the Present* (2018); H. Henrietta Stockel, *Salvation Through Slavery: Chiricahua Apaches and Priests on the Spanish Colonial Frontier* (2008); Amy G. Remensnyder, *La Conquistadora: The Virgin Mary at War and Peace in the Old and New Worlds* (2014); and Natale A. Zappia, *Traders and Raiders: The Indigenous World of the Colorado Basin, 1510–1859* (2014).

Florida has its own historiographical traditions and rich literature documenting the Indigenous peoples of the peninsula, the encounter between Spaniards and Natives, and the efforts of the newcomers to bring the region under Spanish control. This body of scholarship remains underutilized by scholars of North America other than specialists, but its treasures are extensive. One starting point is the observations of the earliest Europeans to arrive, notably René Laudonnière's *Three Voyages*, ed. Charles E. Bennett (2001). As the explorer recognized, he and his shipmates entered a world dominated by strong Native polities. For those populations, see Jerald T. Milanich, *The Timucua* (1996). For the colonial era, see Michael V. Gannon, *The Cross in the Sand: The Early Catholic Church in Florida, 1513–1870* (1965); John H. Hann, *Apalachee: The Land Between the Rivers* (2017) and his *A History of the Timucua Indians and Missions* (1996); Charles Hudson, *The Juan Pardo Expeditions: Exploration of the Carolinas and Tennessee, 1566–1568*, rev. ed. (2005); Eugene Lyon, *The Enterprise of Florida: Pedro

Menéndez de Avilés and the Spanish Conquest of 1565–1568 (1974); Gonzalo Solís de Merás, *Pedro Menéndez de Avilés and the Conquest of Florida*, trans. David Arbesú (2017); Woodbury Lowery, *The Spanish Settlements within the Present Limits of the United States, 1513–1561*, 2 vols. (1901–1905); Robert A. Matter, "Mission Life in Seventeenth-Century Florida," *Catholic Historical Review* 67 (1981); Bonnie G. McEwan, "Colonialism on the Spanish Florida Frontier: Mission San Luis, 1656–1704," *Florida Historical Quarterly* 92 (2014); Jerald T. Milanich, *Florida Indians and the Invasion from Europe* (1995); Susan R. Parker, "St. Augustine in the Seventeenth-Century: Capital of La Florida," *Florida Historical Quarterly* 92 (2014); and J. Michael Francis and Kathleen M. Kole, *Murder and Martyrdom in Spanish Florida: Don Juan and the Guale Uprising of 1597*, American Museum of Natural History Anthropological Papers 95 (2011). George A. Broadwell and Alejandra Dubcovsky, "Chief Manuel's 1651 Timucua Letter: The Oldest Letter in a Native Language of the United States," *Proceedings of the American Philosophical Society* 164 (2023), reveals the early adoption of European-style writing by some Native peoples in North America.

For the Pueblo Revolt, see Charles W. Hackett, ed., *Revolt of the Pueblo Indians of New Mexico and Otermín's Attempted Reconquest, 1680–1682*, 2 vols. (1942); Andrew L. Knaut, *The Pueblo Revolt of 1680: Conquest and Resistance in Seventeenth-Century New Mexico* (1995); Matthew Liebman, *Revolt: An Archaeological History of Pueblo Resistance and Revitalization in 17th-Century New Mexico* (2012); and Michael V. Wilcox, *The Pueblo Revolt and the Mythology of Conquest: An Indigenous Archaeology of Contact* (2009).

Canada

European explorers and colonizers also arrived in Canada, though their numbers were much smaller than the migrations to other parts of North America and so too was their immediate impact on Native peoples, though over the course of the sixteenth and seventeenth centuries widespread demographic change came to the St. Lawrence Valley. The most extensive record can be found in the essential Rueben G. Thwaites, ed., *The Jesuit Relations and Allied Documents*, 73 vols. (1896–1901). The rich documentary record of the region, which sheds light on early encounters between Native peoples in the St. Lawrence Valley, the modern Maritime Provinces, and the region around Hudson Bay, starts even earlier in *The Voyages of Jacques Cartier*, with an introduction by Ramsay Cook (1993), a volume reprinting much of *The Voyages of Jacques Cartier* (1924) and *A Collection of Documents Relating to Jacques Cartier and the Sieur de Roberval* (1930), earlier published by the Public Archives of Canada; Henry P. Biggar, ed., *The Precursors of Jacques Cartier, 1497–1534* (1911); James A. Williamson, ed., *The Cabot Voyages and Bristol Discovery Under Henry VII*, Works Issued by the Hakluyt Society, 2nd Ser., CXX (1962); Joyce Marshall, ed., *Word from New France: The Selected Letters of Marie de L'Incarnation* (1967); David Beers Quinn, ed., *The Voyages and Colonising Enterprises of Sir Humphrey Gilbert*, 2 vols., Works Issued by the Hakluyt Society, 2nd Ser., LXXXIII–LXXXIV (1940); David B. Quinn and Neil M. Cheshire, eds., *The New Found Land of Stephen Parmenius: The Life and Writings of a Hungarian Poet, Drowned on a Voyage from Newfoundland, 1583* (1972); and Gerrit de Veer, *The Three Voyages of William Barents to the Arctic Regions*, trans. William Phillip, ed. Koolemans Beynen, 2nd ed., Works Issued by the Hakluyt Society, 1st Ser., 54 (1876).

Drawing on such sources, modern scholars have produced remarkable works about Canada. Valuable insights about early Canada can be found in Gauvin A. Bailey, *Architecture and Urbanism in the French Atlantic Empire: State, Church, and Society, 1604–1830* (2018); J. Braat,

"Dutch Activities in the North and the Arctic During the Sixteenth and Seventeenth Centuries," *Arctic* 37 (1984); Jennifer S. H. Brown and Elizabeth Vibert, eds., *Reading Beyond Words: Contexts for Native History*, 2nd ed. (2009); Marq de Villiers and Sheila Hirtle, *Sable Island: The Strange Origins and Curious History of a Dune Adrift in the Atlantic* (2004); Louise Dechêne, *Habitants and Merchants in Seventeenth-Century Montreal*, trans. Liana Vardi (1992); David Hackett Fischer, *Champlain's Dream: The European Founding of North America* (2008); William W. Fitzhugh and Jacqueline S. Olin, eds., *Archaeology of the Frobisher Voyages* (1993); Peter N. Moogk, "Reluctant Exiles: Emigrants from France in Canada Before 1760," *William and Mary Quarterly* 46 (1989); Newfoundland Historical Society, *A Short History of Newfoundland and Labrador* (2008); Peter E. Pope, *The Many Landfalls of John Cabot* (1997), and his *Fish into Wine: The Newfoundland Plantation in the Seventeenth Century* (2004); Bruce G. Trigger, *The Children of Aataentsic: A History of the Huron People to 1660*, 2 vols. (1976), and his edited book *Northeast*, vol. 15 of the *Handbook of North American Indians* (1978); and Marcel Trudel, *The Beginnings of New France, 1524–1663*, trans. Patricia Claxton (1973). *Ontario Archaeology* 96 (2016) is an entire issue devoted to the Indigenous peoples of the St. Lawrence Valley. Derek Hayes's *Historical Atlas of Canada* (2002) is an indispensable guide to the ways that early modern Europeans mapped the region.

Northern Canada, including the Arctic, has generated its own share of scholarship. See Ann M. Carlos and Frank D. Lewis, *Commerce by a Frozen Sea: Native Americans and the European Fur Trade* (2011), and Peter C. Mancall, *Fatal Journey: The Final Expedition of Henry Hudson—A Tale of Mutiny and Murder in the Arctic* (2009).

English America

The English arrival on the mainland has received extraordinary attention. Much of the earliest scholarship focused on Virginia and New England, and that emphasis continues despite the great increase in scholarship on other parts of the Atlantic basin where English colonizers arrived. Firsthand observations in North America generated extensive discussion within the realm about what could be found in the Western Hemisphere and what it meant for the realm. See Joyce Chaplin, *Subject Matter: Technology, The Body, and Science on the Anglo-American Frontier, 1500–1676* (2001); Leslie B. Cormack, *Charting an Empire: Geography at the English Universities, 1580–1620* (1997); Mary Fuller, *Lines Drawn Across the Globe: Reading Richard Hakluyt's Principal Navigations* (2023); and Kim Sloan, ed., *A New World: England's First View of America* (2007).

English explorers have also received substantial attention, at the time and since. It is impossible to imagine how historians could have reconstructed the early colonial period without the major collections by the younger Richard Hakluyt and the minister Samuel Purchas. Hakluyt's most important work, including a version of his "Discourse of Western Planting," can be found in E. G. R. Taylor, ed., *The Original Writings and Correspondence of the Two Richard Hakluyts*, 2 vols., Works Issued by the Hakluyt Society, 2nd Ser., 56–57 (1935). There is also a stand-alone version: David B. Quinn and Alison M. Quinn, ed., *A Particuler Discourse . . . Known as Discourse of Western Planting*, Works Issued by the Hakluyt Society, Extra Series 45 (1993). Hakluyt's *Principall Navigations* (1589) and the expanded three-volume edition (1598–1600) as well as Purchas's *Hakluytus Posthumus, or Purchas his Pilgrimes* (1625) are available in modern editions. The 1613, 1614, and 1617 editions of *Purchas his Pilgrimage* are available through EEBO.

Few have attracted as much fascination as Sir Francis Drake, who was active first in the Atlantic basin and then survived a circumnavigation that took him to the Pacific coast. That part of his career inspired the California-based Drake Navigators Guild. For studies of the explorer, see Samuel Bawlf, *The Secret Voyages of Sir Francis Drake, 1577–1580* (2003); Melissa Darby, *Thunder Go North: The Hunt for Sir Francis Drake's Fair & Good Bay* (2019); and Harry Kelsey, *Sir Francis Drake: The Queen's Pirate* (1998). Equally durable has been the interest in Sir Walter Ralegh (Raleigh); see Schmidt, ed., *The Discovery of Guiana by Sir Walter Ralegh, with Related Documents* (2008), and David B. Quinn, *Raleigh and the British Empire*, new ed. (1962). For Ralegh, see Alan Gallay, *Walter Ralegh: Architect of Empire* (2019).

Roanoke and the Chesapeake

For Roanoke, see James Horn, *A Kingdom Strange: The Brief and Tragic History of the Lost Colony of Roanoke* (2010); Karen Ordahl Kupperman, *Roanoke: The Abandoned Colony* (1984); Michael L. Oberg, *The Head in Edward Nugent's Hand: Roanoke's Forgotten Indians* (2008); David B. Quinn, *Set Fair for Roanoke: Voyages and Colonies, 1584–1606* (1985); and David Stick, *Roanoke Island: The Beginnings of North America* (1983). While the colony failed, the visual record it produced, especially in the watercolors by John White, has remained central to historical understanding of the early colonial period. For the watercolors and the rest of White's work, see Paul Hulton and David B. Quinn, *The American Drawings of John White*, 2 vols. (1964).

The foundational documents for the Virginia Company, the primary organizer of colonization along the Chesapeake before 1625, can be found in Susan Myra Kingsbury, ed., *The Records of the Virginia Company of London*, 4 vols. (1906–1935). Other necessary primary sources include Philip L. Barbour, ed., *The Jamestown Voyages Under the First Charter, 1606–1609*, 2 vols., Works Issued by the Hakluyt Society, 2nd Ser., 136–137 (1969); Philip L. Barbour, ed., *The Complete Works of Captain John Smith*, 3 vols. (1986); Samuel Bemiss, ed., *The Three Charters of the Virginia Company of London with Seven Related Documents, 1606–1621* (1957); James Horn, ed., *Captain John Smith: Writings with Other Narratives of Roanoke, Jamestown, and the First English Settlement of America* (2007); Mark Nicholls, "George Percy's 'Trewe Relacyon': A Primary Source for the Jamestown Settlement," *Virginia Magazine of History and Biography* 113 (2005); Henry Spelman, *Relation of Virginia: A Boy's Memoir of Life with Powhatans and Patawomecks*, ed. Karen Ordahl Kupperman (2019); [William Strachey], *For the Colony in Virginea Britannia: Lawes Divine, Morall and Martiall, etc.*, ed. David H. Flaherty (1969); Robert Beverley, *The History and Present State of Virginia, in Four Parts* (1705), now available in an excellent edition by Susan Scott Parrish (2013); Warren Billings, ed., *The Old Dominion in the Seventeenth Century*, rev. ed. (2007); and Michael Leroy Oberg, ed., *Samuel Wiseman's Book of Record: The Official Account of Bacon's Rebellion in Virginia* (2005).

For relations between the region's Indigenous peoples and colonizers, see Linwood "Little Bear" Custalow and Angela L. Daniel "Silver Star," *The True Story of Pocahontas: The Other Side of History* (2007); Martin Gallivan, *The Powhatan Landscape: An Archaeological History of the Algonquian Chesapeake* (2018); Frederic W. Gleach, *Powhatan's World and Colonial Virginia: A Conflict of Cultures* (1997); James Horn, *A Brave and Cunning Prince: The Great Chief Opechancanough and the War for America* (2021); Stephen R. Potter, *Commoners, Tribute, and Chiefs: The Development of Algonquian Culture in the Potomac Valley* (1993), 32–43; James D. Rice, *Nature and History in the Potomac Country: From Hunter-Gatherers to the Age of Jefferson* (2009); Rice, "War and Politics: Powhatan Expansionism and the Problem of Native American Warfare," *William and Mary Quarterly*, 3rd Ser., 77 (2020); and Helen C. Rountree, *Pocahontas's People: The Powhatan Indians of Virginia Through Four Centuries* (1990).

For English colonization, the ideal starting point remains Edmund Morgan, *American Slavery, American Freedom: The Ordeal of Colonial Virginia* (1975), a compelling narrative account of the struggles of the English and their fateful turn to enslaving Africans. Other crucial works include Bernard Bailyn, "Politics and Social Structure in Virginia," in James M. Smith, ed., *Seventeenth-Century America: Essays in Colonial History* (1959); Kathleen M. Brown, *Good Wives, Nasty Wenches, and Anxious Patriarchs: Gender, Race, and Power in Colonial Virginia* (1996); Lois Green Carr and Lorena S. Walsh, "The Planter's Wife: The Experience of White Women in Seventeenth-Century Maryland," *William and Mary Quarterly*, 3rd Ser., 34 (1977); Misha Ewen, *The Virginia Venture: American Colonization and English Society, 1580–1660* (2022); Alexander B. Haskell, *For God, King, and People: Forging Commonwealth Bonds in Renaissance Virginia* (2017); James Horn, *A Land as God Made It: Jamestown and the Birth of America* (2005); James Horn, *Adapting to a New World: English Society in the Seventeenth-Century Chesapeake* (1994); James Horn et al., *Jane: Starvation, Cannibalism, and Endurance at Jamestown* (2013); Ivor Noël Hume, *Martin's Hundred* (1982); William M. Kelso, *Jamestown: The Buried Truth* (2006); Matthew Kruer, *Time of Anarchy: Indigenous Power and the Crisis of Colonialism in Early America* (2021); Allan Kulikoff, *Tobacco and Slaves: The Development of Southern Cultures in the Chesapeake, 1680–1800* (1986); Karen Ordahl Kupperman, *The Jamestown Project* (2007); Theodore Rabb, *Jacobean Gentleman: Sir Edwin Sandys, 1561–1629* (1998); James D. Rice, *Tales from a Revolution: Bacon's Rebellion and the Transformation of Early America* (2012); Darrett B. Rutman and Anita H. Rutman, *A Place in Time: Middlesex County, Virginia, 1650–1750* (1984); Thad W. Tate and David L. Ammerman, eds., *The Chesapeake in the Seventeenth Century: Essays on Anglo-American Society* (1979); and Lorena Walsh, *Motives of Honor, Pleasure, and Profit: Plantation Management in the Colonial Chesapeake* (2010). For the later development of the region, see Allan Kulikoff, *Tobacco and Slaves: The Development of Southern Cultures in the Chesapeake, 1680–1800* (1986).

The 400th anniversary of the establishment of Jamestown, in 2007, and the 400th anniversaries of the arrival of the first enslaved Africans in Viriginia and the origins of the House of Burgesses, both in 2019, produced a flood of scholarship. See, among other anniversary-year volumes, Peter C. Mancall, ed., *The Atlantic World and Virginia, 1550–1624* (2007) and Paul Musselwhite, James Horn, and Peter C. Mancall, eds., *Virginia 1619: Slavery and Freedom in the Making of English America* (2019).

For early Maryland, see Clayton C. Hall, ed., *Narratives of Early Maryland, 1633–1684* (1910); Ronald Hoffman, *Princes of Ireland, Planters of Maryland: A Carroll Saga, 1500–1782* (2000); Edward G. Gray, *Mason-Dixon: Crucible of the Nation* (2023); David B. Quinn, ed., *Early Maryland in a Wider World* (1982); and Antoinette Sutto, *Loyal Protestants and Dangerous Papists: Maryland and the Politics of Religion in the English Atlantic* (2015).

New England

New England, like the Chesapeake, has received extensive treatment for generations. Many of the crucial primary sources are available in modern editions, including William Bradford, *Of Plimoth Plantation*, ed. Kenneth Minkema et al. (2020); Bernard Bailyn, ed., *The Apologia of Robert Keayne . . . The Self-Portrait of a Puritan Merchant* (1965), a text that should be read alongside Bailyn's "The Apologia of Robert Keayne," *William and Mary Quarterly*, 3rd Ser., 7 (1950); Lisa Brooks and Kelly Wisecup, eds., *Plymouth Colony: Narratives of English Settlement and Native Resistance from the Mayflower to King Philip's War* (2022); Richard Dunn, ed., *The Journal of John Winthrop, 1630–1649* (1996); David D. Hall, ed., *Puritans in the New World: A Critical*

Anthology (2004); Sydney V. James Jr., ed., *Three Visitors to Early Plymouth* (1963); Alan Heimert and Andrew Delbanco, eds., *The Puritans in America: A Narrative Anthology* (1985); *The New English Canaan of Thomas Morton* (orig. pub. 1637), ed. Charles Francis Adams Jr., Publications of the Prince Society (1883); and Mary Rowlandson, *The Sovereignty and Goodness of God* (orig. pub. 1682), ed. Neal Salisbury (1997).

Beginning in the 1960s, historians began to produce a series of works analyzing New England at the level of the town. These so-called town studies proliferated and remain valuable. Among the most influential are Charles E. Clark, *The Eastern Frontier: The Settlement of Northern New England, 1610–1763* (1970); George D. Langdon Jr., *Pilgrim Colony: A History of New Plymouth, 1620–1691* (1966); John Demos, *A Little Commonwealth: Family Life in Plymouth Colony* (1970); Philip J. Greven Jr., *Four Generations: Population, Land, and Family in Colonial Andover, Massachusetts* (1970); Kenneth Lockridge, *A New England Town, the First Hundred Years: Dedham, Massachusetts, 1636–1736* (1970); John F. Martin, *Profits in the Wilderness: Entrepreneurship and the Founding of New England Towns in the Seventeenth Century* (1991); and Michael Zuckerman, *Peaceable Kingdoms: New England Towns in the Eighteenth Century* (1970).

These works established a firm foundation, built on analysis of quantifiable records, that has enabled a new generation of scholars to create works that blend town-level analysis with insights about culture, economics, and religion. The best example is Mark Peterson's monumental *The City-State of Boston: The Rise and Fall of an Atlantic Power, 1630–1865* (2019); see also Virginia DeJohn Anderson, *New England's Generation: The Great Migration and the Formation of Society and Culture in the Seventeenth Century* (1991) as well as her "Migrants and Motives: Religion and the Settlement of New England, 1630–1640," *New England Quarterly* 58 (1985); Bernard Bailyn, *The New England Merchants in the Seventeenth Century* (1955); Rhys Isaac, "Order and Growth, Authority and Meaning in Colonial New England," *American Historical Review* 76 (1971); Winifred B. Rothenberg, "The Emergence of a Capital Market in Rural Massachusetts," *Journal of Economic History* 45 (1985); Laurel Thatcher Ulrich, *Good Wives: Image and Reality in the Lives of Women in Northern New England, 1650–1750* (1982); Daniel Vickers, *Farmers and Fishermen: Two Centuries of Work in Essex County, Massachusetts, 1630–1830* (1994); and Helena Wall, *Fierce Communion: Family and Community in Early America* (1990).

These works recognize the powerful force of dissenting faith in the creation of New England's colonial communities. The spiritual ideas that motivated migration of many from England to New England have also elicited serious historical treatment, starting with the work of Perry Miller, whose deep research into the sources of dissenters' faith and actions can be seen in his *The New England Mind: The Seventeenth Century* (1939), *The New England Mind: From Colony to Province* (1953), and *Nature's Nation* (1967). In the years that followed, subtle studies blending intellectual and cultural history interpreted these famous dissenters in works that remain worth reading. The best starting point is Edmund Morgan, *Visible Saints: The History of a Puritan Idea* (1963), but many other works have filled out the picture that Miller and Morgan sketched. See, again among many, Francis J. Bremer, *John Winthrop: America's Forgotten Founding Father* (2003) and his *One Small Candle: The Plymouth Puritans and the Beginning of English New England* (2020); Stephen Foster, *The Long Argument: English Puritanism and the Shaping of New England Culture, 1570–1700* (1991); David Hall, *Worlds of Wonder, Days of Judgment: Popular Religious Belief in Early New England* (1989); Janice Knight, *Orthodoxies in Massachusetts: Rereading American Puritanism* (1994); Susan Hardman Moore, *Pilgrims: New England Settlers and the Call of Home* (2007); Stephen Nissenbaum, *The Battle for Christmas:*

A Cultural History of America's Most Cherished Holiday (1996); Mark A. Peterson, *The Price of Redemption: The Spiritual Economy of Puritan New England* (1997); David J. Silverman, *Faith and Boundaries: Colonists, Christianity, and Community Among the Wampanoag Indians of Martha's Vineyard, 1600–1871* (2005); and Michael P. Winship, *Godly Republicanism: Puritans, Pilgrims, and a City on a Hill* (2012). Of course, even among colonists there were those who did not agree with the dissenters' agenda or their actions and whose actions led them to be exiled; see Peter C. Mancall, *The Trials of Thomas Morton: An Anglican Lawyer, His Puritan Foes, and the Battle for a New England* (2019); Carla G. Pestana, "The Quaker Executions as Myth and History," *Journal of American History* 80 (1993); Ann Fairfax Withington and Jack Schwartz, "The Political Trial of Anne Hutchinson," *New England Quarterly* 51 (1978); and studies of Roger Williams including John M. Barry, *Roger Williams and the Creation of the American Soul: Church, State, and the Birth of Liberty* (2012) and Patricia Rubertone, *Grave Undertakings: An Archaeology of Roger Williams and the Narragansett Indians* (2001).

William Pynchon, his family, and their efforts to transform Agawam into Springfield have inspired a series of works, including Stephen Innes, *Labor in a New Land: Economy and Society in Seventeenth-Century Springfield* (1983); David M. Powers, "William Pynchon, the Agawam Indians, and the 1636 Deed for Springfield," *Historical Journal of Massachusetts* 45 (2017); and Michael P. Winship, "Contesting Control of Orthodoxy Among the Godly: William Pynchon Reexamined," *William and Mary Quarterly*, 3rd Ser., 54 (1997). The remarkable records of the local court he led can be found in Joseph H. Smith, ed., *Colonial Justice in Western Massachusetts (1639–1702): The Pynchon Court Record* (1961).

One of the enduring aspects of New England's history was colonists' periodic obsessions with questions relating to demonic possession and witchcraft. Vital studies of these phenomena include John Demos's foundational *Entertaining Satan: Witchcraft and the Culture of Early New England* (1982); Malcolm Gaskill, *The Ruin of All Witches: Life and Death in the New World* (2021), another study of early Springfield; David D. Hall, ed., *Witch-Hunting in Seventeenth-Century New England*, 2nd ed. (1999); and Carol Karlsen, *Devil in the Shape of a Woman: Witchcraft in Colonial New England* (1987). While it may be tempting to look for the local origins of colonial passions on the topic, residents in New England responded to an understanding of witchcraft that had taken shape in England, Scotland, and across Europe; see, among many works, Stuart Clark, *Thinking with Demons: The Idea of Witchcraft in Early Modern Europe* (1997) and Tracy Borman, *Witches: James I and the English Witch Hunters* (2013). *Contested Continent* concludes before the outbreak of witchcraft accusations in and around Salem in 1692, but the literature for that moment reflects developments from before 1680; see, again among many sources, Mary Beth Norton, *In the Devil's Snare: The Salem Witchcraft Crisis of 1692* (2002).

While studies of New England's colonists and their faith traditions remain active, many scholars have also written about the newcomers' tense and often violent relations with the region's Indigenous peoples. Those hostile emotions arose well before the destructive violence of the mid-1670s. For this literature, see Kathleen Bragdon, *Native Peoples of Southern New England, 1500–1650* (1999); Richard W. Cogley, *John Eliot's Mission to the Indians Before King Philip's War* (1999); Jean M. O'Brien, *Dispossession by Degrees: Indian Land and Identity in Natick, Massachusetts, 1650–1790* (1997) and her *Firsting and Lasting: Writing Indians out of Existence in New England* (2010); Jenny Hale Pulsipher, *Subjects unto the Same King: Indians, English, and the Contest for Authority in Colonial New England* (2005); and Neal Salisbury, *Manitou and Providence: Indians, Europeans, and the Making of New England, 1500–1643* (1982). The era of Metacom's war has produced its own library of interpretations, including Lisa Brooks, *Our Beloved Kin: A New History of King Philip's War* (2018); Katherine A. Grandjean, "The Long Wake of the Pequot War," *Early American Studies* 9 (2011); Yasuhide Kawashima, *Igniting King Philip's War: The John Sassomon Murder Trial* (2001); Jill Lepore, *The Name of War: King Philip's War and the Origins of American Identity* (1998); and Daniel R. Mandell, *King Philip's War: Colonial Expansion, Native Resistance, and the End of Indian Sovereignty* (2010). That war has figured prominently in early American military history; see John Grenier, *The First Way of War: American War Making on the Frontier* (2005). Many colonists may have wanted to remove Native peoples from across New England, but if that was their goal, they failed, a point made by the Pequot historian William Apess, who published the first Indigenous autobiography in the United States, *A Son of the Forest* (1829). His writings are available in Barry O'Connell, ed., *On Our Own Ground: The Complete Writings of William Apess, a Pequot* (1992).

Carolina and the Greater Caribbean

New England and the Chesapeake colonies preoccupied historians of early America for generations, but recently there has been a near-explosion of works about the greater Caribbean, the territory that stretches from the coast of the Carolinas in the northwest to Bermuda in the Atlantic and then southward through the Caribbean to the coastline of modern Venezuela and Brazil. Many of these studies have focused on the history of enslavement and the slave trade. Others concentrate on particular colonial outposts. Much of the primary source literature is available in modern editions or accessible online publications. These include Richard Ligon, *A True and Exact History of the Island of Barbados*, ed. Karen Ordahl Kupperman (2011); [Nathaniel Butler], *The Historye of the Bermudaes or Summer Islands*, ed. J. Henry Lefroy, Works Issued by the Hakluyt Society LXV (1882); Aubrey Gwynn, "Documents Relating to the Irish in the West Indies," *Analecta Hibernica* 4 (1932); Joyce Lorimer, ed., *English and Irish Settlement on the River Amazon, 1550–1646*, Works Issued by the Hakluyt Society, 2nd Ser., 171 (1989); and Alexander S. Salley, ed., *Narratives of Early Carolina, 1650–1708* (1911).

The best introduction to Carolina's early history can be found in Peter Wood, *Black Majority: Negroes in Colonial South Carolina from 1670 Through the Stono Rebellion* (1974) and in James H. Merrell, *The Indians' New World: Catawbas and Their Neighbors from European Contact Through the Era of Removal* (1989). Other important studies include Lars C. Adams, " 'The Battle of Weyanoke Creek': A Story of the Third Anglo-Powhatan War in Early Carolina," *Native South* 6 (2013); Paul E. Kopperman, "Profile of Failure: The Carolana Project, 1629–1640," *North Carolina Historical Review* 59 (1982); William S. Powell, "Carolana and the Incomparable Roanoke: Explorations and Attempted Settlements, 1620–1633," *North Carolina Historical Review* 51 (1974); and M. Eugene Sirmans, *Colonial South Carolina: A Political History, 1663–1763* (1966).

Some recent scholars have offered histories that span much of the region. These include Paul E. Kopperman, "Ambivalent Allies: Anglo-Dutch Relations and the Struggle against the Spanish Empire in the Caribbean, 1621–1641," *Journal of Caribbean History* 21 (1987); Karen Ordahl Kupperman, "Errand to the Indies: Puritan Colonization from Providence Island Through the Western Design," *William and Mary Quarterly*, 3rd Ser., 45 (1988); Carla G. Pestana, *The English Atlantic in an Age of Revolution, 1640–1661* (2004); and David Wheat, *Atlantic Africa and the Spanish Caribbean, 1570–1640* (2016).

For Bermuda, see Virginia Bernhard, "Religion, Politics, and Witchcraft in Bermuda, 1651–55," *William and Mary Quarterly*, 3rd Ser., 67 (2010), and her *A Tale of Two Colonies: What Really*

Happened in Virginia and Bermuda? (2011); Michael Jarvis, *Isle of Devils, Isle of Saints: An Atlantic History of Bermuda, 1609–1684* (2022); and Heather M. Kopelson, "Sinning Property and the Legal Transformation of Abominable Sex in Early Bermuda," *William and Mary Quarterly*, 3rd Ser., 70 (2013).

Barbados has attracted much more sustained attention. See, among other works, Hilary McD. Beckles, *A History of Barbados: From Amerindian Settlement to Caribbean Single Market*, 2nd ed. (2006); Richard S. Dunn, "The Barbados Census of 1680: Profile of the Richest Colony in English America," *William and Mary Quarterly* 26 (1969); David Eltis, "The Total Product of Barbados, 1664–1701," *Journal of Economic History* 55 (1995), and his "Estimates of Exports from Barbados and Jamaica, 1655–1701," *William and Mary Quarterly*, 3rd Ser., 52 (1995); George Gmelch and Sharon Bohn Gmelch, "Barbados's Amerindian Past," *Anthropology Today* 12 (1996); Larry Gragg, *Englishmen Transplanted: The English Colonization of Barbadoes, 1627–1715* (2003); Jerome Handler, "The Amerindian Slave Population of Barbados in the Seventeenth and Early Eighteenth Centuries," *Caribbean Studies* 8 (1969) and his "Amerindians and their contribution to Barbadian Life," *Journal of the Barbados Museum and Historical Society* 35 (1977); and Russell R. Menard, *Sweet Negotiations: Sugar, Slavery, and Plantation Agriculture in Early Barbados* (2006).

For the Bahamas, see Michael Craton and Gail Saunders, *Islanders in the Stream: A History of the Bahamian People* (1992), and W. Hubert Miller, "The Colonization of the Bahamas, 1647–1670," *William and Mary Quarterly*, 3rd Ser., 2 (1945).

For Providence Island, see Karen Ordahl Kupperman, *Providence Island, 1630–1641: The Other Puritan Colony* (1993), and Alison Games, " 'The Sanctuarye of Our Rebell Negroes': The Atlantic Context of Local Resistance on Providence Island, 1630–1641," *Slavery and Abolition* 19 (1998).

For the Lesser Antilles, see Robert Paquette and Stanley Engerman, eds., *The Lesser Antilles in the Age of European Expansion* (1996).

For Jamaica, see the extraordinary volume of work produced by Trevor Burnard, including T. G. Burnard, " 'Prodigious Riches': The Wealth of Jamaica Before the American Revolution," *Economic History Review* LIV (2001) and Trevor Burnard and Kenneth Morgan, "The Dynamics of the Slave Market and Slave Purchasing Patterns in Jamaica, 1655–1788," *William and Mary Quarterly*, 3rd Ser., 58 (2001).

Much of the best work about the greater Caribbean focuses on the development of plantations populated primarily by bound servants and enslaved Africans and their children. See, among others, Trevor Burnard, *Planters, Merchants, and Slaves: Plantation Societies in British America, 1650–1820* (2015); Hilary McD. Beckles, "A 'Riotous and Unruly Lot': Irish Indentured Servants and Freemen in the English West Indies, 1644–1713," *William and Mary Quarterly* 47 (1990); and Tessa Murphy, *The Creole Archipelago: Race and Borders in the Colonial Caribbean* (2021).

Lenapehoking and Iroquoia

The region encompassing the modern Hudson, Mohawk, Susquehanna, and Delaware Valleys spawned multiple names. Some were Native, including Iroquoia, the homeland of the Haudenosaunee, and Lenapehoking, the ancestral territory claimed by Lenapes, Munsees, and related groups. Europeans imposed their own names on this region, including New Netherland, New York, Pennsylvania, and New Sweden. But just as these names overlapped and shifted, so too did peoples move back and forth across the area. The best starting point is, again, in the documentary record, including J. Franklin Jameson, ed., *Narratives of New Netherland, 1609–1664* (1909); Albert C. Myers, ed. *Narratives of Early Pennsylvania, West New Jersey, and Delaware, 1630–1707* (1912); and Adriean van der Donck, *A Description of New Netherland*, trans. Diederick Willem Goedhuys, ed. Charles T. Gehring and William A. Starna (2008).

For Iroquoia, see Allan Greer, *Mohawk Saint: Catherine Tekakwitha and the Jesuits* (2005); Daniel K. Richter, *The Ordeal of the Longhouse: The Peoples of the Iroquois League in the Era of European Colonization* (1992); and Daniel K. Richter, "War and Culture: The Iroquois Experience," *William and Mary Quarterly*, 3rd Ser., 40 (1983).

For the lower Hudson Valley and Long Island, the territory that the Dutch tried to take from the Munsees and Lenapes and then the English took from the Dutch, renaming the primary town from New Amsterdam to New York City, see Anne-Marie Cantwell and Diana diZerega Wall, *Unearthing Gotham: The Archaeology of New York City* (2001); Charles T. Gehring and William A. Starna, "Dutch and Indians in the Hudson Valley: The Early Period," *Hudson Valley Regional Review* 9 (1992); Robert S. Grumet, *The Munsee Indians: A History* (2009); Evan Haefeli, "On First Contact and Apotheosis: Manitou and Men," *Ethnohistory* 54 (2007); Jaap Jacobs, *The Colony of New Netherland: A Dutch Settlement in Seventeenth-Century America* (2005); Sung Bok Kim, *Landlord and Tenant in Colonial New York, 1664–1775* (1978); Nicole S. Maskiell, *Bound by Bondage: Slavery and the Creation of a Northern Gentry* (2022); Donna Merwick, *Stuyvesant Bound: An Essay on Loss Across Time* (2013); Paul Otto, *The Dutch-Munsee Encounter in America: The Struggle for Sovereignty in the Hudson Valley* (2006); Paul Otto, "Common Practices and Mutual Misunderstandings: Henry Hudson, Native Americans, and the Birth of New Netherland," *de Halve Maen* 72 (1999); Paul Otto, "The Origins of New Netherland: Interpreting Native American Responses to Henry Hudson's Visit," *Itinerario* 13 (1994), 22–39; Oliver A. Rink, *Holland on the Hudson: An Economic and Social History of Dutch New York* (1986); Robert C. Ritchie, *The Duke's Province: A Study of New York Politics and Society, 1664–1691* (1977); Susanah Shaw Romney, *New Netherland Connections: Intimate Networks and Atlantic Ties in Seventeenth-Century America* (2014); and Alan Trelease, *Indian Affairs in Colonial New York: The Seventeenth Century* (1960).

For the modern Delaware Valley, see Stellan Dahlgren and Hans Norman, *The Rise and Fall of New Sweden: Governor Johan Risingh's Journal 1645–1655 in Its Historical Context* (1988); Gunlög Fur, *Colonialism in the Margins: Cultural Encounters in New Sweden and Lapland* (2005); Carol E. Hoffecker et al., eds., *New Sweden in America* (1995); Jean R. Soderlund, *Lenape Country: Delaware Valley Society Before William Penn* (2015); and C. A. Weslager, *New Sweden on the Delaware, 1638–1655* (1988).

The Environment

Stories about environmental change form one of the crucial pillars of *Contested Continent*. The ecological issues they raise relate to a major intellectual problem that hovers over all attempts to write the history of this era—the tendency to believe that what happened after 1492 had to happen, as if it were inevitable. There were plenty of people who did see in daily life a scheme that humans could not control. Many of the English Protestant religious dissenters believed that they were less agents of their own control than actors playing parts written by their god. But one need not embrace these Protestant dissenters' views to come to a similar conclusion, though using a more modern idiom. After environmental historian Alfred Crosby introduced the notion of the "Columbian Exchange" in a 1972 book with that title, many presumed that biology drove destiny. Lacking acquired immunities from childhood exposure to death-dealing ailments like smallpox, this argument attests, Indigenous Americans must have been destined for destruction. Plenty of observers over time drew that conclusion. But this is obviously wrong, as the survival of hundreds of Indigenous nations across the Americas proves. While the transfer of disease-bearing microbes did matter at crucial inflection points from 1492 to 1680, pathogens need to be understood in a historical and social context. Immigrants who lacked knowledge of local environments could succumb as quickly as Indigenous facing an unknown disease. Those whose bodies were weakened by violence were more likely to die from an illness than those who had not suffered from others' cruelty. While it is true that even healthy people could succumb during a virulent outbreak like the hemorrhagic fevers that raced through the Valley of Mexico in the 1540s, weakened bodies proved more susceptible. Historians writing about the intersection of disease and mortality sometimes offer challenging technical explanations, but there are some who have written about the early modern human body and what happened to it with clarity. The best over-arching view can be found in John L. Brooke, *Climate Change and the Course of Global History: A Rough Journey* (2014), which situates developments within the Americas into a global context, a crucial focus since pathogens did not respect national boundaries.

Ships from the eastern shores of the Atlantic basin brought hundreds of thousands of people to the Western Hemisphere, many of them against their will. They also brought diseases that devastated Indigenous bodies and reduced Native communities, sometimes, according to observers, destroying them. Study of the transportation of disease-bearing viruses and bacteria began in earnest with Alfred W. Crosby Jr.'s *The Columbian Exchange: Biological and Cultural Consequences of 1492* (1972). In the years since, many more scholars have studied the movement of diseases along with other goods. Excellent works include Crosby's follow-up volume, *Ecological Imperialism: The Biological Expansion of Europe, 900–1900* (1986); Rodolfo Acuna-Soto et al., "Megadrought and Megadeath in 16th Century Mexico," *Emerging Infectious Diseases* 4 (2002); Noble David Cook, *Born to Die: Disease and New World Conquest, 1492–1650* (1998); Philip D. Curtin, "Disease Exchange Across the Tropical Atlantic," *History and Philosophy of the Life Sciences* 15 (1993); Ann F. Ramenofsky, *Vectors of Death: The Archaeology of European Contact* (1987); John W. Verano and Douglas H. Ubelaker, eds., *Disease and Demography in the Americas* (1992); and Herman J. Viola and Carolyn Margolis, eds., *Seeds of Change: Five Hundred Years since Columbus* (1991).

Scholarly understanding of how and why diseases spread as they did advanced dramatically when the medical community confronted HIV/AIDS, which produced studies in virology and epidemiology that transformed interpretations of what happened centuries ago. The best introduction to this literature is David W. Jones, "Virgin Soils Revisited," *William and Mary Quarterly*, 3rd Ser., 60, no. 4 (October 2003) and *Rationalizing Epidemics: Meanings and Uses of American Indian Mortality Since 1600* (2004).

Modern insights into disease-induced stress and mortality help explain the complex relationship between demographic threats and the rise of Indigenous slavery as well. See Paul Kelton, *Epidemics and Enslavement: Biological Catastrophe in the Native Southeast, 1492–1715* (2007); Catherine M. Cameron, Paul Kelton, and Alan C. Swedlund, eds., *Beyond Germs: Native Depopulation in North America* (2015); and Robbie Ethridge and Sheri M. Shuck-Hall, eds., *Mapping the Mississippian Shatter Zone: The Colonial Indian Slave Trade and Regional Instability in the American South* (2009).

The environmental consequences of 1492 also extended to the reshaping of American landscapes. To be sure, the eastward spread of maize agriculture from the Mississippi Valley took place long before Europeans arrived along the continent's shores. But more wide-ranging environmental change followed the arrival of Europeans who sought to extract wealth from American islands, forests, fields, and fisheries. Although the field of environmental history has a tradition that dates back at least as far as George Perkins Marsh's *Man and Nature; or, Physical Geography as Modified by Human Action* (1864), Crosby's identification of the Columbian Exchange helped launch a revolution in studies of early American communities and their relationship to the physical world. The development of the field can be seen in Donald Worster, *Nature's Economy: A History of Ecological Ideas* (1977). The ideal starting point for those interested in the environmental history of colonial North America is William Cronon, *Changes in the Land: Indians, Colonists, and the Ecology of New England* (1983), a book that shaped much of the field. The rich literature focused on early America includes Jennifer L. Anderson, *Mahogany: The Costs of Luxury in Early America* (2012); Brian Donahue, *The Great Meadow: Farmers and the Land in Colonial Concord* (2004); Elizabeth Ganson, *Natural Designs: Gonzalo Fernández de Oviedo and the Invention of New World Nature* (2024); Pekka Hämäläinen, "The Politics of Grass: European Expansion, Ecological Change, and Indigenous Power in the Southwest Borderlands," *William and Mary Quarterly* 67 (2010); Shepard Krech III, *The Ecological Indian: Myth and History* (1999); Peter C. Mancall, *Nature and Culture in the Early Modern Atlantic* (2018); J. R. McNeill, *Mosquito Empires: Ecology and War in the Greater Caribbean, 1620–1914* (2010); Carolyn Merchant, *Ecological Revolutions: Nature, Gender, and Science in New England* (1989); Elinor Melville, *A Plague of Sheep: Environmental Consequences of the Conquest of Mexico* (1997); Robert Morrissey, *People of the Ecotone: Environment and Indigenous Power at the Center of Early America* (2022); Keith Pluymers, *No Wood, No Kingdom: Political Ecology in the English Atlantic* (2021); Timothy Silver, *A New Face on the Countryside: Indians, Colonists, and Slaves in South Atlantic Forests, 1500–1800* (1990); Sam White, *A Cold Welcome: The Little Ice Age and Europe's Encounter with North America* (2017); and Thomas M. Wickman, *Snowshoe Country: An Environmental and Cultural History of Winter in the Early American Northeast* (2018). Wide-ranging ecological change enabled Europeans and colonists to extract wealth, but some among them recognized the dangers associated with the mad rush for profits; see Richard Grove, *Green Imperialism: Colonial Expansion, Tropical Island Edens, and the Origins of Environmentalism, 1600–1860* (1995) and Londa Schiebinger and Claudia Swan, eds., *Colonial Botany: Science, Commerce, and Politics in the Early Modern World* (2005). For England, see Keith Thomas, *Man and the Natural World: Changing Attitudes in England, 1500–1800* (1983).

For human relations with animals (including fish), see Virginia DeJohn Anderson, *Creatures of Empire: How Domestic Animals Transformed Early America* (2004); W. Jeffrey Bolster, *The Mortal Sea: Fishing the Atlantic in the Age of Sail* (2012); Jack Bouchard, *Terra Nova: Food, Water, and Work in an Early Atlantic World* (2025); Richard C. Hoffman, *The Catch: An Environmental History of Medieval European Fisheries* (2023); Peter Mitchell, *Horse Nations: The Worldwide Impact of the Horse on Indigenous Societies Post-1492* (2015); and Marcy Norton, *The Tame and the Wild: People and Animals After 1492* (2024).

For an extensive review of this literature and the primary sources that can be used to write early modern environmental history, see Peter C. Mancall, "Pigs for Historians: *Changes in the Land* and Beyond," *William and Mary Quarterly*, 3rd Ser., 67 (2010).

Index

Note: Figures are indicated by an italic *f* following the page number.